Operations Management

ACTIVEBOOK VERSION 1.0

Mark D. Hanna
MIAMI UNIVERSITY-OHIO
W. Rocky Newman
MIAMI UNIVERSITY-OHIO

Upper Saddle River, New Jersey, 07458

Executive Editor: Tom Tucker
Editor-in-Chief: P.J. Boardman
Director of Development: Steve Deitmer
Developmental Editor: Elisa Adams
Developmental Editor, Active Learning Technologies: John Morley, PhD
Media Consultants, Active Learning Technologies: Isaac Dialsingh, PhD, Scott Erickson, PhD, and Ann Theis, PhD
Assistant Editor: Erika Rusnak
Editorial Assistant: Jisun Lee
Media Project Manager: Nancy Welcher
Marketing Manager: Debbie Clare
Managing Editor (Production): Cynthia Regan
Production Editor: Dianne Falcone
Permissions Coordinator: Suzanne Grappi
Associate Director, Manufacturing: Vincent Scelta
Design Manager: Pat Smythe
Interior/Cover Design: Cheryl Asherman
Cover Illustration/Photo: © 2002 Digital Vision
Associate Director, Multimedia Production: Karen Goldsmith
Manager, Print Production: Christy Mahon
Composition/Illustration: GGS Information Services, Inc.
Printer/Binder: Quebecor/Dubuque

Credits and acknowledgments borrowed from other sources and reproduced, with permission, in this textbook appear on appropriate page within text and on page 560.

Pearson Education LTD.
Pearson Education Australia PTY, Limited
Pearson Education Singapore, Pte. Ltd
Pearson Education North Asia Ltd
Pearson Education, Canada, Ltd
Pearson Educación de Mexico, S.A. de C.V.
Pearson Education–Japan
Pearson Education Malaysia, Pte. Ltd

10 9 8 7 6 5 4 3 2 1
ISBN 0-13-066345-X

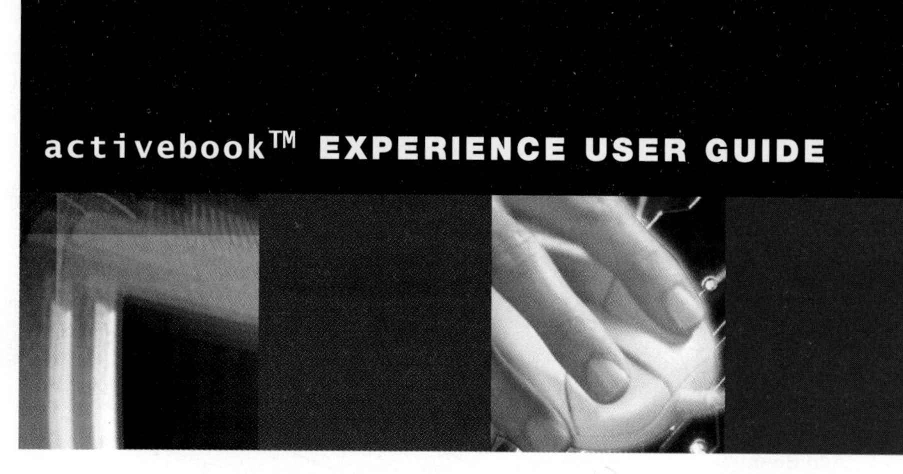

What Is the activebook™ Experience?

The activebook experience is a new kind of textbook that combines the best elements of print and electronic media. In addition to this print version, you'll have access to an online version of your book that is enhanced by a variety of multimedia elements. These include active exercises, interactive quizzes, and poll questions. These elements give you a chance to explore the text's issues in more depth.

How to Redeem Your Access Code

Redeeming your access code is fast and easy. To complete this one-time registration process, go to **www.prenhall.com/myactivebook**. Follow the new user link to register and redeem your access code. Enter the access code bound inside your book, and complete the simple registration form. When you are done, click **submit**. It will take a few minutes to redeem your access code, and then you will be taken to your homepage.

The activebook Experience Homepage

In this section you'll become acquainted with the features of the activebook experience. Once you're familiar with them, you'll be on your way.

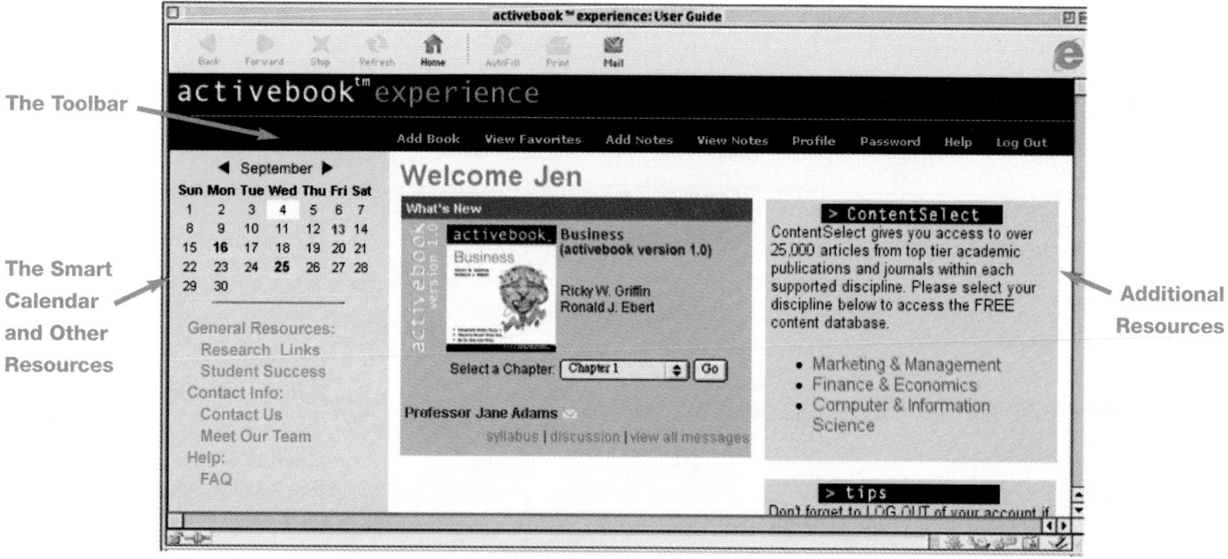

1. The Toolbar

Let's begin with the commands in the toolbar near the top of the homepage. This bar features eight commands: **add book**, **view favorites**, **add notes**, **view notes**, **profile**, **password**, **help**, and **log out**.

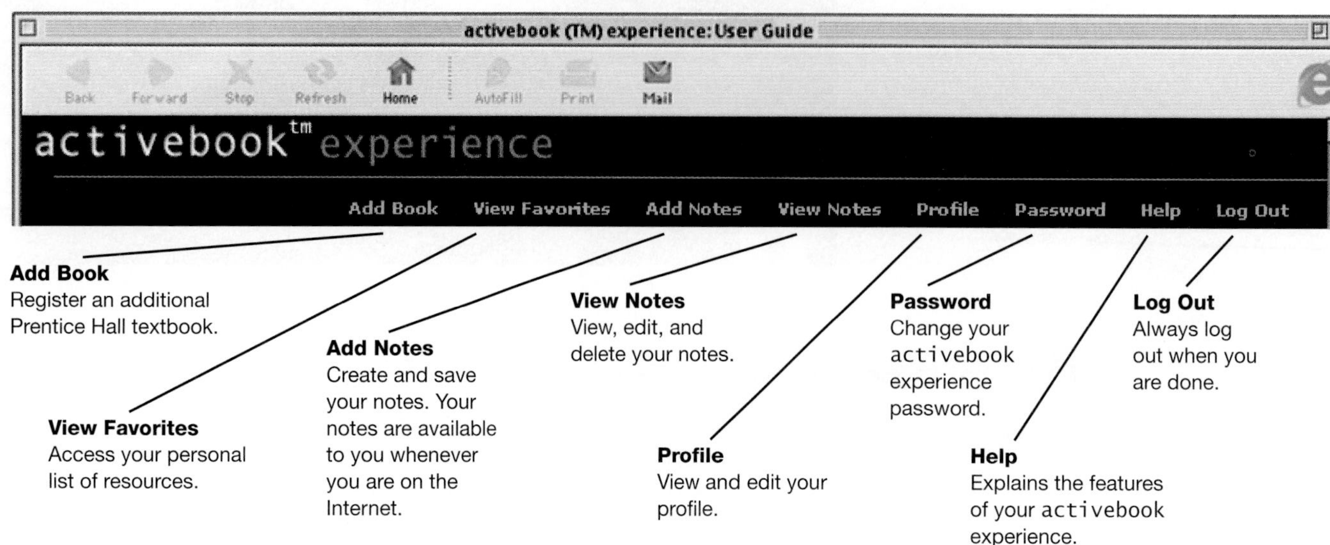

Add Book
Register an additional Prentice Hall textbook.

View Favorites
Access your personal list of resources.

Add Notes
Create and save your notes. Your notes are available to you whenever you are on the Internet.

View Notes
View, edit, and delete your notes.

Profile
View and edit your profile.

Password
Change your activebook experience password.

Help
Explains the features of your activebook experience.

Log Out
Always log out when you are done.

Now let's take a look at the features presented in the navigation bar on the left side of the screen.

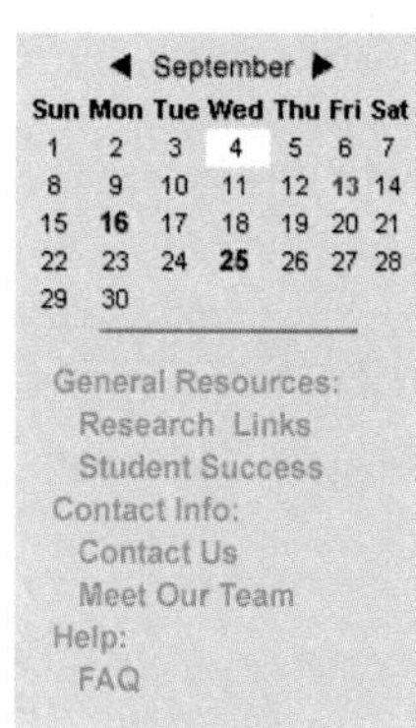

2. The Smart Calendar and Other Resources

The Smart Calendar
Instantly view all the activities for the month by clicking on a date.

Research Links
Provides a selection of annotated links to additional resources and search sites.

Student Success
Links to Prentice Hall's Student Success Web site. You will find numerous features designed to help you through your educational journey (for example, career paths, money matters, and employment opportunities).

Contact Us
Contact Prentice Hall either via telephone or e-mail to share your ideas about your activebook experience or to ask questions.

FAQ
Find answers to frequently asked questions about your activebook experience.

3. Additional Resources

After redeeming your access code, you can make use of the following resources.

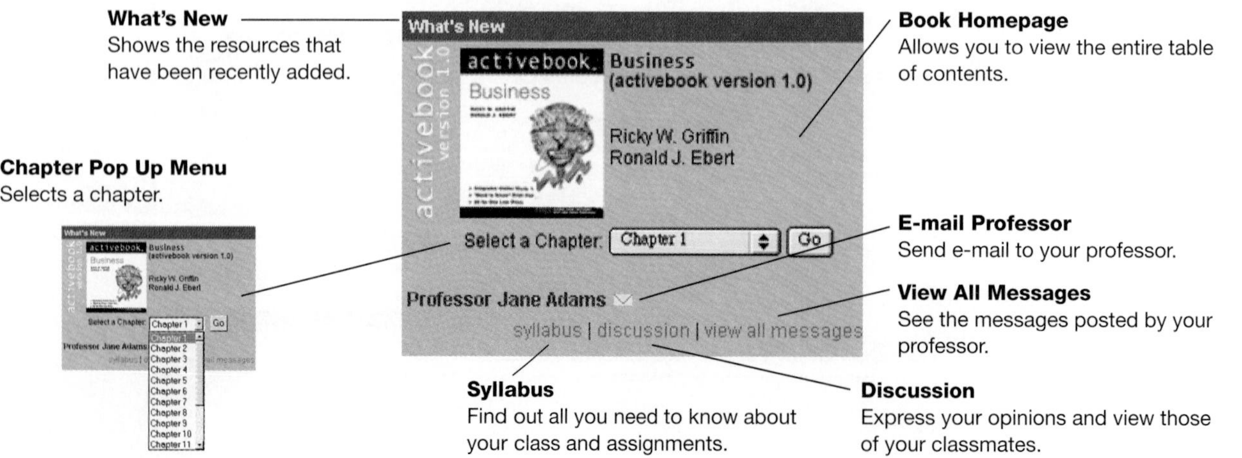

What's New
Shows the resources that have been recently added.

Chapter Pop Up Menu
Selects a chapter.

Book Homepage
Allows you to view the entire table of contents.

E-mail Professor
Send e-mail to your professor.

View All Messages
See the messages posted by your professor.

Syllabus
Find out all you need to know about your class and assignments.

Discussion
Express your opinions and view those of your classmates.

Finding Your Professor

If your professor has posted course material, you can create a link to him or her on your homepage. Once connected to your professor, you can access the **syllabus**, **view messages** from him or her, and **e-mail** him or her.

To Find Your Professor

- Click on **find your professor**.
- Search for your professor's name (using his or her last name or your school's name). Then select it.
- Click **submit** and you will return to your homepage.

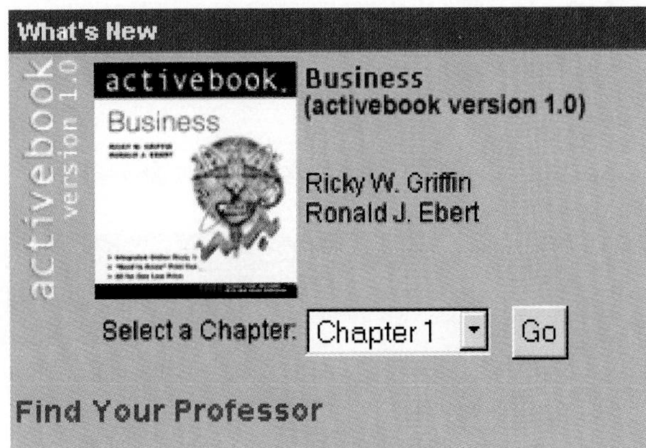

Viewing Your Professor's Syllabus

If your professor is using the **syllabus** feature, click the **syllabus** link to check assignments and course announcements.

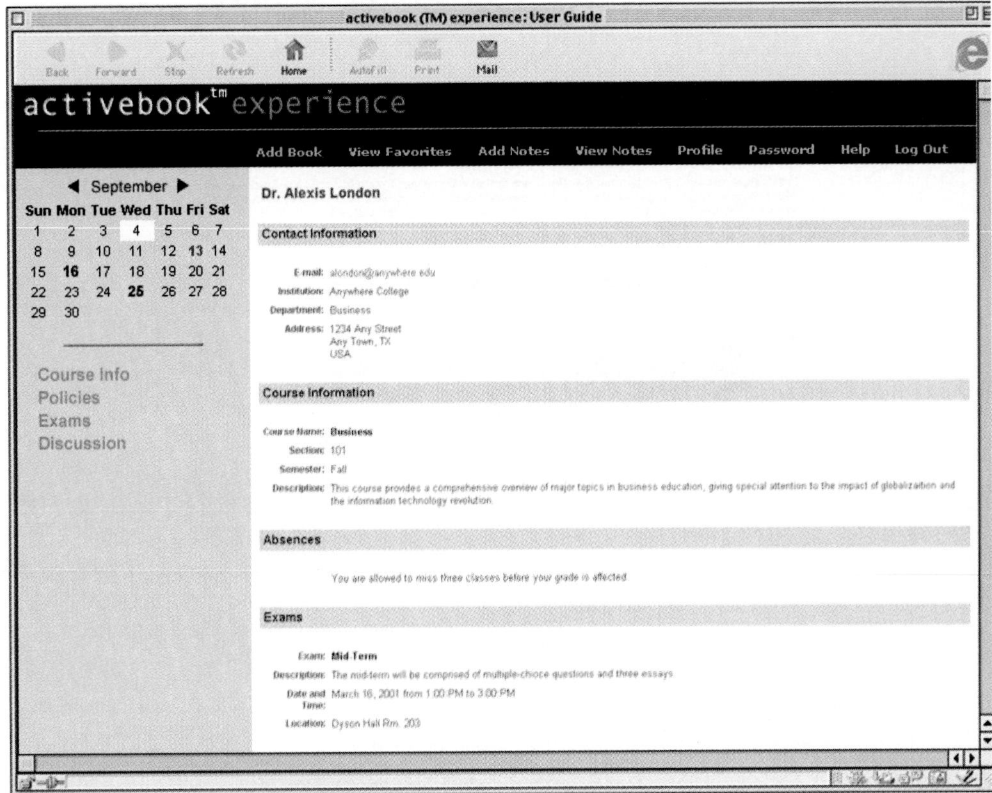

Exploring the activebook Experience

When you're ready to begin, select a chapter. In every chapter you will find: the **what's ahead** section, **objectives**, **active concept checks**, **key terms**, and a **chapter wrap-up**. Each chapter may also include a **gearing-up quiz**, **video examples** or **exercises**, **audio examples** or **exercises**, **active polls**, and **active figures**, **maps**, and **graphs**.

Let's take a look at these elements. Every chapter begins with **what's ahead**. This section tells you what material the chapter will cover.

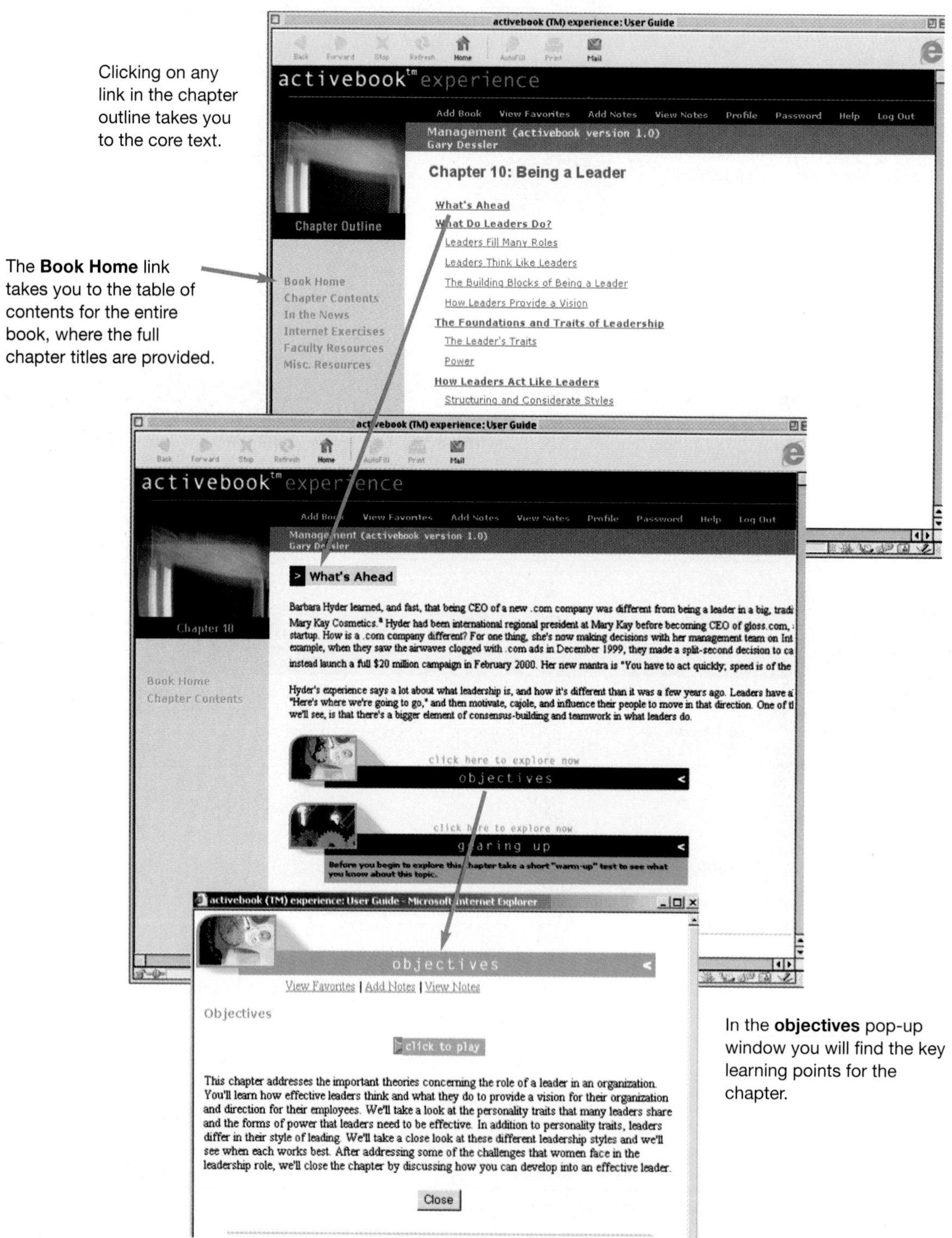

Clicking on any link in the chapter outline takes you to the core text.

The **Book Home** link takes you to the table of contents for the entire book, where the full chapter titles are provided.

In the **objectives** pop-up window you will find the key learning points for the chapter.

Another element that can appear in the **what's ahead** section is the **gearing up quiz**. This quiz is designed to get you thinking about important topics in the chapter.

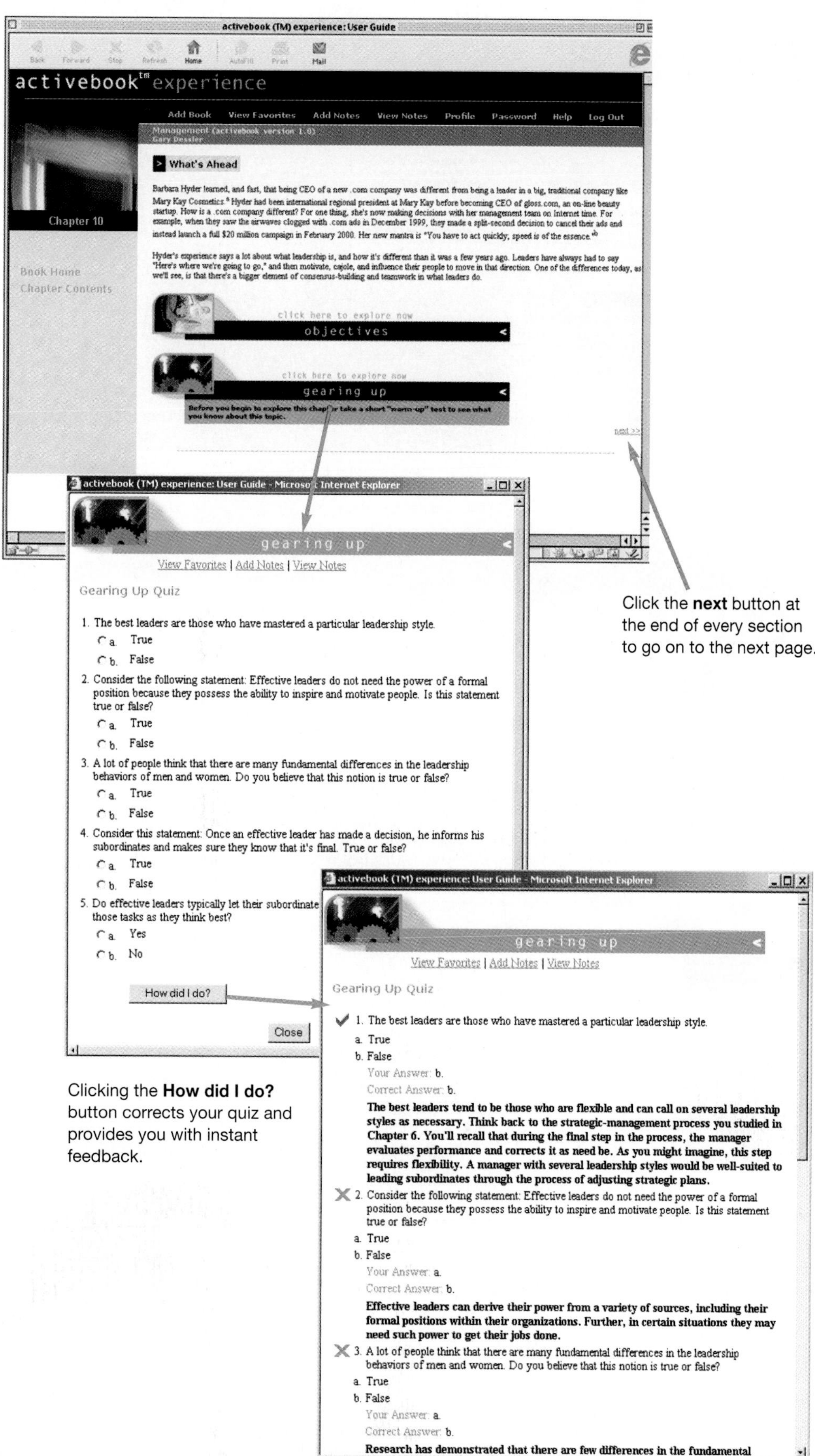

Click the **next** button at the end of every section to go on to the next page.

Clicking the **How did I do?** button corrects your quiz and provides you with instant feedback.

After **gearing up**, you're ready to start reading the chapter. Chapters are divided into major sections.

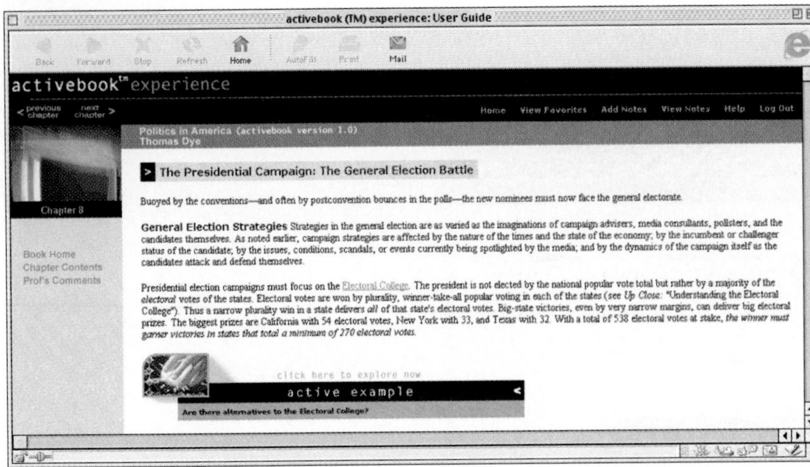

As you read each section, you will encounter the active elements. Let's become acquainted with some of them.

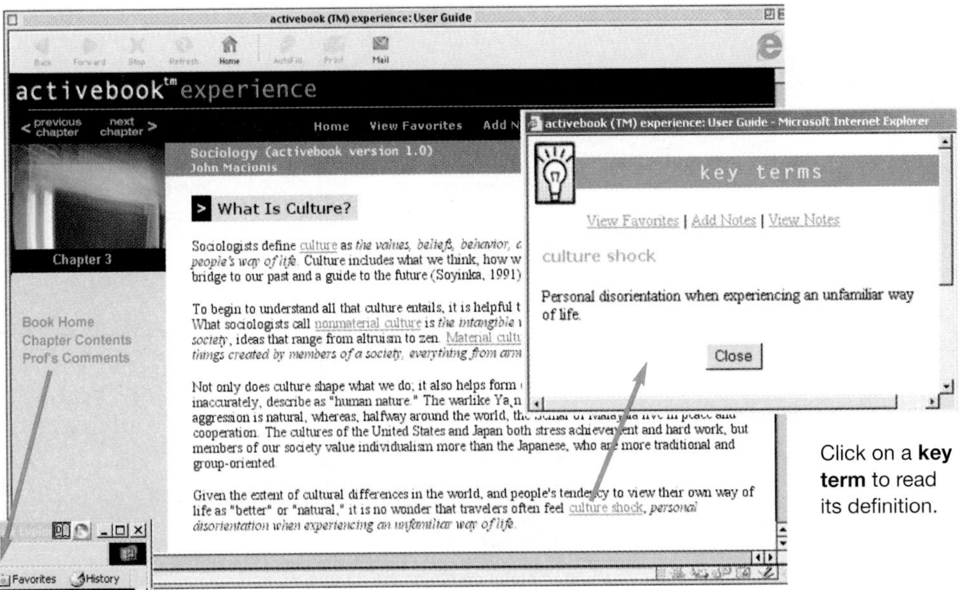

Professor's Comments is where you can find your professor's thoughts on a particular topic.

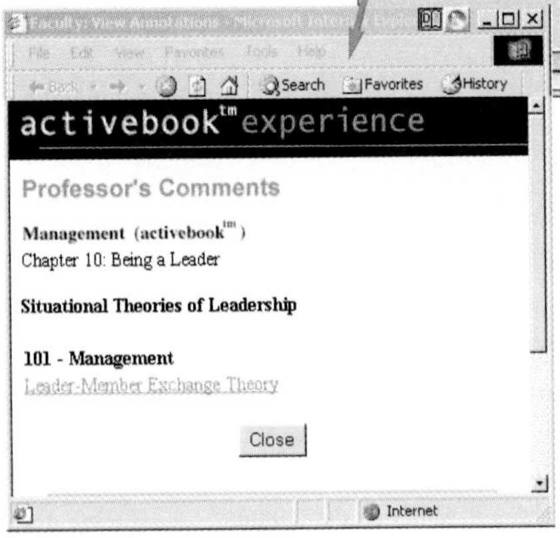

Click on a **key term** to read its definition.

Listen to quotes from key figures by clicking on the **audio example**.

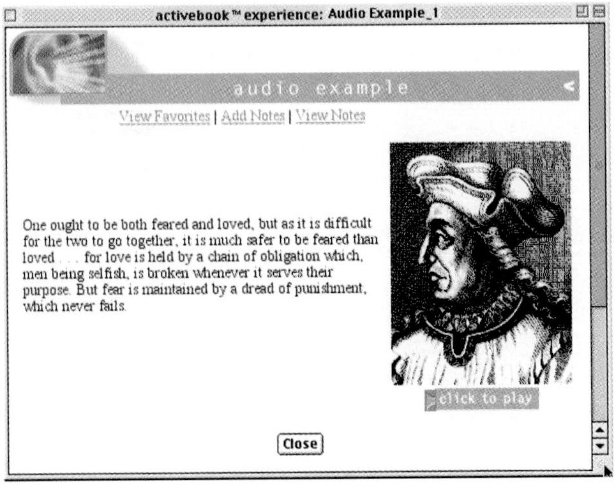

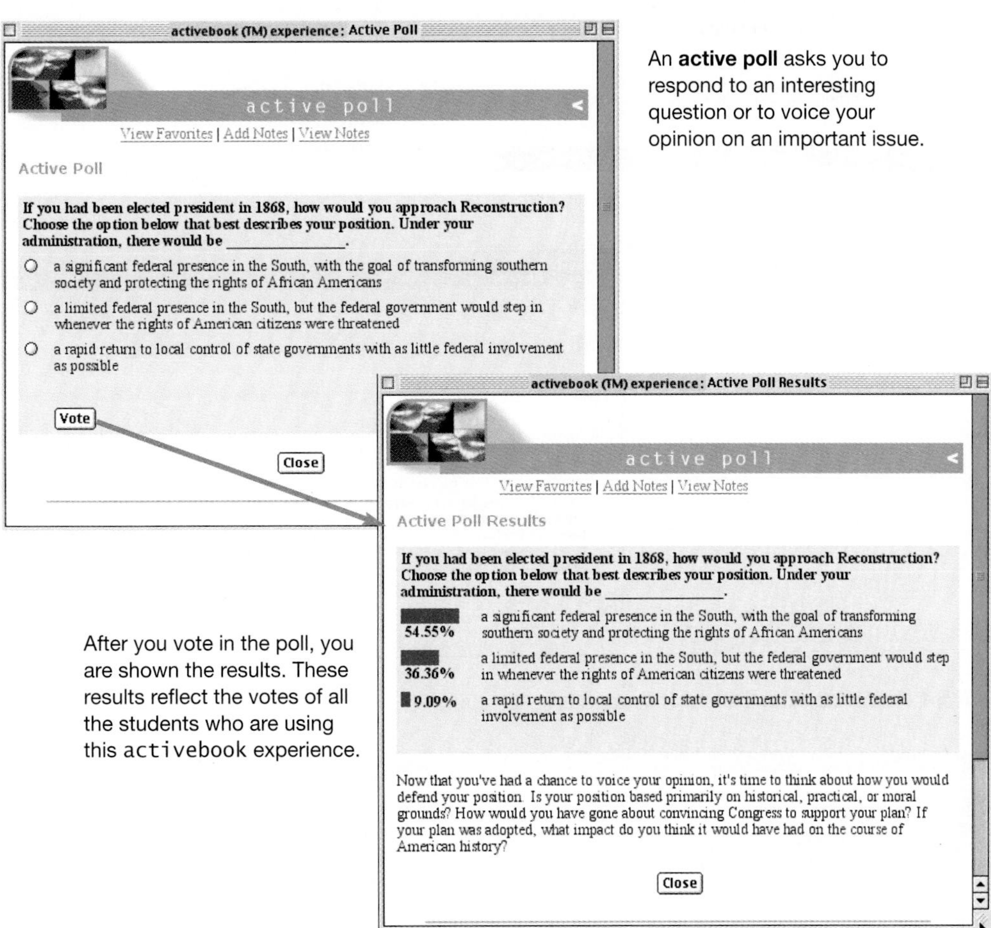

An **active poll** asks you to respond to an interesting question or to voice your opinion on an important issue.

After you vote in the poll, you are shown the results. These results reflect the votes of all the students who are using this activebook experience.

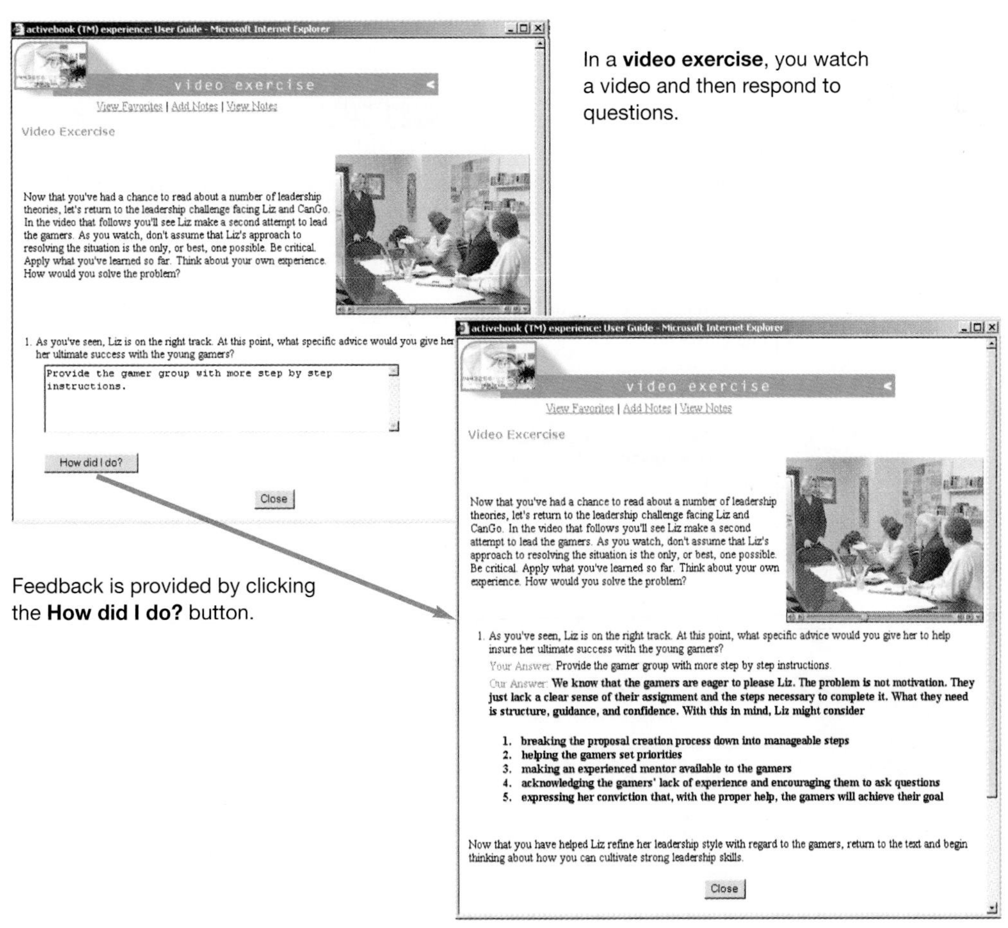

In a **video exercise**, you watch a video and then respond to questions.

Feedback is provided by clicking the **How did I do?** button.

In addition to **video exercises** you might also find an **active exercise** or an **active example**.

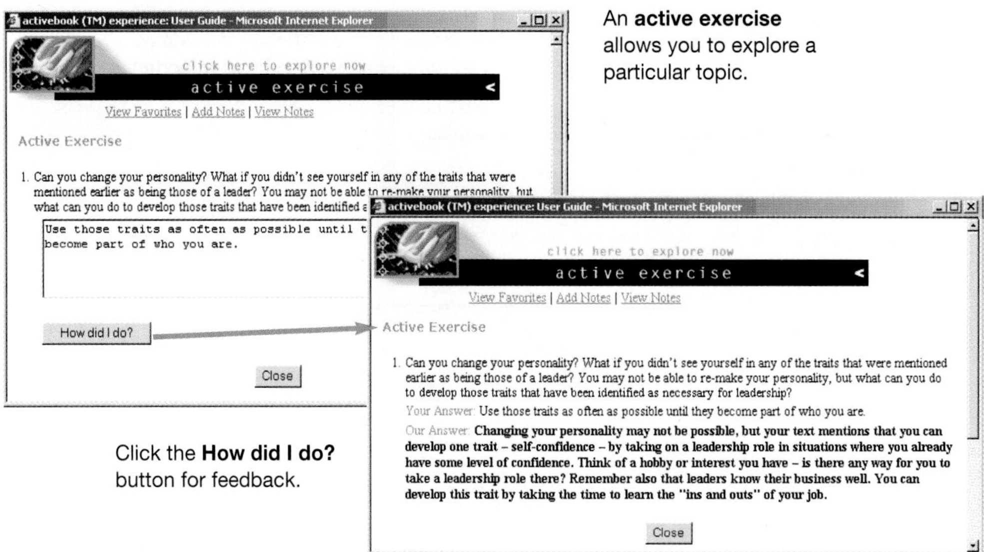

An **active exercise** allows you to explore a particular topic.

Click the **How did I do?** button for feedback.

Active concept checks occur at the end of every major section.

activebook experience: User Guide - Microsoft Internet Explorer

active concept check

View Favorites | Add Notes | View Notes

Concept Check

1. The Electoral College meets in Washington D.C.
   a. True
   b. False
   Your Answer: a.
   Correct Answer: b.
   The Electoral College never meets in a single location. They meet at their respective state capitals. Review the Concept
2. The four states with the most electoral votes are
   a. California, Texas, Florida, and New York.
   b. California, Texas, New York, and Pennsylvania.
   c. California, Texas, Pennsylvania, and Florida.
   d. California, Texas, Illinois, and Florida.
   Your Answer: a.
3. In the past six presidential elections, California has voted for the Democrats four times.
   a. True
   b. False

How did I do?

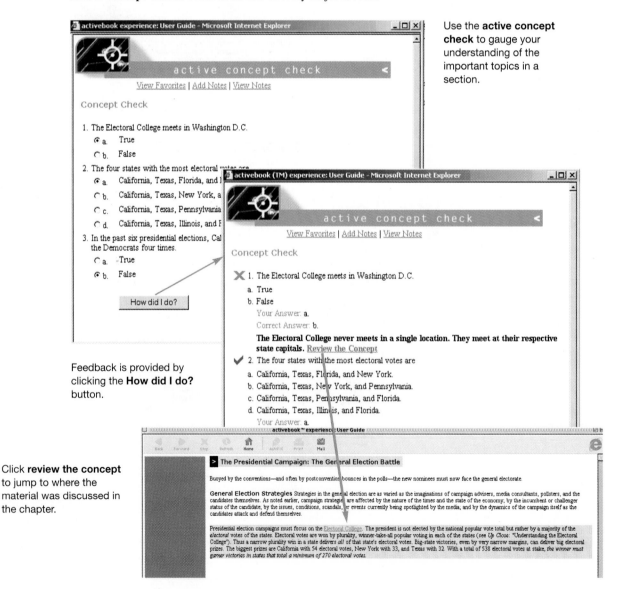

Use the **active concept check** to gauge your understanding of the important topics in a section.

Feedback is provided by clicking the **How did I do?** button.

The Presidential Campaign: The General Election Battle

Buoyed by the conventions—and often by postconvention bounces in the polls—the new nominees must now face the general electorate.

General Election Strategies Strategies in the general election are as varied as the imaginations of campaign advisers, media consultants, pollsters, and the candidates themselves. As noted earlier, campaign strategies are affected by the nature of the times and the state of the economy; by the incumbent or challenger status of the candidate; by the issues, conditions, scandals, or events currently being spotlighted by the media; and by the dynamics of the campaign itself as the candidates attack and defend themselves.

Presidential election campaigns must focus on the Electoral College. The president is not elected by the national popular vote total but rather by a majority of the *electoral* votes of the states. Electoral votes are won by plurality, winner-take-all popular voting in each of the states (see *Up Close:* "Understanding the Electoral College"). Thus a narrow plurality win in a state delivers *all* of that state's electoral votes. Big-state victories, even by very narrow margins, can deliver big electoral prizes. The biggest prizes are California with 54 electoral votes, New York with 33, and Texas with 32. With a total of 538 electoral votes at stake, *the winner must garner victories in states that total a minimum of 270 electoral votes.*

Click **review the concept** to jump to where the material was discussed in the chapter.

All of your end-of-chapter resources and a practice quiz can be found in the **chapter wrap-up** section.

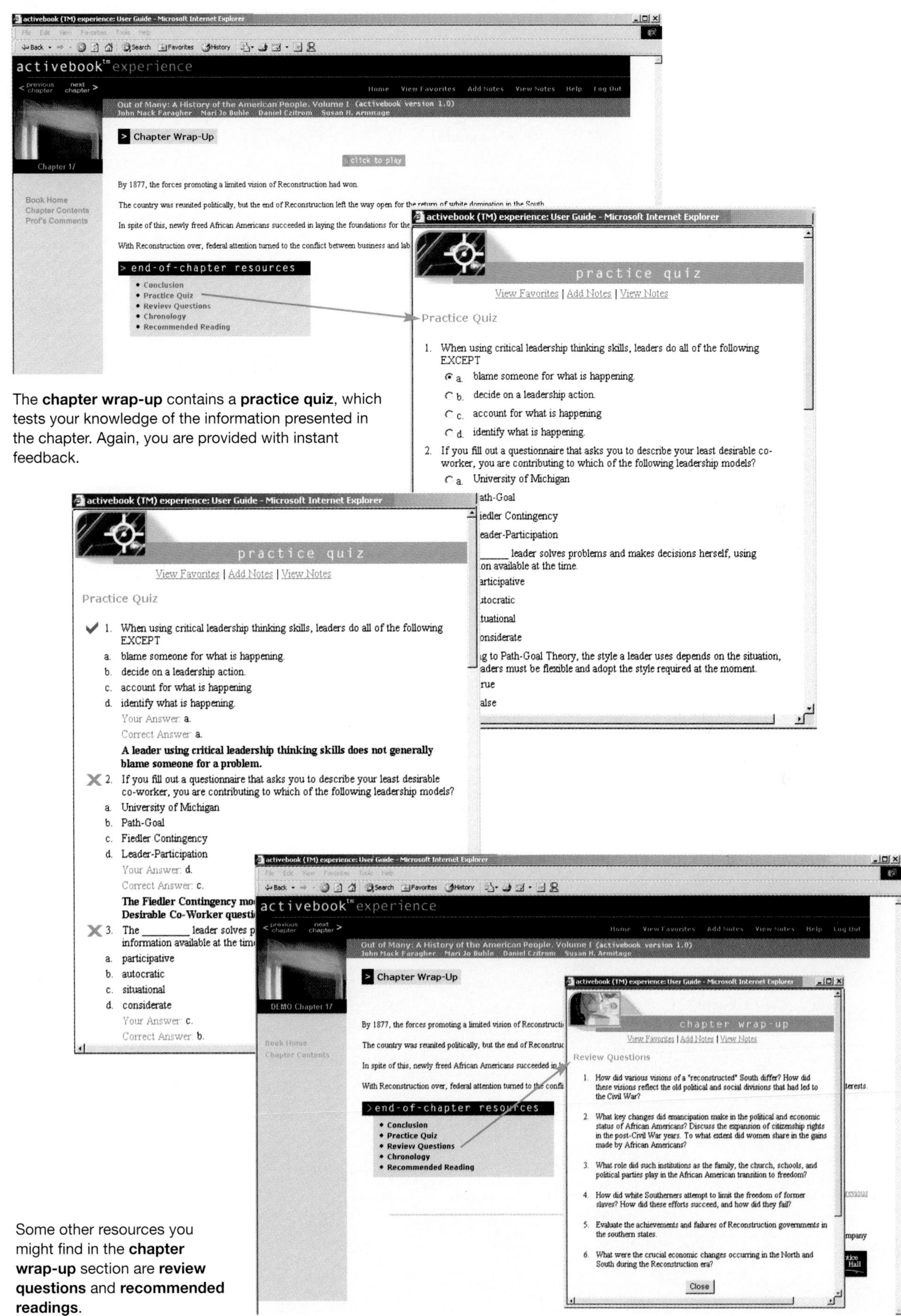

The **chapter wrap-up** contains a **practice quiz**, which tests your knowledge of the information presented in the chapter. Again, you are provided with instant feedback.

Some other resources you might find in the **chapter wrap-up** section are **review questions** and **recommended readings**.

CHAPTER 1

Developing a Customer Orientation

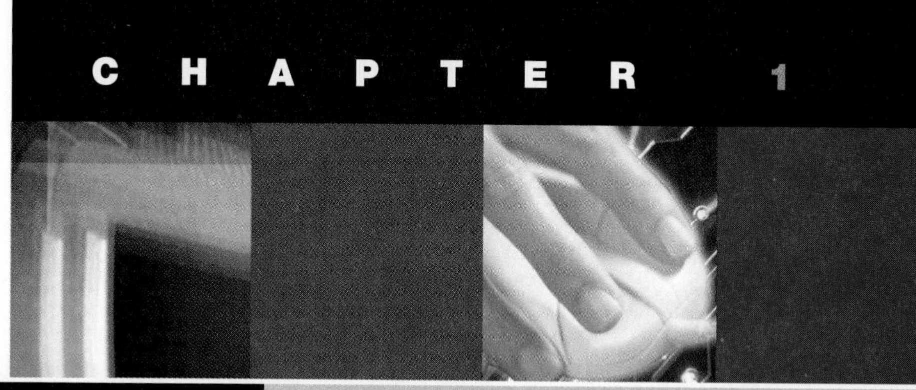

Chapter Outline

What's Ahead

OPERATIONS MANAGERS AT THE RECREATION CENTER

We begin this chapter by introducing you to four managers and their work. The four, Tom Jackson, Cheryl Sanders, Luis Flores, and Fred Silverton, meet early each morning as they work out before heading off to their jobs in a diverse set of industries. They are all members of the same recreational facility on the campus of a nearby university. (The facility is modeled after one on our own campus—so it's probably much like one on your campus, too. We'll call it "the Rec Center" from here on out.) The four, quite different in backgrounds, jobs, and personalities, have formed a common friendship. In addition to their interest in working out, they have found they can share thoughts on a variety of issues. In fact, over the last few months, they have found the issues they face have quite a bit in common. In each of the following chapters of this text, conversations between these managers are used to highlight some of the chapter's topics. We think reading these conversations will provide a context for understanding what the chapter is about and what to look for as you study.

The four managers represent the diversity of jobs that exist in operations management. Two work in service industries and two in manufacturing. Two work in businesses that customize their offerings and two work for operations that have standardized offerings. Both small and large businesses are represented. The managers are at different stages of career advancement. Because the managers and their jobs are so diverse, you'll be able to learn about a lot of different operational issues and gain a broad exposure to the field from their conversations. For example, just reading the biographical sketches at the beginning of this chapter will help you learn what operations management is all about.

TOM JACKSON

Tom Jackson is a 48-year-old chief of operations for a small but growing airline based in the large southwestern city where he lives. Tom, who is married and has two children, has an undergraduate degree in engineering. He earned an MBA part-time at night while serving full time as an Air Force officer. Tom has spent the last 18 years in the reserves, and will retire in two to three years. He has spent his civilian career with two airlines, leaving a larger company three years ago when an old Air Force friend offered him a chance to get in at the ground level of a new start-up.

Tom's new airline is a regional carrier that offers frequent flights on selected routes. The company is always looking for a way to cut costs and pass the savings on to customers. Minimizing frills on frequent flights along high-traffic routes has made the service both inexpensive (by industry standards) and highly reliable—points that the airline exploits in its advertising. But the company is less flexible than other airlines on certain points. For example, though it does not require a Saturday stay as a prerequisite for a discounted fare, it does restrict ticket exchanges when a passenger's plans change at the last minute. While punctual departure and arrival are a top priority, the airline's check-in time is a little earlier than most other airlines', and employees will not hold a plane for anyone. Tom's airline offers only one passenger class on its flights, and restricts carry-on luggage more than most of its competitors.

CHERYL SANDERS

Cheryl Sanders, 32 years old and single, is a hospital administrator at a small general hospital located in the suburbs outside the city where Tom works. The hospital she administers is part of a much larger chain of hospitals and allied health care facilities based in the Southwest. Cheryl has a master's degree in health administration from a well-known eastern school, and an undergraduate degree in business administration. She began her career with the chain seven years ago and transferred to the hospital where she now works, after receiving a major promotion. While Cheryl is gaining experience at this hospital, she will oversee the entire administrative staff.

Cheryl is considered to be a rising star in her corporation. Though she may not have the seniority some of her contemporaries possess, her ability to think across functional boundaries, or "outside the box," has not gone unnoticed by senior managers. Since assuming her new position, Cheryl has begun to feel more and more pressure to control costs while maintaining excellence in the delivery of a wide range of services. She sees the hospital's mission as providing high-quality health care for common health problems, and when necessary, transferring more complicated cases to specialist hospitals.

FRED SILVERTON

Fred Silverton is 40 years old, single, and very wrapped up in his job as the marketing manager for a division of a large electronics firm. Like Tom Jackson, Fred has an undergraduate degree in engineering; he also has an Ivy League MBA, which he occasionally mentions to those he works with. Fred looks much younger than he is, a fact he fears may not be to his advantage in dealing with others. Coworkers sometimes feel he has a chip on his shoulder. Fred's division manufactures low-end versions of three communication products for the cost-conscious segment of the consumer electronics market. Model changeovers are few and far between; production volumes are high. Because all three products require similar steps, including circuit board preparation, insertion of purchased electronic components, flow soldering, and final assembly, the production process has been automated.

Fred has been with this division for almost two years. Before that he worked for a division that manufactured cutting-edge products, with all the newest features. Innovation was not only rewarded but expected, and the pace of product development was exhilarating. Fred dealt with a variety of customers and products on a day-to-day basis, a challenge he truly enjoyed. Adjusting to the new job has been difficult for him. He finds that product designs rarely change, and the only improvement anyone wants to talk about is squeezing pennies from product cost by enhancing the manufacturing process. While Fred understands the need to cut costs to meet the requirements of a cost-conscious market segment, he begrudges the change in attitude he feels he must make in order to succeed in the new division.

LUIS FLORES

Luis Flores is a 27-year-old production supervisor for a small, privately owned furniture manufacturer with revenues of about $8 million last year. He met his wife, a high school teacher, while attending evening classes at the college. Luis, who is in his eighth year with the business, has always been a self-starter with a great work ethic. He spent his first six years with the company as a machine operator on the factory floor, then moved into a supervisory position after completing his degree in business administration. An accounting major in college, Luis realized early that he wanted to be close to "where the rubber meets the road," as he likes to put it; thus his decision to stay on the floor after graduation.

Luis's company manufactures a wide variety of products, primarily of upholstered wood. Recently the owners have looked into other lines of furniture to appeal to what they see as an increasingly cost-conscious market for their products. The company is known for the quality and contemporary styling of its furniture. But in the last few years discount-priced competitors, whose products have traditionally been limited in quality and styling, have been able to expand their product lines and increase quality without raising their prices significantly. At least for now, Luis feels that the superior styling of his company's products will protect the firm's market share; yet no one can predict how long that situation will last.

> objectives

Take a moment to familiarize yourself with the key objectives of this chapter.

> gearing up

Before you begin reading this chapter, try a short warm-up activity.

> Introduction

This introductory chapter sets the stage for the rest of the book by defining and describing operations management (OM). Operations management is about the processes that organizations use to satisfy their customers. It's a critical business function in both service and manufacturing companies. Its historical focus was more centered on measures of resource utilization, such as productivity and efficiency; nowadays, the focus is on satisfying customers by delivering the value they expect.

An important perspective introduced in this chapter is that the primary purpose of most organizations is to provide some service to customers. Making money is the reward for doing this effectively.

When it's the other way around, companies run the risks of losing their focus, angering their customers, and losing the opportunity to stay in business and serve customers. Since OM is the function responsible for the firm's value-adding activities, this view of business suggests that satisfying customers is the most important focus for operations.

Managing operations well can lead to satisfied customers and is one critical element in business success. To manage operations well requires more than functional excellence; it requires effective communication with customers to know what their expectations are. (The beautician with the best hair-cutting techniques and a reputation for being the best stylist in town can still fail in business if a customer's preferences are ignored, the facility isn't appealing, the job takes too long, or customers are treated rudely.) Most service companies have to bundle facilitating goods with their services, and most manufacturers have to bundle facilitating services with their products, to satisfy their customers.

In addition to understanding customer expectations, operations managers must communicate and work effectively with employees in the other functions of their business—such as finance, marketing, engineering, human resources, and accounting. It takes the coordinated value-adding activities of all of these functions to satisfy customers and gain advantages in competitive markets.

active concept check <

Now let's take a moment to test your knowledge of the concepts you have studied in this section.

> Integrating Operations Management with Other Functions

Managing operations well requires effective interaction with the other functional areas of business. When people from the various functions don't work together well, it is very difficult to effectively satisfy customers or even make minor improvements in operations. That's one of the major reasons why virtually all business students—regardless of their major—take a course in operations management. Satisfying customers takes coordinated effort across all functional areas.

In many companies, workers are organized into their jobs and given office space according to their functional area. The marketing people work with other marketing people, have a boss from the marketing function, and don't often see workers from other functional areas. The same holds for financial managers, accountants, human resources professionals, engineers, and operations managers. Figure 1.1 shows the typical organizational chart for companies like this. Notice that the only link between the functional areas is at the very top of the corporate hierarchy. In other words, any interaction between functions only occurs at high levels of the company. Most workers don't understand the activities and work concerns of their colleagues in other functional areas. What's more, they have no way to learn these concerns. It's been said that they are stuck in their *functional silos*. Look at Figure 1.1 and you can see why that term has been used: The functional areas even look like the grain silos found near railroad tracks in agricultural communities or the shipping docks where tankers are loaded. If this chart were on white paper as most are, the white spaces on the organizational chart would hide lots of cross-functional relationships that could be very helpful if they were well managed.

An example of the difficulty of working in functional silos is provided by Claudio, a welder at Cast-Fab, Inc., in Cincinnati, Ohio. Cast-Fab is a foundry where hot molten metal is poured into a mold and cast into various parts. These casings, and other forms of metal, are then fabricated into a variety of applications.

A few years ago, Claudio had a great money-saving idea. One particular machine casing that Cast-Fab made for an industrial customer required a number of internal welds. The casing was a rectangular cube that was completely open on one side and had three compartments separated by internal dividers, as illustrated in Figure 1.2. The internal dividers had to be reinforced once they had been riveted in place, a task that was accomplished by spot-welding the joints on both sides of the dividers. To allow welders to reach the dividers through a closed side of the cube, three holes had to be cut in the metal casing opposite the open side of the cube. When the welders were finished spot-welding the dividers, they welded the three access holes shut. Later on, the welds on the access holes were ground down, and the entire casing was "painted" using an electrolytic coating process. As a result, customers were not aware that the access holes had ever existed.

Since Claudio and all the other welders he knew could actually (and more easily) climb into the casing through the open side to do the spot welding, they usually chose not to use the access holes. The only reason the holes were there was that the product engineer who designed the casing had put

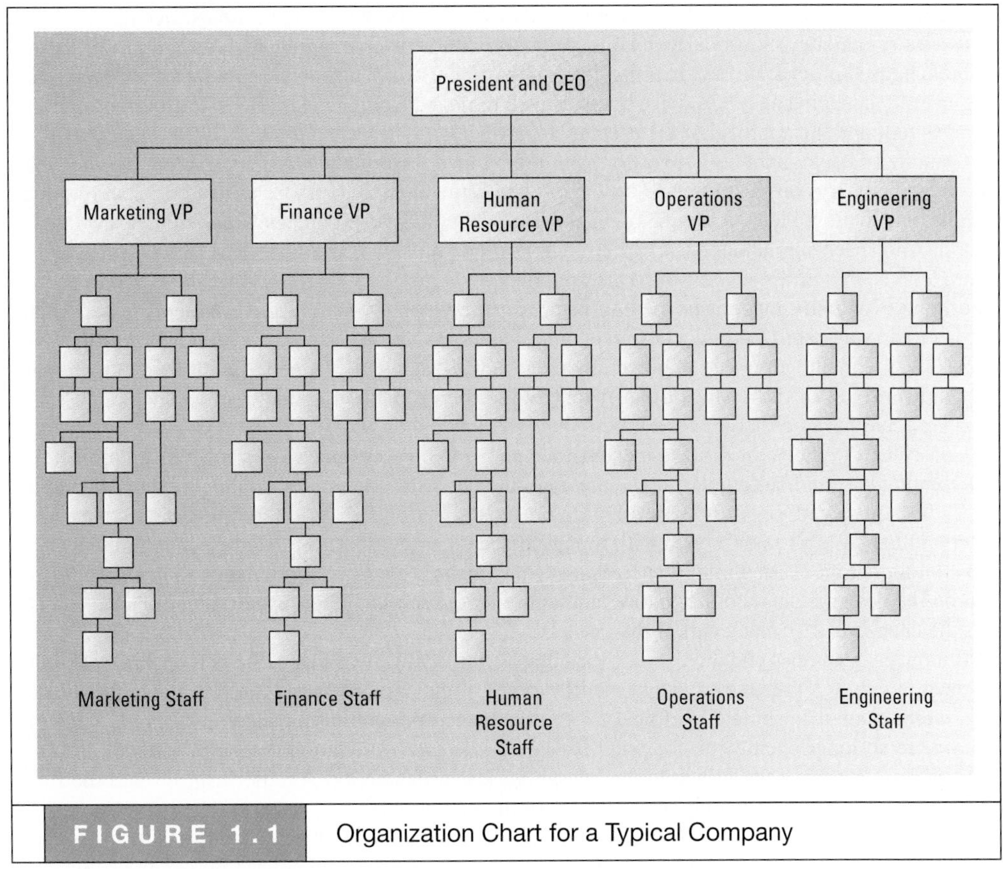

FIGURE 1.1 Organization Chart for a Typical Company

them on the blueprint, quite possibly before a subsequent engineering change resulted in the opposite side wall being removed to make it open (and the no-brainer way to weld the internal dividers!). Since nobody used them, Claudio suggested to his boss that the fabrication department should stop cutting the holes in the casing. Since the customer had no use for the holes, cutting them was a waste of the fabricator's time; welding them shut was a waste of the welder's time; and prepping the holes for coating wasted time in the paint and coating department.

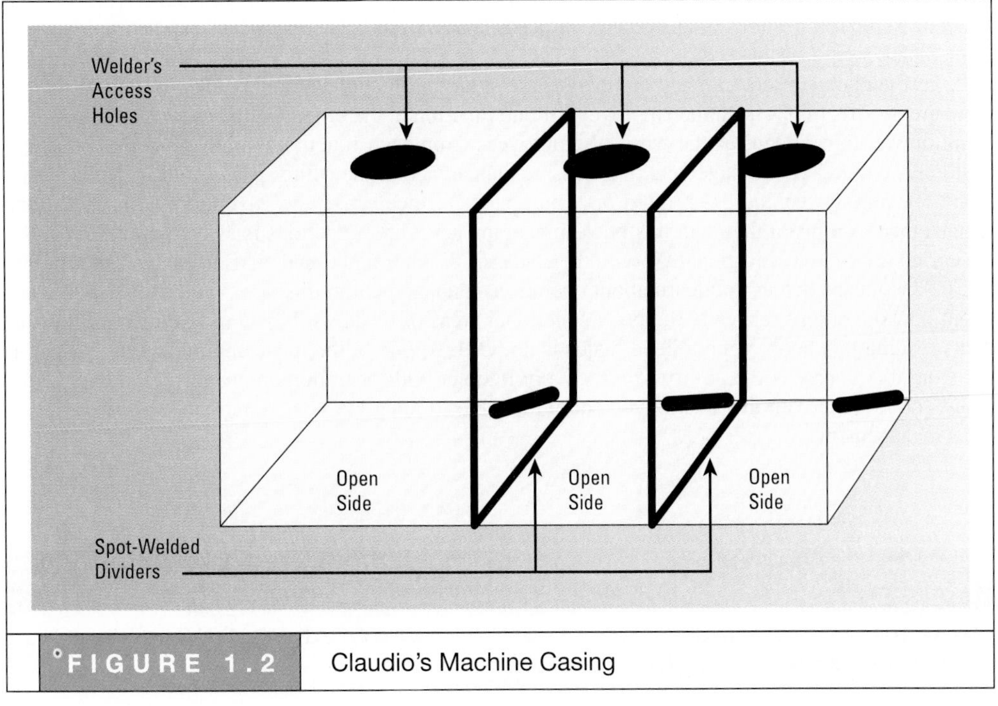

FIGURE 1.2 Claudio's Machine Casing

Figure 1.3 shows a portion of Cast-Fab's organizational structure at that time. Notice that the company was organized traditionally, by function. Not only were finishing, welding, and fabrication workers housed in separate departments; those departments were physically separate from each other. Engineering occupied an office space that was well removed from the plant floor. Furthermore, design changes required the approval of all affected departments.

Claudio's boss thought his suggestion was a great idea. He said he would pass it on, but the welding coordinator was on vacation, and by the time he came back to work, Claudio's boss had forgotten to call back about the idea. A couple of weeks later, Claudio worked on a new casing and saw that his idea had not been implemented. Unlike most workers, however, Claudio didn't give up easily; he reminded his boss of his suggestion. This time his boss's message got through to the welding coordinator, and eventually made it to the engineering supervisor's desk. All the engineering supervisor needed to do was to tell a product design engineer to have a drafter change the master blueprint on the AutoCad system and a process engineer change the work standards (time required for cutting, welding, and finishing of the casing) used in scheduling the production of the casing. The whole set of changes could have been completed in less than 15 minutes.

Unfortunately, the engineering supervisor happened to be very busy with a new design project that was running late, and he forgot to make these simple requests. After several more attempts, Claudio's boss's boss managed to get the part diagram changed—but nobody told the fabrication coordinator. After another casing came through with the usual access holes, another adventure in communication, and a lot more time wasted in the functional silos, Claudio's boss finally managed to get the information on the design change to the folding and cutting workers. Only because of Claudio's persistence was the change finally made part of the process.

But the story doesn't end there. Once the engineering change was made, the person who scheduled production didn't get the message that the next order of the casing would require less time in the cutting, welding, and finishing departments. Then that scheduler got an unwelcome surprise. Since the holes were no longer being cut, the plant had more idle time, utilization of equipment had dropped, and the v.p. for operations was complaining about low productivity! Another trip through the functional silos was required to straighten that side of the matter out.

Cast-Fab's president and CEO, Jim Bushman, was new on the job when Claudio made his suggestion. He had been encouraging workers to make suggestions that would either improve the company's process or enhance the employees' work life. Maybe that's why Claudio didn't give up. Bushman tells Claudio's story in public frequently, because it illustrates the problems companies encounter. Their processes cut through the white spaces of their organization chart, but their people and decision-making systems can't.

Things have changed at Cast-Fab. Today, Claudio can make suggestions at regular meetings of his cross-functional workgroup. The group includes workers from all the various functions—engineers, production planners, and marketing representatives. His team has full responsibility for a particular set of products. The whole team works at the same physical location because all the members have been collocated to the shop floor. Because all functions are represented at the work group meetings and because everyone works at the same location every day, the group members can readily see and understand the implications of any change request. Today, Claudio's suggestions can be implemented immediately.

Like Claudio, workers in many companies are stuck in functional silos. Notice in Figure 1.1 that there are no direct lines from the employees of one function to the other. On the other hand, just satisfying one customer requires the work of employees from each function. In other words, satisfying customers requires the management of processes that cut across the white spaces of the organizational chart. (Assuming the chart is printed on white paper.) Since satisfying customers with operations management is a major theme in this book, managing across the functions is also a major theme. We have tried very hard to integrate OM with the concerns of other functional areas in each chapter of this book. That means that as you learn about operations management in this book, you should also learn about how operations relates to the other functional areas of business. If you're like most of the students reading this book, your college major is not OM, so one of the most important benefits you'll get from this course is the ability to effectively interact with operations managers. In other words, when you're done with this course you should be able to integrate your functional area with operations management.

active concept check

Now let's take a moment to test your knowledge of the concepts you have studied in this section.

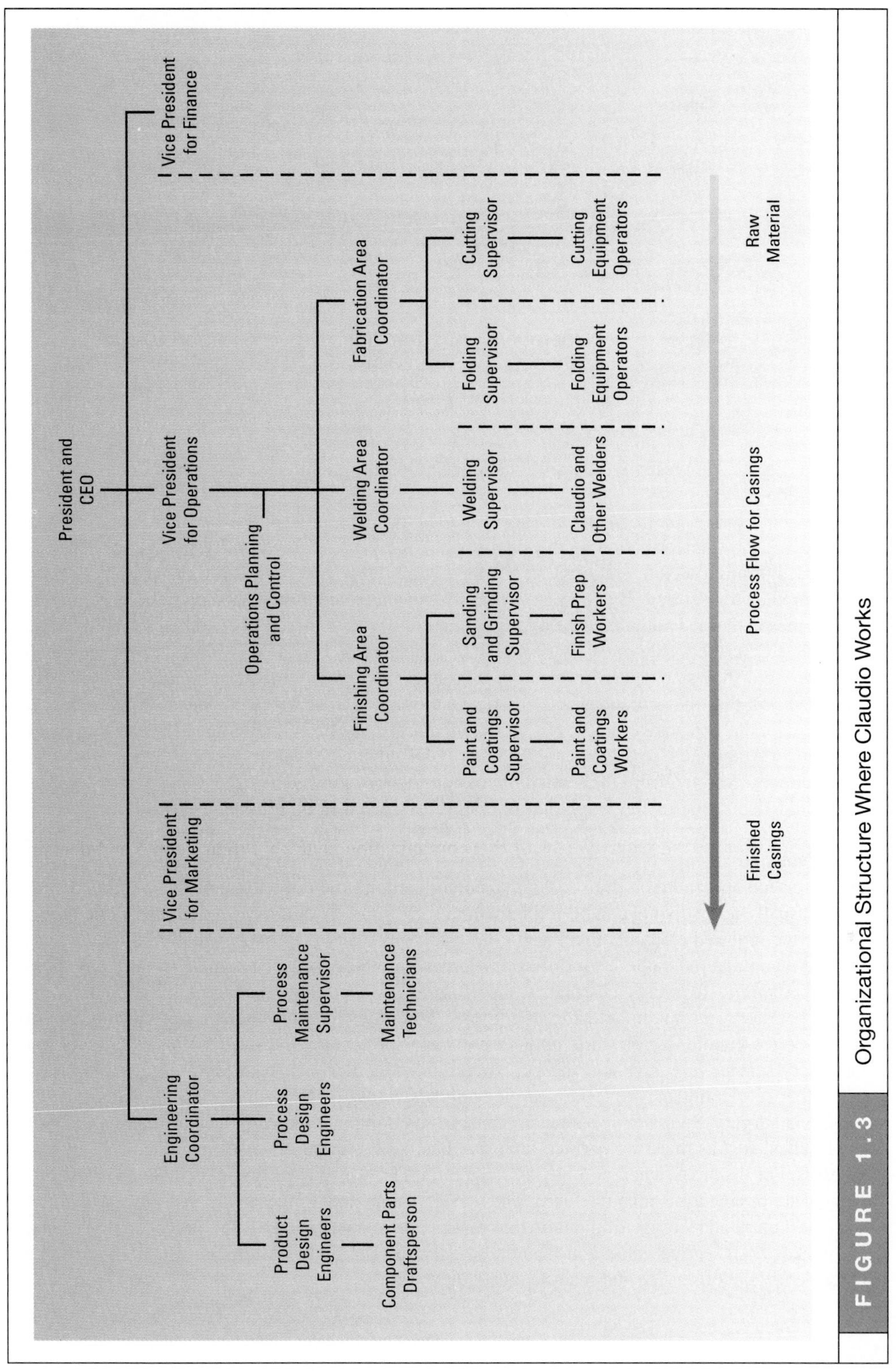

FIGURE 1.3 Organizational Structure Where Claudio Works

What is Operations Management?

Management entails planning, leading, organizing, and controlling an organization's human and capital resources in order to accomplish its objectives. **Operations management** is the administration of processes that transform inputs of labor, capital, and materials into output bundles of products and services that are valued by customers. As such, operations management is not just about how people manage factories; it's just as much about how you run a radio station, municipal park, or special

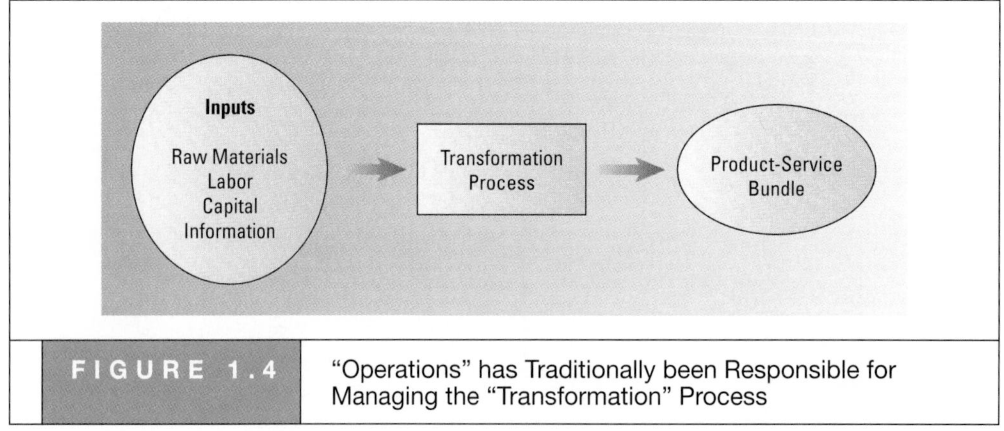

FIGURE 1.4 "Operations" has Traditionally been Responsible for Managing the "Transformation" Process

fundraiser. Figure 1.4 presents the traditional conception of operations management consistent with this definition.

OM is about both *manufacturing* and *services.* The primary value added by manufacturing operations involves the transformation of physical (or tangible) materials into physical goods. The value that is added through such operations can be either stored or transported as long as the physical good can be stored or transported. By contrast, the primary value added by service operations is not tangible. This means that the value created by service operations is generally consumed as the operations are conducted. Services cannot easily be stored or transported. This distinction between manufacturing and services shows up clearly in macroeconomic trends. From a macroeconomic point of view, it has been shown that the percentage of Americans employed in services has been growing in recent decades. Also, the percentage employed in manufacturing has been declining. It is also true that the percentage of American Gross Domestic Product (GDP) that comes from services and the dollar volume of services exported from the United States continues to grow.

Table 1.1 lists some of the ways that operations are used to add value. These include physical change, transportation, storage and distribution, inspection, exchange, information, and physiological change. Notice that some of the ways that value is added seem to fit manufacturing operations and some fit service operations. In most cases, customers require more than one of these forms of value, and they usually don't distinguish between them in their mind. They simply expect the value provider to bundle the required elements together in one package. Customers don't usually buy their service value and manufactured value from different sources. In other words, customers usually buy a *product-service bundle.* To satisfy customers, therefore, most operations managers must focus on both service operations and manufacturing operations. That doesn't mean there's a 50-50 mix in every product-service bundle. If you think about a counselor or psychiatrist for example, the operation is clearly very service intensive and the percentage of value derived from facilitating goods is very small. Other service-intensive product-service bundles would include fitness training, auditing, consulting, and surgery. Such service-intensive businesses dominate the economy in many areas of the United States. Just as there are service-intensive businesses, there are also manufacturing-intensive businesses. For example, when you buy a refrigerator, car, washing machine, or wrench, most of the value you are paying for is manufactured. The service component of these bundles is primarily related to the distribution and storage of the item that makes it available exactly when you need it. Because it usually takes both service value and manufactured value to satisfy customers, this book provides a balanced coverage of service and manufacturing operations.

active exercise

Take a moment to apply what you've learned.

Productivity is the relationship between output and input for any process. Mathematically speaking, that's the ratio of output to input (output ÷ input). Based on the traditional view of OM presented in Figure 1.4, improvements in operations management would provide higher levels of productivity. Higher levels of productivity, in turn, lead to a higher standard of living for those who have a stake in the process. That is a good reason for companies to focus their attention on operations management

TABLE 1.1 Value-Adding Activities

Value-Adding Activity	Definition	For Instance
Physical Change	Physically changing the shape or form of input materials.	• Sawing trees into dimensional lumber. • Baking flour, yeast, and salt into bread. • Cosmetic surgery. • Photo film developing.
Transportation	Transporting material or customers from where they are to where they need to be.	• Commuting on the local mass transit system. • UPS delivering packages. • Flying on an airline. • Shipping coal or grain via the railroad. • Transporting cars from the assembly plant to the local dealership.
Storage/Distribution	Stocking quantities of material until needed by a customer.	• Storing gas at the corner filling station. • Warehousing toys until Christmas. • A vending machine keeping soda cold until you want to buy a can. • Managing the inventory at any retail store.
Inspection	Stratifying, comparing, or verifying some characteristic to a predetermined standard or specification.	• The IRS monitoring the income tax system. • An audit performed by a public accounting firm. • The USDA grading meat before it gets to the grocery store. • Administering the SAT, ACT, MCAT, LCAT, GMAT, or GRE tests.
Exchange	Facilitating the interchange of product-service bundles.	• The New York Stock Exchange. • The classified ads of a local newspaper. • Operating an employment agency or real estate agency. • Operating a consignment shop.
Information	Transferring or disseminating valuable information.	• Advertising. • The class for which you're reading this (we hope!). • Swimming lessons. • Watching CNN. • Calling 1-800-555-1212. • The doctor's office.
Physiological	Improving the customer's physical or mental state.	• Working out at the health club. • Disneyland! • Going to church. • Seeing an eating disorders therapist.

and make certain that their practices are not wasteful. On the other hand, an excessive focus on productivity can be dangerous. Training employees or buying new and superior equipment can lead to decreases in productivity because the input part of the ratio (in the denominator) increases with such actions. As a result, managers who are rewarded for maintaining or improving productivity levels often choose to forego opportunities to invest in training, new equipment, product-service bundle redesign, or other ways to improve the value they deliver to customers. Consequently, improving customer service is a better focus for operations managers than improving productivity.

Measuring productivity can be a challenge in services but is more straightforward in manufacturing. In the case of services, it can be difficult to measure inputs and outputs as discrete units. (How can you measure the fitness you gain from a workout in a gym?) As a result, productivity measures in services are usually geared more toward the availability and utilization of resources. For example, the number of visits to the weight room per day can be used as an indicator of the value generated by that facility.

Operations management is just as relevant to service-intensive businesses as to manufacturing companies. Pictured here is Miami University's new Recreation Sports Center (Rec Center). We use this venue to illustrate many of the concepts presented in this book.

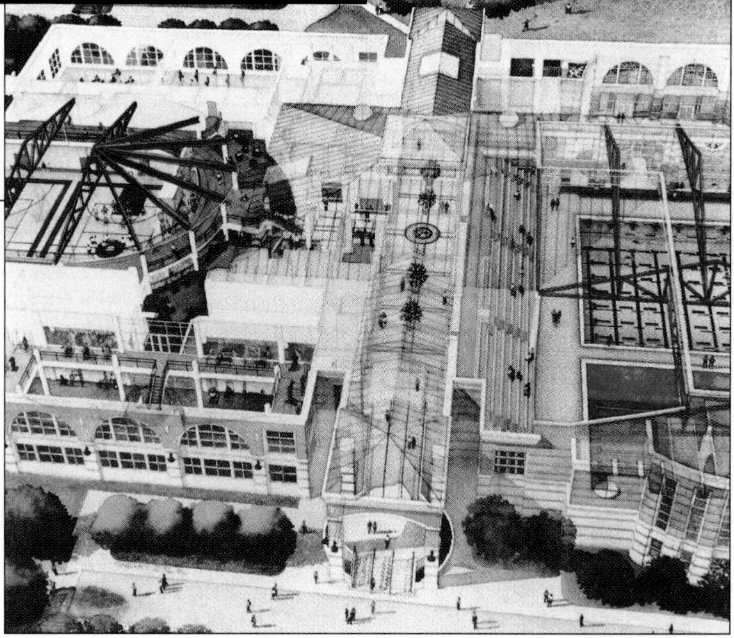

active exercise

Take a moment to apply what you've learned.

active concept check

Now let's take a moment to test your knowledge of the concepts you have studied in this section.

Operations Management in the Age of E-Commerce

E-commerce refers to the integrated set of computer technologies that enables consumers and businesses to conduct business over electronic networks. Today that means doing business on the Internet, whereas in the past companies would use Electronic Data Interchange (EDI) across their own networks with suppliers and/or customers. Web browsers that use the Internet have replaced many of the internal computer systems that companies once used for EDI. Additionally, the Internet boom has made e-commerce a much bigger and more pervasive aspect of business than it was when companies had to spend their own money to create their private EDI networks. The benefits of e-commerce include reduced paperwork, improved decision making, reduced inventory requirements, and more rapid response to customer requirements.

E-commerce activities generally fall into two categories: business to business (B2B) and business to consumer (B2C). B2B e-commerce involves using the Internet to communicate between businesses that are related in a chain of suppliers and customers. This information can then be used to make operational decisions in the individual businesses, and, as a result, the entire chain can be more coordinated. For example, e-commerce allows a vendor company to determine what it needs to supply to its business customers by simply accessing the production schedules of that company—no purchase orders are needed, and no time is required for a decision maker to prepare the purchase order. Further, a vendor company may be able to forecast what will be needed on the basis of sales information made available by its customers. For example, a paper pulp supplier to Proctor and Gamble's tissue-making operation could predict upcoming demand for their pulp by tracking sales information gathered at Wal-Mart's cash registers. Because of the improved coordination, less time elapses between the demand and supply of those items. Consequently, there is less need for businesses to carry extra inventory or excess capacity just in case they need to respond to unforeseen surges in demand.

B2C e-commerce involves using the Internet to market a firm's value offerings to customers and gather information regarding customer preferences and opinion. For example, electronic marketplaces, such as the eBay on-line auction site have become very popular ways to facilitate trade. Companies use their web sites to promote themselves to prospective employees and to advertise the superior aspects of their product-service bundle to customers. Many companies also allow customers to place orders from electronic forms on their web sites and use their web sites to collect payments from their customers.

E-commerce has had a huge impact on the way business is conducted, and this impact is only likely to become greater in the future. In short, it has made business decision making more *integrated* and less functionally oriented. **Enterprise Resources Planning (ERP) systems** are software packages that integrate decision support programs for the various functional areas with a common database. The ability to easily gather and immediately transfer information anywhere in the world at any time has allowed companies to make marketing, operations, and financial decisions based on the same information. They can therefore coordinate their functional areas on a global basis without the delays previously required for the exchange of information. Sales information can immediately be reflected in financial and operational decisions. Operational information—such as capacity, schedules, and inventory levels—can immediately be reflected in marketing and financial decisions. Financial information—such as the cost of capital, production costs, and so on—can immediately be reflected in the decisions of other functional areas. Consequently, OM in the age of e-commerce is much more integrated with the other functional areas of business. Operational decision makers can no longer afford to take a functional perspective when they make decisions; rather, they have to take a business perspective and make sure that their decision fits with the decisions that are being made by others in the organization.

> **active example**

Take a closer look at the concepts and issues you've been reading about.

> **active concept check**

Now let's take a moment to test your knowledge of the concepts you have studied in this section.

> Miami's New Recreation Center: Service-Intensive Operations Management

Recreational athletics have long been a part of most college campuses. Providing for the athletic recreational expectations of several thousand students requires universities to create and manage a significant service operation. Miami University in Ohio is no exception. However, as the interests of students change and develop over time, so do their recreational needs. The old standbys—basketball, running, swimming, racquetball, and weight lifting—are as popular, or more so, on campus as they have ever been, but today's student body wants more: new activities, new spins on old hobbies, and all in a social setting. Mountain climbing has moved indoors in the form of climbing walls. Soccer has also moved indoors and hockey skates have come off the ice and on to roller blades. Steppers and other sophisticated devices can give you a workout faster and more efficiently. Mile after mile on stationary bikes has turned into computer-simulated steppers and road rallies. In many ways, exercise has become high tech. Additionally, other needs of the customer, otherwise known as the student, have become apparent. Working out, recreation, and competition have picked up a "social" twist. The recreational venue is now seen as a place to gather or meet. It is a place to see and be seen by others.

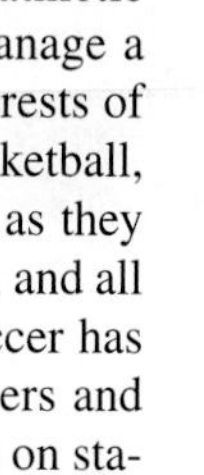

Miami's new Student Recreation Center opened in 1994. It includes an indoor running track, basketball courts, indoor soccer, three pool areas (an Olympic-size pool with 1,200-seat natatorium, a 10m platform diving well, and a leisure pool complete with a wading area for small children and a 14-person hot tub spa), racquetball courts, dance/combative arts rooms, state-of-the-art weightlifting facilities, aerobic exercise equipment, common areas for meeting and socializing, a small snack and sandwich shop where students may also use their meal plans in lieu of cash, a pro shop, and even a big screen TV. Besides local, regional, and even national swimming and diving competitions held there, many other activities use the center as a venue for participants and spectators alike. Along with a dedicated staff, these facilities are operated in such a way as to provide valuable opportunities for students and others from the university community to directly meet their recreational needs.

In a broader sense, the recreation center provides many indirect benefits to the university community. By making the university more attractive to incoming students, more prospective students apply for admission. The more applicants to choose from, the better qualified each incoming first-year class will be. The more qualified students admitted to the university, the higher the level of learning accomplished in the classroom. The higher the level of learning, the better the graduate. The better the graduate, the better the reputation of the school and the value of the degree from that school. In addition, the presence of the recreation center can help with faculty recruitment, which directly influences the quality of the student experience and their value to hiring firms.

It should be clear from the above description that Miami University's recreation center is just as much an operation as a car factory. Operations management is just as relevant to the rec center's managers as it is to a plant manager in a manufacturing company. There are customers to be satisfied—in this case, the customers are students, faculty, university staff, community members, and organizations (such as fraternities, sororities, the NCAA, or other outside groups) who use the facility for special events and competitions. The rec center has inputs (facilities, labor, expertise, and management), outputs (improved client fitness, educational events, formal and informal social events, organized and informal competition, etc.), and processes (for example, maintenance of equipment, scheduling of venues, safety procedures, customer satisfaction measurement, and the individual workout procedures that are facilitated).

Operations management at the rec center involves planning resource capacity (deciding how much of each type of equipment and group fitness activities to provide), scheduling existing resources to demand needs, and monitoring the existing processes—such as check-in, towel laundry, cleaning, and maintenance—to ensure that they are working as they should. In addition, managers must define jobs, train and supervise workers, and manage an inventory of towels, balls, skates, ropes, pro-shop items, food, and equipment.

Operations management at the recreation center does bear many similarities to OM at manufacturing plants, especially those that provide a highly customized product-service bundle. Most of the rec center's customers expect a unique and personalized service each time they come in, thus the workers, schedules, and facilities must be flexible enough to accommodate a wide diversity of customer expectations. (In the water sports area alone, you might find a two-year-old in a wading pool, a world-class athlete completing a training regimen, a physical therapy patient walking against a current, and a group of retirees doing water aerobics.) In addition, there must be enough capacity to meet this highly diverse demand during peak periods without excessive service lead times.

Despite the similarities, OM is clearly somewhat different for this service process than for a manufacturing process. For example, the product-service bundle includes much more intangible value: social events and physical fitness are difficult to inventory! Productivity, too, has to be thought of in different terms. The staff does keep close tabs on the number of guests at each venue on an hour-by-hour basis. Thus, they can monitor productivity in the form of participants per worker hour. When they do a good job of forecasting participant levels, and schedule workers accordingly, they'll reach their productivity targets.

video exercise

Take a moment to apply what you've learned.

Customer Service: The Purpose of Organizations

Many current business leaders believe that the basic purpose of any business is to provide financial benefits to shareholders. We challenge this view.

First, many businesses are nonprofits—companies that have been established to provide some needed service. Your university's local employee credit union may be such a business. It exists to provide employees with a financial service, not to provide owners with a profit. Similarly, the local theater, government agencies, religious organizations, and United Way groups usually provide services without seeking a profit. Profit-seeking companies are not the only type of business organization. Second, profit which derives from both revenue and efficient management is a business reward for satisfying customer needs. Though some individuals may believe that their organization exists primarily for the purpose of rewarding the owners financially, maximized long-run financial performance comes from providing some sustained benefit to the organization's customer(s).

Third, although long-term business survival is based on profitability (among other things), long-term profitability comes from sustained competitive advantage, and that is derived from consistently satisfying customers—not just maintaining a high level of productivity. True, without adequate profit that comes from sufficient levels of productivity, a business sacrifices the ability to meet its customers' future needs. Profit is required to maintain the level of shareholder investment necessary to sustain the business and is therefore essential to the ongoing development of the business. But you need a horse to pull a cart, and you shouldn't put the cart before the horse. Profit is like the cart; satisfying customers is like the horse. If profit is the primary purpose of your business, the cart is before the horse.

For these reasons, we believe that the primary purpose of all organizations, including businesses, is to meet customer needs and satisfy customer expectations. Every organization has a customer, and every customer has expectations regarding that organization's output. This truism holds whether the organization produces a tangible good (such as cars) or provides an intangible service (such as health care), and whether or not it seeks a profit.

The view that business exists primarily for the sake of customers is important to managing well. If a manager believes that the business is there for the customers first, the issue of making a profit will not be overlooked. In fact, making a profit is necessary to staying in business and continuing to satisfy customers. On the other hand, if a manager believes that the business exists to maximize shareholder return, customer satisfaction could easily be sacrificed, over both the short and long term.

IDENTIFYING THE CUSTOMER

A **customer** may be defined as any individual or group that uses the output of a process. From this standpoint, every individual and organization has a number of customers.

Most people would probably define a customer as the target of the service provided by the organization. What they are really thinking of is the **external customer.** For example, a patient who receives medical services in a hospital would be an external customer. But organizations also have **internal customers,** customers who exist within the organization. For instance, a doctor at a hospital may send biological specimens to a lab for analysis. A particular type of analysis may require several procedures performed in sequence by a team of technicians. This situation creates a set of internal customers within the hospital. From the viewpoint of anyone who is seeking to assess the lab's performance, the doctors are external customers, that is, they use the lab's analytical services. But the lab is a customer, too, in that it must use the paperwork the doctors create to provide the desired service. Finally, from the standpoint of an administrator who seeks to measure the effectiveness of the hospital's patient services, the doctor and the lab are both internal customers.

Because the only real value created by an organization is derived through the satisfaction of its customers' needs and expectations, understanding the definition of the customer within all contexts of an organization is critical. Members of an organization tend to identify only the *paying customer* as the customer they must satisfy. This critical consumer is actually the external customer. In many cases, other parties, or *stakeholders* in the organization's output, must also be defined as external customers, even though they may not be direct consumers of the organization's output. Stakeholder groups such as stockholders, government agencies, local communities, and workers and their families are affected by an organization's activities and can therefore be considered customers; they rely in some way on the output of certain organizational processes. For instance, the U.S. Internal Revenue Service (like the tax-collecting agencies in municipalities, states, and other countries) is a customer of the payroll department in most organizations, because it relies on information about employee salaries and withholdings. In today's complicated marketplace, balancing the needs of these other stakeholder groups with those of the direct consumer, whose sense of value determines the maximum price that can be charged for the organization's output, is very difficult. In many cases, meeting the needs of indirect stakeholders adds to the cost of doing business without directly increasing the value to the paying consumer.

While the organization's ability to satisfy the paying customer has been, and always will be, the primary focus of the operations process, contemporary thinking also acknowledges a series of customer-supplier relationships within the organization. When an assembly worker pushes a part down the line to the next workstation, that worker is supplying an internal customer. Internal customer-supplier relationships exist at all levels of the organization. For example, when the vice president of purchasing sits down with the vice president of manufacturing to discuss how parts can be better delivered to the assembly line, the vice president of purchasing is looking for a way to better serve an internal customer. When a chef asks the server to clarify a meal order, the chef is dealing with an internal customer.

A business process usually includes many internal customer-supplier relationships, at a variety of levels. Organizations in which individuals view their jobs independently of those employees with whom they interact will miss many opportunities to improve the way they satisfy the needs of internal customers. Improving both internal and external customer relationships can have a synergistic effect on the cumulative value the firm creates for the paying customer.

Frequently, a network of internal and external customers must work together, coordinating their efforts to satisfy the *ultimate customer,* usually thought of as the consumer. If you ate breakfast at a cafeteria or restaurant this morning, you were the ultimate customer of a farming operation; a meat packaging process; transportation, warehousing, and other wholesaler activities; a food preparation service; a Food and Drug Administration inspector; a garbage collection service; and a host of other service and manufacturing operations. In other words, you were the ultimate customer in a **value chain,** which is a group of sequentially related value-adding activities. The meat packager, on the other hand, was the farmer's external customer. To provide value to the value chain's ultimate customer, organizations must have a clear understanding of what is needed to satisfy a host of internal and external customers.

active exercise <

Take a moment to apply what you've learned.

PROVIDING THE RIGHT GOODS AND SERVICES

To satisfy the ultimate customer, an organization must (1) define a product-service bundle to meet a targeted set of customer expectations; (2) develop a value-adding system capable of meeting those expectations; (3) establish and effectively use an operational performance measurement system; and (4) obtain and effectively respond to customer satisfaction feedback. You could even put this in the form of the following *customer satisfaction equation:*

$$\text{Customer Satisfaction} = (\text{product} - \text{service bundle performance}) - (\text{customer expectations})$$

For example, on a visit to Pittsburgh to attend a conference, one of the authors was absolutely delighted by the service he received as a customer of the Pittsburgh subway system. His delight was due to two factors. First, his expectations of what his experience would be like were extremely low. Visions of a dirty, poorly lit, and potentially unsafe subway station, along with noisy, crowded, and graffiti-covered subway cars, were foremost in his mind as he set out from his downtown hotel and walked to the station. Second, the subway experience turned out to be just the opposite of what he expected. The station was spacious and well lit, with clean white walls (no graffiti!). Soft classical music filled the facility. The cars were quiet, clean, and fast. Signs and train schedules were readily available, and the cost was modest. The customers and service personnel were polite and respectful, and the atmosphere was assuring in terms of personal safety. In short, the difference between high-service performance and low customer expectations was very significant, and the result was a delighted customer.

Define a Product-Service Bundle

Customers expect to get some combination of goods and services with every purchase. A **good** is a tangible object or product that can be created, transferred, or stored and used later. A **service** is an intangible and perishable benefit. Services are created and used simultaneously, or nearly simultaneously. While a service can't be stored for later use, its effect may last over time.

In practice, almost all purchases of goods also include purchases of **facilitating services**—those services that allow the customer to enjoy the benefits of the good's intended use. What does a customer purchase when she hands the auto dealer a cashier's check? If all she really purchases is steel, plastic, and rubber, then she should not care whether she drives her purchase home or carries it in a large number of boxes ("Some assembly required"). Obviously, when a customer purchases a car, she is also buying the facilitating services of the workers who assembled the car, the trucker who delivered it to the dealer, and the mechanic who prepared it for final delivery. Most dealers are more than happy to bundle in a maintenance contract on the new vehicle. Now, with the availability of services like Cadillac's On-Star System, car buyers have the option of bundling in automatic roadside assistance, routing assistance, and a host of other services with the purchase of their car.

Similarly, almost all purchases of services include purchases of **facilitating goods**—those goods that allow for the transfer of a service's value to the customer. Let's say you just bought a pair of athletic shoes. You had to have them. They're the latest rage. They're even endorsed by all three of your favorite professional athletes. Chances are you bought these shoes at a store, which charged you more for the shoes than it paid the distributor (Nike, Reebok, Adidas, etc.). You also paid the store for various services, which probably included a convenient location, on-site storage, and maybe even a guaranteed return policy. In other words, you were seeking a value far greater than the physical value of the rubber, cloth, laces, and binding you received. The store, in turn, paid the distributor for more than the physical value of the rubber, cloth, laces, and binding; it paid for the national promotion campaign (remember the professional endorsements), the availability of an adequate supply of shoes at the beginning of the athletic season, shipping and handling, and the privilege of returning unsold or damaged goods. Finally, the distributor paid some manufacturer (probably in Southeast Asia) more for the shoes than the cost of the materials. It paid for the assembly service, as well as the coordination of work-force schedules and material procurement. In most cases, whether a customer purchases a good or a service, the total value of the purchase usually includes a "bundle" of goods and services. We'll refer to that as a **product-service bundle.**

Because virtually all purchases encompass a bundle of goods and services, focusing solely on managing the physical production of an item may result in poor customer service. For instance, the cost of the physical production of a daily newspaper might be optimized if the publisher were to print one month's supply at a time. The publisher might thereby take advantage of quantity discounts on paper and delivery. But in so doing, the publisher would utterly compromise the effectiveness of the service component of the bundle; the idea of a monthly publication of daily news is absurd.

Managing service operations without considering the linkages to the physical processes that support the service's delivery is equally inadvisable. For instance, you might prefer that your physician come to your home if you are ill or incapacitated. In the past, physicians often made house calls, because they could easily carry the facilitating goods (stethoscope, syringe, bandages, medicine) with them. Today, doctors rely on facilitating goods that are much less portable, including modern diagnostic technologies such as X-rays, CAT Scans, MRIs, EKGs, and sonograms. Considering the value that is added by these facilitating goods, most patients will gladly travel to the hospital or doctor's office to obtain a superior service bundle.

Ultimately, organizations must understand what is important to their customers and create a product-service bundle that will meet the customer's expectations. Even the IRS, which came under a great deal of scrutiny from Congress in 1997 and 1998, has begun to see that it too needs to satisfy customers. The IRS began displaying a new mission statement in its 1998 tax publications, at IRS offices, and on its web site. The mission statement emphasizes service as its major focus. It says that the IRS's

BMW assembles Z3 and M roadsters at their facility in Greer, South Carolina. Most people call this assembly work "manufacturing" and the assembly of bikes at a Wal-Mart or burgers at a restaurant a "service". That suggests that there are many commonalities between so-called service operations and manufacturing operations. In fact, in most cases a product is used to store the service value in the product-service bundle.

mission is to "provide America's taxpayers top quality service by helping them understand and meet their tax responsibilities and by applying the tax law with integrity and fairness to all." This statement contrasts with a statement from the 1980s which pronounced that its primary job was to "collect the proper amount of tax revenue at the least cost."

Naturally, both customer input and the organization's competitive strategy will play a major role in deciding what a firm will provide for customers. In targeting specific customer expectations, smart companies combine products and services to gain customers' attention and keep their loyalty. Focusing only on what has traditionally been referred to as the *service concept* for service firms, or the *key manufacturing task* for manufacturers, is no longer sufficient. Figure 1.5 illustrates the relationship between the definition of the product-service bundle and other basic steps in the development of customer value.

Develop the Value-Adding System

The **value-adding system** is an organized group of interrelated activities and/or processes that creates the product-service bundle and thereby adds the value required by customers. This system includes both the organization's managerial infrastructure and the physical processes it uses. Traditionally, the value-adding system has been referred to as the **service delivery system** in service organizations, or as the *manufacturing process* by manufacturers. The term *value-adding system,* however, reflects the fact that from a competitive and customer-oriented standpoint, the managerial infrastructure, service delivery system, and manufacturing process—as well as the linkages among them—are all critical parts of one system.

As we indicated at the beginning of this chapter, OM has traditionally been defined as the business function with responsibility for management of the "transformation process" an organization uses to

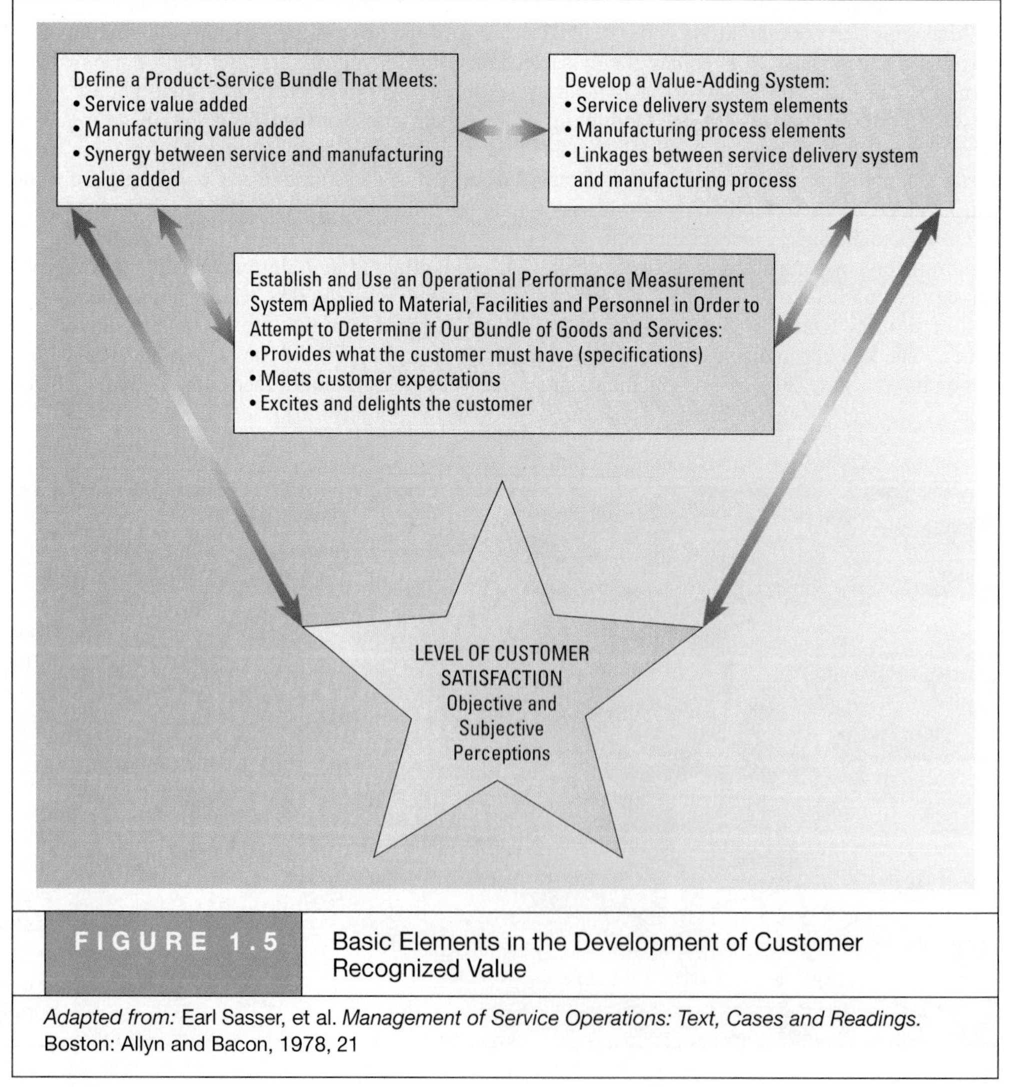

FIGURE 1.5 Basic Elements in the Development of Customer Recognized Value

Adapted from: Earl Sasser, et al. *Management of Service Operations: Text, Cases and Readings.* Boston: Allyn and Bacon, 1978, 21

convert its inputs into outputs. Figure 1.4 illustrates this definition of operations. In the past, this perspective and terminology allowed operations managers to focus on the technical core of the business, or the physical process used to convert inputs to outputs. In car factories, for example, operations managers were responsible for scheduling and coordinating components fabrication and assembly in order to meet goals, such as the number of cars to be made and the cost and quality of the finished product. In banks, operations managers oversaw the back room, where checks were processed, account statements generated, security systems maintained, and monthly mailings collated.

This focus on the technical core often resulted in operations managers who were out of touch with customer expectations, who focused instead on meeting production quotas, keeping costs down, or keeping products "defect free." In other words, the goals of operations managers were related to the things they made and the cost of making them, not to customer satisfaction. Today, the operations function is viewed as a broadly defined system for adding value as customer needs and expectations dictate. Operations professionals don't just change inputs to outputs; they satisfy customers.

Particularly for service-intensive operations, the need for contact with a customer can play an important role in designing the value-adding system. If there is a high need for contact and the customer plays a significant role in the value-adding process, customer needs for information, security, and physical comfort must be considered in designing the value-adding system. If less contact is needed, efficiency can be given greater emphasis when designing the system. Also, if there are parts of the process where customer contact is not as important and these can be removed from the customer's line of sight, these can be designed for efficiency. Thus, you'll find a bank lobby designed for customer comfort and the back room operations (where checks are processed) designed for efficiency. Similarly, airline terminals are designed with comfort in mind, but because the customer doesn't see what happens after they check their bags, the baggage handling services can be designed for efficiency. Table 1.2 provides more information about the impact of customer contact on the design and operation of the value-adding system.

Establish an Operational Performance Measurement System

An **operational performance measurement system** measures the firm's effectiveness in using the value-adding system. This measurement system provides feedback that may be used to monitor, update, and improve the value-adding system. Traditionally, service providers have focused on what they referred to as the *service level,* which was their measure of value added. Manufacturers focused on *product quality specifications.* These are easier to measure and track than is customer satisfaction, and that's probably part of the reason that they are used so widely.

Yet satisfying customers requires more than a high level of service or product quality. The measures that are used to track system performance should reflect what is really important to the customer, rather than what is easy for management to use. In fact, improved performance on any performance measure is meaningless if the customer does not perceive the product-service bundle to be improved. For example, at one time Ford customers expressed concern about the fit of their car doors. Ford responded to their concern by measuring the distance between the door and the fender, as well as the degree to which they closed flush—only to find that what customers really cared about was how easily the door could be opened and what it sounded like when it was closed. Another example is the tendency of fast-food restaurants to add more items to the menu. Instead of boosting product-service bundle value, such decisions threaten the ability to meet critical customer expectations in the areas of speed, quality, and cost.

In service-intensive businesses, both explicit services and implicit services may impact the customer's level of satisfaction. **Explicit services** are the value offerings for which the customer is paying. For example, at a fast food restaurant it's the prepared food, and at a barber it's the haircut. **Implicit services** are the customers' unspoken expectations about how the explicit service will be delivered. Examples of implicit services are friendliness, competence, and trust. Particularly in service-intensive businesses, it's important to recognize customer expectations for implicit services while providing the explicit services of the firm. Implicit services are often the real reason that people choose to do business with particular proprietors.

Obtain Customer Satisfaction Feedback

Many organizations mistakenly think they are measuring customer satisfaction by tracking complaints and warranty claims, which are measures of customer dissatisfaction. Needless to say, customer dissatisfaction is much easier to measure than customer satisfaction. The fact that customer satisfaction may be very difficult to quantify highlights the importance of the operational performance measurement system and reinforces the point that operational measures should be carefully chosen to reflect the values and desires of target customers.

In the mid-1980s, Xerox had a remarkable insight on the measurement of customer satisfaction. In conducting customer surveys, Xerox used a five-point scale for customers to report their level of

TABLE 1.2 The Role of Customer Contact on the Design of Value-Adding Systems

Design Considerations	High-Contact Operation	Low-Contact Operation
Product design	Environment as well as the physical product define the nature of the service.	Customer is not in the service environment.
Quality control	Quality standards often are in the eye of the beholder and hence variable.	Quality standards generally are measurable and hence fixed.
Process design	Stages of production process have a direct, immediate effect on the customer.	Customer is not involved in the majority of processing steps.
Facility location	Operations must be near the customer.	Operations may be placed near supply, transportation, or labor.
Capacity planning	To avoid lost sales, capacity must be set to match peak demand.	Storable output permits setting capacity at some average demand level.
Facility layout	Facility should accommodate the customer's physical and psychological needs and expectations.	Facility should enhance production.
Worker skills	Direct workforce makes up a major part of the service product and so must be able to interact well with the public.	Direct workforce need only have technical skills.
Time standards	Service time depends on customer needs, and therefore time standards are inherently loose.	Work is performed on customer surrogates (e.g., forms), and time standards can be tight.
Wage payment	Variable output requires time-based wage systems.	"Fixable" output permits output-based wage systems.
Forecasting production planning	Forecasts are short-term and time-oriented. Orders cannot be stored, so smooth-ing production flow will result in loss of business.	Forecasts are long-term and output-oriented. Both backlogging and production smoothing are possible.
Scheduling	Customer is in the production schedule and must be accommodated.	Customer is concerned mainly with completion dates.

Source: Richard B. Chase, "Where Does the Customer Fit in a Service Operation," *Harvard Business Review* (November–December 1978): 139.

satisfaction. Customers gave four points if they were "satisfied" with Xerox products and services, and five points if they were "very satisfied." A comparison of individual customer survey responses and whether those customers decided later to purchase more Xerox products showed that those who gave Xerox 5s ("very satisfied") for performance were six times more likely to repurchase than customers who gave the company 4s ("satisfied"). Since this discovery, Xerox has fine-tuned its performance measurement system to use 5s as the only meaningful measure of customer satisfaction.[1]

Brand equity is important from a marketing perspective. The term **brand equity** refers to the general perception of value associated with an organization's product-service bundle. For example, brand equity explains why you will pay more for a pair of Nike's than for some other equally sophisticated

[1]Heskett, Sasser, and Schlesinger, *The Service Profit Chain* (New York: Free Press, 1997), 81.

athletic shoe. Similarly, the concept of brand equity explains why Coca-Cola can charge more for its soft drinks than a manufacturer of generic soft drinks. Brand equity can be measured. In the Coca-Cola example, it's the difference between the price customers will pay for Coke and the price they'll pay for generic drinks. Consequently, brand equity is one indicator of customer satisfaction levels.

John Whitney, professor of management and executive director of the Deming Center for Quality Management at Columbia University, has pointed out that brand equity is both the customer's perception and the delivery system used to back up that perception (Cable News Network, 1995). Brand equity is not just the name of a product or service. Indeed, a successful brand will go downhill quickly if the delivery system changes and the owner can no longer back up the brand's image. A common mistake is to focus on the cosmetic part of brand equity at the expense of the whole. Cadillac, for example, experienced a serious loss of brand equity in the mid-1980s because of quality problems and changes in the product line. The marketing program, which was just as aggressive as ever, had little to do with the loss.

The defined product-service bundle, the value-adding system, and the operational performance measurement system must fit together logically, for that is how customer satisfaction is won and enhanced. Lack of a logical fit among these elements of the whole is the most fundamental hindrance of most efforts to improve customer satisfaction. In this text, the terms *product-service bundle, value-adding system, operational performance measurement system,* and *level of customer satisfaction* are used to emphasize the importance of effectively blending the service and manufacturing operations required to consistently satisfy customers.

If operations managers are focused on providing customer satisfaction, they will take a holistic view of the firm. A firm cannot gain a sustainable competitive advantage without effectively combining the work of various business disciplines (marketing, operations, control, and finance); functional excellence alone will not create a competitive advantage. To use an analogy, sports historians may claim that the New York Yankees of the 1970s were the greatest team money could buy, but they would also agree that the Yankees never lived up to their collective potential. Most sports historians would also agree that the performance of the gold-medal-winning 1980 U.S. Olympic hockey team exceeded the collective potential of the individual players. The team's success may have had more to do with the synergies among the players than with their individual skills. As in sports, the competitive advantage of a business arises as much from the linkages among activities as it does from the individual activities themselves.

In other words, marketing, accounting, and finance professionals must be able to cross functional barriers and develop synergies with operations that will produce a competitive advantage in serving a given set of customers. And operations professionals must also be conversant in marketing, accounting, and finance. Recognition of the importance of these linkages was responsible for the change in manufacturing philosophy that produced the quality revolution of the 1980s in the United States.

> active concept check

Now let's take a moment to test your knowledge of the concepts you have studied in this section.

> Well-Managed Operations: The Source of Customer Satisfaction

To consistently satisfy customers, an organization must deliver a purchase bundle that the customer perceives to have value. Operations management (OM) is directly responsible for the satisfaction of customers through activities that include: (1) the design of the physical transformation processes that provide the specific value a customer desires; (2) the design of systems for planning, scheduling, and controlling the physical work and material flows within those transformation processes; and (3) the design of systems for monitoring and improving the organization's effectiveness in satisfying customers, as well as the effective operation of the planning, scheduling, and controlling systems to create products and services that satisfy customers.

An organization may seek to add value for customers directly or indirectly, through physical alterations, transportation, storage, inspection, exchange, the facilitation of physiological change, the provision of informational services, or other such activities. From the customer's perspective, however, the value created exists only because it is customer, time, or place specific. Customer-specific value implies the creation of value for a particular individual or defined group. Examples of goods or services with customer-specific value include tailor-made suits, prescription eyeglasses, team uniforms, health care, and haircuts. While the creation of value will always have some reference to time, time specificity is most relevant to product-service bundles whose value declines rapidly. A newspaper has time-specific value, as do fresh-cut Christmas trees, the services of a pit crew during an automobile race, and last-minute tax advice during the second week of April. Finally, many service industries may, by definition, place a relatively high level of importance on the place where a service is provided. For instance, civil engineering projects, home repairs, lawn services, and pizza delivery services provide satisfactory customer value only when they are delivered at the exact location the customer specifies.

Most businesses today acknowledge the need to better understand the wants and needs of their customers in order to improve their value-adding systems. We have seen that to be successful, a process must result in products and services that, when bundled together, truly satisfy customer requirements. Customer satisfaction is the true measure of the value-adding system's success. But does "building a better mousetrap" always increase value or customer satisfaction? If so, what does "better" mean? Lower cost? Fewer defects? Even if a product is correctly built to design specifications, is the way it functions an issue? How long it will last? As different as these issues and their implications appear to be, they all might fit some part of the market definition of "better." The successful firm needs to define "better" in terms of the market niche it aims to serve, because improvements that relate to that niche are the only ones the firm will be compensated for.

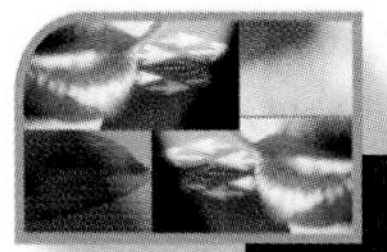

active poll <

What do you think? Voice your opinion and find out what others have to say.

Operations managers who focus on the technical core are in danger of becoming too concerned with the technical excellence of their product or service. They can easily lose sight of what customers expect to receive in the product-service bundle. In 1979, John Delorean tried to launch a stainless steel sports car with a 25-year warranty on key components. While he may well have been ahead of his time (as per Michael J. Fox in the movie *Back to the Future*), he almost surely underestimated the sports car–buying public's reluctance to pay a premium price for a car that would last 25 years. At that time, a 25-year warranty was not part of the market's definition of "better," at least not to the extent that customers would pay for it.

Operations management is important to every business. Operations adds the value that businesses provide to customers. There is little point in achieving excellence in marketing, control, and finance if a business cannot do a good job of managing its operations.

Even for those people who don't manage operations, an understanding of operations management is important. Every organization that has long-term viability conducts some kind of operations, whether or not it groups operations in a separate function or unit. By effectively integrating operational decisions with those in other functions, managers may leverage value creation activities to produce greater customer satisfaction. To use another sports analogy, Joe Montana was an outstanding quarterback because he could think like a receiver; he frequently was able to anticipate the receiver's next move. Jerry Rice, Montana's receiver, was an outstanding receiver because he could think like a quarterback. Because Rice could recognize the pressures that would force Montana to get rid of the ball, he was ready to catch it; he knew what to expect even before the ball was thrown. Just as successful athletic teams depend on players who understand all positions, business organizations need managers who understand the roles and decision-making processes of all functions.

Effective application of OM concepts to other functions in an organization is also critical to business success because of the large number of internal customer-supplier relationships in most businesses. Customer satisfaction can be improved through the application of OM concepts to those relationships, even though they may be outside the operations function. For example, effective scheduling and continuous improvement of operations are critical to the marketing manager, who must coordinate the activities of a sales force with customer information needs and promotional plans; and to the human resources manager, who must coordinate the interviewing and training of job applicants and employees.

Historically, the field of operations management has made significant societal contributions, helping all kinds of organizations to avoid repeating serious mistakes. From this perspective, OM is valuable to managerial decision makers in all functions.

> active concept check

Now let's take a moment to test your knowledge of the concepts you have studied in this section.

> Integrating Operational Decisions

Figure 1.6 presents an overview of this book. You notice that the text can be thought of in three parts. Chapters 1 through 6 deal with issues that pervade any operational decision. The topics covered in these chapters are over-arching considerations to the decisions covered in the remainder of the text. Chapters 7 through 10 cover the structural decisions in operations management. These decisions deal with the physical design of the value-adding system. They have long-term implications because they can't quickly be changed once a facility is built and equipped and personnel are in place. Finally, Chapters 11–16 focus on the infrastructural decisions in OM. These are planning and control decisions about how existing facilities will be used. Obviously, they are constrained by previous structural decisions and have more of a short-term focus.

Figure 1.6 also points out a few of the key relationships between this chapter and other chapters of the text. (It should be obvious that this chapter is foundational to the whole text and there are clearly relationships between material covered in each chapter of this text and material in each of the other

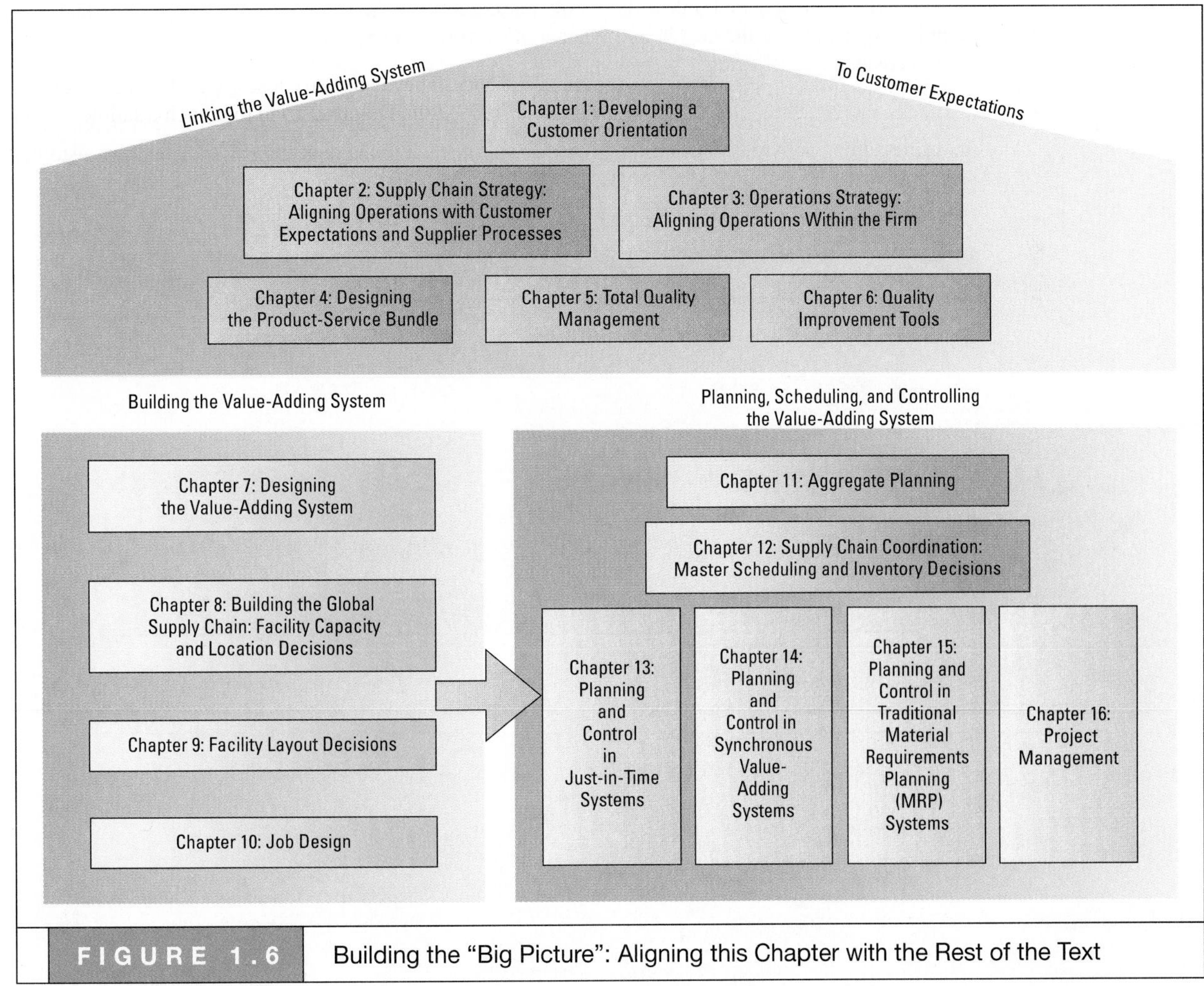

FIGURE 1.6 Building the "Big Picture": Aligning this Chapter with the Rest of the Text

chapters.) This chapter's focus on developing a customer orientation provides an important foundation for our discussion of product-service bundle design in Chapter 4. Without a clear focus on satisfying the customer, it is difficult to effectively evaluate alternatives in the design of product-service bundles. In the same way, this chapter provides an important foundation for Chapter 7, which covers the design of the value-adding system. Finally, Chapter 12 deals with the scheduling decisions that most directly impact when a customer will receive their goods or services. This chapter's discussion of a customer orientation is important in creating such schedules, particularly for companies that might be more interested in something else—such as the efficiency of the schedule or scheduling process.

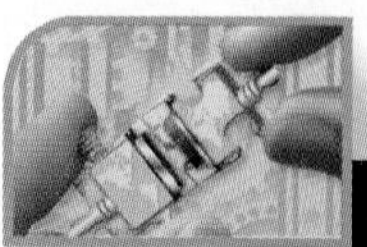

integrated OM <

Take a moment to apply what you've learned.

Chapter Wrap-Up

This chapter has presented an overview of the role of operations management in supporting the long-term success of modern organizations. Traditionally, operations managers were concerned only with managing transformation processes. This led to a narrow focus on the firm's technical core and an emphasis on productivity rather than the firm's broader value-adding system and customer satisfaction.

Today, most customers expect more than a product or service; they expect a product-service bundle and will not be satisfied unless the whole package meets their expectations. Operations management is responsible for the design and management of the value-adding systems organizations use to sustain customer satisfaction.

While operations is vital to the development of customer satisfaction and competitive advantage, it is but one of several vital business functions. The linkages between operational decision making and the value-adding activities of other functions are also critical to the ongoing enhancement of customer satisfaction and competitive advantage.

> end-of-chapter resources

- **Practice Quiz**
- **Key Terms**
- **Discussion Questions**
- **Case 1.1: Mitchellace: Manufacturing Intensive Operations Management**
- **References**
- **Plant Tours**

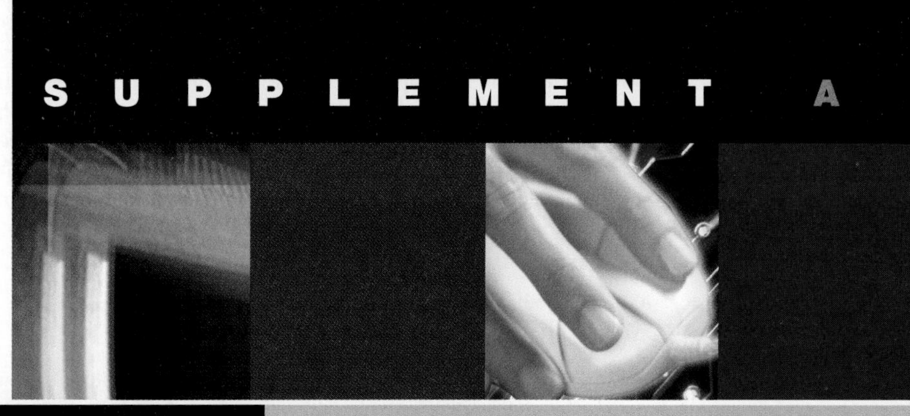

History and Trends in OM

Supplement Outline

Introduction

This supplement presents the historical development of the field of operations management chronologically, beginning with the Industrial Revolution of the late 1700s and moving through to the present. As you might suspect, the field has benefited from developments in many different areas of study and shares its roots with several other fields such as organizational behavior, industrial engineering, management science, statistics, and information systems. Learning about these roots will help you get a better understanding of what you'll be studying as you learn about OM.

This supplement also describes the trends that seem to be influencing the current development of OM. These include the dominance of the service sector as a source of employment, internationalization of business, concerns for the natural environment, and requirements to work synergistically both with personnel from other functions and with individuals from other companies within a chain of sequentially related value-adding activities.

Finally, the supplement concludes with a brief discussion of the professional opportunities in the field of OM.

The Chronological Development of Operations Management

While operations have been managed from the beginning of time, we trace the roots of what we call "operations management" back to the birth of mass production during the Industrial Revolution. In this section, we trace chronological development of the field up to the present. We show OM to be a field that has been influenced by many disciplines, including industrial engineering, industrial psychology and sociology, statistics, management science, management information systems, and others.

THE INDUSTRIAL REVOLUTION: THE BIRTH OF MASS PRODUCTION

Adam Smith popularized the concept of division of labor in England in the late 1700s. He illustrated this concept with the example of pin makers. Working alone, a worker could produce 20 pins a day. When repeatedly performing a limited portion of the work involved in making a pin, a small group of workers could produce 48,000 pins a day. Along with specialization of labor came the concerns of industrialization, including worker motivation and development, worker welfare, the organization of work, tracking of inventory, product design for mass production, and questions regarding the limits of economies of scale (including how many units should be produced at a given time and appropriate rationale for the mechanization of human work).

In *The Evolution of Management Thought,* Daniel Wren states, "Historically, industrialization is a relatively recent phenomenon. Humankind existed for eons before the great advances in power, transportation, communication, and technology that came to be known as the Industrial Revolution. . . . Some people engaged in economic undertakings, but not on a scale to compare with what would emerge as a result of the Industrial Revolution" (Wren 1994). Modern systems for the management of operations have roots in that period. It was the **Industrial Revolution** that made common the mass production of standardized products. At that time, a host of operational complexities and problems were encountered for the first time. As a result, a number of individuals attempted to solve problems related to the methods used and the organization of work, while others focused on the human problems associated with mass production in factories. It soon became clear that piecemeal organization, varied approaches to communication, and nonstandardized information handling were not adequate to meet the needs of business; rather a structured system of management was needed in order to effectively administer large-scale enterprises.

SCIENTIFIC MANAGEMENT: DEVELOPING A TECHNICAL UNDERSTANDING OF WORK

The term **scientific management** refers to the system of management introduced by Frederick W. Taylor in the late 1800s. In fact, scientific management has also been called the Taylor System. **Time study,** a technique used to precisely define an activity or job as a detailed set of repeatable tasks and determine the time in which these are to be done, was the foundation of the Taylor System. By using time study, management could set work standards "scientifically," rather than relying on the past performance of workers to set work standards. Given the ability to independently analyze work, management then gained the opportunity to use a piece-rate incentive plan, to select workers who were best suited to particular jobs, to train workers in the ideal way to complete a task, and to track production costs according to particular classifications for reporting based on the deviations from those standards. In essence, the Taylor System allowed for a separation of the planning of work from the performance of work. Scientific management has been praised due to the increases in worker productivity that it generated. On the other hand, scientific management may have been more suited to a time when a great deal of physical labor was not automated and the level of education of the workforce was extremely limited. Scientific management has been criticized for developing work settings that weren't fulfilling from a human perspective.

As a result of Taylor and others who worked to promote scientific management, this system became widely used in the United States and elsewhere. Since Taylor and many of his disciples were engineers, the ongoing development of scientific management led to a field of engineering now known as industrial engineering. In industrial engineering curricula, much of the influence of scientific management remains. Also, many Japanese authors and managers credit scientific management for providing techniques that they have used to establish their highly effective operational systems. Today, as we are beginning to place greater stress on workplace ergonomics and learn more about the management practices of the Japanese, there is renewed interest in scientific management.

INDUSTRIAL PSYCHOLOGY AND INDUSTRIAL SOCIOLOGY: DEVELOPING A HUMAN UNDERSTANDING OF WORK

The rise in unionization of the American workforce resulted from labor's dissatisfaction with scientific management. Given the criticisms of the Taylor System, many of the developments between 1910 and 1940 were related to the psychology of workers. In 1913, Hugo Münsterberg laid the foundation for the field of industrial psychology with the publication of his work *Psychology and Industrial Efficiency.* In 1912, Lillian Gilbreth completed a dissertation that was later published as *The Psychology of Management: The Function of Mind in Determining, Teaching and Installing Methods of Least Waste.* To be sure, these efforts were presented in the context of the Taylor System and were used to point out the value of understanding human mental processes in the design of work. It was suggested that by considering human factors in the design of work, systems would be developed where workers were both better off and more productive.

As a result of interest in the human behavioral dimensions of work, a series of experiments were performed by Elton Mayo at the Hawthorne plant of the Western Electric Company in the late 1920s and early 1930s. Initially designed to identify optimal environmental conditions for maximized productivity, these well-known experiments led to greater understanding of the implications of social factors for worker productivity. In fact, the very understanding that work systems are also social systems (and that social factors profoundly influence individual work behavior) can be attributed to the **Hawthorne Studies.** The Hawthorne Studies are frequently credited as providing a foundation for the study of human behavior in organizations, which continues today in the field of organizational behavior.

STATISTICAL CONTROL OF QUALITY

Walter Shewhart, a manager at the Hawthorne plant of the Bell Telephone Laboratories in the early 1900s, was the first to develop and use statistical methods to control quality. As early as 1924, he was promoting the use of **control charts.** (A control chart plots the behavior of some system variable of interest to determine whether there are any unusual circumstances in the system.) By 1931 Shewhart had published *Economic Control of Quality of Manufactured Product.* Following this, in the 1930s and 1940s, there were a number of statisticians who contributed methods of sampling, analysis, and control techniques that were useful to managers interested in quality.

Statistical quality control techniques provide an interesting counterpoint to the job design techniques of the Taylor System. The time study, job assignment, and training techniques of scientific management were used to design variability out of a job. They allowed managers to set a standard production rate, or quota, for workers. By contrast, statistical quality control techniques recognize that there is inherent variation in any system. A worker cannot reasonably be expected to produce the very same amount of quality product as every other worker—workers are different. Similarly, a worker will not produce the very same amount of quality product every hour—there are good days and bad days. Based on the ability to estimate the natural variation in the system, quality control techniques are designed to alert managers to unusual variation from system standards.

MANAGEMENT SCIENCE: OPTIMIZING THE USE OF LIMITED RESOURCES

During World War II, the U.S. industrial sector was faced with the challenge of supplying geographically distant troops with food, clothing, armor, munitions, and other supplies that were available in only limited amounts. In short, the demand for products from the industrial sector exceeded the production capacity, transportation capacity, and capacity of the resource supply base. Coordinated decisions had to be made about the use of resources, production capacity, and transportation capacity. At this time, the military relied on mathematicians to develop solutions to their resource allocation problems, and the field of mathematics referred to as **operations research (OR)** was developed. Much of the early development of OR involved refining the operation of radar, estimating war losses, and forecasting enemy strength. [Today, operations research is also known as **management science (MS)**.]

The mathematical tools developed for wartime applications were first applied in business during the 1950s. The tools were particularly useful at that time because of the large backlog of demand for household products that resulted from wartime austerity and postwar economic prosperity. In general, these mathematical decision modeling tools are useful whenever there are some constraints and there is a clear objective influenced by those constraints. This is certainly the case in business where organizations seek to maximize profits or minimize costs in the context of such limitations as budgets, plant capacity, market size, and supply of raw materials.

FUNCTIONALIZATION OF OM: BRINGING IT ALL TOGETHER IN ONE FUNCTION

In the late 1950s, it became clear that factory managers were applying knowledge of the technical aspects of work design, statistical control of quality, human aspects of work, and tools for the optimization of resource allocation. These managers were referred to as production managers, and the field of production management was recognized as a discipline within business schools. Production management was only then recognized as a function within businesses that required understanding work from a variety of perspectives.

In the 1970s, many of the tools of production management were applied in the service sector, and the field came to be referred to as production/operations management (POM). Today, the field is simply referred to as operations management (OM). OM is widely recognized as a business function that is critical to the success of any organization.

THE MRP CRUSADES: COMPUTERIZING OPERATIONAL DECISION MAKING

In many ways, the field of operations management in the United States was stagnant during the 1950s, 1960s, and early 1970s. This was a time in which U.S. business, which had not been faced with the difficulty of rebuilding infrastructure after World War II, faced seemingly unlimited global demand for its seemingly superior products. U.S. business was able to sell anything that was produced with a "made in the USA" label on it. As production management had been only recently recognized as a business function, production managers were given liberty to apply the tools of their trade. With operations managers to take care of the details, other managers seemed to feel that all of the problems of production had been solved. In the United States, OM was not seen as a potential source of competitive advantage. Instead, U.S. businesses built and entrenched bureaucracies that sustained a status quo brought about by prosperity and a false sense of superiority. Some would argue that inertia ruled the day and the concept "if it ain't broke, don't fix it" became a guiding light. Any change that might have occurred in such a setting would be primarily reactive to immediate problems, challenges in the marketplace, or innovations. Proactive change, or improvement, was rare.

The 1960s and 1970s did represent a period of significant progress in the application of computing technologies in industry. Processes were further automated, and since the decision-making tools of production management were widely known, some of them could also be programmed into computer systems to make the production manager's job easier. In fact, the most widely applied computerized production management planning tool was **material requirements planning (MRP)**. The drive to promote MRP in America has been referred to as the MRP crusades. As a result of the MRP crusades, widespread application of automation technologies, and subsequent developments in information technologies, the management of operations now relies heavily on up-to-date information systems.

JIT, THE QUALITY REVOLUTION, AND OPERATIONS STRATEGY

While American business was ignoring production management in the post-war decades, the Toyota production system was being developed in Japan. The Toyota system was a result of a variety of efforts designed to catch up with Western automotive manufacturers without the benefit of massive funds or new production facilities. This system, now referred to as **just-in-time (JIT),** was largely developed to enhance productivity and reduce cost by removing waste from production. Taiichi Ohno, the Toyota executive largely responsible for the development of the JIT system emphasizes that because the Toyota production system was created from actual practices in the factories of Toyota, it is a very practical approach—not just a theory. It's very applicable to actual business operations and well suited for implementation.

Poor quality is a major source of waste targeted by the JIT system. During the 1950s and 1960s, the worker-inspired Japanese industry was able to develop operational systems that were more productive than their American counterparts. In fact, they were able to produce material goods of superior quality at a lower cost. Although Americans such as Armand Fiegenbaum, W. Edwards Deming, and Joseph Juran had provided U.S. business with the insights required for a quality revolution in the 1950s, America experienced the quality revolution out of painful necessity in the 1980s with widespread adoption of *total quality management.* The strong business orientation toward creation and enhancement of customer satisfaction that this text reflects is a result of this quality revolution. Observing the practices of Japanese managers, many of which originated in the United States, has led to an American rediscovery of many of the roots of OM.

As a consequence of the threat posed by international competition, and more particularly the lessons learned from the Japanese, OM has gained worldwide recognition as a key to competitiveness for organizations in the 21st century. In fact, rather than leaving operations professionals to their own

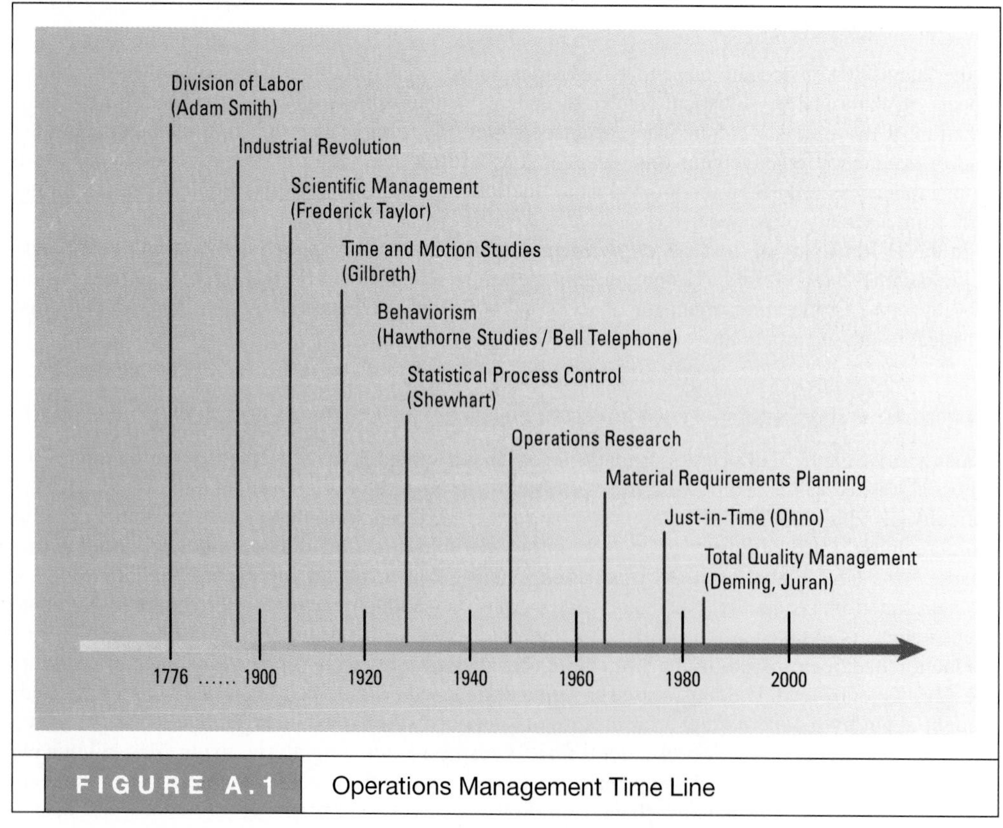

FIGURE A.1 Operations Management Time Line

functional devices, modern organizations rely on operations professionals to integrate their decision-making processes with organizational objectives and competitive realities. This calls for an operations strategy that can guide decision making throughout the operations function. Today's progressive organizations are developing operations strategies that effectively leverage operational excellence into global competitive advantages.

Figure A.1 summarizes the development of OM as we have described it in the above paragraphs.

active exercise

Take a moment to apply what you've learned.

Current Trends Influencing the Field of Operations Management

There are significant trends outside of the field of operations that will influence the evolution of OM in the coming decades. These are the growth and dominance of services, internationalization of the operations function, an increased role for operations in improving environmental quality so that the practices of business may be demonstrably "sustainable," managing cross-functional processes and supply-chain management.

GROWTH AND DOMINANCE OF SERVICES

At one time, the primary employment sector in the U.S. economy was agriculture; with the Industrial Revolution that changed, and manufacturing was the primary employment sector. Today it's services. This is true of other advanced nations as well. For example, the percentage of employment in service sector jobs in 1993 for a sampling of nations was: Canada 75%, United States 74%, Belgium 71%, Israel 68%, France 66%, Italy 60%, and Japan 60%.[1] Today, for most of these countries, the percentage of workers employed by service businesses is even higher.

INTERNATIONALIZATION

Business competition is now global. Improvements in logistical systems, communication technologies along with greater opportunities for international trade have created new opportunities and challenges in the design of value-adding systems. Improved logistical systems allow for greater coordination of geographically distributed operations and reduce the need for large inventories of materials that are transported from one plant to another. Today it is much easier to tie together the work of several manufacturing and service facilities to create the firm's product-service bundle. At the same time, reliable communication networks allow information to be shared widely. Thus, decision making can be decentralized without significant loss in coordination. Along with the opportunities presented by improved logistics and communication come the challenges of greater diversity of customers and suppliers made possible through the elimination of trade restrictions. Today's operations face increasing pressure to be "world class," and product-service bundles need to meet the expectations of diverse customers.

ENVIRONMENTAL QUALITY

Environmental concerns have traditionally not been the focus of operations managers. Increased regulation, public scrutiny, customer expectations, and the concern of employees for their community are beginning to change this. We are beginning to learn that effectiveness in managing operations is just as important to environmental excellence as it is to product quality and cost. As a result, the environmental impact of operational decisions seems to be a growing consideration for business.

CROSS-FUNCTIONAL MANAGEMENT

Organization charts have functional lines of responsibility drawn in black. In between these functions are **white spaces.** Most meaningful work is done in processes, or value-adding systems that span several functions. On the other hand, organizational lines, decision making, and communication systems

[1]Department of International Economic and Social Affairs Statistical Office, United Nations, New York *1993 Statistical Yearbook* (1993): 236–242.

are designed to support functional decision-making hierarchies. Cross-functional management involves integrating the work and decisions of all functions in the value-adding system. Managers are being given responsibility for processes instead of, or in addition to, their functional responsibilities. Cross-functional teams are being used more and more and are clearly a vital aspect of managing the white spaces. **Business process reengineering (BPR)** is a technique frequently used to re-invent processes that are weak because they span functional boundaries in hierarchical organization charts but aren't coordinated across these boundaries. Information systems are being designed to support cross-functional decision making and communication. Workers are being collocated so that their decisions are more likely to support the process and less likely to be dominated by functional turf rivalries. All of these changes suggest that, in contrast to the dominance of functional hierarchies in the 20th century, integrative management that spans the white spaces will become the central business paradigm of the 21st century.

SUPPLY-CHAIN MANAGEMENT

A **supply chain** begins with the extraction of natural resources and extends to the ultimate disposal of the leftover material in landfills, smokestacks, or drains. In the past, companies within a supply chain would vigorously compete for the profit in the chain. A firm would negotiate lower prices with a supplier in order to lower their cost and increase their profits. A firm would price products to their customer based on some profit maximization criteria.

Today, business is concerned with the competitiveness of the entire chain of value-adding activities they use to satisfy their customers. To satisfy customers and to remain competitive in the long run, the entire value chain needs to be competitive. We now recognize that cooperation within the value chain can be very useful and when our customers grow and profit because of the competitiveness of their supply chain, we will grow and profit.

Toyota is seen as one of today's most efficient companies, and it is estimated that less than 30% of the cost in their supply chain is of direct benefit to their customers. They probably couldn't get to 100%; even so there is plenty of room for them to improve. As a result, it is clear that focusing on improving the supply chain, especially by coordinating the value-adding activities of the different companies in the chain, can lead to tremendous improvements in the value provided to customers.

THE EXPLOSION OF E-COMMERCE

Recent developments have made computers a pervasive force in our world. Only 20 years ago, most industrial computer applications ran off of mainframes or minicomputers; the Internet was an unwieldy connection primarily used in large-scale research environments, and personal computers (PCs) weren't much more than toys. Today most businesses are either running sophisticated business software on their PCs or they're using a client-server architecture to enhance their decision-making processes. The Internet has saturated the far reaches of the globe, thereby connecting businesses with their suppliers and customers across the world with instantaneous communication.

The advent of e-commerce has serious implications for the practice of OM. In particular, rather than focusing on decision alternatives that optimize internal performance (within the OM function), operational decisions must be more responsive to other functional areas. Business decisions, whether in OM or any other area, must be more cross-functional and must have a more global focus. Finally, operations managers must use the Internet to more effectively anticipate and respond to the needs of their customers and their customer's customers. They can no longer wait for the paperwork to commit their resources. Rather, by sharing information and profits across a supply chain, they may do business without requiring a financial transaction to trigger operational activities.

CAREERS IN OPERATIONS MANAGEMENT

As you might have guessed from our description of the development of OM, the job of the operations manager is a professional position of increasing significance to a firm's competitive future. It is no longer the blue-collar factory job that fails to tax the capabilities of today's business school graduate. The connotation of a grimy sweatshop is far removed from the reality of a career in operations management. Operations professionals are just as likely to apply their knowledge in the most prestigious management consulting firms, financial institutions, airlines, or hospitals as they are to apply it in a manufacturing company.

Many operations professionals belong to APICS—the Educational Society for Resource Professionals, formerly known as the **American Production and Inventory Control Society (APICS)**. APICS is currently the largest professional organization dedicated only to operations managers. This international organization, founded in the United States in 1957, boasts more than 50,000 members and has provided certification examinations leading the **certification in production and**

inventory management (**CPIM**) since 1972. APICS recently has begun offering a *certification in integrated resource management* (CIRM). There are more than 10,000 APICS members who have earned the CPIM. The existence of a certification program such as the CPIM suggests that there is clear consensus regarding the body of knowledge in which operations professionals should be competent. The existence of a large number of certified professionals attests to a professionalism in the field.

> active exercise

Take a moment to apply what you've learned.

Recently, a number of articles have recommended OM as one of the top career opportunities, offering graduates excellent job prospects, salaries, and growth potential. Common entry-level opportunities for operations management majors include: coordinating the value-adding processes in banks, purchasing materials for manufacturing organizations, scheduling or supervising value-adding activities in any service or manufacturing context, coordinating logistics to ensure that information and materials are available when needed, quality assurance, process improvement consulting, and supply-chain management. The typical company has most of its capital invested in the value-adding processes that are managed by operations managers. As a result, entry-level positions in operations management are especially appealing to individuals who want visibility early in their career. In fact, it is not uncommon for entry-level operations personnel to coordinate and supervise the value-adding activities that use tens of millions of dollars of capital investment and annual purchases of many millions of dollars of materials to create many millions of dollars worth of profit. If they do a good job, they can have a very positive influence on their firm's performance, and that can open many doors for advancement.

Working in the area of operations management is an effective way to move up in a corporation. One study by Heidrick & Struggles, an executive recruiting firm, showed that of 74 individuals promoted to top positions, 60 came up through operations. Many companies have formally defined vice-presidential positions in OM. Operational concerns are very important to senior managers in every organization. In sum, opportunity for rewarding work and professional advancement is abundant within the functional area of operations management.

> Supplement Wrap-Up

Now that you've read a brief history of Operations Management, you may wish to test yourself to see how well you've comprehended the material. In the box below you'll find a number of links. Click on any one of these links to find additional supplement resources.

> end-of-supplement resources

- Practice Quiz
- Key Terms
- Discussion Questions
- References

Supply-Chain Strategy: Aligning Operations with Customer Expectations and Supplier Processes

CHAPTER 2

Chapter Outline

What's Ahead

. . . BACK AT THE REC CENTER

The managers we introduced you to in Chapter 1 are Fred, Cheryl, Luis, and Tom (see the beginning of Chapter 1 if you don't remember their jobs). It is 6 A.M. and the Rec Center has just opened. The early risers who want to get in a workout before heading off to face the day are starting to arrive. Fred was in first today, and he seems to be rushing a bit.

"What's the rush?" asked Tom from a stepper. Fred had passed in front of him for the fourth time now as he paced in between his reps on the bench press machine. "Is your plant burning down or what?" Tom laughed.

"Yeah, right," realized Fred, "I guess I'm a little preoccupied this morning." He stopped and sat down on a bench in between Tom's stepper and the dumbbells Luis and Cheryl were using. "Some stuff going on, you know, I'm still getting used to this new position." Fred had recently moved from a division that manufactured a wide array of customized electronics for a variety of customers to become marketing manager for one that produced a couple of standardized products for a small number of big volume customers. He still wasn't sure he liked the switch. "We used to sit and wait for the phone to ring, take an order, somebody made it, and we shipped it! I had never even known how it was made, just what it could do and how to sell it!" he said.

"So what's the big deal?" asked Luis as he finished some bicep curls and put the dumbbell back on the rack. "I thought you said your life was simpler now, making one model on each line, just keeping a handful of customers happy. I'll bet you're even going home by 5 most nights!" he joked.

"You're right in most ways," Fred replied. "It's the flip side of the coin in some others ways, though. That's the part making life difficult! Might only be a couple but the accounts I deal with now, these people think they own you!" He went on to describe to the group how he was to meet a team from one of his bigger accounts and some outside experts today to go through his process. He can't understand why a good pager isn't enough; now they want to come visit the factory. He did say that it was in connection with a new certification program his company was attempting to implement. "I've got to meet them at the plant this morning. They want to check us out. We told them we're working on the 'ISO 9000' stuff, but they still want to see our process? Why should they care?" he asked, getting annoyed.

"I've read about that 'ISO' thing," said Luis. "It's some sort of deal for doing business in Europe, isn't it? We don't export much so it's not an issue for us right now, but, Tom, weren't you talking about it last week?" he asked.

"Yeah, doesn't mean you're really good, it just means you're really as good as you say you are," replied Tom.

"That's it!" said Fred. "We have 'em coming in to look us over, mostly people from our customers, and the others are some sort of judges or something like that."

"You mean 'registrars'?" asked Cheryl. She had finished her last set of curls and was now listening.

"A hospital worries about ISO 9000?" asked Luis.

"Sure, we went through it already. We had to in order to work with some of the bigger health insurance companies," she added. She explained how some of the bigger insurance companies were becoming more selective in how they managed health care and that steering more patients to fewer hospitals was a form of "putting all their eggs in one basket" as she called it. It simplified things, gave them economies of scale, and it even allowed the insurance companies to offload some of the administrative side of their business to the hospital, which made certain their doctor's referrals stayed inside the network where possible. ISO 9000 was a way of making sure you had the systems in place to help you live up to your end of the bargain.

"I guess that explains some of the other things these customers are asking for," added Fred, reacting to Cheryl's analogy. He talked about how some of the larger accounts also wanted his company to take over a bigger share of their business relationship. In fact, he said one wanted Fred's company to now handle all the logistics between them. Another even wanted Fred's people to actually manage the inventory of his pagers in their warehouses. He also said that most of his current customers used his company as the primary source or in some cases as the only source for the product categories he handled. "I guess they are willing to pay a little more when they ask us to do this stuff, and we get some guarantees," Fred said as he began to convince himself of what he was saying. As he talked, Tom was nodding. They understood what Cheryl was saying about an egg basket.

"That's it," Cheryl said. "We can add those other services when we have that kind of a relationship with an insurance company." She suggested it was the same with a hospital as it was with making pagers. "Fred, when they buy a basic pager from you, your customers are paying you to manage their inventory too," she added.

"They couldn't do that unless we were their only supplier, could they?" asked Fred as he continued to understand. The others were shaking their heads "no" as they agreed with him.

"You know," said Luis looking puzzled, "I always thought that was what you weren't supposed to do, you know, the 'all the eggs in one basket thing'?" He understood he might get a higher return in his retirement fund from putting the same amount of money into a single stock, assuming he picked a good one, but he also knew the risk involved if he picked a bad one. All the things Cheryl and Fred were talking about seemed to contradict that thinking, the idea of diversification to minimize risk, that is.

"I think I see the problem," said Cheryl. "When it comes to the stock market," she continued, "to consider all the things that can influence the stock market, even a single stock, is likely to be impossible to analyze at once," she said as she moved from the leg machine to the incline board and started her ab crunches. In that case, she argued, it made sense to deal with the uncertainty of the market by diversifying. "I think what Fred's customers, the insurance companies, my hospital, and all of our suppliers are doing to get on the same page is called supply-chain management," she added. She stopped her exercises to explain that the more you simplify and assure what you do, how you do it, and with whom you do it, then the more you can view the relationships between business partners with certainty and the less the need for spreading the risk. Basically, she argued that what all of them are working towards, what some people are calling supply-chain management, is about knowing and not guessing or playing the odds. She said it's about knowing what your customer and your customer's customer is going to want from you. It's also about knowing and not guessing, she suggested, what your supplier and your supplier's supplier will do for you. When you know those things for sure, either by working with them or looking for things like ISO 9000 certification, you benefit by dealing exclusively with them.

Fred and Luis were nodding in agreement as they finished their workouts.

"Yup," said Tom getting off the stepper and heading for the showers. "Just like getting on a 737—if you're going to put all your eggs in one basket, make darn sure it's a good basket!" he laughed.

"But Tom, didn't your son call the other morning to say he ran out of gas driving your car to high school?" asked Luis, grinning.

"Yes," Tom answered looking confused. "So?"

"Well, next time I fly your airline, can you get somebody else to check the gas?"

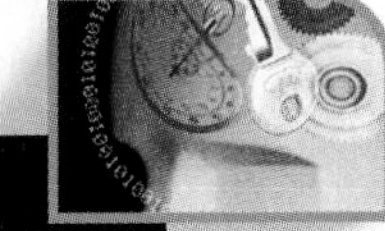

> objectives

Take a moment to familiarize yourself with the key objectives of this chapter.

> gearing up

Before you begin reading this chapter, try a short warm-up activity.

> Introduction

This chapter introduces you to the practices of **supply-chain management (SCM),** which may be defined as the configuration, coordination, and improvement of a sequentially related set of operations. You might recall from Chapter 1 that we defined a customer as anyone who uses the output of a process. Thus, customer's customers are important to an organization that is focused on customer service. Additionally, if a supplier uses a purchase order, that makes them (and ultimately their suppliers) a customer of the purchasing agent's paperwork. Our discussion of supply chain management is, therefore, an extension of the focus on customer service that was introduced in Chapter 1. With SCM, the idea of satisfying an entire chain of customers (and competing with suppliers to win the business of the ultimate customer) becomes reality.

The first major section of this chapter deals with linkages between the material covered in this chapter and other functional areas of business. SCM is a very interdisciplinary topic; thus, it is not hard to point out many key linkages between this chapter and any functional area in business. Bottom line, regardless of your major you should find this chapter extremely relevant.

In this chapter, we describe the historic development of supply-chain management. Specifically, we point out that coordinating sequentially related activities is not really anything new. What is new is our ability to do this in complex environments where customers are given significant choices in regard to the product-service bundle.

Next we provide a general overview of the decisions that comprise supply chain management. Much of this is facilitated by some examples that we present. Specifically, we give an overview of SCM in the auto and health care industries.

This chapter discusses "bricks and mortar" issues in SCM in the section on supply-chain configuration issues. Decisions such as the technology to use, what to make and what to buy, how many vendors to use, where to locate certain types of capacity, and what types of product service bundles to provide all relate to the configuration of the supply chain.

Coordination of the supply chain is also an important part of this chapter. Our primary focus in this section is on the enabling technologies and the ways that firms can more effectively communicate and interact with their upstream suppliers and downstream customers.

Finally, the chapter includes a section on improving supply chains. In this section we present seven principles for supply-chain management that will help you to see the areas where improvement can be pursued via SCM efforts. Obviously, configuring and coordinating supply chains doesn't happen once and for all. Rather, effective SCM entails an ongoing process of continual improvement to existing configurations and coordination processes.

> Integrating Operations Management with other Functions

Figure 2.1 highlights some of the key linkages between the various functional areas of business and the topics covered in this chapter. Recognize that we could put a star in every cell of this matrix; we didn't because we're just trying to highlight some of the most obvious linkages.

Historically, it was the idea of greater customization that has led to a divide-and-conquer approach to issues of coordination across entire supply chains. Giving customers choices has introduced complexity in the form of product variety, demand uncertainty, and the resulting variable capacity requirements. Thus, marketing has played a key role in the historic structure of supply chains. Less complexity allowed for more coordination. Today, there is more opportunity to coordinate activities across the supply chain even in the presence of complexity because of the enabling information systems and communication technologies. The result: Supply-chain management has become a critical aspect of business success and mass customization has replaced mass production in many industries.

All functions are involved in SCM decisions. SCM has direct implications for estimating financial performance for equity markets and for capital allocation decisions. Accounting plays a significant role in SCM through providing cost estimates that drive SCM configuration and coordination issues. Human Resource issues are common in SCM configuration and coordination, whether through questions of labor cost and workforce skill in global sourcing decisions or capacity and scheduling issues in SCM coordination. Marketing plays a key part through its role in coordinating logistical systems, product-service bundle design, and transferring customer intelligence to the organization. Engineering provides significant input to SCM configuration through its involvement in design of both the product-service bundle and the value-adding system. Finally, MIS is responsible for the enabling information system technologies that play such a significant role in coordinating and improving supply chains.

Chapter Topics \ Functional Areas of Business	Finance	Accounting	Human Resources	Marketing	Engineering	Management Information Systems
Integrating Operations Management with Other Functions	●	●	●	●	●	●
Supply-Chain Management: From Henry Ford to E-Commerce				●		●
Supply-Chain Management Decisions	●	●	●	●	●	●
Supply-Chain Configuration Strategies				●	●	
Supply-Chain Coordination Strategies			●	●		●
Improving Supply Chains: Seven Principles	●	●		●		●

FIGURE 2.1 Integrating Operations Management with Other Functions

> Supply-Chain Management: From Henry Ford to E-Commerce

Until quite recently, the ownership of business supply chains was always highly concentrated. For example, craftsmen would generally handle all stages of a process, from the conversion of natural resources through to providing customers with products. Musicians would design and build their own instruments, carpenters would hew lumber from beams and build their products, metalworkers would smelt their own materials and make products from these. Even in the early 20th century, after the Industrial Revolution, the tendency was for capitalists to control large vertically integrated empires. Ford Motor Company, which did everything from mining to final assembly of its Model T vehicles in the early 1900s, is an example of such an empire. This one-company approach allowed Ford to coordinate all of the sequentially related activities and gain very large efficiencies. Every part of the chain became very efficient at doing one thing. The weakness of these systems was that it was very difficult to accommodate product variety or make model changes. It took Ford about $200 million to change all of the tools and systems so that they could make the Model A instead of the Model T. Ultimately, because of the lack of flexibility in the Ford system, General Motors (GM) was able to gain the upper hand in the automobile business at that time. With the added complexity introduced by allowing variation of colors, engines, and interiors within one model of car, an expanded product line including multiple car models produced in varying quantities, and frequent model redesigns, Ford lost the ability to compete while controlling all aspects of production.

As a result of the coordination problems eventually faced by Henry Ford, the typical industrial supply chain has been broken into many pieces which are managed separately. It's a divide-and-conquer solution to the problem. In addition to complexity, some of the factors leading to the division of supply chains are technology, economies of scale, and a need for focus in operations. Regarding technology, it is common to manage high-tech operations and low-tech operations separately. Also, capital-intensive operations are often separated from labor-intensive operations. Regarding scale, it is common to manage operations that produce standardized products or services in large quantities separately from those that produce a greater variety of customized products in smaller volumes. Finally, regarding the need for focus in operations, it is desirable for a business in a supply chain to have a homogeneous mix of products and customers. Where there are mismatches in the product line or customer set, it is common to divide up businesses.

Figure 2.2 describes a supply chain using the metaphor of a river with dams. Each dam represents the interface between one company and another. The water in the river represents material flowing through the supply chain. Actually, the figure is much simpler than a real-world supply chain because there's just one single material flow. A picture of a river with many tributaries and many channels at its delta would be a more fitting analogy. Did you notice the pools behind each dam? These are needed to ensure that the company can respond quickly to the exact material needs of their customer and also protect the company from problems with their suppliers. Having an extra stock of raw materials, work in process inventory, and finished goods helps buffer the operations of the individual companies from the demand and supply uncertainty they face.

One of the weaknesses of a supply chain that has been divided up between multiple businesses is that the businesses are likely to act in their own interests to optimize their own profit. The goal of satisfying an ultimate customer is easily lost and opportunities that could arise from some coordination of decisions across stages of the supply chain could be lost. Many companies recognized this with the advent of Just-in-Time manufacturing in the 1970s and 1980s. Their efforts to reduce waste in internal operations led them to begin working more closely with suppliers and customers. If suppliers could be made more reliable, there would be less need for inventories of raw materials, quality inspection systems, rework, and other non-value-adding activities. Similarly, if customer demand could be leveled and customer needs better understood, there would be less need for finished goods inventory, sales incentives, and so on. Thus, companies were learning the cost of the buffers represented by the pools you see behind the dams in Figure 2.2. **Lean production,** which is an approach to managing operations without massive buffers of inventory, became much more common. By removing the pools of inventory, companies were able to cut costs, improve quality feedback, shorten production leadtimes, and reduce the time required to introduce new products or services. Recent advances in information systems technology now allow many firms to go one step further by looking upstream beyond their suppliers and downstream beyond their customers in attempts to make their supply chain leaner.

> active exercise

Take a closer look at the concepts and issues you've been reading about.

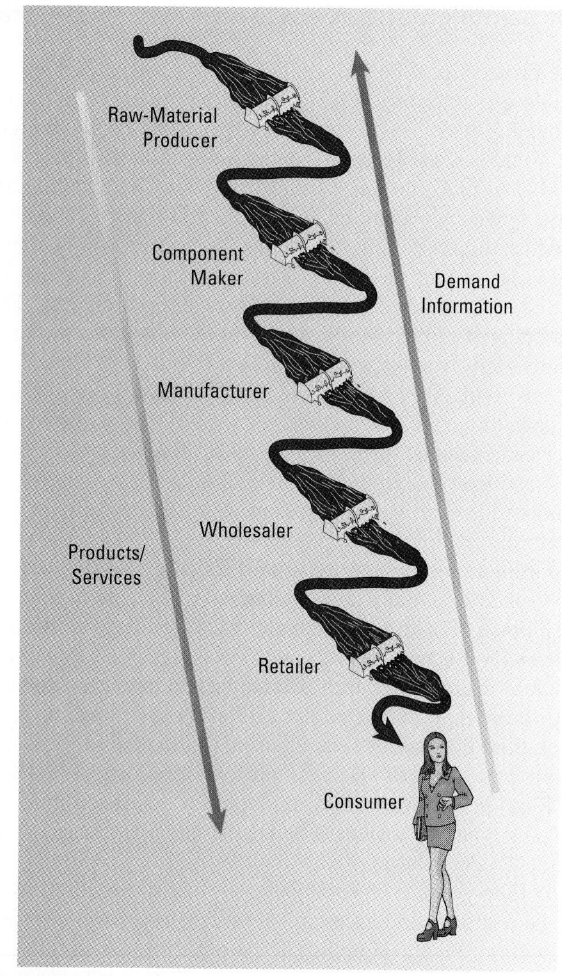

FIGURE 2.2 Supply-Chain Management as a River

active concept check <

Now let's take a moment to test your knowledge of the concepts you have studied in this section.

> Supply-Chain Management Decisions

Earlier we defined supply chain management as the configuration, coordination, and improvement of a set of sequentially related operations. As such, SCM involves three types of activity: configuration, coordination, and improvement. Configuration of the supply chain, from the perspective of individual companies, involves such tasks as determining

- what the product-service bundle will include
- what portion of the bundle's value will be provided by the company and what part will be bought from others
- where facilities will be located and what their capabilities will be
- what technologies will be used

- how communication between customers and suppliers will be handled
- the expectations to which suppliers and customers will be held

Coordination of the supply chain, from the perspective of individual companies, involves such tasks as

- determining when to provide products and services in the bundle and in what quantities
- ensuring that suppliers are able to effectively provide the value required of them in the appropriate levels of quality, cost, and timeliness
- setting appropriate levels for capacity, inventory, and lead time in light of supply-and-demand uncertainty
- communicating demand, performance expectations, and performance results with suppliers and customers

Improvement of the supply chain, from the perspective of individual companies, involves changing the configuration and/or the approach to coordination in order to enhance the overall performance of the chain. As such it can involve

- installing Enterprise Resources Planning (ERP) systems or other information technologies such as bar coding, automated data collection in point of sale (POS) systems, geographic positioning and material tracking systems in logistical systems, and other communication and decision-supporting information technologies
- streamlining the channels of supply by working with suppliers and/or customers to eliminate capacity imbalances between their processes and yours, weeding out under-performing suppliers, creating more effective logistical systems, and so on
- changing technologies or planning systems to improve quality, lead-time, cost, or service
- redesigning the product-service bundle to make it easier to provide or be of greater value to the customer

To give you a more concrete feel for supply-chain management, we will now look at examples from the automobile industry and health care.

SCM IN THE AUTOMOBILE INDUSTRY

Today's supply chain in the automobile industry is much different from the situation Henry Ford faced in the early 1900s, when he could get away with saying customers could have "any color they wanted as long as it was black." Automobile industry supply chains are characterized in Figure 2.3. Companies that assemble cars—such as Ford, GM, Chrysler, Toyota and Honda—usually have the largest capital investment and have the greatest influence over the other companies in the supply chain. The decisions they make in designing the product-service bundle, designing the value-adding system, and operating the value-adding system have a major influence on the level of satisfaction experienced by the ultimate customer and the competitiveness of the entire supply chain. Looking upstream, the most directly affected companies are the assemblers' *first tier suppliers.* These are the companies that sell things like radios, seats, headlamps, and paint to the auto assemblers. Automobile assemblers have incredible leverage because of the amount of materials that they buy, and they exert a huge influence on these companies. First tier suppliers are generally held accountable for the quality and timeliness of the materials that they provide. Since the assemblers produce automobiles in large quantities, the suppliers generally respond to their expectations.

Through their first tier suppliers, assemblers influence their *second tier suppliers.* Examples of second tier suppliers include fabric producers who sell to the companies that make car seats, companies that make electronic components and sell them to the firms that produce dashboard components and radios, and so on. Though Figure 2.3 shows only two levels of supply, in fact there could be several. The influence of the large car assemblers, however, diminishes the farther upstream into the supply chain you move. For example, you could say that the company making the thread that goes into car seat fabric is a third tier supplier, the cotton broker that sells to the thread maker is a fourth tier supplier, the farmer that sells to the cotton broker is a fifth tier supplier, and so on. Since cotton is a commodity and thread is a standardized product with multiple applications, the auto assemblers would have limited ability and little reason to attempt to influence the activities of such firms.

Looking forward, automobile assemblers also have significant influence on the distribution and retail practices in their supply chain. *Distributors* transport the car from the factory to the retailers and often use a regional distribution center where they may hold a large inventory of finished cars. If you've ever bought a car in the United States, you've seen a dealer add on a "destination charge." This cost of distribution is not the same amount for every car on the dealer's lot. Not every automobile

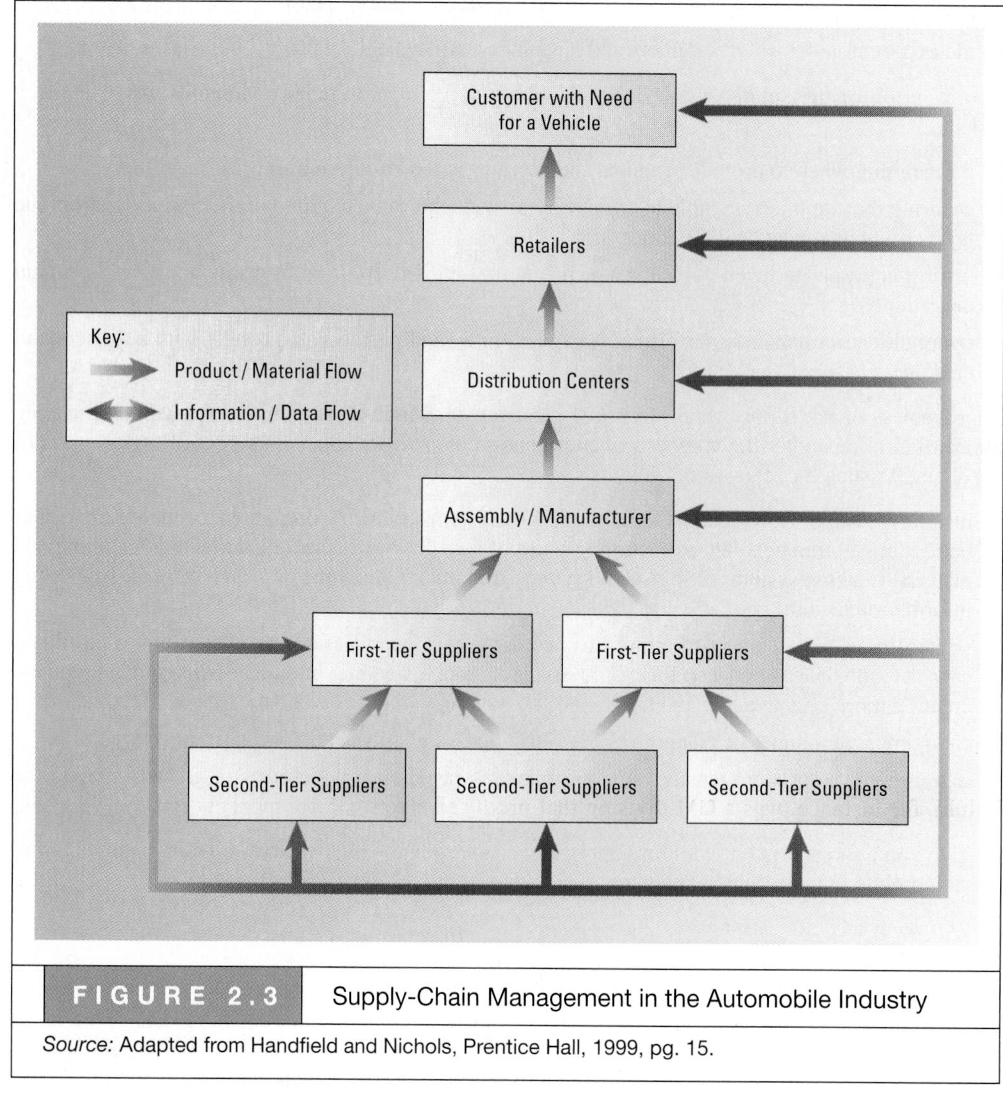

FIGURE 2.3 Supply-Chain Management in the Automobile Industry

Source: Adapted from Handfield and Nichols, Prentice Hall, 1999, pg. 15.

assembler uses the same logistics companies and distribution network. As a result, some companies may have much more inventory in the pipeline than others, some may incur much greater distribution costs, and some may gain some competitive advantage out of their distribution systems. Just as it is with first tier suppliers, auto assembly companies exert a huge influence over the practices of their distributors. Additionally, they control many of the practices of their retailers. Because the auto assembly companies can decide what cars a car dealer (i.e. the *retailer*) gets and when—as well as the difference between Manufacturer's Suggested Retail Price (MSRP) and dealer's invoice cost—it is in the best interests of the retailers to adhere to the guidelines set forth by the assemblers.

Ultimately, in today's world of almost unlimited customer choice, it takes many companies—each with its own unique expertise—to convert things like plastic, metal, glass, and fabric into the car you drive away from a retail showroom. Supply-chain management is the configuring, coordinating, and improving of the activities of all of these firms. This implies establishing and managing both the flow of materials and the flow of information. Material flows are shown in Figure 2.3 as solid lines. Notice in the figure that material flows in only one direction. Actually, that's somewhat simplistic. Because of environmental concerns, unused or damaged materials can be returned from any stage of the supply chain to earlier stages if they are recyclable, reusable, repairable, or remanufacturable. You might realize that money flows in the opposite direction of the material. Financial managers, accountants, and auditors who are concerned with cash flows, monitoring the value of inventory, and predicting earnings are therefore quite concerned with managing the same linkages as those who manage the material flows, only they are managing these from a financial perspective.

Looking at Figure 2.3 you'll notice that information flows from any stage of the supply chain to any other. In the past, this was not possible. Rather, information regarding demand and customer requirements was passed upstream through the supply chain one stage at a time. Customers told retailers what they wanted, retailers ordered vehicles, distributors told the assemblers what was in short supply, assemblers bought what they needed, and so on. The exchange of demand information generally relied on purchase orders, and financial information was exchanged via paper invoice. Because of the inefficiencies of this form of communication, manufacturers at each stage of the chain usually simply forecasted demand, scheduled their facilities based on expected demand, and then met customer demand from stock. If the forecast was wrong, they found ways to liquidate their excess inventories through incentives and other demand management practices. Today, information is frequently exchanged via **Electronic Data Interchange (EDI)**, which is a method of transferring business information such as demand, price, available capacity, and anticipated delivery date between suppliers and customers via a predetermined protocol. In fact, material flows and financial transactions need not rely on paper documents at all. Often, companies provide passwords to suppliers so they can access assembly schedules on their web site and deliver material when needed. There's no need even for a purchase order if a supplier is set up with the program. **Enterprise Resources Planning (ERP)** systems are information systems that allow companies to access the schedules of their downstream suppliers and schedule their own operations so that they are making what will be needed rather than what they think will be needed. Information technologies such as EDI and ERP systems are key enablers of supply chain management.

Each of the major auto assembly companies employs unique strategies in their dealings with their upstream suppliers. The strategies will even vary within a company on the basis of the particular vehicle being built. Chrysler, for instance, buys more of the parts that go into their vehicles than most other auto assembly companies. They buy 100% of the parts that go into the Dodge Viper and Plymouth Prowler. On the other hand, they make most of the critical components that go into the Jeep Wrangler. On average, it is estimated that Chrysler buys 70% of the parts for the cars that they sell. This allows the company to focus on what it wants to be good at—designing and assembling cars—and on leveraging the technological expertise of its suppliers through an ability to manage the supply chain. When Honda and Toyota began making automobiles in North America, many of their suppliers from Japan opened facilities in North America. One of the distinctive features of their supply-chain strategy is their loyalty to their suppliers. GM has historically owned many of its first tier suppliers. Delphi, for instance, was a GM division that produced electronic components for GM vehicles. Volkswagen, perhaps suggesting that it sees itself more as an auto design and marketing company than as a manufacturer, has recently developed a truck assembly facility in Brazil where suppliers assemble their own part of the car on the assembly line. (For example, Bosch employees and not VW employees, put the brakes and fuel injection systems on the truck.)

In this discussion of SCM in the auto industry, we have provided a fairly representative picture of supply chains for most durable goods. Clearly, the dynamics of supply chains are quite different for different types of goods. The picture is quite different for consumer goods, where large retailers such as Wal-Mart generally dictate the delivery requirements and terms of purchase for both large and small suppliers. Generally, suppliers are expected to keep the shelves stocked based on *point-of-sale (POS) information* that Wal-Mart loads into its computer system when items are scanned at cash registers. Often, the suppliers actually don't get paid for their merchandise until after it has been sold by Wal-Mart. Also, where product-service bundles are much less customized, SCM involves much more coordination of design and technical information exchanges and takes on much less of a cost savings orientation. Regardless of the situation, the point of supply-chain management is to configure operational resources in such a way that the needs of the ultimate customer can be competitively satisfied.

In any industrial supply chain, service-intensive operations play a key role. Logistics—including transportation, warehousing, and material tracking services—account for a large portion of most product-service bundles. This is especially true when you consider international or global supply chains. Additionally, information systems provide the critical data processing services needed to coordinate industrial supply chains. Without these two key services, the concept of supply-chain management could never become a reality.

> active poll

What do you think? Voice your opinion and find out what others have to say.

SUPPLY-CHAIN MANAGEMENT IN HEALTH CARE

Based on the above discussion, it might seem that SCM is primarily focused on the product side of the product-service bundle. In reality, however, the concepts can be applied to service facilities as well. Figure 2.4 presents an overview of a health care supply chain. Comparing this figure to Figure 2.3, you'll notice that there is just as much to coordinate in the health care supply chain as there is in an automobile supply chain. One difference is critical: Health care has to be much more customized. As a result, there are many more possibilities for patient flow than can be shown in this simple diagram. Thus, recognize that the diagram only presents typical patient flows and information flows.

The most influential stage of the health care supply chain shown in Figure 2.4 is the insurance company. The role of health insurance companies from a supply-chain perspective is threefold: (1) to configure the network of providers from which customers access health services, (2) to coordinate the decisions made within that network of providers so that cost is contained while a satisfactory level of service is made available, and (3) to economically provide their traditional insurance value by protecting the customer from the risk of health care costs that exceed his or her financial means. Notice from the figure that the insurance company goes between the customer and health care providers. Also, the insurance company serves employers. In many cases, large companies will be "self-insured" in the sense that they actually pay the health care costs their employees incur under their benefits plan. The role of the insurance company is simply to administer the plan, and the money they make comes from administration fees. In other cases, employers aren't large enough to self-insure and choose to pay insurance premiums so that the insurance company will actually assume the risk of the health care costs. In any case, it's important to recognize that employers are customers of the insurance company just as much as individual employees are customers.

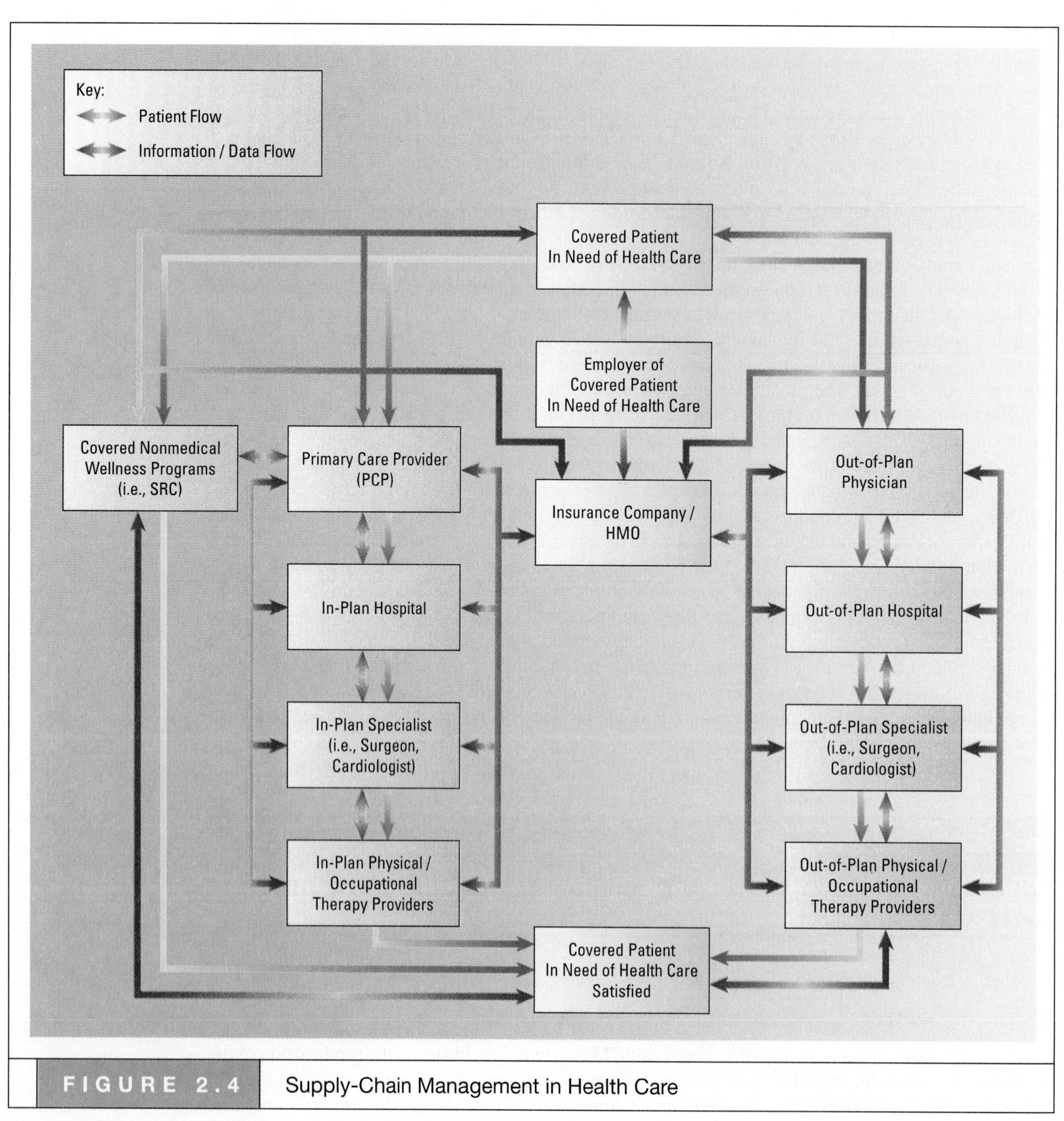

FIGURE 2.4 Supply-Chain Management in Health Care

MIAMI'S REC CENTER AND HEALTH CARE SUPPLY CHAINS

Figure 2.4 includes wellness programs as an operation in the health care supply chain. Miami's Student Recreation Center (SRC) is an example of an operation that can easily be a part of such covered wellness programs. Many hospitals also have wellness programs in which physical conditioning and aerobic activities are prescribed for health plan members as preventive measures. It is believed that promoting healthy lifestyles is one of the most effective ways to economically ensure that clients of health insurance companies don't face health care costs that exceed their financial means. As such, Figure 2.4 provides three sets of sequentially related operations that are managed by insurance companies and/or Health Maintenance Organizations (HMO) to provide patients with access to the needed medical services. The first and perhaps most economic alternative is wellness. The second is a network of "in plan" providers who are chosen because of their willingness to comply with the terms of the established health care plan. Third, the most expensive and least controlled set of operations are out-of-plan professionals.

In order to play a role in the health care supply chain, it would be necessary for the SRC to demonstrate that it has staff with the skill to promote wellness. Enrolling individuals in a wellness program doesn't just mean selling them memberships in the recreation center. Membership does nothing to promote wellness; appropriate exercise programs must also be faithfully carried out by members of the wellness program and rec center. While exercise can be beneficial in reducing exposure to significant health risks, exercise can also lead to injury and significant health care expenditures. As a consequence, wellness programs require administration and follow-through. Given that the SRC focuses mostly on student recreation and education, it has not chosen to build the administrative structure required to pursue an enrollment-based wellness program coordinated with the university's insurance company.

> active concept check

Now let's take a moment to test your knowledge of the concepts you have studied in this section.

> Supply-Chain Configuration Strategies

Supply-chain configuration involves establishing the parameters and boundaries that govern a firm's relationships within its chain of suppliers and customers.

VERTICAL INTEGRATION

What work should the firm do in-house and what should it contract out? These questions are associated with *vertical integration* decisions. Backward vertical integration decisions determine what a firm will make and what it will buy; forward vertical integration decisions determine what a firm will keep for use in subsequent operations and what it will sell. These decisions set the boundaries of the firm's value-adding system. Vertical integration is more frequently pursued in situations in which production volumes are high and firms have the needed expertise to run the supplying process (backward integration) or the customer involvement process (forward integration). Such high-volume operations depend on a reliable supply of materials and dependable channels of distribution.

Table 2.1 indicates when vertical integration makes sense and when it doesn't. If input materials are not related to the current focus of a company's business, nor are they unique or exclusive, vertical integration does not make sense. (Why would General Motors make paper for its photocopiers?) But if producing the input material is consistent with the company's current focus, then vertical integration would be worthwhile only if internal suppliers are more competitive than external suppliers. For example, General Motors might make ball bearings or radios or any number of automotive components and subassemblies, but only if its internal suppliers are competitive with external suppliers. Likewise, if a company holds the exclusive rights to an input, or needs to maintain the uniqueness of an offering on the basis of the uniqueness of that material, vertical integration is always worth considering. For example, Brush-Wellman is a company that makes engineered products from alloys of Beryllium. The company is vertically integrated backward to the mining of Beryllium—it controls the only mine for this metal outside of China and the Commonwealth of Independent States. Thus, vertical integration gives Brush Wellman a significant competitive advantage in the market for engineered products of Beryllium alloys.

TABLE 2.1 Guidelines for Vertical Integration Decisions

Consistency with current business focus / Exclusivity of use	Low	High
High	Make the decision based on the long-term economics of the "supplier" business—e.g. Should McDonald's make their own Happy Meal toys?	This is an obvious candidate for vertical integration—e.g., Should Kentucky Fried Chicken make their own "special blend of spices" for the "original recipe" fried chicken?
Low	This is an obvious situation for purchasing material from an outside supplier—e.g., Should your university make paper for its photocopying and printing needs?	Make the decision based on the competitiveness of the internal supplier—e.g., Should General Motors make car radios?

When an item does not fit with the firm's current focus, the option of vertical integration may still be considered, based on the long-term economic question of the value of the supplier's business. For example, McDonald's might get into the toy-making business in order to stock its Happy Meals with unique toys, but only if the toy-making business promises to be profitable over the long-term. Obviously, an item that is both required by a business and consistent with the firm's current focus provides the strongest incentive for vertical integration.

The terms *basic producer, converter, fabricator,* and *assembler* have been used to distinguish common steps in the creation of value among manufacturers. Common relationships between these steps are illustrated in the network seen in Figure 2.5. **Basic producers** use natural resources such as iron ore, oil, wheat, and minerals as inputs. Their outputs are basic materials such as rolled steel, flour, and plastic powders. **Converters** use basic materials as their inputs and add value by cutting and blending them in various ways. For example, a steel converter purchases rolls of steel in standard widths and thicknesses from steel mills. These rolls of steel are too heavy and too big to be used (or even handled)

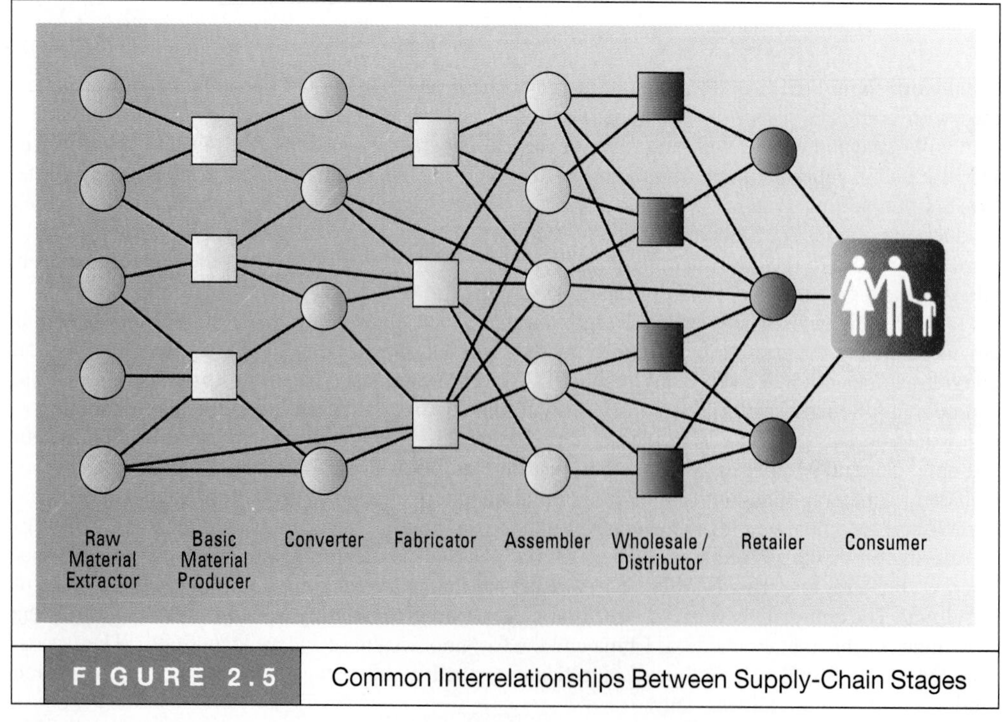

FIGURE 2.5 Common Interrelationships Between Supply-Chain Stages

by the equipment in most manufacturing plants. Thus the converter provides a valuable service by cutting the rolls into sheets and slitting them into smaller rolls on smaller spools, such that it will be suitable for processing. **Fabricators** use the material that is provided by converters to create parts for assembly operations. For example, folding a sheet of steel to make the metal part of a refrigerator door is a fabrication operation. Since basic producers, converters, and fabricators tend to make a variety of outputs from standardized inputs, they are said to have *diverging material flows.* By contrast, **assemblers** bring together a variety of different parts; thus they have *converging material flows.*

Distinguishing between terms like *fabricator* and *converter* is sometimes difficult; occasionally the two terms are used interchangeably. Figure 2.6 should help to clarify the use of this terminology. The figure shows the degree of vertical integration of some real companies as of 1998. Note that the boxes for the more fully integrated companies are wider than the others: They span more stages in the creation of value. For instance, Anheuser-Busch has a high degree of vertical integration; it is engaged in everything from agricultural operations (to secure raw materials) to the distribution of the finished product. Anheuser-Busch also manages a huge recycling operation to secure materials for canning its product. By contrast, AK Steel simply makes (converts) steel; Prince Corporation fabricates automobile parts, to the exclusion of all other activities; and Mad Monk Beer merely distributes its product—the company negotiates contracts for its manufacture.

Table 2.2 shows the range of possibilities in vertical integration, which runs from the hollow corporation at one end of the spectrum, through the use of original equipment manufacturers (OEMs) or subsidiaries for supply or distribution, to full vertical integration at the other end of the spectrum. A **hollow corporation** is a company that does not actually add value to the items it sells, but interacts with a network of supplying companies to sell their products. No material conversions take place in a hollow corporation. Mail-order companies are often hollow corporations. These operations—whose only working assets are a phone bank, a web page, or a mailbox with which to take orders—place items in their catalogs if they believe the supply to be adequate. Ordered goods are then sent directly from the supplier to the customer. In contrast, **original equipment manufacturers** are companies that manufacture components and/or products for sale under some other company's name.

For example, RCA was the first company to introduce digital satellite systems (DSS) for home television, though it has never actually made the systems. Thomson Consumer Electronics is RCA's OEM; it manufactures the DSS systems sold under RCA's label. Thomson benefits from RCA's name recognition, while RCA avoids the expense of developing its own process for manufacturing the

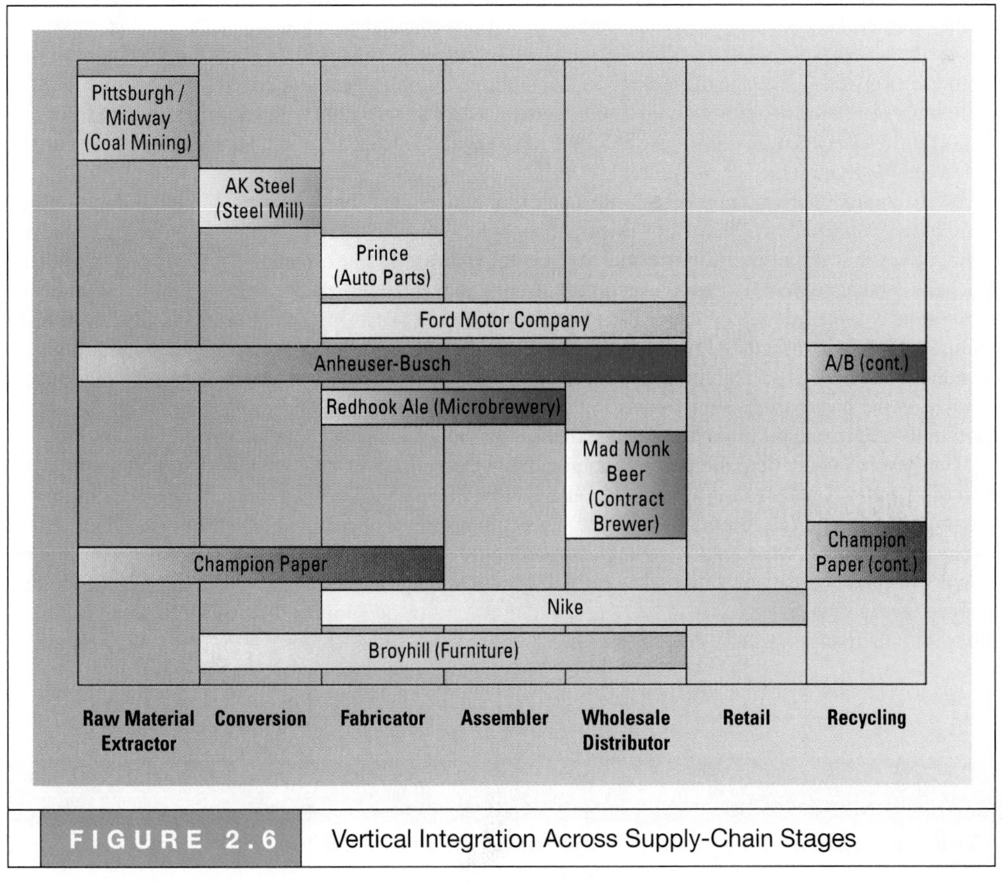

FIGURE 2.6 Vertical Integration Across Supply-Chain Stages

TABLE 2.2 Levels of Vertical Integration

Hollow Corporation	Original Equipment Manufacturer (OEM)	Subsidiary Supplier	Subsidiary Distributor	Full Vertical Integration
Buys and sells but doesn't "make" anything.	"Makes what someone else sells. Degree of backward integration can vary significantly from one OEM to the next.	Extracts raw materials or "makes" parts or subassemblies for a parent company.	Distributes and/ or sells the things that the parent company "makes."	Extracts raw materials, "makes" parts and subassemblies, assembles, "distributes," and "sells" its own products. Does not rely on any other company to add value to the product-service bundle.

complex DSS systems. By integrating backward, companies can create *subsidiary suppliers*. Similarly, by integrating forward, they can create *subsidiary distributors*. For example, Universal Studios is a subsidiary supplier of films for Disney. When Disney bought Capitol Cities/ABC, it created a subsidiary distributor for its media assets.

Finally, fully integrated companies own all the value-adding steps related to providing their product-service bundles. These firms are engaged in everything from raw material extraction to post-sale service activities. During the early part of the 1900s, Henry Ford's manufacturing operations were fully integrated. Ford had rubber plantations, farms, and mines; made the metal, rubber, concrete, and other basic materials; fabricated parts and subassemblies of every type; assembled cars and trucks; and distributed all of these. Today, many of the large paper companies are fully integrated; they own and manage forest land, harvest timber, operate lumber mills, make paper pulp, and manufacture paper products.

Since, for vertically integrated firms, the whole value chain eventually ends up on one consolidated income statement, one negative aspect of vertical integration is the increased exposure to financial risk associated with the business cycle of recession and growth. When companies control more of the assets in a supply chain, they bear more of the economic problems during slow sales periods for the chain's output. When many companies share the supply chain, the economic problems can be spread across these companies. Other drawbacks of vertical integration include a loss of expertise resulting from the consolidation of management and operations (supplies and expertise from companies specializing in one area are generally lost with vertical integration), failure to recognize external market opportunities because of the secure internal market, and a loss of competitiveness because of the secure internal market.

For example, GM might be very good at assembling cars, but that doesn't mean that GM would be good at making tires. If GM were to integrate backward and buy Michelin, managers would find that many issues that are relevant to tire making are not relevant to car assembly. If GM were to replace Michelin's management with auto executives or even to consolidate the management of the two firms, the company would lose key expertise in regard to tire making. Michelin would have less need to compete for GM's orders and might not even pursue outside sales opportunities because of adequate demand from GM. Thus, Michelin would become less competitive, less attuned to consumer needs. Finally, if the car market were to take a downturn, GM would suffer simultaneously in two areas (assembly and tire making) instead of just one (assembly).

The benefits of vertical integration include greater control over product quality, greater coordination of operations across the value chain, access to new technologies and other intelligence of strategic importance, and the potential for larger aggregate profit margins. Ultimately, by weighing what is to be gained against what is to be lost, a company must determine its ideal degree of vertical integration. Firms that choose not to integrate vertically may attempt to gain some of the benefits of vertical integration by devoting significant resources and energy to developing trusting long-term relationships with their suppliers and customers.

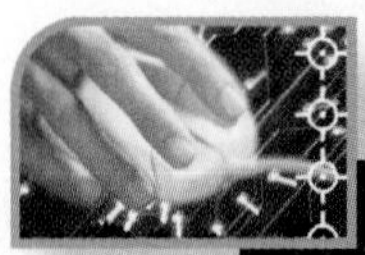

active exercise <

Take a moment to apply what you've learned.

OUTSOURCING

In contrast to vertical integration, **outsourcing** is contracting with a third party to provide some aspect of the product-service bundle. The practice of outsourcing various aspects of the product-service bundle is rapidly growing because of the increased ability to communicate electronically and the availability of modern cost-accounting tools that can be used to compare in-house and supplier costs. One study, published in 1999 by *Purchasing* magazine, indicated that 54% of the companies surveyed had outsourced manufacturing or service activities in the past two to three years and 46% indicated they were intending to increase their outsourcing activity. By contrast only 38% had done no outsourcing and only 4% intended to reduce their outsourcing activity. Other findings of this study were that most companies are satisfied with their outsourcing arrangements, rigorous supplier qualification and monitoring are central to successful outsourcing, and outsourcing decisions are most commonly made by cross-functional teams. Specifically, one respondent indicated that outsourcing decisions were "completely cross-functional" and based on input from "purchasing, technology, quality, marketing, finance, manufacturing, etc."[1]

Outsourcing benefits firms in many ways. It allows a company to focus on what it does best: its *core competencies.* It adds capacity without adding significant fixed costs and overhead. It is often more cost effective, because suppliers may be better at the outsourced activity and they may gain economies of scale through providing the same service or manufacturing value to multiple customers. Finally, outsourcing supports corporate growth and market agility: It allows companies to grow without making large capital investments that would hurt their income levels in the case of an economic downturn.

Many companies referred to as *contract manufacturers* have now emerged and there's no reason to assume that the best and biggest are in the United States. Outsourcing is certainly one factor that puts the "global" in global supply-chain management. The emerging industrial economies of the Pacific Rim have become common locations for contract manufacturers. Singapore, for example, with excellent port facilities, a highly educated and disciplined workforce, and outstanding communications and technological infrastructure has become a major player for electronics contract manufacturing. Singapore-based firms such as NatSteel Electronics Ltd. or Venture Manufacturing Ltd. manufacture products for HP, IBM, Apple, Seagate Technologies, Lockheed Martin, Motorola, Compaq, Iomega, and others from production facilities dispersed around the world. SCI Systems based in Huntsville, Alabama; Solectron Corporation of Milpitas, California; and Jabil Circuit, Inc. are among the largest contract manufacturers in the United States. Jabil's customer list includes such well-known customers as Cisco Systems, Dell, HP, 3Com, Gateway 2000, Nortel Networks, and Ascend Communications. In fact, though Cisco dominates the market for Internet routers, it hardly makes any products itself. The company's vice president is quoted as saying: "We've cleaned up the supply chain. . . . You don't add value by having multiple people touch a product."[2]

Contract manufacturers often describe themselves as *manufacturing services* and are classified as service providers. They aren't necessarily a choice to consider only when your own company is short on capacity. Instead, they may provide much better quality and supply-chain performance. For example, Solectron was ranked number 3 overall in *Business Week*'s 1999 World's Best Performing Information Technology listing. It was listed in the service providers, distributors, and resellers category and was number one in its category. Solectron has won the highly prestigious Malcolm Baldrige National Quality Award twice, illustrating that contract manufacturers are not a lesser choice. Its press releases suggest that "by partnering with Solectron, OEMs can achieve better asset utilization, faster time-to-market and time-to-volume, and the lowest total product costs."

According to *Forbes* magazine, the trend toward outsourcing appears to be gaining momentum. In a 1999 article[3] it suggests that telecommunications equipment makers alone are expected to divest approximately $20 billion in facilities over the next few years. It also suggests that "if recent trends continue, many of the biggest-name companies will someday exit manufacturing entirely and busy themselves with design and marketing.

Channel assembly and *vendor-managed inventory* are value-added services being offered by many logistics companies, which allow companies to outsource activities that would have been unthinkable in the past. Now, rather than transporting a fully assembled product, a number of trucking firms have trained their drivers to assemble products that they frequently transport. This is one example of channel assembly. In this case, the strategy significantly reduces transportation costs and the risk of damage during transportation. Vendor managed inventory is a similar concept, whereby the logistics provider or material supplier keeps track of the materials that are bought by a customer on a regular

[1]Source: Anne Millen Porter, "Outsourcing Gains Popularity," *Purchasing Online: The Magazine of Supply Chain Management* (March 11, 1999). Accessed online.

[2]Neil Weinberg, "Bill Morean's $1.2 Billion Haircut," *Forbes* magazine, June 14, 1999, (on-line edition).

[3]Ibid.

basis. Instead of responding to a purchase order, they just make sure the customer has what they need when it's needed and bill them for what is used. If a logistics provider is managing the inventory, this allows them to decide when to transport the materials on the basis of other shipments that they have to handle and can result in significant savings in shipping costs. If a supplier is managing the inventory, this allows them to see usage patterns and schedule production based on what's best for them instead of waiting for a purchase order to schedule production. *Stockless purchasing* is frequently associated with vendor managed inventory. In this case, a supplier manages inventory that is physically housed in the customer's facility but owned by the supplier. Thus, the inventory is available to the customer but not owned by the customer. From the customer's accountant's perspective, they are stockless. Only when the customer actually uses the inventory does a transaction occur that could be recognized as a sale.

So what should a company outsource? The answer seems to be anything that can be done more effectively by another provider. It is easy to find examples where companies have outsourced all of their manufacturing, production, and assembly of their direct materials (e.g., the VW plant in Brazil we described earlier), indirect materials such as business forms or packaging, logistics, distribution, inventory management, and noncore operations such as a cafeteria on a college campus.

video exercise <

Take a moment to apply what you've learned.

active concept check <

Now let's take a moment to test your knowledge of the concepts you have studied in this section.

> Supply-Chain Coordination Strategies

Supply-chain coordination involves a firm in integrating its decisions with those made within its chain of suppliers and customers.

RELATIONSHIP MANAGEMENT

Both supplier relations and customer relations are key to effective coordination of supply chains. In the past, the interaction between suppliers and their customers was often adversarial and based on negotiated contracts that spelled out all of the terms and conditions to which both parties were required to comply. This might still be a very suitable way for large companies to buy commodities that would be of equal quality regardless of the supplier. On the other hand, many supplier–customer relationships don't work like that any more. Instead, companies are creating long-term strategic relationships with their suppliers and expecting them to provide much more than a product at a particular price. **Sole sourcing** is a practice whereby a company commits to buy all of a particular type of its services or goods from one vendor. In exchange, the vendor becomes a partner in design of new product-service bundles, vendor expertise and knowledge can be shared and leveraged for product and process improvement, the costs of negotiating and administering contracts are reduced, and the planning decisions can be coordinated more closely. **Integrated supply** is one approach to sole sourcing now being promoted by many distributing companies. With integrated supply, a distributor offers to provide a high level of service on an entire line of products at agreed-upon prices in exchange for a guarantee that they will receive all of the distribution business in that product line. Ultimately, such relationships require supply chain partners to trust each other and conduct their business with integrity. Without the ability to trust supply-chain partners, most of the strategies described in this chapter are difficult to use.

Even when sole sourcing is not seen as a viable option, many companies are becoming more aggressive in their attempts to manage their suppliers. One way to do this is through **supplier certification,** which is a practice of requiring suppliers to document certain characteristics in order to obtain business. For example, some companies require their suppliers to maintain certain standards for quality and on-time delivery, have a certain level of financial strength, use a particular approach for electronic exchange of data, use certain workforce management practices, follow certain ethical guidelines, and so on. Many companies don't set their own supplier certification standards but do rely on universal quality standards called *ISO 9000 standards* which were introduced in the late 1980s. Thousands of facilities were certified under these standards during the decade of the 1990s. By requiring suppliers to be ISO 9000 certified, a company could ensure that the practices of the supplier were consistent. This allowed them to base their planning decisions on a known level of quality—and also to eliminate suppliers that provided inconsistent quality. (The automobile industry in the United States requires suppliers to comply with *QS 9000 standards,* which is an expanded version of ISO 9000.) Another set of standards, called *ISO 14000 standards,* allows companies to gain certification for their environmental management systems.

Beyond certification, many customers are working to help suppliers improve their processes. Chrysler Corporation, for instance, spends considerable resources to reduce the costs of its purchased materials through its Supplier Cost Reduction (SCORE) program. In this program, Chrysler sets cost-reduction goals and suppliers make cost-reduction proposals to achieve those goals. Chrysler and the supplier share in the savings. Total savings from the program, which began in 1990, are now estimated to exceed $1 billion.

Relationship management isn't all about customers dictating requirements for suppliers; it's a two-way street. Certainly, suppliers can gain benefits from the preferential treatment they receive. They also need to rethink the way they approach the marketplace. Rather than following a sales-intensive strategy, suppliers may benefit from relationship marketing techniques. Instead of being focused on negotiating the optimal conditions for individual orders, suppliers need to demonstrate their strength and capabilities to gain the trust of their customers. Further, by investing their money, time, and effort to gain a clear understanding of their customer's needs and satisfying these, they gain the preferential treatment they desire.

> **active example**

Take a closer look at the concepts and issues you've been reading about.

> **video exercise**

Take a moment to apply what you've learned.

E-COMMERCE

As was noted in Chapter 1, e-commerce is much more than the on-line stores of larger retailers. In fact, it has become a major component of business-to-business relationships across most manufacturing supply chains. Information technology is a key enabler of supply chain coordination. Table 2.3 illustrates the role of information in making coordination possible without relying heavily on inventory buffers between steps of the supply chain. Essentially, effective use of information technologies allows firms to turn the supply-chain management process upside down. Upstream planning decisions can be based on downstream demand. In the past, these decisions would be based on forecasts, and material availability would be used to influence demand.

Without collecting and sharing information regarding demand, inventory, capacity, and schedules, it is not possible to make coordinated decisions in one company—let alone across an entire supply chain. As a consequence, *Automated Data Collection* (ADC) devices are a critical component of the SCM coordination picture. ADC can be accomplished through point-of-sale systems and other types of bar code scanners; however, more sophisticated technologies are also available. *Radio frequency identification* (RFID) systems work by placing small microchip-based tags and transponders on items, so their location and quantities can always be immediately verified. In the past, RFID has only been economically viable by reusing the tags and transponders. Today, however, disposable and ultra-thin transponders are beginning to be used by airlines in luggage applications. It is likely that RFID

TABLE 2.3 Supply-Chain Information Reverses Coordination Approach

Old supply-chain coordination approach (information used)	E-commerce-based supply-chain coordination approach (shared information)
Step 1: Buy raw materials and schedule capacity. Buy extra inventory or reserve extra capacity in case the forecast is wrong. (Forecasted use of the materials.)	Step 1: Provide a customized product in response to a known customer requirement. (Customer specifications for desired product-service bundle.)
Step 2: Make a finished product or service. Make a little extra and put it in inventory in case the forecast is wrong. (Product/Service Standards fixed by design. Quantities based on demand forecasts.)	Step 2: Deliver products/service based on their consumption. (Customer sales information collected through POS system. Logistics and distribution system responds to actual consumption.)
Step 3: Distribute goods to market. Make sure to have some channel inventory or expediting systems in case the demand doesn't match availability. (Established logistical/distribution system.)	Step 3: Provide no more of the product-service bundles than is justified by known demand. (Value-adding system responds to known consumption.)
Step 4: Sell through retailers. Offer incentives such as rebates or promotional pricing if inventories are too large. (Actual sales information may not be shared with the product-service bundle provider.)	Step 4: Buy materials and schedule capacity based on known demand. (Suppliers respond in the same way and may use POS information rather than requiring purchase orders and demand forecasts.)

Source: Adapted from Rhonda R. Lummus, and Robert J. Vokura, "Managing the Demand Chain through Managing the Information Flow: Capturing 'Moments of Information'." *Production and Inventory Management Journal* 40, no. 1 (1999): 17.

systems will eventually replace many bar code–based inventory tracking systems. Real-time locator systems are now becoming available; they use wall-mounted readers to monitor the movement of materials in a facility based on information from the data tags.

Once data has been collected, it is necessary to provide access and decision support systems to enhance its usefulness. ERP systems that allow companies to communicate demand, inventory, and scheduling decisions with one another can have a big impact on the level of coordination accomplished across the supply chain. Recently, there has been debate over the usefulness of ERP systems because lots of companies have spent lots of money on them, yet obtained mediocre or dismal results. Large ERP systems are expensive. Their implementation usually takes on a high profile in a company. Often their implementation requires the use of outside consulting agencies that may be perceived as unfamiliar with existing company concerns. And their effectiveness may be significantly influenced by the inability or unwillingness of a company to change existing systems and processes to make way for the ERP system. Consequently, when they fail, it's a big deal. On the other hand, where ERP systems are successfully implemented, their value is difficult to understate.

In the late 1990s, many companies struggled to free their computing systems of the so-called millennium (or Y2K) bug. (This refers to a problem with many older computer programs and chips that coded year-related information using two digits to save memory when computer technologies were less advanced than today. For example, "99" meant 1999 and "00" meant 1900. Since both 2000 and 1900 would have to be "00" and computers were programmed to treat "00" exclusively as 1900, time-based calculations would all be wrong after the turn of the century.) One way to deal with the problem was to install new information systems and do away with older systems that were not Y2K compliant. The result for many firms was a rushed implementation of ERP software, with the idea that they could later change the business process to better fit the software. Unfortunately, this is not the ideal approach to change management. Software systems then perpetuate old, potentially ineffective practices. Generally, it would be better to update and improve business processes before installing ERP software and information systems to automate and perpetuate them.

E-commerce has had a large impact on the structure of supply chains. Middlemen, the historic channels for trade of materials and information, are less influential and often not even needed in the supply chain. By contrast, logistics providers and experts on materials processing, warehousing, and transfers (such as UPS, Federal Express, DHL) have grown in their importance, particularly with the globalization of business. Similarly, the channel power of retailers has extended backward throughout entire supply chains. As an example, Wal-Mart has pioneered data sharing, business partnerships that allow suppliers to ensure that their merchandise is fully stocked on the retail shelves, and direct connections via the Internet to those who schedule their vendors' processes. Finally, the Internet has provided an information umbrella in materials auction systems that can allow buyers to pool their orders to obtain volume pricing, while at the same time allowing a wider range of suppliers the opportunity to bid for such orders.

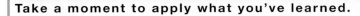

> active exercise

Take a moment to apply what you've learned.

> active concept check

Now let's take a moment to test your knowledge of the concepts you have studied in this section.

> Improving Supply Chains: Seven Principles

Figure 2.7 illustrates the fact that once a supply-chain configuration has been established and once coordination mechanisms are in use, they may still be improved. It also presents seven principles for supply-chain improvement. In some cases, the ideal configuration changes over time with changes in technology and customer preferences. In other cases, technology allows different mechanisms for coordination across the supply chain. At any rate, it is generally advisable for companies to view their supply-chain configuration and coordination systems as worthy of improvement. By making improvements over time, competitive advantages can be gained in the marketplace. When companies think their supply chain has been optimized, they are likely to become resistant to changes that might lead to improvement. Over time, this can lead to a loss of competitive advantage or even to competitive disadvantage. Each of the seven principles is discussed in further detail below:

SEGMENT CUSTOMERS BASED UPON SERVICE NEEDS

Different customers have unique service requirements, and meeting their requirements necessitates different approaches to supply-chain configuration and coordination. Henry Ford's "one size fits all" is clearly not what supply-chain management is all about. Instead, performance can be improved

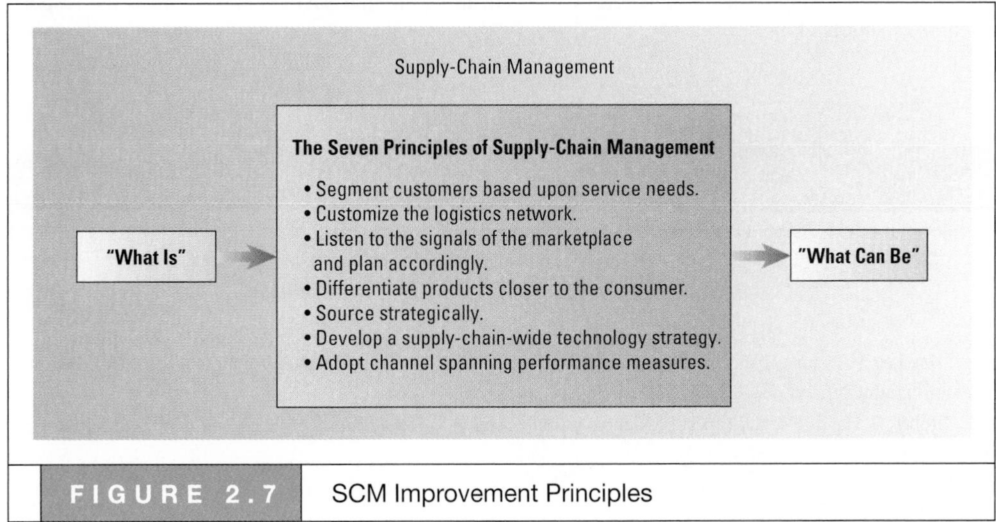

FIGURE 2.7 SCM Improvement Principles

(from the customer's perspective and eventually from a competitive perspective) by more effectively matching what is provided, when it is provided, and in the quantities it will be provided to specific customer requirements. Building a system that allows customers to specify just what their product and service preferences are sounds great, but this does require a certain level of marketing research skill, operational flexibility, and cost accounting sophistication. You need to have a good handle on what specific customer groups want; accurately estimate what that will cost and justify the cost to the customer, and be good enough to follow through on promises to satisfy those preferences.

CUSTOMIZE THE LOGISTICS NETWORK

Logistics is a big part of the supply chain. It's not enough just to be able to make what a customer wants or provide the desired level of service. It's important to be able to distribute the product-service bundle in the quantities and timing requirements determined by the customer. Again, one size does not fit all. For example, the logistics network used to provide replacement parts to a trucking company that maintains its own large fleet of vehicles would be much different than the network used to provide parts to the many independent vehicle repair shops. From the customer's perspective, improvement of the supply chain often implies customization of the logistics network based on the segmentation described in the first step above.

LISTEN TO THE SIGNALS OF THE MARKETPLACE AND PLAN ACCORDINGLY

This involves reversing the traditional practice of listening to demand forecasts created independently by various functions of the business and various businesses across the supply chain and planning according to these forecasts. The result of planning based on independent forecasts is capacity and material imbalances across the supply chain and a phenomenon referred to as the **bullwhip effect.** The bullwhip effect is the tendency of small variations in demand to become larger as their implications are transmitted backward through a supply chain. Handfield and Nichols (1999) describe the findings of a study on this phenomenon[4] as a result of "distorted information from one end of the supply chain to the other" and describe Proctor & Gamble's (somewhat funny) experience as follows:

> "P&G began to explore this phenomenon after a series of particularly erratic shifts in ordering up and down the supply chain for one of its most popular products, Pampers disposable diapers. After determining that it was highly unlikely that the infants and toddlers at the ultimate user level for Pampers were creating extreme swings in demand for the product, the examination began to work back through the supply chain. It was found that distributors' orders showed far more variability than the level of demand represented at retail stores themselves. Continuing through the supply chain, P&G's orders to its supplier, 3M, indicated the most variability of all."[5]

The variability was found to come from updates and changes in demand forecasts, batching orders together in order to reduce transportation and other costs associated with producing and stocking the diapers, price fluctuations that occurred to move inventory close to the end of accounting reporting periods, or quantity discounts and other means of rationing supply across the supply chain.[6] Studies have indicated that stockpiling inventory across the supply chain can result in hundreds of days of inventory. Eliminating such inefficiencies can result in significant savings and improve the responsiveness of supply chains.

active exercise <

Take a moment to apply what you've learned.

[4]Hau Lee, V. Padmanabhan, and Seungjin Whang, "The Bullwhip Effect in Supply Chains," *Sloan Management Review,* (Spring 1997): 93–102.

[5]Robert B. Handfield, and Ernest L. Nichols Jr., *Introduction to Supply Chain Management* (Upper Saddle River, NJ: Prentice-Hall, 1999), 17–18.

[6]Ibid.

DIFFERENTIATE PRODUCTS CLOSER TO THE CONSUMER

Postponement is a strategy that delays customization of the product-service bundle as long as possible. For example, a drug manufacturer could postpone customization by distributing drugs in powder form to pharmacies and allowing the pharmacies to create tablets of various sizes depending on customer dosages (e.g., 500 mg and 1000 mg). Similarly, creating modular product and service designs supports a postponement strategy. One diesel engine manufacturer, for example, produces both V6 and V12 engines from the same V6 engine blocks. The V12 is made of two V6 engine blocks bolted together. Restaurants can customize their beverages or meals in much the same way: When they get the customer's order, they simply have to assemble modules that are prepared in advance. This allows them to provide quick service with acceptable levels of customization. Contract manufacturers that assemble computers based on customer orders also provide a good example of the customization made available through postponement.

SOURCE STRATEGICALLY

Strategic sourcing suggests that suppliers who have demonstrated superior performance deserve customer loyalty and preferential treatment. Clearly, one way to improve the supply chain is to select an excellent set of suppliers—particularly for critical or strategic elements of the product-service bundle—and invest money, time, and effort in making them even better. This also allows the developments and improvements pursued by suppliers to be targeted to the needs of the downstream stages of the supply chain.

DEVELOP A SUPPLY-CHAIN-WIDE TECHNOLOGY STRATEGY

One of the difficulties in implementing mechanisms and tools for supply-chain coordination is that companies make technology decisions independently—then their information systems are not compatible and information is not easily shared back and forth. The flow of information is just as important to supply-chain coordination as the logistical system is to the supply-chain configuration. When technology investments across the supply chain result in compatible information systems, readily available data can be transformed into the useful information that leads to coordinated decision making. When information systems are not compatible, companies are likely to spend a great deal of time, money, and energy in building managerial and software interfaces that span the systems. Even with these interfaces, it may be difficult to get access to the information that would allow coordinated decision making.

ADOPT CHANNEL SPANNING PERFORMANCE MEASURES

One of the biggest difficulties faced by those who are trying to make improvements in supply chains is that individual companies pay decision makers. Their rewards are generally based on functional performance measures and to some extent the financial performance of their company. Improving the performance of the whole chain may not result in improvements of narrow functional measures, especially in the short-term. For example, if you're studying local performance measures for a logistics provider (such as average shipment weight or dollars billed per mile), it might not look good for a logistics provider to carry special shipments for a valued customer on a less-than-truckload basis. On the other hand, if you're looking at a global performance measure (such as days of inventory in the supply chain), this customized treatment would be better.

Even in one business, establishing agreed-upon performance measures that do lead to cross-functional coordination but don't result in sacrifices of long-term performance for short-term results and don't create undesired incentives is difficult. Of course, expanding the development of performance measures to consider an entire supply chain is even more difficult. Nevertheless, if there is no measurement of supply-chain-wide performance, there will be little incentive for supply-chain improvement. Localized decision making will be perpetuated, and the inefficiencies associated with it will not be eliminated. Generally, it does require a strong party—such as a WalMart in the consumer goods supply chain, a large auto company in the automobile supply chain, or a large insurance company in the health care supply chain—to force the adoption of chain-spanning performance measures and objectives.

> active concept check

Now let's take a moment to test your knowledge of the concepts you have studied in this section.

> Integrating Operational Decisions

This chapter is part of the overarching material covered in Chapters 1–6 that describes approaches linking the value-adding system to customer expectations. This initial part of the book provides a context for the structural and infrastructural decisions covered later in the book.

This chapter has direct linkages to virtually every chapter in the book, but especially to Chapters 3, 4, 7, and 12. Chapter 3 covers operations strategy—the supply chain configuration issues faced by a company will depend heavily on their operations strategy. Chapters 4 and 7 deal with design of the product-service bundle and the value-adding system—these decision areas are significant factors in the configuration of supply chains. Finally, Chapter 12 deals with scheduling issues that put flesh around the concept of supply-chain coordination.

All in all, it could be said that this chapter is a sort-of road map to the rest of the book. Specifically, the part of the book that deals with building the value-adding system addresses supply-chain configuration issues from the operations management perspective. The part that deals with planning, scheduling, and controlling the value-adding system addresses supply-chain coordination issues from the operations management perspective. And the part of the book that deals with linking the value-adding system to customer expectations deals with improving the supply chain from the operations management perspective.

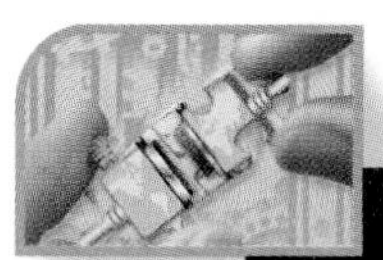

integrated OM

Take a moment to apply what you've learned.

> Chapter Wrap-Up

This chapter has introduced you to the topic of supply-chain management. SCM deals with the configuration, coordination, and improvement of sequentially related operations. It is a cross-functional, cross-business, integrative topic which has gained more and more attention in recent years because of coordination opportunities available as a result of advances in information systems technology and because of the operational benefits observed through lean production methods.

Supply chains will vary from industry to industry. In some industries, such as automobiles, powerful companies with large operational volumes and significant capital drive supply-chain management configuration and coordination approaches. In other industries, such as health care, service providers drive the configuration of the supply chain and all coordination goes through them.

Supply-chain configuration involves design decisions and strategic alignment of an organization's resources with those of other product or service providers in the chain. Companies need to decide what their core competencies will be, become the best in the chain at that, and find ways to get the other members of the chain to effectively provide the other aspects of the product-service bundle. Thus configuration choices could involve either vertical integration or outsourcing.

Supply-chain coordination involves scheduling resources, information exchange, and material flows across the extended enterprise. Relationship management activities, such as supplier development and relationship marketing, are key enablers of supply-chain coordination. Information technologies, such as ADC and ERP systems, are also key enablers of coordinated decision making across the chain.

Typical supply chains present many opportunities for system-wide improvement. We have described seven common ways to improve supply chains in this chapter: Segmenting customers based on their unique service needs, customizing the logistics network for each customer segment, listening to the signals of the marketplace and planning according to these rather than according to independent forecasts, differentiating products closer to the customer through the postponement strategy, sourcing strategically, developing supply-chain-wide technology strategies, and adopting channel spanning performance measurement strategies.

> end-of-chapter resources

- Practice Quiz
- Key Terms
- Discussion Questions
- Case 2.1: Manufacturers Squeeze Retailers
- References
- Plant Tours

Operations Strategy: Aligning Operations within the Firm

Chapter Outline

What's Ahead

. . . BACK AT THE REC CENTER

The four have all arrived early and are in the exercise room, well into their workout, when Fred cuts his stay short, saying, "I'm off to another mind-numbing sales meeting. Somebody has to keep our salespeople from going off the deep end!" Luis looks surprised that Fred is leaving so soon. "Yeah, they all want to keep their numbers up, because the margins in this division are so tight. They all want to bring home that big commission. They'll promise the moon if it gets them the order!" Fred puffs as he climbs off the stepper.

Fred has complained before that his staff is always trying to promise some new color or other feature to prospective customers. Many of those promises create problems for the manufacturing people, who must keep costs low for the division to be profitable. "You know, maybe a company logo on a beeper, some variation in the shell, or maybe even a favor on the shipping time," he continues as his breathing slows a bit. "The problem is that when production sees the order, that stuff really hits the fan." Fred knows the production people want to keep the schedule simple and easy to plan, well in advance of actual production. They want plain vanilla with no surprises. The little favors a salesperson might sneak in for a customer in order to make a bigger sale can be very problematic for them.

"I think it's kind of boring, you know, no bells or whistles, but that's what works in this market. I keep hearing that our customers buy from us because we are the cheapest. The way we squeeze pennies, we must be pretty darn good," he sneers.

"Yeah, our agents deal with a similar situation when they're confronted with passengers who want some slack with check-in time or schedule changes," Tom responds, as he glances at the pulse reading on the monitor of his exercise bike. Like Fred's company, Tom's airline makes its bread and butter on being less expensive than the competition. Last-minute changes and special requests are just the sort of thing that adds to the cost of a ticket. Tom knows that an airline like his, or any other business that focuses on low-cost operation, can't turn a profit on special orders, a wide variety of customers, or a new and untried operating method.

"We go by the book; if we don't, we lose money. If we do, we keep costs down, make a little money on each seat, and make a profit by filling more seats over the long run," continues Tom. "Plain old vanilla might not be too exciting, but if it's good and people can get it fast and when they want it, then we can win them over. If they want 33 flavors, well, they'll be going somewhere else anyway," Tom adds, with enough steam to make the pulse monitor on his bike beep like a warning light in an airplane cockpit.

Fred nods in agreement. "I know what you're saying. It's just that when the customer is in your face, you want to make him happy. I just get frustrated because cost was only an afterthought in my last job. We weren't stupid about costs. We just wanted to suit our customers to a tee. We just passed on whatever costs we felt were justified. Nobody complained as long as we got the product right."

Fred knows he can't do that in his new job. Like Tom's airline, his division is only selling plain vanilla. While in some ways Fred may feel that isn't as exciting as selling 33 flavors, he is gradually starting to see the challenge of cooperating with operations in order to keep production costs down. "It'll take some time, but I can learn," Fred concludes, as he reaches for a towel and wipes the sweat from his eyes.

Luis and Cheryl are listening from across the room as they take turns doing sets on a weight machine. "We're more like your old division at the hospital," Cheryl offers. "People want exactly what they need, they want it now, and they want it to be the best technology can offer. Everybody in our business knows that's not easy, and it certainly isn't cheap. We feel we're winning when we keep costs down to what is reasonable and customary for our type of hospital. We just try to keep them in the ballpark and focus on health care to fit the individual. If cost were a big issue, we couldn't always do what is expected of us. But then, maybe you and I ought to trade jobs for a while. It sounds as if we both like the grass on the other side of the fence."

"We're not like Fred's place, either. We're definitely not the cheapest sofa maker in town," Luis chimes in. "Making the cheapest chair, sofa, or table available doesn't fit in with what we do. To be the cheapest, we'd have to cut out a lot of the services that set us apart from the other guys. That's not what we're in business for. Our problem is getting everybody on the same page. It's as if we all look at the same picture and then go off into our own little groups. There's not a lot of talking between the groups. Eventually we work it out, but it takes time, and it isn't cheap."

Top managers in Luis's company have expressed concern about this issue in the past. They sometimes feel that marketing, finance, and operations aren't always in sync. What's more, workers on the shop floor often feel confused about priorities and sense they are being pulled in different directions. Middle managers like Luis sometimes doubt that the issue of what kind of company the firm wants to be has ever been settled for sure. Luis knows how much time the designers spend coming up with new styles and fresh fabrics, and how hard the sales staff works to ensure a good fit with each customer's needs. He knows his company does a lot of things that customers don't necessarily see on the delivery truck. But he isn't sure that the company always takes the best path. With everybody interpreting their functional goals independently, the results can be very wasteful and frustrating. Ironically, the company is small and closely held by just a few owners. If anybody should be able to get it together, Luis thinks, it should be them.

"Yeah, I've seen some of your more, uh, 'unique' stuff, and the price tags that go with it! Different strokes, I guess," laughs Tom.

"Well, you're right, some of it gets pretty wild, but somebody wanted it, and we knew how to make it. If they can afford to have us do it, they're usually pretty cool with it when they see it. Besides, that's what we're here for," Luis replies, pretending to look insulted.

Fred is nodding again, but this time he is more comfortable with what he is hearing. "Yes, I guess it's sort of like what we want out of this club. Tom and I are here to lose some pounds, keep the ticker in shape, and maybe extend what we have a little longer. We pay the same membership fees as you two, yet you and Cheryl are after something else. You want to add something with those weights. We don't get what we want with the weights, but I doubt you'd leave the weight machine and the mirror long enough to use this stepper! The more I think about it, I need to realize that our goals are different in this new division. I guess that means that the strategy for meeting those goals has to be different."

Fred is beginning to see that the priorities a firm chooses help to shape its strategies. Different priorities, different strategies. Listening to Luis and thinking about his upcoming meeting, he realizes that regardless of the priorities a company chooses, the better they are understood across functional lines, the more competitive the firm will be. "You know me, I'm used to giving customers what they want. Add the features, bells and whistles—newer, neater, cutting edge. But cost? Now they tell me to be the cheapest?" After a pause, Fred concludes, "I need to adjust my thinking."

"You can joke about the mirror all you want, Mr. Aerobics! It's all in the perspective, the big picture," Luis shoots back, as he flexes his arms mockingly. Luis knows that unless everybody sees the same picture, finding strategies that will fit together will be a long and slow process. If you're having a hard time seeing the forest through the trees, he realizes, maybe you need to step back and look at the forest from a broader perspective. Fred, Tom, and Cheryl nod in understanding as they head off to face their day at work.

> objectives

Take a moment to familiarize yourself with the key objectives of this chapter.

> gearing up

Before you begin reading this chapter, try a short warm-up activity.

> Introduction

This chapter introduces the topic of operations strategy. For a company to provide consistent value for their customers and gain a competitive advantage as a result, it is important for its decision makers to be consistent with each other. When their decisions are consistent, you can say they are implementing a clear strategy.

Decisions are made at every level of an organization. There is, therefore, a hierarchy within which decisions fit. At the corporate level, decisions generally answer the question, What business are we in? At the business level they indicate how a firm will compete against others that offer the same kind of products and services. This involves deciding what type of competitive advantage the company will seek in the marketplace and allocating resources in light of that decision. Finally, within the various functions, decision makers have to figure out how they will use their resources to support the pursuit of competitive advantage.

Operations management involves both structural and infrastructural decisions. The structural decisions are about facilities, product and service designs, technology, and how responsibilities will be divided among the various companies involved in a sequence of value-adding activities. In other words, the structural decisions are "bricks and mortar" decisions with long-term implications. Infrastructural decisions pertain to such issues as scheduling, quality assurance, employee supervision, and maintenance of the system. These decisions focus on the use of existing operational resources over the short-term and intermediate-range time horizon.

Companies vary in the degree to which they integrate their operational decisions into the broader strategy of their company. For instance, a company could treat operations as an independent function—with their only expectation being that operations not create any problems; they could expect operations to at least match what competitors are doing; they could expect operations to provide some source of competitive advantage in support of the business strategy; or they could expect the operations function to drive the business strategy by developing unique sources of competitive advantage. The more decisions within operations are integrated and the more operational decisions are integrated with those of the other business functions, the more likely it is that the firm will gain the competitive advantages it seeks in the marketplace.

One area of interest to many companies and their customers is the environmental impact of their ongoing operations. This is one area where we can clearly illustrate the importance of integrating operational decisions with those of other functions. In fact, the last section of this chapter suggests that the more effectively a company integrates its operational decisions with those of other functions, the more likely it is to attain environmental excellence.

> Integrating Operations Management with Other Functions

Can you imagine how frustrating it would be for a salesperson whose marketing department has advertised a new product based on its unequaled design quality to find out that the operations function had tried to make the item as inexpensively as possible? Or what if a service is advertised as the fastest but the operations managers are always delaying jobs to save money and avoid paying overtime? What if a product is marketed as low cost and built inexpensively, but the finance department tries to charge unusually high interest rates to consumers? How do you think a human resources professional, whose job is to recruit engineers and scientists at the cutting edge of their profession, would react when asked by a cost-conscious controller to save money by advertising positions in the local paper instead of a scientific journal? What about the engineer whose research and development budget is cut because of the same cost-conscious controller—just as a technological breakthrough is within reach?

Conflicting situations between individuals in different functional areas, such as the illustrative examples in the last paragraph, are not the least bit uncommon. It's also common for there to be conflicting priorities at different levels of the corporate hierarchy, even within the same function. It is a real challenge for companies to get decision makers—with different educational backgrounds, different performance measures, different pay scales, and different jobs—to make all of their decisions mutually reinforcing. Strategic planning is one way that companies attempt to do this. Through the strategic planning process, companies get managers in every area to figure out how they can contribute to a common mission and vision of their firm. Then, when strategic plans are implemented, the hope is that the frustrating conflicts between functional areas will not arise. Figure 3.1 highlights some of the major relationships between this chapter's sections and various functional areas in business. In reality, this entire chapter on

Chapter Topics / Functional Areas of Business	Finance	Accounting	Human Resources	Marketing	Engineering	Management Information Systems
Integrating Operations Management with Other Functions	●	●	●	●	●	●
What Is a Strategy?	●	●	●	●	●	●
The Strategic Decision Hierarchy	●	●	●	●	●	●
Effective Alignment of Operational Decisions	●	●	●	●	●	●
Strategic Integration of Operational Decisions				●		
Environmental Excellence and Operations Strategy				●	●	

FIGURE 3.1 Integrating Operations Management with Other Functions

operations strategy is focused on linking operations management to other functional areas, so we could have simply put an asterisk in every cell of this matrix. We do, however, believe that the last two sections have a lot to say about the relationship between operations and marketing. Also, the final section deals with many design issues that are significant to the work of engineering professionals.

> video exercise

Take a moment to apply what you've learned.

> What Is a Strategy?

Most successful businesses have a clear mission, set long-term goals that reflect that mission, and then set more specific short-term objectives that reflect those goals. Frequently, mission statements, key organizational goals, and specific objectives are published and given to all employees, as well as to other interested parties. The mission, goals, and objectives of a company are supposed to give a good indication of its strategy. Using these formal statements to establish a strategic direction that is acceptable to most employees helps to keep the company's decisions consistent over time.

In contrast to formal statements of mission, goals, and objectives (which might not reflect the beliefs and attitudes of many employees), a **strategy** is the set of actual decisions made by an organization over time. If the decisions are consistent or follow a defined pattern, the organization is more likely to accomplish its long-term goals.

Not all organizations have the same goals or make similar decisions, even when they are in the same basic industry. For example, decisions made by McDonald's employees may not be consistent with those made at five-star restaurants. Decisions made by the manufacturer of the disposable pen you use to take notes may differ from those of the manufacturer of the fountain pen you got when you graduated from high school.

In every organization, everybody should be pulling together to achieve shared objectives. When employees make decisions that are not consistent, their decisions don't reinforce the work of others, and the organization's progress suffers. Figure 3.2 illustrates this point. The large arrow in Figure 3.2a represents organizational progress, while the small arrows represent the separate directions in which various decisions pull the organization. As Figure 3.2b suggests, consistent individual decisions work together to enhance the organization's progress. Often, consistent decisions reinforce each other to create **synergy,** which is a condition that makes a combined total worth more than the sum of its individual parts. That is, the progress produced by a group of consistent decisions taken together is greater than the progress produced by the same decisions taken without group reinforcement.

Strategic decisions are made on several levels of a business. Taken together, those levels form what is called the strategic decision hierarchy.

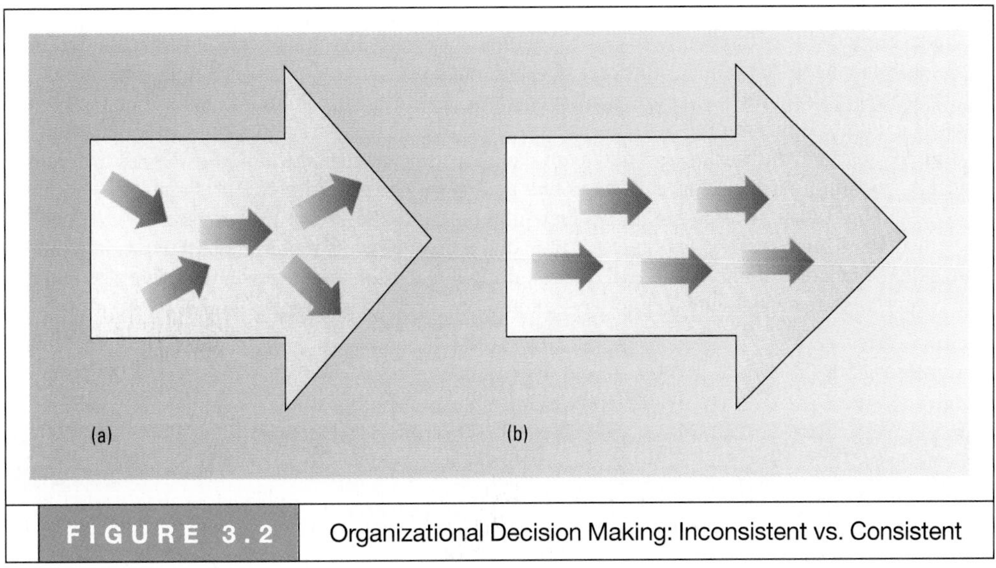

FIGURE 3.2 Organizational Decision Making: Inconsistent vs. Consistent

active concept check <

Now let's take a moment to test your knowledge of the concepts you have studied in this section.

The Strategic Decision Hierarchy

The strategic decision hierarchy is made up of corporate decisions, business decisions, and functional decisions. It is called a hierarchy because functions are found within businesses, and businesses within corporations. Figure 3.3 describes this hierarchy of decisions managers make. Using this figure as a road map, we will discuss each level of the strategic decision hierarchy.

CORPORATE STRATEGY: WHAT BUSINESS ARE WE IN?

Any issue of the *Wall Street Journal* contains news of businesses being started, bought, sold, merged, or shut down under bankruptcy protection laws. Newspapers also report on new products under development and new markets being opened. The press regularly reports that companies have been reorganized or downsized in order to allocate corporate resources to higher-priority projects. The decisions to take such actions, which are made by senior corporate executives, comprise what is frequently referred to as corporate strategy. In essence, a **corporate strategy** is the set of decisions that answer the question, What business are we in?

Two common decision-making patterns exist at the corporate level. One is *conglomerate* (or *unrelated*) *diversification*. Organizations that pursue conglomerate diversification end up owning a wide variety of unrelated business ventures. They may simply be financial amalgamations, or holding companies, that make no attempt to coordinate the strategies of their individual member companies. General Electric (GE) is one example of such a company: It runs a broad portfolio of businesses, including companies that make light bulbs, appliances, jet engines, industrial diamonds, and power turbines. GE also owns a broadcasting company. In conglomerates, the strategies of the corporation's various businesses do not need to be related, and decision making can be fully decentralized.

A second decision-making pattern is *related diversification*. Corporations that seek to coordinate the activities of the companies they own pursue related diversification. Companies may be related in a variety of ways, including common product technologies, process technologies, resource requirements, or markets. Procter & Gamble's corporate strategy is an example of related diversification. Although Procter & Gamble is very large, it sells only consumer products such as soaps, detergents, shampoos, diapers, and pharmaceuticals. As a compromise between conglomerate diversification and related diversification, some large conglomerates may seek to coordinate the activities of certain groups of companies, or divisions, within their portfolios. This approach to organizing corporate resources is called divisionalization.

Under related diversification or divisionalization, corporate policies frequently limit the freedom of business managers to act independently of other companies in the organization. For instance, corporate policy may require that a critical component or a significant volume of material be exchanged among the corporation's businesses. Or a corporation that has constructed a diversified portfolio of new businesses, growing businesses, and mature businesses may manage those businesses differently, treating the mature businesses as cash cows and giving the newer businesses preference for developmental funding. Other such corporate policies might include the use of formal financial hurdles for investment decisions; short-term control of financial performance; a requirement that profitable divisions "share the pain" of unprofitable divisions during a recession; and the establishment of a centralized corporate staff to deal with technology, compliance, and other complex issues.

active exercise <

Take a moment to apply what you've learned.

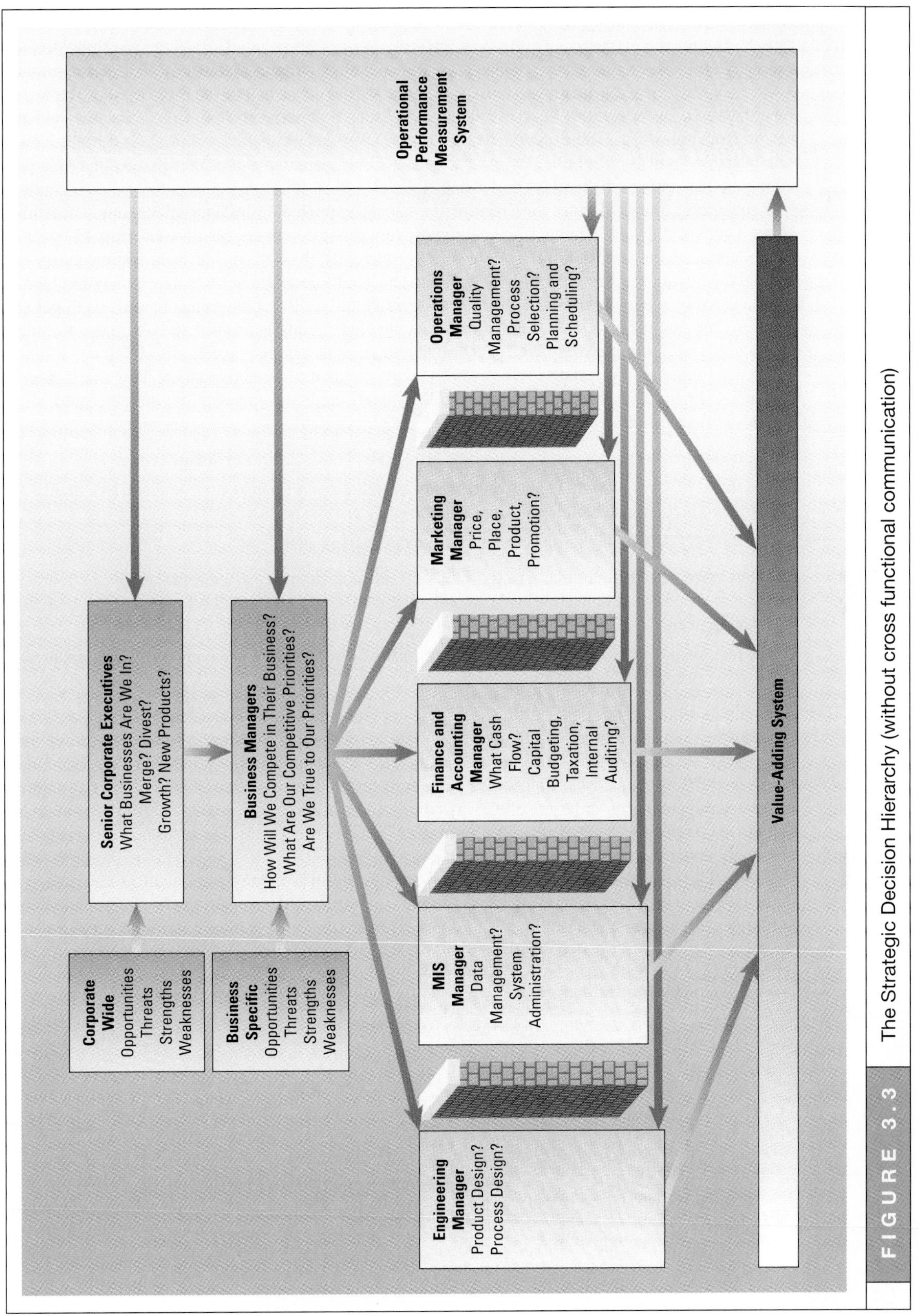

FIGURE 3.3 The Strategic Decision Hierarchy (without cross functional communication)

BUSINESS STRATEGY: HOW WILL WE COMPETE IN THIS BUSINESS?

The development of strategy is a top-down activity. As has been noted, large corporations develop strategies for achieving long-term objectives that may include growth, stability, or long-term return on assets and investments. A **business strategy** is the set of decisions that answer the question, How will we compete in this business? (Keep in mind that for many organizations, the corporation and the business unit are one and the same, in which case the corporate and business-level strategies are the same.) The business strategy should be designed to create some sustainable competitive advantage by providing unique value in the markets the business serves.

A business strategy defines the spirit of the business much as a bumper sticker says something about a car's occupants. To give some examples from the group at the health club, Luis Flores may describe his custom furniture factory's business strategy by saying, "If you want fast or cheap, call them. If you want the best, call us." Cheryl Sanders might describe her hospital by saying, "We're there and ready when you need us." Tom Jackson might offer, "If you're going our way, we'll get you there on time and on budget." Fred Silverton's electronics firm might describe its basic pager this way: "Who needs bells and whistles? We'll get you the message at a price you can afford."

To determine how to compete in a given industry, companies need to analyze their external environments. The five forces that play a critical role in determining the opportunities and threats to which a firm's business strategy must respond are:[1]

- the competitiveness that results from interfirm rivalry (e.g., Chevrolet versus Ford)
- the threat of new entrants (e.g., Could a new business open up next door and sell essentially the same product-service bundle to essentially the same customers?)
- the threat of substitute products (e.g., satellite dish versus cable)
- the relative power of suppliers (e.g., Intel's power as a supplier of microprocessors to computer manufacturers versus the power of a small company that supplies metal screws used in assembling the computers)
- the relative power of customers (e.g., the customer's power in dealing with Wal-Mart versus Wal-Mart's power in dealing with suppliers)

Figure 3.4 summarizes the findings of a survey of 500 chief executive officers of small- and medium-size manufacturers. Of the strategic planning activities the respondents found to be very important, "meeting with the customer to discuss ways to maximize our value" was mentioned most often—by 95% of executives. Eighty-five percent of respondents mentioned including key suppliers in long-term planning in order to solicit ways to improve products and processes. And 62% said that gathering competitive intelligence was important. Clearly, analyzing the external environment is extremely important to business strategists.

Companies need to consider their internal strengths and weaknesses as well as their external threats and opportunities in order to target a sustainable competitive position. As Figure 3.4 shows, executives think there are several ways to do so. They include: (1) setting aside time specifically to

Although these are both Marriott hotels, they are quite different. With different brands like Fairfield Inn, Courtyard by Marriott, Residence Inn, and Marriott, the corporation has established multiple businesses that can pursue different business strategies even if they are located in adjacent lots.

[1]Michael J. Porter, *Competitive Strategy* (New York: Free Press, 1980).

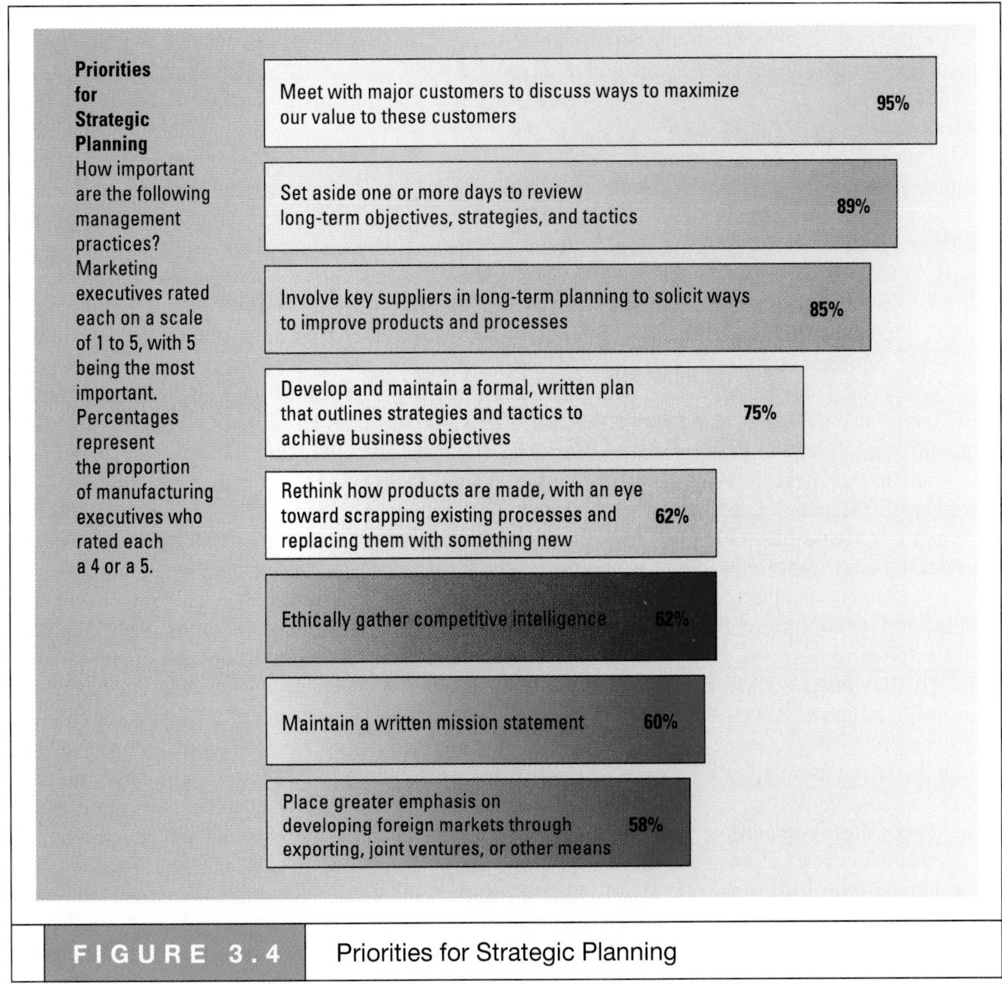
Priorities for Strategic Planning
How important are the following management practices? Marketing executives rated each on a scale of 1 to 5, with 5 being the most important. Percentages represent the proportion of manufacturing executives who rated each a 4 or a 5.
Meet with major customers to discuss ways to maximize our value to these customers
95%
Set aside one or more days to review long-term objectives, strategies, and tactics
89%
Involve key suppliers in long-term planning to solicit ways to improve products and processes
85%
Develop and maintain a formal, written plan that outlines strategies and tactics to achieve business objectives
75%
Rethink how products are made, with an eye toward scrapping existing processes and replacing them with something new
62%
Ethically gather competitive intelligence
62%
Maintain a written mission statement
60%
Place greater emphasis on developing foreign markets through exporting, joint ventures, or other means
58%

FIGURE 3.4 Priorities for Strategic Planning

review long-term objectives, strategies, and tactics; (2) developing a formal written plan that outlines the strategies and tactics to be used in achieving business objectives; (3) rethinking how products are made, with the idea of completely changing the process; and (4) maintaining a written mission statement. Recently, e-commerce has created an entirely new set of opportunities for many businesses and has at the same time threatened the established competitive position of many others. The point of the business strategy is to develop and use internal strengths to capitalize on existing and future opportunities, while preventing the internal weaknesses that expose a company to current and anticipated external threats.

Business unit goals frequently address issues of profitability, market share, and service to other business units within the corporation. Individual business units need to pursue these goals in a way that is consistent with the policies and expectations of the parent corporation. For example, treating customer firms within a holding company differently from customer firms outside the holding company would make little sense. But in a firm that has pursued related diversification, giving preference to other divisions in terms of service schedules, inside information on new designs, and other collaborative benefits often makes sense. In general, the corporate strategy will constrain the business strategy. That is, the strategic options available to a division manager or business unit president will be limited by the corporate policies with which she or he must abide.

The challenge in devising a business strategy is to gain a sustainable competitive advantage in the marketplace. To do so, managers must understand their specific markets' **order-qualifying criteria,** which is what they must do to gain the consideration of targeted customers. They must also know their **order-winning criteria,** which is what they must do to win their business. Order-qualifying and order-winning criteria vary with the market served. Order-qualifying criteria may include a competitive product warranty, a product design that is legally acceptable for customer use, an acceptable price range, a certain set of features, or reliability at or above a specified level. In the case of a restaurant in a small college town, order-qualifying criteria might include a convenient distance from the campus, a brief waiting time for orders, the availability of seating, variety in menu, and a lively atmosphere.

Though business managers cannot afford to overlook order-qualifying criteria, in and of themselves those criteria do not provide a sustainable competitive advantage. Competitive advantage is gained by including order-winning criteria in the product-service bundle. In the case of a restaurant in a small college town, order-winning criteria are probably related primarily to the cost of the product-service bundle.

The general language of corporate- and business-level objectives concerning customer needs and expectations must be broken down into specific directions for developing and operating the value-adding system. Potential conflicts among process technologies, job design, plant layout, and other operational concerns need to be resolved with an eye toward meeting and exceeding customer expectations. Rather than trying to be all things to all people, managers must resolve these conflicts by setting competitive priorities at the business level and sticking to them. A **competitive priority** is a defined emphasis that a business chooses to pursue and which should be supported by the decisions it makes. By setting competitive priorities and clearly communicating them, companies tell decision makers what they should be buying with their decisions. If the decisions a company makes consistently emphasize the same set of competitive priorities, the business has a good chance of gaining a competitive advantage in those priorities. For example, if on every day and in every way, all a company's employees make decisions that help the company to keep costs down, that company is likely to become a cost leader and thus win the business of cost-conscious customers.

When a business has a clearly focused set of competitive priorities, managers of that business understand better what the business is and what it is not. *Quality, flexibility, timeliness,* and *low cost* form a reasonably complete set of competitive priorities, although each of these could be pursued in a variety of ways by different companies. For example, quality could be pursued through improved product reliability, improved customer service, improved conformance to design specifications. Similarly, flexibility could be pursued through value-adding systems that provide a wide range of offerings or a limited range of offerings in a variety of volumes. Timeliness could be pursued through improved product development speed, improved on-time delivery performance, or reduced service response times. Formulating a business strategy involves choosing to emphasize a limited combination of low cost, flexibility, quality, and timeliness in making business decisions. Because of the trade-offs between these competitive priorities, a firm can seldom be all things to all people.

The people at NASA provide an interesting example of competitive priorities. After the failure of several massive projects in the late 1980s (e.g., the original failure of the Hubble telescope, the multi-billion dollar failure of the Mars Observer program, and the disastrous space shuttle Challenger explosion), they adopted a new mantra, Better, Faster, Cheaper. (In other words, they were simultaneously pursuing the three priorities of quality, timeliness, and low cost.) Now, illustrating the fact that not all priorities can be maximally achieved at once, some of the employees jokingly say, "Better, faster, cheaper: pick two." For example, the Mars Voyager could probably have been made better by taking more time and spending more money. Or the project might have been done faster with more employees and bigger budgets—thus trading faster for cheaper.

A survey of competitive priorities among U.S. manufacturers administered by the Boston University Manufacturing Roundtable in 1996 found that quality was the top-ranked priority, followed by timeliness and low cost. Respondents to the survey from the European Union had similar rankings for the competitive priorities. Interestingly, the Japanese respondents had somewhat different rankings: They gave low price the top place.

active exercise

Take a moment to apply what you've learned.

FUNCTIONAL STRATEGIES: HOW CAN WE FUNCTION WITHIN THE WHOLE?

Because each function and support area in a business—marketing, finance, accounting, engineering, human resources, management information systems, and operations—is responsible for a particular set of decisions, managers need to develop functional objectives that are consistent with and supportive of the business unit's goals, to guide decision makers in each function. From an operational perspective, this task entails making decisions about the value-adding system (the business's processes and decision-making infrastructures) that will create value for the business's internal and external customers.

Often, such decisions are made independently of their impact on other functions. As organizations grow and evolve over time, the walls that separate thinking and decision making in one function from thinking and decision making in other functions can become very rigid. Figure 3.3 emphasizes the fact that as managers in a given function work within the guidelines of a defined business-level strategy, they frequently do so without cross-functional thinking and communication. There are real physical barriers between the functions—these may include geographic distances. For example, marketing might be done out of regional sales centers, finance out of corporate headquarters, and operations from centralized facilities. Even when the functions are all combined under one roof, the functions are usually housed on separate floors or wings of the building. In their own office suites, employees relate only to people from their own function. In such settings, cross-functional communication only happens at the highest executive levels. To get a message over the wall, it has to go up first. As a result, managers and workers don't know what is happening in other areas and they really cannot work together. Many business people call this phenomenon, in which organizational barriers prohibit communication between functions, the *silo effect* or the *smokestack effect.* In so doing, they are comparing each functional area to a silo or smokestack—the only way to get a message in or out is through the top.

When managers within each function focus on only those issues that are relevant to their own function or department, a business is not as likely to reach its goals. For example, when Fred's salespeople promise customers a variety of colors in an effort to make their monthly sales quota, their company's ability to keep costs low is compromised. And if the engineers who work with Luis were to reorganize the factory layout to reduce the cost to manufacture a particular type of table, they might destroy some of the flexibility the factory needs to produce the wide array of other products the company must build.

Today, though many companies are mired in the silo syndrome, many progressive firms also appear to be moving toward the cross-functional thinking illustrated by Figure 3.5. They are finding ways to break down the barriers between functions. One simple way is simply to collocate workers from different functions. Why not put a salesperson's office close to the office of the operations manager who schedules the service being sold? Why not let the members of a cross-functional team share the same office suite?

Another approach to managing across the white spaces is to build a formal matrix structure that gives members of management teams responsibility for an entire product-service bundle in addition to their functional responsibility. Since business processes (such as designing, building, marketing, and servicing a product-service bundle) span the functions of the typical organizational chart, a focus on processes is a good way to create teamwork across functional barriers. One noted example of this exists at Chrysler Corporation where, in addition to the traditional hierarchy, there are "platform teams" that are responsible for specific vehicle types. Thus if you were a financial manager at Chrysler you would have at least two bosses: your supervisor in the finance department and your supervisor on the platform team. When Chrysler created this matrix structure, they were so committed to managing cross-functional processes that they also built a new corporate headquarters to reflect their new way of doing business. Chrysler's headquarters in Auburn Hills, Michigan (called Chrysler Technical Center) is built around hubs. Functional areas are located together on the same wing of the building, and platform teams are generally on the same floor. At each hub of the building, there are many meeting rooms; teams need not reserve a meeting room—one will always be available. Thus, physical barriers to cross-functional decision making and communication are removed and it is easier to manage across fuctional boundaries.

To obtain the desired mix of competitive priorities, decision makers in the various functions must pull together rather than oppose each other. Cross-functional decisions can have a positive and synergistic relationship that should be pursued. Other decisions may also have a negative relationship because of tradeoffs between functional goals and outcomes. Tradeoffs between functional preferences need to be evaluated in terms of the business's competitive priorities. Thinking through the relationships with a matrix like the one in Figure 3.6 can help managers come to agreement when there are differences between the functions and can help them identify areas where they are working together well. A bullet in any cell of this figure suggests a strong linkage between the competitive priority and functional decision represented by the cell.

> active poll

What do you think? Voice your opinion and find out what others have to say.

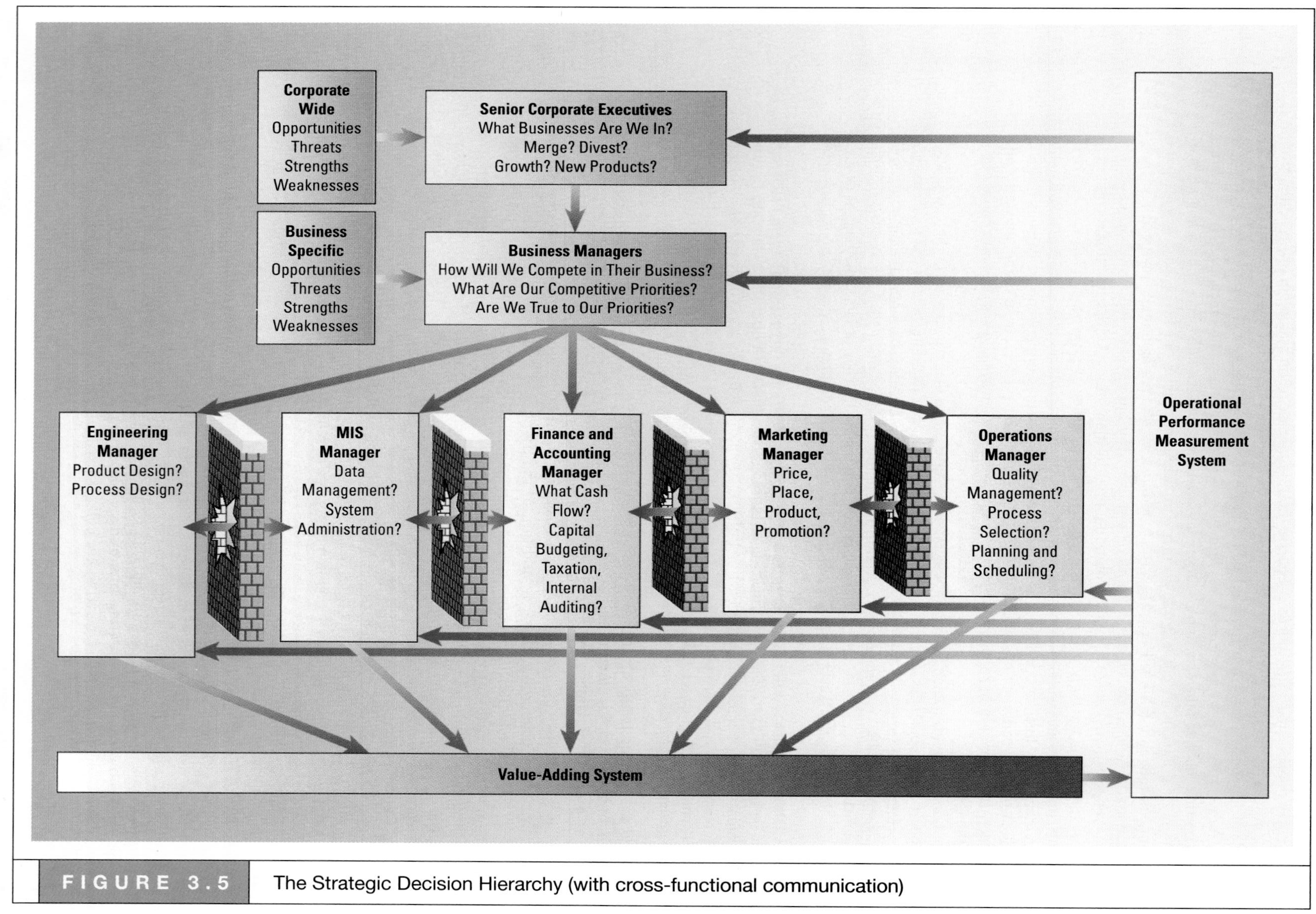

FIGURE 3.5 The Strategic Decision Hierarchy (with cross-functional communication)

	Marketing	Product Range	Selling Price	Promotion	Availability / Delivery Time	Finance	Cash Flow	Capital Investment	Accounting	Costing Accuracy	Taxation Burden	Internal Auditing Complexity	Engineering	Product Design / Change	Process Design / Change	Operations	Make / Buy Mix	Facility Capacity & Location	Technology Mix	Process Layout	Planning & Scheduling	Quality Assurance	Supervisory Policies	Maintenance Management	Human Resources	Staffing	Employee Relations	Compensation / Benefits	Management of Information Systems	Information System Design	Information System Operation
Low Cost			●		●			●		●				●	●		●		●	●		●	●			●					
Flexibility		●												●	●				●	●	●					●				●	●
Quality		●			●									●	●						●	●				●	●				
Timeliness				●	●													●		●	●									●	●

FIGURE 3.6 Impact of Functional Areas on Competitive Priorities

If you were thinking about your prior work experience, you might fill in the cells of Figure 3.6 differently than we have. Of course, the key relationships between functional areas could vary depending on the business. We were thinking about Fred Silverton's comments at the beginning of this chapter when we filled in the cells (and trying to identify some commonly important linkages). You may recall that Fred was having trouble reconciling the way success was measured in his old position with the way it is measured in his new position. (Remember that each division of a conglomerate may be viewed as a separate business unit.) Fred's old division focused on customization and cutting-edge product design. Its competitive priorities emphasized flexibility and quality over low cost and delivery speed, the focus at the new division. Given the strong direct linkages between the flexibility and quality rows in Figure 3.6 and the product range column, the competitive priorities in Fred's last division are understandable. So is the heavier emphasis on low cost and delivery speed in the new division—both priorities that are directly related to competitive pricing and wide availability.

Within operations, the increased customization requested by the marketing function would have several effects. Customized orders would result in a larger number of unique product types and would therefore complicate production planning and scheduling. Such product design changes would almost certainly make quality assurance and supervision more difficult. Should those changes require modification to the production process, the impact on the technology mix and process layout would need to be examined. Changes to the production process could strain the facility's capacity enough to force a relocation.

All in all, if a firm is to maintain a consistent strategic direction, its managers must understand the interfunctional relationships described in Figure 3.6. To be competitive in the 21st century, companies must be able to make functional decisions with a full understanding of their cross-functional impact on the entire organization.

> active exercise

Take a moment to apply what you've learned.

> active concept check

Now let's take a moment to test your knowledge of the concepts you have studied in this section.

Effective Alignment of Operational Decisions

In many, if not most, organizations, the operations function is central to the creation of value. On average, the operations function is estimated to control roughly 70% of a business's assets. Clearly, making operational decisions that are consistent with the business's strategy is important. The set of decisions made in a firm's operations management function is its **operations strategy.**

The set of decisions that is the firm's operations strategy may be divided into two categories: structural decisions and infrastructural decisions. **Structural decisions,** which establish the design, or "bricks and mortar," of the value-adding system, have long-term significance because they are not easily changed. Their outcomes also determine the firm's range of options in making **infrastructural decisions,** which determine the procedures, systems, and policies that coordinate the firm's operations. Infrastructural decisions are more easily reversed or changed than "bricks and mortar" decisions.

STRUCTURAL DECISIONS

Structural decisions may be divided into four major categories: the "make or buy" question, facility capacity and location choices, the technological mix decision, and process type and layout choices. The following sections examine some of these key structural choices in operational decision making.

Make or Buy Choices

These decisions answer questions such as the following: When there is a choice, should the firm make a component or subassembly in house or buy it from a supplier? How does this decision influence the firm's cost structure, product quality, flexibility, profitability in times of recession and economic expansion, risk of excess capacity, and overall level of profitability? Do the firm's make or buy choices support its competitive priorities?

Make or buy decisions extend to service environments where managers must decide whether to use outside services as part of the overall package. For example, many organizations outsource food services and janitorial services to organizations that have developed expertise in these areas. While a hospital or school may manage these services in-house, they often find that companies like Aramark (food service) and ServiceMaster (janitorial services) deliver superior performance at reasonable cost. Outsourcing in such cases permits the hospital to focus on health care and the school to focus on education—their respective areas of primary competency.

Facility Capacity and Location Choices

These decisions relate to questions such as the following: Can the firm satisfy the demand for its products and services? Has its ability to do so changed over time? Will it change in the future? Does the firm purposely keep its capacity low or high? If so, what does that choice imply about its cost structure, profitability, service level, flexibility, workforce policies, and product quality? In light of the firm's competitive priorities, is the firm making the correct capacity decisions?

Firms must decide how many facilities they need, how big those facilities should be, and where they should be located. To make such decisions, managers need to think about the focus of specific facilities and how they are organized into groups or divisions. Facilities might be grouped by process similarities, product-service bundle commonalties, technology, or scale. For example, a hospital might choose to put all its lab facilities in one area, because of process similarities, but to keep its emergency room separate from the surgical and long-term care areas, because of product-service bundle differences. These decisions will have clear implications for cost, service level, workforce policy, production planning and control, and quality and should therefore be evaluated in light of the firm's competitive priorities.

Technological Mix Choices

From a wide array of technologies, managers must select those that are most supportive of the organization's competitive priorities. Their choices are not limited only to technologies that have been tested and are immediately available. In fact, many technological choices set a standard that influences the compatibility of a firm's products, services, and processes with yet-to-be-developed cutting-edge technologies. Thus, a technological choice must be viewed as having long-term implications for the firm's competitiveness.

As such, a technological choice cannot be made effectively without first establishing some guiding standards and principles in an overall technology strategy. Obviously, decision makers must weigh the tradeoffs between new and mature technologies, between slowly changing and rapidly expanding

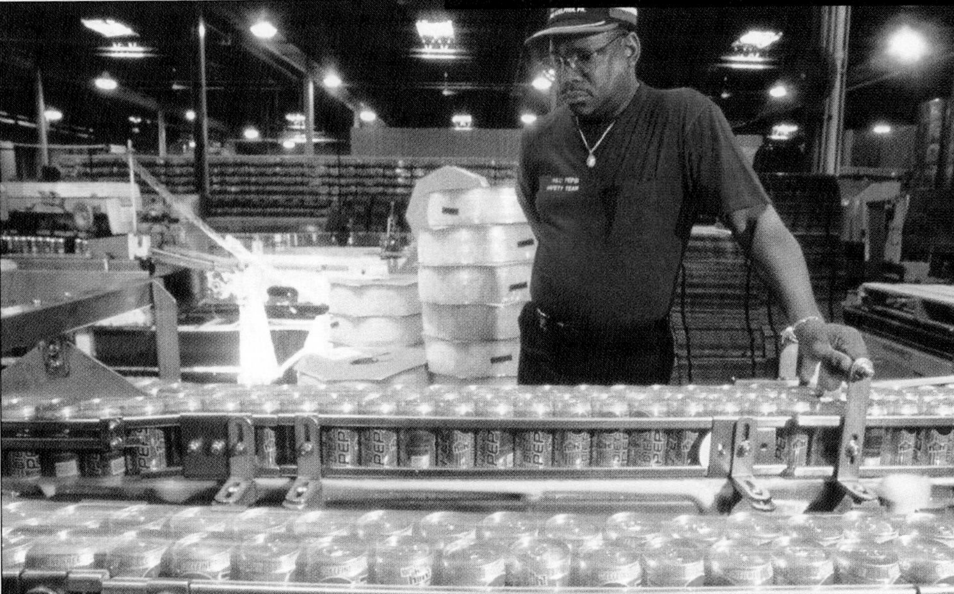

This Pepsi-Cola bottling/canning plant utilizes a continuous flow process in a product-oriented layout to fill millions of (hopefully) identical beverage cans each year.

technologies, and between predictable technologies and those whose future is uncertain. Other factors an organization should consider include:

- the degree to which work should be mechanized
- the degree to which equipment should be automated
- the desired extent of specialization of equipment
- the choice between in-house technology and that of outside vendors
- setup and changeover requirements
- the skills required to use a new technology versus those available in-house
- maintenance requirements

The implications of the new technology for the firm's investment, service levels, production planning, product quality, risk, cost structure, and break-even levels will all weigh heavily on the firm's future competitiveness.

Service Process Type Choices

Figure 3.7 presents a model for categorizing service organizations called the service process matrix. The model uses two dimensions to characterize different service delivery processes. The first dimension is the degree of labor intensity, which is the ratio of labor cost to capital cost. Service-intensive processes with high labor intensity include department stores, universities, dental offices, and law firms. Services with low labor intensity include airlines, railways, resorts, and hospitals.

The second dimension is the degree of interaction and customization, which measures the degree of individual attention required by the customer. While doctors and auto repair businesses must customize their diagnoses and prescriptions for individual clients, airlines and schools can package and deliver standardized services for large groups of customers.

When combined, the two dimensions of the service process matrix create four categories of service environments, each with its own set of management challenges. These challenges are identified in Figure 3.8. For example, an airline is categorized as a **service factory** (service-intensive processes with low labor intensity and low customization) because it routinely flies hundreds of passengers at a time on a Boeing 747 between Chicago and Tokyo nonstop. The airline managers must pay special attention to the timing and selection of new aircraft purchases, the planning of promotions to fill plane capacity during off-peak periods, the scheduling of flights, the need for standard operating procedures to reduce uncertainty, and the need to make customers feel comfortable despite the standardized nature of the environment.

Service shops (service-intensive processes with low labor intensity and high customization) such as hospitals present managers with concerns over capital expenditures, such as MRI equipment. Other challenges include: managing hospital capacity by emphasizing outpatient services instead of building

Degree of Labor Intensity	Degree of Customer Interaction and Customization: Low	High
Low	*Service Factory* Airlines Trucking Hotels Resorts & Recreation	*Service Shop* Hospitals Auto Repair Printing Shop Other Repair Shops
High	*Mass Service* Retailing Wholesaling Schools Retail Aspects of Commercial Banking	*Professional Service* Doctors Lawyers Accountants Architects

FIGURE 3.7 The Service Process Matrix

Source: Adapted from "How Can Service Businesses Survive and Prosper?" by Roger Schmenner, *Sloan Management Review,* V. 27, n. 3, 1986, p. 25

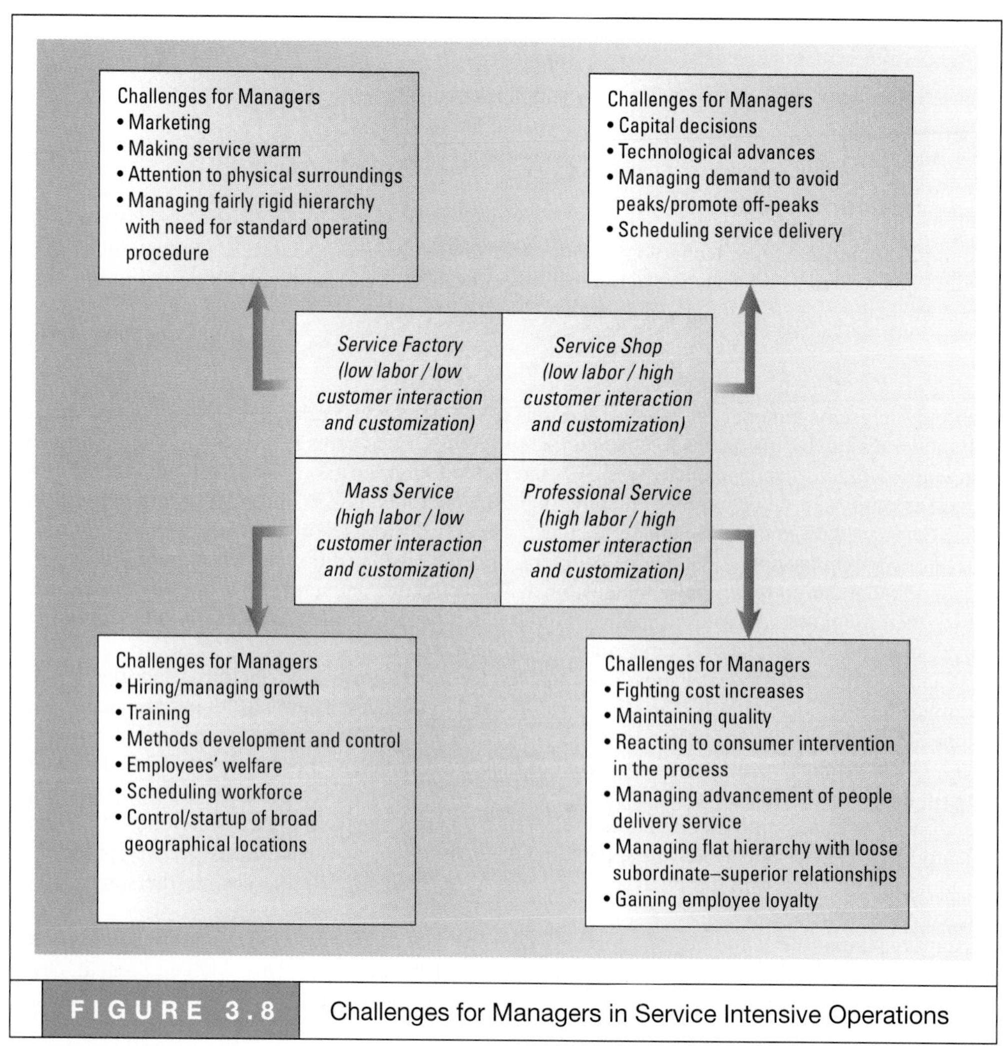

FIGURE 3.8 Challenges for Managers in Service Intensive Operations

more hospital rooms; scheduling elective surgeries during times of low demand; pushing decision-making power down to lower levels of the hierarchy to satisfy individual patient needs; and seeking ways to keep costs down while maintaining quality care.

Mass services (service-intensive processes with high labor intensity and low customization) such as universities present administrators with challenges such as: ensuring a qualified and motivated faculty; scheduling classes to match student needs with classroom availability; developing new programs while dropping others to keep services relevant and costs low; and promoting the unique aspects of the university despite its overall standard design.

In **professional services** (service-intensive processes with high labor intensity and high customization) such as law offices, managers must nurture the expertise of the partners, associates, and staff, maintain a flat hierarchy to be responsive to individual clients, and devote attention to hiring, training, and motivating personnel, while developing procedures and schedules that make efficient use of personnel.

By identifying their service environment as one of the four types in the service process matrix, managers can develop a strategy that supports the decision areas critical to success. Other service-intensive processes in the same category can be studied for innovative ideas, which managers can apply to their own company. For example, bank managers can study the customer relations approach of Wal-Mart (both Wal-Mart and banks are in the mass service category) and adopt a new customer-friendly image. As a result, they might end up wearing polo shirts to be visible and accessible, smiling a lot to be welcoming, and yet maintaining a highly standardized array of financial services.

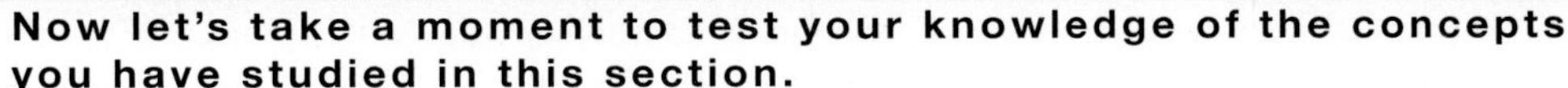

Now let's take a moment to test your knowledge of the concepts you have studied in this section.

Miami's Student Recreation Center—A Hybrid Service Process

It is hard to be everything to all customers at all times and to do it cost effectively. The operational strategy of the Student Recreation Center (SRC) is consistent with that of the university as a whole. Decisions on scheduling, programming, and future capital expenditures must all be made with an eye to making more options available, with less wait and on a reasonable budget. Specifically, the operational strategy of the SRC is to offer a large variety of popular health enhancing recreational opportunities in one location and in as timely a fashion as is possible within existing budgetary constraints.

The SRC offers a wide variety of choices for individual recreation and social interaction with the option of a personal trainer for an additional fee. From that perspective, the rec center is a service shop. It also offers a number of classes oriented to physical and mental development and provides the venue for major aquatic sports competitions. From that perspective, the center is a mass service. As such, we would call it a *hybrid* service operation.

In hybrid operations, managers have to balance the competitive requirements of two (or more) different kinds of processes. On the one hand, it is a service shop, so SRC administrators are concerned with making the best choices for equipment purchases, managing capacity and demand by establishing variable time limits at different times of the day, scheduling competitive major events during university holidays and weekends, training the staff to quickly respond to customer needs, and seeking ways to keep costs down while maintaining a wide variety of recreational opportunities. On the other hand, it is as mass service, so administrators are concerned with ensuring a qualified and motivated staff, scheduling recreational events and competitions to match demand and facility availability, developing new programs while dropping others to keep the offerings current and costs low, and promoting the unique aspects of the facility. The two types of services do sometimes come into conflict. For example, from the mass service perspective, the ideal time to schedule swimming competitions is during university breaks. From the service shop perspective, however, there are a number of local residents—including some faculty and students—for whom the best time to get a workout is when the university is on a break. Similarly, the best time to have an intramural competition is in the late afternoon and evening, but that's also the time that many students are looking for pick-up games. Balancing the service shop and mass service aspects of the rec center's service is one of the biggest challenges managers face.

video exercise

Take a moment to apply what you've learned.

Manufacturing Process Type and Process Layout Choices

Manufacturing processes may be classified along a continuum ranging from project, job shop, and batch processes to repetitive manufacturing and continuous-flow production. These are the generic options in terms of process type. The choice of manufacturing process is a basic structural decision which must be consistent with the firm's competitive priorities. The decision should also be consistent with other structural decisions so as to produce synergies in pursuit of the firm's strategic objectives. Because these structural decisions cannot be reversed quickly, they have long-term implications. They establish the set of options available to the decision makers who must run the firm day to day.

Projects are operations that complete "one-of-a-kind" goods and services. Examples include class projects, major research and development initiatives, and the design and construction of a bridge, building, tunnel, network, communications system, or training program. Projects represent a unique managerial challenge: They are usually costly, time-consuming, and of vital strategic importance to the customer.

Because many projects are unique, there is frequently a great deal of uncertainty in project management. Often, a project represents work that has never been done before and will never need to be done again. Although budgets and deadlines are very important in project management, predicting exactly how long a project will take and what it will cost is extremely difficult. Thus, projects are frequently completed late and over budget. Furthermore, the workers assigned to a project are in some cases under pressure to "work themselves out of a job." Thus, workforce considerations are also unique in project management.

Most of the time, the resources used to complete a project are organized around a *fixed-position layout.* That is, since most projects produce large, one-of-a-kind deliverables, the material, equipment, and other resources for the project are brought to the construction site instead of being moved through a factory. Building construction sites are the best example of a fixed-position layout, but ships, airplanes, and many large machines are also produced in permanent facilities using a fixed-position layout.

A **job shop** is a production process that is designed to produce small volumes of highly customized products. The job shop uses general-purpose equipment and skilled workers to produce items such as the machine tools that are used to produce other products; product testing prototypes; replacement parts for antiquated equipment; and other items produced in very small volume. This type of process is the natural choice for firms seeking to provide flexibility, customization, and low fixed cost, possibly at the expense of conformance quality, delivery speed, and unit (or variable) cost.

A **batch process** is a production process that produces groups of items that are essentially identical, called production lots or batches. The size of a production lot is usually a function of the time required to ready the equipment for production and the near-term demand for the item. At home, for example, cookies are usually baked in batches large enough to be worth the expense and effort, but not so large that they will go stale and be wasted. Batch production may be required by technical factors such as fermentation (for instance, in wine making), color uniformity (in fabric printing), or customer demand (for group tours, for example). Items such as clothing, furniture, and many food products are commonly manufactured in batches. In a batch process, flexibility and product customization are lower than they are in the job shop. On the other hand, consistency, unit (variable) cost, and delivery speed are improved.

Job shop and batch processes usually employ a *process-oriented,* or *functional, layout.* In this type of layout, all equipment of similar function or type is grouped together in departments or sections. For example, in Cheryl Sanders's hospital lab, all the radiological facilities might be located in one place, all the biochemical testing equipment in another place, and so forth. In Luis's furniture factory, general-purpose equipment for cutting, sanding, and polishing wood, cutting fabric, and assembling the finished product would be located in separate areas. Products move from department to department along a route dictated by the item's processing requirements. Because general-purpose equipment is used, skilled workers are needed to meet the specific requirements of each customer's order.

The functional layout provides a great deal of flexibility and enhances the development of function-specific skills. On the other hand, functional layouts are not as efficient as other types of layout. If you have ever been to an amusement park, you will remember how much time you had to spend waiting in line. The same is true for parts moving through a facility using a functional layout. As much as 90% of a part's production time may be spent waiting in queue to be processed. To simplify what can be a logistical nightmare, entire batches are generally completed at a single work center before being moved, all together, to the next work center. Imagine how long it would take a group of 55 children (a typical busload) to go through all the rides in an amusement park if no one in the group could go on to the next ride until the last person finished the previous ride! Slow, yes; efficient, no. But think how easily the progress of the group could be tracked and how readily its plans could be changed.

When most people think of manufacturing, they think of a **repetitive process,** which is a system used to make large volumes of standardized products. The traditional assembly line, whether worker paced or machine paced, is the most common example of repetitive manufacturing or processing. In this type of process, low-skilled workers use dedicated equipment installed at a high fixed cost. In the age of mass production and global consumer marketing, repetitive manufacturing has provided a large volume of highly standardized products of consistent quality, at a very low unit cost.

The assembly line is actually a *repetitive discrete* manufacturing process. **Discrete processes** produce products that can be counted in integer units and are functional only in their completed form. Cars, appliances, audio equipment, and Easter baskets are all examples of products that are likely to be made using a repetitive discrete manufacturing process.

In contrast, nondiscrete manufacturing processes produce items that cannot be counted in integer units, such as chemicals, pharmaceuticals (though aspirin can be counted in units, two half units are just as valuable as one whole), petroleum products, and most agricultural commodities, such as flour and sugar. Repetitive nondiscrete manufacturing systems are called **continuous-flow processes** and are used to make these types of products. While most are eventually packaged in discrete (countable) units that can be bought off the shelf, during production they are handled in nondiscrete form.

Repetitive and continuous-flow manufacturing generally employ a *product-oriented layout.* This is the type of environment in which Fred Silverton is employed. In these cases, the demand for a single product or family of similar products is sufficient to warrant the use of a dedicated process. Equipment is laid out according to the processing sequence required for a particular product or product family. With a single flow-through process, the logistics are simply compared to the process-oriented layout. Thus, while the size of the production batch may be much larger (theoretically reaching infinity when one product is all that is ever made using a particular process), products flow through the process individually, step by step. The level of automation and other economies of scale usually found in product-oriented layouts provide extremely low unit cost and high conformance quality. But these capabilities are achieved at the expense of product flexibility and require a high commitment of capital up-front (i.e., a high fixed cost).

In sum, the order-winning criteria for job shops are high flexibility, a wide range of design capabilities, and fast delivery. Reasonably low cost is one common order-qualifying criteria in job shops. As one moves to the other end of the spectrum of process types, demand for product volume increases and the ability to provide product variety decreases. In the continuous process, low cost is a common order-winning criteria. Order qualifiers include sufficient flexibility, established design capability, and reasonable delivery speed. These relationships among order-winning criteria, order-qualifying criteria, and process choice are illustrated in Figure 3.9. (The project process choice is not included in Figure 3.9 because each project will have its own unique order winners and order qualifiers.)

> video example

Take a closer look at the concepts and issues you've been reading about.

> active exercise

Take a moment to apply what you've learned.

INFRASTRUCTURAL DECISIONS

The ongoing decisions required to put the firm's structural decisions into action, referred to as infrastructural decisions, include matters such as policies, procedures, information support systems, and definitions of responsibility. Because infrastructural decisions often pertain to issues that are less tangible than the bricks and mortar of structural decisions, their impact is usually less permanent. In

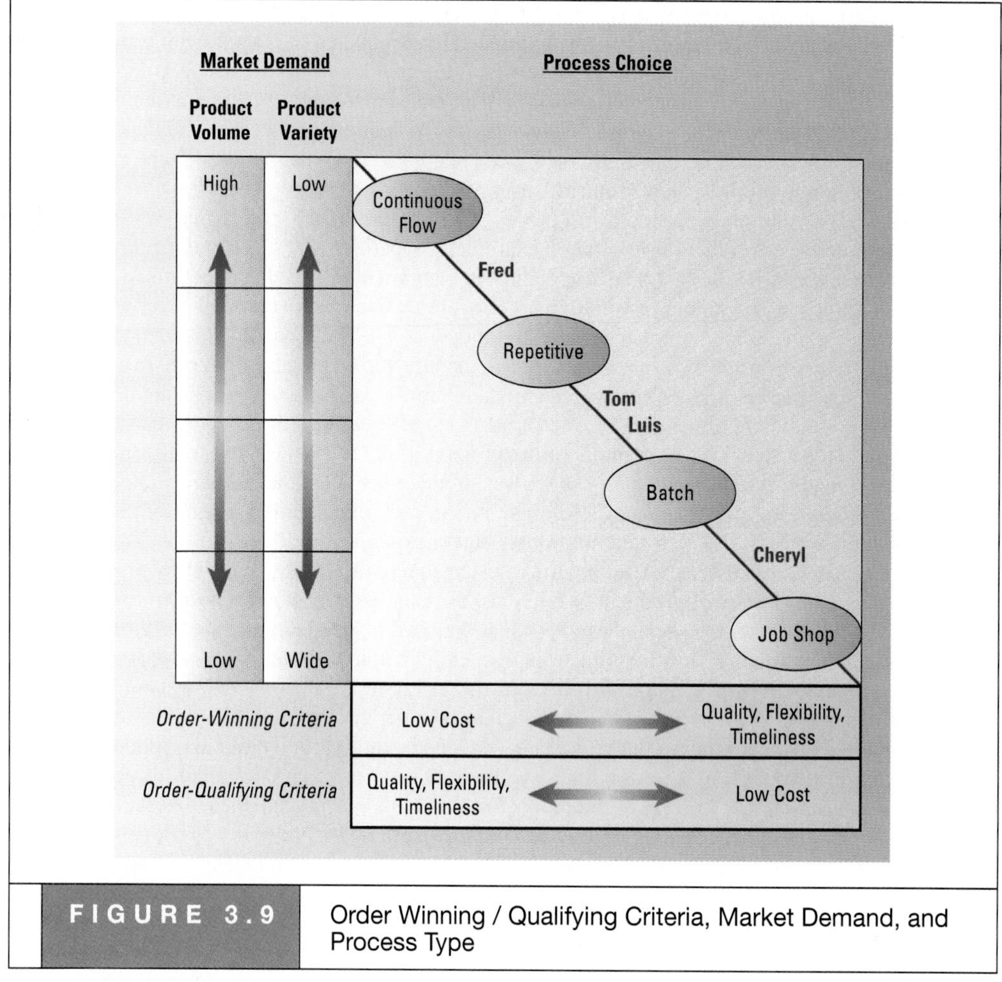

FIGURE 3.9 Order Winning / Qualifying Criteria, Market Demand, and Process Type

operations, infrastructural decisions cover production planning and control, quality assurance, supervision policy, and maintenance management.

Production Planning and Control Choices

Most organizations use a planning system to buy materials and deploy process resources in order to meet customer demand. Such systems allow decision makers to check the availability of resources and schedule the resources that are needed to satisfy customer orders, forecasted demand, or some combination of the two. Control systems must be used to monitor actual production performance against planned schedules.

The variety of demands placed on firms using project, job shop, and batch processes can be quite wide. Forecasting the demand for a wide variety of customized products far enough in advance to have the products ready and waiting on the shelf when the customer needs them is very difficult. Consequently, many firms apply a **make-to-order** policy to such products—that is, they do not actually start the production process until the customer places an order. Maintaining the proper balance of competitive priorities in such an environment can be a challenge. With a large number of customer orders sharing the firm's process resources simultaneously, devising a suitable production planning and control system is a key factor in achieving successful operations.

In contrast, a company that wants to allow for immediate product availability by building inventories of finished product based on forecasted customer demand is using a **make-to-stock** policy. This approach usually makes sense for companies that produce a narrow range of products and services repetitively or continuously using a product-oriented layout. In such setups, production planning and control is less challenging, and a simpler system may be used.

Today, given the competitive challenges of a changing marketplace, a growing number of companies are considering hybrid versions of the make-to-order and make-to-stock policies called **assemble-to-order** policies. A pizzeria that readies the ingredients of a pizza in advance of the customer's call (mixing the dough, letting it rise, and even in some cases putting it on the pan and adding the sauce and cheese), then adds the toppings and bakes the pizza after the order has been taken is following an assemble-to-order policy. Other examples include the truck factory that builds the basic shells and drive trains, then outfits each vehicle to customer specifications; and the baker who keeps a stock of undecorated birthday cakes at the ready for last-minute orders. The assemble-to-order policy is a compromise between the competitive priorities of delivery speed and product variety. While this approach may require increased flexibility in process design, it does help a company maintain a wide variety of product offerings. By simplifying much of the production planning and control, it also keeps delivery time to the customer within competitive ranges.

Quality Assurance Choices

Policies and procedures must be established to guarantee that an organization's processes meet customers' needs and expectations for product design, quality conformance, reliability, and value. Traditional approaches to quality have focused primarily on the inspection of process output in order to sort out nonconforming units. But in contemporary business, quality assurance has become a pervasive issue whose ramifications affect decision making throughout the organization at every level. Operationally speaking, a system must be in place to address quality concerns proactively and to respond to problems detected during production or service or from a complaint by a customer.

Supervisory Policy Choices

Today's workforce is more educated than that of the past. As a result, highly structured, centralized decision making is being questioned at many firms. Policies and organization structures that decentralize decision making and push decisions to the lowest possible level in the organization are becoming more common. For instance, *team-based management* has replaced employee supervisors with autonomous work teams in many organizations. *Employee involvement (EI)* programs, which allow employee teams to make improvements in their own workplaces, and cross-functional problem-solving teams are also finding their way into the managerial infrastructure of most organizations.

Maintenance Management Choices

Inadequate maintenance of equipment creates numerous operational problems, including unplanned downtime, long setups, reduced operating speed and efficiency, poor employee morale, increased numbers of defects, and accelerated aging of equipment. Yet maintenance is often conducted by an outside department or vendor and is therefore viewed by many managers as an intrusive activity. Balancing the intrusiveness of regularly scheduled preventive maintenance against the inconvenience and potential disaster of process failures, which require corrective maintenance, is an important aspect of a company's infrastructure. While no one wants to tighten the availability of important resources to allow for scheduled "tune-ups," developing a systematic approach to preventive maintenance has been very beneficial to many companies. As a rule, companies that stress preventive maintenance are moving away from a policy of "If it's not broke, don't fix it" and toward a policy of "A stitch in time saves nine."

Total productive maintenance (TPM) recognizes that machine operators frequently "know" their equipment better than any outside maintenance staff ever could. The TPM approach stresses that workers should help to maintain their own equipment. In such a program, specialists in the maintenance department are responsible for advising the firm on equipment purchases, training workers to perform routine maintenance, and performing major equipment overhauls. The idea is to ensure that equipment is always in peak performance condition, rather than to focus only on preventing or correcting breakdowns.

> active example

Take a closer look at the concepts and issues you've been reading about.

DECISION AUDITING

Wickham Skinner, a leader in the development of the field of operations strategy, once wrote:

> The most typical serious condition in most manufacturing plants is that of inconsistencies existing within the infrastructure. Different sectors of manufacturing policy are implicitly set up to accomplish conflicting objectives. It is as if an automobile engine were designed for Indy racing, the transmission for fuel economy, the tires for comfort, the suspension for road race maneuverability and the trunk space for camping." (Skinner 1985, 96)

Skinner encouraged companies to conduct what he called a manufacturing strategy audit on a regular basis. In a manufacturing strategy audit, manufacturing managers detail the strategic priorities and biases suggested by the way decisions are made in each of the structural and infrastructural decision categories. They then share the information with top management, who might ask why a certain approach has been used and what the alternatives are. A manufacturing strategy audit may reveal a less-than-optimal alignment of decision-making priorities, perhaps caused by organizational change, growth, customer pressure, or new technologies. It may also reveal a need for a change in operations or suggest new organizational possibilities based on the development of new operational capabilities.

active concept check

Now let's take a moment to test your knowledge of the concepts you have studied in this section.

Strategic Integration of Operational Decisions

Most firms move through four distinct stages as they develop their ability to manage operations strategically (Hayes and Wheelwright 1984). Beginning with the internally neutral stage, they progress through an externally neutral stage, then to an internally supportive stage, and finally to the externally supportive stage.

The motto of an *internally neutral* firm might be "We want to be as good as we have been in the past." Such organizations manage their operations reactively, failing to see the proactive strategic contribution operations can make. They tend to stress goals and measures that emphasize the avoidance of surprises. The general attitude is that operations can have a significant negative impact on the firm through its mistakes—but little positive impact. Thus, the management of operations is left to functional experts who receive little strategic direction.

Occasionally, firms in the internally neutral stage will realize that their competitors have managed to gain a competitive edge based on the advancement of their operational capabilities. Having awakened to the threat, the firm's strategic managers recognize that operations can play a strategic role—at least to the extent that it controls costs. At this point, decision makers will set goals for operations: namely, that the firm should follow industry practice and achieve industry standards. Essentially, the focus has moved from internal neutrality to external neutrality. The motto of the *externally neutral* firm might be "We want to be as good as the competition." When external neutrality is the firm's focus, managers will more readily approve the capital investments needed to make significant changes in infrastructure or process technology, provided that the investments will put the firm on a par with the competition.

In organizations that have attained external neutrality, managers may eventually realize that the firm's strategy is different from that of other firms; hence, following industry practice will not provide any lasting competitive advantages. In such firms, managers may begin to align their operational decisions with the organization's competitive priorities and strategic goals. These firms have moved from a focus on external neutrality to a focus on *internally supportive* operations. In this stage, managers realize that a proactive OM strategy can play a synergistic role in the firm's overall strategy. Their motto might be "We want operational decisions to match up with and play a forward-thinking role in our business strategy, so that we don't waste time and energy on the wrong questions."

The final stage in the integration of operations strategy is the *externally supportive* stage. This stage differs from the internally supportive stage in that operations becomes a full-fledged, proactive partner in setting the firm's strategic direction. Whereas in the prior stage, operational decisions had to conform to corporate strategy, in this stage they can influence and set the direction for corporate strategy. Thus, an operations-based competitive advantage that could not have been envisioned in an earlier stage may be targeted and gained in this final stage. For example, operations may discover a unique approach to providing a service that allows the organization to bundle other services at no additional cost. If the organization is focused on the development of a competitive advantage through such innovations, it has reached the externally supportive stage.

Hayes and Wheelwright suggest that a firm cannot move directly from stage one to stage four. Organizational learning must take place in the process of moving from one stage to the next. Changes in decision-making procedures, changes in corporate structures and infrastructures, and even changes in personnel may be necessary to prepare for movement to a more advanced stage. Failure to lay the groundwork that is usually put in place in the process of evolving to a higher level of integration could produce only the well-meant goal of externally supportive operational decision making, without the people, perspectives, and systems necessary to support such an expectation.

> video exercise

Take a moment to apply what you've learned.

> active example

Take a closer look at the concepts and issues you've been reading about.

Environmental Excellence and Operations Strategy

In recent years, society has made increasing demands for social responsibility on the part of business. Today, companies must comply with a host of local, state, national, and international regulations, many of them dealing with the preservation of our natural environment. In the United States over the past 30 years, concern for the natural environment has led to the creation of the Environmental Protection Agency and a large body of environmental legislation that affects business. At the national level, these legal requirements include the reporting of toxic releases that result from the manufacture, use, or transportation of any of more than 300 chemicals named in Title III of the Superfund Amendments and Reauthorization Act (SARA), also called the Emergency Planning and Community Right to Know Act. In addition, the Comprehensive Environmental Response, Compensation, and Liability Act (CERCLA), which created the Superfund, established joint and several liability for the cleanup of environmental problems created in the past (meaning that you are responsible if you ever owned the property in question, whether or not you did the damage). U.S. businesses are also required to comply with the Clean Air Act, the Clean Water Act, the Toxic Substances Control Act, the Resource Conservation and Recovery Act, and many other national, state, and local statutes.

Many facilities such as this recycling plant are emerging to provide businesses with an alternative to the landfill for the disposal of their solid waste materials. If they only reclaim the materials they are often called demanufacturing operations; if they also reconstruct products from previously used but refurbished parts they are called remanufacturing operations.

Beyond these legislative hurdles, companies must respond to customer, employee, community, and shareholder pressure for environmental excellence. One critical incident, such as the Bhopal disaster or the grounding of the Exxon Valdez, can have significant implications both for the environment and for the long-term profitability of a business organization. Given the risks and the potential impact of environmental issues on profitability, environmental issues now play a significant role in the corporate and business-level strategy of many firms. Since operations is directly responsible for the creation of the goods and services customers value, it is also directly responsible for the creation of the wastes they abhor. As a result, it is imperative that companies integrate the requirement for environmental excellence into their operations strategies.

Effective operations management can have a significant impact on the firm's environmental performance. In a recent survey (Newman and Hanna 1996), firms were asked questions about their environmental awareness and the degree to which operations had been strategically integrated in the firms' strategy. Firms in the early stages of strategic integration did not report high levels of environmental awareness. Only those firms in the later stages of strategic integration reported high levels of environmental awareness. Based on the results of this survey, on the research of others who have studied the relationship between operational performance and environmental excellence, and on what is known about how organizations develop capabilities over time, it seems likely that operational excellence is a necessary prerequisite to environmental excellence.

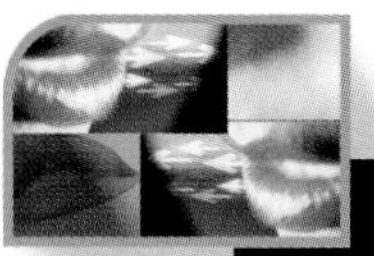

active poll <

What do you think? Voice your opinion and find out what others have to say.

active concept check <

Now let's take a moment to test your knowledge of the concepts you have studied in this section.

> Integrating Operational Decisions

This chapter has focused on aligning operational decisions with one another and with the decisions made in other areas of the firm. While the considerations of this chapter are related in some way to everything else in the book, you might notice key linkages with this chapter's material as you consider Chapters 2, 5, 7, and 11. Chapter 2 was about making operational decisions fit with entities outside of the firm. Along with this chapter, it provides the context for operational decision makers. Chapter 5 focuses on total quality management. When this approach is a part of a company's way of doing business, it requires all managers to be on the same wavelength and reinforces the customer-oriented strategic direction of the firm. Chapter 7 deals with the design of the value-adding system. Clearly, the strategy of the firm dictates many aspects of the value-adding system's design. Finally, Chapter 11 deals with aggregate planning. The competitive priorities of the firm will have a big influence on the way in which companies plan to meet demand. (i.e., how they'll balance inventory, backlogs, overtime, and changes in the workforce size).

integrated OM <

Take a moment to apply what you've learned.

> Chapter Wrap-Up

An operations strategy is a pattern of decisions that are made in the operations function. When the decision pattern is consistent and is well aligned with a business's competitive priorities, operations is likely to be in tune with customer expectations and to make significant contributions that place the firm in a position of competitive advantage.

Since decisions are made at every level of each organization and strategy is a pattern of decisions, there is a strategic decision hierarchy. Decisions made by top corporate managers determine what businesses a company will pursue. These decision makers allocate resources based on the potential they see for shareholder rewards. Within the context of the resource picture that develops from corporate strategy decisions, business managers, such as divisional presidents, have to determine how they will seek to satisfy customers and create competitive advantages. Finally, managers in the functional areas make the decisions that actually create the value envisioned by the business strategy.

Operations strategy includes both structural and infrastructural decisions. Structural decisions establish the system that is used to add value for customers. These decisions, which have long-term significance, constrain the firm's infrastructural decisions, which determine how the value-adding system will be run on an ongoing basis. Though infrastructural decisions generally have only short-term significance, the pattern of infrastructural decisions that develops over time can influence the firm's structural requirements.

This text provides insight into a variety of OM decisions. Any OM decision should pull together with other OM decisions, as well as with the decisions made in other functions to support the business strategy. Some firms treat the operations function as an independent decision-making entity and do not effectively integrate the area with the rest of the business. Other firms actually use their operational strengths to drive the company's pursuit of competitive advantage. The degree to which operational decisions are integrated with the business strategy plays a significant role in building customer satisfaction and competitive advantage.

There are significant benefits that come from consistent decision making between operations and other functional areas. Significant synergies can be gained. For this reason, it is important for firms to figure out how they can break down communication barriers between the functions. Managers in the functional areas need to focus on the business objectives and the need to satisfy customers. That takes working together across functional boundaries.

Significant environmental benefits can be derived from the development of operations management capabilities. When operations are more efficient they waste less and therefore pollute less. Operations managers who can effectively manage a firm's resources to create competitive advantages in terms of cost, quality, flexibility, or speed, are also likely to be able to address environmental concerns. This is one area that illustrates the importance of operational excellence and cross-functional cooperation as a basis for the pursuit of company objectives.

> end-of-chapter resources

- Practice Quiz
- Key Terms
- Discussion Questions
- Case 3: Motel 6 is Still a Cheap Sleep, but with New Strategies
- References
- Plant Tours

Decision Analysis

SUPPLEMENT B

Supplement Outline

The Components of a Decision Problem

The three basic components of a decision problem are the decision alternatives; the possible **environments,** conditions, or states of nature within which a decision is to be implemented; and the **outcomes** or payoffs that will result from each possible combination of alternatives and states of nature.

The *decision alternatives* are those actions from among which the decision maker must choose. That is, they are the aspects of the decision situation over which the decision maker has direct control.

The **states of nature** are those aspects of the decision situation over which the decision maker does *not* have direct control. They certainly include things over which there is no control, such as the weather, the general state of the economy, or actions taken by the national government. They may also include things which can be influenced to some extent but not completely. The market response to a new product (which is partly determined by the price charged and advertising) or a competitor's actions (which may be at least partly determined by choices made by the decision maker) are conditions the decision maker cannot determine completely.

Making a decision and implementing it within a state of nature will result in some outcome, which may be either a gain or a loss. The **payoff function** specifies what that outcome is for every possible alternative/state-of-nature combination. The payoff function may be given either as an equation or, when the possible decision alternatives and states of nature are relatively limited, as a **payoff table** or *matrix.* For example, Table B.1 shows a payoff table for a proposed cardiac catheterization service at Cheryl's hospital.

Example B.1

Cheryl has been approached by the head of the hospital's cardiac care unit about the possibility of starting a cardiac catheterization service at the hospital. Doing so would require either the conversion of existing space in the hospital (which would allow the development of a small unit) or the construction of an addition (which would make a larger unit possible). Additional equipment would also have to be purchased. Before taking this idea to the capital expenditure review committee for the chain that owns the hospital, Cheryl gets information on the costs of the two possibilities from the hospital architect and asks the hospital's marketing department for a preliminary assessment of the possible levels of demand for this type of service. Putting this information together, Cheryl creates the payoff table in Table B.1. The hospital chain uses a five-year planning horizon for major capital expenditures. The five-year returns shown in the table are stated in millions of dollars of net present value over that time horizon.

TABLE B.1 Payoff Table for Cardiac Catheterization Service

Demand Level			
Alternative	**Low**	**Medium**	**High**
Build addition	−3	1	7
Convert space	−1	2	5
Do nothing	0	0	0

active exercise <

Take a moment to apply what you've learned.

Types of Decision Problems

There are three basic types of decision problems, each with its own mode of analysis:

1. **Decision making under certainty:** *In this type of problem, the state of nature is known, so the payoff table has only one column. In principle, the analysis is simple: Choose the alternative with the best payoff. In practice, it is not always that easy, since an "alternative" may actually represent the values for many decision variables. However, solution procedures have been developed for many problems of this type. For example, Supplement C presents an introduction to linear programming, a popular technique for decision making under certainty.*
2. **Decision making under uncertainty:** *In this type of problem, decision makers have the payoff table, but no information on the relative likelihood of the states of nature. A number of approaches to this type of problem are possible, several of which will be discussed in this supplement.*
3. **Decision making under risk:** *In this type of problem, in addition to the payoff table, decision makers have the probabilities for the different states of nature. The standard approach is expected value analysis, which will be discussed in this supplement.*

DECISION MAKING UNDER UNCERTAINTY

As noted above, in decision making under uncertainty we have a payoff table but no information about the relative likelihood of the different states of nature. A number of procedures have been developed for choosing an **alternative** under these conditions, each based on a different philosophy about what constitutes a good choice. We shall consider four: maximax, maximin, equal likelihood, and minimax regret.

Maximax Procedure

The **maximax** procedure (called the **minimin** procedure if the payoffs are costs or losses rather than profits or gains) is an optimistic approach. It assumes that no matter what alternative we choose, "nature" will smile favorably on us and choose the state of nature that will benefit us the most (or hurt us the least). Thus, we choose the alternative with the largest maximum gain (or the smallest minimum loss).

Example B.2

Find the maximax solution to Cheryl's cardiac catheterization service problem described in Example B.1.

Solution:
From Exhibit B.1, the maximum payoffs for the decision alternatives are:

Build addition:	7
Convert space:	5
Do nothing:	0

The largest maximum payoff is 7, so the "maximax" decision is to *build an addition.*

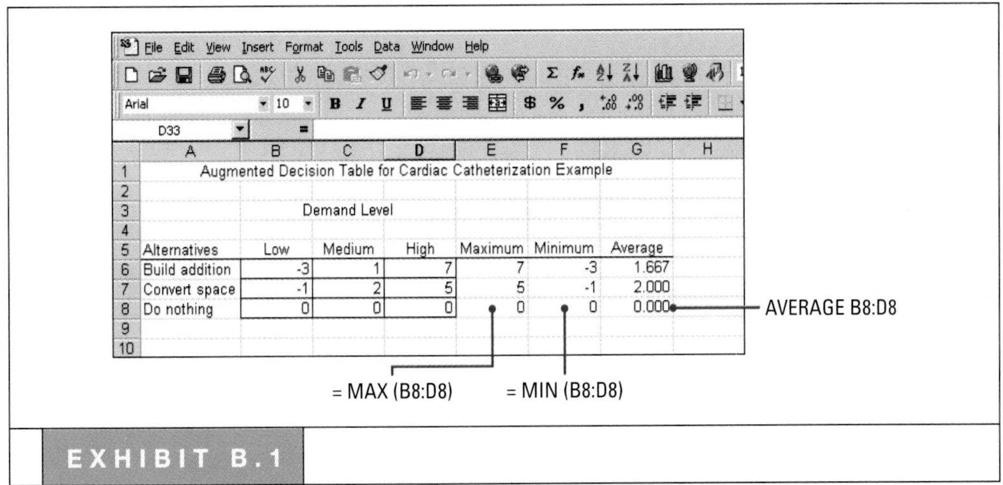

	A	B	C	D	E	F	G	H
1	Augmented Decision Table for Cardiac Catheterization Example							
2								
3		Demand Level						
4								
5	Alternatives	Low	Medium	High	Maximum	Minimum	Average	
6	Build addition	-3	1	7	7	-3	1.667	
7	Convert space	-1	2	5	5	-1	2.000	
8	Do nothing	0	0	0	0	0	0.000	
9								
10								

EXHIBIT B.1

> active exercise

Take a moment to apply what you've learned.

Maximin procedure

The **maximin** procedure (called the **minimax** procedure if the payoffs are costs or losses) is a pessimistic approach. It assumes that, no matter what alternative we choose, "nature" will choose the state of nature that benefits us the least (or hurts us the most). Thus, we choose the alternative with the largest minimum gain (or the smallest maximum loss). In fact, if "nature" is a competitor who gets to choose his alternative after we have chosen ours, this could be a very good strategy. (This gets into an area called *game theory,* which we will not discuss.)

Example B.3

Find the maximin solution to Cheryl's cardiac catheterization service problem described in Example B.1.

Solution:
From Exhibit B.1, the minimum payoffs for the alternatives are:

Build addition:	−3
Convert space:	−1
Do nothing:	0

The largest minimum payoff is 0, so the "maximin" decision is to *do nothing.*

> active exercise

Take a moment to apply what you've learned.

Equal Likelihood Procedure

One criticism of the maximax and maximin strategies is that they focus on only one payoff for each alternative, ignoring all other states of nature and their payoffs. The **equal likelihood** procedure is based on the assumption that if we cannot determine the relative likelihood of the states of nature, then it is rational to presume that they are equally likely. If this is the case, then we should choose the alternative with the largest average payoff (or the smallest average payoff for losses).

Example B.4

Find the equal likelihood solution to Cheryl's cardiac catheterization service problem described in Example B.1.

Solution:
From Exhibit B.1, the averages of the rows of the payoff table are:

Build addition:	1.667
Convert space:	2.000
Do nothing:	0

The largest average payoff is 2.0, so the "equal likelihood" decision is to *convert space.*

active exercise 

Take a moment to apply what you've learned.

Minimax Regret Procedure

We have all had the experience of making a decision and then, after observing the result, wishing that we had made another choice instead, so that our payoff would have been better (or less bad). That is the concept behind the **minimax regret** procedure: We choose the alternative that will yield the smallest possible maximum regret. The procedure has two steps:

1. *Construct a regret table by subtracting each payoff from the maximum payoff in its column. (For a loss table, subtract the smallest loss in each column from each entry in its column.)*
2. *Apply the minimax procedure to the regret table: Find the maximum regret in each row; then choose the alternative with the smallest maximum regret.*

Example B.5

Find the minimax regret solution to Cheryl's cardiac catheterization service problem described in Example B.1.

Solution:

Step 1: Construct the regret table from the payoff table in Table B.1. As shown in Exhibit B.2, this is done in two steps. First, as shown in Exhibit B.2(a), find the maximum entry in each column of the payoff table. Second, as shown in Exhibit B.2(b), each payoff table entry is subtracted from the maximum in its column to get the regret table.

Step 2: Find the maximum regret for each alternative, as shown to the right of the regret table in Figure B.2(b). The alternative with the smallest maximum regret is to *convert space,* with a maximum regret of 2.

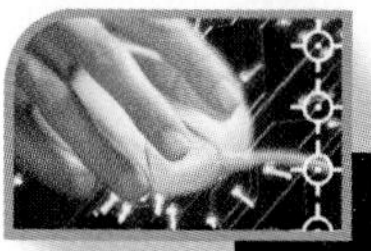

active exercise 

Take a moment to apply what you've learned.

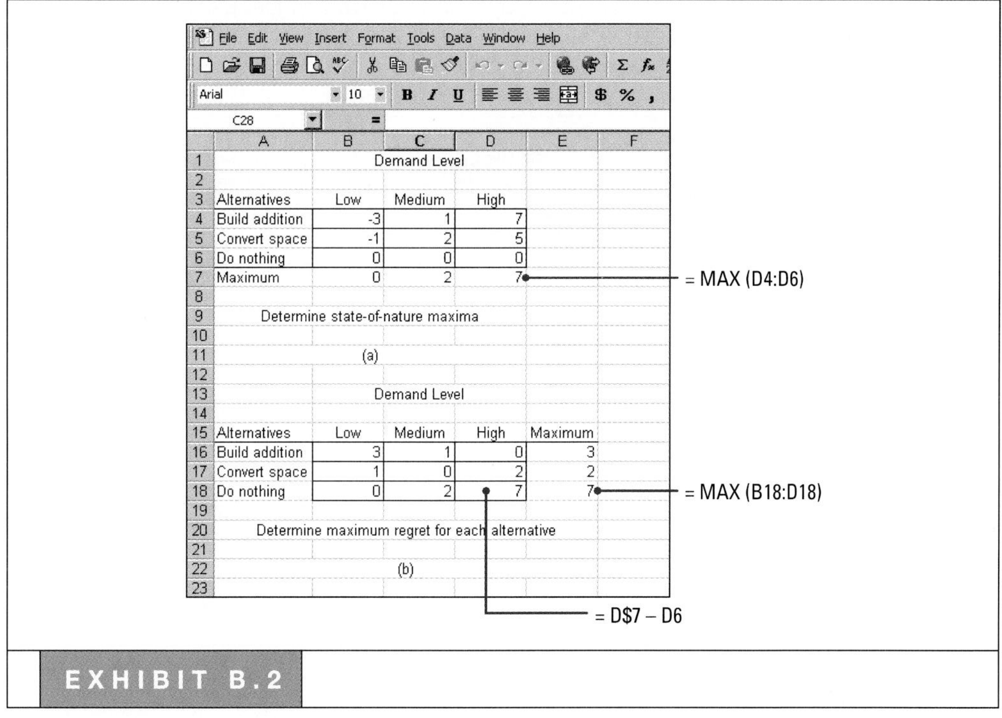

	Demand Level		
Alternatives	Low	Medium	High
Build addition	-3	1	7
Convert space	-1	2	5
Do nothing	0	0	0
Maximum	0	2	7

Determine state-of-nature maxima

(a)

	Demand Level			
Alternatives	Low	Medium	High	Maximum
Build addition	3	1	0	3
Convert space	1	0	2	2
Do nothing	0	2	7	7

Determine maximum regret for each alternative

(b)

EXHIBIT B.2

DECISION MAKING UNDER RISK

There are two basic approaches to decision making under risk: (1) maximizing expected gain or minimizing expected loss, and (2) minimizing expected regret.

Maximizing Expected Gain

Under some reasonable assumptions about the characteristics of a rational decision maker, it can be shown that when probabilities for the states of nature are known, the alternative that maximizes the expected gain (or minimizes the expected loss) is the appropriate decision. To determine the expected value of a decision alternative, multiply that alternative's payoff under each different state of nature by that state of nature's probability and sum the resulting products.

Minimizing Expected Regret

As an alternative to using the payoff table to maximize the expected gain (or minimize the expected loss), we can choose the alternative that minimizes the expected regret. As shown in Examples B.6 and B.7, the two approaches lead to the same decision.

Example B.6

(Refer to Example B.1.) Cheryl has gone back to the hospital's marketing department to get some additional information about the relative likelihood of the different levels of demand for the proposed cardiac catheterization service. After review of their marketing research, the department gives Cheryl the following probability estimates: P(low) = .2, P(medium) = .7, P(high) = .1. Using these probabilities, determine which alternative maximizes the expected value return to the hospital.

Solution:
The projected returns are given by the rows of Table B.1. The expected returns for the three alternatives are:

$$\begin{aligned}\text{Build addition: } & .2(-3) + .7(1) + .1(7) \\ &= -.6 + .7 + .7 = .8 \\ \text{Convert space: } & .2(-1) + .7(2) + .1(5) \\ &= -.2 + 1.4 + .5 = 1.7 \\ \text{Do nothing: } & .2(0) + .7(0) + .1(0) = 0\end{aligned}$$

The alternative with the highest expected payoff is to *convert space.* Exhibit B.3 shows the Excel computation of the expected values.

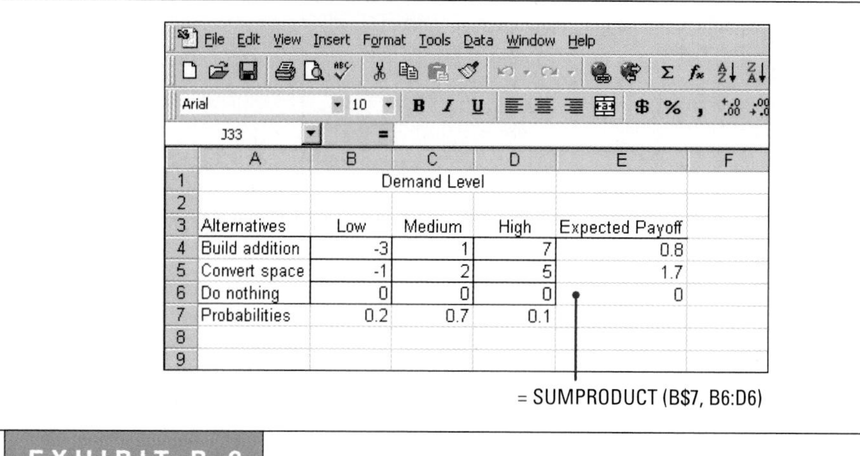

	A	B	C	D	E	F
1			Demand Level			
2						
3	Alternatives	Low	Medium	High	Expected Payoff	
4	Build addition	-3	1	7	0.8	
5	Convert space	-1	2	5	1.7	
6	Do nothing	0	0	0	0	
7	Probabilities	0.2	0.7	0.1		
8						
9						

EXHIBIT B.3

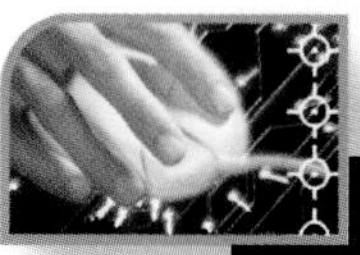

active exercise

Take a moment to apply what you've learned.

Example B.7

(Refer to Example B.1.) The regret matrix for the cardiac catheterization lab decision problem was developed in Example B.5. Determine which decision alternative minimizes the hospital management's expected regret.

Solution:
Using the regret matrix from Exhibit B.2(b) and the probabilities given in Example B.6, the expected regrets for the three decision alternatives are:

$$\begin{aligned}\text{Build addition: } & .2(-3) + .7(1) + .1(0) \\ & = -.6 + .7 + 0 = 1.3 \\ \text{Convert space: } & .2(-1) + .7(0) + .1(2) \\ & = -.2 + 0 + .2 = .4 \\ \text{Do nothing: } & .2(0) + .7(2) + .1(7) \\ & = 0 + 1.4 + .7 = 2.1\end{aligned}$$

The alternative with the lowest expected regret is to *convert space.*

active exercise

Take a moment to apply what you've learned.

Comparing the expected **regrets** found in Example B.7 with the expected **payoffs** in Example B.6, we see that, for each pair of alternatives, the difference between the values of the expected gains and the difference between the values of the expected regrets are identical. For example, the difference between the expected gains for "build addition" and "convert space" is 1.7 − .8 = .9. The difference between the expected regrets for the same pair is 1.3 − .4 = .9. This finding is not specific to this particular example, but is a general result.

The Expected Value of Perfect Information

If, before having to make a final decision, we could find out exactly what the state of nature was going to be, we could improve the quality of the decision. The **expected value of perfect information (EVPI)** is a measure of the expected *current* worth to the decision maker of being able to find out, just before having to make the decision, what the state of nature will be. It combines the current assessments of the probabilities of the states of nature with the improved value of knowing the state of nature. Thus, the EVPI is computed as the difference between the expected value of making the decision with perfect information (EWPI), given by the weighted combination of the best payoffs for each state of nature, and the expected value of the best decision with current information.

Example B.8

(Refer to Example B.1.) Assuming it would be possible to find out the demand level for the cardiac catheterization service before making a final decision about whether to introduce the service and, if so, how large a unit to build, determine the current expected value of having this perfect information.

Solution:
The best decisions for each state of nature (demand level) and their values, as given in Exhibit B.1, are:

Demand	*Best Decision*	*Value*
Low	Do nothing	0
Medium	Convert space	2
High	Build addition	7

Using the probabilities of the demand levels given in Example B.6, the expected value with perfect information (EWPI) is:

$$\text{EWPI} = .2(0) + .7(2) + .1(7) = 0 + 1.4 + .7 = 2.1$$

The best decision without having perfect information, as found in Example B.6, is to convert space, which has an expected value of 1.7. Thus, the expected value of perfect information is:

$$\text{EVPI} = \text{EWPI} - \text{E(best decision)} = 2.1 - 1.7 = .4$$

That is, the hospital could increase its expected net present value by $.4 million if it were able to find out what the demand for this new service would be before committing to whether and how to provide it.

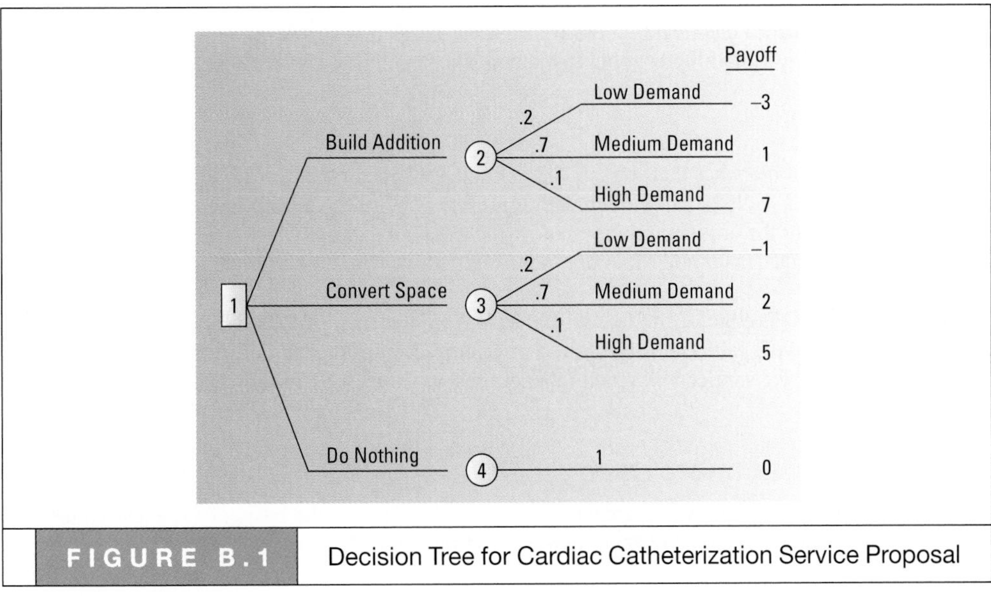

FIGURE B.1 Decision Tree for Cardiac Catheterization Service Proposal

active exercise <

Take a moment to apply what you've learned.

Note that the expected value of perfect information in Example B.8 is exactly the same as the expected regret from Example B.7. Given that EVPI and expected regret are both computed by comparing, for each state of nature, the value of a specific decision with the value of the best decision for that state of nature, this result is not an accident. It will always be the case.

Since it is never possible (at least legally) to get perfect information before having to make a decision, the expected value of perfect information is useful mainly as an upper bound on the *expected value of sample or imperfect information* (such as market surveys or economic forecasts), which is often available before a final decision must be made.

DECISION TREES: AN ALTERNATIVE TO PAYOFF TABLES

An alternative to using a payoff to compute the expected values of decision alternatives is to use a **decision tree.** As shown in Figure B.1, a decision tree consists of two or more stages or levels, shown in *time order* from left to right.

Nodes and Branches

Each level of a decision tree consists of *nodes* (the squares and circles) and *branches,* which represent alternatives. The square nodes represent decision points; each branch from a decision node represents one of the decision alternatives available at that point. The circles, or **chance nodes,** represent problem features that are determined by chance or probability, such as the states of nature.

Figure B.1 is actually the decision tree for Cheryl's problem of whether to propose starting a cardiac catheterization service and, if so, how large a unit to build. The nodes have been numbered to facilitate the description of the tree.

- Node 1 is the **decision node.** There are three alternatives, represented by the three branches: (1) build an addition, (2) convert existing space, and (3) do nothing.
- Node 2 is a chance node representing the possible states of nature that might follow a decision to build an addition. There are three possibilities: (1) low demand, which has a probability of .2, (2) medium demand, which has a probability of .7, and (3) high demand, which has a probability of .1. Notice that each state of nature's probability has been written next to its branch.
- Node 3 is another chance node, representing the possible states of nature that might follow a decision to convert existing space. The branching is identical to the one for node 2.
- Node 4 is the chance node that represents what might happen after a decision to do nothing. While it could have branches identical to those for nodes 2 and 3, it is simpler to represent this way. That is, with probability 1, nothing is going to happen since no action is being taken.

Paths and Payoffs

A connected series of branches that starts at the extreme left side of the tree (node 1) and goes through all levels of the tree is called a *path.* Each path represents one of the possible sequences of decisions and chance results for the problem represented by the tree. For example, "build addition" from node 1 and "medium demand" from node 2 is one possible path or decision alternative and demand level sequence.

At the extreme right edge of the tree is the net payoff for each of these possible paths, as given originally in the payoff table in Table B.1. For example, building an addition and experiencing medium demand for the service will result in a net present value of $1 million.

ANALYZING A DECISION TREE

The standard approach to analyzing a decision tree is to choose on the basis of expected value. The procedure for doing this is called **averaging out and folding back.**

Averaging out means replacing each branching by a single number. For a chance branching, the number used is the expected value, which is found by multiplying the probability of each branch by the value at its right end and summing. For a decision branching, the number used is the value of the best alternative in the branching.

Folding back means that this process starts at the right-hand edge of the tree and proceeds back to the start of the tree, working from right to left.

Example B.9

Use the process of averaging out and folding back to analyze the decision tree shown in Figure B.1. Determine which decision alternative maximizes the expected return for the cardiac catheterization decision problem described in Example B.1.

Solution:
The first round of averaging out consists of replacing each chance branching in the right-most level of the tree by its expected value:

- The chance branching from node 2 is replaced by its expected value:

$$.2(-3) + .7(1) + .1(7) = -.6 + .7 + .7 = .8$$

- The chance branching from node 3 is replaced by its expected value:

$$.2(-1) + .7(2) + .1(5) = -.2 + 1.4 + .5 = 1.7$$

- The chance branching from node 4 is replaced by its expected value, which is 0.

The result of this first round of averaging out is the reduced tree shown in Figure B.2(a), in which each second-level chance branching has been replaced by its expected value.

We now back up one level in the tree (folding back). In the second round of "averaging out," node 1, which is in the new right-most level of the tree of the reduced tree shown in Figure B.2(a), is replaced by the value of the best alternative, which is 1.7 for "convert space." To show this, the value of the alternative chosen has been written above the decision node and the branches not chosen have been marked out with slashes as shown in Figure B.2(b).

Since the tree now has only one decision node, we can readily see that the decision strategy that maximizes the expected return to the hospital over the planning horizon is: Convert space for an expected net present value of $1.7 million.

In practice, we would consolidate the entire analysis process into a single decision tree rather than redrawing successively smaller trees after each round of averaging out and folding back. To do this, the result of each averaging out is written above the node to which it applies, with, as suggested in Example B.9, the decision alternatives not chosen being marked out with slashes. The result of applying this summarization process to the analysis in Example B.9 is shown in Figure B.3, with the averaging out results being shown in red.

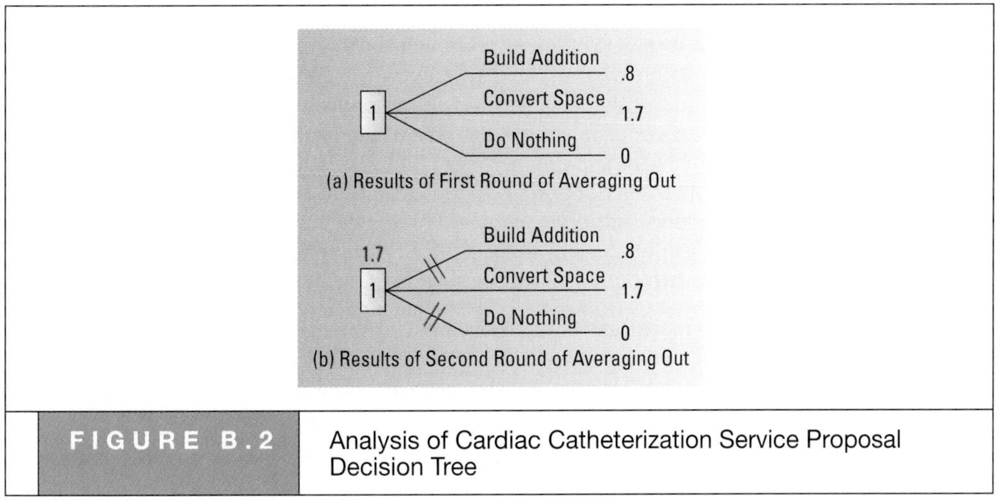

FIGURE B.2 Analysis of Cardiac Catheterization Service Proposal Decision Tree

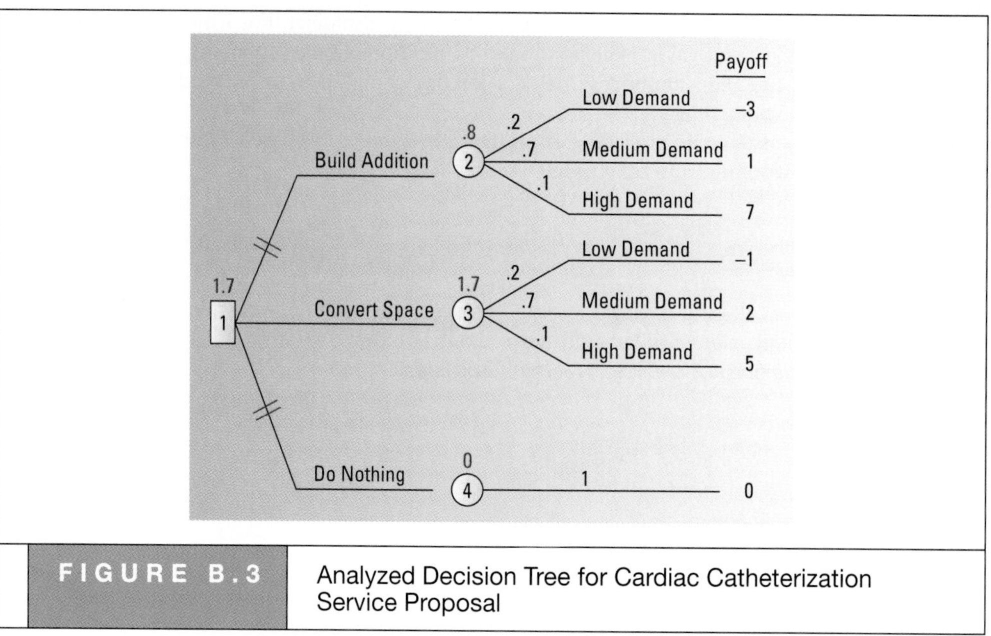

FIGURE B.3 Analyzed Decision Tree for Cardiac Catheterization Service Proposal

active exercise

Take a moment to apply what you've learned.

MULTISTAGE DECISION TREES

While we can certainly use a decision tree to analyze a one-decision problem, as just illustrated for Cheryl's cardiac catheterization service proposal, we really will not gain anything we could not get from a payoff table analysis. The real benefit of using a decision tree comes in more complicated problems with multiple levels of decisions or states of nature, particularly if the decision alternatives, the states of nature, or their probabilities depend on what precedes them in the tree. While we could still use payoff tables to analyze these types of problems, structuring the tables would be difficult. A tree shows the structure and relationships in such a problem much better than a table does.

Example B.10

Fred has just returned from a weeklong trip to China, where he was part of a team sent by his company to explore a joint venture with a Chinese company to manufacture and market consumer electronics in China and Southeast Asia. Part of the decision about whether and how to enter into the arrangement is the decision about the size of the facility to build. The two alternatives discussed were (1) to build a large plant initially or (2) to build a small plant and then, if warranted, expand later or, if business is not good enough, sell out to the Chinese partner.

The possible decisions—along with preliminary estimates of the sales levels, their probabilities, and the resulting net present values of the different combinations—are shown in the decision tree in Figure B.4. Notice two particular features of this tree:

- It is possible to have two or more successive chance nodes, as in the "high" result of node 2 (sales level during the first two years) being followed by node 4 rather than a decision. (Technically, there is a decision to "stay" or "sell out," but the decision is obvious and is not included in the analysis.)
- The probabilities of the states of nature for nodes 4, 8, 9, 10, and 11, all of which deal with the sales level during years 3–5, depend on the sales level during the first two years. That is, the later years' sales probabilities are conditional on the earlier years' results.

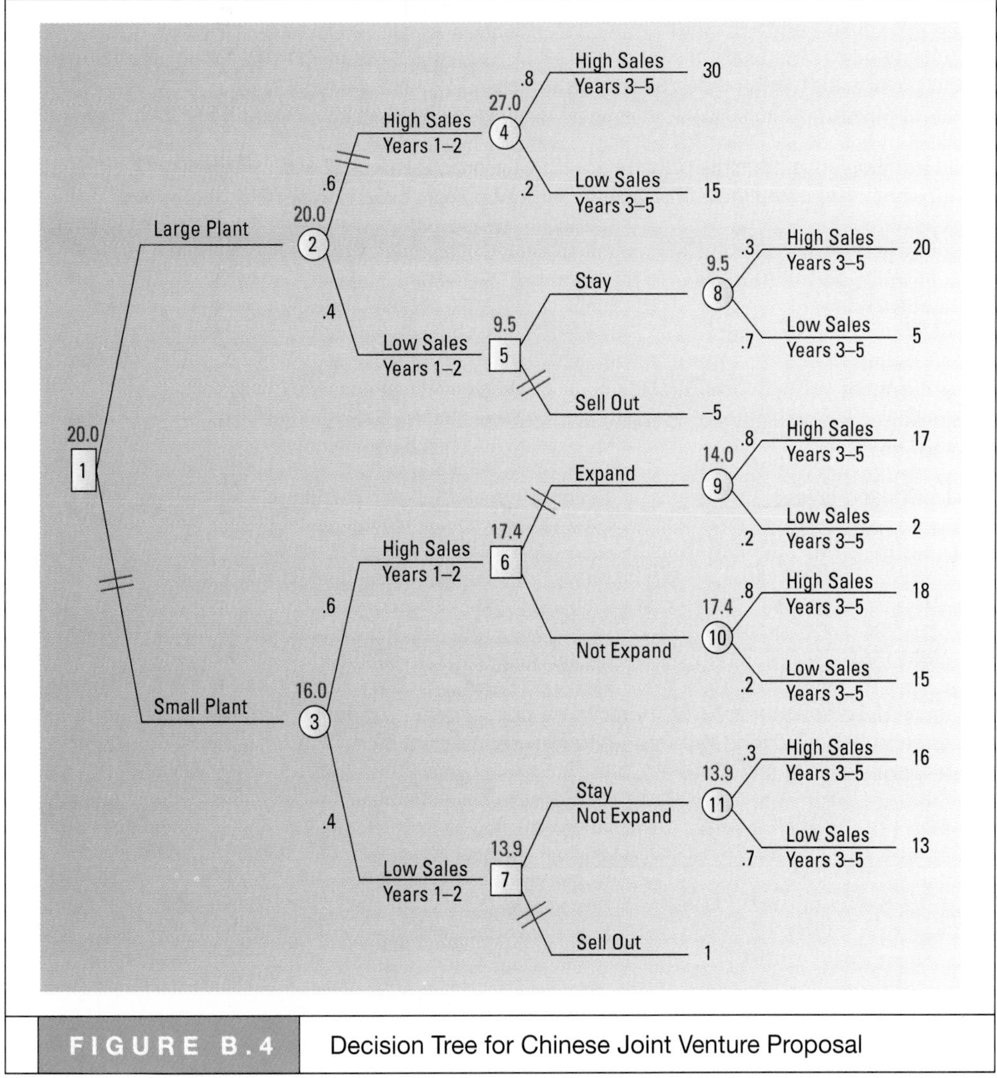

FIGURE B.4 Decision Tree for Chinese Joint Venture Proposal

Determine what Fred's strategy should be. That is, determine whether they should initially build a large or small plant and, subsequently, what to do after the end of the first two years.

Solution:
The averaging out and folding back analysis of this decision is shown in red on the tree in Figure B.4. The best strategy is to build a large plant (node 1 choice) and, whether the first two years' sales are high or low (node 4), to stay with the project. The overall expected net present value from following this strategy is $20.0 million.

> **active exercise**

Take a moment to apply what you've learned.

OTHER APPROACHES TO ANALYZING A DECISION TREE

While expected value analysis is the standard approach to analyzing a decision tree, it is not the only method possible. Two alternative approaches are **risk analysis,** which recognizes the various possible outcomes and their probabilities, and extreme case analysis, which, like the maximax and maximin strategies, takes either an optimistic or pessimistic view rather than working with probabilities. Explanations of both approaches follow.

Example B.11

Refer back to the decision tree in Figure B.1. Construct cumulative probability distributions for the payoffs for the three decision alternatives.

Solution:
"Build addition" has possible payoffs of −3, with probability .2, 1 with probability .7, and 7, with probability 1. The cumulative probability distribution for "build addition" is, therefore:

Value	*Cumulative Probability*
−3	.2
1	.9
7	.1

Similarly, the cumulative probability distributions for the alternatives "convert space" and "do nothing" are:

Convert space		*Do nothing*	
Value	*Cumulative Probability*	*Value*	*Cumulative Probability*
−1	.2	0	1.0
2	.9		
5	1.0		

Figure B.5 shows graphs of these three cumulative probability distributions. The decision maker can choose among the three alternatives by comparing the cumulative distributions on whatever basis he or she prefers.

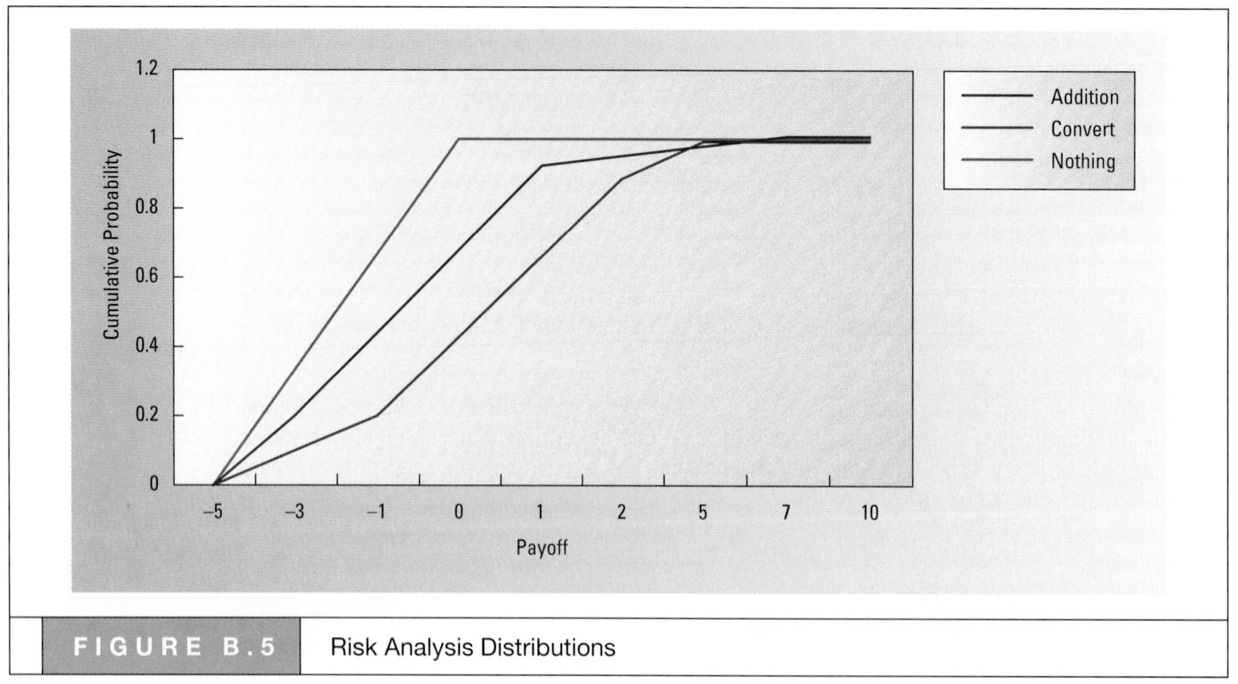

FIGURE B.5 Risk Analysis Distributions

active exercise

Take a moment to apply what you've learned.

Risk analysis

This approach to analyzing a decision tree recognizes each possible decision combination and the set of possible payoffs and their probabilities. These are then converted into a cumulative probability distribution and graphed for comparison purposes.

Extreme Case Analysis

This approach combines the averaging out and folding back approach described for expected value analysis with the procedures used earlier for decision making under certainty. The folding back part is the same, but in averaging out, rather than replacing a chance branching by its expected value, use the highest branch value (for the "best case" analysis) or use the lowest branch value (for the "worst case" analysis).

Example B.12

Refer back to Figure B.1. Perform a "best case" analysis on the cardiac catheterization service problem. (The "worst case" analysis will be left for the problems.)

Solution:
The results of averaging out and folding back for a best case analysis are shown in red in the tree diagram in Figure B.6. The probability values from Figure B.1 have been eliminated since they are not relevant for a best case analysis.

In the first round of averaging out:

- The branching from node 2 is replaced by 7, the value for high demand.
- The branching from node 3 is replaced by 5, the value for high demand.
- The branching from node 4 is replaced by 0, which is the only possible payoff.

The second round of averaging out uses the results from the first round. Since node 1 is a decision node, its branching is replaced with the value of the alternative chosen. Given that we are following a maximax or "best case" approach, that alternative is "build addition," with value 7.

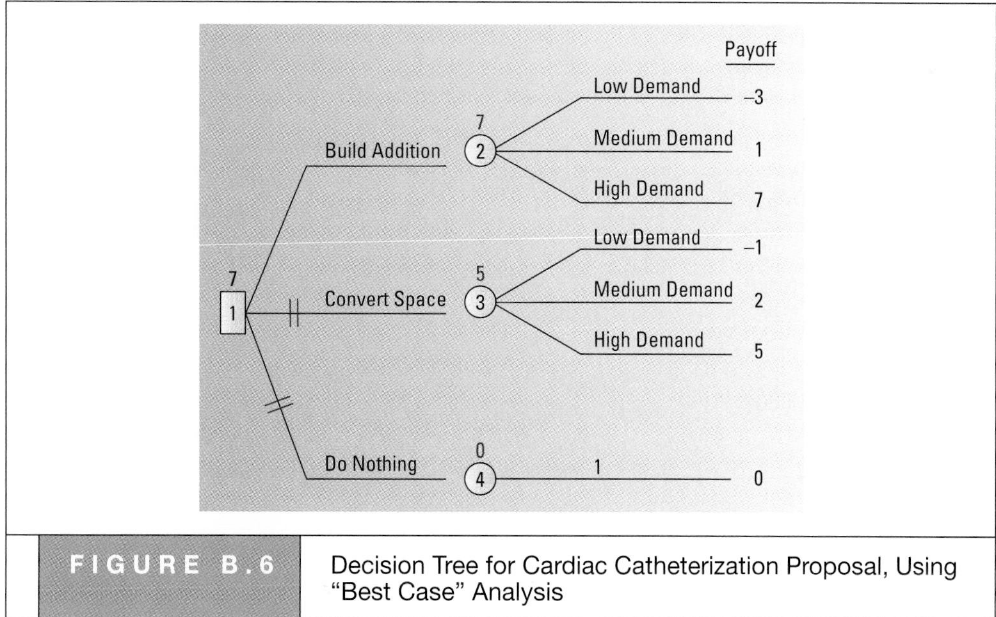

FIGURE B.6 Decision Tree for Cardiac Catheterization Proposal, Using "Best Case" Analysis

> active exercise

Take a moment to apply what you've learned.

Utility: An Alternative to Dollar Value

In some decisions, money is not an appropriate measure of the quality of the various outcomes. For example, how could you put a dollar value on losing your health or winning the top international award in your field? In other cases, the dollar value of an outcome may have implications beyond its monetary significance. A big loss, for example, may result in the bankruptcy of the organization, which is more significant than the dollar value of the loss.

When dollar value alone is not an adequate measure of the value of an outcome, an alternative measure, **utility,** may be used. How to determine values for a utility function for a given situation is outside the scope of this supplement. However, a fairly complete discussion may be found in any text on decision theory, such as Raiffa, *Decision Analysis: Introductory Lectures on Choices Under Uncertainty* (Addison-Wesley, 1970). Making decisions based on utility, however, is no different from making decisions based on money, as described in this supplement.

Supplement Wrap-Up

All decision problems have three basic components: decision alternatives, implementation environments or states of nature, and a payoff function that gives the gain or loss for each alternative/state-of-nature combination.

In decision making under uncertainty, we assume that these three components are all that are known. A number of procedures based on different philosophies of what constitutes a good approach—maximax, maximin, equal likelihood, and minimax regret—were presented and illustrated.

Maximization of expected value or minimization of expected cost is the standard procedure for decision making under risk, in which probabilities for the states of nature are known in addition to the three basic components described.

An alternative to using payoff tables for decision making under risk is the decision tree, in which branchings represent either the decision alternatives or the states of nature relevant at a given point in the process. Decision trees are more flexible than payoff tables and can be more easily used to represent multistage decision problems and situations in which the probabilities of the states of nature depend on what has happened up to that point in the tree. The standard analysis approach for a decision tree with probabilities is averaging out and folding back, in which, starting at the right-most side of the tree, each branching is replaced by a single number—the expected value of a chance branching or the value of the alternative chosen in a decision branching. Two other possible approaches to analyzing a decision tree were also presented: risk analysis and best case or worst case analysis.

end-of-supplement resources

- Practice Quiz
- Key Terms
- Solved Problems
- Discussion Questions
- Problems

Designing the Product-Service Bundle

Chapter Outline

What's Ahead

. . . BACK AT THE REC CENTER

Everyone else had already worked up a good sweat by the time Luis arrived at the club on Monday morning. When Luis is more than a few minutes late, it's usually a sign that something has gone wrong over the weekend, prompting an early morning call from the third-shift supervisor around 5:00 A.M. (Many three-shift operations start the week on Sunday night or Monday morning.) But on this day, Luis seemed in a great mood.

"Hit it hard this morning, folks; Gatorade's on me!" he offered happily, as he burst through the door doing his best "air guitar" routine. "They were rockin' on the third shift last night, and I just got the gold record!"

"Whoa, hold on there! What's the big celebration?" asked Fred, wondering what was going on. "Did you hit the lottery?"

"Nope, nothing like that," Luis assured the group, continuing to smile. "I got a call from the folks on the third shift just after they started using that new latex stain this morning." Luis was referring to a new stain to be used on a best-selling line of bedroom furniture. He had worked very hard with one of his company's better suppliers to develop the stain. The supplier had never produced anything like it, certainly not in the small quantities and wide array of colors Luis had asked for. He was very proud of the project, which had turned out well for the supplier, for Luis's company, and for Luis himself. "They called to tell me it was working great. I was pretty sure everything was on track for the launch when I left on Friday, but they called just to tell me the first parts are out of the spray booths, and everything looks great!"

"Wait a minute. You're this excited about some new kind of paint?" Fred asked.

"It isn't just new paint," Luis replied, with some exasperation. "It's a stain that seals wood as well as anything we can get, but compared to the oil-based stuff, it's easier to use, easier to clean up, and it comes in more colors, too. The best part, though, was how we worked with the supplier to develop it. No quality problems at all."

"Luis, you've talked about problems with paint before. They always seem to work out in the end. Why is this stain any different?" Cheryl asked.

Fred interrupted, saying, "Come on, you get word to your suppliers, tell them what you want; they each put a bid together, and the best price wins!" In Fred's mind, that's how it happens. In his mind, the supplier's marketing representatives find out what the customer wants; then they send the specifications to the engineers. The product engineers use the specs to design the product. When they're finished and they get the contract, they send the specs to the process engineers; they design the process. Then the process engineers come up with a set of operating procedures and give them to folks like Luis, who manufacture the product. After all that, marketing tries to deliver the new product to the customer on time. If the product isn't right, the customer sends it back to the factory and it all starts over. Eventually, everyone gets the specs straight and the customer is satisfied. You just work out the kinks and move on.

"That's how we used to do it," Luis replied. "Remember how I told you awhile back that the EPA had been on our backs about solvent emissions? Remember the hassle we had with that other supplier, you know, when we were switching to latex-based paints because they didn't need the solvents to clean them up? Well, I made sure we didn't make the same mistake twice now that we're looking for stains!"

A year or so earlier, the EPA had really put the pressure on Luis's company to cut its emissions. Managers had decided that one way to comply would be to reduce the need for the solvents that were used to clean up oil-based paints during color changes in the spray booth. They had turned to their suppliers for a latex-based paint that could be cleaned up with soap and water. They also wanted to schedule smaller and more frequent deliveries to keep paint inventory lower. A purchasing manager, the owner's nephew, had gone about obtaining a source for the paint much the way Fred had suggested it is done. A representative from the company that had been supplying the oil-based paint came in, listened to what he wanted, and told him she would be back in a couple of months with something Luis's company could use.

After almost eight months, the representative came back complaining about the formula for the paint and the delivery schedule the nephew had asked for. As it turned out, the representative could have been back much sooner if people at her company could have used their own expertise to come up with the right formula. Instead, bound by what they thought engineers and managers at Luis's company had wanted, they struggled for months to come up with an acceptable solution. Not only did the supplier's delay throw off the introduction of the new contemporary furniture collection; the colors didn't match the metal and plastic parts that held the furniture together. The whole process had to be done over again.

"I guess nobody was too happy with that the first time. I remember you talking about all the damage control," Cheryl admitted.

"I never did ask you what the problem was. What took them so long to get the formula right? Why was the delivery schedule a problem?" Tom asked, finishing a set of leg extensions.

"We told them up front what we wanted the paint to look like, and what we wanted it to do. But I guess a lot of what we wanted got lost in the translation. If we had talked directly to their engineers from the start, it would have worked out a lot better," Luis answered. "It was like a game of Telephone; the story changes each time it's retold. By the time the product design people formulated the stuff and the process people reengineered the production lines to make it, the consistency of the paint was way too heavy. The colors didn't match the samples. The new setup times killed them. Turns out they just didn't ask the right questions."

When the supplier tried to set up the production line, the change in formula and the heavier consistency complicated the setup and slowed production time whenever the color was changed. With a more expensive setup, the small quantities they were asking for would be unprofitable. The whole project ground to a halt while the marketing rep tried to negotiate a higher price to cover the higher cost. It turned out that the heavier consistency was caused by an additive that was no longer needed in the latex-based formula. Only after a lot of back and forth was the issue resolved. "The whole deal with longer setups became a non-issue" Luis laughed.

"Well, what you just described sounds typical for us," Fred offered, as he grabbed a drink of water and headed toward the treadmill. "What was so special about the way you dealt with the stain this time? What did you or your supplier do differently?"

"I've heard a lot about teams and concurrent engineering in my evening classes. After the paint problem, I convinced my boss to try a different approach with the stain. I wanted to get everybody talking up front," Luis replied. "One thing I did was to get together a team to meet with the supplier's people. We included representatives from purchasing, engineering, operations, even marketing. We met with a similar group from the supplier to talk the whole thing through. The combined groups talked about what we need from them and what the supplier needs from us, realizing that using a team approach could help when it came to putting a new product together."

"Did you listen to each other? Did it work?" asked Cheryl. "I mean, I guess you must have, if this morning's news was so good."

"Yeah, we did. With everybody working off the same page, they got us a prototype sample much faster than before. As a matter of fact, one of their production guys called us after one of their team meetings to tell us that their engineers were trying to work out the consistency issue with our people, so we could avoid the problems we had with the paint. Turned out that, like the paint, we really don't need the additive. They got rid of it, and the stain was fine. That helped their changeover problem, too. It would take some time, but in the meantime it was easy for us to change the quantities we bought, to give them a chance to adjust. We made everybody look like rocket scientists!" he said happily. "It sure would have saved a lot of headaches and delays if we had used this process when we were getting the paint deal together! Now we know better. We even got some surprise benefits: Taking the additive out made it easier to get the color and tone of the samples right and reduced the cost. There were lots of positive spinoffs like that."

"Well, I guess everything needs to happen faster these days. What happened to 'Slow and steady wins the race'?" asked Fred.

"I think somebody saw you on the treadmill and rewrote the story!" chided Luis.

> objectives

Take a moment to familiarize yourself with the key objectives of this chapter.

> gearing up

Before you begin reading this chapter, try a short warm-up activity.

> Introduction

> active exercise

Take a moment to apply what you've learned.

As you begin this chapter, take a moment to look around you. What products do you see? Over the past several days, what services have you used? Have you bought anything to eat or drink, to wear or listen to? List at least 10 products and services you have used, and answer the following questions: What is unusual or unique about each item on your list? What are the standard features of each? If you purchased the items, why did you buy them rather than competing products or services? If you begin to evaluate products and services in this way, before long you will be asking questions like, Why did they make or plan it that way? What could they have been thinking when they designed that? or, Hey—that's pretty cool; I wonder how they thought of that?"

Asking questions about products and services is not just something you should do when you are reading an OM book. While you may not be aware of it, as a consumer you are always evaluating the design of the products and services you buy. For example, long before your meal at a restaurant is finished, you form a number of opinions regarding the food and service you receive. Hours or even days after you finish your meal, your evaluation could change based on new information you gain from conversations with friends or from media reports.

Look back at your list of goods and services. There's a good chance that it includes some goods or services you wouldn't have dreamed of 20 years ago. Does your list include a videotape recorder, a CD player, a personal computer or anything related to it, a cellular phone, a cash machine, a quick oil change, an electronic card catalog search, an overnight mail service, a facsimile machine, a diet soft drink sweetened with NutraSweet, or a soft drink in a can with no throwaway tab? These items, which we tend to take for granted today, weren't available just 20 years ago. In some cases, they weren't even anticipated!

Can you think of some goods and services that you are only beginning to anticipate, ones that might make a list of everyday items in the next 10 to 15 years? Will new cars routinely include Global Positioning Systems and interactive road maps? Will your telephone number be assigned to you and travel with you wherever you go, instead of being assigned to a specific location, as it is now? Will you rent movies over the Internet instead of at a video store? Will you still buy CDs, or will you buy network access to their content from an on-line library? Will you buy electricity the way that you currently buy long-distance telephone service? Will cars, appliances, and medical devices like pacemakers have built-in maintenance monitors that are in constant contact with the producer, to signal the need for a repair before a breakdown occurs? Will college professors give quizzes on a web page instead of in class? No doubt 10 years from now, you will be taking for granted countless goods and services that you can't even imagine today! These are the issues faced by designers of product-service bundles, and this chapter describes how they do their job.

Designing product-service bundles is greatly facilitated if companies can manage the white spaces between the functional areas of their business. Marketing research might identify an idea for a product or service, but before they get a chance to sell it to a customer, many other departments will have impacted the resulting product-service bundle. Research and development departments will have developed the product-service bundle and assessed its feasibility, process engineering departments will have created equipment and systems used to produce and deliver the package, purchasing and operations will have added the specified value, and finance will have created the needed budgets for capital acquisition and ongoing operations. In addition to all of these functional areas, customers and suppliers could have been involved in the development of the product-service bundle.

Development of a product-service bundle requires the completion of a defined set of tasks—identifying a financially viable market opportunity, physically designing the product-service bundle, designing required value-adding processes, developing systems for supply and operation of those processes, and establishing sales and service procedures.

Traditionally, the design of product-service bundles has been seen as the job of marketing experts and product designers. But because the design of products and services often dictates the way in which they are made and delivered, design is also critical to operations management and other functions. All of the functions involved in transforming an idea into a revenue-generating reality have done their part in the process independently and only when their turn came. Earlier work would be turned over from one department to the next until the design was complete.

The modern business environment presents many challenges to the traditional approach to designing product-service bundles. Global markets require designs that satisfy a large and diverse set of customer requirements. Global competition requires ever higher levels of quality, performance, and cost competitiveness. Technology and competitive strategies force business to respond quickly to changing customer requirements. Customers are more and more aware of their alternatives and are less likely to accept partial satisfaction of their requirements. Finally, more and more customers are requiring turnkey solutions to their needs that effectively match manufactured products and services. In today's business world, the traditional approach that allows business functions to make independent decisions regarding design of the product-service bundle will still get the job done—but it may be too late or too far off targeted customer expectations and thus result in less-than-desirable commercial success.

A team-based approach that concurrently includes the perspectives of all business functions is better suited to designing product-service bundles in the current business climate. This approach generally results in product-service bundle designs that are less expensive to make, are more in line with customer expectations, use more current technologies, and reach the market more quickly.

Many decision-making tools are used in the design process. This chapter discusses a number of these, including quality function deployment, computer-aided design, and various product-costing methods. In addition, the supplement to this chapter describes statistical tools that are useful for making decisions in the presence of uncertainty.

Not every technological breakthrough or idea for a product improvement is a technical or financial success. There are plenty of white elephant stories to go around—and a lot of companies keep the prototypes around to laugh about. These products or services may have sounded great on paper, but though they were technically elegant, they were hard to manufacture or deliver. Or, like the peanut butter and jelly that came in the same jar, the idea just never caught on. This should help you realize that product-service bundle design is an ongoing activity in many organizations. Even the failures are beneficial from the standpoint that most companies learn something about the design process, technology, and customer preferences with each new product-service bundle they design.

> active concept check

Now let's take a moment to test your knowledge of the concepts you have studied in this section.

Integrating Operations Management with Other Functions

Figure 4.1 presents a matrix that highlights the main linkages between the topics in this chapter and other functional areas in business. Historically, the functions most involved in designing products and services were marketing and engineering. Marketing was involved in identifying customer requirements and determining the extent to which various design proposals met those needs. Engineering was involved in actually developing the product-service bundle. The parts of this chapter that deal most directly with the traditional approach to designing product-service bundles will, therefore, be most closely linked to decisions made in those functional areas.

Chapter Topics \ Functional Areas of Business	Finance	Accounting	Human Resources	Marketing	Engineering	Management Information Systems
Integrating Operations Management with Other Functions				●	●	●
Tasks Involved in the Design of Product-Service Bundles				●	●	
The Traditional Approach to Design of Product-Service Bundles				●	●	
Challenges of the Traditional Approach				●	●	
The Modern Approach to Design of Product-Service Bundles	●	●	●	●	●	●
Tools That Are Useful in Designing Products and Services	●	●				●

FIGURE 4.1 Integrating Operations Management with Other Functions

Modern design processes generally draw upon cross-functional teams. In addition, they recognize that separating design from other operational decisions in a business can hinder efforts to satisfy customer requirements. Rather, product-service bundle designs play a significant role in the activities of each function. Indeed, every functional area, as well as outside parties such as customers and suppliers, is influenced by the design of the product-service bundle. It is important to consider all of these viewpoints in design decisions, and cross-functional teams are commonly used in the design process today. The section of this chapter that discusses the modern approach to design of product-service bundles is, therefore, closely related to the decisions made in every functional area.

The final section of this chapter describes a representative set of tools that are used in design processes. Among these are break-even analysis, cost accounting, and computer-aided design tools. Thus, Figure 4.1 indicates strong linkages between the content of this section and the functional areas of finance, accounting, and management information system (MIS).

Personnel from the various functional areas in a business do need to work together to evaluate design tradeoffs and create design synergies for the firm to satisfy customers and gain competitive advantage—but that's not a one-time event. Managing across the functions on an ongoing basis provides the needed understanding and trust to make design decisions on new product-service bundles. Consequently, businesses frequently redesign their products and services. Just as originally designing a product-service bundle requires cooperation across functions, so does the redesign effort.

As Figure 4.2 indicates, product life-cycles are getting shorter and shorter. While this does allow companies to gain time-based competitive advantages from their modern design processes, it also requires the various business functions to work together more effectively. Each time a new or redesigned product is introduced, marketing needs to both promote the new and sell the remainder of the old. OM has to begin producing the new to satisfy demand, while maintaining an adequate but not excessive supply of the old item. This transition requires excellent understanding of specific market requirements to be transferred from marketing professionals to OM decisions. Otherwise it is possible that a large quantity of obsolescent inventory will be produced.

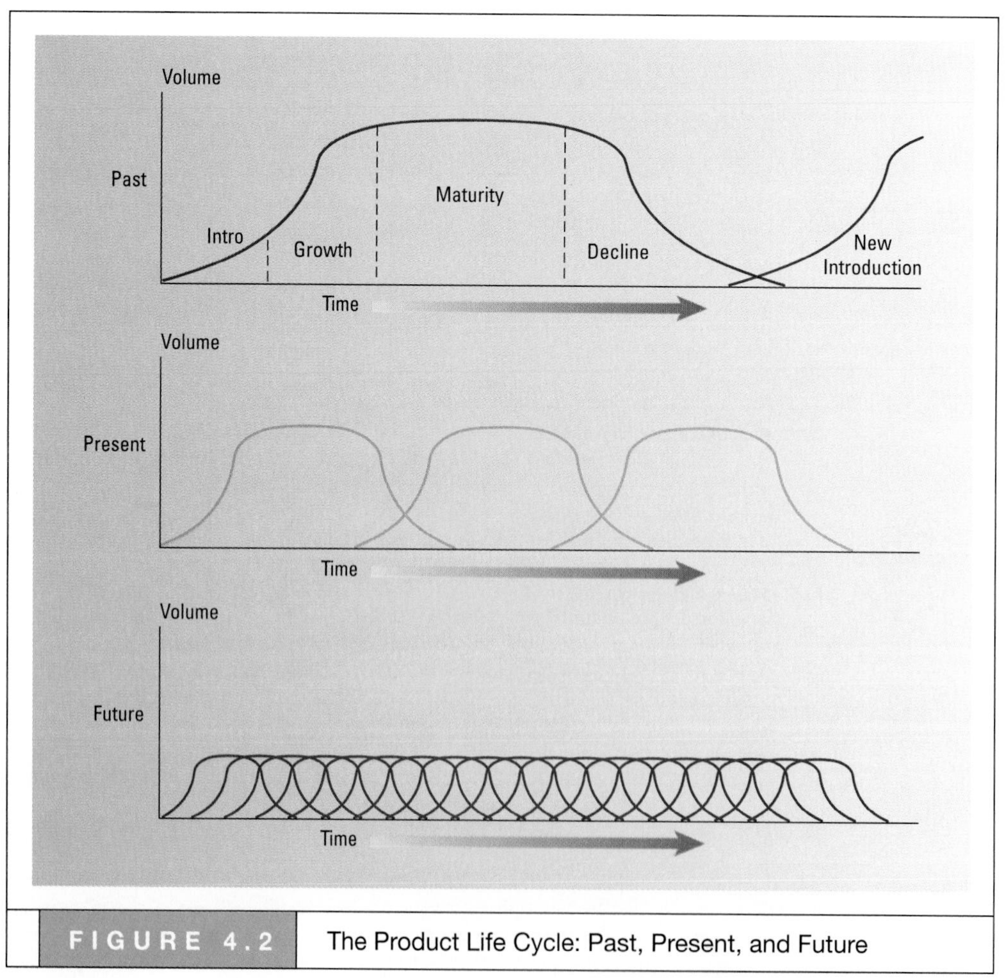

FIGURE 4.2 The Product Life Cycle: Past, Present, and Future

> video exercise

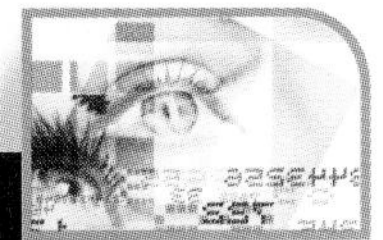

Take a moment to apply what you've learned.

> active concept check

Now let's take a moment to test your knowledge of the concepts you have studied in this section.

> Designing a Product-Service Bundle at Miami's Rec Center

More and more outdoor enthusiasts are taking to the trails on their mountain bikes every year. While by no means limited to any age group, mountain biking is one of the fastest-growing outdoor activities for rec center patrons in their 20s and 30s. With appropriate equipment, the thrill of challenging gravity, the terrain, and your own endurance (not to mention pain threshold!) can be a safe, healthy, and ecologically benign activity. However, mountain biking along Miami's hiking trails, primarily intended for those on foot, has also been increasing just as fast. Problems with safety, erosion, and trail maintenance have been an increasing source of contention. As hiking trails may be the only currently available venue for bike enthusiasts, the obvious solution is the development of trails designed primarily for mountain biking.

University communities are quite often a market where demands for mountain bikes and appropriate off-road trails are concentrated. The Outdoor Pursuits Center (OPC) at Miami University's Student Recreation Center is no exception. Some possibilities do currently exist but are not viewed as sufficient to meet demand. A state park approximately 40 miles away has successfully developed a rigorous series of trails yet most are very "technical" (meaning they are designed for the most experienced mountain biker). A second state park, only 15 minutes away, also developed trails to keep bikers off of their hiking trails. At this location, however, the trail length was very limited and insufficient to fully satisfy demand. While bikes can be rented at either location, most users ride their own.

Seeing the need to prevent degradation of hiking trails and conflict between mountain bikers and other trail users, the OPC approached Miami University about developing a less-technical course somewhere on campus. A plan was developed in conjunction with a local bike shop that has been a long-time supplier to the university community of a variety of upscale bikes and biking accessories. Through the advice and cooperation of the OPC and the local bike shop, the university chose some undeveloped woodlands adjacent to Miami's Peffer Park, a part of the greenbelt on the edge of campus.

The insight of bike shop employees was important to the development of the Peffer Park trails. Because they have daily interaction with the local biking crowd, they were able to provide perspectives on the skill levels of the typical rider, local conditions of concern to bikers (how muddy will trails get and what kind of erosion prevention is appropriate, what kinds of problems do bikers face with poison ivy or thorns and briers, what level of topography do bikers need and want, etc.), and the extent to which technical challenges were needed to attract riders to the trail. The OPC used this insight to prepare a proposal that became a business plan for the trail. The proposal included the various product-service bundles they might offer (i.e., the different types of trails, sponsored events to be held at the site, maintenance concerns, safety concerns), the estimated demand for those trails, and the equipment needs of the OPC. In the end, the university agreed with the proposal and a trail was developed. This made it easier for the university to keep bikers off of designated hiking trails, reducing the maintenance costs on these trails as well as the risk of conflict between trail users. At the same time, mountain bikers were provided a convenient venue for the pursuit of their thrills, without interference from other types of trail users.

What can we learn from the SRC's experience in developing the trails at Peffer Park? First, the development process used in this situation required cross-functional thinking to meet the needs of campus mountain bikers. Expertise for the development of the trails came from outdoor enthusiasts, city business people, and campus administrators. Second, it is difficult to separate the product-service bundle in this situation from the value-adding system. By making the trail available in a setting that can be easily accessed by rec center patrons and campus security (and ensuring that it is well suited to the bikes and maintenance readily available in town), the rec center is creating elements of both the product-service bundle and the value-adding system. As it is with the mountain bike trail, it is often difficult for service operations to separate the product-service bundle from the value-adding system. Third, the design process involved both customers and suppliers. The customers are the bikers and other park users whose input was sought in the trail design process. Suppliers included the university administrators responsible for upkeep of the park and greenbelt, university security personnel, city security personnel, and the owners of the bike shop. Finally, when the design process included all of these stakeholders, a win-win design resulted. Rec center customers got a new facility where they could pursue their outdoor sport interests. The rec center got a facility they could use to promote outdoor sports. The bike center got a facility to which they could direct their customers, which could help them to build their business. Finally, the university enhanced the range of educational and social opportunities that could be pursued by its students.

video example <

Take a closer look at the concepts and issues you've been reading about.

> Tasks in the Design of Product-Service Bundles

The extent to which the design of product-service bundles is an everyday part of a firm's activity depends to some degree on the strategic decisions discussed in Chapter 2. The flexibility needed to continually introduce and maintain a wide variety of product-service bundles may be a major part of the strategy for a business like Luis's furniture factory or Cheryl's hospital. Or the business strategy might be to maintain a narrower range of products and services in a cost-effective fashion, as in Fred's electronics business and Tom's airline. Figure 4.3 relates the rate of new product introduction to a firm's process type, level of dedication of its process technology, and order winners and qualifiers.

For firms on the right side of the scale in Figure 4.3 (batch processes and job shops), new product introduction is a more common aspect of daily operations. General-purpose technology is used to produce a wide and changing array of low-volume products and services in a job or batch process. For example, every day the Parker-Hannifin Corporation plant in Brookville, Ohio, makes customized hydraulic tube fittings to match unique blueprints representing new product designs. Similarly, most fine restaurants introduce new entrees and customize existing ones to customers' tastes on an ongoing basis. On the right side of the figure of the scale, the firm's design capability, the ease with which its output mix can be changed to match customer demand (in other words, the firm's flexibility), and the speed with which the firm can get new and customized products to the marketplace are key order winners. Cost, conformance, and delivery reliability need only meet levels necessary to qualify for the business. In such situations, the introduction of new products is an ongoing part of the business and is generally integrated into most, if not all, systems, technologies, and other resources the firm employs.

Unlike the fine restaurants just mentioned, where new products are common, at fast-food restaurants like McDonald's, the introduction of a new sandwich is usually announced with fanfare. Similarly, most car manufacturers must shut down for two weeks each summer just to retool for the relatively minor changes in product line from one model year to the next. Most auto companies consider they are doing a great job if they can introduce a totally new product in less than three years, from drawing board to showroom floor. In fact, many experts attribute much of Chrysler's resurgence during the 1990s to the ability to introduce a new product line about once a year, after about 30 months incubation time. These firms, shown on the left side of Figure 4.3 (continuous and repetitive processes), use dedicated technology in a line or continuous process to mass-produce large quantities of standardized products and services. They win orders with low cost, conformance quality, and reliable delivery schedules. Criteria such as flexibility, delivery speed, and design capability are usually defined by the market, and must be met in order for the firms to qualify to be considered for the business. In these situations, the nature of the dedicated resources and technologies that are usually employed makes the introduction of a totally new product or service design a major undertaking.

Figure 4.3 illustrates clearly that some firms engage heavily in product design and redesign to satisfy small market segments, while others redesign their offerings less frequently to satisfy large demand volumes. That does not mean that all companies on the right side of Figure 4.3 are small or that all companies on the left side are large. Microsoft Corporation, quite a large business, is con-

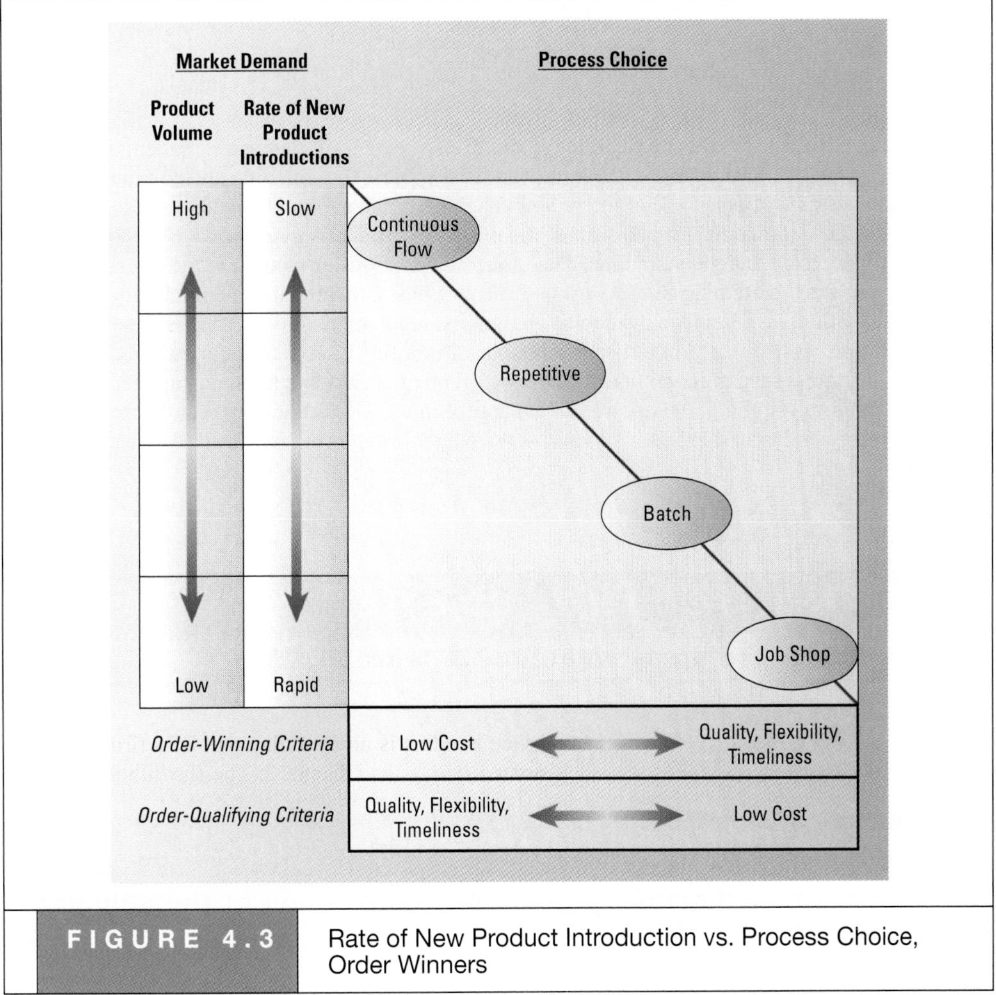

FIGURE 4.3 Rate of New Product Introduction vs. Process Choice, Order Winners

stantly adding to the mix of software and related product-service bundles offered, while many small pizza places offer only a single product, pizza, in a limited number of sizes.

Depending on the firm's operational strategy, the magnitude of the tasks that must be accomplished in designing a new product-service bundle may vary, but in most cases a common set of tasks must precede production. Typical tasks in designing product-service bundles and getting them to market may include:

- Doing market research to identify an opportunity.
- Performing basic scientific research needed to develop the breakthroughs an opportunity depends on.
- Choosing or developing a technology required to translate scientific breakthroughs into commercial concepts.
- Developing specific applications, systems, and products and services.
- Testing the performance of new applications, systems, and products and services.
- Testing customer response to new applications and products and services.
- Creating a value-adding system that is capable of delivering the new applications, systems, and products and services. This task includes the design and development of manufacturing processes to make specific product elements of the bundle; the development of service delivery systems to provide the service elements of the bundle; the development of systems to deliver maintenance and support services; the development of systems to deliver allied services and products (for example, toner for copiers); the development of supplier capabilities; and the development of an appropriate distribution system.
- Ensuring the legal and regulatory compliance of new applications, systems, and products and services.

- Obtaining patents, trademarks, and copyrights, as appropriate.
- Developing a marketing plan and marketing the new applications, systems, and products and services. Such a plan must address the traditional marketing considerations of place, price, and promotion, as well as customer education.

Many of these tasks are sequentially related. Many also seem to fit within the domain of a specific function. For example, the marketing department does the marketing research and planning, the legal department takes care of patents, and the product engineering department oversees product development. As a result, in functional organizations, the design of product-service bundles has traditionally been accomplished one function at a time. The sequential relationship of the tasks, however, does not mean that the issues pertaining to the various tasks are best considered sequentially. For instance, firms should be thinking about the availability of quality suppliers early in the development of a specific application, system, or product-service bundle. As a result, cross-functional product design teams, which address several functional issues concurrently (as Luis and his stain supplier's staff did) are becoming more common. The organizational approach used does not significantly change the set of core tasks required to design a new product-service bundle and bring it to market, however.

active exercise

Take a moment to apply what you've learned.

active concept check

Now let's take a moment to test your knowledge of the concepts you have studied in this section.

The Traditional Approach to the Design of Product-Service Bundles

The traditional approach to the design of products and services, which is a natural byproduct of the functional silos that are present in most companies, might be described as an *over-the-wall* approach (see Figure 4.4). The design process begins when a market opportunity is identified. Once senior management has decided to pursue the opportunity, preliminary conceptual development is performed, perhaps by a research and development department. The result of this work is a design concept that provides a general description of the product-service bundle and the technologies required to produce it. The design concept is then passed on to design engineering, the department that is responsible for the actual design of the product. As the expression *over-the-wall* suggests, until the design concept has been approved, the design department has no access to or influence over it. Similarly, once the project has been tossed over the wall, the research and development department does not expect to have anything more to do with it.

Once completed, the physical design of the product or service is delegated to a design engineering team, along with a deadline for completion of the design specifications. Within this department, the design engineering task might be divided between creative staff (designers) and design testing staff (product engineers). Such an arrangement allows the creative staff to exercise their skill in the development of product aesthetics without hindrance from the product engineers, who are responsible for developing the technical specifications and testing the product or service's performance. Since the design department usually has multiple projects under development, those projects whose deadlines are approaching tend to receive the most attention. In general, design departments are biased toward creativity and the use of new, cutting-edge technologies.

When the design has been finalized at last, the design engineering department passes responsibility for the new product or service on to the process engineering department. Again, the expression *over the wall* signifies that until the design department is finished and the design specifications have been passed on, the process engineering department has no access to the design and no influence over

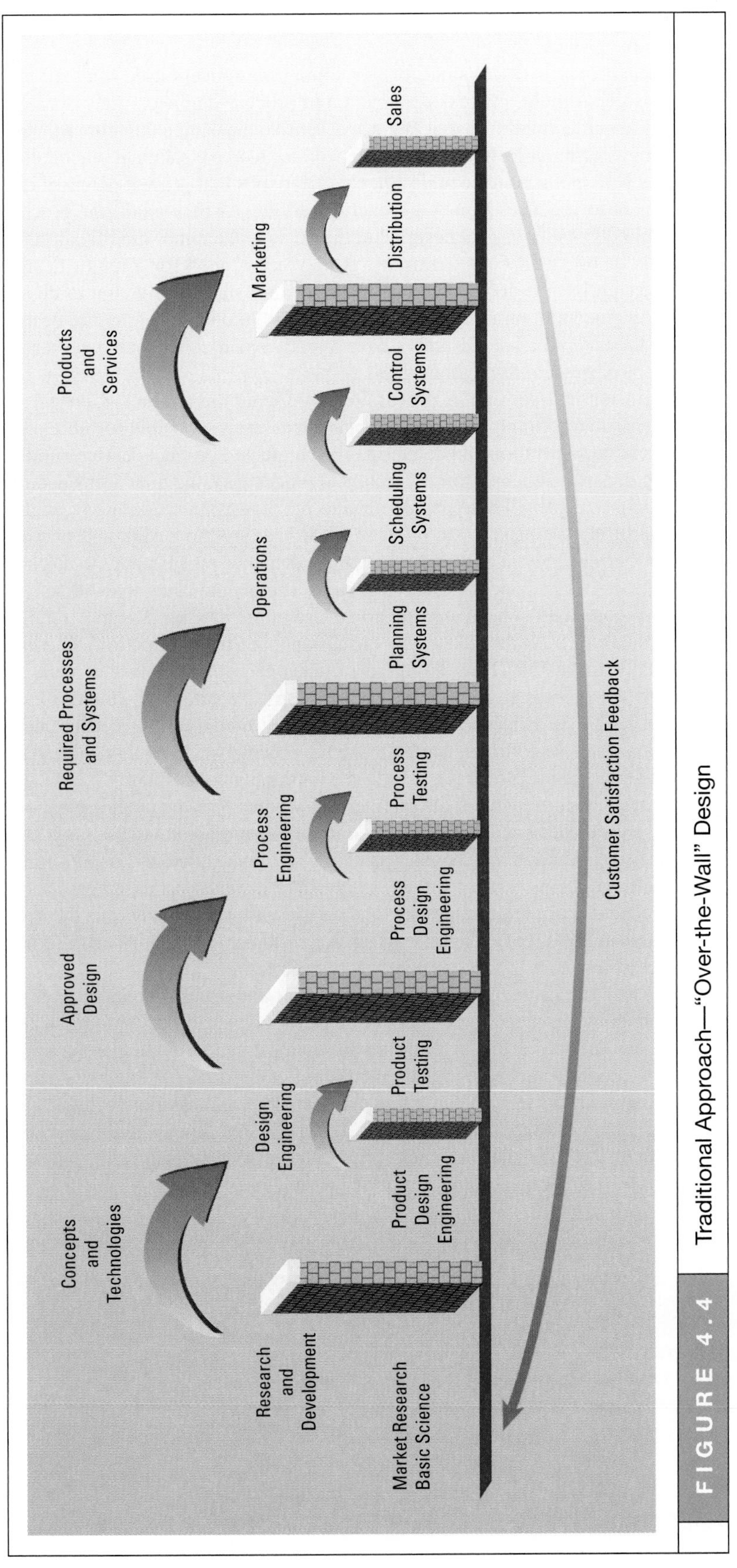

FIGURE 4.4 Traditional Approach—"Over-the-Wall" Design

it. Likewise, once the project has been tossed over the wall, the design department does not expect to have anything more to do with the project.

The process engineering department is responsible for developing the process used to create the product or service. Within this department, process designers and process engineers may actually build and install the equipment specified by the design engineers. Unlike the design department, with its creative bias, the process engineering department has a decided bias toward technical practicality. Chances are, process engineers will spot a number of design characteristics that present practical difficulties in making the equipment to produce the new product or service. As they work, the process engineers will attempt to accommodate the original design, but they may make minor modifications to the design based on economic or practical considerations. If they see a need for a major design change, they might send the design back to its originators. There is a strong incentive not to do so, however, because the process engineers have a deadline, too—and who knows how long the design department will take to make the changes. The designers have already spent considerable resources testing the design and will not be eager to rethink their ideas.

Ultimately, the process engineers will deliver the process for producing the product or service to the operations management department. Employees in this department are responsible for obtaining raw materials, putting the process into operation and delivering the completed product-service bundle. Unlike the process engineering department's bias toward technical practicality, the operations department has a bias toward working practicality. These people need to put together a working system for planning, scheduling, and controlling the production process, as defined by the design and process engineering departments. New hurdles may need to be crossed. A particular process may look good on paper but might not be workable from an operational perspective. The maintenance schedule might be unrealistic, or unforeseen worker safety concerns might arise. Use of the new process may require significant training. Finally, meeting both the design specifications and the production schedule simultaneously may be practically impossible. Thus, employees in the operations department could be tempted to return the process to the process engineers for modifications. Unfortunately, there is usually so much invested in a project by the time it reaches operations that modifications become economically infeasible. Thus, operations has to find a way to make the process work. At this point, they may simply throw the product-service bundle over the wall to the marketing department.

The marketing department must distribute and sell the services and products created by the operations department. Depending on the various decisions that have been made since marketing first suggested design changes or proposed the new product-service bundle (including the product-service bundle's function, the accompanying services, and its appearance, reliability, availability, and cost), workers in this department may find that the product-service bundle does not (and perhaps never did) really meet the need it was intended to satisfy. Unfortunately, it takes a long time to receive customer feedback—and the delay can put a firm at a significant disadvantage in today's competitive marketplace.

Today most managers recognize the value of a long-term focus, of building market share through customer satisfaction. They recognize the need to be more effective in converting new products and services to commercial successes. In fact, a number of trends have converged to challenge the traditional over-the-wall approach to production. These include increasing globalization of business, rapid technological change, shortening product life cycles, e-commerce and other information technologies that facilitate the integration of customer concerns in each aspect of the design process, growth in customer sophistication and awareness, and the need to bundle service and manufacturing value together.

active concept check <

Now let's take a moment to test your knowledge of the concepts you have studied in this section.

> The Modern Approach to the Design of Product-Service Bundles

As we have seen, the design of product-service bundles has traditionally included a set of sequentially related tasks, each represented by a different function. In the past, the sequential relationship of the tasks led to an over-the-wall approach to design, with each function working more or less in isolation from the others. Figure 4.5(a) profiles this traditional approach to the design of product-service bundles.

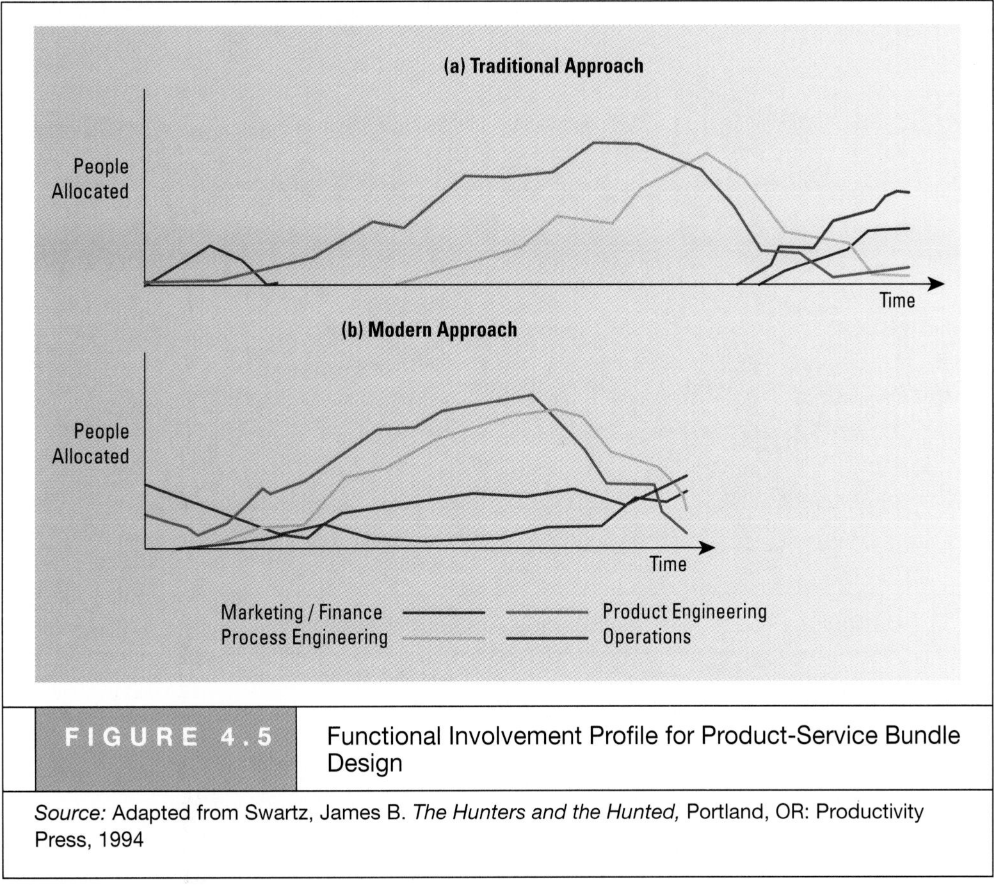

FIGURE 4.5 Functional Involvement Profile for Product-Service Bundle Design

Source: Adapted from Swartz, James B. *The Hunters and the Hunted,* Portland, OR: Productivity Press, 1994

As the figure shows, an over-the-wall approach simply spans the gaps between functions; it doesn't *manage* them. Modern approaches to designing the product-service bundle place much greater emphasis on effective management of all functions throughout the design process. Figure 4.5(b) profiles the modern approach to designing the product-service bundle. In modern design projects, a cross-functional design team typically manages the entire design process, in which all functions participate concurrently. Thus the process is frequently referred to as the concurrent team approach. The next section describes the modern approach to design in greater detail.

TEAM STRUCTURE INSTEAD OF FUNCTIONAL STRUCTURE

Figure 4.6 contrasts the traditional over-the-wall approach to designing product-service bundles with the modern concurrent team approach. In Figure 4.6a, which shows the traditional approach, each function "spins off" its contribution to the product-service bundle's design. Once its work, which is seen as functional output, has been completed, the function's job is finished. The customer is seen only as the initiator of the project and a potential user of the final product or service. At each stage of the design process, the emphasis is on only one functional stakeholder's priorities.

In Figure 4.6b, which shows the modern approach, each function "spins in" its contribution to the cross-functional design team that has been established for the duration of the project. The customer is seen as a part of the design team throughout the design process. Each function is represented on the design team, so that its concerns can be reflected in those decisions that are heavily influenced by the other functions. Together, the functional "spin ins" and the customer-driven market opportunity move the design process forward. Though functional excellence remains an important goal, it is subordinated to customer satisfaction, the dominant concern of the entire team and the common goal that unifies its efforts. Because of the increased emphasis on consideration of all stakeholder concerns, and on the development of consensus solutions that will deliver customer satisfaction, no surprises should arise in the process of making and selling the new product-service bundle.

Despite its seeming simplicity and apparent advantages, the concurrent team approach is not always easy to implement. Typically, teams go through a life cycle of their own. In the beginning there is usually significant conflict. Goals are not always clear. Individuals bring their own functional

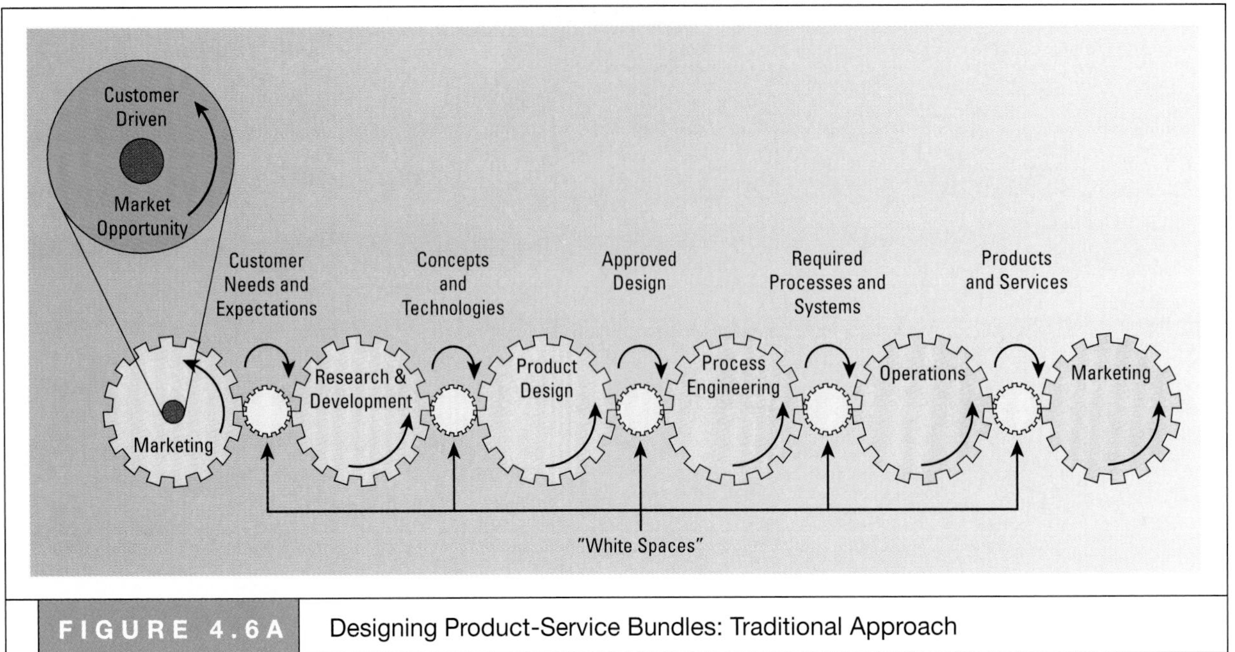

FIGURE 4.6A Designing Product-Service Bundles: Traditional Approach

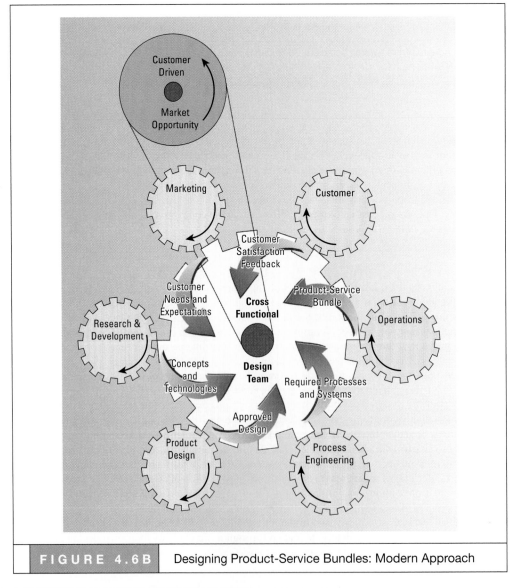

FIGURE 4.6B Designing Product-Service Bundles: Modern Approach

perspectives to the team and tend to be intolerant of the perspectives of others. Trust may be lacking. Particularly in organizations with strong functional barriers, team members may fear that their allegiance to the team will hurt them in their own departments.

Putting such fears to rest can be difficult. As the team works through initial conflicts, the project may seem to flounder. Unless team members work through these initial conflicts, however, they may never develop a common perspective on the project, and a joint understanding of how it should proceed. Even when a team has effectively worked through its initial differences, honest differences based on functional biases may keep the group from coming to a clear consensus on key project decisions. At such times strong team leadership, that can move the project forward without allowing mutual trust among team members to break down, is vital.

One aspect of successful design teams is the ability of members to make significant contributions to decision making at each stage of the design process. In other words, when the design team is working effectively, an operations manager or supplier can make relevant suggestions very early in the design process. This requires an ability to interpret the meaning of early design choices on their functional area later in the design process and effectively communicate this to others. When teams have this kind of capability, they are able to concurrently consider multiple perspectives. The result is usually faster completion of superior designs.

CONCURRENT ENGINEERING INSTEAD OF SEQUENTIAL/HIERARCHICAL ENGINEERING

Concurrent engineering is an approach to product-service design in which the concerns of more than one function are considered simultaneously. Examples include: design for manufacturability; design for procurement; design for environment; and design for disassembly.

Design for manufacturability (DFM) is a product development approach that explicitly considers the effectiveness with which an item can be made during the initial development of the product-service design. This approach is based on the belief that the cost of developing and running the value-adding system is as important as the functionality and aesthetics of the product-service bundle. **Taguchi methods**—statistical studies that can be used to ensure that product design specifications are wide (or narrow) enough to accommodate likely levels of process variability—are a key component of DFM. Obviously, a baker would want to be sure that bread will be sliced thinly enough to fit easily into the customer's toaster; a quick lube shop would want to make sure that its garage door is wide and high enough to accommodate even the biggest vehicles. In the same way, when Motorola designs the various parts of their pagers, it needs to be certain that the parts can be easily assembled. Thus, manufacturability is considered concurrently with more traditional design criteria and becomes a key criterion in evaluating the designers' work.

Another strategy used in concurrent engineering is **design for procurement,** which is the explicit consideration of component parts supply during the initial development of a product-service design. What is the supply base for the required component parts? What is the capacity of that supply base? At what cost can parts be made and at what levels of conformance quality? Design for procurement extends the DFM concept to the early stages in the creation of value, before in-house production begins.

Design for environment is a product development approach that broadens the concept of design for manufacturability even further to include the environmental impact of a design, from the extraction of raw materials to their disposal. This strategy is based on the concept of **sustainability,** which encourages companies to meet the needs of today's consumer without compromising the ability of future generations to meet their needs. **Life-cycle analysis** is a tool used by designers in an attempt to determine the environmental impact of a product from cradle to grave. In designing a new refrigerator, for example, manufacturers should be concerned with the availability of appropriate metals from new and recycled sources; the availability and effectiveness of chlorofluorocarbon-free insulating materials; the availability and effectiveness of CFC-free cooling agents; the environmental impact of the processes that are used to manufacture, distribute, and service the refrigerator; the energy costs and other environmental impacts associated with the consumers' use of the refrigerator; the recyclability of the refrigerator and its components; and the ultimate disposal of those materials.

Though the concepts of life-cycle analysis and sustainability are useful and appealing, universally accepted methodologies for life-cycle analysis do not exist. Furthermore, managerial incentives seldom take into account environmental risks; nor has society developed many economic incentives to encourage the practice of sustainability. From a practical perspective, designing for the environment is still a major challenge.

Another strategy, *design for disassembly,* has become increasingly important in the context of the extensive environmental regulations with which businesses must now comply. More and more, manufacturers are beginning to understand and accept the fact that they are responsible for the items they make, from start to finish. In Germany, a law has been passed that requires manufacturers to recover all the nonconsumable materials used in their products. Soft drink and beer makers have had little difficulty in meeting the requirement, but automobile manufacturers have found it to be a problem. As a result of the legislation, BMW has designed the first completely recyclable car. To give another example, in the United States, many manufacturers cannot shut down or sell their obsolescent manufacturing plants because of the site remediation costs and environmental liabilities associated with their disassembly. (Environmentally speaking, some things are best left alone.) Using a design-for-disassembly philosophy today can help to prevent such environmental liabilities in the future.

active exercise

Take a moment to apply what you've learned.

GROUP TECHNOLOGY, MODULAR DESIGN, PRODUCT SIMPLIFICATION, AND E-COMMERCE

Like design for disassembly, group technology, modular design, and product simplification have all been used primarily in a manufacturing context. Each can be used in a team approach to concurrent engineering to speed the design process and create product-service bundles that involve simpler value-adding activities and are more easily managed.

Group technology is an engineering and manufacturing strategy based on the development and exploitation of commonalities among parts, equipment, or processes. For instance, a company that makes metal parts might group its products according to shape and the type of metal or alloy they are made of. Doing so allows a designer who is choosing shapes and materials to see whether an off-the-shelf part might work just as well as a newly designed part. The designer can also determine what types of shapes are compatible with what types of materials. By taking advantage of group technology, a design team can enhance the manufacturability of a design, speed up the design cycle, improve the company's profit margins, and save the customer money.

Modular design is an approach that allows designers to consider an item's components or subsystems independently. Because these independent modules can be installed and replaced individually, the concept is beneficial when requirements vary from one customer to the next and when customer needs may change over time. In addition, it is useful in complex assemblies, because technological improvements to subsystems usually do not develop at the same rate. By using a modular design strategy, designers can update selected subsystems and components with newer modules. Thus, the firm can extend the usefulness of key technologies, while giving customers the benefit of the most recent technological developments. For example, Ford was able to use a transmission developed in the early 1990s in trucks and vans designed in the 1980s, because the transmission was designed as a replaceable module. Modular design doesn't just make sense for manufacturers—it's useful in many service settings as well. Software development services, for example, rely particularly heavily on modular design. By putting together the right set of modules, or subroutines, an off-the-shelf information system can be tailored to fit many different unique customer applications. (See this chapter's boxed insert which provides an example of this concept designed jointly by Federal Express and the software developer SAP.)

Product simplification is a design (or redesign) strategy that improves the manufacturability, serviceability, or reliability of a product or service by reducing the complexity of its design. Often a product or part may be needlessly complex because of a designer or product engineer's bias toward technological sophistication or perhaps because of incremental design changes that have been made over a period of years. By reducing the number of parts or materials used, or changing the way in which parts are assembled, designers can realize significant benefits. For instance, in a product simplification effort made during the design of the 1992 Seville, Cadillac cut the number of parts used by 20%. This resulted in cost savings, quality improvement, ergonomic gains, and shorter cycle times.

E-commerce can now play a big role in the design process. For example, several firms in the auto industry use the engineering services of MSX. MSX has offices in 23 countries and chooses to locate very close to its customers' facilities, so the auto companies can be assured of a consistent and global solution to their engineering requirements. At the same time, since MSX uses computer-aided engineering tools, the auto companies can easily outsource design tasks that previously would have been kept in-house. Ford Motor Company, for example, uses MSX as a supplier of engineering drawings, and MSX keeps track of all of Ford's part designs. When Ford engineers want a part drawing, they get it from MSX and not internally. In a similar way, several auto companies use MSX to manufacture their design prototypes so that their existing assembly capacity can be devoted to the production of current models. MSX can easily undertake these jobs because they are equipped to receive the designs electronically.

> **active example**

Take a closer look at the concepts and issues you've been reading about.

We have just discussed a long list of strategies that can contribute to the work of design teams using the concurrent team approach. These include design for manufacture, design for procurement, design for the environment, group technology, product simplification, design for disassembly, and more. What is the bottom line of all of these approaches? The customer. A concurrent design team will be successful only if it spins off a product-service bundle that delights the customer, both now and in the future.

> **active concept check**

Now let's take a moment to test your knowledge of the concepts you have studied in this section.

Tools That are Useful in Designing Products and Services

There are many ways companies can funnel customer-driven needs and expectations into the design of their products and services. These tools are used to understand customer needs and expectations, to evaluate design tradeoffs, to enhance communication between members of the design team, to better communicate the rationale behind design decisions to outside parties, and to determine the financial feasibility of design alternatives. The following tools are a representative subset of the many tools that could be useful in the process of designing product-service bundles.

THE KANO MODEL

Figure 4.7 shows the Kano model, a diagram of the relationship between the extent to which a customer's needs (or requirements) are met by a hypothetical product characteristic and the level of satisfaction the customer derives from that characteristic. In this model, there are three types of product characteristics: must-do characteristics, expected characteristics, and excitement characteristics.

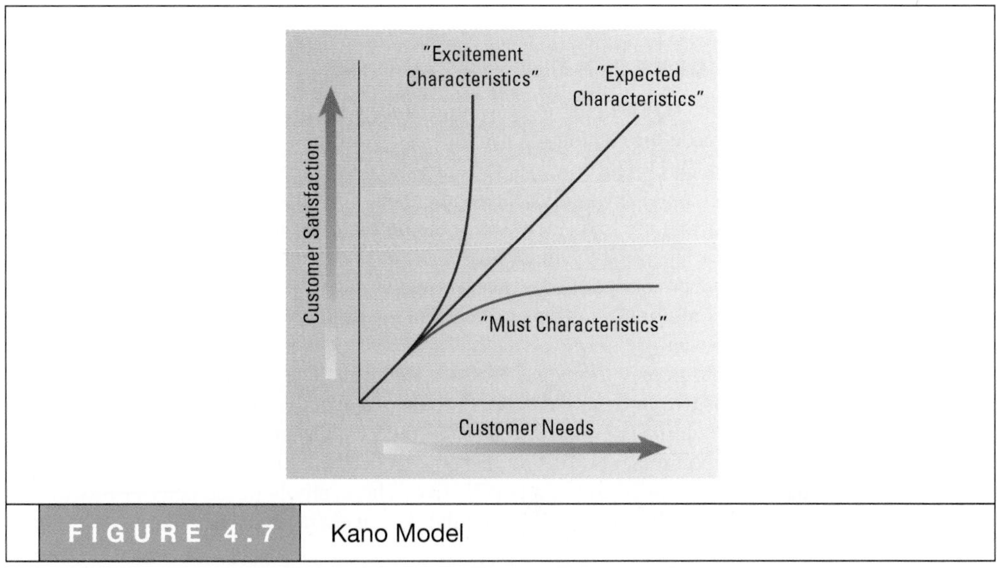

FIGURE 4.7 Kano Model

Must-do characteristics are those that meet a customer requirement but whose enhancement beyond a certain saturation point adds little value. Once the customer's need has been met, customer satisfaction is not enhanced by these product characteristics. For example, the typical consumer would not value reductions in the emission levels of a new automobile that already satisfies all federal and state regulations. Similarly, improving the sound quality in the speaker at the Wendy's drive-up window, or increasing the insulation on a household extension cord will satisfy customers only up to a given threshold; beyond that point it will not enhance customer satisfaction.

On the other hand, enhancing an *expected* characteristic will always increase customer satisfaction. Providing more of an expected feature always meets more of the customer's needs. Other things being equal, a car tire that lasts longer, a fishing line that holds more weight, and a hamburger patty that fills a larger bun all meet more of a customer's needs. With such product characteristics, one generally gets what one pays for.

Can you remember a time when you were blown away by your first experience with a product? Customers may not always be able to articulate the characteristics of a product which, if available, would really turn them on. These hard-to-express characteristics, called *excitement characteristics* in the Kano model, add more than the usual amount of satisfaction to the customer's experience. As more of these features are added to the product bundle, they provide increasingly higher returns on the customer satisfaction scale.

Asked to identify the excitement features in a potential product or service, customers often can say only, "I'll know it when I see it." If designers are successful in identifying those characteristics that excite the customer, however, a large amount of customer satisfaction can often be generated through modest changes in the product-service bundle. Examples of recent successes include a second set of car stereo controls (on the steering wheel); a remote control that beeps when the owner claps, making it easy to find in a typical dorm room; dorm-room connections to the campus PC network; a Michael Jordan autograph on a basketball; and a 10-minute oil and lube service that includes a vacuuming of the car's interior and window wash.

Today's excitement characteristics can easily become tomorrow's expected characteristics and may eventually become must-do characteristics. For example, the automatic redial function on a touch-tone phone, an excitement characteristic of the 1970s, became an expected feature in the 1990s. Automobile safety features such as seat belts, 5 mph bumpers, antilock brakes, and air bags were once excitement characteristics for safety-conscious consumers. But later, as the technology became more widespread and public concern for safety increased, those features became must-do characteristics, in many cases because of legislation. Similarly, the mouse, the CD-ROM, high-resolution color screens, and fax technologies, which were originally excitement features, became expected or must-do features in succeeding generations of personal computers.

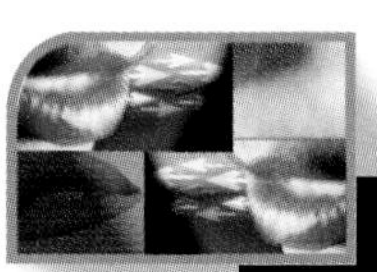

active poll <

What do you think? Voice your opinion and find out what others have to say.

QUALITY FUNCTION DEPLOYMENT (QFD)

Quality function deployment (QFD) is a design methodology that is used to integrate customer expectations with decisions made throughout the product design process. Figure 4.8 shows a generic *house of quality* as it is used in QFD. The porch on the left side of the house lists the customer requirements, called "whats," in horizontal rows. These customer requirements are the must-do, expected, and excitement characteristics that are to be included in the product-service bundle. The porch on the right side of the house identifies the relative importance of each of these features, and presents a competitive assessment of the product-service bundle. Each column under the roof of the house represents a design characteristic that is required in order to meet one or more of the customer requirements. These design requirements are called "hows."

A triangular co-relationship matrix forms the roof of the house. The cells of this matrix provide information regarding the positive or negative tradeoffs between specific design characteristics. The main room of the house of quality is a matrix that is formed by the intersection of the customer requirements and the design requirements. This matrix provides critical insight into the importance of each design characteristic from the customer's perspective. The symbols in the cells of this matrix provide information regarding the importance of particular design characteristics to the satisfaction of

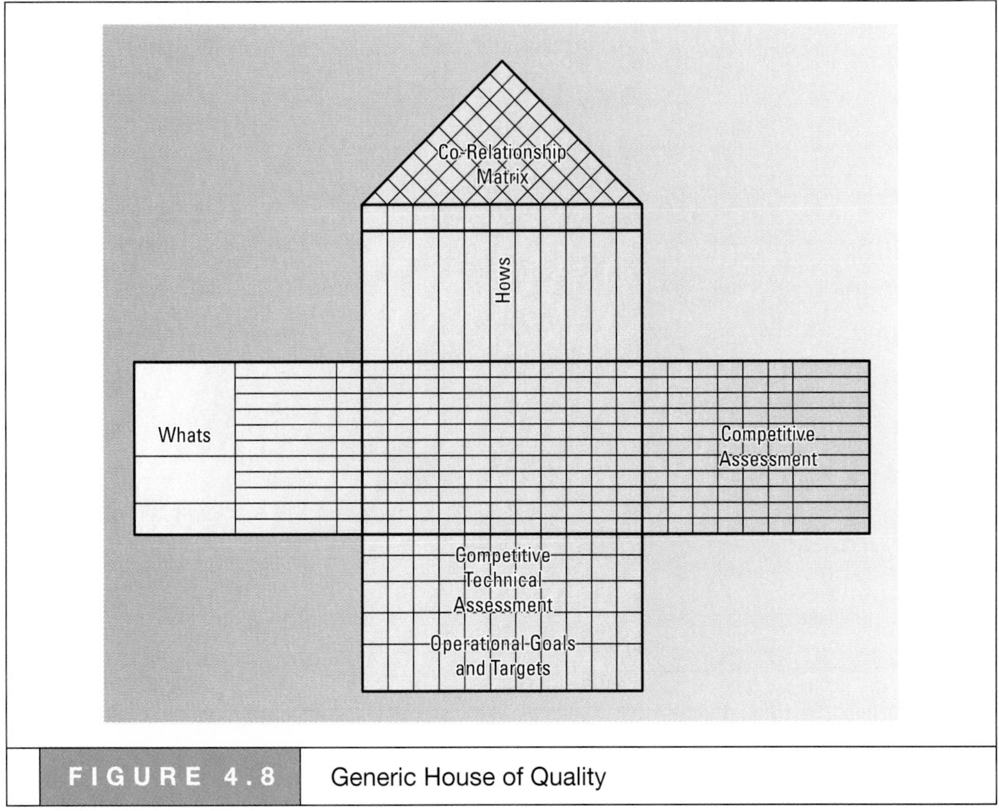

FIGURE 4.8 Generic House of Quality

the particular customer expectations the cells represent. The basement of the house provides information that is useful in technical assessment of the product-service bundle.

Once a product has been designed, its parts and subassemblies have to be designed. As a result, each column of the house of quality becomes a row in a new house that represents the design of a part or subassembly. In other words, the design requirements of the product-service bundle form internal requirements for the parts and subassemblies. For example, the house of quality for a warehouse might have a row that identifies a storage capacity requirement and a column that specifies a rack system to meet that need. A design house for the rack system would show the requirements for the rack in the rows and the construction specs for the rack in the columns.

Once the product, its subassemblies, and its parts have been designed, the processes to make them must also be designed. The rows of a process house can be derived from the columns of a part house. In this way, the design requirements of a part form the internal requirements for the process that is used to make the part. If the rack system for the warehouse was designed of steel, for instance, then a particular type of process would be needed to build the racks. The process design characteristics would specify the required labor, equipment, method of transporting materials, and so on.

Once a process has been designed, operational procedures must be developed to run the process. The rows of the operations house are derived from the columns of the process house. In other words, the design requirements of the process house become the internal customer requirements for the operational systems that are used to run them. In the case of the process used to make warehouse racks, the operations house would determine how workers are scheduled, what training they receive, where they are located, how equipment is maintained, when materials are ordered and in what quantities, where materials are stored, and so forth.

The overlapping series of houses of quality produced in this process is shown in Figure 4.9. The figure shows graphically that the central focus and overriding theme of all the decisions made in the QFD process is the development of products, parts, processes, and operational systems that are responsive to customer expectations, and that will ultimately provide customer satisfaction. If at any point in the design or operation of a production system an individual is not sure why he or she is performing a particular task, that person should be able to ask a series of "why" questions that establish a meaningful relationship between the task and a customer expectation.

QFD *could* be used in an over-the-wall design process, to help those who are performing each successive function to understand the reasoning behind earlier design decisions. But QFD is particularly

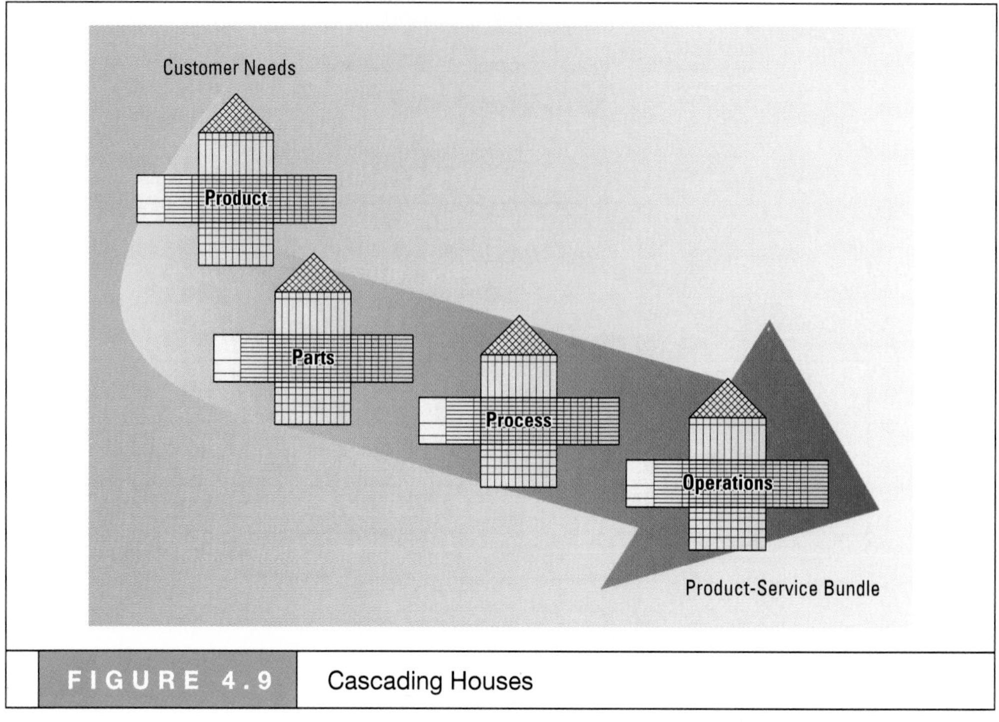

FIGURE 4.9 Cascading Houses

useful in concurrent design, because it gives structure to the design process. By working either forward or backward through the series of overlapping houses, teams can see the impact of early design decisions on other functions.

Competitive and Technical Analysis

Because QFD is geared toward the development of customer satisfaction, gathering information on customer satisfaction is a critical step in this method. Information may come from a competitor's customers as well as from the firm's present, past, and potential customers. Such information is used to develop a competitive analysis (the right porch of the house of quality) and a technical analysis (the basement of the house), both of which will guide design decisions. Further input can come from analyzing a competitor's product-service bundle. By purchasing the competitor's outputs and disassembling them, employees can use *reverse engineering* to learn more about the product and the technological strategies used to produce it. They may also obtain useful information about reliability and performance capabilities and may even gain clues about the competitor's plan for the future. The design team can then use this information to establish design targets that position the product-service bundle to best advantage from a competitive standpoint.

Design Targets

Figure 4.10 shows how competitive and technical design targets were set for the WriteSharp pencil. As you can see, the competitive analysis compares the ability of both the product-service bundle and benchmark competing products to satisfy customer needs. This analysis helps the design team to set its competitive targets. Similarly, the technical analysis compares the functional performance of the product-service bundle with that of benchmark competing products. It is used to set technical targets. In QFD, both the technical and the competitive targets are set by consensus of the design team. Though the targets need not always meet or exceed the competitive benchmarks on all criteria, they should add up to a composite target that is clearly superior to the competition. Performance profiles or arithmetic factor-rating can be used to assess the targets.

The competitive analysis performed in Figure 4.10B applies arithmetic factor-rating to the WriteSharp pencil example. The customer-determined importance rating is multiplied by the satisfaction rating the customers gave each pencil. Adding the score achieved for each "what" yields an overall rating. Note that while the current WriteSharp design has the highest overall rating, customer perception is that competitor X has the reputation for the highest quality, while competitor Y is the low-cost producer. Looking at the quantitative analysis in Figure 4.10B or the competitive performance profiles in Figure 4.10C, it is clear that WriteSharp is as good as or better than competitor X on

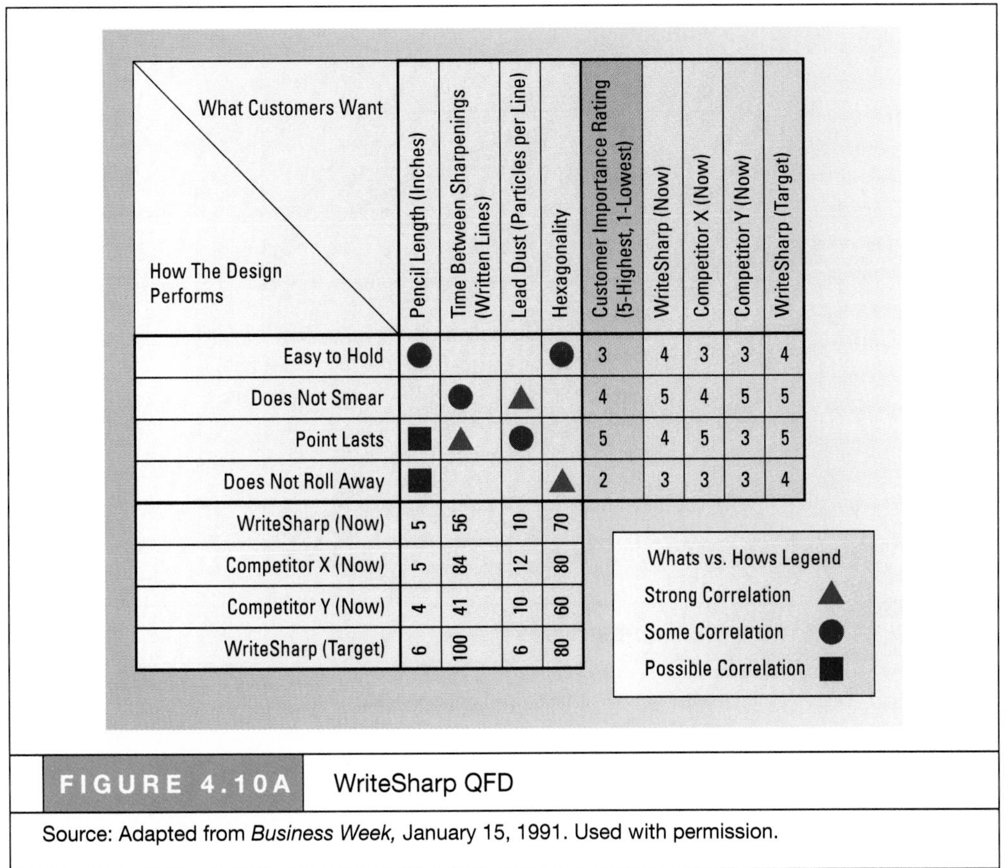

What Customers Want / How The Design Performs	Pencil Length (Inches)	Time Between Sharpenings (Written Lines)	Lead Dust (Particles per Line)	Hexagonality	Customer Importance Rating (5-Highest, 1-Lowest)	WriteSharp (Now)	Competitor X (Now)	Competitor Y (Now)	WriteSharp (Target)
Easy to Hold	●			●	3	4	3	3	4
Does Not Smear		●	▲		4	5	4	5	5
Point Lasts	■	▲	●		5	4	5	3	5
Does Not Roll Away	■			▲	2	3	3	3	4
WriteSharp (Now)	5	56	10	70					
Competitor X (Now)	5	84	12	80					
Competitor Y (Now)	4	41	10	60					
WriteSharp (Target)	6	100	6	80					

FIGURE 4.10A WriteSharp QFD

Source: Adapted from *Business Week,* January 15, 1991. Used with permission.

Whats Importance Rating (5=highest)	WriteSharp (Now)	Competitor X (Now)	Competitor Y (Now)	WriteSharp (Target)
3	3 × 4 = 12	3 × 3 = 9	3 × 3 = 9	3 × 4 = 12
4	4 × 5 = 20	4 × 4 = 16	4 × 5 = 20	4 × 5 = 20
5	5 × 4 = 20	5 × 5 = 25	5 × 3 = 15	5 × 5 = 25
2	2 × 3 = 6	2 × 3 = 6	2 × 3 = 6	2 × 4 = 8
Overall Rating	58	56	50	65
Market Price	$0.15	$0.18	$0.14	$0.16
Market Share	16%	12%	32%	20%
Profit (per unit)	$0.02	$0.03	$0.02	$0.04

FIGURE 4.10B Competitive Analysis

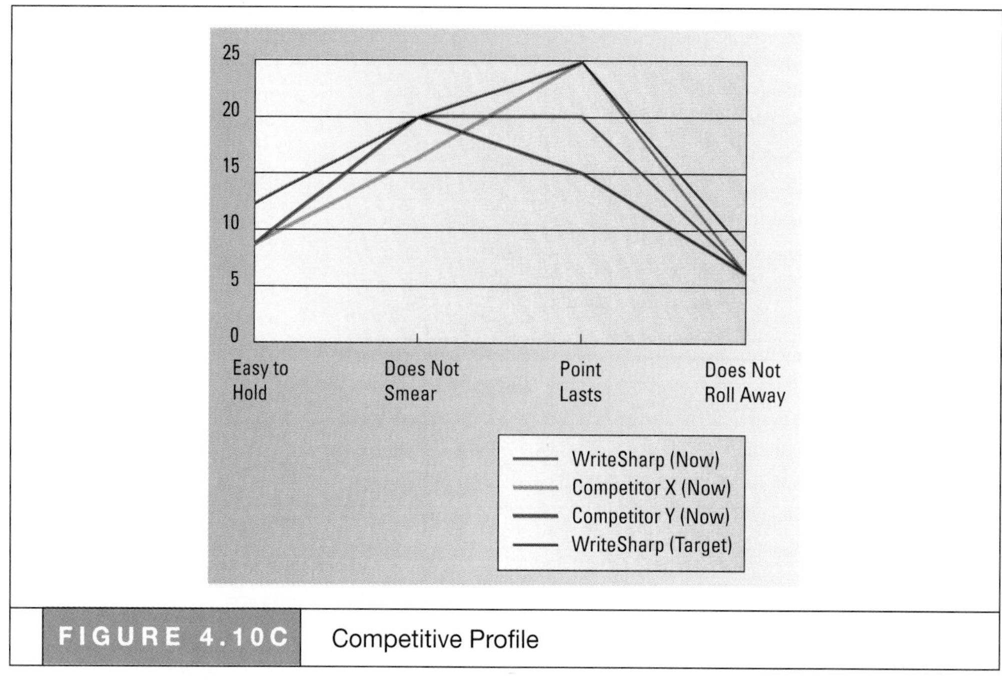

FIGURE 4.10C Competitive Profile

all the "whats" except the most important: how long the point lasts. WriteSharp is also even with or ahead of competitor Y on all "whats," yet it makes the same profit per unit.

A similar factor-rating analysis could have been performed on the "hows." Using some estimate of the technical feasibility of the desired improvement for weight (analogous to the customer importance rating in Figure 4.10A), as well as the performance data in the basement of the house, an overall feasibility rating could be created for each "how." A technical performance profile could also be graphed from such data.

After looking at the relationships between the "whats" and the "hows" in Figure 4.10A, WriteSharp managers established a design team to investigate the most significant "how" related to the durability of the point, as measured by the time between sharpenings. The aim was to close the *performance gap* between the WriteSharp design and that of competitor X. A second team was set up to examine the pencil's shape, in an attempt to differentiate WriteSharp's design from that of the low-cost competitor, Y, and create a positive performance gap in the process.

The first team found that a better lead formulation was the key to increasing the time between sharpenings and eventually focused on the binder, or glue, used to form the lead. A new polymer was found that would wear down more slowly. This formulation also reduced the dust level by retaining more moisture, somewhat like a crayon. Thus, two customer concerns were addressed. Though the new binder was more expensive, it allowed for tighter production controls and actually cut production costs by $.01 per unit.

The second team examined the effect of switching from cedar to oak for the wood casing around the lead. When that idea did not work, the team decided to tighten production controls on the existing cedar design and improved the quality of the pencil's hexagonal shape, thereby reducing the likelihood of its rolling off the user's desk. Together, the two teams arrived at a design that met the target levels described in Figures 4.10A–C, and in the process increased the value to the customer enough to justify a $.01 price increase. Combined with the $.01 cost reduction, their work doubled the profitability of the product and was projected to increase market share.

COMPUTER-AIDED DESIGN (CAD)

Computer-aided design (CAD) is an approach that uses computer software and hardware applications to generate digitized models representing a product's structural characteristics and physical dimensions. The models can then be analyzed using special software, represented and examined from a wide variety of perspectives on a computer screen, and printed out on a blueprint plotter or some other output device.

The Boeing 777 is one of the largest manufactured items ever designed using CAD. The technology allowed approximately 7,000 specialists to collaborate on one model. By using CAD software, Boeing significantly reduced rework and cut estimated total project costs by 20%. To give another example, Atlanta's committee for the 1996 Olympic Games used CAD to design the Georgia Dome.

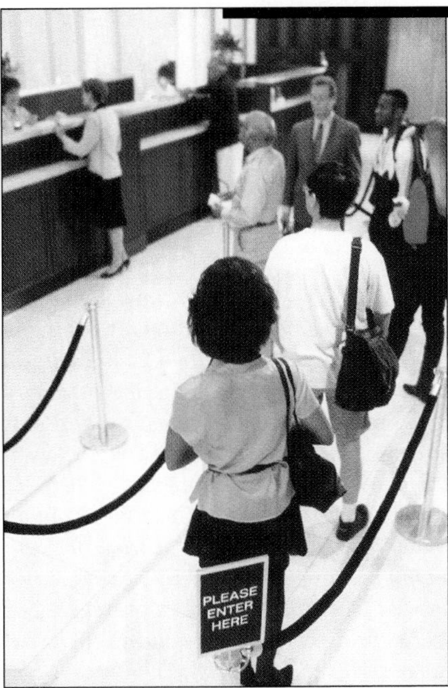

While the "back room" operations of a bank that take care of check clearing and payment processing can be organized to enhance efficiency, the teller services are generally organized to enhance the ability of customers to effectively communicate their requirements as they interact with the bank's representatives. The single queue requires that the first customer to arrive is also the first served—which helps customers to feel that they are being treated fairly even if they have to wait.

Using the computer model to experiment with various seating configurations before the stadium was actually built allowed the committee to add thousands of extra seats (and sell thousands of extra tickets), to finalize security plans early, and even to identify the best places to locate television photographers.

When CAD is linked to a computer-aided manufacturing (CAM) system, designing for manufacturing considerations becomes even simpler. With a *CAD/CAM system,* a set of alternative CAD designs can be run through the CAM system to generate the programs that would be used to make the items with automated equipment. If one of the proposed part-manufacturing programs is longer than another by a thousand lines of code, engineers can easily select the design which requires a shorter part-manufacturing program.

Going one step further, interfacing CAD with programs that simulate the value-adding system used to deliver the product-service bundle will allow the design team to assess the technical feasibility, economic feasibility, and manufacturability of a design. Such simulation programs help designers to understand the impact of various design variables—such as dimensional specifications, materials, and product structure—on performance variables, including processing times, work-in-process inventory requirements, and process capacity requirements. Without simulations, these design variables would have to be tested using actual prototypes and processes, which would be far more costly.

You'd probably be interested to know that modern roller coaster designers rely heavily on CAD technology to build the world's most exciting and safe rides. In Minnesota, Valleyfairs's "Wild Thing" takes riders up 200 feet before sending them hurtling through more than a mile of steel track at speeds up to 74 miles per hour. To design the $10 million ride, engineers created computer simulation models that show the effects of speed and force on riders, cars, and track. With this instant computer information, engineers were able to build a roller coaster with the sharpest possible curves and the steepest inclines and create the greatest illusion of imminent danger. With CAD tools now available, roller coaster designers are limited only by the additional fright the average rider is able to endure.

CAD is also particularly useful in the context of group technology and modular design, because of the ease with which modules can be cut from one design and pasted onto another via computer. Design software is a critical building block of computer integrated manufacturing systems that facilitate e-commerce. Linking CAD with CAM and other information systems that assist with day-to-day operational decision making can provide significant synergies throughout a supply chain. Although CAD provides significant benefits on its own, its potential is not fully realized until it is linked with other information technology-based systems.

> active example

Take a closer look at the concepts and issues you've been reading about.

SERVICE BLUEPRINTING

Chase's customer contact model is a valuable tool for designing the product-service bundle. High customer contact elements can be identified and enhanced to deliver personal satisfaction to the customer. Low contact elements can be separated from high contact elements to drive down costs through standardizing, prioritizing, and automating.

The customer contact model's practical value comes from applying it to existing service environments to improve performance. Design improvements of existing services can be conducted through the following four steps:

1. *Blueprint the service.* A **service blueprint** *is a visual diagram—usually a flowchart—that depicts all of the activities in the service delivery process. These include activities involving information processing, customer interactions, and employee decisions. Figure 4.11 presents an example of a service blueprint. The flowchart is analyzed to identify the fail points in the delivery system. Fail points are steps in the service delivery process where meeting customer expectations is critical and perhaps more difficult to achieve. Resources, employee training, and management attention must be provided to these fail points to ensure that customer needs are met.*
2. *Identify customer contact points and reduce contact where appropriate. Customer contact activities are identified by a "line of visibility" that separates steps in the service delivery process where customers are present or actively participate. These contact activities should be examined to determine if some elements may be removed from the customer's presence. For example, perhaps a bank teller conducts unnecessary data processing activity during each customer transaction. Such processing activities should be reassigned to "backroom" areas where they don't interfere with customer service and where they can be more efficiently completed.*
3. *Improve the quality of contact. Where contact is critical to the service, opportunities to enhance the customer's experience should be identified. Some examples include express lines in grocery stores, weekend and evening hours for dentists and car repair shops, and hiring and training people to deliver great customer service.*
4. *Improve efficiency in low contact operations. In low contact operations, costs can be reduced by standardizing work procedures, prioritizing jobs, and adopting computerized and automated processing systems.*

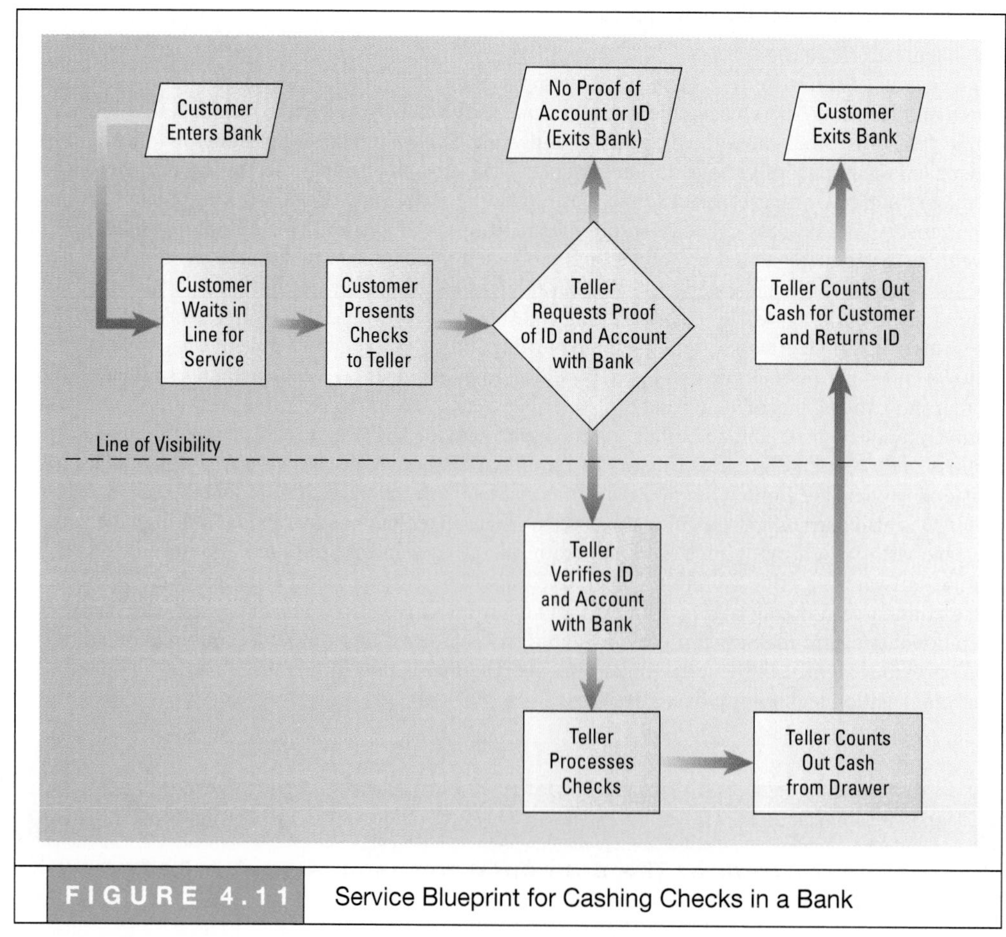

FIGURE 4.11 Service Blueprint for Cashing Checks in a Bank

PRODUCT COSTING METHODS

As much as 85% of a product's lifetime costs are locked in before the first unit is ever produced. Accurate product costing is therefore a critical design issue. Whether one is designing a new product-service bundle or modifying an existing design, some understanding of the cost implications of the decisions that are made is vital. The cost of providing the product-service bundle is critical from the standpoint of both profitability and customer satisfaction.

Activity-Based Costing

A product-service bundle's cost is usually described as some combination of direct costs, which are related to the manufacture and delivery of the bundle, and indirect costs, which represent administrative overhead. Many of the product-costing techniques used today were developed at a time when product life cycles were longer, direct labor was the primary cost driver next to materials, firms emphasized strategies designed to attain economies of scale. An **economy of scale** is a reduction in variable cost per unit that can be used to justify higher fixed costs. As a result, the overhead costs generated in the product design, administrative, and sales departments were typically allocated to products based on their labor content. Many firms, however, have now begun to stress strategies based on economies of scope. An **economy of scope** is an economic advantage obtained through process flexibility. In today's highly automated business world, with its greater emphasis on economies of scope, modular design, and group technology, the traditional product costing approach does not always make sense. In certain industries, the cost of direct labor may be as small as 5%, while overhead may represent more than half a product's cost.

Today, financial software makes it easier to trace overhead costs back to the products that required them. One alternative, **activity-based costing (ABC),** is an accounting method that allocates costs to the product-service bundle based on overhead activities performed. For instance, using a dedicated machine to make a large volume of an old component may require very little direct labor. Using traditional cost-accounting practices, such an item would be allocated very little overhead cost. Yet that component might not fit with a new group technology. Trying to make the item work with a new design could require considerable engineering design time, additional assembly time, and so on. In contrast, a new component that requires more direct labor but works with group technology and can be made on more flexible equipment, would be allocated rather high overhead cost using traditional accounting methods. Yet the new approach might actually consume far less overhead, and provide significant economies of scope to boot.

Break-Even Analysis

Cost-volume break-even analysis is a financial tool that may be used to justify a new product-service bundle or a change to an existing one. This tool uses cost estimates of the type discussed above (whether derived through ABC or more traditional cost allocation approaches). Consider the following example:

A computer manufacturer is proposing a change to its memory configuration. The manufacturer currently offers 8 megabytes of memory, delivered via an old memory board designed to accept two 4-megabyte chips. But increasing software memory requirements and the declining cost of memory may have made a change in system architecture worthwhile. The company is considering switching to 8-megabyte memory slots. It has estimated that the up-front design cost of such a change in system architecture is approximately $5,000 per week, amortized over the system's three-year life. The average cost of memory is estimated at $45 per 8 megabytes if bought in 8-megabyte increments, or $55 per 8 megabytes if bought in 4-megabyte increments. The company assumes that no other costs will be influenced by the proposed design change.

Cost-volume break-even analysis can be used to compare these two alternatives and determine the weekly volume at which either alternative would be preferable. The relevant cost of the new alternative would be $5,000 per week plus $45 per unit. The relevant cost of continuing with the old design would simply be $55 per unit. By setting these two costs equal, we can find the *break-even volume* for the new design:

$$\begin{aligned} \$5000 + \$45X &= \$55X \\ \$5000 &= \$10X \\ 500 &= X \end{aligned}$$

If the volume is expected to be greater than 500 units per week, changing the system design makes sense. Otherwise, the computer maker should stick with the old design.

Chrysler makes only a few thousand Vipers a year. Its ability to rapidly design, produce, and market this car in small volumes with a profit comes from its cross-functional team structure and has provided marketing benefits that spill over to its high-volume production models.

The break-even volume can also be found graphically. The cost of the new alternative can be graphed using the equation Y = \$5,000 + \$45X; the cost of the existing approach would be Y = \$55X. Figure 4.12 illustrates the resulting graph. The *break-even point* is the point where weekly volume is 500 units and weekly cost is \$27,500—that is, (500, 27,500).

\$ Cost
60000
50000
40000
30000
20000
10000
5000
0
Old System Architecture
Break-Even Point
Break-Even Cost (\$ 27,500)
New System Architecture
Breakeven Volume
0 100 200 300 400 500 600 700 800 900 1000
Units/ Week
Volume
Volumes at Which the Old Alternative Is Better
Volumes at Which the New Alternative Is Better
Y = 55X
Y = 5000 + 45X

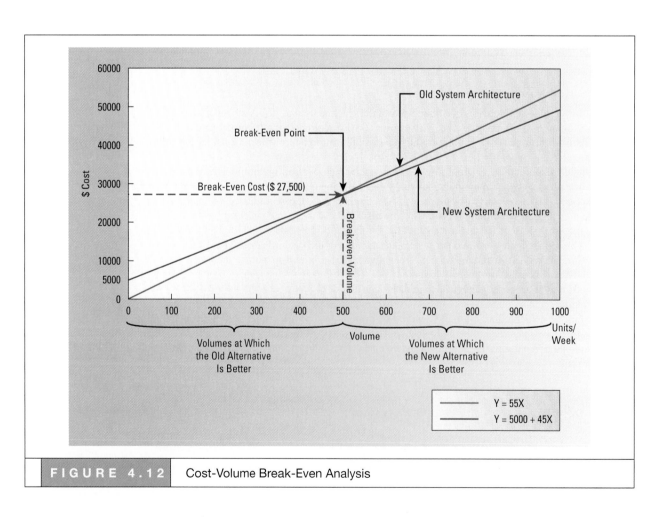

FIGURE 4.12 Cost-Volume Break-Even Analysis

While break-even analysis is very useful in estimating the viability of proposed design changes, it relies on inexact demand and cost estimates. Most organizations must therefore go further in justifying design projects that require significant capital outlays. More detailed and complex techniques are covered in cost accounting and managerial finance classes; they are beyond the scope of this book.

> active example

Take a closer look at the concepts and issues you've been reading about.

> active concept check

Now let's take a moment to test your knowledge of the concepts you have studied in this section.

> Integrating Operational Decisions

There is some connection between this chapter and every other chapter in the text, but in this section we're just pointing out some of the chapters most directly related to this one. The material in this chapter is included as a part of the content that overarches decisions about how to structure and run the operational system.

Naturally, decisions regarding the design of the value-adding system (Chapter 7) will be closely linked to the product-service bundle design decisions covered in this chapter. Indeed, we have spent considerable time in this chapter discussing the need to reflect process design and manufacturability concerns in the design of the product-service bundle. Similarly, decisions about capacity and master schedules, covered in Chapter 8, can have a big impact on the value that customers receive. For example, if the product-service bundle is highly customized and short lead times are a part of the bundle, there are clear implications for capacity and scheduling. Specifically, it will be beneficial to have excess capacity to enhance responsiveness, and scheduling will need to reflect individual orders.

Quality function deployment, a technique we have discussed in this chapter, is one tool that formalizes the linkages discussed in the previous paragraph. The first house in the QFD approach deals directly with the product-service bundle's design. The second deals with component part designs. The third deals with processes by which the product-service bundle will be created and delivered, thus it covers many of the decisions discussed in Chapter 6. Finally, the fourth house deals with the operation of the process, thereby covering many of the decisions to be addressed in Chapters 11 and 12.

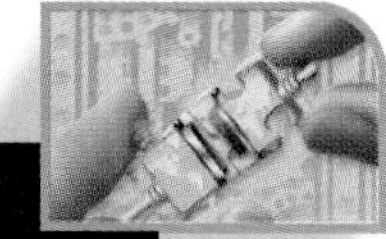

> integrated OM

Take a moment to apply what you've learned.

> Chapter Wrap-Up

This chapter has covered issues in the design of product-service bundles including: the specific tasks involved, the traditional approach, challenges to the traditional approach, the modern approach, and representative tools that are useful in the design process.

The tasks included in the process of designing the product-service bundle range from concept development to delivery of the first unit. In the traditional approach, these tasks are accomplished in functional silos, and work is passed over a series of walls until the design sequence has been completed. The traditional approach is not well adapted to the modern business climate, which is heavily influenced by time-based competition and frequently offers better returns through economies of scope than through economies of scale.

An approach that is better suited to the current competitive environment, concurrent engineering, relies on input from all functions throughout the design process. This modern approach stresses design for manufacture, design for procurement, and design for the environment. Other modern design concepts include group technology, modular design, product simplification, and design for disassembly.

Regardless of the approach that is taken to organizing the design process, certain tools may be used to enhance its effectiveness and efficiency. They include computer-aided design/computer-aided manufacturing (CAD/CAM) systems, quality function deployment (QFD), and a variety of cost estimation and project justification techniques, such as cost-volume break-even analysis.

> end-of-chapter resources

- **Practice Quiz**
- **Key Terms**
- **Solved Problems**
- **Discussion Questions**
- **Problems**
- **Case 4.1: Real Queasiness in Virtual Reality**
- **References**
- **Plant Tours**

CHAPTER 5

Total Quality Management

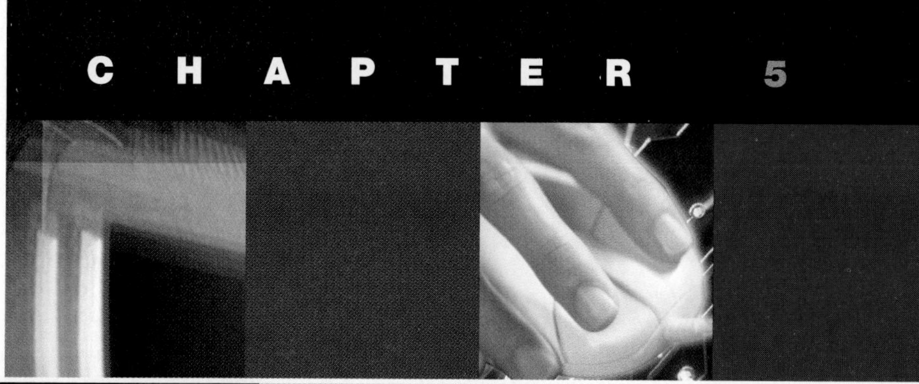

Chapter Outline

> What's Ahead

. . . BACK AT THE REC CENTER

About 6:30 on Friday morning, near the end of another work week, Luis, Cheryl, and Tom arrived at the health club. They were surprised to find Fred already in the exercise room, furiously pumping away on the stepper. He didn't look happy.

"Fred, if that's not the look of somebody who's frustrated, then I'm running for president!" offered Luis. "Has something got you worked up at the office? You don't look like a guy who's getting ready to have a good time this weekend."

"Weekend—what weekend?" snarled Fred. "For years I've had customers wanting the best. Now they want cheap. And now my biggest account is beefing about our defect rate!" he added. Fred was obviously frustrated by some of the differences between his old job and his new one. He had spent several years marketing a premium-priced product with innovative design, cutting-edge features, and custom fit. Now, just as he was finally getting used to marketing a low-end, standardized product for the cost conscious, his customers had begun to demand high quality, too! The representative for his biggest account had just told him that if Fred's company couldn't cut its defect rate by 10 percent per year, she could no longer do business with Fred.

"We just undercut our competition to grab all of this account's business, and then BOOM, she hit us with the defect rate. She can't be serious!" Fred objected, getting off the stepper. For almost a year, his division had been cutting its costs to the bone to keep the delivered price to this account competitive. Fred felt the defect rate was reasonable; they hadn't been shipping any more defective products than they used to. In fact, they had shipped fewer defective pagers than the competition and at a better price, too! Inspectors always checked the products as they went out and scrapped a fair share of them, but nobody can catch everything. "The way I always heard it was, you get what you pay for! She's asking for cake and wants to eat it, too!" he concluded.

"Consumer electronics is a tough business, Fred, no doubt about it. Maybe you need to think about what your customers want from you—not your old ones, but your new ones," Tom responded. "What you're talking about sounds a lot like our last year or two. We went as far as to bring in some total quality management consultants. They helped us to see who our customers were and how we could serve them better and cut costs, too."

Tom recalled how strange it had seemed to him the first time he heard it. But the consultants argued that even an airline could do better by customers and actually lower costs at the same time, if marketers really knew what the customers wanted. Specifically, as a relatively new carrier, Tom's outfit didn't have to unlearn as much as other airlines might have to. The consultants told Tom that his people needed to define their customers' needs, identify a market niche whose needs they could satisfy, and focus on constantly improving their ability to meet those needs.

It wasn't easy. "We took a look at what we do, who we are, and who our customers are. We figured our customers were travelers who need on-time service to places where the only alternative to our service is driving. Those customers want service without frills, at a low cost," he added. "We collected data on our customers' needs, how well our process meets those needs, and how we compared to the competition. We used all that information to improve our performance."

"For example," Tom went on, "we always fly the same type of plane, avoid crowded airports, and keep frills down. We realized that standard equipment can make servicing the plane easier, quicker, and more predictable. We don't even handle interline baggage. Do you know how much a plane can earn per hour flying? How much do you think it can earn sitting on the ground while we shuffle seats around or the ground crew tries to remember where the fuel goes or how much gas the tank holds?

"We also realized that flying to older, smaller, less-crowded urban airports is usually cheaper. They're only a quick cab ride to most business destinations anyway. If you don't need to connect, why fly into a busy airport?" Tom asked. "By moving away from larger, more crowded airports out in the suburbs, we can keep costs down and avoid long, irritating delays on arrival or departure." He also said they realized that on short flights, serving food or offering reserved seating is unnecessary. "Guess how much it costs to take a can of soda to 30,000 feet, serve it, and collect the empty cup?" Tom asked rhetorically.

"Well, I know where Fred is going with this," replied Luis, as he took off his sweats. "When a customer specifies a high-end piece of furniture, one with all the frills, she knows it's going to cost more than the cheaper model. She also knows that if you want it to be cheaper, buy the basic model out-of-stock inventory," he said. "That's just the way business is done. You can't stay in business long by letting everybody have their cake and eat it, too!" he laughed as he picked up a towel from the pile of clean ones by the water cooler.

"Come on, guys, it may be 6:30 in the morning, but I can see that all three of you are right. It's just that you're in different businesses," Cheryl added, after listening patiently as the other three blew off steam. "Fred, you and Tom sell the low-cost, off-the-shelf, no-frills basic model. Luis, you sell high-end stuff with all the extras, and you tailor it to the customer's specifications. That's different." Cheryl understands that Fred and Tom deal with high-volume production of a relatively standard output. If they focus on minimizing variation and waste from the production process, they can offer the same or better benefit to their customers at a lower cost. As long as they are disciplined in what they do, they can have their cake and eat a little, too.

Cheryl said her hospital is more like Luis's furniture factory, in that each patient, like a customer looking to buy a custom-tailored table or chair, has different needs. Not all patients can be treated the same way. At the hospital, meeting patients' needs comes first; minimizing waste comes second. Cheryl knows that if managers at the hospital, like those at the furniture factory, can accurately determine what patients truly need and what they don't, then they can still keep costs reasonable.

She also said that in many ways the job is easier for Tom or Fred. They can sit in an office or a lab and get all the help they need figuring out the next month's schedule or what the newest pager will look like. In Cheryl's business, or any other business in which unique customer service is part of the total package, customer needs have to be assessed on the fly a lot of the time. That's tough—especially when a mistake could kill someone.

"But in a lot of ways, we're the same," Cheryl continued. "We're all concerned with getting waste out of the system. In our case, and I'm sure the same goes for Luis, we balance flexibility and effective treatment with efficiency," she said. They may reorganize doctors', nurses', and technicians' duties to increase the productivity of all concerned, but they won't do it at the expense of safe and effective patient care. "A key for us would be to improve communication between our processes and our patients," Cheryl explained. "But the automated phone-answering system that works for Tom's airline won't cut it in ER."

"You're right. If people want to buy the pagers I sell now, they don't look for extras," Fred agreed. "But how can we meet their expectations for quality, too?" he asked.

"By collecting data about what your customers need and how you deliver it, just like Tom's airline does!" Cheryl replied. "We do the same thing to improve our processes. Feedback is important. It just keeps us focused on our customers' needs," Cheryl continued, as she began doing sit-ups on the inclined bench. "I say it's a question of commitment and discipline. Sort of like working out: If you stay with it, the payoffs will come."

"It's a people thing, too," Tom added. "We give our people a lot of room to make things better. Everybody is included, not just management. You know, we cut out a lot of red tape and get people excited about the program." he said. Tom's past experience has shown him that much of the time, the person on the shop floor is the one who finds the solution to the operating problem, who eliminates waste or unnecessary complications in a product's design.

"Wait a minute," Fred interrupted. "If we let everybody run around changing everything, we'll never get anywhere, and nothing will work. Not if everybody's going every which way!" he pleaded.

"No, you're only seeing the superficial part," Tom reassured him. "The whole idea is based on everybody being on the same page." Tom has spent a lot of time instilling a set of shared values in workers. He knows from experience that those shared values foster a commitment to the customer and to quality. "If everybody is looking in the same direction, you'll be surprised what they can do when they're turned loose," he suggested. Nodding, they all got back to working out.

> objectives

Take a moment to familiarize yourself with the key objectives of this chapter.

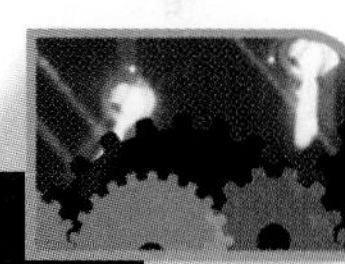

> gearing up

Before you begin reading this chapter, try a short warm-up activity.

> Introduction

In a 1956 article in the *Harvard Business Review,* Armand Feigenbaum identified three new trends that would have significant implications for the management of quality. First, customer expectations for quality were rising sharply. The post–World War II era of high demand and low capacity was sure to end, and with it the day when providers of goods and services could specify their own levels of quality. Customers would eventually be able to hold out for their preferred levels of quality. Second, quality practices and techniques, which had been in use since the early days of the industrial revolution, were outmoded. They required large inspection departments and emphasized standards for the quantity rather than the quality of output. Third, costs arising from poor quality had become very high, limiting the competitive strength of American companies. Taken together, these three trends suggested that firms would have to improve the quality of their output at the same time that they reduced the costs.

Feigenbaum proposed a solution to these problematic trends, which he called total quality control (TQC). The major difference between TQC and prior practice was that in TQC, quality was everyone's job. Feigenbaum had noticed that quality improvement efforts died quickly when the responsibility for quality was located in one department. As he put it, "These experiments have had a life span of as long as six months—when the job incumbent had the advantage of a strong stomach, a rhinoceros hide, and a well spent and sober boyhood. Others not similarly endowed did not last even that long" (Costin 1999, 85).

The danger in making quality everyone's job is that it is easy to assume that someone else is taking care of it. To make sure that quality did not become "nobody's job," Feigenbaum suggested that firms maintain a functional unit that specialized in quality and quality alone, across all operations. The unit would be responsible for the control of new designs, incoming materials, production, and process improvement. In this context, quality control would include the observation of completed work, to determine whether it met prespecified standards, as well as the coordination of efforts to ensure and improve quality.

Feigenbaum's proposal was based on a thorough acquaintance with the production process. In most organizations, the marketing personnel are in close contact with customers; they understand customer requirements better than others in the organization. But to effectively satisfy customers' expectations, operations personnel must understand the quality standards customers require. Likewise, to set appropriate technical parameters for products and services, design engineers must rely on information provided by marketing and operations. All functions within the system, including but not limited to marketing, design, and operations, must interact effectively in a coordinated effort to satisfy the customer. Clearly, quality *is* everyone's job.

The first two sections in this chapter, "Committing to Total Quality" and "Shifting Paradigms of Management," provide a fuller perspective on the issues introduced in Chapters 1–3. The third section, "Leaders of the Quality Movement in the United States," provides a historical perspective on Total Quality Management (TQM), including three theoretical frameworks on which the TQM philosophy is based. The fourth section, "Quality Awards and Certifications," provides a discussion of ways that companies can validate their quality systems based on external review; one way is through quality awards such as the Malcolm Baldrige National Quality Award; another is via certifications, such as the ISO 9000 certification, granted after investigation by outside reviewers.

active concept check

Now let's take a moment to test your knowledge of the concepts you have studied in this section.

This group of Mercedes employees form a work area team involved in process improvement projects.

Chapter Topics \ Functional Areas of Business	Finance	Accounting	Human Resources	Marketing	Engineering	Management Information Systems
Integrating Operations Management with Other Functions	●	●	●	●	●	●
Committing to Total Quality	●	●	●	●	●	●
Shifting Paradigms of Management			●			
Leaders of the Quality Movement in the United States						
Quality Awards and Certifications				●		
Quality Management and the Environment				●	●	

FIGURE 5.1 Integrating Operations Management with Other Functions

Integrating Operations Management with Other Functions

Figure 5.1 highlights the major linkages between this chapter's sections and the primary functional areas in most firms. You'll notice that the most obvious connections are early in the chapter. First of all, this section is a reminder that it's important for managers to interact effectively across functional boundaries. Simply making the "best" decision from a functional perspective seldom accomplishes the overall competitive objectives of a firm. This is especially true when it comes to the quality of the product-service bundle, because the value that customers receive comes from the contributions of many functional areas. For example, the ability to finance a purchase is often a key determinant of customer satisfaction with automobile dealership services. This ability and the speed with which it is made available (loans while you wait), in turn, is influenced by information systems that generate credit histories and process loan application paperwork. The marketing function relies on these systems when they determine the way that customers will be attracted to a dealership. Further, operations scheduling is influenced by the marketing plans, and the timing of the plans can be influenced by advice from accountants regarding inventory taxes. When these functions are all coordinated effectively, the product-service bundle can be much more appealing to the car buyer. When the functions make their decisions independently, there are bound to be times when the decisions benefit the functional area rather than the customer.

The second section of the chapter deals with the commitments of total quality management. The whole organization must reflect these commitments in their decision making if a company wants to claim that they are using TQM. As such, it's important for personnel in each functional area to understand how these commitments can influence the way they do their work.

With a few exceptions, the cross-functional linkages from remaining sections of this chapter are less obvious. The exceptions are highlighted in Figure 5.1. Specifically, the shifting paradigms highlighted in this chapter have had a significant impact on the practice of human resource management. Also, attaining quality awards and certifications or reducing a company's environmental impact through quality improvement methods can have significant marketing benefits. Finally, particularly in manufacturing companies, opportunities for enhancing a company's environmental friendliness often rely on technical support from the engineering function.

Committing to Total Quality

The need to follow through on one's commitments is at the heart of total quality management. The **total quality management (TQM)** system is based on four fundamental commitments:

1. Commitment to the customer's total satisfaction
2. Commitment to understanding and improving the organization's processes
3. Commitment to employee involvement
4. Commitment to data-based decision making

The relationships among these four commitments are illustrated in Figure 5.2. The first two commitments represent outcomes; the third and fourth represent methods that provide the foundation for achieving the desired outcomes. Together, these four commitments form the TQM system.

A shared vision and values provide the basis for making these commitments. (Without a shared vision and values, individuals would find it difficult to agree to any commitment, much less act on it.) Because the four commitments often require behavior that is not customary to managers, in most organizations, unusual steps must be taken to ensure that workers and customers do not perceive the commitments as hollow promises. In addition to verbal commitments, financial resources must be allocated, appropriate reward systems established, human resource management practices altered, and training provided. Finally, once the new system has been put in place, it must be given time to produce results.

Commitment 1: A Commitment to the Customer and Total Customer Satisfaction

The very purpose of organizations is to meet customer needs and satisfy their expectations. Whether the customer is internal or external, making a true commitment to customer satisfaction requires managers to follow through in at least three ways:

1. They must establish an ongoing process that effectively measures the level of satisfaction customers are receiving from the firm's product-service bundle.
2. They must maintain excellent communication between employees and the customers they serve.
3. They must design processes and product-service bundles that delight customers, both by responding to customers' concerns and by anticipating customers' needs and expectations.

The importance of committing to the customer cannot be overemphasized. The willingness to solicit input from customers and to respond in tangible ways allows companies that are pursuing TQM to remain competitive, even in the face of intense global competition.

active example

Take a closer look at the concepts and issues you've been reading about.

Commitment 2: A Commitment to Understanding and Improving the Firm's Process

All value is added through some kind of process. Every worker has a direct supplier and a direct customer, whether that worker has a clerical job, a manufacturing job, a service job, or a managerial job. Unfortunately, not all workers understand their processes. Fewer have the opportunity to discuss their work requirements with their suppliers and customers, and fewer still have the opportunity to improve their processes.

Thus the second major commitment of TQM is to develop an understanding of the operations system as a whole, one that is shared by all employees who are part of that system. Firms that are committed to TQM recognize that in an ever-changing business environment, no process can be perfect. They stress process improvement continually, even when there is no danger of producing defective items, because process improvement is the foundation on which customer satisfaction is built.

Flow charts provide a visual model of a process that allows workers to see how they fit into the big picture. Many other analytical tools can also be used to help workers understand their processes (Chapter 6 is devoted to describing a number of these). Thus, firms that are committed to understanding and improving their processes will train all their employees to use a wide variety of techniques to

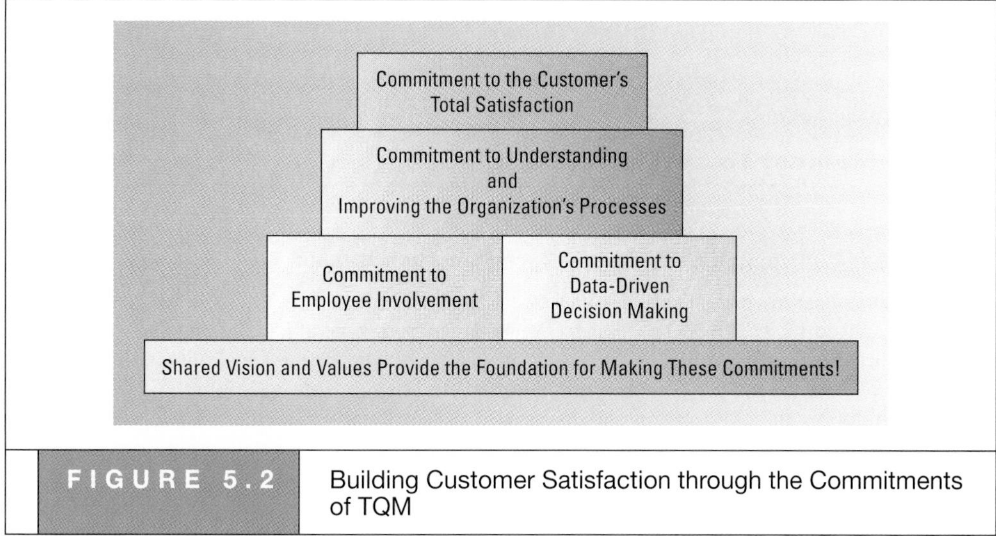

FIGURE 5.2 Building Customer Satisfaction through the Commitments of TQM

analyze data and make informed decisions about the processes where they work. Unlocking the creativity of the workforce, the third commitment in TQM, is a critical foundation of the ongoing improvement of a process.

> **video exercise**
>
> **Take a moment to apply what you've learned.**

Commitment 3: A Commitment to the Firm's Employees and to Total Employee Involvement

There is a subtle distinction between the traditional view of the worker and the perspective promoted by TQM. Traditionally, a worker was viewed as a person who completes a task. In that context, it was easy for workers to "check their brains at the door" when they arrived at work. But in TQM, the worker is viewed as the source of process improvements. Thus, rather than seeing this week's production quota in the worker's hands, managers need to see the company's future in the worker's minds. For many firms seeking to pursue total quality, this kind of mental adjustment may require considerable change on the part of managers as well as employees.

Employees, in fact, are as much a part of a business process as are the machines they use and the work procedures they follow. Thus, a focus on improving the process must include improvements in the skills and knowledge of employees. Every person in the organization represents a link in the process, a source of ideas for improvement. Furthermore, the cooperation of all employees is essential to the effective implementation of positive change. Because the people who work in the system every day are the best equipped to understand and improve the system, they must be empowered to do so.

One way to empower employees to improve their processes and satisfy customers is to create a team spirit that is strong enough to overcome the professional, functional, or position-related barriers to teamwork. Managers must take the first step in this effort; workers are much more likely to step out of their own comfort zones when they have a positive example to follow. Managers must also work hard to make sure that all employees understand and buy into the firm's mission, vision, and values. And they must assure workers that they will not lose their jobs because of improvements in the efficiency of the process. In sum, a climate of trust is necessary for teamwork to flourish.

Employee involvement (EI) is a formal approach to creating a spirit of teamwork that will lead to widespread process improvements. Typically, workers are encouraged to make suggestions that will produce improvements in their workplace, including reduced costs, higher quality, greater safety, better ergonomics, more effective environmental safeguards, enhanced decision making, more efficient use of space, and the like. Once a suggestion has been approved by managers, a team of volunteers is asked to work on developing a specific approach to implementing the suggestion. Members of the team receive any training they need to follow the project through to its completion.

active exercise

Take a moment to apply what you've learned.

Commitment 4: A Commitment to Data-Based Decision Making

Managers almost always make their decisions based on some kind of data. Often, however, they do not process the data correctly, they base their decisions on the wrong type of data, or they interpret the data incorrectly because of personal biases. Managers may also fail to understand the limitations of the available data and the ramifications of those limitations (in other words, they may jump to conclusions).

Statistical tools can help decision makers to process data correctly, so that they rely less on their own gut feelings. While they shouldn't overlook their intuition (that's a data point, too), whenever possible they should validate their intuition with appropriately generated statistical results, so that their biases will not keep them from making the best decisions. Quality experts are in universal agreement that the effective use of statistical tools is critical to the improvement of processes, products, and customer satisfaction. Thus a commitment to data-based decision making implies a need to train all employees in the appropriate use of statistics. As an example, consider Table 5.1 which presents some quality indicators that could be used to generate objective data and enhance administration in a university context.

active concept check

Now let's take a moment to test your knowledge of the concepts you have studied in this section.

> Committing to the Customer at the Student Recreation Center

Who are the Student Recreation Center's (SRC) customers and what do they want? While this may seem like an easy question, they do call it the student recreation center, so customers must be students who want recreation—but there is much more to the question than meets the eye. An amazing amount of data was collected through surveys and interviews with students during the planning and design stages of the SRC's development. Committees composed of students, faculty, local community members, and university administrators all combined to anticipate what the "customers" would want in terms of basic services and how best to design a facility that could deliver them. The basic design that resulted is state of the art and has been very successful, but continued attention to customer satisfaction is still a major commitment.

The "customers" of the SRC come from many places. While it's true that the majority of the patrons coming through the turnstiles are traditional college students, many faculty, staff, and their families also come on a regular basis. Local community members not affiliated with the university can also purchase memberships. Outside organizations, like the NCAA which held its national swimming and diving championships there, are also customers. Internally, many on-campus organizations (i.e., fraternities and sororities) and departments (i.e., intramural sports, residence halls, admissions) also use the SRC for various functions and events and would also be considered internal customers.

Working at the SRC is considered one of the more desirable jobs on campus. Prospective employees typically have a shared appreciation for the synergies between physical and mental health. They also need to understand the heavy emphasis on customer service that is part of the intended culture. Ongoing in-service training is a major part of building that intended culture; each employee will spend anywhere from two to four hours per month in training, with some specialized jobs requiring significantly more. When you add in the SRC's growing prominence as a social hub on campus, the employees of the SRC see it as a fun place to work and good experience.

Data collection is a major part of the SRC's commitment to customer satisfaction. Customer comment cards are collected from several locations around the SRC on a regular basis. In addition, surveys and feedback cards are solicited from all major events and functions held at the SRC. The data is

TABLE 5.1 Quality Measures For a University

Product-Service Bundle Feature	Attribute or Requirement	Measures	Corrective Action for Nonconformance
Supporting facility	• Appearance of campus	• Visibility of appropriate signs, volume of uncollected or loose trash, landscaping appeal	• Maintenance, paint, litter collection processes, sign replacement programs
	• Classrooms and offices	• Room temperature, lights working, volume of uncollected or loose trash	• Repair, replace, and clean
Facilitating goods	• Textbooks	• Percentage of required books and class materials that are in stock	• Improve coordination between faculty and bookstore managers
	• Computers	• Average age of machines in labs, waiting time for machines during peak usage	• Establish a replacement schedule and process, improve lab scheduling, set usage limits
	• Campus food	• Survey student satisfaction with meal plan, sales of meals to non-plan students	• Train cooks and servers, select superior vendors, etc.
Explicit services	• Professors	• Percentage with doctorates	• Adapt hiring criteria and pay scales
	• Academic programs	• Accreditation, journal rankings	• Use resources according to accreditation or ranking criteria
Implicit services	• Safety	• Crime statistics	• Increase patrols, promote awareness
	• Social and entertainment opportunities	• Number and quality of programs vs. comparable universities	• Hire competent staff, commit resources

routinely analyzed with an eye toward trends or themes. A Student Staff Advisory Committee (SSAC) meets weekly with SRC administrators to talk about issues that come up in the data or those issues that arise through their day-to-day interactions with customers. The SSAC is comprised of representatives from all departments of the SRC (the aquatic center, pro shop, the Outdoor Pursuits Center, fitness center, aerobic sports and dance, etc.). They discuss ways to deal with unique situations that arise in the data and many times decide to collect more specific data to follow up on a trend or theme. For example, a recent survey was administered in the fitness center concerning the type of music to play at different times of the day. A similar approach was taken in the aerobic sports and dance center with respect to offering kick-boxing classes. Finally, specific input from customers in the aquatic center was solicited in order to improve the scheduling of activities and the most desired pool temperature! In each case, data collected from customers was used as a basis for decision making.

SRC administrators also point to this type of ongoing data collection as a way of better understanding the product they offer customers. They now know that lap swimmers want the 50m pool cooler (80 degrees) than the senior citizens who do water aerobics in the recreational pool (86 degrees), yet divers prefer something in the middle for the diving well. They also understand that patrons using the fitness center prefer a softer, more relaxing station in the morning during their indoor walks around the track; but afternoon customers want to jog to a faster beat. All in all, according to senior management, having a process in place to continually improve the way customer needs are met is the key.

active concept check <

Now let's take a moment to test your knowledge of the concepts you have studied in this section.

Shifting Paradigms of Management

A **paradigm** is a way of thinking, a pattern or model that serves as an example. Making the commitments required by TQM has forced organizations to radically change the way they view the world and conduct their business. In short, it has forced a paradigm shift in managerial thinking, from the traditional functional paradigm to the TQM paradigm. Table 5.2 summarizes several aspects of this change in thinking.

ANALYTIC VERSUS HOLISTIC THINKING

In the *analytic approach* used in traditional management, complex problems are broken down into independent subproblems that can be understood more easily. The idea is that if each part works correctly, the whole system will work correctly. Focusing on a small portion of the problem at a time also permits a more detailed analysis of subsystem variables. Thus the analytic approach enhances a manager's understanding of subsystems, improves their efficiency, or better controls the portion of a problem that is under study. In using the divide-and-conquer strategy to solve problems, however, decision

TABLE 5.2 The Paradigm Shift to Total Quality Management

Traditional Approach	Total Quality Approach
Analytic thinking • Functional management • Local performance measures	Holistic thinking • Process management • Global performance measures
Focus on acceptability • Meeting specifications • Performance plateaus	Focus on desirability • Pursuit of perfection • Continuous improvement
Focus on short-term financial performance • Financial control • Results oriented	Focus on long-term market share • Managerial leadership • Process oriented
Reactive response to customers • Add on treatments for symptoms • Focus on product elegance	Proactive solutions for customers • Addressing the root cause • Focus on customer satisfaction
Competitive sourcing • Large base of suppliers • Bidding for contracts • Buyer mandates • Short-term, contract-focused relationship	Supply-chain management • Select set of suppliers • Single-supplier sourcing • Supplier input in design decisions • Long-term, improvement-oriented relationship
Class-conscious thinking • Hourly versus salaried • Labor versus management • Skilled versus unskilled • Functional classifications and competition	Team thinking • Focus on teamwork • Focus on system improvement • Focus on satisfying internal customers • Functional excellence supportive of system improvement

makers may fail to recognize that an understanding of each part does not necessarily confer an understanding of the whole.

Because all parts of a system must interact to form a cohesive whole, the whole is much more than the sum of its parts. Perhaps you have heard a world-class orchestra perform in concert. Though you may have been impressed by the talent of a brilliant virtuoso soloist, you would not have enjoyed the evening nearly so much if all the musicians had played their parts one at a time. In the *holistic approach* to problem solving, subsystems are studied in the context of a clear understanding of the system as a whole.

Building a system out of the parts (the analytic approach) is substantially different from building the parts for a system (the holistic approach). To fully understand their processes, firms that implement TQM must take advantage of both approaches. For many companies, that means deemphasizing functional management and local performance measures (such as departmental reject rates) in favor of process management and global performance measures (such as customer satisfaction).

> active exercise

Take a moment to apply what you've learned.

ACCEPTABILITY VERSUS DESIRABILITY

The Ford Motor Company's experience illustrates the practical implications of these two orientations. In the late 1970s and early 1980s, Ford executives believed that their business encompassed four essential tasks: (1) the design, (2) parts manufacture, (3) assembly, and (4) distribution, sales, and servicing of automotive products. Based on an extensive analysis, Ford managers had concluded that the majority of the company's problems originated in parts manufacture. As a result, Ford executives had become convinced that they would have to improve the company's part-making capabilities significantly and were seriously considering outsourcing the majority of parts.

As an experiment, Ford managers decided to "clone" a Mazda transmission plant at their facility in Batavia, Ohio. Because of Ford's partial ownership of Mazda, Ford's designers were able to copy exactly the Japanese firm's technology, organization, layout, and product specifications. After the new plant went online, Ford used transmissions from both plants in its vehicles. Despite the similarity of the two plants, transmission-related warranty costs were roughly ten times greater for the transmissions that were made in Ohio than for those made in Japan.

What was the difference between the Japanese- and American-made transmissions, and why was the performance of the Mazda transmissions significantly superior to that of the Ford transmissions? First, Ford found that American employees defined a quality part as one that was built to specifications. A *specification,* or "spec," defines the boundary between that which is acceptable and that which is not. When asked where the specifications had come from, employees pointed to the process engineers. The process engineers, too, defined quality as conformance to specifications, but they maintained that those specifications came from the product engineers. The product engineers defined quality as the precision of specifications—but there was no science to setting specifications. Furthermore, the product engineers believed that making a specification more precise would raise both manufacturing costs and quality. They wrote their specifications so as to achieve acceptable cost and quality levels.

In contrast, Mazda's Japanese engineers defined quality in terms of appearance and functionality. When thinking of quality, they were more likely to consider a part's reliability and ultimate usefulness. They were also more willing to deviate from specifications (i.e., sacrifice acceptability) in order to satisfy their internal customers (i.e., enhance desirability). For example, they would readily shorten a part so that it would fit better with other parts or lengthen it so that it would attach more easily. In fact, in studying Mazda's parts, Ford's engineers found that they were roughly four times more likely to deviate from specifications than Ford's American-made parts. But though Mazda parts satisfied specifications less frequently, there was much less variability from part to part. The holistic thinking of the Japanese workers appeared to be the primary reason for the significantly superior performance of the Mazda transmissions.

In the context of acceptability, performance tends to improve only because problems arise, forcing change in the system. In contrast, the drive for continuous improvement is rooted in a focus on desirability. For example, while accepting America's top prize for quality in manufacturing in 1989, Xerox Chairman David Kearns explained, "We are in a race without a finish line. Because, as we improve, so does our competition. And the better we get, the more our customers expect from us."

SHORT-TERM PERFORMANCE VERSUS LONG-TERM MARKET SHARE

In the West, managers are frequently evaluated, rewarded, and promoted on the basis of short-term financial performance, partly because of the analytic orientation of Western culture and partly because of the tendency of stockholders to transfer their assets into companies whose shares are appreciating in value. The practice of rewarding short-term financial performance is widely seen as an obstacle to quality improvement efforts. Decisions that are made to generate short-term gains can send signals that overpower any or all of the four TQM commitments. For example, the desire to generate quarterly profits can lead to a decision to put off an improvement that everyone knows is necessary. Such a decision is inconsistent with both a commitment to the customer and a commitment to the process.

Japanese firms tend to place greater emphasis on garnering long-term market share, and they frequently sacrifice short-term profits in pursuit of that goal. Their emphasis on long-term market share is consistent with the commitment to customer satisfaction, continuous process improvement, employee involvement, and data-based decision making. Indeed, if a company expects its market share to grow, long-term investments in these areas are justifiable.

Brian Joiner, a well-known quality consultant, and his coauthor, Peter Scholtes, have pointed out the following negative outcomes of short-term managerial control:

- Measurable short-term accomplishments get attention, even though organizational survival may depend on unmeasurable activities with long-term consequences.
- Short-term control systems always intensify organizational conflict. For example, to make a sale in order to reach a monthly quota, marketing personnel might make a promise that production personnel cannot keep.
- When measurable controls are not practical or feasible, workers and managers play games with performance numbers to make themselves look better.
- Playing games closes down open communication and can lead to dishonesty, finger pointing, blame games, and excuse making.
- Blame games may cause "covering your rear" to become more important than doing the job.
- Employees are motivated by fear.
- Management focuses inward rather than on the customer.

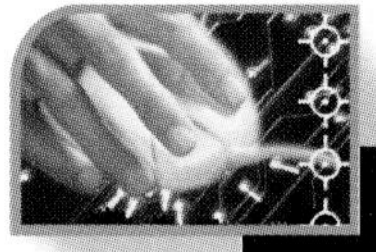

active exercise <

Take a moment to apply what you've learned.

REACTIVE RESPONSE VERSUS PROACTIVE SOLUTIONS

If an organization has not made the four commitments of TQM, it is likely to pursue objectives that are stated explicitly in financial terms. By the time customer problems or unique requests get the attention of managers, the matter has usually become urgent. As a result, managers are often willing to pay dearly for a quick fix. Pressured to get rid of the problem no matter what the cost, they will usually opt for some fancy technology or other expensive solution. After all, they need to have something to show for their investment.

One way that proactive quality efforts pay off is in repeat business, that is, when satisfied customers return to purchase more. Repeat customers are less expensive to attract than first-time customers, they require less effort and expense to acquaint with existing service processes, they are inclined to spend more on additional items and services, and they spread the positive word of mouth that is the lifeblood of any organization. The following list[1] provides several additional reasons for managers to proactively focus on long-term quality improvement:

- The average business only hears from 4% of its dissatisfied customers. Of the 96% who do not bother to complain, 25% have serious problems.
- The 4% who complain are more likely to stay with the supplier than the 96% who don't complain.
- About 60% of the complaining customers would stay as customers if their problems were resolved; 95% would stay if the problems were quickly resolved.

[1]From: James A. Fitzsimmons and Mona J. Fitzsimmons, *Service Management,* 2nd ed., Burr Ridge, Illinois: Irwin McGraw-Hill, 1994, p. 304.

- A dissatisfied customer will tell from 10 to 20 other people about his or her problem, but a customer whose problem has been resolved will only tell approximately five people.

These statistics regarding the impact of dissatisfied customers on future sales suggest that it is very important to have a recovery plan for the times when a customer is dissatisfied. This is especially important in service environments where customer contact is high. The term **service recovery** refers to converting a customer who is dissatisfied with a service into one who is satisfied. Unlike warranty-based product replacements that could occur months after a purchase, service recovery often has to happen at the time the service is being provided. For example, a patient receiving treatment from a physician might not get the relief she expected, even though the office featured the best equipment and techniques. Or perhaps an office staff member unknowingly made an insensitive comment to the patient. (Such situations can happen even in the best service facilities.) An organization without a service recovery plan might not even have a way to find out that the customer is dissatisfied, and if they do learn of the dissatisfaction might simply chalk up the dissatisfaction to a "you can't win them all" philosophy. An organization with a proactive approach to service recovery will seek to find out if their customers are satisfied and will act quickly to rectify any problems.

Key elements of a service recovery program include:

1. Recruiting, hiring, training, and promoting employees for excellence in service recovery.
2. Actively seeking customer complaints through such tools as toll-free customer service phone numbers, follow-up phone or mail surveys, and questioning customers about the service during service delivery.
3. Measuring the costs of dissatisfied customers and matching investments in quality improvement to the level of these costs.
4. Giving authority to front-line employees to take corrective action immediately upon learning of a customer's dissatisfaction.
5. Making managers easily available to customers.
6. Rewarding employees for superior service recovery efforts.
7. Including service recovery as part of the business strategy.
8. Committing top managers to strive for both service perfection and effective recovery plans.

When customer satisfaction is the key focus of the organization, managers will be proactive about customer service objectives in addition to their financial goals. In such companies, customer concerns have management's attention continuously, not just when things get out of hand. Therefore, managers are proactive in eliminating the root cause of potential problems, in order to prevent problems from occurring or recurring. Quick fixes and expensive solutions don't impress managers in these companies. Instead, they seek solutions that add value from the perspective of the customer.

> video exercise

Take a moment to apply what you've learned.

COMPETITIVE SOURCING VERSUS SUPPLY-CHAIN MANAGEMENT

Companies that frequently put their contracts up for bid in order to make their suppliers compete with one another generally find it difficult to get anything extra from their suppliers. That might be okay if the company is Boeing and they are buying candy to give away at trade shows. It might not be such a good idea if the company is Boeing and they're buying jet engines or a critical avionic instrument for their airplanes. It doesn't make sense for short-term suppliers to get involved in design projects with their customer, invest significantly in information systems linkages to their customer's facilities, or make capacity and facility plans favorable to their customers. The benefits that come from such cooperation are available only to customers who are willing to accept long-term relationships with suppliers. Obviously, the benefits coming from cooperative suppliers often outweigh the short-term material cost advantages that might come from awarding business on the basis of a competitive bidding system.

In the pursuit of quality, many firms are choosing to move toward a single supplier or a very select group of suppliers, for one item. Over the 1980s, for example, Xerox reduced the number of its suppliers from more than 5,000 to approximately 400. This approach may limit the buying organization's ability to bargain for the most competitive price. It also exposes the buying firm to the risk of supply shortages. On the other hand, it gives the buying firm time to investigate the costs of producing the item and to justify the price requested. It also enables buyers to work with suppliers in order to modify product or component designs, processes, or buyer–supplier linkages. By concentrating on improving the supply chain rather than administering contracts, firms can reduce both waste and the total cost of sourcing. The improved relationship with the supplier allows the firm to generate improvements over the long term. This is also true in service businesses; even McDonald's could be used as an example of a company that pursues long-term relationships with its suppliers.

The benefits of a cooperative supplier–purchaser relationship accrue not just to the buyer, but to the supplier as well. Suppliers receive many benefits in return for their cooperation, including long-term business commitments, more competitive customers, better information for use in planning and control, advance notice of new product designs and technologies, and assistance in making improvements.

CLASS THINKING VERSUS TEAM THINKING

Consider the view expressed by Kaoru Ishikawa:

> Companies exist in a society for the purpose of satisfying people in that society. This is the reason for their existence and should be their primary goal. . . . If people do not feel happy and cannot be made happy, that company does not deserve to exist. . . . The first order of business is to let the employees have adequate income. Their humanity must be respected, and they must be given an opportunity to enjoy their work and lead a happy life. The term "employees" as used here includes employees of subcontractors and affiliated sales and service organizations. . . . Customers come next. They must feel satisfied and pleased when they buy and use goods and services. . . . The welfare of shareholders must also be taken into consideration. . . . Each company must make sufficient profit to provide stock dividends for shareholders (Ishikawa 1985, 97–99).

The quality paradigm emphasizes that first and foremost, employees are human and must be treated with respect because of their humanity. It emphasizes the importance of each individual and the need for a team-oriented work environment. A person's job classification—salaried or hourly, management or labor—simply signals that he or she is an internal customer whose requirements must be met. At the very least, therefore, every employee should receive the same amount of respect as the firm's customers. Every function must contribute its unique expertise, not just to improve the system, but to satisfy the *person* who is the firm's ultimate customer. The focus shifts from job classes to teamwork, from organizational position to process improvement, and from cross-functional competition to cross-functional cooperation.

active concept check <

Now let's take a moment to test your knowledge of the concepts you have studied in this section.

> Leaders of the Quality Movement in the United States

The movement toward total quality management in the United States can be attributed to the enduring work of three crusaders: W. Edwards Deming, Joseph M. Juran, and Philip Crosby. In fact, these men preached quality as ardently as any religious leader. In recognition of the fact that they were attempting to change both managerial beliefs and corporate practices, they are commonly referred to as quality management *gurus*—a term that is used to communicate great respect for a person's wisdom and teachings.

W. EDWARDS DEMING

W. Edwards Deming (1900–1993) was born in Sioux City, South Dakota, and raised in Iowa and Wyoming. After earning a doctorate in mathematical physics from Yale in 1928, he taught statistics and served as a consultant for the rest of his career. As a result of his work in Japanese industry, Deming is often credited with sparking the revolution in Japanese manufacturing practice that made that nation a global competitor. Indeed, one of the highest honors a contemporary Japanese businessperson or company can win is the Deming Prize. Deming received the Order of the Sacred

Treasure from the Emperor of Japan in 1960. Later, as a result of the success of Japanese industry, he gained a following in the United States and in 1987 was awarded the National Medal of Technology by President Reagan. Deming continued his efforts to transform American industry until his death in 1993.

In the fall of 1927, Deming met Dr. Walter Shewhart of Bell Laboratories. Deming later attributed much of the content of his books, as well as the philosophy he presented in his seminars, to Shewhart's teachings. Deming's major idea, the Deming chain reaction (see Figure 5.3), was that quality improvement is not a costly business option but a strategic imperative that is essential to business survival. If quality improves, productivity will improve, because fewer defects imply less waste. Productivity improvement, in turn, confers the ability to lower prices. Coupled with higher quality, lower prices can lead to increased market share, which implies the ability not only to stay in business but to provide more jobs. This message, while it sounds quite reasonable in retrospect, was once a revolutionary one to American managers, who have traditionally focused on cost containment for the sake of enhanced short-term financial performance.

The **P-D-C-A cycle** (also called the Shewhart cycle, or the Deming cycle) is a set of steps to be repeated in the pursuit of continuous improvement. It includes four steps: Plan, Do, Check, and Act (see Figure 5.4). Both Japanese and American managers now apply this cycle to specific processes, as well as in their general approach to running their organizations. They do so by first *planning* an improvement, then *doing* what they have planned, perhaps on a test basis. They then *check* to see if the results are consistent with their expectations. When they are convinced that a plan is working, they *act* to fully implement it. They then improve the newly implemented plan by putting it through another P-D-C-A cycle.

Deming is best known for his 14-point philosophy, which is summarized in Table 5.3. The 14 points should not be seen as a menu from which managers may pick and choose. Rather, they represent a complete package in which each individual point is essential to the whole. Deming designed the 14 points to counter what he called the "seven deadly diseases" and "other serious obstacles" to improvement (see Table 5.4). For most traditionally managed organizations, the 14 points represent an alternative business paradigm. (To put this paradigm into perspective, it is helpful to remember that Deming was a statistician. His work promotes constancy of purpose, and thereby the reduction of process variation.)

Many American managers find Deming's philosophy difficult to accept. For example, American managers tend to rely heavily on work standards to establish pay scales for workers. Yet Deming's 11th point says to do away with them. Whether or not a manager accepts Deming's advice, he or she should recognize that worker performance will vary from day to day and hour to hour. A worker who is doing his best will meet the standard at times but will not meet it at others. Unfortunately, the work

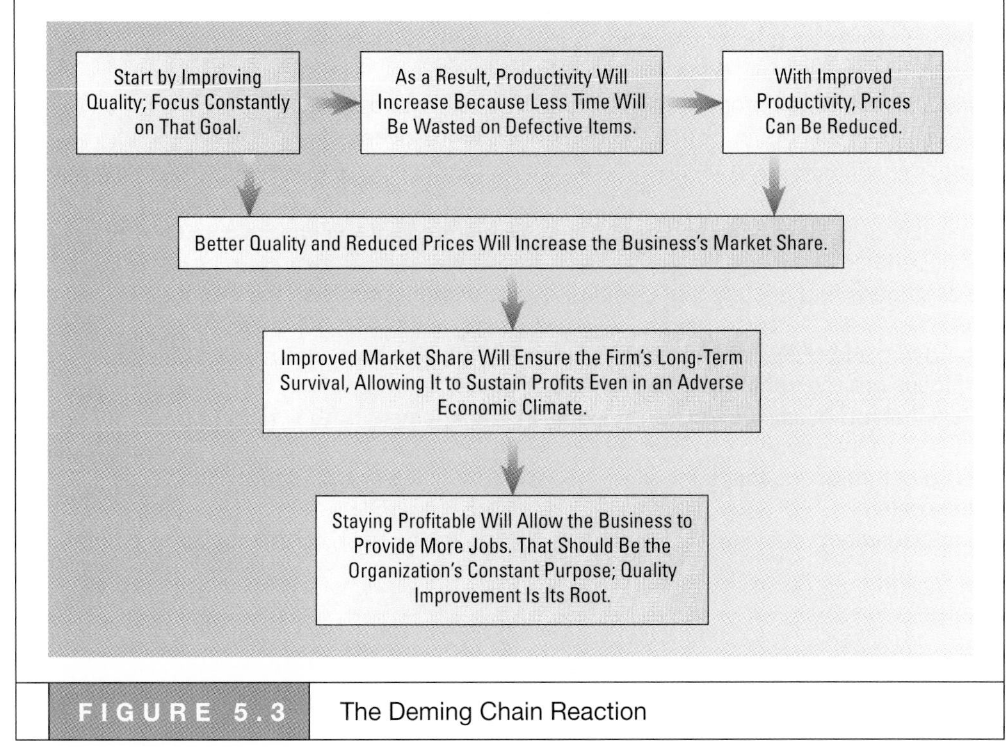

FIGURE 5.3 The Deming Chain Reaction

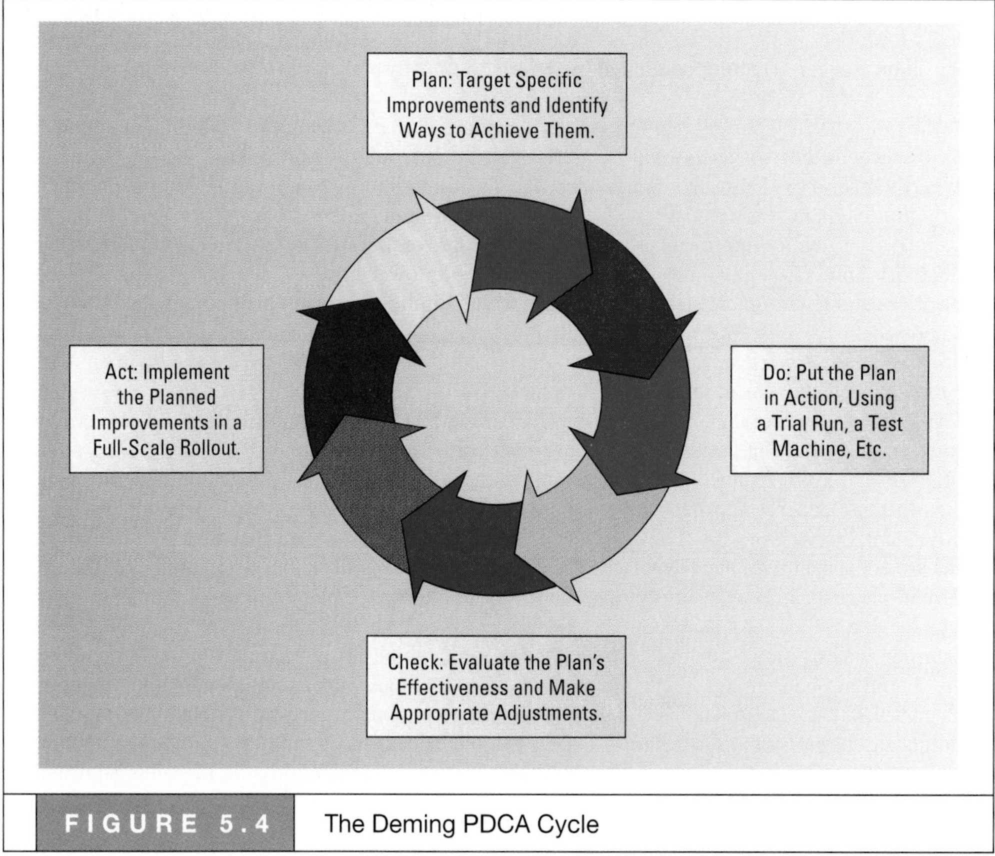
Plan: Target Specific Improvements and Identify Ways to Achieve Them.
Do: Put the Plan in Action, Using a Trial Run, a Test Machine, Etc.
Check: Evaluate the Plan's Effectiveness and Make Appropriate Adjustments.
Act: Implement the Planned Improvements in a Full-Scale Rollout.

FIGURE 5.4 The Deming PDCA Cycle

TABLE 5.3 Deming's Fourteen-Point Philosophy

1. Create constancy of purpose for continual improvement of products and service with a plan to become competitive, stay in business, and provide jobs.
2. Adopt the new philosophy in its entirety. We are in a new economic age.
3. Cease dependence on mass inspection by building quality into the system.
4. End the practice of awarding business based on the price tag alone.
5. Improve constantly and forever the process for planning production and service.
6. Institute ongoing training on the job for both management and employees.
7. Institute leadership. Management must create an environment that helps workers to do their job well.
8. Drive out fear.
9. Break down organizational barriers based on department or hierarchical level and establish effective cross-functional cooperation.
10. Eliminate the use of slogans and posters that demand quality without providing the methods for improvement.
11. Eliminate work standards and management goals that are unchanging and arbitrarily applied to everyone. Instead focus on leadership for improvement of quality.
12. Remove the barriers that rob hourly workers and people in management of their right to pride of workmanship.
13. Institute a vigorous program of education for all employees. Improving knowledge will lead to improvement of the system.
14. Demonstrate top management commitment to the new philosophy by pushing the above 13 points every day.

TABLE 5.4 The Seven Deadly Diseases and Other Obstacles to Improvement

Seven Deadly Diseases:

1. Lack of constancy of purpose.
2. Focus on short-term profits—it prohibits constancy of focus and improvement.
3. Performance appraisal systems—they reinforce number 2 and prevent number 1.
4. Job hopping—it reinforces number 2 and number 3 and prevents number 1.
5. Using only visible figures—they may not be meaningful and can easily be manipulated in the short-term.
6. Excessive medical costs (in the United States)—lead to a bias for technology and against the worker and is a societal problem that must be dealt with. (The medical insurance cost for a machine is $0.00; the cost for a worker is much higher and somewhat difficult to project over the long-term; so when a machine can replace a worker, management will lean toward the machine.)
7. Excessive costs of liability—the legal issues can prevent good faith efforts to improve and handcuff management leaders. (For example, management might decide not to study and document the certain quality characteristics in a process that makes airbag triggers for fear that the results might eventually be used against them in a lawsuit.)

Other Obstacles:

1. Hoping for or expecting a quick fix.
2. Believing that automation, new technologies, or solving problems will transform industry and make it competitive.
3. Relying on examples instead of theory. It's better to understand and apply theory than to copy examples.
4. "That won't work here" attitudes.
5. Obsolescence in schools of business.
6. Poor teaching of statistical methods in industry.
7. Inspecting materials after production instead of focusing on improvement.
8. Delegating quality problems to the "quality control department."
9. Blaming the workers for quality problems.
10. Relying on techniques and programs instead of knowledge.
11. Using computers but not the information they can provide.
12. Thinking that it's enough to meet the specifications and focusing on producing zero defects.
13. Inadequate testing of prototypes—these are only made once (i.e., they're "one-offs") and can't tell you about process variation.
14. Thinking that only "experts" that understand our business can help.

standard fails to accommodate this natural variation in human performance. Therefore, using a work standard may seem generous to the worker at times and oppressive at others. If managers fail to understand the natural variations in worker performance and use work standards blindly, their insensitivity may actually prove harmful to workers' morale.

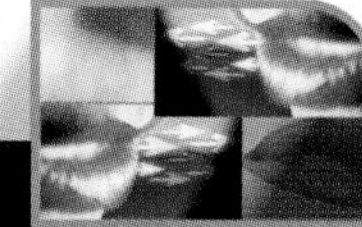

> active poll

What do you think? Voice your opinion and find out what others have to say.

JOSEPH M. JURAN

Joseph M. Juran (1904–) began his career as an industrial engineer in the inspection department at the Hawthorne Plant of the Western Electric Company. At that time, one out of every eight employees at the plant was an inspector! While at Hawthorne, Juran prepared the pamphlet *Statistical Methods Applied to Manufacturing Problems* and used it to teach Shewhart's concepts in evening courses for workers. By 1937, Juran had been promoted to corporate industrial engineer and had transferred to Western Electric's New York headquarters. In 1941, following U.S. entry into the Second World War, he left Western Electric to serve his country as an administrator.

When the war ended, Juran chose not to return to Western Electric. Instead, he embarked on a career of helping managers to understand quality issues and improve their systems. To that end he compiled *Juran's Quality Control Handbook* (1951), a classic which is still in print and is regarded as the most exhaustive reference book on quality management. In 1979, he founded the Juran Institute, which today provides training and consulting services throughout the industrialized world.

Like Deming, Juran had great success in working with Japanese industrial clients in the 1950s and 1960s. Later, in the 1970s and 1980s, he became influential in the American quality revolution. He, too, has been awarded the Order of the Sacred Treasure by the Emperor of Japan and has received the U.S. National Medal of Technology. But while Deming approached the subject of quality as a statistician, Juran approached it as an engineer and a manager. Juran thought that quality improvement issues should be presented in the language of management, which is primarily a financial language. Furthermore, he saw quality itself as a financial issue. Quality costs can be measured, and quality improvement projects represent investment opportunities whose returns often cannot be matched by other types of investments.

Quality Costs

Juran suggested that quality costs be divided into four categories: internal failure costs, external failure costs, appraisal costs, and prevention costs. **Internal failure costs** are expenditures associated with products, subassemblies, or components that are not fit for use and have not yet been transferred to the customer. The cost of scrap, rework, and avoidable process losses (like container overflow), as well as the cost of dealing with scrap and rework—such as reinspection, downgrading, and failure analysis costs—are all internal failure costs. **External failure costs** are expenditures associated with items that are not fit for use but have nevertheless been transferred to the customer. Warranty charges and the costs of investigating customer complaints, returning and replacing materials, and making concessions to customers are all external failure costs. **Appraisal costs** are expenditures associated with the inspection and testing of materials and services at any point in a value-adding process. **Prevention costs** are expenses accrued in efforts to prevent failure and appraisal costs. Process control costs, as well as the cost of product design reviews, quality audits, supplier evaluations, training, and quality planning, are prevention costs.

Juran's four quality costs relate directly to service environments as well as manufacturing environments. For example, a credit union incurs prevention costs in the areas of quality planning, recruitment and selection, training programs, computer system backups, credit checks on loan applicants, and quality improvement programs. Appraisal costs cover activities such as periodic inspection of equipment, monitoring service performance (such as the average time it takes to serve a customer during the lunch hour), daily balancing of accounts, periodic auditing, and collecting data regarding customer satisfaction. Internal failure costs include scrapped paperwork, adjusting for incorrect teller transactions, redoing paperwork and government reports with errors, the cost of writing-off or collecting-on delinquent loans, and equipment downtime. External failure costs involve interest penalties, time involved in tracking down the cause of a customer-reported transaction error and making adjustments, negative judgments arising from lawsuits against the bank, payments made to external collection agencies for delinquent loans, and lost future business.

In manufacturing settings, the obvious costs of poor quality include reprocessing, production and disposal of rejects, sorting and inspection, warranty programs, customer claims, and product downgrades. But those costs are likely to be minor compared to the hidden costs of poor quality, which could include lost sales, lost goodwill, process downtime, overtime to correct errors, extra inventory, delays in delivery, penalties for late delivery, lost discounts, damage to other goods, inventory obsolescence, extra charges for expedited delivery services such as overnight shipping, extra process capacity, and the costly adjustments customers make to overcome supplier errors. Although estimating the exact cost of poor quality is difficult, an attempt to do so can be helpful in setting priorities for improvement. Though data are difficult to obtain, common estimates suggest that product-service complexity has a strong influence on these costs, which may range from 5% to 35% of sales for manufacturing companies, and 25% to 40% of operating expenses for other companies.

In recent years, it has become clear that in many settings, companies can achieve 100% conformance to quality specifications through the use of modern technologies and the effective design of products and processes. [Conformance to a quality specification simply means meeting the specification. A company with 100% conformance over a given period has experienced no nonconforming (or defective) items during that time.] The long-term goal of most organizations is to achieve 100% conformance. Figure 5.5(a) illustrates the relationship among prevention, appraisal, and failure costs in such a setting. Efforts to eliminate defects through prevention and appraisal become more costly as

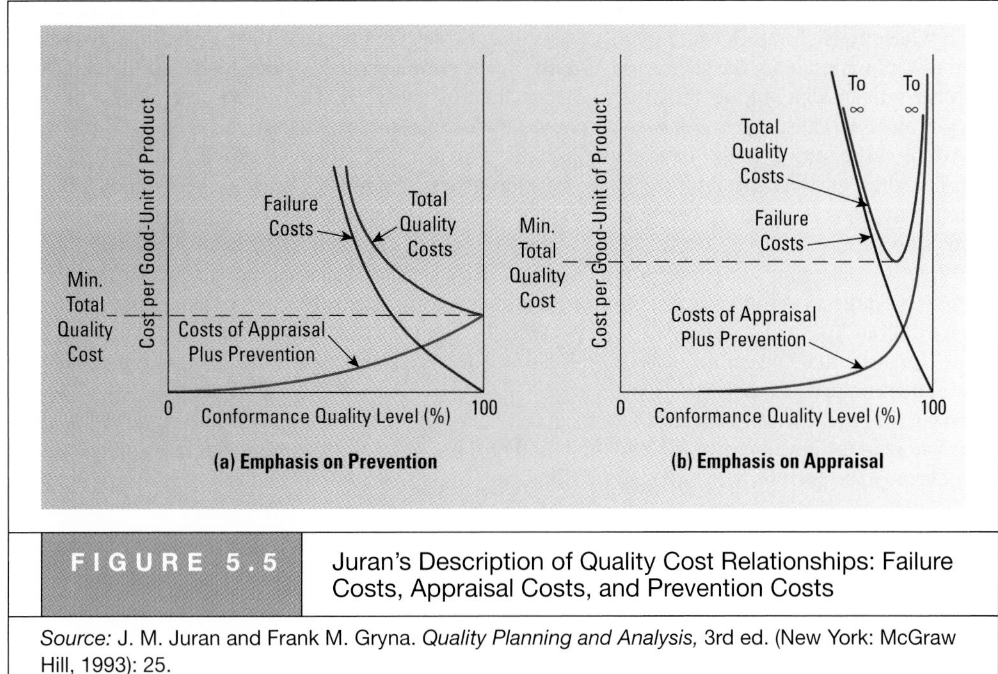

FIGURE 5.5 Juran's Description of Quality Cost Relationships: Failure Costs, Appraisal Costs, and Prevention Costs

Source: J. M. Juran and Frank M. Gryna. *Quality Planning and Analysis,* 3rd ed. (New York: McGraw Hill, 1993): 25.

100% conformance is approached, yet failure costs continue to decline. As a result, the total quality costs are at their lowest when the company attains 100% conformance.

In certain situations 100% conformance may not be feasible, especially in the short run. Figure 5.5(b) illustrates this second situation. If an organization is operating to the left of the minimum point on the total quality cost curve, managers will be motivated to spend more on appraisal and prevention because a small expense in these areas can lead to significant savings in failure costs, thus lowering the total quality costs. If an organization is operating to the right of the minimum point, managers are likely to cut back on inspection or product testing or find other ways to reduce appraisal and prevention costs. Realizing that failure costs are likely to increase with such an action, they will look for ways to scale back the appraisal and prevention costs that have the smallest impact on failure costs. Organizations that are operating close to the minimum point on the total quality cost curve will try to continue balancing appraisal and prevention costs with failure costs in the way that led them to this minimum point.

Once an organization has performed a cost-of-quality analysis, managers will begin to think of quality improvement in financial terms. In fact, they might realize that quality improvement projects offer a far superior return than stock buy-backs, the purchase of equity in other firms, or new product development. Thinking about quality in financial terms also helps top managers to see the importance of their own participation in quality-related activities.

> active exercise

Take a moment to apply what you've learned.

Quality Management

Because top management is intimately familiar with the three basic financial management activities—financial planning (budgeting), financial control (budget monitoring), and financial improvement (increasing income and reducing costs)—Juran suggested that the management of quality include the same three managerial processes: quality planning, quality control, and quality improvement. **Quality planning** means defining the organization's mission regarding quality, identifying customers' needs regarding quality and translating those needs into developed products, and developing the processes for ensuring quality and transferring those processes to operations. **Quality control** means determining whether the organization's quality plans are achieving the desired outcomes and taking remedial action when they are not. Because quality control processes identify sporadic problems, they are oriented toward maintaining the status quo. **Quality improvement** means reducing costs and increasing customer satisfaction, product reliability, and product longevity. Quality improvement happens project by project. Because it reduces costs, it plays a major role in changing the status quo.

To help companies organize their activities in order to promote quality improvement, Juran devised what he called the *breakthrough sequence* for eliminating chronic waste in the production process. Table 5.5 outlines Juran's breakthrough sequence. The organizational approach he described was not meant to be applied to the "useful many" projects, which can be carried out by empowering all employees to make improvements within their own work areas or departments. Nor was it intended to address sporadic problems, which should be addressed through process control. Instead, it was designed to address the "vital few" system-wide problems, which are usually cross-functional in nature. Changes that correct this sort of problem frequently produce quantum leaps in organizational capabilities and productivity.

Today Juran is recognized, especially by quality management professionals, as one of the leading contributors to the development of the field. His contributions to the development of useful techniques and generally accepted principles has had a significant impact on the way quality concerns are actually

TABLE 5.5 Juran's Breakthrough Sequence

1. **Prove the need for breakthrough and management's willingness to support necessary changes.** Management must recognize its responsibility for the system and the competitive importance of improvements that eliminate chronic waste. Quantum leaps in quality performance can only come from management-sponsored system changes. A Quality Council of the top executives of the company should be formed. The Quality Council should include representation of all key business functions. A Diagnostic Group composed of quality professionals and analysts should also be formed to aid the Quality Council.
2. **Identify desirable projects and prioritize them.** "Pareto analysis" should be used by the Diagnostic Group to help the Quality Council distinguish between the vital few projects and the useful many. Oftentimes the vital few will be cross-functional in nature and require the Quality Council's sponsorship. The useful many projects will frequently pertain to only one department. They do not require the direct attention of the Quality Council since they can be implemented within the improvement plans of the department affected.
3. **Organize project teams.** It is important to publish the projects and team members selected and to make the projects part of the business plan. This provides rights for the teams to call meetings, get help from experts, request sensitive information and the like. Each team has its own organizational structure—a leader, members, rules for attendance, etc. A team should have a sponsor since it is not a part of the organizational hierarchy.
4. **Verify the project need and mission.** Each team should be supervised by a mission statement, which may be drafted by the Diagnostic Group, but must be approved by the Quality Council. Team members should begin by documenting the specifics of the situation for which their mission gives them responsibility.
5. **Diagnose the causes.** The team must begin with a "diagnostic journey" involving analysis of symptoms, developing theories as to the causes of the problems, testing the plausible theories, and finally establishing the root of the problem being addressed.
6. **Provide a remedy and prove that it works effectively.** The diagnostic journey is followed by a "remedial journey" that requires the development of alternative remedies for the problem, testing the various options to select the preferred solution, testing the selected solution in simulated conditions, testing the remedy in real world conditions, and establishing controls for the new situation.
7. **Deal with resistance to change.** Anticipate that the remedy will be met with natural resistance to change—and will be new to everyone outside of the team unless the team has worked hard to build bridges that others can cross. It is important to treat people with dignity, provide for participation, provide ample time for consideration, work with recognized leaders, include no excess baggage, and clearly establish the need for the change. Resistance to change must be addressed directly. Negative attitudes that sabotage improvement efforts must be overcome.
8. **Institute controls to hold gains.** Process changes should be designed to be irreversible, and the new system should be sustainable under real operating conditions. New operating procedures must be developed and appropriate training provided to those who are affected by the change.

managed. Additionally, his books are still widely read, and the Juran Institute continues to provide useful guidance to clients all over the world.

PHILIP CROSBY

Unlike Juran and Deming, Philip Crosby (1926–) began his career in quality as an inspector and worked his way up through the ranks of quality professions. Along the way he was also a tester, assistant foreman, junior engineer, reliability engineer, group engineer, section chief, manager, director, and corporate vice president. (He ended his corporate career as ITT's vice president of quality.) According to Crosby, this tour of duty helped him to see quality management in terms of who does what specific job and to view these concepts in a people-oriented way. It comes as no surprise, then, that he felt one of the most important components of a quality improvement program was training. In 1979, he formed the Crosby Quality College to train managers in quality improvement. The practical suggestions included in Crosby's training programs have been found useful by hundreds of managers.

> active concept check

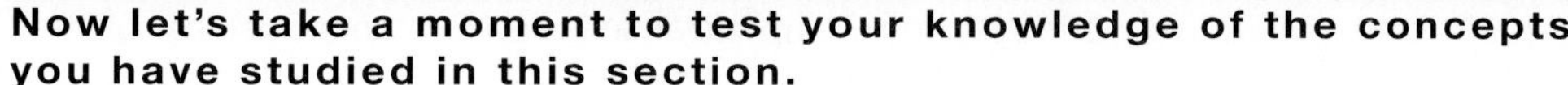

Now let's take a moment to test your knowledge of the concepts you have studied in this section.

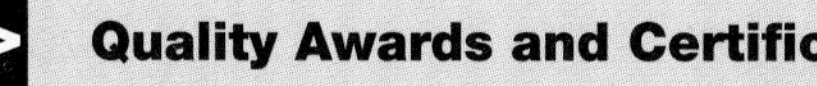

Quality Awards and Certifications

There are numerous quality-related awards and certifications that companies might choose to pursue. Some of these are industry specific, while others are available within only one state or country. In this section we describe America's most prestigious quality award which applies to virtually all industries, and the ISO 9000 certification program which has a global reach in all industries.

THE BALDRIGE AWARD

The **Baldrige Award** is the United States's national quality award. Created by an act of Congress in 1987, it is believed to have played a significant role in promoting quality management practices. The award was named after Malcolm Baldrige, U.S. Secretary of Commerce from 1981 to 1987, whose managerial excellence is credited with long-term improvements in the efficiency and effectiveness of the U.S. government.

The purpose of the Malcolm Baldrige National Quality Award is to highlight the performance of firms that have attained excellence in quality management. The award could be given to no more than two firms in each of three categories: manufacturing, service, and small business in any given year until 1998. At that time the program was expanded to include education and health care. Table 5.6 lists the winners of the Baldrige Award from 1988 through 1999.

> active example

Take a closer look at the concepts and issues you've been reading about.

The Baldrige Award has already paid dividends for American business. It has heightened corporate awareness of state-of-the-art quality management practices. Applying for the award can be expensive and time consuming, so that relatively few firms decide to apply each year. Nevertheless, more than 1 million copies of the award criteria were distributed between 1987 and 1995. Many firms, perhaps thousands, conduct internal assessments of their quality practices based on the Baldrige Award criteria. They then use the information they have obtained to identify opportunities for improvement. All told, the Baldrige Award has done a great deal to enhance quality improvement efforts in American companies.

TABLE 5.6 Baldrige Award Winners, 1988 to 1999

Year	Winning Companies
1988	• Motorola Incorporated • Westinghouse Electric Corporation, Commercial Nuclear Fuels Division • Globe Metallurgical Incorporated
1989	• Milliken & Company • Xerox Corporation, Business Products and Systems
1990	• Cadillac Motor Car Division • IBM Rochester • Federal Express Corporation • Wallace Co. Incorporated
1991	• Solectron Corporation • Zytec Corporation • Marlow Industries
1992	• AT&T Network Systems Group—Transmission Systems Business Unit • Defense Systems & Electronics Group • AT&T Universal Card Services • The Ritz-Carlton Hotel Company • Granite Rock Company
1993	• Eastman Chemical Company • Ames Rubber Corporation
1994	• AT&T Consumer Communication Services • GTE Directories Corporation • Wainwright Industries
1995	• Armstrong World Industries' Building Products Operation • Corning Telecommunications Products Division
1996	• Trident Precision Manufacturing • Custom Research • Adac Labs • Dana Commercial Credit
1997	• 3M Dental Products Division • Merrill Lynch Credit Corporation • Solectron Corporation • Xerox Business Systems
1998	• Boeing Airlift and Tanker Programs • Solar Turbines, Inc. • Texas Nameplate Company, Inc.
1999	• STMicroelectronics, Inc.—Region Americas • BI • The Ritz-Carlton Hotel Co., L.L.C. • Sunny Fresh Foods

Table 5.7 identifies the criteria and scoring for the 1999 Baldrige Award. According to the administrators of the award, world-class companies should be able to achieve and maintain a score of over 70%. To do so, (1) the firm's performance must be good to excellent in most key areas; (2) it must sustain most of its improvement trends or performance levels; and (3) in many, if not most, areas of performance and improvement, the firm must lead or compare very well to benchmark companies.

The Baldrige Award is Americas top quality award. See their web site at http://www.quality.nist.gov/.

For most American companies, a score of 25% would be an accurate evaluation. Such a score would suggest that a company is beginning to establish a systematic approach to dealing with the evaluation criteria. That is, it is beginning to move away from a reactive approach to quality and toward the continuous improvement of processes. Because the firm is just beginning to develop quality management capabilities, major gaps exist in its managerial approach. Figure 5.6 presents the Baldrige Award criteria framework, which shows the interrelationships among the examination criteria. To learn more about the Baldrige Award, check out the following web site: http://www.quality.nist.gov/

> active exercise

Take a moment to apply what you've learned.

ISO 9000 CERTIFICATION

The International Organization for Standardization is a worldwide federation of national standards organizations. The United States's representative is the National Institute for Standards and Technology (NIST), which is part of the U.S. Commerce Department. One division of NIST, the American National Standards Institute (ANSI), is responsible for developing the standards used by American industry. ANSI maintains the American version of the ISO 9000 standard (titled ANSI/ASQC Q90-1987) in cooperation with the American Society for Quality Control (ASQC). Because local standardization authorities differ, most countries have local versions of (and local names for) the ISO 9000 standards.

The International Organization for Standardization established its uniform quality standards in 1987. The **ISO 9000 standards** are actually a series of standards, including:

- ISO 9000—A summary and guide to the other standards in the series. (The American equivalent is ANSI/ASQC Q90-1987.)
- ISO 9001—The most comprehensive standard; includes 20 system requirements for design, development, production, installation, and servicing. (The American version is ANSI/ASQC Q91-1987.)
- ISO 9002—A standard that includes 18 system requirements for manufacturing and installation. It does not include requirements dealing with design and after-sale service which are a part of ISO 9001. (The American version is ANSI/ASQC Q92-1987.)

TABLE 5.7	1999 Baldrige Award Categories, Items and Point Values	
1999 Categories/Items	**Point Values**	
1.0	**Leadership**	**125**
1.1	Organizational Leadership	85
1.2	Public Responsibility and Citizenship	40
2.0	**Strategic Planning**	**85**
2.1	Strategy Development	40
2.2	Strategy Deployment	45
3.0	**Customer and Market Focus**	**60**
3.1	Customer and Market Knowledge	30
3.2	Customer Satisfaction and Relationships	30
4.0	**Information and Analysis**	**85**
4.1	Measurement of Organizational Performance	40
4.2	Analysis of Organizational Performance	45
5.0	**Human Resource Focus**	**85**
5.1	Work Systems	35
5.2	Employee Education, Training, and Development	25
4.4	Employee Well-Being and Satisfaction	25
6.0	**Process Management**	**100**
6.1	Product and Service Processes	55
6.2	Support Processes	15
6.3	Supplier and Partnering Processes	30
7.0	**Business Results**	**450**
7.1	Customer-Focused Results	115
7.2	Financial and Market Results	115
7.3	Human Resource Results	80
7.4	Supplier and Partner Results	25
7.5	Organizational Effectiveness Results	115
	Total Points	**1000**

Source: Malcolm Baldrige National Quality Award 1999 Criteria for Performance Excellence at http:www.quality.nist.gov.

- ISO 9003—A standard for final inspection and testing that includes 12 system requirements. (The American equivalent is ANSI/ASQC Q93-1987.)
- ISO 9004—A guideline for the development of quality management systems.

The primary benefit of ISO certification is the market access it provides. ISO certification was originally intended as a requirement for doing business in certain industries within the European Community (EC) and with the governments of EC countries. The idea was that a common standard would prevent a company from having to comply with separate standards in every country where it did business. Even outside the EC, obtaining such certification frequently allows firms to avoid meeting the requirements of various supplier certification programs promoted by their customers. In fact, many firms now require their suppliers to be ISO-certified, and even more prefer ISO-certified suppliers over those that are not certified.

You might have guessed that ISO is an acronym for International Organization for Standardization, but it is not. *ISO* comes from the Greek word *isos,* meaning "equal." It has the same meaning as the

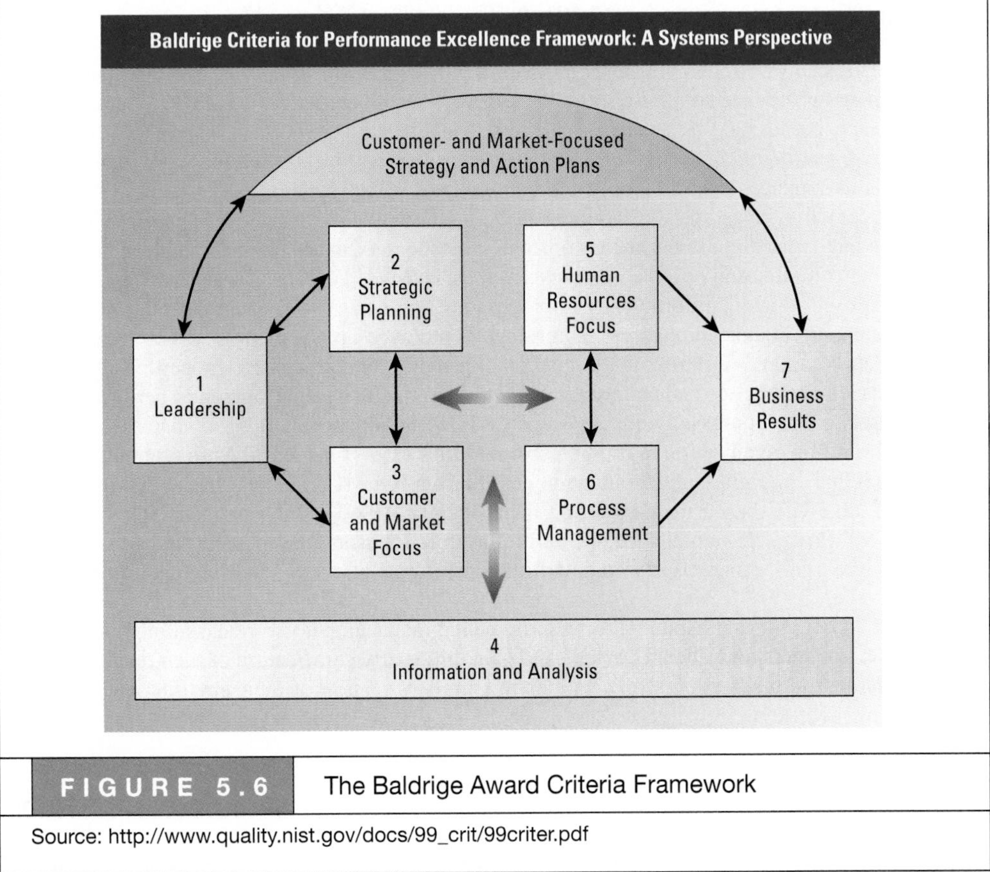

FIGURE 5.6 The Baldrige Award Criteria Framework

Source: http://www.quality.nist.gov/docs/99_crit/99criter.pdf

prefix that is used in the terms *isosceles triangle*, *isobars* (on a weather map), and *isometric exercise.* Certification under the ISO 9000 standards, then, simply means that a registered third-party examiner has determined that the procedures actually used by the certified organization are the same as the procedures described in their own documentation.

The ISO standards received stiff criticism in the 1990s. Juran has been known to complain, "There is nothing in ISO 9000 about continuous quality improvement, customer satisfaction, or employee involvement" (*Quality Progress,* October 1993, 63–65). Bergman and Klefsjö have estimated that a company could get as few as 250 points on a Baldrige Award examination and still become ISO 9001 certified! As a result of these criticisms, the ISO quality standards have recently been revised to focus more on customer satisfaction and process improvement. The new standards are currently being referred to as ISO 9000: 2000.

> active exercise

Take a moment to apply what you've learned.

> active concept check

Now let's take a moment to test your knowledge of the concepts you have studied in this section.

Quality Management and the Environment

In recent years, many customers have begun to expect organizations to provide products and services without damaging the natural environment or creating significant safety hazards to humans. Since customers expect a business to be environmentally friendly, environmental performance is a quality issue for firms that define quality in terms of customer satisfaction. In fact, there are many linkages between quality management and the natural environment. Quality management allows firms to produce fewer defective items and thus to generate less environmental waste. (This point is especially important in industries that use hazardous or toxic substances.) Quality management can also be used to develop more durable and reliable products and thus to reduce landfill. Quality management procedures can be used to maintain efficiency in process operations and to prevent emissions of environmentally damaging liquids and vapors. Increasingly, employee involvement teams are being used to allow workers to address environmental concerns in their work processes. Indeed, virtually every quality management practice can be leveraged to enhance the firm's environmental performance.

Some firms are so impressed with the value of TQM in addressing environmental concerns that they have formed an organization to promote **Total Quality Environmental Management (TQEM),** called the Global Environmental Management Initiative (GEMI). GEMI's membership is mostly made up of large U.S.-based manufacturing firms such as Allied Signal, Amoco, Anheuser-Busch, Boeing, AT&T, Proctor & Gamble, Merck, and Johnson & Johnson. The focus of TQEM is to make it every employee's job to proactively find and implement cost-effective environmental improvement solutions.

The ISO 14000 series of standards for environmental management was released in 1996. Much as the ISO 9000 standards now allow companies to gain third-party certification of their quality systems, the **ISO 14000 standards** allow organizations to gain certification of their environmental management systems (EMS).

active concept check

Now let's take a moment to test your knowledge of the concepts you have studied in this section.

Integrating Operational Decisions

This chapter is in the part of the text where we're building the overarching concepts within which operational systems are developed and run. Obviously, you could find a linkage between the material in this chapter and every other chapter in this book. This chapter on total quality management is closely linked to Chapters 4 and 7, which deal with the design of the product-service bundle and value-adding system. This linkage highlights the perspective of Deming and Juran that it is the system responsible for delivering quality and satisfying customers. Once the product-service bundle's design is finalized, the opportunity to improve customer satisfaction is limited. Similarly, once the value-adding system's design is finalized, large-scale changes to enhance customer satisfaction are difficult to make. Chapter 6, which presents quality improvement tools, is obviously closely linked to this chapter because it is a glimpse into the methodologies that can be used to make data-driven decisions that enhance quality.

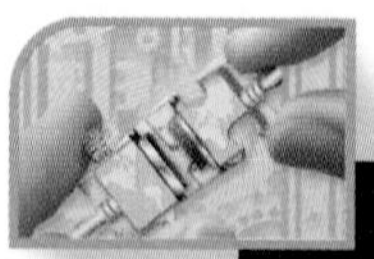

integrated OM

Take a moment to apply what you've learned.

> Chapter Wrap-Up

In the 1950s, visionary thinkers such as Joseph Juran and W. Edwards Deming helped Japanese managers learn how to manage their operations so as to increase quality. Along with Armand Fiegenbaum, Juran and Deming warned American businesspeople that in a consumer society, quality would become more and more important to their success. Quality management practices, on the other hand, would actually make firms more efficient. Not until the late 1980s did their approach catch on in the United States. Since then American business has gone through a period of revitalization so significant that it has been termed the "Second Industrial Revolution." Total quality management was at the heart of that revitalization. Partly because of the success of TQM, American business leaders now have a renewed understanding of the importance of operations management to business success. In fact, Juran has predicted that just as the 20th century was the century of productivity, the 21st will be the century of quality.

For most American firms, adopting TQM required significant changes in their usual way of thinking and doing business. Those changes represented a paradigm shift in managers' understanding of the importance of customer satisfaction, process improvement, employee involvement, and data-based decision making. They also increased managers' appreciation for holistic thinking, single sourcing, a long-term focus on market share, the pursuit of perfection, the proactive treatment of quality issues, and respect for the humanity of workers.

The total quality management movement has now spread well beyond the manufacturing sector. Quality awards, such as the Baldrige Award, the Deming Prize, and the European Quality Award, are offered in several classes, including services. Government, educational institutions, and other public entities are under strong pressure to improve their operational performance using TQM principles, and quality awards have been established to recognize their achievements. The growing importance of standards such as the ISO 9000 series shows that quality has become a globally accepted requirement for market entry.

Quality management applies to much more than the products companies produce; it is central to the work life of employees, including their safety, health, and morale. Recently, forward-thinking managers have recognized that quality management may also help to improve the environmental performance of business and thus to preserve our natural heritage for future generations.

> end-of-chapter resources

- **Practice Quiz**
- **Key Terms**
- **Discussion Questions**
- **Case 5.1: Quality and Customer Service At The IRS**
- **References**
- **Plant Tours**

C H A P T E R 6

Quality Improvement Tools

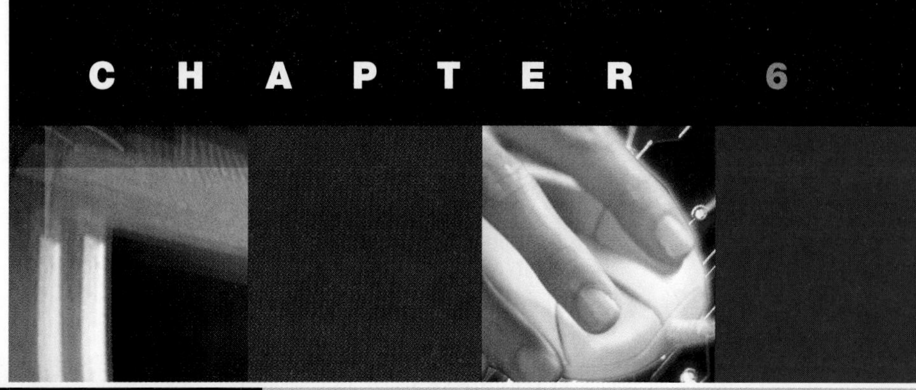

Chapter Outline

What's Ahead

. . . BACK AT THE REC CENTER

"The club is a little busier than usual this morning," noted Luis, as he and Fred left the locker room to get started.

"I guess a lot of people need to vent their frustration this morning," Fred replied, remembering how a few weeks earlier he had felt the need to get up before sunrise when a client was pressing him on his defects rate. "For a lot of these people, this must be a great way to clear the head for the day's trials and tribulations. We've had our customers on our heels for a month or so over our defect rates. I was really upset about it last month, and coming here to 'work it out,' so to speak, helped a lot."

"Well, you seemed to get a lot of advice last month. Did it do you any good?" Luis asked.

"It's still too early to tell," Fred responded. "We've got a long way to go to get to where we're comfortable, but I heard some of the things Tom and Cheryl said about quality. It's starting to really hit home."

"Oops! There they are. Let's not let them get too big-headed," Luis joked, pointing Tom and Cheryl out to Fred. "Time to pay homage to the health club TQM gurus."

"Hey, I heard that!" Cheryl said, without looking up from the leg press station. "Just because you thought Juran and his brother were part of a rock group from the 80s!"

"Yeah, you thought Crosby played a TV doctor named Huckstable—I won't even ask about Deming," Tom joked, as he and Cheryl each finished a set of ab crunches.

"It's been awhile since we talked about it, but now that you bring it up, Fred, how's it going with all that quality stuff your customers were hassling you about?" asked Tom. He wondered whether Fred or his company had given any real thought to the things that the group had discussed while working out last month.

"Yeah, some," Fred replied. "Luis and I were just saying that it was starting to take shape." Fred said that their advice has been helpful, too. At least now he knows what he needs to do. He was referring to his company's efforts to redefine the customer's needs and expectations and decide how to deal with them. Fred and his coworkers know that low cost is important, but so are consistent performance and the value they add through some of the little things they do to compete—like making smaller, more frequent deliveries inside tighter time windows. "I guess it's kind of like we put a new coat of paint on the building and then stuck a sign in front that says 'new and improved.' Now we have to back it up!"

"The way you were talking earlier, I thought you had actually started to change some things," noted Luis.

"Well, we have done more," Fred went on, growing more confident about the topic as he went along. As an example, he mentioned that there had been a lot of complaints about the fit between the pager casings and the buttons on top of the pager. His customers said they were "sticky," so he did some checking, and now he's looking at the suppliers for the casings and the buttons. He made sure the suppliers understood the specifications for the part and started to look into hiring some more inspectors. "You know, to make sure we're getting what we asked for," Fred said.

"My question is, who's going to pay for the inspectors?" Tom asked.

"Well, maybe we should just tighten the specs we send the suppliers—sort of ask for the moon and hope for something we can use? " Fred suggested.

"Hold on a minute," Luis interrupted. "I heard you guys saying that better quality is usually *more* cost effective, and now Fred is talking about hiring more inspectors? Which way is it?"

"In the short run, you do what you have to do to detect the problem, or maybe I should say the problem's symptoms. You deal with the lesser of the two evils," Cheryl said. "But if you stop there, it's like just sweeping the dirt under the rug or like the pastry chef eating his mistakes. The problem is still there, and in time things will begin to bulge—the rug, the chef, and eventually the costs!"

"That makes sense. Sometimes that bulge messes up our whole syyyysss . . . system," Luis gasped, as he realized he had too much weight on the bench press bar. "When we reject something—a truckload from our lumber supplier, a batch of components, whatever—it screws up our whole schedule. Sometimes we have some extra inventory sitting around just in case, but that's expensive, too," he continued, after Tom, who was spotting him, helped him up with the bar.

"You're both on track, from what I've seen, but are you satisfied with where you are? Are you there yet?" Tom asked, as he eased the bar back into its resting place. "Detection is a first step, but it's reactionary unless it becomes feedback to the original process. That's the key: Don't just sweep it back under the rug or onto the truck. Cheryl said it a second ago: Most of the time you see symptoms, not problems."

"But how do you know the difference—I mean, between symptoms and problems?" Fred asked.

"Well, there are tools that can help you connect the dots," Tom replied, as he got ready for another set. "It takes some snooping and digging." He suggested that self-directed teams, maybe drawing from more than one work area, were a good way to start. He liked them to use tools like control charts, histograms, flow charts, stuff like that. "We train all our people to use those tools," said Tom, adding that a lot of them are based on statistics, but all of them are pretty intuitive. Most of the time, just asking why some symptom happens is a good start. When you find out the answer, ask why the answer happens, and when you find that out, ask why again. "When you can't find an easy answer to a 'why,' you've probably landed on the root cause, " said Tom.

"It's too early in the morning for this. You lost me at the first 'why' in the road!" Luis complained.

"Yeah, yeah, let's do it this way. Hypothetically, let's say Fred was late today for the sixth time in the last two weeks," Cheryl jumped in, seizing the opportunity to needle Fred. "If he said that he slept through the alarm. . ."

"You don't need to dig any further. Get him a louder alarm," Luis suggested, interrupting Cheryl.

"No, I would ask him why he slept through the alarm, and he would say he was up real late," Cheryl replied.

"Give him a curfew?" Luis asked.

"No, I'd ask him why he was up so late. Assume he says he was up late wondering about important things, like why we drive on parkways and park on driveways, or whether his headlights would work if his car were going the speed of light. Then the problem is obvious.

To keep asking why is not going to get you any further. Fred doesn't need an alarm clock, he needs a girlfriend!" Cheryl concluded, poking Fred in the ribs as he walked by on his way to get a drink of water.

"That's going to take some real problem solving!" laughed Luis.

"Well, yes, that's one example!" Tom said with a smile. "We call that one the 'five why's and a how'." He mentioned how his airport staff forms teams and uses a process called the "QI story" to work toward identifying problems and suggesting solutions. He said it provides a structure for improving a process. "Some of our best solutions come from folks on the front line," he said.

"Give us an example, Tom. If I'm not following this, then I know Fred isn't," Luis said, smiling at the dirty look Fred shot at him.

"Okay, that's easy. We used to think our late departure times were due to some piece of equipment not being available when we needed it. But our ground people did a QI analysis and found the cause was largely our check-in procedures. While other airlines might have spent a bundle trying to fix a symptom—you know, having a lot of expensive equipment sitting around idle most of the time, just to get away from the gate on schedule—we used the ideas the agents generated to streamline our check-in system. We found the real problem and solved it. Now we leave the gate on time, make passengers happy, and save a bundle, too!" Tom boasted. "Once we begin to deal with the really pressing things our passengers tell us about, we can go on to the things that might win us more business. Really, that's the third part of all this, continuous improvement. We can always get better."

"Okay, I hear what you're saying, and it sounds as if I shouldn't get ahead of the game here," sighed Fred. "We've got a lot of work ahead of us, but it seems like we're on the right path. Maybe we need to talk with our shop floor people and our suppliers about this pager issue. There may be more to it than just more inspection or what specs we look at."

"Sounds like maybe you'll be dragging in here after some late nights after all, girlfriend or not," chuckled Luis.

> objectives

Take a moment to familiarize yourself with the key objectives of this chapter.

> gearing up

Before you begin reading this chapter, try a short warm-up activity.

> Introduction

Traditionally, experts in the field of quality control have relied heavily on statistical tools that describe a process and its output based on an analysis of samples taken from incoming materials, work in process, finished goods, or other process variables. Yet clearly, effective quality management benefits from other types of tools as well. Today, the study of quality may be included in a variety of courses—operations management, marketing, organizational behavior, engineering, and statistics. All these disciplines have contributed useful tools for improving quality.

This chapter focuses on tools that are useful in analyzing and improving the firm's value-adding system. It continues the discussion of customer-defined quality and value-adding systems that began in Chapter 1, by describing the tools firms use to fulfill the demands of a customer orientation. Specifically, it details tools for detecting quality problems, tools for preventing quality problems, and tools for promoting ongoing improvement. In the process, it answers a question many people ask after being introduced to the philosophy of total quality management (TQM): "It sounds great, but what do I do differently when I get back to work on Monday morning?"

The detection and prevention of quality problems relate to ongoing improvement in much the same way as diagnostic and preventive medicine are related to fitness and wellness programs. Diagnostic medicine involves determining the malady from which a patient suffers. It involves gathering samples (specimens and measurement of metabolic variables such as temperature, blood pressure, and pulse rate) and analyzing these to determine the conditions which must be present in the body from which the samples were taken. Once a diagnosis has been rendered, in many cases it is possible to prevent recurrence of a patient's problem. For example, seizures can be prevented by prescribing certain drugs. In other cases, inoculation, exercise, or dietary changes are used to prevent undesirable physical conditions and illness. Still, many people who are, by all appearances, perfectly healthy will consult doctors, nurses, and other health care professionals for help with establishing lifestyles that further enhance their current health. The focus of these wellness programs is not simply to prevent future illness, but to improve the patient's current quality of life. As it is with health care, so it is with ensuring the quality of a company's products or services. One must first find and stop the bleeding, then take steps to immunize the firm against future problems. Otherwise, plans to enhance quality may never materialize.

active concept check

Now let's take a moment to test your knowledge of the concepts you have studied in this section.

Integrating Operations Management with Other Functions

Figure 6.1 highlights some of the most important linkages between the sections of this chapter and other functional areas of business. Obviously, the work conducted in each functional area is done using some process and has some level of quality. We could easily discuss the quality of work done by a marketing department or advertising agency, the quality of work done by an engineering department or design firm, the quality of work done by an accounting department or auditing company, and so on. As such, the tools covered in this chapter are directly applicable and highly relevant to any business student.

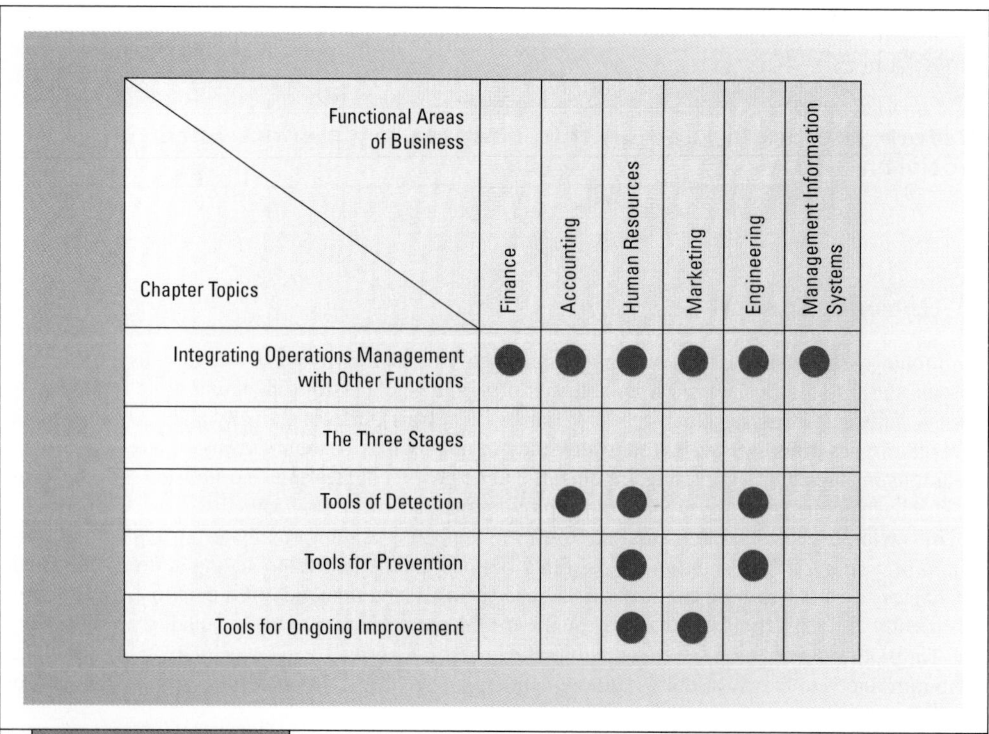

Chapter Topics / Functional Areas of Business	Finance	Accounting	Human Resources	Marketing	Engineering	Management Information Systems
Integrating Operations Management with Other Functions	●	●	●	●	●	●
The Three Stages						
Tools of Detection		●	●		●	
Tools for Prevention			●		●	
Tools for Ongoing Improvement			●	●		

FIGURE 6.1 Integrating Operations Management with Other Functions

Beyond the obvious relevance of this chapter to all functional areas, described in the last paragraph, some of the tools we describe have more immediate applicability to a particular major. Accountants are often conducting audits and will find our discussion of testing and inspection (in the section of the chapter dealing with detection of quality problems) particularly relevant. Human resources majors will recognize that all of the tools must be used in a work context by employees and will recognize the key role that they play in setting up the personnel systems that provide training and the opportunities for employees to use the tools. Marketing majors, who are naturally concerned about effectively linking operations with customer expectations, will notice the marketing potential of the tools for ongoing improvement. Finally, engineering majors will recognize that they will be expected to use all of the tools for prevention of defects, regardless of the engineering job they hold upon graduation from college.

> Three Stages of Quality Management

The discussion of total quality management in Chapter 5 may have suggested to you that most companies are proactive in developing and implementing systems to ensure customer satisfaction. They aren't. More often, an organization will become concerned about quality because of serious problems. In most cases, the problems aren't new. In fact, firms usually take responsibility for problems only after the symptoms of the problems have been clear for some time. A complaint from a customer is not a quality problem; it is a symptom. So also are rejected parts, escalating warranty costs, loss of market share, and an inability to meet customer delivery dates. They are all are symptoms of some underlying problem that might be related to quality.

When a problem first arises, organizations may be blind to the symptoms. Firms (and individuals, for that matter) may remain in a state of denial for quite a while, ignoring the symptoms, denying the problems, or denying responsibility for the problems. Only after a significant loss of market share, the loss of an important customer, a rapid escalation in quality costs, or even a brush with bankruptcy may an organization admit the existence of underlying problems with quality. What follows, in most organizations, is a developmental process that has three stages: detection, prevention, and ongoing improvement. This chapter focuses on the tools that have particular applications at various stages in the development of a total quality management system.

People who work for an organization that has not documented the symptoms of underlying quality problems will naturally be reluctant to take responsibility for them. Finding ways to measure and document the symptoms that suggest the existence of underlying problems is a natural starting point for an organization that is moving out of denial and beginning to grapple with issues of quality. This early stage in the development of quality management capabilities is called the *detection phase.* In the detection phase, quality management is still reactive; typically, the primary focus is the discovery of *nonconforming* (or *defective*) items before they reach the customer. The quality management tools that are used during this stage reflect this focus.

Eventually, as a result of improvements made through remedial actions in the first phase, problems may begin to crop up less frequently. As the benefit of the firm's detection efforts is realized less frequently, the cost of detecting problems becomes quite expensive on a per-problem basis. At this point, most organizations shift from a reactive approach to quality management based on detection to a proactive approach based on prevention. During the second phase, called the *prevention phase,* organizations attempt to control the critical steps in their processes, so that process changes that could produce undesired results will be noticed and corrected before nonconforming products or services are created. They do so by reducing the variation in their processes and by making their product designs more "robust," so that they can accommodate higher levels of process variation without creating nonconforming goods or services.

Ultimately, the quality management system may develop to the point where processes are capable of operating for long periods of time without generating nonconforming output. When it does, the organization may move from the prevention phase to the ongoing improvement phase. Firms in this third stage of development realize that even if a process is not creating nonconforming output, it can always be improved. A product or service may not be considered "defective,"[1] but any variation from design targets represents some loss of quality, increase in the cost to society, or both. Since there is some natural variation in every process, every process can be improved.

[1]Quality professionals don't like to use the terms "defects" and "defective" any more. Instead, they use the terms "nonconformities" and "nonconforming" (and we will, too). These terms carry less negative baggage, and they are more specific—an item might be "nonconforming" from the perspective that it misses its design specification. From a customer's perspective, however, the product may work just fine and not have any visible problems. In fact, the product might be nonconforming because it is better than the design.

TABLE 6.1	The Three Stages of Quality Management
Stage of Development	**Typical Source of Improvement**
Detection	Reacting to problems as they arise, especially if getting to the root of the problem and solving it is recognized as the lesser evil
Prevention	Taking care of special cases by removing assignable or identifiable causes of system variation
Ongoing improvement	Taking care of everyday cases by reducing common or natural causes of system variation; focusing on reducing waste and better meeting customer expectations.

Ultimately, improvement includes any change that enhances the value provided to customers. Thus, firms in the ongoing improvement phase will use their quality management processes to accomplish a wide range of desirable outcomes, such as eliminating waste, increasing product reliability, enhancing the appearance of products, improving the delivery of a service, customizing the product or service to the needs of specific customers, sharpening worker training programs and skills, enhancing the work life of employees, increasing safety in the work place, and reducing the firm's environmental impact.

Table 6.1 summarizes the three stages of development in the management of quality and the sources of improvement in each.

The following sections present some of the major tools that are used in quality improvement efforts, in the order in which a firm that is following the developmental pattern just discussed might encounter them. The first section presents tools that are likely to be used in the detection phase; the second section, tools that are likely to be used in the prevention phase. The chapter closes with a discussion of tools that are commonly used during the ongoing improvement phase.

active concept check 

Now let's take a moment to test your knowledge of the concepts you have studied in this section.

 Tools for Detection of Quality Problems

Every organization, even those that don't seem to be particularly concerned about quality, learns about quality problems in some way. They may learn about their problems when customers complain, when they are handed a lawsuit, when other companies win their customers, or when their market share dips low enough that profitability suffers. This section describes approaches companies can take to learn about the quality of their work before it ever gets into the customer's possession, including (1) testing and inspection, (2) acceptance sampling, and (3) statistical process control based on attribute measures.

active example 

Take a closer look at the concepts and issues you've been reading about.

TESTING AND INSPECTION

In business today, one often hears the saying "You can't inspect quality into the product." This is a true statement, particularly if quality is defined in terms of customer satisfaction and the inspection occurs after the product is complete. Yet inspection is a skill that is critical to any quality program. In an age in which data-based decision making lies at the heart of quality management, inspection is critical

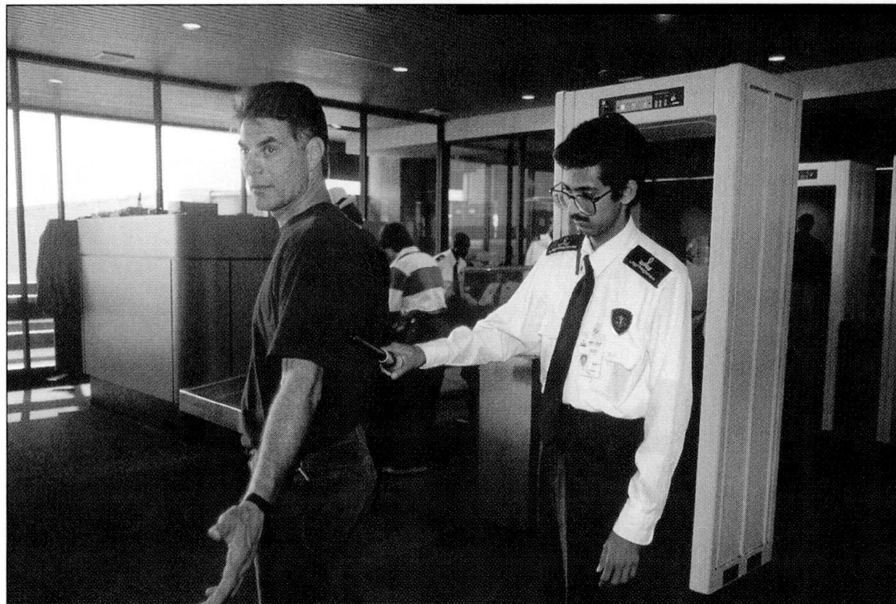

The security inspection you undergo at an airport provides attribute data. From the airline's perspective, either you are a security risk or you aren't (and if you've passed the inspection you aren't).

because it is the source of the data used in any decision-making application. Without reliable data gathered under a well-reasoned plan for inspection, even the most sophisticated statistical techniques are useless.

Inspection generally refers to the process of comparing the characteristics of a product or service with the characteristics that define its acceptability. Historically the term has been used to refer to the measurement of certain dimensional or physical characteristics that represent important properties of component products and service outcomes. Dimensional properties describe a product's size and weight, including measures such as length, diameter, ground clearance, or liquid volume. Physical characteristics include the color, density, or porosity of an item, the legibility of printed matter, the fit of a joint, the cleanliness of a facility, the duration of a telephone service encounter, and the presence or absence of a handshake, eye contact, or a smile in a personal service encounter.

Physical and dimensional characteristics can be **attribute measures** (which are measured in categories), but they provide more information when they are **variable measures** (which are measured on a continuous scale). Obtaining a variable measurement usually costs more than an attribute measurement; hence, the choice of measurement must be based on the need for the data. For example, a child's height is measured as an attribute at amusement parks, where a quick comparison with a cutoff point marked on a measuring stick indicates whether a child is tall enough for a particular ride. In that setting, there is no reason to take the time to measure the exact height of each customer. Obviously, to properly assess the child's growth, a pediatrician would measure a child's height as a variable, not an attribute.

Historically, inspection has been distinguished from **testing,** which refers to the measurement of the performance of complex assemblies and service systems. We speak of the test weight of fishing line, lie detector tests, IQ tests, missile tests, tests of the reliability of a computer system, or the "torture chamber" test used to try the durability of an automobile's paint job.

In an academic setting, professors typically use both testing and inspection to determine the grade that best reflects a student's performance. Taking attendance or giving a fixed number of points for participation in a particular exercise amounts to inspection. Many true/false and multiple-choice questions are arguably forms of inspection, in that they measure only whether or not the student knows (or can guess from a limited set of choices) the meaning of a term or acronym. On the other hand, complex homework problems, spreadsheets, programming assignments, and integrative essay questions represent a testing of the student's performance. They can be used to evaluate the level of development of some combination of skill and understanding. Whether the information on a student's performance comes from inspection or testing, it is valuable only to the extent that it is relevant to the learning objectives set out in the course syllabus. That is why professors rely primarily on objective test questions in survey courses, which are designed to provide broad exposure to a particular topic, and on subjective questions in upper-level courses, which are designed to explore a subject in depth.

Today, the terms *testing* and *inspection* are often used interchangeably. Both are sources of the data used in quality management. In fact, without inspection, there could be no assessment of quality and no data-driven decision making. Each week many firms manufacture thousands of items or experience thousands of service encounters, implying that some clear plan for inspection is critical. Whatever the plan, it must be cost effective, and it must provide the data needed for the managerial purposes of detection of nonconformities, prevention of nonconformities, and process improvement.

active exercise <

Take a moment to apply what you've learned.

ACCEPTANCE SAMPLING

Acceptance sampling is a tool that uses information gained from a sample of finished items to determine whether or not to accept the entire batch from which the sample was taken. This type of sampling should be used only when the supply process is unstable and the cost of acceptance sampling is less than the cost of 0% or 100% inspection. (When the supply process is stable, 100% or 0% inspection will always be less expensive than sampling.)

Sampling Plans

Using acceptance sampling, inspectors may reject a batch of thousands of items based on the presence of a small number of nonconforming items in a sample. In the sampling plan shown in Figure 6.2A, a production batch of 10,000 items is evaluated by taking a sample of 200 items. The letter c is usually used to represent the acceptance number or the cutoff point between acceptance and rejection of the entire batch. In this example, $c = 5$, meaning that if five or fewer of the 200 items are found to be nonconforming, the entire batch will be accepted, but if six or more of the items are found to be nonconforming, the entire batch will be rejected. Depending on the costs of inspection and of the items being inspected, a rejected batch would then be subjected to 100% inspection or it would be discarded.

For example, let's say that Fred buys electronic chips from a supplier in Southeast Asia. Waiting for a replacement for a rejected batch might disrupt his production schedule. In that case, Fred would have to pay local inspectors, either in his own company or in an outside firm, to go through the entire batch and sort out the problem chips. (If Fred's supply contract provided for such a circumstance, he might even be able to charge the supplier for the cost of inspecting the batch, as well as the cost of the rejected chips.) Nonconforming items found during the 100% inspection would be set apart for repair or disposal. Finally, because errors can occur even in a 100% inspection, the batch might have to be inspected once again using acceptance sampling.

The acceptance sampling plan shown in Figure 6.2A is called a *single sampling* plan, because the decision to accept or reject the lot is based on just one sample. Figure 6.2B shows a *double sampling* plan that is comparable to the single sampling plan presented in Figure 6.2A. In this plan, the sample size (n) is 125, and there are two cutoff points for the first sample, an upper limit of five and a lower limit of two nonconforming items. If the number of nonconforming items in the first sample is two or less, inspectors will accept the entire lot; if it is five or more, they will reject the entire lot. If the num-

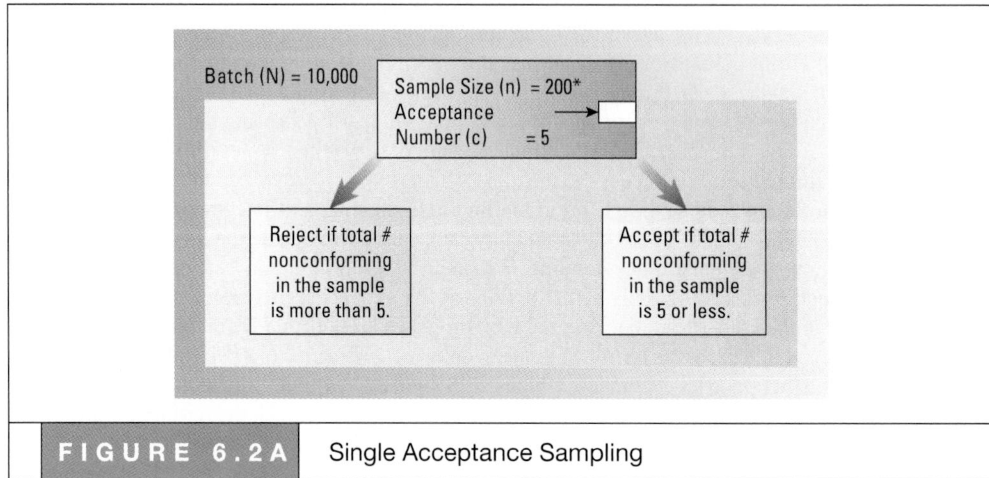

FIGURE 6.2A Single Acceptance Sampling

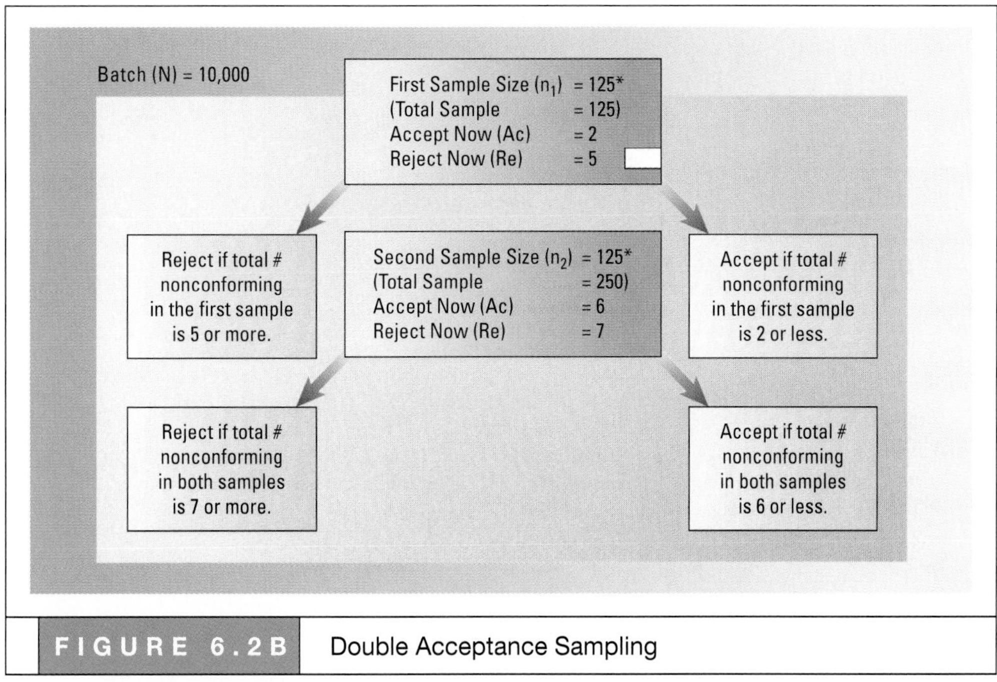
Batch (N) = 10,000
First Sample Size (n_1) = 125*
(Total Sample = 125)
Accept Now (Ac) = 2
Reject Now (Re) = 5
Reject if total # nonconforming in the first sample is 5 or more.
Second Sample Size (n_2) = 125*
(Total Sample = 250)
Accept Now (Ac) = 6
Reject Now (Re) = 7
Accept if total # nonconforming in the first sample is 2 or less.
Reject if total # nonconforming in both samples is 7 or more.
Accept if total # nonconforming in both samples is 6 or less.

FIGURE 6.2B Double Acceptance Sampling

ber of nonconforming items falls between two and five, the plan suggests that the inspector dig a little deeper and take a second sample of 125 items (making the total sample size 250). Note that in the second sample, the cutoff points, six and seven, refer to the *total* number of nonconforming items in *both* samples.

When quality is typically either very good or very poor (that is, when it is bimodal), double sampling may be more cost-effective than single sampling because decisions will often be made based on the initial sample and the second sample will not be taken. But when the distribution of lot quality is *not* bimodal, double sampling can be more expensive than single sampling because both samples will have to be taken in order to make a conclusion regarding the quality of the batch. (Recall that the single sampling plan was based on a sample size of 200 rather than 250.) For example, Fred's chip supplier might have two different factories—one in Indonesia and another in Malaysia—but one central distribution center in Singapore. Let's say the chips from Malaysia typically meet Fred's acceptance criteria, but the chips from Indonesia typically do not. If Fred has no way of knowing the source of the chips he receives, he might be able to tell the difference based on a very small sample. Occasionally, he might need a second sample to make a final determination regarding the acceptability of a lot. Since he typically makes his decision based on the first sample, he'll save money over time by using double sampling.

Another type of plan, *sequential sampling,* extends the process of double sampling through several iterations. Figure 6.2C shows a sequential sampling plan. Note that the entire lot could be accepted or rejected on the basis of a first sample size of just 50 items.

If single, double, and sequential sampling plans seem confusing to you, you might think about the way you decide to buy a new CD. If certain artists have always appealed to you, you probably have all their disks and will buy their new disks without even listening to them first. In the unlikely event that you get home and find you don't like the new disk, you can always recover some of your cost by reselling it or returning it to the store. Similarly, there are some artists whose work you know is not for you. When you see their new CDs on a promotional rack, you pass by without buying. Thus, when artists have a "stable" style, your sampling policy is 0% inspection.

There are other artists whose musical styles vary from disk to disk and track to track. If you know that you like some of their work but tend to listen only to selected tracks on their CDs, you will probably listen to several tracks before you decide to buy one of their new CDs. This approach is analogous to single sampling. Still other artists' works vary quite a bit from disk to disk but not from track to track. If you have really enjoyed some of their disks but can't stand others, you might listen to one track or part of a track on a new CD. That would probably be enough to tell you whether you should add the new disk to your already oversized collection. If the track is all right but not great, you might listen to another couple of tracks, just to be sure of your conclusion. This approach would be analogous to double or sequential sampling.

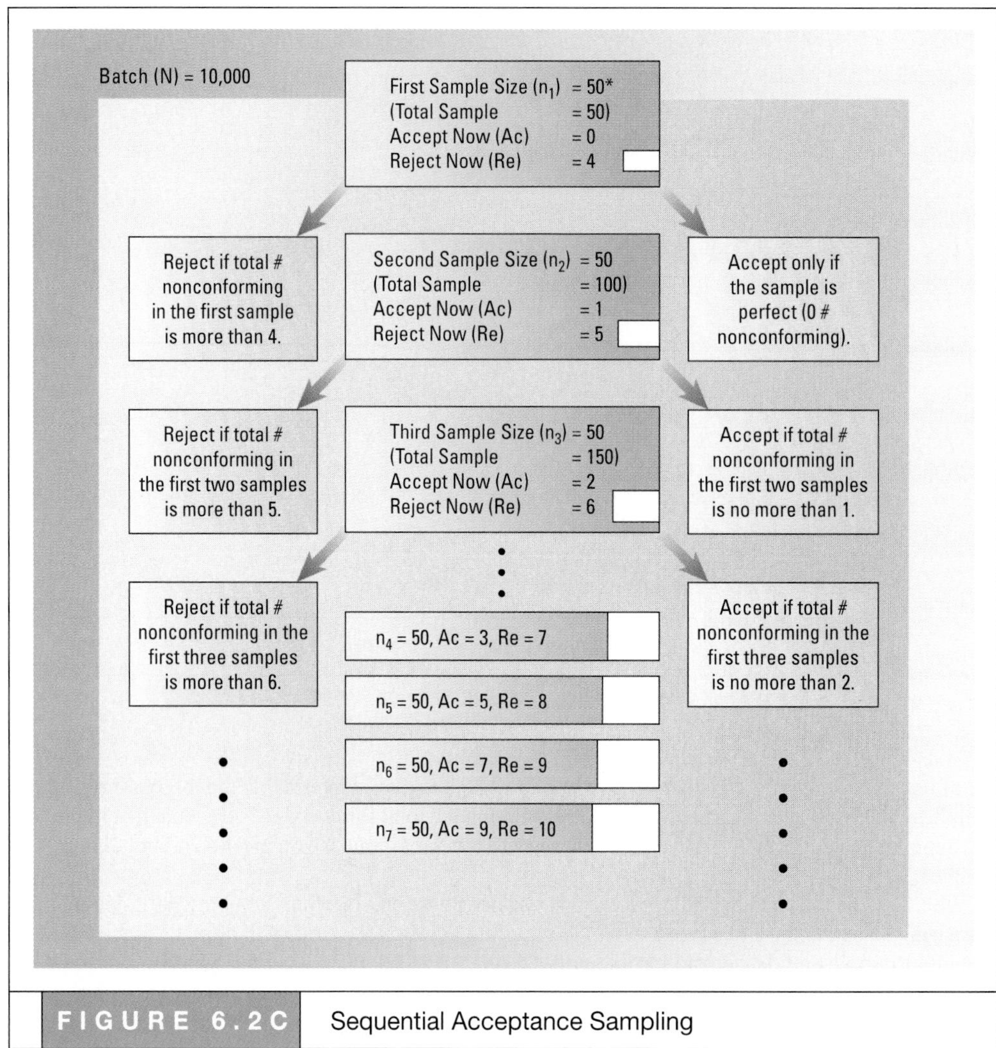
Batch (N) = 10,000
First Sample Size (n_1) = 50*
(Total Sample = 50)
Accept Now (Ac) = 0
Reject Now (Re) = 4
Reject if total # nonconforming in the first sample is more than 4.
Second Sample Size (n_2) = 50
(Total Sample = 100)
Accept Now (Ac) = 1
Reject Now (Re) = 5
Accept only if the sample is perfect (0 # nonconforming).
Reject if total # nonconforming in the first two samples is more than 5.
Third Sample Size (n_3) = 50
(Total Sample = 150)
Accept Now (Ac) = 2
Reject Now (Re) = 6
Accept if total # nonconforming in the first two samples is no more than 1.
Reject if total # nonconforming in the first three samples is more than 6.
n_4 = 50, Ac = 3, Re = 7
n_5 = 50, Ac = 5, Re = 8
n_6 = 50, Ac = 7, Re = 9
n_7 = 50, Ac = 9, Re = 10
Accept if total # nonconforming in the first three samples is no more than 2.

FIGURE 6.2C Sequential Acceptance Sampling

Error, Risk, and Tolerance Levels

Acceptance sampling is not a foolproof procedure. Inspectors can reject lots that should be accepted and accept lots that should be rejected using acceptance sampling. Such mistakes may result from errors in sampling or inspection or both. A **sampling error** occurs when a sample is biased, or unrepresentative of the batch. An **inspection error** occurs when the measurement that is applied to the sample is observed, recorded, or interpreted incorrectly.

When a lot that should be accepted is rejected, a **type I error** has occurred. The risk of making type I errors, which is referred to as **producers risk,** is represented by the Greek letter α (alpha). When a lot that should have been rejected is accepted, a **type II error** has occurred. The risk of making a type II error, which is called **consumers risk,** is represented by the Greek letter β (beta). Figure 6.3 summarizes the potential errors and risks associated with acceptance sampling.

To define the proportion of nonconforming items that is acceptable in a batch, statisticians have devised a parameter called the **acceptable quality level (AQL**). This is the level of quality the customer would expect to be rejected only very infrequently (recognizing the limitations of a supplier's process, the limitations of acceptance sampling, and the cost of obtaining higher levels of quality). With regard to the AQL, Juran and Gryna have written:

> It should be emphasized to both internal and external suppliers that *all* product submitted for inspection is expected to meet specifications. An acceptable quality level does not mean the submission of a certain amount of nonconforming product is approved. The AQL simply recognizes that, under sampling, some nonconforming product will pass through the sampling scheme. (Juran and Gryna, 1993, 466–467)

As the following illustration points out, the use of the term *acceptable* in AQL is not entirely consistent with common usage of the term. In the early 1980s, IBM decided to try purchasing manufac-

Batch Really Is: / We Decide to:	Accept	Reject
Good	Correct decision....	**Type I Error (Producer's Risk)**
Bad	**Type II Error (Consumer's Risk)**	Correct decision....

FIGURE 6.3 Sampling Errors

tured parts from a Japanese supplier. Engineers at IBM established specifications for the parts and set a limit, three parts out of 10,000, on the number of nonconforming parts that would be considered acceptable. With the first delivery, the Japanese supplier enclosed a letter stating, "We Japanese have a hard time understanding North American business practices. But the 3 defective units per 10,000 have been included and wrapped separately. Hope this pleases" (*Toronto Sun,* April 25, 1983, p. 6).

The **lot tolerance percent defective (LTPD),** sometimes called the rejectable quality level, is the level of quality that the customer would expect the sampling plan to accept very infrequently (recognizing that such a failure rate could disrupt production schedules, damage other inventory, and otherwise harm the product's quality).

Figure 6.4 illustrates both the LTPD and the AQL as a percentage of nonconforming items in a lot. The higher the value on the horizontal axis, the poorer the quality of the lot. The probability of acceptance of lots of various quality levels can be shown on an **operating characteristics (OC) curve.** OC curves can be used to describe the risk of type I and type II errors in an acceptance sampling plan. The ideal OC curve is shown in Figure 6.4(a). (Again, notice that the higher the value on the horizontal axis, the poorer the quality of the lot.) This discontinuous curve represents a perfectly discriminating plan that allows no type I and type II errors. The probability that acceptable lots will be accepted is 1.0, and the probability that unacceptable lots will be accepted is 0. With such an acceptance plan, the AQL need not be distinguished from the LTPD; the only relevant issue is the quality threshold that marks the difference between what is acceptable and what is not.

Unfortunately, because of sampling error and inspection error, there is no acceptance sampling plan that is perfectly discriminating. No real-world sampling plan has the OC curve shown in Figure 6.4(a). Figure 6.4(b) presents a realistic OC curve, which is essentially defined by the two points (AQL, 1-α) and (LTPD, β). The probabilities α and β represent the producer and consumer risk, respectively—in other words, the risk of error in the sampling or inspection process. Note that from zero to the AQL on the horizontal axis, lots are seldom rejected; beyond the LTPD level, lots are seldom accepted. Between the AQL and the LTPD, the chance that the lot will be accepted declines as the percentage of nonconforming items rises. If the curve in Figure 6.4(b) were steeper, both α and β would be smaller, as would the range of quality levels between the AQL and LTPD. Steeper OC curves represent more discriminating sampling plans; from that perspective, they are desirable. On the other hand, an OC curve may be made steeper only by increasing the size of the sample; thus, the more discriminating the plan, the more costly.

If the sample size is held constant, the steepness of the OC curve cannot be changed. But by changing the acceptance number (c), buyers can increase α and decrease β, or vice versa. Increasing the acceptance number makes it easier for inspectors to accept rejectable lots and more difficult for them to reject acceptable lots. Therefore, it increases the risk of type II Error, β, and reduces the risk of type I error, α. Conversely, decreasing the acceptance number will increase the risk of type I error, α, and reduce the risk of type II error, β.

Ultimately, the consumer will pay for the sampling plan and for both types of error, because producers pass their costs on to consumers. It is therefore important that industrial buyers consider the risks and costs associated with various acceptance sampling plans when choosing an acceptance plan.

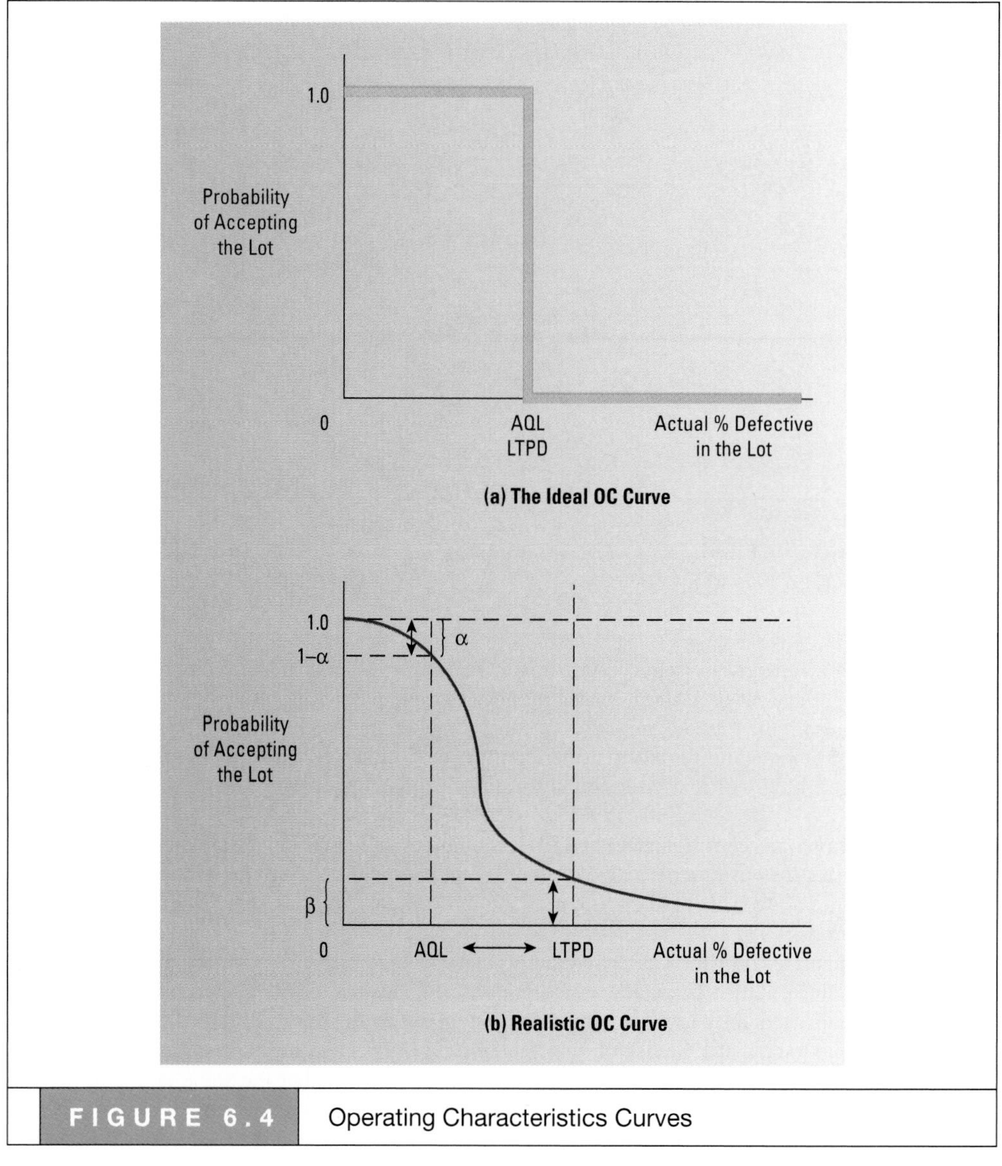

FIGURE 6.4 Operating Characteristics Curves

Studying and comparing the OC curves and the costs associated with various plans will help buyers to select an appropriate plan.

Psychological Effects of Sampling

There is an interesting psychological effect associated with acceptance sampling. From the production worker's perspective, management is willing to reject all the labor invested in making a lot of, say, 10,000 items because as few as six nonconforming items were found. One message of that procedure is that quality is extremely important. But another, hidden message may be that management doesn't care enough about the worker's efforts to look at the whole picture. How would you feel if your professor asked you to solve a hundred problems, then chose one problem at random and reported a semester grade of pass or fail on the basis of that one problem? Would you bother to do all the problems or would you try to guess which one was going to be graded? Particularly when workers' wages, and thus their livelihoods, depend on their productivity rates, the consequences of using acceptance sampling may actually prove harmful to quality efforts.

For these reasons, Deming was strongly opposed to the use of acceptance sampling, which he saw as a means of quality *control* that could inhibit quality *management.* As a result, acceptance sampling has fallen out of favor in recent years. Deming was also well known for his mathematical proof that when a production process is stable, either 100% inspection or no inspection (all or none) is always more cost efficient than sampling. (A stable process is one in which the proportion of items produced out of conformance is known.) Figure 6.5 presents Deming's recommendations for using acceptance sampling. This figure makes the point that there is a very specific and legitimate use for acceptance

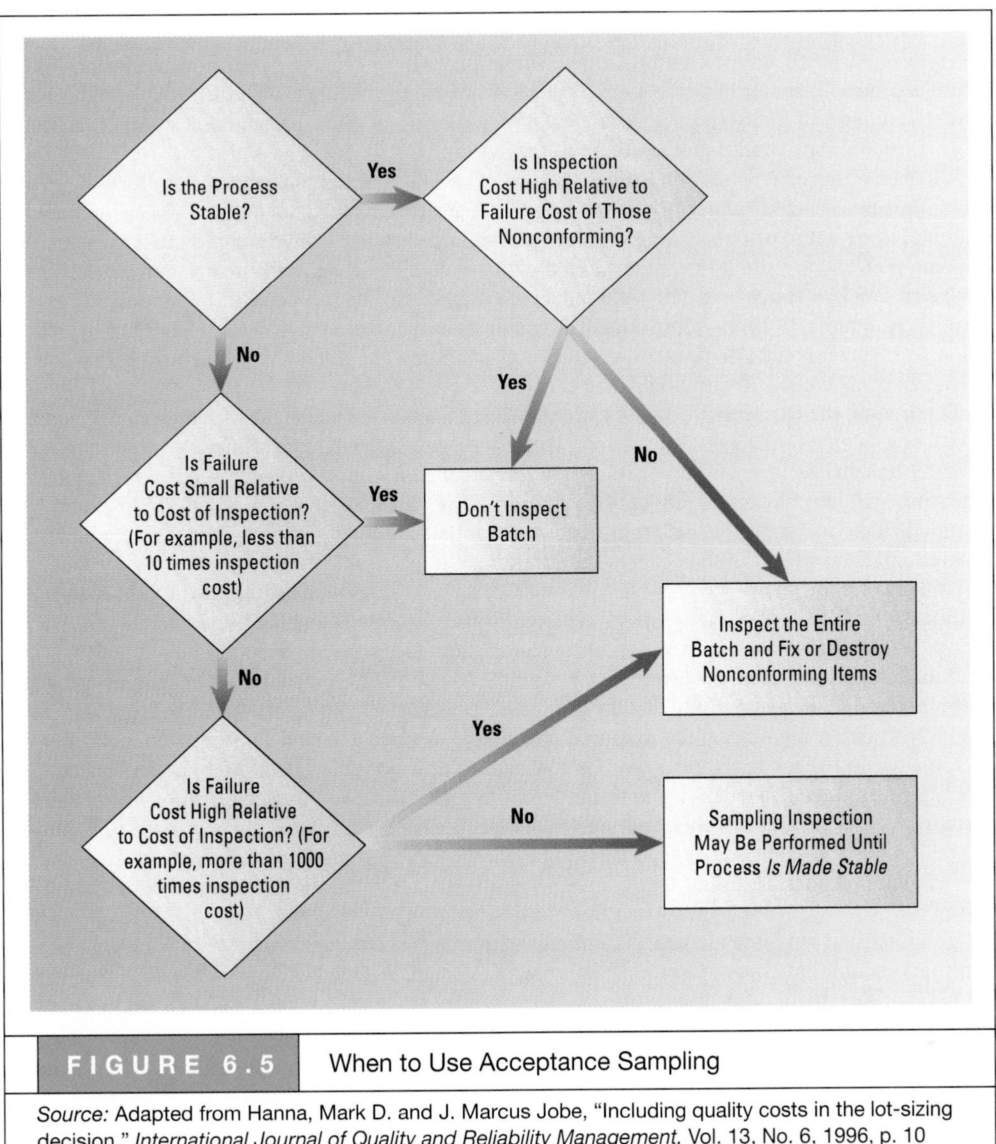

FIGURE 6.5 When to Use Acceptance Sampling

Source: Adapted from Hanna, Mark D. and J. Marcus Jobe, "Including quality costs in the lot-sizing decision," *International Journal of Quality and Reliability Management,* Vol. 13, No. 6, 1996, p. 10 (Figure 1).

sampling, but that it is not appropriate for widespread use. When acceptance sampling is used, the firm should focus on improving and stabilizing the process whose output is sampled, so that the procedure may eventually be discontinued.

STATISTICAL PROCESS CONTROL

In contrast to acceptance sampling, in which inspection is used to decide whether to accept or reject finished output, process control inspection is used to decide whether or not a production process is operating as expected. Rather than waiting until a production batch has been finished, inspectors use process control techniques to detect the symptoms of problems while a batch is being produced; they then make any necessary adjustments.

Process control may be accomplished through real-time inspection of 100% of the product passing through some control point, or it may be done using a mechanical device that automatically adjusts for process changes. For example, some firms in the paper industry use Measurex™ machines to continuously monitor the thickness of paper in process and automatically adjust process controls. An alternative to 100% inspection is to take samples at specified time intervals. For example, in beer brewing, certain variables need only be monitored at specific intervals in the fermentation process. When processes are monitored and adjusted on the basis of sample data, **statistical process control (SPC)** is being used. SPC helps managers determine what type of variation is present in the process they are monitoring.

Types of Variation in a System

One type of variation, called **common cause variation** (also referred to as **random variation**), is the natural variation inherent in any system. It arises from a large number of unidentifiable and random causes. Deming and Juran have suggested that 85% of the variation in a production system is common cause variation that is built into the design of the system.

When common cause variation is the only type of variation present in a system or process, the system or process is said to be in **control,** meaning that management need not take any special action. For example, if the cause of outstanding or poor performance is some unidentifiable random event, outstanding performance should not be rewarded with a bonus, nor poor performance punished. Instead, managers should attempt to identify and reduce the root cause. Juran's breakthrough sequence can be used to make radical system improvements, by attacking the vital few causes on a project-by-project basis. Worker teams can also be empowered to make ongoing incremental improvements, by attacking the useful many causes of variation.

Think about the teaching evaluations you may have filled out at the end of a semester. The scores a professor gets on any one question will vary from student to student, from section to section, and from semester to semester. Even if the instructor follows identical routines in each section each semester, the scores will show a certain amount of variation. This variation in scores, which is an example of common cause variation, results from many factors that are difficult to trace, each of which contributes only a small part of the observable variation.

Unlike common cause variation, the presence of **special cause variation** (also called **assignable variation**) usually reflects a significant change in the system. Typically, the root cause of such a change is identifiable; managers and workers should therefore seek to identify it.

If the unusual symptom is desirable (for example, much fewer nonconformities than usual), managers should find a way to ensure that the root cause is preserved and incorporated in the system at all times. A worker's job description might be changed and a bonus added for consistent and effective performance of the job in the new way. Or particularly efficient equipment might be duplicated elsewhere. For example, Tom Jackson's airline might find that at one airport, departures have been late much less often than usual. In searching for a special cause for this desirable variation, managers might find that the standard baggage-handling machine has been replaced with a newer model. If so, they should consider installing that baggage-handling machine at all the other airports the airline serves.

If the unusual symptom is undesirable (for example, many more nonconformities than usual), managers should find a way to eliminate the root cause. A disgruntled worker who is unwilling to perform according to his job description or is purposely undermining the system might be fired. Inefficient equipment might be removed. If, for example, Tom Jackson's airline found that at one particular airport, departures have been late much more often than usual because a particular baggage-handling machine has been breaking down frequently, the appropriate response would probably be to replace that machine.

In the example of teaching evaluations, you might have figured out what a special cause variation might be. Teaching the course a new way, using a new book, or giving a particularly difficult test the day before evaluations are done could all produce special cause variations in teacher evaluations. All are identifiable factors that can cause positive or negative changes in the results of an evaluation.

When managers respond to a common cause variation by taking some special action, they introduce more variation into the system. The cause of this type of variation, which is assignable to management, is referred to as **tampering.** For example, an instructor who teaches a course the same way she or he always has but attempts to improve student evaluations by giving students an A or extra credit just before distributing the evaluation forms, would be guilty of tampering. Tampering amounts to playing games with the measurement system.

A fourth type of variation, **structural variation,** is caused by patterns in the system. For example, workforce performance may vary by shift; an individual worker's performance may vary by the time of day; and a machine's performance may vary with the maintenance interval or the plant's ambient temperature. In a teaching evaluation, an instructor who receives high ratings for morning sections and low ratings for afternoon or evening sections would be manifesting a structural variation in performance, which could have implications for the best time to schedule the class.

video exercise

Take a moment to apply what you've learned.

Sampling Distributions

How do managers distinguish among the different types of variation in a production system? One way is to examine the sampling distribution for the process. A **sampling distribution** identifies the probability that a particular sample statistic will take on a given value if common cause variation is the only type of variation present in the system. In other words, the sampling distribution answers the question, What are the chances that this process is operating as expected? By taking a sample and calculating the statistics for which the sampling distribution is known, managers can make inferences about the likely nature of the system from which the sample was taken. If both the sample and the sampling distribution suggest that the behavior of the system is unusual, managers can conclude that special cause variation is present. That is, the process is not operating as expected; either the results are too good to be true, or there is some problem that must be dealt with.

For example, the well-known central limit theorem, which describes the sampling distribution of means, states that if a population has a mean of μ and a standard deviation of σ, and if all possible samples of size n are taken and their means ($\bar{X}$s) calculated, the sampling distribution of those means will have a mean of μ and a standard deviation of $\sigma/\sqrt{n}$, and as n increases the distribution will approach normality. Figure 6.6a illustrates the central limit theorem. In Figure 6.6(b), we apply the theorem by setting the mean, μ, equal to 50; sample size, n, equal to 9; and standard deviation, σ, equal to 5, which implies that the sampling distribution of means has a mean, μ, of 50 and a standard deviation ($\sigma_{\bar{X}}$) of $5/\sqrt{9} = 1.67$. Now, suppose we took a sample of nine observations from this theoretical system and obtained a sample mean higher than 55. Given very low risk of a type I error, we could conclude that special variation exists in this system.

To give a more common example, think about the distribution of height measurements among the students in your class. Unless you are attending a special class for basketball players, there is probably quite a lot of variation in height among your classmates. If you were to place your classmates into groups of two, three, four, and so forth, and average the heights of the members of those groups, the averages would vary much less than the individual heights, because the tall people and the short people would tend to cancel each other out. The same logic can be applied to the output of a production system.

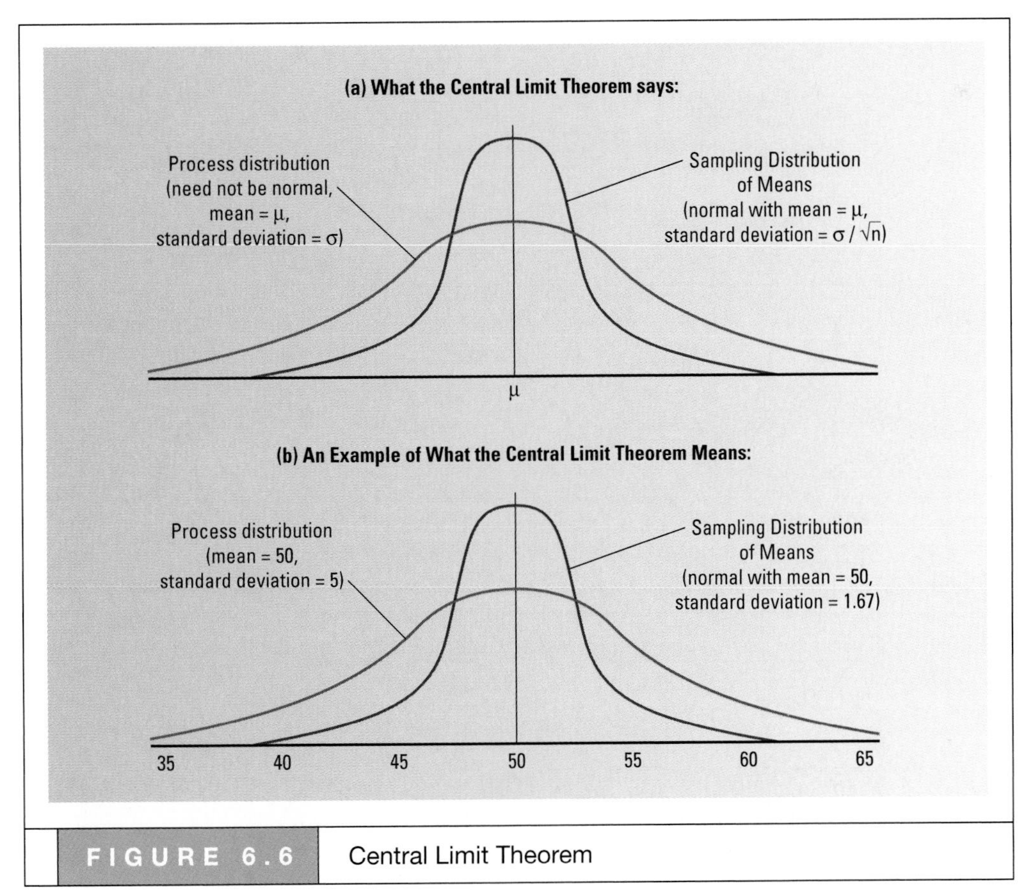

FIGURE 6.6 Central Limit Theorem

Control Charts and Rules of Run

Control charts are statistical tools that allow decision makers to distinguish processes that are in control from those that are out of control. Walter Shewhart, who has been called the father of statistical quality control, was the first to use such charts. As Figure 6.7 shows, a control chart has a *center line (CL)*, an *upper control limit (UCL)*, and a *lower control limit (LCL)*, all of which are calculated using information about the sampling distribution for the statistic plotted on the chart. (A **control limit** is a value used to distinguish between commonly expected and unusual values for a sample statistic.) Sample statistics are plotted against these limits; any point that falls outside the limits is considered an indicator of special cause variation in the system that generated the sample.

As Figure 6.7(a) shows, the distance of the upper and lower control limits from the center line determines the risk of both a type I error (concluding that the process is out of control when it is really in control) and a type II error (concluding that the process is in control when it is not). Figure 6.7(a) also shows that when a process is in control, the probability of a value falling outside either of the control limits is very small. Figures 6.7(b) and (c) show that the probability of a type II error is a function of both the degree of shift in the process statistic being monitored and the distance of the control limits from the center line. A small shift may not be of as much practical significance as a large shift. Fortunately, as the shift in the process increases, the probability of a type II error decreases.

Shewhart suggested that control limits that are 3 standard deviations (of the appropriate sampling distribution) away from the mean. In theory, there is no reason why 3 sigma control limits should be preferred to limits of some other distance from the center line. Rather, the relative costs of making type I and type II errors should determine the distance of the control limits from the center line. In the United States, however, 3 sigma control limits are commonly used.

We have seen that any point that falls outside a control chart's limits may indicate that some special cause variation is affecting the process. In practice, however, that is not the only rule that is used to conclude that a process is out of control. The other rules, which are referred to as *rules of run*, are based on patterns in the control chart. Using these rules reduces the chance of making type II errors. Figure 6.8 summarizes some commonly used rules of run.

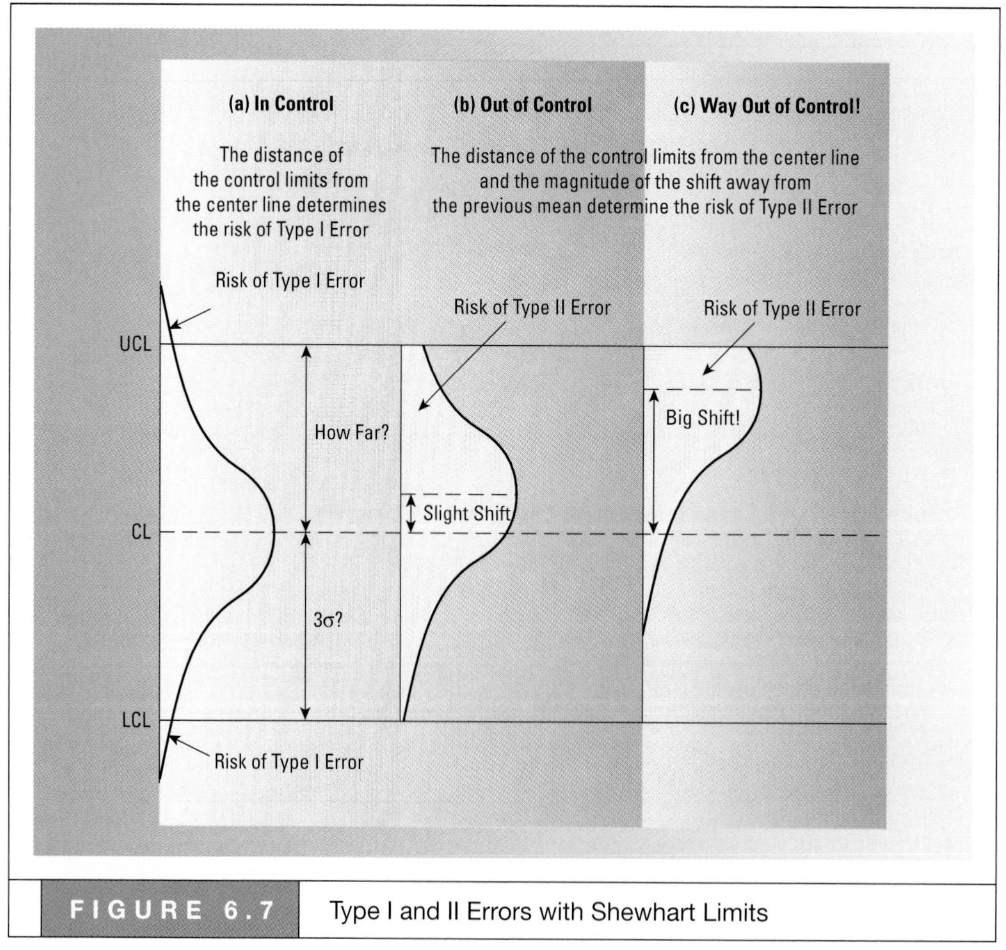

FIGURE 6.7 Type I and II Errors with Shewhart Limits

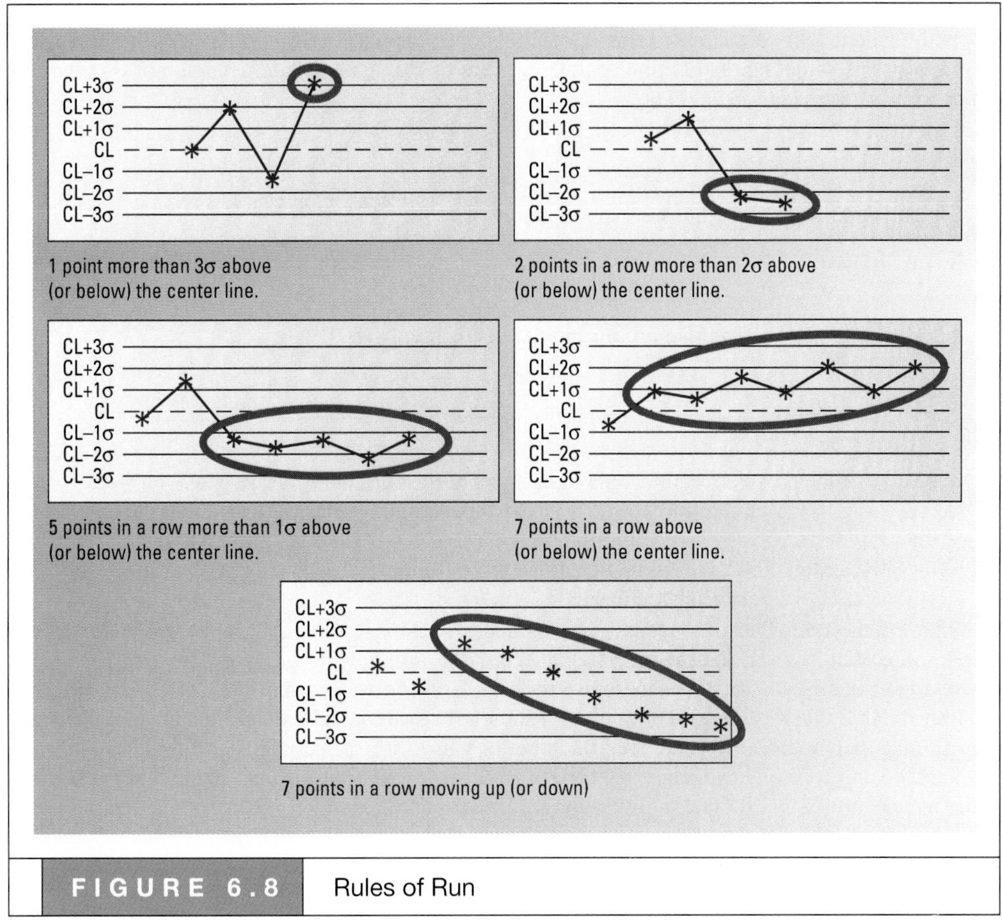

FIGURE 6.8 Rules of Run

Attribute Control Charts

Attribute control charts rely on sample statistics generated from inspections yielding results that can assume only a fixed number of values. For example, the proportion of nonconforming items in a sample of 100 items can be one of only 101 numbers (0.00, 0.01, 0.02 . . . 0.99, 1.00). Similarly, the number of nonconformities must be an integer. Common attribute control charts include *p-charts,* which are used to study the proportion of nonconforming items, and *c-charts,* which plot the number of nonconformities.

The* p*-Chart Suppose you are Tom Jackson, working for an airline. You might have noticed that over the past three years, the proportion of passengers who are told to go to the wrong gate for departure has averaged 2%. The ability to direct passengers to the correct gate is a critical process attribute for several reasons. On the ground, an airplane makes no money; therefore, airline employees will not hold a plane for a passenger who fails to reach the gate by departure time. At the same time, the airline's goal is to satisfy customers completely, and passengers are never completely satisfied until both they and their luggage have reached their destination on time.

If you found that in a sample of 500 passengers, 20 had been given faulty instructions, what would you think? Is this an unusual situation that needs to be investigated? Should the person at the information desk be reprimanded or trained better? Or is this just a normal variation in the complex process of assigning planes to gates and communicating those assignments to passengers through computer monitors and airline personnel? What would you think if on each of the last four days, samples of 500 passengers yielded only one faulty instruction? Would you consider that result too good to be true? Or would you think there had been some real improvement in your airline's service—or that someone is covering up his errors?

Unless you know the distribution of the percentage of faulty instructions the airline has experienced in the past, you cannot answer these questions. Knowing that the average has been 2% (or 10 out of 500) is not sufficient information. What you must know is whether the deviation from the mean represented by a sample with 20 faulty instructions is a common deviation or an unusual one. The same statement applies to the samples with only one faulty instruction.

Fortunately, statistical theory can provide a picture of the distribution of the percentage of faulty instructions, called the sampling distribution of the proportion nonconforming, or the sampling distribution of p. The sampling distribution of p has a mean of $\bar{p}$ and a standard deviation of σ_p. The formulas for these variables are:

$$\text{Sample size} = n$$

$$\text{proportion nonconforming in } i^{th} \text{ sample} = p_i = \frac{\#\ nonconforming\ in\ sample\ i}{n}$$

$$\text{average proportion nonconforming} = \bar{p} = \frac{\sum_{i=1}^{m} p_i}{m}$$

$$\text{standard deviation of proportion nonconforming} = \sigma_p = \sqrt{\frac{\bar{p}\,(1-\bar{p})}{n}}$$

In the case of the process for informing passengers of the correct departure gate, you were given $\bar{p}$ (it was 2%, or 0.02). You can now find σ_p. Using this formula, you discover that σ_p is 0.0062609. Since the proportion of nonconforming instructions in the sample with 20 faulty instructions was 20/500 = 0.04, and $\bar{p}$ is 0.02, the proportion nonconforming for that sample is (.04 − .02) / 0.0062609 = 3.194 standard deviations from the mean.

What are the odds that no unusual circumstances will exist when a sample attribute is 3.194 standard deviations from the mean? The value for the number of standard deviations from the mean is the z-score, which allows us to use the standard normal distribution. (Z is the continuous random variable that represents the number of standard deviations away from the mean in the standard normal distribution.) If you check the table of values for the standard normal distribution at the back of this text (see Appendix 1), you will discover that the probability is approximately equal to (1 − .99929) = 0.00071. Given this information, you are likely to conclude that you need to find the root cause of the dramatic increase in the percentage of faulty instructions. If you find the root cause, you will attempt to institute system changes that will prevent a repetition of the problem.

What about the situation in which for four straight days, only one out of 500 instructions was faulty? Here p = .002; thus, z is (.002 − .02) / 0.0062609 = −2.874, or 2.874 standard deviations below the mean. Using the standard normal distribution table, the probability of your sample having such a low proportion nonconforming when $\bar{p}$ is 0.02 is approximately 0.0021. This seems unlikely, but if it had happened only once you might not worry. The probability of the same result occurring four times in a row can be found using the rule of probability, $P(A \cap B) = P(A) \times P(B)$. Therefore, the probability of obtaining four consecutive samples with only one faulty instruction is equal to $(0.0021)^4$, which amounts to less than two chances in 100 billion. In this case, you would again conclude that something unusual must be going on. Since you like the results, you will want to discover the root cause of such excellent performance and institute controls to ensure that it continues.

Control charts, more specifically p-charts, help managers and workers to deal with the kinds of problem we have just discussed. Instead of going to the standard normal distribution table and looking up a z-score every time they take a sample, they use a control chart to decide whether or not a variation is unusual by comparing $\bar{p}$ for the sample to the limits of the p-chart. Charting the values over time also allows managers to see any patterns, or runs, in the data.

Since this chapter follows American practice, which is based on Shewhart's suggestion of 3σ limits, the formulas for the upper control limit (UCL), center line (CL) and lower control limit (LCL) on a p-chart are as follows:

$$UCL_p = \bar{p} + 3\sigma_p = \bar{p} + 3\sqrt{\frac{\bar{p}(1-\bar{p})}{n}}$$

$$CL_p = \bar{p}$$

$$LCL_p = \bar{p} - 3\sigma_p = \bar{p} - 3\sqrt{\frac{\bar{p}(1-\bar{p})}{n}}$$

To return to the airline example, suppose you took 10 samples of 500 departure instructions each and found the following numbers of incorrect instructions in each sample: 10, 12, 6, 14, 11, 9, 4, 14, 13, 10. You could construct a p-chart and plot these observations as follows. The chart's limits are CL = 0.02, UCL = 0.02 + 3 (0.0062609) = 0.0387829, and LCL = 0.02 − 3 (0.0062609) = 0.001217. Figure 6.9 shows the finished p-chart.

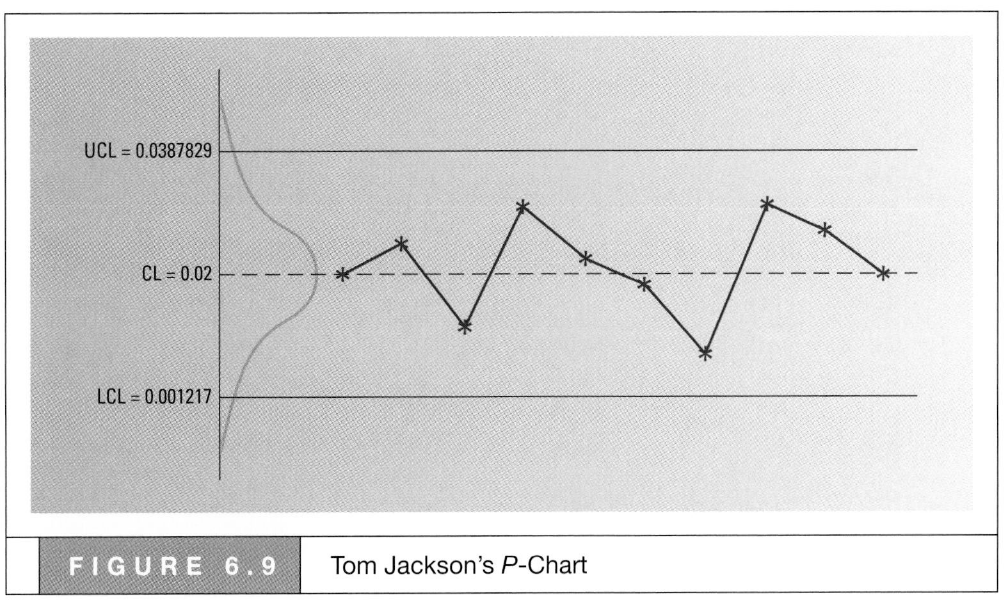

FIGURE 6.9 Tom Jackson's *P*-Chart

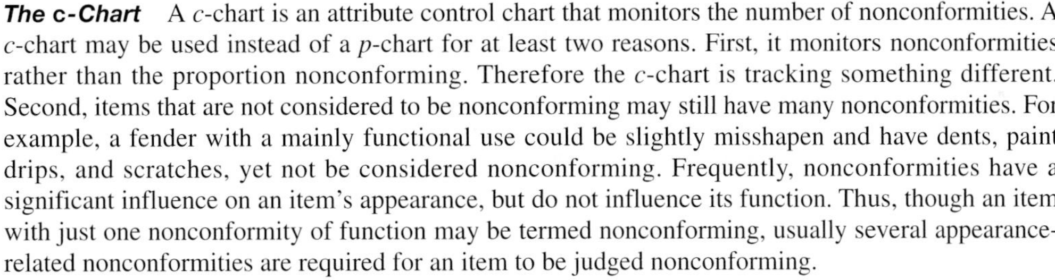

The c-Chart A *c*-chart is an attribute control chart that monitors the number of nonconformities. A *c*-chart may be used instead of a *p*-chart for at least two reasons. First, it monitors nonconformities rather than the proportion nonconforming. Therefore the *c*-chart is tracking something different. Second, items that are not considered to be nonconforming may still have many nonconformities. For example, a fender with a mainly functional use could be slightly misshapen and have dents, paint drips, and scratches, yet not be considered nonconforming. Frequently, nonconformities have a significant influence on an item's appearance, but do not influence its function. Thus, though an item with just one nonconformity of function may be termed nonconforming, usually several appearance-related nonconformities are required for an item to be judged nonconforming.

Formulas for the *c*-chart are:

$$UCL_c = \bar{c} + 3\sigma_c = \bar{c} + 3\sqrt{\bar{c}}$$

$$CL_c = \bar{c}$$

$$LCL_c = \bar{c} - 3\sigma_c = \bar{c} - 3\sqrt{\bar{c}}$$

Suppose Luis is evaluating a new supplier of fabric for his popular Southwestern-style furniture collection. He has requested 15 separate production runs of the same pattern in order to evaluate the supplier's ability to produce the design with consistency. Critical nonconformities in a bolt of fabric would include a color that did not match the standard, a flaw in the weaving, a margin that is narrower than specified (making the fabric difficult to stretch in cutting), and loss of color when the fabric is subjected to dry cleaning. Let's assume that Luis is particularly concerned about flaws in the weaving. In inspecting the 15 bolts the supplier has provided, he finds the following numbers of flaws on each bolt:

BOLT #	1	2	3	4	5	6	7	8	9	10	11	12	13	14	15
# of nonconformities	25	32	51	63	44	42	39	45	47	32	58	43	44	28	40

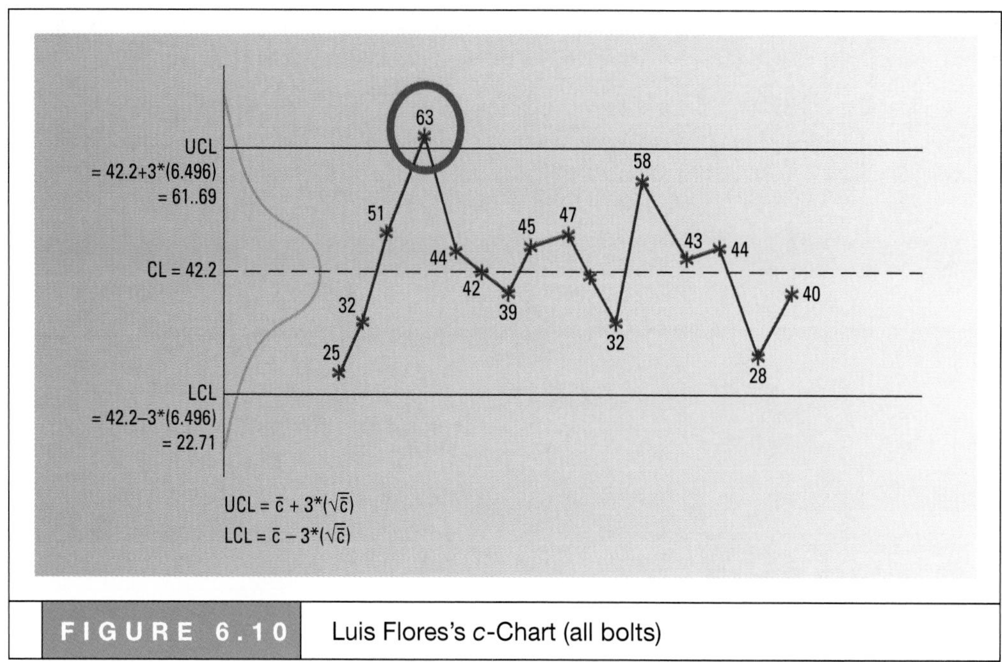

FIGURE 6.10 Luis Flores's *c*-Chart (all bolts)

Using these data, Luis would find $CL_c = \bar{c} = 42.2$, $UCL_c = 61.69$ and $LCL_c = 22.71$. The resulting *c*-chart is presented in Figure 6.10. It shows some indication of a lack of control: Bolt number four has 63 nonconformities, which is just above the upper control limit. Thus, Luis should investigate the value for bolt number four. Was the bolt inspected correctly? If so, where on the bolt were the nonconformities? Can the supplier identify the cause of the nonconformities on this bolt? If so, can the root cause of the nonconformities be eliminated, and when? Based on the answers to these questions, Luis may decide that bolt number four is not representative of the supplier's output when the process is in control. He could then eliminate that bolt from consideration and construct a new *c*-chart based on the 14 remaining bolts, which appear to be representative of the supplier's process when it is in control.

Luis's new *c*-chart would have the following values: $CL_c = \bar{c} = 40.71$, $UCL_c = 59.86$ and $LCL_c = 21.57$. Since the new chart has no indications of a lack of control, Luis may conclude that this supplier's fabric will have an average of 40.71 nonconformities per bolt. Unless there is some special cause of variation in the supplier's process, individual bolts will have between 22 and 59 nonconformities. If this level of quality, along with the supplier's other capabilities, meets the needs of Luis's company, Luis should feel free to proceed with the contract negotiations.

active exercise <

Take a moment to apply what you've learned.

video exercise <

Take a moment to apply what you've learned.

active concept check <

Now let's take a moment to test your knowledge of the concepts you have studied in this section.

Tools for Prevention of Quality Problems

As processes improve, they become less apt to produce nonconformities, or nonconforming items. As a result, the tools that were used during the detection phase become obsolete. Using a tool that relies on nonconforming material is expensive when nonconformities are difficult to identify.

Suppose, for instance, that a machine that fills 1-gallon milk jugs is being monitored with a *p*-chart. Let's say a nonconforming jug is defined as one that has more than 1.02 gallons or less than .98 gallons. That means that 1.02 is the *upper specification limit (USL)* and 0.98 is the *lower specification limit (LSL).* (A **specification limit** is the minimum level of conformance to a design target required for an item to be deemed conforming.) Inspecting just one milk jug may cost as much as $1, because in addition to the actual cost of the inspection, the inspected jugs cannot be sold. What would be the implications of an improvement in the proportion nonconforming, p, from 0.01 to 0.005?

If p is 0.01, the sample size would probably be at least 400, because when only one in a hundred items is nonconforming, inspectors usually need to look at several hundred items to get a good estimate of p. (The actual sample size required depends on the amount of variation in the sampling distribution of p; it could be much higher than 400.) With an inspection cost of $1 per item, then, obtaining just one point to plot on the *p*-chart would cost at least $400. If p were improved to 0.005, the required sample size to get a reasonable estimate of p would double, as would the cost of using the *p*-chart. This simple example clearly illustrates that as a process improves, attribute control techniques become more expensive. Indeed, for very good processes, the cost of using attribute control may be prohibitive.

STATISTICAL PROCESS CONTROL BY VARIABLE

One alternative to attribute control is variables control. In the case of the machine that fills 1-gallon milk jugs, the machine's performance can be monitored by tracking the volume of the milk that is placed in the jugs. A reasonable estimate of the average amount of milk being placed in the jugs could be obtained by inspecting only a fraction of the 400 jugs needed to plot one point on a *p*-chart when $p = 0.01$. In fact, inspectors might well need to examine only five jugs. Since obtaining a data point for the control chart would be far less expensive using this approach, inspectors might also take samples more frequently. Finally, if the common cause variation in the process is small enough, the information provided by these samples might even allow inspectors to recognize situations in which the machine is starting to drift away from its target of 1.000 gallons per jug long before any nonconforming jugs are created. Variables control, then, has the potential to *prevent* the creation of nonconforming products or services.

The most commonly used variables control charts plot sample means and ranges and are called $\overline{X}$ *and R-charts.* Two statistics, the sample mean and the sample range, are plotted for each sample. The three σ control limits for the $\overline{X}$ and the *R*-charts may be found using computational factors that are based on estimates of the relationship between the average range, $\overline{R}$, and the process standard devia-

SPC is effective only when the control scheme is designed based on appropriate data stratification. It may also require workers to gather data consistently across multiple shifts, days, and work centers. It is important not to overlook this human aspect to the effective use of SPC.

TABLE 6.2 Computational Factors for the $\overline{X}$ and R-Chart

n	A_2	D_3	D_4
2	1.880	0.000	3.267
3	1.023	0.000	2.575
4	0.729	0.000	2.282
5	0.577	0.000	2.115
6	0.483	0.000	2.004
7	0.419	0.076	1.924
8	0.373	0.136	1.864
9	0.337	0.184	1.816
10	0.308	0.223	1.777
11	0.285	0.256	1.744
12	0.266	0.284	1.716
13	0.249	0.308	1.692
14	0.235	0.329	1.671
15	0.223	0.348	1.652
16	0.212	0.364	1.636
17	0.203	0.379	1.621
18	0.194	0.392	1.608
19	0.187	0.404	1.596
20	0.180	0.414	1.586
21	0.173	0.425	1.575
22	0.167	0.434	1.566
23	0.162	0.443	1.557
24	0.157	0.452	1.548
25	0.153	0.459	1.541

Source: Table B_2 of the *A.S.T.M. Manual on Quality Control of Materials,* p. 115. Used with permission.

tion (see Table 6.2). As a rule, at least 20 samples are required to get a good estimate of $\overline{R}$ if the computational factors are used to estimate variability.

The equations for the $\overline{X}$ and the R-chart are:

$$UCL_{\overline{X}} = \overline{\overline{X}} + 3\sigma_{\overline{X}} \approx \overline{\overline{X}} + A_2\overline{R}$$
$$CL_{\overline{X}} = \overline{\overline{X}}$$
$$LCL_{\overline{X}} = \overline{\overline{X}} - 3\sigma_{\overline{X}} \approx \overline{\overline{X}} - A_2\overline{R}$$
$$UCL_R = \overline{R} + 3\sigma_R \approx D_4\overline{R}$$
$$CL_R = \overline{R}$$
$$LCL_R = \overline{R} - 3\sigma_R \approx D_3\overline{R}$$

Table 6.3 presents sample computations for an $\overline{X}$ and R-chart based on the example of the machine that fills milk jugs. The chart itself, which was computed using the factors in Table 6.2, appears in Figure 6.11.

It might have been better if the $\overline{X}$ and R-chart had been named the R and $\overline{X}$-charts, because the R-chart should always be interpreted before the $\overline{X}$-chart. The R-chart monitors a system's variability; thus an R-chart that is in control indicates that the system's precision has not changed. Since the control limits on the $\overline{X}$-chart are a function of the system's variability, they should be used only when that variability is known with some confidence—and that can be the case only when the R-chart shows no indications of a lack of control. When the R-chart demonstrates a process variability that is in control, the $\overline{X}$-chart provides an indication of the system's accuracy.

The difference between precision and accuracy is subtle. Figure 6.12 illustrates the two concepts in terms of a bulls-eye target. Assume that the points on the targets represent the performance of machines that center watermarks on paper stationery. Part a of Figure 6.12 shows the precision and accuracy of a machine that is demonstrating only common cause variability. Both the $\overline{X}$ and the R-chart for this machine are in control. Part b shows the performance of a machine whose R-chart is out

TABLE 6.3 Computations for an Example $\bar{X}$ and *R-Chart*

	Observation (Milk Jug)					Sample	Sample
Sample	**1**	**2**	**3**	**4**	**5**	**Mean($\bar{x}$)**	**Range(R)**
1	1.005	1.008	1.000	0.999	1.003	1.0030	0.0090
2	1.004	1.004	1.010	0.998	1.004	1.0040	0.0120
3	1.000	0.997	0.998	1.003	1.001	0.9998	0.0060
4	0.996	0.999	0.989	1.001	0.999	0.9968	0.0120
5	1.002	0.998	0.997	0.993	1.003	0.9986	0.0100
6	0.993	0.995	0.994	0.997	0.999	0.9956	0.0060
7	1.000	1.005	1.002	0.998	0.998	1.0006	0.0070
8	0.997	0.998	1.004	1.006	0.994	0.9998	0.0120
9	0.996	1.006	1.004	1.005	1.002	1.0026	0.0100
10	1.003	0.995	0.998	0.999	0.991	0.9972	0.0120
11	1.012	1.015	1.006	1.007	1.008	1.0096	0.0090
12	1.005	1.006	1.009	1.000	0.999	1.0038	0.0100
13	0.997	0.996	0.995	0.999	1.000	0.9974	0.0050
14	0.999	1.000	1.005	1.003	0.997	1.0008	0.0080
15	0.987	0.990	0.994	0.990	0.989	0.9900	0.0070
16	1.000	1.002	0.995	0.994	0.999	0.9980	0.0080
17	1.003	1.003	1.002	1.004	0.998	1.0020	0.0060
18	0.992	0.997	1.008	0.998	0.999	0.9988	0.0160
19	0.994	1.006	1.003	1.005	1.000	1.0016	0.0120
20	1.006	1.003	1.000	1.000	0.995	1.0008	0.0110
21	1.011	1.008	1.000	1.004	1.001	1.0048	0.0110
22	0.999	0.991	0.995	1.000	1.001	0.9972	0.0100
23	0.998	0.988	1.000	1.001	1.002	0.9978	0.0140
24	0.999	1.000	1.001	1.002	1.001	1.0006	0.0030
25	0.998	0.995	0.993	0.998	0.999	0.9966	0.0060
					Averages	$\bar{\bar{X}}$=0.9999	$\bar{R}$=0.0093
					UCL	1.0053	0.0196
					LCL	0.9946	0.0000

Factors from Table 6.2

A2	D3	D4
0.577	0.000	2.115

of control, but whose $\bar{X}$-chart is in control. Though this machine's precision has been lost, its performance is still reasonably accurate.

Now suppose inspectors identify and remove the special cause of the variation—maybe it was a loose bolt—shown in Figure 6.12(b). Suppose further that the operator learns that the customer would prefer to have the watermark appear in the upper right-hand quadrant of the paper. Figure 6.12(c) shows the results after the machine's precision has been brought under control and the process retargeted. Based on the *old* specifications, this process is precise but not very accurate. In Figure 6.12(d), the process has moved out of control on the $\bar{X}$-chart, though the watermarks appear to be placed with greater precision than normal. If the precision remains this good, eventually a run will fall below the center line of the *R*-chart, leading to an investigation into the cause of the variation. New limits will be established for the two charts based on the new target and the reduction in variability.

Now return to Figure 6.11, which illustrates the performance of the machine that fills milk jugs. Notice that none of the rules of run illustrated in Figure 6.8 have been violated on the *R*-chart in Figure 6.11. Consequently, we can go on to interpret the $\bar{X}$-chart for this machine. We see immediately that two points are out of control. These indicators of a shift in the mean should be investigated and corrected, as should all special cause variations.

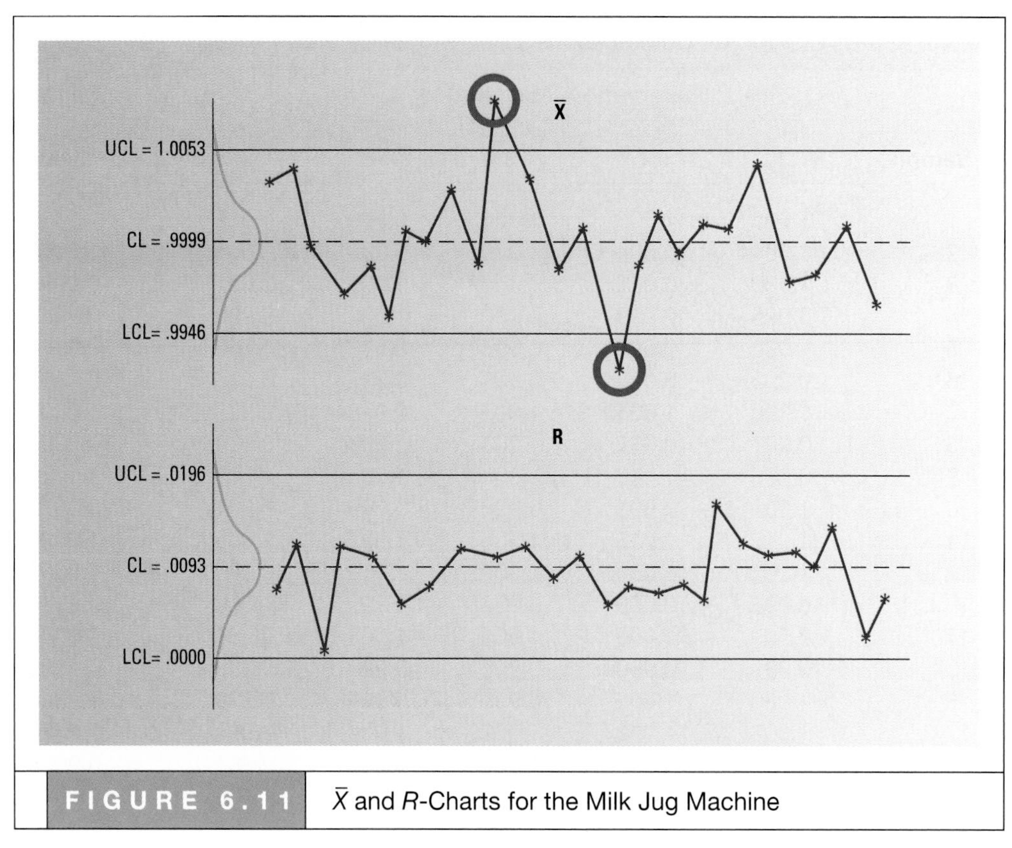

FIGURE 6.11 $\bar{X}$ and *R*-Charts for the Milk Jug Machine

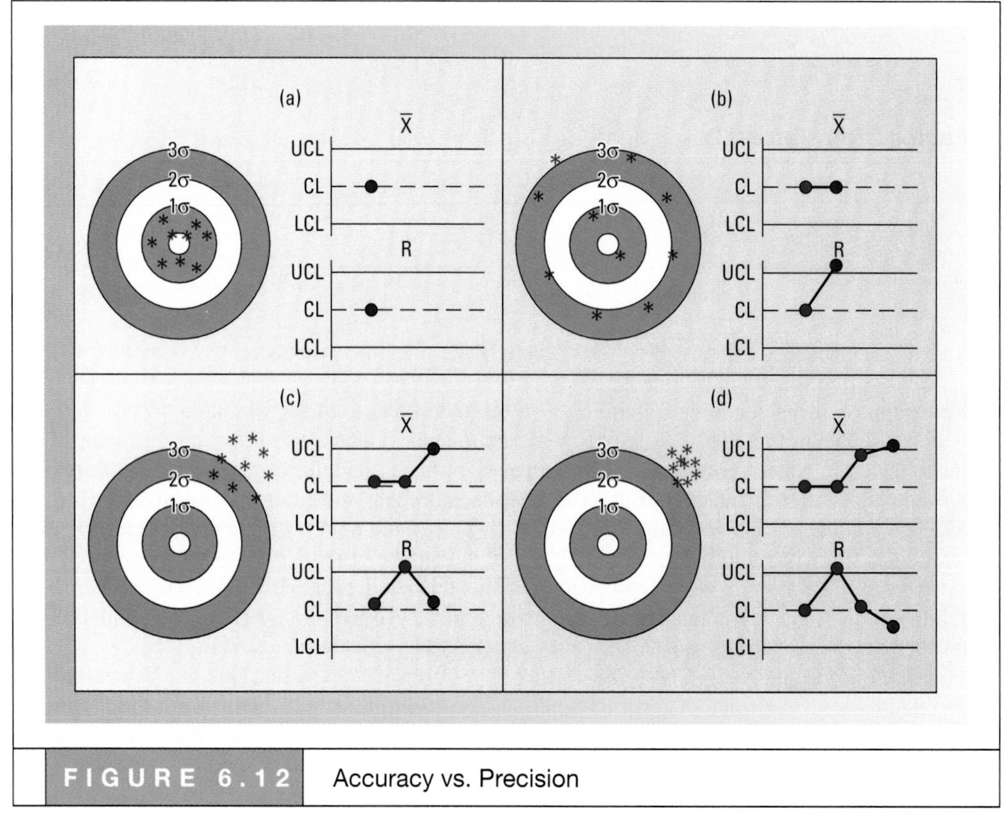

FIGURE 6.12 Accuracy vs. Precision

Does being in control mean that a machine is not producing any nonconforming items? Certainly not! It means only that there is no special cause variation in the process. A process that is in control may or may not produce nonconforming items. As we shall see in the next section, the relationship between the variation in the process and the tolerance for variation represented by the product specifications determines whether or not a process that is in control is capable of nonconformity-free operation.

> active exercise

Take a moment to apply what you've learned.

CAPABILITY INDEXES

The ability of a process to meet specifications, called **process capability,** is measured by comparing the variation in the process with the allowance for variation provided by the specifications. A *capability index* expresses the concept of process capability in numeric terms. Four commonly cited capability indices are the C_p index, the C_{pk} index, the CPU index, and the CPL index. They are computed as follows:

$$C_p = \frac{(USL - LSL)}{6\sigma}$$

$$C_{pk} = min\left\{\frac{\overline{\overline{X}} - LSL}{3\sigma}, \frac{USL - \overline{\overline{X}}}{3\sigma}\right\}$$

$$CPU = \frac{USL - \overline{\overline{X}}}{3\sigma}$$

$$CPL = \frac{\overline{\overline{X}} - LSL}{3\sigma}$$

Each of the capability indexes yields different information. The C_p index indicates the process's *potential* capability, because it assumes that the distribution of process output is centered perfectly between the specification limits. Large values are desirable on the capability indexes. Thus, a C_p of 1.0 would mean that about 3 parts in 1,000 can be expected to be "out of spec"; a C_p of 1.33 would mean that about 64 parts per million (PPM) can be expected to be out of spec; and a C_p of 1.67 would indicate a nonconformity rate of about 1 PPM. In general, a process with $C_{pk} \leq 1.0$ is said to be "not capable"; a process with $C_{pk} \geq 1.0$ is said to be "capable." Figure 6.13 summarizes and illustrates this information. It shows that as process capability improves, the use of quality control tools such as final goods inspection, acceptance sampling, and statistical process control should decline.

When a process is centered between the LSL and USL, the C_p index and the C_{pk} index will have the same value. The C_{pk} index indicates the *actual* capability of a process, whether or not its mean is perfectly centered between the USL and LSL. Since in reality, process output distributions frequently are *not* centered between the product specifications, most large industrial companies use the C_{pk} index to describe their expectations of process capability in supply contracts. For example, Cummins Engine Company told suppliers in the early 1990s that they had to demonstrate process C_{pk}s above 1.33 and C_{pk}s of 1.67 or above by 1998.

The difference between the values of the C_p index and the C_{pk} index indicates how much the actual process capability could be improved by moving the mean to the center of the specification limits, without reducing variation in the process. This information is valuable, because changing the mean of a process is usually much easier than reducing process variation.

The CPU and the CPL are used less frequently than the C_{pk}. They are of particular interest only with one-sided specifications or when managers are concerned about either the LSL or the USL.

You might have heard about a concept called 6σ quality, meaning that specification limits are six standard deviations away from the process mean. Major companies like Motorola and General Electric have made the concept of 6σ quality famous. This standard equates to a C_p index of 2.0. In a process with an output distribution centered between the specifications and $C_p = 2.0$, the proportion nonconforming would best be measured in parts per billion! In processes in which shifts in the process average are common, 6σ design is particularly useful. Even if the output distribution of a 6σ process were to move off center by $\pm\ 1.5\sigma$, only 3.4 PPM would be out of spec.

The 6σ quality concept is just as applicable to service output as to manufacturing output. For instance, the FAA might say that "on time" means arrival within 15 minutes of schedule. This concept is important for air traffic control purposes, for being early is just as problematic as being late from the

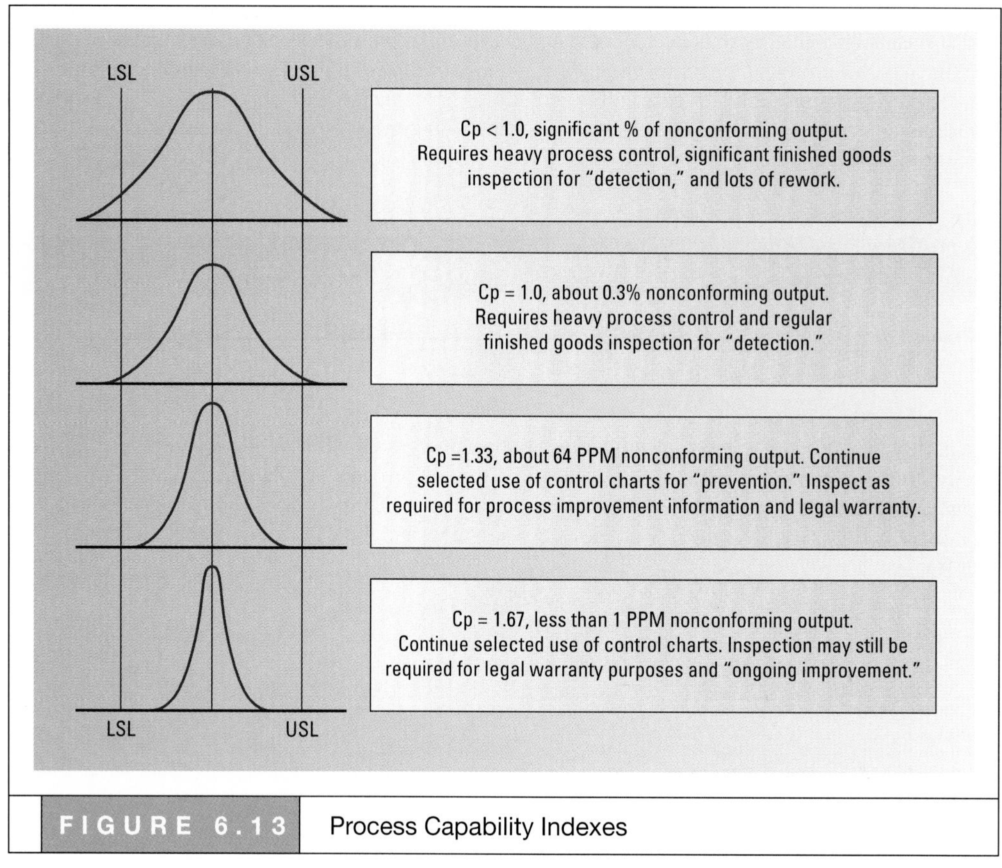

FIGURE 6.13 Process Capability Indexes

controller's point of view. If Tom Jackson's airline were to find a way to ensure that on average, flights arrived at the scheduled time, with a standard deviation equal to 2.5 minutes or less, it would achieve 6σ quality. Managers would be able to tell the FAA that the airline's planes are always "on time" and that tracking the airline's performance is a waste of the FAA's resources.

FAILPROOFING METHODS

In all the methods of statistical analysis discussed so far, nonconformities are prevented through a process of sampling and monitoring. At best, these techniques provide only partial assurance that the proportion nonconforming will be acceptable and that special cause variation will be spotted. But the real goal of most companies is zero nonconformities. Obviously, to produce no nonconformities, a process must be unable to fail. Failproofing a process is therefore a much better form of nonconformity prevention and process control than is statistical process control.

The Japanese term for "failproof" is **poka yoke.** As an example, a *poka yoke* device used at the Cummins Engine Company makes sure the correct transmission is placed in the company's midrange diesel engines. Electric eyes on the supply rack at the workstation check to "see" what type of transmission parts (automatic or manual) the assembly worker at the station picks up. The assembly line is also monitored by a computer program that keeps track of each engine during its assembly, based on the engine's bar-coded serial number. Before the computer allows the engine to advance to the next workstation, it checks the specifications for this particular engine. If the worker takes parts for an automatic transmission out of stock when the engine is supposed to have a manual transmission, the engine will not advance to the next point on the assembly line. In fact, it will not advance until the correct transmission parts have been removed from stock. Other examples of failproofing in manufacturing environments include warning lights when tools are worn or out of tolerance, master templates to match production samples against, and checklists which specify exact steps to complete a process.

The concept of failproofing a production process was first introduced by the Japanese operations expert Shigeo Shingo. Though Shingo devised the idea of *poka yoke* devices for use in manufacturing processes, the concept is applicable to service processes as well. For example, in some states, driver's licenses show individuals under 21 years of age in profile rather than full face. The practice is intended to fail-safe the process of checking a person's age before the sale of alcohol and tobacco. It essentially eliminates the likelihood that a person who is checking the age of a minor will read a birthdate incorrectly or calculate the individual's age incorrectly. Other examples of failproofing in services include signs along customer waiting lines that list information and items the customer will need to receive service (e.g., Cash Only), the McDonald's french fry scoop that measures a consistent quantity of fries, warning messages generated while executing computer software programs, motion detectors that turn off lights when people exit a room, reminder telephone calls for appointments, and beepers on ATM machines to remind people to remove their card.

> active poll

What do you think? Voice your opinion and find out what others have to say.

> active concept check

Now let's take a moment to test your knowledge of the concepts you have studied in this section.

Tools for Ongoing Improvement

Because of advances in process capability, nonconformity prevention eventually loses its appeal as a focus for quality improvement efforts. The ability to satisfy customer requirements today, however, does not imply an ability to satisfy customer expectations in the future, because customer expectations change over time. Nor does the fact that a process is capable of producing without nonconformities mean that it cannot be improved. Finally, processes that are not improving may be eroding.

For all these reasons, the focus of quality improvement efforts may eventually shift from prevention to ongoing and continuous improvement. Focusing on ongoing improvement is a way of preparing to meet customers' future expectations, whether they can be anticipated or not. Even when customers' future expectations are unforeseen and unforeseeable, a focus on continual improvement can lead to the development of capabilities that will prepare a firm to meet new expectations.

In Chapter 5 we suggested that the continuous improvement of processes is one of the key commitments of TQM. Ongoing, continuous improvement of processes requires a company to establish a climate in which everyone focuses on delighting the customer. Thus, the tools and methods that are used to foster ongoing improvement are meant not just for quality professionals, but for everyone. They are most useful in the context of an organizationwide focus on customer satisfaction consistent with the four commitments of TQM.

Table 6.4 presents an example of a continuous improvement process. This table was developed by Cummins Engine Company and printed on laminated three-by-five-inch index cards for easy reference by employees. It illustrates the greater context in which the tools and methods for achieving ongoing, continuous improvement should be used.

THE QUALITY IMPROVEMENT (QI) STORY

The **QI story** is a structured process that allows a group to use both numeric and subjective data to solve problems. It provides a way for group members to organize their interactions, collect and analyze data, and monitor their progress. This method was originally conceived as a technique for communicating the rationale a group used in arriving at a proposed solution. In reality, groups that use the QI story are able not only to communicate their solutions; they are also better able to obtain input from nonteam members and are more productive in their problem solving.

The QI story is composed of seven logical steps taken in sequence. The first step establishes the groundwork for the second, the second for the third, and so forth:

Step 1. Establish the reason for improvement: Select a theme.

Step 2. Describe the current situation, including gaps between the existing state and the desired state.

Step 3. Analyze and identify possible root causes, and rank their impact on the project theme.

Step 4. Identify countermeasures, rank them, and establish a plan for testing them.

TABLE 6.4	Cummins Engine's Continuous Improvement Process

1. Define Customers and Products (internal and external)
Describe products/services provided to customers
Identify important features/characteristics
Establish feedback mechanism for improvement

2. Define Suppliers and Products (internal and external)
Describe product/service required for your process
Identify suppliers and important features/characteristics
Establish feedback mechanism for improvement

3. Define Internal Process
Describe internal work flow
Identify connecting or supplying work flows
Document the work flow

4. Establish Improvement Goals/Focus on Trouble Spots
Identify bottleneck operations
Identify incapable operations
Look for excessive inventory levels
Eliminate waste wherever it is found
Simplify process while maintaining reliability/consistency
Benchmark best system
Continuously improve capability of all operations
Use above data to define improvement goals

5. Implement Improvements
Identify areas to be improved first
Establish work teams for improvement
Select and train work group leaders
Train work group members
Problem solve and implement improvements
Support/reward work groups
Celebrate successes and failures
Define what was learned and improve improvement work

6. Define Improved System
Fail-safe improved operations
Revise and document improved work flow
Formalize in total quality system where appropriate

7. Evaluate and Improve
Audit products/processes/systems
Plan for improvement without losing gains
Measure and track product/process performance
Revisit benchmark
Plan next level of improvement

Step 5. Test the countermeasures with a prototype, trial period, or trial department. If the countermeasures fail, go back to step 4. If the plan works, move on to step 6.

Step 6. Standardize the solution and ensure that processes do not revert to the status quo.

Step 7. Continue the improvement cycle with another theme.

These steps will be easy to remember if you think about the last time your roommate confronted you over a pile of dirty laundry left unattended too long. Your roommate's nose identified the need for improvement and, chances are, located a mound of evidence that documented the situation. As you began to look through the clothing, you probably did some analysis and figured out how long it had been since your last trip to the laundromat, how many times you had exercised since then, and so forth. Based on this analysis, you would have developed a plan to prevent the problem from recurring. If your analysis showed that the most offensive items were also those that had been in the pile the longest, your plan might have called for the two of you to take turns doing each other's laundry once a week, so that no items would remain unlaundered for more than four days. If the offensive items were exercise clothes, your plan may have specified the timing of your trips to the laundromat relative to the timing of your exercise sessions and may have called for a different storage procedure as well.

If your plan worked, you probably kept it up. If it did not work, you obviously needed to think of another plan. When you finally solved the problem, you had responded to a critical need identified by your roommate. The next time a domestic problem arises (say, an alarm clock that always goes off five times before your roommate gets up), this problem-solving experience will help both of you to address the issue in a constructive way. Even if the next problem is much more complex, you will trust each other more and be able to build on your earlier success. With each new experience in team problem solving, your effectiveness as a team will grow.

By this point in your college career, you should be familiar with, and may have used, many of the tools for data collection and analysis that are used by quality improvement teams. The tools themselves are shown in Figure 6.14, parts A–K. The following bullet list summarizes those tools in the context of the QI story. Figure 6.15 on page 184 places some of the tools shown in Figure 6.14 in the context of the QI story.

- **Checklists:** A checklist is a guide to accomplishing a task. It is particularly useful to standardize the way that routine tasks are done and make note of any unusual occurrences in the process. If the completed checksheet is signed by the worker and saved, it can provide an audit trail for the work that was done. For example, a "knock off" checklist at a restaurant could list the various cleaning tasks and machine shutdowns that have to be done before going home. The manager would know, by looking at the completed checklist, that it is okay to let employees "knock off."
- **Checksheets:** Much like a checklist, a checksheet is more oriented toward collecting data and less oriented toward guiding activity. A checksheet is a template that provides the structure used to record data. For instance, a checksheet used to record nonconformities on windshields might include spaces for the inspector to record the batch inspected and the equipment used for inspection and could have a picture of the windshield to illustrate the location of observed nonconformities.
- **Brainstorming:** Brainstorming is a well-known technique used to generate an extensive list of ideas pertinent to a particular problem. You could brainstorm to identify root causes or to suggest possible solutions. While brainstorming, no judgment of the value of any idea should take place, for this could inhibit input. Brainstorming is a particularly effective way of gathering subjective data.

Setup Approval Checklist

Product to be made ______
Customer ______
Quantity to be made ______
Fixtures needed ______
Machine tool needed ______
Setup Operator ______

OED Prep Activities: Time/Initial
Die inspection ______
Die maintenance ______
Fixture maintenance ______
Setup tool retrieval ______
Fixture retrieval ______
Begin checklist for setup ______
Prepare toolkit for setup ______
Get material needed for production ______

Name ______
Date ______
Begin time ______
Location ______
Machine ID ______

Signature

IED Activities: Time/Initial
Machine maintenance ______
Tool removal ______
Tool installation ______
Batch prototype ______
Prototype inspection ______
Approval request ______
Production go ahead ______

OED Wrap-up Activities: Time/Initial
Die inspection ______
Die maintenance ______
Fixture maintenance ______
Tool storage ______
Fixture storage ______
File checklist for setup ______

FIGURE 6.14A Checklist

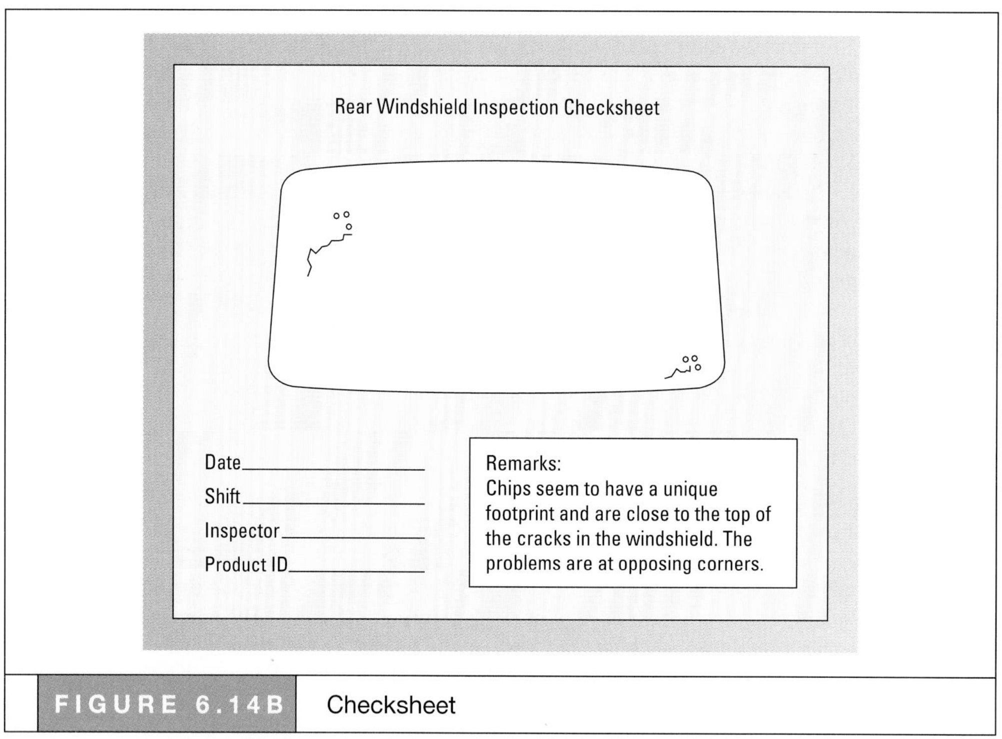

FIGURE 6.14B Checksheet

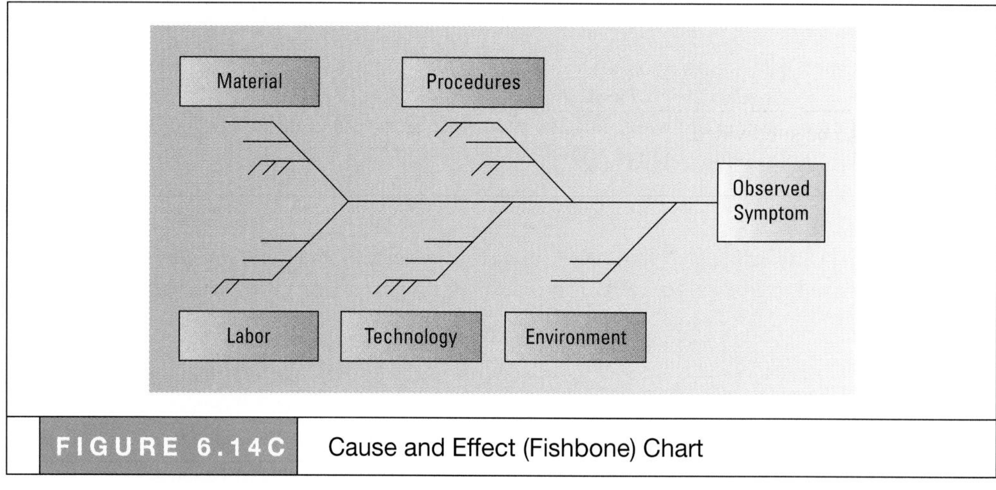

FIGURE 6.14C Cause and Effect (Fishbone) Chart

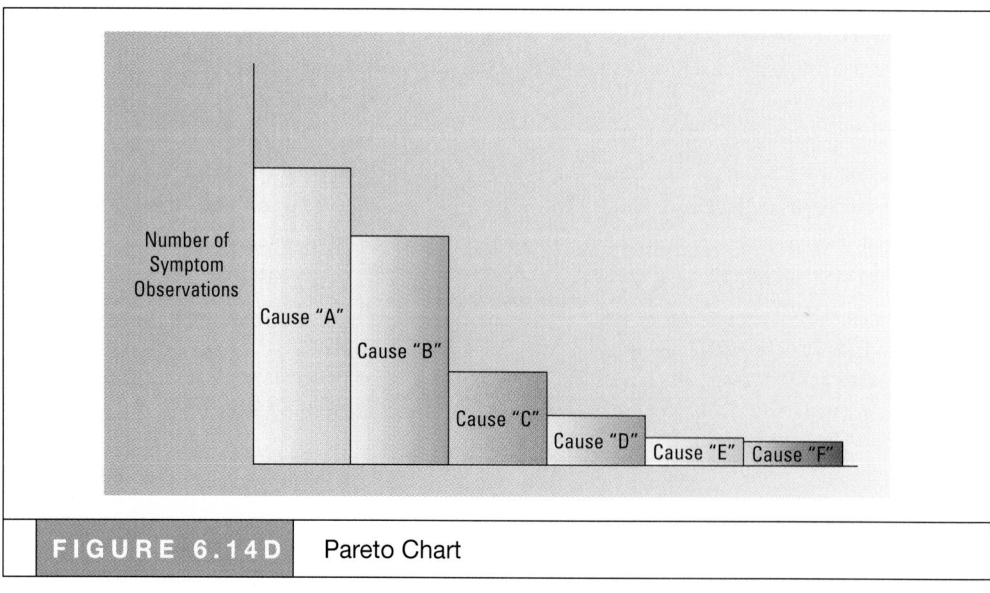

FIGURE 6.14D Pareto Chart

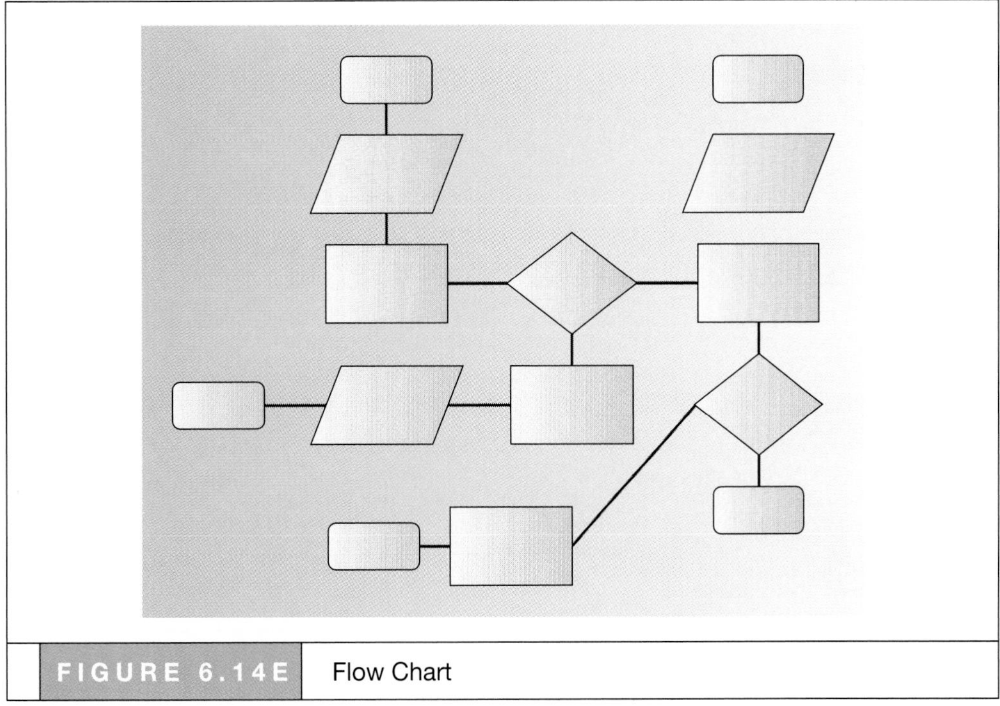

FIGURE 6.14E Flow Chart

- **Cause and effect diagrams (fishbone charts):** Fishbone diagrams categorize the potential reasons for a situation that is observed. These diagrams might take a list of causes of a problem that come out of a brainstorming session and group them broadly into groups such as "material," "method," "man," and "machine." The main groups form the major vertebrae of the "fish," and these can also be subdivided.
- **5 Ws and H:** The 5 Ws and H are a set of questions that can help identify the root cause of a problem. This approach can be used to determine if a fishbone diagram is correctly constructed. When a problem arises, by asking a series of "why" questions we can move to the root cause on a fishbone. For example, if a FedEx delivery was late, we ask **why.** If it's that a sorting machine broke down at the Memphis distribution hub, we again ask **why.** If it's because it overheated, we again ask **why.** If the wrong type of lubricant had been used, we again ask **why.** If the lubricant labels had been changed by the supplier to meet new environmental labeling requirements, we need not ask why again. Instead we would ask **how** we can make sure the problem doesn't arise again. Maybe we would ask the supplier to educate the maintenance department about their new labeling scheme.

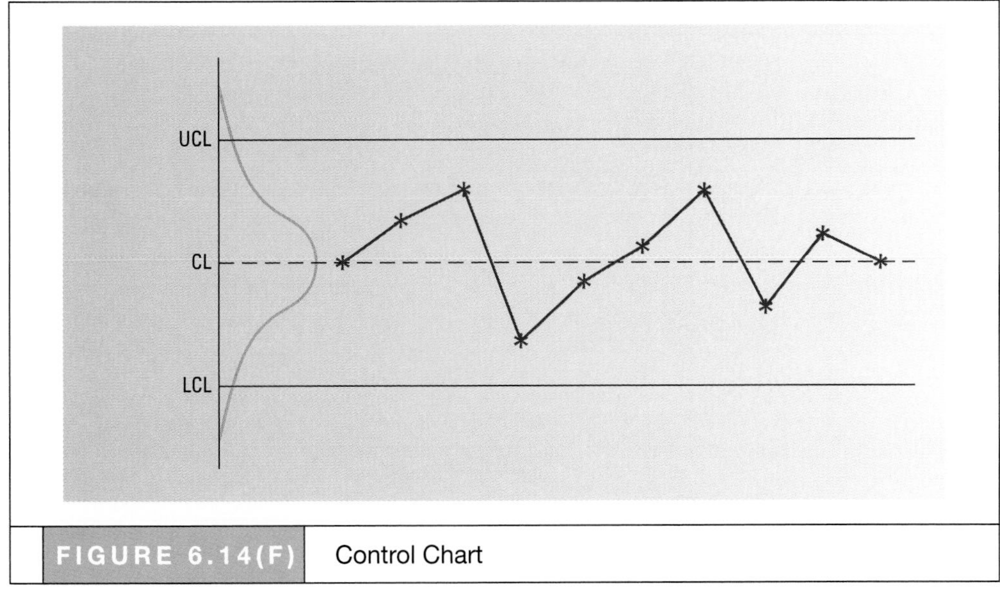

FIGURE 6.14(F) Control Chart

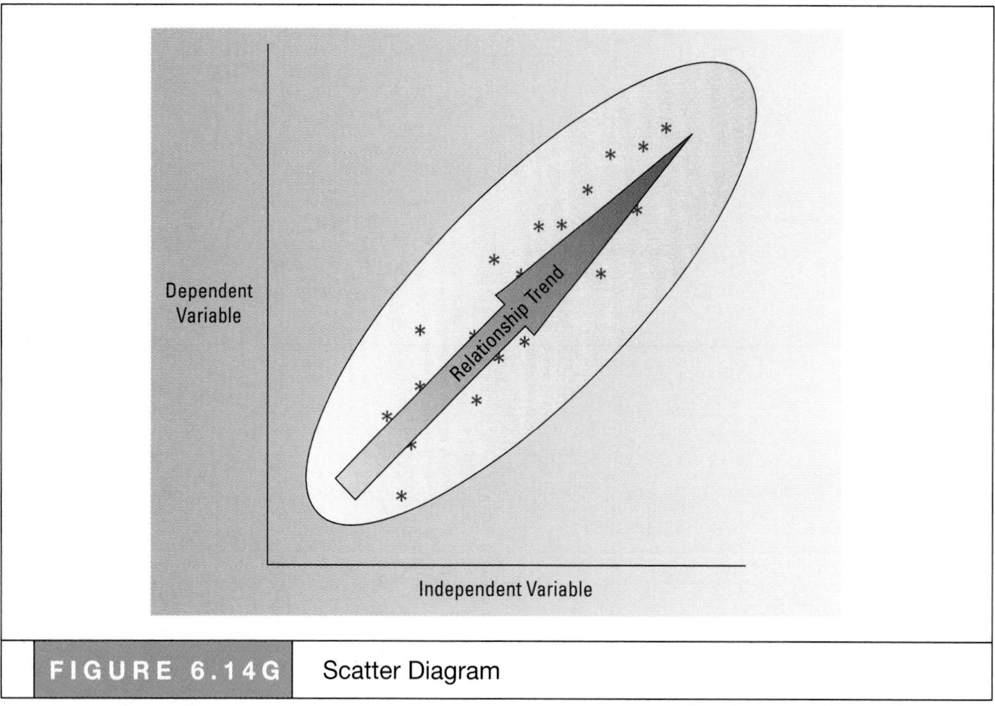

FIGURE 6.14G Scatter Diagram

- **Pareto charts:** Pareto charts are bar charts used to distinguish "the vital few from the trivial many." They are based on the Pareto principle, also known as the "80/20 rule." In terms of quality, the 80/20 rule would say that 80% of the problems come from 20% of the causes. Pareto charts typically deal with category data.
- **Histograms:** A histogram is a bar chart that presents a frequency distribution. Unlike the Pareto chart that uses category data, it can be used to characterize the relative frequency of process output along a scale that is divided into equal regions. A histogram can tell us if product output is "skewed" in any particular direction, if it is "bimodal," or if it is balanced around the distributions mean.
- **Flow charts:** Flow charts are tools that are especially effective in describing a process by graphically depicting all of the steps in the process in sequence. In operations, we stress the importance of using flow charts to understand both product flows and information flows. You can use flow charts to highlight the places where problems are most likely (or opportunity for improvement is greatest) by comparing a flow chart of the process as it is with a flow chart of the process as it would be under ideal circumstances.
- **Control charts:** Control charts have been discussed at length in this chapter. These are used to determine whether or not there is special cause variation in a process.

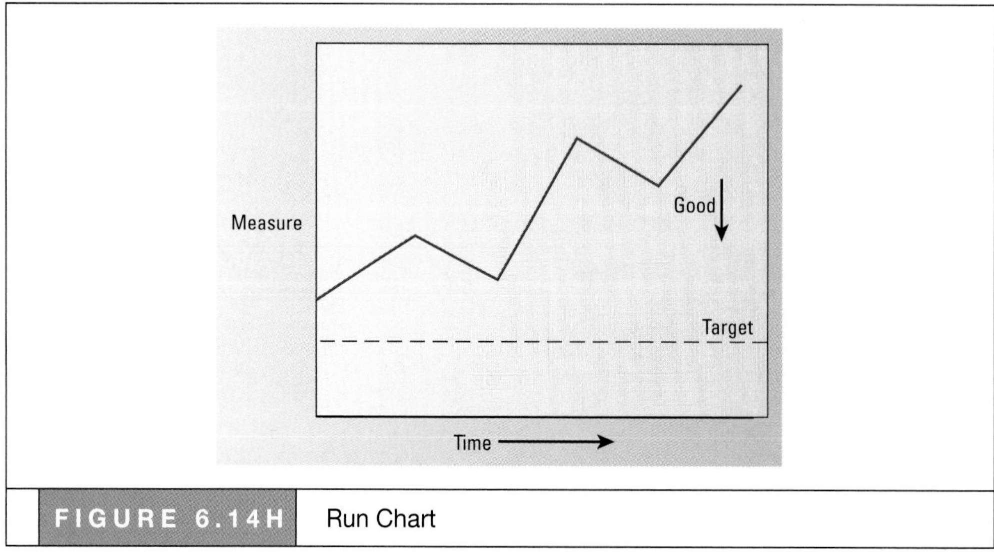

FIGURE 6.14H Run Chart

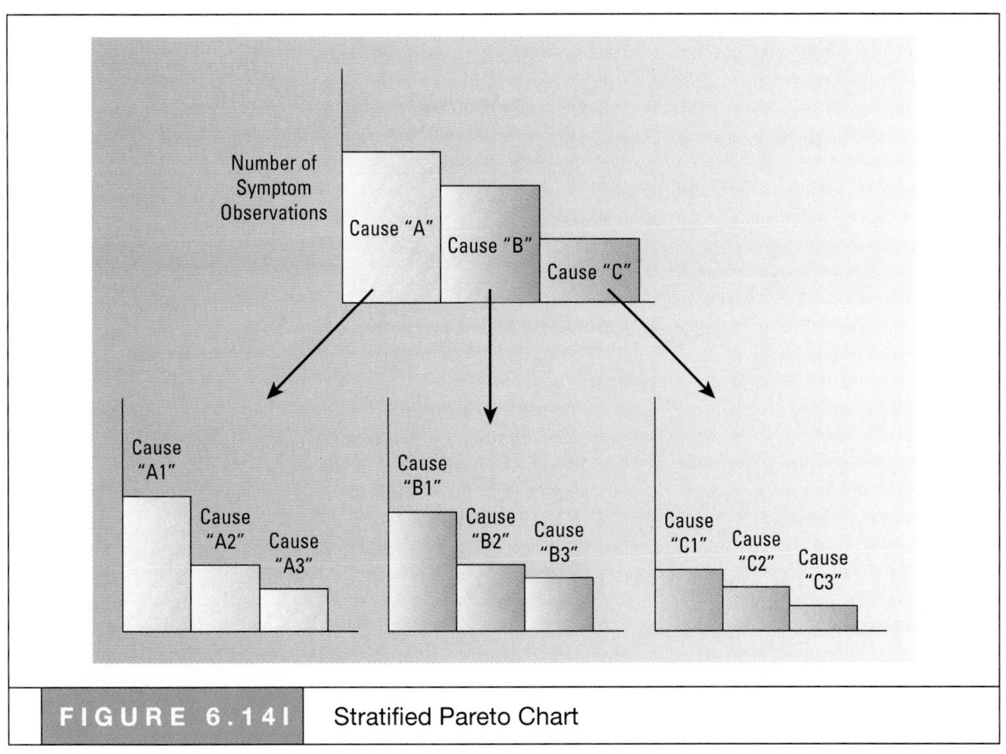

FIGURE 6.14I Stratified Pareto Chart

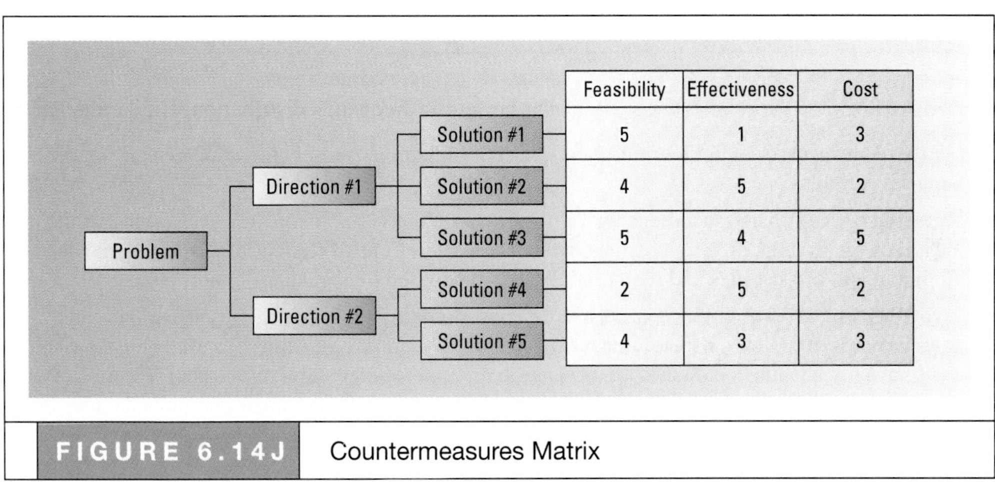

	Feasibility	Effectiveness	Cost
Solution #1	5	1	3
Solution #2	4	5	2
Solution #3	5	4	5
Solution #4	2	5	2
Solution #5	4	3	3

FIGURE 6.14J Countermeasures Matrix

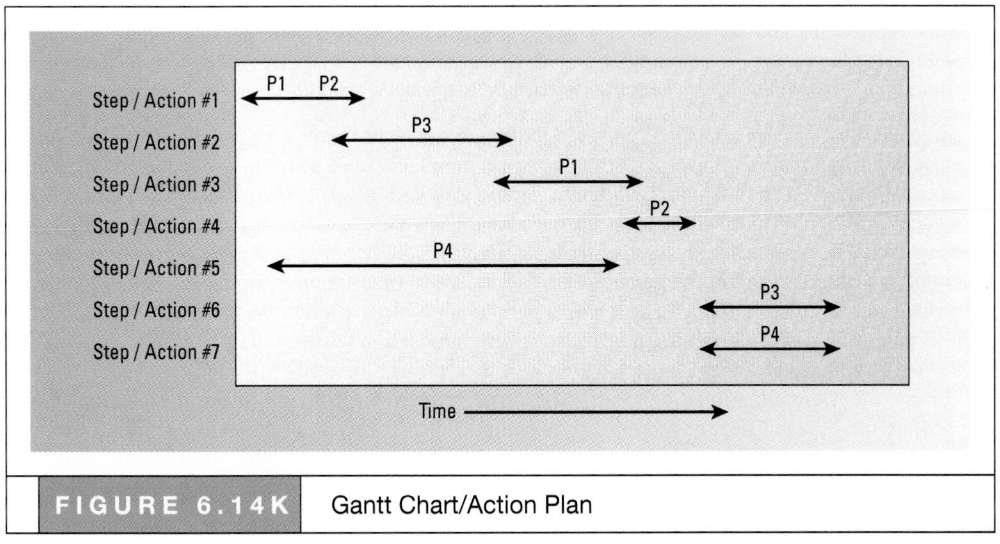

FIGURE 6.14K Gantt Chart/Action Plan

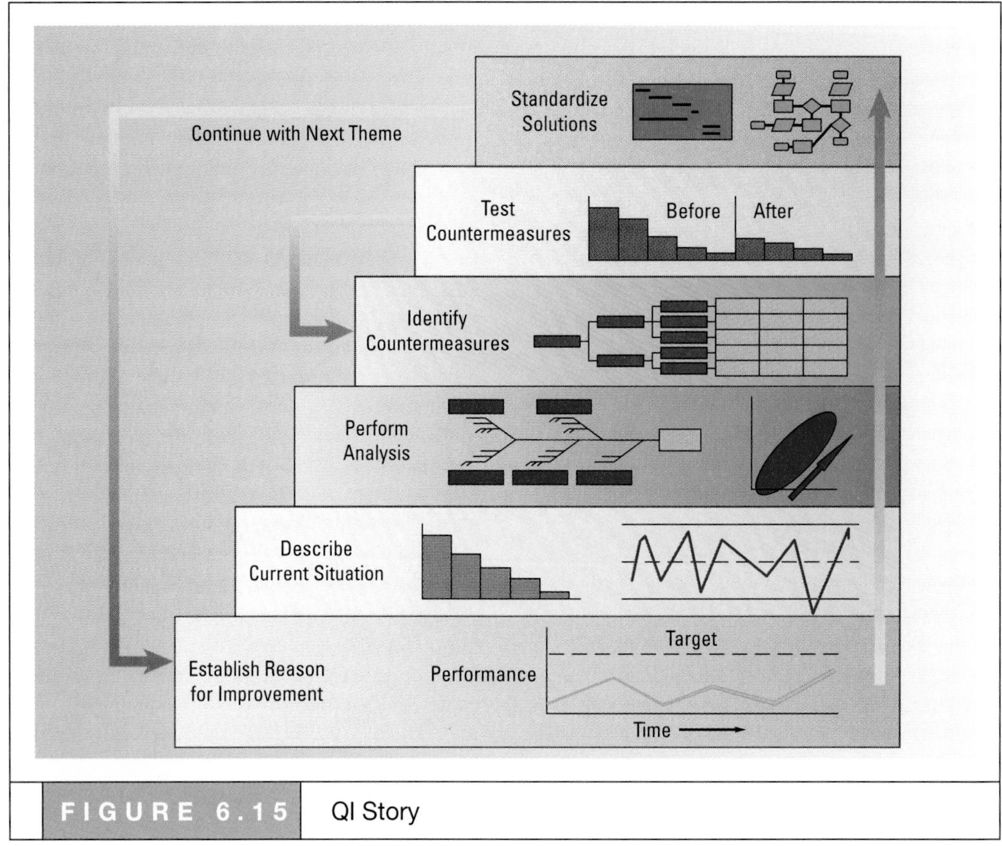

FIGURE 6.15 QI Story

- **Scatter diagrams:** Scatter diagrams can be used to pictorially present the underlying relationships between variables.
- **Run charts:** Run charts document the value of a particular variable over time. Like a control chart, they allow us to track process changes over time. Unlike control charts, they usually are based on all output and not samples and they don't have limits based on some past experience.
- **Stratification:** Stratification is a way of breaking data down by category. When data has been aggregated, it often loses its usefulness. For example, in most cases the percentage of the popular vote that a presidential candidate obtains is probably not so interesting to political scientists. When this percentage is broken down by state, county, income level, sex, or profession, the data becomes much more useful.
- **Countermeasures matrix:** This matrix provides a way of ranking a variety of possible solutions on a variety of criteria such as effectiveness, feasibility, safety, environmental impact, and cost. By giving weights to the various criteria, preference for one of many solutions can be established.
- **Gantt chart:** A Gantt chart is used to display planned (and actual) progress over time. Displaying planned timing of activities on a time line helps team members recognize what activities are really critical and how well they are keeping up with their project's schedule.

Although most managers are well prepared to use tools such as these, the typical hourly wage earner may not be. Many may not have performed well academically, and some may not have high school diplomas or may even be functionally illiterate. Training should therefore be made available to workers, so that they will be able to use these tools. Besides the tools themselves, training should cover skills such as interpersonal communication, effective writing, effective collaboration, and group decision making—skills that are often lacking in the general workforce. Just-in-time training should also be available, in case a team needs special training to deal with a particular problem or simply requires a refresher course. (Just-in-time training is not training about just-in-time production systems, but is training given at the time when a team needs to learn something to move their project forward.)

Finally, most organizations make a facilitator available to QI teams, often the person who is responsible for the employee involvement program. The facilitator can act as a sounding board for teams and can also monitor their progress, put them in touch with experts from other functions or divisions when necessary, and help them to work through interpersonal conflicts.

> active concept check

Now let's take a moment to test your knowledge of the concepts you have studied in this section.

Solving the Music Dilemma at the Student Recreation Center

The QI story approach to ongoing process improvement can be used in a variety of settings and is limited neither to manufacturing nor for-profit enterprises. In fact, the Fitness Center (FC) at Miami University's Student Recreation Center (SRC) recently used a very similar approach to solving a problem regarding music.

Not long after it opened in 1994 and over the period of several weeks, SRC staff noticed a common theme through a number of complaints and suggestions turned in by patrons. It seems that the choice of music played in the FC left much to be desired according to a lot of the people who work out there. The FC is the section of the SRC where a wide variety of students and community people work out on weight machines, lift free weights, ride stationary bikes, climb steppers, and use a variety of other types of exercise machinery. The music helps pass the time while working out on a solitary station, as well as adds to the social atmosphere of the FC.

The sound system's volume and FM radio station choice is controlled from the staff station in the center of the FC. Originally, there were no policies for music selection. Student staff workers were allowed to choose the station according to their tastes, as long as volume was kept to a level where conversation was possible. However, given the diverse nature of the people who use the center, some diverse opinions of what type of music should be played appeared inevitable. It was not uncommon for a dozen people to ask for a change of station during the two-hour shift of a student staff worker. The number of people who were dissatisfied with the music selection seemed significant. Staff, anxious to be helpful, would change stations when requested, only to find that one change led to another request and another and another—seemingly endlessly.

SRC administrators noticed the issue when periodic reviews of the complaints and suggestions took place. The Student Staff Advisory Committee (SSAC) met on the issue and decided to take the QI story approach to handling the issue. Figure 6.16 describes the steps taken in this effort.

Given a reason to look into the issue, the SSAC brainstormed through some possible assessments of the situation. They decided to develop a survey and collect the data needed to make a recommendation. In looking at the comments, the SSAC came to the conclusion that, while many patrons mentioned one station or another by call letters or frequency, they would solicit preferences based on station format. They also looked at the time a person worked out and even asked, based upon a couple of comments from patrons, whether they should just turn the system off and let users bring in their own CD players and headphones.

Over a three-week period, 285 surveys were collected from students and community patrons. SSAC members felt the breakdown between students (224) and community users (61) was fairly close to the normal mix of users. A Pareto chart was compiled to illustrate the results. The results were inconclusive at first. As Figure 6.17 shows, no clear winner was found. In fact, even if the top three were chosen, more than 40% of the respondents' preferences would be overlooked. After further discussion, the Pareto chart was stratified by the time period in which the respondent usually worked out. The resulting Pareto charts are also shown in Figure 6.17. Now, the results were much more informative.

When the student team looked at the results stratified by the time periods that typify the demand patterns of the FC, they saw some useful patterns. For example, the early morning crowd is older, more from the community. Among this group, 95% preferred country, oldies, or light rock. By contrast the late-night crowd is student dominated and 86% of this group of patrons preferred light rock, classic rock, or alternative. In fact, when the SSAC looked at all the results by the remaining time blocks, the top three stations in each block got at least 90% of the votes. This made planning a solution to the music selection problem straightforward. The staff set a policy where the play list for each time block was set by the top three vote getters. They decided only to change stations on a staff shift change (every one to two hours). They also set a plan in place to review the lists with follow-up surveys once a year to monitor any changing preferences. The results are shown in Figure 6.18. After a few weeks of the new policy, the number of comment cards critical of the music played in the FC was significantly reduced from the levels turned in before the play lists were implemented.

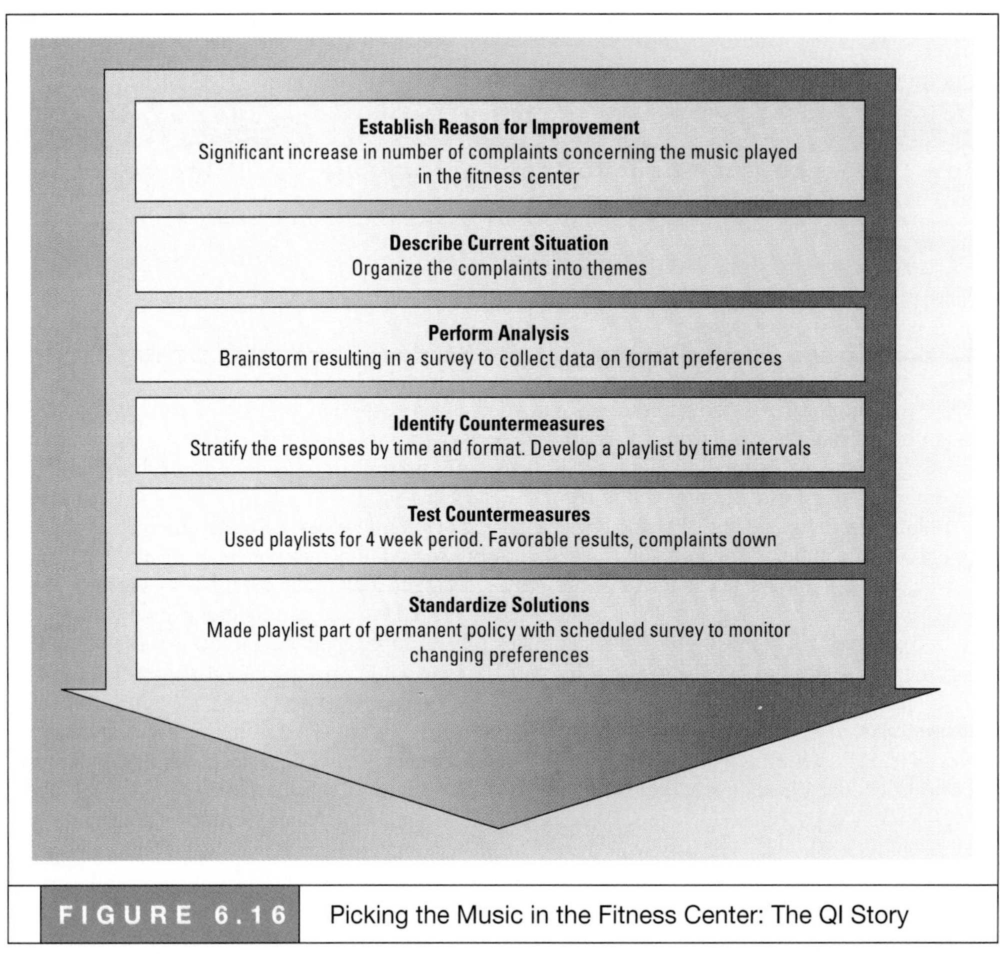

FIGURE 6.16 Picking the Music in the Fitness Center: The QI Story

TABLE 6.5 Music Format Survey at the SRC

We Want Your Musical Opinion!

Throughout the semester, we constantly get questions and comments concerning the music that is played in the fitness center. Please complete the following survey and help us try to improve your satisfaction with the music we play. We'll compile the results and make adjustments according to the survey results.

Gender: Female Male
Status: Student Community

What would you think of having no music in the Fitness Center and having the option of providing your own source of music (i.e., headphones)?	Good Idea	Dislike the Idea	No Opinion				
How many times a week do you use the Fitness Center?	1–2	3–5	6–10	More than 10			
What time of day do you prefer to use the Fitness Center?	6–10 AM	10 AM–2 PM	2 PM–6 PM	6 PM–10 PM	10 PM–2 AM		
What type of music do you prefer to work out to?	Pop/Rock	Alternative	Country	Light Rock	Oldies	Classical	Classic Rock

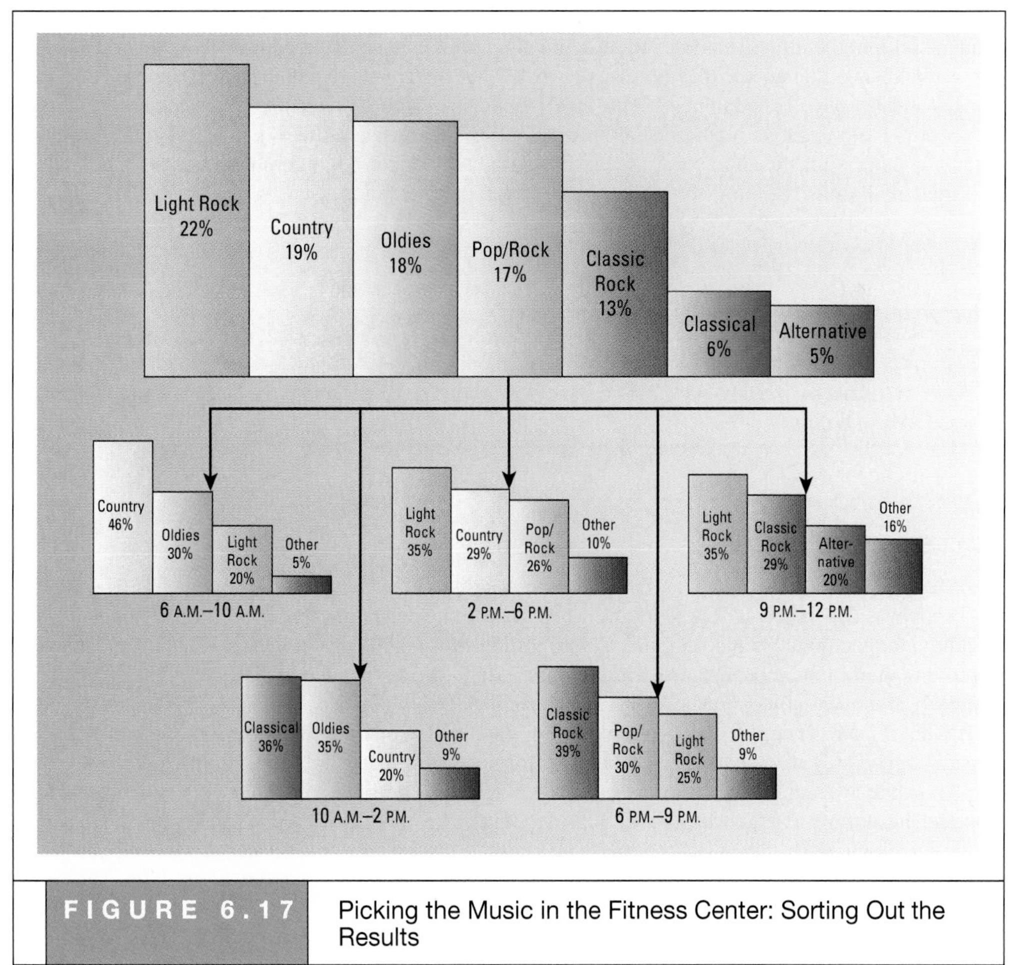

FIGURE 6.17 Picking the Music in the Fitness Center: Sorting Out the Results

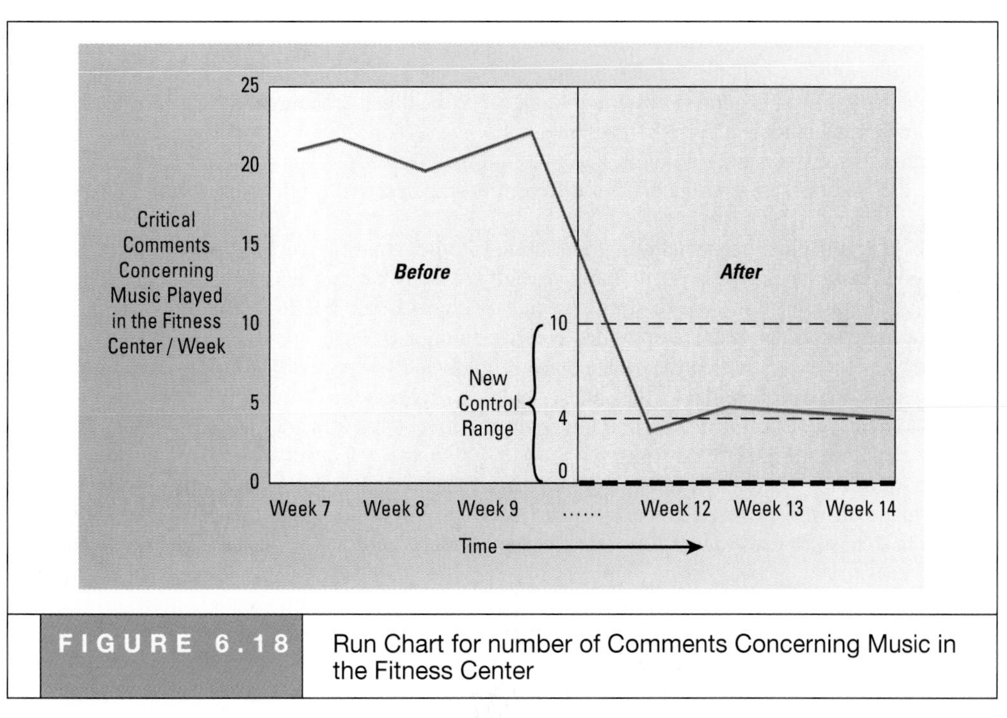

FIGURE 6.18 Run Chart for number of Comments Concerning Music in the Fitness Center

Notice in Figure 6.18 that the students have created a *c*-chart so that they can tell if there are any sudden shifts in the effectiveness of their new music policy. If negative comments go higher than 10 per week, this would indicate that there has probably been some change in the effectiveness of the policy. The managers will need to investigate to see if they can identify a reason for this change and institute controls to prevent its recurrence. Conversely, if there are several weeks in a row with zero complaints, managers may wish to see if the numbers are being doctored, if comment cards are being lost, or if there really have been no complaints regarding music selection.

video example

Take a closer look at the concepts and issues you've been reading about.

KAIZEN WORKSHOPS

Kaizen is a Japanese term that can be translated roughly as "continuous improvement." The Kaizen workshop was developed at Toyota in the 1950s to promote active ongoing, continuous improvement. Recently, the technique has been gaining recognition in the United States as a valuable approach to improving operations. For instance, DaimlerChrysler is promoting the technique aggressively, both internally and externally, with suppliers.

A *Kaizen workshop* is an action-oriented three-to-five-day on-site event that focuses on improving a specific process. Participants in the workshop form a cross-functional team that includes both those who know the process well and those who can provide fresh perspectives. This team is given the mission and the authority to take immediate action to revise the process in order to achieve breakthroughs in quality, productivity, inventory reduction, manufacturing cycle time, and floor space utilization.

The workshop begins with a short training session that is usually only a few hours long. The group then proceeds to study the process and undertake changes. Typically, the team will make small improvements immediately. Improvements that require no more than two or three days of concentrated effort will generally be made before the end of the workshop. Other improvements will be left with the "owner" of the process, to be completed by clearly specified dates. A follow-up meeting is held a few months after the workshop to ensure that short-term gains have been sustained and that longer-term improvements have been accomplished. Table 6.6 outlines a typical schedule for a Kaizen workshop.

CROSS-FUNCTIONAL QUALITY IMPROVEMENT TEAMS

Earlier in this chapter, we stressed that all functions in a business have a significant contribution to make to any quality management system, though each functional area might stress different kinds of quality improvement tools. Given the fact that quality is everyone's problem, getting a variety of people together to solve a quality problem makes a lot of sense. People with different backgrounds and training will see the same problem from different perspectives and will think of different ways to solve the problem.

Compared to the homogeneous workforce in many other countries (notably Japan), the American workforce is very diverse—a strength that is partially responsible for the famous "Yankee ingenuity." Because of the presence of diverse strengths and weaknesses, a cross-functional team of American workers can be expected to come up with a creative solution to virtually any problem when empowered to do so. However, the creativity that comes from diversity brings with it a slowness in moving to consensus. (When everyone thinks the same way, creativity may be limited but consensus is easy to achieve.) Therefore, learning how to communicate effectively and to work together in groups is much more important to the American workforce than to the Japanese. Conversely, learning to be creative, to think "outside the box," and to avoid groupthink is more important for the Japanese workforce. While American workers have to work hard to build a consensus around their best ideas, Japanese workers have to work hard to make sure they have considered alternative perspectives and to generate creative ideas.

Since the goal of any improvement is ultimately to improve customer satisfaction, no function can be disinterested in continuous improvement projects. In fact, most solutions to quality problems that have not been solved within a function will require coordinated changes in several functions. This is another fundamental reason why cross-functional quality improvement teams are needed.

TABLE 6.6	Generic Schedule for a Kaizen Workshop
Time	**Activities**
Before the workshop	Select a project Set project objectives Select a team leader and team members Take care of the logistical issues Inform affected employees of the upcoming workshop
Day 1	Deliver any training Study the process as it is and gain an understanding of the workshop's key objectives
Day 2	Analyze the process Brainstorm for improvement ideas Develop solutions
Day 3	Implement solutions Refine the solutions/improve the process further Monitor the new process Begin to prepare a presentation
Day 4	Confirm results of the changes implemented Complete a presentation Make a presentation to management
After the workshop	Conduct a 30-day follow-up audit Complete a follow-up report for management

> active concept check

Now let's take a moment to test your knowledge of the concepts you have studied in this section.

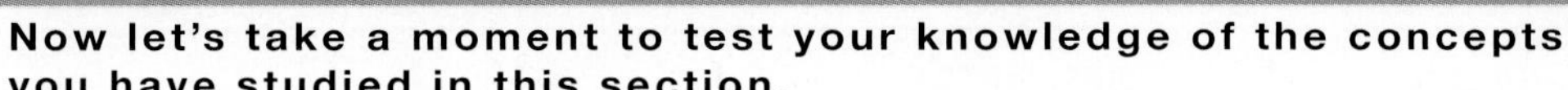

> Integrating Operational Decisions

> video exercise

Take a moment to apply what you've learned.

Of course, this chapter about quality improvement tools is directly tied to the earlier chapter on total quality management. Additionally, the tools discussed in this chapter have many potential applications in other operational decision-making areas. The most obvious of these are design decisions. Thus the chapters on design of the product-service bundle and design of the value-adding system closely linked to this chapter.

This is the last chapter in the part of the text where we have been covering the overarching concepts of operations management. In the first six chapters of this book we have

- defined OM, described its historic development, and established the importance of customer-driven decision making to successful management of operations;

- described the importance of managing the flow of materials and information in order to effectively coordinate decision making throughout extended enterprises referred to as supply chains, which involves aligning operations with both customer expectations and supplier processes;
- described strategic management, clarified the role of strategy in operational decision making, and brought into focus the role of operations strategy in creating competitive advantages in the marketplace;
- described traditional and modern team-based processes for the design of product-service bundles while presenting techniques, such as quality function deployment, that are useful in this design process—in other words, we've described what it takes to make certain that what you bring to market matches the set of customer expectations that have been strategically targeted;
- described total quality management and developed an understanding of the managerial commitments required in its pursuit—and in doing so, we have presented an approach to management that formally recognizes the importance of both employee and customer stakeholders;
- described tools that can be used to support efforts to improve customer satisfaction.

These chapters provide the backdrop for the remaining parts of the text where we describe structural decisions involved in building a value-adding system and infrastructural decisions involved in running such a system. Specifically, you should keep in mind the following themes, developed in these first chapters, as you proceed through the rest of this text:

1. All operational decisions can influence customer satisfaction and should be customer driven.
2. Customers usually buy both product and service value together in a product-service bundle. Therefore, we shouldn't think about operations management as being about providing either goods or services. Rather, OM is usually about providing both goods and services. Effectively managing operations involves effectively managing service and production processes.
3. Operational decisions are made in the context of business strategies and should be effectively aligned with decisions that are being made in other functional areas of business and other stages of the supply chain. Most business processes require the involvement of multiple functions across multiple stages of value creation. Companies that are good at managing the white spaces of their organizational charts and good at aligning resources through an entire supply chain are the best at satisfying their customers. In fact, functional excellence alone is seldom sufficient to ensure competitiveness. It takes both functional excellence and effective management of the white spaces (cross-functional coordination of business processes) to remain competitive in today's marketplace.

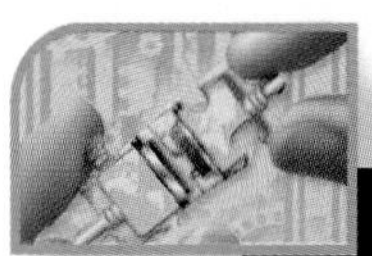

integrated OM <

Take a moment to apply what you've learned.

> Chapter Wrap-Up

An old American proverb states "If the job is too hard, you must be using the wrong tool." This chapter has presented a variety of tools that can be useful to firms in improving customer satisfaction. Obviously, which tool to use depends on the result the company wants to produce. Companies that are trying to find nonconforming material will use tools based on some sort of end-of-pipe inspection—acceptance sampling, 100% inspection of process output, or attribute control. These companies are using the tools for detection purposes.

Companies that are trying to prevent nonconformities might use *poka yoke* devices to failproof their processes. Also they might use variables control charts, like the $\overline{X}$ and R-charts discussed in this chapter, to identify the likelihood of the presence of special cause variation. They might even use capability indexes to monitor the ability of their processes to operate without producing nonconformities.

Finally, even the most capable processes can be improved by putting all employees to work in quality improvement teams using a wide variety of tools within the QI story or Kaizen workshop methodology. This clearly requires a company to build a personnel system that provides workers with the needed training, motivation, and time to contribute to process improvement. Further, workers need to be assured that they won't lose their jobs if the improvements they make enhance productivity to the extent that fewer workers might be needed.

Many of the tools we've discussed in this chapter were developed by statisticians, and many of the tools were first applied in production operations. That doesn't mean that they aren't applicable in many other environments. Their use is certainly widespread in service operations. If you look closely enough, you'll probably even find some employees at your university using them. Indeed, as a set, the tools that we have described in this chapter are suited for application in virtually any operational setting.

> end-of-chapter resources

- Practice Quiz
- Key Terms
- Solved Problems
- Discussion Questions
- Problems
- Case 6.1: AAA Seeks to Reduce Roadside Assistance Costs
- References
- Plant Tours

CHAPTER 7

Designing the Value-Adding System

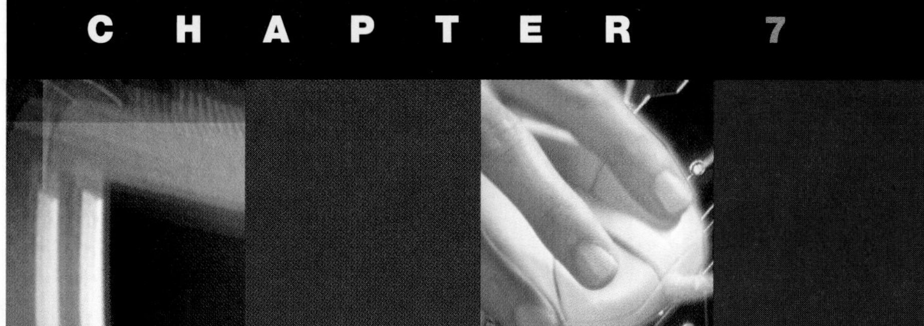

Chapter Outline

What's Ahead

. . . BACK AT THE REC CENTER

Early one Monday, as everyone was finishing up the day's workout, Luis picked up the business section of the morning paper. "Look at this. It says here that today is the day they finally start up the baggage-sorting machine at that big new western airport," Luis said loudly. He was talking about an article that described a high-tech computer-controlled system that was supposed to be flexible, fast, accurate, and cost effective. However, the system had had some well-publicized glitches, delays, and cost overruns. "I'll bet they're keeping their fingers crossed. If that thing goes belly up again, heads could roll!" Luis crowed, glancing in Tom's direction.

"Why do they have so many problems, anyway? They're just sorting suitcases. What do they need flexibility for?" Fred asked. "They fly the same routes every day. They should have it down by now!"

"Better them than you, Tom, but isn't this new sorter something the airport has been planning for a long time, anyway?" Cheryl asked from the treadmill.

"Well, yeah, but with all this new high-tech stuff, you can never take anything for granted. They've been trying to get it right for a couple of years now," Tom explained, as he shot a dirty look at Fred. Fred and Luis had obviously hit a sore spot.

"From what I've heard, it sounds as if they didn't think it through," Cheryl said. "Have they really thought about the changes in an airport over the last few years? You guys are a good example of what's changed. How different is the new system, anyway?" she asked.

"Well, I've heard a little about what they were doing. They just automated a bigger version of the old system. It's based on what was put into airports 30 years ago. It wouldn't fit us very well," Tom answered.

"This sounds like that TV commercial, the one with those software guys who say things like, 'We have new solutions to old problems'," Luis chuckled. "Sounds like they may be using an old solution to a new problem!"

"But what's the big deal with baggage, anyway? How hard could it be to stack the stuff away in the same type of plane every time?" Luis asked again.

"You're right. That part of our business—flying the same routes, using the same planes—yeah, that part's pretty standard. But with a whole planeload of passengers, each one coming from and going to different places, other parts of the business can get really difficult to manage," replied Tom. "I never thought it could get so complicated, but it sure has! The bottom line is, we don't make money with our planes on the ground."

Tom and the group have talked many times before about this issue. They understand that anything that will help the airline to get a plane back into the air more quickly will improve its performance. "I don't know that we need a baggage sorter just like the one in the paper. We'd want to look into it. But whether it's that or something else that makes the sorting process faster and more reliable, well, it reduces delays and it could cut handling costs, too," Tom added.

"It still sounds easy compared to what we deal with," argued Luis.

"It's not as easy as you'd think, Luis. In our business, we're always under pressure to raise service level and lower our costs. Something like this new baggage sorter might be a good bet on both counts!" Tom replied.

Fred had been listening while resting between sets on the bench. "I know that feeling," he said. "Over the last two years we've put about $15 million into our main pager facility to cut costs and, yes, Luis, to improve our flexibility!" Historically, Fred's division had used automation to lower its costs and increase its reliability. But the accountants would say that more production volume was needed to justify the automation that had just been put in, and that usually meant lowering costs further—which required more automation, and so on.

"But don't you make zillions of just one thing?" Luis asked, somewhat confused.

"Yeah, exactly, but things have changed for us, too," responded Fred. "The difference between the technology we're putting in now and what we used to put in 10 years ago is the way it handles a new product line. It seems we have to go from one generation of our pager to the next much faster than we used to, so now we have to look at a piece of equipment in terms of more than once around the block." Fred picked up the weights again. His company used to write off an investment in equipment on a single model; now it needs to be stretched out over several models. That makes equipment flexibility—at least, enough flexibility to handle differences in product design from one generation to the next—a growing issue, even to his company.

"Well, all that is fine, but I'd like to see you handle the things we have to deal with. Every order is different!" Luis exclaimed. "Even when it's a piece we've made before, one that's on our basic product list, it's going to go to somebody different or it hasn't been made in a long time. After a while, the folks on the floor forget the best ways to make a product, and they have to learn them all over again. And talk about complex! We've got tons of orders open and on the floor, all at the same time!" he added, referring to the hundreds of different furniture pieces that were moving through different stages of production on any day. "Try keeping track of that!" He threw both hands in the air in exasperation.

"Yeah, you lead a rough life over there," Tom laughed, as he played an imaginary violin in mock sympathy. "But people recognize you for being a custom manufacturer, and you make a good penny doing it!"

"Whoa, not so fast. We can't get the margins we used to get. Things have changed for us, too, you know!" Luis said in his own defense.

"Yeah, well anyway, that's part of what you sell. Nobody squeezes costs out of your process the way the competition forces us to squeeze 'em out of ours," said Tom. Luis knows people expect to pay for a custom fit. In Tom's eyes, Luis has it easy. "With home computers, toll-free numbers, and travel agents online, anybody who knows the difference between an airport runway and a bowling alley knows when we're a dollar over the other guy's price!" Tom said. He was referring to the constant price wars and other forms of competitive behavior that have kept the cost of an airline ticket low in his market. In fact, his airline was usually the one that started them. It's hard to compete that way, but they do. "The thing is, though, low price might get the customers on the plane the first time, but being on time, reliable, and having a lot of flights to choose from will keep them coming back. That just means we're always looking to make our process better," Tom added.

"Okay, but we still have to offer the same customized fit. It's just that now they want it faster and cheaper!" Luis persisted. "Our company is as flexible as it's ever been, but now there's a lot more pressure than there used to be to keep costs low. There's always someone out there who claims to be everything we are, but faster or cheaper. It's been easy up till now. We could always point out what we could offer that the other guys couldn't. It's just that they've narrowed the gap, and that puts pressure on our margins. Good quality at a reasonable price and in a reasonable time frame used to be enough. Now the customers want their cake, and they want to eat it, too!"

Luis's process is labor intensive, involving highly skilled people using general-purpose equipment to make just about anything anybody could want in the way of furniture. With all the different models the company makes, predicting capacity needs is difficult, and that means a lot of in-process inventory to keep everyone busy. Lots of inventory means a job takes even longer to get through to the customer. The process that used to work isn't good enough anymore, and Luis isn't sure what to do about it. It won't be easy or cheap, but somehow they have to compete!

"Have you looked into automation?" asked Cheryl. "I mean flexible high-tech stuff?"

"A few months ago we put some computer-controlled machines into a couple of departments," Luis responded. "The people who sold us the equipment said it would cut our labor costs and increase our speed and reliability, too." Luis sounded a little sarcastic. "The salespeople also told us we could switch back and forth between models faster, and that meant we wouldn't have to batch our orders. That we really liked!" Many times, to avoid unnecessary setups, Luis had waited until enough orders for a particular model accumulated before setting up a machine. But those batches of combined orders tended to flow through the shop together, increasing the amount of work in process inventory.

"You know," said Tom, "what you're talking about sounds a lot like the new airport systems, sort of like what Fred was describing, too."

"I guess Cheryl is right. Making choices about the technology we use isn't a simple either-or situation anymore," said Fred, as he summed up his view of the morning's conversation.

"I agree," Tom said. "It seems that modern technology is changing the way we all look at the systems we use to provide our products and services. Unless we want to end up with a process like the new baggage system in the newspaper, we can't just focus on the technology. Sometimes we have to work on the system, too!"

"Right! Yeah, you're both right. I just hope that when Luis goes back to work and looks at the way his tables are made, he doesn't think we were pulling his leg!" added Cheryl, as she headed for the locker room.

> objectives

Take a moment to familiarize yourself with the key objectives of this chapter.

> gearing up

Before you begin reading this chapter, try a short warm-up activity.

> Introduction

In the past, little thought was given to the role of operations in the firm's overall strategy. Nor was much attention given to the customer's role in designing the product-service bundle or the value-adding system. Today things are different, in two ways. First, the customer is at the center of decisions that have to do with process selection and the design of the service delivery system. Second, the design of processes and product-service bundles is addressed concurrently, in cross-functional teams that draw heavily on customer-driven definitions of quality.

This chapter describes the way in which companies commit their resources to value-adding systems that will deliver product-service bundles according to competitive priorities. The first section links this chapter's material to other functional areas. Simply put, a company's value proposition requires a system to back it up. That system, in turn, includes a significant role for employees in every functional area. As a consequence, it is very simple to draw connections between value-adding system design considerations and every functional area of business.

The chapter describes the competitive considerations involved in designing the value-adding system. We focus on four main areas: flexibility, technology choices, customer involvement, and supply-chain configuration. While a process that does not support a well-defined strategy is of limited value, a process that is ill-suited to provide the intended product-service bundle is worth even less. Therefore, system design decisions need to be driven by the competitive position a company wants in the marketplace.

Technology is a critical component of any value-adding system. It can be used to make processes more efficient. It can be used to improve the conformance quality of process outputs. It can even be used to make processes more flexible. Information technology has become a particularly pervasive aspect of value delivery in both manufacturing and services. In manufacturing, it can be used for process control and provides real time information that allows managers to plan their operations and communicate their decisions more effectively. In services, it actually allows customers to add the value for themselves, in the ways they prefer, at the times they find most convenient.

Many analytical tools could be used by those who have to choose between alternative technologies in designing value-adding systems. Among these, and perhaps the most commonly used, is cost-volume break-even analysis (CVBA). This simple tool allows managers to determine the demand volumes at which various alternatives provide the greatest profit. An extension of CVBA is cost-volume-flexibility break-even analysis (CVFBA). This technique allows managers to determine demand volumes and levels of output variety for which particular alternatives provide the greatest economic advantage. CVFBA is more fit for analyzing alternatives where one of the benefits under consideration is system flexibility.

The potential impact of technology on system performance depends on the type of process. For this reason, we've added a section in this chapter that relates technology issues to competitive concerns in job shop, batch, repetitive, and continuous processes.

There's also a section on facility focus, another critical issue in system design. Firms with a variety of product-service bundles need to decide whether they will have a limited number of large multi-purpose facilities or a larger number of smaller facilities that are more focused.

Value-adding systems aren't designed and forgotten. Rather, they should be continuously improved by making incremental changes. Occasionally, despite efforts at ongoing improvement, some part of an existing value-adding system may need to be scrapped and completely redesigned. Business process reengineering is an approach well suited to such situations.

In many ways, then, process selection and the design of the service delivery system are pivotal components in OM. After all, they focus on the development of the organization's value-adding system.

active concept check

Now let's take a moment to test your knowledge of the concepts you have studied in this section.

Integrating Operations Management with Other Functions

Figure 7.1 highlights some of the critical linkages between the operational issues involved in value-adding system design decisions and other functional areas. This part of the chapter is obviously important to all business majors, because it indicates the way that professionals from various functional areas relate to the issues addressed in this chapter.

Most of this chapter is likely to be of particular interest to marketing and engineering majors. Marketing professionals play a large role in determining the best competitive position for a firm and explaining this to the rest of the organization. Thus, they are the conduit by which customer preferences become the driver of system design decisions. Engineers, on the other hand, must communicate the potential of alternative technologies to meet these competitive requirements. Changes in technology can open competitive opportunities, and a company's technical staff must be the conduit by which managers become aware of such opportunities.

The part of this chapter detailing system design factors has widespread applicability to other functional areas. The relationship with finance is highlighted because of the role of financial managers in

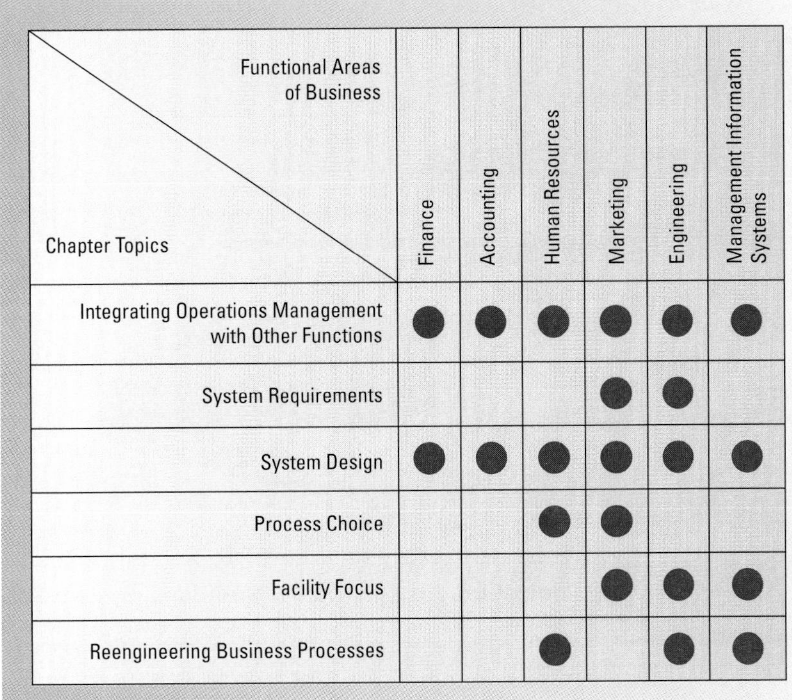

Chapter Topics \ Functional Areas of Business	Finance	Accounting	Human Resources	Marketing	Engineering	Management Information Systems
Integrating Operations Management with Other Functions	●	●	●	●	●	●
System Requirements				●	●	
System Design	●	●	●	●	●	●
Process Choice			●	●		
Facility Focus				●	●	●
Reengineering Business Processes			●		●	●

FIGURE 7.1 Integrating Operations Management with Other Functions

allocation of capital for system development and improvement. Ultimately, systems have to be financially viable, and tools for justification of system alternatives are discussed in this section. Human resources issues in this section focus on the skills and skill levels required—appropriate staffing plans and HR strategies must be based on the mix of design factors selected. As indicated in the previous paragraph, the knowledge base of marketing and engineering personnel will greatly facilitate the choices made in system design. Finally, information systems requirements will vary depending on the choices made in system design.

Business process reengineering is an approach businesses use to redesign existing systems. It's a way of changing people's jobs so that the company can compete more effectively. That makes it of particular significance to the human resources function. It's also very important to technical people such as those found in engineering and management information systems departments because advances in their areas can lead to opportunities for significant improvement through process redesign.

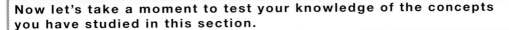

> active concept check

Now let's take a moment to test your knowledge of the concepts you have studied in this section.

> Determining System Requirements

No business can be all things to all customers. Businesses must therefore set competitive priorities that rank the importance of factors such as low cost, flexibility, high-quality design, and speedy delivery. Establishing a clear set of competitive priorities is a critical part of strategic planning at the business level. It helps to define what the firm is and what it is not.

Along with clear competitive priorities, a clear definition of the product-service bundle is an important starting point in the design of any value-adding system. As Figure 7.2 shows, the definition

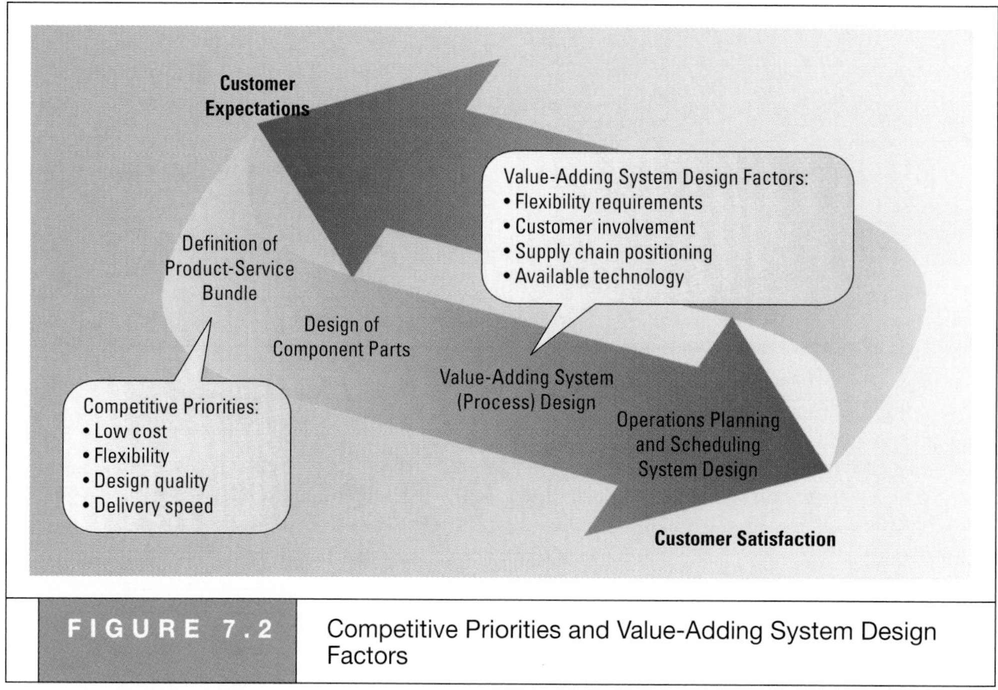

FIGURE 7.2 Competitive Priorities and Value-Adding System Design Factors

of the product-service bundle sets in motion a series of related decisions, from the design of component parts and the process in which they are used to the system's day-to-day operation.

In the past, system design decisions were made after the product design had been completed. In fact, product engineers were likely to be both physically and functionally separated from the process engineers. As Figures 4.4 and 4.6(a) illustrated, interaction between these groups usually occurred when an approved product design was thrown over the functional wall, or across the white spaces on the organizational chart, from design engineering to process engineering. We saw in Chapter 4 that this approach led to a sequential consideration of design decisions. Important process design decisions were often constrained to less desirable alternatives, because the design of the product-service bundle had already been finalized.

Figure 4.6(b) illustrated the modern approach to system design, in which a cross-functional team uses concurrent engineering to select the value-adding system best suited to the product-service bundle. A certain amount of information on the design of the product-service bundle is necessary for work on the process design to begin, because the process must be capable of providing the bundle. But the product-service bundle need not be finalized for work on the system to begin. As the product-service bundle moves from design concept to prototype through testing and toward final approval, the process requirements become clearer.

Using an iterative approach that allows designers to address process design issues in greater and greater detail as the product-service bundle's design becomes clearer makes sense. Such an approach allows product designers to modify the product-service bundle based on feedback from the process designers. They can evaluate various alternatives based on manufacturability, the implications for procurement (sometimes called "component sourceability"), and marketability. Designers can ask the question, From the customer's perspective, is the added value of this design characteristic worth the cost? Often a very small change to a product-service bundle's design can have a significant impact on the process design. Without such ongoing two-way communication, product designers might as well be working blindfolded; they cannot really know the implications of their decisions for the process and for customer satisfaction.

Finally, as we saw in Chapter 4, concurrent consideration of product design and system design issues significantly reduces the time to market for both new and modified items.

active concept check

Now let's take a moment to test your knowledge of the concepts you have studied in this section.

System Design Factors

Designing the value-adding system requires decisions about the system's flexibility, customer involvement, supply-chain configuration, and technology. These characteristics of the value-adding system are called system design factors. **Flexibility** refers to the system's ability to respond to uncertainty and variability in the business environment. **Customer involvement** pertains to the customer's role in creating or customizing a particular product-service bundle. **Supply-chain configuration** defines the relationships between value-adding activities, both within and outside of the company. This includes *vertical integration decisions,* which focus on the determining extent of the value chain that a company's value-adding system will span. In backward vertical integration, the process includes upstream activities in the value chain (that is, activities that are close to the raw material source). In forward vertical integration, the process includes downstream activities (those that are closer to the ultimate consumer). Finally, **technology selection** refers to a variety of issues, including the degree and type of automation and the supplier of the equipment.

The choice of process type, or system type, includes alternatives such as the job shop, batch process, line flow, and continuous flow. As Figure 7.3 shows, this choice is determined largely by decisions about the design factors just discussed.

The four design factors cannot be considered independently; they are interrelated. For example, an inflexible system that is based on significant backward vertical integration and extensive automation could not deliver a high degree of customer involvement. Any customer who tried to influence such a system would quickly become frustrated. (Can you imagine a beauty shop where the stylists treat customers as if they were cars on an assembly line? Or imagine trying to get into one of GM's assembly plants so you can tell workers how to make the Camaro you just ordered. Do you think they would let you bring your own stereo and speakers, so the line workers could install them in the car?)

Obviously, the value-adding system needs to be designed in such a way that it will be capable of delivering customer satisfaction according to the firm's competitive priorities. Taken together, decisions on the four design factors must make sense. If they do, they can create a synergy that has the potential to satisfy the customer. If they do not, the system will not be able to satisfy the customer.

FLEXIBILITY

In the past, companies that wanted to build flexibility into their value-adding systems relied on general-purpose equipment and skilled workers. The per-unit variable cost of production was relatively high and fixed costs were low. Because companies were using general-purpose equipment, they could provide a wide variety of items. Flexibility was further enhanced by the fact that equipment could readily be sold, traded, or acquired as needed; by definition, general-purpose equipment can be used to produce a wide array of outputs. In a typical day, firms with flexible processes might have made

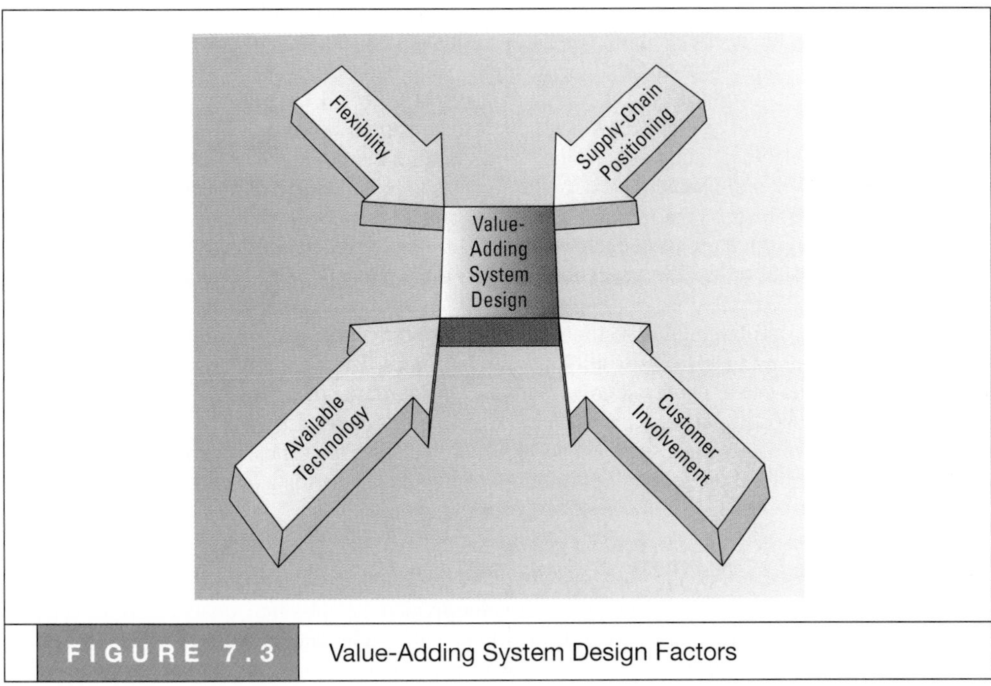

FIGURE 7.3 Value-Adding System Design Factors

only a few units of a variety of items and justified the higher prices of those items as a legitimate reward for the firm's flexibility. Because prices were high and the product-service bundle could be provided with general-purpose equipment, barriers to entry were low in the market segments these firms served.

In the past, companies that chose *not* to build high levels of flexibility into their processes would have chosen to produce standardized goods and services, in volumes large enough to justify the expensive special-purpose equipment required. To the extent that their volumes would support it, they would assume higher fixed costs to automate their processes. The automation of dedicated equipment, which is referred to as **hard automation,** adds very specialized capabilities to equipment. With hard automation, the fixed costs of production are high and the per-unit variable cost of production is low. Thus, hard automation typically provides economies of scale. This benefit, however, is obtained at the cost of reduced system flexibility.

In a typical day, such firms would produce a large quantity of only one item. Because the goods were standardized, customers would not pay a premium for them. Instead, firms would generate a profit as a reward for their ability to produce large volumes at a cost slightly below the low prices customers were willing to pay. Because of the low prices and high fixed costs, barriers to entry in such market segments were high.

Today the availability of **flexible automation** technologies, which are capable of controlling equipment that produces a variety of goods, makes the discussion of the value-adding system's flexibility much more complex than it once was. Designing the flexibility of a process is no longer simply a matter of deciding between low-fixed-cost, general-purpose equipment, and high-fixed-cost, dedicated equipment. Indeed, given the trend toward shortened product lifecycles, production volumes are often insufficient to warrant processes that use hard automation. Moreover, the availability of flexible automation technologies allows firms with general-purpose equipment to consider trading higher fixed costs for lower per-unit variable costs without giving up flexibility. Thus, they can often provide considerable variety in their product-service bundles or even customize their bundles at unit costs not much higher than those of firms that use hard automation. Similarly, firms using hard automation can trade a small increase in per-unit variable cost for increased flexibility and thereby raise their prices.

Building a flexible system depends on more than just equipment choices; a variety of other structural and infrastructural decisions influence flexibility. In fact, the flexibility that arises from equipment is better referred to as **machine-level flexibility**. The flexibility of the system as a whole is referred to as **facility-level flexibility.** Besides machine-level flexibility, factors such as design and engineering capabilities, adequate capacity in resources, effective inventory management policies, short lead times, short setup times, high quality of conformance (which reduces the need for rework), and the ability to readily change schedules all contribute to facility-level flexibility.

Workforce considerations play a key role in facility-level flexibility. Cross-training workers so they can perform multiple tasks allows a company to change the product mix on an hourly basis, to quickly resolve bottlenecks and other capacity shortages, and to improve customer service. But there are barriers to the development of a flexible workforce. Fear of change or the loss of status, pride or the rivalries associated with trade or work group affiliations, and work standards that reward workers for speed and efficiency are all detrimental to the development of a flexible workforce. But the most formidable barrier is the restrictive collective bargaining agreements that are designed to provide job security for specific trades by giving them a monopoly of work in that trade.

In plants where such work rules have been included in a collective bargaining agreement, a simple one-hour maintenance task can take days. Suppose a small part of a cooling system pump needs to be replaced. First, the electrician has to be called to ensure that the power is off; that could take a day, depending on the worker's schedule. Next, a plumber has to be scheduled to disconnect the pipes and shut off all the fluid flows to the pump. Then maintenance technicians must be called in, trade by trade. If any special repairs are needed, workers from the appropriate trades must be scheduled. Finally, the plumber has to be called back to reconnect the piping and the electrician to reconnect the power.

Many times the contribution that a single flexible resource makes toward facility-level flexibility can be rendered moot by a lack of flexibility in other resources. There are nine positions on a baseball team; if the best hitter can only play shortstop, the fact that several other players on the team are flexible enough to play shortstop in addition to their other positions doesn't matter. A lack of facility-level flexibility becomes obvious when the team needs better defensive skills at shortstop than the best hitter can offer—especially if the second-best hitter can only play shortstop as well.

CUSTOMER INVOLVEMENT

You may recall several occasions when your instructor divided the class into small groups to perform an exercise or discuss a particular concept. Rather than deliver a lecture, at which you would be only an observer, the instructor instead chose an educational process that would actively include you.

Involving customers can simultaneously improve their level of satisfaction and reduce the provider's costs. When designing systems to involve customers, businesses need to make certain that access is provided for all of their customers including those with disabilities. Also, the appropriate level of security and monitoring must be provided. Here, a 90-year-old customer is seen using a self-service scanning station at a Kroger store in Atlanta.

Putting you into a small group made your participation critical to the learning process. It probably helped you to get more out of the class and may have allowed you to think about some topics that were important to you, but which otherwise would not have been on the instructor's agenda.

In many situations, the customer must be an integral part of the value-adding system. Including the customer in the process can improve the tailoring of the product-service bundle to the customer's expectations and reduce costs (see Table 7.1). For example, obtaining a patient history at the doctor's office helps the doctor to tailor his or her health care service to a specific patient. Working with a patient on an outpatient basis to build a healthier lifestyle may help to reduce the risk of costly hospital stays later on.

Situations in which the primary value is added to the product part of the product-service bundle are illustrated in the right-hand column of Table 7.1. Self-service at the gasoline pump is an example of the use of customer involvement to reduce the cost of a product-service bundle. Selling goods with "some assembly required" also helps to reduce the cost of the product-service bundle, as well as to increase the possibility for customization and reduce potential losses from quality problems during assembly. For example, computer desks that can be assembled at home can be shipped in compact flat boxes, with very little chance of damage during transit. This product-service bundle provides enough

TABLE 7.1 Examples of Customer Involvement

	Primary Source of Value Added:	
Customer Involvement Results from Emphasis on:	**Service Aspects of the Product-Service Bundle**	**Product Aspects of the Product-Service Bundle**
Low Cost	• Soda fountain at a fast food restaurant • Automated teller machine • Laundromat • Co-op daycare	• Self-service gasoline • "Pick your own" strawberries • Backyard swing set sold unassembled • TV dinners
High Level of Customization	• Personal fitness consultant • Psychotherapist • Full-service stock broker • Formalwear rental	• Personally designed greeting card kiosk • "Naked" furniture • "Tailor-made" clothing

savings and requires a simple enough task (or so the assembly instructions suggest) that many customers opt not to buy preassembled desks.

When the primary value is added to the service portion of the product-service bundle, customer involvement is frequently required rather than optional. Making sure that the customer is consulted at the right times is therefore critically important. For example, in medicine, a doctor cannot possibly diagnose a patient's needs without feedback from the patient, nor can the doctor effect a long-term cure without significant action on the patient's part. Still, at times the dentist will give Novocain and the surgeon will use anesthetics to prevent customer involvement (and feedback) at inappropriate times. Similarly, lawyers, sports agents, advertising firms, and financial service institutions must rely on input from their clients in order to conduct their business effectively. The type of customer involvement will be dictated partially by provider preferences, customer and provider expertise, technical requirements, and customer needs; but the timing and location of a service may well be dictated by the customer.

SUPPLY-CHAIN CONFIGURATION

Numerous supply-chain configuration issues arise in designing value-adding systems. Among these are the structure of information flows, the structure of material flows and distribution networks, and degree of vertical integration.

Information about demand and customer preferences must be made available to operational decision makers throughout the supply chain. This information flows from customers to suppliers in the opposite direction of material flows. Providing access to this information requires the design of interfaces that allow businesses to share information. Standards for the reporting and exchange of information—including security standards—must be established. Thus, information systems and communication technologies are a critical aspect of configuring a supply chain.

Just as important as designing the avenues of information exchange, material flows need to be thought out—especially in the case of manufacturing supply chains. This aspect of value-adding system design requires companies to think about where value will be added, how much capacity is needed at various stages in the creation of value, and how materials will be transferred between the stages of value creation.

Associated with the design of material flows is the design of the distribution networks that transfer materials between facilities that are sequentially related in the creation of value. Particularly with the advent of lean production systems, which don't provide for large quantities of excess inventory between stages of value creation, the reliability of the distribution network is crucial. The logistical system must be designed so that it is capable of consistently transferring material through the supply chain at the pace of material use in downstream operations. Without such logistical capabilities, inventory must be warehoused to protect against material shortages resulting from logistical disruptions.

Finally, supply-chain configuration also involves vertical integration and outsourcing decisions. Companies must establish their core competencies and determine the extent to which they will own operations other than these. For instance, an insurance company might outsource the claims processing part of their business in order to focus on the sale of policies. By outsourcing these operations, the companies limit their own financial risk and may reduce their costs by gaining access to greater economies of scale experienced by the supplying firms. By contrast, some companies will choose to buy, or internally develop, companies that are their suppliers or customers. Such vertical integration is likely to provide greater profit margins and may allow the company to more effectively control quality, material flows, and security.

TECHNOLOGY SELECTION

In the course of doing business, most companies will see opportunities to use new technology, either because of a need to improve their operations or because of promotional activity by vendors. There are three stages in the process of bringing new equipment and process technologies on-line; Figure 7.4 summarizes them. In the first stage, managers define feasible technological alternatives and estimate their costs and benefits. This fact-finding exercise might include the use of a relatively simple break-even analysis, or it might require more complex analytical models or computer simulations. In the second stage, managers use their cost-benefit analysis to select the most desirable alternative. Their financial calculations will generally include a discounted future cash flow analysis, which can yield a net present value (NPV), or an internal rate of return (IRR). Worst-case estimates, likely estimates, and optimistic estimates should be presented for each alternative, along with information on the environmental impact and other risks associated with each new technology. These figures are usually included in a formal proposal that is presented to managers who hold line responsibility for profit and loss.

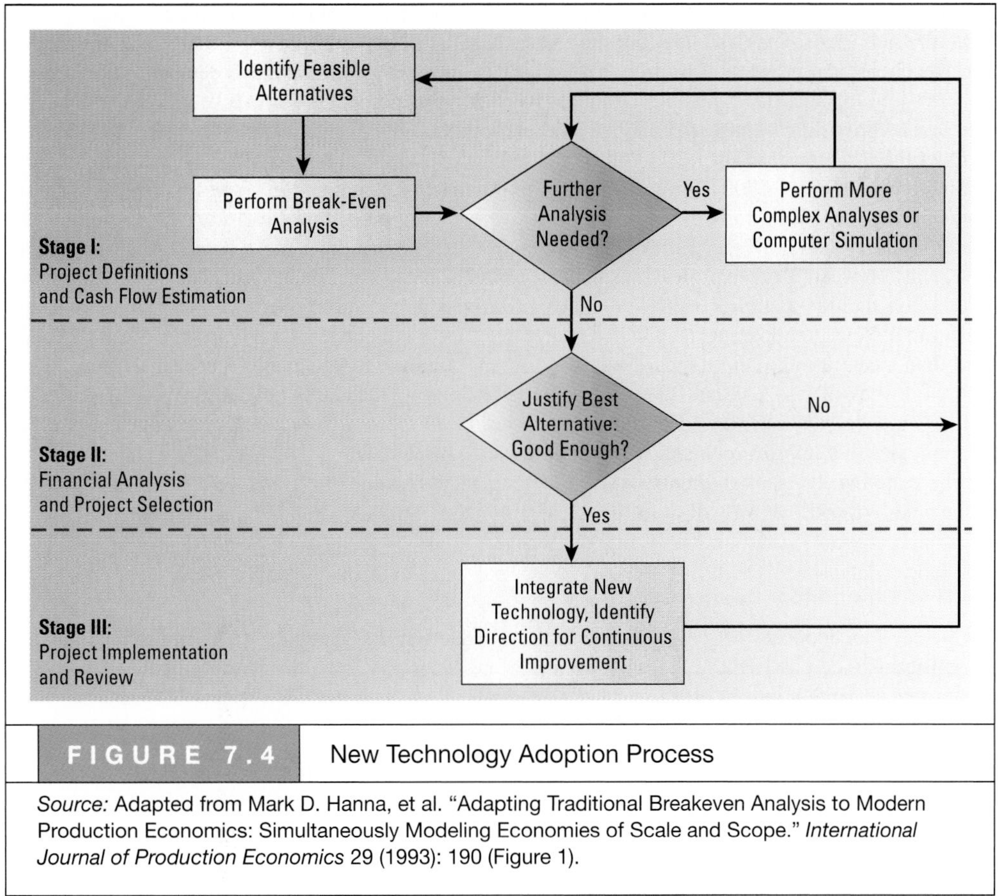

FIGURE 7.4 New Technology Adoption Process

Source: Adapted from Mark D. Hanna, et al. "Adapting Traditional Breakeven Analysis to Modern Production Economics: Simultaneously Modeling Economies of Scale and Scope." *International Journal of Production Economics* 29 (1993): 190 (Figure 1).

After its approval by management, a new technology must be integrated into the existing system. In the third stage of the new technology adoption process, as the technology is implemented, new opportunities for improvement may present themselves. For instance, once a new bar code system has been adopted for storage and retrieval of inventory, managers might want to use it to track units as they move through the plant, in order to generate information useful for scheduling and control purposes. Or a university that has adopted a single-card system for access to athletic events, recreational facilities, cafeterias, and ATM machines might find that with only slight modifications, the card could be used to allow access to students' dorm rooms as well. In many cases, new opportunities such as these could not have been anticipated without an initial investment in the new technology. Before they are fully implemented, new uses for an installed technology must be analyzed thoroughly—meaning that managers must return to stages I and II of the new technology adoption process.

Many North Americans harbor strongly negative opinions of automation. They believe that automation threatens their job security and is therefore antilabor. Skilled workers fear that their craftsmanship and other creative skills that they have traditionally passed down the generations through various forms of apprenticeship may be lost forever because of automation. As their skills become rare, they become expensive, providing further incentive for companies to automate. At one Ford plant, demand for skilled work generated enough overtime that about half the 240 skilled tradespeople made more than $100,000 per year in 1995. In the United States as a whole, about 28,000 of the 11 million precision production and craft workers earn more than $100,000 per year.[1] Thus workers almost always oppose managerial attempts to improve a company's competitiveness by automation. Particularly in an era of corporate downsizing, when nobody's job is secure, managers should demonstrate their concern for the very real human costs that accompany a decision to automate.

Those who have a favorable opinion of automation believe that asking a worker to perform any task that can be done by a machine is disrespectful. In their thinking, respect for humanity means viewing workers as thinkers and problem solvers in a complex value-adding system. Whenever possi-

[1] Aaron Luchetti, "An Auto Worker Earns More than $100,000, but at a Personal Cost," *The Wall Street Journal* (August 1, 1996): page A1.

ble, they feel, routine, dull, and dangerous tasks should be performed by machines. These people agree that job security is desirable, but they note that it is not guaranteed by the absence of automation. Technological progress is a force that will not be stopped by a manager's decision to preserve a worker's job. Job security is better guaranteed by making use of technology to keep a company competitive and providing training to enhance workers' problem-solving skills.

Over the long term, adjustments will be made in the labor markets, and society will benefit from automation. In the late 1700s, 95% of the U.S. population was engaged in some form of agricultural work; during the 1800s, railway and road work were highly labor intensive. Today, technology has rendered these economic sectors less labor intensive, freeing up the human capital that our society now relies on to staff other professions critical to our standard of living. Other long-term results of automation include a shorter workweek and a relatively high employment rate (about 94% at any given time). Your grandparents may well remember a time when the standard workweek was 48 hours. Less than a century ago, the standard workweek was 72 hours; today, many Europeans enjoy a standard workweek of just 32 hours. Over the same period, living standards have improved dramatically. Technological advances and automation are responsible in part for these positive changes, as well as for many positive improvements in worker health and safety.

There are two types of automation, fixed (or hard) and flexible, each of which has its advantages. In the next two sections we will examine those benefits in detail.

Fixed Automation for Economies of Scale

In Chapter 4 an economy of scale was defined as a reduction in variable cost per unit that can justify a significant fixed cost. Traditionally, automation has been possible only with dedicated equipment that produced large volumes of standardized product. In essence, then, any technology that replaced labor was adopted because of its potential to reduce variable costs.

Cost-Volume Break-Even Analysis **Cost-volume break-even analysis (CVBA)** is a capital investment justification tool that is well suited to modeling the costs associated with fixed automation. By graphing the total costs of various process options against the cumulative volume produced (or customers served), the analyst can determine the break-even volume for those options. The break-even volume is that volume at which the total costs of the two options are equal; it is found at the intersection between the two cost-volume lines. The break-even point may also be found algebraically, by setting the fixed costs plus variable costs for the two alternatives equal. For example:

$$\text{FC}_\text{A} + \text{VC}_\text{A} \times \text{Volume} = \text{FC}_\text{B} + \text{VC}_\text{B} \times \text{Volume}$$

Solving for the volume in this equation yields the following expression for the break-even volume:

$$\text{Break-even volume} = \frac{\text{FC}_\text{A} - \text{FC}_\text{B}}{\text{VC}_\text{B} - \text{VC}_\text{A}}$$

Because graphs give analysts a feel for the sensitivity of a particular technology to changes in volume, drawing a break-even graph is usually a good idea, even if an algebraic solution has been used to find the break-even volume.

Consider the following example that we've constructed using some information in a *The Wall Street Journal* article about Gillette and some guesses on our part. Gillette makes 1.8 billion razors a year, and the firm's board of directors recently approved an expenditure to test a laser welding system for manufacturing the Sensor. (Therefore, though there probably were other fixed costs, we will assume the difference in fixed costs between the old and the new system is $FC_A - FC_B = \$10$ million.) If engineers had determined that Gillette could save, say, four-tenths of a cent ($VC_B - VC_A = \$0.004$) per razor blade by investing \$10 million to modify the production process, then Gillette would have needed to sell 2.5 billion (\$10 million / \$0.004) razor blades to break even on the investment. Figure 7.5 shows the break-even graph for this example.

Today, information technology is having a significant impact not just on the manufacturing sector, but on the service sector as well. One industry that exemplifies the impact of technology on services is the financial services sector. At one time in the banking industry, automation referred to the computerization of the machines that count money. But deregulation, the movement toward a cashless society, and electronic record-keeping, funds transfer, and trading in stocks, bonds, and commodities have had a significant effect on this industry. There is now no particular benefit to having a savings account in a "hometown" bank. If you live in Miami, you can access money that has been deposited in a Seattle bank just as easily as money deposited in a local bank. In either case, you would use the nearest ATM.

As a result, today no U.S. bank can consider its competitive arena to be the "local" market. Large banks have generated tremendous economies of scale by leveraging their investments in electronic technologies to serve a larger customer base. Similarly, discount brokers and financial services insti-

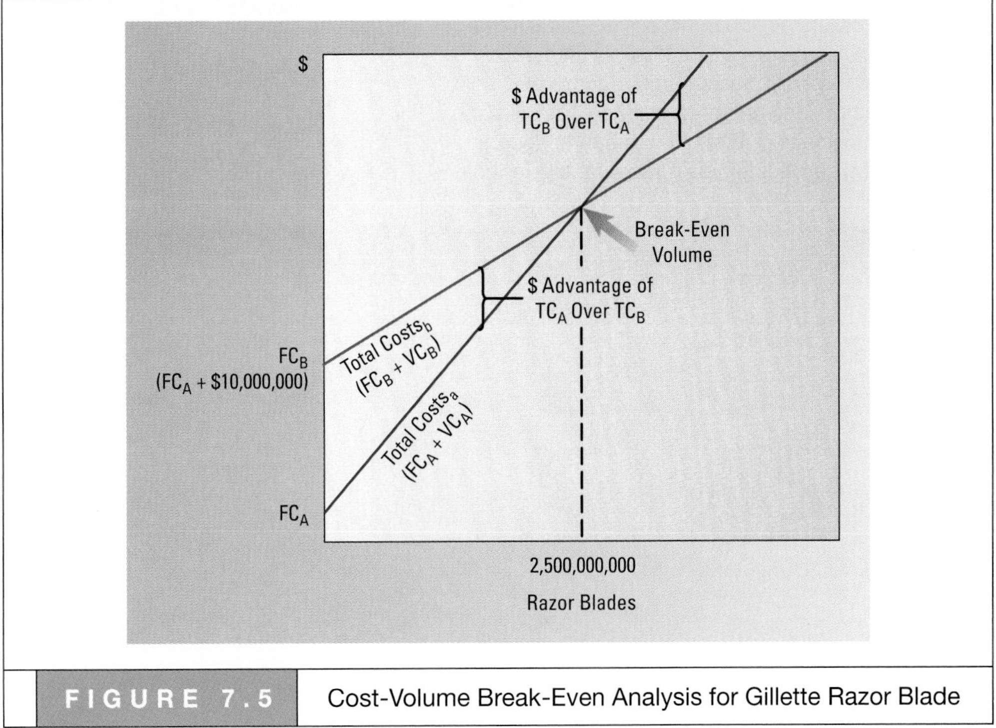

FIGURE 7.5 Cost-Volume Break-Even Analysis for Gillette Razor Blade

tutions have gained significant advantages over local stockbrokers by using technology to generate economies of scale.

In sum, making the right technological choices is critical to success in any business. Hugh McColl, CEO of Bank of America, recently stated. . . . "This thing (technology) is like a tidal wave. If you fail in the game, you're going to be dead." We agree. Attempting to use processes that go against the tide of technological change has led to the competitive failure of many businesses. On the other hand, riding the wave of technological change can lead to exceptional success.

> active example

Take a closer look at the concepts and issues you've been reading about.

Flexible Automation for Economies of Scope

In recent years, computer-based technologies have become available that make feasible the automation of processes that do not produce large volumes of standardized products. One basic foundation of such technologies is the concept of numerical control. A **numerical control (NC)** machine is one that can be programmed to operate automatically using coded instructions. The earliest forms of numerical control used punch cards or circular paper tapes on which machining instructions had been encoded in the form of punched-out dots. One pass through the cards or one revolution of the tape on the numerical control machine would produce one unit of an item. (The unique set of machining instructions for making a particular item is called its part program.) Later, magnetic media such as cassette tapes and disks replaced punch cards and tapes. Numerically controlled general-purpose equipment can be used to produce low-volume items with higher levels of precision, consistency, and productivity than operator-controlled equipment.

Today, numerical control is often integrated into production equipment. A **computerized numerical control (CNC)** machine is a piece of equipment that has been outfitted with a computer that can store part programs. If a part has been made on such a machine in the past, its part program is likely to be stored in the computer. The machine operator only has to instruct the machine to make that particular part; that person doesn't have to load a new part program into the machine each time a different part is made.

Application of information technologies has supported a wave of consolidation in the banking industry and has allowed banks to become much more efficient while also improving customer service. Diebold and NCR are now making ATMs that enhance security by identifying cardholders using the pattern in their eyes' iris.

Distributed numerical control (DNC) (also called direct numerical control) refers to the use of a group of networked CNC machines run from a common server. The server is a computer that can download and store part programs from a centralized mainframe or server. It can also collect performance statistics and monitor the status of all of the machines in the network. With DNC, all part programs need not be stored on each CNC. Part programs for items that are made on only one machine can be stored on that machine's CNC. Programs for items that are made using several different machines can be stored on the local network server. Part programs for items that are manufactured in many different geographic locations can be stored on the mainframe computer. Figure 7.6 illustrates the concepts of numerical control, computerized numerical control, and distributed numerical control.

Besides material processing equipment, material handling and storage systems can be automated. An *automated storage and retrieval system (AS/RS)* makes use of bar code technology to identify materials that have arrived for storage. It places them in storage automatically and records their location in a computerized memory bank. When the materials are needed, the AS/RS automatically

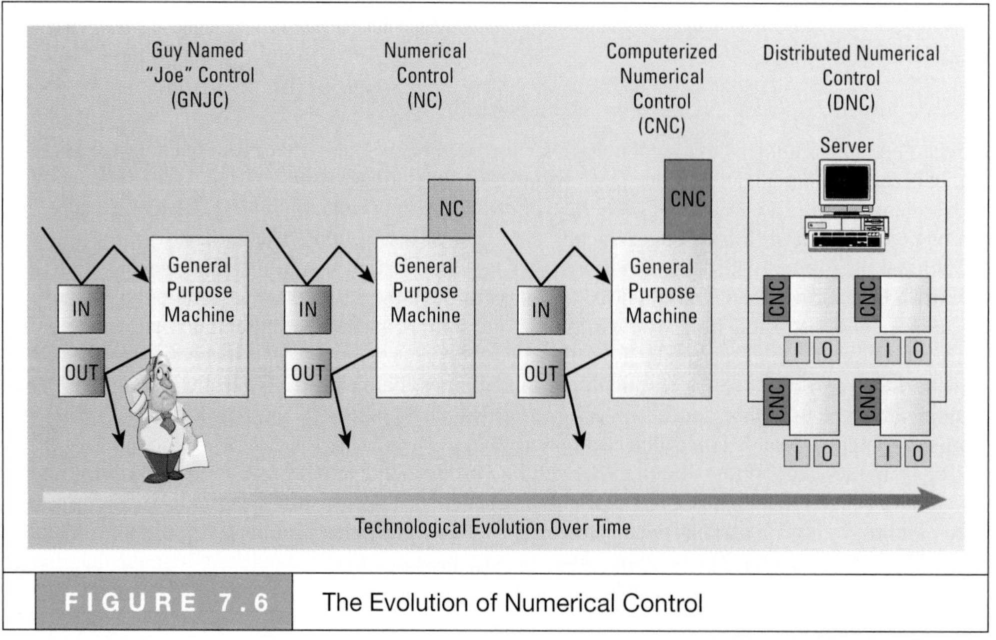

FIGURE 7.6 The Evolution of Numerical Control

removes them from storage. AS/RS systems not only provide accurate information about inventory on a real-time basis; they are programmed to "learn" patterns of material usage, so that commonly used items can be retrieved quickly and easily, and less frequently used items stored in out-of-the-way locations.

To transport materials without using forklifts with human drivers, engineers developed the *automated guided vehicle (AGV)*. These vehicles can be programmed to avoid collisions and can be operated in environments considered unsafe for human material handlers. In many plants today, a grid of wires beneath the floor allows an AGV to "know" where it is and be instructed (by wireless transmission from a host computer) where to go next. In other settings, particularly where a standardized product is made in high volumes, AGVs follow a preprogrammed route along a line on the floor.

Group technology (GT) is an approach to product and process design that is based on commonalities among parts. In this approach, similarities in the shape, size, material, or routing of parts are used to create product families. For instance, in an existing product mix, a particular group of products may use the same resources. If it does not, a number of items may be redesigned in order to create a group that can use the same resources.

As for new products, they should not be designed from the ground up, because that approach might lead to new routings, new material sources, equipment needs, or the like. Designing each part from the ground up also produces a proliferation of designs, which can make the storage and retrieval of product designs difficult or expensive. Instead, whenever possible, new product designs should make use of existing components and design standards and should be made to fit into a specific product family. Since in group technology, each part within a group has the same routing and structural characteristics, companies that use GT can dedicate manufacturing cells to a particular product family. Dedicated cells offer great advantages in terms of product cost, quality of conformance, and delivery speed, in exchange for only a small loss in flexibility.

A **flexible manufacturing system (FMS)** is essentially an automated manufacturing cell—a group of interconnected, numerically controlled machines with automated material-handling capabilities and a shared control system. The automated material-handling system must be capable of loading and unloading materials on the NC machines, as well as transporting parts between them. An FMS, then, is capable of making a wide variety of parts, even in small quantities, without human intervention. Although flexible manufacturing systems are very expensive, they can frequently be justified in the context of group technology. Without group technology, an FMS is likely to be underutilized and eventually to be removed. Figure 7.7 illustrates the typical evolution of group technology cells and flexible manufacturing systems in a job shop or batch process. Part (a) shows a production setting in which similar equipment is placed together. For example, if work center A is a place where metal is cut, all metal-cutting equipment would be kept in that one work center. Note that there are four work centers in part (a): A, B, C, and D. Each work center has a number of general-purpose resources that could be either operator controlled or numerically controlled. Since the equipment in each work center is not specialized, the system is capable of producing just about anything. Although the picture shows the routing A–B–C–D, the number of possible routings through the shop is limitless, since a route could have any number of stops.

A flexible manufacturing system is an automated manufacturing cell comprised of numerically controlled machines (such as these Cincinnati Milacron machining centers) linked by a central computer and tied to an automated handling system.

While this setup is flexible, it is not very efficient, nor is it well coordinated: Individual jobs are handled independently. If a firm found that much of a product mix could be produced using one common route, managers might use some of their general-purpose equipment to create a dedicated GT cell. Some companies might even redesign certain products to make them suitable for production in such a cell. Part (b) of Figure 7.7 shows such an arrangement. Note that the common route for the group of parts made in the GT cell is A–B–C–D. Finally, some firms might contemplate establishing an FMS. Part (c) of Figure 7.7 shows an FMS that is an automated version of the GT cell in part (b).

Computer integrated manufacturing (CIM) combines automated process and material handling technologies with other computer-based manufacturing technologies, so that computers everywhere in the company can "talk" to one another. Chapter 4 introduced computer-aided design (CAD) systems; later chapters will introduce computerized planning and control systems. A CIM system provides interfaces between these various systems. Figure 7.8 illustrates the role of CIM in linking product design, process design, and operations planning and control systems. As we saw in Chapter 4,

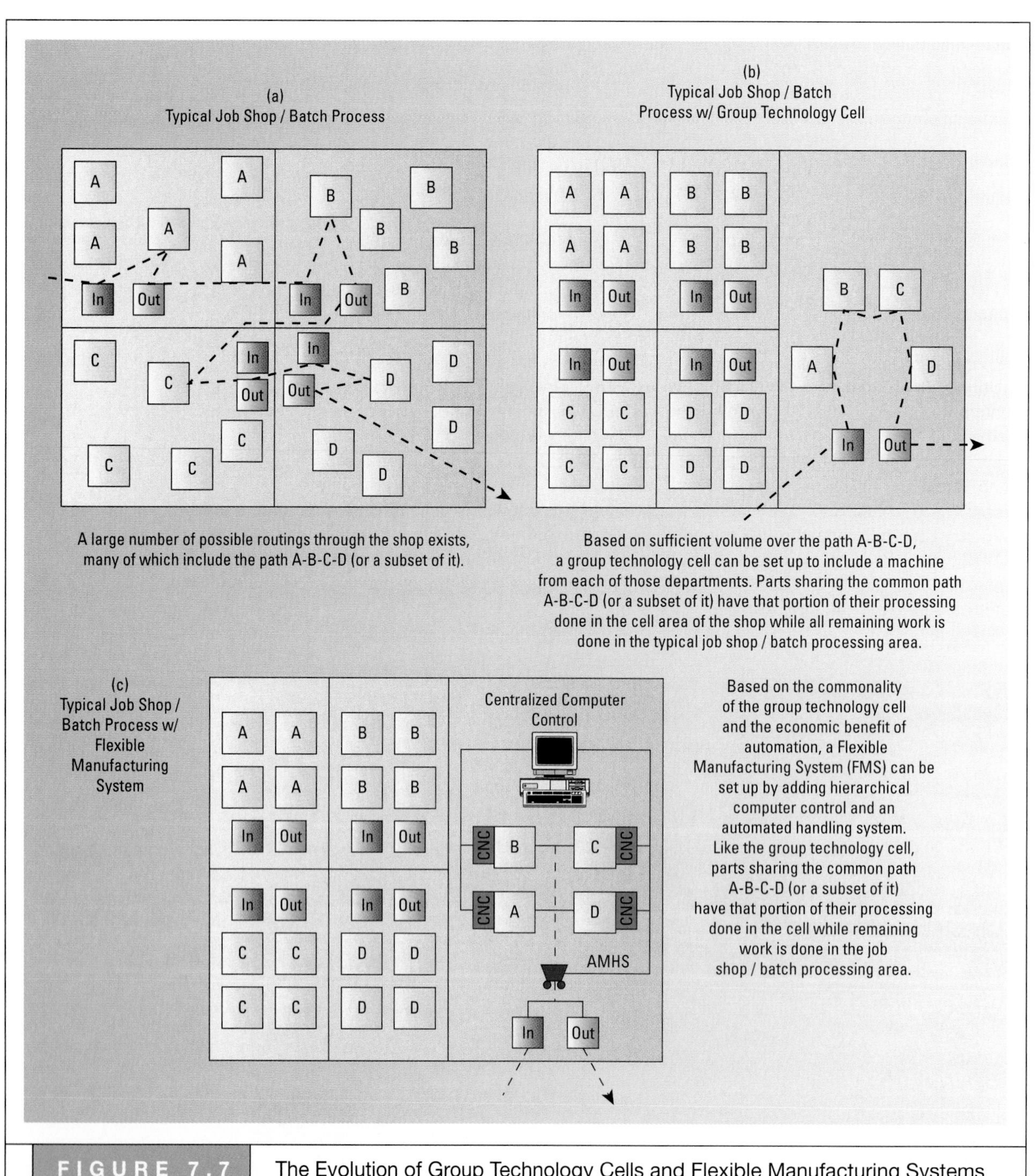

FIGURE 7.7 The Evolution of Group Technology Cells and Flexible Manufacturing Systems

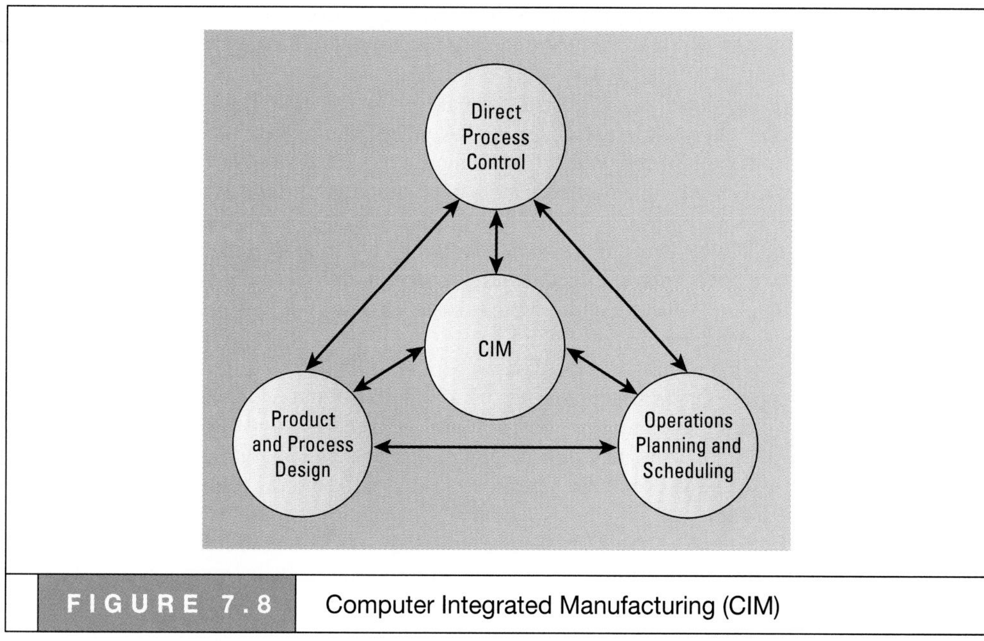

FIGURE 7.8 Computer Integrated Manufacturing (CIM)

there are significant benefits to such integration. Product design changes can quickly be tested for manufacturability, and accurate data on process performance can be made available for use in planning and control decisions. Moreover, the system architecture bridges functional boundaries, allowing managers in one function to gain a better understanding of the impact of their decisions on other functions.

Unlike fixed automation, the technologies used in flexible automation are not designed to generate economies of scale. Rather, they provide economies of scope or scale, depending on the competitive priorities they support. (Recall that in Chapter 4, an economy of scope was described as an economic advantage that is obtained through process flexibility.) Cost-volume break-even analysis is therefore not well suited to describing the costs and benefits of flexible automation. **Cost-volume-flexibility break-even analysis (CVFBA),** by contrast, is a tool that can be used to evaluate the economic tradeoffs in technology investments that may pay off through economies of scope. In CVFBA, instead of finding a break-even volume, the analyst finds several break-even lines that represent combinations of volume and variety for which the process alternatives are equally attractive. A more complete discussion of CVFBA is provided in the next section of this chapter.

Cost-Volume-Flexibility Break-Even Analysis In the past, manufacturers focused almost exclusively on one of two competitive strategies: either low cost or flexibility and customization. A low-cost strategy usually meant using highly automated technology to mass produce a standardized product-service bundle. When a more customized fit was called for in order to differentiate a product-service bundle, a manufacturer would use a more labor-intensive technology to provide the necessary flexibility in the manufacturing process.

Today this type of either-or situation is becoming less and less common. Competing on the basis of a totally standardized product is becoming more and more difficult, no matter how competitive the price. Customers are beginning to expect a better match with their specific needs, whether in terms of timing, variety, or quantity. For example, if you want your hamburger served without a pickle at a fast-food restaurant, the manager cannot afford to treat you as if you come from outer space. Granted, in the past he might have suggested politely that "at our low prices, you can't ask for special favors." But today, the competing store next door will tell you that you can "have it your way" and make good on the statement quickly and at almost the same low price. To give another example, as recently as 1983, Anheuser-Busch, the world's largest brewer, produced only six varieties of beer in a handful of package options. Now, through product proliferation and licensing agreements with international companies, the firm produces several times that many products in about twice as many packaging options. The bottom line is that, except for a few rare markets (e.g., toothpick manufacturing, currency printing or coin minting, and oil refining), customers are demanding increased variety and customization in markets that have traditionally been highly cost competitive.

A similar situation is developing in markets in which companies have traditionally competed on the basis of flexibility. In these markets, companies are now being pressed to be more cost competitive. The health care industry, express delivery services, and the machine tool industry are all good examples. In these industries, though the ability to provide a product-service bundle that precisely meets a specific customer's expectations is still the primary reason a company wins business, cost is no longer an afterthought.

Traditionally companies have used CVBA to evaluate a new process technology, followed sometimes by a more detailed analysis. In essence, a CVBA yields the point of intersection between the total cost curves of competing process alternatives, which shows the break-even volume, or the point at which the two alternatives are equally attractive. In most situations in the past, a CVBA model adequately captured the tradeoff between the higher fixed costs of hard automation and the lower variable costs that resulted from labor savings. Because flexibility was not an issue, the model did not need to include some measure of the economic effect of variety in the product-service bundle on the choice of process. More often than not, when flexibility was an issue, cost was not. The need to justify technology from that perspective did not exist.

Today, business isn't that simple. In most cases, a firm must consider the economic effect of variety in the product-service bundle when choosing a process. With today's flexible automation, the increased fixed costs of automation may be "buying" more than economies of scale, achieved through lower variable costs per unit. They may also be purchasing economies of scope, achieved through lower flexibility costs. In a significant number of cases, higher fixed costs cannot be justified based only on economies of scale.

Fortunately, the CVBA model can be modified to include the economic impact of both volume (economies of scale) and flexibility (economies of scope). This modified model is CVFBA. By including both volume (variable costs) and flexibility (setup costs), we can define the total costs of two alternatives as:

$$\text{Total Costs} = \text{Fixed Costs (FC)} + \text{Variable Costs (VC)} + \text{Setup Costs (SC)}$$

Recall that modeling only two variables, fixed costs and variable costs, yields a total cost line for each alternative; the intersection of the total cost lines represents the volume at which the total costs of two alternatives are equal. Modeling *three* variables for each option (fixed costs, variable costs, and flexibility costs) yields a total cost *plane.* Just as the floor and wall of your classroom meet along a line, two total cost planes will intersect along a similar line. The points along that line represent the set of volume and flexibility combinations for which the combined total costs of two alternatives are equal. In this three-way break-even case, an entire line rather than a single point becomes the relevant equality. Combinations of volume and flexibility that fall to either side of the line are better served by one of the two alternatives.

For example, in a hospital, the fixed cost of a manually operated diagnostic testing machine might be $1,000 per week. The cost to set up the machine for a different type of test might be $25. A second option might be a machine that incorporates a higher degree of flexible automation. The more automated machine might have a fixed cost of $2,500 per week, but because a computer controls it, setup for a different type of test might be much more efficient, at an estimated cost of only $15. The more automated process might also be expected to reduce volume-related variable costs to only $3 per test, compared to $5 per test for the manually operated machine.

In making this decision, an analyst could model the total costs of each machine and set them equal to each other. Using traditional CVBA, one would see that a volume of 750 tests per week would be necessary to justify purchase of the automated machine based on volume alone ($\$1{,}000 + \$5 \times 750 = \$2{,}500 + \$3 \times 750$). On the other hand, if looking only at flexibility or at the reduced setup cost, one would find that at least 150 different setups per week would be necessary to justify the automated option ($\$1{,}000 + \$25 \times 150 = \$2{,}500 + \$15 \times 150$). But if the analyst considers both volume and flexibility, the results will be different. In the following equation, CFVBA is used to combine fixed costs with both volume and flexibility costs. The resulting relationship can be graphed as the line that separates those combinations for which one alternative is more economically advantageous than the other (see Figure 7.9).

$$\$1000 + \$5 \times \text{Volume} + \$25 \times \text{Setups} = \$2500 + \$3 \times \text{Volume} + \$15 \times \text{Setups}$$

or

$$\text{Volume} = 750 - 5 \times \text{Setups}$$

Graphing this relationship, we see that a volume of 750 tests per week, 150 setups per week, or some combination of the two is needed to equate the use of the two machines. Any point to the upper right-hand side of the diagonal line would represent such a combination. Assuming that approximately 450 tests are done each week, a traditional break-even analysis based on volume alone would not justify purchase of the automated machine ($\$1{,}000 + \$5 \times 450 < \$2{,}500 + 450 \times \$3$). Assuming that the tests are done in batches of five similar tests each, the machine would be set up about 90 times a week. Again, an analysis based on economy of scope alone would not justify purchase of the more automated process ($\$1{,}000 + \$25 \times 90 < \$2{,}500 + \$15 \times 90$). But

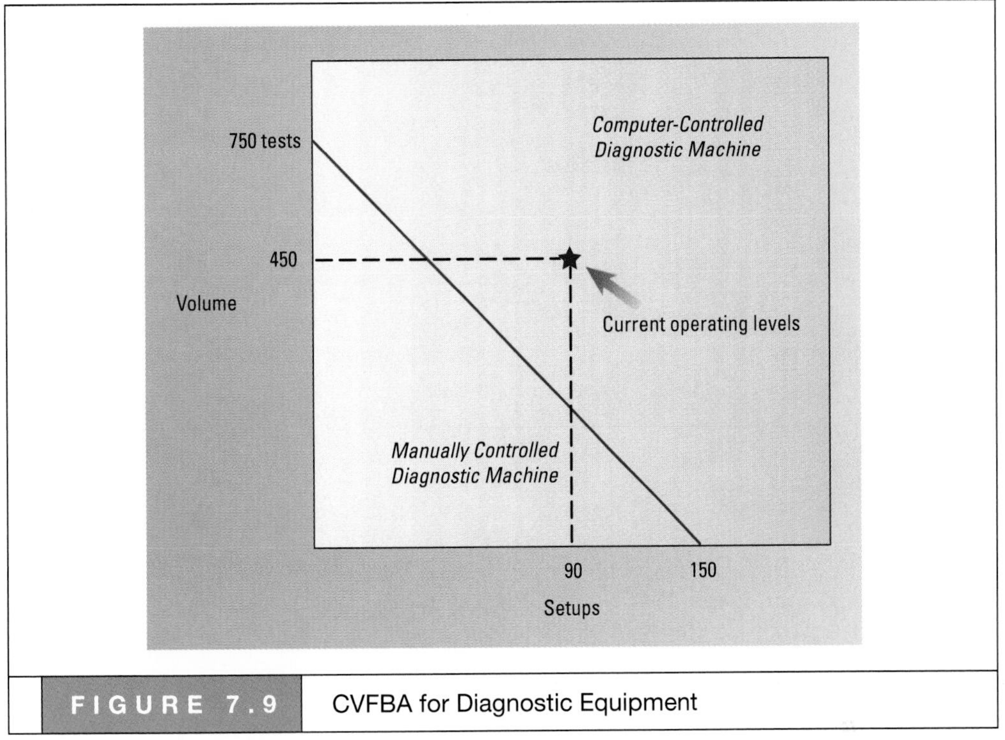

FIGURE 7.9 CVFBA for Diagnostic Equipment

when the analysis is based on volume and flexibility combined, the variable cost savings on 450 tests plus the setup cost savings on 90 setups are more than enough to justify purchase of the automated machine.

This approach can be helpful in making other types of choices. In a more traditional situation (one having to do with hard automation), lower variable costs might be obtained at the expense of higher fixed costs and flexibility costs. While in the past, low cost and high levels of flexibility rarely coexisted, that is not necessarily the case today. Consider the selection of an injection molding machine. One alternative might be a highly automated machine, with fixed costs of $150,000 per year, that can mold the outer shell of a pager out of hard plastic for about $.25 a unit. Retooling this machine to make a different model is estimated to cost about $15,000—very expensive. A smaller, less automated machine has a fixed cost of just $90,000 per year but a higher variable cost of $.45 per unit. Retooling this machine would be easier than the other and would cost only $6,000. The firm currently produces 450,000 units per year of a single model. However, as product life cycles grow shorter, workers on the factory floor are switching to new models more and more often. Managers expect they will have to change models at least five times a year over the foreseeable future. What should they do?

Using traditional CVBA, only 300,000 units a year are needed to justify using the larger machine. However, that analysis ignores the cost of retooling to produce new models. Ten years ago, retooling costs might not have been an issue, but in today's competitive environment, flexibility costs cannot be ignored. Using the more comprehensive CVFBA model, managers could estimate the total costs of each injection-molding machine and set them equal to each other. The resulting relationship could then be graphed as the line that separates those combinations for which one alternative would be more economically advantageous than the other:

$$\$150{,}000 + \$.25 \times \text{Volume} + \$15{,}000 \times \text{Tooling} = \$90{,}000 + \$.45 \times \text{Volume} + \$6{,}000 \times \text{Tooling}$$

or

$$\text{Volume} = 300{,}000 + 45{,}000 \times \text{Tooling}$$

If we graph this relationship (as in Figure 7.10), we can see a clear distinction between the two alternatives. If no additional retooling is required, any volume over 300,000 units per year would favor the larger machine. However, each new model raises the level of volume required to justify the larger machine by 45,000 units. Assuming that five new models are introduced in the coming year, a volume of 525,000 units would be required to justify use of the larger machine. Given that the plant's expected volume is only 450,000 and given the likelihood of an increasing need for flexibility over time, the firm is probably better off staying with the smaller machine.

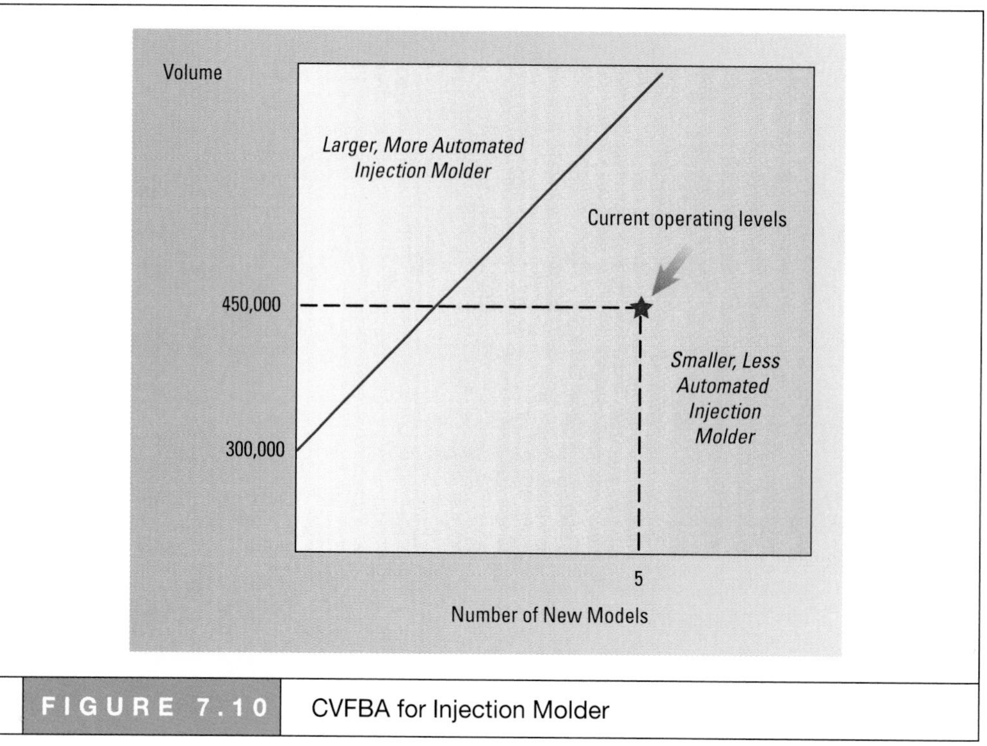

FIGURE 7.10 CVFBA for Injection Molder

active exercise

Take a moment to apply what you've learned.

active concept check

Now let's take a moment to test your knowledge of the concepts you have studied in this section.

System Design Factors at Miami's Rec Center

As has been noted in earlier chapters, Miami's Rec Center is a highly integrated facility which provides a full range of personal fitness and recreational opportunities under one roof in a location centrally located relative to the residential student population. The design of this facility has played a central role in its success. It has shown that you can make a big splash, even when you're not really offering anything new, by redesigning your service facility.

Prior to building the rec center, Miami University offered most of the recreational opportunities currently available there. (The only exceptions are the indoor track, climbing wall, and the current in the recreational pool.) The difference was that these recreational activities were dispersed around the campus. There were no synergies between the facilities, and their administration was decentralized. When the rec center was built, the design brought all of the campus's fitness and recreational resources under one roof. As a result, synergies were created that gave the recreational opportunities a high profile on campus, attracted potential students, allowed the university to provide therapy services in conjunction with local medical establishments, generated revenue by meeting a community need, and created new opportunities for healthy social interaction. From a client perspective, you could now get all of the recreational opportunities in one package, for one price, at one place.

The success of the rec center can be attributed, at least in part, to the consistent way in which the design factors of flexibility, customer involvement, supply-chain configuration, and technology were applied in the rec center's design:

- ***Flexibility:*** The venues and equipment in the rec center are best characterized as general purpose. Thus, the equipment provides a high degree of flexibility to the center. The facility can be used to meet the entire spectrum of fitness, recreation, and therapy needs of the university community. More specialized equipment was a better fit in the context of the multiple specialized recreation venues that were replaced by the rec center.
- ***Customer Involvement:*** The rec center design provides for a high degree of customer involvement. The only place there's an observation deck is above the aquatic center, where competitions are held. Otherwise, the floor space of the center is designed for client activity. The facility's location is central to the student residence area, it is open from early in the morning until late at night, hygiene needs such as food and towels are provided, and the access halls are wide. All of these elements of the facility's design combine to funnel clients to the resources they will use. The design's central characteristic is ready access to allow client involvement in the activity of their choice.
- ***Supply-Chain Configuration:*** The rec center is more than a place for people to work out. It is a place for people to learn about recreational alternatives; the rec center offers fitness classes, has personal trainers, and provides many of the resources needed for basic physical therapy. In this sense, the rec center has vertically integrated its services.
- ***Technology:*** The rec center has integrated its technology with campus access and payment systems. Student ID cards are used to allow students access to the center and for equipment check-out. These cards are also used by students on the campus meal plan to pay for food from the snack bar. Faculty who buy memberships also use their university ID cards at the rec center. The result: Familiar technology is used to enhance security and customer access to the facility. The limited use of technology serves the purpose of integrating the rec center with other campus systems.

Taken together, the design of the value-adding system at Miami's rec center demonstrates that aligning system design factors around a common design objective can enhance the effectiveness of the facility. Particularly for service facilities like the rec center, the design of the facility determines the service experience of the customers. Thus, the facility design is potentially difficult to distinguish from the design of the service itself.

> video exercise

Take a moment to apply what you've learned.

Process Choice

The choice of a production process was first discussed in Chapter 3. Figure 7.11 summarizes the distinctions among the four major process types: the job shop, batch process, repetitive process, and continuous process. They include clear differences in the source of demand information, in the variety of inputs and outputs, and in the volume of the output. Managers of a *job shop* receive job specifications directly from their customers; they use general-purpose equipment to create a wide variety of outputs from a wide variety of inputs. Managers of a *batch process* limit the variety of specifications they will accept from a customer but do allow customers to specify volume and certain other characteristics of the output. Like the job shop, the batch process uses general-purpose equipment, but there is less variety of input and output and the volume of output is somewhat larger. In contrast, a *repetitive process* and *continuous flow processes* produce standardized outputs from standardized inputs using dedicated equipment. The only way that customers can "specify" what they wish to receive is by adjusting their rate of consumption.

Return for a moment to Figure 7.3, which indicates that, taken together, decisions regarding the design of the value-adding system (flexibility, technology, vertical integration and customer involvement) imply the choice of a particular type of process. That is, a particular set of decisions about the four major system design factors will lead to the choice of a job shop, another to the choice of a batch process, and others to the choice of a repetitive or continuous process. Figure 7.12 summarizes the

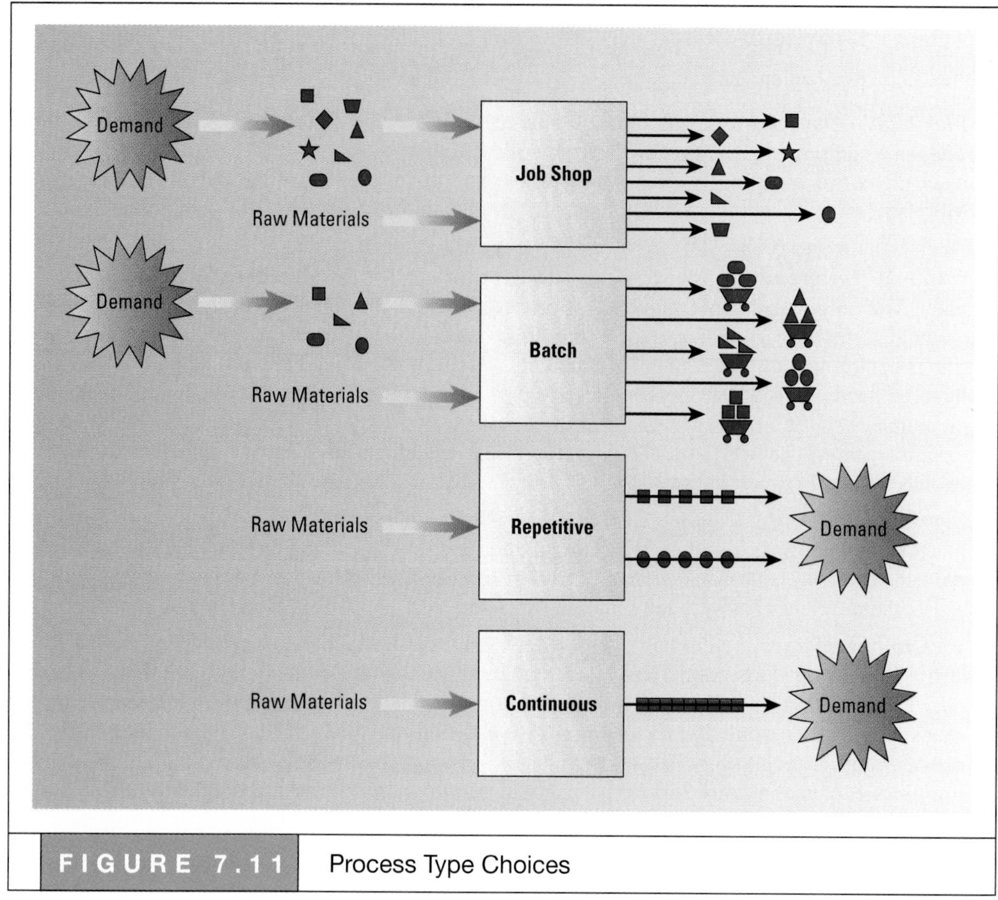

FIGURE 7.11 Process Type Choices

relationship between the choice of process type and the design of the value-adding system. Generally speaking, job shops and batch processes are appropriate for systems in which orders are won on the basis of flexibility, design capacity, and delivery speed. Thus, the decision to use a job shop or batch process is associated with little vertical integration, considerable flexibility in product and process, and customer input in developing the product-service bundle. Conversely, a repetitive or continuous flow process would be preferred when the primary order winner is low cost. Those processes place more emphasis on vertical integration and dedicated process technologies (to reduce costs) and little emphasis on flexibility and customer involvement.

As Figure 7.12 shows, when competitive priorities have been neatly defined in terms of order-winning and order-qualifying criteria, system design factors have traditionally provided a clear set of either-or tradeoffs, making the choice of a process type relatively simple. In some cases, however, the choice is not so simple. Some combination of process types, such as a group technology cell within a job shop, might be a beneficial hybrid. Multiple process types are combined in a **hybrid process.** For example, beverages are frequently prepared in a batch process and then canned in a continuous-flow process.

The advent of flexible automation technologies has further complicated the choice of process type (see Figure 7.13). Producing a single unit of 12 different items will probably never cost less than producing 12 units of a single item. Thus, the tradeoff between flexibility and cost will probably always be with us. Through CIM, however, job shops and batch processes in which flexibility, design capacity, and delivery speed are the order winners can now qualify for some orders on the basis of unit cost. Similarly, repetitive and continuous flow processes that normally win orders on the basis of cost, can now use CIM to qualify for some orders on the basis of flexibility, design capacity, and delivery speed.

In short, the boundaries of the competitive playing field have become blurred. No longer can manufacturers that use flexible processes ignore the price differential between their product-service bundles and those of manufacturers using dedicated processes (or vice versa). Indeed, flexible producers may now be capable of providing product-service bundles at a low enough price to take some business away from low-cost producers. Likewise, the low-cost producers may be able to offer enough customization to take some business from even the most flexible producer.

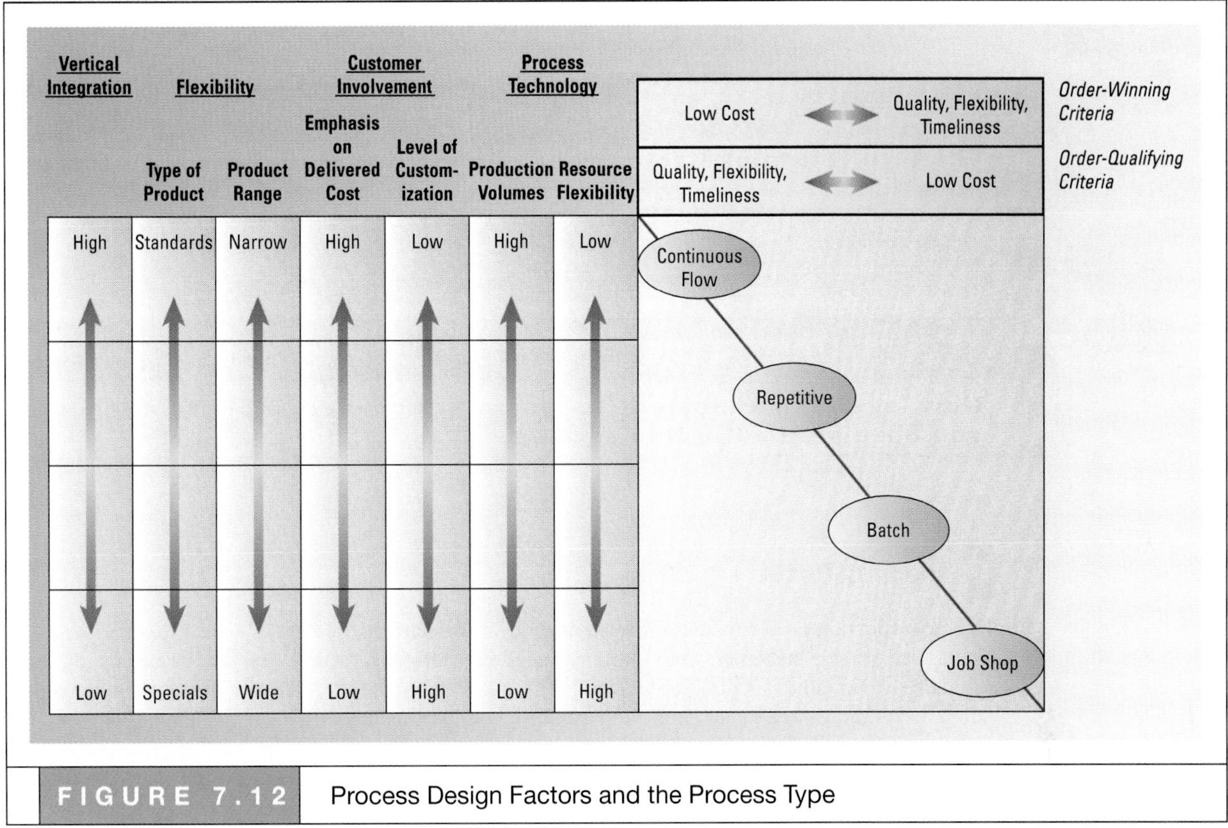

FIGURE 7.12 Process Design Factors and the Process Type

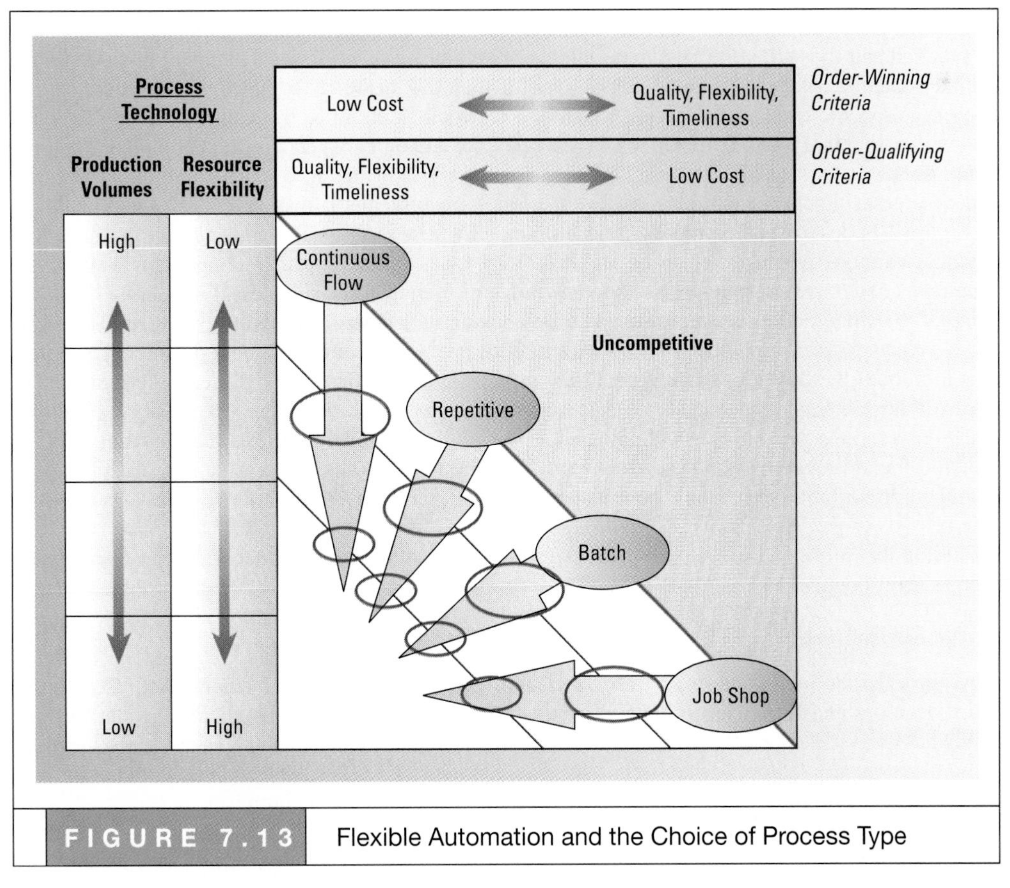

FIGURE 7.13 Flexible Automation and the Choice of Process Type

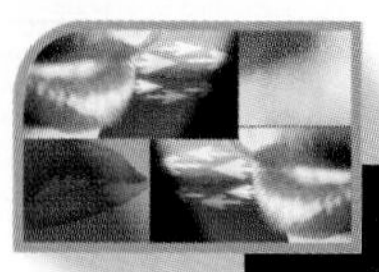

active poll <

What do you think? Voice your opinion and find out what others have to say.

active concept check <

Now let's take a moment to test your knowledge of the concepts you have studied in this section.

> Facility Focus

The most common problems in a value-adding system arise from the lack of a clear *facility focus.* No facility can provide customers with unlimited choice, the highest quality, and the lowest cost on short schedules and in either small or large quantities—all at the same time. In other words, a single facility cannot be all things to all customers, at least not if it is to perform well.

Lack of focus makes a value-adding system complex and impossible to manage effectively. Size, the diversity of product-service bundles produced, logistics, the number of customers, and the number of suppliers are just a few sources of the complexity of an unfocused facility. Because complexity has many root causes, new strategic options should always be weighed against the complexity they may introduce to the value-adding system. Many times, the KISS principle (Keep It Simple, Stupid) is applicable. To be the lowest-cost provider, a facility must produce on a large scale; thus, the diversity of the product-service bundle must be held in check. To produce a diversity of bundles or small quantities of bundles, a facility must de-emphasize cost.

A facility may be focused by establishing a homogeneous set of customer expectations that must be satisfied and by setting uniform expectations across the value-adding system. Because the value-adding system in a focused facility is less complex than that of other facilities, there is more repetition, more specific expertise, less conflict among viewpoints and objectives, and a greater ability to deal with particular types of problems. When it comes to customer expectations, everyone in the facility is "on the same page." The focused facility, then, can be expected to be particularly good at a limited set of tasks. Focused facilities provide superior competitive performance.

Figure 7.14 describes the process of developing a focused facility. The starting point is the firm's business strategy, because decisions about facility focus must support management's efforts to develop a competitive advantage. So that the choice of focus will be realistic, the current characteristics of the value-adding system must also be considered at the outset. Not all facilities are new, and even new facilities employ workers with a set of preexisting attitudes, beliefs, and capabilities. Based on both the business strategy and the current characteristics of the system, then, managers must establish a homogeneous set of customer expectations, quality targets, key success factors, scale of operations, and process technologies for the facility. To achieve or maintain a facility focus, decisions regarding all five of these "focus variables" must generally be consistent, though for technological or competitive reasons, one of the focus variables may receive more emphasis than the others.

During this process of developing the focused facility, managers will need to answer questions such as the following:

- Will regional or local facilities supply the firm's entire product line?

  When each facility produces an entire product line focused on a homogeneous set of customer expectations and quality levels are consistent across the entire product line, there is no clear advantage to large-scale operations. Similar technologies can be used for all elements of the product line, and key success factors can transcend the entire product line. For example, each restaurant in a fast-food chain produces most, if not all, of the standard menu on the premises.

- Will regional facilities supply only those parts of the product line that use common process technologies?

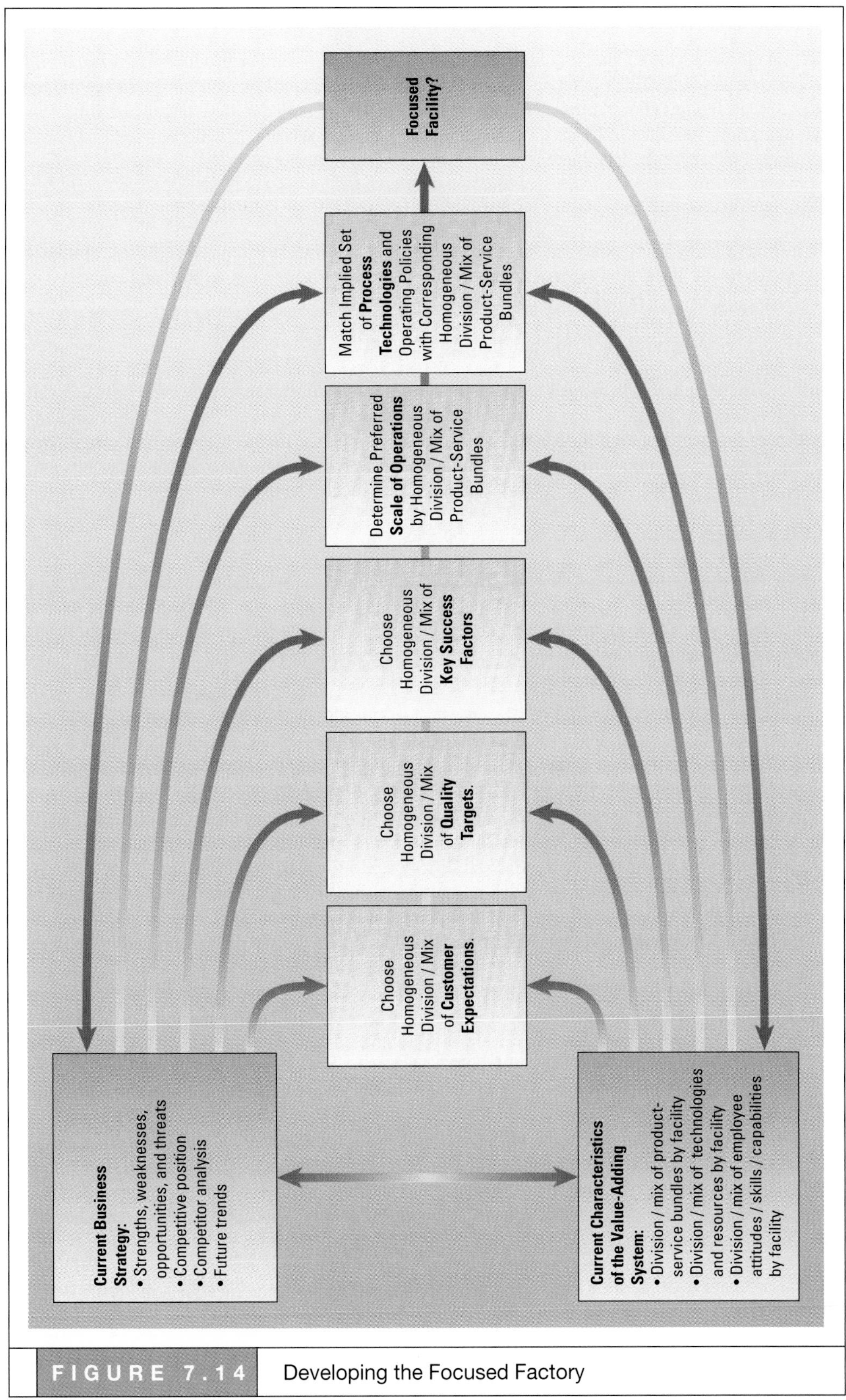
Current Business Strategy:
• Strengths, weaknesses, opportunities, and threats
• Competitive position
• Competitor analysis
• Future trends
Current Characteristics of the Value-Adding System:
• Division / mix of product-service bundles by facility
• Division / mix of technologies and resources by facility
• Division / mix of employee attitudes / skills / capabilities by facility
Choose Homogeneous Division / Mix of Customer Expectations.
Choose Homogeneous Division / Mix of Quality Targets.
Choose Homogeneous Division / Mix of Key Success Factors
Determine Preferred Scale of Operations by Homogeneous Division / Mix of Product-Service Bundles
Match Implied Set of Process Technologies and Operating Policies with Corresponding Homogeneous Division / Mix of Product-Service Bundles
Focused Facility?

FIGURE 7.14 Developing the Focused Factory

In some cases, it makes sense for each facility to focus on a subset of the product line that shares a common set of technologies or other resources. For example, Proctor & Gamble (P&G) makes Ivory Snow bar soap in selected facilities, along with other products that are made on similar machines (e.g., Irish Spring); Folgers coffee (another P&G product) is processed at a different facility.

- Will regional facilities supply only those parts of the product line that have similar quality targets?

  While the Ford Motor Company builds Lincolns and Fords on similar product platforms, it builds them in separate facilities in order to accommodate the increased demand for quality in the more luxurious Lincolns. For example, the Lincoln Mark VIII is built on the Cougar platform. While Cougars are assembled in Detroit, the Mark VIII is built in a Wixom, Michigan, plant that is better equipped to handle the labor-intensive assembly of luxury interiors.

- Will small-scale regional facilities complement a few large-scale centralized facilities?

  Wal-Mart's many local stores are served by a few large regional distribution facilities. Similarly, a large, vertically integrated steel company might make steel in one big facility and convert it into various products in a number of smaller regional facilities.

- Will facilities be divided according to their key success factors?

  Most hospitals put their emergency rooms in a different location from the quiet, tightly controlled environments required for most of their other services. Managers at Parker-Hannifin's Eaton, Ohio, tube fittings plant noticed that small orders simply got lost in their normal mix of large-volume business. So the company built another plant in Brookville, Ohio, designed to focus only on small, unique orders and the factors that determine success in that market segment.

- Will one large-scale, all-purpose facility supply the entire product line to all regions?

  When the demand for a homogeneous group of product-service bundles is compared to the natural economies of scale for a process, a single facility may be indicated. For example, the Treasury Department prints U.S. currency of all denominations in a single facility for distribution throughout the nation and the world. The Hill-Rom Company builds hospital beds for more than 90% of the U.S. market in a single facility in Batesville, Indiana.

In some cases, a highly focused facility like Parker-Hannifin's Brookville, Ohio, plant cannot be justified economically, because of the fixed cost of building and maintaining that sort of value-adding system. In other cases, a large multipurpose facility cannot be sold, and employees cannot be transferred or terminated. Even if the facility could be sold and the employees terminated, the cost of replacing one big facility with a number of smaller plants might be prohibitive. The economics of sharing the same roof, parking lot, support staff, and other forms of fixed overhead cost may render the cost of physically separate facilities prohibitive. In such cases, a facility focus may be developed through an approach called the **plant within a plant,** or a plant that is physically located under the same roof as another plant or plants but has its own organization, employees, and facilities. Some companies have even built physical walls to separate various processes according to their focus.

This concept is not limited to manufacturing. Without realizing it, you have probably dealt with many focused service industries. Maybe it was a separate area in a local supermarket, set aside for renting movies, complete with its own inventory system, cash registers, and staff. Or perhaps the auto repair section in your local Wal-Mart or Kmart has been separated from the rest of the store. What is shared, what is kept separate, and what synergy is gained by combining these services under one roof?

You might even have applied the concept of facility focus to your living arrangements. There are many solid economic reasons for sharing an apartment with a roommate, even after college, while one is young and single. For similar reasons, you may live at home with your parents, or your parents or grandparents may someday live with you. If you and your parents, grandparents, or roommate have compatible lifestyles, such an arrangement works well. But if not, how do you make it work? By identifying dissimilarities and separating certain key resources or living areas. For instance, dividing up closet space and finishing off a garage apartment or second bathroom allows for a more focused use of living space.

active concept check

Now let's take a moment to test your knowledge of the concepts you have studied in this section.

Business Process Reengineering

The primary focus of this chapter has been the design of the process that is used to create a firm's product-service bundle. All too often, managers tend to focus their improvement efforts on the *physical* transformation process. Perhaps that is because the physical process is visible or because managers associate it more closely than other processes with improvements to profitability. Or perhaps it is because management is usually not directly affected by efforts to improve the physical process.

A newer approach to process improvement focuses primarily on *managerial* processes. This recent phenomenon recognizes that all work is done in some process and that every employee, regardless of rank, has a customer and a supplier. As such, the processes of hiring employees, paying bills, identifying suppliers, providing computer services, marketing products, raising capital, and many other business activities are reasonable targets for improvement. Moreover, customer dissatisfaction and the inability to improve customer satisfaction often stem more from a company's business processes than from its physical processes. In fact, that is the reason for emphasizing the product-service bundle, rather than just products or services, in a course on operations management.

As Table 7.2 shows, efforts to improve business processes may be focused on making localized, incremental improvements or on making radical improvements with widespread consequences. The

TABLE 7.2 Reengineering Versus Continuous Improvement

(a): Degree and Breadth of Change Desired

	Breadth of areas addressed:	
Degree of Change	**Global and Broad in Scope**	**Local and Narrow in Scope**
Revolutionary	Process reengineering	May be suboptimal and doomed to die on the vine. Many times constrained by issues outside its scope. Might not fit with the rest of the business. Like working to put a five-year supply of ink in a disposable pen that usually ends up lost, broken, stolen, or sat on within 3–4 weeks.
Incremental	Many times not worth the effort. Like getting an entire army lined up and in sync just to march a few yards.	Continuous improvement

(b): System Complexity and Breadth of Change Desired

	Breadth of areas addressed	
System Complexity	**Global and Broad in Scope**	**Local and Narrow in Scope**
Complex with many interrelated parts	Process reengineering	Continuous improvement
Simple with few interrelated parts	Should be obvious, should be done. "No-brainers" like moving from the telegraph to the telephone or from the typewriter to the word processor.	Continuous improvement

Source: Adapted from J. Chris White, "Reengineering and Continuous Improvement," *Quality Digest,* July 1996: p. 31–34.

process of making localized, incremental improvements using the techniques of business process analysis is typically referred to as **continuous improvement.** Continuous improvement is useful in both complex systems with many interrelated parts and simple systems with few interrelated parts. In contrast, reengineering (or **business process reengineering**) is a "blow it up and start over from scratch" improvement approach. Reengineering doesn't make much sense on a local scale or with very simple systems, because simple systems and local subsystems are constrained largely by outside factors. Thus, a complete redesign of a small subsystem can create many problems, yet has the potential to make only incremental improvements.

Many business processes are truly cross-functional. Some have evolved over a significant period because of business and personnel changes. When managers examine them closely, they often wonder, "Why would anyone in his right mind do things that way?" Changing such processes is very difficult because of the tendency of employees in functional silos to maintain their resources, status, and power base. Business process reengineering is one approach to developing new ways to manage cross-functional improvement efforts.

Because many business processes were poorly designed or were designed when conditions were vastly different, there is a great need for managers who can successfully lead change efforts. There is also a great need for frameworks, techniques, and methods that managers can employ in their efforts to adapt organizational processes to current realities. Business process reengineering (BPR) is one such technique. BPR has been defined as "starting over," or more formally "the fundamental rethinking and redesign of business processes to achieve dramatic improvements in critical contemporary measures of performance such as cost, quality, service, and speed" (M. Hammer and J. Champy 1993). In contrast to the "employee involvement" and "continuous improvement" approaches of the total quality management system that try to make lots of small improvements, BPR seeks to accomplish rapid radical redesign of broad cross-functional business processes. BPR is a higher risk approach that "bets the farm" on a whole new way of doing things.

active example <

Take a closer look at the concepts and issues you've been reading about.

CONVERSION PROCESSES VERSUS BUSINESS PROCESSES

Conversion processes are the physical systems used by manufacturers and services to create their product-service bundle. For example, the system used at the cafeteria to prepare and deliver your most recent meal is a conversion process. So, too, are processes that make paper from wood chips, assemble cars from parts, and print tickets for a concert. Process reengineering (or process design) has been around for a long time if we are talking about conversion processes. Business process reengineering has a different focus. It uses process design tools to address administrative processes that accomplish such tasks as paying suppliers, distributing finished goods, designing product-service bundles, buying materials, hiring employees, and scheduling workers. For such processes BPR answers questions like: Exactly what needs to be done? Who should do it? How? Where? When? For how long?

WIDESPREAD USE OF E-COMMERCE TOOLS

The advent of management information systems that use centralized databases has significantly changed the set of possible approaches organizations can use to make decisions. Today, managers and other decision makers frequently use data that they did not collect themselves. Data is available, frequently on a real-time basis, from many sites all over the world. Decisions that were once centralized because of the need of a hierarchy to collect and aggregate data can now be decentralized and made more quickly. As a result, BPR has often been called an MIS technique. We agree that MIS is frequently central to the success of BPR, and technology frequently does drive organizational change. MIS is an *enabling technology* for many positive process changes generally associated with e-commerce. Information systems are only tools to accomplish some objective. The sophistication of information systems is meaningless unless it improves organizational performance in some way. Thus, BPR is much more than an MIS technique.

A REENGINEERING ALGORITHM

Since each reengineering effort has unique goals, is shaped by a different team of individuals, and addresses a unique process, every project will proceed along a different course. The creativity of team members and their ability to direct the development of their project should never be compromised by setting up a procedure or set of steps that they must follow. Nevertheless, there are some fairly common patterns that can be seen if you look at a cross-section of reengineering projects. These patterns are what we present below in the form of an algorithm, or set of sequentially related steps.

Step 1: Prioritize Processes for Reengineering

To get going with BPR there has to be a process to change. A company's leaders are responsible for determining which processes to reengineer and when. Processes that are performing poorly and have significant impact on customer satisfaction and competitiveness are obvious candidates. It's very common for a small percentage of the business processes to account for a majority of the problems experienced by customers. Pareto analysis can be used to determine which processes are most important to address. When a firm is just beginning to use BPR, it is a good idea not to pick the most difficult reengineering project. Instead, many companies choose to "pick the low-hanging fruit" while they gain experience with BPR. This allows leaders to demonstrate early successes and helps to build support for other reengineering efforts.

Step 2: Organize and Educate

Reengineering is done by people. The people you choose to be on a reengineering team are a major factor in determining the impact of the team. Most commonly, the people required are those that are involved in the process being changed. Since most business processes cut across several functions, most reengineering teams are cross-functional teams. It is very important for the team members to be representative, or at least respected and accessible, in their home function. If an important group of people is left out of the effort, important insights may be missed and the project may be strongly opposed in that area. The team members also need to be creative risk-takers who can communicate well. They might have to decide to eliminate their own work areas and sell that decision to their colleagues. Experts suggest that these team members be exempted from most, if not all, of their normal duties and assigned full time to the reengineering effort.

Top-level managers whose power and authority can be leveraged to support the requests of the team also need to be assigned to the reengineering effort. The idea of letting workers make their own decisions about their own work area is great in the context of continuous improvement, but in the context of BPR top management sponsorship is essential. Top management also needs to lead in the implementation of BPR plans. Some respected consultants and authors recommend devoting at least 20% of the chief executive's time to the project during the design phase of a BPR project and 50% during the implementation phase. Allocating an additional 50% of another senior executive's time during the implementation phase is also recommended. BPR must be driven by customer priorities and it has to be strategically important—it's the "big time"—and to be successful, it must be provided visible senior management leadership.

It's not enough to just put the right people on the reengineering team. They have to have a place to meet, they have to get paid despite the fact that they may not be assigned to any particular function, they may need to travel to get ideas from other firms, and they will probably need support staff such as MIS professionals to help them carry their project forward. In short, they need a budget and other resources with which to operate. As the BPR project progresses, an implementation budget will likely be developed by the team. This, too, needs to be provided if there is any chance for the project to be successful.

If you pick the best set of people for a reengineering team, you still can't be sure that they are all ready for the task at hand. A team member's former work experience may not have exposed him or her to every part of the broader process the team is getting ready to change. They also need to learn the company's goals for the project so that their decisions will be consistent with the strategies of the firm and they will know when they have completed their task.

Step 3: Document the Current Process

Reengineering teams have to start with the existing process. To start with, they must understand the process as a system. Later, they must be able to communicate and defend their suggested changes to others. As a result, it is important to document the process at the beginning of a reengineering effort. There are at least two major ways in which a process can be documented: (1) Flow charts indicate what happens to information and material as it moves through a process, and (2) Performance measures indicate the effectiveness of the process. This documentation, if well done, can be used as a baseline from which to measure the impact of a reengineering team.

Step 4: Develop a Vision for the Future Process

A reengineering team needs goals. These goals provide a shared vision for the team; without such a shared vision, there can be little hope for success. In fact, a team's success should be measured against their goals, not only against the baseline of past performance. For example, a team reengineering a payroll system might begin with a process that employs 100 people, processes paychecks and tax payments with 99% accuracy, and accommodates voluntary deductions to as many as four different accounts. A team that reduces head count by 50%, eliminates 50% of the paycheck and tax payment errors, and increases the capability to handle voluntary deductions by 50% would seem to be very successful when compared to prior performance. In reality, this same reengineering effort might have really failed. If the team's goal had been an improvement of 90% in all of these areas, a 50% improvement would be a failure.

How do reengineering teams set appropriate goals? Clearly, benchmarking other processes is one important aspect of the goal-setting process. By benchmarking other processes, a team may be able to challenge arguments that their goals are impossible. In fact, the existence of benchmark performances demonstrates not only what is possible, but what has actually been achieved. Having this information available helps the team to come together in support of goals that are truly ambitious.

Once benchmarks have been established, the team needs to consider the differences between their process and the benchmark, the theoretical extent of improvement possible, and the extent of improvement that customers and competitive factors would require. All of these issues play a role in the final determination of the group's goals.

Step 5: Starting with the Current Process, Design the Future Process

Once a group has goals for the process they are reengineering they can begin to think about what process changes need to take place in order for the goals to be met. No doubt they will have many ideas that may have come from benchmarking other processes and attempting to set project goals, as well as from years of frustration with existing processes and the suggestions of others. These ideas must now be studied objectively. The best must be chosen for implementation. Teams use a wide variety of analytical and conceptual tools to design the future process. Included among these are tools such as service blueprinting, value-added analysis, process simulation, flow charting, and other tools discussed in Chapter 5.

Step 6: Develop an Implementation Plan

Before actually implementing the changes called for by the design of the future process, managers need to think about the way in which the changes will be made. It is natural to encounter resistance to change. In fact, it is healthy for employees to question the value of change. Managers and redesign teams need to determine the impact of their proposed changes on current employees. In most cases, process redesign results in a loss of jobs, a loss of employee status, or a major change in the social environment. Managers need to communicate the rationale for the changes and the benefits that will accrue to the employees who are most affected by the plan.

The implementation plan must spell out the time line for process changes and the roles of particular individuals. Senior managers will need to devote significant time to the project—it is important for the implementation plan to spell this out so that managers commit to this schedule and include it in their performance objectives. Prior to widespread application of the redesign, the plan should include a period of time for measuring and testing results, potentially in a pilot study. Generally, the pilot study should be followed by some sort of training on a wide-scale basis. Changes cost money. An implementation plan should anticipate the financial costs and establish an adequate budget and should consider how progress will be communicated. Implementation teams need to provide regular progress reports to both senior managers and to employees affected by the change. Finally, the last step in the implementation plan needs to be establishing mechanisms for control in the new process. If the process is meeting objectives, those who take over its management on an ongoing basis need to maintain the gains that have been achieved and not allow any aspect of the process to revert to prior norms.

Step 7: Implement the Plan

Once a plan is in place, it can be implemented. During this phase of the reengineering project, the demands on managerial time and the rate at which money is spent will be very high. It has even been suggested that as much as 50% of a senior manager's time, in addition to 20% to 50% of the chief executive's time, could be consumed during the implementation phase. At any rate, it is critical that managers and reengineering teams devote significant time and energy. They must take a hands-on approach. If they don't keep up with the details, critical elements of the process change may be overlooked. Worse yet, employees may feel that management is not committed to the change. Inertia can easily overtake a reengineering project and lead to dismal results.

Step 8: Measure, Evaluate, and Report Results

For process changes to last, it must be demonstrated that the changes are beneficial. Just like a person on a diet needs to have scales and use them regularly, process redesign efforts need a comprehensive measurement system that reports changes in quality, cost, flexibility, cycle time, and other variables of interest. Without such a system, it will be difficult to tell whether the changes are leading to the desired improvements. Also, without an effective performance measurement system, it will be difficult to determine what aspects of the new process are not working as expected.

REENGINEERING PRINCIPLES

Michael Hammer has suggested a number of principles of reengineering that should be used by process redesign teams as they move through the process outlined above. These principles are as follows:

1. *Organize around outcomes, not tasks.* This means that people need to think of themselves more in terms of what their process is accomplishing than by what their department is or what task they perform.
2. *Have those who use the output of the process perform the process.* For example, companies can use computer technology to allow customers to input the information regarding their purchase. Or departments can use available data in purchasing their own materials rather than having a purchasing department buy materials for them.
3. *Subsume information-processing work into the real work that produces the information.* For example, rather than having a salesperson prepare monthly sales reports, sales reports could easily be generated by information systems that schedule the operations resulting from sales.
4. *Treat geographically dispersed resources as though they were centralized.* For example, a company with 50 different plants could have one central purchasing department that generates economies of scale by combining the orders required for each of the plants.
5. *Link parallel activities instead of integrating their results.* For example, when college students register for classes, they have to decide what classes to take and they have to clear their fees. In many universities, the two parallel activities are handled separately but the results eventually come together. Registration is not complete until fees are cleared on the basis of courses scheduled. At other universities, the fee calculation and scheduling activities are integrated in one process.
6. *Put the decision point where the work is performed, and build control into the process.* In other words, let employees have responsibility for their own work decisions—instead of a boss who's across the building, hidden by a door and behind a desk. The old departmentalized, hierarchical approach made more sense when employees had less education and training, and it doesn't fit the process orientation suggested in step number one.

> active concept check

Now let's take a moment to test your knowledge of the concepts you have studied in this section.

Integrating Operational Decisions

This has been the first chapter in the part of the text (Chapters 7–10) that focuses on building the value-adding system. Along with Chapters 8, 9, and 10, this chapter describes the decisions that lead to the operating structure of a company. Structural decisions deal with the physical characteristics of the operation: how many facilities, what kinds of technologies, arrangement of resources within facilities, design of worker jobs, and so on.

The decisions discussed in this chapter are closely related to decisions covered in Chapters 2, 3, and 4. Indeed, the value-adding system's boundaries are a function of supply-chain considerations (Chapter 2), its design must reflect the operational strategy of the firm, and its characteristics must follow directly from product-service bundle design decisions (Chapter 4). This chapter's material is also closely linked to Chapters 9 and 12. Chapter 9 discusses layout decisions. Layout choices and types will reflect process choices made in the design of the value-adding system. Master scheduling approaches are also a function of the type of process (Chapter 12).

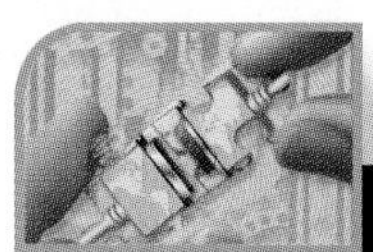

integrated OM <

Take a moment to apply what you've learned.

> Chapter Wrap-Up

This chapter has introduced many considerations in the design of value-adding systems. It is important to remember the contrast, first introduced in Chapter 4, between sequential, over-the-wall design processes and concurrent team design processes. Clearly managers need information about the product-service bundle in order to design an appropriate value-adding system. But knowledge of the choices available to designers of the value-adding system can significantly improve the competitiveness of the product-service bundle. For this reason, the system design issues covered in this chapter should be approached from the perspective of a cross-functional design team that also has influence over product-service bundle designs.

Based on the firm's competitive priorities, those who design the value-adding system must make choices regarding the system's flexibility, customer involvement, degree of vertical integration, and technological options. Those choices will ultimately determine the type of process—job shop, batch, repetitive, or continuous flow—the value-adding system will use to deliver the product-service bundle. Since, over time, a facility can lose the clear focus it may originally have had, the issue of facility focus must constantly be revisited. To remain competitive, a firm must regularly review the priorities behind each of the decisions that were made regarding its value-adding system. Managers must verify that the decisions are mutually supportive and serve a common set of objectives.

Over time, both competitive conditions and value-adding systems will change. Business process reengineering is an important way of maintaining the ongoing competitiveness of a firm's value-adding system. Any company that recognizes the importance of its value-adding system will have an ongoing process that is geared toward continuous improvement of the system. At some point, revolutionary improvements may need to be made to an existing value-adding system. Business process reengineering will prove valuable to both corporations and public institutions that need to make large leaps in competitiveness by redesigning their value-adding systems "from the ground up."

> end-of-chapter resources

- Practice Quiz
- Key Terms
- Solved Problems
- Discussion Questions
- Problems
- Case 7.1: Having Fun Flying Southwest Airlines

Building the Global Supply Chain: Facility Capacity and Location Decisions

CHAPTER 8

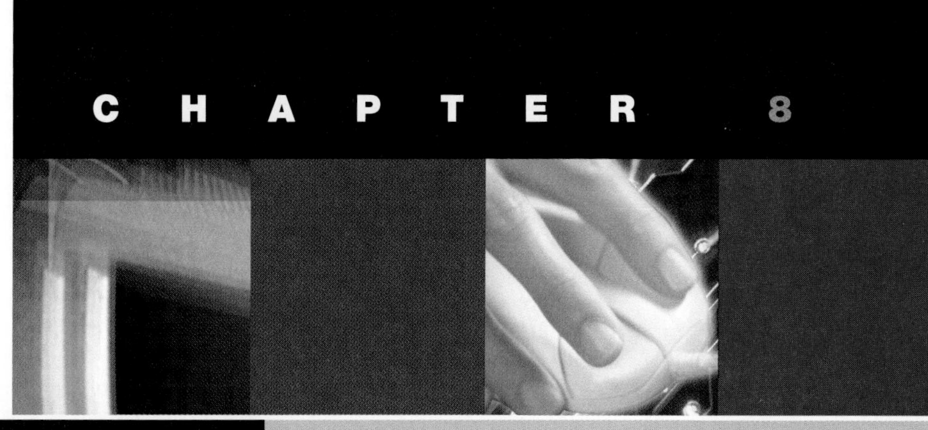

Chapter Outline

What's Ahead

. . . BACK AT THE REC CENTER

"I can't believe they're making such a fuss over where to put the new baseball stadium in Cincinnati!" said Luis, as he skimmed the sports section one morning while riding the air bike.

"I know what you mean. It seems like a big deal over just a couple of blocks," agreed Fred, as he rode along next to Luis. Fred had just finished the sports section and passed it on to Luis. "Whether it's on the river front or up the street a couple of blocks seems pretty minor to me, but remember, it's a baseball park, not a stadium!"

The city of Cincinnati had just approved a substantial increase in the countywide sales tax, to raise the funds to build a new baseball park for the Reds and a new football stadium for the Bengals. The mere fact that a majority of the voting public was willing to support the two projects spoke volumes about the importance of where the franchises were located.

"I heard the whole thing started when both the Reds and the Bengals threatened to leave if they didn't get new facilities," said Tom, as he worked out on a stepper. "The fans lose when a team leaves, but so does the league. It leaves a big hole in the market."

"You're right," injected Luis. "Just look at what happened to Cleveland! How could the NFL not be in Cleveland those four years?"

"Not every city is going to get a major league sports franchise," countered Fred. "Everybody has fast food, a dry cleaner, and even one of those quick oil-change places, but not everybody has an NFL franchise!" And when people do have one, the exact location of the stadium isn't such a big deal. Fans will always find the place, and besides, all the games are on TV. I always know where my TV is!"

"When you say location is no big deal, are you just talking football or are you talking fast food and everything else you mentioned?" asked Tom.

"Everything, all of it!" Fred replied. "The whole location thing is overblown. Provide a good product, with good promotion, price, and delivery—that'll bring the customers in. That's all you need. This side of the highway or that side, this neighborhood or that one—it all seems too petty for a baseball park. I guess, that sort of stuff makes sense for a fast-food restaurant, but we're talking about the Cincinnati Reds, not the Riverfront Reds, the Fourth Street Reds, or the Broadway Commons Reds! What difference does it make, as long as the team's in Cincinnati?"

Cheryl had been quiet through this exchange. Like Tom and Luis, she sometimes liked to give Fred enough rope to hang himself. And he usually obliged. The friendly sparring amongst the group was one of the reasons Cheryl liked to come in so early for her workouts. "No, I think you're wrong, Fred," said Cheryl. "Location can be a big deal for Major League Baseball or for fast-food restaurants! Their perspectives may vary, but the issues are the same."

While Luis loved to give Fred a hard time, he had brought the issue up in the first place and he could see Fred's point. "What difference would a couple of blocks make?" he asked. "It's still the same city."

"That's part of it," Cheryl replied. "I'd even say that in some cases, location is part of what they're selling. You know, 'Let's root, root, root for the home team.' But you'd be surprised, especially in these cases. What would happen if they crossed the Ohio River into Kentucky? Would you still call them the Cincinnati Reds? Look how upset New Yorkers got over the Jets and the Giants playing in New Jersey!"

"It sure seemed like a big deal in Charlotte," agreed Tom. "I heard both North and South Carolina wanted the Panthers. I'll bet calling them the Carolina Panthers was a political compromise."

"I'm sure the NFL has to look at the big picture when it comes to locating an expansion team or deciding whether existing teams can move," said Luis. "I agree that market size and potential customer base is a big issue—but the detailed stuff?"

"Well, fast food is different from major league sports," Cheryl argued. "The economics are different. It makes sense to have hundreds or even thousands of small stores spread around the country, as opposed to just 30 franchises spread over major markets." The others were beginning to see her point. Nobody would want to drive as far for fast food as they would to see one of the 30 best football teams in the country. And the economic benefit and prestige of having a major league franchise close by was obvious to them. Cheryl continued: "But deciding which 30 markets is just the first step. What cities to choose might be the next step. Then someone has to decide the exact spot for each stadium or ballpark."

"That last part, the specific site, now that's just like fast food, right?" asked Luis.

"Yes," replied Cheryl. "At that point they look at the same stuff."

"It's funny," Luis said. "When the NFL awarded expansion franchises a few years back, who got'em? Carolina and Jacksonville did. St. Louis and Baltimore were the runners-up. Now they've got teams and so does Cleveland." This comment seemed to reinforce Cheryl's point about the league considering the big picture.

"New team or not, if I'm Art Modell, I haven't been spending much time in Cleveland lately!" said Tom, referring to the infamous owner who had—like Robert Irsay moving the Colts from Baltimore to Indianapolis 13 years earlier—moved the Browns from Cleveland to Baltimore to bail out his financial problems.

"I still want to know what makes any of this like fast food!" interrupted Fred.

"Right, well if you think about it, somebody like McDonald's is in every major market—in fact, they're in just about every city or burg with more than a couple of hundred people," laughed Cheryl. "All that high-level big-picture stuff is kind of moot for them. But the idea of what makes a specific location good or bad, traffic flow, access, property cost, that kind of stuff. Just like the Carolina Panthers."

"She's right. There was a lot of talk in the paper about exactly where the stadium would go when the league decided to put the team in North Carolina," added Tom. "I heard it came down to Charlotte, North Carolina, or York County, in South Carolina. York County would have been a lot more expensive, even though the two sites are practically right next to each other."

"Why was that? What difference would it have made?" asked Fred, glancing skeptically at Tom.

"For one thing, York County didn't have the little things—the paper called them 'infrastructure'—to support the stadium," replied Tom. "The roads and highways in and out of the possible sites were more congested. Parking, mass transit—all that stuff would have had to be upgraded. For big bucks, too. And getting up to the speed necessary to handle the extra traffic flow would have taken a lot longer."

"I heard it would have taken two years," Cheryl said.

"Couldn't they have played somewhere else in the meantime?" asked Fred.

"They did that, anyway," exclaimed Tom. "They played at Clemson for a year, as it was!"

"Didn't the paper also mention an NFL rule that says a stadium has to be cleared within 30 minutes after a game is over?" Cheryl asked. "Seems as if that would have been easier in North Carolina. You know, the access roads and what not."

"You know, we look for the same things when we locate in a new city," added Tom, in support of Cheryl's last point. "We try to avoid crowded, expensive airports, especially the ones that are dominated by a single carrier." When Tom's airline wants to get into a particular market, managers check out all the options. Many times a region has several airports to choose from. "For example, in Chicago, we fly in and out of Midway Airport, downtown, and avoid O'Hare, out in the suburbs," Tom added.

"But aren't the big, new airports the most convenient to get in and out of?" asked Luis. "My in-laws live in Virginia, near D.C. Dulles is a great place to fly into. You just get onto the new access highway and boom, you're on the beltway in no time. Now National Airport, that's a different story. It's in the middle of town!"

"Okay, but a lot of our passengers are commuters—you know, business travelers taking the same small hop on a regular basis. They like coming in to downtown," Tom countered. "And besides, when you fly into somebody else's hub, you get stacked up behind their flights and circle for a long time. When those big places get busy, you really chew up extra time."

"So?" asked Luis, "That's the airline's problem. What does it have to do with me?"

"It is the airline's problem," responded Cheryl, motioning at Tom. "But they've got to look at the big picture." Cheryl sees that the airline's ability to satisfy a customer's need for timely transportation is a function of many factors. While fighting traffic between the suburbs and a smaller, less crowded downtown airport is time consuming, flying in and out of that location might actually be quicker door to door, given the possibility of delays at the larger, more crowded, suburban airport.

"Just what he wants—more time with the in-laws!" quipped Fred.

"Okay, I see your point about location," Fred conceded. "But you have to admit that airlines and sports teams deal with the consumer. For us, we just look for the best place to put a factory, to find the skilled labor and materials we need, and the shipping."

"Yeah, there aren't a lot of walkups on game day at the ol' pager factory!" Luis laughed.

"Very funny, but you're right," Fred admitted. "Most of our location decisions are made by looking at costs."

"Sorry, it's just that we're not looking to grow that fast or move, so it's easy for me to be sarcastic," Luis admitted. "But as long as we're on the subject, Tom, can you get my wife a deal on some tickets to D.C.?"

> objectives

Take a moment to familiarize yourself with the key objectives of this chapter.

> gearing up

Before you begin reading this chapter, try a short warm-up activity.

> Introduction

In designing any value-adding system, one of the first and most important issues to address is the required long-term capacity. For example, an executive who is planning a new hospital wing or manufacturing plant would immediately ask how big it should be. For the hospital, the answer could be stated in terms of number of beds, number of nursing stations, number of patients served per day, square footage, or some other measure. For the manufacturing plant, size could be stated in terms of the number of units produced in a month, the dollar volume of sales per month, or the volume of raw materials used per month. The demand for the product-service bundle is the obvious starting point for any such discussion. The "size," or capacity, that decisions makers settle on may in turn help to determine the best location.

video exercise

Take a moment to apply what you've learned.

This chapter begins by addressing the strategic issues in capacity decisions. For example, which is better: a small number of large facilities, each of which serves a fairly large region (like the 12 Federal Reserve banks), or a large number of smaller facilities, each of which serves a local area (like the local branches of a big-city library system)? This fundamental question has a bearing on both capacity and location decisions. Industry factors play a role, too. Clearly, deciding where to put a large auto assembly plant presumes a different set of concerns than deciding where to put a fast-food store.

Next the chapter considers the economics of capacity decisions. Here we describe tools used to evaluate capacity alternatives and discuss the economic tradeoffs that come into play when choosing between large-scale facilities and smaller alternatives.

Following the section on the economics of capacity decisions, the chapter presents concepts relevant to making location decisions. A decision hierarchy, ranging from choice of country right down to selection of a specific site, is presented, along with the factors that most influence location decisions at each level of the hierarchy.

Finally, the chapter presents a number of tools that help decision makers decide where they should locate facilities. These include information systems (IS) tools, quantitative methods, market analysis techniques such as trade area studies, and so on. The idea is not that decision makers should pick just one of these tools to determine the location of a facility. Rather, by using a combination of these tools, managers from a variety of business functions can work together to ensure that the entire range of relevant considerations is included in the location decision.

Integrating Operations Management with Other Functions

Figure 8.1 highlights some of the major relationships between material covered in this chapter and other business functional areas. Obviously, this part of the chapter is important to all majors, because it indicates the way that professionals from their functional areas relate to the issues addressed in this chapter.

The next section of the chapter addresses long-term capacity decisions. These decisions have a significant impact on the profitability and competitiveness of any business. As a result, financial analysts include long-term capacity issues in the performance forecasts they use to guide investment decisions, and conversely the financial justification of capacity decisions is based on such forecasts. Similarly, long-term forecasts prepared in the marketing function are used to support capacity decisions, and capacity decisions make long-term planning possible in the marketing function. Through the corporate strategic planning process, capacity decisions require the marketing, finance, and operations functions to be very closely linked.

The section of this chapter that describes the economics of capacity decisions is closely tied to the finance, accounting, and engineering functions. This section includes a description of financial tools that are useful in capacity decisions, which use information generated by the accounting function. We suggest that the section is particularly useful to personnel from the engineering function, because these individuals must frequently use the tools we describe.

Figure 8.1 suggests that location decisions are closely linked to the finance, accounting, human resource (HR), and marketing concerns. All of these linkages should be very obvious. From a financial perspective, operational costs, insurance requirements, property-related liability concerns, and capital requirements are all critical issues in a location decision. Accountants know well that tax laws and accounting standards can vary greatly from location to location and will seek to locate facilities in the most advantageous municipality, state, and country. From an HR perspective, companies making facility location decisions have to consider the availability of needed workers, regional attitudes toward (and participation rates in) labor unions, quality of work life, cost of living for transferred workers, and so on. From a marketing perspective, location often plays a critical role in access to customers.

Chapter Topics \ Functional Areas of Business	Finance	Accounting	Human Resources	Marketing	Engineering	Management Information Systems
Integrating Operations Management with Other Functions	●	●	●	●	●	●
Long-Term Capacity Issues	●			●		
The Economics of Capacity Decisions	●	●			●	
Locations Decisions	●	●	●	●		
Decision-Making Tools for Locating Facilities				●		●

FIGURE 8.1 Integrating Operations Management with Other Functions

Finally, Figure 8.1 links the section of this chapter that describes decision-making tools to the marketing and management information systems (MIS) functions. A number of the tools we describe in this section are used in these functions or at least require the assistance of these functions to be used. For example, trade area analysis is commonly seen as a marketing tool. Whether it is done by marketing personnel or not, it does rely on demographic information most likely to be generated by the marketing function. Similarly, geographic information systems have become a very sophisticated and widely used MIS application to support location decisions.

> Long-Term Capacity Issues

How many seats should a new major league baseball or football stadium have? A new church? What size moving van should a transfer and storage company buy? How many checkout registers should a grocery store have? How many copies per hour should a copy machine produce? How many cars per shift should an assembly line turn out? And what bandwidth will a new communications network require? All these questions address long-term capacity decisions.

From an operational perspective, **capacity** is defined as the maximum rate of output from a process. It can be easy to state from a theoretical perspective, but difficult to realistically estimate. For example, the *theoretical capacity* of an 8-ounce beverage glass is obvious—8 ounces. But you can't expect a table server in a busy restaurant to deliver 8 ounces to the customer's table in a reasonably short period of time in an 8 ounce glass. Thus, the *effective capacity* is less than 8 ounces and difficult to estimate. The effective capacity of an 8-ounce glass depends on how busy the restaurant is, how experienced the server is, what type of beverage is involved, how far the server must walk, and other factors. Just like the restaurant glass, it can be easy to state the theoretical capacity of a service or manufacturing process, but a host of real-world considerations can make it hard to know the effective capacity of a process.

Long-term capacity choices are difficult to make because they must be arrived at in the face of great uncertainty about future demand, future costs, technological change, and competitors' capacity plans. What is more, a poor decision by one company can often cause significant long-term losses for an entire industry. For example, if there were two NFL teams in Cincinnati, filling both stadiums on the same day would be difficult and both teams would suffer. Similarly, if an airline were to acquire more planes than it could fill, managers might try to cover fixed costs by discounting passenger fares, provoking a price war that would hurt the entire industry. Conversely, wise decisions about capacity can produce significant profitability and sustained competitive advantage over long periods.

Since capacity choices have a significant impact on financial performance, almost any well-done financial analysis of a company's performance will include an assessment of long-term capacity. The following examples from the Value Line Investors Survey are representative of the way in which capacity plans are addressed in financial analyses.

- Regarding the Norway-based Petroleum Geo-Services, a company that specializes in gathering data from marine seismic surveys to create maps of the geology beneath the ocean floor, the report dated November 29, 1996, states: "Petroleum Geo-Services has ordered two more Ramform vessels. Due to their impressive operating results, the company has ordered the construction of two additional vessels of this same design at a total cost of about $160 million, to be delivered in 1998. . . . Demand is increasing and survey prices are steady to up. This applies even more so to the Ramform vessels, since their increased efficiency flows directly to the bottom line."
- Regarding the ATM and point of sale (POS) system manufacturer Diebold, Inc., the report dated January 24, 1997, states: "The backlog at September 30th was $238 million, 41% above the year-ago level, and total orders were likely 30% higher in 1996 than in the previous year. Diebold is in the process of adding three domestic manufacturing facilities to meet the increased demand. . . . We also look for production efficiencies at the new factories to bolster the gross margin towards the close of 1997."
- Regarding the oil exploration and drilling services company Helmerich & Payne, Inc., the report dated November 29, 1996, states: "Land-based drillers, like Helmerich, have more recently begun to enjoy heavy demand. Dayrates (the amount it costs to rent a rig for a day), though rising, are still too low to justify the construction of new rigs. Thus the number of available rigs is not increasing, while demand for oil and gas is going up. We think the limitation on the number of rigs will keep dayrates moving ahead, along with results at Helmerich."
- Regarding Linear Technology Corporation, a company that designs and manufactures analog integrated circuits, the January 24, 1997, survey states: "The company has almost completed the testing phase of its Camus, Washington, plant. It will probably go online by the end of the March quarter and should reach full production a few quarters thereafter. Linear will then transfer some of the production from Milpitas to Camus, which is more efficient and whose capacity can be easily increased. Start-up expenses will probably slightly offset the gains over the next three quarters, knocking margins down temporarily. Further out, though, the new plant will reduce cost and provide a means to increase total production as demand grows beyond Milpitas's capacity, which is between $90 million and $100 million per quarter."

Clearly, long-term capacity decisions have strategic implications.

CAPACITY STRATEGY

Capacity decisions encompass more than expansion; they can also include the closing or downsizing of facilities, the transfer of existing facilities, and the creation of brand-new facilities or prototype systems. Generally speaking, changing levels of demand or a need to become more competitive motivates all these decisions.

Compared to the relatively smooth pattern of demand changes, capacity changes typically come in large increments. Even though consumers buy airline tickets, cars, dishwashers, and gasoline in small quantities, the airports, stadiums, factories, and oil tankers that provide these product-service bundles are all large-scale facilities. Even small, labor-intensive facilities expand and shrink their capacity in much larger increments than those in which they sell. Over time, therefore, imbalances between capacity and demand are bound to develop.

active example

Take a closer look at the concepts and issues you've been reading about.

Deciding how much to increase or decrease capacity, and when, is a strategic choice. The set of long-term decisions a firm makes about the size of its plants and equipment is its **capacity strategy.** Figure 8.2 illustrates a number of possible decision-making patterns. Based on industry factors and competitive strategy, a company will lean toward one of the three strategies shown in the figure.

Capacity decisions for waiting lines, ticket windows, the monorail, and each attraction are an important aspect of the design of Disney's Magic Kingdom in Orlando, Florida. The waiting lines grow and shrink to cover temporary differences between a resource's capacity and demand. If the resource's capacity is too small, the lines get too long and customers will be forced to seek out other attractions.

Figure 8.2(a) illustrates a *capacity cushion strategy* that is used in many service operations to ensure that demand can be met from existing resources. Firms that cannot create an inventory or a demand backlog must have excess capacity in order to deal with the extremes of demand. For example, the fire department in a small town may possess several fire trucks that are seldom, if ever, on call all at once. Similarly, an electrical utility needs enough capacity to meet peak demand, which usually occurs early in the evening during the hottest part of the summer. A bank needs enough teller windows

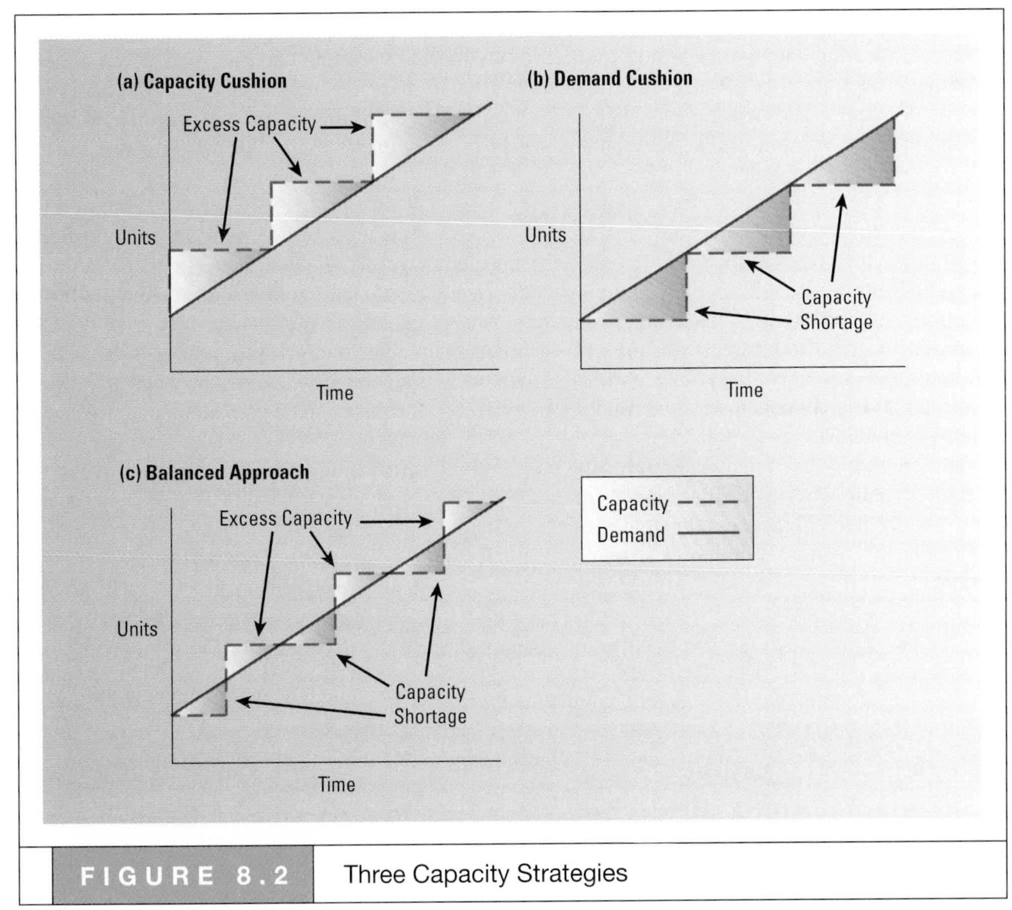

FIGURE 8.2 Three Capacity Strategies

to handle traffic on the busiest days, like the Friday before the Fourth of July (which is a payday for many employers and retirement systems, a dividend payment time for many publicly owned companies, and the start of many workers' vacations). Finally, an Internet service provider such as America Online needs to have an adequate number of connections, so that customers will not cancel their accounts because of an inability to access the network.

A capacity cushion strategy is also useful in the growth stage of the product life cycle. Firms that seek to obtain first-mover advantages—as well as those that seek to gain the competitive advantages associated with flexibility, speed, and superior service—frequently adopt this strategy. Petroleum Geo-Services's decision to order two more Ramform vessels (see page 315) is a good example of that use of the cushion strategy. A capacity cushion also works well with limited reliance on finished goods inventory, aggressive sales and marketing efforts, the use of customer incentives, and a great deal of product variety. Clearly, capacity decisions cannot be made in isolation by operations managers alone. Rather, they must fit the firm's business strategy as well as decision making in other functions, such as finance and marketing.

Financially, adding new capacity in anticipation of market growth can be risky. If the demand does not materialize, or if it is slower to materialize than expected, the fixed costs of the new capacity are not likely to be covered. For example, Petroleum Geo-Services's two new ships could end up sitting in the harbor, being sublet as party boats, if the company cannot generate enough orders for marine geographic surveys. The fact is, demand does not always grow. The same capacity cushion that provides a first-mover advantage in a growing market can provide a last-mover disadvantage in a declining market. And the firm that seeks to create a capacity cushion is likely to have higher fixed costs, which will limit its ability to harvest profits in the later stages of the product life cycle.

Figure 8.2(b) illustrates a *demand cushion strategy,* in which fixed costs are more easily covered. Firms that use demand cushions tend to maintain high inventory levels or large demand backlogs. They often compete on the basis of price and are likely to outsource certain noncritical tasks. These firms are less likely than others to try to be first to market with new products and features, and they generally invest less money in aggressive marketing campaigns.

Diebold is an example of a company that maintains a demand cushion in the form of a large demand backlog. Though having excess demand may seem to be a luxury, problems can arise when a demand cushion is too large. For example, if there is a demand cushion for the OM course at your school and no additional sections are made available, some of those students who are unable to register for the class might find a way to take the class elsewhere. In the worst case, the capacity shortage could prevent some students from graduating on time. Situations like this one would eventually become public, and your school would find recruiting more difficult and costly. With fewer students and a higher recruitment expense, the school might have to increase tuition. As a consequence, firms should take care to add new capacity before their demand cushions become too large. If Diebold's demand backlog becomes too large, customers may become dissatisfied with the long wait for the firm's ATMs and POS systems, and Diebold may lose sales to competitors.

Figure 8.2(c) shows a third capacity strategy, the *balanced capacity strategy.* Firms that compete in cyclical industries and firms that are in the maturity stage of the product life cycle are likely to adopt this strategy. Such firms endeavor to match their capacity as closely as possible to near-term demand. Depending on the economic climate, they carry either excess capacity or excess demand. During recessions they will tend to have excess capacity; during economic expansions they may develop shortages. To such firms, effectively anticipating changes in the economic cycle is very important, as is flexibility in capacity. They may prefer to lease rather than own, rely on temporary employees rather than hire a permanent staff, or find alternative uses for their capacity by developing complementary businesses.

Helmerich & Payne is an example of the balanced capacity strategy. Notice that the firm is not planning to build any new drilling rigs, even though it seems to have a demand cushion. Instead, it is benefiting from the higher rig rents that result from increased demand. (A few years earlier, this firm had a capacity cushion. It did not destroy or recycle its spare rigs just because they weren't in use at that time.)

active example

Take a closer look at the concepts and issues you've been reading about.

CAPACITY UTILIZATION

Capacity utilization is the ratio of capacity used during a fixed period of time to the available capacity during that same time period. Figure 8.3 shows the aggregate capacity utilization rate for American manufacturers in recent years. Published by the Federal Reserve, the manufacturing capacity utilization rate is watched closely by economists, because it is a useful indicator for forecasting long-term interest rates. It is calculated as the ratio of actual manufacturing output to potential full-capacity output.

The higher the capacity utilization rate rises above some benchmark level—say, 85%—the tighter the plant capacity and the more difficulty factories will have meeting their orders. Under such conditions, labor shortages and equipment breakdowns tend to lead to supply shortages and higher production costs. The cost increases, in turn, trigger a rise in the level of inflation, higher long-term interest rates, and lower levels of capital investment. Pressure mounts for manufacturers to expand their capacity—which is why aggregate capacity utilization rarely rises above 90%.

The capacity utilization rate falls during recessionary periods, such as the shaded ones in Figure 8.3. If it drops too low, manufacturers have difficulty covering their fixed costs and operating profitably. Pressure mounts to close down plants and lay off workers. As a result, the utilization rate rarely falls below 70%.

As you might imagine, the quality of long-term capacity decisions depends in large part on the quality of the economic forecasts on which they are based. Long-term forecasting is therefore one of the primary challenges for managers who make capacity decisions.

LONG-TERM FORECASTING

No one knows for certain what the future holds; the further into the future one looks, the less certain one can be. While you probably have a good idea where you will be and what you'll be doing tomorrow, you may have more questions about where you will be in a month's time. You may not even be able to guess where you will be and what you'll be doing 10 years from now. But in a manufacturing

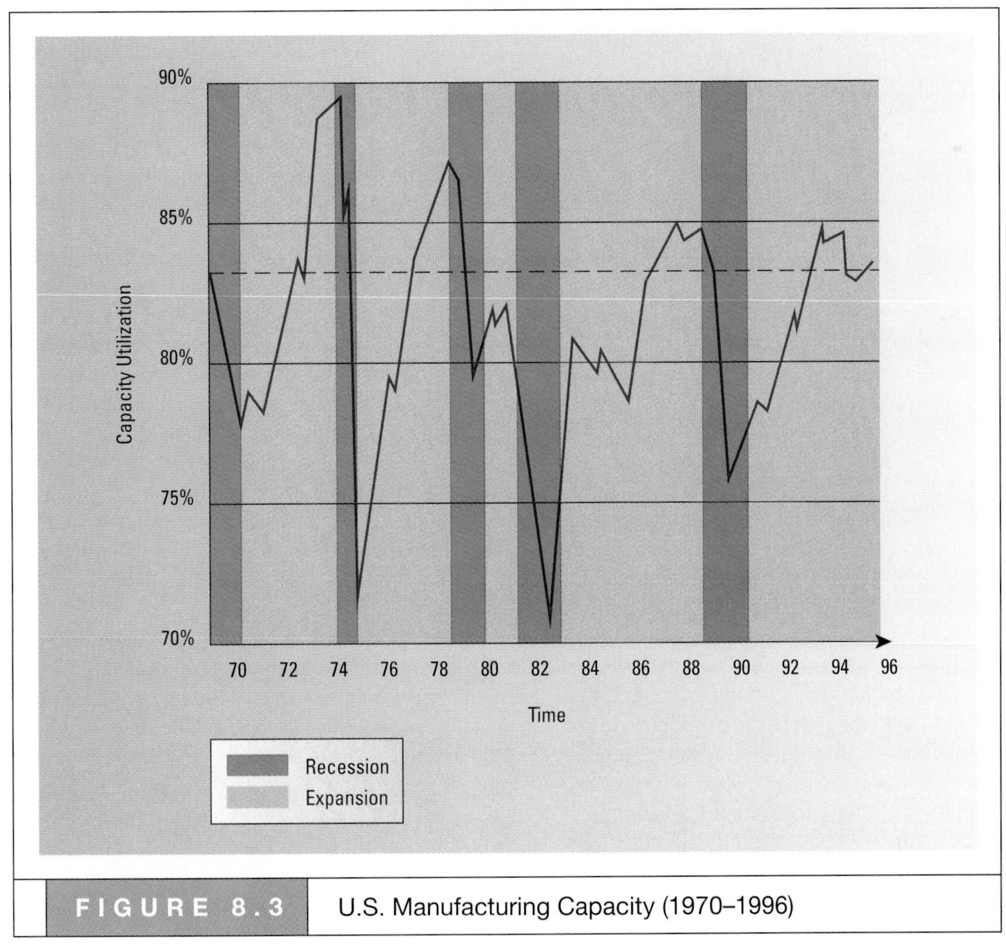

FIGURE 8.3 U.S. Manufacturing Capacity (1970–1996)

Because of the energy required to heat the metal, steel mills must be designed with enough capacity to roll the slabs they form from the red-hot liquid. If more metal is heated than rolled, a great deal of energy is wasted. Therefore, balanced capacity is designed into the system and is very difficult to change.

or service facility, the equipment, processes, and technologies that are installed today must be useful over a time frame that is measured in decades. Because the decision to build, expand, or shut down facilities has long-term implications, it must be based on a long-term forecast.

In forecasting, the future is predicted on the basis of past occurrences. (Predictions that are not based on past experience—for instance, those that are based on the way a Coke bottle is pointed when it stops spinning—cannot be called forecasts.) The future can be predicted in a variety of ways. If you were on a weekly class schedule, you would probably forecast where you will be at 10:00 A.M. tomorrow by looking at where you were at that time six days ago. To forecast what you'll be doing six months from now, you will probably have to look at more information. For example, if you are a junior, you might ask a number of seniors in your major what they did on a typical day last term.

Forecasting what you will be doing in five years is far more difficult. Many other factors, such as your health, your attitude toward risk, and your goals—together with technological changes, the economic climate, your employer's financial strength, and your coworkers' plans—will have some bearing on that forecast. Similarly, long-term forecasters try to assess the impact of a broad range of factors on a firm's capacity needs. They do not rely solely on the projections made by quantitative models. Instead, they examine qualitative and subjective information obtained from experts in various disciplines who understand past relationships among the many factors that could influence capacity.

Perhaps the best-known approach to generating forecasts from expert opinion is the **Delphi method,** in which the forecaster uses a series of surveys to develop a consensus of expert opinion on a subject. For example, a paper company might need to project paper usage in the years 2010 to 2030 in order to decide whether or not to build a new manufacturing plant. In the Delphi method, the forecaster would first develop a panel of experts, including leaders in the industry; leaders of supplying industries, such as forestry; leaders in customer groups, such as printers and publishers; representatives of competing technologies, such as the computer industry; and other relevant experts, such as economists, demographers, and futurists. This panel would be asked to respond to a series of questions relevant to the level of paper demand during the period of interest, usually in a mail survey. If the experts agree, their views can be used as a consensus forecast.

Chances are, experts from such diverse fields will hold different viewpoints; they usually will not agree on all questions. If that were the case, the forecaster would summarize the experts' views according to their fields of expertise, and then provide the information to the entire panel. Along with the feedback, the forecaster would provide another survey for the experts to complete. As the process is repeated, some degree of consensus among the experts might develop. Once a consensus has been reached, or if after several successive surveys it becomes clear that a consensus will never be attainable, the Delphi method should be stopped.

In another forecasting method, **scenario planning,** long-term planners deal with uncertainty by preparing for a variety of possible situations. By testing the performance of several alternative long-term plans under a wide range of potential scenarios, managers can gain a feel for the risks associated with each plan. They can then select the plan that represents the smallest exposure to negative consequences, or the greatest likelihood of good results, or the best results under certain circumstances.

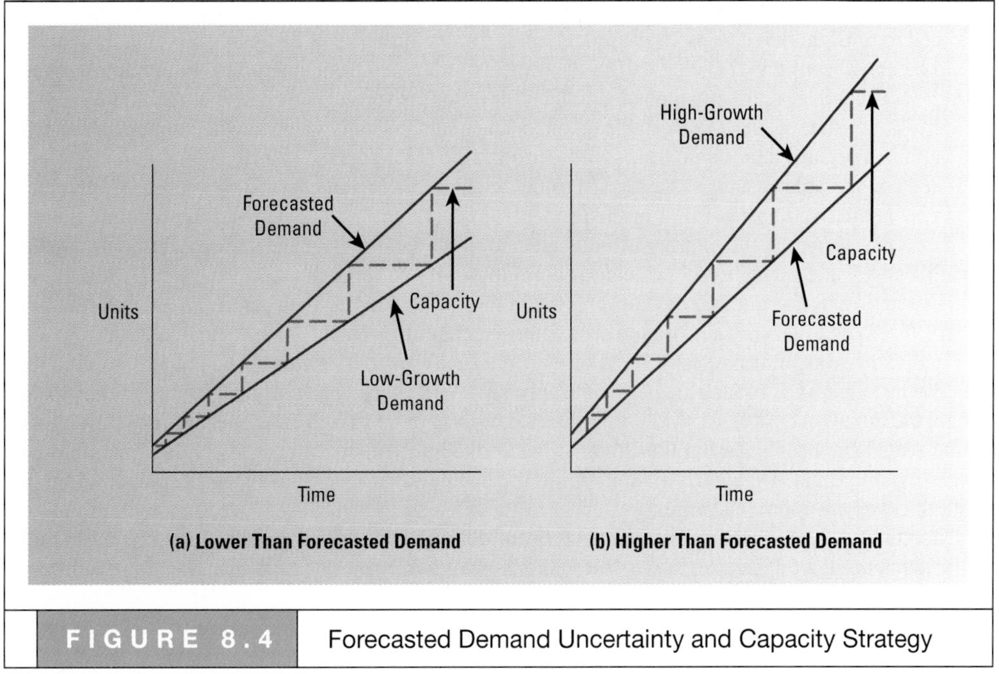

FIGURE 8.4 Forecasted Demand Uncertainty and Capacity Strategy

Their decision will reflect their willingness to take risks, as well as their beliefs about the likelihood of various scenarios.

Figure 8.4 illustrates the impact of uncertainty on two capacity strategies. Notice in Figure 8.4(a) that a strategy that is intended to provide a demand cushion, given forecasted demand, could result in a capacity cushion, given lower-than-expected demand. Similarly, in Figure 8.4(b), a capacity cushion strategy could yield a demand cushion if actual demand were to be higher than forecasted demand. As a result, long-term forecasters (and managers who make decisions that have long-term implications) are usually more interested in the range of possibilities than in consensus, or middle-of-the-road, projections.

> active concept check

Now let's take a moment to test your knowledge of the concepts you have studied in this section.

The Economics of Capacity Decisions

Once a capacity strategy has been settled on, managers must address the economics of the capacity decision. What are the capacities of various facilities, and what are the costs and benefits associated with each? Seven different types of cost enter into a capacity decision. They are: fixed costs, variable costs, total cost, average fixed cost, average variable cost, average unit cost, and marginal cost.

Fixed costs are the costs of inputs to the product-service bundle that cannot be changed over the short run. For example, a steel company has a quantifiable capital investment in each of its manufacturing plants, one that cannot be changed over the short run. Similarly, a doctor's office has to pay utility bills and salaries for employees at the front desk, regardless of the number of patients cared for in a given month. An airline has to make the lease payments on aircraft, maintain all equipment, and pay employees in the air and on the ground, whether it serves 1,000 or 10,000 passengers per day. The total fixed cost for a facility is the sum of all its fixed costs over a particular period. Over the long run, facilities can be shut down, downsized, or expanded, so the concept of fixed costs is not applicable to long-run cost functions.

Variable costs are the costs of inputs to the product-service bundle that vary with the number of units (or volume) produced or served. Over the short run, these costs may vary because of quantity discounts for large purchases, the relative size of production runs or shipments, the particular costs prescribed in collective bargaining agreements, and so on. For instance, Tom's airline probably buys less food for a flight that carries 30 passengers than for one that carries 80 passengers; thus, food costs would be considered a variable cost. The costs of raw materials frequently vary. For example, Fred's factory will spend less money on plastic pellets if it produces fewer pagers. The total variable cost for a facility is the sum of all of its variable costs for the given period's volume. The sum of *all* the fixed and variable costs for a facility over a given period is the **total cost.**

Fixed and variable costs may be used to calculate the average unit costs for the period. The average fixed cost is the fixed cost per unit of the product-service bundle. It is calculated by dividing the total fixed cost per period by the number of units created in the facility over the same period. The **average variable cost** is the variable cost per unit. It is computed by dividing the total variable cost for the volume in a period by the number of units created in the facility during the period. The sum of the average fixed cost and the average variable cost is the **average unit cost.**

Finally, the **marginal cost** is the cost of providing *one additional unit* of the product-service bundle. For instance, if Tom's airline has an empty seat on a plane that is flying from Phoenix to San Diego, the marginal cost of serving one additional passenger on that flight would be very small. But if all the seats have been sold and the flight is overbooked, the marginal cost of serving one more passenger would be much greater. At some point, the airline might even have to schedule an additional flight to cover one more passenger.

Once the costs of various facilities have been identified, managers can use them to analyze the costs and benefits of each alternative. We will examine two methods of choosing among facilities of different capacity: simple break-even analysis and returns to scale.

Simple break-even analysis is one way to estimate the volumes at which various facilities provide the most economical returns. An estimate of fixed costs and variable costs must be made for each facility. Once those estimates have been obtained, they can be plotted on a graph that shows which alternatives are better at various volumes. This technique was described in detail in Chapters 4 and 7, thus we will not devote further attention to the topic in this chapter.

A second method of determining the best capacity is based on an analysis of returns to scale. Since the fixed costs of operating a facility cannot be changed in the short-run, businesses need to operate at a sufficient volume to cover those costs. When a firm is operating at low volumes, it may experience increasing returns to scale, meaning that the average unit cost of producing $(n + 1)$ units is lower than the average unit cost of producing (n) units. Put another way, increasing returns to scale exist when a facility's average unit cost curve is downward sloping. For example, the average cost per patient in a 300-bed hospital is much lower when all 300 beds are full than when only 200 are full. Similarly, on an assembly line that has been designed to produce one car every two minutes, the production cost per vehicle will be lower at a production rate of 240 cars per eight-hour shift than at a rate of only 200 per shift.

The law of diminishing returns suggests that a facility cannot produce increasing returns to scale indefinitely. As volume rises, coverage of costs that are fixed over the short run may no longer dominate in the computation of average unit cost. Instead, variable costs may begin to rise, due to problems associated with higher volumes. Thus, **decreasing returns to scale** set in: The average unit cost of producing $(n + 1)$ units rises above the average unit cost of producing (n) units, and the average unit cost curve begins to slope upward. For instance, maintaining a steady level of 400 patients in a 300-bed hospital would probably require significant overtime expenditures, along with equipment rental costs and other unusual expenses. So, too, producing 400 cars per eight-hour shift on an assembly line designed to make just one car every two minutes would take an economic toll. Figure 8.5 illustrates the concepts of increasing and decreasing returns to scale.

The volume, or scale of operations, at which average total cost per unit is minimized is called the facility's **best operating level.** The point marked BOL in Figure 8.5 shows the best operating level.

active exercise

Take a moment to apply what you've learned.

Suppose Tom's airline offers a daily flight from Ontario Airport in southern California to a small airport close to some ski resorts in British Columbia. Service on the route is maintained year round, even though monthly ticket sales range from a low of about 500 in the summer months to a high of approximately 5,500 in December and January. Table 8.1 provides information on the monthly costs associated with the airline's facilities in British Columbia. Tickets sell for $190 (column 2), and monthly fixed costs total $200,000 (column 3). (The fixed costs include such items as lease payments on the aircraft that are locked in by contract, gate rentals, the fuel cost required to fly an empty plane

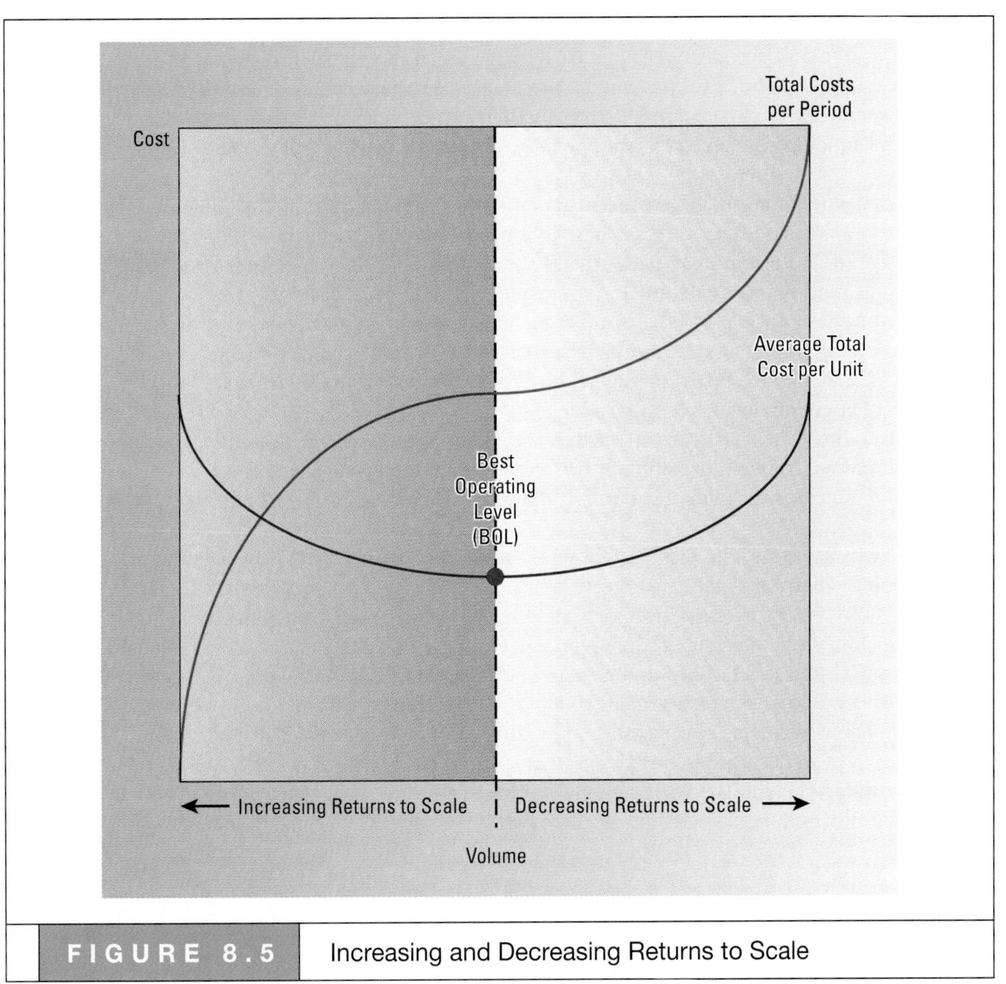

FIGURE 8.5 Increasing and Decreasing Returns to Scale

TABLE 8.1 Monthly Costs and Profits for the B. C. Airline Route

Vol. (1)	Price per Unit (2)	Fixed Cost (3)	Variable Cost (4)	Total Cost (5)	Per Unit Marginal Cost (6)	Average Fixed Cost (7)	Average Variable Cost (8)	Average Total Cost (9)	Total Profit (10)	Profit per Unit (11)
500	$190	$200,000	$30,000.00	$230,000.00	$60.00	$400.00	$60.00	$460.00	-135000	($270.00)
750	$190	$200,000	$45,000.00	$245,000.00	$60.00	$266.67	$60.00	$326.67	-102500	($136.67)
1000	$190	$200,000	$60,000.00	$260,000.00	$60.00	$200.00	$60.00	$260.00	-70000	($70.00)
1250	$190	$200,000	$75,000.00	$275,000.00	$60.00	$160.00	$60.00	$220.00	-37500	($30.00)
1500	$190	$200,000	$90,000.00	$290,000.00	$60.00	$133.33	$60.00	$193.33	-5000	($3.33)
1750	$190	$200,000	$105,000.00	$305,000.00	$60.00	$114.29	$60.00	$174.29	27500	$15.71
2000	$190	$200,000	$120,000.00	$320,000.00	$60.00	$100.00	$60.00	$160.00	60000	$30.00
2250	$190	$200,000	$135,000.00	$335,000.00	$60.00	$88.89	$60.00	$148.89	92500	$41.11
2500	$190	$200,000	$150,000.00	$350,000.00	$60.00	$80.00	$60.00	$140.00	125000	$50.00
2750	$190	$200,000	$165,000.00	$365,000.00	$60.00	$72.73	$60.00	$132.73	157500	$57.27
3000	$190	$200,000	$180,000.00	$380,000.00	$60.00	$66.67	$60.00	$126.67	190000	$63.33
3250	$190	$200,000	$225,000.00	$425,000.00	$180.00	$61.54	$69.23	$130.77	192500	$59.23
3500	$190	$200,000	$270,000.00	$470,000.00	$180.00	$57.14	$77.14	$134.29	195000	$55.71
3750	$190	$200,000	$315,000.00	$515,000.00	$180.00	$53.33	$84.00	$137.33	197500	$52.67
4000	$190	$200,000	$360,000.00	$560,000.00	$180.00	$50.00	$90.00	$140.00	200000	$50.00
4250	$190	$200,000	$405,000.00	$605,000.00	$180.00	$47.06	$95.29	$142.35	202500	$47.65
4500	$190	$200,000	$450,000.00	$650,000.00	$180.00	$44.44	$100.00	$144.44	205000	$45.56
4750	$190	$200,000	$540,000.00	$740,000.00	$360.00	$42.11	$113.68	$155.79	162500	$34.21
5000	$190	$200,000	$630,000.00	$830,000.00	$360.00	$40.00	$126.00	$166.00	120000	$24.00
5250	$190	$200,000	$720,000.00	$920,000.00	$360.00	$38.10	$137.14	$175.24	77500	$14.76
5500	$190	$200,000	$810,000.00	$1,010,000.00	$360.00	$36.36	$147.27	$183.64	35000	$6.36

over the route, and staffing for gates and flights at the minimal level required to offer the service.) At a marginal cost of $60 per ticket (column 6), average variable cost is estimated at $60 per ticket (column 8) up to a volume of 3,000 passengers (column 1). (Variable cost covers such items as the additional fuel required per passenger, per passenger airport use fees, commissions paid to travel agents, and food and supplies consumed by passengers.) What is this facility's best operating level? Its profit-maximizing level?

Notice that at volumes of 3,000 passengers or less, per unit profit (column 11) increases. Thus, the airline enjoys increasing returns to scale at volumes of 3,000 passengers or less. Beyond 3,000 passengers a month, the airline may need to add some additional crew members or it may have to pay overtime to ground support personnel. As a result, marginal cost (column 6) grows to $180 per passenger for volumes between 3,000 and 4,500 passengers. In other words, at passenger volumes above 3,000, decreasing returns to scale set in. The increase in volume reduces per unit profit (column 11) when volume rises above 3,000 passengers a month. For the route to British Columbia, then, this facility's best operating level is 3,000 passengers.

Figure 8.6 shows the short-run cost curves obtained from the data in Table 8.1. Notice that average total cost continues to decline as long as it is greater than the per unit marginal cost. Thus, the minimum point on the average total cost curve is the point where marginal cost and average total cost are equal.

Notice from Table 8.1 that profit is not necessarily maximized at the best operating level. Indeed, up to the point where marginal cost exceeds marginal revenue, or price per unit (column 2), the airline will make more money by carrying more passengers. Beyond 3,000 passengers the airline does not make as much money on each additional passenger, but it still makes a profit as long as it carries no more than 4,500 passengers. With more than 4,500 passengers a month, marginal cost reaches $360 per ticket, which exceeds the marginal revenue per ticket. Since marginal cost exceeds price per unit, total profit begins to decline. The profit-maximizing level is therefore 4,500 passengers.

You may be wondering why an airline would consider booking beyond the profit-maximizing level. Over the short term, booking beyond the best operating level, or even the profit-maximizing level, is not uncommon. The airline sacrifices short-run profits to build customer satisfaction and ensure long-run profitability. A business may incur costly overtime or weekend labor costs if it gets an

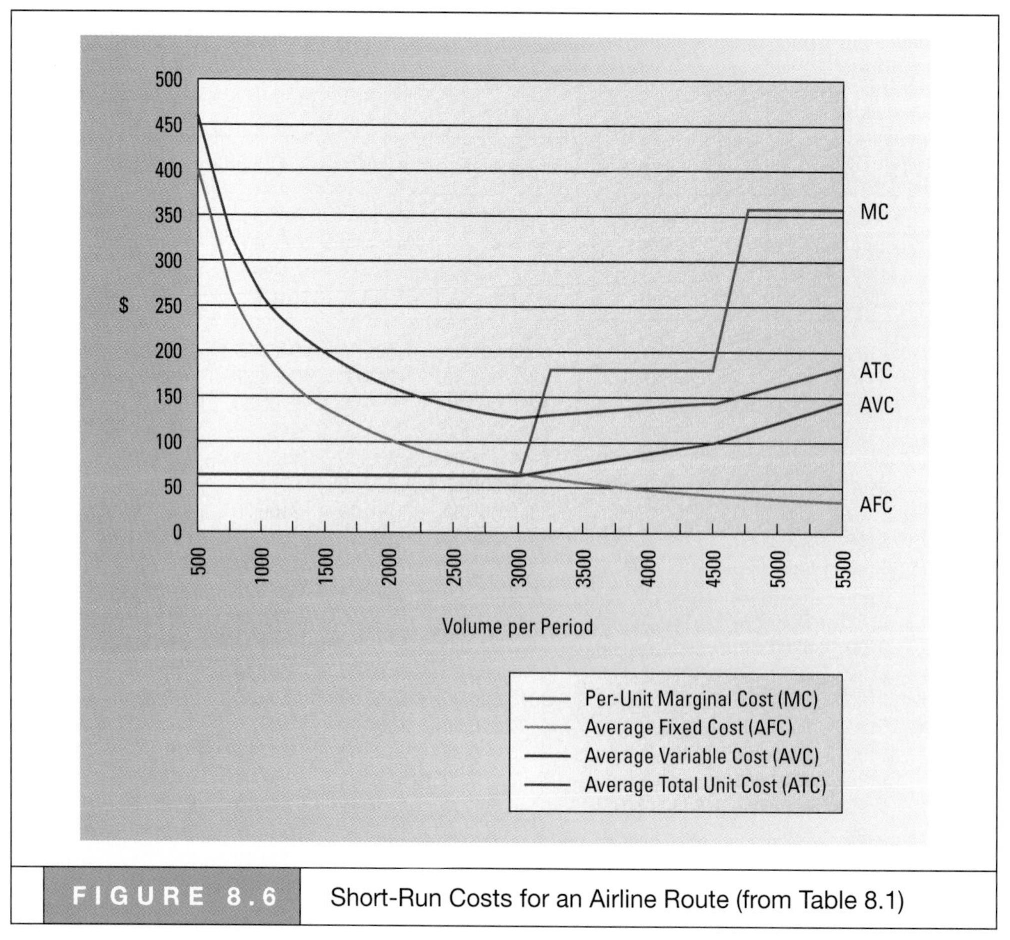

FIGURE 8.6 Short-Run Costs for an Airline Route (from Table 8.1)

order out for a big or important customer. In fact, Tom's airline overbooks on purpose, offering a seat to everyone possible during the peak season, in order to build a loyal customer base during the off-season. Sometimes the airline has to offer travel vouchers or hotel rooms to compensate passengers who have been bumped from an overbooked flight—a practice that obviously raises its costs.

Clearly, the scale on which a business operates has an economic effect on the business's returns. An **economy of scale** is the economic advantage that is often associated with the ability to operate at higher volumes. High levels of demand or required capacity, purchase discounts for large volumes, the practice of carrying large inventories, and the use of dedicated equipment to produce standardized product-service bundles can all provide economies of scale. The reverse of an economy of scale, a **diseconomy of scale,** is an economic *disadvantage* associated with operating at higher volumes. Low levels of demand, high costs for finished goods transportation, an inability to carry large inventories due to a limited shelf life, and the costs of paperwork and bureaucracy can produce diseconomies of scale.

Over the long run, based on expected demand, businesses will adjust their capacity to avoid diseconomies of scale and obtain economies of scale. Tom's airline could shut down, downsize, expand, or maintain the size of its current facilities in British Columbia. Such long-term capacity choices represent a variety of possible short-run cost curves.

Tom's airline is considering upgrading its facility in British Columbia. At the airline's current terminal in British Columbia, Facility A, passengers must disembark via an outdoor stairway and walk to the terminal. The costs associated with this facility were summarized in Table 8.1. At the proposed Facility B, passengers could disembark via a covered walkway that connects directly to the terminal. Facility B would have relatively high monthly fixed costs of about $500,000 (see Figure 8.7a) but

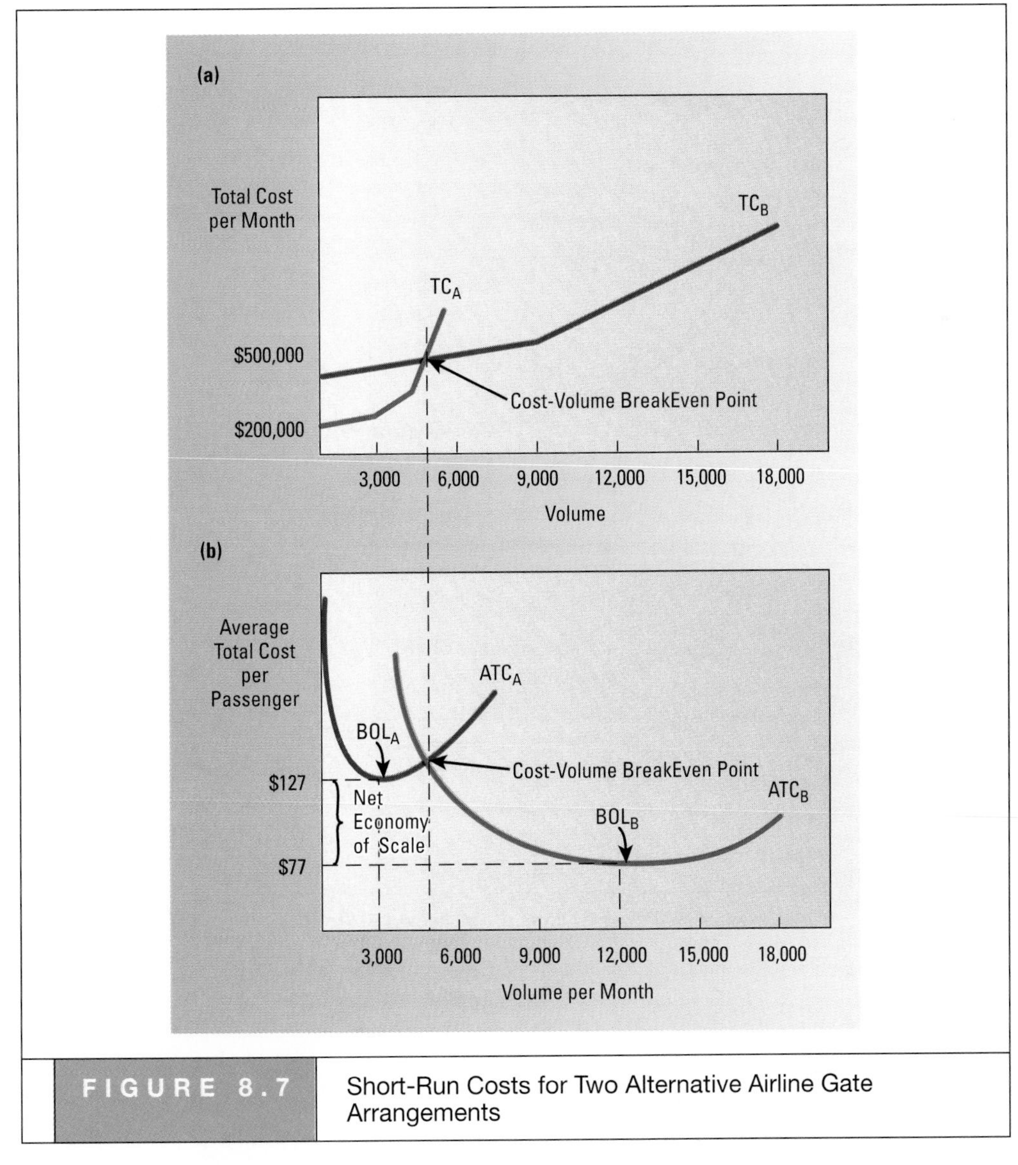

FIGURE 8.7 Short-Run Costs for Two Alternative Airline Gate Arrangements

would lower variable costs to $40 per ticketed passenger, up to a monthly total of 9,000 passengers. Beyond that point, they would rise to $80 per passenger up to a maximum capacity of 18,000 passengers per month. What is the best operating level for each facility? The break-even volume?

Figure 8.7(b) shows that the best operating level for Facility A, $BOL_{A,}$ is 3,000 passengers at the minimum average total cost of $127 (also seen in Table 8.1). This passenger volume is much lower than the best operating level for Facility B, $BOL_{B,}$ which turns out to be 12,000 passengers at the minimum average total cost of $77. The break-even volume—where the two average total cost curves, ATC_A and $ATC_{B,}$ intersect—is about 4,600 passengers.

Thus, if the airline's long-term forecasts suggest a growth in demand on the route to British Columbia, managers might consider expanding the terminal's capacity. The *net economy of scale* associated with the move would be the difference between their best operating levels, about $50 per ticketed passenger. However, managers probably would not make the change unless they expected monthly demand to be higher than the break-even volume. If the demand for tickets to this destination grows beyond the break-even point during the off-season, managers should look into the larger facility.

Figure 8.8 shows a set of short-run average cost (SRAC) curves, which yield a long-run average cost (LRAC) curve. On this long-run curve, economies of scale are gained up to a certain point by changing processes, which means moving from one short-run average cost curve to another. After a certain point, diseconomies of scale would cause long-run average costs to increase. Ideally, managers would avoid operating at a volume that is large enough to incur diseconomies of scale. Because of the relationship between the product life cycle (PLC) and long-run capacity decisions, the pattern of the

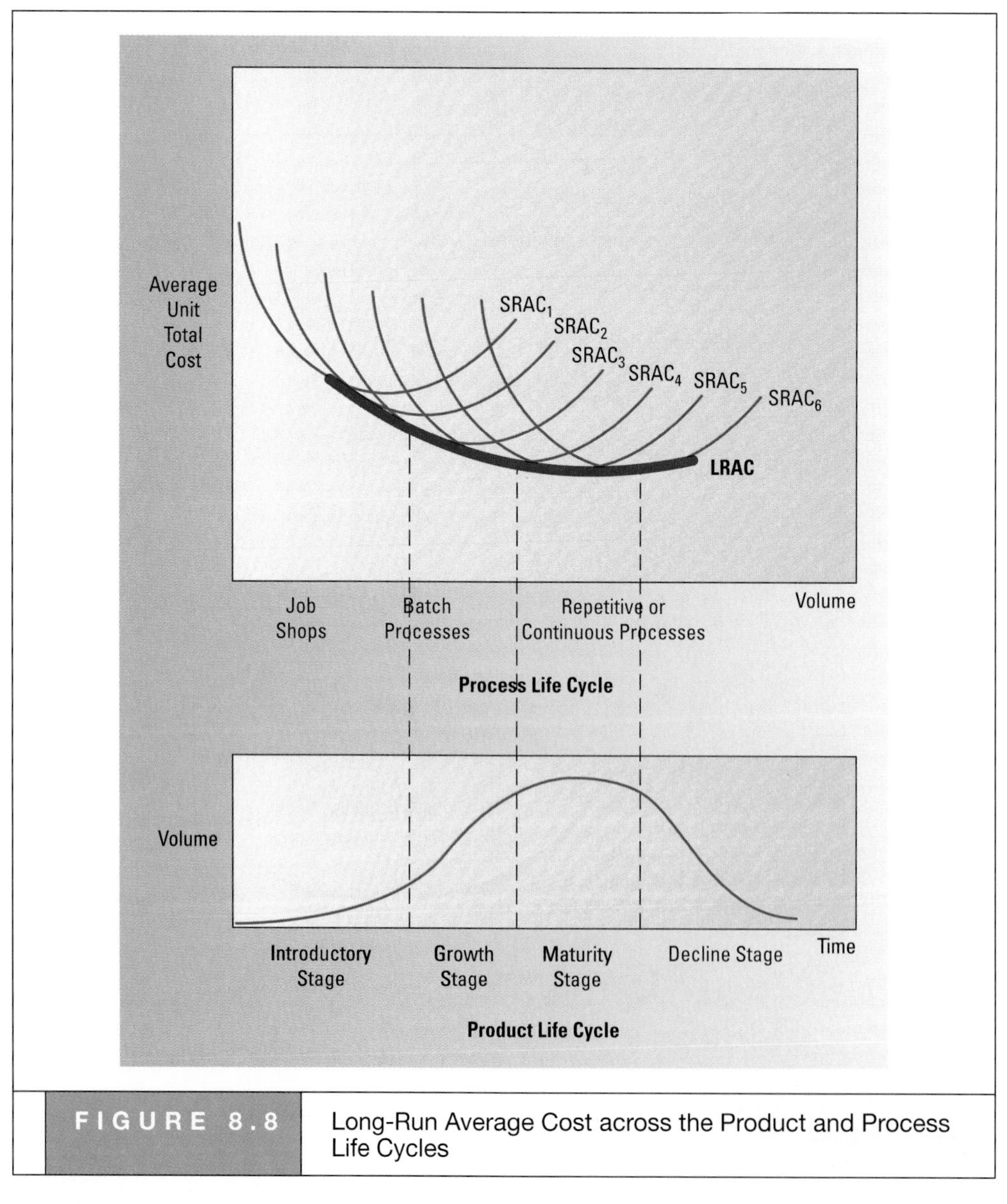

FIGURE 8.8 Long-Run Average Cost across the Product and Process Life Cycles

long-run average cost curve is rather predictable up to the maturity stage. During the introductory stage of the product life cycle, demand is small, technological standards are less than certain, and customer preferences are still unclear. As a result, job shop and batch production facilities, which have low fixed costs and high variable costs, are best suited to this stage. During the growth stage of the cycle, firms begin to move to larger facilities with higher fixed costs and lower variable costs. This trend continues into the maturity stage, until product volume begins to decline, at which point large facilities with high fixed cost and low variable cost become less efficient. As the market continues to decline and volumes drop, the large facilities may be replaced with smaller facilities that have higher variable costs but lower fixed costs (such as batch processes and job shops). This cycle of process changes, which results from product life cycles, is referred to as the **process life cycle (PSLC)**.

Like the process life cycle, a firm's facility strategy will have a major impact on its long-run average cost curve. A facility strategy determines whether a firm will have a small number of large facilities or a larger number of small facilities, as well as what combination of product variety and geographic range its facilities will supply. For instance, facilities might supply:

- a wide range of products on a global, regional, or local basis
- a narrow range of products on a global, regional, or local basis
- some combination of these options

Figure 8.9 shows how process and industry factors help to determine a company's facility strategy. The horizontal scale in this figure represents the extent to which manufacturing adds value to the product-service bundle. Product manufacturers appear at the far left; pure services at the far right. The vertical scale represents the extent to which industry factors do or do not provide economies of scale. Where markets are large, product-service bundles are standardized, production volumes are high, and extensive personal interaction with the customer is not required, bigger facilities are usually better. In these cases, the economic benefits of a large-scale operation usually outweigh the economic drawbacks. This rule applies to services as well as to products. For example, NFL franchises, catalog distribution centers, and automobile assembly plants all benefit from economies of scale and all employ large facilities (see Figure 8.9). Similarly, bakeries, copy shops, and fire departments all experience diseconomies of scale. They are likely to be small and local in nature.

As this discussion suggests, a facility's capacity is closely related to its location. In the next section we will examine the issues managers must consider in selecting a location for a new facility.

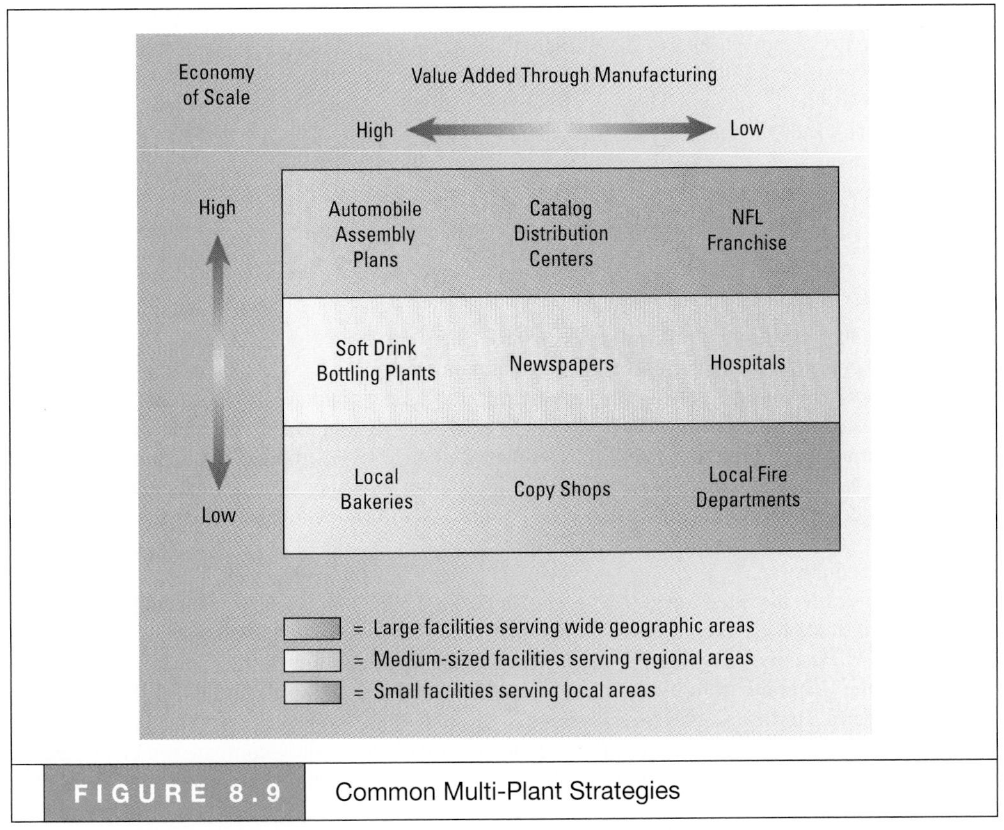

FIGURE 8.9 Common Multi-Plant Strategies

active concept check

Now let's take a moment to test your knowledge of the concepts you have studied in this section.

Location Decisions

If you have an address of your own, chances are you have made a *location decision.* Your complete address indicates your country, region (the first three digits of your zip code), state, city, street, and the exact location of your residence. Notice that the order of your address represents a clear hierarchy. When you chose your location, you probably didn't have to decide on all levels of the hierarchy. You probably took the country where you would live for granted, and you may have had a clear preference for a particular region or state, based on your family and personal relationships. If you had already chosen a college or a particular job, even the city of your residence may have been predetermined. Thus, not all location decisions require explicit consideration of each level of the hierarchy. As individuals, we get into the decision-making loop at a particular level, then move to more and more specific levels.

Businesses, too, get into location decisions at varying levels of the location hierarchy. We have seen that bakeries, copy shops, and fire departments tend to be small-scale facilities that serve local areas. Their location decisions are dominated by local and site-specific concerns. Soft drink bottlers, newspapers, and hospitals are medium-sized facilities and must therefore consider regional issues as well as local and site-specific concerns. Large-scale service and manufacturing facilities, such as automotive assembly plants, catalog distribution centers, and NFL teams, must consider national and international issues as well as regional, local, and site-specific concerns.

The problem of locating a major league sports franchise or stadium is a good example of the hierarchical considerations in location decisions. Although the National Football League (NFL) may someday consider locating a franchise outside the United States, to date it has been unwilling to do so. To maintain a strong following throughout the United States, however, the NFL tries very hard to be even-handed in locating new franchises. In deciding where to start new franchises or where to allow existing franchises to relocate, the NFL has considered regional demographics, business demographics (indicative of the market for luxury boxes among corporate clients), and the distribution of existing franchises. Local factors, such as a city council's willingness to fund the construction of a new stadium, are also important. Finally, before awarding a franchise to a city, the NFL must be certain that it has a suitable site for a stadium. Thus, the franchise location decision is an effort to obtain the best mix of regional, local, and site-specific factors.

In the following sections we will consider each of the categories in the *location decision hierarchy.* Then we will address the question of whether to locate near suppliers or customers and the recent trend toward collocation with the customer.

THE LOCATION DECISION HIERARCHY

Table 8.2 lists the major issues in location decisions, categorized by their level in the location hierarchy. We will begin with the highest level global-international concerns.

Decision makers who are considering expanding into a new country or geographic region must consider macroeconomic, demographic, and political issues of long-term significance. They must consider international trade issues, such as currency exchange risks, import-export quotas, and balance of trade. Access to a country's or trading block's market may also be important. The availability of skilled labor, materials, and support services; political, cultural, and legal concerns; and quality-of-life issues—all these *global-international issues* must be considered prior to a significant investment in a new country.

Once the decision has been made to locate a facility in a particular country or trading block, decision makers must choose a region based on *regional issues* like geographic, demographic, or cultural differences. For example, the geography, culture, and demographic trends of the southeastern United States are quite different from the geography, culture, and demographic trends of the Midwest, Southwest, Pacific Northwest, and New England.

Companies that want to locate close to their customer base commonly compare regions based on market characteristics, such as customer quality, customer quantity, and customer value. **Customer**

TABLE 8.2	Considerations in the Location Decision by Levels in the Location Hierarchy
Level in the Location Hierarchy	**Considerations That Are Usually Important to the Decision Maker**
Global-International	• International trade issues (currency exchange risk, balance of trade, quotas, tariffs, etc.) • Market access issues (free-trade agreements like NAFTA, consumer sentiment toward imported goods, etc.) • Labor issues (availability, wages, skills and training, regulations) • Supply issues (availability of raw material, local content laws, etc.) • Political concerns (stability of current regime, risk of asset nationalization, local ownership laws, etc.) • Cultural issues (compatibility of business practices and products with local culture) • Legal issues (environmental regulations, accounting and reporting requirements, etc.) • Quality-of-life issues (desirability as a place to live)
Regional	• Supply issues (availability of material inputs) • Market and demographic factors • Economic conditions • Costs of key inputs and advertising media • Labor climate • Quality-of-life issues
Community	• Transportation options and costs (by river, sea, rail, truck, pipeline, and air) • Utility options and costs • Civil services • Financial incentives • Legal climate and community receptiveness • Environmental concerns
Site specific	• Fixed costs (land, construction, taxes, etc.) • Operating costs (maintenance, transportation, utilities, labor, etc.) • Access concerns (for customers, suppliers, utilities, etc.) • Work environment (crime statistics, nearby eating establishments, etc.) • Key questions (what mix has worked well for the firm in the past?)

quality refers to the portion of the market that matches the customer profile for which a product-service bundle is designed. It indicates how hard a company will have to work to get customers. **Customer quantity** is an indicator of market size, stated in terms of the total number of buyers—for example, number of households, number of individuals in a particular demographic category, or number of companies that use a product-service bundle. **Customer value** describes the spending potential of a spending unit. Average household expenditure, average disposable income, and average production volume (for industrial customers) are measures of customer value.

Once a firm has identified the right region for a new facility, it must find one or more specific communities in which to locate the facility. In evaluating various communities, decision makers will look at specific community issues, such as the cost of inputs and transportation, the quality of the infrastructure, environmental regulations and other legal issues, and so on. Frequently, communities will offer significant tax abatements and infrastructural improvements to a particular site, in the hope of attracting a new facility. When BMW chose to build an automotive assembly plant in Spartanburg, South Carolina, it received economic incentives worth more than $150 million from the state, county, and city and from local businesses, including millions of dollars worth of infrastructural improvements, from the purchase and removal of nearby residential buildings to the construction of new roads and utility pipelines. (To date, the economic benefits of these incentives to residents of the state of South Carolina, in the form of increased tax revenues and economic activity, have far exceeded their cost.)

Occasionally, rather than selecting a locality where support services are already in place, a company will look for an undeveloped area where it can start from scratch. Such facilities are called *greenfields.* The idea is to build exactly what the firm needs, rather than to live with the results of past decisions. The Saturn plant in Springhill, Tennessee, is a greenfield facility.

Companies tend to learn from their experiences in site selection. Often, two or three sites that seem to have identical location profiles yield vastly different operational results. After looking at many existing sites, managers begin to see what makes a location good for their specific purposes. They find that a good site for a McDonald's franchise isn't necessarily a good site for a Wendy's. The best approach to site selection is to analyze the demographic and performance characteristics of the firm's existing sites and select new sites based on those factors most closely associated with superior operational results.

Virtually no detail is irrelevant to a site selection. You might not think that the side of the road makes much difference, but if the breakfast business is really important to your fast-food service, you will have a strong preference for the right side of the road on major commuting arteries. Or perhaps you think that the previous ownership and use of land doesn't matter. But in fact, under current law, property owners are liable for environmental remediation costs, even if an environmental problem was created by a past owner. Thus, the financial strength of previous owners, as well as the previous uses of the land, are of critical importance. These and other *site-specific issues*—such as land and building costs, utility costs, safety, and property taxes—are of great importance in selecting a location for a facility.

active exercise

Take a moment to apply what you've learned.

active concept check

Now let's take a moment to test your knowledge of the concepts you have studied in this section.

Locating Miami's Student Rec Center

In many ways, choosing the location of the Student Recreation Center (SRC) was like that of placing a hospital or McDonald's in a city. National-, regional-, or even community-specific issues were moot; the university was not going to move. In this case, selecting a site from a limited set of feasible alternatives was the only concern.

Locating the SRC was mostly a matter of accessibility and convenience for its patrons. Thus the facility had to be central to the student body from a residential perspective, easy to access by nonstudent community members, and at a site that wouldn't adversely impact other university services and infrastructures. For example, the capacity of the existing centralized campus cooling and heating system would have to be considered, and the site had to fit within the long-run campus master plan.

The actual site selected was on the extreme southwestern portion of the campus. This was central to the student body, though not central to the campus because many students live off campus to the south and west and inter-collegiate athletes who have facilities of their own occupy many of the dorms on the north side of campus. The location on the edge of campus facilitated special event access by large groups of out-of-town guests with minimal disruption to campus services and infrastructure. Finally, one of two cooling towers for the system used to heat and cool most campus buildings is located close to the site of the rec center. The efficiency of this system drops as the distance between the chiller and the buildings it serves increases. At the time the SRC's location was under consideration, a plan was also put in place to expand the nearby cooling tower. This allowed the university to rebalance the load between the two cooling towers and achieve improved efficiency. A final benefit of the selected site was the fact that it could share a parking lot with married student housing. This reduced the amount of campus green space lost to the new facility.

LOCATING NEAR SUPPLIERS OR CUSTOMERS

We have seen that proximity to supplies and markets frequently dominates facility location decisions. But because the major markets for a company's products are rarely located in the same area as its raw materials, decision makers must often decide whether to locate close to their suppliers, close to customers, or somewhere in between.

During the early 1980s when General Motors (GM) was planning the Saturn Corporation, location issues were obviously very important for them to consider. Both the need for economies of scale in automobile manufacturing and the unique Saturn concept made location important. For political reasons, the plant had to be located in the United States. For logistical reasons, potential supplier locations and geographic proximity to the U.S. market were critical. Therefore, GM narrowed the location to the Midwest. Governors from no less than nine states made pitches with economic incentives to attract the new company. By the time GM announced the choice of Spring Hill, Tennessee, in July 1985, it had looked at possibilities in all nine states, a number of cities, and numerous sites. Availability of skilled labor, economic incentives, and, most importantly, good logistical access for inbound supplies and outbound cars were all keys to the final choice.

Shipping weight, an indicator of transportation time and cost, is a critical factor in such decisions in manufacturing facilities. Some facilities add weight to a product, while others reduce it. **Weight-added operations** tend to use converging material flows to produce items that are much more costly to transport than the supplies from which they are made. For example, a bridge or other construction project is a weight-added product. Naturally, the facilities that are used to build a bridge must be located at the bridge. By contrast, mining, agriculture, and refining are **weight-reduced operations,** which use diverging material flows to stratify objects according to their market value. Transporting the dirt that clings to iron ore or copper over great distances makes little sense. Similarly, lumber is usually cut to standard dimensions and dried prior to shipment over long distances. Thus, mining and lumber facilities are located close to suppliers. Figure 8.10 illustrates the spectrum of weight-added and weight-reduced operations in manufacturing.

A parallel consideration to the weight-added, weight-reduced spectrum helps to explain the location of service facilities. In services the material logistics issues are replaced with the logistics of access. Convenient access to the demand source or the source of supply becomes more critical than the cost of moving things. For example, locating a fire department or doctor's office close to the customer is much more important than locating it close to a training facility or to the homes of staff members. In these cases, a small force of professionals serves a large number of customers, most of whom would not want to pay taxes for a facility located an hour from home. By contrast, at a research hospital, a large number of professionals serves a relatively small group of patients. Traveling a day or two to such a facility is worthwhile if a patient gets the benefit of the expertise of so many specialists. Similarly, since films can be easily distributed once they have been created, movie studios usually locate close to the sources of acting and editing talent (i.e., Hollywood).

> **active example**
>
> **Take a closer look at the concepts and issues you've been reading about.**

A quick look at some maps will demonstrate the significance of the weight-added, weight-reduced spectrum in facility location decisions. Figures 8.11 and 8.12 show the locations of facilities in the wood and forest products industries. (Note that these maps are based on aggregate economic data and may not reflect the concentration of facilities for any one firm.) Figure 8.11 shows that the greatest concentration of logging activity is in the southeastern and western states. Sawmills, planing mills, hardwood dimension mills, and flooring mills all house weight-reducing activities. They convert raw timber of varying shapes, lengths, and water content into dried lumber cut to standard dimensions. Most such plants are concentrated close to the timber sources in the Southeast. Wood products—for example, cabinets—that are made from the output of these lumber mills are manufactured closer to customers, in the Midwest and West, because they are heavy and bulky to ship (weight added).

Figure 8.12 shows the distribution of facilities that make and use paper products. Once more, notice that logging activity is concentrated in the Southeast and West. Paper mills, on the other hand, are concentrated in the Midwest and Northeast—a distribution very different from that of the sawmills (see Figure 8.11). The wood chips and dried pulp used in paper making (whether they are the product of logging, a byproduct of lumber milling, or recycled material) can be transported easily, with no concern for damage. Paper, on the other hand, must be protected from the elements, because it can

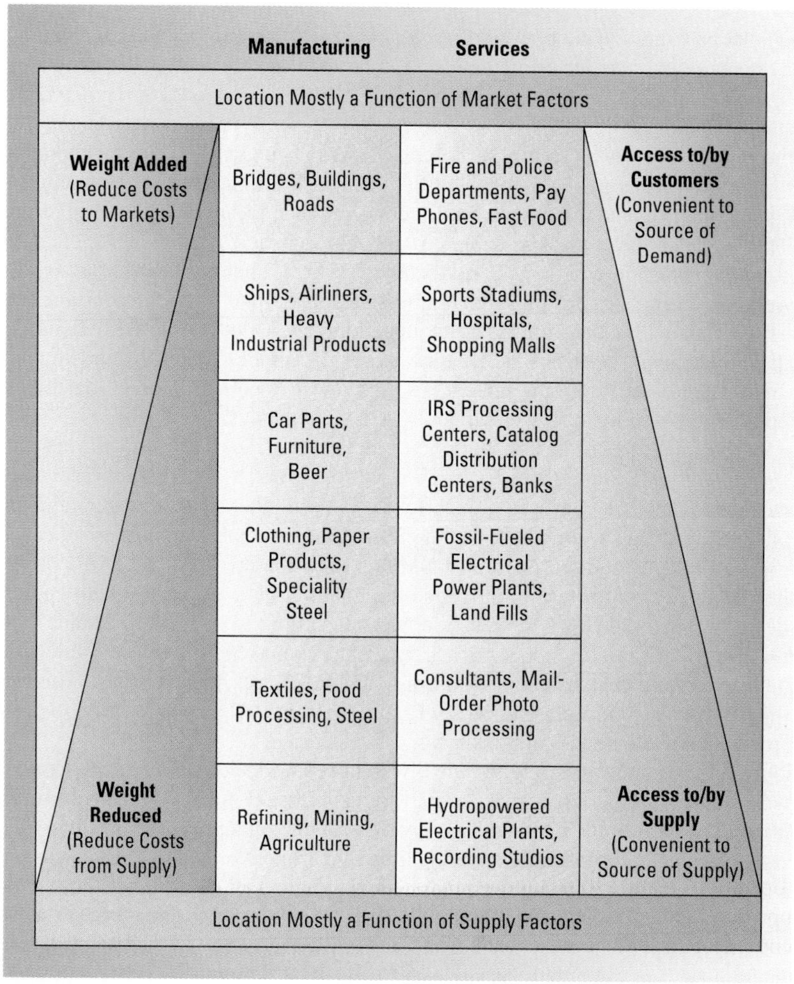

	Manufacturing	Services	
Location Mostly a Function of Market Factors			
Weight Added (Reduce Costs to Markets)	Bridges, Buildings, Roads	Fire and Police Departments, Pay Phones, Fast Food	**Access to/by Customers** (Convenient to Source of Demand)
	Ships, Airliners, Heavy Industrial Products	Sports Stadiums, Hospitals, Shopping Malls	
	Car Parts, Furniture, Beer	IRS Processing Centers, Catalog Distribution Centers, Banks	
	Clothing, Paper Products, Speciality Steel	Fossil-Fueled Electrical Power Plants, Land Fills	
	Textiles, Food Processing, Steel	Consultants, Mail-Order Photo Processing	
Weight Reduced (Reduce Costs from Supply)	Refining, Mining, Agriculture	Hydropowered Electrical Plants, Recording Studios	**Access to/by Supply** (Convenient to Source of Supply)
Location Mostly a Function of Supply Factors			

FIGURE 8.10 The Weight/Access Spectrum of Operations

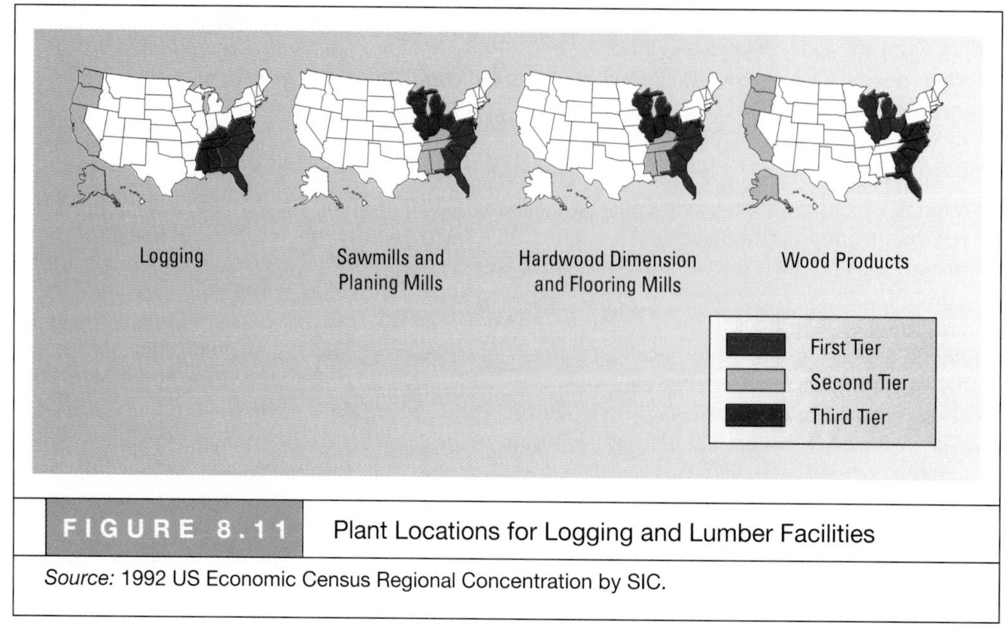

FIGURE 8.11 Plant Locations for Logging and Lumber Facilities

Source: 1992 US Economic Census Regional Concentration by SIC.

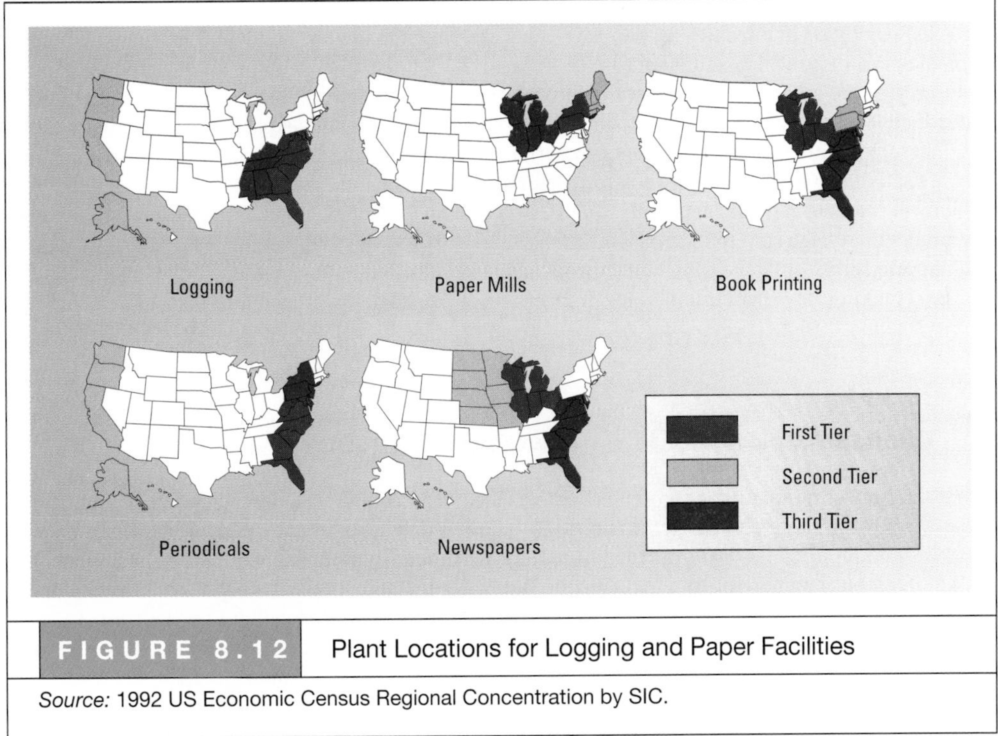

FIGURE 8.12 Plant Locations for Logging and Paper Facilities

Source: 1992 US Economic Census Regional Concentration by SIC.

easily be damaged in storage and transit. Consequently, paper-making facilities are concentrated close to the areas where paper is used to print books and newspapers.

Service operations feature some unique approaches to the location decision. **Competitive clustering** is an approach used by motels and automobile dealerships to locate close to competitors. Motels cluster around major airports because that's where the customers are. Auto dealerships anticipate consumer behavior by locating close to one another, making the comparison and bargaining process easiest and quickest for both customers and dealers.

Saturation marketing is an approach (used by Au Bon Pain, a croissant sandwich restaurant chain and others) that segments high-density urban areas into small, focused markets such as shopping malls and office buildings. Au Bon Pain restaurants may be located within very short distances of one another. While some sales cannibalization among restaurants can occur with this strategy, extremely close proximity to customers (shoppers and office workers) is viewed as the key to increased sales.

Substituting technology for physical proximity is a strategy used by some health care clinics in delivering services to remote areas and some prisons. High-resolution cameras and real-time communications equipment permit physicians to diagnose problems and prescribe remedies without being physically present. Automatic payroll deposits and deductions, and banking by computer and telephone reduce the need for bank customers to travel to bank offices. University distance learning programs provide education access to people for whom traveling to campus is inconvenient. In these cases, technology enables organizations to increase their customer base and geographic reach without substantially increasing costs.

SUPPLY-CHAIN MANAGEMENT AND COLLOCATION

Clearly, the way in which suppliers and customers interact is an important consideration in facility location decisions. Businesses have been moving toward more cooperative *supply-chain management,* in the interest of providing greater value to the customer. Rather than locate an operation near the customer, they may choose to locate *inside* a customer's facility. In fact, a Volkswagen facility in Brazil took this idea to an extreme. At this plant, suppliers are completely responsible for assembling that portion of the vehicle in which their material is used.

While locating one's assembly workers under a customer's roof is not yet common, stationing personnel with other responsibilities there is. Suppliers' design personnel are often located at the customer's facility, where they are full-fledged members of the product design team. Much of the task of designing new products and services is in effect outsourced, without any proprietary information leaving the facility. Likewise, quality personnel routinely work at suppliers' and customers' plants, in order to perform inspections and resolve problems quickly. Rather than stationing transportation and logistical personnel in a facility of their own, they are better located in the facilities where shipments originate or in those where shipments are sent.

Finally, suppliers frequently do not receive purchase orders telling them what to ship and when. Instead, their inventory planning and control personnel make those decisions at the customer's facilities. These people know the customer's material requirements and are responsible for making sure they are satisfied. Given the ability to electronically share sales information gathered by point-of-sale systems in retail establishments, many suppliers now "own" their part of an assembled product until that product has been sold to the consumer.

All these forms of *collocation* help firms to manage across functions and improve customer service. By breaking down communication barriers, they facilitate joint problem solving and process improvement.

Decision-Making Tools for Locating Facilities

Given the impact of location decisions, managers will use every tool at their disposal in an effort to make the best possible choices. In this section, we will discuss a limited number of representative decision-making tools that are useful in locating facilities. In studying and using these decision-making tools, it is important to remember the old maxim, "Garbage in, garbage out." Regardless of the tool they are using, managers must have accurate and current information in order to make good decisions. In fact, the quality of the information that is used may have a much more significant impact on the quality of the decision than the choice of decision-making technique.

Typically, managers will tap at least three sources of data in making a facility location decision. One source, **syndicated data,** is found in existing databases and provides demographic information about the lifestyles, needs, and expectations of potential customers. Syndicated data generally does not provide all the information managers need, and it may not be current or accurate. In that case, managers must be willing to incur the expense of gathering and maintaining the additional data they need. **Primary research** involves managers in gathering the specific information they need about past and potential customers. Though this type of data is more expensive than syndicated data, it may be more meaningful, since the manager can choose the individuals to include in the study and the exact questions to be asked. Finally, **point of sale (POS) data,** which is captured when the customer actually makes a purchase, is even more valuable than primary research because it indicates what customers do, not just what they say they do. Rather than suggesting what the firm's customer base could be, POS data shows what the customer base really is.

In the sections that follow, we will examine five decision-making tools which are essentially methods of manipulating syndicated, primary research, and point-of-sale data.

GEOGRAPHIC INFORMATION SYSTEMS (GIS)

An estimated 80% or more of business data has some spatial context—a street address, plant name, or ZIP code. Until recently, however, most computer databases did not include information about location. But the development of systems for storing and sharing large amounts of data, tagging data by location, and displaying it visually has put a wealth of information at decision-makers' fingertips.

A **spatial data warehouse** is a database including geographic information that can be accessed by users of a client-server computer system. Such databases contain information that is useful to a wide range of users. They may receive input from and transmit data to remote locations, either stationary or mobile, via communication links such as phone lines and digital satellite transmission. Thus, instead of building and maintaining a number of separate databases, companies can build one large database. In 1997, data warehousing was an estimated $15 billion industry, growing at a rate of 10% to 15% a year.

The **global positioning system (GPS)** is a highly effective mechanism for location identification. Its value is enhanced when decision makers can integrate GPS outputs with the data values stored in a spatial data warehouse. Developed by the military to guide missiles, the satellite-based GPS can identify a location's latitude, longitude, and altitude within a few millimeters. The applications are almost endless. Using a GPS receiver, a farmer can gather data on crop yields during harvest, in order to identify fields with low and high yields. Such information is useful in preparing fields and planting them the following year. Similarly, businesses can use the GPS to identify the location of rental cars, trucks, and service and maintenance vans, or the location of billboards carrying a particular advertisement. This type of information allows managers to make real-time decisions about staffing, routing, and the effectiveness of an advertising campaign. Over time, it can become the foundation for long-term decisions on facility location and capacity.

Information that is gathered through a global positioning system is often used in a **geographic information system (GIS),** a software tool that is used to improve spatially oriented decisions. A GIS can display the relationship between business variables, like sales, and location variables, like customer residence. For instance, a GIS can be used to display sales data on a map, a format that is much easier to understand than the usual column-and-row approach. Cost factors, transportation times, and service quality issues can also be linked to specific locations. For example, Tom Jackson's airline could use a GIS to identify those airports where ground services are performed most cost effectively, and then use that information in routing, scheduling, and purchasing decisions. Figure 8.13 suggests some of the elements that might be part of such a system.

Geographic boundaries are lines of demarcation that allow spatial data to be categorized. Without these, data cannot be displayed and analyzed geographically. In the United States, many different approaches are used to define geographic boundaries. They include:

- *Physical geography:* the natural boundaries established by surface and subterrestrial features, such as mountains, watersheds, forests, underground aquifers, soil, and so on.
- *Census geography:* block group, census tract, city, county, metropolitan statistical area, state, and township.
- *TIGER streets:* short for the Census Bureau's topologically integrated geographic encoding and reference file, a set of computerized maps that provide the locational context for every street, highway, bridge, and tunnel in the United States.
- *Congressional districts:* information on a multitude of demographic variables can be found in many different databases.

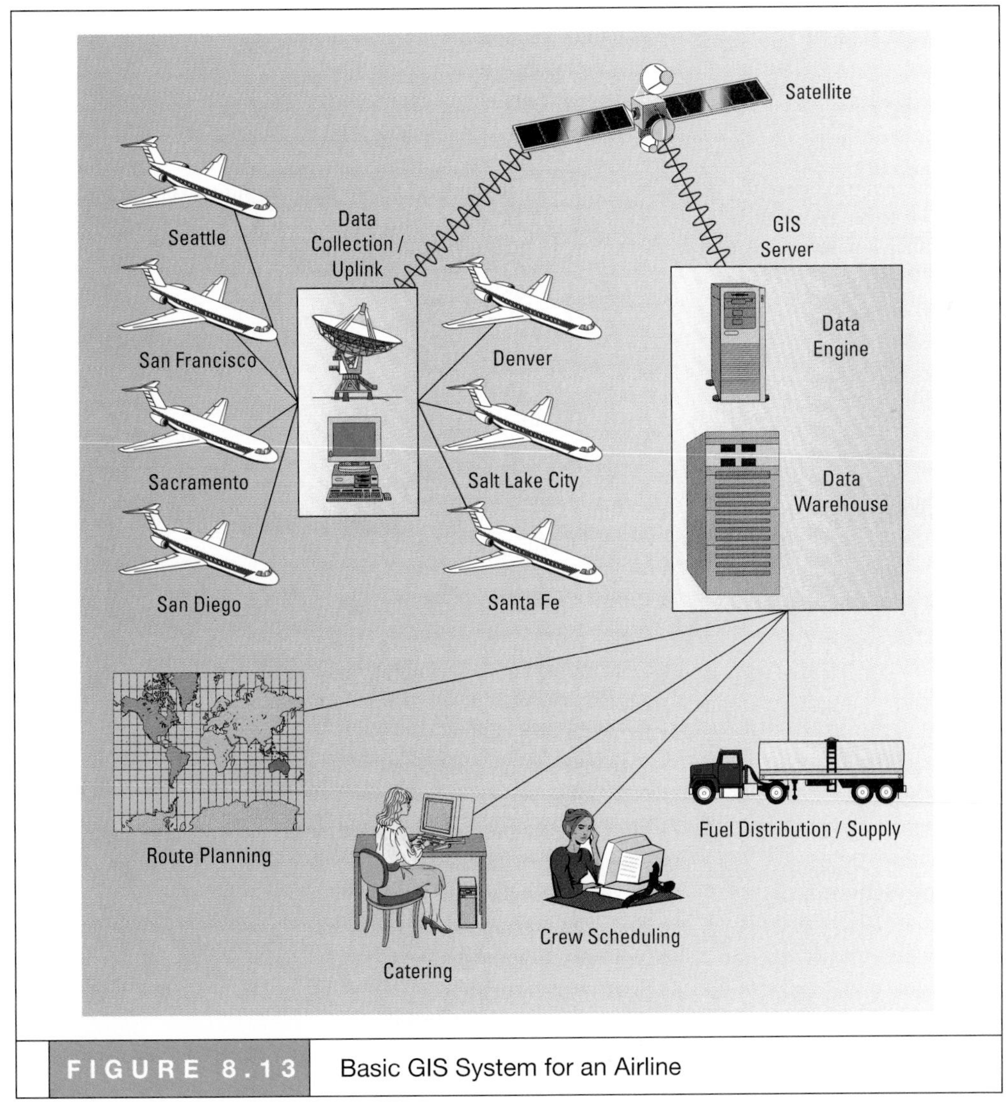

FIGURE 8.13 Basic GIS System for an Airline

- *Landmarks:* airports (about 600 commercial airports in the United States), universities (several thousand), population centroids for incorporated places (more than 20,000), and so forth. A GIS can identify and plot the location of all airports serving more than 100,000 travelers per year, all colleges with an OM major, and all cities with a hospital.
- *Media geography:* geographic areas defined on the basis of broadcast media coverage—radio and television, cable systems, distribution of periodicals and directories such as the Yellow Pages, and so on.
- *Postal geography:* the regions defined by the three- and five-digit ZIP codes.
- *Highway infrastructure:* major interstates, federal and state highways, and county roads.
- *Utility infrastructure:* electrical lines, water mains, gas pipelines, and so on.
- *Street intersections:* tens of thousands of geographic points with which data may be associated.
- *Telephone service geography:* telephone exchanges, area codes, and designated prefixes.

GIS technology has many different uses. Table 8.3 categorizes some of them by business function. As the technology gains acceptance, more and more of the software for traditional decision-making

TABLE 8.3 GIS Applications Categorized by Business Function

Functional Area	GIS Applications
Finance and Accounting	• Accounting for environmental liabilities and the risks of weather and crime-related losses • Disaster planning • Loss management • Underwriting • Analyzing the flow of financial resources • Asset and inventory management • Locating financial service outlets, such as ATMs and branches
Marketing	• Sales territory design • Sales forecasting • Sales district performance analysis • Marketing research • Direct marketing • Product development • Media planning • Emerging market analysis
Operations Management	• Facility location (site selection, land economics, real estate demographics) • Facility layout • Facility network analysis and planning • Emergency management • Distribution system planning • Mobile asset management • Routing analysis
Human Resources	• Compensation planning • Social issues • Interorganizational networking and information flow • Demographic issues
Management Information Systems	• Systems development • Database design • Network planning • Data warehousing • Electronic data interchange • Privacy and security

tools will be integrated with GIS software, and the supply of spatial databases to support them will increase. The use of GIS specifically to locate facilities is expected to grow rapidly in the coming years.

CENTER OF GRAVITY METHOD

The center of gravity of a physical object is the point on which its entire weight could theoretically be balanced. With regard to facility location, the center of gravity is that place that best balances the transportation demands associated with operating a facility. The **center of gravity method,** then, is a mathematical technique that gives decision makers a rough idea of the most suitable location for a new facility.

Suppose you own a laundry service based at several storefront locations. You decide to build a new central facility that will service all those locations. One way to find the center of gravity would be to paste a map on a board and drill holes where each of the storefronts is located. If you thread a string through each of the holes and attach a weight representing the volume of work handled at each location, then tie all the strings together and let go, the knot that joins all the strings together will land at the center of gravity.

The center of gravity can also be found mathematically. If you place a coordinate plane over the map and identify the coordinates of each of the storefronts, you can compute the coordinates of the center of gravity using Equations 8.1 and 8.2. Assuming n storefronts, each located at some point identified by the coordinates (x_i, y_i) and doing a weekly volume of business equal to v_i, the center of gravity would be the point (x_{cg}, y_{cg}).

$$X_{cg} = \frac{\sum_{i=1}^{n} x_i v_i}{\sum_{i=1}^{n} v_i} \qquad \text{Equation 8.1}$$

$$y_{cg} = \frac{\sum_{i=1}^{n} y_i v_i}{\sum_{i=1}^{n} v_i} \qquad \text{Equation 8.2}$$

Suppose an employment agency has obtained a contract to place 550 summer employees with a large company that has service facilities in Detroit, Toledo, and Cleveland. Of the employees, 350 will be assigned to Cleveland, 150 to Detroit, and 50 to Toledo. After reviewing a large number of applications, the firm's managers have decided to conduct a two-day screening of 175 students from Miami University (Ohio), 100 from Ohio State University, and 275 from Ohio University. On the first day, screenings will be conducted off campus; on the second day, at one of the three facilities where the new employees will work. Each student will be reimbursed for mileage, and all must be present at one location for the first day of screening. Use the center of gravity method to determine the most cost-effective location for the first day's screening.

Figure 8.14 shows the solution to this problem graphically. The data are summarized in Table 8.4. The computations are also shown in the figure. Based on this method of analysis, managers should look for a site near the point marked *X* on the map in Figure 8.14.

While the center of gravity method is used most often to find a specific site, it can also be used on higher levels of the location hierarchy. For instance, if a company intends to serve several regions with a new facility or to receive materials from several regions, the center of gravity method could be used to identify the most suitable region.

One caveat: The ideal location may not be a feasible location. Murphy's Law suggests that the center of gravity location will probably fall right in the middle of the local forest preserve or in a neighborhood with a residential zoning. Even when the center of gravity location is feasible, it should be seen only as the starting point in the search for a location. Managers should consider a variety of alternatives before selecting any one location.

> active exercise

Take a moment to apply what you've learned.

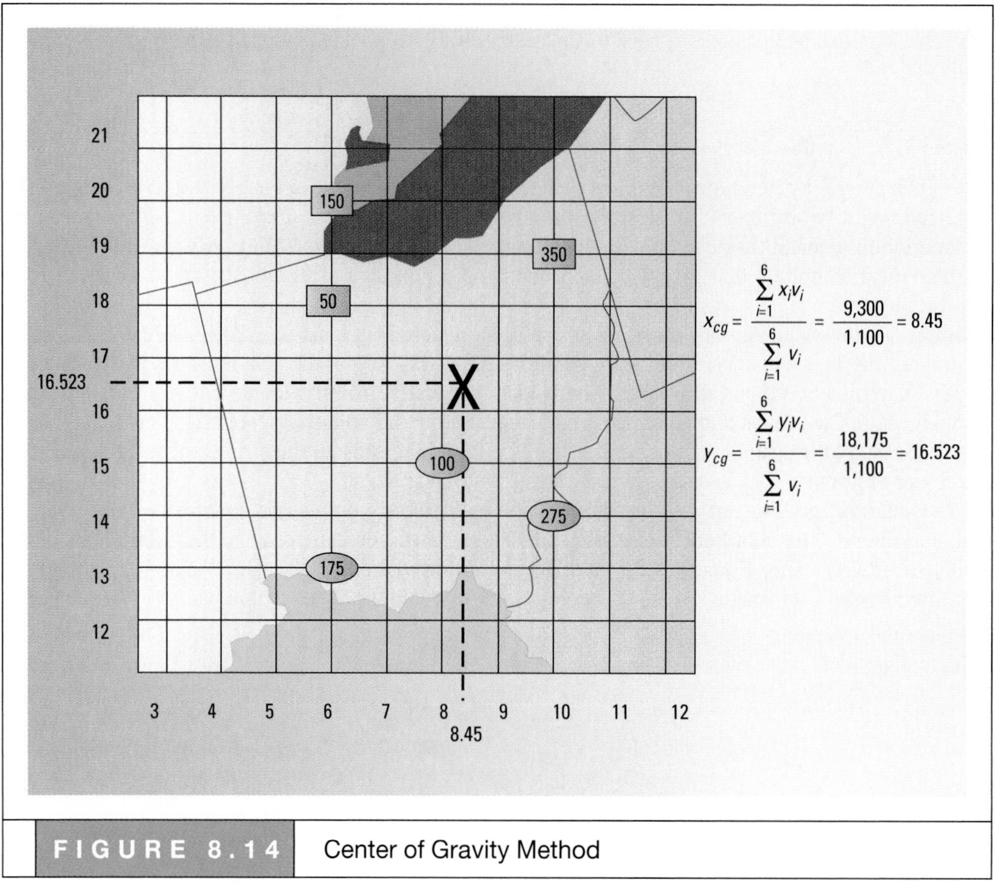

FIGURE 8.14 Center of Gravity Method

TRADE AREA ANALYSIS

Trade area analysis, which determines the impact of one facility on the business of others, is especially important for service franchises because it can be used to ensure that a new facility will not take significant business from existing facilities. Managers can then target the new facility at customers located within an area that is underserved. Table 8.5 presents some information that could be used for a trade area analysis.

One way to perform such an analysis is to graph the percentage of customers the business could serve as a function of their distance from the site. Such information can also be displayed on a map of the trade area (see Figure 8.15). Managers can then examine the map to see where customer concentrations are heaviest.

Figure 8.16 shows the distance decay curve obtained from this data. Clearly, significant business could be lost if a new facility is built within five miles of the existing facility. The accompanying map shows that most of the customers from outside the 70% ring do not reside in the northeastern quadrant, even though household incomes in that quadrant seem similar to those inside the 70% ring. If other demographic factors do not contradict this information, the distance decay curve and map sug-

TABLE 8.4 Market and Source Data for the Center of Gravity Method

Raw Material Source / Market Concentration	Volume (V_i)	X_i	Y_i
Miami University	175	6	13
Ohio State University	100	8	15
Ohio University	275	10	14
Cleveland Market	350	10	19
Detroit Market	150	6	20
Toledo Market	50	6	18

TABLE 8.5 Data for Distance Decay Report in Trade Area Analysis

Distance from Site (Miles)	Cumulative Number of Customers	% Customers
0.9	57	5
1.5	200	15
1.9	377	25
2.6	499	35
3.1	566	40
3.4	637	45
3.7	681	50
4.0	752	55
4.4	851	60
4.8	890	65
5.6	956	70
6.7	1023	75
8.0	1095	80
9.9	1162	85
12.3	1232	90
16.9	1302	95
45.8	1370	100

Source: Adapted from Jim Laiderman, "Site Selection Basics," in *Business Geographics* (February, 1997): 20–23, and http://www.geoplace.com/bg.

gest that locating a new facility in the northeastern quadrant could significantly expand sales without a major reduction in sales at the existing facility.

MULTIPLE-FACTOR RATING SYSTEMS

We have seen that a variety of factors are important to decision makers at each level of the location decision hierarchy. What is their relative importance, and which factor is most important? The answers to these questions vary from one decision to the next; there may be no precise answer. But rating the factors according to their general importance can help decision makers to avoid placing too much emphasis on the wrong factors. **Multiple-factor rating systems** can be used to compare the attractiveness of several locations on the basis of more than one criteria.

The relative attractiveness of a given location can be estimated mathematically using equation 8.3. In this equation, the rating of location i on factor j is referred to as $r_{ij,}$ and the weight assigned to factor j is referred to as $w_{j.}$ The number of different factors is assumed to be m.

$$\text{Location attractiveness for location } i \ \sum_{j=1}^{m} r_{ij} w_j \ = \text{Equation 8.3}$$

A young entrepreneur named Sparky wants to open a fireworks stand in a small Southern town. He is considering three different locations. One is in the town square, which offers many amenities for workers but suffers from inadequate parking for customers. Another location is next to a lake, on the outskirts of town. The lakeside location has plenty of parking and is the safest place to store fireworks, but it has few amenities for workers and is out of the way for customers. A third location is the parking lot for the veterinary center, on the main highway that links the town to the larger metropolitan area. Its primary drawback is the lack of amenities for workers. Use multiple-factor rating to help Sparky select the best location.

Table 8.6 shows the factor ratings and weights for the three locations. Notice that the third location got the highest location attractiveness score, even though it got only medium ratings on most factors. Decision makers are sometimes surprised by the results of weighted-factor ratings, especially if they are not fully aware of their biases. For example, the decision maker who subconsciously feels that sales is the most important issue in locating a business would have located Sparky's stand in the town square.

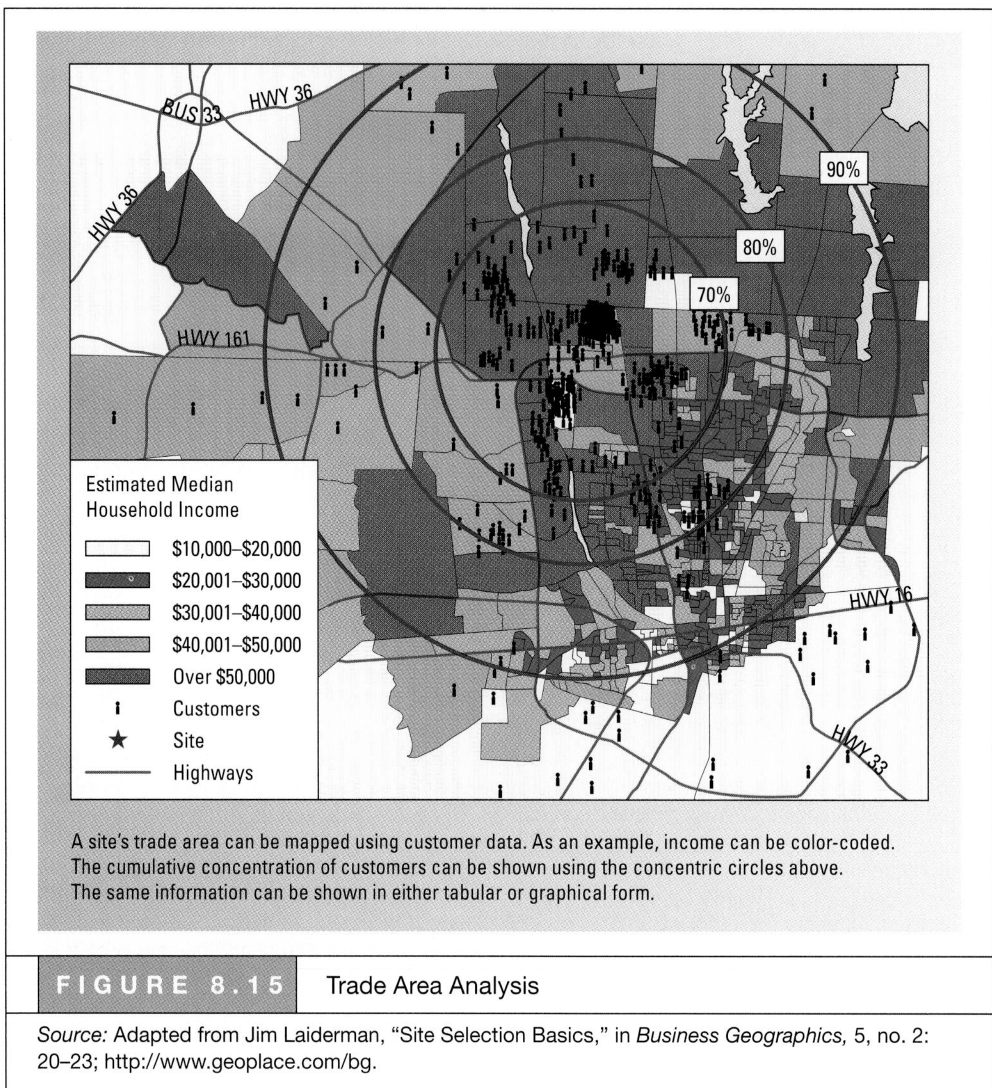

A site's trade area can be mapped using customer data. As an example, income can be color-coded. The cumulative concentration of customers can be shown using the concentric circles above. The same information can be shown in either tabular or graphical form.

FIGURE 8.15 Trade Area Analysis

Source: Adapted from Jim Laiderman, "Site Selection Basics," in *Business Geographics,* 5, no. 2: 20–23; http://www.geoplace.com/bg.

Obviously, factor-rating systems can be used only when certain overriding factors will not eliminate some locations from consideration. Sparky might have eliminated several locations at the outset, based on overriding factors such as projected income or the availability of a retail permit. Perhaps safety should be an overriding concern for a fireworks business. If so, Sparky need not compute attractiveness ratings based on all the factors; instead, he should locate his fireworks stand at the lake.

video example

Take a closer look at the concepts and issues you've been reading about.

MATHEMATICAL MODELING AND COMPUTER SIMULATIONS

Before computers became widely available, decision-making models had to be simple enough to be solved using slide rules. The mathematical techniques managers used were not much more complex than simple break-even analysis. Based on a limited number of variables and a small number of equations, of necessity they aggregated many variables into one. By today's standards these *mathematical modeling* tools were crude.

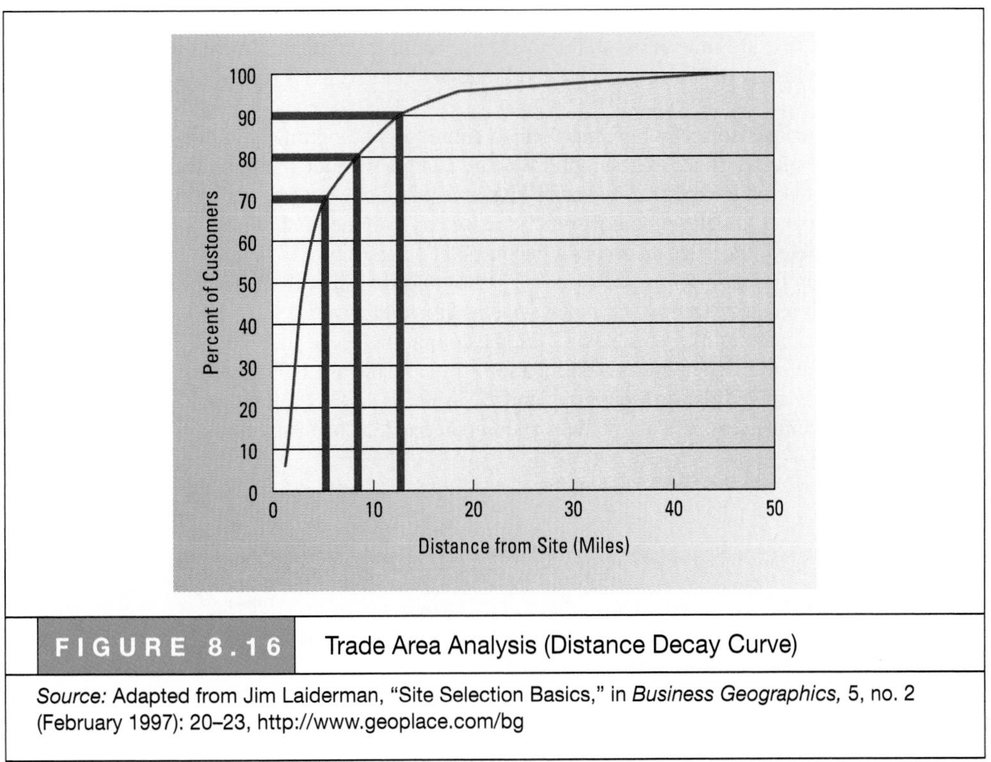

FIGURE 8.16 Trade Area Analysis (Distance Decay Curve)

Source: Adapted from Jim Laiderman, "Site Selection Basics," in *Business Geographics,* 5, no. 2 (February 1997): 20–23, http://www.geoplace.com/bg

Over time, as computing power became less expensive, decision-making models became more sophisticated. Today, computers can solve models with thousands of equations and variables. Decision makers can choose from a variety of mathematical techniques for maximizing service potential or minimizing costs. Generally speaking, however, these models do not effectively incorporate contingencies and uncertainty. For example, the weekly volume of shipments between two facilities is

TABLE 8.6 Factor Ratings for the Three Location Alternatives for Sparky's Fireworks

	Factor weight (On a scale of 1 to 10, how important is this factor? 1 is bad, 10 is good.)	**Location Rating** Converted from any previous measurement to a scale of 1 to 10, where 1 is bad and 10 is good.)		
Factor		**Town Square**	**Beside the Lake**	**Vet's Parking Lot on Hwy 27**
Safety	10	2	10	8
Convenience for customers	5	4	1	6
Cost of operation	7	1	7	6
Convenience for workers	3	8	2	2
Availability of workers	5	8	4	5
Forecasted sales volume	7	10	2	4
Impact of sales taxes on margin	4	1	10	10
Location Attractiveness Score (sum of the ratings multiplied by each corresponding factor weight)		185	234	251

often treated as a constant, rather than a variable. What is more, decision-making models usually quantify variables that are inherently qualitative. For instance, the quality of the water supply for a soda bottler or the loss of the customer's goodwill due to slow service is often translated into a financial cost.

Seldom is the answer to a complex problem so simple as one optimal solution. Decision makers need to know how much a model's assumptions could change without changing the optimal solution. This kind of information is provided by **sensitivity analysis.** For example, sensitivity analysis would allow a decision maker to determine how much the weekly volume of shipments between two facilities can increase before the selected location becomes less than optimal.

Though *computer simulation* models generally do not provide optimal solutions, they do allow decision makers to model extremely complex systems and to incorporate probabilistic and qualitative variables as well as quantitative variables. Given the computing speed that is available to virtually all businesses today, the user friendliness of simulation software, the availability of vast amounts of relevant information in spatial data warehouses, and the benefits of GIS, more and more managers are making their location decisions with the help of computerized decision support software.

active concept check <

Now let's take a moment to test your knowledge of the concepts you have studied in this section.

> Integrating Operational Decisions

The issues covered in this chapter—long-term capacity planning, facility location, and the tools for making decisions on facility location—are linked to the material covered in previous chapters. Chapter 2 introduced the topic of supply-chain management. This chapter focuses on the most obvious structural decisions, capacity and location decisions, that are required to build any link in a supply chain. Indeed, without insight into downstream customer expectations and upstream supply capabilities, long-term capacity and facility location decisions are difficult to make with any degree of confidence. In addition, the design of both the product-service bundle and the value-adding system (discussed in Chapters 4 and 7) directly impact capacity and location decisions. This is especially true for services where location and speed of response may serve as defining characteristics of the value offered to customers.

As for future chapters, this chapter's material is most closely related to that in Chapters 9, 10, and 11. As we point out in Chapter 9, layout decisions can have a large impact on the effective capacity of a facility. Chapter 10 describes job design issues including worker selection which can impact location decisions. Finally, Chapter 11 deals with intermediate range capacity planning decisions. These are naturally constrained by the longer-range capacity and location decisions of the firm.

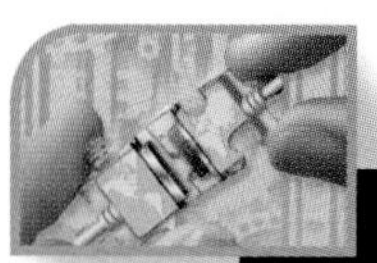

integrated OM <

Take a moment to apply what you've learned.

> Chapter Wrap-Up

This chapter describes the location and capacity decisions. These have long-term implications for the operating structure and profitability of every organization. Deciding how large a facility should be or where it should be located requires the attention of personnel in all of the functional areas of business, for such decisions have significant implications for every function in the business. Mistakes can damage the firm's profitability for decades, while good decisions can ensure a sustained competitive advantage. The uncertainty surrounding long-term forecasts complicates the decision-making task considerably. To safeguard against faulty decisions, some firms adopt a demand-cushioning or capacity-cushioning strategy. Others use scenario planning to identify capacity and location options that will prove workable in a variety of situations.

In selecting a place to do business, companies must consider global, regional, community, and site-specific issues. This range of issues is referred to as the location decision hierarchy. Firms whose operations add weight to their product-service bundle, either literally or metaphorically, often choose to locate close to their customers. Firms whose operations reduce the weight of the product-service bundle often locate close to their suppliers. A variety of supply-chain management issues enters into such decisions.

Capacity decisions are very closely related to location decisions. For instance, a company that has chosen to build a large plant in order to generate economies of scale is not likely to maintain a large number of locations. Firms that seek economies of scope rather than economies of scale might choose to maintain a large number of plants. The scale of an organization's facilities also helps to determine what elements of the location decision hierarchy are relevant to the decision.

Recently, geographic information systems have become available to managers who must choose facility locations. These tools allow managers to visualize the impact of their decisions through maps. They provide a much more effective method of analysis and communication of spatial data than the models available to decision makers in the past and are likely to be widely used. Other tools that are useful in making location decisions are the center of gravity method, trade area analysis, factor rating, mathematical modeling, and computerized simulation.

> end-of-chapter resources

- **Practice Quiz**
- **Key Terms**
- **Solved Problems**
- **Discussion Questions**
- **Problems**
- **Case 8.1: Contrasting Location Decisions for American and German Firms**
- **References**
- **Factory Tours**

Mathematical Optimization

SUPPLEMENT C

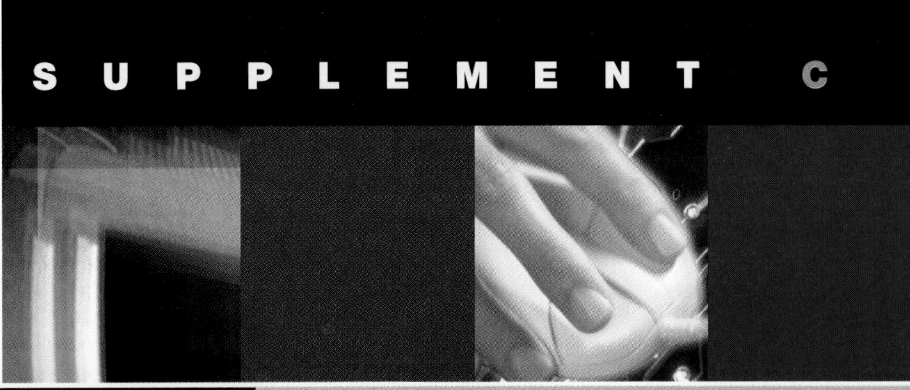

Supplement Outline

Introduction

Any decision-making situation involves two basic issues: What are we making decisions about, and how do we know that one decision alternative is better than another? Of increasing importance in management decision making is the use of mathematical models as part of the process of organizing data, generating decision alternatives, and evaluating those alternatives.

One particular type of mathematical model that has proven itself useful over and over again is **mathematical programming**. In this model type, values of one or more decision variables are chosen to maximize or minimize the value of an **objective function,** a mathematical expression that states how the variables contribute to achieving the decision maker's objective. Many types of mathematical programming models exist, some more useful in practice than others. In this supplement we will consider two: linear programming, which is an extremely powerful and widely used general model; and the transportation model, a special case of the linear programming model that has particular relevance to the facility location decision.

Linear Programming

Linear programming (LP) is a special type of mathematical programming model. It is used to determine the values of decision variables that will maximize or minimize the value of a linear objective function, subject to a set of linear equation or inequality constraints. A mathematical expression is linear if it is the sum of terms, each of which is a constant times a variable. For example, $5X + 3Y$ is a **linear expression,** but $3X^2 + 4XY - 6/Y$ is not, because it includes a square, a product of two variables, and a quotient.

While restricting both the objective function and the constraints to linear expressions may seem to limit the usefulness of linear programming, that is not the case. The relationships in many problems are sufficiently close to being linear that linear programming has been used extensively and profitably in practically every functional area of business.

A small-scale example of a very popular type of application—the product mix problem—will be used to illustrate the basic ideas of linear programming. In this application, the problem is to determine how many of each of several products to make so as to maximize their total contribution to profit and overhead, without overusing limited resources.

MODEL FORMULATION

Building a linear programming model begins with defining *decision variables* and formulating the objective function that is to be maximized or minimized. In addition, the *constraints* that limit the decision maker's freedom to choose values for the decision variables must also be formulated.

Example C.1

The furniture company for which Luis works has introduced a new, higher quality line of wooden office furniture, which has proven to be so popular that the company can sell all that it can produce. Unfortunately, from the company's perspective, the special type of wood used for this line is in limited supply, as are the special skills required for its manufacture. But the profit contribution on this line of furniture is higher than it is on the company's other lines. Management would like to maximize the line's profit contribution by producing the best possible combination of the two products in the line: desks and conference tables.

Profit contributions and resource usage for the two products in the line are as follows: Each desk requires 3 units of wood, 4 hours of assembly time, and 4 hours of finishing time and returns $110 to profit and overhead. Each table requires 2 units of wood, 2 hours of assembly time, and 6 hours of finishing time and returns $160 to profit and overhead. Ten units of wood, 15 hours of assembly time, and 24 hours of finishing time are available per day.

Formulate a linear programming model to determine how many desks and conference tables Luis's company should produce each day.

Solution:

First, define the decision variables as:

D = the number of desks to produce each day

T = the number of conference tables to produce each day

The objective function to be maximized is total contribution to profit, so:

$$\text{Maximize } 110D + 160T$$

Three resources are available only in limited supply: wood, assembly time, and finishing time. Set up a constraint for each, stating that the amount of resource used will be no more than the amount available.

$$\text{Wood: } 3D + 2T \leq 10$$

$$\text{Assembly: } 4D + 2T \leq 15$$

$$\text{Finishing: } 4D + 6T \leq 24$$

To illustrate the rationale of these constraints, let us consider the wood constraint in detail: Each desk produced requires 3 units of wood; thus, the total amount of wood used in making D desks is 3D units. Similarly, each table produced requires 2 units of wood, so the total amount of wood used in making T tables is 2T units. Adding these together, the total amount of wood used in producing D desks and T tables is $3D + 2T$ *units.* Since only 10 units of wood are available, the company must choose values for D and T that will result in $3D + 2T \leq 10$.

The reasoning behind the assembly and finishing constraints is similar.

Finally, producing negative quantities of these two products obviously makes no sense, so add two non-negativity constraints:

$$D \geq 0, T \geq 0$$

active exercise

Take a moment to apply what you've learned.

GRAPHICAL SOLUTION

When a linear programming problem has only two decision variables, we can solve it graphically. This is obviously not important for solving realistic problems, but the graph helps us to understand some of the basic ideas associated with the solution process and the solution.

Example C.2

Solve the problem in Example C.1 graphically.

Solution:
First set up a two-dimensional solution space with variable axes at right angles to one another, as in Figure C.1. Since the decision variables must have nonnegative values, we only need to concern ourselves with the upper right-hand or nonnegative quadrant of the space, which is shown by leaving only that area unshaded.

The next step is to graph each of the constraints, which is done in the first three panels of Figure C.2. To graph an inequality constraint, first graph the equation and then shade the part of the space that does not satisfy the inequality. For example, in Figure C.2(a), for the wood constraint, graph the line for the equation $3D + 2T = 10$. To determine where the line crosses the D axis, set $T = 0$ and solve the equation to get $D = 3.333$. To determine where the line crosses the T axis, set $D = 0$ and solve the equation to get $T = 5.0$. Next, determine which side of the line satisfies the inequality $3D + 2T < 10$. The easiest way to do this is to check whether the origin, where $D = T = 0$, satisfies the inequality. It does, so all the points on the line and in the space below it satisfy the constraint, and all the points above the line do not. Shade the area above the line, as in Figure C.2(a), to show that those points do not satisfy the constraint. Parts (b) and (c) of Figure C.2 are done the same way.

Since the solution must satisfy all the constraints, all three lines should actually be drawn on the same graph. The three individual constraints are combined into one graph in Figure C.2(d). The unshaded part of that diagram, along with its edges, represents the **feasible set** for the problem—that is, the set of points that satisfy all the constraints.

The next step is to use the objective function to identify which feasible solution is *optimal.* Since the objective function is not an equation or an inequality, it cannot be graphed. However, if we set the objective function equal to a specific number, we can graph that equation. Figure C.3

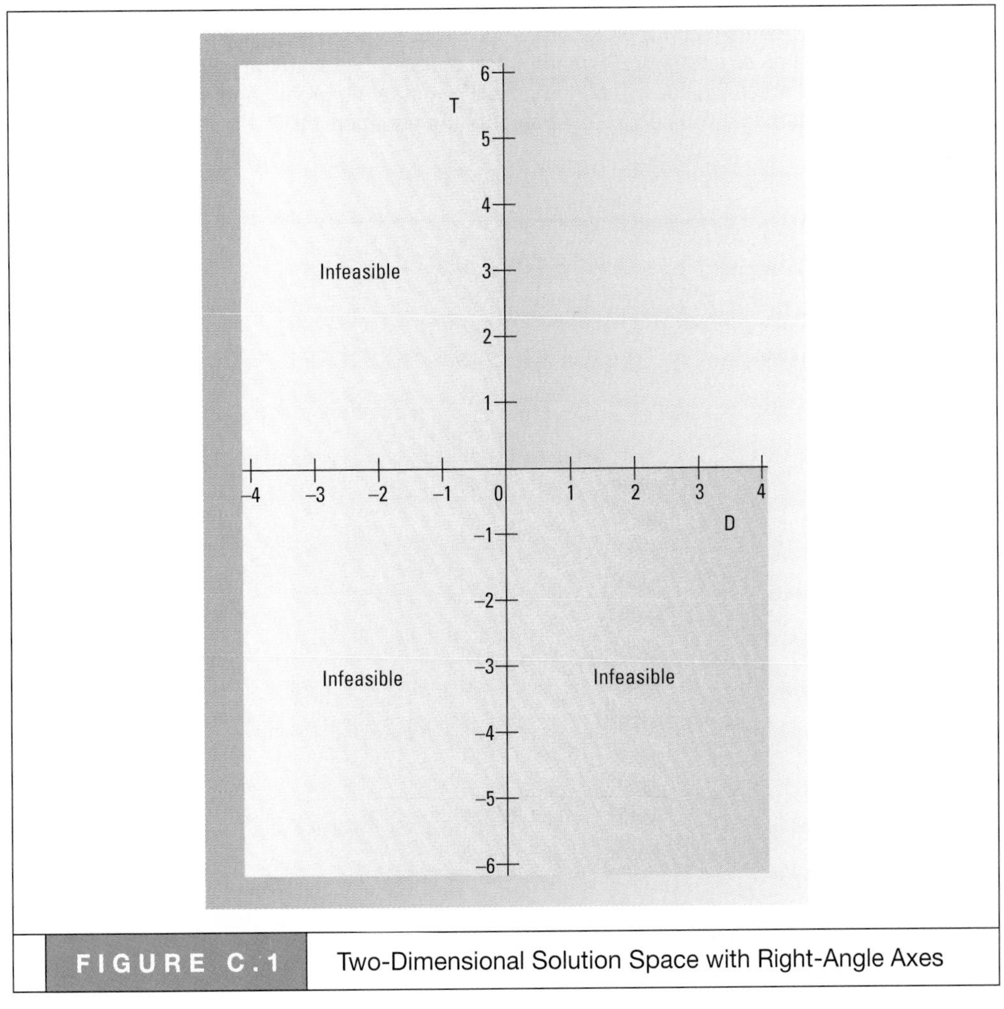

FIGURE C.1 Two-Dimensional Solution Space with Right-Angle Axes

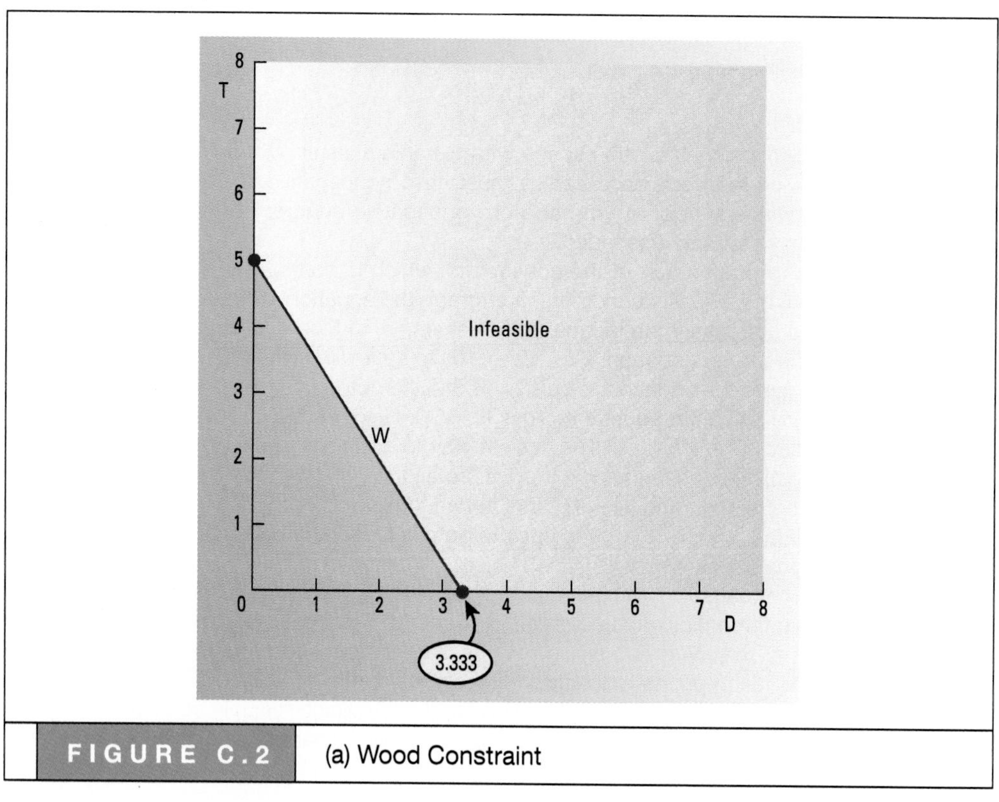

FIGURE C.2 (a) Wood Constraint

shows the feasible set along with three possible objective function lines. The line closest to the origin, labeled 320, represents the equation $110D + 160T = 320$. Any point on that line represents a solution that gives a total profit contribution of \$320. Because the line lies within the feasible set (unshaded area), we know that it is possible to attain a profit contribution of \$320. The line farthest from the origin, labeled 800, represents the equation $110D + 160T = 800$. Because

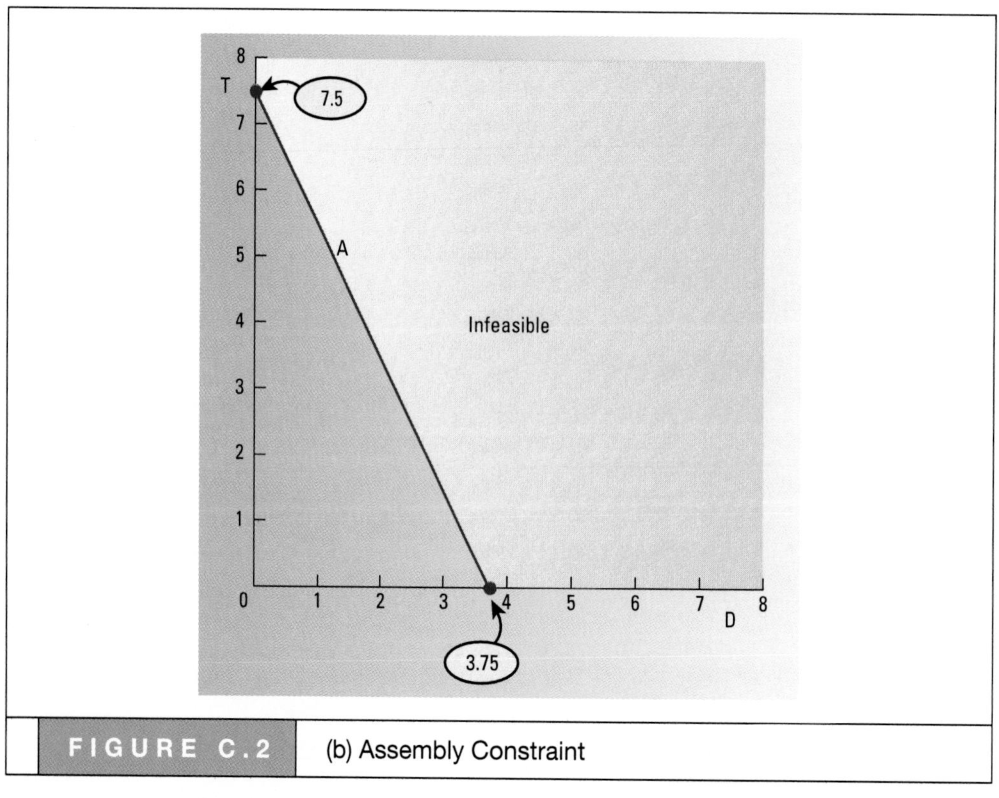

FIGURE C.2 (b) Assembly Constraint

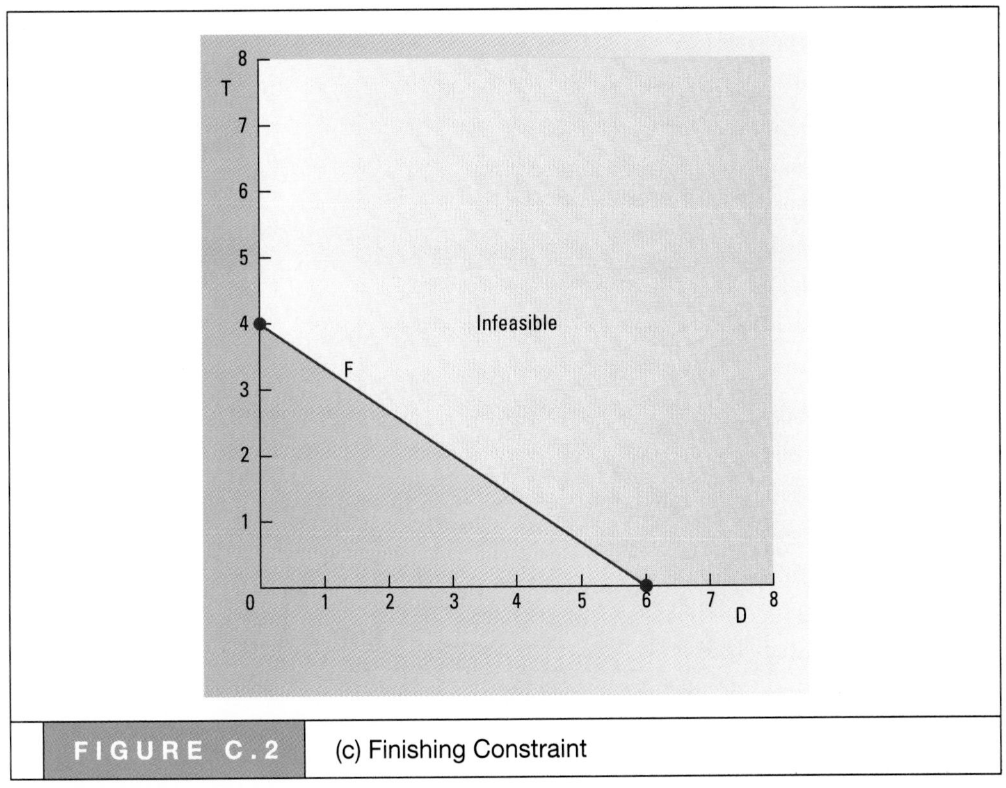

FIGURE C.2 (c) Finishing Constraint

this line lies entirely outside the feasible set, we know that a total profit contribution of $800 is not possible.

These two lines show us two other things that are crucial to determining the location of the optimal solution. First, they are *parallel,* which means that any other line $110D + 160T = number$ will be parallel to them. Second, the line with the higher number on the right side lies farther from the origin. To maximize the value of the objective function, we must find a line that is between

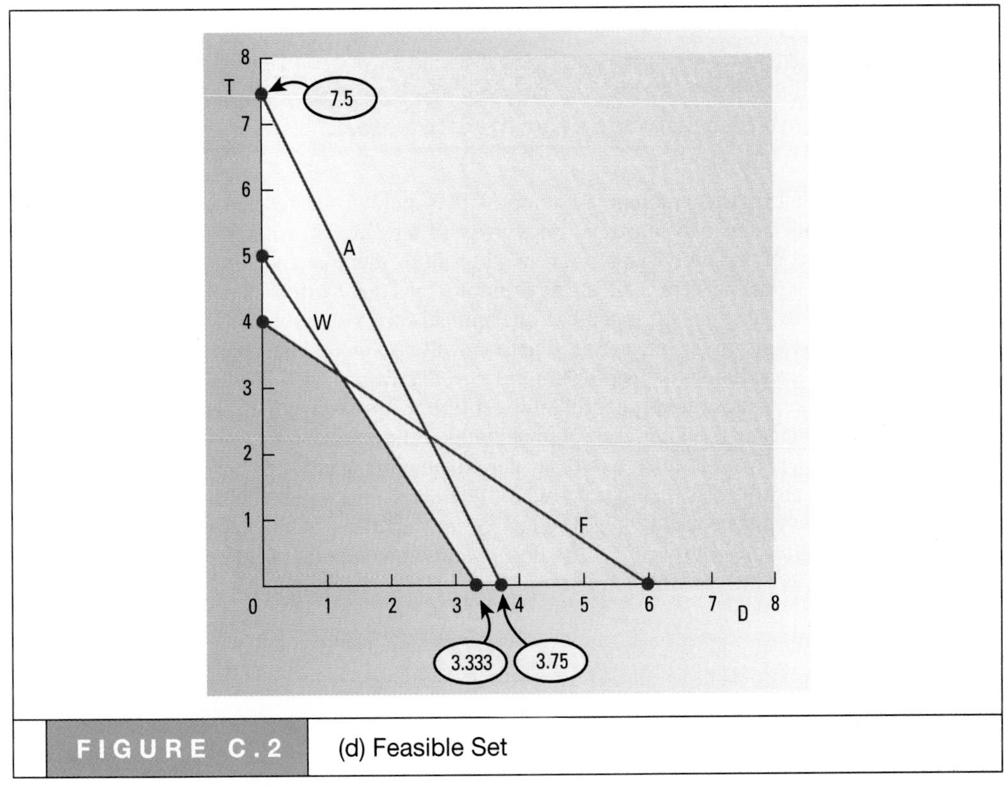

FIGURE C.2 (d) Feasible Set

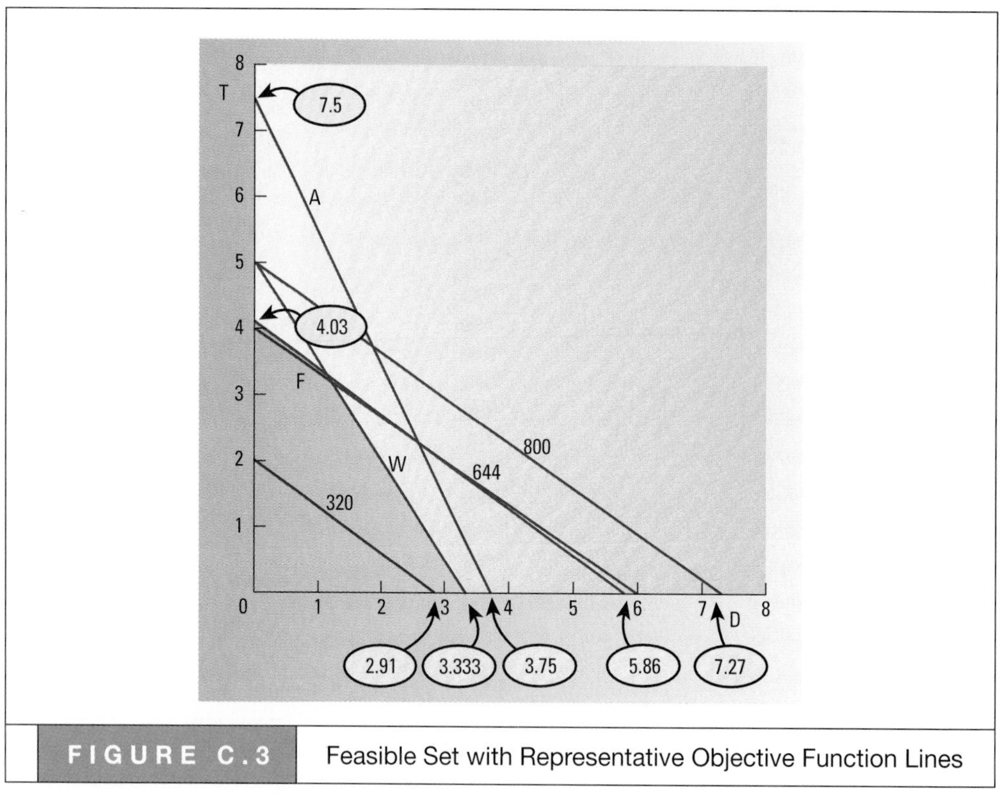

FIGURE C.3 Feasible Set with Representative Objective Function Lines

and parallel to these two, as far from the origin as possible, but still passes through some part of the feasible set. That line is the third line on the graph, labeled 644. The point where that line passes through a corner of the feasible set, at the intersection of the W (wood) and F (finishing) equation lines, is the optimal solution to the problem. Solving the W and F equations simultaneously gives the optimal solution: D = 1.2, T = 3.2, which gives a profit contribution of $644.[1]

active exercise

Take a moment to apply what you've learned.

Note that the solution to the problem in Example C.2 is that it is located at a corner of the feasible set—that is, at a point where two constraint lines cross. (There are five constraint lines: the two axes plus the lines labeled W, A, and F.) This is a general result: If there is an optimal solution (and there will always be one, as long as there is a feasible solution), then there will be one at a corner of the feasible set. In some cases there may be more than one optimal corner solution; if so, they will be at adjacent corners and all points on the line connecting them will also be optimal solutions.

Note also that in the solution to this problem, *the variable values are not integers*. For purposes of actually using a linear programming problem's solution, this may or may not be a problem. Obviously, Luis's company cannot make fractional units of furniture, so the optimal solution cannot be implemented on a daily basis. Over a five-day period, however, Luis could implement this solution by making 6 desks and 16 tables. In other problems, fractional units will make sense. Although linear programming does not always yield integer values for the variables, an extension of linear programming, called *integer linear programming* (IP), does. Many LP computer packages can solve IP problems, although they will be more restricted in size and will take longer to solve.

[1]Verify that the solution D = 1.2 and T = 3.2 is a feasible solution and does give a total profit contribution of 644 by substituting those values into the three constraints and the objective function.

USING EXCEL'S SOLVER

If a linear programming model includes more than two decision variables, then a systematic, computerized solution procedure is needed. The standard computerized LP solution procedure is a variation of the simplex method, in which the search for the optimal solution starts at the origin and follows a path from corner to adjacent corner of the solution space until it reaches a corner that it recognizes as being optimal. At that point it stops. Excel's **Solver** uses a different search procedure, a variation on a more general procedure that can also be used with nonlinear mathematical programming problems.

Using Solver to solve a linear programming problem is a straightforward procedure. First, set the problem up in a spreadsheet. Next, select Tools from the menu, select Solver from the pull-down menu, and fill in the dialog box. In addition to identifying the *target cell* and the *changing cells,* you must also fill in the *constraints* box. This is done by clicking on the Add button next to it and marking a constraint, repeating the process as many times as necessary. Once the dialog box is complete, click on the Options button and check Assume Linear Model. Click OK and then click Solve. When the Solver Results box appears, mark the reports you wish to receive and click OK.

Example C.3

Use Excel's Solver to solve the LP model in Example C.1. Determine how many desks and conference tables to produce and what the total profit contribution will be. Also determine how much of each resource is used and how much is left over.

Solution:
First set up a spreadsheet, as shown in Exhibit C.1. Columns C and D correspond to the two products, with the changing cells (decision variables) for desks in cell C5 and for tables in cell D5. The products' profit contributions are shown in row 8. Rows 15 through 17 contain the resource information, with the amounts used per unit of product in columns C and D of those rows. The total amount of each resource used by the solution in cells C5 and D5 is shown in a cell in column E. Cell E15 shows the amount of wood used by the solution in cells C5 and D5. The formula in cell E15 is *=SUMPRODUCT($C$5:$D$5,C15:D15),* which translates into *3 × DESKS + 2 × TABLES.* This formula is then copied into E16 and E17, so that cell E16 shows the amount of assembly time used and cell E17 shows the amount of finishing time used. The available amounts of the resources are given in F15 through F17. Finally, the total contribution to profit and overhead is given in the target cell F6, the formula for which is *=SUMPRODUCT(C5:D5,C8:D8).*

Next click on Tools on the menu bar and select Solver. The results of filling in the Solver dialog box are in Exhibit C.2. The top part should be obvious. The target cell is F6, where the for-

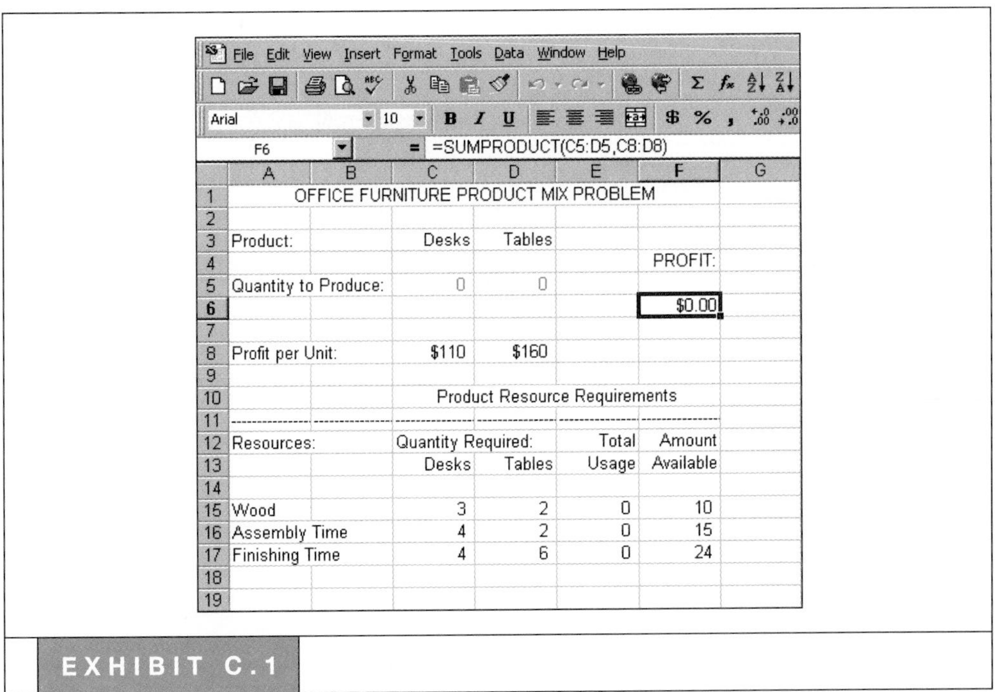

	A	B	C	D	E	F	G
1	OFFICE FURNITURE PRODUCT MIX PROBLEM						
2							
3	Product:		Desks	Tables			
4						PROFIT:	
5	Quantity to Produce:		0	0			
6						$0.00	
7							
8	Profit per Unit:		$110	$160			
9							
10			Product Resource Requirements				
11							
12	Resources:		Quantity Required:		Total	Amount	
13			Desks	Tables	Usage	Available	
14							
15	Wood		3	2	0	10	
16	Assembly Time		4	2	0	15	
17	Finishing Time		4	6	0	24	
18							
19							

EXHIBIT C.1

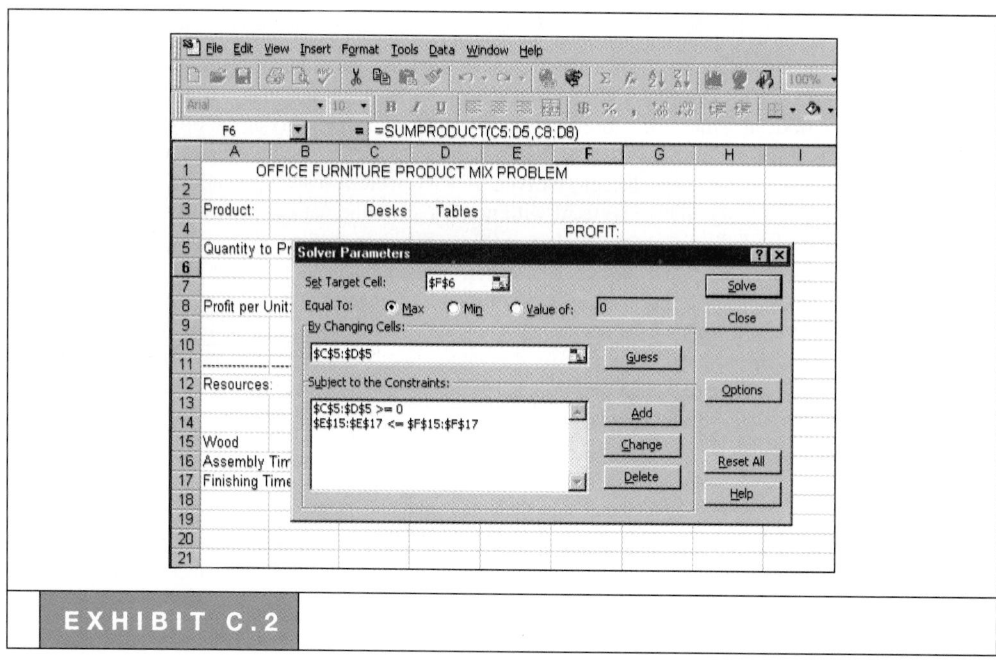

EXHIBIT C.2

mula for the total profit contribution is located, and the changing cells are C5 and D5, where the values for the amounts of desks and tables to produce appear. The Constraints box is filled in as follows: Click Add. Then click in the left panel, mark E15:E17, select <= from the relationship box, click in the right panel, and mark F15:F17. Doing this sets up the three resource constraints. To include the nonnegativity constraints, click Add again. Then click in the left panel, mark C5:D5 (the changing cells), select >= from the relationship box, click in the right panel, and type 0.

You are now ready to solve the problem. Click on Options, check Assume Linear Model, click OK, and click Solve. In the Solver Results box, mark Keep Solver Solution and select the Answer and Sensitivity Reports; click OK. The resulting spreadsheet is shown in Exhibit C.3, which gives the optimal solution, as does the Answer Report shown in Exhibit C.4. The optimal solution, which yields a total profit contribution of $644, is to produce 1.2 desks and 3.2 tables. In Exhibit

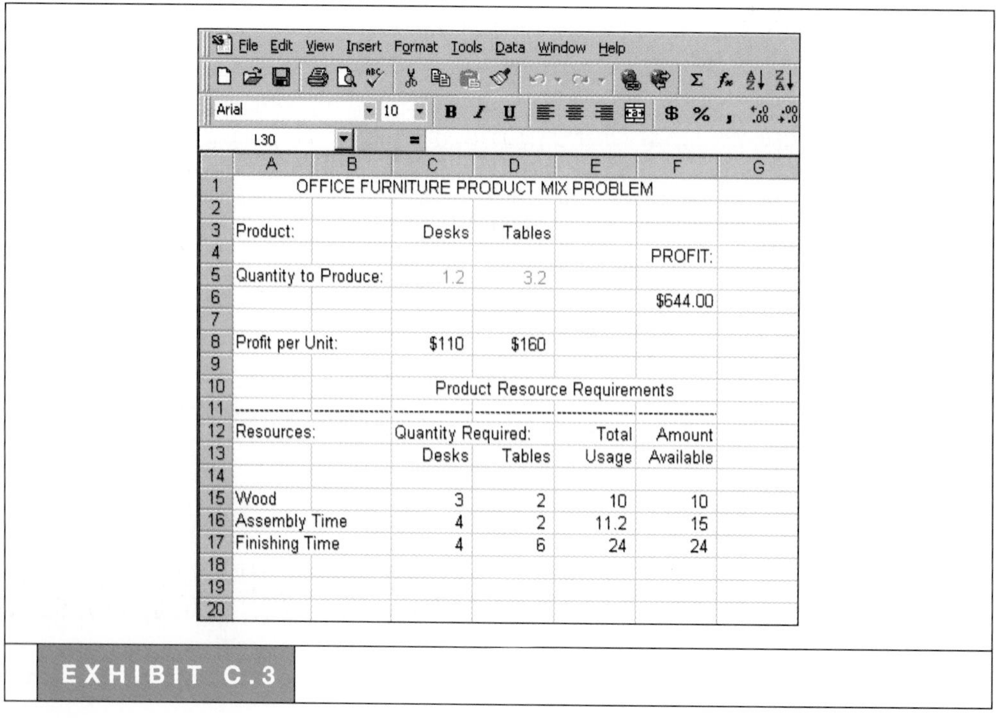

	A	B	C	D	E	F	G
1	OFFICE FURNITURE PRODUCT MIX PROBLEM						
2							
3	Product:		Desks	Tables			
4						PROFIT:	
5	Quantity to Produce:		1.2	3.2			
6						$644.00	
7							
8	Profit per Unit:		$110	$160			
9							
10			Product Resource Requirements				
11							
12	Resources:		Quantity Required:		Total	Amount	
13			Desks	Tables	Usage	Available	
14							
15	Wood		3	2	10	10	
16	Assembly Time		4	2	11.2	15	
17	Finishing Time		4	6	24	24	
18							
19							
20							

EXHIBIT C.3

Microsoft Excel 8.0a Answer Report
Worksheet: [Furniture.xls]Sheet1
Report Created: 8/10/98 8:15:54 AM

Target Cell (Max)

Cell	Name	Original Value	Final Value
$F$6	PROFIT:	$0.00	$644.00

Adjustable Cells

Cell	Name	Original Value	Final Value
$C$5	DESKS	0	1.2
$D$5	TABLES	0	3.2

Constraints

Cell	Name	Cell Value	Formula	Status	Slack
$E$15	Wood Usage	10	$E$15<=$F$15	Binding	0
$E$16	Assembly Time Usage	11.2	$E$16<=$F$16	Not Binding	3.8
$E$17	Finishing Time Usage	24	$E$17<=$F$17	Binding	0
$C$5	DESKS	1.2	$C$5>=0	Not Binding	1.2
$D$5	TABLES	3.2	$D$5>=0	Not Binding	3.2

EXHIBIT C.4

C.4 we see that this solution uses all 10 units of wood, so that the amount of wood left over (the slack for wood) is 0. Further, the amount of assembly time used is 11.2 hours, with assembly time slack = 3.8 hours, and the amount of finishing time used is 24 hours, with finishing time slack = 0 hours.

> active exercise

Take a moment to apply what you've learned.

SHADOW PRICES AND SENSITIVITY ANALYSIS

While all the numbers in a linear programming model are treated as though they are exact and known for certain, that is often not the case in reality; they are only estimates or may change over time. As is the case for any decision model, we are interested in knowing how much these numbers can change without changing the solution and what the implications of changing any of these numbers would be. That is, we are interested in the *sensitivity* of the solution to the numbers used. We will be looking at three questions:

1. How much can we change a decision variable's objective function coefficient value before it would change the solution?
2. How would changing the limit (right-hand side value) of a constraint affect the value of the objective function?
3. By how much can we change that limit and still have the same effect?

OBJECTIVE FUNCTION SENSITIVITY

Looking at the graph for the furniture problem (Example C.1) in Figure C.3, it should be obvious that if we make the objective function line slightly flatter or steeper, we will still get the same feasible set corner as the optimal solution. The objective function line will become flatter if we decrease the coefficient of D (desks) to less than $110 or increase the coefficient of T (tables) to more than $160. Similarly, the objective function line will become steeper if we do the opposite—increase the coefficient of D or decrease the coefficient of T.

Looking more closely at Figure C.3, we can see that the maximum amount by which we can flatten the objective function line and still get the same optimal solution is to make it coincide with line F. If the objective function line gets any flatter than line F, the location of the optimal solution will shift to the point where line F crosses the vertical axis, and the new optimal solution will be D = 0 and T = 4. In the same way, we can also see that the steepest we can make the objective function line and still get the same optimal solution is to make it coincide with line W. If the objective function line gets any steeper than line W, the location of the optimal solution will shift to the point where line W crosses the horizontal axis, and the new optimal solution will be D = 3.333 and T = 0.

The slope of a straight line (that is, how flat or steep it is) is determined by the ratio of the coefficients of its two variables. Assuming that we do not change the objective function coefficient of T (keeping it at $160), the smallest we can make the coefficient of D without making the objective function line flatter than line F is $106.667—a (maximum) decrease of $3.333 from the current value of $110. Similarly, the largest we can make the coefficient of D without making the objective function line steeper than line W is $240—a (maximum) increase of $130 from $110. These maximum decrease and increase values may be found in the desks line of the Sensitivity Report from Solver shown in Exhibit C.5. Thus the **insensitivity range** for the desks objective function coefficient is $106.667 to $240. As long as the profit contribution of a table stays at $160, the profit contribution of a desk can be anywhere in this range and the optimal solution will still be to produce 1.2 desks and 3.2 tables. The *total* profit contribution will, of course, change to reflect the new unit contributions.

We can apply exactly the same analysis to the tables line in Exhibit C.5. Assuming we keep the objective function coefficient of D at $110, the maximum amount by which we can decrease the coefficient of T (from $160) without making the objective function line steeper than line W is $86.667 to $73.333. Similarly, the maximum amount by which we can increase the coefficient of T without making the objective function line flatter than line F is $5 to $165. Thus, the insensitivity range for the desks objective function coefficient is $73.333 to $165. As long as the profit contribution of a desk stays at $110, the profit contribution of a table can be anywhere in this range, and the optimal solution will still be to produce 1.2 desks and 3.2 tables.

Microsoft Excel 8.0a Sensitivity Report
Worksheet: [Furniture.xls]Sheet1
Report Created: 8/10/98 8:15:54 AM

Adjustable Cells

Cell	Name	Final Value	Reduced Cost	Objective Coefficient	Allowable Increase	Allowable Decrease
$C$5	DESKS	1.2	0	110	130	3.333333333
$D$5	TABLES	3.2	0	160	5	86.66666667

Constraints

Cell	Name	Final Value	Shadow Price	Constraint R.H. Side	Allowable Increase	Allowable Decrease
$E$15	Wood Usage	10	2	10	2.375	2
$E$16	Assembly Time Usage	11.2	0	15	1E+30	3.8
$E$17	Finishing Time Usage	24	26	24	6	10.66666667

EXHIBIT C.5

CHANGING A CONSTRAINT'S LIMIT: THE SHADOW PRICE

Looking again at the graph for the furniture problem in Figure C.3, it is obvious that changing a constraint's limit or right-hand side, which will move that constraint's equation line, may or may not make any difference in the solution, depending on which line is moved.

Since the location of the current optimal solution is the point where the W and F constraint lines cross, moving either of those lines by changing the amount of either wood or finishing time available will lead to a new optimal solution. This new solution will have a different objective function value. The value will be better if the change in the constraint increases the size of the feasible set, so that a new, better solution can be found; it will be worse if the change reduces the size of the feasible set, so that the previously optimal solution is eliminated.

On the other hand, the current optimal solution is well inside the feasible area for the assembly time constraint (there is assembly time slack), so moving line A in toward the origin a little (by reducing the available assembly time slightly) or moving line A away from the origin (by increasing the available assembly time) will not make a new optimal solution necessary. Since the optimal solution will not change, the objective function value will not change either.

The change in the value of the objective function that results from a one-unit change in the right-hand side of a constraint (while holding everything else constant) is called the constraint's shadow price, marginal cost, or marginal value. The shadow price of a constraint is very useful because it tells us the maximum amount we should be willing to pay for a resource, *over and above the price* used in determining the objective function coefficient values, either to get an additional unit of that resource or to avoid losing one.

Graphically, the shadow price can be found by regraphing the problem with the new constraint line given by the new value of the resource's availability, resolving the problem, and computing the amount by which the objective function value has changed. *Within limits,* we would find that the change is *exactly the same* (although of opposite sign) whether the right-hand side of the constraint is increased or decreased.

If Excel's Solver is used to solve the model, the shadow price can be found in the Constraints section of the Sensitivity Report. For example, in Exhibit C.5 the shadow price for wood is $2 per unit; the shadow price for finishing time is $26 per hour. The shadow price for assembly time is 0, since changing the location of line A slightly will not change the optimal solution or the objective function value.

CHANGING A CONSTRAINT'S LIMIT: THE RANGE

While increasing the amount of wood available from 10 units to 11 would increase the total profit contribution by $2 (from $644 to $646) and a second increase from 11 units to 12 would further increase the total profit contribution by an additional $2 (to $648), a third increase from 12 units to 13 would *not* raise the total profit contribution to $650. The graph in Figure C.4 makes the reason clear: There is not enough assembly time to take full advantage of that 13th unit of wood. In fact, given that there are only 15 hours of assembly time available, the maximum amount of wood that could be used by the optimal solution when 13 units of wood are available ($D = 2.625$ and $T = 2.25$, for a profit of $648.75) is only 12.375 units. Thus, the maximum increase in the amount of available wood for which the shadow price will be $2 is $12.375 - 10 = 2.375$ units. Similarly, by moving the W line closer to the origin, we find that the maximum decrease in the amount of available wood for which the shadow price would be $2 per unit is 2 units (from 10 down to 8).

Just as the shadow price for a constraint can be found in Solver's Sensitivity Report, so also is the range within which that shadow price holds. Referring to the "allowable increase" and "allowable decrease" columns in Exhibit C.5, the range for the wood constraint goes from a minimum of $10 - 2 = 8$ units to a maximum of $10 + 2.375 = 12.375$ units. Assuming nothing else changes, any change in the amount of wood available within that range will have a marginal value of $2 per unit. The results for the finishing time constraint are determined in the same way.

The situation with the assembly time constraint is a little different. Since only 11.2 of the 15 available assembly time hours are actually being used by the current solution, a reduction in the available assembly time to that level will have no effect on the objective function value (the shadow price will be 0). The maximum reduction for a constraint with slack is equal to the amount of slack, in this case, 3.8 hours, for a lower limit of 11.2 hours. Increasing the amount of assembly time available will have no effect at all, other than to increase the slack on a one-for-one basis. Thus, the upper limit for the assembly time constraint's range is ∞.[2]

[2]Excel shows ∞ as 1E+30, a very large number (1 followed by 30 zeros).

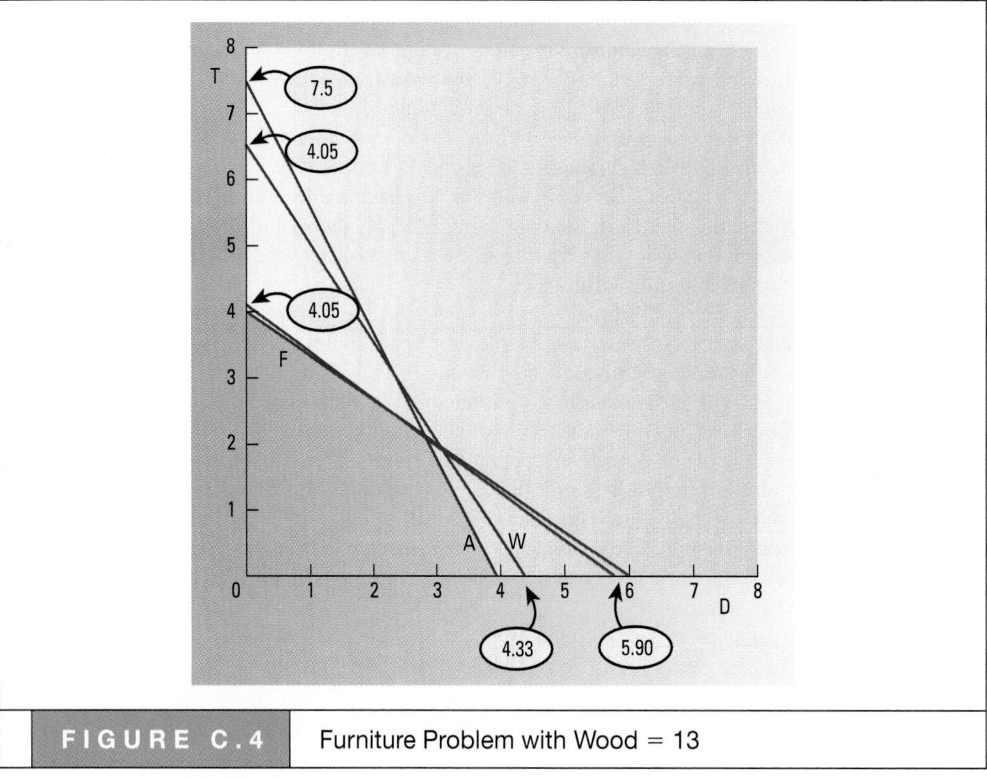

FIGURE C.4 Furniture Problem with Wood = 13

Example C.4

(Refer to Example C.1.) Luis's company would like to increase the production of the new office furniture line and the profit contribution from it. While the supplier cannot provide additional wood in the near future, employees can be asked to work overtime. What is the maximum amount the company should pay for overtime in the two departments, and how much overtime should be worked in each?

Solution:

From the Sensitivity Report in Exhibit C.5, we find that there is already slack in the assembly time constraint, with a shadow price of 0; working any overtime in assembly makes no sense. For finishing time, the shadow price is $26 within a range of 13.333 (24 - 10.667) to 30 (24 + 6) hours. Paying an overtime premium of up to $26 per hour for a maximum of 6 additional hours of finishing time would make sense.

active exercise

Take a moment to apply what you've learned.

The Transportation Model

Many companies produce the same product at several factories and distribute it through a number of different warehouses. In such systems, a basic problem is to determine how much of the product to ship from each of the factories to each of the warehouses. The **transportation model** is a special type of linear programming model that can be useful in solving this type of problem.

The basic structure of a transportation model is as follows: A given product is available in specific limited quantities at each of a number of sources (for example, factories) and is required in specified amounts at each of a number of **destinations** (for example, warehouses). The cost of shipping a unit from each source to each destination is known and is the same for every unit shipped on that route.

The problem is to determine how much to ship from each **source** to each destination so as to minimize the total shipping cost.

MODEL FORMULATION

Because of the relatively simple nature of the problem, a special format—called a **transportation tableau**—is used to summarize the information for a transportation model. A transportation tableau is a matrix with a row for each source and a column for each destination. Written in each cell of the matrix is the cost of shipping a unit from the row's source to the destination's column. Written to the right of each row is the availability at that row's source, and at the bottom of each column is the requirement at that column's destination.

Example C.5

Fred's company produces pagers at three plants in the Southwest (SW), Midwest (MW), and Southeast (SE). The SW plant has a capacity of 100,000 units per month, while each of the other two plants has a capacity of 150,000 units per month. The products are distributed nationally through warehouses in California, which has monthly demand of 70,000 units, Texas (40,000), Michigan (50,000), North Carolina (70,000), and Pennsylvania (90,000). The cost (in $100) of shipping 1,000 units from each plant to each warehouse is given in Table C.1. Formulate a transportation tableau to summarize the information about the production and distribution of pagers in Fred's company.

TABLE C.1 Unit Transportation Costs for Example C.3

	Warehouse				
Plant	CA	TX	MI	NC	PA
SW	10	8	13	16	18
MW	12	7	6	9	9
SE	17	12	10	5	9

Solution:
There are three sources (SW, MW, and SE) and five destinations (CA, TX, MI, NC, and PA), so we need a three-by-five matrix, as shown in Figure C.5. The plants' capacities, in thousands of units, appear along the right edge of the matrix. The warehouses' requirements, also in thousands of units, appear along the bottom edge of the matrix. The unit costs from Table C.1 appear in the squares in the upper right corner of each cell of the matrix. (At this point ignore the red numbers.)

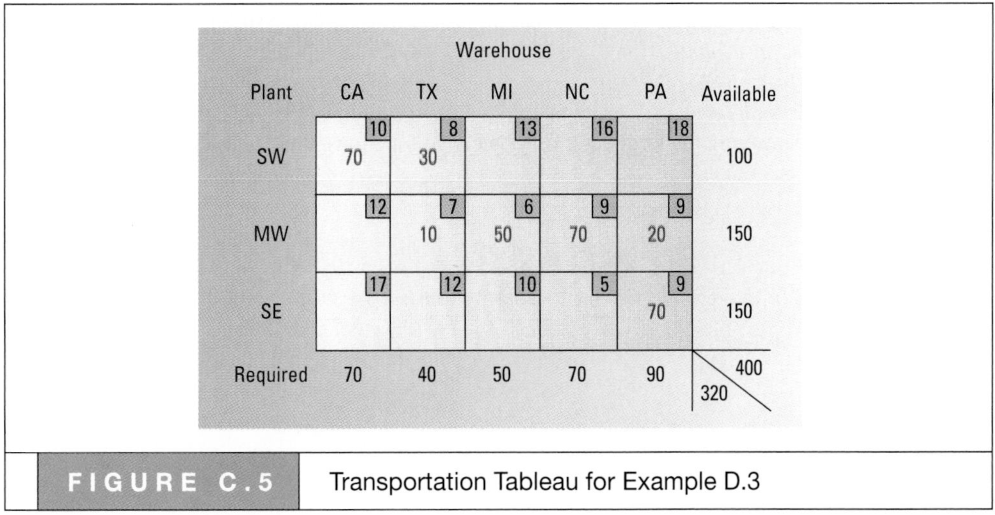

FIGURE C.5 Transportation Tableau for Example D.3

active exercise <

Take a moment to apply what you've learned.

If the total units available at the sources equals the total units required at the destinations, a transportation model is said to be *balanced.* The model in Example C.2 is *unbalanced* because the total units available (400) is more than the total units required (320). If we wished, we could transform the tableau in Figure C.5 into a balanced tableau by adding a sixth column, called a *dummy* destination, that would absorb the excess supply of 80 units. The costs for that column would all be 0 since "shipping" from a real source to the dummy destination means not actually producing and shipping those units. (Similarly, if the total units available at the sources were less than the total units required at the destinations, then we could add a dummy source to provide the shortage, again with 0 costs. "Shipping" from the dummy source to a real destination would then represent failing to meet demand.) We will not include the dummy destination here because it is not needed for our solution procedure.[3]

MODEL SOLUTION

To solve a transportation model, we must assign values to the cells of the transportation tableau (the source/destination shipments) that meet the following two criteria:

1. The sum of the values assigned to a row is equal to the row's availability (less than or equal to if total supply exceeds total demand).
2. The sum of the values assigned to a column is equal to the column's requirements (less than or equal to if total demand exceeds total supply).

The red values in the cells in Figure C.5 constitute a solution to the problem in Example C.5. By multiplying each shipment by its unit cost and summing we get a total cost of $2,750. As we shall soon see, however, this solution is not optimal.

While it is possible to find an optimal solution to a relatively small transportation model like the one in Example C.5 by hand, the work can become tedious. We will instead solve this problem using Excel's Solver.

The first step in using Solver to find an optimal solution is to set up a spreadsheet that contains the relevant information and spaces for the solution. Instead of the tableau in Figure C.5, in which both the unit shipping costs and the shipping amounts were entered into the same cell, we will use two matrixes, one for the costs and one for the shipments. The spreadsheet in Exhibit C.6 contains the information for the problem in Example C.5. The unit cost matrix, taken from Table C.1, is in B6:F8, with the plant names in column A and the warehouse names in row 5. The shipment matrix, which will be the changing cells for Solver, is in B13:F15, with the plant names in column A and the warehouse names in row 12. The total amounts shipped from the plants will be shown in G13:G15; each is the sum of the shipment cells on its left. The units available are shown in the cells next to these in H13:H15. The total amounts shipped to the warehouses will be shown in B16:F16; each is the sum of the shipment cells above it. The requirements are shown below them in B17:F17. Finally, the total cost, which will be the target cell for Solver, is shown in B19. The formula in that cell is *=SUMPRODUCT(B6:F8,B13:F15).*

Once the spreadsheet has been set up, the procedure for using Solver to get the optimal solution is basically the same as for a regular LP problem, as described earlier. Click on Tools and Solver and fill in the dialog box, identifying the target cell (the objective function), the changing cells (the decision variables), and the constraints.

Example C.6

Refer to Example C.5. Use Excel's Solver to determine the optimal distribution pattern for pagers at Fred's company.

[3]However, you will find it included in many software packages for solving transportation models.

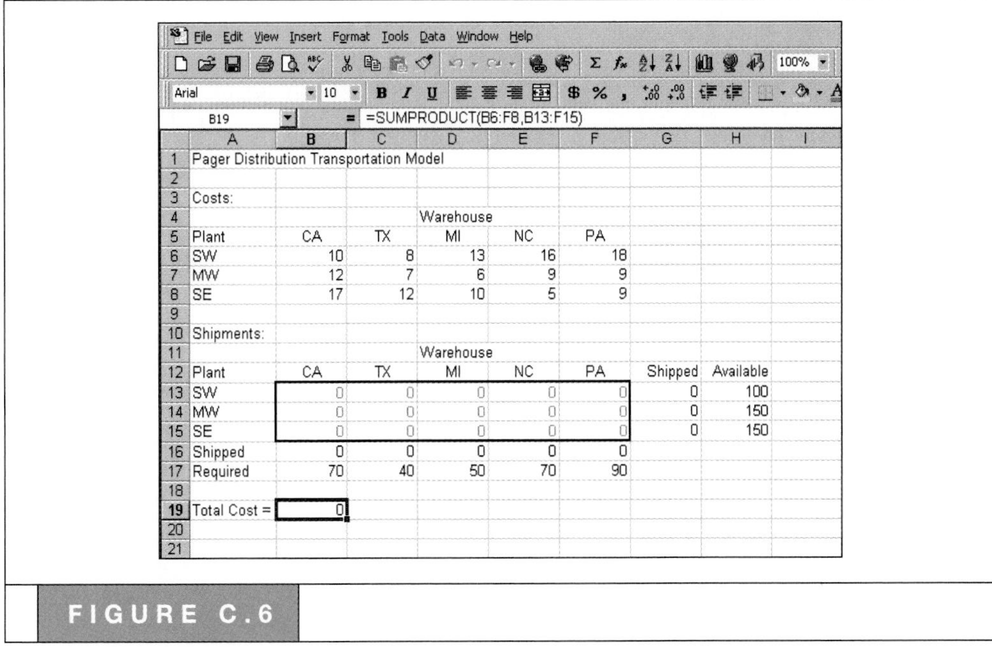

	A	B	C	D	E	F	G	H
1	Pager Distribution Transportation Model							
2								
3	Costs:							
4				Warehouse				
5	Plant	CA	TX	MI	NC	PA		
6	SW	10	8	13	16	18		
7	MW	12	7	6	9	9		
8	SE	17	12	10	5	9		
9								
10	Shipments:							
11				Warehouse				
12	Plant	CA	TX	MI	NC	PA	Shipped	Available
13	SW	0	0	0	0	0	0	100
14	MW	0	0	0	0	0	0	150
15	SE	0	0	0	0	0	0	150
16	Shipped	0	0	0	0	0		
17	Required	70	40	50	70	90		
18								
19	Total Cost =	0						

FIGURE C.6

Solution:
The completed dialog box for the problem in the spreadsheet in Exhibit C.6 is shown in Exhibit C.7. The target cell is B19, the total cost. The changing cells are B13:F15, the shipment matrix. There are three sets of constraints:

1. Do not ship more units from a source than are available there. This constraint is handled by specifying that *G13:G15 <= H13:H15.*
2. Ship to each destination the number of units required there. This constraint is handled by specifying that *B16:F16 = B17:F17.*
3. All variables must be nonnegative. This constraint is handled by specifying that *B13:F15 >= 0.*

Once the dialog box has been filled in, click on Options, check Assume Linear Model, and click OK; then click on Solve. Choose the Solver Reports desired (Solution and Sensitivity) and click OK.

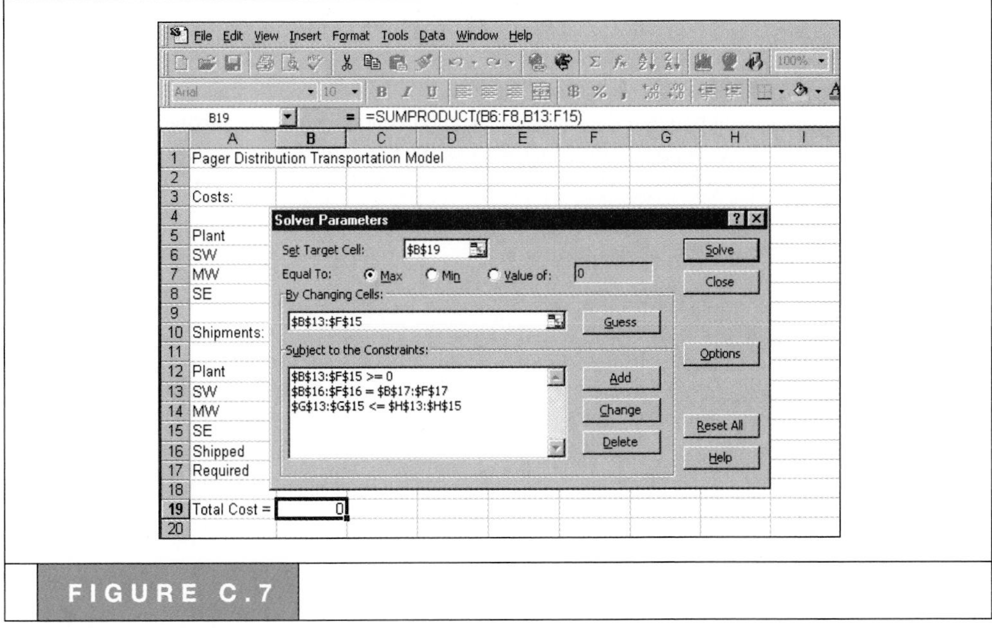

FIGURE C.7

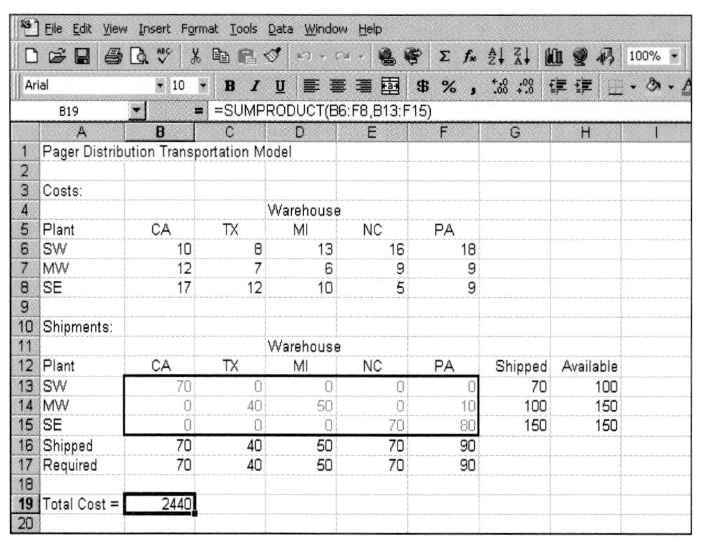

B19 =SUMPRODUCT(B6:F8,B13:F15)

	A	B	C	D	E	F	G	H	I
1	Pager Distribution Transportation Model								
2									
3	Costs:								
4				Warehouse					
5	Plant	CA	TX	MI	NC	PA			
6	SW	10	8	13	16	18			
7	MW	12	7	6	9	9			
8	SE	17	12	10	5	9			
9									
10	Shipments:								
11				Warehouse					
12	Plant	CA	TX	MI	NC	PA	Shipped	Available	
13	SW	70	0	0	0	0	70	100	
14	MW	0	40	50	0	10	100	150	
15	SE	0	0	0	70	80	150	150	
16	Shipped	70	40	50	70	90			
17	Required	70	40	50	70	90			
18									
19	Total Cost =	2440							
20									

FIGURE C.8

The solution is shown in Exhibit C.8. The optimal solution, which has a cost of $2,440, calls for shipping 70 (thousand) units from SW to CA, 40 from MW to TX, 50 from MW to MI, 10 from MW to PA, 70 from SE to NC, and 80 from SE to PA. Note that all warehouses will receive their full requirements. The SE plant will be used to its full capacity, but the SW plant will use only 70 of its 100-unit capacity and the MW plant only 100 of its 150-unit capacity.

active exercise

Take a moment to apply what you've learned.

SENSITIVITY ANALYSIS

Since a transportation model is a special type of linear programming model, the same **sensitivity analysis** information is available. In particular, we can find, for each source/destination combination, the range within which its unit cost can vary without changing the optimal shipping pattern. For each unused combination, we can find the *reduced cost,* the amount by which the unit cost would have to be reduced before that route should be used. In addition, we can find, for each source and destination constraint, the shadow price and the range within which that shadow price holds. For a source, the shadow price indicates by how much the total cost would decrease (increase) if one more (less) unit were available at that source. For a destination, the shadow price indicates by how much the total cost would increase (decrease) if one more (less) unit were required at that destination.

Example C.7

Refer to Example C.6. Fred's company's management is interested in the following two questions: (1) Management will shortly be negotiating a new contract with the trucking company that makes deliveries from the SW plant. By how much would the unit cost for shipments to California have to increase before it would change the shipping pattern? (2) Management is considering increasing the capacity of one or more of its pager plants. Which plant, if any, should have its capacity increased?

Solution:
The Sensitivity Report for the problem in Example C.6 is shown in Exhibit C.9. The answers to both questions can be obtained from that output.

1. In the adjustable cells portion of the Sensitivity Report, the maximum amount by which the objective coefficient of cell B13 (the SW/CA shipment variable) can be increased without

Microsoft Excel 8.0a Sensitivity Report
Worksheet: [Electronics.xls]Sheet1
Report Created: 8/10/98 8:29:11 AM

Adjustable Cells

Cell	Name	Final Value	Reduced Cost	Objective Coefficient	Allowable Increase	Allowable Decrease
$B$13	SW CA	70	0	10	1.999999995	1E+30
$C$13	SW TX	0	0.99999993	7.999999998	1E+30	0.999999993
$D$13	SW MI	0	6.99999998	13	1E+30	6.999999998
$E$13	SW NC	0	11	16	1E+30	11
$F$13	SW PA	0	9	18	1E+30	9
$B$14	MW CA	0	1.999999995	12	1E+30	1.999999995
$C$14	MW TX	40	0	7.000000005	0.999999993	1E+30
$D$14	MW MI	50	0	6	4	1E+30
$E$14	MW NC	0	3.999999999	9	1E+30	3.999999999
$F$14	MW PA	10	0	9	3.999999999	0
$B$15	SE CA	0	6.999999999	17	1E+30	6.999999998
$C$15	SE TX	0	4.999999995	12	1E+30	4.999999995
$D$15	SE MI	0	4	10	1E+30	4
$E$15	SE NC	70	0	5.000000001	3.999999999	1E+30
$F$15	SE PA	80	0	9	0	3.999999999

Constraints

Cell	Name	Final Value	Shadow Price	Constraint R.H. Side	Allowable Increase	Allowable Decrease
$G$13	SW Shipped	70	0	100	1E+30	30
$G$14	MW Shipped	100	0	150	1E+30	50
$G$15	SE Shipped	150	0	150	10	50
$B$16	Shipped CA	70	10	70	30	70
$C$16	Shipped TX	40	7.0000000005	40	50	40
$D$16	Shipped MI	50	6	50	50	50
$E$16	Shipped NC	70	5.0000000001	70	50	10
$F$16	Shipped PA	90	9	90	50	10

FIGURE C.9

changing the currently optimal shipping pattern is $2, to a total of $12. If the unit cost increases to more than $12, the optimal solution will be different.

2. The constraints portion of the Sensitivity Report shows that neither the SW or MW plant is using all of its existing capacity, so neither should have its capacity increased. Although the SE plant is operating at full capacity, its shadow price is 0 within the range of *150 − 50 = 100* to 150 + *10 = 160.* There is no economic rationale for increasing the capacity at the SE plant, either.

active exercise

Take a moment to apply what you've learned.

Supplement Wrap-Up

Any decision-making situation involves two basic issues: What are we making decisions about, and how do we know that one decision alternative is better than another? One useful approach to answering these questions is mathematical programming. Decision variables are defined and an objective function is used to decide which combination of decision variable values is best. We considered two types of mathematical programming models: linear programming and the transportation model, both are readily solved with Excel's Solver.

Linear programming is widely used in all functional areas of business. The problem is to determine the values for the decision variables that maximize or minimize the value of a linear objective function while satisfying a set of linear constraints. While problems with only two variables can be solved graphically, solving realistic problems requires the use of a computer package. In addition to providing the optimal values of the decision variables, the computer package will also provide sensitivity analysis information. Shadow prices for the constraints indicate the marginal values or costs for changes in the amounts of resources or other constraints in the problem. The sensitivity analysis also shows the range for which that shadow price holds and the range within which a variable's objective function coefficient can change without changing the optimal solution.

The transportation model is a special type of linear programming model. In its classic form, the problem is to determine how much of an item to ship from each of the sources at which it is available in limited quantities to each of the destinations at which it is required in specified amounts. Since a transportation model is a type of linear programming model, all the same sensitivity analysis information is available from the solution.

end-of-supplement resources

- Practice Quiz
- Key Terms
- Solved Problems
- Discussion Questions
- Problems

Facility Layout Decisions

CHAPTER 9

Chapter Outline

What's Ahead

. . . BACK AT THE REC CENTER

Luis had arrived with everybody else this morning, but he seemed more interested in socializing than in exercising. Now, about 10 minutes ahead of usual, he was getting ready to head for the lockers.

"What's the rush? You hardly worked out this morning," noted Tom. "You have a big day coming up at work, or what?"

"No, not really," Luis replied. "I'm just a little drained this morning. I went to one of those really big health clubs last night. A guy at work has been talking about this new circuit training he's doing there, and I wanted to check it out."

"Oh, I get it. You don't like us anymore! You're going to leave us high and dry," Fred chimed in, with as maudlin a look as he could muster. He was pretty sure Luis had no intention of leaving the group. He knew Luis liked the early morning workouts at the small facility where they had all met. In fact, he had discussed the other health club with Luis the previous week. He was just giving Luis some good-natured ribbing, with his visit to the larger club serving as the excuse.

"No, no, no," Luis interrupted defensively. "That's not it at all. My friend keeps talking about how he gets such a great workout in such a small amount of time. It sounded interesting. He kept asking me to join him, so finally I said okay. I'll try anything once."

"Well, what did you think? Was it what you expected?" asked Cheryl.

"Yes and no," replied Luis. "Most of the equipment is grouped by type, just like it is here. All the bikes were in one place, the steppers in another—even the weight stations were clustered. It was set up the same way we group our machines at work, by department—you know, by what they do."

There was a lot of similarity between the way the two health clubs were organized. In fact, both were laid out much the same way as the machines in Luis's factory. Luis had always heard his factory referred to as a functionally organized job shop, so he assumed that the layout of the health clubs could be called the same. When it came to getting a workout, it seemed that both clubs were just as inefficient and time consuming as his factory was in making a batch of tables. Though Luis realized he came to the club for more than just an efficient workout, he had thought he might as well check out the other club's setup. Maybe he'd learn something about getting a good workout and running a factory at the same time.

"But how is that different from what we have here?" asked Fred, interrupting Luis. "I've seen the place you're talking about from the street. It looks huge! They must have twenty of everything. We're lucky to have two of anything! Besides size, what's the big deal?"

"Yes, it's very big! The different areas, or sections, all had a staffer who specialized in one activity. It was pretty cool. They really knew their stuff." He told the group about how aerobics were held in a separate room that was closed off during classes. You could still have a conversation, even when there was a class in session; no boom box drowned you out. He told them the club even had a couple of rooms just for daycare. "But all that's not really why I went," he said. "I went to try an area where they had a sequence of stations set up for circuit training."

Luis realized that there might be some advantages to the size of the club (the specialization and all), but he was sure it took a lot of memberships to pay for such a huge operation. As big as the club was, Luis had noticed that some sections were particularly crowded, with a lot of people waiting to get on the machines. Those parts didn't seem to move any faster than they did at the smaller club. In fact, in the smaller club, you could look across the room to see whether the upcoming stations or machines were busy and reshuffle the order of your workout accordingly. In the larger club, Luis had noticed that some of the machines he liked to use were at opposite ends of the building. While he didn't mind the walk, by the time he got there and found out a machine was busy, it was a pain to go look for something else to do. Besides, when he got out of line to check another area, he lost his spot in the place where he had been working out. That part of the new club didn't seem any more efficient than the old one—maybe even less so. But that was not what Luis had gone there for. "What I really went there for was the circuit training," he repeated.

"I've heard something about that kind of stuff, but not much," Cheryl said, curious. "What was it like?"

"Pretty nice," Luis answered. "They had a series of stations set up in a fixed sequence. You went from one to the next in two-minute intervals. What you did at each one took about a minute to a minute and a half. You got a few seconds to recover and then went right on to the next one. First it was some easy stretching stuff, then a strider, a bike, some weights for the legs, bench press—a lot of stuff. By the time we were done, we had really pretty much hit all the bases. Right down the line. Real quick and to the point! I was really feeling the burn in about 30 minutes."

"What if you wanted to skip something or go in a different order?" asked Tom.

"Yeah, that sounds like trying to get a McDonald's hamburger without a pickle!" added Fred.

"It sounds like the same tradeoff you might make in a fast-food restaurant, a factory, or even a hospital," interjected Cheryl. She knew from experience that flexibility and efficiency don't often go hand in hand. "You get through the circuit predictably as long as you want to do the same basic stuff—you know, use it the same way as everybody else. Try to get some variety—take a slower pace than the rest of the crowd or go back to get something you forgot—well, I bet that's different!"

"Yeah, kind of like ordering that burger without the pickle from the drive-up window. I can hear the horns blowing now!" laughed Luis.

"You're right, you can't do that on the circuit—not without a hassle, anyway. I guess if you want variety or something unique, you need to use those specialized sections you mentioned earlier," she said to Luis.

"I see what you mean," said Tom. "The circuit is a great idea if there are enough people who want the same type of workout at the same pace. Kind of like having enough people who are willing to buy the same type of car, hamburger, or even a seat to Dallas six times a day! You set up an assembly line," he added.

"Sounds like our pager assembly," added Fred. We make them all with pickles, six pieces of rehydrated onion, 3 grams of ketchup, 2 grams of mustard, and a 1.5-ounce patty!" he said. "You can have them any way you want them, as long as it's the one way we make them!"

"But like Tom said, that's not a problem if there's enough demand for that particular pager. You can keep the costs down when you do it that way, right?" said Cheryl, explaining her point further.

"Costs down?" asked Luis. "That place of Fred's costs bizillions! How can that be cheap?"

"Volume, volume, volume!" replied Fred. "Just like the airlines, we spread it out over volume. Everything we do, we do to get the numbers up! That means we keep the cost down. But we wouldn't do that unless we knew the numbers were there. This new club must figure a lot of people want that type of circuit training."

"Maybe somebody should open up a club just for circuit training?" asked Tom.

"Well, for now, this may be a good compromise—you know, until they see the interest is going to last," Cheryl replied. She recognized that management could always move the circuit machines back to the areas they came from. From the description, it sounded as if the club had not spent much money on things that couldn't easily be undone with a few carts, dollies, and some strong employees.

"Yeah, but when it's all said and done, this deal reminds me of what I like about my factory and this club," summarized Luis. "It's flexible enough to give me what I need, even if I do have to wait for Tom to quit hogging the treadmill once in a while!"

"Right, and it's small enough to be comfortable!" added Cheryl. The others agreed. Tom grinned at Luis as he added five more minutes to the treadmill timer.

> objectives

Take a moment to familiarize yourself with the key objectives of this chapter.

> gearing up

Before you begin reading this chapter, try a short warm-up activity.

> Introduction

In this chapter we introduce a variety of general layout types, describe the impact of layout decisions on competitiveness, summarize the considerations that drive layout decisions, and present a number of quantitative tools that can help managers who make layout decisions.

As the conversation at the health club suggests, the choice of a layout for a factory or service operation is a significant one. Such decisions are particularly crucial in big cities, where office rents are extremely expensive. Average annual occupancy costs[1] in Bombay, Hong Kong, Tokyo, and London have run at $143, $105, $95, and $95 per square foot, respectively. (In some of these cases, rents have actually declined from higher levels.) Consider what the occupancy cost for *prime* office space could cost in these cities. Surely, Lloyd's of London could easily charge 10 times the average rent in London to insurers wishing to rent an office or cubicle in its headquarters.

Think about the practical implications of these costs for layout planners. Using valuable floor space for a wastebasket costs an additional $100 per month. A large desktop with space for horizontally stored files costs a great deal more than an upright filing cabinet. All in all, layout decisions can have a significant impact on the cost of operating a facility, the effectiveness of employees from all functional areas, and the ability of the facility to meet the firm's operational goals.

Moreover, though moving furnishings within a facility is easier than relocating the entire facility, layout decisions are usually seen as long-term decisions. Once a facility has been set up in a particular way, it tends to stay that way for some time, because changing the layout will disrupt the firm's operations. You may have noticed this tendency in your own home. It has probably been awhile since you last rearranged your bedroom, den, or home office.

[1]As of the first quarter of 1997.

Integrating Operations Management with Other Functions

Figure 9.1 highlights some of the major relationships between material covered in this chapter and other business functional areas. Obviously, this part of the chapter is important to all majors, because it indicates the way that professionals from their functional areas relate to the issues addressed in this chapter.

The next section of the chapter describes a variety of general layout types. The obvious cross-functional linkages to the finance and human resources (HR) functions are highlighted in Figure 9.1. Both the capital intensity and the worker skill requirements vary significantly between layout types. Thus, the capital budgeting processes of financial managers and the staffing, evaluation, and promotion processes of HR managers will be quite different across the spectrum of process types.

The section of the chapter describing the impact of layout decisions on competitiveness has natural linkages to the finance and marketing functions. In this section, we illustrate the potential of layout decisions to impact the income and valuation of a firm. We also illustrate the impact that marketing decisions can have on facility layout.

The next section of the chapter describes the range of considerations that can drive layout decisions. Concerns from any functional area can influence layout choices, however engineers and information systems professionals may have the greatest influence. Structural designs of buildings and the design of equipment that must be placed within them, coming from the engineering function, together limit the set of choices available when facility layout decisions are made. Similarly, the advent of personalized computing has provided alternatives that allow people to work together without necessarily being in close physical proximity. Thus, the location of data ports, Internet connections, and so on (which wasn't even an issue 10 years ago) has become a much larger consideration in the layout of facilities.

The final two sections of the chapter present tools that are useful to managers who actually make layout decisions. Figure 9.1 suggests that these sections will be of particular interest to individuals from the engineering and accounting functions. The linkage to engineering is obvious; it is frequently engineers who are charged with using these tools. As for accounting, particularly in the case of process-oriented layouts, the information they provide through their cost accounting practices provides the data needed to utilize these tools.

Chapter Topics \ Functional Areas of Business	Finance	Accounting	Human Resources	Marketing	Engineering	Management Information Systems
Integrating Operations Management with Other Functions	●	●	●	●	●	●
General Layout Types	●		●			
Layout Decisions and Competitiveness	●			●		
Considerations that Drive Layout Decisions					●	●
Tools to Help with Process-Oriented Layouts		●			●	
Line Balancing For Product-Oriented Layouts					●	

FIGURE 9.1 Integrating Operations Management with Other Functions

> General Layout Types

Regardless of a firm's competitive priorities, the *layout* of its facilities will impact the way those facilities are run and therefore the firm's competitiveness over the long haul. Different layouts present different managerial challenges, as well as different opportunities to satisfy unmet customer needs. As a result, a strategic perspective, geared toward customer satisfaction, is required to make the right layout choices. In the following sections, we will examine the advantages and disadvantages of five basic layouts.

> **video example**
>
> **Take a closer look at the concepts and issues you've been reading about.**

FIXED-POSITION LAYOUTS

In a **fixed-position layout,** value-adding resources travel to the customer or need. Unlike other layouts, materials do not travel through a value-adding system. A fixed-position layout is used to film a movie or video on location; to repair or manufacture a boat in dry dock; to build a house or assemble a swing set in the back yard. In addition, manufacturers of large industrial equipment frequently use a fixed-position layout for final assembly, either immediately prior to shipment or at the customer's manufacturing facility.

The benefit of a fixed-position layout is that highly specialized experts, materials, and resources can be brought in to work on the product-service bundle. When you build a new house on site, you can bring in any subcontractor you choose to customize it to your taste. But when you build a house using prefabricated parts shipped from a factory, your choice of materials, resources, and expertise is much more limited. The disadvantages of the fixed-position layout include a lack of efficiency, difficulty in scheduling and communicating with widely dispersed resources, and a potential for significant cost overruns and quality problems.

PRODUCT LAYOUTS

In a **product layout,** the value-adding resources are arranged in the order in which materials or customers must flow to complete the product-service bundle. The resources in the product layout are dedicated solely to the creation of one product-service bundle; they cannot be used for other purposes. This layout is typically used in mass-production assembly operations. For example, Fred's electronic products assembly operation uses a product layout. If you have ever had the feeling of being herded through a crowded airport, you will recognize the typical airport as a product-oriented layout. Ultimately, the only value the airport facility adds is to assemble planeloads of passengers and move them through check-in, seat assignment, and boarding, while the ground crews service the aircraft. Figure 9.2 shows a rough sketch of Redhook Ale's product layout. Though the diagram doesn't

This Boeing 747-400 freighter is being assembled to carry the Air Force's flying laser. Using a fixed position layout makes it easier for Boeing to customize the aircraft.

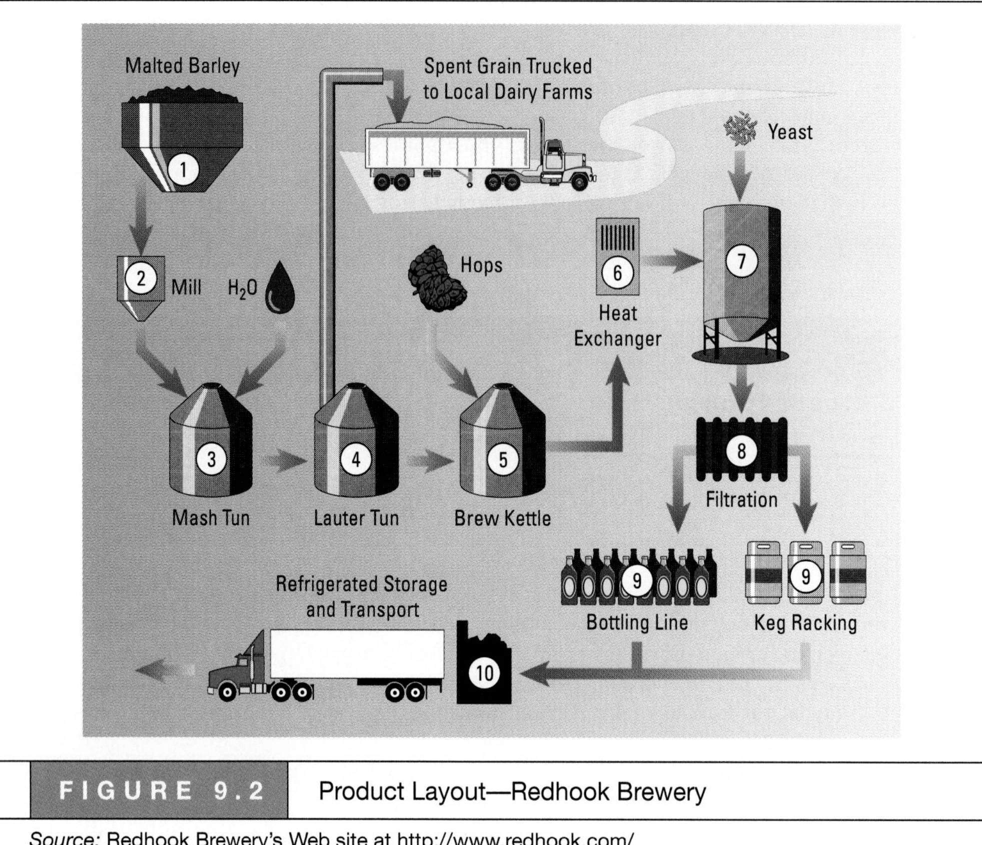

FIGURE 9.2 Product Layout—Redhook Brewery

Source: Redhook Brewery's Web site at http://www.redhook.com/

include the square footage allocated to each step in the process or the location of inventory and offices, which are also a part of the layout, it gives a good idea of what a product layout looks like.

Using product layouts allows production and material-handling tasks to be automated, thus reducing the need for skilled labor. If demand is large enough, a product layout will enable the production of large quantities of the same item at very low cost. This advantage is particularly important when customers are willing to accept a standardized product-service bundle but demand low prices and high quality. From a financial perspective, the outcome of such high-volume operations can be large profits.

The disadvantage of a product layout is its lack of flexibility. Fred's pager assembly operation is a good example. To introduce a new model, Fred's company must make a significant investment in new tooling, the installation of which disrupts the production line. Moving to a new product (not just a new model) presents an even bigger problem in terms of cost and disruption. When customer preferences change or substitute product-service bundles become available, demand declines and the company has difficulty spreading its high fixed costs over a large number of units. The dual problem of high per-unit costs and unattractive offerings reduces the company's profits—in extreme cases driving it into bankruptcy. From a human perspective, the result is usually reduced income or widespread layoffs for workers. (These wage losses and layoffs usually affect those workers who are least equipped to handle them—namely, those with low-skill jobs.)

active example

Take a closer look at the concepts and issues you've been reading about.

PROCESS LAYOUTS

In a **process layout,** also called a **functional layout,** value-adding resources are arranged in groups based on what they do. All the resources that perform similar tasks are located together, so that mate-

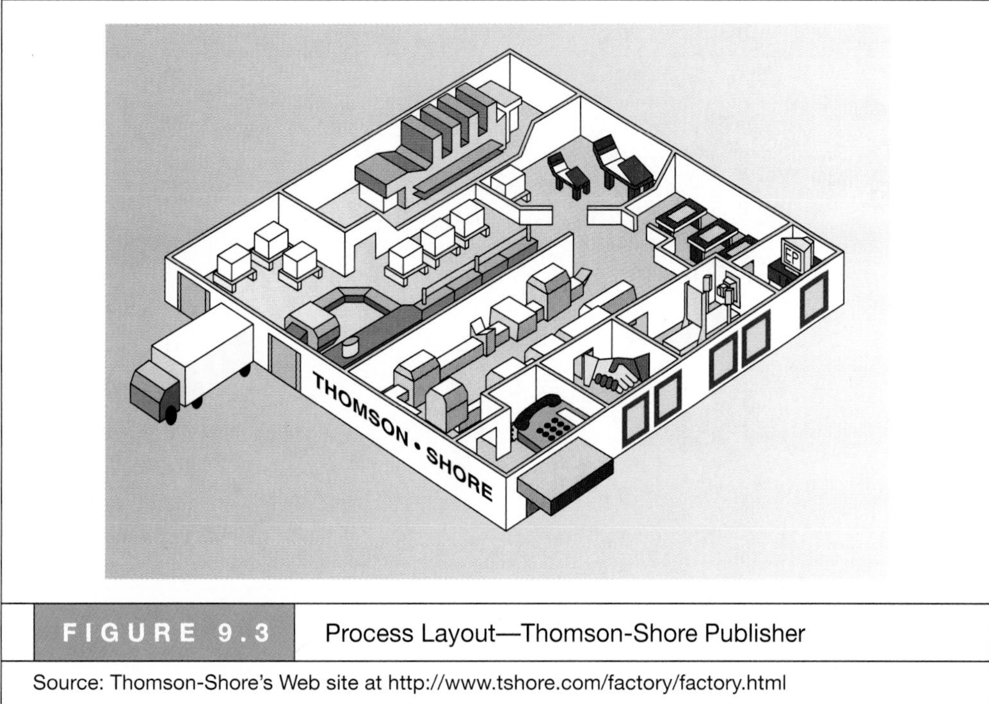

FIGURE 9.3 Process Layout—Thomson-Shore Publisher

Source: Thomson-Shore's Web site at http://www.tshore.com/factory/factory.html

rials can be routed through the resources in any order. The small health club where Cheryl, Fred, Luis, and Tom meet has a process layout, as does Luis's furniture factory. Cheryl's hospital, like many others, is supported by a process layout in which medical professionals are grouped by specialty. Figure 9.3 shows the process layout used by a book publisher.

Because the process layout is flexible, it can be used to provide highly customized product-service bundles. It also fosters an environment in which functional excellence can flourish. In a process layout, skilled workers are likely to learn from each other and take pride in their technical capabilities. However, this flexibility and functional excellence come at the expense of efficiency and quick response time and bring with them a complex managerial environment. Coordinating a set of diverse jobs is a tremendous challenge in an environment in which workers tend to think of themselves as a part of a functional work area rather than as a part of a broader value-adding system. Employees in this type of environment might be more loyal to their department than to the company, or they might be more concerned with technical excellence than with customer satisfaction.

> active exercise

Take a moment to apply what you've learned.

CELLULAR LAYOUTS

The conversation that opened this chapter described an exercise circuit that had been added to a large health club with a process layout. The exercise circuit was actually a value-adding cell—a place in which general-purpose resources are dedicated to a particular group of products, parts, subassemblies, or services. A facility made up entirely of such cells would be said to have a **cellular layout.** Each cell in such a layout is, in effect, a pseudo product layout.

Figure 9.4 shows the cellular layout used at a Harley-Davidson plant. Cellular layouts are designed to obtain much of the efficiency of a product layout without sacrificing flexibility. Using many cells, a facility with such a layout can make a variety of items. Cellular layouts can be much more flexible than product layouts and much more efficient than process layouts. Depending on the way they are run, they can deliver a mixture of the advantages and disadvantages of process and product layouts.

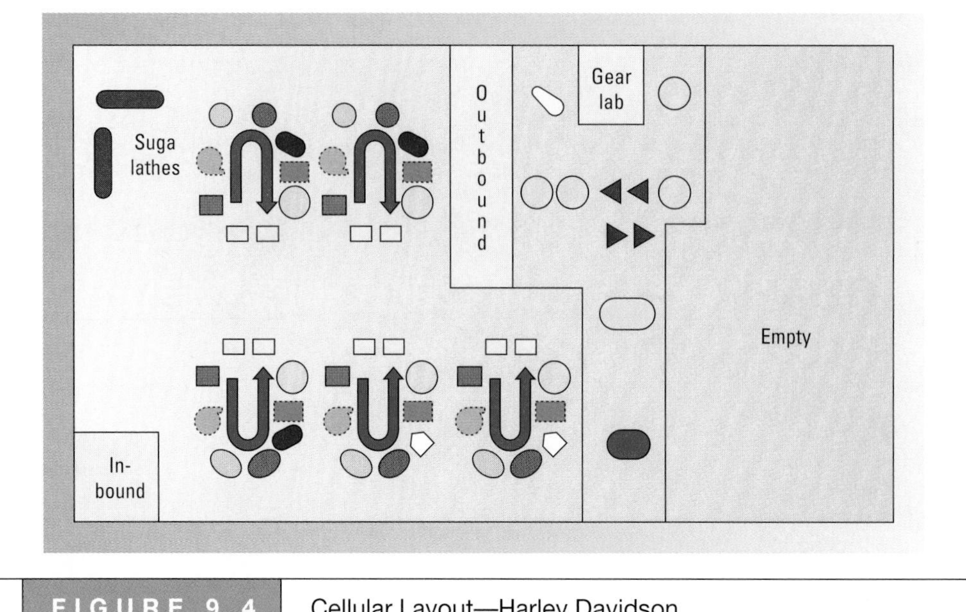

FIGURE 9.4 Cellular Layout—Harley Davidson

Source: Peter Reid, *Well-Made in America* (New York: McGraw-Hill, 1990), copyright © 1990.

video example

Take a closer look at the concepts and issues you've been reading about.

HYBRID LAYOUTS

Many facilities have multiple purposes. For instance, the Honda of America plant in Marysville, Ohio, both makes parts and assembles cars. The large health club Luis visited in the opening of this chapter was experimenting with circuit training in the midst of its process layout. Such facilities are said to have **hybrid layouts,** which are combinations of product, process, and cellular layouts.

Figure 9.5 shows the layout of a manufacturing plant owned by Mazak, a machine tool manufacturer in northern Kentucky. Mazak fabricates its parts in one of six cells, assembles the major parts for large machines in fixed assembly stations, and does the final assembly at the customer's site. Note that the part of the plant where the assembly takes place has a fixed-position layout. Mazak indicates that the fabricating cells provide 95% of the firm's part-making value added. This figure suggests that the company has used the cellular layout within its hybrid layout effectively.

video example 

Take a closer look at the concepts and issues you've been reading about.

active concept check

Now let's take a moment to test your knowledge of the concepts you have studied in this section.

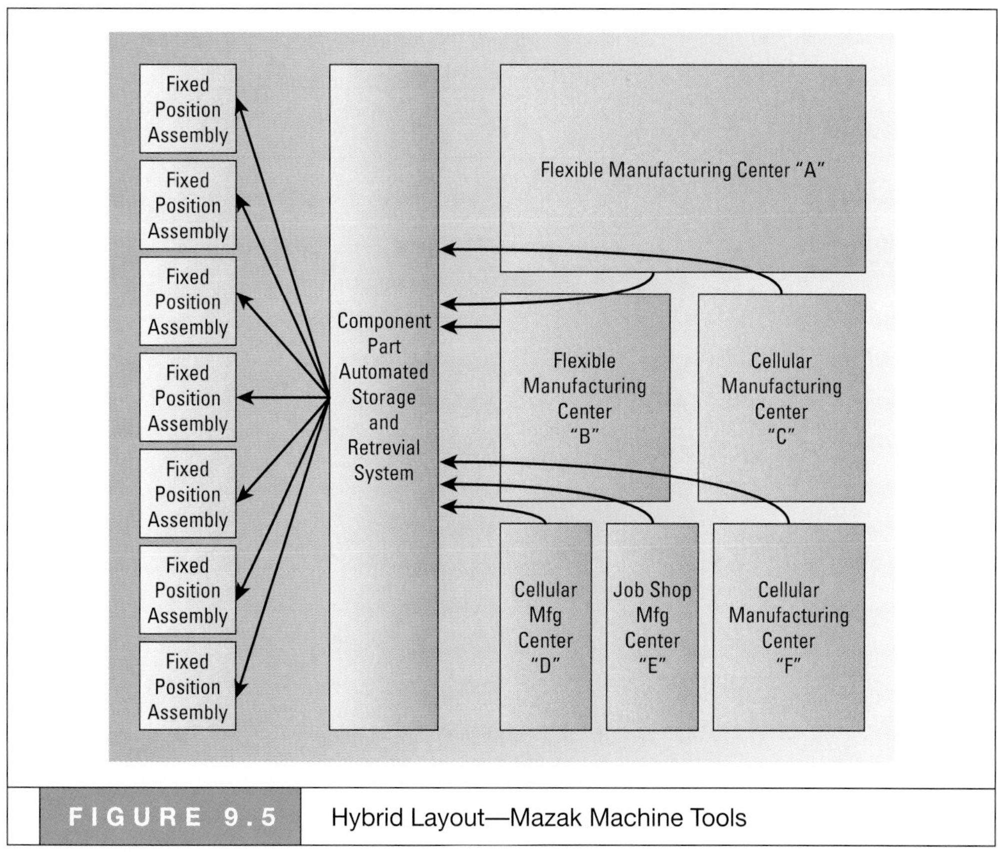

FIGURE 9.5 Hybrid Layout—Mazak Machine Tools

Layout Decisions and Competitiveness

You have probably come to the conclusion that process layouts are well suited to job shops and batch processes, while product layouts lend themselves to continuous flow and repetitive processes. If so, you're exactly right. The reason for this relationship is simple: The firm's competitive priorities should be reflected in all its operational decisions, including those that have to do with the layout of its facilities. If the firm's product-service bundles require customization, then process flexibility, design capability, and delivery speed are of paramount importance. A process-oriented layout will help the firm to attain those strategic advantages. Conversely, a product-oriented layout will provide

Workers in this Honda of America stamping area are inspecting the stamped side panels that have been produced from rolled steel by giant metal presses.

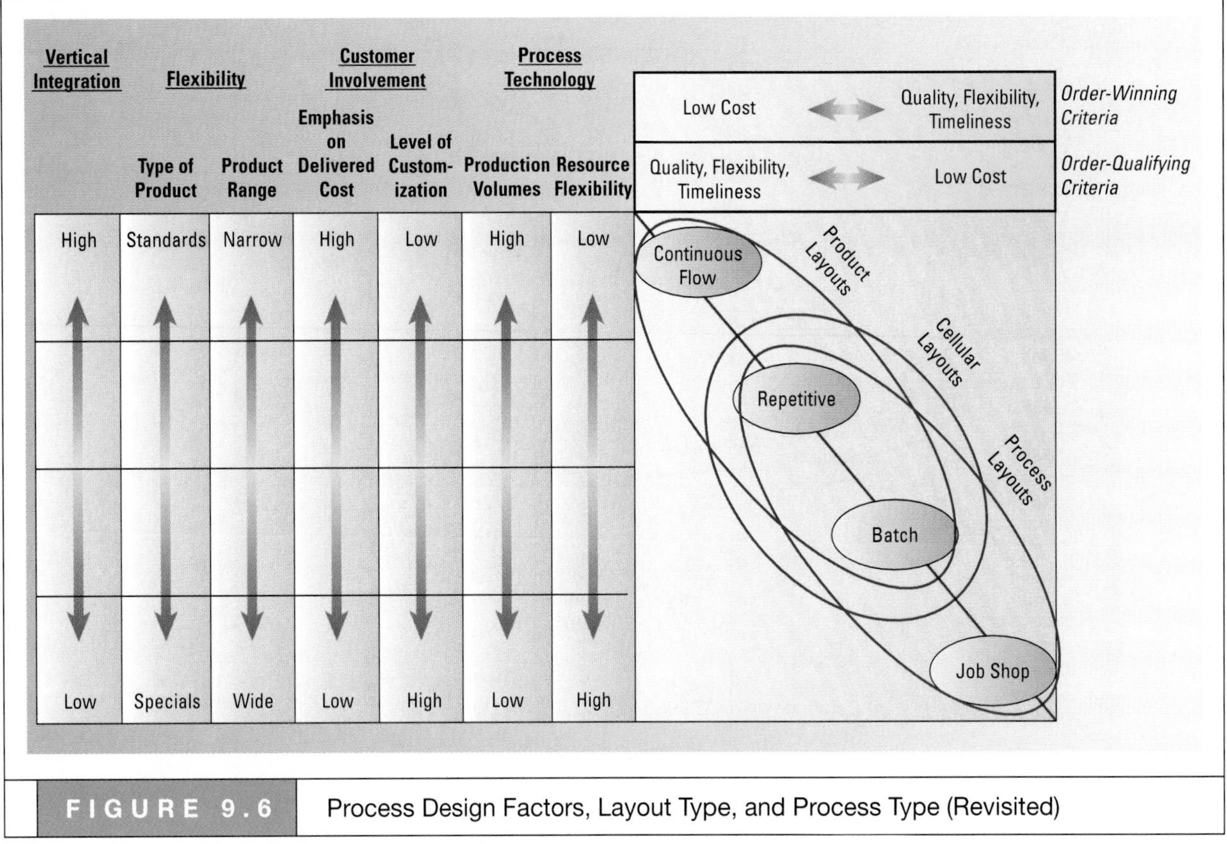

FIGURE 9.6 Process Design Factors, Layout Type, and Process Type (Revisited)

highly standardized, low-cost product-service bundles on a fixed schedule. Figure 9.6 revisits the discussion of process choice in Chapter 7 from the perspective of layout type rather than process choice. Notice that though the correlation between process type and layout is strong, more than one type of layout can be used in any type of process.

Facility layout decisions do have a significant impact on competitiveness. One of the authors of this book once worked for a printing firm called Dependa Graphics. Figure 9.7a shows the initial layout at one of the company's facilities. As you can see, there was very little room for inventory in that

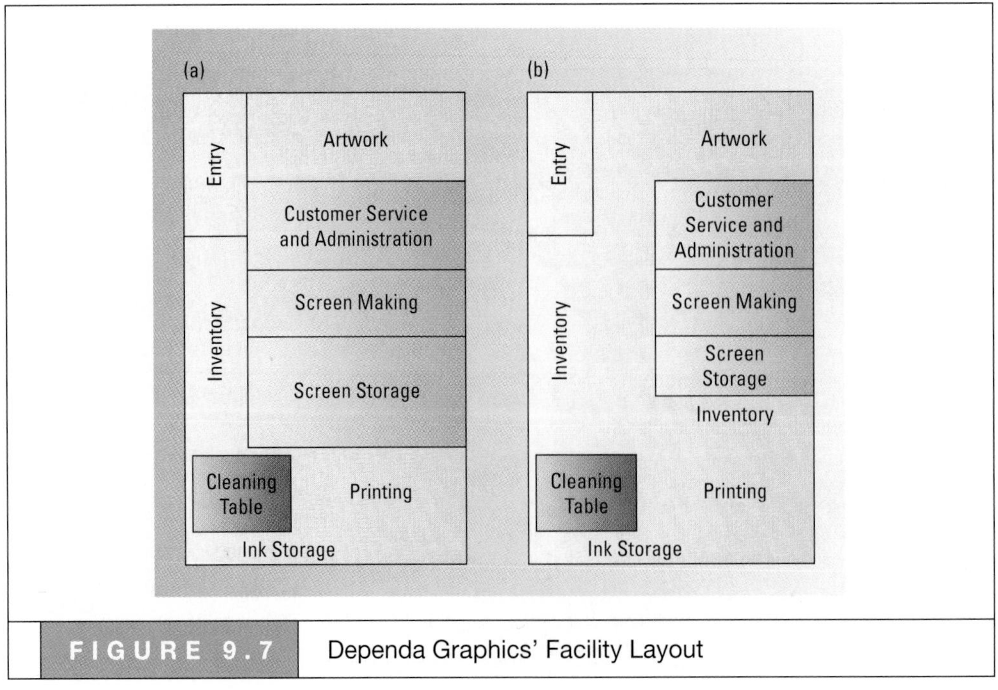

FIGURE 9.7 Dependa Graphics' Facility Layout

process layout. Basically, unused materials were kept in boxes in the hall. If materials were ordered too long before they were to be printed or were not picked up immediately after printing, the facility faced a significant space shortage. During busy periods, the business could not meet the needs of all its customers, and jobs over a certain size simply were not feasible. Because the business could not grow, its profitability was severely limited.

When the layout of the Dependa Graphics facility was modified as shown in Figure 9.7b, the firm experienced a large increase in both the volume of its business and its profitability. One year after the change, the owner sold the business at a substantial profit—a result he could not have achieved without the positive financial performance enabled by the change in layout.

This example illustrates two other points. First, layout decisions can't always be made starting with a clean sheet of paper. Often, the ideal layout cannot be accomplished because of existing structural realities. The building might be too small, a load-bearing wall might be in the wrong place, or the required investment might be too large. Even so, a company should not overlook opportunities to make incremental improvements to a layout. Second, a company shouldn't automatically write off a new business opportunity just because it doesn't fit the existing layout. Dependa Graphics was able to significantly expand the range of job sizes it could handle by making a small change in layout.

Another example of this point is the Ford Motor Company's auto assembly operations, which use a product-oriented layout. In the early 1980s, when T-tops became popular, Ford's Mustang assembly line could not accommodate that product option. Until the line could be revamped, managers set up an off-line functional work area in which fully roofed car bodies could be converted to T-tops. For a short period, Ford's layout was less than ideal, but the company nonetheless took advantage of a significant new market opportunity and satisfied an unexpected customer requirement.

In addition to competitiveness, facility layout can have a large impact on service rates and customer satisfaction. For example, in the early 1990s, the layout of carry-on luggage security stations at the Minneapolis/St. Paul (MSP) airport was causing significant delays for passengers who transferred to connecting flights. The security stations were located at the entry to each concourse. This ensured that any person on a concourse had been through the security checkpoint. Those who weren't on a concourse weren't forced to undergo needless inspection. Unfortunately, it also caused unnecessary delays for passengers who deplaned on one concourse and needed to board a plane on another concourse. Since these passengers had already passed through a security checkpoint at their airport of origin, it was redundant to check them again for connecting flights. When it was determined that about 40% of the people passing through the checkpoints were doing so to make flight connections, the security stations were moved to the airport's ticket counters. Connecting passengers no longer have to pass through security checkpoints. The layout change virtually eliminated the security checkpoint bottleneck and improved the satisfaction of both the travelers whose flights originated at MSP and those who were making connecting flights.

> Considerations That Drive Layout Decisions

What considerations are important in making a layout decision? Obviously, the answer to this question will not be the same in all situations. As a rule, though, the needs of customers and employees will play a significant role in any decision. Some of those needs are included in the partial list that follows:

- *To reduce unnecessary activities,* including non-value-adding activities such as material handling, packaging, and removal of packaging.
- *To prevent damage to inventory* through material handling, packaging, and removal of packaging.
- *To enhance communication* among individuals, groups, or departments. For example, the Chrysler Technology Center in Auburn Hills, Michigan, is designed to enhance teamwork among functions. Each function has its own wing in the building, and each platform team its own floor. The building has several hubs where the wings come together, each with a public area containing displays of mutual interest to the various functional groups in the adjoining wings. A ring of meeting rooms surrounds each hub. Thus, the whole layout of the Chrysler Technology Center reflects Chrysler's matrix organizational structure and its emphasis on teamwork. (For another example of this need, see the boxed insert that describes the unusual layout used by the candymaker Mars, Inc., to enhance communication in its facilities.)

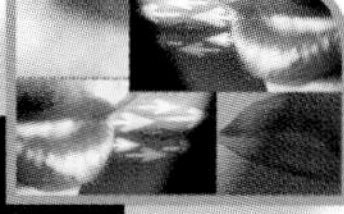

> active poll

What do you think? Voice your opinion and find out what others have to say.

- *To prevent rework.* Frequently rework results from poor communication about requirements. Getting the job done right the first time has a great deal to do with effective communication of expectations between and among functional groups—which is enhanced by an appropriate layout.
- *To discourage communication* between particular individuals, groups, or departments. A single facility might house the value-adding systems for several different product-service bundles. If competitive priorities and customer expectations differ significantly from one bundle to the next, companies with multiproduct facilities might use an arrangement like the *plant within a plant* to keep employees focused on the relevant customer expectations. Some common examples of the plant-within-a-plant layout are the pharmacy at the grocery store, the snack bar at the discount store, and the cosmetics counter in a large department store.

Similarly, when incompatible processes or materials are housed under the same roof, they need to be separated. For example, finishing wooden or metal items usually requires some kind of dust-producing operation followed by a color coating. If the two processes were not physically separated, the dust from the first operation would spoil the second. Thus, great care is always taken to seal off the paint booth from other operations. So, too, a darkroom is usually separated from the seating and display area in a photographic studio. And you probably recall that your high school band room wasn't located next door to the library.

- *To provide privacy.* Because privacy discourages unwanted communication, separating certain departments, such as payroll or human resources, from others makes sense. Furthermore, in certain service environments, privacy is a luxury that can be used to generate significant additional revenues. The luxury box at the ballpark, the private hospital room with attached toilet and shower, and the separate banquet hall all command a premium price. Here's a "first-class" example: In 1996, British Airways (BA) won a number of prestigious design awards for its redesigned first-class area on Boeing 747-400 aircraft used on long intercontinental flights. Individual cabins, including double units for couples traveling together, replaced the original configuration of seats in rows. Yacht interior architects designed the cabins. They can be used as a private office, mini-meeting room, entertainment center, dining room for two, or a bedroom complete with a flat 6-foot-6-inch bed. (At the touch of a button, the compartments—trimmed in pear wood and suede—change from work area to bedroom or anything in between. The personal entertainment system includes a video player and a fiber optic light on a flexible stem to allow for reading, work, or sleep.) Changing the rules and thinking outside of the box allowed BA to develop a layout that provides passengers with a great measure of privacy. It also helped the company achieve the competitive edge as it claims to now provide "the ultimate luxury in overseas flights."
- *To provide for safety* of employees, customers, and neighbors. The pharmaceutical company that makes both aspirin and morphine obviously needs to keep the two processes and packaging operations separate. Similarly, the part of a facility that makes or uses explosives will not be located near the smoking lounge.
- *To provide for security* of resources. For example, a movie theater that stays open later than the neighboring retail stores will be located on the perimeter of the mall and have separate access. So, too, an ATM that is accessible after hours must be carefully placed.
- *To enhance labor skills and functional excellence* through specialization. For example, professors in the accounting department will be located in the same area, so that they can interact and keep up-to-date in their field.
- *To enhance the quality of work life.* Cummins Engine Company's Mid-Range Engine Plant, which is located close to Columbus, Indiana, provides an interesting example of this need. The parking lot for this manufacturing facility is on the roof, and most of the exterior is covered with windows. Thus, the interior is filled with natural light, and workers gaze out on flora and fauna rather than on parking lots and cars. Though employees must still perform repetitive tasks, they have less reason to dread going to work in the morning.
- *To provide for customer involvement* in the value-adding process. Particularly in service operations, individual customers often need to be included in the value-adding process. For this reason, the psychologist has a counseling office, not a counseling classroom. Similarly, at better restaurants customers are served at the table rather than on a cafeteria line.

> Tools to Help with Process-Oriented Layout Decisions

Planners often think of layout decisions in horizontal terms, which is fine if a facility has only one floor. Many facilities, however, are housed in buildings with more than one floor or level. Retail establishments, office buildings, factories, restaurants, aircraft, ships, and trains are just a few examples. In such cases, thinking of alternative layouts one floor at a time is a temptation, because the spaces and distances are easier to visualize that way. Doing so is something like taking the roof off a dollhouse or architect's model in order to view the interior.

Though thinking of multiple-story facilities in terms of three-dimensional space is very helpful, until recently it has been difficult to do. But today, planners can use computer modeling tools to visualize three-dimensional spaces from a variety of angles and perspectives. Doing so helps to eliminate problem layouts and tends to produce better layouts than those that are planned one level at a time. Particularly when the creation of the product-service bundle requires a high degree of customer interaction, computer modeling can help to optimize the design of a facility from the customer's perspective. It allows layout planners to ask themselves, How will this layout look and feel to the customer?

> active example

Take a closer look at the concepts and issues you've been reading about.

SIMPLIFIED SYSTEMATIC LAYOUT PLANNING

Simplified Systematic Layout Planning (SSLP) is a tool used to develop process-oriented layouts in service organizations and other settings where the need for proximity between departments is influenced by a number of qualitative factors. The first step in this approach is to classify the need for each department to be adjacent to other departments. Planners generally use an A-E-I-O-U-X taxonomy, as follows:

A—adjacency is *absolutely* necessary
E—adjacency is *especially important*
I—adjacency is *important*
O—*ordinary* closeness is okay
U—proximity is *unimportant*
X—proximity is *undesirable*

Obviously, these classifications should not come out of the blue. Rather, the eventual users of the facility, including the department heads who will operate and maintain it, should be consulted regarding the real need for proximity and distance between various departments.

Once department pairs have been rated using the A-E-I-O-U-X taxonomy, planners must attempt to develop a layout that is consistent with those ratings. The second step in the SSLP is therefore to build department clusters based on the A, or absolutely necessary, requirements. In the third step,

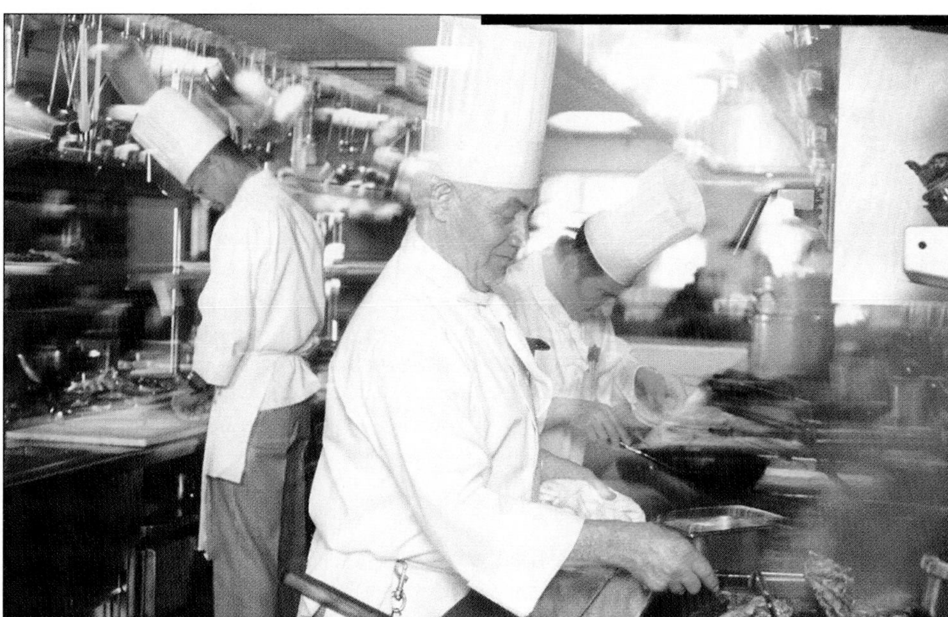

The layout of a chef's kitchen should provide flexibility and immediate access to utensils and uncooked food storage facilities. Utensils are not cleaned in the cooking area.

planners add to these A clusters based on the E (especially important) requirements, and so on, until all the requirements have been included. The result is a set of clusters that indicates the preferred location of departments relative to each other.

Once the relative location of departments has been determined, the actual layout can be planned. At this point, planners begin to deal with variations in the amount of space required from one department to the next. Taking these into account, planners attempt to develop several alternative layouts, all based on the relative locations they have developed. (If you have ever looked in a mirror, you will understand a basic implication of symmetry: that there may be several different ways to arrange departments without changing their relative locations.) In the sixth and last step, planners select one of those alternatives and finalize the layout.

The recently completed Miami University (Ohio) Recreational Sports Center was planned using SSLP. Table 9.1 shows the adjacency requirements for the various departments in the facility. This table, called a REL chart, shows the relationships among departments (REL is short for "relationship"). In Table 9.2, which shows only the As from Table 9.1, the rows and columns have been sorted to clarify the clustering that results from a consideration of the A requirements. Figure 9.8 shows the clusters obtained in this second step of the SSLP. Note that there are five separate clusters and that a number of departments are not included in any of them. For convenience, we will call these five initial clusters water sports, public access, Fitness Center, courts, and Outdoor Pursuits.

Table 9.3 adds the E requirements to the A requirements in Table 9.2. The clusters obtained in this third step of the SSLP are shown in Figure 9.9. (To distinguish among the various requirements, three lines connect the A requirements, two lines the E requirements, and one line the I requirements.) Notice that another cluster, which we will call the locker rooms, has been added. The public access and water sports clusters have been joined at the natatorium spectator gallery (NSG), and a Recreational Sports Office has been added to the public access cluster.

Table 9.4 adds the I requirements to the A and E requirements in Table 9.3. Figure 9.10 shows the clusters after this fourth step in the SSLP. The picture has been simplified so that only one line represents all the I requirements between any two clusters; otherwise, the lines would have begun to look like spaghetti. At this point, all areas have been attached, and it has become clear that the locker rooms should be centrally located. Because all areas have been included in Figure 9.10, it is not necessary to draw another figure showing the clustering after consideration of the O requirements.[2]

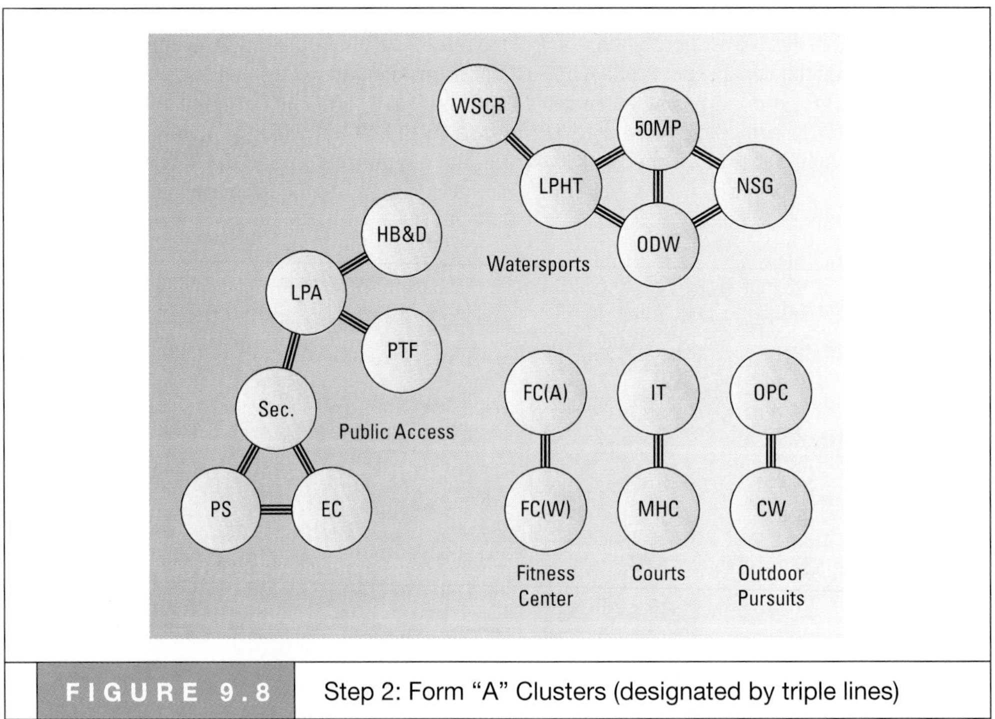

FIGURE 9.8 Step 2: Form "A" Clusters (designated by triple lines)

[2]Often, layout planners will use four, three, two, and one lines to represent the A, E, I, and O requirements, respectively. Since we chose not to show the O requirements, we began with three lines. In addition, some planners use colors or different line weights or styles to distinguish among the types of requirement.

TABLE 9.1 Adjacency Requirements (REL Chart)

	Recreational sports office	Pro shop	Men's locker room and toilets	Women's locker room and toilets	Family locker room and toilets	50 meter pool	Olympic diving well	Natatorium spectator gallery	Recreational pool and hot tub	Multipurpose hardwood courts	Indoor track	Racquet courts	Exercise performance rooms	Watersports classroom	Fitness Center (aerobic)	Fitness Center (weightlifting)	Equipment checkout	Security	Lounge and public areas	Public toilet facilities	Outdoor Pursuit Center	Climbing wall	Health Bar & Deli
Recreational sports office																							
Pro shop	E																						
Men's locker room and toilets	X	X																					
Women's locker room and toilets	X	X	E																				
Family locker room and toilets	X	X	E	E																			
50 meter pool	X	O	I	I	I																		
Olympic diving well	X	O	I	I	I	A																	
Natatorium spectator gallery	X	U	U	U	U	A	A																
Recreational pool and hot tub	X	O	I	I	I	A	E	U															
Multipurpose hardwood courts	X	O	I	I	I	X	X	X	X														
Indoor track	U	O	I	I	I	X	X	X	X	A													
Racquet courts	U	O	I	I	I	U	X	X	U	U	U												
Exercise performance rooms	O	O	I	I	I	U	X	X	U	U	U	U											
Watersports classroom	O	O	I	I	I	E	E	U	A	U	U	U	U										
Fitness Center (aerobic)	X	O	I	I	I	X	X	X	X	U	I	U	U	U									
Fitness Center (weightlifting)	X	O	I	I	I	X	X	X	X	U	I	U	U	U	A								
Equipment checkout	E	A	I	I	I	U	U	X	U	I	U	U	U	U	U	U							
Security	E	A	I	I	I	U	U	E	U	U	U	U	U	U	U	U	A						
Lounge and public areas	I	E	O	O	O	U	U	E	U	U	U	U	U	U	U	U	U	A					
Public toilet facilities	I	O	I	I	I	U	U	E	U	U	U	U	U	U	U	U	U	U	A				
Outdoor Pursuit Center	I	U	U	U	U	U	U	U	U	U	U	U	U	U	U	U	U	U	U	U			
Climbing wall	U	U	I	I	I	U	U	U	U	U	U	U	U	U	U	U	U	U	U	I	A		
Health Bar & Deli	I	O	U	U	U	U	U	E	U	U	U	U	U	U	U	U	U	U	A	U	U	U	

TABLE 9.2 Adjacency Requirements ("A's")

	50 meter pool	Olympic diving well	Natatorium spectator gallery	Leisure pool and hot tub	Watersports classroom	Pro shop	Equipment checkout	Security	Lounge and public areas	Public toilet facilities	Health Bar & Deli	Recreational Sports Office	Fitness Center (aerobic)	Fitness Center (weightlifting)	Multipurpose hardwood courts	Indoor track	Outdoor Pursuit Center	Climbing wall	Men's locker room and toilets	Women's locker room and toilets	Family locker room and toilets	Racquet courts	Exercise performance rooms
50 meter pool																							
Olympic diving well	A																						
Natatorium spectator gallery	A	A																					
Leisure pool and hot tub	A																						
Watersports classroom				A																			
Pro shop																							
Equipment checkout						A																	
Security						A	A																
Lounge and public areas								A															
Public toilet facilities									A														
Health Bar & Deli									A														
Recreational Sports Office													A										
Fitness Center (aerobic)																							
Fitness Center (weightlifting)																							
Multipurpose hardwood courts														A									
Indoor track																							
Outdoor Pursuit Center																A							
Climbing wall																							
Men's locker room and toilets																							
Women's locker room and toilets																							
Family locker room and toliets																							
Racquet courts																							
Exercise performance rooms																							

TABLE 9.3 Adjacency Requirements ("A's & E's")

	50 meter pool	Olympic diving well	Natatorium spectator gallery	Leisure pool and hot tub	Watersports classroom	Pro shop	Equipment checkout	Security	Lounge and public areas	Public toilet facilities	Health Bar & Deli	Recreational Sports Office	Fitness Center (aerobic)	Fitness Center (weightlifting)	Multipurpose hardwood courts	Indoor track	Outdoor Pursuit Center	Climbing wall	Men's locker room and toilets	Women's locker room and toilets	Family locker room and toilets	Racquet courts	Exercise performance rooms
50 meter pool																							
Olympic diving well	A																						
Natatorium spectator gallery	A	A																					
Leisure pool and hot tub	A	E																					
Watersports classroom	E	E		A																			
Pro shop												E											
Equipment checkout						A						E											
Security			E			A	A					E											
Lounge and public areas			E			E		A															
Public toilet facilities			E						A														
Health Bar & Deli			E						A														
Recreational Sports Office																							
Fitness Center (aerobic)																							
Fitness Center (weightlifting)													A										
Multipurpose hardwood courts																							
Indoor track															A								
Outdoor Pursuit Center																							
Climbing wall																	A						
Men's locker room and toilets																							
Women's locker room and toilets																			E				
Family locker room and toliets																			E	E			
Racquet courts																							
Exercise performance rooms																							

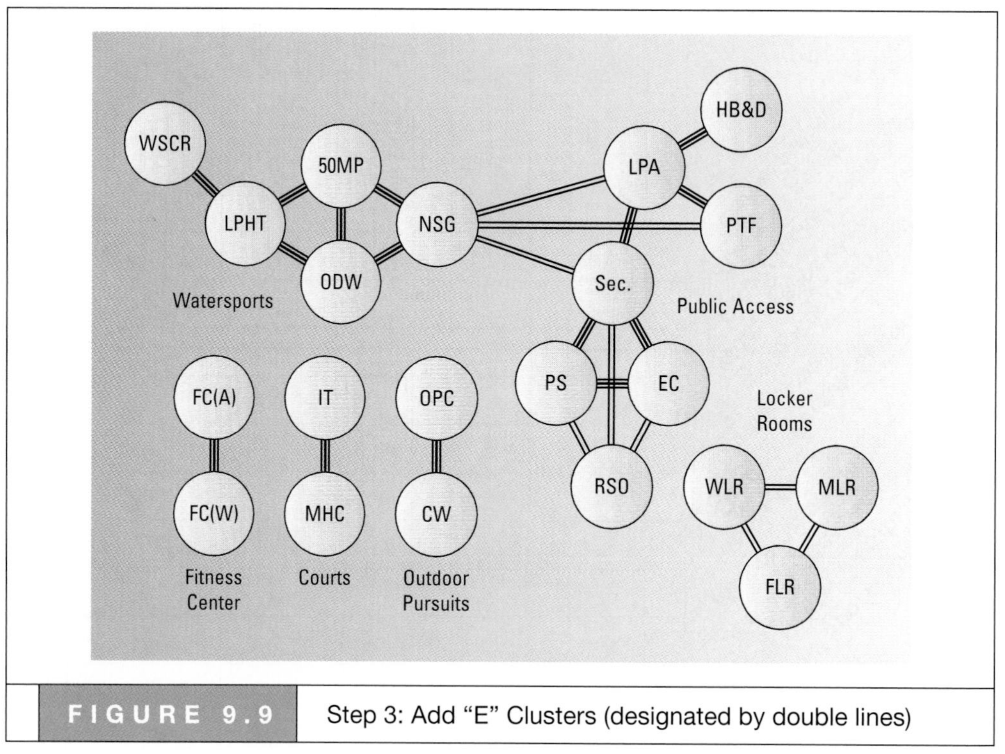

FIGURE 9.9 Step 3: Add "E" Clusters (designated by double lines)

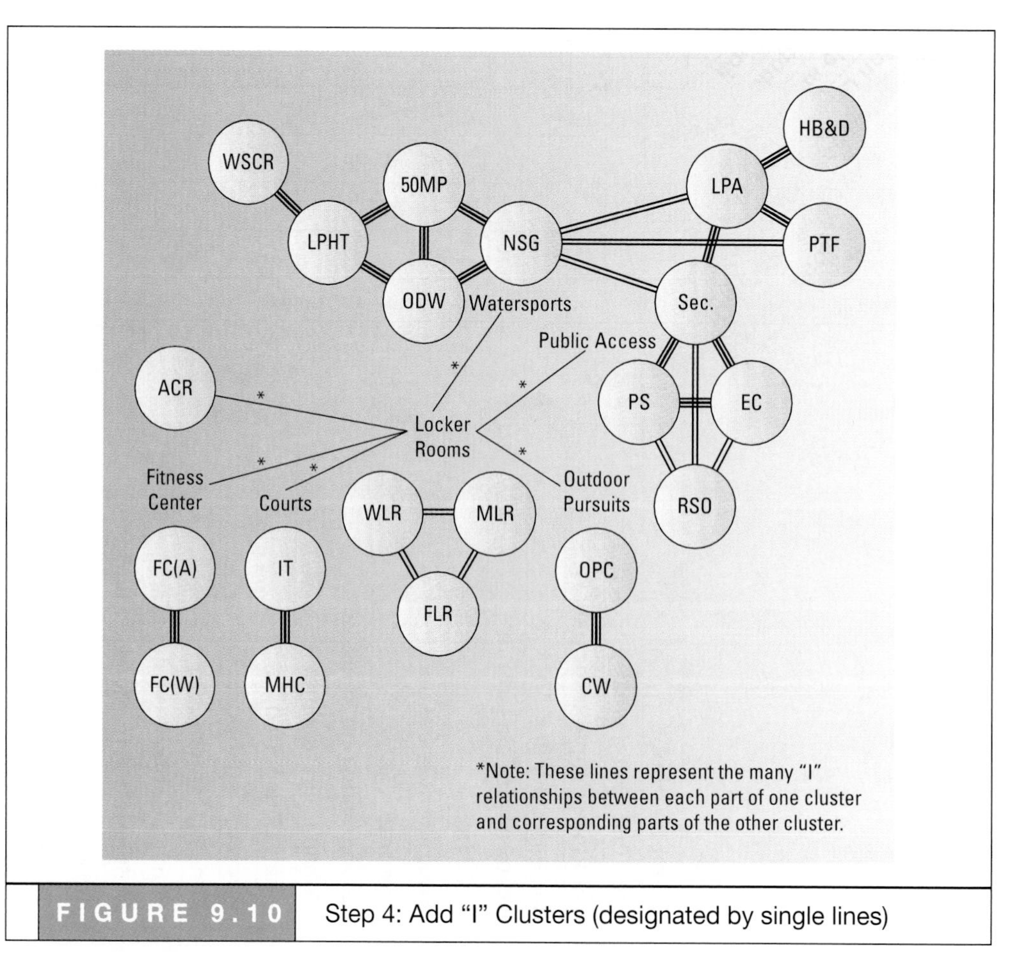

FIGURE 9.10 Step 4: Add "I" Clusters (designated by single lines)

TABLE 9.4 Adjacency Requirements (“A’s, E’s, & I’s”)

	50 meter pool	Olympic diving well	Natatorium spectator gallery	Leisure pool and hot tub	Watersports classroom	Pro shop	Equipment checkout	Security	Lounge and public areas	Public toilet facilities	Health Bar & Deli	Recreational Sports Office	Fitness Center (aerobic)	Fitness Center (weightlifting)	Multipurpose hardwood courts	Indoor track	Outdoor Pursuit Center	Climbing wall	Men’s locker room and toilets	Women’s locker room and toilets	Family locker room and toilets	Racquet courts	Exercise performance rooms
50 meter pool																			I	I	I		
Olympic diving well	A																		I	I	I		
Natatorium spectator gallery	A	A																					
Leisure pool and hot tub	A	E																	I	I	I		
Watersports classroom	E	E		A															I	I	I		
Pro shop																							
Equipment checkout						A						E			I				I	I	I		
Security			E			A	A					E							I	I	I		
Lounge and public areas			E			E		A				I											
Public toilet facilities			E						A			I							I	I	I		
Health Bar & Deli			E						A			I											
Recreational Sports Office																							
Fitness Center (aerobic)																I			I	I	I		
Fitness Center (weightlifting)													A						I	I	I		
Multipurpose hardwood courts																			I	I	I		
Indoor track															A				I	I	I		
Outdoor Pursuit Center																							
Climbing wall																	A		I	I	I		
Men’s locker room and toilets																							
Women’s locker room and toilets																			E				
Family locker room and toliets																			E	E			
Racquet courts																			I	I	I		
Exercise performance rooms																			I	I	I		

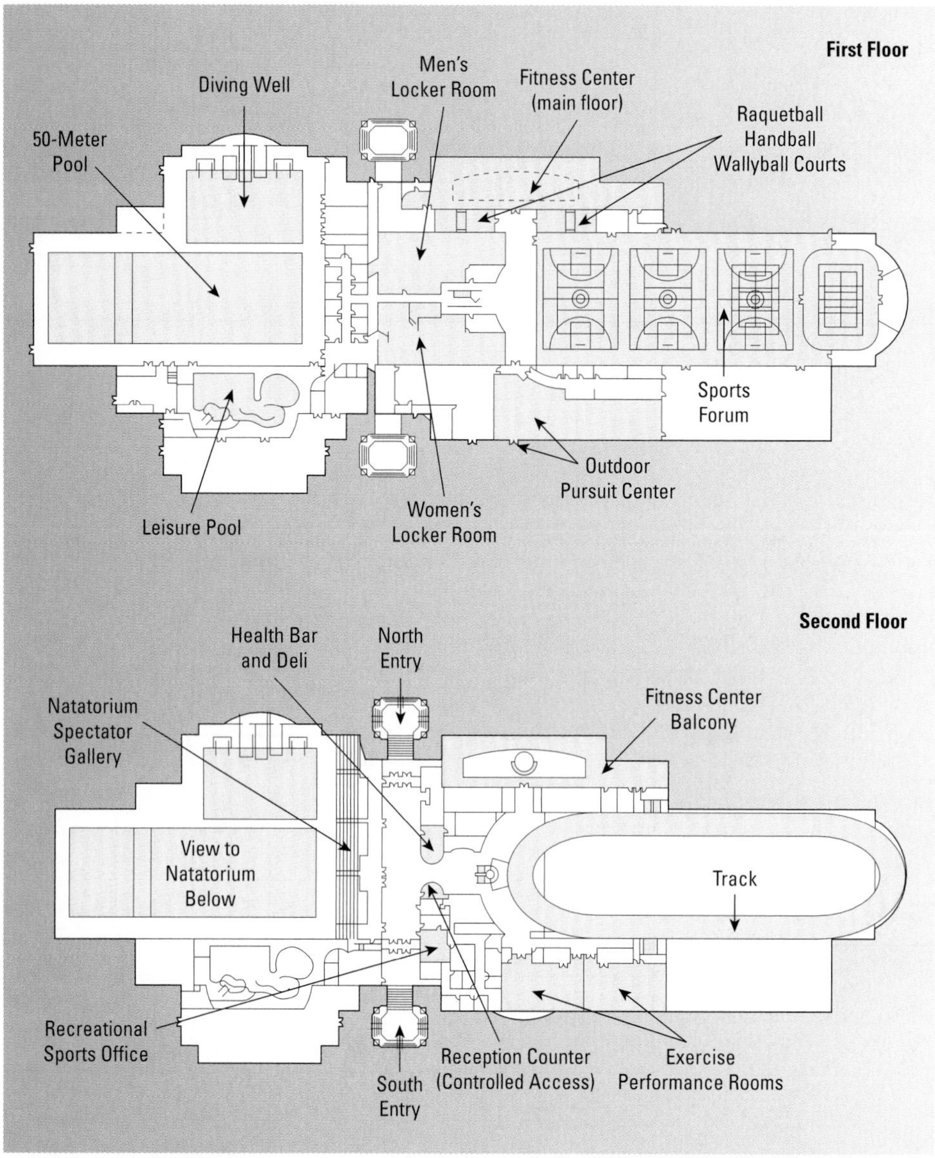

FIGURE 9.11 Final Floor Plan for Student Recreation Center

Based on the information developed in the first four steps of the SSLP, planners considered a number of possible layouts (step 5) before selecting a final layout. Figure 9.11 shows the final layout for this facility. The Miami University Recreational Sports Center, as it is now called, was one of six winners of *Athletic Business* magazine's Facility of Merit award in 1995. It has been used by the Japanese national swim team in preparation for the 1996 Olympic Games and has hosted several national swimming meets, including the 1997 Women's National Collegiate Athletic Associations Finals.

video exercise

Take a moment to apply what you've learned.

DISTANCE- AND LOAD-BASED DECISION-MAKING TOOLS

In developing process-oriented layouts, the costs of material and customer movement should be considered. Using mathematical modeling techniques based on assumptions about future demand for various product-service bundles, it is possible to minimize the distance customers must travel or the pound-feet of materials that must be moved. However, process-oriented layouts must usually be developed in the face of significant uncertainty about future demand. Therefore, decision makers commonly use a cut-and-try approach to develop a layout that will accommodate a variety of possible demand patterns.

For example, assume that a manufacturer of specialty papers has recently had some problems with overtime and timely delivery of materials. Managers have decided to evaluate the plant's existing layout, to see if alterations might improve performance. Figure 9.12 shows the plant's current layout. The only physical walls inside the facility are located around the roll-paper storage and papermaking areas; the lines between other functional areas represent aisles that are used for transporting materials. Paper pulp and paper rolls are received via rail and truck. The pulp goes to the roll paper machine, where it is made into rolls of a variety of colors and weights. These rolls are then sent to roll paper storage, where they are kept along with rolls from outside vendors. Defective rolls go into recyclable paper storage.

When a customer such as a greeting card company, a publisher of annual reports, or some other specialty printer orders paper for a production run, the stock is pulled from roll storage and converted as necessary in the laminating, embossing, and cutting centers. (Laminating or embossing must be done before cutting.) Depending on their size, the leftover rolls are sent either to roll paper storage or recyclable paper storage. Nonlaminated paper that is wasted due to cutting is also sent to the recyclable paper storage area, for eventual use in making new rolls. Customer orders are assembled in the assembly area prior to packing and shipping. All outbound shipments are placed on a railcar, which is dispatched daily to the distribution center across town.

Table 9.5 shows the distance (in meters) between each pair of work centers, as they are currently arranged. Table 9.6 indicates the average weekly volume shipped between each pair of work centers over the past six months. Multiplying the distance by the volume for each pair of work centers provides the distance-volume figures shown in Table 9.7. Notice that although the layout shown in Figure 9.12 makes sense from the perspective of materials flow, the volume of paper being embossed or laminated is small relative to the amount being cut. The weekly shipment from roll storage to cutting

TABLE 9.5 The Paper Co. Distance Matrix (Current)

	Receiving	Papermaking	Roll Paper Storage	Recyclable Paper & Pulp Storage	Laminating	Embossing	Cutting	Packaging	Shipping
Receiving									
Papermaking	60								
Roll Paper Storage	60	50							
Recyclable Paper & Pulp Storage	50	70	20						
Laminating	75	30	20	55					
Embossing	85	50	30	50	20				
Cutting	105	40	60	80	20	25			
Packaging	125	100	60	100	30	20	40		
Shipping	100	130	40	40	60	30	115	45	
Assembly	140	110	85	120	50	30	25	25	90

TABLE 9.6	The Paper Co. Volume Matrix

	Receiving	Papermaking	Roll Paper Storage	Recyclable Paper & Pulp Storage	Laminating	Embossing	Cutting	Packaging	Shipping
Receiving									
Papermaking	15								
Roll Paper Storage	75	75							
Recyclable Paper & Pulp Storage	0	25	5						
Laminating	0	0	10	0					
Embossing	0	0	30	2	0				
Cutting	6	0	105	12	10	30			
Packaging	0	0	0	0	0	0	0		
Shipping	0	0	0	7	0	0	0	150	
Assembly	0	0	0	0	0	0	150	150	0

of 6,300 ton-meters is significantly greater than other shipments to and from roll storage. This imbalance indicates a potential source of improvement in materials handling.

Figure 9.13 shows an alternative layout for this plant. Notice that only the cutting, embossing, and laminating areas have been moved. The new distance matrix is shown in Table 9.8, and the new distance-volume matrix in Table 9.9. Notice that the number of ton-meters traveled between roll storage

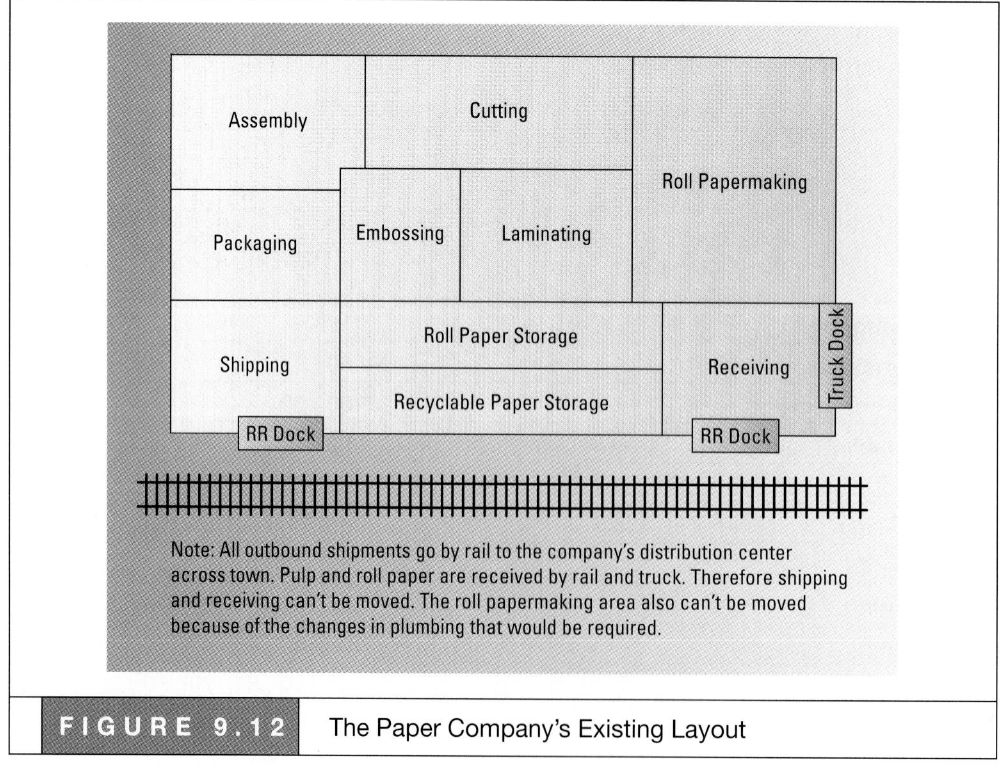
Assembly
Cutting
Roll Papermaking
Packaging
Embossing
Laminating
Shipping
Roll Paper Storage
Recyclable Paper Storage
Receiving
Truck Dock
RR Dock
RR Dock
Note: All outbound shipments go by rail to the company's distribution center across town. Pulp and roll paper are received by rail and truck. Therefore shipping and receiving can't be moved. The roll papermaking area also can't be moved because of the changes in plumbing that would be required.

FIGURE 9.12 The Paper Company's Existing Layout

TABLE 9.7 The Paper Co. Distance * Volume Matrix (Current)

	Receiving	Papermaking	Roll Paper Storage	Recyclable Paper & Pulp Storage	Laminating	Embossing	Cutting	Packaging	Shipping	TOTALS
Receiving										
Papermaking	900									900
Roll Paper Storage	4500	3750								8250
Recyclable Paper & Pulp Storage	0	1750	100							1850
Laminating	0	0	200	0						200
Embossing	0	0	900	100	0					1000
Cutting	630	0	6300	960	200	750				8840
Packaging	0	0	0	0	0	0	0			0
Shipping	0	0	0	0	0	0	0	6750		7030
Assembly	0	0	0	0	0	0	3750	3750	0	7500
										35570

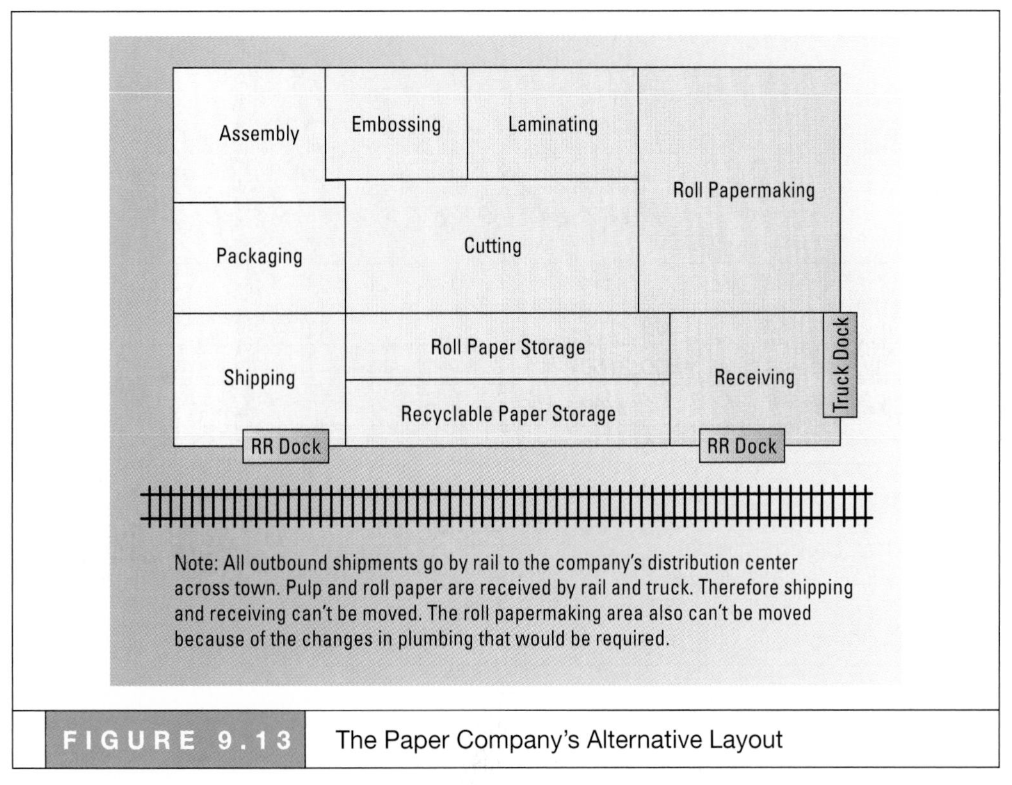

FIGURE 9.13 The Paper Company's Alternative Layout

TABLE 9.8 The Paper Co. Distance Matrix (Alternative)

	Receiving	Papermaking	Roll Paper Storage	Recyclable Paper & Pulp Storage	Laminating	Embossing	Cutting	Packaging	Shipping
Receiving									
Papermaking	60								
Roll Paper Storage	60	50							
Recyclable Paper & Pulp Storage	50	70	20						
Laminating	100	35	60	75					
Embossing	110	55	70	90	20				
Cutting	80	40	20	40	20	25			
Packaging	125	100	60	100	30	20	40		
Shipping	100	130	40	40	60	30	115	45	
Assembly	140	100	85	120	50	30	25	25	90

TABLE 9.9 The Paper Co. Distance * Volume Matrix (Alternative)

	Receiving	Papermaking	Roll Paper Storage	Recyclable Paper & Pulp Storage	Laminating	Embossing	Cutting	Packaging	Shipping	TOTALS
Receiving										
Papermaking	900									900
Roll Paper Storage	4500	3750								8250
Recyclable Paper & Pulp Storage	0	1750	100							1850
Laminating	0	0	600	0						600
Embossing	0	0	2100	180	0					2280
Cutting	480	0	2100	480	200	750				4010
Packaging	0	0	0	0	0	0	0			0
Shipping	0	0	0	280	0	0	0	6750		7030
Assembly	0	0	0	0	0	0	3750	3750	0	7500
										32420

and the embossing and laminating centers has risen. In fact, jobs that are embossed or laminated are now traveling much farther than they did before. This increase is more than offset, however, by the reduction in travel distance for jobs that require only cutting. Note that the total weekly material handling (in ton-meters) has fallen almost 10%.

> active concept check

Now let's take a moment to test your knowledge of the concepts you have studied in this section.

Line Balancing for Product-Oriented Layouts

In contrast to the process-oriented layouts we have been considering, product-oriented layouts are designed to be especially efficient in the creation of a standardized product-service bundle. In product-oriented layouts, including *assembly lines,* all value-adding resources are arranged in a suitable sequence; tasks are performed repetitively, with little variation in processing time; and virtually no inventory is kept between workstations. Thus, stations cannot operate independently, and the pace of the slowest workstation determines the pace of the entire system. (You've heard the old saying, "A chain is only as strong as its weakest link"; similarly, an assembly line is only as fast as its slowest workstation.) The difference between the pace of the slowest workstation and the pace of other stations represents wasted time.

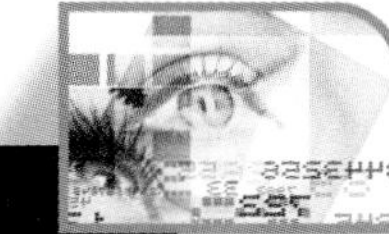

> video exercise

Take a moment to apply what you've learned.

On an assembly line, the time allowed for each workstation to complete its portion of the work on one unit of output is called the **cycle time.** Typically, the cycle time is determined either by the rate at which the product-service bundle is consumed in the marketplace or by the time the slowest workstation requires to complete its assigned tasks. The total time a unit spends on the line, which can be found by multiplying the line's cycle time by the number of workstations on the line, is called the **production lead-time.** The ratio of the time a workstation requires to complete its assigned tasks to the cycle time is called the **workstation utilization.** The average utilization of workstations on the line, which is the ratio of the total time to complete all tasks on the line to the production lead-time, is called the **utilization of the line.**

To illustrate these key terms, let's look at a very simple example of an assembly line. Suppose you and two friends decide to help a local mayoral candidate by stuffing, sealing, and labeling envelopes. You've been given the folded letters, preprinted labels, and envelopes preprinted with a return address and postal permit number. To minimize the amount of time spent on the task, you decide to use an assembly line. One of you stuffs an envelope, then passes it to the next person, who seals it and passes it on to the third person, who labels it. The process is illustrated in Figure 9.14. Stuffing, sealing, and labeling take 5.1, 6.0, and 3.8 seconds, respectively. Obviously, one envelope can be completed every 6.0 seconds. If you chose to work at that pace, your cycle time would be 6.0 seconds. Assuming that it is, the production lead-time for one envelope will be 18 seconds (6.0 seconds times 3 workstations). The utilization of the three workstations will be $5.1/6.0 = .85$, $6.0/6.0 = 1.00$, and $3.8/6.0 = .63$, respectively. The total time required to complete all tasks is $5.1 + 6.0 + 3.8 = 14.9$ seconds. Therefore, utilization of the line is $14.9/18 = .8278$.

Is there any way to improve on these measures? In the very simple assembly line just described, probably not. But in more complex operations, tasks might be divided among workstations so as to minimize the line's cycle time. **Line balancing** is a procedure that can be used to optimize the assignment of tasks to work centers. In real-world assembly operations, line-balancing procedures, or *heuristics,* are very complex. They must encompass many thousands of **elemental tasks**—operations that cannot be divided, because of technical reasons or managerial preference—each with variable processing times. As a result, line-balancing heuristics do not guarantee optimal task assignment. Because of their complexity, they are typically built into computer programs; only simple assembly operations are balanced with paper and pencil. To help in visualizing the line, planners often draw or

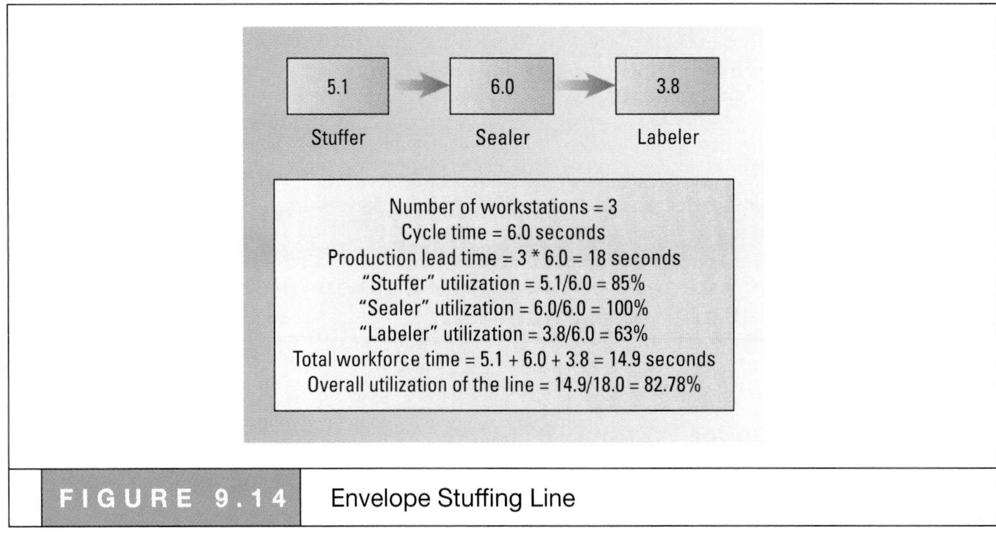

5.1
6.0
3.8
Stuffer
Sealer
Labeler
Number of workstations = 3
Cycle time = 6.0 seconds
Production lead time = 3 * 6.0 = 18 seconds
"Stuffer" utilization = 5.1/6.0 = 85%
"Sealer" utilization = 6.0/6.0 = 100%
"Labeler" utilization = 3.8/6.0 = 63%
Total workforce time = 5.1 + 6.0 + 3.8 = 14.9 seconds
Overall utilization of the line = 14.9/18.0 = 82.78%

FIGURE 9.14 Envelope Stuffing Line

print out a **precedence diagram**—a schematic drawing that shows the order and duration of the required tasks.

Since there is no guarantee that a given heuristic will maximize utilization of the line, managers tend to assign tasks based on rules that they believe will work well. An **assignment rule** is a heuristic that establishes the basis for choosing an elemental task for assignment to a workstation. For example, one common assignment rule is the Longest Task Time rule. The logic of this rule is that once the tasks that take a long time have been assigned to workstations, adding tasks of shorter duration should be easy. Conversely, assigning the shortest tasks first may make the assignment of longer tasks difficult without creating additional workstations. (This approach is something like packing the biggest things in a suitcase first, then filling in with smaller items.)

To illustrate how line balancing is done, suppose the manager of a department store has decided to employ college students on winter break to assemble Radio Flyer wagons for sale during the holiday season. The assembly tasks are listed in Table 9.10 (page 412); a drawing of the parts to be assembled is shown in Figure 9.15 (page 412). The manager expects to sell 800 assembled wagons over the holiday season but would like to employ the students for only one 40-hour week at the beginning of their winter break. She wants to set up an assembly line that will be capable of assembling 800 wagons in 40 hours, using the smallest possible number of workers. The line-balancing process for this operation may be summarized as follows:

TABLE 9.10 Tasks, Duration, and Precedence for the Toy Wagon

Task	Description	Duration	Immediate Predecessor(s)
1	Unpack box and distribute parts	2.00	None
2	Inspect wheels	1.00	1
3	Place tires on wheels	2.00	2
4	Attach first wheel to axles	0.50	3
5	Attach second wheel to axles	0.50	8, 9
6	Attach hubcaps	1.00	5
7	Inspect tray	0.50	1
8	Attach front axle to tray	0.50	4
9	Attach rear axle to tray	0.50	4
10	Inspect handle	0.50	1
11	Attach handle to tray	0.50	7, 10
12	Lubricate axles	0.50	8, 9
13	Lubricate handle	0.25	11
14	Attach decals	0.50	7
15	Inspect and test wagon	0.75	13, 8, 9
16	Remove assembled wagon to storage	2.00	15
		13.50	

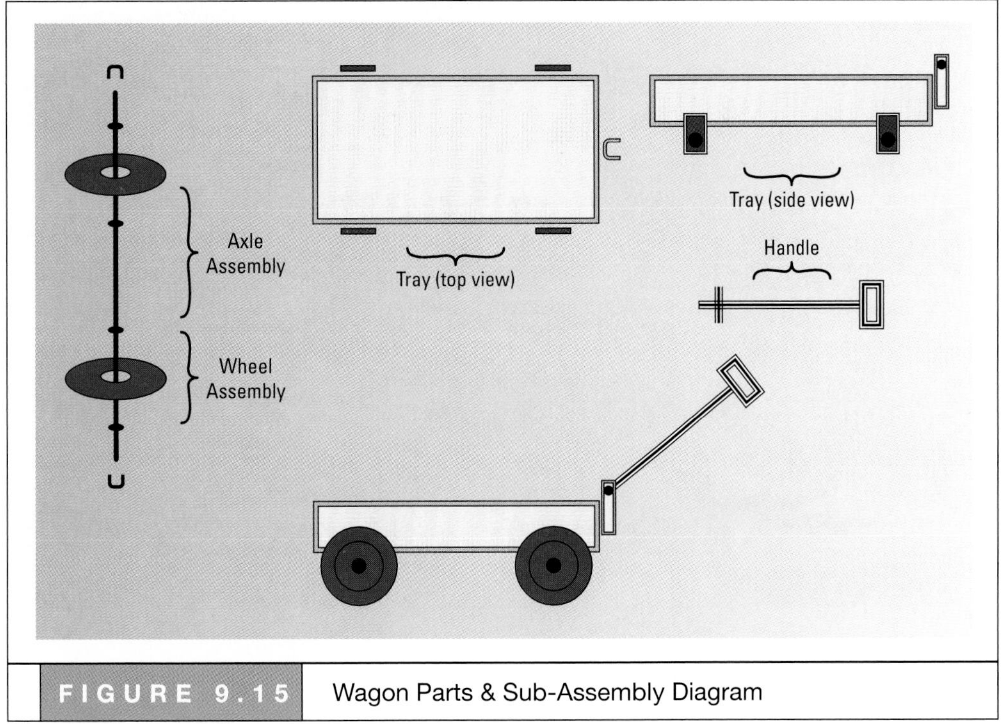

FIGURE 9.15 Wagon Parts & Sub-Assembly Diagram

Step 1: Draw the precedence diagram.

Figure 9.16 (page 413) shows the precedence diagram for the wagon assembly line. All the information required to draw the diagram is found in Table 9.10.

Step 2: Find the required cycle time.

To assemble 800 wagons in 40 hours, workers will need to put them together at an average pace of 1 per 3.00 minutes. ([40 hrs × 60 min/hr] / 800 units = 3 min/unit).

Step 3: Find the *theoretical minimum number of workstations.*

The total time required to assemble each wagon is 13.5 minutes. Since the work must be accomplished within the cycle time of 3 minutes, at least 5 stations will be required (13.5 min / 3 min/station = 4.5 stations, or 5, rounded up to the next highest integer). Thus, if the work can be divided more or less evenly, the manager will be able to accomplish her goal of assembling 800 wagons in one week using only five workers. But if the work is not evenly divisible, more than five workers or one week might be required to get the job done. One indivisible task may take a long time, or a set of tasks, each with a duration just long enough to prevent its combination with other tasks, may complicate the process.

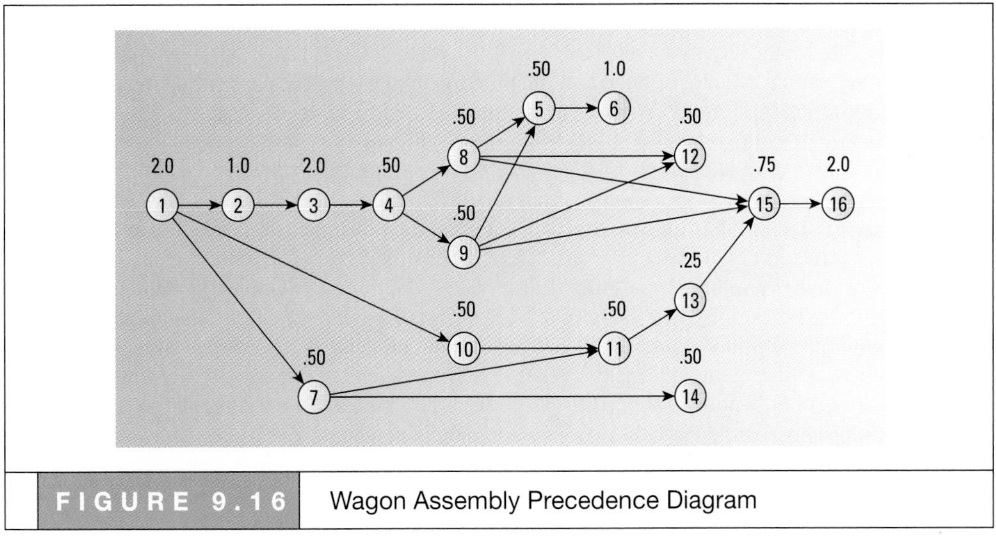

FIGURE 9.16 Wagon Assembly Precedence Diagram

The cycle times of individual workstations must be balanced on an assembly line. Ergonomic concerns are also very important. Because of the nature of the work repetitive stress injuries are common.

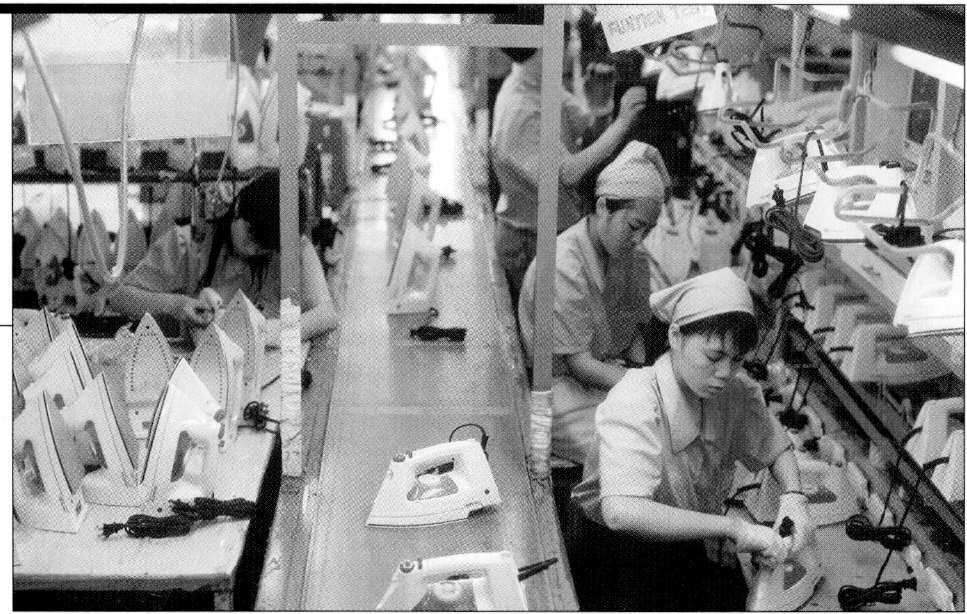

Step 4: Assign the tasks to work centers.

Tasks are assigned to workstations using a priority rule. Most planners start with the first tasks in the sequence; they place them in the first workstation, as many as can be added without exceeding the required cycle time. In this example, when more than one task is adjacent to tasks already assigned to a work center, we will use the Longest Task Time priority rule. In other words, we will add the task of longest duration to the work center first. When two or more such tasks are of the same duration, we will add the task that is followed by the greatest number of activities.

Table 9.11 shows this assignment algorithm at work. When we begin, no tasks have been assigned to any station. At that point, the only task with no unassigned predecessors is task 1. Thus, the only assignable task for workstation I is task 1.

Once task 1 has been assigned to workstation 1, tasks 2, 7, and 10 become assignable. Each has a duration less than or equal to the remaining 1.00 minute at workstation I, and none has an unassigned predecessor. We select task 2 because it takes the longest time. At that point, no more time remains to be assigned at workstation 1.

We can now begin to assign tasks to workstation II. We continue assigning tasks to stations until all the tasks have been assigned. Notice that by the end of Table 9.11, we have managed to assign all tasks to only five workstations, the theoretical minimum number of stations. Figure 9.17 shows the precedence diagram for this operation. We now know that the manager can accomplish her goal of assembling 800 wagons in one week using just five workers.

Unfortunately, the process of line balancing doesn't always work out as well as it did in Example 9.0. In the example, we were able to divide the work evenly enough to achieve the theoretical minimum number of stations. Often, task times do not fit together so neatly, and additional workstations are needed to achieve the required cycle time.

Furthermore, you might have noticed that the time required to complete a work assignment varied from one workstation to the next. Workers at stations I, II, and III had to complete 3.00 minutes of work, while those at stations IV and V had to do only 2.50 and 2.00 minutes of work, respectively. What do you think would happen if you hired five college students for a week, paid them the same wage, and made three of them work substantially harder than the others? Unless they were unusual people, assigning jobs in this way would produce a great deal of dissension. Job dissatisfaction and low levels of motivation could be the result. Clearly, there is a great deal more to job design than assigning tasks to workstations. (Job design is discussed more thoroughly in the next chapter.)

Caution should be exercised in using and interpreting the results of line-balancing heuristics. Planners should question the assumptions made during the process: How did they come up with the time required to do the elemental tasks? What if demand were to change so that the cycle time becomes too long, or utilization of the workstations becomes too low? What if the product needs to be modified in some way: Would the facility need a completely new line? Moreover, one must remember that though the estimates of demand and task times used in line-balancing heuristics are constants, they represent variables with probabilistic distributions. Practically speaking, a real-world assembly line is not going to operate like clockwork, no matter how well it has been balanced.

Job Design

CHAPTER 10

Chapter Outline

What's Ahead

. . . BACK AT THE REC CENTER

"I just don't understand people," muttered Luis, mostly to himself as he pumped away at one of the weight stations. The others, arriving at the normal time, had noticed his disposition and had been giving him more space than usual. After a few more minutes of working out his frustrations, Luis looked around and began to notice the impact his mood was having on the group's normally friendly atmosphere. "Okay, I'm sorry," he said, a little sheepishly. "It's just that I've got a mess on my desk to face when I get in, and I'm not really looking forward to it. But hey, I'm okay now. I won't bite!"

"Well, I wasn't sure for a while," laughed Tom. He was just finishing some sit-ups and had turned around on the inclined bench to take a short breather. "I wasn't going to get too close."

"So, what's the mess you have to clean up? Yours or somebody else's?" Cheryl asked from the treadmill across the room.

"Actually, it's both. I've been trying to get my people to think for themselves a little—you know, give them some room to do what they need to do," Luis replied. He said some of them took to it "like ducks to water," but others didn't want anything to do with the idea." Luis was sitting now, having worked up a good sweat. He went on to describe his efforts to share decision making with the people who work on the shop floor. He called the idea empowerment, something he had heard about in the Organizational Behavior class he was taking in a part-time MBA program. "Some of them just don't want to make any decisions—you know, go out on a limb," he complained. "They just want to be told what to do!"

"So?" asked Fred. "I've got a lot of people like that, it works out just right." Fred was sitting on an air strider next to Luis. "I don't want the guy who's putting the board in the pager to just up and change something some morning. That could mess up my whole line!" In Fred's mind, creativity was not something that belonged on the assembly line. The others nodded—except Luis.

"It's not the same," answered Luis. "I run a job shop. We make decisions about work order changes on the floor all the time. Sometimes we change the quantity; sometimes we bump a job to let another go ahead. Sometimes we rethink how we're going to make something, who's going to do what when, or what the thing's going to look like." Luis paused for a moment to get a drink from the water fountain. "What was it you said a couple of weeks ago—'you make all plain vanilla'?" he asked with a laugh.

"Okay, okay, I'll give you that," Fred replied. "We think it all through, set up the process, and then train the line workers. We get it together up front and then practice until everyone knows the drill. There aren't a lot of decisions to make on the fly."

"Well, we have a different situation. We have to make decisions," said Luis. "And we need to figure out who decides what. I don't want to have to make all the decisions, especially not when the workers are closer to the problem than I am."

"We've been down this road, too," replied Cheryl. "We don't want orderlies filling prescriptions! But what happened?"

"Oh, yeah. Well, we had a problem in the staining booth yesterday," explained Luis. An operator had stained a batch of 1,500 spindles a very dark color. Earlier in the day, the same operator had stained 300 seats for the kitchen stools he knew those spindles were meant for—only he had stained them a much lighter shade. When Luis questioned him about it, he admitted he had been aware of the difference in color and had thought it was odd. But as Luis explained, "He said he didn't think much about it, but when he did, well, he figured the best thing to do was to follow the work order." Luis was upset that the worker hadn't used some common sense. Why hadn't he stopped and checked it out? Now Luis was sitting on a large batch of seats that didn't match the spindles. He might not need spindles in that shade for months, if ever. He was also likely to be late in delivering the order of kitchen stools, which had come from a good customer. "I just can't believe the guy didn't check it out!" Luis exclaimed, exasperated.

"Well, what do you pay him to do?" asked Tom.

"Well, umm, I—I mean, we pay him to run a painting and staining booth," said Luis. He was somewhat taken aback by the question, which seemed to have such an obvious answer. "Why, what are you getting at?"

"I mean, it seems to me that you pay him for painting and staining a wide variety of things," suggested Tom. "I'll bet he never heard his job was to second-guess the system!"

"Well, he knows we don't make vanilla either!" said Luis.

Tom knew Fred would object and he did. He had an answer ready. "You've told us how standardized the work is on your line, how automated it is, and most is pretty routine—in fact, too routine, to hear you tell it," said Tom.

"Well, that's what we do, we mass-produce pagers, all alike," said Fred. "That's the only way it'll work. Come on, don't tell me you haven't heard of Adam Smith and his pin makers, Eli Whitney and interchangeable parts. Heck, I saw an old silent movie of Henry Ford just last night, actually pulling a 1913 Model T down the assembly line with a rope!" he said, with a bit of extra ummph to his voice. "What should I be paying them to do?"

"Yeah," added Luis, "and what am I doing wrong? Who elected you genius?"

"I think I see where Tom is going with this," said Cheryl, as she stopped her treadmill. "Let me ask you a question, Luis. Have you ever fired someone for doing what the work order said to do?"

"No," Luis answered.

"Have you ever fired someone for *not* doing what the work order said to do?" she asked next.

"Probably," Luis answered. "I don't know about just once, but maybe if it's a chronic problem. It's definitely not going to get anybody a raise, though!"

"Well, maybe it should, " Cheryl replied.

"I suppose I should give raises, too—you know, to people who don't do what we assign them to do!" Fred said, his voice loaded with sarcasm.

"No, not at all," said Cheryl. "I'm just saying that if you want to empower people to do something, make it part of the job. Reward them for it." She pointed out that in Luis's job shop, an immediate improvement in either the product or the process design is more likely to be noticed on the floor than in the manager's office. In a job shop, responsibility and authority can be built into a job to reward workers for facilitating improvements. That was the kind of change in job design she thought Tom was really talking about. "If you want someone to look beyond the blinders of the work order, make it part of his job," said Cheryl.

"Exactly," added Tom. "You need to design jobs so that you get what you want from the workers."

Everyone agreed that on Fred's assembly line, making an immediate change in either the process or product design might not work. There the physical composition and layout of the process was a reflection of the product. You couldn't change the product design without serious implications for what was usually a big capital investment, at least not in Fred's case. Rarely could an individual line worker see enough from the vantage point of his workstation to appreciate all the implications of a change he might suggest. The individual worker's part in the process was just a small slice of the pie. But a line worker might well see the potential for streamlining the process and quite possibly the interface with stations up and down the line.

"In your case, Fred, you might want the line workers' job description to include keeping their eyes open and making suggestions to improve the process. Just make sure *somebody* is looking at the big picture," added Tom. "In your case, focus on the process. In Luis's case, maybe focus on both the process and the product. You might even think about getting people into groups or teams with different perspectives." Tom got off the inclined board and moved to another station.

"Seems to me," said Cheryl, "that the important thing is to structure the job descriptions and reward system to encourage what you want from workers and still give them what they need. Empowerment is an important issue, but there's a lot more to it than making people feel good by talking about it! Some people are going to need it more than others. Some situations will call for it more than others. Bringing them all into line with each other is a tough assignment. You guys ought to see how tough it gets in the hospital. We've got to empower and reward our people in a way that allows them to balance what the patients think they should be getting with what we think they should be getting. I can't imagine you have it any easier, Tom."

"No, you're right. The presence of a customer makes the game tougher to play," Tom answered. "I mean, should a flight attendant recheck the headcount so the plane can take off on time, or help a passenger to find someone to swap seats with? We can't anticipate every conflict and tell the attendants what they should do in every case. They have to make the call."

"Well, I'm beginning to see what you're getting at," said Fred, sliding under the bench press station, which seemed a bit overloaded for him. "With all this talk about job design, empowerment, and who does what, do you think I can empower this?" He attempted, without much success, to move the bar.

"Well, between plain old inertia and plain old gravity," laughed Cheryl, "you've got your job cut out for you, big guy!"

> objectives

Take a moment to familiarize yourself with the key objectives of this chapter.

> gearing up

Before you begin reading this chapter, try a short warm-up activity.

> Introduction

In modern history, Adam Smith's experiment with the manufacture of pins may have been the starting point for the purposeful design of work. You might recall from Appendix A that Smith popularized the concept of the division of labor, or job specialization, in England in the late 1700s. Working alone, he showed, a worker could produce 20 pins a day. But a small group of workers, each of whom repeatedly performed a limited portion of the work of making a pin, could produce 48,000 pins a day.

More recent developments in job design have included the use of time and motion studies to develop work standards for repetitive jobs—guidelines for what must be done, the technique to be used, and the time allotted for completion. Time and motion studies are very mechanistic, focusing primarily on the physical aspects of jobs. Researchers using other, more behavioral approaches have sought to enhance the motivational characteristics of work. Often, a worker's rate of output is determined less by the physical ability to complete a task correctly in a given period than by the desire and willingness to do so.

Socio-technical systems theory was developed to match the mechanical with the human elements of the work environment. This theory emphasizes the impact of the production process on workers' social structure. Employees have many objectives besides the creation of a product-service bundle; thus, it is important to consider their social needs when designing a job. Likewise, employee involvement programs seek to unleash workers' creativity. Such programs allow workers to shape their own work environment, solve persistent problems, and respond to opportunities for improvement that others seldom notice.

Integrating Operations Management with Other Functions

Figure 10.1 highlights some of the major relationships between material covered in this chapter and other business functional areas. Looking at the figure, you'll note that this particular section is important to all majors. Also, the section describing employee involvement practices is linked to all business functions because these practices pervade the design of jobs in all areas of a business in many of today's companies.

The next section of the chapter, describing work standards approaches to job design, is most closely linked to decisions made in the human resources (HR) and engineering functions. This section actually describes techniques that were developed by industrial engineers to help improve efficiency

Chapter Topics \ Functional Areas of Business	Finance	Accounting	Human Resources	Marketing	Engineering	Management Information Systems
Integrating Operations Management with Other Functions	●	●	●	●	●	●
Work Standards Approaches			●		●	
The Job Characteristics Model			●			
The Socio-Technical Systems Approach			●		●	●
Employee Involvement and the High-Performance Workplace	●	●	●	●	●	●
The Service Profit Chain	●	●	●	●		
Job Design and Competitive Priorities			●	●		

FIGURE 10.1 Integrating Operations Management with other Functions

and ergonomics through time and motion studies. While the techniques are applied by industrial engineers, they also have implications for HR decisions, such as worker selection and compensation.

The section of this chapter describing the job characteristics model is most directly linked to the HR function. In this section we present one widely accepted behavioral model as it includes many of the behavioral considerations that arise in job design. This model helps explain the relationships among job design, motivation, and worker behavior. It thus helps managers understand how to modify job designs to enhance worker performance.

In today's workplace, most workers interact with other workers as well as technology. Often new technology, such as machines or information systems, fails to deliver all of the expected benefits because it does not fit within the existing social structure. The general idea of socio-technical systems theory is that job designs should be based on an understanding of the social and technical systems within which they exist. As such, engineers and management information systems (MIS) professionals who develop and install new technologies and systems, might benefit by first understanding the social context in which their machines and programs will be used. HR professionals can play a role in adapting the social structure of work to its technical requirements through their recruitment, selection, promotion, retention, and compensation decisions.

The service profit chain is a model that describes the role employees play in developing cycles of success and failure for their employer. This model ties together job design considerations, financial issues such as productivity, profitability, and revenue growth, and marketing concerns such as customer loyalty. It explains why the design of jobs, especially in service-intensive businesses, provides either the foundation for ongoing success or the basis for intractable problems.

The final section of the chapter deals with the relationship between competitive choices a firm might have made and the design of jobs. Since competitive positioning is highly relevant to marketing, we've suggested that this section may be most closely linked to that business function.

> Work Standards Approaches

If you have ever held a job, you probably remember a time when another worker said something like, "Slow down or you're going to make us all look bad." Often, this comment will be made during your first few days on the job and continue until you adapt your pace to that of the leading bully in your work area. This social pressure to perform your work in a particular way is called **worker soldiering.** Through such social mechanisms, workers determine the rate at which work will be done. When they do, they take over part of management's traditional role in *job design.*

While Frederick Taylor, the father of scientific management, was taking night classes in mechanical engineering, he worked the day shift in a steel mill. There Taylor observed that worker soldiering played a major role in determining the rate at which work was done. He felt strongly that instead of allowing workers to determine production rates, managers should use quantitative and motivational techniques to determine and control the pace of work. Later, Taylor and his fellow researchers, Frank and Lillian Gilbreth, suggested the use of time and motion studies in setting job standards.

STANDARD TIMES

In **time and motion studies,** job standards are determined by breaking a task down into its basic movements and measuring the time required to complete those movements. The Gilbreths identified 14 such motions, which they called *Therbligs* (*Gilbreths* spelled backward). Therbligs included activities such as grasping with a hand, searching visually or with a hand, selecting one part from among several, moving an item by hand, moving an empty hand, mental planning, and resting to overcome fatigue. The Gilbreths theorized that by eliminating unnecessary motions and training workers to perform only required motions, they could standardize any job for all capable workers. The time required to complete the job could then be computed by adding the times allowed for each of the Therbligs in the job. Thus, a **work standard** is a defined procedure for completion of a task and includes a clearly stated task duration. In another approach to setting work standards researchers timed workers with a stopwatch as they performed the various tasks that made up their jobs. They then used the distribution of times observed to determine an acceptable work standard.

Work sampling is a technique used to establish work standards for less structured jobs such as those held by librarians, policemen, or sales managers. In **work sampling** employees record their allocation of time to their various responsibilities and this information is used to determine future staff requirements and compensation.

Obviously, a work standard is useful only if workers can be made to conform to the standard. Determining an appropriate standard is far easier than imposing it on workers, however. Thus, companies that use work standards must find a way to get workers to accept them. The most common

Athletes often cover a fixed distance faster during a timed workout than during a game. Similarly, work-studies in industry often underestimate the time required to complete a job because the conditions of the study were not the same as typical work conditions.

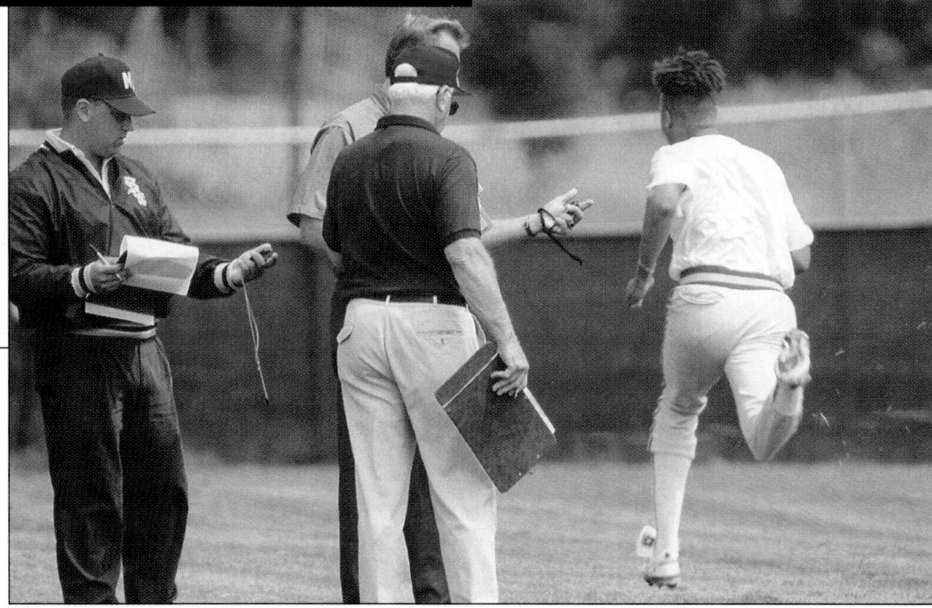

approach has been to select those workers who are best suited to the task, train them to complete the task in the manner required to achieve the standard, and motivate them to achieve the standard using some piece rate system. Taylor, who suggested the approach, favored a piece rate pay system for those who accomplished the standard and a bonus for those who exceeded it.

One advantage of work standards is that they allow managers to separate the planning and doing of work. If managers can effectively estimate the rate at which work will be done, they can also plan schedules, estimate the labor requirements for a given period, tell customers how long a job will take, estimate the labor cost attributable to a particular product-service bundle, and so on. This advantage was particularly important in the past, when managers dealt with a large pool of workers with limited reading, writing, and analytical skills. On the other hand, managerial systems that separate planners from doers tend to reinforce "we versus they" attitudes. Workers often complained about managers who pushed them to achieve a standard while "sitting up in their air-conditioned office without lifting a finger to help." Indeed, managers were often so concerned with the standards, they seemed uninterested in the workers' feelings. They saw the imposition of a work standard much as the process of setting a knob on a machine. But while a work standard is fixed, human strength and concentration vary over time and environmental conditions. From the worker's perspective, work standards were not a very caring approach. Not surprisingly, Scientific Management techniques provoked a strong worker backlash in the early decades of the 20th century. Indeed, many scholars attribute the growth of unions in the first half of the century to the failure of Scientific Management.

STANDARD PROCEDURE

Eventually, the field of industrial engineering grew out of scientific management. Together, these two approaches to the management of work contributed many of the advances in operational efficiency that support our current consumptive lifestyle. Even today, industrial engineers conduct time and motion or work sampling studies. Because most workers today can read, write, and perform many of the analytic tasks once reserved for managers, separation of the planning and doing of work is now not so essential. Instead, members of a work group in a repetitive manufacturing environment might ask an industrial engineer to help them design the jobs in their work area. In fact, in many work places, autonomous groups of workers bear full responsibility for staffing, scheduling, and improving their work processes. Even unionized blue-collar workers in heavy industry have accepted this approach.

Much of the foregoing discussion of work standards focused on the rate at which work should be completed. In other words, a work standard tells *how much* work a worker should be expected to do in a given period. Originally, when jobs tended to be quite repetitive, that focus might have been relevant. If a worker was expected to complete 60 defect-free pieces in an hour, he or she could be reprimanded for completing only 55 or rewarded for completing 65. Quality was inspected after the fact, and consistency was ensured through the worker's familiarity with the work.

But today, most repetitive jobs have been automated. Not many jobs require a worker to repeat a one-minute task for eight hours. Instead, workers have been cross-trained to perform a variety of tasks in any given day; they are multiskilled. As a result, work standards now focus on the question of *how* a task should be completed. Job standardization provides uniformity of procedure, even though most procedures are conducted by a variety of employees. If a job is done wrong, a mistake is made, or production rates become excessively slow, the question managers ask is, Have we been following the standard procedure? Producing 60 units an hour rather than 55 is less important than following standard procedure.

ISO 9000 certification requirements, which have become essential in many manufacturing firms, reinforce this emphasis on the standardization of work procedures. To become and remain ISO 9000 certified, workers must know and follow the standards for the jobs they perform. They must also be able to look up the documentation for the standards if they have questions.

THE HUMAN FACTOR IN JOB DESIGN

To illustrate the importance of the human factor in job standards for routine work, the Gilbreths developed some experiments that focused on the activities of individual workers. Though their experiments have not been widely used in the West, since the 1930s they have been used extensively by Japanese managers. The Japanese call these experiments *table top experiments,* because they can be done at a desk.

For example, one experiment shows that workers' familiarity with a task makes a big difference in the rate at which they can perform it. The experiment requires the worker to write the words *industrial engineering* 10 times. An observer provides the subjects with blank cards and times them. Naturally some improvement occurs, but since the task is familiar and simple, the improvement is not significant. The workers are then told that their work is being "cut in half": They must write *industrial engineering* 10 times, leaving out every other letter. (The result should be "idsra egneig.") Again, an observer provides blank cards and times the subjects, this time exhorting them not to slack off or create defects.

As you might imagine, subjects take much longer to do "half of the work," making more errors in the process. They also reveal an interesting pattern of learning. They typically complete the first card faster than the second and third, yet take significantly less time to complete the last card. Experimenters theorize that subjects take longer to complete the second and third cards because they feel a need to go back and check what they have written.

In other experiments, workers were asked to write the words *production engineer* backward, as they would appear in a mirror. These and other experiments illustrated the significance of a worker's familiarity with the task standard, the order of tasks, and the way in which tasks are learned. Scholars now believe that some of these experiments, along with lessons learned from Henry Ford and other key U.S. industrial figures, became the foundation for the Japanese management system in the latter half of the 20th century.

JOB SPECIALIZATION AND SKILL SET STRATIFICATION

Whether a business is using work standards or not, if a job requires more than one skill a manager may want to take advantage of **job specialization,** which divides work according to the type of skill or knowledge required for its completion. Designing jobs so as to optimize worker skills makes sense, particularly in the delivery of services that require a highly skilled worker to be supported by less-skilled workers. Examples of job design by *skill set stratification* can be found at doctors' offices, restaurants, repair services, and even beauty salons. You may have noticed that at certain beauty salons, some stylists only cut and style hair, while other employees make appointments or shampoo, dry, and sweep up hair. Designing jobs by skill set optimizes the salon's income. You may prefer to go to a barber or beautician who does it all—shampoos, cuts, styles, dries, and sweeps. If so, the price you pay will be higher than elsewhere, or the business will be making less money than other salons, because you will be paying a skilled stylist to do tasks that don't require much skill.

> active example

Take a closer look at the concepts and issues you've been reading about.

active concept check

Now let's take a moment to test your knowledge of the concepts you have studied in this section.

The Job Characteristics Model

The primary shortcoming of the Scientific Management approach to job design is clearly its mechanistic treatment of workers. Workers have feelings; no matter how well they are selected, trained, and paid, if they are treated like machines they will resent it. Workers' feelings about their work and their motivation to perform it are stressed in the *job characteristics model* of work proposed by Hackman and Oldham (1976); see Figure 10.2. This model summarizes a long stream of behavioral research into the relationship among job design, worker motivation, and job performance.

According to the job characteristics model, the job design variables that are important to worker motivation are:

Skill variety—the extent to which a job includes different activities requiring different skills and talents.

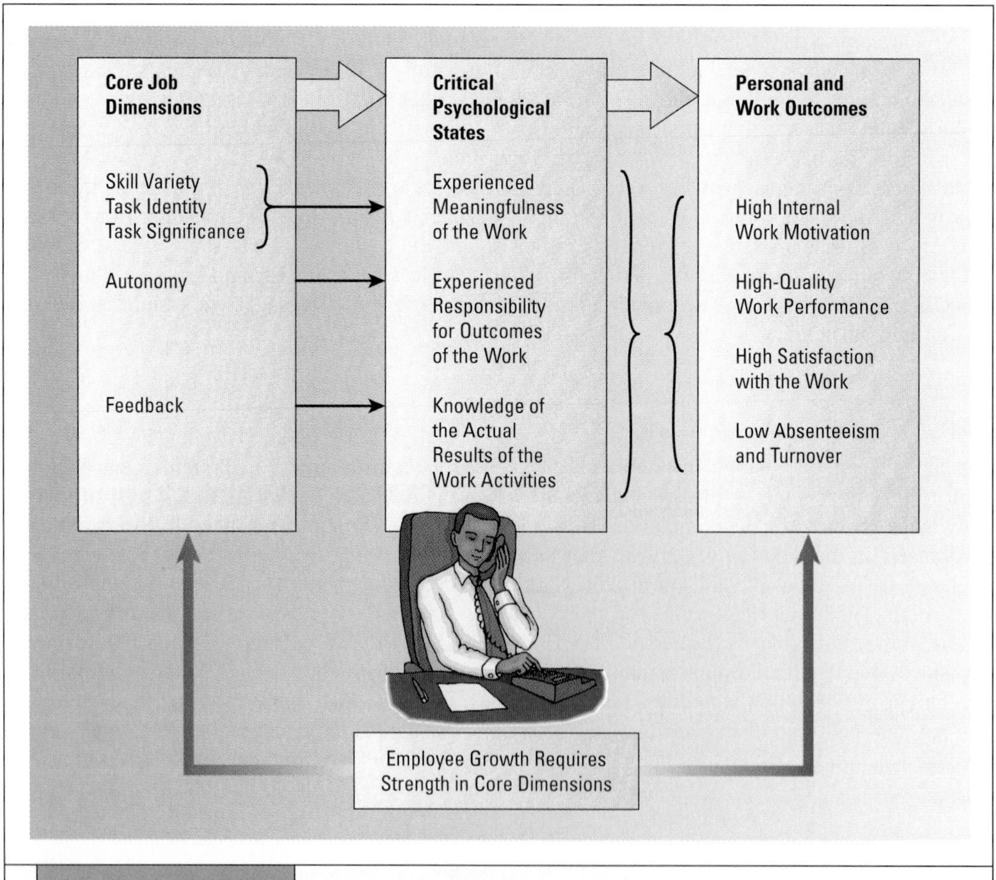

FIGURE 10.2 The Job Characteristics Model

Source: Hackman, J. R. and G. R. Oldham. "Motivation through the design of work: Test of a theory." *Organizational Behavior and Human Performance* 16 (1976): 250–279.

Task identity—the extent to which a job requires the completion of a recognizable product-service bundle. In other words, can the worker tell the customer that she or he is responsible for the product-service bundle just purchased?

Task significance—the extent to which a job impacts other people, including fellow employees, customers, community members, and so on.

Autonomy—the extent to which a worker is free to do a job in her or his own way. The ability to schedule a job, determine the techniques and procedures to be used, and judge the quality of the finished work all add autonomy to a job.

Feedback—the extent to which a worker is informed about her or his effectiveness on a routine basis.

The job characteristics model suggests that job design, in and of itself, can motivate workers by altering their psychological state. Some job designs are more apt than others to provide experiences through which workers attribute meaningfulness to their work, assume responsibility for their work, and gain feedback on the results of their work. Jobs that provide these psychological benefits are more likely than others to produce positive personal and work outcomes, including higher levels of motivation, higher performance levels, higher satisfaction with work, and lower rates of absenteeism and turnover. Furthermore, research suggests that for most of these outcomes, the impact of improved job design will be more significant if individual workers possess a strong need or desire for personal growth.

THE MOTIVATING POTENTIAL SCORE

The motivational potential of a particular job, called its motivating potential score (MPS), may be calculated using Equation 9.1.

$$\text{Motivating Potential Score } (MPS) = (\text{skill variety} + \text{task identity} + \text{task significance}) \times \text{autonomy} \times \text{feedback} \quad \text{(Equation 9.1)}$$

Since the MPS is a multiplicative combination of job dimensions, a job design will not motivate workers if feedback, autonomy, or a combination of skill variety, task identity, and task significance is missing. That means workers will have to be motivated by other means, such as a combination of rewards, punishment, and their own internal desire to do the work. Conversely, the more of the five core job dimensions a job design includes, the greater the job's motivating potential.

Consider the work of a short-order cook at the Awful Waffle, a fast-food restaurant. The establishment offers a limited menu of similar items, all prepared in the same manner; thus, skill variety is low. Furthermore, the cook doesn't buy materials and in many cases doesn't even mix up the batter, but just heats it up. Task identity is low then, too. Though the cook's work is very important to the customer, his recipes aren't going to be printed in culinary magazines. Task significance is therefore low. Autonomy is nonexistent in the short-order cook's job: He is told when to come to work, when to leave, and is given no choice in what to prepare and when. Finally, no formal feedback loop requires customers to compliment the cook's efforts. Little wonder that the classifieds are filled with help-wanted ads for short-order cooks! Turnover is high because the job's motivating potential score is close to zero—and its extrinsic rewards aren't significant, either.

Now consider the job of head chef at a five-star restaurant. Because the chef must prepare a variety of desserts, entrees, appetizers, seasonal dishes, and drinks, skill variety is high. Task identity is high, too, since the chef buys the ingredients, determines how to prepare and season each dish, and even takes care to arrange the items attractively on the plate. Because a five-star restaurant has a reputation, the chef's recipes will be regarded as proprietary information until they are published and may even win awards. The rich and famous are likely to patronize the chef. Thus, task significance is high. The chef is also autonomous, preparing the foods he or she chooses when and how he or she wishes. Diners are expected to relay their compliments to the chef via the garçon or maitre d'. For all these reasons, the MPS of the head chef's job is high. Turnover and absenteeism are low; a chef might remain at one restaurant for decades.

> active example

Take a closer look at the concepts and issues you've been reading about.

IMPROVING A JOB'S MOTIVATING POTENTIAL

Ideally every job should include some combination of the five core job characteristics. Fortunately these job design variables can be manipulated in a number of ways. Common strategies for improving a job's motivating potential score include the following:

Job enlargement adds skill variety through the addition of new tasks.

Job rotation adds skill variety by moving workers through a series of different jobs over a prescribed period.

Job enrichment adds task significance and enhances autonomy by combining some planning and controlling with the doing of work. For example, a job can be enriched by allowing workers to decide what methods to use, train new hires, schedule their own work, solve their own operational problems, and control part of their budget. The establishment of responsibility for internal and external customer relationships provides task significance, task identity, and feedback.

Job-contained feedback channels provide private, timely, and accurate data on job performance. For example, if client relationships and quality evaluation requirements are built into a job, workers will get feedback straight from the customer's mouth. This type of feedback is generally superior to any feedback a supervisor could provide. Moreover, when feedback comes from a supervisor, the employee will seek to satisfy the supervisor; but when feedback comes from the customer, the employee is more likely to satisfy the customer.

active concept check

Now let's take a moment to test your knowledge of the concepts you have studied in this section.

Designing Jobs at the Student Recreation Center

The Student Recreation Center (SRC) is not unlike most service-intensive facilities. It is a labor-intensive facility that requires a large staff on the floor, in the pool, and behind the counter to facilitate the varied programming activities that it schedules. Considering the very large number and variety of tasks and responsibilities that must be divided into manageable jobs, defining "who does what" can be a formidable challenge. SRC job design, like that of other organizations, must be sufficiently specialized to match the skills of the available staff and yet be challenging in such a way as to appeal to the staff member and be intrinsically rewarding. The various tasks and responsibilities within the SRC have a broad range of skill requirements that must be considered during the process of designing staff jobs. In addition, students staff most of the SRC's nonadministrative or supervisory positions. Since high turnover is typical among student workers, this further complicates job design.

The job characteristics model has helped with job design at the SRC. Wherever possible, skill variety, task identity, and task significance are emphasized. Autonomy and feedback are built into the SRC's infrastructure as well. Broadening the responsibilities for floor supervisors and cross training workers in several positions at the front desk enhance skill variety. Ongoing on-the-job training, which emphasizes the interdependent nature of positions at the SRC, helps address the identity and significance of the tasks that make up each job. A student worker team (see "Solving the Music Dilemma at the Student Recreation Center" in Chapter 6) that meets weekly to address continuous improvement suggestions from workers or patrons adds an element of feedback. Most staff have been empowered with decision-making autonomy that fits their specific job.

There are two types of jobs at the SRC: those that require a distinct skill, such as being a lifeguard or officiating games, and those that are task-oriented, such as clerical or janitorial positions. The core job dimensions of the job characteristics model vary by the type of job. While task-oriented jobs can use job rotation or other forms of horizontal job enlargement to improve the motivating potential of the job, this is not as easy for jobs based upon skill groups. For example, lifeguards have high levels of autonomy and task identity, but a rotation between stations on a quick basis is about all that can be done to address the limited variety of skills required most of the time they are on duty. Intramural game officials have high levels of autonomy and skill variety, but their authority is often challenged when somebody doesn't like a call. The authority vested in the official's job description goes a long way toward providing task significance and identity.

The use of student workers can present difficulties for campus facility administrators. Because student workers generally place a higher priority in their studies than their jobs, many only work as much as they absolutely have to. While understandable, this makes it hard to schedule and retain students. Jobs in the SRC do have some advantages over washing dishes in the dining hall, yet working to design attractive jobs—with high enough motivating potentials that students compete for them—has benefited both the student workers and SRC administrators.

The Socio-Technical Systems Approach

According to *socio-technical systems theory,* there are two systems in any workplace: a social system and a technical system. The technical system has only one purpose: to create a product-service bundle that will satisfy customers. The social system, on the other hand, may have numerous objectives, only one of which is creating the product-service bundle. Other objectives may include providing for the material needs of workers' families, uplifting the community's quality of life, keeping the environment clean, and making life at work more enjoyable. Often, these other objectives are much more important than the first to the people who make up the social system.

Figure 10.3 illustrates a common situation. On the one hand, the technical system is designed to be highly effective at meeting a product's design specifications. The social system, on the other hand, has evolved over time to meet the interests and needs of the employees. Because the social system's objectives do not match the technical system's objectives, the socio-technical system is not particularly well suited to providing the product-service bundle the customer desires. The idea behind socio-technical systems theory is that in any organization, there is a best match between the technical system and the social system. That match, which is best suited to satisfying customer requirements, is a critical aspect of job design.

While automation is usually seen as a change in the technical system, in reality, any change in the technical system will change the social system as well. The decision to automate a worker's job creates a new type of job to support the new technology. Changing the makeup of the workforce also creates fear of job loss, mistrust, and insecurity in the workforce. Often, managers will automate a process to achieve higher levels of productivity, trusting that their goal can be met solely through a

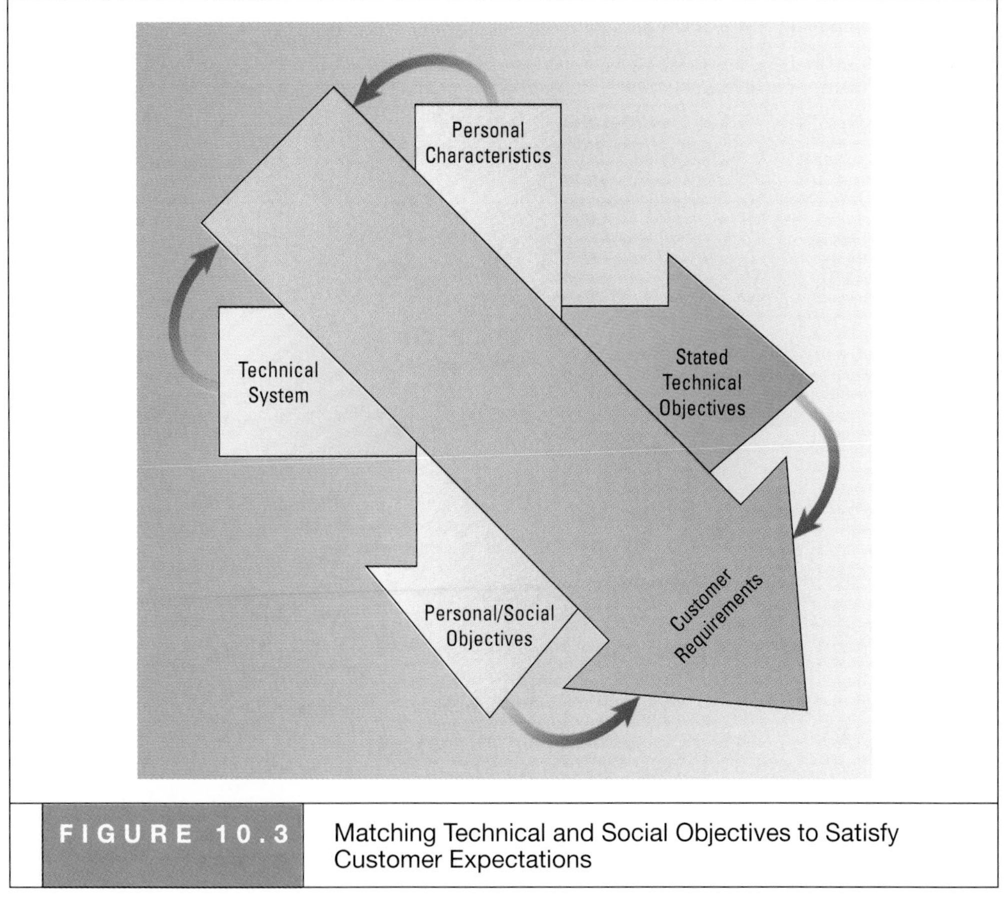

FIGURE 10.3 Matching Technical and Social Objectives to Satisfy Customer Expectations

Hospital nursing stations are designed to provide both the social interactions and the technical resources needed to enhance the service nurses provide.

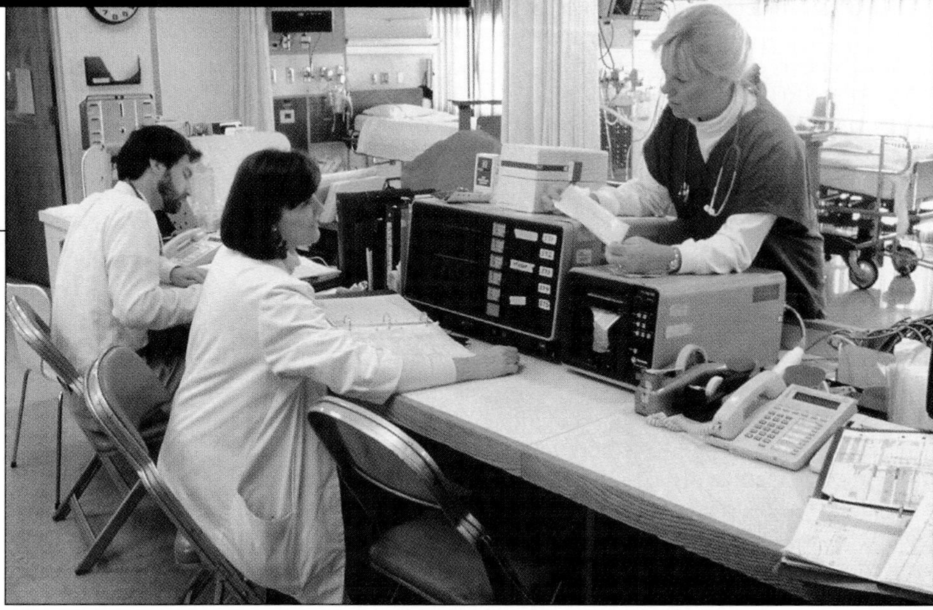

change in the technical system. Later, when they cannot use the new technology effectively because it does not fit the existing social system, they realize they have made a costly blunder.

Just as the changes in the technical system can force changes in the social system, changes in the social system can drive technical considerations. Two examples are the increasing concern for ergonomics and worker safety. Automating jobs that are dangerous or highly repetitive makes a great deal of sense. Indeed, workers might tend to avoid dangerous, monotonous, or difficult jobs through tardiness, absenteeism, and other social mechanisms. Where these problems exist or where operational equipment is not designed with the user in mind, managers should use technology to remedy the social problem.

Figure 10.4 illustrates the constant pressure for change in job design. While all managers hope that the existing job design and work organization are consistent with company strategy, structure (building and equipment), and infrastructure (decision making, training, procedures, and systems), those relationships cannot be set in concrete. Technological change, change in customer preferences, and social change will eventually create mismatches that require jobs to be redesigned.

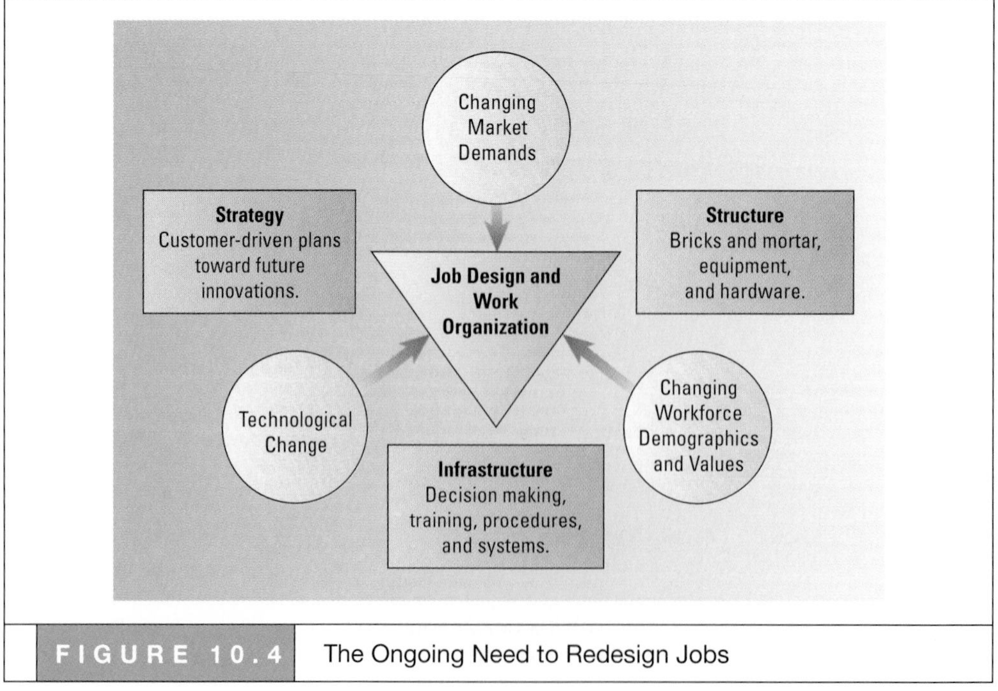

FIGURE 10.4 The Ongoing Need to Redesign Jobs

active example

Take a closer look at the concepts and issues you've been reading about.

Employee Involvement and the High-Performance Workplace

Today, most employers realize that to remain competitive, they need to capitalize on the brain power and creativity of their workforce. Job designs that include only physical tasks and treat workers like machines are on the way out. If the physical tasks in a job are so repetitive that they do not require worker creativity, the job is frequently automated. Similarly, the notion that management plans and controls what workers do is falling out of favor. As a value-adding system resource, workers are notably different from machines in that they can adapt, learn, interact with others, and grow. Machines can't make suggestions that will improve customer service, worker safety, product reliability, or environmental performance. Workers, on the other hand, can make hundreds of suggestions each year, and they can cooperate with others to make the improvements they have suggested a reality.

Employee Involvement (EI) is a management approach that allows allow workers to participate regularly in the operating decisions that affect them, including planning, job design, process improvement, goal setting, performance measurement, and problem solving. Designed to give employees more pride, responsibility, and reward for their companies' success, EI has been an extremely effective approach, because it places the power to address both problems and opportunities in the hands of those workers best able to do so.

ENCOURAGING TEAMWORK

One of the most common ways to harness the mental power of workers is to form worker teams. Teams are used in just about every area of business and at just about every organization. They are the engine behind any successful effort to implement the Total Quality philosophy and rely heavily on quality tools, such as the Quality Improvement story.

Regardless of the context of teamwork, the assignment of workers to teams has a significant impact on the design of their jobs. Communication, analytical skills, functional knowledge in multiple areas, goal-oriented behavior, and consensus-based decision making all become critical to job performance. Teamwork also means that job performance cannot be fully described, measured, or rewarded solely in terms of hourly output. In a team environment, therefore, managers must act as leaders who value employee input and participative decision making. They cannot simply oversee administrative procedures and guard the status quo.

Teams are a way of life at many organizations today. The job design tools and techniques described in this chapter are often used by teams themselves to design their own jobs. As a result, the benefits of teamwork are now widely recognized. As a former president of Ford Motor Company has said, "No matter what you're trying to do, teams are the most effective way to get the job done."[1] Some of the specific benefits teams have generated for their companies include:

- cost reductions in materials, overhead, and labor;
- improvements in product reliability and usefulness;
- process improvements, including reduced setup and operating time, improved flexibility and quality of conformance, a reduction in unexpected downtime, and improved reliability of delivery;
- the reduction or elimination of waste, including transportation, rework, shrinkage, packaging, storage cost, and paperwork;
- improvements in worker safety, health, knowledge, engagement, skill, and morale;
- improved environmental performance; and
- improved supplier, customer, and community relations.

Companies that are serious about EI design the system so as to facilitate and reward worker participation. Typically, in each facility, managers called **facilitators** support the teams' efforts and respond

[1]This comment was made in a presentation by Thomas Page at the dedication of Miami University's Page Center for Entrepreneurship, September 26, 1994.

to workers' suggestions for improvement. The facilitator's job is to provide any necessary training, which often includes coaching in problem solving and communication. Facilitators can also put teams in touch with functional experts, customers, or outside vendors who have the knowledge and information they need. Having enough facilitators to support the level of team activity present in a facility is critical. Frequently, facilitators will report to a director of EI, who reports in turn to a corporate vice president for quality.

One of the keys to successful teamwork is the knowledge and skill of team members. Consequently, most successful EI programs provide significant training to employees. Performing effectively as a team member will be difficult if an employee's reading, writing, speaking, listening, or basic data analysis skills are limited. Understanding group dynamics—how to conduct meetings, develop a consensus, and include less-outgoing members—is also important. Team members must understand the proper roles of leaders, facilitators, and others in the group, as well as the importance of preparing for a meeting. All these general skills must be built into the workforce; one cannot assume that a new hire has them.

In addition to general skills, team members might require training specific to a project. For example, a team that is trying to reduce setup time on a specific machine might need training in the Single-Minute Exchange of Dies (SMED) system for reducing setup time. Similarly, a team that is trying to prevent equipment breakdowns might need training by the manufacturer of the equipment or training in total productive maintenance. Or a team might need help in comprehending the production process as a whole. Process-oriented experiments (similar to table top experiments, except that they are applied to a whole process) can help team members to understand the dynamics of a complex production process, including the impact on productivity of bottlenecks, inventory buffers, quality problems, and process disruptions. Experimentation of this nature is particularly useful for teams that design their own jobs and work as an autonomous group. It not only helps members to better understand and design their jobs, but it improves the effectiveness of the group as a whole.

active exercise <

Take a moment to apply what you've learned.

REWARDING EMPLOYEE INVOLVEMENT

As for rewards, most companies compensate workers generously for their participation. At Honda of America Manufacturing (HAM), for example, workers who make suggestions for improvement and then serve on teams to implement their suggestions receive small cash bonuses. Every bona fide suggestion is compensated with a $3, $6, $20, $50, or $100 bonus in the next paycheck. Simple, run-of-the-mill suggestions are evaluated by supervisors and facilitators and rewarded at the lower levels. Suggestions that have a significant impact beyond the local work area are forwarded to higher levels of management. The higher a suggestion goes, the greater the monetary reward. In addition to small bonuses, employees can earn between 10 and 50 points for each suggestion, and 50 points for completing a team project, such as investigating, planning, and implementing a suggestion.

As workers accumulate points, they begin to receive prizes. Workers who reach the 300-point milestone receive a plaque from the plant manager. At 1,000 points, they receive an $800 cash bonus. At the 2,500-point milestone, the participating employee can choose a new Honda Civic or pay the difference and get an Accord. At 5,000 points, the grand prize includes a new Accord, a paid two-week trip for two anywhere in the world, and a cash bonus worth four weeks' pay! Honda also pays monthly bonuses for perfect attendance and on-time arrival, as well as an annual profit-sharing bonus based partly on the company's profitability and partly on the employee's performance. Because of this voluntary program, a large percentage of Honda's workforce is highly motivated to improve the company's operating system. Though the work may be monotonous and all workers have the same title and receive the same wage, without regard to seniority, Honda of America turns away thousands of job applicants each year.

To recognize groups of employees, most large companies hold team competitions. Honda, for example, has one competition for supplier teams and another for internal teams. Teams present their projects and showcase the problem-solving processes they used, allowing all employees to learn from their experiences. The winners at each facility go on to a national competition; the national winners compete internationally. Organizations such as the Association for Quality and Participation (AQP) and state manufacturers' organizations also sponsor team competitions. The travel and recognition that are associated with these competitions are a significant reward for the workers who participate.

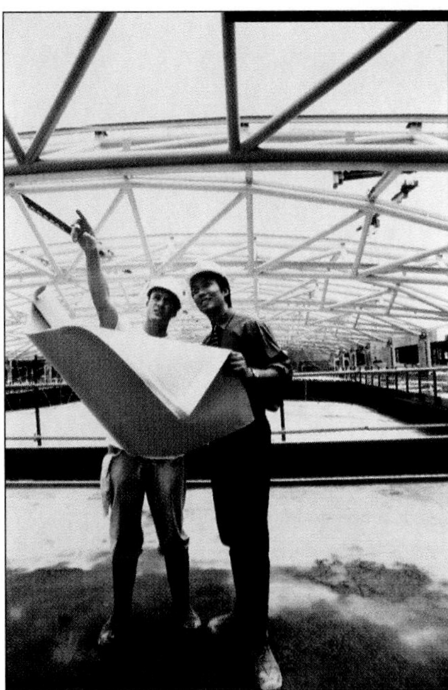

With increasing use of Employee Involvement in business, effective communication among workers is an important part of any job. In the management of projects such as this construction site in Hong Kong and in process facilities that do customized work, it is virtually impossible to satisfy customers without frequent communication facilitated by visual aids such as these blueprints.

Given the key elements of a well-designed EI program—excellent facilitators, readily available training, a well-designed reward system—one can see that teamwork requires a significant investment in the workforce. Does it pay? Many companies are convinced that it does. Honda of America executives believe they get back more than five dollars for every dollar they spend on the EI program. In many cases, the financial return is ongoing, because while the improvements are paid for only once, they last for many years. Large organizations may generate more than a million worker suggestions a year; many estimate the combined return on their suggestion and EI programs to be roughly 100 to 1. In other words, for every penny they spend, they are getting back roughly a dollar.

In the United States, some legal objections have been raised to certain manufacturers' EI programs. Union leaders may suspect that manufacturers might be using EI programs to thwart or even replace the unions' role in meeting workers' needs. Thus, companies must be careful to ensure that teams in their EI programs do not violate national labor law. Generally speaking, team activities may be illegal if they (1) address labor issues that affect employees who do not belong to the team; (2) address matters such as wages, grievances, hours, or working conditions; (3) include deals with management on certain issues; or (4) represent employees being "led through the hoops" by managers, rather than operating autonomously.

> active example

Take a closer look at the concepts and issues you've been reading about.

> active concept check

Now let's take a moment to test your knowledge of the concepts you have studied in this section.

> The Service Profit Chain

Heskett, Sasser, and Schlesinger (1987) developed the concept of the service profit chain. Illustrated in Figure 10.5, the model suggests that employees drive service value, which drives customer satis-

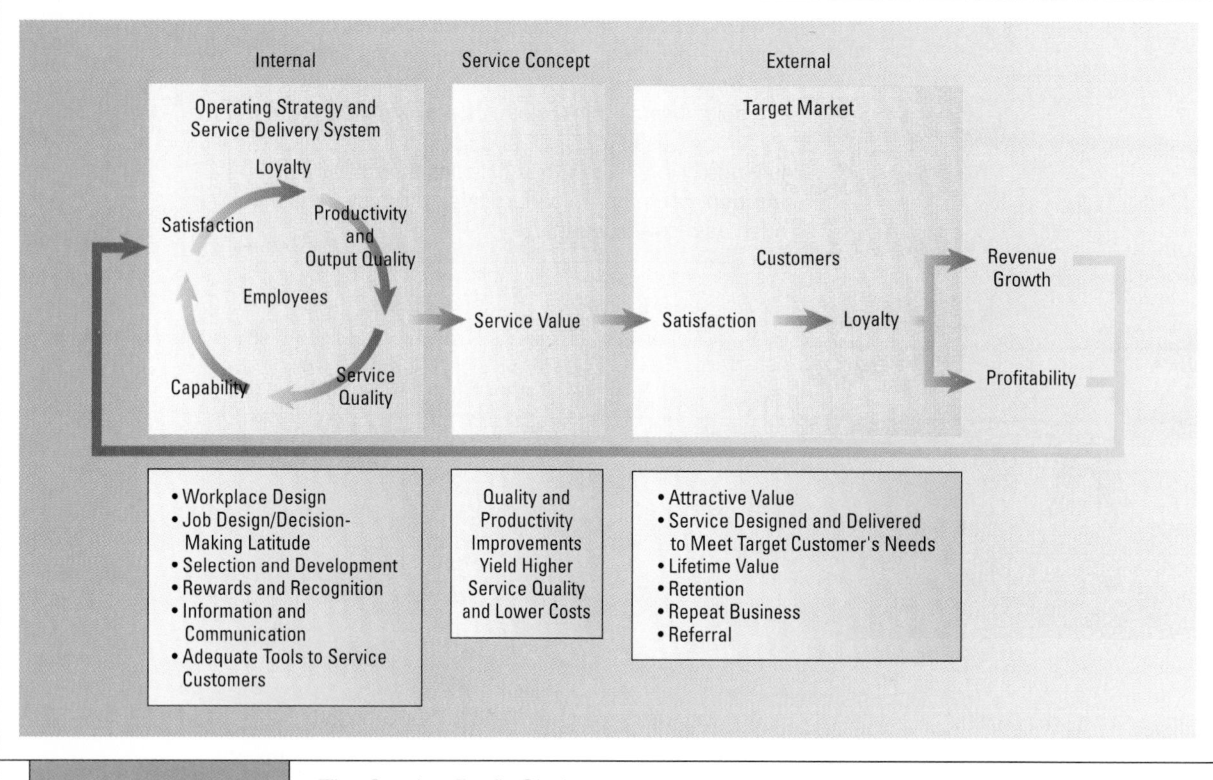

FIGURE 10.5 The Service Profit Chain

Source: The Service Profit Chain, Heskett, Sasser, and Schlesinger, Free Press, 1987, p. 19.

faction and loyalty, which drives revenue and profit growth. In short, the service profit chain recommends that primary attention be paid to the role of employees as a key driver of profits. This concept, despite its name, is not limited to service environments. Whether an organization primarily manufactures a product or delivers services involving high customer contact, its employees are critical to quality and financial performance.

In Figure 10.5, the box labeled "Operating Strategy and Service Delivery System" encompasses the elements of employee performance. "Capability" refers to recruiting, hiring, and training employees who can do the work and find fulfillment in the work. "Satisfaction" comes from a work environment that provides both extrinsic financial rewards and intrinsic rewards.

Employees who are equipped to accomplish excellence and are satisfied with the rewards that come from high performance will become loyal to the employer. They will be less likely to quit and look for work elsewhere. This is because employers who devote proportionately more resources to employee hiring, training, and motivating than competing area employers quickly become known in the community as "employers of choice." Word spreads fast among potential job applicants when an employer offers higher-than-average wages, health and dental benefits, and such perks as on-site daycare facilities. Employers of choice enjoy a larger pool of better-qualified job applicants because they are the most desirable employer in the community. Employee turnover rates at employers of choice can be as low as 1% to 2% annually.

Loyal employees become more productive employees over time. They learn more skills, they become experts in the organization's product-service bundle, they help train new employees, and they often develop important relationships with customers and suppliers. The result is high service quality delivered by employees. The circle of arrows in the "Employees" box in Figure 10.5 indicates the synergy that is created through the interaction of the different elements of employee performance.

video exercise

Take a moment to apply what you've learned.

The middle box labeled "Service Concept" is the combination of low costs and high service quality that result from an effective employee strategy. The customer, as depicted in the "Customers" box on the right ultimately determines service value. High service value means that customers will be satisfied with their purchases, will become loyal, and will spread positive word of mouth in the community. Repeat customers are cheaper to serve and tend to purchase more per transaction. New customers, by contrast, are more expensive to attract and serve, and tend to spend less per transaction.

The output of the service profit chain model is revenue growth and profitability. It represents a "breakthrough" strategy for organizations that are frustrated by industry convention. The fast-food industry provides a good context for applying the service profit chain model. Fast-food restaurants are plagued with low pay, low morale, boring work tasks, and high employee turnover. Fast-food employers claim they can't pay more because they must keep their costs in line with competitors. The result is that no employer is an employer of choice. To job applicants, one employer is the same as another and no reason for loyalty exists. Customer service is frequently slowed because of worker shortages, poor worker attitudes, or inadequate levels of worker training. Poor customer service, in turn, leads to lower service value, lower customer satisfaction, lower loyalty, and less revenue growth and profitability. With less revenue and profitability, it becomes more difficult to improve worker wages and training. This self-perpetuating mess is called the "cycle of failure."

Several years ago, the croissant sandwich restaurant chain Au Bon Pain tried to turn the cycle of failure into the cycle of success. Their new approach slashed the number of part-time employees and created full-time positions that promised a 50-hour weekly work schedule, with 10 hours paid as overtime. This arrangement provided the financial incentive for the new full-time employees to be loyal to their Au Bon Pain jobs. The overtime provided an incentive to avoid missing work, since a missed day meant a loss of the 10 hours of overtime pay. The full-time employees became more knowledgeable, faster, and more accurate in filling customer orders. Customer "regulars" became acquainted with employees who worked the same shifts every day. The result was a high level of comfort and familiarity for the customers. This led to repeat business, positive word of mouth, increased store sales, and greater profits. Through the service profit chain, Au Bon Pain did, in fact, turn the cycle of failure into the cycle of success.[2]

> active exercise

Take a moment to apply what you've learned.

> active concept check

Now let's take a moment to test your knowledge of the concepts you have studied in this section.

> Job Design and Competitive Priorities

The modern worker and work environment are quite different from the workers and factories of the past. Today even the least educated workers are better educated than workers were 40 or 50 years ago: Most are high school graduates. Furthermore, today's workers enjoy a great deal of job mobility; the idea of spending one's entire life doing just one job is a thing of the past. Temporary workers ("temps") are used much more widely today than in the past. Finally, the present focus on satisfying a firm's internal and external customers makes the current workplace very different from the workplace of times past.

As a result of these changes, job design has changed. While specialization and scientific management, which stressed the separate planning and execution of work, did improve productivity significantly in the early 20th century, today managers recognize that jobs can become too specialized.

[2]This information on the service profit chain is adapted from: James L. Heskett, Thomas O. Jones, Gary W. Loveman, W. Earl Sasser, Jr., and Leonard A. Schlesinger, "Putting the Service Profit Chain to Work," *Harvard Business Review* (March–April, 1994): 166; and W. Earl Sasser Jr., and Lucy Lytle, "Au Bon Pain: The Partner/Manager Program," Case No. 9-687-063, Boston: Harvard Business School Publishing Division, 1993.

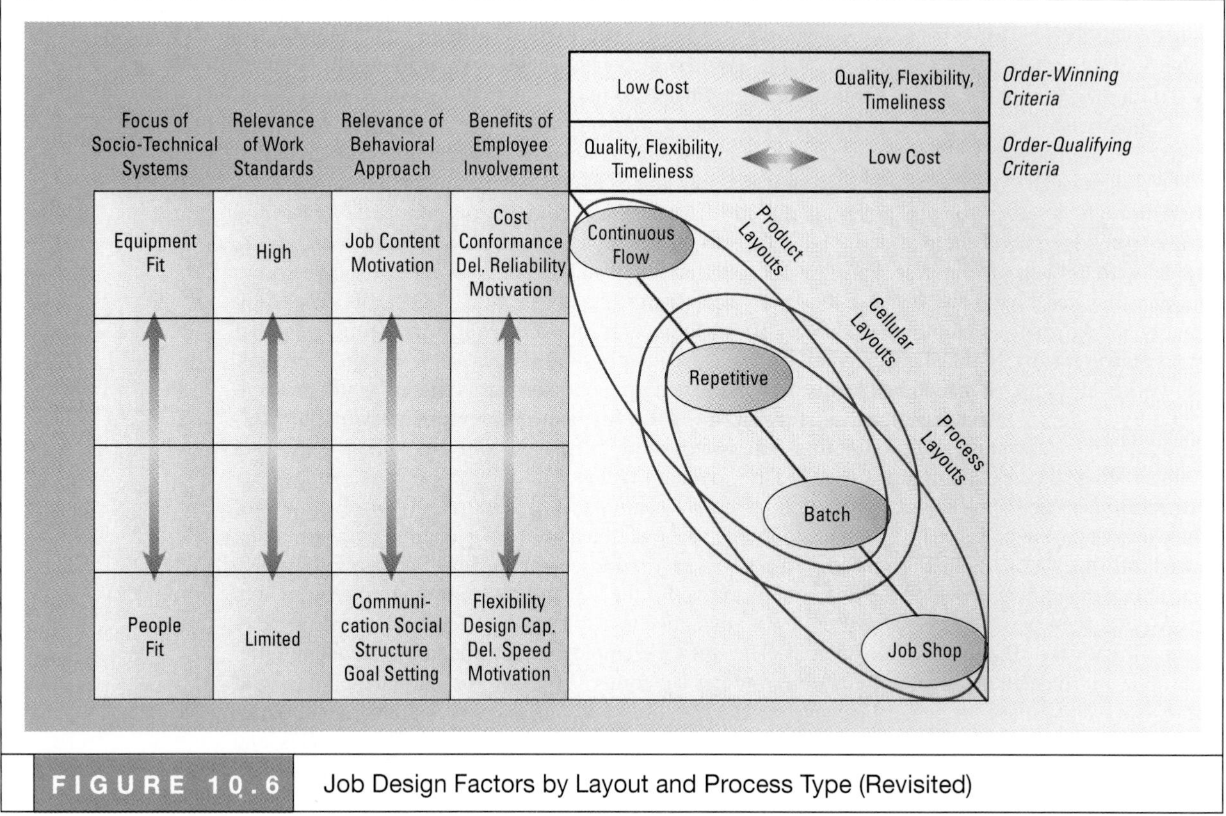

FIGURE 10.6 Job Design Factors by Layout and Process Type (Revisited)

Improving a single worker's productivity, for example, may harm the production flow and overall system performance. With too much specialization, a company might lose sight of customer satisfaction. Given the dynamics of today's workforce, cooperation and teamwork may be more important than individual performance. In working together as a team, individuals may need to sacrifice their own productivity to improve the overall productivity of the system. The team approach also helps to overcome some of the problems associated with a transient workforce. That is not to suggest that the tools once used in job design are irrelevant today, but those tools must be used selectively by workers themselves.

Figure 10.6 shows that not all job design considerations are of equal importance in all operational settings. Work standards, which first became popular in the age of mass production, are still highly relevant in companies that win orders on the basis of cost, conformance, and reliable delivery. But with the growing importance of customization and the increasing flexibility of operational systems, such standards are becoming far from universal in their application. Though work standards may not be valuable to firms that compete on the basis of flexibility, the behavioral and socio-technical systems approaches to job design are. In continuous flow or repetitive manufacturing environments, the behavioral approach to job design focuses primarily on improving job content in order to enhance worker motivation. In batch processes and job shops, however, the behavioral approach to job design focuses more on communication, social structure, and goal setting. Finally, though the EI approach seems applicable to any production environment, the focus of employee teams will depend on the firm's competitive priorities. Note that for each type of production process, the benefits of EI programs are the same as the order-winning criteria for that process.

> Integrating Operational Decisions

This is the final chapter in what might be called the bricks-and-mortar section of this book. Job design is a structural aspect of the value-adding system. Thus, this chapter is closely linked to earlier chapters that dealt with nuts-and-bolts issues, including process design and layout (Chapters 7 and 9). This chapter, however, addresses the flesh-and-bones issue of the role of workers. What will workers do? What responsibilities will they be given? How will they be compensated? As you have seen in this chapter, all these questions are related to the technology issues covered in Chapters 7 and 9 and product-service design covered in Chapter 4. The chapter is also closely tied to Chapter 11, because the design of jobs has a significant impact on the flexibility of labor and the latitude that is available to those managers who make intermediate-range labor plans.

> integrated OM

Take a moment to apply what you've learned.

> Chapter Wrap-Up

Employees' jobs are part of the value-adding system, so customer satisfaction depends to some degree on the design of those jobs. Throughout this book, we have emphasized that the value-adding system should fit a company's competitive priorities. The jobs that employees are asked to do should support the company's operations strategy. Where the competitive priority is cost, jobs will be designed to provide efficiency. Where the competitive priority is flexibility, jobs will be designed to enhance creativity, innovation, and communication.

The work standards approach to job design makes sense in operations in which workers do not have the analytical skills to make decisions about their own work, or in which the production of a highly standardized product-service bundle cannot be automated. Traditionally, work standards have focused on *how much* work should be done in a given period. Workers were motivated with extrinsic rewards. Today, work standards are used to standardize tasks and procedures that are performed by many different workers. This approach, which facilitates job rotation, requires a more broadly skilled workforce but adds interest to workers' lives.

The job characteristics model, which represents a behavioral approach to job design, focuses on the need to motivate workers. The motivating potential score measures a job's motivational ability—the extent to which the job provides skill variety, task identity, task significance, autonomy, and feedback. Because low-MPS jobs are associated with turnover, absenteeism, and even quality problems, employers should try to eliminate those positions whenever possible.

Socio-technical systems theory emphasizes the need to effectively match the mechanical and human elements in the work environment. Too frequently, jobs must be made to fit the technical constraints of machines designed by engineers who are more concerned with technological sophistication than with user-friendliness. When workers must adjust to a machine's shortcomings, they lose their motivation and pride of workmanship. This theory, then, suggests that the design of both machines and jobs should focus on satisfying customer requirements.

Today employees are expected to assist in the improvement and ongoing operation of the systems in which they work. This expectation has altered both the jobs workers do and the way in which they are managed. Employee Involvement is an approach that emphasizes the use of teams to leverage workers' brainpower. As workers become decision makers, management's role evolves from direct supervision to facilitation of teamwork.

The service profit chain is one model that effectively links job design to the ongoing performance of firms. When jobs are well designed, one should expect higher levels of productivity, output quality, service quality, performance capability, employee satisfaction, and loyalty. Thus customers receive greater value, are more satisfied, and become more loyal. Consequently revenue can more easily be grown and profitability can be enhanced. These business results allow managers to further enhance the workplace and satisfaction of employees, which continues the cycle. An ongoing and sustainable cycle of success, therefore, can begin with the effective design of jobs. By contrast, poor design of jobs can lead to a cycle of failure that is very difficult to escape.

The options available to a firm in regards to job design are constrained by the competitive choices that they have made to position their product-service bundle in the marketplace. As mentioned in Chapter 3, the value-adding system and the product-service bundle must fit the competitive priorities of the firm. Since job design is a part of the value-adding system's design, job design choices must fit a firm's competitive priorities. Companies that are trying to compete on the basis of cost are more likely to pursue cost efficiency, quality of conformance, and delivery reliability while designing jobs. By contrast, companies that compete on the basis of flexibility are more likely to pay attention to issues such as communication, social structure, and skill development.

> end-of-chapter resources

- Practice Quiz
- Key Terms
- Discussion Questions
- Case 10.1: Attitude Adjustment in East LA (A True Story)
- References
- Factory Tours

Aggregate Planning

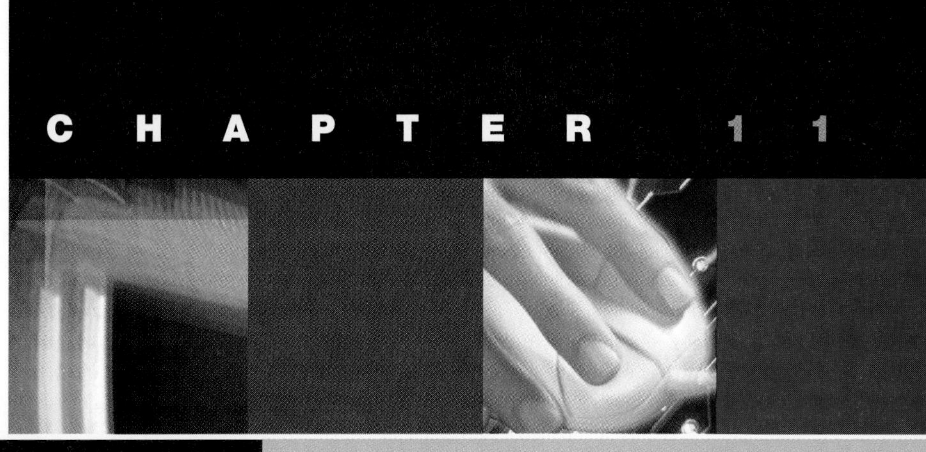

Chapter Outline

What's Ahead

. . . BACK AT THE REC CENTER

The day after Thanksgiving, everyone at the club was feeling slow and overstuffed. A lot of the regulars had the day off and were sleeping in. But Cheryl, Fred, Luis, and Tom were there already, working off yesterday's feast.

Tom had arrived first. He had to work that day, and he wanted to get in early; Thanksgiving was the busiest holiday of the year in the U.S. airline industry. Fred and Luis were just starting to stretch and warm up. They were probably there out of habit; both had the day off. Cheryl was riding a stationary bike. She was on her way to the office to catch up on some paperwork that had piled up while she was away on a trip to San Diego.

"Hey, Tom, I flew home on one of your flights Wednesday," Cheryl said. "The flight was on time, as usual, but I was really impressed with how smoothly things went on the ground, given the number of people traveling and the bad weather forecasts. I just couldn't get over the crowds. The San Diego airport was packed! It was wall-to-wall people when I got back here, too. Everything went great, though.

Tom, seeing a chance to brag a bit between bench presses, explained that Fridays and Sundays were usually the busiest days of the week. All the business travelers and vacationers ending or beginning their trips could really jam things up. But the day before Thanksgiving was just like a Friday; given the short workweek and when you factored in the large number of people traveling over such a short period, it became the busiest day of the year. Most of the airports his airline flew in and out of weren't equipped to handle those numbers every day, he went on, but once a year wasn't too bad, especially when the forecasters could see it coming. It just meant a lot of overtime and some sore feet.

"That's what I like about our factory," interjected Fred, as he finished stretching. He was referring to the factory that supplied his division with mass-produced, standardized pagers. "We crank 'em out at whatever pace the annual plan calls for, pile 'em up at the end of the line, and ship 'em when we sell 'em. If we run out for a week or two, we back order," he said, with obvious satisfaction. "Planning is easy. Get the monthly numbers from the marketing people, adjust the line, get some lunch, and call it a day. What a life!"

"I don't think it's quite that easy, even in *your* business," Luis doubted aloud.

"Yeah," suggested Tom, "even though a lot of the decisions are hardwired into the production line, it can't be easy to rebalance the jobs all the way down the line every time marketing wants to change the pace."

"It isn't, and that's why we don't do it very often. It's cheaper to let inventory build up. Nobody likes back orders, either, but we do it when we have to," said Fred.

"That's okay for a pager or a cell phone, but you can't use inventory to set a broken leg or get someone home for the holidays!" laughed Luis, as he got up on a stepper. "You can't inventory services!"

"Right, Luis, but you know, you're a lot more like us than you are like Fred," said Cheryl. "You guys do most of your work to order. You don't inventory much finished furniture either."

"You're telling me!" Luis responded. "And have you seen how many different pieces of furniture we make? With all the labor we use, we could never keep our line as smooth as Fred's." We still plan ahead, though: hiring, layoffs, raw materials, overtime, temps—all that stuff. We put it all together with our forecasts and make everything line up for the next few months. We can't just change everything over breakfast and have it on the floor by lunch! Just the time it takes to hire a machine operator—all said and done, we're looking 8 to 10 weeks down the road."

"We make only a couple of different pagers, so plugging in the right numbers based on a new forecast is pretty straightforward," Fred responded, as he looked around the room. With so many people staying home this morning, he had more stations to choose from than usual. "How do you know what your orders will be if you do as much custom work as you say you do?" he asked Luis.

"It's hard," said Luis. "We don't know what our orders will be until we get them. We do forecasts, though. We just add up the labor hours we'll need to get the stuff out the door. For us, labor is the hardest thing to plan. If we can estimate our total needs—you know, a monthly head count over the next year or so—we can figure out what we need each day when the time comes."

"It's funny, we do sort of the same thing," replied Tom, who had moved over to the biceps curl station. "It's a little different, though. We're planning for personnel and equipment. We forecast all the demand on each flight over the next year or two—booked flights and forecasts together. Then we boil them down into one big number per month, as far ahead as we can see." Tom took one last pull on the bar. "We talk about total passengers and passenger miles. We can't sweat the specifics at that point—too much can happen. We don't assign equipment, personnel, or gates until much later."

Tom had just finished his second set on the weight machines, so he decided to take a break and concentrate on what he was saying. "We try to match total available equipment, personnel, and airport resources to the demand forecast for each month. It'd be hard for us to pile up inventory the way Fred does," he laughed. "We can't just go out and buy a plane or hire a pilot the same morning, either. Just like at Cheryl's hospital, some of our months are heavier than others. We need to look way down the road to adjust our capacity. We hire temps, lease equipment, manage our vacation times, and move scheduled maintenance around so that most of the time the totals match up. It's not so bad when we can see a crunch coming—when people book tickets well in advance and future ticket orders are predictable. Then we can usually handle it. The two things we can't control are the weather and who actually shows up for the ride. But again, we build in some room to maneuver, so that with planning it all tends to work out. We usually manage to get people where they want to go."

The conversation moved on to other issues: leftover turkey, football games, and the like. A minute or two later, Tom's look of confidence had vanished, as he remembered the unpleasant task he had to deal with that day. "You know what we were just talking about? How well we plan and schedule our flights? Well, it doesn't always work out that well," Tom said. "I have to call Boeing this morning and try to work out some problems with them." He was referring to the world's largest manufacturer of jet airliners. Tom's airline owned more than 200 jets, all of them Boeing 737s. "We ordered a few new 737s awhile back. Nothing special, just what we always order. But now everything is delayed. They have a real logjam up there, I guess. Everything is six months behind schedule."

"I think I read something about that in *The Wall Street Journal,*" said Cheryl. "It sounded as if they just missed the boat on their planning."

"*Plane,* they missed the *plane!*" interrupted Luis.

"Good one," laughed Tom. "That's exactly what they did." He explained that Boeing's forecasting people had predicted a period of slow demand. Thinking it would be a good time to make some changes, top management had decided to downsize and restructure some business processes. The people at the top also thought it would be a good time to install some new technology and implement a production quality system that had been in the works for some time. "The only problem was, after a good part of the workforce had been laid off in preparation for the changes, the orders for new planes just took off!" said Tom.

"Booo, that was bad," laughed Cheryl and Luis.

"Well, in any case, they've got a huge backlog in the factory, and they think it'll be a year or more before they can catch up," Tom said. "It's kind of like shutting down a lane on the freeway in the middle of the night, when you think nobody's out. Then, wham! Cars come out of nowhere. Suddenly you've got a big traffic jam that could take hours to undo." The pileup was having an effect on Boeing's suppliers as well as its customers. Besides downsizing their own employees, Boeing's managers had cut back on multiple suppliers of certain parts or components. Now the firm had fewer suppliers to turn to and was leaning very hard on the ones that were left. "It's not good for anybody," Tom concluded, as he headed for the locker room. "It's going to be an interesting few months."

"Makes you wonder about those forecasts, doesn't it?" asked Luis, as he started on his second set.

"It sure does. Makes me wonder about this weekend, too," said Fred, philosophically.

"Huh?" asked the rest of the group in unison.

"I really need to clean out my garage—probably as much as Boeing needed to reengineer some processes and systems," Fred replied.

"I'm still missing the point," said Tom.

"Well, if they can misread their forecasts that badly, I'm definitely going to check the weather before I start moving everything out to the driveway!" said Fred with a smile.

"The best-laid plans of mice and men," mused Cheryl.

"Yeah, but Shakespeare never tried to buy an airplane, or clean out his garage the day after Thanksgiving!" laughed Fred.

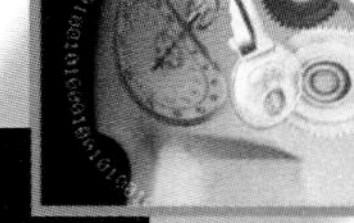

> objectives

Take a moment to familiarize yourself with the key objectives of this chapter.

gearing up

Before you begin reading this chapter, try a short warm-up activity.

Introduction

Up to this point in the text we have been discussing strategic issues in operations and the design of new value-adding systems. We have looked closely at the operational decisions that determine the structure within which a company operates. Such decisions are generally related to long-term demand forecasts, which are updated at least once a year based on projections many years into the future. These decisions have long-term implications; they typically take years to implement, affect the entire range of a company's product-service bundles, and cannot easily be reversed.

You've probably noticed that many classrooms at your college or university have 40 or fewer seats. Class size is considered to be a factor in the quality provided by an educational institution: the smaller, the

better. If the biggest classroom at a school has only 40 chairs, professors must satisfy the demand for a popular course through several small sections rather than one large lecture class. Thus, a bricks-and-mortar structural decision that was made years ago has a direct impact on today's scheduling decisions.

Or consider a hotel at a large resort. When it was built, demographic projections and other long-term forecasts suggested that with expected growth in convention and tourist business, 3,000 rooms could eventually be filled during peak periods. Now the housekeeping and administrative staff must be able to meet the needs of such a large capacity, particularly on days when all the rooms are occupied. Thus, structural operating constraints establish the boundaries for intermediate-range operational plans. The hotel knows how many housekeepers to hire, and the college or university knows how many sections to schedule, because of structural characteristics that are relatively permanent.

From here forward, we will focus on the operation of *existing* systems. In particular, this chapter will concentrate on intermediate-range issues in the operation of value-adding systems. As usual, the chapter begins with a section describing the linkages between the operational concepts covered here and the various functional areas of business. The decisions we describe in this chapter set the stage for more detailed planning in every functional area. For example, cash flow projections in finance, sales projections in marketing, and hiring plans in human resources must all take into account the overall capacity plans of the firm.

Intermediate term operational plans focus on ensuring that resources are in place to meet overall demand 6 to 18 months into the future. In the university, this kind of work is usually done by department chairs, who must determine how many sections will be taught by their department and develop suitable staffing plans. Since the planning considers all sections taught by the department as equal—and doesn't distinguish between specific classes—the task is called *aggregate planning.* The actual scheduling, which matches individual instructors to specific class sections, can be done later.

Aggregate planners have a very limited set of variables to use. They can change workforce size through hiring and layoff decisions. They can make plans to extend the hours contributed by each worker through such mechanisms as overtime. In some situations they can shift capacity to a later month by building inventory or shift demand to a later month by extending a back order. Finally, in some cases subcontracting can be used to expand capacity.

In service environments, the options are often more limited than in manufacturing. It's often not possible to inventory, subcontract, or backlog a service. Consequently, we discuss strategies for managing demand and supply that are employed in various service environments.

Aggregate planners may pursue a variety of different strategies in their attempt to match resource availability to expected demand. In this chapter we describe strategies that (1) keep capacity stable at an average demand level, (2) match capacity to expected changes in demand, (3) ensure adequate capacity for peak demand periods, and (4) combine the other three strategies in some way. The strategy selected by an aggregate planner is generally a function of their business, process type, and competitive strategy.

Numerous quantitative methods have been suggested and used by aggregate planners. In this chapter we describe methods that model manager decisions, optimizing methods, and the spreadsheet-based cut and try approach. While it might seem that managers would use techniques that provide an optimal solution, this is often not the case because of the uncertainty surrounding demand projections. In fact, the cut and try approach is the most used technique and, as such, we describe this approach in the greatest detail.

This chapter identifies ways that e-commerce and supply-chain management (SCM) practices have had a positive influence on the effectiveness of aggregate planning. In particular, SCM and e-commerce have created closer linkages and greater trust between an organization and its customers. This information and trust can result in plans that are both more effective and more stable.

active exercise

Take a moment to apply what you've learned.

Integrating Operations Management with Other Functions

Figure 11.1 highlights some of the critical linkages between the operational issues involved in aggregate planning decisions and other functional areas. This part of the chapter is obviously important to all business majors, because it indicates the way that professionals from their various functional areas relate to the issues addressed in this chapter.

Chapter Topics \ Functional Areas of Business	Finance	Accounting	Human Resources	Marketing	Engineering	Management Information Systems
Integrating Operations Management with Other Functions	●	●	●	●	●	●
Planning for the Intermediate Term	●	●	●	●	●	●
Aggregate Planning Variables			●			
Special Aggregate Planning Considerations in Service Environments			●			
General Aggregate Planning Strategies	●	●	●	●		
Aggregate Planning Methods		●				●
E-Commerce, Supply-Chain Management, and Aggregate Planning				●		●

FIGURE 11.1 Integrating Operations Management with Other Functions

Intermediate-range plans, by their very nature, have to take into account the considerations of all functions, because the more detailed plans in each area have to fit within this plan. The cash flow projections and working capital plans prepared by financial managers must be consistent with the aggregate plan for operations. Accountants have to prepare pro forma statements, allocate costs, and value operating assets, such as inventories, in a way that is consistent with the intermediate-range plans of the firm. Human resource professionals must make necessary adjustments to workforce size and contracts based on the aggregate plan. Marketing programs, including advertising and promotional budgets, are generally critical to accomplishing the aggregate plan and must be consistent with it. Engineering changes applied to products and processes must be timed correctly and play a role in intermediate-range performance expectations. Finally, management information systems need to be capable of providing the same information to managers in all functional areas. When managers are all working with the same data and operational plans, their decisions are more likely to be consistent and they are more likely to accomplish the results they desire. Thus, Figure 11.1 shows the section of this chapter that describes intermediate-range planning to be very closely linked to decisions that are made in each functional area.

As the chapter moves into more detailed coverage of operational issues in aggregate planning, the most obvious linkages are with the human resources function (HR). Workforce size adjustments and other personnel contract issues arise from the aggregate planning process and require follow-through on the part of HR. This may be particularly true in certain services where inventories cannot be used to prepare for demand increases and the only way to adjust capacity is through personnel changes.

The aggregate planning strategies we describe in this chapter have different implications for competitiveness. A level strategy, for instance, could help a company to operate efficiently with a stable workforce and easily track costs but limit its responsiveness to customer preferences. A chase strategy, by contrast, might allow a firm to be quite responsive to customer preferences at the cost of efficiency, workforce stability, and cost accounting simplicity. Thus, the section of the chapter dealing with aggregate planning strategies will be of particular interest to finance, accounting, human resources, and marketing majors.

Figure 11.1 links the part of the chapter dealing with aggregate planning methods to the accounting and management information systems functions. All of these methods rely on cost estimates that must be provided—in some form—by the accounting function. Many of these techniques require the application of computational technologies.

The final section of the chapter addresses the impact of recent business trends, namely e-commerce and supply-chain management, on the practice of aggregate planning. This section specifically points out the importance of marketing initiatives, such as relationship marketing, to develop the trust needed for managers to base their internal aggregate planning decisions on customer needs for capacity that have not been expressed in terms of actual orders. Additionally, this section's content on the impact of e-commerce on aggregate planning activities suggests the linkage to the MIS function.

Planning for the Intermediate Term

Intermediate-range planners typically look 6 to 18 months forward; they plan in monthly increments and generally revise their plans each month based on intermediate-range forecasts. Some firms look further forward than others, depending on their time frame for decision making. For example, Boeing relies on a skilled workforce and therefore cannot rapidly change its production plans. Its intermediate-range plans cover a relatively long period. A fast food restaurant, on the other hand, need not look so far forward.

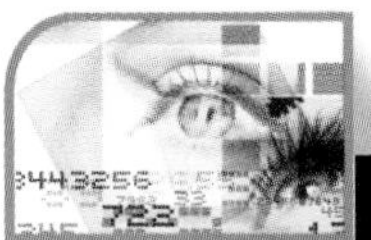

video example

Take a closer look at the concepts and issues you've been reading about.

In the intermediate range, separate plans are made for groups of product-service bundles with similar value-delivery characteristics or marketing requirements. Resources are then allocated to product groups according to those plans. For example, Pepsi could plan in terms of the number of gallons produced per month, rather than in terms of cans versus 2-liter bottles or bulk packs. Carpet companies could aggregate their demand according to major carpet types, such as Berber, plush, pile, and indoor-outdoor. The intermediate-range forecast would indicate how many million square yards of carpet would be needed in each category, but the aggregate plan would not specify specific colors or patterns. Similarly, a large accounting and consulting firm would aggregate its personnel or billable hours by group or division, such as auditing, tax accounting, and process consulting.

Because demand is considered in the aggregate, the intermediate-range planning task is often called *aggregate planning*. An **aggregate plan** indicates the ways in which existing resources will be used to meet expected levels of demand for product groups over the intermediate range. It sets target levels for the size of the workforce, the extent of subcontracting, the monthly production rate, and the level of inventory. These decisions must typically be made several months in advance.

In contrast, short-term plans address day-to-day decisions with relatively short lead times. In this type of operations planning, time is divided into weekly or daily increments, and plans must continually be revised. The short-term plan includes a **master schedule**, or detailed description of the product-service bundles scheduled to be completed over the near term. It also indicates how workers and equipment will be used, how the in-house creation of various parts of the product-service bundle will be coordinated, and how outsourced materials and services will be procured. Figure 11.2 summarizes the differences between short- and intermediate-range planning.

The firm's competitive priorities determine what is included in its intermediate- and short-range plans. Companies that emphasize customization of their product-service bundles must cope with a great deal of complexity and uncertainty in their planning. Every job is different; each goes through a different set of work centers, and no one knows how long its passage through the factory will take. For companies that emphasize low-cost delivery of a standardized product-service bundle, planning and control of operations is much simpler. Because the product is standardized, the process is as well; the main task is to schedule operations at a flow rate that matches the level of demand.

Short-term plans must be closely monitored to ensure their feasibility. Managers may be tempted to make unrealistic commitments in order to please customers, but in most organizations, there is usually very little flexibility in short-term capacity. As a result, companies need to be effective in their short-term scheduling and very careful about the promises they make to customers regarding delivery dates.

Regardless of the time frame, operations planning is based on a **rolling planning horizon**, which is a planning period whose beginning- and endpoints slide forward with the passage of time. At least once a year, the long-range plan will be updated, across both the product and process life cycle. Of

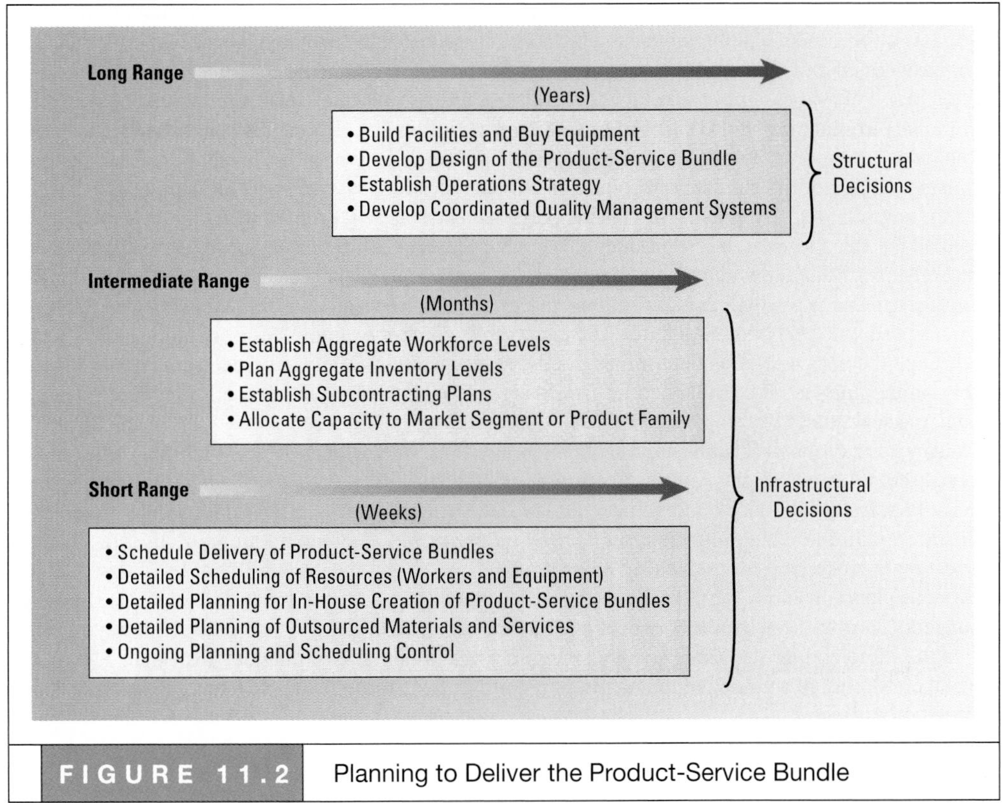

FIGURE 11.2 Planning to Deliver the Product-Service Bundle

course, the definition of *long range* varies from one industry to the next; the product life cycle for a new computer chip is much shorter than the life cycle for potato chips. So while a five- to 10-year plan might seem very long range to Intel, a forest products company such as Georgia Pacific or Weyerhauser would need to look at least 30 years forward.

Intermediate-range plans are updated more frequently than the long-range plan, often on a monthly basis. Companies must pay particular attention to their staffing plans over the intermediate term. If more skilled workers are needed and the labor market is particularly tight, the time horizon for the intermediate-range plan may need to be longer than a year. If labor is readily available, the intermediate-range plan might not extend so far forward. Production lead-times also affect the length of the intermediate-range plan. A ship builder or large aircraft manufacturer can reliably predict workforce requirements several years ahead, because such products are always in production for several years. A specialty clothing manufacturer will not have the same luxury, however. Once fashion trends have become clear, the manufacturer must respond rapidly to staffing needs.

Short-range plans are updated on an ongoing basis, daily or weekly. If the cumulative lead-time required to provide the product-service bundle is six weeks, schedules will need to be revised at least once a week, looking at least six weeks forward. In that case, planners will usually create a tentative schedule that looks forward more than six weeks (say, 10 to 20 weeks), so that the company will be prepared for an unusually busy or slow period.

Since the short-range, intermediate-range, and long-range plans all pertain to the same set of resources, they must fit together. A small change in the long-range plan, such as the decision to delay an expansion, could produce very different scenarios over the short and intermediate range. Similarly, a decision by intermediate-range planners to limit the use of overtime could cause significant capacity shortages and reduce flexibility over the short run. Finally, short-range decisions can affect the intermediate- and long-range plans. For instance, week-to-week scheduling that produces a continually growing backlog may lead to heavier use of subcontracting over the intermediate range or even to a decision to expand capacity.

Different types of processes produce vastly different levels of complexity in short-term scheduling. From a planning standpoint, job shops and batch processes that produce customized product-service bundles are a highly complex environment. At the most detailed level, that of a job shop, planners must deal with a varying number of jobs, each of which is unlike any other that has been done in the past. Because each job follows its own unique route through the facility, the planner can only estimate processing times in the various work centers. Because each work center may have a number of jobs queued up for processing, the waiting time at each work center is usually unpredictable. Despite the inherent uncertainty, job shops must give customers some indication of when their jobs will be completed. In contrast, planning and control for a continuous or repetitive process such as an assembly line is quite simple. All the inputs and outputs are standardized, so the only real question planners must answer is, How fast should we run the process?

For high-volume assembly lines that create standardized product-service bundles, *deterministic approaches* to planning and control are most useful. In these environments, the schedule is "hard-wired" into the process, so that it represents a firm commitment to a rate of production. The planner's task is simply to specify the rate of production for each product-service bundle. Then, on the basis of the resulting schedule, suppliers will provide parts, supervisors will prepare work and overtime schedules, and the sales force will sell product-service bundles. A Saturn dealer, for example, can tell customers the exact day on which the car they have ordered will be delivered. So, too, Saturn's suppliers do not have to be told which parts to ship on any given day; they can determine that information from Saturn's production schedule. An automatic car wash is another example. Since the time a car takes to go through the car wash is predetermined, a customer's waiting time can be determined easily based solely on the number of cars queued up for service. This type of production environment is easy to model and schedule.

Whenever a group of jobs must compete for limited resources, however, the planning environment becomes complicated. Highly complex environments like the job shop, where many different product-service bundles are produced and value is added in a variety of ways, cannot be modeled in a deterministic way. In these environments, *probabilistic approaches* to planning are more useful. Planners first estimate processing times, waiting times, transfer times, and the probability of breakdowns. They then make planning and control decisions based on expected processing times and lot sizes. But while managers can indicate when they expect a job to be completed, delays can occur for many reasons. When the value-adding steps are executed, they may take more or less time than expected. The schedule is therefore more a guideline than a binding commitment, and time buffers are built into most job completion estimates.

To better appreciate why a complex business environment cannot be modeled deterministically, think about an amusement park. Imagine one person trying to plan out a day at Six Flags, Disneyland, or some other park—what rides to take, in what order, and at what time. Now imagine trying to do the same for all the visitors on a given day. Consider the timing of employees' breaks, unexpected absences, the length of waiting lines, and the possibility of equipment breakdowns. Such an environment can be modeled effectively only in a probabilistic way.

Figure 11.3 illustrates the relationships between intermediate- and short-range planning and control in various environments that we have just discussed and helps you to understand how the chapters that follow relate to the material we will cover in this chapter. Chapter 11 covers aggregate planning for all environments. Chapter 12 covers the supply chain–related issues of inventory management and

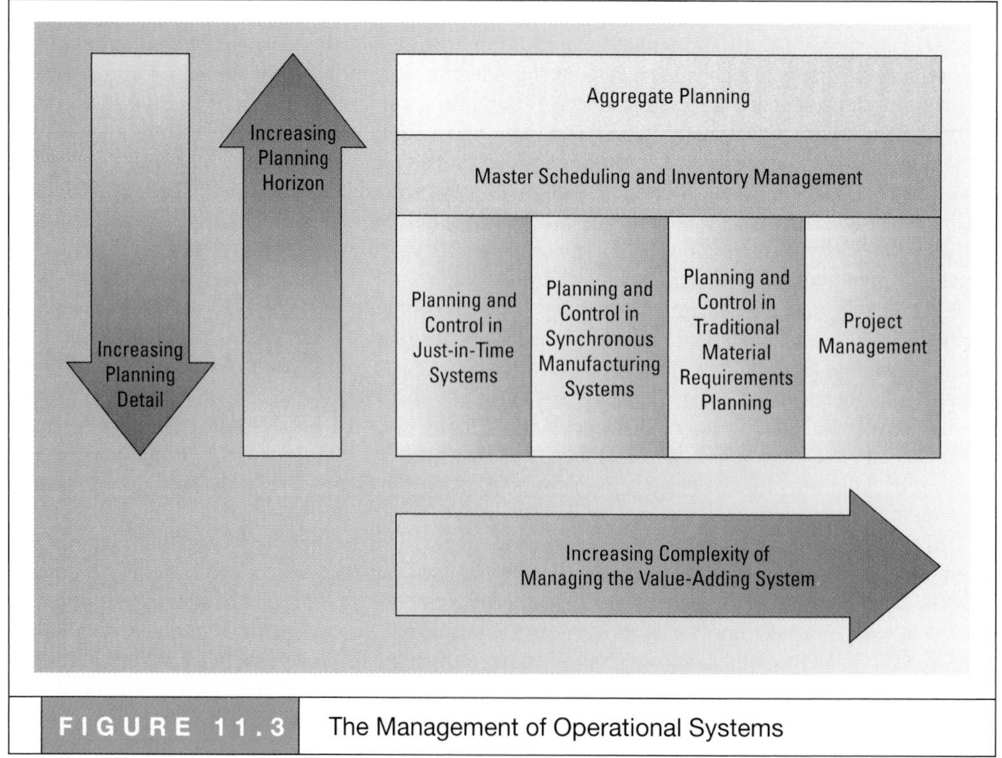

FIGURE 11.3 The Management of Operational Systems

master scheduling for all environments. Chapters 13–16 deal with detailed planning and scheduling issues one environment at a time, starting with simple environments in Chapter 13 and moving to greater and greater levels of complexity.

> active concept check

Now let's take a moment to test your knowledge of the concepts you have studied in this section.

> Aggregate Planning Variables

Aggregate planning, or the development of a month-by-month intermediate-range schedule for families of product-service bundles, is based on an intermediate-term demand forecast. To understand aggregate planning, then, one must first have at least a basic understanding of the forecasting process. (Forecasting methods are covered in more detail in the supplement to this chapter.)

To begin with, because demand follows patterns, future demand is predictable, or "forecastable." However, the precision with which future demand can be predicted decreases the farther into the future one attempts to look.

Depending on the planning system a business uses, this characteristic of forecasting may be more or less significant. Some companies use make-to-order planning and control systems; others, make-to-stock or assemble-to-order systems. In a **make-to-stock** system, the entire schedule is based on forecasted demand figures. In contrast, in **make-to-order** systems, managers have purchase orders in hand when they are planning, so they know the demand for products and services at least as far forward as their processing lead-times. Looking several months forward, however, their forecasts may be based primarily on predicted orders. **Assemble-to-order** systems are a combination of the make-to-stock and make-to-order approaches: Production of customer orders are scheduled using components and subassemblies that have been made to stock.

> active example

Take a closer look at the concepts and issues you've been reading about.

Fortunately, the precision of a forecast can be estimated. Thus, an aggregate plan can be based on expected demand, best-case scenarios, and worst-case scenarios. As more information becomes available, forecasts should be updated. The aggregate plan is effectively based on a moving target.

Typically, in the intermediate time frame, no new facilities can be built, no old facilities can be shut down, and no productivity improvement programs can have their full effect. These kinds of structural changes simply take too long to plan and implement. For example, several years would be required to construct a new wing at a hospital, and the lead-time from order to delivery of a new airplane is several years. Though the firm's structure is fixed in the intermediate term, the demand for each family of product-service bundles is likely to vary from month to month. Aggregate planners must therefore determine how to vary monthly volumes in order to meet demand in the most effective way.

The set of planning variables available to the aggregate planner is quite limited: It includes only the inventory account, the monthly production rate, the size of the workforce, and the extent of subcontracting. Of course, not all these variables are equally available to all businesses. Like many other service businesses, a hospital cannot inventory services; the freedom to hire and fire staff may also be limited in many skill categories. In capital-intensive processes such as steel making, production rates and workforce requirements are largely fixed.

The inventory account, if there is one, may be positive or negative. A positive inventory account indicates that the plan is to have materials on hand. A negative inventory account indicates a planned production **backlog**, or a deliberate amount of unmet demand. The planned level of the inventory account can be changed by producing more or less in any given month than the forecasted level of demand. This goal may be accomplished in several ways. The planned monthly production rate can be changed by varying the number of overtime hours worked in a month. (At General Motors, two recent strikes were caused by this use of overtime.) The planned size of the workforce can be changed by hiring or laying off workers. For instance, to meet demand during a holiday rush, retailers often hire temps to staff their stores and catalog operations. Finally, subcontracting plans can be changed, within certain limitations and for a limited time.

To the aggregate planner, each of these variables has a cost. No checks are actually written to cover the cost estimates associated with an aggregate plan; rather, the figures are used to compare the opportunity cost of meeting demand through various approaches. The cost of carrying inventory, for instance, is much higher than the investment income lost on money tied up in warehoused goods. It includes items such as the rental fee for warehouse space, the administrative expense associated with monitoring and tracking the extra inventory, potential loss from damage to goods in storage or transit, tax and insurance costs, and the risk that the warehoused materials will become obsolete while they are in storage. By comparison, the cost of a planned backlog includes sales lost due to delays in customer service, the administrative expense associated with keeping track of unfilled orders, and the cost of maintaining the systems that respond to customer inquiries about orders. Changing the production rate by adding extra overtime typically inflates the hourly cost of labor at least 50 percent. Hiring or laying off workers obviously requires a significant amount of administrative time and record keeping. New workers must be trained and oriented; laid-off workers usually receive some severance pay or outplacement services or both. Finally, subcontracting requires extra administrative effort and may erode profit margins or the quality of customer service.

Ultimately, the aggregate planner's goal is to meet customer requirements, based on some forecasted demand pattern, through whatever mix of inventory, overtime, workforce size, and subcontracting minimizes the firm's costs. An alternative goal, particularly when the service component of the product-service bundle is significant, might be to ensure sufficient capacity to meet the expected peak level of demand. For example, the aggregate plan for a hospital emergency room should ensure that enough doctors are scheduled to handle the highest expected level of monthly demand. In a small college town, that would probably mean scheduling more doctor-hours during the academic year than during summer vacation. In operations in which service is not a significant part of the product-service bundle—such as a factory that makes a standardized, mass-produced product—maintaining a level workforce might be important. In those cases, inventory might be varied in order to level production.

active concept check <

Now let's take a moment to test your knowledge of the concepts you have studied in this section.

Special Aggregate Planning Considerations in Service Environments

Aggregate planning in service environments is especially challenging because services typically cannot be inventoried in anticipation of future demand. Planning sufficient service capacity is the main approach to satisfying customer demand. The benefits of satisfied customers, however, must be weighed against the risks and costs of excess capacity. We describe several strategies that help service operations managers keep demand and supply in balance below.

STRATEGIES FOR MANAGING SERVICE DEMAND

1. Segmenting customers. An orthodontist group serves both adults and children. The group schedules short checkups (15 minutes or less) for children in the early morning before school starts and in the late afternoon after school is out. Adult patients may come in for short checkups anytime. However, both children and adults must schedule long appointments for mid- to late morning and early afternoon. Since orthodontia patients have many more short appointments than long ones, this scheduling policy minimizes the frequency of children missing school to attend an appointment. It also maintains high flexibility in short appointments to accommodate adult schedules, while keeping capacity utilization consistently high by forcing long appointments into the middle of the day.

2. Differential pricing. Most of us are familiar with the strategy of using price discounts to encourage customers to purchase services at nonpeak times. Utilities offer special rates for off-peak electricity and phone usage. Restaurants promote "early bird specials" to fill tables before peak dining hours. Movie theaters sell discount tickets for matinee shows. Resorts reduce their rates for periods when business is slow. Some organizations have highly sophisticated pricing strategies, where different service "packages" can be priced at different rates. For example, Chicago's Shedd Aquarium divides its facilities into (1) regular exhibits of species from around the world, (2) the dolphin and beluga tanks, and (3) special shows such as a traveling exhibit of sea horses; various ticket packages provide different amounts of access to the aquarium's facilities. Pricing can be an effective tool to maintain high capacity utilization and maximize total revenue.

3. Counterseasonal products and services. Many services suffer from demand seasonality. Summer resorts, universities, bicycle shops, and other specialty retailers all suffer from excess capacity when the peak sales season passes. Adding counterseasonal services is one way to combat this problem. In recent years, scores of summer resorts in Minnesota have insulated their cabins and now offer winter accommodations to snowmobile and cross-country skiing enthusiasts. Universities offer group retreats and sports camps during the summer months. In northern states, specialty bicycle shops sell ice skates and skis during the fall and winter months, while motorcycle dealers sell snowmobiles.

4. Complementary products and services. A common strategy for Las Vegas hotels is to offer a complete package of services to keep guests (and their money) in the hotel's complex and away from competing facilities. A full service Las Vegas hotel offers reasonably priced rooms, multiple restaurant and bar options, extravagant Broadway shows, and of course, extensive gambling opportunities.

5. Reservation systems. Airlines, hotels, restaurants, hair salons, and numerous other services use reservations to match future service capacity with future demand. Customers who request reservations that are already filled often can adjust to other options, thereby smoothing demand across a broader range of service capacity. Reservations are convenient to both customers and service providers. Problems with this strategy include customers who don't show up for their appointment and providers who overbook their services and cannot serve everyone with a reservation. One way of dealing with customer "no-shows" is to collect the service payment in advance and not issue refunds to no-shows. For example, airlines sell nonrefundable tickets. Another approach is to charge a minimum fee if the customer does not cancel a reservation or appointment within 24 hours. Overbooking costs the service provider money in compensation paid to inconvenienced customers and the loss of future business when customers are alienated.

STRATEGIES FOR MANAGING SERVICE SUPPLY

1. Schedule employees to match demand patterns. No customer at a fast food restaurant will deny that it makes sense to schedule a sufficient number of employees to meet demand peaks that occur at breakfast, lunch, dinner, and perhaps a late-night "bar rush." However, it is critical for controlling labor costs that some workers finish their shifts at the end of these demand peaks.

2. Customer participation. Customers provide their own service when they bag their own groceries, check themselves out of the library, complete loan applications prior to meeting with a loan officer, cut their own Christmas trees, and fill their cars with gasoline. Problems can occur with this approach when customers lack sufficient training in procedures or equipment operation. Customers may also cause problems if they try to cheat the system (e.g., drive away without paying for gas) or by causing quality problems (e.g., contaminating bulk foods in the grocery store).

3. Contingent employees. Part-time and temporary full-time workers are called "contingent" employees. They benefit the company by quickly filling supply gaps that occur when demand picks

Today, highly skilled and educated workers are provided by a variety of Professional Employment Organizations (PEOs). Such organizations make it easier for their customer companies to balance their aggregate capacity and demand through changes in workforce size.

up. Contingent workers are used in both service and manufacturing environments. Retail stores hire contingent workers during the busy holiday sales seasons, and universities hire fixed-term professors to fill in for professors who are on leave.

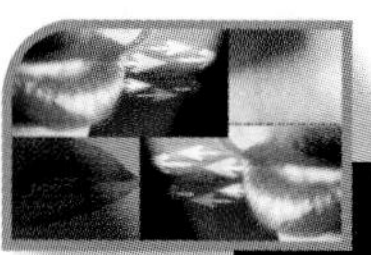

active poll

What do you think? Voice your opinion and find out what others have to say.

4. Adjustable capacity. A favorite saying with fast food managers is, "If you've got time to lean, you've got time to clean." During slack periods between meal rushes, employees spend their time conducting supportive tasks such as cleaning, staging food supplies, and replenishing napkin and condiment dispensers. When the peak periods begin, the workers can be reassigned to focus on essential tasks in serving customers. University classrooms are sometimes separated by floor-to-ceiling partitions, which can be removed to create large lecture rooms, then easily repositioned for smaller classes. Sports stadiums may be designed to accommodate multiple sporting and entertainment events in a variety of configurations.

5. Shared capacity. Airlines that overbook often can move "extra" passengers to flights on competing airlines. Hotels have similar arrangements with one another to handle overbooking problems. Accounting firms often outsource work during the busy tax season. During periods of excess capacity, an airline may lease its aircraft to other airlines or freight shipping businesses. Universities and colleges may lease classroom space to other institutions that conduct special workshops, programs, and classes.

active concept check

Now let's take a moment to test your knowledge of the concepts you have studied in this section.

> Aggregate Planning at Miami's Student Rec Center

The Student Recreation Center's (SRC) location—on a college campus (Miami University) in a small town (Oxford, Ohio)—leads to very defined resource demand and availability patterns. Essentially, demand varies among holidays, summer academic terms, and regular academic terms. During holidays, demand is high in the morning but very low all through the day. During summer terms, demand is relatively even throughout the day at a moderate rate. During the regular terms, demand is moderate in the mornings and at peak levels through the afternoon and evening hours. Because the demand pattern is so stable, the rec center employs an aggregate planning strategy that provides daily staffing at fixed levels for holidays, summer academic terms, and regular academic terms. The staffing level is set based on the philosophy that clients should not have to wait in line to receive assistance or to begin their workout. Specific hourly worker schedules are not a concern at this point. (Actual scheduling and assignment of workers to specific tasks can be done later, based on worker preferences and staffing needs.)

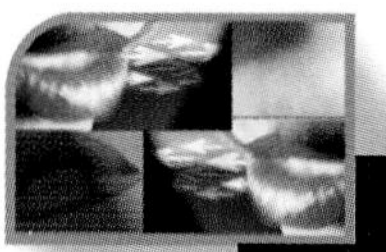

active poll

What do you think? Voice your opinion and find out what others have to say.

Since the rec center cannot inventory workouts, the primary aggregate planning variables they use are workforce related. For aggregate planning purposes, the workforce is divided into three groups:

aquatics staff, who serve primarily as lifeguards; instructors, who teach fitness classes of all types and serve as personal trainers; and area monitors, who work in facility access, equipment and towel checkouts, the pro shop, and fitness areas. The task in aggregate planning is to ensure that there will be adequate staffing to meet peak levels of demand in all three areas. Total daily worker hours in each of the staffing areas (aquatics, instructors, and monitors) are fixed for each of the demand periods. The monthly worker hour requirements can be readily computed and aggregate staffing plans developed.

SRC staffing comes in two forms: permanent employees and student workers. Student workers are readily available for regular terms, somewhat difficult to obtain during summer terms, and virtually unavailable during holiday periods. As a consequence, staffing needs are met by adjusting the number of available student worker hours whenever possible. Regular workers are given overtime assignments only during periods when student workers are not available.

Since the university works on a fiscal year that begins July 1, rec center managers must determine their staffing needs for the coming year each June. These staffing projections are used to prepare budgets that cover wages for student workers as well as overtime costs that are incurred by the regular staff. The budget preparation period, however, is not the only time that staffing plans can be made. Aggregate planning is an ongoing activity. As demand projections change during the course of the year, the rec center managers update their staffing plans and modify their staffing levels accordingly.

SRC managers employ many of the strategies for managing service demand and managing service supply, described in the last section. Demand for rec center services is managed by hosting counter-seasonal events. For example, NCAA swimming competitions are hosted during spring break, and other aquatic events and Outdoor Pursuit Center trips are offered during student holidays. Complementary services are offered: personal trainers, healthy lifestyle classes, intramural competitions, and physical education. Reservation systems are used for high-demand facilities such as racquetball courts and treadmills. Employees are scheduled to match the demand pattern. Contingent workers—the student workers—are a critical aspect of the rec center's capacity adjustment system. Finally, the fitness area monitors provide adjustable capacity since they are used to doing a variety of tasks—equipment maintenance, equipment checkout, pro shop sales, and recreation area supervision.

> General Aggregate Planning Strategies

Aggregate planners may employ several strategies to meet expected customer demand. For instance, in a **level production strategy,** demand is met by altering only the inventory account. In a **chase demand strategy,** demand is met by matching planned monthly production with forecasted demand, while the inventory account is held constant. In a **peak demand strategy,** particularly useful in service settings, capacity is varied to meet the highest level of demand at particular times. Planners can also combine aspects of these approaches. The strategy that planners select should depend on the company's competitive priorities and the ways in which its product-service bundles add value for customers. Table 11.1 summarizes four aggregate planning strategies discussed in detail in the following pages.

With a continuous flow operation and fixed capacity, this Exxon Refinery in Baton Rouge, Louisiana uses a level production strategy. Capacity is stored in the form of inventory to cover future surges in demand.

TABLE 11.1 Aggregate Planning Strategies

Strategy	Variables Used	Compatible Competitive Priorities	Environments Where Most Common
Peak Demand Strategy	• Undertime or Excess Capacity* • Subcontracting	• Delivery Speed • Conformance Quality • Flexibility	• Emergency Services • Easily Obtainable Substitutes • Cost of Back Orders High
Level Production Strategy	• Inventory/Backlog	• Low Cost • Design Quality • Delivery Speed**	• Repetitive Manufacturing • Continuous Processes • Highly Skilled Professionals • Cost of Capacity Changes High
Chase Demand Strategy	• Workforce Size • Overtime/Undertime • Subcontracting	• Flexibility • Design Quality • Delivery Speed	• Pure Service • Job Shops • Batch Manufacturing • Cost of Inventory High
Mixed Strategies	• Inventory/Backlog • Workforce size • Overtime/Undertime • Subcontracting • Excess Capacity*	• Any	• Somewhat balance cost tradeoffs

*Planned buffers of resources other than labor

**Based upon the use of accumulated inventory

THE LEVEL PRODUCTION STRATEGY

In the level production strategy, changes in the inventory account are used to balance mismatches between monthly demand and output. Workforce size, production rates, and subcontracting are held constant. This strategy boosts worker morale, because it eliminates the disruptions in employment associated with changing production rates. From the employer's viewpoint, it also eliminates the cost and paperwork associated with the hiring and laying off of workers, while providing a low-cost, high-quality production system. But other benefits are lost in a level production strategy, including flexibility, the ability to provide a high level of customization, and the ability to always satisfy all a customer's requirements.

The level production strategy is especially desirable in businesses that can afford to hold inventory or carry backlogs. Capital-intensive businesses, such as steel manufacturers and other basic materials producers, are often forced by the nature of their processes to use this strategy. The strategy is also compatible with make-to-stock planning and control systems. However, many service businesses cannot employ a level production strategy, because most of the value they add cannot be held in inventory or back ordered.

Table 11.2 shows an aggregate plan for Fred's pager factory. The upper lefthand corner of the spreadsheet displays a group of fixed production parameters, including the desired safety stock, the production rate in units per worker hour, the number of regular time (RT) hours in a month, the normal wage per hour, and other costs. The main portion of the spreadsheet shows the level production plan and the costs associated with it. At the beginning of May, Fred expects to have 12,000 units in inventory (column 1). Beginning inventory in other months will depend on production and usage after this starting point. The expected demand column (column 2) shows the demand forecasts for pagers.

TABLE 11.2 Fred's Pagers

Level Production Strategy

Safety stock desired	12000
Units/worker hour	20
RT hours/month	160
RT wage/hour	$12
OT wage/hour	$18
Subcontract cost/unit	$2.50
Hiring cost/worker	$500.00
Layoff cost/worker	$1,500.0
Inventory cost/unit/month	0
Back ordering cost/unit/month	$0.05

Total Cost = $364,125.00

	(1)	(2)	(3)	(4)	(5)	(6)	(7)	(8)	(9)	(10)	(11)	(12)	(13)	(14)
Month	Beginning Inventory	Expected Demand	Production Required	Worker Hires (layoffs)	Workforce Size	Reg. Time Hours	Overtime Hours	In-House Production	Subcontracted Production	Cumulative Production	Cumulative Demand	Ending Inventory	Hiring Cost	Layoff Cost
May	12,000	28,500	28,500	0	10	1,600	0	32,000	0	44,000	28,500	15,500	0	0
June	15,500	28,500	25,000	0	10	1,600	0	32,000	0	76,000	57,000	19,000	0	0
July	19,000	28,500	21,500	0	10	1,600	0	32,000	0	108,000	85,500	22,500	0	0
August	22,500	33,000	22,500	0	10	1,600	0	32,000	0	140,000	118,500	21,500	0	0
September	21,500	33,000	23,500	0	10	1,600	0	32,000	0	172,000	151,500	20,500	0	0
October	20,500	33,000	24,500	0	10	1,600	0	32,000	0	204,000	184,500	19,500	0	0
November	19,500	33,000	25,500	0	10	1,600	0	32,000	0	236,000	217,500	18,500	0	0
December	15,800	38,000	31,500	0	10	1,600	0	32,000	0	268,000	255,500	12,500	0	0
January	12,500	32,000	31,500	0	10	1,600	0	32,000	0	300,000	287,500	12,500	0	0
February	12,500	28,500	28,000	0	10	1,600	0	32,000	0	332,000	316,000	16,000	0	0
March	16,000	28,500	24,500	0	10	1,600	0	32,000	0	364,000	344,500	19,500	0	0
April	19,500	28,500	21,000	0	10	1,600	0	32,000	0	396,000	373,000	23,000	0	0
May	23,000	30,000	19,000	0	10	1,600	0	32,000	0	428,000	403,000	25,000	0	0
June	25,000	30,000	17,000	0	10	1,600	0	32,000	0	460,000	433,000	27,000	0	0
July	27,000	30,000	15,000	0	10	1,600	0	32,000	0	492,000	463,000	29,000	0	0
August	29,000	35,000	18,000	0	10	1,600	0	32,000	0	524,000	498,000	26,000	0	0
September	26,000	35,000	21,000	0	10	1,600	0	32,000	0	556,000	533,000	23,000	0	0
October	23,000	35,000	24,000	0	10	1,600	0	32,000	0	588,000	568,000	20,000	0	0
													0	0

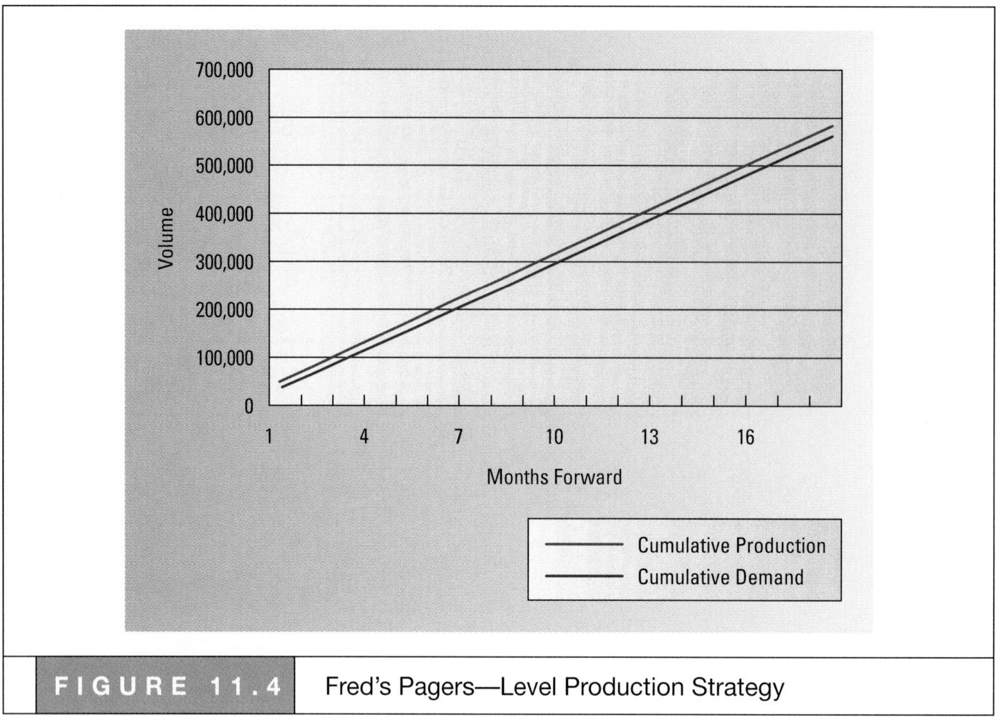

FIGURE 11.4 Fred's Pagers—Level Production Strategy

Fred's factory has 10 workers at the beginning of May (column 5); the size of the workforce in any given month will depend on the amount of firing and hiring that occurs after this point. The number of regular time hours in the month (column 6) is a function of the workforce size. The assumption is that each worker works and is paid for all the regular time hours in the month. Overtime and subcontracted hours (columns 7 and 9) are numeric values plugged in by the aggregate planner.

Monthly in-house production is simply a function of the production rate (units per worker hour) and the number of regular time and overtime labor hours in the month. Ending inventory (column 12) is equal to cumulative production minus cumulative demand (column 11). Notice that monthly production stays the same, while the inventory account (whether beginning or ending) changes from month to month. Costs are a direct function of the aggregate plan. Thus, the last seven columns in Table 11.2 relate directly to the cost parameters in the upper left-hand corner.

It is sometimes useful to graph cumulative production and cumulative demand. Figure 11.4 illustrates the mismatches between the rate of production and the rate of demand in a level production strategy. By studying this type of graph, aggregate planners may be able to improve their monthly plans.

active exercise <

Take a moment to apply what you've learned.

THE CHASE DEMAND STRATEGY

In the chase demand strategy, changes in the use of overtime and the size of the workforce are used to adjust monthly output to match changes in forecasted demand. Inventory levels are held constant. This strategy is suitable for both manufacturing and service operations in which holding inventory or keeping a backlog is costly or impossible. It is particularly appropriate in operations that produce highly customized product-service bundles, as well as in make-to-order environments in general.

Table 11.3 shows an aggregate plan for Luis's furniture factory. This spreadsheet was generated using the same set of formulas as that used in Table 11.2; however, in this plan, the goal was to match monthly production with monthly demand. Notice that the inventory account does not change from month to month, but the size of the workforce and the amount of overtime vary, depending on forecasted demand. Figure 11.5 shows the close relationship between cumulative production and cumulative demand in a chase demand strategy.

TABLE 11.3 Luis' Metal Frame Sofas Chase Demand Strategy

Chase Demand Strategy

Safety stock desired	0	**Total Cost = $193,620.00**
Units/worker hour	0.1	
RT hours/month	160	
RT wage/hour	$18	
OT wage/hour	$27	
Subcontract cost/hour	$30.00	
Hiring cost/worker	$500.00	
Layoff cost/worker	$1,500.00	
Inventory cost/unit/month	$20.00	
Back ordering cost/unit/month	$4.00	
Maximum overtime/month	100 hours	

Month	Beginning Inventory	Expected Demand	Worker Hires (layoffs)	Workforce Size	Reg. Time Hours	Overtime Hours	Subcontracted Hours	Total Production	Cumulative Production	Cumulative Demand	Ending Inventory	Hiring Cost	Layoff Cost
May	28	75	0	4	640	100	10	75	103	75	28	0	0
June	28	56	(1)	3	480	80	0	56	159	131	28	0	$1,500
July	28	48	0	3	480	0	0	48	207	179	28	0	0
August	28	40	(1)	2	320	80	0	40	247	219	28	0	$1,500
September	28	40	0	2	320	80	0	40	287	259	28	0	0
October	28	35	0	2	320	30	0	35	322	294	28	0	0
November	28	45	0	2	320	100	30	45	367	339	28	0	0
December	28	100	4	6	960	40	0	100	467	439	28	$2,000	0
January	28	80	(1)	5	800	0	0	80	547	519	28	0	$1,500
February	28	40	(3)	2	320	80	0	40	587	559	28	0	$4,500
March	28	30	(1)	1	160	100	40	30	617	589	28	0	$1,500
April	28	40	1	2	320	80	0	40	657	629	28	$500	0
May	28	35	0	2	320	30	0	35	692	664	28	0	0
June	28	40	0	2	320	80	0	40	732	704	28	0	0
July	28	50	1	3	480	20	0	50	782	754	28	$500	0
August	28	40	(1)	2	320	80	0	40	822	794	28	0	$1,500
September	28	40	0	2	320	80	0	40	862	834	28	0	0
October	28	40	0	2	320	80	0	40	902	874	28	0	0
												$3,000	$12,000

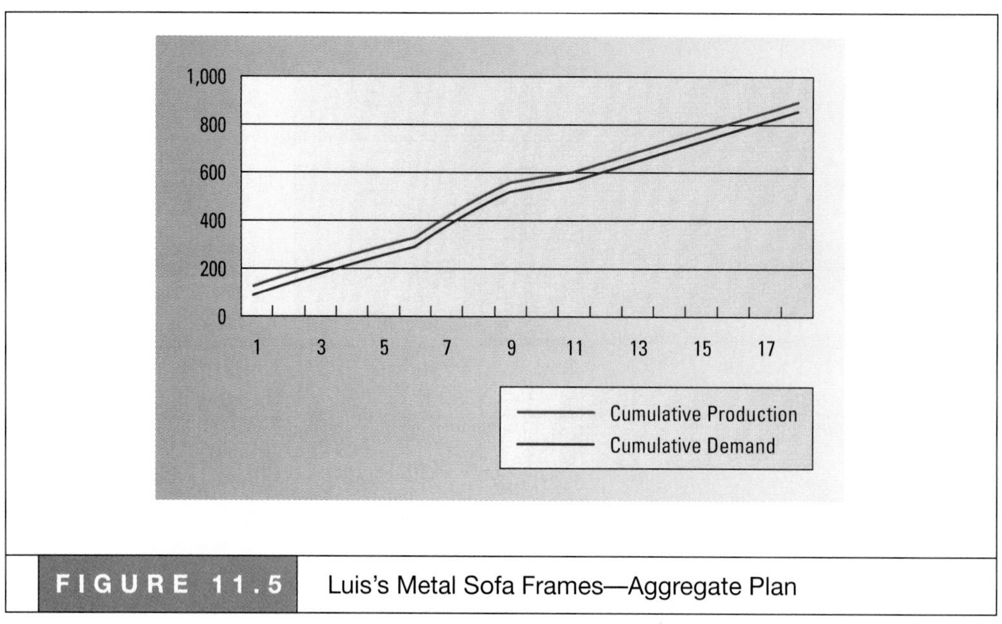

FIGURE 11.5 Luis's Metal Sofa Frames—Aggregate Plan

THE PEAK DEMAND STRATEGY

In the peak demand strategy, changes in overtime and in the size of the workforce are used to match monthly capacity to the anticipated maximum monthly demand. This strategy is generally used in service operations in which the immediate availability of customized service is critical. The lonely Maytag repairman just might be needed someday, so he waits patiently for the customer's phone call. So do firefighters, pizza makers, and physicians in an emergency room. In fact, many services are useless unless they are available on demand. Because these types of service cannot be inventoried, the peak demand strategy may be thought of as a special case of the chase demand strategy. (If there is no inventory, then obviously there can be no variation in inventory.) The peak demand strategy is particularly appropriate in operations in which the product-service bundle is highly customized.

Table 11.4 shows an aggregate plan for Cheryl's emergency room; along with Figure 11.6, it illustrates the chase demand strategy. Notice that there is no inventory at any time. (How could emergency health services be inventoried?) Apart from the absence of inventory, however, the arithmetic in this spreadsheet is identical to that in Fred and Luis's spreadsheets (see Tables 11.2 and 11.3). While the inventory account doesn't change, the size of the workforce and the amount of overtime vary from month to month, depending on forecasted demand. In months in which the size of the workforce is more than adequate to meet demand, the emergency room simply carries extra capacity—just in case it is needed.

The only aggregate planning strategy that really makes sense for emergency services is a peak demand strategy.

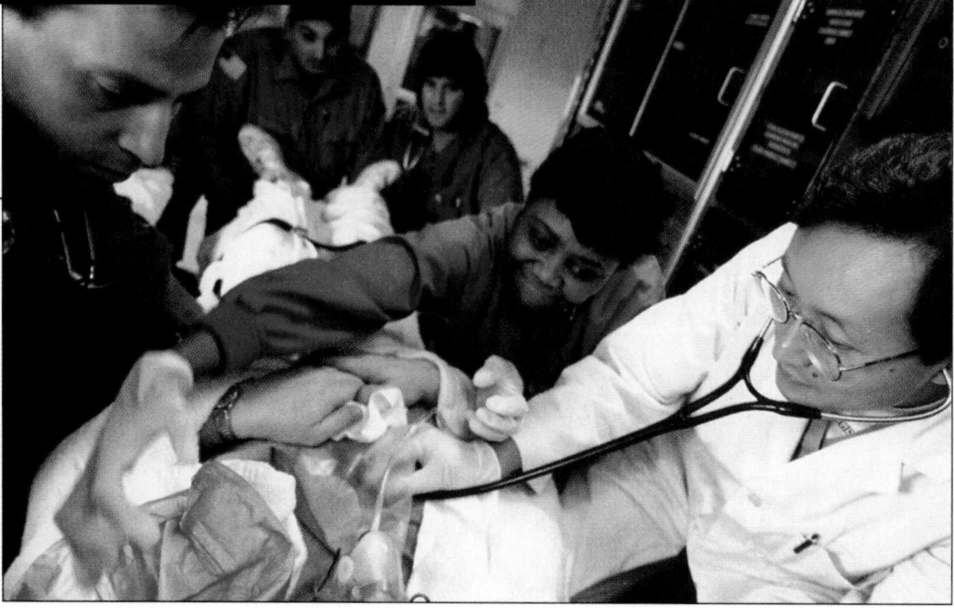

TABLE 11.4 Cheryl's Emergency Room

Peak Demand Strategy

Patients/doctor hour	3
Hours/month for staff doctors	168
Doctor on duty wage/hour	$200.00
Doctor call fee per patient (OT pay)	$100.00
Hiring cost/doctor	$2,500.00
Layoff cost/doctor	$2,500.00
Current staffing level (doctors)	10

Total Cost = $4,947,280.00

Month	Expected Patient Load	Doctor Hires (layoffs)	Staff Size	Staffed Hours	Staff covered Patients	On-Call Patient Load	Cumulative patients Covered	Cumulative expected load	Hiring Cost	Layoff Cost	On-Call Cost
May	5,000	0	10	1,680	5,040	0	5,040	5,000	0	0	0
June	5,200	0	10	1,680	5,040	160	10,240	10,200	0	0	$16,000
July	6,000	1	11	1,848	5,544	456	16,240	16,200	$2,500	0	$45,600
August	5,500	0	11	1,848	5,544	0	21,784	21,700	0	0	0
September	5,000	0	11	1,848	5,544	0	27,328	26,700	0	0	0
October	4,000	(3)	8	1,344	4,032	0	31,360	30,700	0	$7,500	0
November	3,500	(1)	7	1,176	3,528	0	34,888	34,200	0	$2,500	0
December	5,000	3	10	1,680	5,040	0	39,928	39,200	$7,500	0	0
January	5,000	0	10	1,680	5,040	0	44,968	44,200	0	0	0
February	3,000	(4)	6	1,008	3,024	0	47,992	47,200	0	$10,000	0
March	3,000	0	6	1,008	3,024	0	51,016	50,200	0	0	0
April	4,000	2	8	1,344	4,032	0	55,048	54,200	$5,000	0	0
May	5,000	2	10	1,680	5,040	0	60,088	59,200	$5,000	0	0
June	5,200	0	10	1,680	5,040	160	65,288	64,400	0	0	$16,000
July	6,500	3	13	2,184	6,552	0	71,840	70,900	$7,500	0	0
August	5,600	(2)	11	1,848	5,544	56	77,440	76,500	0	$5,000	$5,600
September	5,100	(1)	10	1,680	5,040	60	82,540	81,600	0	$2,500	$6,000
October	4,000	(2)	8	1,344	4,032	0	86,572	85,600	0	$5,000	0
									$27,500	$32,500	$89,200

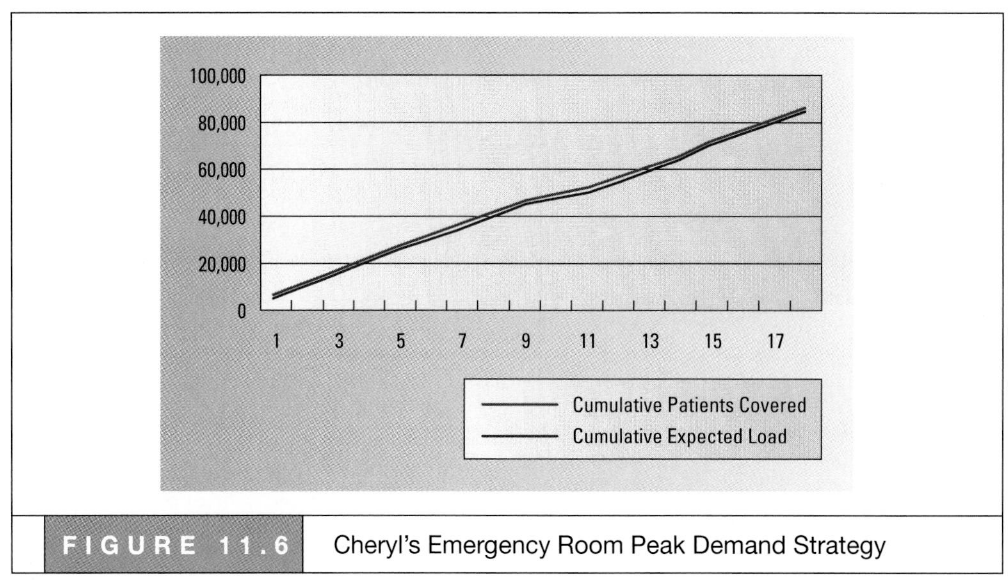

FIGURE 11.6 Cheryl's Emergency Room Peak Demand Strategy

MIXED STRATEGIES

In *mixed strategies,* changes in subcontracting, the production rate, and the size of both inventory and the workforce are used to adjust monthly output. By manipulating all these variables, planners can often significantly reduce costs, minimize the disruption of operations, enhance customer service, or otherwise improve on an aggregate plan based on a pure strategy. For example, the hiring costs associated with a chase demand strategy might be significantly reduced by holding a small quantity of inventory for a month or two. Or the well-timed use of temporary personnel could offset a significant amount of the inventory holding cost or back-ordering cost associated with a level production plan, with no reduction in quality or customer service. Mixed strategies may be used in both manufacturing and service operations in which some form of inventory (perhaps only partially complete) can be held.

Table 11.5 shows a revised aggregate plan for Fred's pager factory. Note that the level production strategy shown in Table 11.2 has been adapted by allowing some variation in hiring, layoffs, and overtime. This plan is not based on a chase demand strategy, because the inventory levels vary.

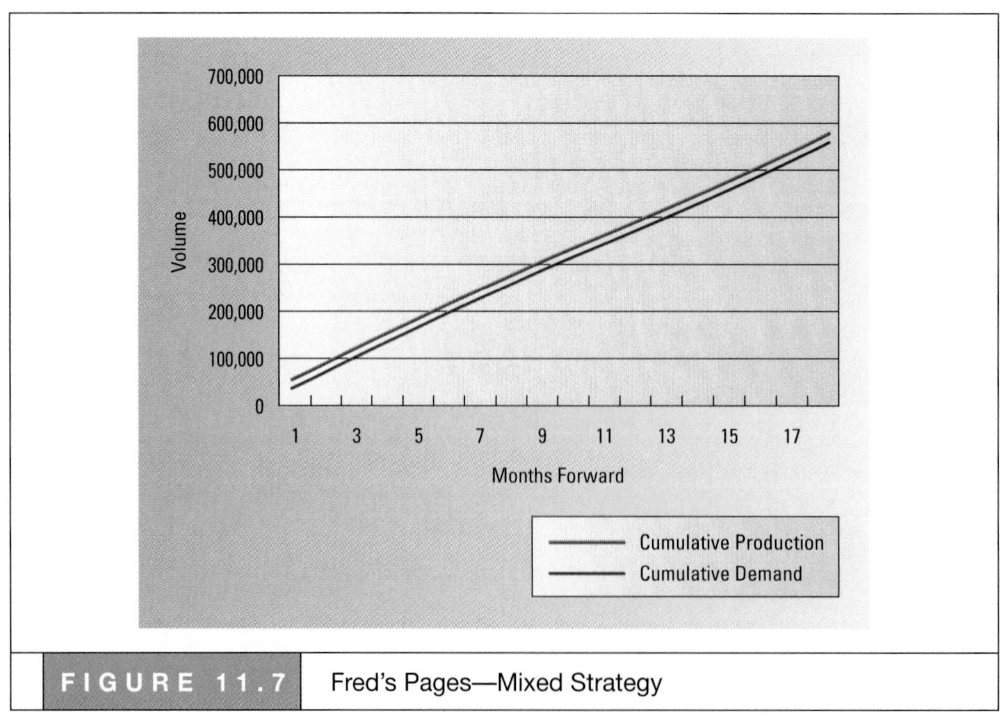

FIGURE 11.7 Fred's Pages—Mixed Strategy

TABLE 11.5 Freds' Pagers

Mixed Strategy

Total Cost = $360,240.00

Worker Hires (layoffs)	Work-force Size	Reg. Time Hours	Overtime Hours	In-House Production	Sub-contracted Production	Cumulative Production	Cumulative Demand	Ending Inventory	Hiring Cost	Layoff Cost	Inventory Cost	Backlog Cost	Sub-contracting Cost	Reg. Time Cost	Overtime Cost
−1	9	1,440	0	28,800	0	40,800	28,500	12,300	0	$1,500	$615	0	0	$17,280	0
0	9	1,440	0	28,800	0	69,600	57,000	12,600	0	0	$630	0	0	$17,280	0
0	9	1,440	0	28,800	0	98,400	85,500	12,900	0	0	$645	0	0	$17,280	0
1	10	1,600	5	32,100	0	130,500	118,500	12,000	$500	0	$600	0	0	$19,200	$90
0	10	1,600	50	33,000	0	163,500	151,500	12,000	0	0	$600	0	0	$19,200	$900
0	10	1,600	50	33,000	0	196,500	184,500	12,000	0	0	$600	0	0	$19,200	$900
0	10	1,600	50	33,000	0	229,500	217,500	12,000	0	0	$600	0	0	$19,200	$900
0	10	1,600	300	38,000	0	267,500	255,500	12,000	0	0	$600	0	0	$19,200	$5,400
0	10	1,600	0	32,000	0	299,500	287,500	12,000	0	0	$600	0	0	$19,200	0
−1	9	1,440	0	28,800	0	328,300	316,000	12,300	0	$1,500	$615	0	0	$17,280	0
0	9	1,440	0	28,800	0	357,100	344,500	12,600	0	0	$630	0	0	$17,280	0
0	9	1,440	0	28,800	0	385,900	373,000	12,900	0	0	$645	0	0	$17,280	0
0	9	1,440	15	29,100	0	415,000	403,000	12,000	0	0	$600	0	0	$17,280	$270
0	9	1,440	60	30,000	0	445,000	433,000	12,000	0	0	$600	0	0	$17,280	$1,080
0	9	1,440	60	30,000	0	475,000	463,000	12,000	0	0	$600	0	0	$17,280	$1,080
2	11	1,760	0	35,200	0	510,200	498,000	12,200	$1,000	0	$610	0	0	$21,120	0
0	11	1,760	0	35,200	0	545,400	533,000	12,400	0	0	$620	0	0	$21,120	0
0	11	1,760	0	35,200	0	580,600	568,000	12,600	0	0	$630	0	0	$21,120	0
									$1,500	$3,000	$11,040	0	0	$334,080	$10,620

A similar mixed strategy could be used in Luis's furniture factory, if inventory could be built up in periods preceding an anticipated surge in demand. (Even though Luis doesn't make furniture in high volumes, partially completed furniture could be inventoried for later finishing. For example, a sofa frame could be used to make a variety of different sofas.) In periods following a surge in demand, the backlog could be worked off.

As was mentioned earlier, a graph of cumulative demand versus cumulative production can be very helpful in determining how to improve an aggregate plan; that is certainly the case with a mixed strategy (see Figure 11.7). The distance between the two curves shows the size of the inventory or production backlog. If the graph for a level production plan shows that the inventory (or backlog) is growing rapidly, then clearly layoffs (or hiring) are likely. Similarly, a rapid change in the slope of the curve for a chase demand plan indicates a period in which inventory might be used to significantly reduce costs. Inventory is selectively used to level out significant changes in the slope of the cumulative production line.

active concept check 

Now let's take a moment to test your knowledge of the concepts you have studied in this section.

Aggregate Planning Methods

OPTIMIZING METHODS

Optimizing methods are used to minimize the cost of an aggregate plan. There are several optimizing methods, including the linear decision rule, the search decision rule, and various forms of linear programming. In *linear decision rule (LDR)* models, the costs of the aggregate plan are represented in the form of quadratic equations, and differential calculus is used to find the lowest-cost plan. In *search decision rule (SDR)* models, a mathematical search process is used to find the best plan among thousands of possible alternatives. In *linear programming (LP)* models, algebra is used to build and optimize mathematical models of the aggregate planning problem.

active example

Take a closer look at the concepts and issues you've been reading about.

While they may sound impressive, these optimizing methods are optimizing only to the extent that they fit the real situation. Since the aggregate plan is based on relatively imprecise forecasts and is updated regularly, many managers question the practical value of so-called optimal plans.

METHODS THAT MODEL MANAGER DECISIONS

The *management coefficients method (MCM)* is another technique used in aggregate planning. In this method, the assumption is made that past managerial decisions have been good, and multiple regression is used to develop a model of those decisions. The regression weights, called *management coefficients,* can then be used as a basis for future decisions or for an evaluation of the consistency with which managers pursue a given aggregate planning strategy. Like the optimizing methods, however, MCM is complicated and difficult to use.

THE CUT AND TRY METHOD

How do managers actually come up with their aggregate plans? Most often, seasoned managers rely on experience to develop a trial plan and then adapt that plan by tinkering. The tinkering involves using spreadsheets such as those that are shown in the section of this chapter describing aggregate planning strategies. By considering alternative plans, managers can evaluate the cost implications of their decisions to hire, layoff workers, use overtime, build inventory for demand in later months, and so on. In addition, they can compare alternative plans under a variety of demand scenarios—such as unexpected declines and sudden increases in demand. By doing so, they are likely to develop a plan that performs well in many situations and is acceptable in a worst-case scenario. This approach is called the *cut and try method.*

The cut and try method doesn't sound scientific, but for many reasons it is a very workable approach. Its primary strength is its reliance on years of managerial experience in planning and running operations. In most cases, managers have seen a similar forecasted demand pattern before. No amount of technical sophistication can replace the insights they have gained through experience with that demand pattern. Furthermore, the aggregate plan is based on a forecast, and forecasts are always uncertain. Managers are not likely to invest the time and energy required to optimize a plan that is based on uncertain numbers. Given the level of uncertainty most businesses face as they look forward 6 to 18 months, a plan that performs well in many situations and has an acceptable worst-case outcome may be better than a plan that minimizes costs based on the assumption that demand forecasts are correct.

What is more, the aggregate plan is typically updated on a monthly basis. Forecasts will change as more information becomes available; inventory levels will change based on actual events; personnel decisions will change the composition of the workforce. Because of the dynamic nature of the value-adding system, managers recognize the necessity of taking an adaptive approach to aggregate planning. They are not overly concerned with developing an optimal plan based on the data available at a given time. Finally, an "optimal" solution often has a narrow focus that renders it problematic. For example, most optimizing methods attempt to minimize the costs associated with an aggregate plan. Sometimes that requires a lot of hiring and firing—clearly not an ideal plan from the standpoint of worker morale. Minimizing the costs of an aggregate plan may also reduce the company's ability to respond effectively to customer expectations based on competitive priorities such as quality and flexibility.

> active concept check

Now let's take a moment to test your knowledge of the concepts you have studied in this section.

> E-Commerce, Supply-Chain Management and Aggregate Planning

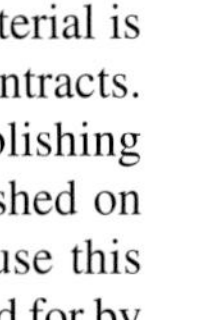

> video example

Take a closer look at the concepts and issues you've been reading about.

Recent developments in supply chain management and e-commerce have some bearing on aggregate planning practices. In particular, rather than sending individual purchase orders each time material is required, it has become more common to work with suppliers on the basis of long-term contracts. Many firms now establish bulk capacity agreements with their suppliers. Rather than establishing capacity levels on the basis of expected demand, the available capacity levels can be established on the basis of the customer's contractually stated requirements for capacity. Suppliers then use this capacity as demand occurs, often without any purchase orders, by simply producing what is called for by the customer's electronically accessible production schedules. Suppliers are responsible for handling the scheduling details and ensuring that there's adequate capacity to provide the needed materials when required by their customers. Customers, likewise, are responsible if there's a lack of balance between the amount of capacity they reserved and the amount they have used. These arrangements provide aggregate planners with much better knowledge of the intermediate-range demand to which their aggregate plan must respond, resulting in more effective and stable plans.

E-commerce requires a lot more than electronic connections between a customer and supplier. It takes a high degree of trust for a supplier to establish capacity levels (for example, by hiring workers) and commit its capacity to a customer, without any formal orders. It also takes trust for a customer to enter bulk capacity agreements and give up the detailed scheduling of component delivery. The relationship between companies becomes broader than one based on business transactions alone—thus relationship marketing takes on a significant role for the supplier, and vendor development becomes important to the customer. The value provided by the supplier is much greater than that of the physical product: It includes the service of synchronizing deliveries and fitting in with the customer's system. For this value to be fully developed and the connection between the two value-adding systems to become seamless, some level of integration between the vendor's and customer's information systems is generally required.

video exercise

Take a moment to apply what you've learned.

Integrating Operational Decisions

The context for the decisions covered in this chapter is set by the structural decisions discussed in earlier chapters. Chapters 4, 7, and 9 are particularly important because product-service bundle designs, value-adding system designs, and facility layouts determine what can be aggregated and what must be kept separate in the process of creating intermediate-range plans.

The decisions discussed in this chapter will then provide the boundaries for, or constraints on, the more detailed short-term scheduling issues covered in the Chapters 12–16. Chapter 12 describes operational planning activities for specific deliverables in the product-service bundle. It breaks apart the aggregate plan into specific plans that will lead to the satisfaction of specific customers. Chapters 13–16 cover the most detailed operational planning decisions in different operational environments. The aggregate planning strategy used varies by operational environment. The level strategy is most useful in the planning environment described in Chapter 13, and its usefulness declines as the environments of Chapters 14, 15, and 16 are covered. By contrast, the usefulness of the chase demand strategy increases as you move from the environment of Chapter 13 forward toward Chapter 16. Mixed strategies, obviously, are more likely to be used in the environments of Chapters 14 and 15 than in those of Chapters 13 and 16.

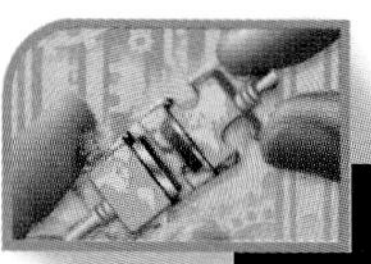

integrated OM

Take a moment to apply what you've learned.

Chapter Wrap-Up

The aggregate plan is an intermediate-range plan that indicates the available capacity for a family of product-service bundles. This kind of planning is an important function of senior managers, such as plant managers, group vice-presidents, and product managers. If it is done well, there should be sufficient money in budgets, adequate arrangements for subcontracting, and a large enough workforce to meet customer expectations, even at busy times. If the aggregate plan does not provide a way to meet a rise in demand, operations managers will be limited in their ability to respond. As a result, customers may experience unusual delays in service, or cost and quality may become problematic. Similarly, if the aggregate plan does not provide a way to adjust for periods of unusually low demand, excess capacity and significant economic loss could be the result. The operations management tasks described in the following chapters cannot be effectively carried out without some sort of aggregate planning.

To create an aggregate plan, companies must rely on forecasts. The aggregate plan determines how capacity will be adjusted in response to forecasted variations in demand. Adjusting capacity in the intermediate term may mean changing the size of the workforce, planning for overtime, subcontracting some tasks, or varying the level of inventories or backlogs. Typically, senior managers will revise the aggregate plan once a month based on their experience and a trial-and-error technique referred to as the cut and try method.

Managers generally prefer different aggregate planning strategies for different business environments. For instance, in service businesses that cannot hold inventory or in businesses in which inventory is expensive to hold, does not keep well, or becomes obsolete quickly, planners are likely to prefer a chase demand strategy. In each period they will try to provide sufficient capacity to meet demand. In other environments, perhaps those in which skilled labor is difficult to obtain and labor agreements limit overtime, managers will prefer a level production strategy, in which changes in inventory or backlog levels are used to even out differences between capacity and demand. In still other cases, economic criteria, competitive priorities, or customer service objectives will require some combination of the chase demand and level production strategies. These combination strategies are called mixed strategies.

Recent developments, including movement toward supply-chain management and e-commerce have had an impact on aggregate planning practices. Because of these trends, information used by aggregate planners is likely to be superior to forecasted demand values that are generated within the company. Thus, the aggregate plans more effectively match supply to demand and need less revision.

> end-of-chapter resources

- Practice Quiz
- Key Terms
- Solved Problems
- Discussion Questions
- Problems
- Case 11.1: America Online Underestimates Demand
- Factory Tours

Forecasting

SUPPLEMENT D

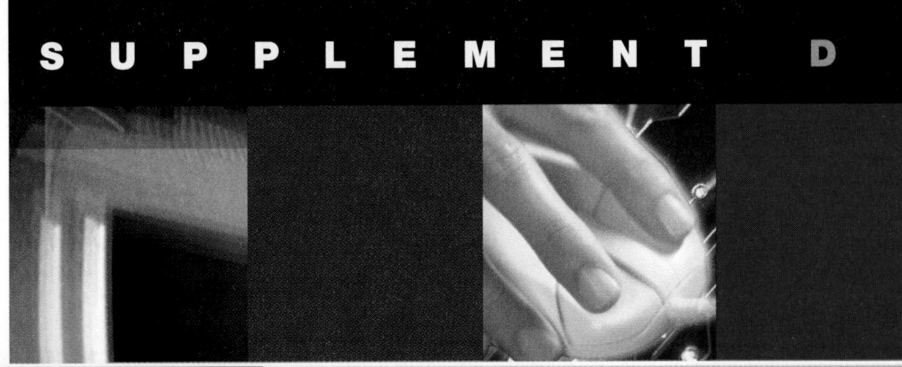

Supplement Outline

> Introduction

An important consideration in any decision-making situation, regardless of whether it is for the long-intermediate-or short-term, is the determination of the conditions under which the decision is to be made. When the relevant conditions are in the future, as is generally the case, this means forecasting. Since forecasts tend to be close, rather than exactly right, we need to consider not only what the forecast is, but also some estimate of how far off it is likely to be.

Choosing a Forecasting Method

The first, and possibly most important point, is that no forecasting system will be best, or even good, for all possible situations. Choosing an appropriate forecasting method involves matching the characteristics, strengths, and weaknesses of the situation with those of the method.

When considering the situational characteristics, the most important is what is being forecasted. Are we interested in the value of a variable at some point in time; in the time at which a series will change direction; or in the time when some event of particular interest (for example, the next generation of some technology) might occur? Besides this overriding consideration, the other situational characteristics usually considered important include:

***1.** The time horizon for the forecast, divided generally into short-term (up to about three months), intermediate-term (from three months to two years), or long-term (over two years). These time divisions are somewhat arbitrary and may vary considerably from industry to industry.*

2. The level of detail, or how much aggregation there will be. For example, are we talking about a product, a product line, a company's division, or the entire company?
3. The number of items. If we are developing forecasts for thousands of items on a monthly basis, we will probably want a simpler technique than if we are forecasting the demand for only one or two items once or twice a year.
4. The stability of the situation. If we can assume basic patterns that held in the past will continue to hold in the future, we can use a different approach than if we are attempting to deal with a great deal of change.

> Forecasting Model Types

We can categorize forecasting models in two general ways:

- quantitative versus qualitative
- time series versus causal

Quantitative models use one or more equations to turn a set of numerical or categorical inputs into a forecast of a value or set of values for one or more variables.

Qualitative models are subjective. They are based on the subjective assessments of individuals, working separately or in groups, rather than on formal equations. Probably the best-known of the qualitative methods is the Delphi technique, discussed in Chapter 8. Given the amount of time and the cost required to use the Delphi technique, it is most often used for long-range decisions with significant implications for capital expenditures or the organization's future direction. At the other extreme, a qualitative method sometimes used for annual demand forecasting is the grass-roots method, in which individual salespeople estimate next year's sales for their territories and the results are added up (with or without adjustment for perceived bias) to get sales for the district, the region, and the company.

Time series models are based on extrapolating the historical pattern for the variable of interest into the future. The model's inputs may include all or selected past values of the variable and, possibly, the forecast errors for all or selected past periods. Time series models are most often used for short time frames; they will be our primary focus.

Causal models estimate the value of the variable of interest, called the *dependent* variable, on the basis of a second set of variables, called the *independent* variables, that are believed to determine the value of the dependent variable. For example, a school system can do a very good (but not perfect) job of forecasting its kindergarten enrollment by looking at the number of births five years earlier. (Why might this approach not give a perfect forecast?) Two popular modeling techniques for causal models are regression and simulation.

Time Series Components

A time series is a time-ordered series of values of some variable. Examples are the monthly, quarterly, or yearly sales of a product or the daily number of passengers for an airline or daily number of cases seen at a hospital emergency room. The variable's value in any specific time period is a function of four factors: (1) trend, (2) cyclic effects, (3) seasonality, and (4) randomness.

TREND

Trend refers to a general pattern of change over time. A few of the many possible basic trend patterns are shown in Figure D.1. The most basic pattern is level or horizontal, shown in Figure D.1a. This pattern implies that there is no basic change expected over time. Figures D.1b and c show increasing and decreasing linear trends. A linear trend implies a constant *amount* of change from one period to the next. Figures D.1d and e show exponential growth and decay patterns. An exponential pattern implies a constant *percentage* change from one period to the next. Figure D.1f is an S-shaped growth curve. Typical of the cumulative demand for a product over its lifetime, it shows a pattern of slow growth, followed by a period of rapid growth, and, finally, slow growth again as the product nears the end of its life cycle.

CYCLIC EFFECTS

Cyclic effects arise from changes in the economy as it moves through the phases of growth and decline in the business cycle, a process that generally takes several years. For any particular item,

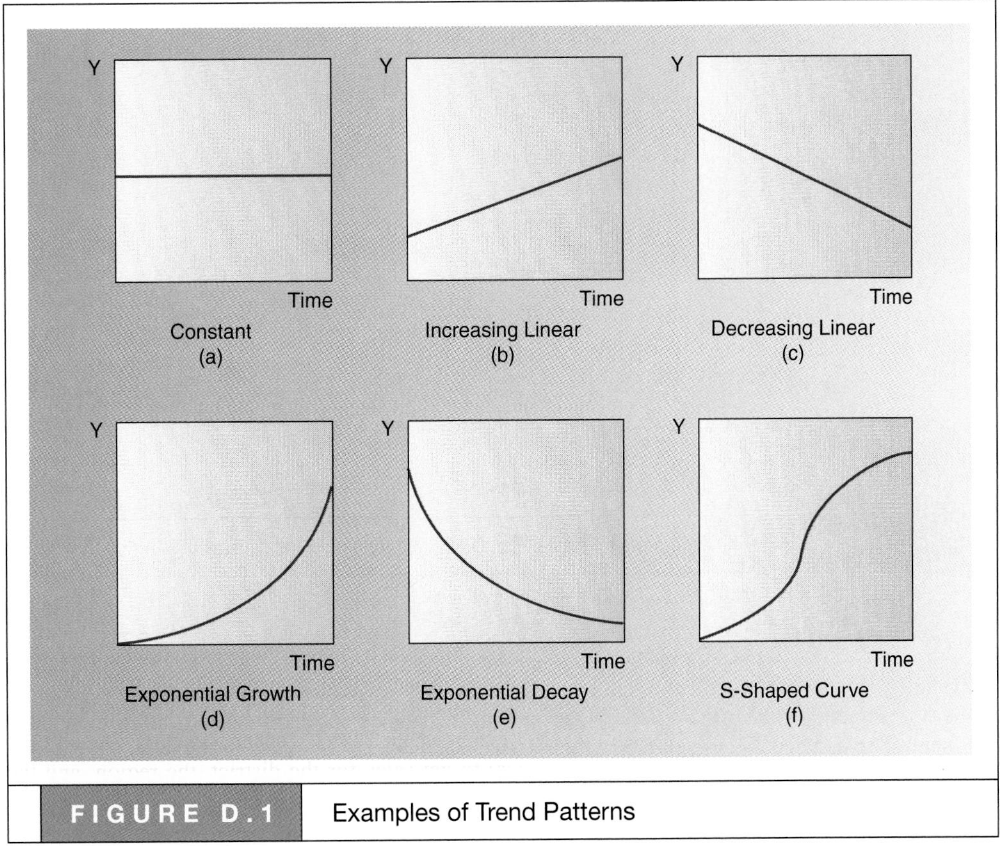

FIGURE D.1 Examples of Trend Patterns

cyclic effects may be very important or not important at all, depending on whether the item is or is not influenced by the phases of the business cycle. Figure D.2 shows a wavelike cyclic effect superimposed on an increasing linear trend.

Incorporating cyclic effects into a forecasting model is extremely difficult because it requires the ability to forecast the timing of the turns in the business cycle and the rates of growth and decline between those turns. Experience has shown that doing so is extremely difficult, if not impossible, in spite of the enormous amounts of money that have been spent on the development of macroeconomic forecasting models. For this reason, cyclic effects are often ignored, at least in those models that forecast only a few months or quarters ahead.

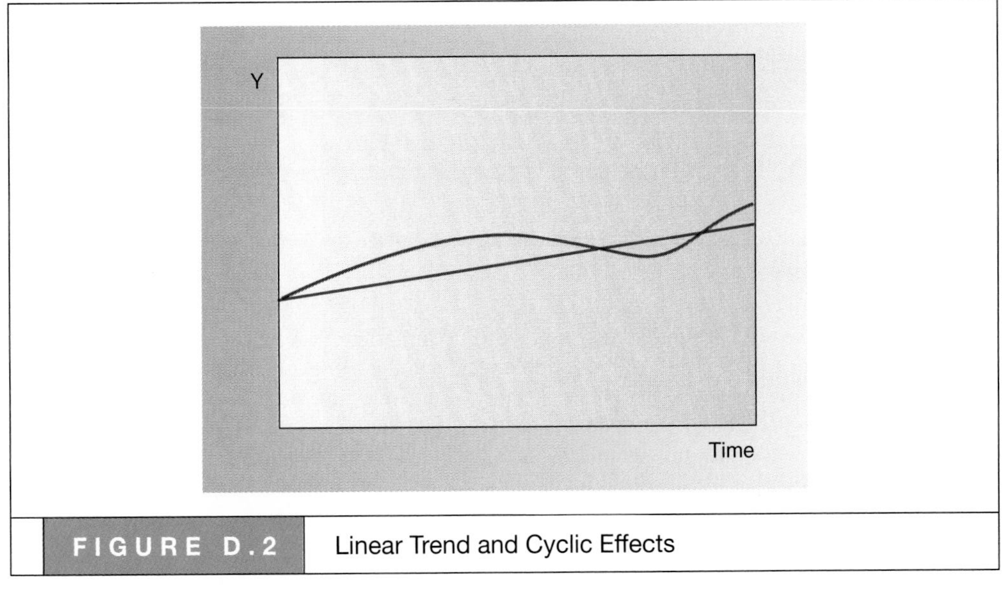

FIGURE D.2 Linear Trend and Cyclic Effects

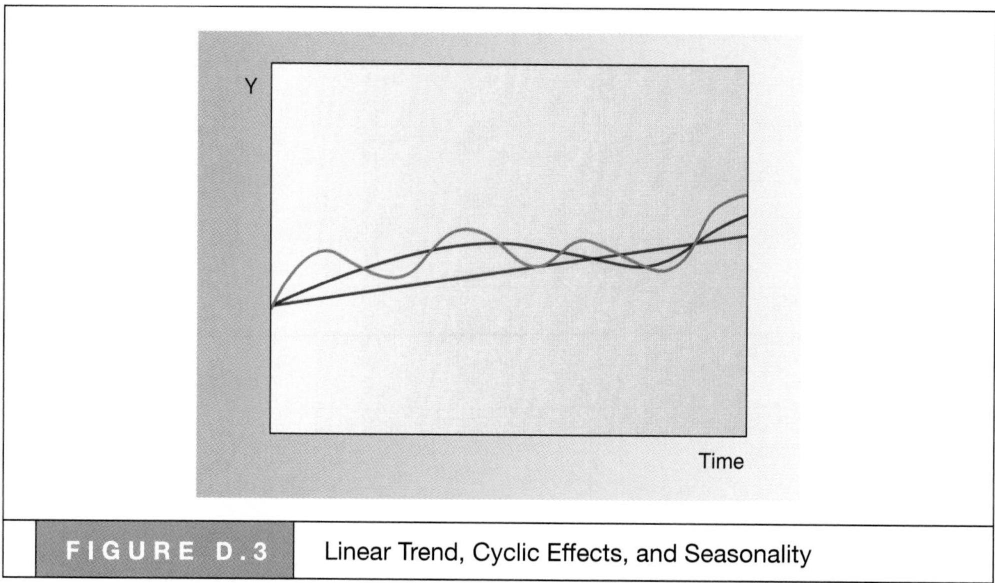

FIGURE D.3 Linear Trend, Cyclic Effects, and Seasonality

SEASONALITY

Seasonality refers to any regular pattern recurring within a time period of no more than one year.

Seasonality effects are often related to the seasons of the year (hence the name), as, for example, the increase in demand for snow tires in the winter and for air conditioners in the summer. Another time-of-year effect is the heavy demand for air travel over the Thanksgiving weekend (see ". . . Back at the Rec Center" at the start of Chapter 12). However, such effects may occur in a time frame of less than a year and may be based on causes that have nothing to do with the yearly seasons or holidays. For example, banks experience regularly recurring patterns in the level of deposits, based on the monthly, semimonthly, biweekly, and weekly pay schedules of their corporate customers. Hospital emergency rooms and police departments experience weekly demand patterns based on the typically increased level of accidents on weekend nights. And 911 operators experience a fluctuating pattern of calls over the course of a day.

Regardless of the nature or cause of the pattern, its recognition can make a forecasting model considerably more accurate. In Figure D.3, an annual seasonal pattern has been added to the trend and cyclic effects of Figure D.2.

RANDOMNESS

Randomness refers to all other factors that cause the actual observed value of a variable to differ from that predicted by the trend, cyclic, and seasonal effects.

active exercise <

Take a moment to apply what you've learned.

> Short-Term Forecasting

When there is no trend in a time series, a naive (but sometimes useful) short-term forecasting approach is to assume that the value of the variable will be the same next period as it is this period. Of course, this approach ignores the effect of seasonality, if it is relevant, but it also causes the forecasts to jump around from period to period in response to the randomness.

One way to compensate for this jumpiness in the forecasts is to use averaging. Two popular time series models for averaging when there is no seasonality[1] are the **simple moving average (SMA)** and

[1]As we shall see later, both methods can be adapted to work with seasonal data.

TABLE D.1	Monthly Demand for Chairs				
Month	**Demand**	**Month**	**Demand**	**Month**	**Demand**
1	122	7	105	13	99
2	90	8	105	14	107
3	131	9	118	15	114
4	87	10	135	16	139
5	123	11	108	17	80
6	127	12	91	18	119

simple exponential smoothing (SES). Both forecast the value for next period simply by estimating the height or level of the horizontal line (see Figure D.1a) around which the actual values are randomly scattered.

SIMPLE MOVING AVERAGE

If we could assume that the height of the line around which the actual values are randomly scattered has always been the same, then the simplest way to estimate it and forecast the value for the next period would be to average all past values of the variable. Since we cannot always make this assumption, a reasonable compromise is to use the average of the last few periods. This approach is called the simple moving average model. Letting F_t be the forecast for period *t* and Y_t be the actual value, the n-period SMA forecast for period t+1 is:

$$F_{t+1} = \frac{Y_t + Y_{t-1} + \ldots Y_{t-n+1}}{n}$$

Example D.1

The demand for a particular type of chairs at Luis's furniture company has been fairly stable. The actual numbers of chairs ordered for the past 18 months are given in Table D.1 and graphed in Exhibit D.1

Find the six-month simple moving average forecasts for months 7 and 8.

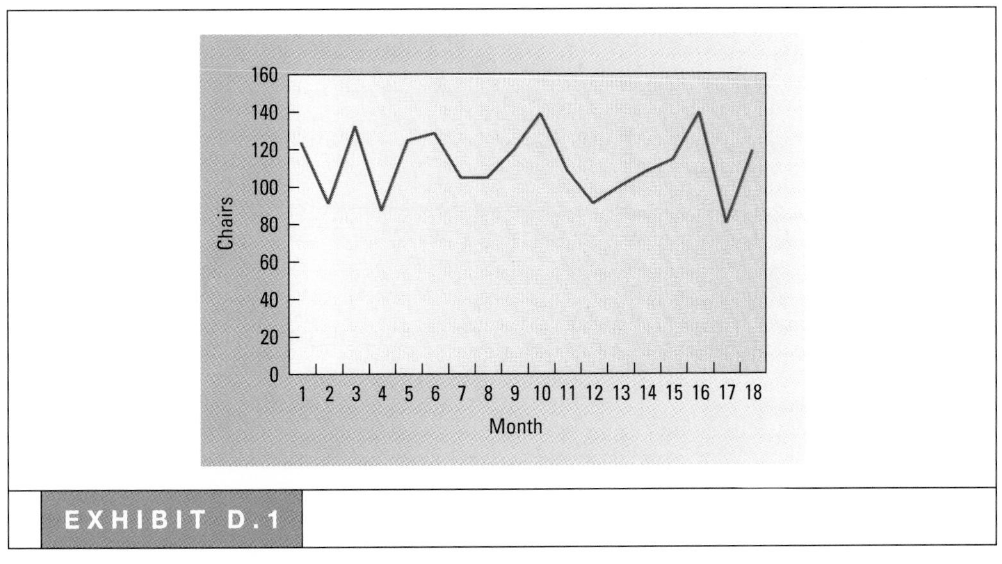

EXHIBIT D.1

Solution:

The six-month SMA forecast for month 7 is:

$$F_7 = \frac{Y_6 + Y_5 + Y_4 + Y_3 + Y_2 + Y_1}{6}$$

$$= \frac{127 + 123 + 87 + 131 + 90 + 122}{6}$$

$$= \frac{680}{6} = 113.333$$

The six-month SMA forecast for month 8 is:

$$F_8 = \frac{Y_7 + Y_6 + Y_5 + Y_4 + Y_3 + Y_2}{6}$$

$$= \frac{105 + 127 + 123 + 87 + 131 + 90}{6}$$

$$= \frac{663}{6} = 110.5$$

active exercise

Take a moment to apply what you've learned.

A comparison of the two equations in this example shows why this model is called a simple *moving* average. As the period to be forecasted moves up by one, the periods for which the actual values are averaged also move up by one; the oldest data value is dropped and replaced by the new one.

This simple model is easy to automate with a spreadsheet, either by building the equation into the sheet directly or by using the spreadsheet's built-in procedure. Exhibit D.2 shows the results of applying the moving average procedure from data analysis in Excel to the data in Table D.1.[2] Notice that there are no forecasts for the first six months, since we can't get an average until we have six months of data. Also notice that, because of the averaging, the line for the forecast does not bounce around as much as the line for the actual data. If we used more periods in the average, the forecast line would fluctuate even less.

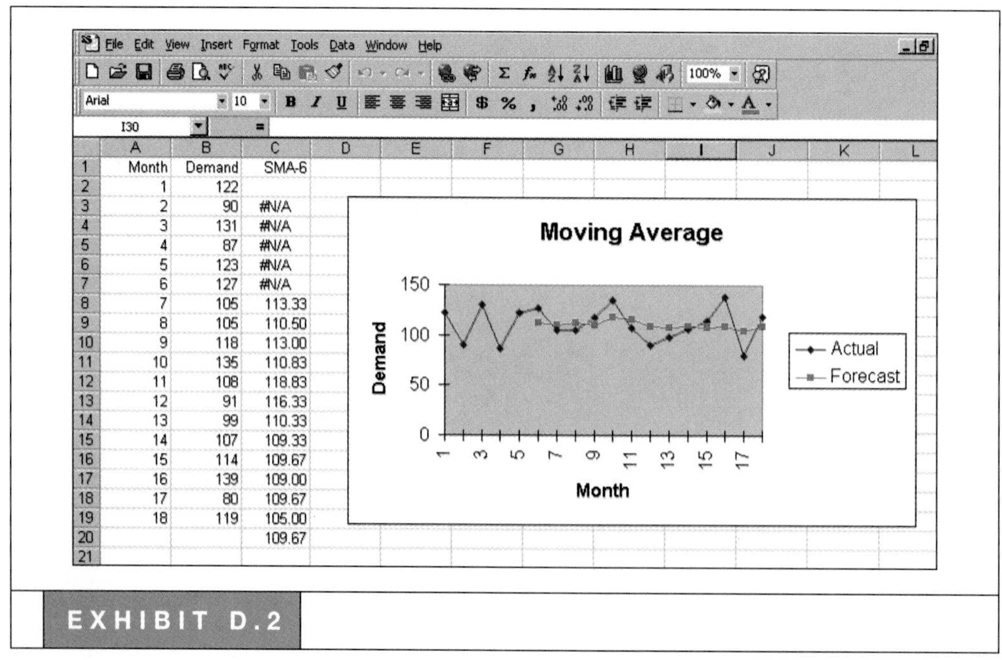

Month	Demand	SMA-6
1	122	
2	90	#N/A
3	131	#N/A
4	87	#N/A
5	123	#N/A
6	127	#N/A
7	105	113.33
8	105	110.50
9	118	113.00
10	135	110.83
11	108	118.83
12	91	116.33
13	99	110.33
14	107	109.33
15	114	109.67
16	139	109.00
17	80	109.67
18	119	105.00
		109.67

EXHIBIT D.2

[2]Excel lines the SMA value up with the last period in the average rather than with the next period. Thus, the SMA column was started in row 3 to be used as a forecast for the next period.

SIMPLE EXPONENTIAL SMOOTHING

While the simple moving average forecast is easy to compute and the concept is easy to understand, it has two possible drawbacks: (1) it treats all values used equally, regardless of their age, and 2) it requires a fair amount of storage (although this drawback becomes less of a problem as computer storage gets cheaper). An alternative to the SMA model is simple exponential smoothing (SES), which differs from SMA in three important respects:

1. The model implicitly uses the entire past history of the time series, not just the most recent periods.
2. The weights assigned to the values decrease[3] with the age of the data, rather than being 1/n for each.
3. Less storage is required: Only the value of the smoothing constant (α in the equations to follow) and the most recent forecast are needed.

There are two alternative, but equivalent, forms of the SES model. The first,

$$F_{t+1} = \alpha Y_t + (1\text{-}\alpha)F_t$$

says that the new forecast is simply a weighted average of the most recent actual value, Y_t, and the old forecast, F_t. The **smoothing constant,** α, is a number between 0 and 1. A value close to 0 produces a lot of smoothing (similar to a large value for *n* in an SMA model), while a value close to 1 yields a forecast that responds quickly to changes in the data pattern.

By doing a little algebra on the equation above, we get the second form of the equation:

$$F_{t+1} = F_t + \alpha(Y_t - F_t).$$

This equation shows that the new forecast is simply the old forecast corrected by a percentage of the amount by which that forecast was in error $(Y_t - F_t)$.

Just as the *n*-period SMA model could not produce a forecast before period n+1, so the SES model cannot give a forecast for period 1 unless, for some reason, there are values for F_0 and Y_0. Common practice, then, is to let $F_1 = Y_1$ and start the forecasts with t = 2.

Example D.2

Refer to Example D.1. Find the SES forecasts for months 2 and 3. Use $\alpha = .3$.

Solution:
Letting $F_1 = Y_1 = 122$ (from Table D.1), the SES forecast for chairs in period 2 with $\alpha = .3$ is:

$$F_2 = \alpha Y_1 + (1-\alpha)F_1 = (.3)(122) + (.7)(122) = 122$$

The forecast for period 3 is:

$$F_3 = \alpha Y_2 + (1-\alpha)F_2 = (.3)(90) + (.7)(122) = 112.4$$

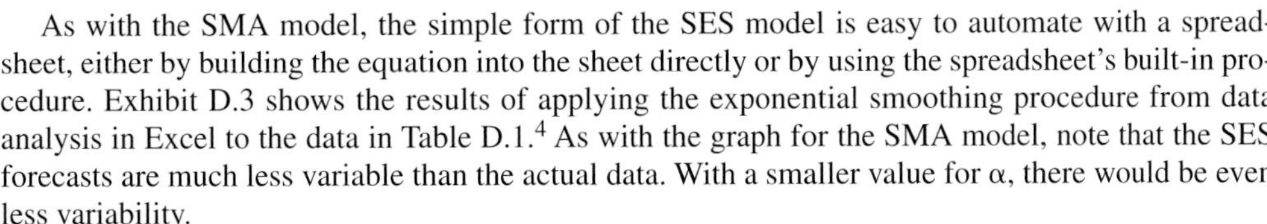

As with the SMA model, the simple form of the SES model is easy to automate with a spreadsheet, either by building the equation into the sheet directly or by using the spreadsheet's built-in procedure. Exhibit D.3 shows the results of applying the exponential smoothing procedure from data analysis in Excel to the data in Table D.1.[4] As with the graph for the SMA model, note that the SES forecasts are much less variable than the actual data. With a smaller value for α, there would be even less variability.

[3]While we will not go through a derivation, the reason this model is called simple *exponential* smoothing is that each period's weight is a constant percentage of the weight for the next (later) period's weight. That is, the weights decline exponentially with the age of the data values.

[4]Excel's Exponential Smoothing dialog box asks for the value of the *damping factor,* which is 1-α, rather than the smoothing constant, α.

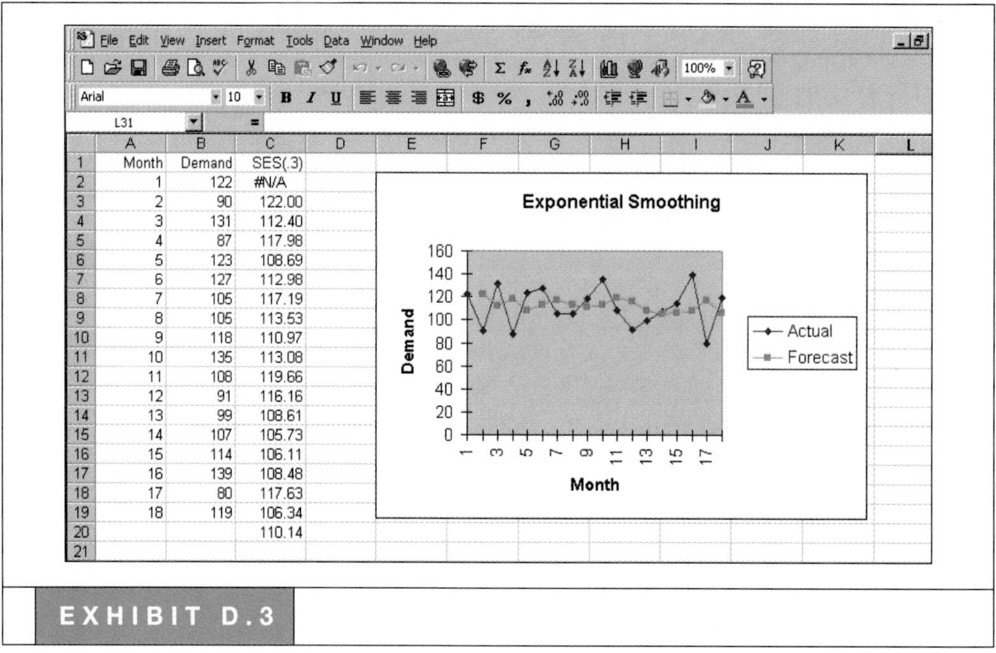

Month	Demand	SES(.3)
1	122	#N/A
2	90	122.00
3	131	112.40
4	87	117.98
5	123	108.69
6	127	112.98
7	105	117.19
8	105	113.53
9	118	110.97
10	135	113.08
11	108	119.66
12	91	116.16
13	99	108.61
14	107	105.73
15	114	106.11
16	139	108.48
17	80	117.63
18	119	106.34
		110.14

EXHIBIT D.3

FORECASTING MORE THAN ONE PERIOD AHEAD

Since the basic data pattern assumed for the SMA and SES models is random scatter around a horizontal line, the forecast is simply the estimated height of that line. Although the equations given above for these models assume that we are forecasting only one period ahead (F_{t+1}), we can just as easily use them to forecast two, three, or as many periods ahead as desired by using the same value. Of course, as with any model, the further into the future we attempt to forecast, the larger our forecast error is likely to be.

OTHER SHORT-TERM FORECASTING MODELS

The two short-term forecasting models discussed are both designed for situations where the basic data pattern is random scatter around a horizontal line. Of course, in many cases we will have either trend or seasonality (or both). How to incorporate seasonality into these models will be discussed later, after we have shown how seasonal factors can be estimated. There are also moving average and exponential smoothing models that build the estimation and use of trend effects directly into short-term forecasts. These models are beyond the scope of this book, but the models are available in many software packages. In particular, exponential smoothing with trend is available in the Excelpom package.

Measuring Forecast Accuracy

An important consideration in the selection and use of a forecasting model is how well it will perform, i.e., how close the forecasts come to the actual values of the variable of interest. Three popular measures of **forecast accuracy** are the **mean squared error (MSE)**, which is analogous to a sample variance in basic statistics, the **mean absolute deviation (MAD)**, and the **mean absolute percentage error (MAPE)**. All three start with the same basic forecasting error measurement:

$$e_t = Y_t - F_t$$

The MSE, MAPE, and MAD actually tell us about the average magnitude of error terms. Any of these three accuracy measures can be used as the basis for comparing forecasting models or as the basis for selecting parameter values for a given model type. Either the MSE or MAD, with appropriate adjustments, can be used for finding forecast intervals (similar to confidence intervals in basic statistics).

The average error term, also called the **mean forecast error (MFE)**, doesn't tell us how accurate our forecast is. The MFE can, however, tell us if our forecast consistently over or under estimates demand. (For this reason the MFE is also called the *forecast bias.*) Forecast bias is considered large when its magnitude is a significant percentage of the MAD. Large negative values for the MFE indicate that our forecasts are consistently higher than demand. By contrast, large positive values suggest that our forecasts are consistently low.

The presence of bias is an indicator of at least three possibilities. First, a large bias indicates that the forecasting technique can be improved; any consistent pattern in the forecast error terms can be analyzed and exploited to improve the forecast. Second, if a forecasting technique becomes biased over time but was not biased to start with, the underlying demand pattern must have changed. (For example, there could have been a turning point in a product life cycle, a new seasonal effect could have developed, and so on.) Third, bias may result from deliberate attempts to manipulate forecasts. For example, marketing personnel or valued customers might attempt to inflate demand forecasts to guarantee the availability of supply. In reality, such attempts are counterproductive because they foster uncertainty, undermine trust, and hinder integrated cross-functional decision making. Decision makers in all functions rely on forecasts to make their decisions. They should all be using the best information available. Rather than manipulating forecasts to influence decisions, managers should get the best forecast possible, then consider their range of options to make the most effective decision. There is ample opportunity for cross-functional influence on decisions once an unbiased forecast has been developed.

MEAN SQUARED ERROR (MSE)

Similar to the procedure for measuring variation in a sample in basic statistics, the mean squared error compensates for the problem of positive/negative error cancellation by squaring the forecast errors, summing them, and then taking their average.

$$MSE = \frac{\Sigma e^2_t}{n} = \frac{\Sigma(Y_t - F_t)^2}{n}$$

Just as we take the square root of a sample variance to get the standard deviation, which is used in finding a confidence interval in statistics, we can take the square root of the MSE, called the **root mean squared error,** and use it as the basis for a forecast interval:

$$RMSE = \sqrt{MSE}$$

Following the basic approach for finding a confidence interval in statistics, a forecast interval for any particular level of confidence can be found as:

$$\text{Forecast} \pm Z(\text{standard error of forecast})$$

Example D.3

Use Excel to compute the mean squared error and root mean squared error for the simple exponential smoothing forecasts with $\alpha = .3$ for the chair demand data found in Example D.2. Use the results to find an approximate 95% forecast interval for chair demand in month 19.

Solution:

The spreadsheet in Exhibit D.4 shows the use of Excel to compute the MSE and RMSE for the chair demand data in Table D.1. (The forecast values from using SES with $\alpha = .3$ come from

File Edit View Insert Format Tools Data Window Help

Arial 10 B I U $ %

H29 =

	A	B	C	D	E	F	G	H
1	Month	Demand	SES(.3)	error	error^2	|error|	|error/Demand|	
2	1	122	#N/A					
3	2	90	122.00	-32.00	1024.00	32.00	35.56	
4	3	131	112.40	18.60	345.96	18.60	14.20	
5	4	87	117.98	-30.98	959.76	30.98	35.61	
6	5	123	108.69	14.31	204.89	14.31	11.64	
7	6	127	112.98	14.02	196.55	14.02	11.04	
8	7	105	117.19	-12.19	148.50	12.19	11.61	
9	8	105	113.53	-8.53	72.77	8.53	8.12	
10	9	118	110.97	7.03	49.40	7.03	5.96	
11	10	135	113.08	21.92	480.49	21.92	16.24	
12	11	108	119.66	-11.66	135.86	11.66	10.79	
13	12	91	116.16	-25.16	632.98	25.16	27.65	
14	13	99	108.61	-9.61	92.38	9.61	9.71	
15	14	107	105.73	1.27	1.62	1.27	1.19	
16	15	114	106.11	7.89	62.26	7.89	6.92	
17	16	139	108.48	30.52	931.67	30.52	21.96	
18	17	80	117.63	-37.63	1416.29	37.63	47.04	
19	18	119	106.34	12.66	160.18	12.66	10.64	
20	19		110.14					
21								
22			Sum =		6915.58	295.98	285.86	
23			Average =		406.80	17.41	16.82	
24				RMSE =	20.17			
25								

EXHIBIT D.4

Exhibit D.3). We see that the MSE is *6915.58/17 = 406.80* and the RMSE is 20.17. Using this value for the RMSE and, from the spreadsheet, the forecast value of 110.1 for $t = 19$, we can get an approximate 95% forecast interval of:

$$F_{19} \pm 2(\text{RMSE}) = 110.1 \pm 2(20.17) = 110.1 \pm 40.34$$
$$= (69.76, 150.44)$$

We could say that we are roughly 95% sure that the demand for chairs in month 19 will be between 70 and 150.

active exercise 

Take a moment to apply what you've learned.

MEAN ABSOLUTE DEVIATION (MAD)

An alternative approach to compensating for the positive/negative error compensation problem is to take the absolute values of the errors and average them to obtain the mean absolute deviation:

$$\text{MAD} = \frac{\Sigma|e|}{n} = \frac{\Sigma|Y_t - F_t|}{n}$$

As we can see by comparing the values of MAD and RMSE in Exhibit D.4, the mean absolute deviation is generally smaller than the root mean square error. However, it has been found that, for a normal probability distribution, MAD tends to be just about 80% of the standard deviation, so we can get a good estimate of the standard deviation of forecast errors by using 1.25MAD.

Example D.4

Use Excel to compute the mean absolute deviation for simple exponential smoothing forecasts with $\alpha = .3$ for the chair demand data found in Example D.2. Use the results to find an approximate 95% forecast interval for chair demand in month 19.

Solution:
Exhibit D.4 also shows the computation of the value of the MAD for the chair demand data in Table D.1, using SES with $\alpha = .3$. From the spreadsheet, we see that the sum of the absolute values of the forecast errors = 295.98 and *MAD = 295.98/17 = 17.41.*

Using this value for MAD and, from the spreadsheet, the forecast value of 110.1 for $t = 19$, we can get an approximate 95% forecast interval of:

$$F_{19} \pm 2(1.25\text{MAD}) = 110.1 \pm 2.5(17.41) = 110.1 \pm 43.525$$
$$= (66.575, 153.625)$$

We could say that we are roughly 95% sure that the demand for chairs in month 19 will be between 67 and 154. This interval is, of course, not exactly the same as the one found above using RMSE, but that is to be expected since neither RMSE nor 1.25MAD is exactly equal to the true standard deviation of forecast errors.

active exercise 

Take a moment to apply what you've learned.

MEAN ABSOLUTE PERCENTAGE ERROR (MAPE)

A large forecast error is less of a problem when the value being forecasted is large than when it is small. An alternative to using the actual error is to use the *relative* or *percentage* error, which is found by dividing the error by the value being forecasted and, if desired, multiplying the ratio by 100. The absolute percentage errors can then be averaged to get the mean absolute percentage error or MAPE:

$$\text{MAPE} = \frac{\Sigma 100 \times (e_t)/Y_t}{n} = \frac{\Sigma 100 \times (Y_t - F_t)/Y_t}{n}$$

While useful as a way of comparing alternative forecasting methods or comparing different parameter values for a particular forecasting method, MAPE does not lend itself to serving as the basis for constructing forecast intervals.

Example D.5

Use Excel to compute the mean absolute deviation for simple exponential smoothing forecasts with $\alpha = .3$ for the chair demand data found in Example D.2.

Solution:
Exhibit D.4 also shows the computation of the value of the MAPE for the chair demand data in Table D.1, using SES with $\alpha = .3$. From the spreadsheet, we see that the sum of the absolute percentage forecast errors is 285.86 and *MAPE = 285.86/17 = 16.82.* That is, the forecast is, on average, in error by 16.82% of the demand value.

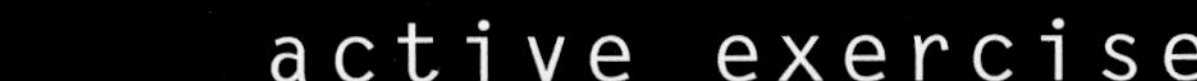

Take a moment to apply what you've learned.

Estimating Trend

While some time series can be expected to stay at a relatively constant level, at least for the near future, others will show a consistent pattern of growth or decline. Many different patterns are possible. Computer programs for forecasting have built into them a variety of trend equations, including the ones in Figure D.1.

The simplest form of trend equation is linear, for which the data is randomly scattered around a straight line, given by the equation

$$T_t = b_0 + b_1 t.$$

In this equation, t is the period number; T_t is the forecasted value that has been adjusted for trend for period t (we'll call it the "trend value" or "trend" for short); b_0 is the intercept, corresponding to the trend value in period 0; and b_1, the slope of the line, gives the change in the trend value from period to period.

Example D.6

A year ago, as part of its community wellness program, Cheryl's hospital started a Saturday morning aerobics program. Since then, the average number of registrants per week has been growing steadily, as can be seen in Exhibit D.5.

Use regression analysis from data analysis in Excel to estimate the trend equation for these data and interpret the results. Use the equation $T_t = b_0 + b_1 t$ to forecast average weekly attendance for the next six months.

Solution:
The regression results are shown in Exhibit D.6. From that output we see that the estimated trend equation is:

$$T_t = 20.114 + 3.069t$$

With $R^2 = .97$, the line fits the data very closely, as shown by the straight line in the graph in Exhibit D.5. The slope coefficient is $b_1 = 3.069$, which means that, on average, the hospital can expect the average weekly number of registrants to increase by a little over three per month.

Assuming that the trend will remain the same (a big assumption), the hospital can use the same equation to forecast the average number of registrants per week for the next six months, as follows:

Month	*Trend*
13	20.114 + 3.069(13) = 60.01
14	20.114 + 3.069(14) = 63.08
15	20.114 + 3.069(15) = 66.15
16	20.114 + 3.069(16) = 69.22
17	20.114 + 3.069(17) = 72.29
18	20.114 + 3.069(18) = 75.36

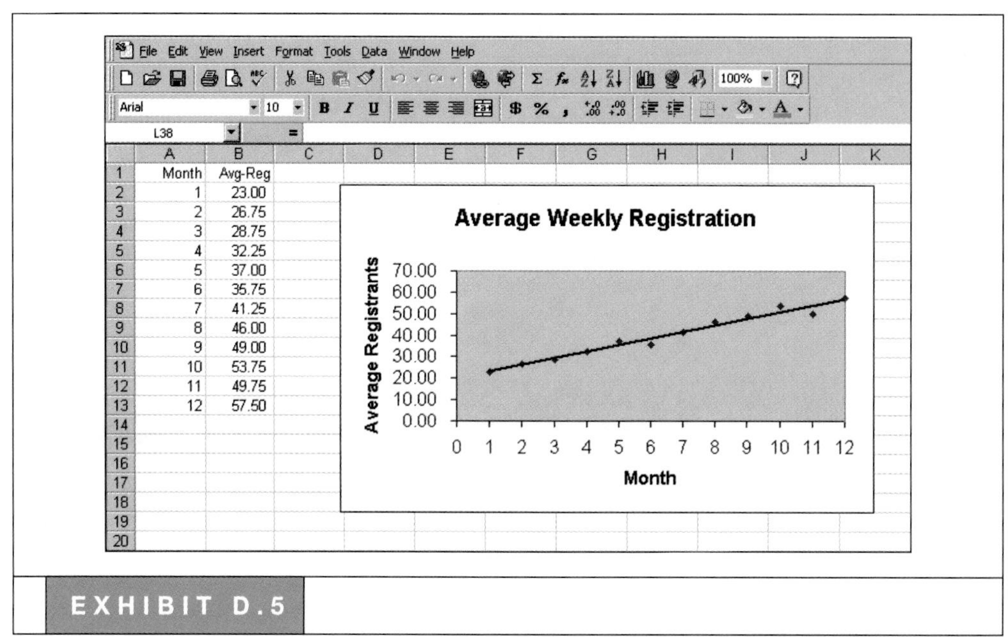

Month	Avg-Reg
1	23.00
2	26.75
3	28.75
4	32.25
5	37.00
6	35.75
7	41.25
8	46.00
9	49.00
10	53.75
11	49.75
12	57.50

EXHIBIT D.5

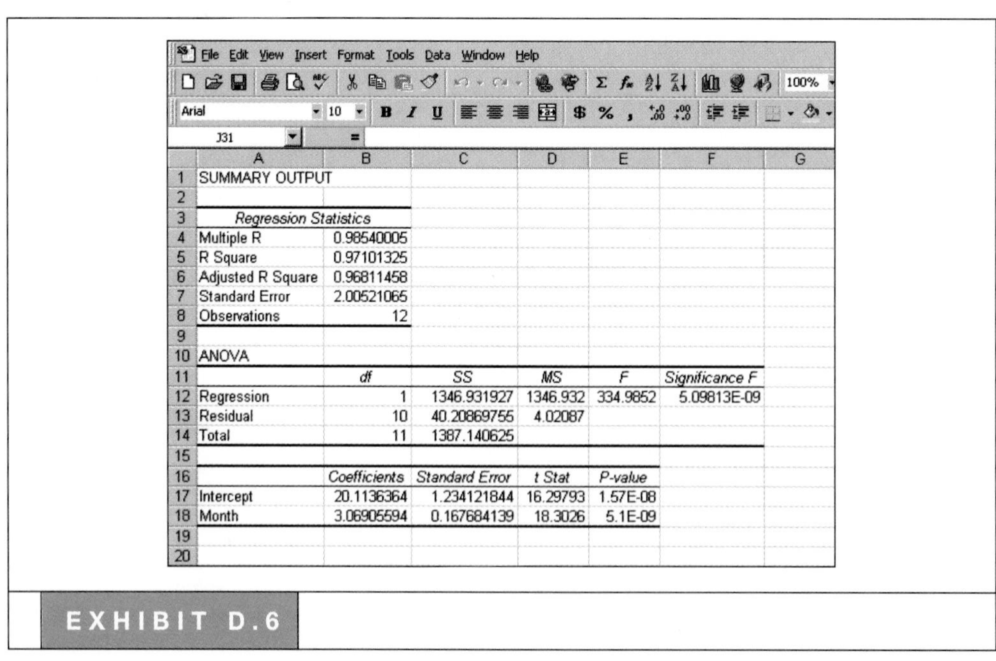

SUMMARY OUTPUT

Regression Statistics	
Multiple R	0.98540005
R Square	0.97101325
Adjusted R Square	0.96811458
Standard Error	2.00521065
Observations	12

ANOVA

	df	*SS*	*MS*	*F*	*Significance F*
Regression	1	1346.931927	1346.932	334.9852	5.09813E-09
Residual	10	40.20869755	4.02087		
Total	11	1387.140625			

	Coefficients	*Standard Error*	*t Stat*	*P-value*
Intercept	20.1136364	1.234121844	16.29793	1.57E-08
Month	3.06905594	0.167684139	18.3026	5.1E-09

EXHIBIT D.6

active exercise

Take a moment to apply what you've learned.

> Estimating and Using Seasonal Indexes

As discussed earlier, seasonality refers to any regular pattern recurring within a time frame of no more than a year. Although seasonal indexes may be either *additive* or *multiplicative,* we shall focus here on the more commonly used multiplicative type.

A **multiplicative seasonal index** is the expected ratio of the value of a time series in the period for which the index applies to the value as called for by any trend and cyclic components. For example, if the seasonal index in a period is 1.0, the value of the time series in that period is expected to be exactly what the trend and cyclic components call for. If the seasonal index is 1.25, the value is expected to be 25% larger than what trend and cycle call for. If the seasonal index is .90, the value is expected to be only 90% of (10% lower than) what the trend and cycle call for. Since seasonal indexes show how to adjust the values of individual periods up or down from "normal," they must average 1.0 across a full set of seasons.

ESTIMATING SEASONAL INDEXES

The basic multiplicative time series model says that the value of the variable is the product of its four component parts: trend, cycle, seasonality, and randomness. That is:

$$Y = T \times C \times S \times R$$

This leads to a four-step process for estimating multiplicative seasonal indexes:

1. Estimate the value of T×C in each period.
2. Divide the value of Y by the estimate of T×C in each period, giving an estimate of S×R for that period.
3. Average the S×R values for all periods of the same type or season to get raw seasonal indexes.
4. Average the raw seasonal indexes. If the average is not 1.0, divide the raw indexes by the actual average to get adjusted seasonal indexes.

There are a number of ways to implement this process. They differ in the way in which the T×C estimates are obtained (step 1). We will consider two approaches, one for basically horizontal data patterns and one for trend. Both approaches assume that cyclic effects are negligible and can be ignored.

HORIZONTAL DATA PATTERNS

If the basic data pattern is horizontal, then its level can be estimated simply by averaging the values for all time periods (step 1 of the process described above). To make this estimate as valid as possible, the same number of each type of season should be included in the average. For quarterly indexes, the average should be based on 4, 8, 12, etc. periods. For monthly indexes, the average should be based on 12, 24, 36, etc. periods.

Example D.7

Exhibit D.7 shows a department store's quarterly sales of lightweight men's pajamas over a period of three years. The graph shows that the basic pattern is horizontal, but with a pronounced up and down quarterly pattern.

Use Excel to estimate the quarterly multiplicative seasonal indexes.

Solution:

Exhibit D.8 shows an Excel spreadsheet for calculating the seasonal indexes. The actual sales values in column C are divided by their average (in C15) to obtain the quarterly ratios in column D. These ratios are grouped by year in columns G-I; the quarterly averages are shown in column J. Since these raw indexes average 1.0, they can be used as seasonal indexes.

TREND DATA PATTERNS

If the basic data pattern exhibits a trend, then the basic trend value for a period can be estimated from the appropriate trend equation (step 1 of the process described above). The seasonality ratio for each period is then found by dividing Y_t, the actual value for that period, by T_t, the trend estimate (step 2 of the process).

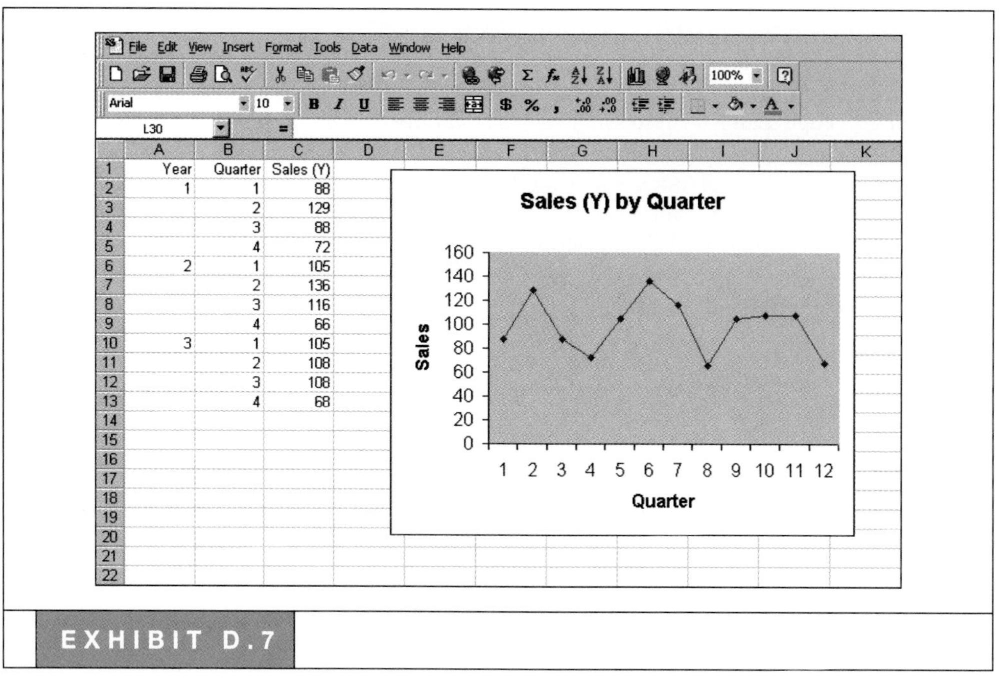

Year	Quarter	Sales (Y)
1	1	88
	2	129
	3	88
	4	72
2	1	105
	2	136
	3	116
	4	66
3	1	105
	2	108
	3	108
	4	68

EXHIBIT D.7

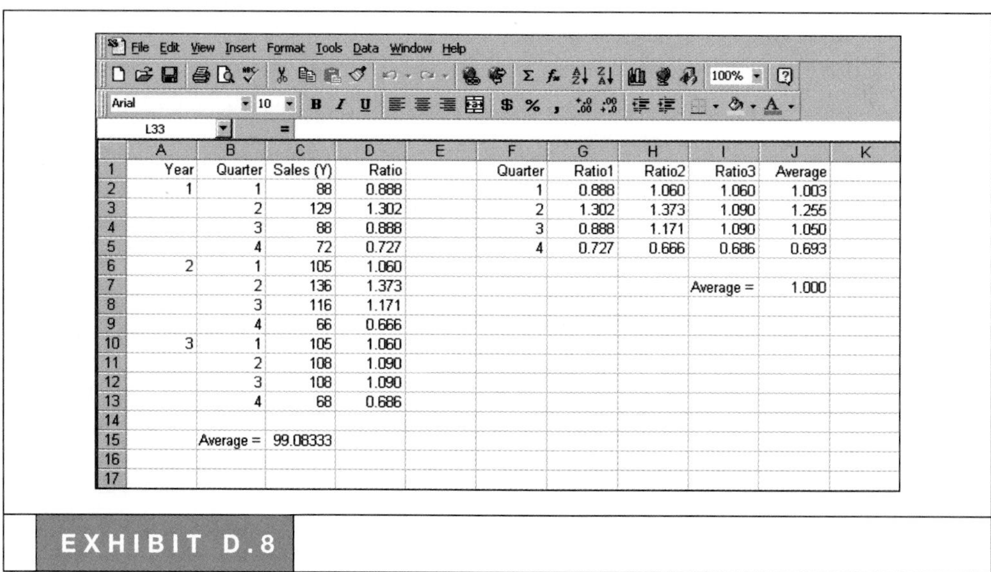

Year	Quarter	Sales (Y)	Ratio
1	1	88	0.888
	2	129	1.302
	3	88	0.888
	4	72	0.727
2	1	105	1.060
	2	136	1.373
	3	116	1.171
	4	66	0.666
3	1	105	1.060
	2	108	1.090
	3	108	1.090
	4	68	0.686
	Average =	99.08333	

Quarter	Ratio1	Ratio2	Ratio3	Average
1	0.888	1.060	1.060	1.003
2	1.302	1.373	1.090	1.255
3	0.888	1.171	1.090	1.050
4	0.727	0.666	0.686	0.693
			Average =	1.000

EXHIBIT D.8

Example D.8

Exhibit D.9 shows the quarterly demand for in-house continuing education at Fred's company over the past two years. The basic data pattern exhibits both upward trend and quarterly seasonality. Estimate the linear trend equation and quarterly multiplicative seasonal indexes.

Solution:

The results from Excel's regression analysis procedure in data analysis are shown in Exhibit D.10, along with the computed trend values for each period and the ratios of actual to trend values. The seasonal indexes are computed as follows:

Quarter	*Quarterly Seasonal Index*
1	$S_1 = (0.909 + 0.966)/2 = 0.938$
2	$S_2 = (1.014 + 1.149)/2 = 1.082$
3	$S_3 = (1.225 + 1.281)/2 = 1.253$
4	$S_4 = (0.715 + 0.737)/2 = 0.726$

Because these raw indexes average 1.0 (to three decimal places), no adjustment is needed.

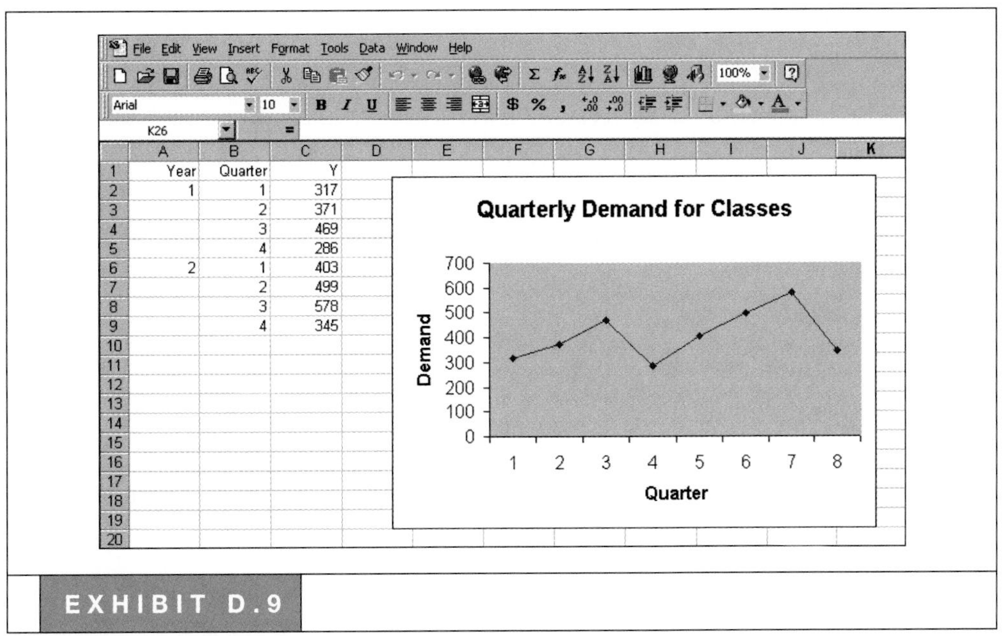

	A	B	C
1	Year	Quarter	Y
2	1	1	317
3		2	371
4		3	469
5		4	286
6	2	1	403
7		2	499
8		3	578
9		4	345

EXHIBIT D.9

Regression Model

	Coefficients	Standard Error	t Stat	P-value
Intercept	331.464	76.026	4.360	0.0048
t	17.119	15.055	1.137	0.2989

Period (t)	Y	Trend	Ratio
1	317	348.583	0.909
2	371	365.702	1.014
3	469	382.821	1.225
4	286	399.940	0.715
5	403	417.060	0.966
6	499	434.179	1.149
7	578	451.298	1.281
8	345	468.417	0.737

EXHIBIT D.10

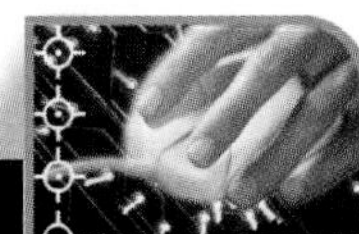

> active exercise

Take a moment to apply what you've learned.

USING SEASONAL INDEXES

Seasonal indexes are used for two purposes:

1. To deseasonalize raw data, in order to compare values from different seasons or to use them in a basic forecasting model
2. To incorporate seasonality into a forecast made by a basic model that does not include seasonal effects

Deseasonalizing Raw Data

Since the multiplicative model incorporates the seasonal effect by multiplying by the seasonal index, seasonality is removed by the reverse process, dividing. That is, you can **deseasonalize** a data value by *dividing* the actual value by the appropriate seasonal index.

Example D.9

Refer to Example D.7. Suppose the sales of lightweight men's pajamas during the four quarters of the next (fourth) year are:

Quarter	*Sales*
1	95
2	116
3	89
4	73

Use simple exponential smoothing with $\alpha = .2$ to find the base level forecast for the first quarter of year 5. Assume the base level forecast for the first quarter of year 4 was 99.1.

Solution:
First use the seasonal indexes found in Example D.7 to deseasonalize the raw data for year 4. Then use these deseasonalized values in an SES model with $\alpha = .2$ to obtain a base-level forecast for quarter 1 of year 5. These operations have been carried out in the spreadsheet in Exhibit D.11, which shows that the base level forecast is 96.75 units. Note that, since the exponential smoothing procedure in Excel assumes that $F_1 = Y_1$, we had to trick it into using a different value for F_1. This was done by inserting a period 0, with $Y_0 = 99.1$, the value we want to use for F_1.

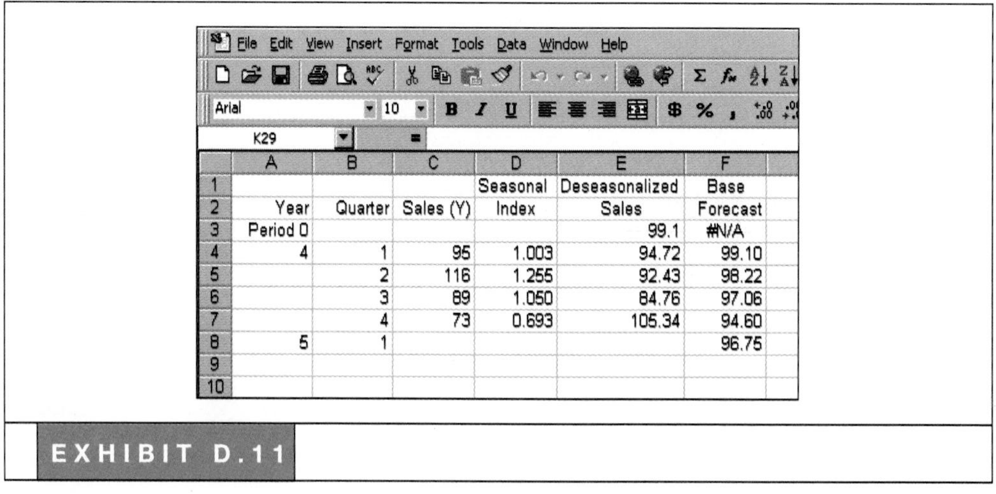

	A	B	C	D	E	F
1				Seasonal	Deseasonalized	Base
2	Year	Quarter	Sales (Y)	Index	Sales	Forecast
3	Period 0				99.1	#N/A
4	4	1	95	1.003	94.72	99.10
5		2	116	1.255	92.43	98.22
6		3	89	1.050	84.76	97.06
7		4	73	0.693	105.34	94.60
8	5	1				96.75
9						
10						

EXHIBIT D.11

Incorporating Seasonality

To use multiplicative seasonal indexes to *incorporate seasonality* into a forecast made with an unseasonalized model, *multiply* the basic value by the appropriate seasonal index.

Example D.10

Refer to Example D.8. Forecast the demand for in-house continuing education classes at Fred's company for the four quarters of next year.

Solution:
Use the trend equation found in Example D.8, $T_t = 331.464 + 17.119t$, to determine the trend value for each of the four quarters. Then multiply the trend values by the seasonal indexes found in Example D.8, to get the forecasts, as follows:

Quarter	t	Trend	x Index =	Forecast
1	9	331.464 + 17.119(9) = 485.535	0.938	455.4
2	10	331.464 + 17.119(10) = 502.654	1.082	543.9
3	11	331.464 + 17.119(11) = 519.773	1.253	651.3
4	12	331.464 + 17.119(12) = 536.892	0.726	389.8

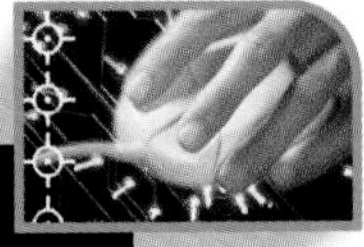

> active exercise

Take a moment to apply what you've learned.

> Supplement Wrap-Up

Two basic ways of categorizing forecasting models are quantitative versus qualitative and time series versus causal. Quantitative models use equations to estimate the value of the variable of interest, while qualitative forecasts are based on the subjective judgment of knowledgeable people. Time series models identify a pattern in the past values of the variable and project it into the future, while causal models estimate the value of the variable of interest on the basis of the values of other variables that are assumed to affect it.

The basic components of a time series are: trend, which is a general pattern of growth or decline; cyclic effects due to the general economic cycle; seasonality, which is a pattern that repeats itself within a time period of no more than a year; and randomness.

Two approaches to short-term forecasting when there is no trend or seasonality are simple moving averages and simple exponential smoothing. A simple moving average uses the average of the last few periods' values as the forecast for the next period. In simple exponential smoothing, the forecast is updated from period to period by adding a percentage of the amount by which the last forecast was in error.

The simplest approach to estimating trend is by using regression. When the trend to be estimated is linear, simple linear regression may be used.

There are a number of ways of estimating multiplicative seasonal indexes. They are all based on averaging, for a set of comparable periods, seasonality ratios found by dividing the actual time series value by a base-level estimate determined by the trend and cyclic components of the model. Multiplicative seasonal indexes are used to incorporate seasonality into a forecast by multiplying the base value by the index, and to deseasonalize data by dividing the actual value by the index.

Three popular measures of forecast accuracy are the mean squared error, found by averaging the squared forecast errors for a number of periods; the mean absolute deviation, found by averaging the absolute values of the forecast errors for a number of periods; and the mean absolute percentage error, found by averaging the absolute values of the forecast error divided by the actual value. A standard deviation to be used as the basis for a forecast interval can be estimated by using either the square root of the mean squared error, called the root mean squared error, or by using 1.25 times the mean absolute deviation.

> end-of-supplement resources

- Practice Quiz
- Key Terms
- Solved Problems
- Discussion Questions
- Problems

Supply-Chain Coordination: Master Scheduling and Inventory Decisions

CHAPTER 12

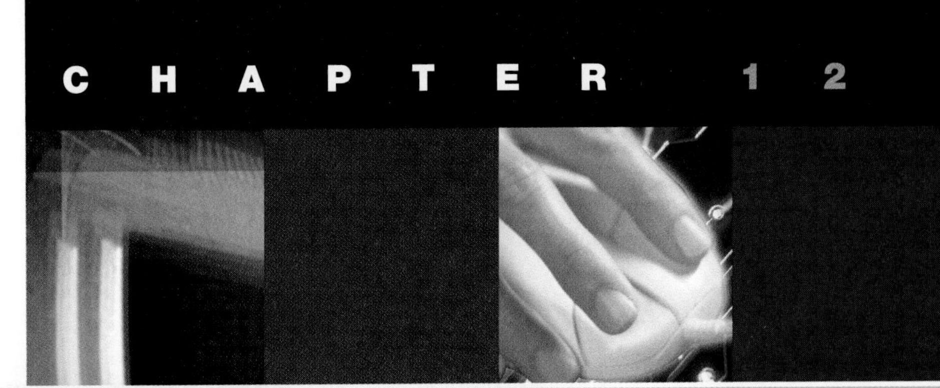

Chapter Outline

What's Ahead

. . . BACK AT THE REC CENTER

It's a Monday morning late in the year. The group has been working out regularly for several months now and their relationship is no longer limited to the early morning workouts at the health club. In fact, Luis and his wife just hosted the group at their house for a dinner the previous Friday. It was the first time the foursome and their significant others had finally met the people they had heard so much about. The evening had gone well. During the workout, talk turned to the wine served with dinner.

"We're neither one a connoisseur," Luis said breathing heavy, "but it's been real easy for both of us to learn. We found this great little shop just a few doors down here in the strip mall. We've been picking the owner's brain for suggestions. Some have been better than others, but everything she's suggested has been really good. Being here by the club, it's easy to stop on the way home from work. We'll pick up a bottle to have with dinner, sometimes a couple extra, you know, if people are coming over, maybe stock up a bit if something we like is on sale. Actually, we bought it a few weeks ago. We tried it and liked it enough to buy a case. That was one less thing we had to worry about in getting the dinner together!"

"Well it worked out great!" said Cheryl. "I just wish I could stock up on nursing hours like you do the Merlot!" she added as she finished her arm curls and exhaled deeply. "I could use a case or two of nursing hours this week!"

"Did you have to mention work?" asked Fred with a pained look.

"I'm sorry," said Cheryl. "I'm thinking shop again!"

Everyone realized, though, that this is one of the benefits of the group. Bouncing problems and ideas off each other, sometimes just letting off steam.

"It's just that coming up with a schedule this week is going to be tough. I'm short people on all three shifts from scheduled vacation and to top it off, I had two more first-shift nurses called in on jury duty! I'm short staffed in the labs as well," she lamented. "Even when you know it's coming, planning to make do with overtime, temps, and juggling people between departments can be tough. Then boom! Jury duty!"

Tom nodded in agreement, but Fred and Luis were a little slow to see the issue. "That's what makes your job so easy," Cheryl said, now turning the table to give Fred a hard time. "You and Luis, you two can see this sort of stuff coming and work ahead. You know, build your inventory. A couple of squirrels, putting away nuts for the winter!" The other three laughed. "You just can't store up your extra nurses and lab techs when things are slow, then pull them out in the winter!"

Tom stopped to listen to Cheryl. "Yeah, we have the same problem with empty seats. It'd sure be nice if we could bank a few to use on those Friday and Sunday flights when we're way overbooked!" he said.

"Hey, wait a minute, we're trying to apply some just-in-time thinking, getting rid of inventory, shorter quality feedback loop, and all that. Don't forget that, you know," replied Luis.

"Yeah, but even in the best cases, you still use inventory to some extent," said Cheryl. "Maybe it's a popular chair you keep so you have it when a customer calls. Maybe it's raw material you bought in bulk to get a great deal, WIP just in case something happens. There are lots of times when you can try to be as JIT as the best of 'em but you still have the option of inventory when it makes sense. Tom and I don't have that option. You can't inventory a service too easily! It's sort of like the wine you served at dinner," Cheryl said, almost as an afterthought.

"Okay, let's see where you're going with this one," Luis said with a grin.

"Well you said a minute ago you sometimes buy a couple of extra bottles when there is an occasion or something, right?" Cheryl asked.

"Yeah, so?" replied Luis.

"Simple, if you were really into JIT at home as you say you are trying to be at work, you'd always buy one bottle at a time just when you need it. You'd never buy a case or any extra for later," Cheryl said.

"I guess you're right. I just never looked at what we buy at home the same way as what we deal with at work," Luis said. "I have to admit we stock up at home on a lot of things because neither of us really likes to shop. Maybe we just dislike shopping more than the hassle of finding a place to put everything! But let's go back to Cheryl's point. I think she's right. My wife and I both enjoy stopping at the wine shop. We like talking wine with the owner and, like I said, it's real convenient for either of us."

"So?" said Fred.

"It's easy," said Tom. "Luis is saying that the hassle of shopping for this particular item is pretty much zero—in fact, it sounds like he actually enjoys it. That means he only buys what he needs that day or for that occasion. There's no need to stock up! You make zillions of one pager because of the hassle of switching your lines between models. You don't like changeovers; Luis likes shopping for different varieties."

"But Luis, you said you sometimes buy a case?" asked Fred.

"Yes, we've done that when we've had a big occasion like last Friday," Luis answered. "We've also bought a case when the owner of the shop wasn't sure how often they could get what we like in again. Actually, that was what happened last time, with that case of Merlot we had some of it last Friday. But the owner also gave us a 10 percent discount on buying by the case, you know, 12 bottles at a time. I'm just not sure if that is worth it."

"Well, if you set aside the fact that you like going to the store and just look at the investment side of buying in quantity, it might be a good idea," answered Cheryl. "That is to say, if you would be drinking wine at dinner regularly, like say a bottle a week. If that's the case—oooh, bad pun— you'd drink it long before it would ever go bad. Then it's just a little money and space that you'd have tied up in the wine until you finish it off."

"Okay, so even if I'm not planning something big where we'll use it all, you're saying buying by the case is a good 'inventory' policy!" laughed Luis. "Does that mean we need to start buying those big 10-pound packs of ground beef as well? You know, the ones where you save 10 cents a pound by buying in bulk?"

"I suppose you could," said Tom, "but as fast as the two of you are likely to go through it, the green you'd be saving after a week or so might be growing in your refrigerator and not your bank account!"

> objectives

Take a moment to familiarize yourself with the key objectives of this chapter.

> gearing up

Before you begin reading this chapter, try a short warm-up activity.

> Introduction

As we saw in Chapter 11, a master schedule indicates the planned delivery time for the product-service bundles a company sells. In Fred's case, the master schedule is the schedule for the assembly of pagers; in Luis's case, it is the schedule for the assembly of the furniture customers have ordered. Cheryl's hospital may have a number of separate master schedules for the delivery of particular services, such as the customer schedule in the outpatient clinic. At Tom's airline, the master schedule would show the flights on which customers can make bookings.

Master scheduling decisions are constrained by capacity decisions that are made in the aggregate planning process described in the last chapter. As a result, master schedulers should not commit to accomplishing work for which they do not have sufficient capacity. Part of master scheduling involves attempts to keep capacity requirements as level as possible from week to week. Heavy use of capacity can lead to problems with worker morale, equipment failure, quality, and customer service. It can also reduce efficiency. Low use of capacity leads to low levels of productivity and can have an influence on worker morale, customer service, and quality.

In manufacturing firms like Fred and Luis's, there is a strong link between master scheduling and inventory, because the way to change the inventory balance is to increase or decrease scheduled production. Because of the link between scheduling and inventory, no chapter on master scheduling would be complete without some discussion of inventory decisions. The last three sections of this chapter address competitive considerations in inventory management, describe several of the most common inventory models, and highlight some recent trends in inventory management. The supplement at the end of the chapter provides a more detailed consideration of quantitative models for inventory management.

> Integrating Operations Management with Other Functions

Figure 12.1 highlights some of the major linkages between the sections of this chapter and other functional areas of business. This part of the chapter is obviously important to all business majors, because it indicates the way that professionals from their various functional areas relate to the issues addressed in this chapter.

The next portion of the chapter describes master scheduling activities. These activities are the focal point for many interactions between operations and the marketing and finance functions. Marketing—and especially sales—personnel are particularly interested in the master schedule to determine when their customers will receive the goods and services they have purchased. The amount of work included on this schedule is an indicator of both the future costs and revenue. Thus, finance personnel rely heavily on the master schedule to estimate future earnings for the benefit of outside investors and to support internal financial management decision makers.

It is possible to estimate capacity requirements in greater detail based on a master schedule than is possible with an aggregate plan. In fact, capacity implications need to be considered before a master

Chapter Topics \ Functional Areas of Business	Finance	Accounting	Human Resources	Marketing	Engineering	Management Information Systems
Integrating Operations Management with Other Functions	●	●	●	●	●	●
Master Scheduling: Supply-Chain Coordinating Decisions	●			●		
Rough-Cut Capacity Planning			●			
Independent Demand Inventory: Competitive Decisions	●	●		●		
Independent Demand Inventory-Models	●	●		●		
E-Commerce-Based Improvements to Master Scheduling and Inventory Management		●				●

FIGURE 12.1 Integrating Operations Management with Other Functions

schedule is finalized. Ideally, the capacity used from week to week should be relatively stable over the short-term—thus limiting the strain on workers that comes with particularly busy weeks and reducing the productivity losses that can come in slow weeks. Because of the work scheduling implications that arise from capacity issues in the master scheduling process, Figure 12.1 highlights a linkage between the human resources function and the "Rough Cut Capacity Planning" section of this chapter.

Inventory decisions directly influence company competitiveness. First of all, inventory is reflected on a company's balance sheet as an asset. Its value has to be established and monitored by the accounting function. As an asset, the inventory represents one of many possible investments for a company's capital. Thus, from a financial analysts perspective, changes in the levels of inventory must be reflected on the balance sheet of the firm and need to have a rational explanation. For example, growth in inventory could result from reduction in sales and indicate problems in the company's competitiveness—yet the inventory would be reported as an asset on the balance sheet. Alternatively, growth in inventory could result from increasing sales and the need for materials to satisfy the increased demand. The level of inventory that is maintained can influence a company's responsiveness, flexibility, performance in regard to customer satisfaction, and numerous other competitive variables. Inventory decisions need to reflect the competitive priorities with which the company goes to market. For all of these reasons, Figure 12.1 links the "Independent Demand Inventory: Competitive Considerations" section of this chapter to the finance, accounting, and marketing functions.

Figure 12.1 also links the "Independent Demand Inventory Models" section of this chapter to the finance, accounting, and marketing functions. From a financial perspective, an understanding of these inventory models can certainly help managers estimate the returns generated through investments in inventory, as well as the cash flow implications of their scheduling decisions. From an accounting perspective, knowledge of these models can be used to assist in cost accounting. Finally, from a marketing perspective, knowledge of the independent demand inventory models is useful because of the competitive implications surrounding their use (described in the previous paragraph). For example, one possibility that the models allow for is inventory shortages, called *stockouts*. A stockout has significant implications for customer satisfaction and customer loyalty that would be very important from a marketing perspective.

The final section of the chapter shown in Figure 12.1 is titled "E-Commerce-Based Improvements to Master Scheduling and Inventory Management." The figure highlights the direct linkages between this section and the accounting and management information systems (MIS) functions. From an accounting perspective, we describe recent changes in cost accounting practices that have had an impact on inventory management practices. As for MIS, we describe the way that computer systems have become a key facilitator to inventory and scheduling decisions by providing real time information regarding inventory levels and usage throughout the supply chain to decision makers at each stage of value creation.

> video exercise

Take a moment to apply what you've learned.

> Master Scheduling: Supply-Chain Coordination Decisions

The master schedule is an important document for virtually every function in a company. In make-to-order (MTO) companies, salespeople need access to the master schedule in order to tell customers when their purchases will be available. In make-to-stock (MTS) companies, marketing people will want to ensure that the timing and quantities of planned output effectively meets forecast demand. Finance people will be concerned with the master schedule in order to project earnings for investors and make appropriate preparations for the cash flows associated with the plans. When agreeing to a particular master schedule, the purchasing and operations functions are essentially saying they can get the job done. In other words, the master schedule is the game plan and a critical linking point for all functions.

The master schedule is also an important linking point between a company and its customers and suppliers. The demand on the master schedule is there because it will be needed eventually to satisfy some customer's requirements (and perhaps the requirements of a customer's customer). Similarly, many of the parts, components, and services that are needed to satisfy the demand on the master schedule will come from suppliers and suppliers of suppliers. The scheduling decisions of one company can have huge consequences on customer satisfaction throughout an entire chain of value-adding customers and suppliers. Ultimately, the long-term competitiveness of each company depends on the effectiveness of the entire supply chain as much as on its internal operations. For this reason, many companies practice supply-chain management, or the coordination of decisions across a series of suppliers and customers in order to more effectively satisfy the needs of end-users of the product-service bundle. Since master scheduling is one of the strongest points of linkage between companies, as well as between the various functions of a single company, it is a critical activity in virtually every organization.

Figure 11.3 compares various planning and control systems. Notice that master scheduling decisions have a shorter planning horizon than aggregate planning. The aggregate plan is typically revised monthly based on a 6- to 18-month planning horizon. Master schedules are typically revised at least once a week, and though they may look forward six months or more, the emphasis is on agreement about satisfaction of near-term customer requirements. Typically, a **freeze window** will be established on the master schedule. This is a fixed period of time at the beginning of the schedule for which the master schedule is final and not subject to revision.

Master scheduling decisions require a higher level of detail than the aggregate planning decisions discussed in Chapter 11. In fact, as Figure 12.2 suggests, master scheduling requires *disaggregation* of the aggregate plan. Aggregate plans set the stage for the execution of a master schedule by making funds available for overtime, subcontracting, changes in workforce size, and the accumulation of inventory to meet periodic surges in demand. Thus, the level of demand accommodated in the master schedule needs to match the level of demand anticipated in the aggregate plan. For example, Luis's aggregate plan might have called for 100 hours of overtime in a particular month; the master schedule would then specify the product-service bundles to be made with that capacity. The aggregate plan is disaggregated further during planning for the timely availability of parts for the product-service bundle (see Chapters 13, 14, 15, and 16). In the end, if aggregate planning has been done well, a company is likely to be able to meet the demand for its products and services effectively.

Figure 12.3 provides a view of the relationships between material decisions, demand forecasts, and capacity decisions. Demand forecasts provide guidance at each stage of the planning process.

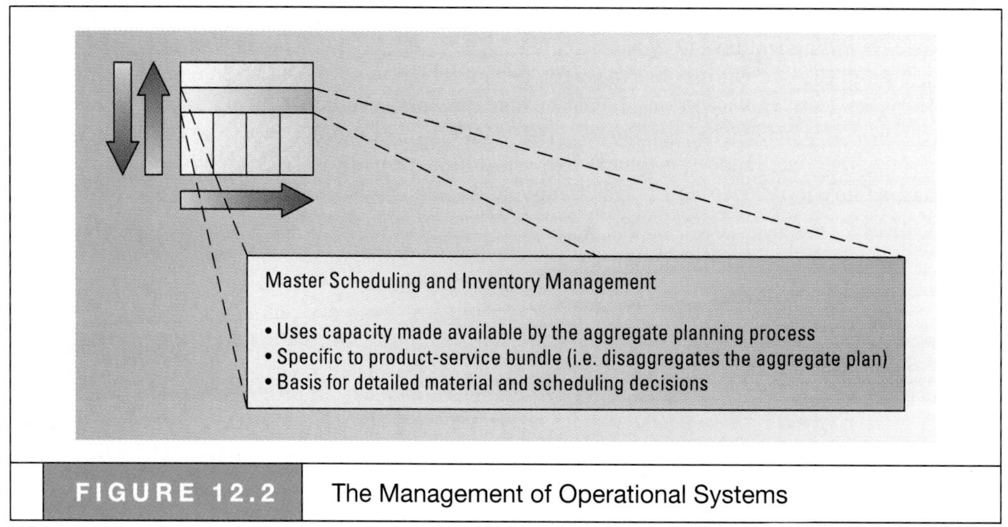

FIGURE 12.2 The Management of Operational Systems

Material Decisions | Demand Forecasts | Capacity Decisions

Product Design and Supplier Relations

Long Range (new markets, market growth, and market share)

Process Design and Supplier Relations

Intermediate (product-service bundle groups)

Aggregate Resource Planning

Short Term (detailed by product-service bundle)

Master Scheduling

Rough-Cut Capacity Planning

Detailed Material/Resource Planning

Detailed Capacity Planning (CRP)

Purchase Orders

Detailed Scheduling (dispatching)

Operational Expectations (loading)

Outsourced Capacity (subcontracting)

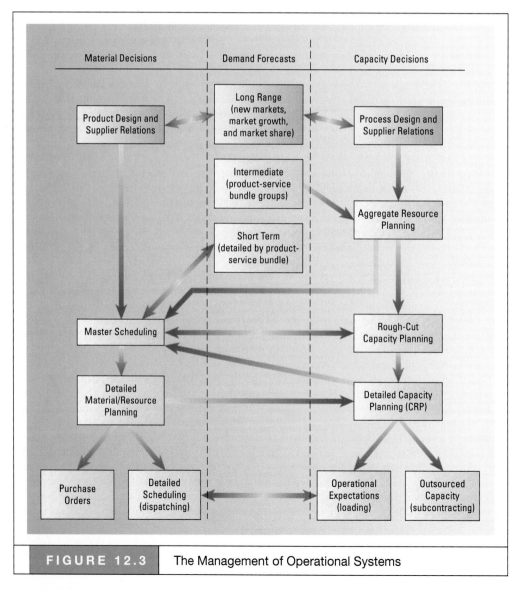

FIGURE 12.3 The Management of Operational Systems

Long-range forecasts, whether qualitative or quantitative, play a significant role in the design of product-service bundles (a material decision) and the other structural decisions of the firm (such as process design). Infrastructural decisions are made within the context established by these structural decisions and rely on intermediate and short-range forecasts. Aggregate planning, for instance, relies on intermediate-range forecasts of demand for groups of products. Likewise, master scheduling, a material decision, relies on detailed product-service bundle demand forecasts. Across the board, material planning decisions and capacity planning decisions have to be synchronized with each other and with demand projections. You cannot schedule operations without available capacity at the required resources. Therefore, master scheduling relies on capacity planning decisions, ranging from aggregate resource planning to detailed capacity plans.

Not all companies are able to make scheduling decisions, project the most detailed capacity implications of these decisions, and then make adjustments to schedules based on capacity utilization issues. Thus, not all of the linkages depicted in Figure 12.3 will be present in all operational planning systems. Regardless of the operational setting and the sophistication of the decision-making system, the goal in master scheduling is to create a material plan that is feasible in light of capacity considerations. You cannot make detailed capacity allocations until material requirements are known. Later chapters in this section of the text will demonstrate the way that material decisions result in actual capacity allocations through **loading decisions** that assign work to resources and **dispatching decisions** that determine the sequence in which that work will be completed.

BUILDING THE MASTER SCHEDULE

Figures 12.4, 12.5, 12.6, and 12.7 present sample master schedules for a variety of environments. At the recreational complex, described in Figure 12.4, the master schedule simply indicates the number of hours that each of the venues is to be open. It could also indicate the specific events that have been scheduled for the various venues in the facility. For the cosmetic surgery department at Cheryl's hospital (Figure 12.5), the schedule indicates the number of times each type of procedure is to be conducted in a given week. Figure 12.6 indicates the planned production of each of the pagers that is produced in Fred's factory, and Figure 12.7 shows the planned production of furniture in Luis's factory.

In these master scheduling examples, the time increment is weekly and the information refers to specific product-service bundles. Thus, the focus has narrowed from the aggregate plan, which dealt with entire product lines and monthly capacity requirements. Nevertheless, there must be a fit

	Week of						
	10/1	10/8	10/15	10/22	10/29	11/5	
Basketball Court	70	70	70	60	70	70	•••••
50-Meter Pool	56	56	56	48	56	56	•••••
Diving Well	32	32	32	16	32	32	•••••
Racquetball Courts	112	112	112	98	112	112	•••••
Snack Bar	70	70	70	60	70	70	•••••
Front Desk	112	112	112	98	112	112	•••••
Pro Shop	56	56	56	48	56	56	•••••
	⋮	⋮	⋮	⋮	⋮	⋮	
Total Staff Hours	508	508	508	428	508	508	•••••

FIGURE 12.4 Master Schedule of Staff Hours for the Student Recreation Center

	Week of 12/1	12/8	12/15	12/22	12/29	1/5	
Liposuction	10	12	12	18	20	12	•••••
Nose Reconstruction	15	15	15	15	15	15	•••••
Face-Lifts	10	10	10	15	30	12	•••••
"Tummy" Tucks	5	5	5	8	8	5	•••••
Skin Grafts	12	12	12	12	12	12	•••••
	⋮	⋮	⋮	⋮	⋮	⋮	
Total Nursing Hours	52	54	54	68	85	56	•••••

FIGURE 12.5 Master Schedule of Nursing Hours for the Surgical Department at Cheryl's Hospital

between the aggregate plan and the master schedule: The total monthly demand for the items shown on a master schedule should be close to the demand anticipated in the corresponding aggregate plan. In master scheduling, however, the actual demand might not be distributed evenly from week to week. (Having 160 hours of capacity a month doesn't necessarily mean you can schedule 80 hours for two weeks and take two weeks off.) As a result, there is a need to assess the feasibility of the master schedule more directly.

The weekly requirements included on the master schedule will come from a detailed forecast. For make-to-order companies, this forecast will be based largely on customer orders expected over the near term. Looking further into the future, however, orders will be less specific and the master schedule will be based more on forecasted demand for the product-service bundle. Figures 12.5 and 12.7 fit the MTO category, as do parts of Figure 12.4. For instance, customized training programs, group

	Week of 1/6	1/13	1/20	1/27	2/3	2/10	
Model 37b (Basic Numeric)	2,000	2,000	4,000	4,000	6,000	6,000	•••••
Model 37c (Deluxe Numeric)	3,000	3,000	3,000	3,000	1,000	1,000	•••••
Model 47b (Basic Alpha-Numeric)	2,000	2,000	3,000	3,000	2,000	3,000	•••••
Model 47c (Deluxe Alpha-Numeric)	1,000	1,000	1,000	1,000	1,000	2,000	•••••
	⋮	⋮	⋮	⋮	⋮	⋮	
Total Line Minutes*	6,000	6,000	7,500	7,500	6,000	7,500	•••••

*Line cycle is approximately 1 minute for deluxe model and 30 seconds for basic models.

FIGURE 12.6 Master Schedule for the Pager Line in Fred's Factory

	Week of						
	10/1	10/8	10/15	10/22	10/29	11/5	
Tbl-h36r-oak	150	150	150	150	150	150	•••••
Tbl-h48r-oak	0	0	0	300	200	200	•••••
Tbl-h48x66-ov-oak	0	0	0	200	200	200	•••••
Tbl-k36r-chy	400	450	400	200	150	100	•••••
Tbl-k48r-chy	500	500	500	100	100	100	•••••
Tbl-k48x66-ov-chy	100	100	100	300	300	300	•••••
Tbl-k48x72-ov-chy	200	200	200	200	200	200	•••••
	⋮	⋮	⋮	⋮	⋮	⋮	
Total Tables	1,350	1,400	1,350	1,450	1,300	1,350	•••••

FIGURE 12.7 Master Schedule for Tables in Luis's Furniture Factory

activities such as the ropes course at the Outdoor Pursuit Center, and group reservations of facilities would all be made to order. In an MTO setting, the freeze window should include the entire production lead-time. That way, there will be no chance of canceling or changing an order once processing has begun.

In make-to-stock organizations, the demand shown on the master schedule is based on forecasted rates of demand for the various product-service bundles. Figure 12.6 and Figure 12.4 both illustrate an MTS environment. The recreation facility is staffed and remains open based on projected usage; thus the open schedule for walk-in customers is the MTS part of the center's master schedule. Whether the center is empty or full—that is, whether the facilities are used or not—it is available to patrons during regular hours. So, too, the pagers Fred's factory makes may or may not be sold, but they are available for shipment to customers. In MTS environments the freeze window on the master schedule should be at least as long as the time suppliers need to respond to purchase orders.

> active exercise

Take a moment to apply what you've learned.

FITTING THE MASTER SCHEDULE TO COMPETITIVE PRIORITIES

Master scheduling is clearly linked to a company's competitiveness. More specifically, decisions made in master scheduling should fit the firm's competitive priorities and promote customer satisfaction in a way that is consistent with the company's other operational decisions. In building a master schedule that will satisfy customers, it is critical to consider the number and frequency of orders or product-service bundles that can be accommodated; the level of uncertainty in demand forecasts; and the impact of scheduling decisions on the firm's competitive priorities. In some cases, firms might need to reconsider their inventory approach. MTO systems are appropriate in settings where flexibility is important and general purpose equipment is available. Such systems can handle frequent orders and are better able to deal with demand uncertainty. Thus, the size of the production run and service delivery options can be based on customer requirements. On the other hand, the MTO approach can have negative consequences on cost, quality of conformance, and delivery reliability, because of lower capacity utilization, schedule changes, and the coordination costs associated with high variety.

If the demand forecast is reasonably certain, an MTS approach is a good fit for companies that emphasize low cost and high quality of conformance and provide mass-produced, standardized product-service bundles. In these companies, the finished goods inventory provides a *buffer* or *decoupling point* between the producer and the customer. Therefore, the system can operate independently of individual customers' demand patterns. This independence from the customer allows the company to choose efficient scheduling alternatives, to order inputs and produce outputs with less frequency, and to level the firm's output rates over time. It also allows the use of dedicated, specialized equipment that is capable of meeting high quality specifications.

> Rough-Cut Capacity Planning

The right-hand side of Figure 12.3 shows three different types of capacity decisions that may be a factor in master scheduling, in order of increasing detail: aggregate planning, rough-cut capacity planning, and detailed capacity planning. The aggregate plan provides for adequate monthly capacity to meet demand, but that doesn't mean that a master schedule based on the same level of monthly output is feasible. (In the same way, 16 credit-hours might seem feasible to you until all your professors schedule major assignments to be completed on the same day.) As a consequence, the feasibility of master schedules must be verified, a process that is called **rough-cut capacity planning.**

Rough-cut capacity planning typically relies on overall estimates of capacity requirements. For instance, a large accounting firm might estimate the data entry, legal, auditing, and tax accounting hours required for a standard audit of a firm with revenues between $500 million and $1 billion. Then, in developing a master schedule, managers would determine the projected weekly totals of data entry, legal, auditing, and tax accounting hours needed. If the results indicate that the schedule is feasible, does their rough estimate mean that all the firm's audits will be completed on schedule and under cost? Of course not; clearly, each audit is unique, and rough-cut capacity planning gives only a general sense of the schedule's feasibility.

Ultimately, a master schedule that looks feasible based on rough-cut capacity planning might not be feasible because of the processing requirements associated with various components and subassemblies. For example, making the body parts for one type of Indy car might take just one week, while manufacturing the body parts for another type might take two weeks. Therefore, leveling the schedule for assembly of the cars, so that 10 cars are assembled each week, might throw off the schedule for parts fabrication. Once a detailed materials plan has been done and a procurement plan for the components and subassemblies completed, however, a detailed capacity check can be constructed. At this point, businesses with highly sophisticated planning and control systems can engage in **closed loop planning,** a process in which information from detailed capacity planning is used to level (and ensure the feasibility of) the master schedule.

A simple example from your own experience will illustrate these three levels of capacity planning. As a freshman you no doubt looked over your program to get an idea of how many hours you could and would take per semester. At that point you weren't thinking much about the specific courses you would take in particular semesters; you were just trying to get an idea of how you would spread your program over a certain number of semesters. This first look at your schedule was analogous to aggregate planning.

At some point you registered for the current semester and decided exactly what courses you needed to take. This second step was analogous to master scheduling. As you scheduled your courses, however, you probably looked at a weekly calendar and tried to divide your coursework between Tuesday/Thursday (TR) and Monday/Wednesday/Friday (MWF) time slots. If your TR schedule looked too crowded with required courses, you probably tried to find electives given on MWF. Even though you probably hadn't seen the syllabus for any of these classes, you were nevertheless making decisions about the feasibility of your schedule. Based on those decisions, you made adjustments to even out your schedule and finally settled on a plan that seemed satisfactory. This course-scheduling activity is analogous to rough-cut capacity planning.

At the beginning of the semester you received a syllabus for each of your classes. At that point you began to look at the specific assignments required in each class, and you dedicated specific blocks of time throughout the semester to those activities. This last step is analogous to detailed capacity planning. Looking at your daily planner for the coming week, you can probably identify specific blocks of time that you set aside to complete specific assignments. But though you tried to level your schedule for the semester, you may have some weeks in which the workload on specific days is well beyond feasible. In those cases, you might ask for extensions on particular projects or you might request your assignments ahead of time, so you can get an early start on your work. In a worst-case scenario, you might actually have to drop a course or take an "incomplete." The fact is, very few students can figure out all the implications of a schedule early enough in the semester to both drop and add courses. Those who can are able to close the loop between their detailed capacity planning and their course scheduling. In other words, they can consider detailed information about their courses (the timing and requirements of assignments, the timing of tests, and so forth) in setting up their semester schedules.

In MTO companies, the master schedule is built by incrementally adding orders to an existing schedule. Planners cannot just add new orders indiscriminately; rather, they must first check to see if there is adequate capacity for the order. Usually this check is based on an overall estimate of the time required to process the order in each work center. Much as when you registered for this semester's classes, not all the details are considered at this point. When customers are particularly time sensitive, the master scheduler will usually attempt to add the order as early as possible, in the hope that it can be completed within a satisfactory period. This practice is referred to as **forward scheduling.**

In MTS companies, planners typically use **backward scheduling** to develop the master schedule. They determine from the forecast when a stock of outputs will be needed, then place orders on the master schedule so as to ensure the availability of outputs by that time. When all of the anticipated demand has been scheduled, the rough-cut capacity planning can be done. Just as in an MTO company, this rough-cut check is based on an overall estimate of the time required to process the orders in each work center. If the initial schedule is not feasible, adjustments can be made by splitting orders so as to defer the production of some items; or the schedule can be leveled in other ways.

> video exercise

Take a moment to apply what you've learned.

> active concept check

Now let's take a moment to test your knowledge of the concepts you have studied in this section.

Independent Demand Inventory: Competitive Considerations

The inventory that is addressed by the master schedule is referred to as **independent demand inventory,** because it is material that the firm produces for sale. Typically, some or all of this type of demand must be forecast. **Dependent demand inventory,** by contrast, is the material that goes into the things the firm sells. This demand can be calculated once the master schedule has been agreed on.

NEGATIVE ASPECTS OF INVENTORY

Earlier chapters have emphasized many of the negative consequences of an over-reliance on independent demand inventory. Those adverse consequences include the following problems:

- Overdepending on inventory can prohibit meaningful feedback on the quality of the product-service bundle. With large inventories, there is usually a long delay between the creation of an item and its use. Thus, when problems are discovered, it is usually too late to investigate and remedy the causes.
- Large inventories hide operational problems that might be solved if they were discovered. When a worker finds a nonconforming item and inventory provides an immediate replacement, the worker has very little incentive to communicate the fact that a defective item was created. Indeed, the cost to the worker of reporting the defective item might exceed the cost of replacing it with conforming inventory.
- There is a financial cost to carrying excess inventory. It includes the lost opportunity to invest the money tied up in the inventory, as well as the rental cost for the space used to house the inventory (including utilities, security, and insurance on the structure and the inventory itself).
- There is some risk of damage to goods held in inventory. The larger the inventory, the more likely items are to be handled before shipment. Often, warehouse workers have to move and replace large quantities of inventory just to find a specific item. Each time an item is handled, there is some chance that it will be damaged.

- There is a cost to tracking and accounting for inventory. Inventory records are often quite inaccurate; thus, accountants and auditors frequently must spend days locating and counting specific items. Much productivity is lost because of time wasted searching for inventory that has been moved without updating warehouse records. Though the bar-coding systems that have become commonplace in almost every business do help in keeping track of inventory, the technology is not without cost. Systems currently under development will allow an entire warehouse to be scanned at one time, alleviating the necessity of having to run each item across a bar-code reader. But while these new systems should significantly improve the capability of firms to track their inventory, they will be even more costly than bar code-based tracking systems.
- Large inventories are associated with a risk of product obsolescence and losses due to depreciation.
- Large inventories can have a significant impact on the flexibility of the value-adding system. When a firm has invested in particular technologies and inventories, it must use them until the inventories are depleted. Technological advances and product innovations cannot be adopted while preexisting inventories appear on the balance sheet.

audio exercise

Take a moment to apply what you've learned.

POSITIVE ASPECTS OF INVENTORY

Clearly, carrying more inventory than is needed is not advisable. On the other hand, inventory is listed on the balance sheet as an asset, and it does have a positive impact on operations when used in moderation. Sometimes managers find it hard to draw the line between inventory that adds value (or facilitates the adding of value) and inventory that is needed only to cover some solvable problem in the value-adding system. Following are some of the potential benefits of inventory that managers might consider:

- Inventory allows managers to decouple operations. That is, placing inventory between two work centers, or between a customer and a supplier, allows them to operate independently. Thus, the two separate value-adding processes can each operate in the most efficient manner, based on local considerations. Decoupling operations also allows producers to set aside material for later use by customers, and customers to receive immediate delivery of in-stock items. In this sense, inventory is particularly useful in complex systems. On the other hand, using inventory to decouple operations might discourage managers from creating mechanisms to reduce the need for inventory or from otherwise solving operational problems.
- Inventory protects one part of an operating system from disruptions in other parts of the system. When a worker at one work center calls in sick or a machine requires maintenance, others can continue to work if inventory is available. (At the same time, the presence of inventory might encourage managers to accept preventable disruptions rather than eliminate them.)
- Inventory can be used to reduce the number of times orders are placed or the number of setups required to meet demand. Thus, time and money spent in preparation to meet demand can be reduced. (On the other hand, the willingness to carry inventory might keep managers from looking for ways to handle setups and logistics more efficiently.)
- Inventory can provide a hedge against inflation. (On the other hand, inventory held for this reason will prevent managers from looking for superior substitutes.)
- Some inventory, such as pipeline inventory, is an integral part of the system. The Alaskan oil pipeline, for instance, is 800 miles long and 4 feet in diameter. That's a "bazillion" barrels of oil inventory that are just part of the system! (If you remember your high school geometry, you could determine that the pipeline can actually hold about 9.778 million barrels. Assuming the pipeline is full and the spot price for crude oil is $25 per barrel, that oil is worth over $244 million. If the money could have been invested elsewhere with a 10% rate of return, the opportunity cost of holding that oil is about $24 million a year.) The same output rate could be achieved with a pipe diameter half the size, at a flow rate twice as fast. The system cost of the additional oil inventory contained in the 4-foot pipe must be lower than the operational costs associated with higher flow rates in a smaller pipe.

- Inventory allows firms to take advantage of quantity discounts from suppliers. (If used for this purpose, however, the availability of inventory might reduce the supplier's incentive to provide small shipments more efficiently.)
- Inventory allows firms to meet unexpected demand. (On the other hand, this safety net allows firms to be less proactive in their attempts to understand customers' needs and to use supply-chain management to coordinate their relations with downstream customers.)

FINDING THE RIGHT INVENTORY LEVEL

Just as carrying excess inventory is not wise, holding inadequate inventory is also inadvisable. Operations are much easier to run when some inventory is available. Financial managers and controllers commonly question the use of inventory, because they are concerned about tying up funds in this way and unsure of the benefits. But operations managers know that inventory, if strategically used, can simplify operations, and they see it as an asset. Salespeople, too, like to be able to satisfy customers immediately.

Thus, companies often debate the question, How much inventory is enough? The answer clearly depends on the level of uncertainty surrounding demand, the potential for system disruptions, and the characteristics of the operating system. The greater the degree of uncertainty surrounding demand and the greater the potential for system disruptions, the more inventory is required to effectively satisfy customer requirements. In the long term, companies should work with customers to reduce this uncertainty.

Fortunately, at least as far as the short term is concerned, the uncertainty surrounding demand can be estimated. One way to do so is to use the error statistics from demand forecasts, such as the mean absolute deviation (MAD), mean forecast error (MFE), or mean squared error (MSE). A similar approach is to simply compute the standard deviation of periodic demand. The potential for system disruptions can also be estimated using measures such as the variability of the time required to complete orders or the variability of the time required for suppliers to fill orders.

In MTS environments, firms will hold inventories of raw materials, work-in-process, or finished goods. In MTO environments, firms are likely to stock only commonly used raw materials. The more flexible operating systems typically require less inventory. Figure 12.8 illustrates the relationship between uncertainty of demand, operational flexibility, and buffers such as inventory. Where the operating system is not very flexible and demand is uncertain, or the potential for system disruption is significant, companies tend to use buffers of inventory, capacity, or lead-time. For example, Wendy's

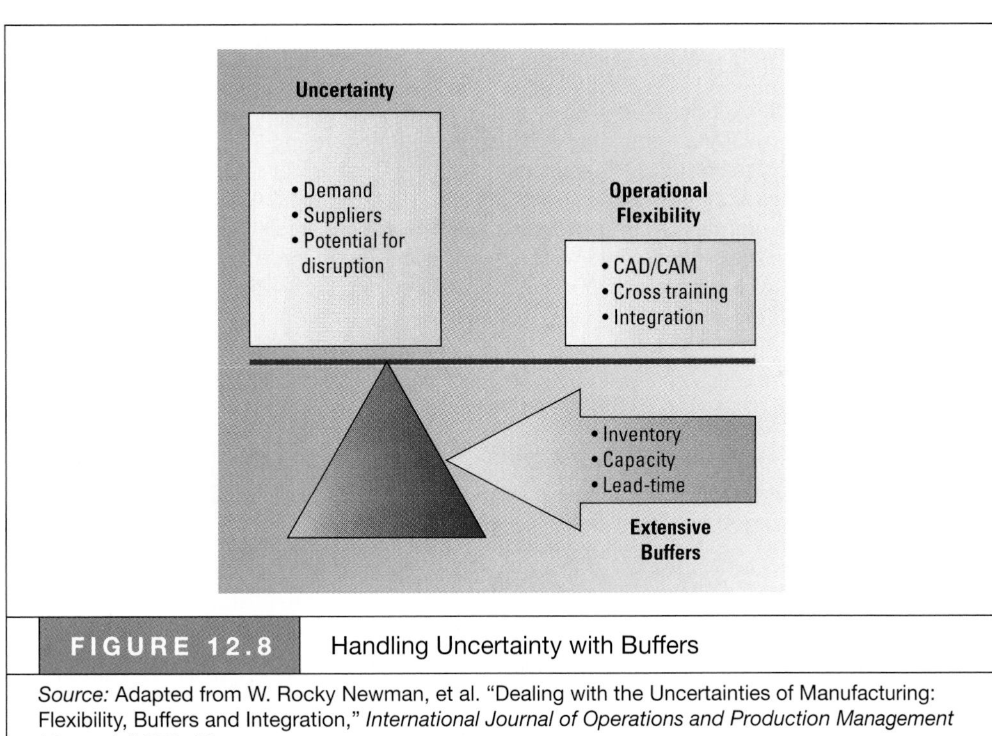

FIGURE 12.8 Handling Uncertainty with Buffers

Source: Adapted from W. Rocky Newman, et al. "Dealing with the Uncertainties of Manufacturing: Flexibility, Buffers and Integration," *International Journal of Operations and Production Management* 13, no. 1 (1993): 25.

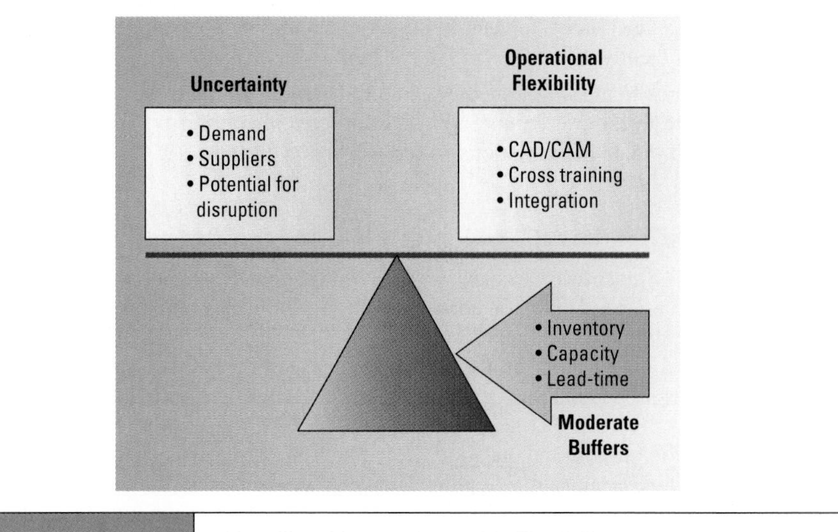

FIGURE 12.9 Handling Uncertainty with Flexibility

Source: Adapted from W. Rocky Newman, et al., "Dealing with the Uncertainties of Manufacturing: Flexibility, Buffers and Integration," *International Journal of Operations and Production Management* 13, no. 1 (1993): 25.

might ask customers to place their orders while waiting in line. This practice moves the waiting line along more quickly, by eliminating some of the uncertainty about what customers want and thus reducing the time they spend at the cash register. Rather than increasing lead-time, Wendy's could choose to improve the flow in the system by carrying excess capacity—for example, by opening another cash register. Or Wendy's could use inventory to take up the slack, by preparing burgers of every variety in advance. (McDonalds, which doesn't encourage customers to customize their orders as Wendy's does, uses the last strategy.)

Buffering the operating system with inventory allows a firm to satisfy customer requirements without investing in system flexibility; thus, a company can avoid the cost of product redesign, automation, or cross training of workers. However, carrying inventory to compensate for uncertainty or inflexibility can actually lead to greater uncertainty and a greater need for capacity, lead-time, or inventory buffers.

When operational flexibility is sufficient to accommodate the levels of uncertainty a firm faces, there is less need for standby inventory, capacity, and lead-time (see Figure 12.9). As was noted in Chapter 7, there is a cost to creating and maintaining a highly flexible value-adding system. In industries where rapid change and time-based competition are a part of life, however, that cost might be a necessity for long-term profitability. In such situations, managers might rely temporarily on buffers of inventory, capacity, and lead-time while working on system improvements. The long-term focus should be on reducing uncertainty and buffers and increasing flexibility, as dictated by the firm's competitive priorities.

video exercise

Take a moment to apply what you've learned.

Inventory at Miami's Rec Center

While inventory is not often thought of as central to the value-adding system in services, the reality is that many times inventory is used in critical ways to facilitate the service. The Student Rec Center (SRC) is no exception: Maintaining a proper level of consumable or nondurable goods throughout the center is critical to patron satisfaction.

Several support areas within the SRC function like other retail organizations and inventory is a central issue. The food court makes decisions regarding inventory of a number of items on a regular basis, as does the pro shop. While not directly linked to use of any specific venue at the SRC, availability of inventory in these areas plays a significant role in the center's product-service bundle. Other consumables that may play a more direct role in SRC activities include many items in the Outdoor Pursuit Center and even a stock of clean towels for the locker rooms.

In other situations, maintaining or replacing inventories of nondurable equipment is critical to SRC use. A stock of various types of balls, racquets, pool cues, Ping-Pong balls and paddles, climbing harnesses, kick boards or other flotation aids, and even jump ropes needs to be monitored and maintained. These items aren't purchased or consumed by patrons, and they're not considered a capital investment. They may, however, wear out or get lost or stolen, or the relative demand for them may change over time. An adequate availability is necessary for effective use of the facility.

Finally, maintenance, repair, and operation inventories (MRO) are required for a steady and efficient operation of the center. While not directly related to the actual product-service bundle, a stock of office supplies, paper towels, soap, pool chemicals, and spare parts for the exercise machines are all necessary for the center's operation.

The SRC is no different than any large service facility in that not much inventory may change hands in the form of the product-service bundle, but it is essential to the value-adding system. Hospitals, airlines, hotels, universities, and even hair salons will maintain inventories in ways similar to the SRC. Most, if not all, of the issues and concerns discussed in this chapter relate to their operations as well as a manufacturer's.

> active concept check

Now let's take a moment to test your knowledge of the concepts you have studied in this section.

Independent Demand Inventory Models

Inventory modeling is a well-established part of operations management. In fact, if you looked in your school's catalog, you would be likely to find a number of courses dealing with inventory modeling. The next few pages will introduce some of the most commonly known and used inventory models, including ABC analysis, several variations of the fixed order quantity model, and fixed order interval models. Regardless of the particular business function you have chosen for a major, you will probably find a general knowledge of these models useful. Further detail on these models is presented in the supplement at the end of this chapter.

ABC INVENTORY ANALYSIS

ABC inventory analysis is a form of *Pareto analysis,* which is based on the rule that 20% of the items in inventory will account for 80% of the value of inventory. You can probably think of lots of examples of the 80/20 rule, right down to the clothes you wear. Have you ever noticed that you wear 20% of your clothes 80% of the time, and the other 80% of your wardrobe only 20% of the time? In this text, Pareto analysis was first mentioned in the context of quality management (see Chapter 6). In that context, it was used to distinguish between the vital few sources of potential improvement and the useful many. In the context of inventory management, Pareto (ABC) analysis is used to distinguish between highly important inventory items and those that are less important. "A" inventory items require tight control policies and close managerial scrutiny, including frequent policy review and **cycle counting,** a periodic audit of inventory quantities to ensure accuracy. Typically *A* items are so designated either because they are critical items or because they represent an unusually high dollar value (see Figure 12.10). *B* inventory items, which are of moderate importance, receive less frequent managerial attention than *A* items. The *C* classification is reserved for items that are inexpensive, infrequently used, or do not otherwise significantly impact customer satisfaction.

Figure 12.11 presents a simple example of ABC analysis at Lainey's Lectronics, a small electronic products retailer. Table (a) lists 20 inventory items; Table (b) ranks those items by annual dollar volume. The far righthand column of Table (b) divides the inventory items into four A items, six B items, and 10 C items. At Lainey's store, the A items are displayed, but the customer must get them from a

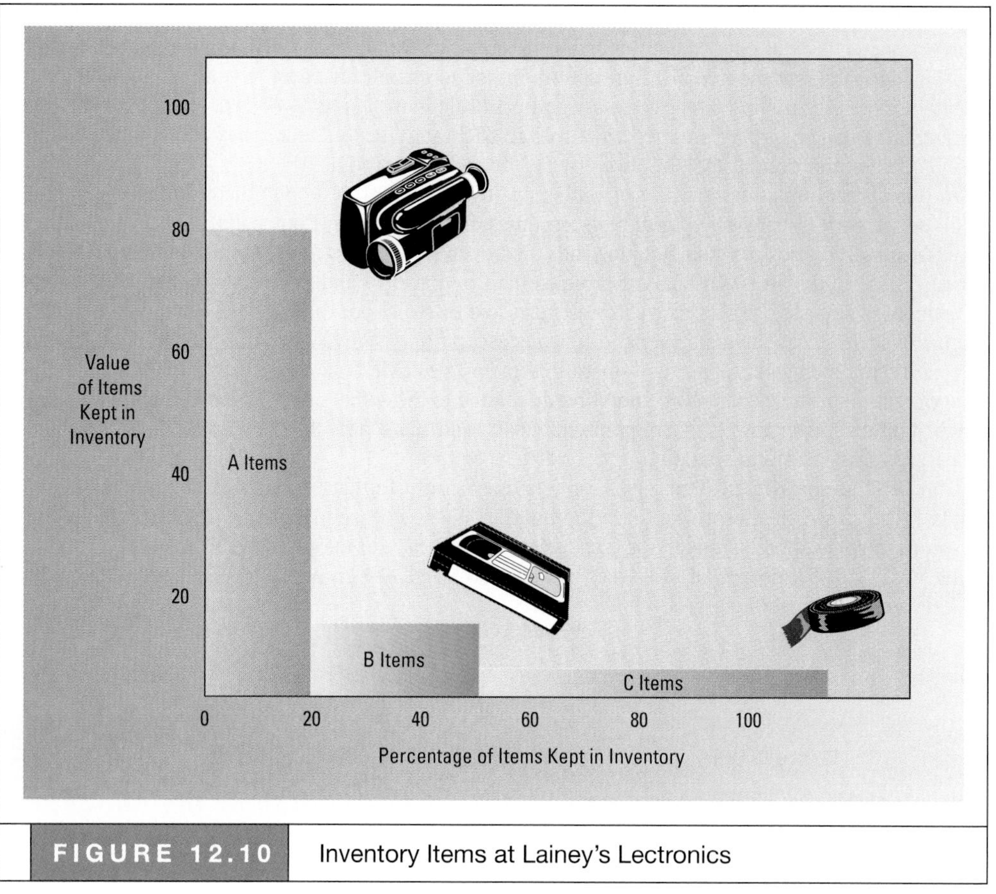

FIGURE 12.10 Inventory Items at Lainey's Lectronics

secured stockpoint. These items are restocked immediately, unless the manufacturer is planning to introduce new models in the near future. The B items are displayed in cases and on shelves within clear view of the cash register; their inventory is replenished each week. The C items are dispersed throughout the store on shelves; replenishment orders are placed monthly.

The ABC classification Lainey's uses is not an irreversible decision. Rather, since demand patterns change over time, certain A or C items could become B items, and vice versa. No doubt outdoor antennas were once a popular item, but with the advent of cable television, Lainey's doesn't seem to be selling many of them.

THE BASIC FIXED ORDER QUANTITY MODEL

Ultimately, the required level of independent demand inventory comes down to customer demand for those items and the timing of their production, as planned in the master schedule. Figure 12.12 presents a basic model for determining the timing and quantity of orders for independent demand inventory items. The graph illustrates a fixed-quantity ordering system with constant demand and lead-time. In this situation, the time to place an order is when inventory has been reduced to the point at which it is sufficient to cover only the demand during lead-time. This level of inventory, which is referred to as the **reorder point,** is simply the product of the demand per day and the lead-time in days. Clearly, to use such a model, a manager must have a perpetual record of on-hand inventory, such that he or she is aware when the reorder point has been reached. Not all inventory items are vital enough to warrant such close scrutiny. Rather, this model is most applicable to A inventory items.

We will refer to the order quantity as Q, the annual demand as D, the daily demand as d, and the lead-time as L. The average inventory is simply one-half the order quantity ($\frac{1}{2}Q$), and the annual holding cost is $(\frac{1}{2}Q)H$, where H is the cost to hold a unit for one year. The number of orders placed in a year is D/Q, and the annual ordering cost is $(D/Q)S$, where S is the cost to place an order (including order preparation, handling, shipping, and receiving costs). Figure 12.13 graphically illustrates the relationship among order size, annual holding costs, and annual ordering costs.

(a)

Item	Monthly Volume	Item Value($)
VCRs	125	$150.00
TVs	75	$375.00
TV Cable (50′)	150	$28.00
T160 VCR Tapes	400	$2.00
T120 VCR Tapes	2,500	$2.00
Stereos	75	$300.00
Speaker Wire (100′)	300	$6.00
Patch Cables	75	$3.00
Indoor TV Antenna	75	$305.00
Deluxe T120 VCR Tapes	1,000	$4.00
D-Cell Batteries	50	$.80
Camcorders	100	$600.00
Camcorder Batteries	250	$30.00
Cable Splitters	25	$2.00
C-Cell Batteries	100	$0.80
AudioTape (90 minute)	2,000	$1.10
Audio Tape (60 minute)	2,500	$0.50
AC/DC Converters	150	$20.00
AAA-Cell Batteries	2,000	$1.00
AA-Cell Batteries	100	$0.50

(b)

Item	Monthly Volume	Item Value($)	Volume($)		
Camcorders	100	$600.00	$60,000.00		
TVs	75	$375.00	$28,125.00		
Stereo	75	$300.00	$22,500.00	"A" Items	
VCRs	125	$150.00	$18,750.00	$129,375.00	78.79%
Camcorder Batteries	260	$30.00	$7,500.00		
T120 VCR Tapes	2,500	$2.00	$5,000.00		
TV Cable (50′)	150	$28.00	$4,200.00		
Deluxe T120 VCR Tapes	1,000	$4.00	$4,000.00		
AC/DC Converters	150	$20.00	$3,000.00	"B" Items	
Indoor TV Antenna	75	$35.00	$2,625.00	$26,325.00	16.03%
AudioTape (90 minute)	2,000	$1.10	$2,200.00		
AAA-Cell Batteries	2,000	$1.10	$2,200.00		
Speaker Wire (100′)	300	$6.00	$1,800.00		
Audio Tape (60 minute)	2,500	$0.50	$1,250.00		
T160 VCR Tapes	400	$2.00	$800.00		
Patch Cables	75	$3.00	$225.00		
C-Cell Batteries	100	$0.80	$80.00		
Cable Splitters	25	$2.00	$50.00		
AA Cell Batteries	100	$0.50	$50.00	"C" Items	
D-Cell Batteries	50	$0.80	$40.00	$8,495.00	5.17%

FIGURE 12.11 ABC Analysis at Lainey's Lectronics

Using differential calculus, it can be shown that the cost-minimizing order quantity is the amount that perfectly balances annual ordering costs and annual holding costs. This amount, referred to as Q^* in Figure 12.13, is frequently referred to as the **economic order quantity,** or **EOQ.** The formula for the EOQ is given in Figure 12.14.

How do managers use this model in the real world? Let's say that the purchasing agent at Cheryl's hospital is reviewing the inventory policy for the scrub kits surgeons and other operating room personnel use. She estimates the annual demand for these items to be roughly 40,000. The annual

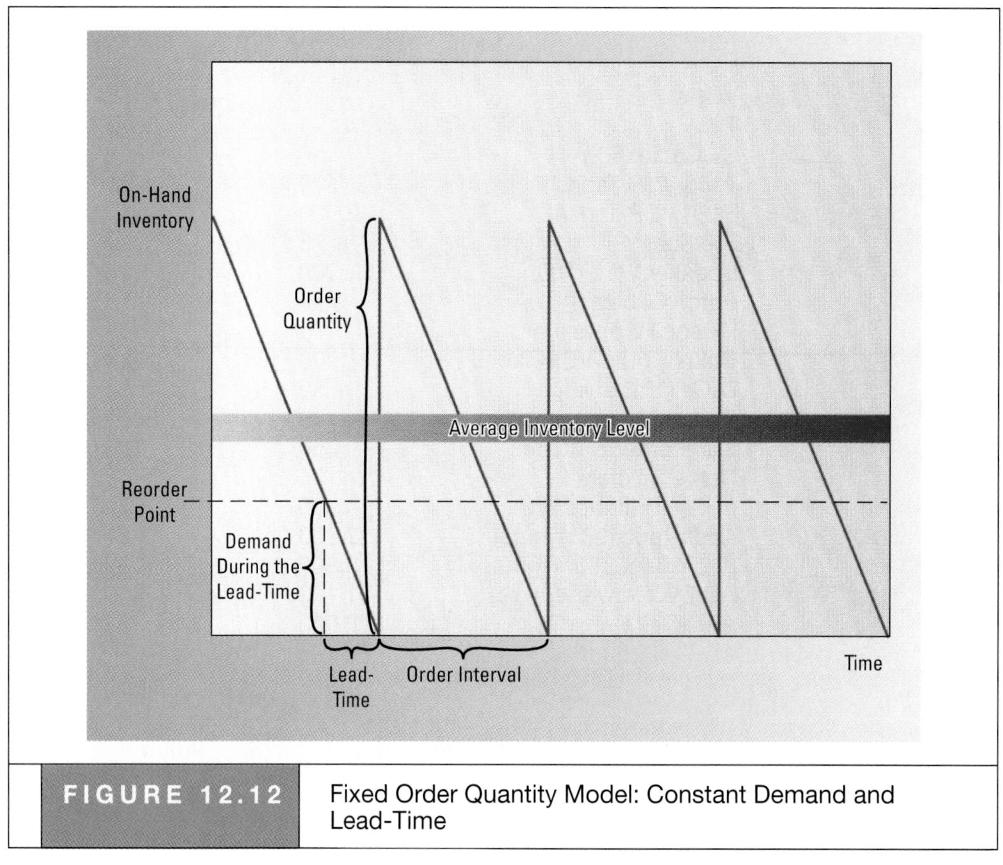

FIGURE 12.12 Fixed Order Quantity Model: Constant Demand and Lead-Time

holding cost is about $0.50 per kit per year, and the ordering cost is roughly $100 per order. The supplier can fill an order in five days. In this situation, the daily demand (d) is 40,000/365 = 109.589 units; therefore the purchasing agent should place an order whenever the inventory level drops to 5 times 109.589, or 548 units. The optimal order quantity, or EOQ, is 4,000 units, computed using the formula

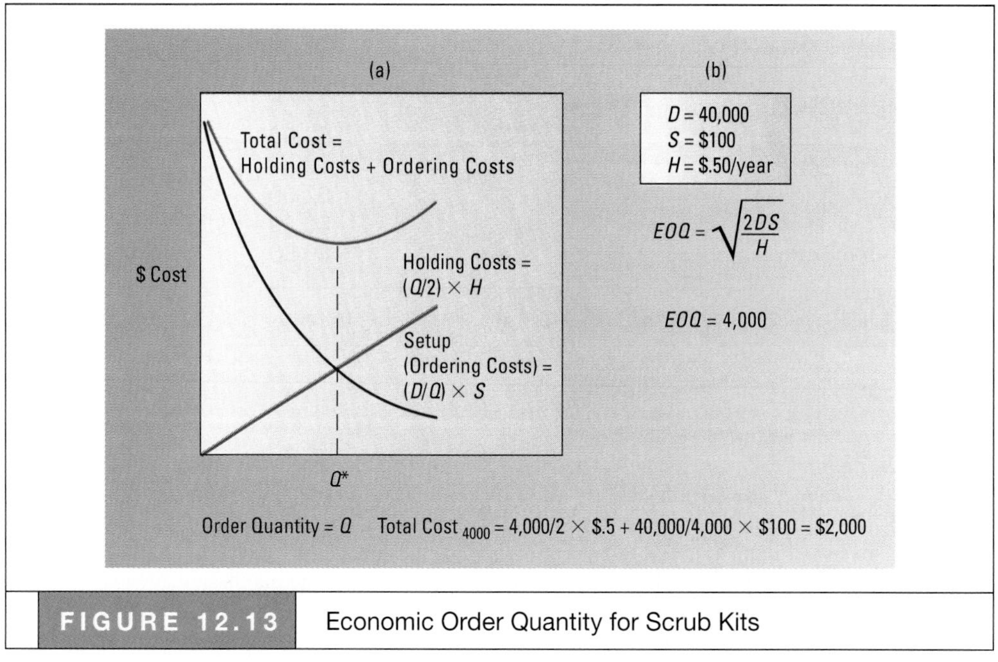

FIGURE 12.13 Economic Order Quantity for Scrub Kits

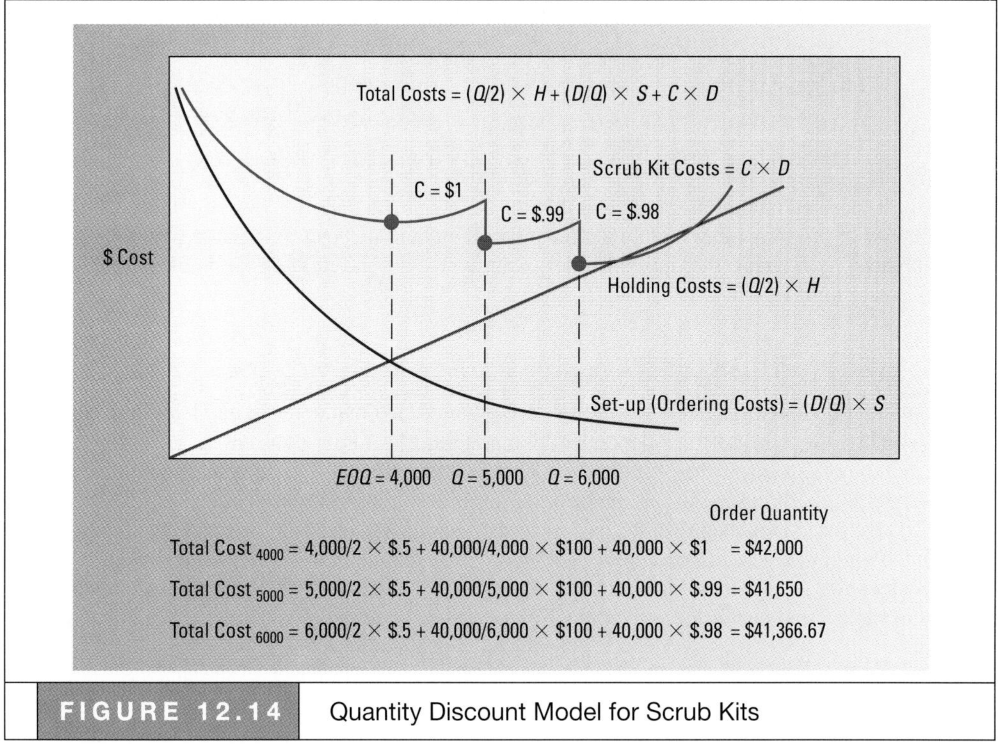

FIGURE 12.14 Quantity Discount Model for Scrub Kits

in Figure 12.13b. Since the usage rate is constant, the period between orders can also be calculated. It will take Q/d days to use the inventory that has been ordered; thus, the order interval is 4,000/109.589, or 36.5 days.

> active poll

What do you think? Voice your opinion and find out what others have to say.

FIXED ORDER QUANTITY WITH PRICE DISCOUNTS

Now let's suppose that the supplier is willing to offer discounts that reduce the per item price from \$1.00 to \$0.99 for orders of 5,000 or more, and to \$0.98 for orders of 6,000 or more. Would it make sense to order the EOQ of 4,000 units or should the purchasing agent buy 5,000 or 6,000 at a time? Figure 12.14 illustrates this situation. Letting C represent price, we have added the annual purchase cost of the item (price times annual demand, or CD) to the total cost function given in Figure 12.13. Note that because of the price breaks, the total cost curve is not continuous.

When price discounts are available, inventory models can be used to calculate the potential of inventory as an investment. (See "Integrating OM: Satisfying Customers Requiring Financial Advice" regarding financial advisor Andrew Tobias' recommendation that customers take full advantage of price discounts for items they are certain to use over time.)

Without price breaks, we know that the total cost curve is a monotonic decreasing function at quantities less than the EOQ, and a monotonically increasing function at quantities greater than the EOQ. (Whoever said you'd never use calculus?) Monotonic *decreasing* means that as you move farther to the right on the horizontal axis, the value of the function on the vertical axis only decreases. Monotonic *increasing* means that as you move farther to the right on the horizontal axis, the value of the function on the vertical axis only increases. Consequently, we need only consider ordering the EOQ versus ordering the *minimum* quantities required to receive the price breaks at quantities greater than the EOQ. In our example, that means comparing the total cost of ordering 4,000 units at a price of \$1 each to the cost of ordering 5,000 units at a price of \$0.99

each or 6,000 units at a price of \$0.98 each. Using the formula given in Figure 12.14, the total costs may be computed as follows:

$$TC_{4000} = (40{,}000/4{,}000)\times 100 + (4{,}000/2)\times 0.50 + 1.00\times 40{,}000 = \$42{,}000.00$$
$$TC_{5000} = (40{,}000/5{,}000)\times 100 + (5{,}000/2)\times 0.50 + 0.99\times 40{,}000 = \$41{,}650.00$$
$$TC_{6000} = (40{,}000/6{,}000)\times 100 + (6{,}000/2)\times 0.50 + 0.98\times 40{,}000 = \$41{,}366.67$$

Based on these computations, it is clear that the savings from the price discount and a reduction in the frequency of ordering more than offset the increase in holding costs associated with the 6,000 unit order quantity. As a result, the optimal order quantity would be 6,000 units, and the order interval would increase to *6,000/109.589,* or 54.75 days.

FIXED ORDER QUANTITY WITH VARIABLE DEMAND AND LEAD-TIMES

The fixed order quantity model shown in Figure 12.12 assumed that demand and lead-time were constant. In reality, the demand for independent demand items is rarely constant. Lead-times might be known, but they frequently vary. As a consequence, managers usually do not set the reorder point at the expected usage during lead-time. Instead, they set it a bit higher to maintain a certain margin of safety. To give a common example of this approach, most people refill their gas tank well before they are about to run out of gas. In the same way, managers are more comfortable with an inventory model that includes some safety stock, such as the one presented in Figure 12.15. Notice that the lead-time in this figure varies from one order to the next. So, too, does the usage rate. The order quantity remains constant.

To accommodate the uncertainty of demand and lead-times in Figure 12.15, managers have added safety stock to the on-hand inventory. Thus, the reorder point is the sum of the safety stock and the expected demand during lead-time. Without safety stock there is about a 50% chance of running out of inventory before a new order comes in (based on a number of assumptions made more clear in the supplement to this chapter). When the safety stock is added to the reorder point, the average inventory level increases by the amount of the safety stock, and the chance of a stock-out decreases. In short, the safety stock protects against shortages that could occur due to higher demand rates or unusually long lead-times.

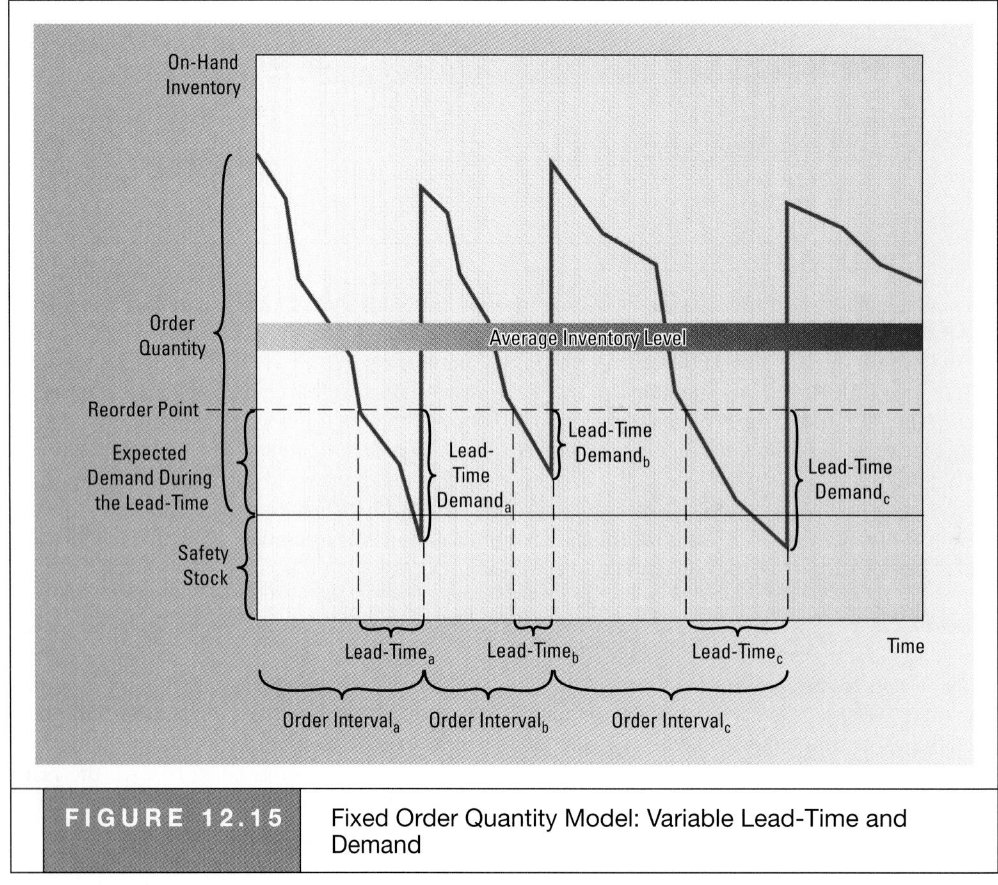

FIGURE 12.15 Fixed Order Quantity Model: Variable Lead-Time and Demand

The amount of safety stock to carry can be determined probabilistically, such that stock-outs will occur in only a certain percentage of order cycles. Alternatively, the level of safety stock can be set such that a certain percentage of demand is satisfied from stock. Detailed information regarding the calculation of safety stock quantities is included in the supplement at the end of this chapter.

The variability of demand and lead-time requires constant monitoring of the level of available inventory. If demand rates were constant, predicting the time when the next order should be placed would be easy. But since demand is variable, the only way to know when to place an order is to keep a perpetual count of inventory. Doing so makes sense for very expensive or important A inventory items, but, for other items, the cost or effort required to keep track of on-hand quantities is prohibitive.

Simple alternatives, such as inventory reserves and two-bin systems, have been developed to keep track of less-important inventory items. A departmental secretary who keeps a stock of overhead transparencies in a locked desk drawer is using a reserve system. When a faculty member complains that the department has run out of transparencies, the secretary simply places the reserve transparencies in the supply closet. The reserves should be adequate to cover the department's needs during the lead-time for reordering the transparencies. Thus, the reserves provide built-in notification that the time to reorder transparencies has arrived. (As a side benefit, the secretary gets to look like a lifesaver.) This approach is similar to the banks' system for notifying customers that they need to reorder checks. A coupon at the front of the last book of checks reminds the customer to reorder; there is no need for a usage tracking system.

A two-bin system like the one illustrated in Figure 12.16 works in a similar way. When users of the copy machine get near the bottom of the pile of paper shown in the figure, they reach a layer of blue paper, which automatically notifies them to reorder. You have probably seen a two-bin system in use at local retail outlets, particularly hardware stores. An open box holds items available for purchase; underneath sits a full, unopened box of the same item. When the top box is emptied, the second is opened, and the label from the empty box is used to order a replacement. The reorder point is reached when the top box is empty. Again, there is no need for daily counts or a usage tracking system.

FIXED ORDER QUANTITY WITH NONINSTANTANEOUS REPLENISHMENT

When goods are purchased from an outside vendor, it is reasonable to expect the entire order to be delivered at once. The fixed order quantity model in Figure 12.12 assumed instantaneous replenishment. But internal orders for parts might not be received all at once; rather, the materials are likely to become available as they are produced. In this situation, each order cycle will be composed of two distinct periods: a period during which both production and usage occur, and a period during which only usage occurs. Figure 12.17 illustrates this situation. It's similar to the situation that develops when you bake four dozen cookies but have only three dozen left when you're done, because some of them got eaten in the process.

Because material is used while it is being produced, the average inventory level is lower when replenishment is noninstantaneous and the optimal production order quantity is slightly larger than the EOQ. In fact, as Figure 12.17 shows, the average level of inventory is $[Q(1-d/p)]/2$, where p is the

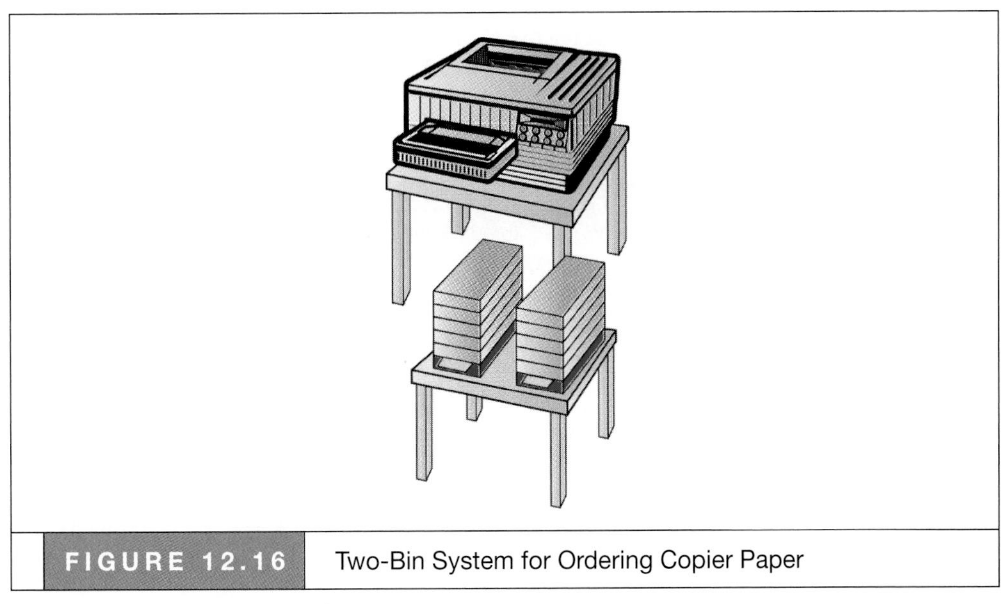

FIGURE 12.16 Two-Bin System for Ordering Copier Paper

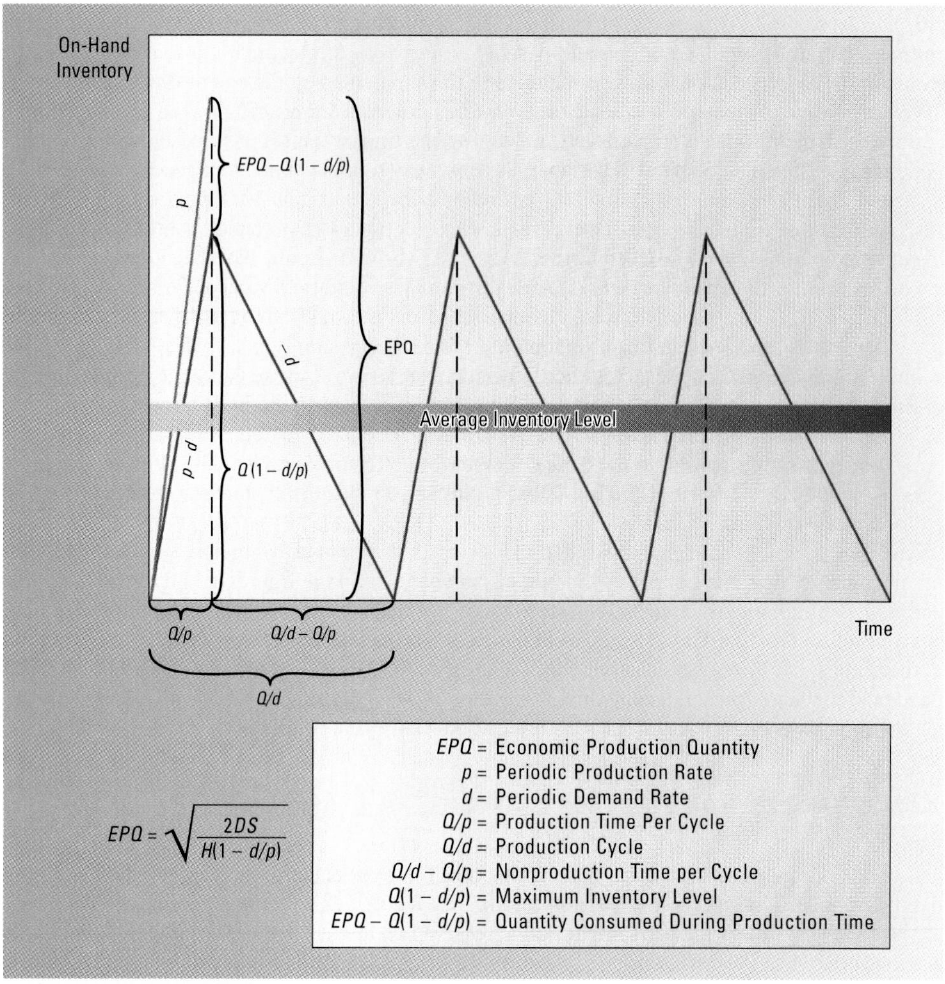

$$EPQ = \sqrt{\frac{2DS}{H(1 - d/p)}}$$

EPQ = Economic Production Quantity
p = Periodic Production Rate
d = Periodic Demand Rate
Q/p = Production Time Per Cycle
Q/d = Production Cycle
$Q/d - Q/p$ = Nonproduction Time per Cycle
$Q(1 - d/p)$ = Maximum Inventory Level
$EPQ - Q(1 - d/p)$ = Quantity Consumed During Production Time

FIGURE 12.17 Fixed Order Quantity Model: Non-Instantaneous Replenishment

periodic production rate (for example, the number of units produced per day). The cost-minimizing production order quantity is frequently referred to as the **economic production quantity, or EPQ.**

The instantaneous and noninstantaneous replenishment models are really not different. In fact, the term *instantaneous* simply means that an order is received before any more stock can be used. In other words, the production rate, *p*, is really fast relative to the usage rate, *d*. That makes the ratio *d/p* close to zero, in which case the formulas for the EOQ and the EPQ are identical.

active exercise

Take a moment to apply what you've learned.

FIXED INTERVAL MODELS

With a steady rate of inventory usage, the EOQ may be considered the amount of on-hand inventory required for a fixed period. Thus, we can talk about an optimal order interval. For example, Cheryl might know that at her hospital, the optimal order quantity for latex gloves will last about two weeks. In that case, it's probably easier to establish a standing order for delivery every two weeks rather than to place a special order whenever the reorder point is reached. If Cheryl does so, she will probably carry a bit of safety stock to cover the surges in demand that might occur during any two-week period.

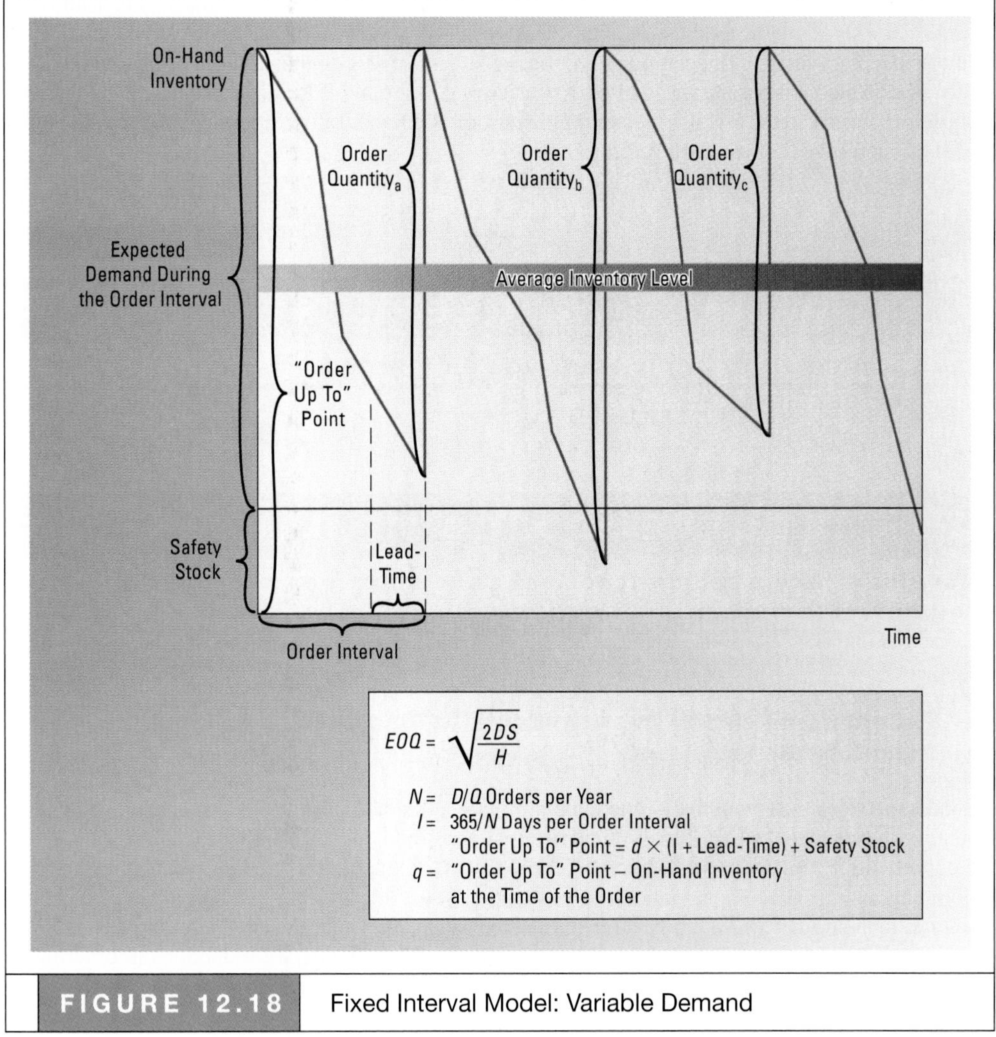

FIGURE 12.18 Fixed Interval Model: Variable Demand

Figure 12.18 presents a number of equations, starting with the formula for the optimal order quantity, which can be used to convert the optimal order quantity to the optimal order interval.

Many salespersons are aware that ordering items regularly every one, two, or three weeks is much easier than planning to order a fixed quantity and tracking the use of inventory until the next order point. They know the economics behind their customers' purchase quantities and visit their customers at fixed intervals that are convenient for reordering. This approach gives customers confidence in the salesperson's ability to meet their needs. It also provides some assurance that their orders will be placed at stock levels reasonably close to the reorder point.

Many companies receive their shipments from suppliers on a fixed interval schedule. Each shipment replaces only those items that have been used since the last shipment. This situation is particularly common in retailing, especially among chain stores and franchises that receive most or all of their independent demand inventory from a central warehousing facility. The local fast food establishment knows when the next truck will be arriving and places its order in time to ensure that items used since the last shipment will be replaced. Figure 12.18 illustrates the fixed interval model.

If demand varies and the order interval is fixed, the quantity that is ordered will vary, depending on the inventory that is on hand at the time the order is placed. The amount that is ordered will be the amount needed to replace the stock used since the last order. Typically, the amount of inventory on hand immediately after an order is received should be sufficient to last through an entire order interval, including lead-time, plus safety stock and minus on-hand inventory. Thus, the order quantity would be:

$$q = \text{average daily demand} \times (\text{order interval} + \text{lead time}) + \text{safety stock} - \text{on hand inventory}$$

Fixed interval models are not often used with A inventory items. Inventory management policies based on these models don't require a perpetual inventory record or close managerial scrutiny; they simply require an inventory check prior to placement of an order. Items that are reordered on a fixed interval model are therefore subject to stock-out at any time during the order interval or lead-time. This risk of a stock-out necessitates higher levels of safety stock than would be required with a fixed quantity inventory model. The combination of a higher risk of stock-out and higher required levels of safety stock is not appropriate for vital or expensive A items. Only if the savings that can be realized by ordering several items together outweigh the cost of additional safety stock would a fixed interval model be appropriate for use with A items.

active exercise <

Take a moment to apply what you've learned.

active concept check <

Now let's take a moment to test your knowledge of the concepts you have studied in this section.

E-Commerce-Based Improvements to Master Scheduling and Inventory Management

Business practices that span many functional areas are at the heart of many of the recent changes in inventory management. Advances in information systems and communication technologies provide the opportunity for greater coordination of decisions among marketing, operations, purchasing, and accounting within one company and across company boundaries within a supply chain. Enterprise resources planning (ERP) systems facilitate this coordinated decision making. Similarly, improving processes that cut across functional boundaries often results in significant reductions in ordering or setup costs and stock-out risks. This allows firms to reduce their order quantities and reorder points and results in leaner inventory policies.

ENTERPRISE RESOURCES PLANNING SYSTEMS

Today most corporate information systems are based on client server technology, whereby many personal computer users can share the same information. This means that the computers in the marketing department share information back and forth with those in finance, OM, purchasing, accounting, logistics, and so on. In other words, up-to-date information regarding sales is readily available to decision makers who forecast earnings, schedule operations, purchase materials, and track costs. Similarly, information regarding operations schedules is available to those who sell, purchase, forecast earnings, and track costs. Really, it is hard to imagine a functional decision that does not benefit from current business information coming from other functional areas. From an inventory management perspective, this information allows firms to more effectively plan the location, quantity, and timing of material availability to more effectively satisfy their customers with lower total inventory costs.

ERP systems don't only span functional areas, they also span geographic distances and potentially multiple businesses in a supply chain. This means that business decision makers can factor the plans and activities of their customers and suppliers—from any location in the world—into their current decisions. It means that they can more easily see inventory throughout their supply chain and compare the efficiency of facilities. As a result, many companies have been able to improve the coordination of their supply chain and dramatically reduce redundant or excessive inventories, planning lead times, working capital requirements, while increasing bargaining power with suppliers, and improving customer service. At the same time, the middle managers whose job it was to accumulate data and pass it through the hierarchy have seen their jobs become obsolete. By re-engineering their scheduling and inventory management systems to take advantage of ERP system capabilities, therefore, companies not only become more efficient, they also become less bureaucratic and more responsive to customer needs. Numerous large companies have credited ERP systems with annual savings in excess of $100 million a year.

The market for ERP software is itself a multibillion dollar market. To date it has been dominated by the German firm SAP. Other mainstream ERP system providers include Oracle, J. D. Edwards, PeopleSoft, and Baan. Figure 12.19 provides a simple overview of the way that SAP's R/3 software

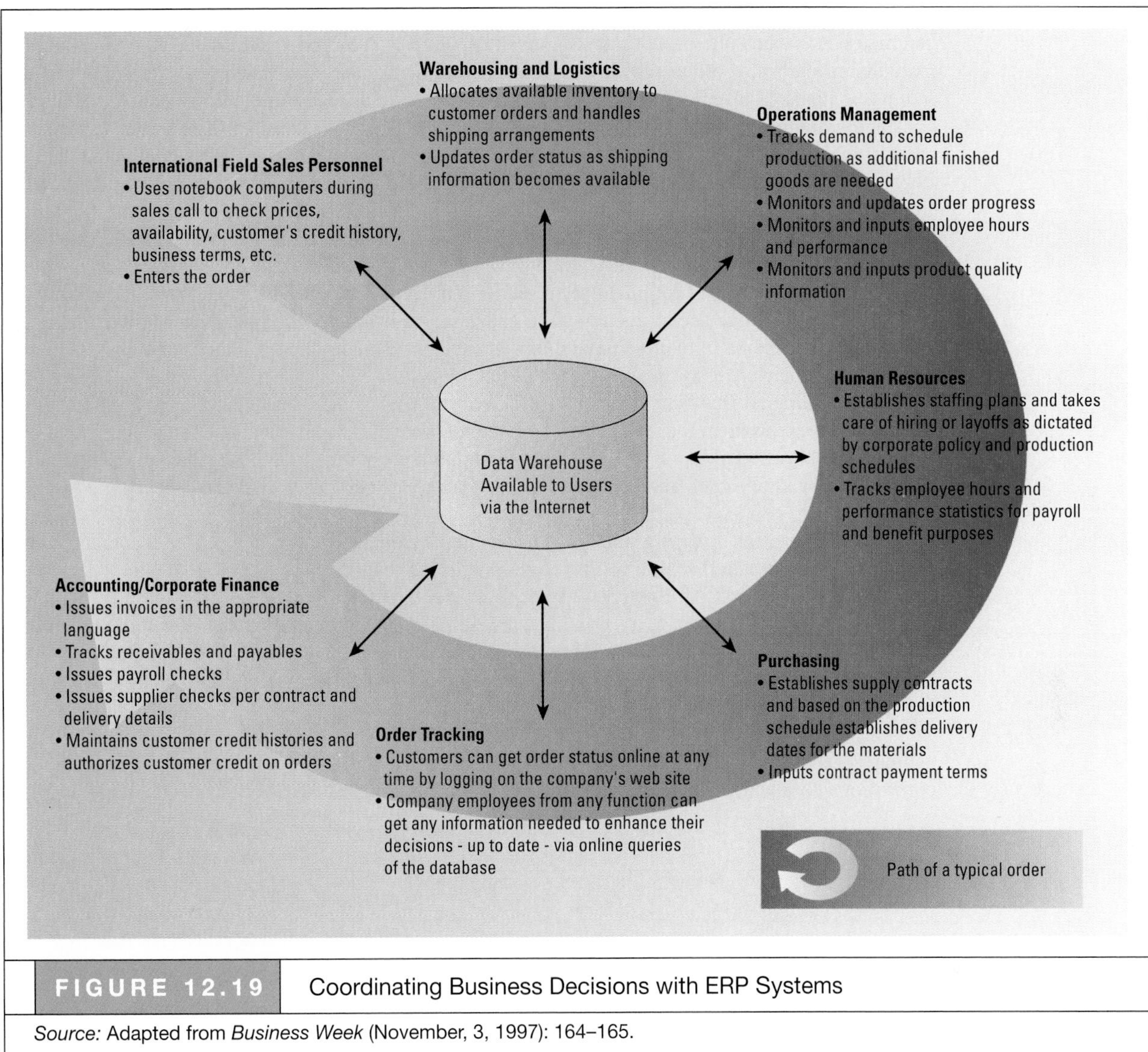

Warehousing and Logistics
• Allocates available inventory to customer orders and handles shipping arrangements
• Updates order status as shipping information becomes available
Operations Management
• Tracks demand to schedule production as additional finished goods are needed
• Monitors and updates order progress
• Monitors and inputs employee hours and performance
• Monitors and inputs product quality information
International Field Sales Personnel
• Uses notebook computers during sales call to check prices, availability, customer's credit history, business terms, etc.
• Enters the order
Data Warehouse Available to Users via the Internet
Human Resources
• Establishes staffing plans and takes care of hiring or layoffs as dictated by corporate policy and production schedules
• Tracks employee hours and performance statistics for payroll and benefit purposes
Accounting/Corporate Finance
• Issues invoices in the appropriate language
• Tracks receivables and payables
• Issues payroll checks
• Issues supplier checks per contract and delivery details
• Maintains customer credit histories and authorizes customer credit on orders
Purchasing
• Establishes supply contracts and based on the production schedule establishes delivery dates for the materials
• Inputs contract payment terms
Order Tracking
• Customers can get order status online at any time by logging on the company's web site
• Company employees from any function can get any information needed to enhance their decisions - up to date - via online queries of the database
Path of a typical order

FIGURE 12.19 Coordinating Business Decisions with ERP Systems

Source: Adapted from *Business Week* (November, 3, 1997): 164–165.

could be used to coordinate an order fulfillment process for a hypothetical sneaker company spanning several functions, facilities, and time zones.

Despite the potential benefits of ERP systems, they are no magic bullet. It is clearly possible for companies to spend millions of dollars on new computer systems—without making any change in their underlying operational and decision-making processes. The result is an expensive system that becomes the scapegoat for ongoing business problems.

IMPROVING ON "OPTIMAL" ORDER QUANTITIES

In the past, the attitude that analytically determined order quantities were optimal led many companies to accept large lot sizes. Recently, managers have come to realize that inventory management policies are closely linked to improvement efforts. As a consequence, they have begun to focus on changing the cost structure that lies behind the EOQ calculations. The EOQ is the optimal lot size only for a given set of costs.

Recently, many firms have made a concerted effort to reduce the transaction costs associated with placing purchase orders or the setup costs associated with in-house orders. When a system has bottlenecks, setup times and costs should not be a deterrent to small lot sizes. Activity-based costing (ABC) might be used to estimate the actual cost of the setup, which is probably close to zero if the firm has extra capacity. Furthermore, a better understanding of the drawbacks associated with holding large inventories has highlighted hidden costs that are not accounted for in the classical EOQ model. As a result, "optimal" order quantities are being reduced, and firms are experiencing fewer of the negative consequences associated with large orders and high inventory levels.

When inventory items are managed using a fixed order quantity model, electronic technologies can be used to reduce the cost of tracking inventory. In fact, it has become much easier to maintain a perpetual inventory record with today's information systems and stock tracking systems that identify individual items of inventory with an inexpensive bar code or electronic chip. As such, the cost of constantly monitoring inventory levels is decreasing. Other improvement programs that can also be used to reduce inventory and improve customer service include electronic data interchange (EDI); improved logistics capabilities and less-than-truckload (LTL) transfer arrangements available from freight carriers; and improvements in supplier processes, such as supplier setup-reduction programs.

As Figure 12.20 shows, ordering costs can also be reduced in fixed interval systems, as can the setup costs for internal orders. Thus, the "optimal" order quantity determined using an inventory model should be viewed as optimal only over the short run. Firms need to take a long-term focus on improving customer service by reducing their reliance on inventory. They can do so by reducing the potential for disruption in their value-adding systems, by reducing the uncertainty that they face, and by improving their ordering and setup capabilities.

Recently, suppliers have questioned the efficiency of the classical EOQ model. Figure 12.21 illustrates the type of problem that can arise when one member of a supply chain adheres rigidly to a particular inventory model. Marshall's bike shop assumes a constant demand for bicycles, its independent demand inventory item. Yet its ordering policy can create very lumpy demand patterns for its parts suppliers.

Thus the "optimal" ordering policy, when applied by one company, can produce boom-and-bust cycles (no pun intended) for suppliers. To deal with the resulting variations in demand, a supplier must carry excess capacity (which is rather inefficient), offer a high level of flexibility (which is costly to develop and maintain), or provide a low level of customer satisfaction. Recognizing that the customer will ultimately pay the supplier's costs, none of these alternatives is very appealing. Chapter 2 on supply-chain management also details recent trends in decision making that recognize the joint interests of all value-adding firms in a supply chain.

In the final analysis, recent trends support the view that the more managers know about the value-adding system and the role of inventory within it, the more likely that their inventory decisions will be consistent with other decisions and will support the firm's competitive priorities. Extending this logic,

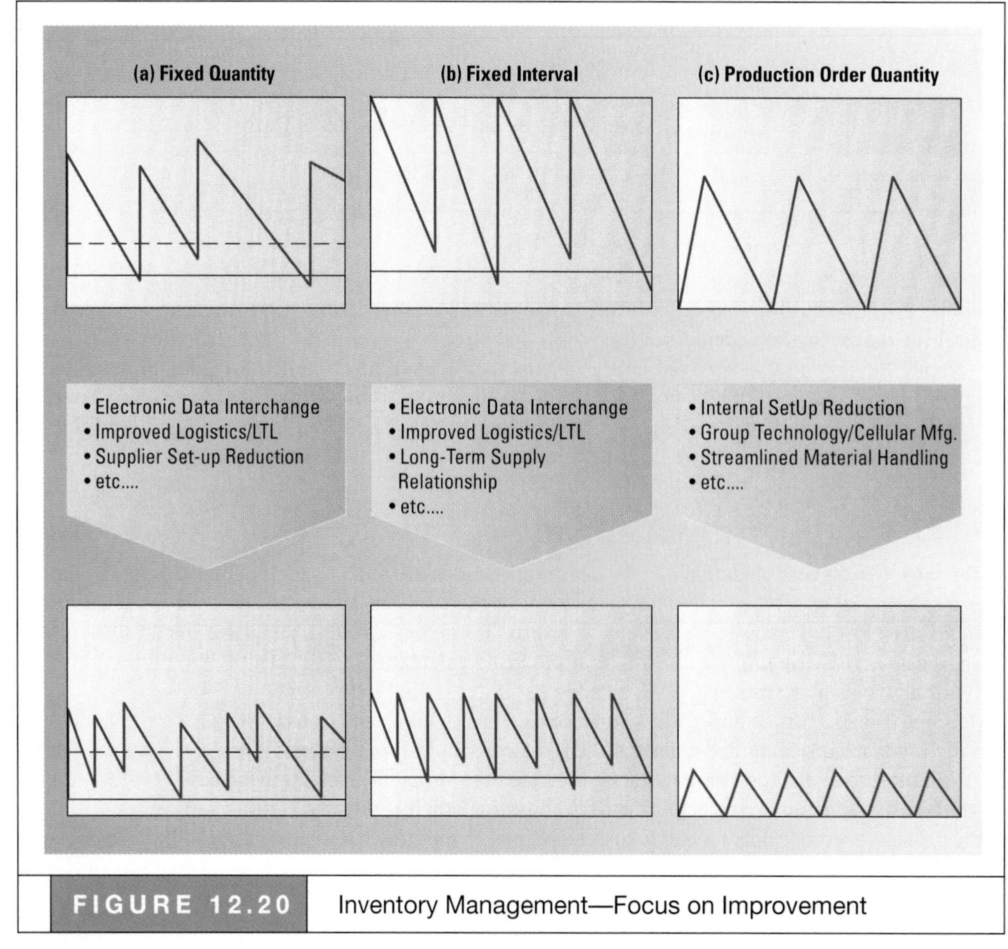

FIGURE 12.20 Inventory Management—Focus on Improvement

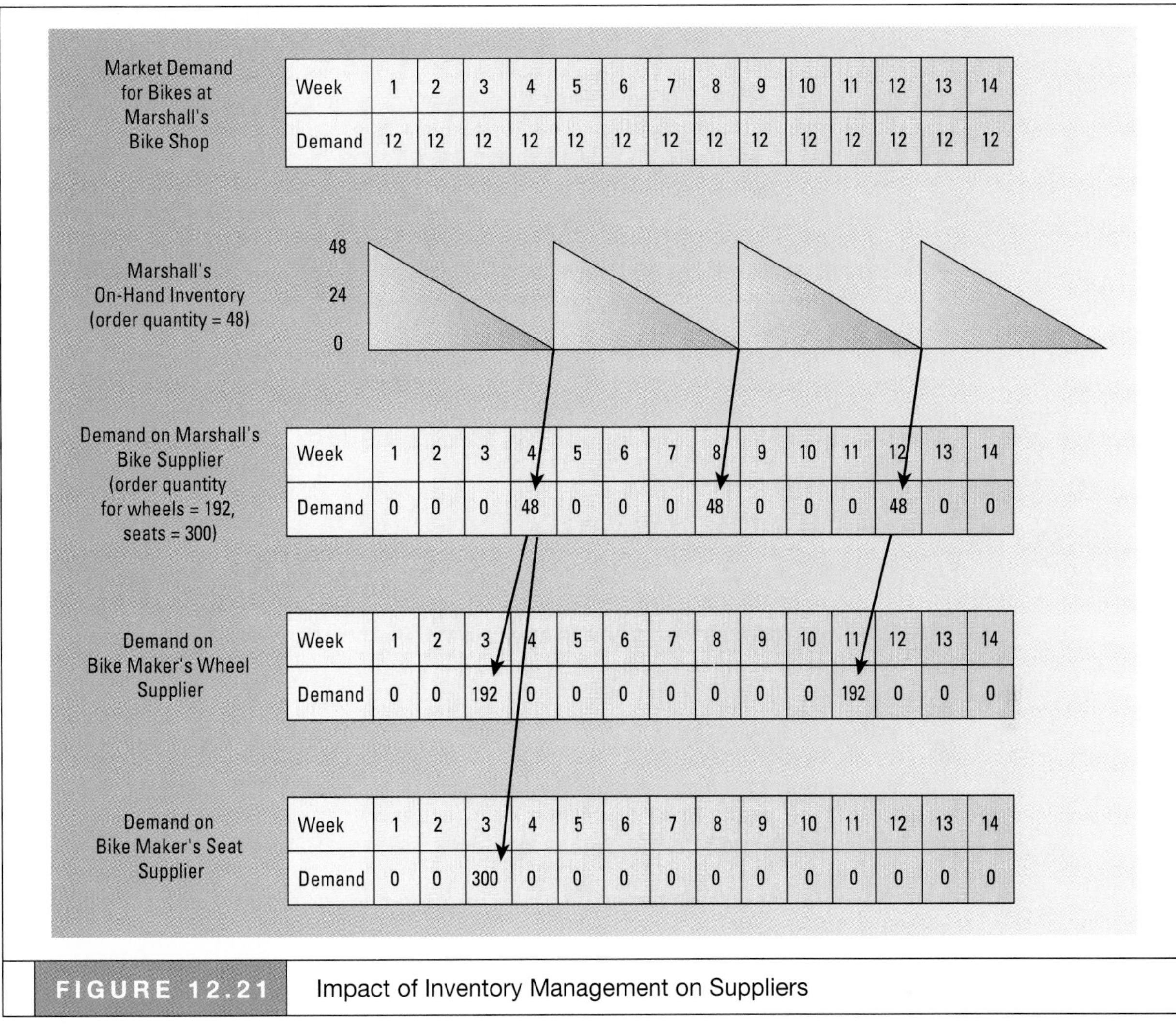

FIGURE 12.21 Impact of Inventory Management on Suppliers

the more managers know about the supply chain upstream and downstream, the better they will be able to make inventory and scheduling decisions that enhance customer satisfaction. Consequently, the recent surge in use of e-commerce applications has the potential to result in improved master scheduling and inventory management decisions.

> active exercise

Take a moment to apply what you've learned.

> active concept check

Now let's take a moment to test your knowledge of the concepts you have studied in this section.

> Integrating Operational Decisions

This chapter's most obvious and direct linkages are to the other chapters in this section of the text including Chapters 11 and 13-16. Chapter 11, on aggregate planning, was a transition between the strategy and design of operations and the operation of existing systems. In this chapter, we have taken the intermediate-range focus of the aggregate plan and broken down the decisions made at that level into the more detailed near-term challenges of getting product-service bundles to customers. Chapters 13-16 describe the material planning and detailed scheduling activities that are required to execute the master schedule in a variety of operational settings. Decisions made in master scheduling provide direct input and direction to the more detailed shorter term planning and control systems discussed in the remainder of this section.

Chapters 2, 3, 4, and 7 also provide information about decisions that are closely linked to those covered in this chapter. Chapter 2 focuses on supply-chain management. Since this chapter deals directly with scheduling delivery of the product-service bundle, it is the internal operation planning activity most closely linked to supply-chain management. Our coverage of ERP systems in this chapter directly reflects this linkage to the material in Chapter 2. In Chapter 3 we discussed the importance of selecting competitive priorities. The approach a firm takes to master scheduling will depend directly on the competitive priorities it has selected. Inventory management strategies can also be used to leverage a firm's competitive advantage and enhance its ability to meet customer needs. This is especially emphasized by recent trends discussed in this chapter. On a more detailed level, many of the parameters within which master scheduling decisions are made are defined by the design of the product-service bundle and value-adding system (Chapters 4 and 7).

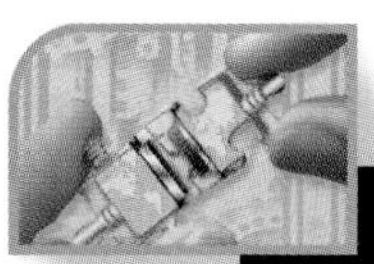

integrated OM <

Take a moment to apply what you've learned.

> Chapter Wrap-Up

This chapter has described master scheduling and inventory management decisions. These decisions are all about how existing capacity (established by long-term value-adding system design and the aggregate plan) will be used to satisfy customers. Master scheduling determines the planned timing of completion for the firm's product-service bundles—what is to be done and when. This activity is central to the satisfaction of customers and as a result becomes a critical linking point among marketing, operations, finance, and purchasing. If master scheduling is done right, scheduling decisions will be consistent with those of all other functions and operations. This achievement allows a firm to set itself apart in the customer's eyes. Being able to give customers what they want when they want it leads to competitive advantage.

Inventory decisions are closely related to scheduling decisions, because inventory is often needed to conduct scheduled activities and, at least in manufacturing operations, is created by scheduled activities. We've discussed a number of inventory models in this chapter, including ABC analysis, fixed quantity models, and fixed interval models. These models are covered in more detail in the supplement following this chapter.

Recently, some of the negative consequences of excessive reliance on inventory have become clear. As a result, firms are looking for ways to do without large stocks of material. They are using technologies to enhance their flexibility and reduce the uncertainty they face. They are also beginning to coordinate their systems across entire supply chains. This strategy allows firms to remove many of the uncertainties that necessitate inventory in the first place.

> end-of-chapter resources

- Practice Quiz
- Key Terms
- Solved Problems
- Discussion Questions
- Problems
- Case 12.1
- References
- Plant Tours

SUPPLEMENT E

Stochastic Independent Demand Inventory Models

Supplement Outline

Lead-Time and the Reorder Point

As Chapter 12 noted, when delivery lead-time, L, and the daily inventory usage rate, d, are fixed and known, it is simple to determine the appropriate **reorder point.** An order should be placed when the amount of inventory available for use during the **lead-time** exactly equals the amount that will be required during the lead-time.

To be more explicit, we will break the analysis down into two cases: one in which the lead-time is shorter than the length of an inventory cycle, and another in which the lead-time is longer than the length of an inventory cycle.

SHORT LEAD-TIME

If the lead-time is shorter than the length of an inventory cycle, then an order should be placed when the amount of inventory *on hand* will exactly cover the demand during the lead-time, as shown in Figure E.1a. That is:

$$R = Ld \qquad \text{Equation E-1}$$

where R = the reorder point, L = the lead-time in days, and d = the daily usage rate.

LONG LEAD-TIME

If the lead-time is longer than the length of an inventory cycle, then an order should be placed when the amount of inventory *on hand* or *on order* (called the *book inventory* or *inventory position*) will exactly cover the demand during the lead-time. Since the on-hand inventory will never be enough to cover all the demand during the lead-time, we must order during one cycle for delivery during a later cycle, as shown in Figure E.1b. The reorder point is still given by Equation E-1 if we base it on the *book inventory* or the *inventory position.* But if we want to base it on on-hand inventory, then:

$$R = Ld - n^*Q^* \qquad \text{Equation E-2}$$

where R, L, and d are as in Equation E-1, Q^* is the order quantity, and n^* is the maximum integer value less than or equal to Ld/Q^*. That is, subtract from Ld as many full-order quantities as possible (to recognize the orders placed during earlier inventory cycles that have not yet been received), and the remainder is R, the reorder point in terms of on-hand inventory.

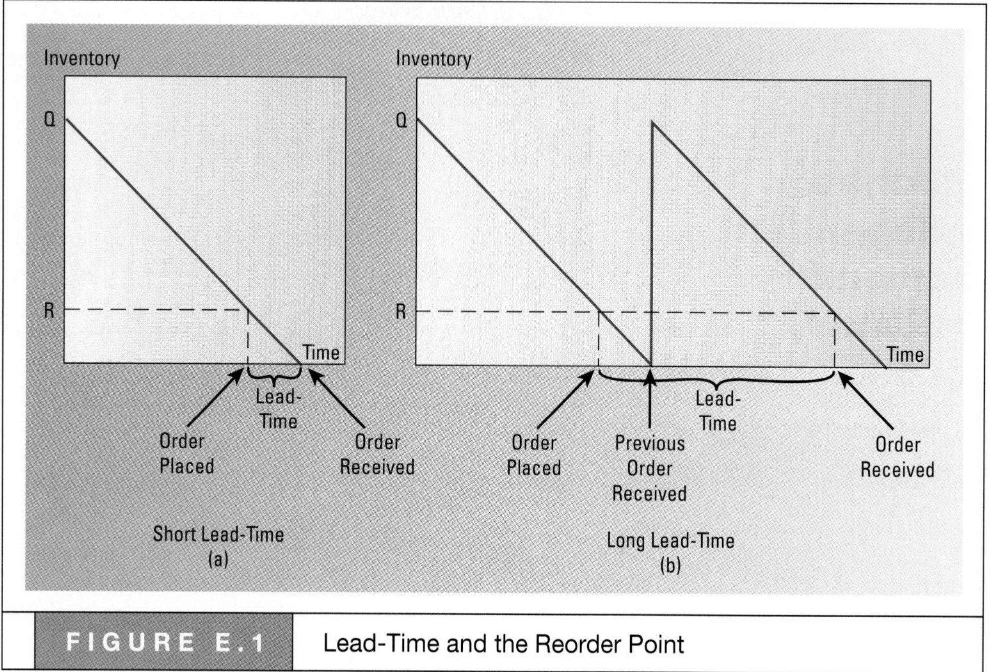

FIGURE E.1 Lead-Time and the Reorder Point

Example E.1

Cheryl's hospital uses approximately 1,000 boxes of nonsterile disposable examining gloves per year. Usage is fairly regular from day to day. The hospital pays $5 per box for the gloves. The accounting department has estimated the cost of placing and receiving an order for this item to be $40 and uses a 20% annual carrying rate for nonperishable inventory (which means the annual holding cost is 20% of the price.) The company that supplies examining gloves to the hospital quotes a delivery time of two weeks (14 days). Determine the reorder point for gloves.

Solution:
Using formulas from Chapter 12 you can determine that the EOQ = 283 boxes, which gives a cycle length of 103.3 days. Since the lead-time (14 days) is shorter than the cycle length, the reorder point is:

$$R = Ld = 14(2.74) = 38.36 \text{ or } 39 \text{ boxes}$$

active exercise <

Take a moment to apply what you've learned.

Determining the Reorder Point When Demand Is Probabilistic

In the preceding discussion, the reorder point was computed under the assumption that the length of the lead-time and the rate at which demand occurs are both known with certainty. Realistically, that will not be the case; either or both of those parameters will be random variables. Rather than the situation pictured in Figures 12.12 and E.1, in which we can order the new material in time to receive it exactly as the existing inventory runs out, we will more likely experience the situation in Figure 12.15. When the demand during the lead-time is a random variable, it will sometimes be less than expected, so some inventory is still left when the next order is received. At other times it will be more than expected, so that a **stockout** will occur.

As is suggested in Figure 12.15, one way of coping with this uncertainty is **safety stock,** which is extra inventory that is held to reduce the chance of a stockout. Then:

$$R = \mu_{DDLT} + SS \qquad \text{Equation E-3}$$

where R is the reorder point, μ_{DDLT} is the expected demand during lead-time, and SS is the safety stock.

There are a number of ways to determine the amount of safety stock to carry. We shall consider two: a policy-based approach and a cost-based approach. First, we need to consider the idea of a *desired service level.*

DESIRED SERVICE LEVEL

The *service level* of an inventory system is a measure of how well it meets demand. One of two approaches, which are somewhat related, is typically used:

1. The probability that a stockout will not occur during an inventory cycle, i.e., the probability that all demand during an inventory cycle will be filled from stock.
2. The probability that a unit of demand will be filled from stock.

The first measure relates directly to the graph of inventory level in Figure 12.15. In the second inventory cycle shown in that figure, the demand during lead-time was low, less than the reorder point, so there would not have been a stockout even if there were no safety stock. During the first and third inventory cycles in Figure 12.15, the demand during lead-time was higher than expected; there would have been a stockout if the safety stock had not been fairly high. If there had only been half as much safety stock, there would have been no stockout during the first cycle, but there would have been a stockout during the third cycle when the demand during lead-time was higher. Thus, within the three cycles shown in Figure 12.15, one of three possible outcomes might have resulted, depending on the level of safety stock:

- With no safety stock, there would have been a stockout during two of the three cycles.
- With a moderate level of safety stock, there would have been a stockout during one of the three cycles.
- With a high level of safety stock (the actual case), there were no stockouts.

The second measure of the service level indicates the *amount* of demand facing a stockout rather than whether or not there is a stockout. This is a fairly common measure of service level in practice; many inventory control departments track their *fill rate,* which is the percentage of demand filled from stock.

These two measures of service level are obviously related: A stockout occurs (measure 1) whether one unit of demand or many cannot be filled from stock (measure 2). The second measure is more complicated, since it not only recognizes the existence of a stockout, but also indicates how much demand goes unmet during the stockout.

While either stockout measure can be used to set the safety stock level, the second measure requires more complicated analysis than we will deal with here. We will focus on the first measure: the probability that a stockout will not occur during an inventory cycle.

A POLICY-BASED APPROACH TO SETTING SAFETY STOCK

A policy-based approach to setting safety stock specifies the maximum allowable probability that there will be a stockout during an inventory cycle. To do this, we must have a probability distribution of **demand during lead-time (DDLT).** There are a variety of ways to develop such a probability distribution. One approach would be to develop a relative frequency distribution based on past history. A second approach would be to use a forecasting system like simple exponential smoothing to estimate the mean demand during lead-time and base the standard deviation on the forecast error measure (see Supplement D).

If we can assume that the lead-time is a constant, with the only variability in demand during the lead-time coming from the variability in day-to-day (or week-to-week, etc.) demand, and further assume that demand is independent from day to day, then determining the mean and standard deviation of demand during lead-time is simpler. From basic probability theory, we get:

$$\mu_{DDLT} = L\mu_d \qquad \text{Equation E-4 (a)}$$

$$\sigma_{DDLT} = \sigma_d\sqrt{L} \qquad \text{Equation E-4 (b)}$$

where μ_d and σ_d are the mean and standard deviation of daily demand.

Regardless of how the probability distribution of demand during lead-time is estimated, we can then determine the reorder point (and safety stock) that would give the desired maximum allowable probability of stockout, as shown in Figure E.2. If we can assume that demand during lead-time has a normal distribution, as shown in Figure E.2, then the reorder point is given by:

$$R = \mu_{DDLT} + Z_\alpha\sigma_{DDLT} \qquad \text{Equation E-5}$$

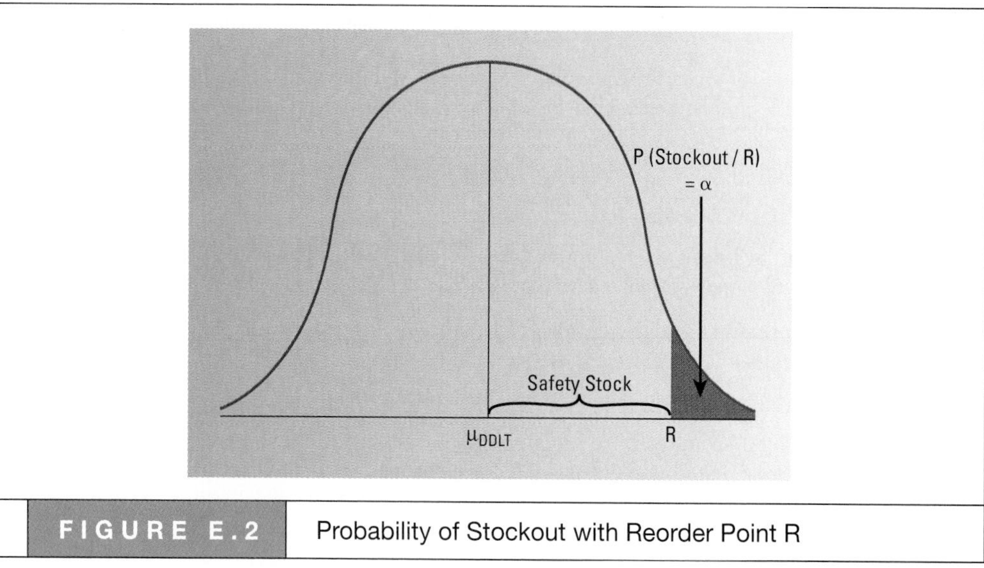

FIGURE E.2 Probability of Stockout with Reorder Point R

where R is the reorder point, μ_{DDLT} is the expected demand during lead-time, σ_{DDLT} is the standard deviation of demand during lead-time, and Z_α is the value of Z, the standard normal variable that gives α, the allowable probability of a stockout.

Example E.2

While the company that supplies examining gloves to Cheryl's hospital (Example E.1) does average 14 days for delivery, as quoted, historical records indicate that demand during lead-time has a standard deviation of 5.3 boxes. Assume demand during lead-time has a normal distribution.

a. What should the reorder point be if the hospital is willing to accept a stockout in one cycle out of 20, on average?

b. What will the safety stock be with this reorder point?

Solution:

a. Averaging one stockout out of 20 cycles means that P(stockout) = .05 for any given cycle. The value of Z that gives $\alpha = .05$ is $Z_\alpha = 1.645$. From Example E.9, the expected demand during a lead-time averaging 14 days is 38.36 boxes. Using Equation E.5, the reorder point is:

$$R = \mu_{DDLT} + Z_\alpha \sigma_{DDLT} = 38.36 + 1.645(5.3) = 38.36 + 8.72 = 47.08 \text{ boxes}$$

This result can be rounded down to 47 boxes, which will raise the probability of a stockout to a little more than .05, or be rounded up to 48 boxes to guarantee the desired service level.

b. If R = 47, the safety stock is 47 − 38.36 = 8.64 boxes.

active exercise

Take a moment to apply what you've learned.

A COST-BASED APPROACH TO SETTING SAFETY STOCK

If it is possible to determine the cost of incurring a stockout, then it is possible to determine what the probability of a stockout *should* be in order to balance the cost of carrying extra inventory (more safety stock) against the expected cost of stockouts without that extra inventory. The simplest approach to determining what the reorder point and safety stock should be in order to balance these costs is to use a payoff table (see Supplement B) and conduct marginal analysis on the reorder point level.

	1-P (Stockout IR) Not Needed	P (Stockout IR) Needed
Do note increase	0	V
Increase	H(Q/D)	H(Q/D)

FIGURE E.3 Payoff Table for Decision about Whether or Not to Increase Reorder Point and Safety Stock

The payoff table for marginal analysis on the reorder point level is shown in Figure E.3. Suppose that the reorder point is R. The question is, Should it be increased to R+1? The two decision alternatives are: (1) do not increase, and (2) increase. There are also two states of nature: (1) Unit R+1 is not needed, and (2) unit R+1 is needed. The probability that unit R+1 is needed is P(stockout|R), i.e., the probability that there will be a stockout if the reorder point is kept at R. The probability that unit R+1 is not needed is simply 1 − P(stockout|R).

The costs for the four cells in Figure E.3 may be explained as follows:

- If unit R+1 is not stocked and not needed, then there is no cost.
- If unit R+1 is not stocked but is needed, then there will be a stockout, which will cost V.
- If unit R+1 is stocked but is not needed, then unit R+1 will have been carried in inventory for the entire length of the inventory cycle. Carrying this unnecessary unit of inventory will cost a fraction of H (defined in Chapter 12 as the annual holding cost per unit of inventory). This fraction of H would be the length of an inventory cycle relative to the length of a year. The demand during an inventory cycle averages Q units, relative to the demand during a year averaging D units, so the relevant fraction is Q/D.
- If unit R+1 is stocked and is needed, then unit R+1 will have been carried in inventory for *almost* the entire length of the inventory cycle, since we are considering the last unit stocked. Rather than try to determine the little bit by which the holding cost could be reduced, we will simply use the same carrying cost shown in the lower left corner of the table.

Using this payoff table, we can see that the reorder point should be increased if the expected cost of an increase is less than or equal to the expected cost of no increase. That is, if:

$$H(Q/D) \leq V{*}P(\text{stockout}|R) = V{*}P(\text{DDLT} > R)$$

Doing a little algebra on this inequality, we get the following result: Set the reorder point at the highest value R for which:

$$P(\text{stockout}) = P(\text{DDLT} > R) \leq \frac{H(Q/D)}{V} = \frac{HQ}{VD} \qquad \text{Equation E-6}$$

Example E.3

Refer to Example E.2. Cheryl's hospital has worked out an arrangement with neighboring hospitals to back each other up in the event that any of them runs out of commonly used supplies. If a hospital stocks out of examining gloves, the materials management department director will send a van to one of the neighboring hospitals to pick some up. When the new order comes in, the borrowed boxes will be replaced. The cost of the emergency restocking procedure is estimated to be \$50. Given this information, what should the reorder point and safety stock be?

Solution:
From the information presented here, V = \$50. From Example E.1, we find that H = \$1 per box per year, D = 1,000 boxes per year, and Q = 283 boxes per order. Using Equation E-6, the desired probability of a stockout is:

$$P(\text{stockout}) = \frac{HQ}{VD} = \frac{(1)(283)}{(1{,}000)(50)} = \frac{283}{50{,}000} = .0057$$

From a normal distribution table, $Z_\alpha = 2.53$ for $\alpha = .0057$. Using Equation E-5:

$$R = \mu_{DDLT} + Z_\alpha \sigma_{DDLT} = 38.36 + 2.53(5.3) = 38.46 + 13.41 = 51.77$$

The reorder point should be 52 boxes, and the safety stock will be 52 − 38.46 = 13.64 boxes.

active exercise <

Take a moment to apply what you've learned.

> Periodic Review Systems

All the models considered so far have been for continuous review or reorder point systems in which the amount ordered is a constant and the time between orders is variable. We will now consider periodic review systems, in which the time between orders, T, called the *review period,* is a constant, and the amount ordered varies to reflect the varying usage between review times.

While it is possible to determine the optimal length of the review period, as suggested in Figure 12.18, T is usually based on the frequency with which a supplier's representative makes deliveries. The issue we deal with here is how to determine the desired **stocking level,** S, when the demand rate is variable.

The basic idea in determining the desired stocking level, S, in a periodic review system is similar to that in determining the reorder point, R, in a continuous review system: The amount of stock available should be sufficient to cover expected demand until the next order arrives, plus an allowance to cover uncertainty. The main difference between the two models is in the safety stock. As shown in Figure 12.15, in a fixed quantity system, the safety stock needs to supply stockout protection for the relatively short time between placing and receiving the order, which is the lead-time, L. In a periodic review system, however, the time between placing orders is fixed, not variable. The safety stock must supply stockout protection for the relatively long time between placing an order and receipt of the *following* order, since that is the next time it will be possible to cover any unusually heavy demands. That is, the safety stock must cover the uncertainty of demand over the time interval T + L, not just L. As a result, the safety stock will be larger than in a periodic review system, even if the average time between orders, the lead-time, and the variability in daily demand are the same.

DETERMINING THE DESIRED STOCKING LEVEL, S

As just stated, the basic concept in determining the desired stocking level is: The amount of stock available should be sufficient to cover expected demand until the next order arrives, plus an allowance to cover uncertainty. Since the time until the next order arrives is T + L—the time until the next order will be placed, T, plus the time until that order is delivered, L—the desired stocking quantity is:

$$S = \mu_d(T + L) + SS \qquad \text{Equation E-7}$$

where μ_d is the expected daily demand, T is the length of the review period in days, L is the lead-time in days, and SS is the safety stock. Since some inventory is likely to exist at the time the order is placed, the actual order quantity will be given by:

$$Q = S - I \qquad \text{Equation E-8}$$

where Q is the order quantity and I is the existing inventory.

DETERMINING THE SAFETY STOCK

Other than the length of time for which the safety stock must provide stockout protection, the process of determining the amount of safety stock to carry in a periodic review system is the same as in a reorder point system. The desired safety stock can be determined with a policy-based approach or a cost-based approach; the procedures are identical to those used previously except for the probability distribution used. As stated, the safety stock must provide stockout protection for the period T + L, so the probability distribution used must be for that amount of time rather than L.

In particular, if we can assume that L, the length of the lead-time, is a constant, as is the length of the review period, T, and the only variability in demand during the period T + L comes from the variability in day-to-day demand; and if we can further assume that demands from day to day are independent, then as in Equation E-4, the mean and standard deviation of demand during the time period T + L are given by:

$$\mu_{T+L} = (T + L)\mu_d \qquad \text{Equation E-9 (a)}$$

$$\sigma_{T+L} = \sigma_d \sqrt{T + L} \qquad \text{Equation E-9 (b)}$$

where μ_d and σ_d are the mean and standard deviation of daily demand. Then, for a desired stockout probability α, the stocking level S is given by:

$$S = (T + L)\mu_d + Z_\alpha \sigma_{T+L} \qquad \text{Equation E-10}$$

Example E.4

Oxygen and other gases are delivered to Cheryl's hospital every Thursday. The quantity delivered is based on an order called in by the hospital on Monday, three days before. The average daily usage of oxygen is 6 tanks, with a standard deviation of 1.2 tanks.

a. Determine the desired stocking level if the hospital wishes to take no more than a 2% chance of running out of oxygen between orders.
b. If there are 10 tanks on hand on a given Monday, what should the order be?

Solution

a. We are given that T = 7 days (review every Monday) and L = 3 days (the Monday order is delivered on Thursday). The mean daily usage is μ_d = 6 tanks and the standard deviation of daily usage is σ_d = 1.2 tanks. The allowable stockout probability is given as α = .02, which, from a normal distribution table, gives a Z value of Z_α = 2.05. From Equations E-9 and E-10, the desired stocking level is:

$$\begin{aligned} S &= (T + L)\mu_d + Z_\alpha \sigma_d \sqrt{T + L} \\ &= (7 + 3)(6) + 2.05(1.2)\sqrt{7 + 3} \\ &= 60 + 7.78 = 67.78 \end{aligned}$$

which we round up to 68.
b. On the Monday when there are 10 tanks on hand, the order should be for 68 − 10 = 58 tanks.

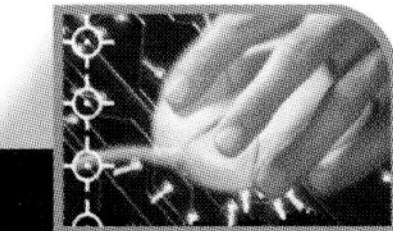

> active exercise

Take a moment to apply what you've learned.

Supplement Wrap-Up

There are two basic decisions to be made in any inventory control system: when to order and how much to order. In a periodic review system, the decision of how much to order is made at regular intervals; in a continuous review or reorder point system, an order is triggered when the available inventory reaches a certain level, the reorder point. The amount ordered can be fixed at a level Q or it can vary, being enough to raise the inventory to a desired stocking level, S.

When the delivery lead-time is known and demand occurs at a constant rate, the reorder point can be easily computed as the amount of demand during lead-time, adjusted, if necessary, for outstanding orders. If, however, either the lead-time or the daily demand is variable, the reorder point can be increased to reduce the chances of a stockout before the order is received. The increased inventory to avoid stockouts is called safety stock. The safety stock level may be determined by specifying the allowable probability of a stockout or by balancing the added cost of safety stock against the reduced cost of expected stockouts.

In a periodic review system with a desired stocking level, S, the value of S can be determined as the expected use between the time one order is placed and the following order is received. As with the reorder point for the continuous review system, this level can be increased by safety stock to reduce the chance of a stockout. In a periodic review system, the amount of safety stock needed to provide a given level of stockout coverage is larger than that required in a continuous review system since the time period for which protection is to be provided is the review period plus the lead-time, not just the lead-time.

> end-of-supplement resources

- Practice Quiz
- Key Terms
- Solved Problem
- Discussion Questions
- Problems

Planning and Control in Just-in-Time Systems

Chapter Outline

What's Ahead

. . . BACK AT THE REC CENTER

"What a weekend!" said Luis as he came into the fitness center just after the rest of the group had arrived one spring Monday morning. "I think I worked harder this weekend than I do in a month at my real job!"

"What do you mean work?" asked Fred as he got on a stepper. "I thought you were getting things started with your little league team?"

Fred was thinking back to the conversation when Luis told them he had volunteered to coach a little league team of 10- to 12-year old kids. Luis didn't have any kids yet, but everybody in the group knew how much he likes kids and loves baseball. Luckily, the others were fans as well and didn't mind too much when he started talking about his favorite team, Cleveland. Coaching a team seemed like a natural fit.

"No, not 'work' work, fun work, I got up early on Saturday . . ." Luis replied but was interrupted.

"Sorry, Luis, you have your words mixed up. Work is work and fun is fun" Fred laughed from the stepper. "You let your boss think you like your job too much and they won't pay you. Nobody gets a paycheck for going to 'fun'," he said.

"Come on! It was for the little league team—it was the pancake day fundraiser I was pushing tickets for last week!" Luis laughed. "I haven't work so hard in years! It was a regular production line!"

"Oh! That's right! I bought the ticket but forgot to go! How was it?" asked Fred.

"I thought it was great," Tom said. "The lines went quick and you even had three kinds of pancakes. Look out IHOP!" Tom's kids, now older, had gone through the same league. While he never was the coach, he had flipped his share of pancakes and poured a lot of coffee during that time.

"It is a lot of fun once you get things up and running," said Tom. "It's like a small factory, everybody running around and making things! A lot of confusion at first, though. Yet after a while, everybody sort of falls into a system or routine. But we never had more than one type of pancake. Wow, from what I remember, you must have had total chaos back there!"

"You flipped flapjacks too?" asked Cheryl, who was sitting down to do leg extensions.

"Oh yeah!" Tom answered. "Pancake Day craziness has been going on for some time now. No organization, too much batter here, not enough there, cold sausage and coffee, long lines of people waiting to get in, and volunteers standing around up to their elbows in stuff, but not the right stuff. And waiting, a lot of waiting."

"Well, I had heard some horror stories from people who had done it before," said Luis. "But as the new guy, I didn't know what to expect. The more I heard about it in the planning committee meetings, the more I thought it would be fun to try and run it like a factory."

Luis took a pen hanging from a clipboard on the wall and started to draw on the back of a signup sheet for an upcoming racquetball tournament. "Here let me show you how we laid it out. It was really pretty simple," Luis said with pride. "I'm not sure how it was done before, but I heard they tried to wait till people came in to do anything, almost like, made to order or something. When that didn't work and lines were too long, people tried to guess what they would need and made up big batches of sausage and batter. Everybody had different ideas how much was enough, how long was too long; it got confused. We simplified it a lot," he said as he finished drawing and leaned over to show them his "floor plan" (see Figure 13.1).

They bought the batter in big 5-gallon pails from a supplier but still had to stir it up with a mixer before it could be used at a griddle. In the past, they kept a big pail at each griddle and dipped in pitchers with which they poured the batter onto the griddle. This year, they kept a pail or two at the mixer. They would fill up a pitcher at the mixer station and run it up to the griddle, where they made the pancakes as people came in. It was slow at first, but they started to keep the griddles full as things got more crowded. In the past, people waited as the pancakes cooked on the griddle. This year they put trays to the side of the griddle, the same trays they use to serve the sausage, to hold a few pancakes made up in advance when things were slow. The trays kept them warm, and having them waiting helped keep the lines moving when the place got busy. "When we filled a tray, we stopped cooking. They stayed

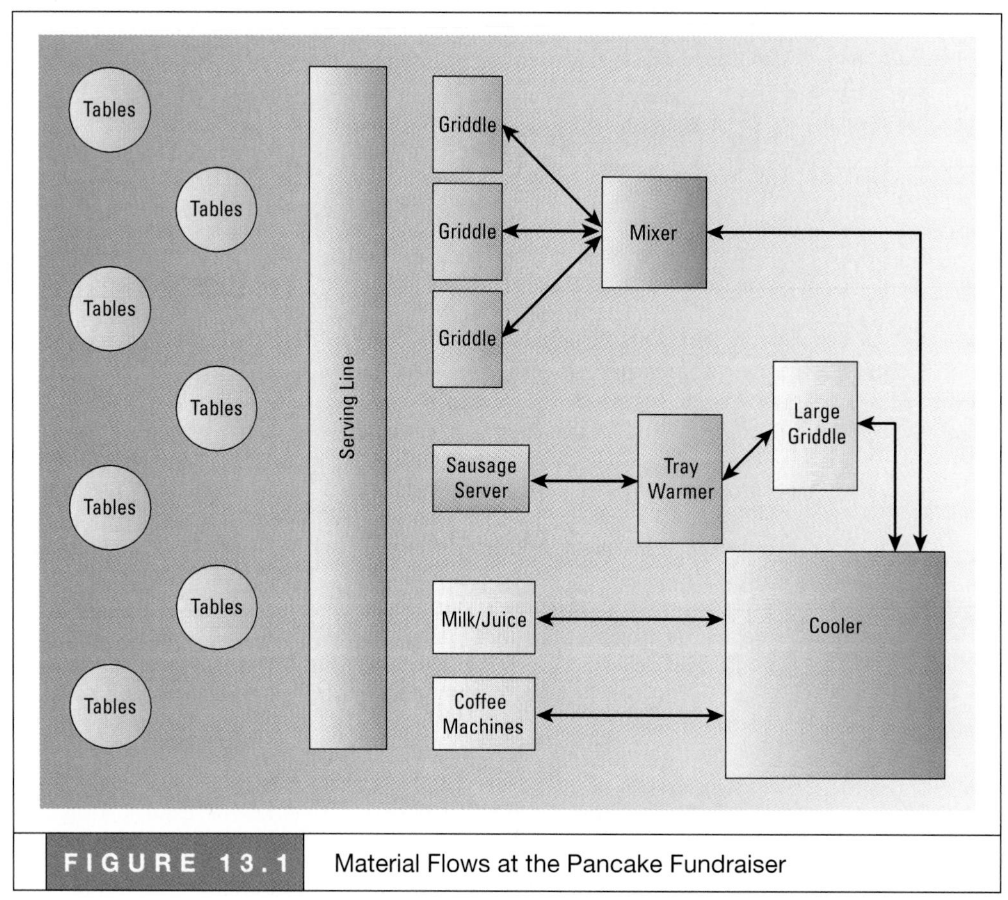

FIGURE 13.1 Material Flows at the Pancake Fundraiser

warmer and fresher." he said. As the pitchers used at the griddles were emptied, little leaguers would bring the empty ones back to the mixer, where they were refilled from the more central location and taken back to the parents and coaches who were running the griddles. "We just decided to stir some blueberries or chocolate chips directly into the pitchers with a big spoon, right there at the griddle. It was really just an afterthought that worked out well," said Luis.

"Didn't that mean a pitcher of each type batter at each griddle?" asked Fred.

"Yes," said Luis, "but that's a lot easier to handle than a 5-gallon pail at each griddle, let alone three pails. The best part was when it got really busy, we just got a few more pitchers out. As it slowed down, we would take a few away. It was really easy to keep everybody up and flippin', and we could keep the batter fresher."

"What happened when the mixer was out of stuff?" asked Tom.

"We had lots of kids to do the running back and forth," answered Luis. "When the mixer emptied a pail, we'd send a kid back to the cooler with the empty one. They would bring a full one back."They generally had one pail at the mixer already stirred up that they used to fill pitchers and one more on the mixer being stirred. As things got busy, they put a third and fourth pail into the system. That way, one could be used to refill the pitchers, a second on the mixer being stirred, a third pail could be opened and ready to go on the mixer, and finally a fourth pail would be "in transit" back to the cooler. Near the end, things slowed down and they could scale it back to where they had one pail refilling the pitchers and when it was empty, what was in the pitchers could hold them till the empty one could get to the cooler and the replacement was brought back to the mixer and stirred up.

Talk shifted to sausages. He said that they buy them frozen from a distributor down the street from the school. Since they didn't have access to a freezer in the school where the breakfast was held, they made a couple trips down to the distributor during the day and put it in the cooler until it needed to be cooked. The sausage was cooked on a large grill. Each batch of sausage was cooked all at once, as the grill was too expensive to keep running all day—not to mention how hot it got in the kitchen when it was turned on. They stored the cooked sausage in a tray warmer rack that held about 25 trays. When a tray was emptied on the serving line, the empty one was taken back to the rack and a full one taken back to the serving line. "We got smart this year," Luis said. "When we went to the supplier to get the sausage, we brought back only what would fit in the tray warmer and no more!" said Luis.

"Plus a little for what the cooks eat along the way?" asked Cheryl with a smile.

"Uh huh!" replied Luis with a grin. "I think they factor in a little 'shrinkage' along the way!" They all groaned. "So, we sent somebody up the street when we got down to the last couple trays. It didn't take long to be back, just a few minutes. Popped it on the grill and got it in the warmer in about 15 minutes, half hour tops if you count the time back and forth from the distributor. If things slowed down while we were going to get more, we'd put it in the cooler for a few minutes." He said it didn't hurt for it to thaw as long as they ended up cooking it. "But we didn't want to have much left over at the end," Luis added.

"Did you do drinks the same way as we used to?" asked Tom.

"Yes, milk and juice were all donated in gallon jugs. We just kept them in the cooler till they were needed," Luis answered. He said they used the empty jugs as a signal here as well. "We put the recycling container near the cooler," he said. "That way, when we took the empties back to throw them away, we brought up the same number of full ones. When things slowed down, though, we didn't keep as many jugs up front."

"It all sounds like you had a good handle on it—better, in fact, than we probably did," said Tom. "But what about the coffee? That was always a pain. When that big 80-cup percolator was empty, it seemed to take forever to brew another pot. The lines got real long and everybody got sick of waiting."

"It's funny you should ask," Luis responded. "That big ol' monster was DOA this year. I saw them taking it out of a box, and it was huge but it wouldn't turn on. Something must have happened since last year, but it was really old looking." He said the committee wanted to get another one just like it but another parent, who worked for Fred's company as it turned out, suggested maybe two to three smaller ones would be better. "They said that way somebody could be changing one while the other percolates and a third is being used. That way, fewer people wait for coffee and it is fresher," Luis added.

"Well your whole system sounds like a 'just-in-time' system to me," said Fred, "just like making pagers."

"Yeah, but you don't smell like maple syrup till the fourth of July when you make pagers all day!" laughed Luis.

"Baseball, pancakes, and the fourth of July," laughed Tom. "Has a nice ring to it!"

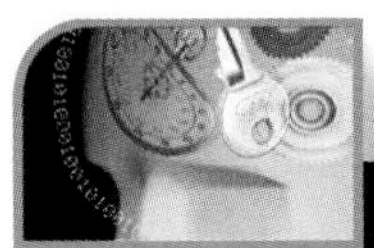

objectives

Take a moment to familiarize yourself with the key objectives of this chapter.

gearing up

Before you begin reading this chapter, try a short warm-up activity.

Introduction

Chapters 11 and 12 began a discussion of how planning, scheduling, and controlling the operation of the value-adding system becomes the interface between the value-adding system and the customer. This chapter continues that discussion on a more detailed level. Specifically, it covers detailed planning and control in just-in-time operational systems. In this chapter, we are particularly concerned with how a JIT company can translate the plans in the master schedule into a detailed operational plan, to the point where every employee knows exactly what to do with which resources at any point in time. In other words, we are concerned with the planning through which commitments to customers are converted into detailed plans for action.

The system a company uses to make detailed planning and control decisions, be it JIT or any other system, has implications for the conduct of work in every functional area of the firm. Since many companies have recently adopted JIT systems, it is easy to describe the systems' implications for other functional areas in terms of the changes that occurred when JIT was adopted. This chapter highlights many of these changes in its attempt to bridge the white spaces from operations management to the other functions.

This chapter's content coverage of JIT begins with an overview that includes a description of the systems' historic development at the Toyota Motor Corporation. The overview also describes JIT's positive impact on business performance and competitiveness with an example from Harley-Davidson motorcycle company and summarizes the general approach to detailed material planning and capacity decisions.

JIT systems rely on a level scheduling approach. Level scheduling ensures that inventory levels remain stable, value is added close to the time that customers purchase value, and the level of managerial effort required to coordinate system activities is quite low.

Material planning in a JIT system is quite simple because level scheduling is used. If the schedule is the same for any hour of the week (or month), then the materials required to execute the schedule are also the same for any hour or the week or month. Essentially, then, the level master schedule creates a rate at which components and other material supplies are consumed. Material planning simply involves ensuring that supplies of these items are replenished at the rate at which they are consumed.

Kanban systems are one way that JIT systems tell workers what to do to replenish materials that have been used. By placing cards or other visual cues in work centers to signal the need for replenishment of materials, it takes very little effort for managers to control inventories and regularly provide detailed work assignments to employees.

JIT systems were developed in a manufacturing environment, have been most commonly implemented by manufacturers, and have had the greatest impact in manufacturing operations. This does not, however, suggest that JIT is not used in services or that elements of the JIT philosophy are not useful in service operations. This chapter describes a number of JIT practices that have been beneficial in service-intensive businesses.

Integrating Operations Management with Other Functions

As large numbers of companies have adopted JIT, the way business is conducted has changed significantly, not just in operations and purchasing, but in all functions. For example, *Business Week* (April 4, 1994) suggested that the adoption of JIT practices in the 1980s "may help explain why the recession of 1990–91 was fairly mild and why the economy was so slow getting back up to speed. In the long run, the trend to lean inventories should act as a kind of wonder drug for the business cycle, boosting the lows and tempering the highs." In the past, when the economy was strong and sales were high, manufacturers had stockpiled inventory in anticipation of even higher demand. When the economy slowed, though, workers had to be laid off, and they weren't rehired until all the old inventory had been consumed. Such managerial decision making amplified the impact of the natural economic cycle of growth and contraction.

Marketing practices changed, too, as a result of JIT. A regional manager of The Pillsbury Company indicated that prior to the company's adoption of JIT, she had worked with the sales force to get "good" demand forecasts for products several weeks into the future. The information was generally gathered from managers or buyers at the grocery stores. If the forecast was a little high, warehouse space was adequate to store the extra items produced. Clearly that was better than experiencing shortages. Consequently, managers and salespeople had an incentive to pad their forecasts.

When the company adopted JIT, the sales force toured the production facility to gain confidence in the new approach to planning and control, which was said to be capable of responding to customers' requirements within a day. They saw the refrigerated warehouse that would no longer be needed under the new system. Because store managers no longer needed to estimate demand weeks into the future, sales representatives stopped padding their forecasts. Instead, just two days prior to delivery they submitted their actual orders.

Store managers later began to wonder why the special pricing deals and store displays they had used to attract customers had disappeared. Pillsbury's sales manager had to explain that periodically lowering the price also lowered the margin on the product and therefore was not good business practice. Furthermore, the whole reason for the price "blow-outs" had been the need to liquidate warehouse inventories accumulated as the result of incorrect forecasts or large lot production. Clearly, for Pillsbury and many other companies, the movement to a JIT planning and control system had a significant impact on marketing and customer relations.

The movement to JIT has had significant impact on the finance and accounting functions as well. During the 1980s, warehouse space requirements were significantly reduced by the adoption of JIT. Prior to that time, mortgages backed by warehouse space had been a major component of virtually every private bond fund. Indeed, fund managers associated that sector of the mortgage market with high performance and low risk. With the advent of JIT, the mortgages on those warehouses suddenly became high-risk investments. Today, the declining use of inventory and the ever-present possibility of further reductions in inventory have discouraged many financial managers from investing in warehouse space.

As far as accounting is concerned, the process of making payments for purchases and receiving payment for the delivery of product-service bundles has begun to change. Even the question of who owns the inventory has become debatable. For example, many suppliers own and maintain stocks of materials in their customers' plants. In some cases, materials are purchased when the company that assembles the product-service bundle uses the material. In other cases, the supplier owns the material until the product-service bundle is actually sold. As a result, paperwork is minimized; the supplier is paid based only on the products that have been sold.

For example, a company that assembles hospital beds knows that if it has sold 100 beds, it has used 100 mattresses. If inventory is low and demand is strong, why not pay suppliers on the basis of deliveries to customers? Suppliers who might be tempted to push overproduced stock onto the customer will not be paid until that stock is actually sold. If inventory is kept too lean and stockouts occur, then the supplier's revenues suffer.

Clearly, these changes in supplier and customer relationships have interesting implications for accountants. If the inventory is under some other company's roof, and formal purchase orders and other contractual paperwork are de-emphasized, when and how should audits be performed? What are the tax, security, and insurance implications of such arrangements? How often should inventory counts be taken?

Finally, the human resources function is handled very differently in JIT companies. In unionized environments, employees can take concerted actions, such as strikes, slowdowns, and protests, which disrupt the value-adding system. Even in nonunionized environments, without inventory buffers and extra capacity, disgruntled individuals and small groups of employees can create serious problems. Teamwork, improvement, coordination, and cooperation all require a participative workforce. Consequently, distinctions between white-collar and blue-collar jobs, excessive reliance on job classification schemes, and traditional piece rate incentives are out of place in a JIT company.

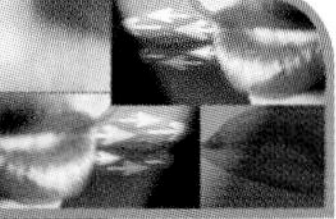

> active poll

What do you think? Voice your opinion and find out what others have to say.

Chapter Topics / Functional Areas of Business	Finance	Accounting	Human Resources	Marketing	Engineering	Management Information Systems
Integrating Operations Management with Other Functions	●	●	●	●	●	●
Overview of JIT Systems	●	●	●	●	●	●
Scheduling and Capacity Management in JIT Systems			●	●		
Material Planning		●				●
Kanban Systems						●
JIT in Services	●	●	●			●

FIGURE 13.2 Integrating Operations Management with Other Functions

Figure 13.2 highlights some of the major linkages between the content of this chapter and other functional areas in business. Obviously, this section of the chapter is directly linked to all of the functional areas of business. So, too, the next section of the chapter that provides an overview of the JIT system has significant implications for each function. Each area of a firm is influenced by changes to the planning and control system. As such, it is important for professionals in each functional area of a company that uses JIT to have a good understanding of the general characteristics of their company's planning and control system. The figure suggests that the importance of linkages between the remaining sections of the chapter will vary for the various functional areas. The section on level scheduling and capacity issues is particularly relevant to marketing and human resources professionals because of its obvious implications for staffing, compensation, and sales, promotion, and customer service decisions. The section on material planning is of particular relevance to the accounting and management information systems functions because of the role these areas play in gathering and providing the information that supports the decisions described. Finally, the section dealing with JIT in services is of particular relevance to functional areas such as finance and accounting, which provide service value and are often core strengths in professional service firms.

Overview of JIT Systems

It's been said that as a young man, Eiji Toyoda (heir to the Toyoda industrial establishment) was sent to learn the management practices of Henry Ford. Yet one of his most inspiring lessons came from a grocery store. Mr. Toyoda was amazed that despite the large variety of items the store carried, the shelves were always completely restocked when he returned the following day. He realized that the store handled more parts than are required to build an automobile and wondered why his family's production facilities always suffered from parts shortages and excesses. His observation, along with the effectiveness with which Ford had synchronized the manufacture of parts and the assembly of cars, provided the seed bank from which the just-in-time system would one day be developed.

Following World War II, executives at the Toyota Motor Company became particularly interested in narrowing the gap between their firm's capabilities and those of the Western automotive industry. They didn't have a cash hoard to invest and their facilities weren't fancy or new, so they focused on reducing costs, eliminating waste, and improving productivity. Over many years of trial and error, under the direction of Taiichi Ohno, Shigeo Shingo, and other visionary leaders, Toyota tested a number of unique approaches which together came to be known as the Toyota Production System. After the oil crisis of 1973, which sparked a crisis of survival in many Japanese firms, the Toyota Production System spread to other industries. In the 1980s, during similar crises resulting from international competition, companies all over the world began to use the system, now called the *just in time (JIT)* system. The JIT system is a way of planning operations that reduces variability of demand, enhances responsiveness of operational resources, and attempts to conduct value-adding operations as close as possible to the time that value is consumed.

Obviously, detailed plans that specify what workers must do must also provide for the needed materials and equipment capacity to get the job done. Figure 13.3 shows the relationships among the master schedule, material decisions, and capacity decisions. The portion of the figure in the upper left shows the broader scheme of operations planning and control systems discussed in Chapter 12. The main part of this figure shows the short-term planning and control tasks and describes their characteristics in a JIT environment. This chapter, then, deals primarily with dependent demand inventory issues. The decisions are not based directly on forecasts, which are probabilistic estimates of demand. Rather, since the master schedule has been set, the decisions are based on an agreed-upon schedule. As the figure indicates, JIT systems rely on a level approach to master scheduling. This is important because it makes the more detailed planning decisions much simpler. If the master schedule is level, material and capacity requirements are also stable and easily calculated. Furthermore, the most detailed decisions about who should do what, and when, can be made without a great deal of management supervision because people will be doing standardized work in a repetitive way.

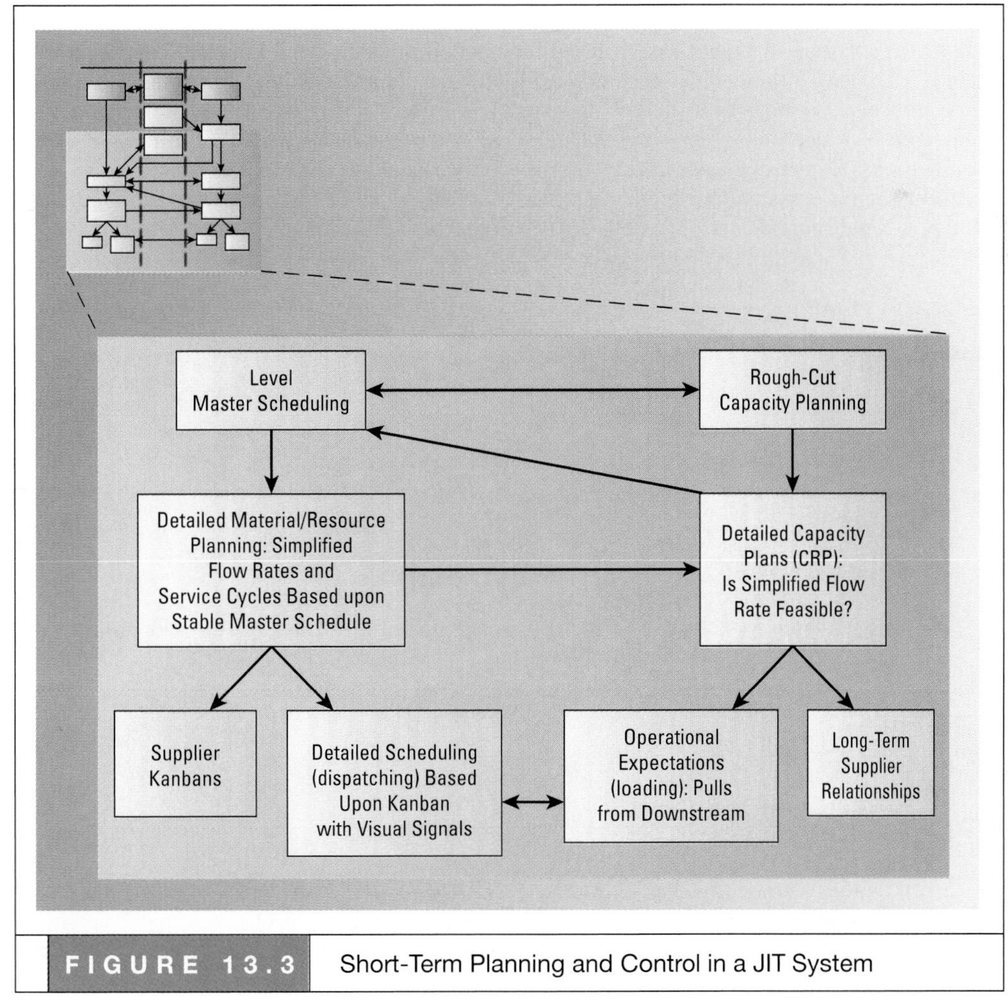

FIGURE 13.3 Short-Term Planning and Control in a JIT System

THE ENORMOUS IMPACT OF JIT

The improvements that resulted from the change to JIT were impressive. Harley-Davidson, which called its JIT system *material-as-needed* (MAN), claimed that over the first few years of its use, the system reduced inventory by 70%, scrap by 50%, warranty claims by 70%, and rework by 90%. As a result, productivity increased by 40%, and the company regained 15% of the American motorcycle market and survived the most significant crisis in its 80-year history. This level of improvement is typical of companies that adopt JIT. In fact, according to a leading OM consultant, in the 1980s companies that adopted JIT reported three-to-five- year improvements as follows:

- manufacturing cycle time reductions of 80%–90%
- inventory reductions of raw materials of 35%–70%, work-in-process reductions of 70%–90%, and finished goods reductions of 60%–90%
- labor cost reductions of 10%–50% of direct labor category and 20%–60% of indirect labor
- space requirement reductions of 40%–80%
- quality cost reductions of 25%–60%
- material costs reductions of 5%–25%

THE APPLICABILITY OF JIT

Despite the benefits of JIT, it is not an appropriate planning and control system for all companies and business environments. Figure 13.4 summarizes the system characteristics for which use of a JIT planning and control system would make sense. If these characteristics aren't present, some different planning and control system (discussed in a later chapter) might be a more logical choice. Typically, JIT systems are a good fit when demand is reasonably stable and high-volume repetitive value-adding systems can be used to make standardized product-service bundles. Effective use of JIT also requires the cooperation and coordination of employees and suppliers.

The JIT system is most effective in settings like Toyota's, where a repetitive value-adding system is in use and product variety is limited. These qualities allow for a balanced capacity throughout the value-adding system. If capacity is balanced throughout the system and product variety is limited, there is little need for day-to-day and moment-to-moment adjustments to the system. The planning and control decision boils down to how many units the system will create in a given period, not how many units of what. Simply removing the "of what" makes the planning and control task more like turning a knob to control the rate of flow from a garden hose.

Interestingly, very complex product-service bundles are frequently created using JIT systems. Most of us would consider an automobile a complex assembly. Touring an automobile assembly plant,

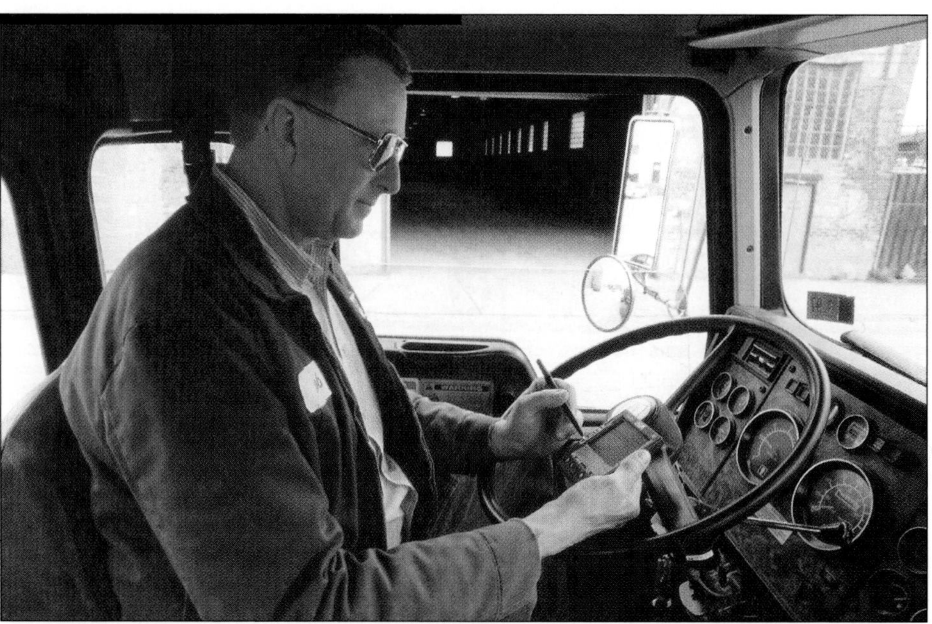

Widespread adoption of JIT has created a boom for the trucking industry. Logistics providers now have the more complex task of handling more frequent and smaller shipments. Advances in communications technologies provide truckers with real-time information and have helped trucking companies to have more flexible routing patterns and providing better service than would have otherwise been possible.

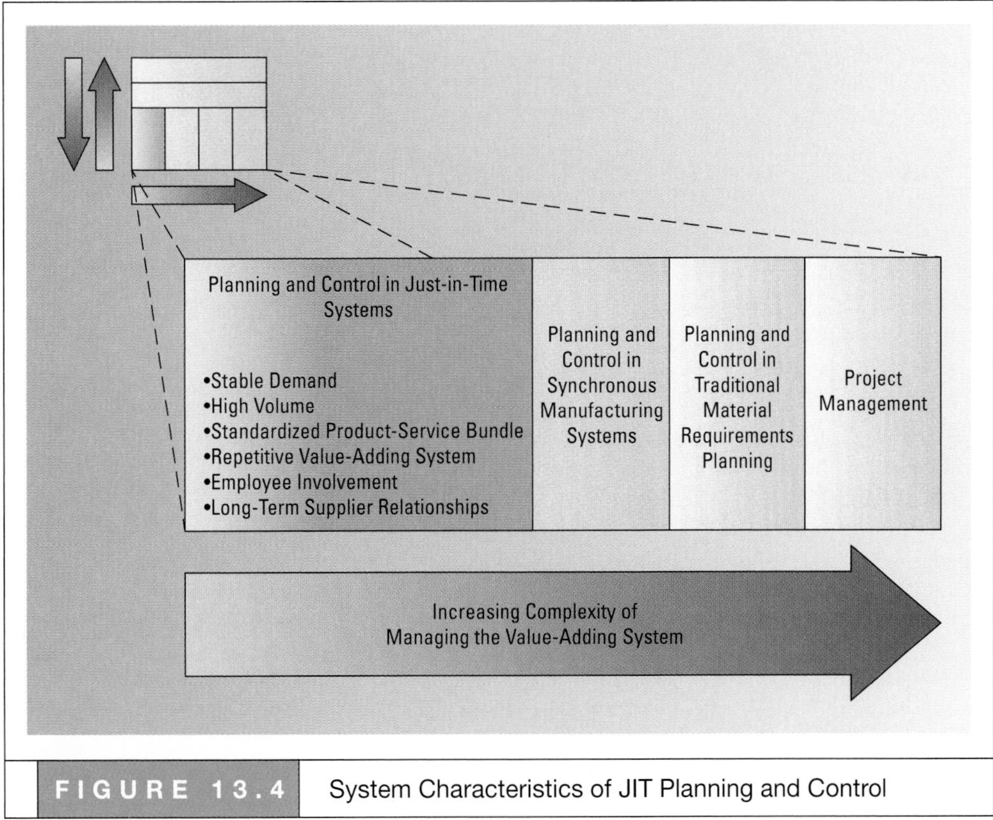

FIGURE 13.4 System Characteristics of JIT Planning and Control

we'd probably say that the value-adding system was complex as well. Yet, we've just described JIT as a system that works well in *simple,* not complex, environments. To understand this seeming paradox, we must distinguish between complexity in the product-service bundle, complexity in the value-adding system, and complexity in planning, scheduling, and controlling the operation of the value-adding system. When you make only one model of a vehicle, with a very limited set of options, the system you create should be very good at making that model. In turn, many of the decisions to be made can be built into the repetitive system. Consequently, the planning and control environment becomes simple.

Complex planning and control environments are those in which there is significant uncertainty regarding demand and in which a great deal of product variety is accommodated with general-purpose equipment. JIT is not well suited to such environments. Lots of customers, lots of suppliers, lots of differently designed (or heterogeneous) products, or lots of options or varying features can greatly complicate the operation of the value-adding system. Many of the decisions that are hardwired into simpler systems must be dealt with on a case-by-case basis. As the complexity of planning, scheduling, and controlling the system increases, dealing with those decisions deterministically becomes more difficult, and managers may need to take a more probabilistic approach. (The next two chapters will deal more with those types of systems.) Figure 13.5 graphically illustrates the differences between operating a simple and a complex value-adding system.

Continuous improvement and employee involvement are core aspects of the JIT system: Every worker is responsible for making sure that things are working right and finding ways to make things work better.

Suppliers of JIT companies are often required to provide shipments on one-, two- or three-hour cycles with materials loaded so that they come off the truck in the order in which they will be used. As a result, it is very helpful if the supplier can operate its processes in sync with those of customers. **Takt time** is the rate at which material is used by the customer's value-adding system. Suppliers will have much greater success in satisfying a JIT customer if their systems also operate at that rate. Since manufacturing cells can be made to operate in takt time, a cellular manufacturing arrangement is an ideal characteristic of JIT suppliers.

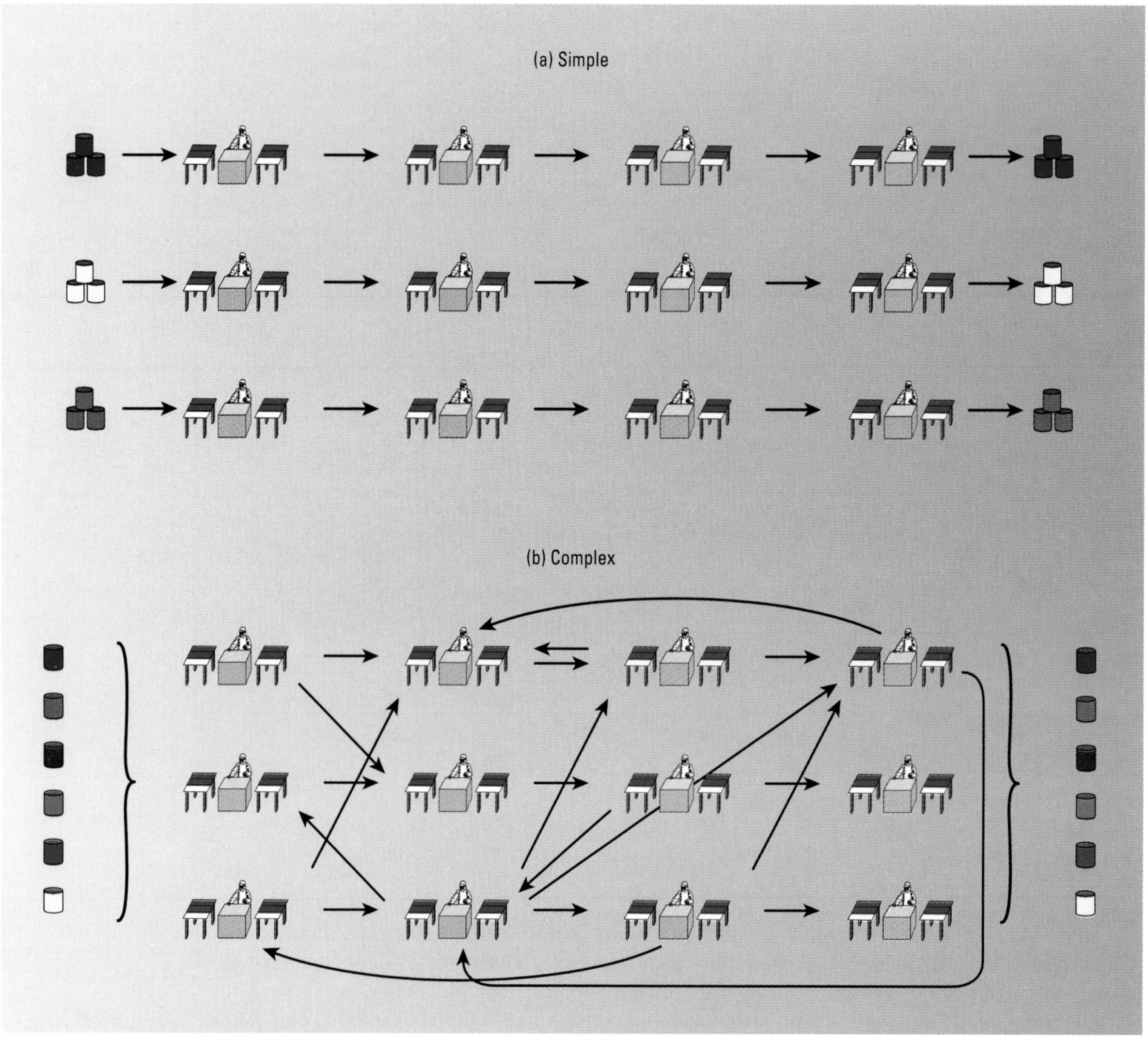

(a) Simple

(b) Complex

FIGURE 13.5 Simple Versus Complex Value-Adding Systems

active exercise <

Take a moment to apply what you've learned.

active concept check <

Now let's take a moment to test your knowledge of the concepts you have studied in this section.

Scheduling and Capacity Management in JIT Systems

This section of the chapter discusses the JIT approach to master scheduling, capacity decisions, inventory decisions, and business relationships with suppliers and customers. In particular, JIT planning and control relies on a level master schedule, prefers excess capacity to excess inventory, and works with suppliers and customers to reduce complexity and uncertainty while simultaneously improving the system's responsiveness to customer requirements.

LEVEL SCHEDULING

JIT planning and control relies on a **level master schedule,** or one in which the same mix of product-service bundles is created repeatedly over the period for which the master schedule has been frozen. For example, if in a given week the United States Mint had only one printing press and had to print 25 million one-dollar bills, 10 million five-dollar bills, 5 million 10-dollar bills, and 1 million 20-dollar bills, the most level schedule they could envision would be to print the following sequence of bills a million times:

1-1-5-1-1-5-1-10-1-1-5-1-1-5-1-10-1-1-5-1-1-
5-1-10-20-1-1-5-1-1-5-1-10-1-1-5-1-1-5-1-10

If this were the sequence in which the money was printed, even if the bill a customer needed was not available from existing stock, it would be printed within one millionth of a week. That places the creation of value and its consumption very close to one another. You could even say that the money is printed just in time. (Now, of course the mint *doesn't* print bills this way, but the idea is interesting; see Discussion Question number 1 at the end of this chapter.)

The independent demand inventory models that were presented in the last chapter based the determination of order quantities on the idea that overall costs are minimized when ordering and holding costs are balanced. The economics presented in Chapter 12 are just as valid for JIT systems as for any other type of system. Note that the schedule for the mint just presented would mean frequently changing over from printing one-dollar bills to five-dollar bills and so forth. In fact, that approach to scheduling would require 31 million setups each week. At the other extreme, if the whole week's demand for each demarcation (or printed piece of currency) were printed before moving on to another demarcation, only four setups per week would be required. However, a holding cost would be incurred since at least a week's supply would need to be on hand whenever the printing of a given demarcation had been completed. (The Federal Reserve Bank wouldn't want to run out of one-dollar bills because of supply problems at the United States Mint.)

JIT PERSPECTIVES ON INVENTORY

Figure 13.6 presents the JIT view of inventory. Problems in a value-adding system are illustrated as rocks at the bottom of the lake. Inventory is the water. If we have enough inventory just in case we

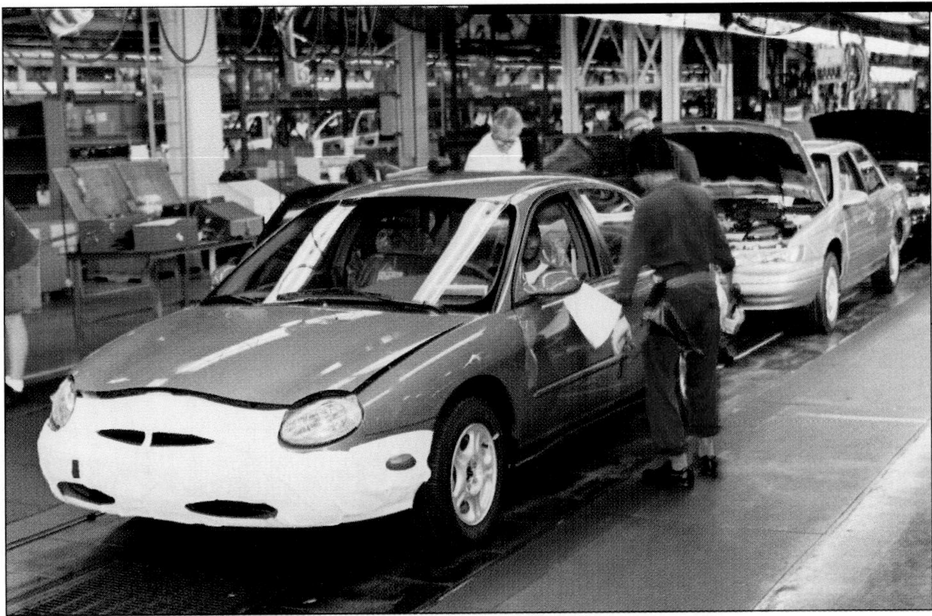

Level scheduling at this automobile plant means that cars aren't assembled in identical batches. Suppliers, therefore, must provide the needed parts in small quantities at fixed intervals, rather than providing large batches all at once.

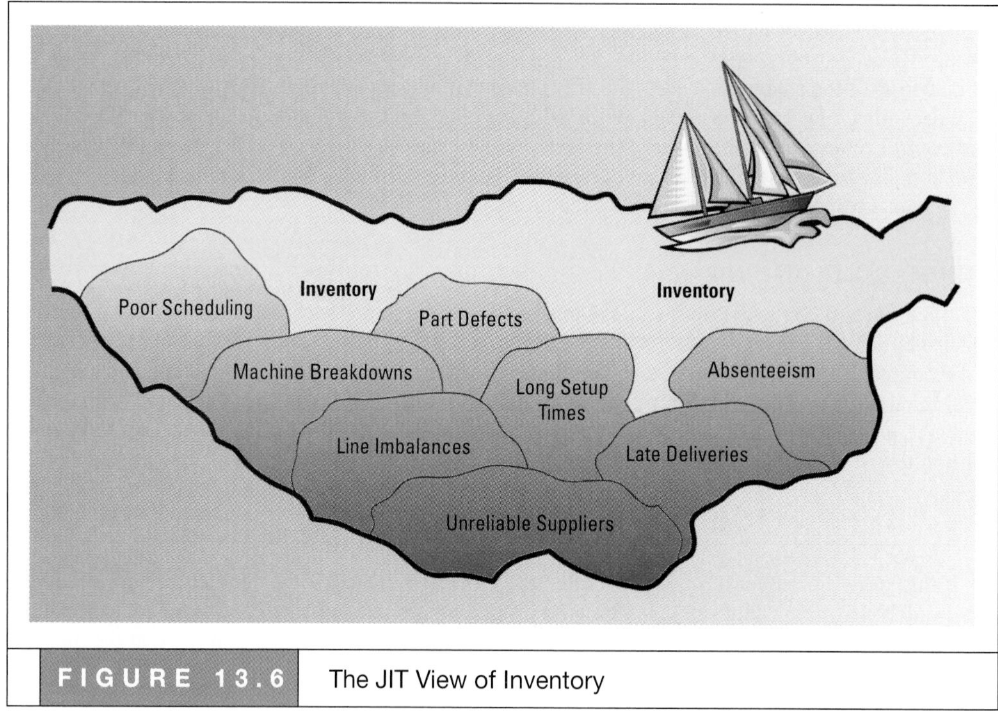

FIGURE 13.6 The JIT View of Inventory

might hit a rock, we can sail through just about any system—despite all the problems that might exist just below the surface. In fact, the inventory will not only keep us from noticing the problems, it will keep us from solving the problems. If a schedule doesn't synchronize what we're doing with customer demand, then *just-in-case inventory* can save the day. If we receive a shipment of bad parts, then a stash of *just-in-case* inventory can save the day. If a machine breaks down, a worker is absent, a supplier fails to come through, a truck gets delayed in transit, a process is idle for a long time, or a capacity imbalance develops, just-in-case inventory can save the day. If, on the other hand, we don't have just-in-case inventory, we expose the problems in our value-adding system and develop a strong incentive to eliminate them. The problems listed in this figure are examples of common ways in which a firm could improve its system. Without inventory to hide these problems, firms experience the problems, but they also gain an understanding of the weaknesses of their system. Nobody likes to hit a rock; managers start running around with worried looks on their faces. But the point is to hit any given rock only once: find it, fix it. Thus, JIT is a philosophy that not only helps managers to find their problems but motivates them to find remedies. With inventory to cover up the problems, managers may never even notice, much less address them.

Figure 13.7 ties problem covering, or just-in-case inventories, to a model first introduced in Chapter 12 (see Figure 12.15). There we saw that safety stock is often used to provide a margin of safety against disruptions in the supply of independent demand inventory items. There are multiple reasons why this margin of safety is needed in any environment. Among these are:

- *Supply uncertainty.* Keeping some inventory just in case a shipment from a supplier is late or full of bad parts. In order to reduce the need for this aspect of the margin of safety, a company needs to be sure that their suppliers have adequate capacity, processes capable of delivering the required quality, input into planning decisions (whether monthly, weekly, or daily), availability from their suppliers, positive employee relations, and so on.
- *Operational complexity/uncertainty.* This is inventory in the system due to long setup or production lead-times. In order to reduce the need for this part of the safety margin, companies should seek ways to simplify product and process designs through the use of group technology; reduce lot sizes; and gain a better understanding of their customers' demand patterns.
- *Infrastructural inertia.* This portion of the safety margin results from policies such as piece rate pay systems, layoff policies, idle labor policies, equipment justification issues, volume purchase discounts, communication policies, and incentive systems that emphasize full utilization of resources. It's hard to overcome the "We do it that way because we've always done it that way" mindset. Nevertheless, companies should recognize the impact that such policies have on their inventory levels. It takes real courage and leadership for a manager to change policies like these and overcome inertia.

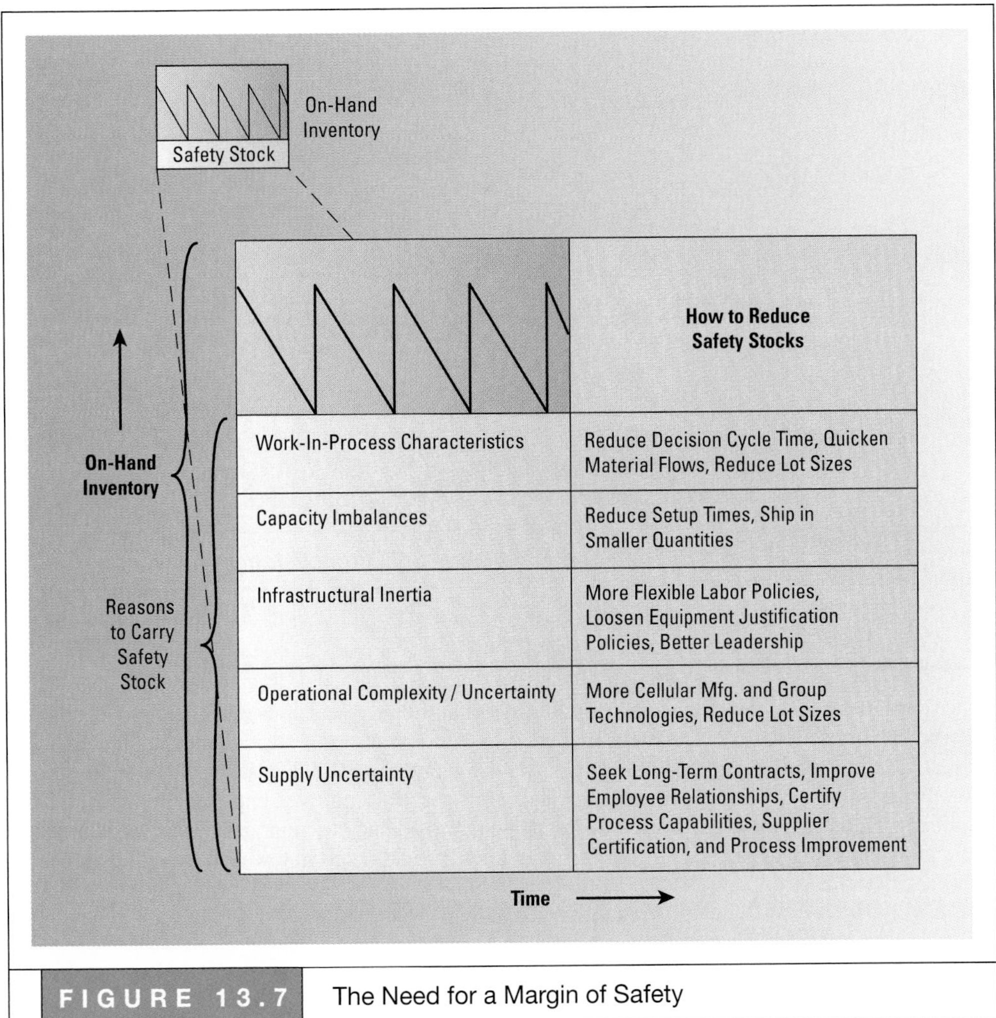

On-Hand
Inventory
Safety Stock
On-Hand
Inventory
Reasons
to Carry
Safety
Stock
How to Reduce
Safety Stocks
Work-In-Process Characteristics
Reduce Decision Cycle Time, Quicken Material Flows, Reduce Lot Sizes
Capacity Imbalances
Reduce Setup Times, Ship in Smaller Quantities
Infrastructural Inertia
More Flexible Labor Policies, Loosen Equipment Justification Policies, Better Leadership
Operational Complexity / Uncertainty
More Cellular Mfg. and Group Technologies, Reduce Lot Sizes
Supply Uncertainty
Seek Long-Term Contracts, Improve Employee Relationships, Certify Process Capabilities, Supplier Certification, and Process Improvement
Time

FIGURE 13.7 The Need for a Margin of Safety

- *Capacity imbalances.* Most carpet stores don't have room for full truckloads, let alone entire production runs of every color they sell. Full truckload shipment preferences and mismatches between the capacity of suppliers and customers can lead to artificially inflated production lot-sizes and transfer lot-sizes. That in turn can lead to redistribution costs, warehousing, and extra handling and rehandling.
- *Work-in-process (WIP) characteristics.* The amount of WIP in the system reflects a number of factors, including the cycle time for decisions and paperwork, labor and material flow reporting, lot sizes, quality levels, packaging requirements, and so on. As noted earlier in the chapter, the JIT system has been extremely effective in reducing the levels of WIP inventory.

Inventories such as safety stock buffers are built in throughout the value-adding systems of many industries. As soon as inventory is added at one point in the system, an element of supply uncertainty or operational complexity is created, to which other parts of the value-adding system respond by adding inventory. The JIT system emphasizes improving and simplifying the value-adding system so that inventory can begin to be removed from the system and the rest of the supply chain. When inventory is removed, thus eliminating an element of supply uncertainty or operational complexity, other parts of the value-adding system can respond by eliminating their inventory. Figure 13.8 illustrates this point.

> active exercise

Take a moment to apply what you've learned.

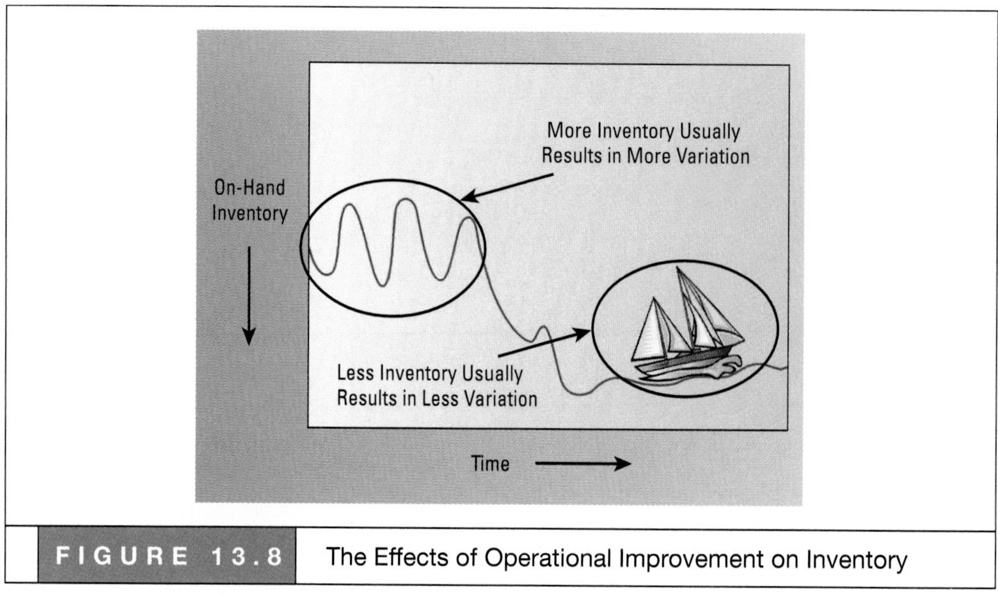

FIGURE 13.8 The Effects of Operational Improvement on Inventory

SUPPLY CHAIN AND E-COMMERCE CONSIDERATIONS IN JIT

Since decisions at one point in the value-adding system influence decisions elsewhere, it is worth considering the impact on customers and suppliers of a company's use of JIT planning and control. This impact is summarized in Figure 13.9. Companies that choose to use JIT systems will attempt to work with their suppliers to effect both structural and infrastructural improvements. On the structural side, suppliers will be encouraged to improve their responsiveness and efficiency via group technology and cellular manufacturing. Reduced inventory at suppliers should result in lower space requirements and

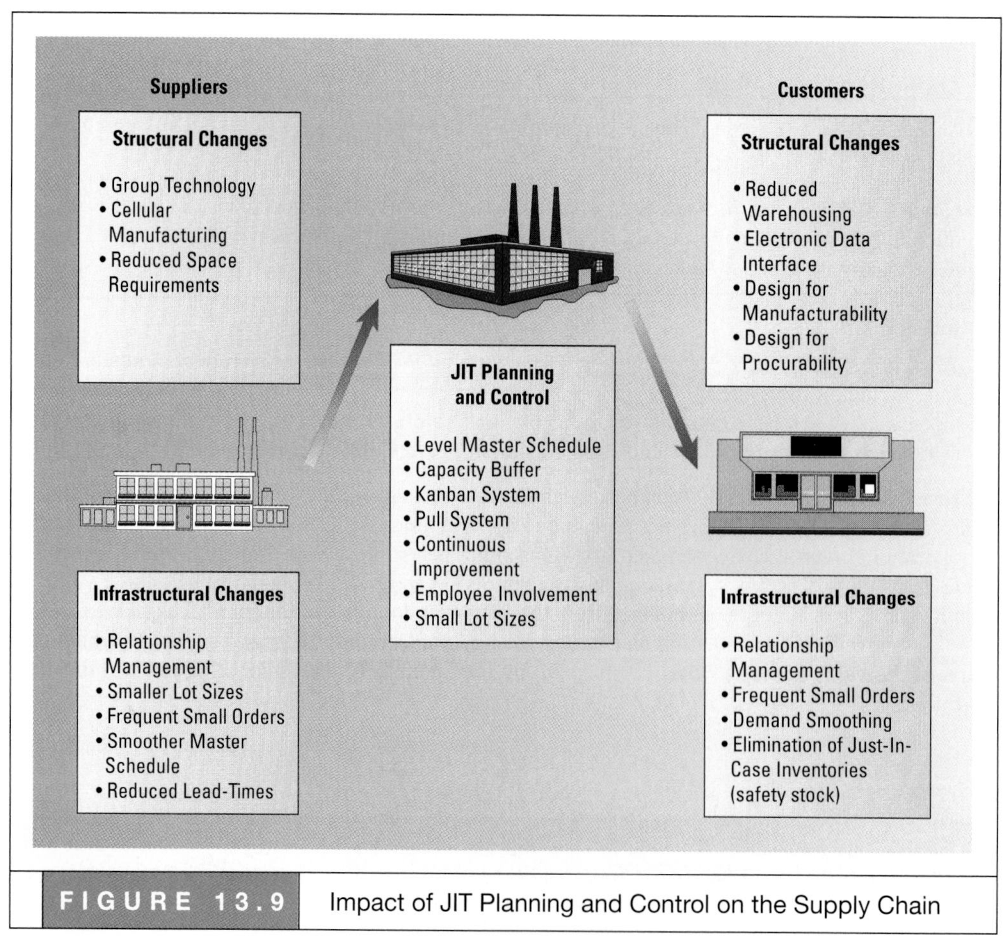

FIGURE 13.9 Impact of JIT Planning and Control on the Supply Chain

therefore lower fixed costs. On the infrastructural side, the emphasis will be placed on maintaining a relationship that is beneficial to both parties. Communication lines need to remain open at all times: Information regarding costs, quality, and process capability needs to be shared without reservation. Along with relationship management, the suppliers of JIT companies will need to be capable of providing product-service bundles in small quantities with frequent deliveries. They will have smoother master schedules and will need to provide short lead-times. When improvements are made, all parties in the supply chain, as well as the customer, should share the benefit of these improvements through higher profit margins and lower costs.

Relationship management is also critical to customers of JIT users. From an infrastructural perspective, they will be expected to place frequent small orders, eliminate their just-in-case inventories, and work with their customers to establish smoother demand patterns. From a structural standpoint, they will be encouraged to design their product-service bundles for manufacturability and procurement, establish electronic data interchange (EDI) systems to remove demand uncertainty, and reduce their inventories of purchased materials.

In reality, it is quite difficult to use JIT at only one stage in the creation of value. Variability and complexity travel through a supply chain much like waves in a slinky hanging vertically from your hand. Let it hang there until it stops bouncing, then wiggle your hand just a little. What happens? The effect ripples through the entire length. In the same way, if only one company in a supply chain introduces variability or complexity, even just a bit, the slight change creates a big bounce at the bottom of the supply chain. Fortunately, just the opposite can happen, too. That is, smoothing the schedule for independent demand product-service bundles can lead to significantly smoother schedules in the work centers or supplier companies that provide materials for that bundle. This slinky illustration describes what we first introduced in Chapter 2 as the bullwhip effect.

Figure 13.10 illustrates the bullwhip effect. As demand becomes more variable, as is the case for companies at the top of the supply chain in Figure 13.10, more and more capacity is needed to maintain a particular service level. This increase in capacity has a significant cost in efficiency, which in turn leads companies to produce larger (more efficient) quantities. The change in strategy introduces uncertainty elsewhere in the supply chain, sending the wave back through the slinky in the other direction.

To summarize, JIT planning and control works best with a level master schedule that is well within the range of feasibility, given the capacity of the supply chain. It requires working with suppliers and customers to reduce complexity and uncertainty, while simultaneously improving the system's ability to support level scheduling and rapid response.

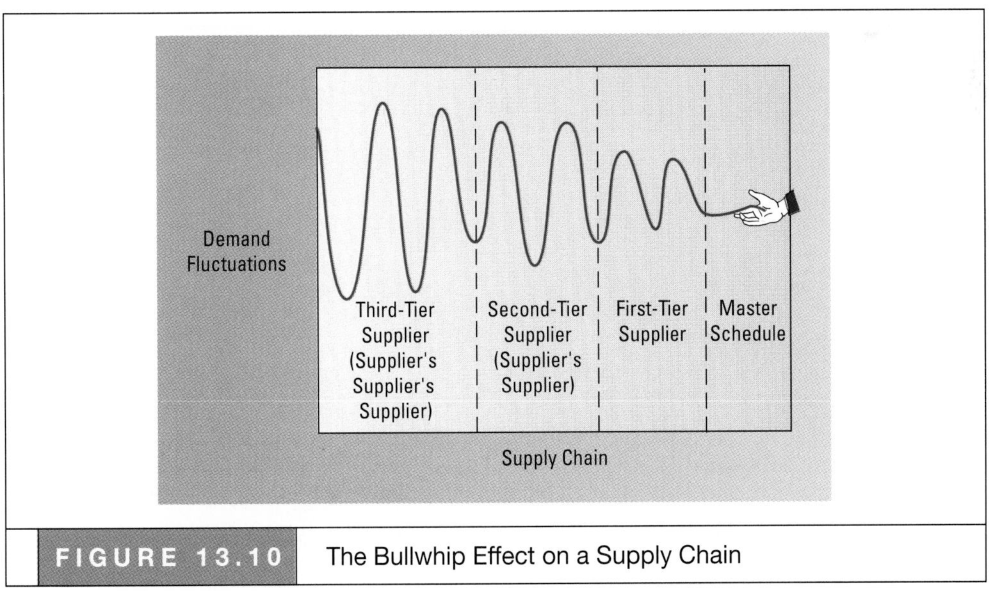

FIGURE 13.10 The Bullwhip Effect on a Supply Chain

> active concept check

Now let's take a moment to test your knowledge of the concepts you have studied in this section.

> Material Planning

To the extent possible, JIT planning and control systems rely on a level master schedule. As a result, daily (or even hourly) material requirements may be identical throughout the week. In that case, detailed material planning means establishing a daily (or hourly) *flow rate* for dependent demand aspects of the product-service bundle. For example, you might find suppliers delivering identical shipments on a two-hour cycle. With frequent shipments, lot sizes need not be large and setups must not take long.

Naturally, service aspects of the value-adding system, such as the transportation of parts, also have to operate on that same cycle. If the capacity of the value-adding system is adequate to sustain the material flow rate and service cycle times established by the leveled master schedule, then facilities can be loaded and scheduled using a system of built-in signals, such as empty storage bins, to "pull" replenishments of materials from one work center to another. This approach is much like Luis's pancake day system of using empty pitchers to signal that more batter is needed at the griddle. (We will discuss pull scheduling in detail in the next section, kanban systems.) By relying on long-term supplier contracts and trustful relationships, managers can guarantee adequate capacity and replenishment of materials from outside as well as inside suppliers and vendors.

LOT SIZES AND SETUP TIME

Based on a level master schedule, JIT requires the preparation of the various aspects of the product-service bundle as needed. For suppliers, whether in-house or external, this requirement implies the need to provide materials in very small quantities on a regular basis. That's impossible if setup costs (or ordering costs) are too high. In Chapter 12 we noted that the optimal lot size is one that balances ordering and holding costs. To accommodate small orders, setup costs have to be drastically reduced. Figure 13.11 summarizes the economics. In the general situation described in Chapter 12, the optimal order quantity was that which balanced holding and setup costs. In a JIT setting, with its bias against holding inventory, the idea is that holding costs are probably higher than estimated because of the negative repercussions associated with inventory. That alone would make the "optimal" lot size smaller, but some method of reducing setup costs would still be needed to get to small-lot production.

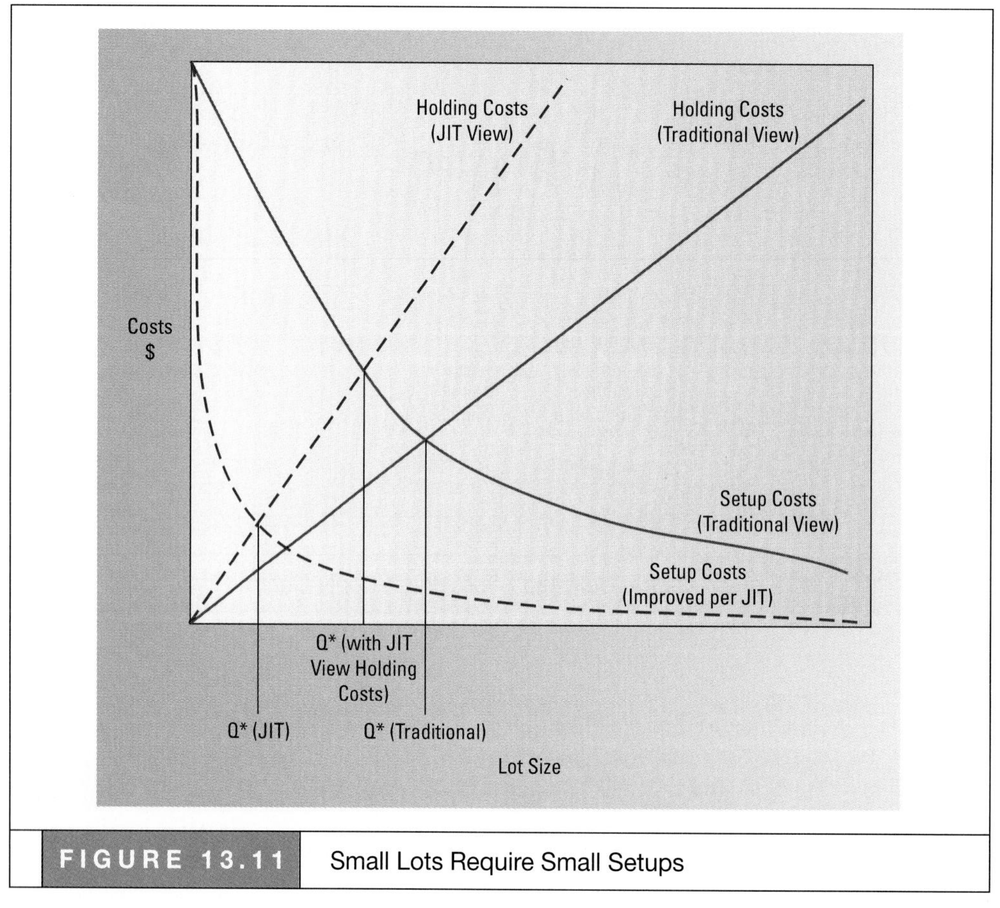

FIGURE 13.11 Small Lots Require Small Setups

The story of a team of workers at a Cadillac plant nicely illustrates the reduction in setup times that can be achieved with JIT. Cadillac has always been known as a maker of high quality luxury automobiles, but in the early 1980s, due to quality problems and some questionable design decisions, the Cadillac name had begun to lose much of its luster. In 1987 a team of workers was formed at a stamping operation and became part of a quality-based turnaround at Cadillac. Stamping is a process in which metal is cut or folded into various shapes using a hydraulic press that can be fitted with various dies. In setting up the press, workers must remove one die and install another that matches the shape to be stamped. To improve the quality of the operation, Cadillac's stamping team decided to reduce its setup time, which averaged 8 hours and 11 minutes. (Long setup times can lead to large production runs and large inventories, which tend to inhibit feedback on quality.) Their project was approved by managers, who arranged for the workers to receive training in setup reduction techniques.

The team returned from training and set a goal: to achieve a certified setup time of less than 5:00 minutes. By 1989 they had demonstrated a consistent time of 4:59 minutes. But having had some training in statistics, team members realized that they had not achieved their goal. Statistically speaking, 4:59 minutes is not significantly different from 5:00 minutes. They went back to work and by 1991 established a standard setup time of 3:37 minutes.

You may be wondering why Cadillac would ever have taken eight hours to accomplish something that could be done in less than five minutes. The reason is that managers didn't think it could be done in less than five minutes. Setups had always taken a long time. Typically, when a large production run was finished, workers were tired and wanted to take a break. They usually hadn't thought about what the next task would be. When they finally got started on the next setup, they realized they had to find the appropriate die for the next job. (The die might not have been put away correctly following its last use, because workers or managers may have been anxious to demonstrate some productivity. And it might not have received the necessary maintenance after its last use.)

Once the workers found the correct die and ascertained that it was fit to use, they "tore down" the last setup and began to build the new one. The new die might have come from a different supplier and might therefore have required different fixtures. (Since dies are expensive—as much as $300,000—they are usually bought through a competitive bidding process. Different suppliers might follow slightly different design conventions, so that their dies might attach to the press in different ways.) Once the old die had been removed and the new die attached, the appropriate raw material had to be located. Finally, a preproduction run of a few parts would be completed, and the parts inspected to ensure that they met specifications. Depending on how busy the quality control lab was, the inspection itself could take some time.

> active exercise

Take a moment to apply what you've learned.

The idea that a setup can and should be done in a matter of minutes was proposed in the 1960s by Shigeo Shingo, a Japanese management consultant. The Shingo system for quick setups, called the **single minute exchange of die system, (SMED)**, reduces setup time in the following ways:

- A distinction is made between **inside exchange of die (IED)** and **outside exchange of die (OED)** activities. IED activities are those which can be done only while a machine is stopped. For example, a die cannot be removed from a machine until a production run has been completed, and a new die must be placed on the machine before a new production can begin. In the SMED system, die maintenance is considered an OED activity. There is no good reason not to have the next die ready and waiting for use prior to the start of a setup.
- Whenever possible, IED activities are converted to OED activities. A simple example of this tactic can be seen in a doctor's office. With only one examining room, one patient must be moved out and the next moved in before a new examination can begin. Vital signs must be taken, and a screening interview may have to be conducted. With two examining rooms, however, the exchange of patients, collection of vital statistics, and screening can be done while the doctor is attending another patient. Adding a room allows the doctor's staff to convert IED activities to OED activities.
- IED activities are streamlined or eliminated. For instance, Figure 13.12 shows several ways to standardize dies and fixtures. Doing so usually means that setup can be done correctly the first time, thus eliminating the need for a preproduction quality assurance check. Using a setup kit with tools prepared and lined up in the order in which they are needed is another way to streamline IED activities. Setup teams often videotape their setups to discover sources of wasted time.

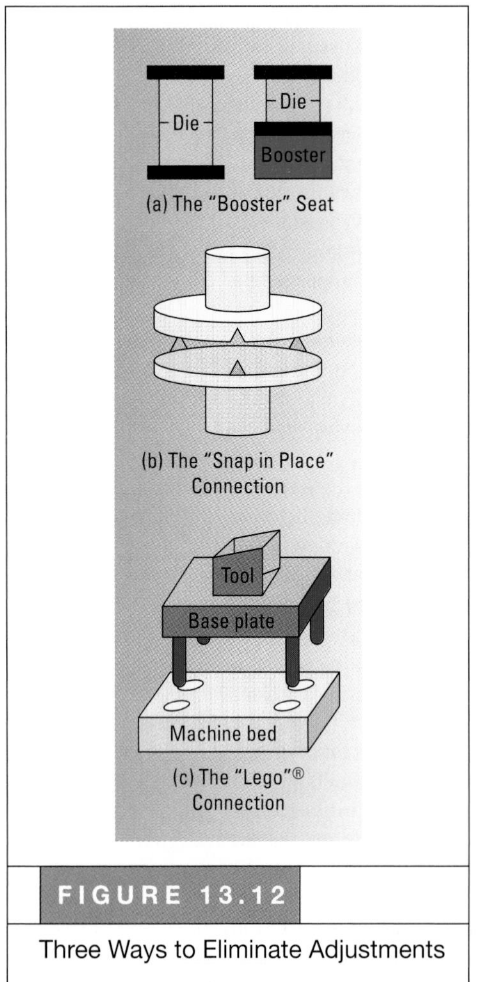

FIGURE 13.12

Three Ways to Eliminate Adjustments

- OED activities are streamlined or eliminated. When the IED portion of the setup time is shortened, it might fall below the OED portion, limiting the impact of further reductions in setup time. If a doctor's exam takes less time than screening and setting up new patients, the doctor will experience costly downtime. Likewise, if a die can be changed in 3:37 minutes, and the whole production run takes only 20 minutes, it's important that the OED portion of the setup not take more than 23:37 minutes.

Reducing setup time can be just as important in service operations as it is in manufacturing. Airline managers have come to realize that planes don't make money while they're on the ground. Customers, too, find that delays in boarding mean they aren't able to get their business done in one day. That means the airlines have got to come up with ways to make quick turnarounds. According to the *Wall Street Journal* (August 4, 1994), USAir recently improved its turnaround time on one hundred 737-200s to the point where those planes could fly seven trips a day rather than six. In doing so, the airline was able to sell an additional 12,000 seats per day.

Some other techniques the airlines have used to speed turnaround times include:

- The "10-minute rule," which requires passengers to board 10 minutes or more before departure time. In SMED terminology, boarding the aircraft is an IED activity, so this rule is part of an effort to streamline IED.
- The carryon luggage "sizer box," which is used to determine whether a passenger's carryon bags are too large before boarding actually begins. This technique converts an IED to an OED activity, reducing the time spent handling unusual carryon items and thus streamlining the boarding process.
- Reliance on a single type of aircraft, which, like die standardization, allows an airline to know exactly what equipment and personnel will be needed for changeovers.
- Cleaning of cabins on an as-needed-only basis. This technique eliminates an IED activity.
- In-flight inventorying and reporting of drink and snack stocks by flight attendants. Thus, caterers know exactly what supplies will be needed before a plane lands. This tactic converts an IED to an OED activity.

active exercise <

Take a moment to apply what you've learned.

OUTSIDE SUPPLIERS AND LOGISTICAL ISSUES

JIT planning and control requires trustworthy suppliers. Letting supply contracts out for bids has serious drawbacks in the JIT environment. By allowing for multiple sources of material inputs, it introduces variability and reduces the customer's ability to interact with the supplier. It also eliminates any possibility of cooperation between manufacturer and supplier in the creation of the synergies and distinctive competencies that lead to a competitive advantage. For these reasons, a long-term relationship with trustworthy suppliers is best suited to the JIT system.

This aspect of the JIT system may be easier to implement in countries like Japan than in the United States. Geographically, Japan is quite small relative to the United States, and its culture places a heavy emphasis on cooperation, trust, and long-term relationships. Many Japanese corporations belong to a *Kieretsu,* or a group of companies that cooperate with one another. For example, Mitsubishi's *Kieretsu* includes a merchant banker, a shipping company, a steel manufacturer, several electronics companies, an automobile maker, and several other companies. A large portion of the stock of each company is held by other companies in the *Kieretsu,* and the directors of the companies meet regularly. In addition, small companies that do not belong to the *Kieretsu* often align themselves with the group. At Toyota City, for instance, there are a large number of small businesses whose primary reason for existence is to provide supplies for Toyota.

Though the U.S. business culture emphasizes independence, and legal barriers forbid anticompetitive practices, working closely with suppliers is still important. Indeed, the geographic distance between manufacturer and supplier may require it. For example, getting regular two-hour shipments to a facility in Detroit from a supplier in Mexico City is a great challenge. To meet such challenges, U.S. companies have developed two significant innovations: the *in-plant supplier* and *sole source logistics* providers.

The Bose Corporation of Boston pioneered the concept of the in-plant supplier. In planning Bose's new facilities, managers added extra office space for the company's suppliers, so that those employees could work on-site. Bose would provide the office space and the necessary support; the supplier would provide the employee's compensation. Today, the in-plant supplier may work full-time at the Bose facility or may be there only a certain number of days each week. Suppliers' personnel often mix with Bose personnel in meetings and during cafeteria breaks. The constant interaction between the two improves coordination with suppliers. The result is greater certainty about the supply of materials and greater efficiency throughout the supply chain.

Product design also benefits from the presence of in-plant suppliers. Even if an engineer from a supplier spends just one or two days a week at the Bose facility, at the very least that person will meet Bose design engineers during cafeteria breaks. When Bose designs a new stereo system, the design engineers will already know what technologies are available from the supplier off the shelf. Often, they will be able to avoid designing a new component from scratch, because something that was used in another application is available. Time, money, and energy would have to be expended in developing such components without the in-plant supplier's presence.

One of Bose's in-plant suppliers, Yellow Freight, is also Bose's *sole source logistics provider,* meaning that it handles all inbound and outbound freight. Since Yellow Freight attends schedule meetings and has complete knowledge of Bose's schedule, there is no need for Bose employees to arrange for the shipment of purchased materials and finished goods—Yellow Freight takes care of it automatically. In fact, Yellow Freight can anticipate Bose's needs and ensure more efficient shipment of supplies. For example, if the Yellow Freight representative knows that a shipment of raw materials will be available at a Bose supplier in California in two hours, the rep can delay an eastbound truck long enough to carry those materials and reroute the truck to ensure that the pickup and delivery take place. The result is greater efficiency in transportation services. Yellow Freight runs more smoothly, Bose gets better service, and a lot less paperwork is required.

Since the advent of JIT, the sole sourcing of logistical services has become common. Most major freight lines now offer turnkey solutions for manufacturers, meaning that they use their logistical expertise, their knowledge of cost factors, and their sophisticated computer models to benefit the manufacturer. Thus, they can provide much more economical service than would be available if manufacturers were to try to determine shipping quantities, schedules, and routes themselves. Work is reduced for both suppliers and their customers, and service improves throughout the supply chain. Note that in this sense, JIT manufacturing relies on a service operation for much of its success.

Figure 13.13 illustrates one of many potential benefits that could arise from improved logistical services. Often, to keep things simple, managers make transfer batches the same size as production batches. In other words, all the work on a particular order will be completed before any of it is transferred from one work area to another. This rule frequently holds true whether the work is being transferred from suppliers to customers or from one work area to another. The top half of the figure shows an order for six units being transferred and processed all at once. If the processing time at each of eight work stations is one hour per unit and the processed goods will not be transferred until all are finished, 24 hours will pass before any finished goods become available. But if the items can be transferred one at a time (bottom half), some finished goods will become available in just eight hours. (Remember that on-hand inventory is proportional to the time a product takes to go through the process.) The producer who uses the latter system can afford to be more responsive and adaptive to customer requirements.

> active concept check

Now let's take a moment to test your knowledge of the concepts you have studied in this section.

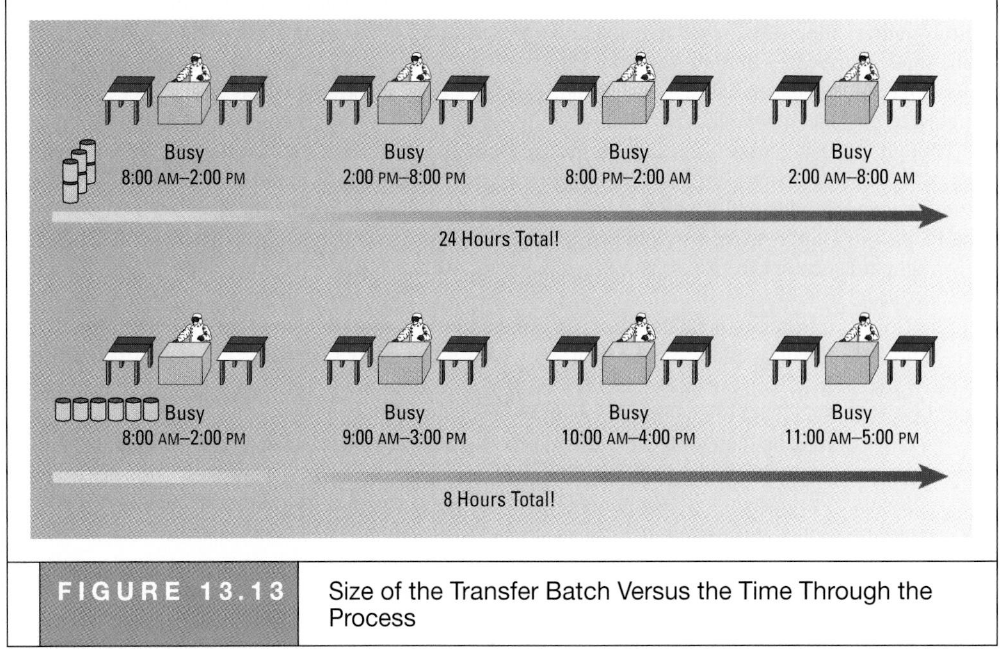

FIGURE 13.13 Size of the Transfer Batch Versus the Time Through the Process

Kanban Systems

Sooner or later, in any operation, one must determine who should do what with which resources on a moment-to-moment basis. In JIT systems, detailed scheduling is often taken care of using a **Kanban system.** *Kanban* is the Japanese word for "card"; in the context of detailed scheduling, a kanban is simply a signal that something needs to be done. The kanban system is a **pull scheduling** system, meaning that work is pulled through the value-adding system by signals from end users. Unless a downstream customer uses a material, its production and replenishment will never be reauthorized.

Figure 13.14 illustrates a simple two-stage kanban system. Department 24K receives material that is described on the card labeled "A" and converts it into something labeled "B." Department 97X converts the material called "B" into something called "C." In the figure, when a customer uses up a bin full of part C, a chain reaction pulls more of that material through the system. When the customer needs the part, he or she takes the material and leaves the kanban behind. Workers in Department 97X see the *free kanban* and replace the used material according to the instructions shown on the card. In doing so, they will use up a bin of part B, leaving the B kanban free. Workers in Department 24K will then use a bin of part A to make a bin of part B, freeing the A kanban and drawing more of that material into the system. Thus, the kanbans authorize workers to perform specific tasks, translating customer needs into work orders without management intervention.

Though cards are typically used in modern kanban systems, there are many other ways to signal workers. As Figure 13.15 shows, an empty space can serve as a kanban. For instance, in the pancake breakfast described at the beginning of this chapter, empty pitchers were used as kanbans, to signal the need for more pancake batter. In other situations, kanbans can be transmitted electronically to employees' workstations.

CONTROLLING INVENTORY LEVELS WITH KANBANS

Management can control the amount of inventory in a value-adding system by adding or removing kanbans. Notice that in Figure 13.14, there were two A kanbans, two C kanbans, and three B kanbans. As a rule, only enough kanbans are needed to ensure that users of a particular material do not suffer stock-outs. The following formula is useful in establishing the number of kanbans needed:

$$\text{\# Kanbans} = [d(L + \propto)] / c$$

where:

d = the leveled pull rate experienced at the workstation

L = the expected lead-time (time from use of the material to its replenishment)

$\propto$ = the safety stock factor, to cover foreseeable variability in L

c = the container or bin size (i.e., the number of units authorized by each kanban)

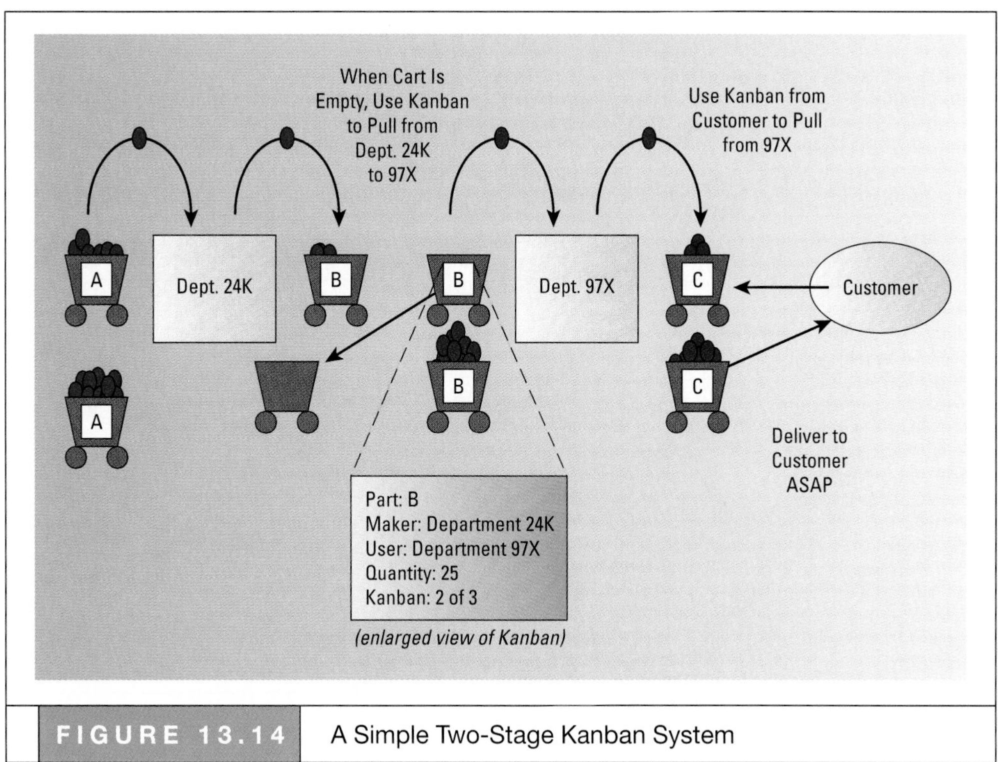

FIGURE 13.14 A Simple Two-Stage Kanban System

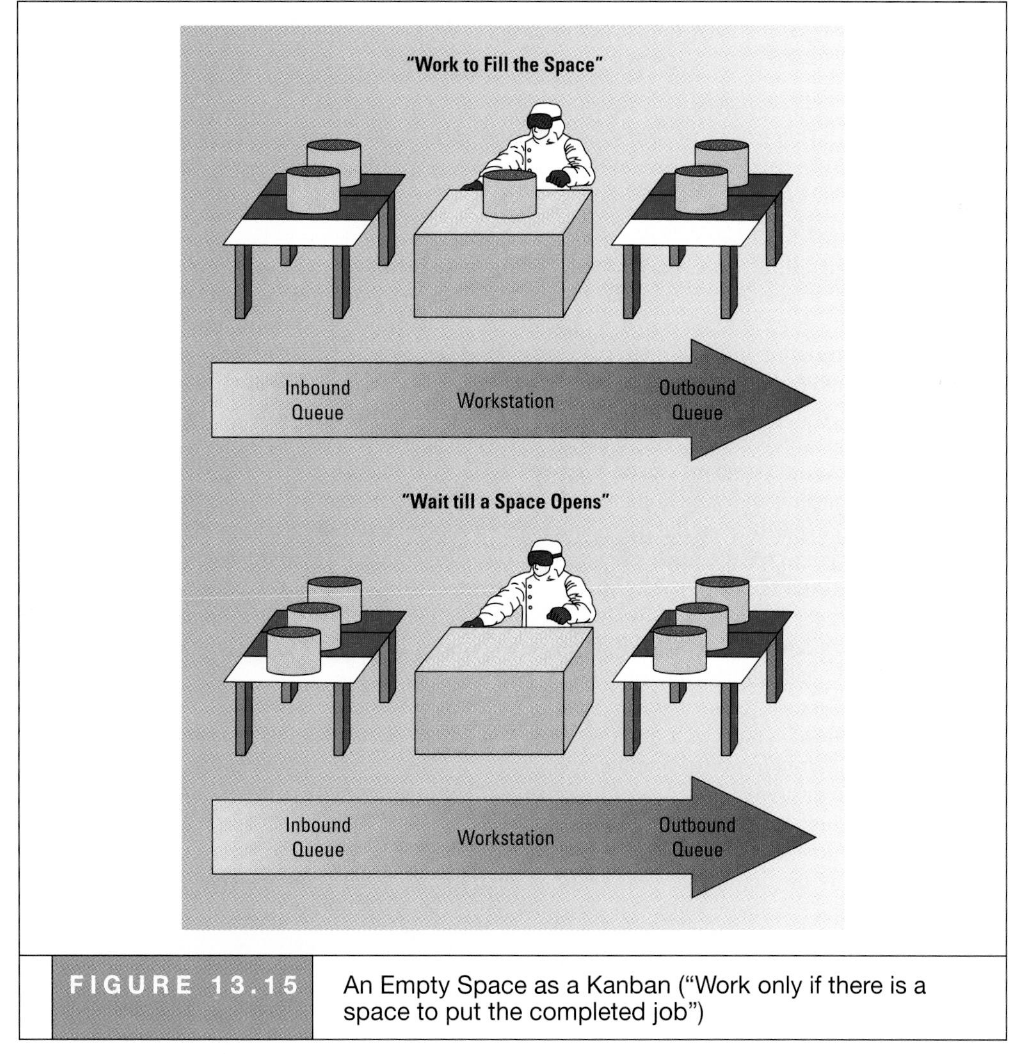

FIGURE 13.15 An Empty Space as a Kanban ("Work only if there is a space to put the completed job")

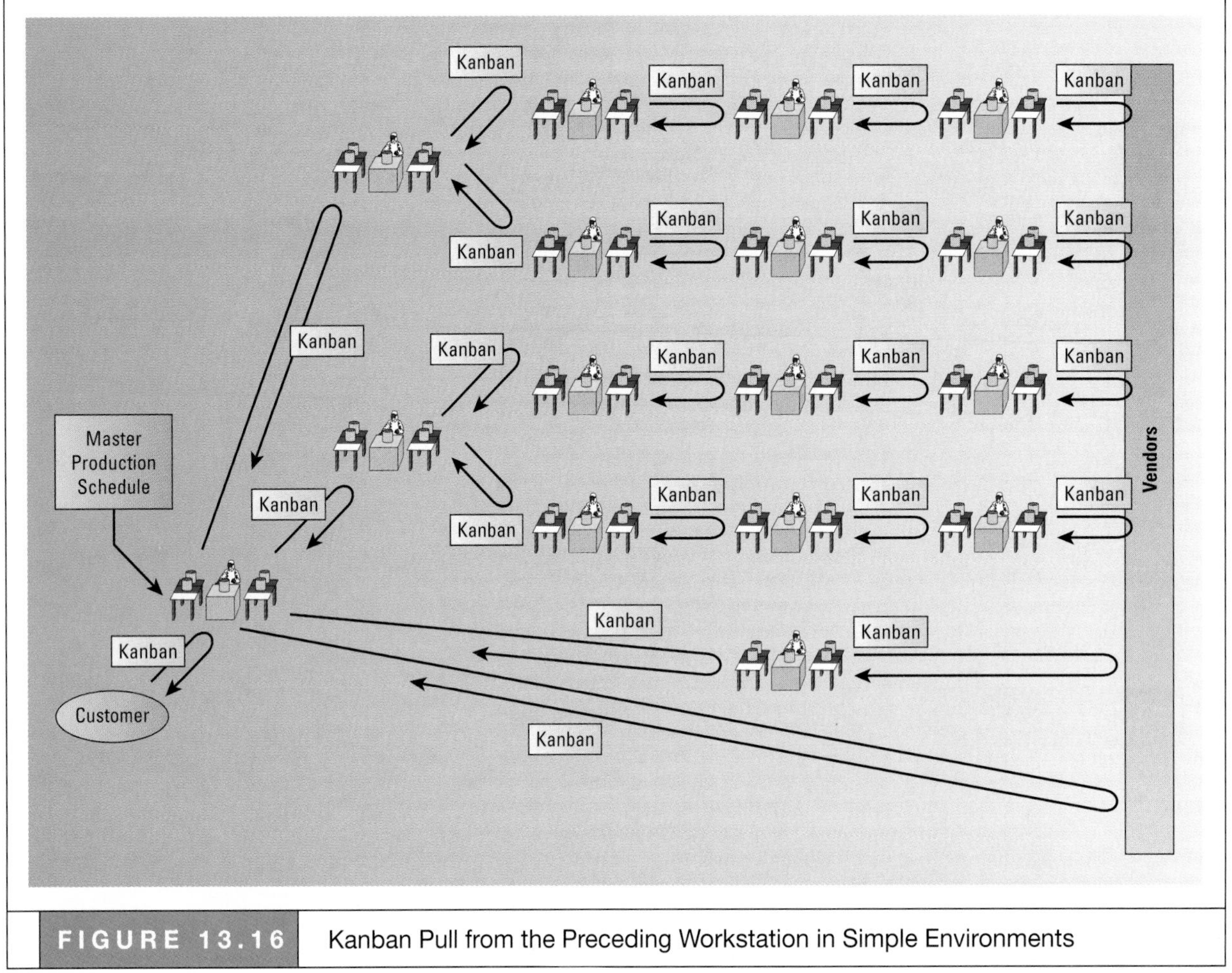

FIGURE 13.16 Kanban Pull from the Preceding Workstation in Simple Environments

As Figure 13.16 illustrates, the kanban system works extremely well in simple environments in which the master schedule has been effectively smoothed and workstation capacities essentially balanced. The beauty of the system is that it can provide all the necessary information about work priorities to each workstation in the system without managerial intervention. It does so based on the pull rate of internal and external customers, so that no workstation will get ahead of others and no unnecessary inventory will accumulate. If a workstation has no free kanbans, workers will not create more inventory—indeed, they cannot. But that doesn't mean that their time is wasted. Downtime that is caused by a lack of free kanbans can be used to help other workers—particularly if the reason for not having a free kanban is that some other work center has experienced a disruption. Alternatively, free time can be used to perform productive maintenance or to pursue ideas for improvement.

The kanban system breaks down when the demand pull comes from multiple sources, when workstation capacities aren't balanced, or when demand is not level. Figure 13.17 (page 588) illustrates this situation. Adding the complexity of multiple customers and suppliers to just one workstation introduces the question of which kanban will receive top priority and why. This weak point will eventually cause the whole system to unravel.

Finally, on an assembly line in which workers perform the same task over and over again using the same materials, there is no need to put routine instructions on kanbans. That doesn't mean that workers don't need information regarding their progress, but simply that they need less detailed information less often. In this type of operation, andon boards are often used. An **andon board** is a large electronic sign that indicates operational performance information. Typically andon boards communicate the daily production goal, current progress toward that goal, whether the assembly line is ahead of or behind target, and the amount of time that has been lost to work stoppages. When work has been stopped, the andon board also tells where the disruption occurred. Workers are allowed, even encouraged, to stop the assembly line when they find a quality problem or experience some other disruption. When they do, other workers can identify the location of the disruption and aid in an effort to eliminate the problem.

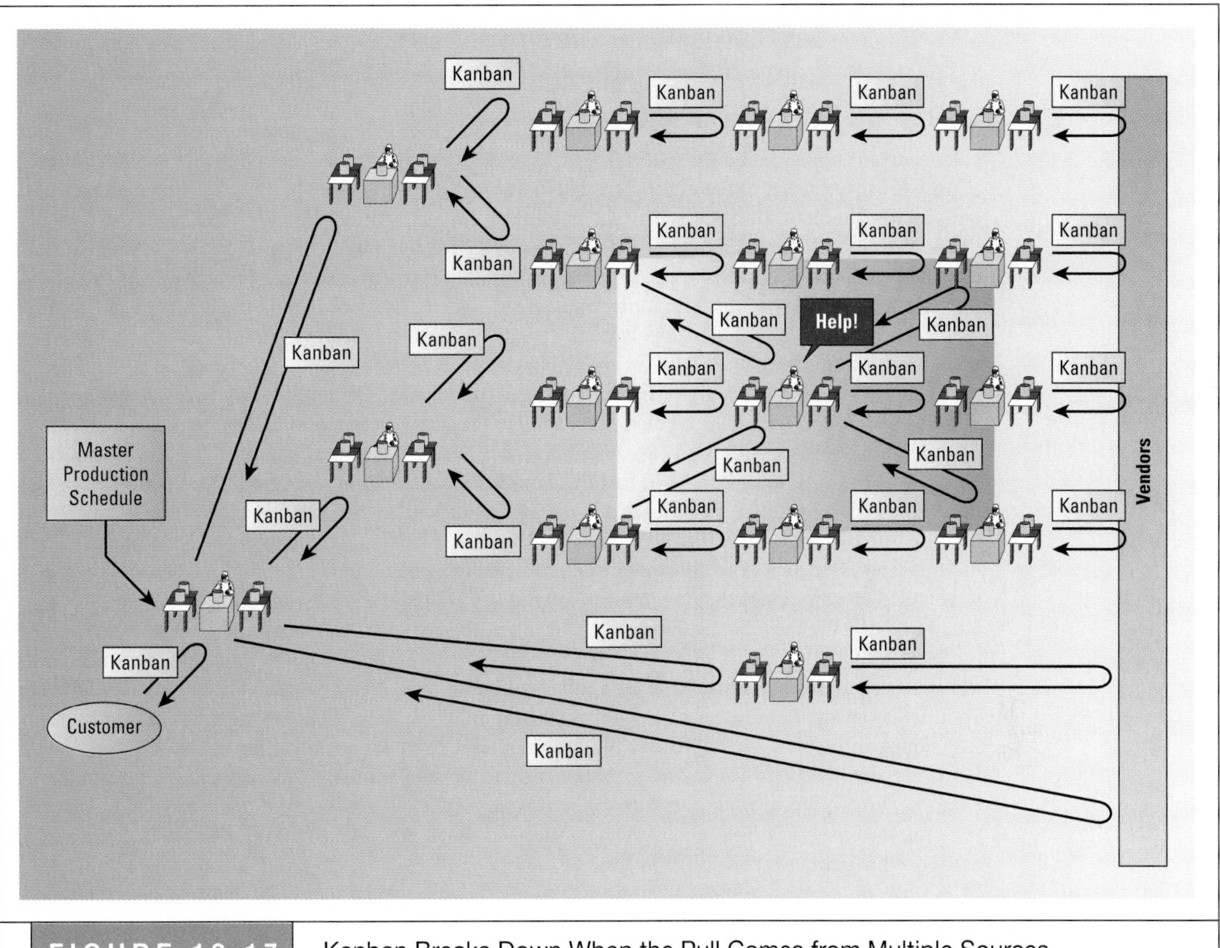

FIGURE 13.17 Kanban Breaks Down When the Pull Comes from Multiple Sources

> video exercise

Take a moment to apply what you've learned.

> active concept check

Now let's take a moment to test your knowledge of the concepts you have studied in this section.

> Two Kanban Systems at the Student Recreation Center

While kanban systems are primarily used to control the flow of material through manufacturing operations, it is not unusual to find kanban-like systems controlling the flow of customers through service-oriented value-adding systems like the Student Recreation Center (SRC). For example, the number of harnesses available on the climbing wall will obviously limit the number of climbers who can use the wall at one time. The number available can be adjusted to fit the current configuration of the wall (e.g., the level of difficulty affects the speed at which a climber progresses and therefore the number of people who can be using it safely) or the number of SRC staff on-hand. In another case, the number of stepping stools available in the step aerobic room controls the size of the "drop-in" class.

There are, however, two examples where a kanban approach can be seen controlling the flow of material, rather than patrons, through the SRC. The SRC provides clean towels at no charge for patrons to use while inside the facility. When they leave, patrons are asked to toss the used towels into a large laundry basket at the equipment checkout area near the exit. In the past, the staff would wait until a large batch of towels was dirty, then call the university trucking office to have them transferred to the university's main laundry facility. The laundry washes these towels along with towels, bed and table linens, athletic uniforms, and other types of laundry from all other university facilities. To keep the transfer costs down, the SRC only transferred large batches of towels to and from the laundry. It would take a few days to get towels back from the laundry; meanwhile, the SRC maintained large inventory of both clean and dirty towels.

Recently a new system was implemented. At the laundry facility, clean towels are strapped into bundles and coded with colored tags that indicate the number of towels in the bundle. While the size of the bundles varies with the "customer," the recreation center gets red tag bundles, which contain 100 towels each. When a bundle of towels is opened, its red tag is placed on a peg near the baskets of used towels. Baskets containing used towels are picked up and bundles of clean towels are delivered daily by the laundry's delivery service from each campus location that uses towels. While at the SRC, the delivery van driver delivers the bundled towels that are on the truck that day and collects the dirty towels and loose red tags that are hanging on the peg. Later at the laundry facility, the dirty towels are laundered and the tags are used to load the truck with the next day's delivery.

With daily deliveries, it takes less than two days from the time a tag is removed from a clean bundle of towels until it returns to the SRC attached to another clean bundle. The recreation center uses about 20 towels per hour over the 15 hours per day that it is open. This means that a bundle lasts about five hours, three bundles would last about a day, and from six to seven tags must be in the system. However, the number of tags can be adjusted up or down for out-of-the-ordinary circumstances. For example, on a holiday when the laundry is closed but the SRC is open, it takes as many as five days for a tag to come back. To plan for this situation, 15 or 16 tags are put into the system a couple of days earlier—that's the original 6–7 plus 9 or 10 extra.

A second use of a kanban-like system is in the pro shop. When the SRC first opened, the pro shop operated as a separate profit center dealing with four main distributors of sporting equipment and apparel, independent of the bookstore and other areas on campus that also dealt with the same distributors. Because their volume was low relative to the other outlets on campus, the pro shop couldn't get as favorable business terms from its suppliers. For instance, lead-time on orders was sometimes as long as two weeks, payment terms were less desirable, and fewer price discounts were available. They also had to limit their variety more than they wanted. After a year of operation, a student employee who had worked in the bookstore before coming to the SRC suggested that they piggyback onto the bookstore system. After some investigation, a new system was developed: The athletic products carried at the bookstore and pro shop were standardized. The "athletic" subset of the bookstore's inventory contains all of the items available at the pro shop. The inventory of the pro shop is now pulled out of the bookstore. Sales recorded on the point of sales (POS) terminal at the pro shop are tallied on the bookstore's computer. Replenishments are sent via university mail couriers on a daily basis. In this case, the POS terminals essentially are sending an electronic kanban with each pro shop transaction. Management can adjust the total number of items available in the pro shop as special events occur or seasonal factors cause demand fluctuations. The combined volume of the bookstore and the pro shop has increased their "clout" with the suppliers. The pro shop can now offer a wider variety of items, keep prices competitive, and carry less inventory due to the daily delivery.

> JIT in Services

As we have described, JIT is a companywide philosophy that relies heavily on continuous improvement and employee involvement. It works best in environments with little uncertainty because uncertainty requires inventory and time buffers that cost money and can reduce customer service performance. JIT systems are designed to drive out uncertainty and to adapt to sources of uncertainty that can't be totally eliminated.

Service-intensive environments can benefit from the perspective of JIT as a broad-based management philosophy. For instance, developing JIT delivery relationships with suppliers of materials used by service businesses is one aspect of JIT in services. McDonald's is a good example; meat, buns, containers, wrappings, condiments, and the like must be delivered at the right time in the right quantities to the right franchisee. But JIT as a philosophy goes deeper than the on-time delivery of tangible goods. Below we identify 10 ways that services can adopt the JIT cornerstones of continuous improvement, employee involvement, and reduced uncertainty.

1. *Organize continuous improvement teams.* The utility company, Florida Power and Light (FP&L), creates teams to address specific problems and customer complaints. The teams use QI story method and tools described in Chapter 6. Most importantly, when improvements are made, policies and procedures are permanently changed to ensure that the new level of performance is sustained. For example, an FP&L team determined that cars hitting utility poles—especially those on the outside of curves—was a major contributor to customer outages. The team helped the company change the location of existing poles and revised the company's method for locating new poles.
2. *Reduce employee absenteeism and turnover.* A major source of uncertainty in service environments is employee absenteeism and turnover. Creating incentives and compensation programs to improve employee reliability and loyalty helps to keep experienced employees on the job. Fairfield Inn provides extra paid vacation days for employees who have no absences. Employees may arrange with other employees to cover their shifts and not have it count as an absence. The program provides some freedom for employees while providing the reliability the company requires.
3. *Cross train employees.* Productivity is enhanced when employees can be assigned to a variety of tasks, depending on the immediate needs of the organization. Cross-trained employees can handle a greater variety of customer requests, fill in for absent coworkers, and improve their compensation and job satisfaction.
4. *Blueprint the service process.* Blueprinting plays a key role in identifying and removing waste in the system. For example, waiting is a common problem for students who visit their university's walk-in health clinic. The reasons for long delays in the clinic's process can be pinpointed by identifying and timing the steps involved, including check-in, chart retrieval, triage, treatment by a care provider, and supplemental services such as x-rays and lab work. Blueprint analysis helps identify service bottlenecks and sources of unnecessary delays.
5. *Update equipment and process technology.* Technology can improve service responsiveness while containing costs. Target stores place telephone call boxes throughout the store so customers can call for assistance. Call boxes help maintain customer service while keeping labor costs down. Target also uses intercom headsets so store employees can communicate with one another without blaring announcements that could annoy customers over a public-address system. As another example, tolls are now collected in some areas via automatic readers that scan vehicles as they drive past. Drivers receive a monthly bill for the tolls they incurred.
6. *Level demand.* Demand is a major source of uncertainty for any business environment. Leveling demand allows companies to reduce inventories or improve response time. One-hour photo labs usually have higher prices for the one-hour service and lower prices for next-day and two-day service. Pricing helps segment demand and spread it more evenly throughout the day. The shops can therefore schedule labor and developing machines with more certainty. Costs are kept low and customer expectations are met consistently.
7. *Have a service recovery plan.* Since uncertainty can't be completely eliminated in most businesses, companies should have a service recovery plan to minimize the impact on customers when things go wrong. One of the authors of this book was shopping at Target on a busy Saturday when all computerized cash registers went down. The store manager immediately announced the temporary outage over the public-address system and requested the customers to be patient. Announcing the incident to all shoppers immediately lowered their expectations regarding the checkout service. It prevented customers from being surprised and disappointed if when they arrived at the registers. Two or three store managers were stationed in the register area handing out $3 vouchers to every customer and apologizing for the delay. The managers also assigned all store personnel to the registers (note the use of cross-trained employees) so customers could be served as quickly as possible once the registers were back on-line. After 15 minutes the registers began operating and the customer backlog was quickly processed. Ideally, Target would like the registers to be reliable, but not all contingencies can be prevented. In this case, what could have been a customer service nightmare turned out to be a minor incident.
8. *Eliminate unnecessary activities.* Understanding customer priorities is the key to eliminating activities that the customer doesn't care about. Bagging your own groceries became popular in many stores when managers recognized that customers associated self-service bagging with lower prices. It also saved the stores in resources. Some stores allow customers to price-scan their own groceries—a move that allows customers with fewer items an alternative to checkout lines.

Remote diagnostic equipment can be used to automatically page a doctor on the basis of a patient's condition. In fact, doctors' schedules, and those of others who require pagers for professional purposes, are generally demand driven.

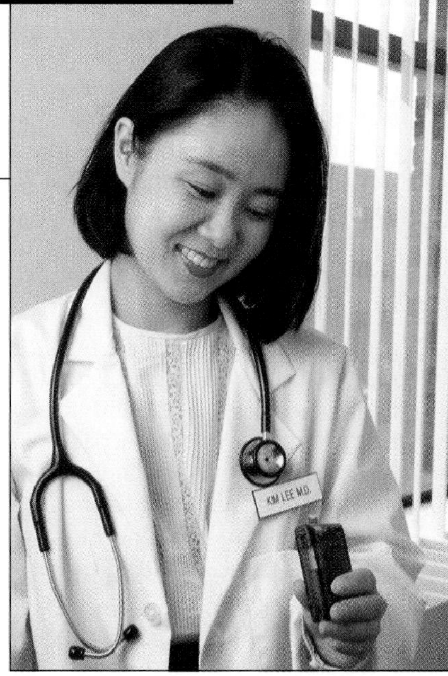

9. *Change the facility layout.* Customers can often be better served and costs saved by simply changing the layout of the service facility. For example, banks that use a single line for waiting customers provide better service than those that use multiple waiting lines because demand is distributed evenly among the tellers. Various congregations have removed bolted-down church pews in favor of movable seating solutions that allow their facility to be used for multiple functions.
10. *Use demand-pull scheduling.* Service technicians, retail store personnel, real estate agents, and funeral home employees are among the numerous service sector employees who provide on-call services. When customer demand arises, these employees can be notified by pager or phone of the need for their services. Another example is paper copiers, which can be evaluated over the phone lines and visited by repair personnel only when maintenance and repair are needed.

active exercise <

Take a moment to apply what you've learned.

active concept check <

Now let's take a moment to test your knowledge of the concepts you have studied in this section.

> Integrating Operational Decisions

This chapter is closely linked to Chapter 4 and Chapter 7 because decisions about the design of the product-service bundle and the value-adding system determine the level of complexity inherent in planning and control of the system. If product designers use modular designs and limit variety in the product line through such mechanisms as group technology, the simple approach to planning and control discussed in this chapter will be more applicable. Similarly, if the value-adding system makes use of cellular or repetitive processes, there is a greater likelihood that the JIT approach to planning and control will work effectively. This chapter is also closely tied to Chapters 11 and 12. These linkages should be obvious: The broader resource planning and scheduling decisions covered in Chapters 11 and 12 establish the level of resources available and what must be accomplished in the short- to intermediate-range. This chapter continues the planning and control process at a more detailed level. It describes the way that JIT systems accomplish the detailed scheduling activities that ensure the requirements of the master schedule are met.

> integrated OM

Take a moment to apply what you've learned.

> Chapter Wrap-Up

In this chapter we have described short-range planning and control for dependent demand items in repetitive value-adding systems. In recent years, the JIT system has become one of the most common approaches to handling material and capacity decisions in such environments. JIT was developed by Toyota Motor Company in the 1950s and 1960s, and took root in the rest of the world by the late 1980s. Its use has influenced the practice of business in virtually every function.

The simpler the value-adding system, the better the JIT system works. JIT is not well-suited to complex value-adding systems, such as batch processes or job shops. JIT emphasizes the reduction of wasteful inventories through the improvement of processes and the elimination of uncertainty. Lower levels of inventory are often achieved through smaller lot sizes that are made possible by extremely low setup costs. Low setup costs are often achieved through a setup-time reduction technique referred to as SMED.

The JIT approach to planning and control relies on a leveled master schedule for independent demand inventory items. A level schedule can be seen as a completion sequence for all of the items that are on the master schedule for a specific planning period. The sequence is repeated until all of the requirements on the master schedule have been met. The more rapidly the sequence can be completed, the more level the schedule. With a more level schedule, inventory levels can also be kept lower, because value can be added at a rate that is consistent with its consumption.

Day-to-day and moment-to-moment scheduling of the JIT environment is accomplished with visual signals such as kanbans and andon boards. The kanban system is designed to allow workers to respond to the demand pull of downstream customers. Thus, workers do not need managers to tell them what to do next. In fact, much of the power and efficiency of the JIT system comes from simplifying the system to the extent that it can run itself. This approach eliminates the need for an army of middle managers to handle production planning and control, and renders the operational system flexible, efficient, and responsive to customer requirements.

The JIT philosophy that stresses employee involvement, uncertainty reduction, and continuous improvement has many applications in service-intensive businesses. Services may try to reduce uncertainty through such mechanisms as demand pull scheduling, employee cross training, and incentive systems based on employee skills, length of service, and attendance record. Continuous improvement in services often comes from employee teams, applications of technology, service blueprinting, changes in facility layout, and elimination of unnecessary activities.

> end-of-chapter resources

- **Practice Quiz**
- **Key Terms**
- **Solved Problem**
- **Discussion Questions**
- **Problems**
- **Case 13.1: Madame Alexander Dolls Moves Toward JIT With Kaizen**
- **Factory Tours**

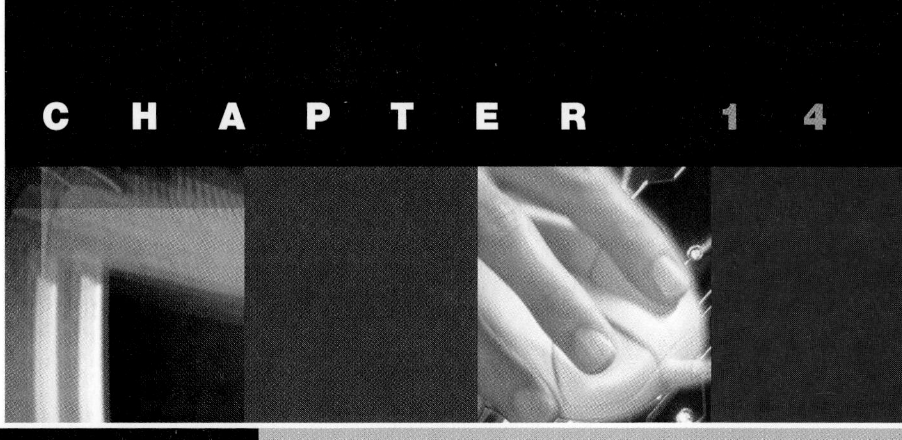

CHAPTER 14

Planning and Control in Synchronous Value-Adding Systems

Chapter Outline

> What's Ahead

. . . BACK AT THE REC CENTER

"Hey Fred, did you get a chance to use the new bike machines with the road race simulators?" asked Luis. It was barely past 6:00 AM and Luis was just coming in. Fred was already on a regular stationary bike. There were only a few people in the center. The rec center had just purchased three bike machines with computerized simulations of various types of road races that the user can choose from as they work out. Riders can pick the style of race and watch a very good graphical simulation of themselves racing another computer-generated rider over very realistically simulated courses. Riders can even pick how good the opponent is in order to make the "race" competitive. Just as with many new pieces of equipment when first introduced, the machines are very popular now and in heavy demand. In fact, until the "newness" wears off, people wanting to use the bikes need to sign up for 20-minute time slots. The rec center has even had to schedule an additional student supervisor to keep the schedule and monitor the use of the machines. The lines had been getting really long, and sometimes people were staying on for an extended period of time, which only made the lines worse.

"They're really cool. You kind of forget you're working out and get caught up in the race on the screen!" Luis added. "What a great way to work out!"

"No, I haven't had a chance to try one yet," said Fred, somewhat disappointedly. "I couldn't get a time slot that fits my schedule until next week. I went over to look at them, and even though there was only one person waiting, the student supervisor told me I had to sign up for a time slot." He looked up and saw Cheryl and Tom coming in. Tom seemed to be looking in the direction of the new bikes as he walked in. "Don't even think about it unless you have an appointment," said Fred.

"So those are the new ones I had been hearing about!" Cheryl said admiringly. "I guess it makes sense to set up a schedule on them while they're the hot ticket. That'll give more people a chance to try them out and will keep anybody from hogging them. Remember when they opened the new racquetball courts?"

"Yes I do," Tom said with an annoyed tone. He was just sitting down to start stretching. "What a mess that was. They had it first come, first serve and then made it a challenge court, winner stays and takes on all comers. The wait got really long and even then, who knew how long you would stay on? A lot of people got discouraged and never even tried to get on."

"That's right," said Cheryl. She remembered how word got around about the wait, which scared people off, and the courts actually sat empty during the late morning and afternoons. "A sign-up sheet does make sense, at least until something else becomes the hot ticket. By that time, people who want to use it can just get a feel for the typical wait at the times they want to come in and plan accordingly." She used Tom's routine as an example. He likes to come in and do six different stations in his workout. Most of the time there is a small wait for a spot on a machine or stepper to open up before he can get on. All total, he plans on about 15 minutes for each station. So with a few minutes spent talking with his friends in the group and a quick shower, he probably needs between an hour and a half and two hours each morning. If he has to be at work by 8, he needs to be at the rec center by 6 AM.

"I do come in earlier sometimes, that is, if I want to do something extra," said Fred. "That's why I got here early today. I wanted to try those bikes."

"Well, the bikes are a bottleneck right now and this makes the most sense until that changes," said Cheryl. "It keeps the bikes busy and the lines short."

"But what happens when somebody signs up for a time slot and then doesn't show?" Fred asked. "I don't even think the next person showed up this morning."

"Well, that's not right," said Tom. "Never let the hot ticket sit idle! That's why we'll overbook a flight when it gets full. Somebody invariably doesn't show and we only make good money when the seats are full."

"But you lose when more people than you expect show up. Don't those vouchers for getting bumped add up?" asked Fred.

"Sure they do," said Tom, "so we have to be careful and try and balance the amount we overbook with the cost of giving out vouchers and flying empty seats on a heavily demanded flight. We've always got a few people wanting to fly standby, too."

"Wouldn't you really rather just have the people who book the flight just show up or cancel in time for you to sell the seats to somebody else?" asked Cheryl.

"That would be nice, too," said Tom. "It sort of gets at the root of the problem. All these new computers we have to hook us up to travel agents, ticket agents, the Internet, other airlines, the whole ball of wax—well, that gives us a better idea of what we need than we used to get in the old days. Someday maybe we'll get it all figured, but for now that's still too complicated. We just play the percentages and hope for the best."

"Well, nobody likes getting bumped at the airport and nobody really wants to find they're double-booked on a bike at 6 AM!" laughed Cheryl. "There are other ways to keep the bottleneck moving."

"Yeah," said Luis, "maybe they could do what the restaurant my wife and I were at last night does." He told them how the restaurant inside a local shopping mall had a waiting line estimated to be 30 to 45 minutes long. The staff gave everyone who was waiting a small pager that only worked within a couple hundred yards of the restaurant. That way those people waiting were free to shop around the mall and could come back to the restaurant when their table was ready by responding to the page. "It was great," laughed Luis. "We didn't have to sit around waiting, and the other stores in the mall liked it, too. They must have—we spent more money in the other stores 'waiting' than we did for dinner!"

"This bottleneck issue happens here, too," Tom replied. Sometimes you can't plan it, you just go with the flow. Every once in a while, there'll be a long line at one of the machines I want to go to next on my circuit. I just try to work around it." If the line at the next station looks long, he'll try a different one. Many times the line at the busy station will be down when he goes back to it. Sometimes he just keeps an eye on the busiest machine for a break in its use. "Sometimes I've even cut it short on one machine to get over to the busiest-looking machine when I can sneak in between other users. I can always go back to the less-busy machines," he said.

"That's not too different than what we do now with our furniture," said Luis. "We look at the master schedule to try and see where we need more capacity, or less, whatever it takes."

"But don't things change?" asked Tom. "If one department or machine is tight this week, what's to say it won't be something else next week? How do you know what the bottleneck is?"

"Well, we can't always," Cheryl replied. Some situations, like the ER, are so complex that by the time they find the bottleneck, it's shifted somewhere else before they can do anything to make the most of it. "That's where you try and deal with the uncertainty as best you can," she said.

"I see," said Luis. "When it comes to the unexpected, you just plan based upon the averages plus a little extra just in case."

"Well, average or not, I want a crack at those new bikes!" laughed Fred.

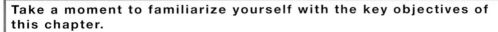

> objectives

Take a moment to familiarize yourself with the key objectives of this chapter.

> gearing up

Before you begin reading this chapter, try a short warm-up activity.

> Introduction

This chapter covers planning and control issues in **synchronous value-adding systems**—systems whose effective management, because of the presence of a bottleneck, requires that the timing of value-adding activities be coordinated (or synchronized) throughout the system. From an operational point of view, a **bottleneck** is any resource that has insufficient capacity to satisfy requirements. It's usually easy to find a bottleneck, because of the large number of customers or jobs waiting for service. For example, at rush hour many commuters avoid the primary bridge out of the city, because they've come to expect traffic to be backed up there. (The bridge is the bottleneck, and the commuters are customers waiting for service.) When a value-adding system has a bottleneck and other activities aren't coordinated with that resource, the bottleneck's capacity might be wasted, unnecessary inventories might be created, and customer service may suffer.

Not all systems are plagued by bottlenecks. If you went to a public elementary school, you were probably never closed out of a course. That's because everyone moved together, in lock step, through a standardized curriculum. The value-adding system was the same for each pupil, and if capacity had to be increased in a particular grade, the need would be clear from the number of students in the next lower grade. Typically, there were no enrollment problems, because potential bottlenecks could be anticipated and eliminated by appropriate staffing decisions. Essentially, the students flowed through the system together, with no special arrangements made for any particular group of students. Planning and control for this type of system was covered in Chapter 13.

But in high school, or more recently in college, you probably experienced difficulty getting into a class you wanted to take. Students at these academic levels may take electives, and they can change their program of study at will. Thus, the level of certainty regarding the demand for particular course offerings is much lower than at an elementary school. Though student demand patterns are continually changing, the faculty of academic departments does not change quickly. As a result, enrollment bottlenecks will crop up in various course sequences, and department chairs must manage them by shifting teaching assignments or limiting enrollments. If, for example, a high school principal anticipates a limited staff for algebra II, she might consider limiting the enrollment in algebra I in earlier semesters and directing some of the closed-out students into geometry or logic courses. The dean of a business school with excess demand for a senior level advertising class might attempt to solve the problem by canceling a section of the introductory marketing prerequisite and shifting the professor's assignment to the senior level course. If you've ever been closed out of a course you needed to graduate on time, you know how important it is for academic administrators to synchronize course offerings.

You'll better understand the concept of a synchronous value-adding system if you briefly consider the contrast, **asynchronous value-adding systems,** which are systems that allow separate value-adding activities to be scheduled independently. A local community college with a high continuing education enrollment and many part-time students who take courses only occasionally cannot synchronize the course offerings in nondegree programs. Administrators won't even try. Instead, they compile a list of offerings and hope for adequate enrollments. Each course faces a go/no-go decision based on current demand. Chapter 14 deals with planning and control issues in asynchronous value-adding systems.

This chapter begins with an explanation of the relevance of bottlenecks to employees in all functions in a synchronous value-adding system. To effectively manage such a system, the functions must be well coordinated across the board. A description of a simple synchronous value-adding system follows. Then, from the standpoint of environmental characteristics, we consider where this approach works best; it's not a tool for every setting. Next, we present an overview of this system, with the emphasis on how to measure performance, account for costs, and manage operations. The chapter closes with a description of a scheduling method called the drum-buffer-rope system, which is useful in dealing with system bottlenecks.

> Integrating Operations Management with Other Functions

Figure 14.1 describes the relationships between the sections of this chapter and other functional areas of business.

Any functional area of any business can include a bottleneck or make decisions that create a bottleneck. Marketing policies that reward a sales force with commissions based on the dollar volume of sales generated, for example, can lead to large sales of low-margin items that are time consuming to produce. Financial management policies that require detailed expense reporting can tie up employee time; to the extent that such policies keep employees from value-adding activities, the paperwork itself may become a bottleneck. Investment policies that require a particular localized rate of return can prevent a company from expanding its capacity at a bottleneck, even though the expansion would improve the firm's profitability. Budgetary policies that limit cash flow can make the financing process a bottleneck in and of itself.

Information systems often limit a firm's capability. For example, many retail companies use bar code readers to determine customer bills at cash registers and point-of-sale (POS) terminals, but their

Chapter Topics / Functional Areas of Business	Finance	Accounting	Human Resources	Marketing	Engineering	Management Information Systems
Integrating Operations Management with Other Functions	●	●	●	●	●	●
An Example of Decision Making in a Synchronous Value-Adding System	●	●		●		
Where Does the Theory of Constraints Make Sense?	●	●	●	●	●	●
Overview of Synchronous Systems and the Theory of Constraints				●	●	
Supply Chain Impact of Synchronous Planning and Control						●
Detailed Scheduling Using the Drum-Buffer-Rope System				●		●

FIGURE 14.1 Integrating Operations Management with Other Functions

information processing capacity is insufficient to use the data for reordering. That is why, even though the checkout register "knows" what has been sold, you may still see clerks going through the aisles of some grocery stores with handheld scanners. The operations function itself often contains one or more bottlenecks. The problem might be inadequate parking space for a service facility, too few examination rooms in a doctor's office, a machine with temporarily insufficient capacity in some part of the value-adding system, a limitation in the availability of some highly demanded material, a shortage of skilled or unskilled labor, or insufficient space for inventory storage. When a company has unused capacity because of low levels of demand, the market itself is the system bottleneck.

Regardless of where a bottleneck is located, decision makers in other functions can do their company harm if they aren't aware of the bottleneck and its implications. An operations manager who doesn't know about a market bottleneck might make too much of the wrong product-service bundles and not enough of the right ones. A salesperson or marketing manager might promote low-profit items, which are difficult and time consuming to make at a bottleneck work center, because they are easy to sell and generate high commissions. Financial managers who are unaware of a bottleneck in another part of the firm are likely to overestimate the revenue potential from investment opportunities that depend on the bottleneck. In fact, one can imagine a host of scenarios in which decision makers' lack of awareness of bottlenecks in other functions results in regrettable choices, from the perspective of the firm or its customers. Clearly, effective management of a synchronous value-adding system presupposes effective management across the white spaces of the organizational chart.

The key to effective management of such systems is to recognize and exploit a system bottleneck wherever it exists. From a marketing perspective, that means selling what is most profitable, not necessarily what carries the highest commission. It even means refusing an order if a bottleneck will limit the firm's ability to profitably deliver the product-service bundle to the customer's satisfaction.

General guidelines for the various functions might be stated as follows:

- Operations should make whatever is most profitable for the firm, not what generates the best local performance results or piece rate bonuses.
- Finance should support efforts to improve performance at the bottleneck. When traditional capital justification techniques are used, the system return on improvements to bottleneck performance is usually understated, because those techniques look at resources in isolation. On the other hand, one must be careful about expecting a return on an investment in a nonbottleneck work center; there is no financial benefit to improving performance at an underutilized resource. Finally, financial managers who are responsible for creating operational budgets need to recognize that in many firms, cash flow problems create operational bottlenecks.
- Engineering, operational, financial, and marketing personnel who serve on design teams need to design (or redesign) product-service bundles for manufacturability. That means they need to be aware of existing and potential bottlenecks and create designs that can bypass these system constraints.
- Accounting must approach cost and performance measurement in nontraditional ways. Activity-based costing, the balanced scorecard (page 615), and other recently developed performance measurement methods that focus on systemwide rather than local performance are necessary if cost information is to adequately support managerial decision making in a synchronous value-adding system.
- Management information systems personnel need to clearly understand the information requirements of managers. Particularly in complex value-adding systems, synchronizing operational, marketing, purchasing, and financial decisions frequently requires the use of decision support systems.

> A Simple Synchronous Value-Adding System

Figure 14.2 illustrates a fairly simple screen-printing operation. The printing process requires that a screen be prepared for each color of a print. Screen preparation and setup takes 30 minutes per screen (5 of those minutes are devoted to setup). The screen is then set up on one of two presses, the garments printed, and the ink cured in the firm's single oven. (A conveyor belt runs through the oven, so curing the ink isn't as much work as it would be in your kitchen oven.) The time required to accomplish each of these operations is indicated in Figure 14.2, along with the available capacity at each of the resources.

Two employees are required to run this operation: an artist-screen maker, who makes the screens and does setups, and a printer, who uses the presses to print the garments. Both these employees are expected to be available for 2,400 minutes each week. The company can't change the available capacity of any of its resources, human or capital, in the short-term—they're fixed. The mix of jobs in the facility, however, will vary from one week to the next, depending on customer needs.

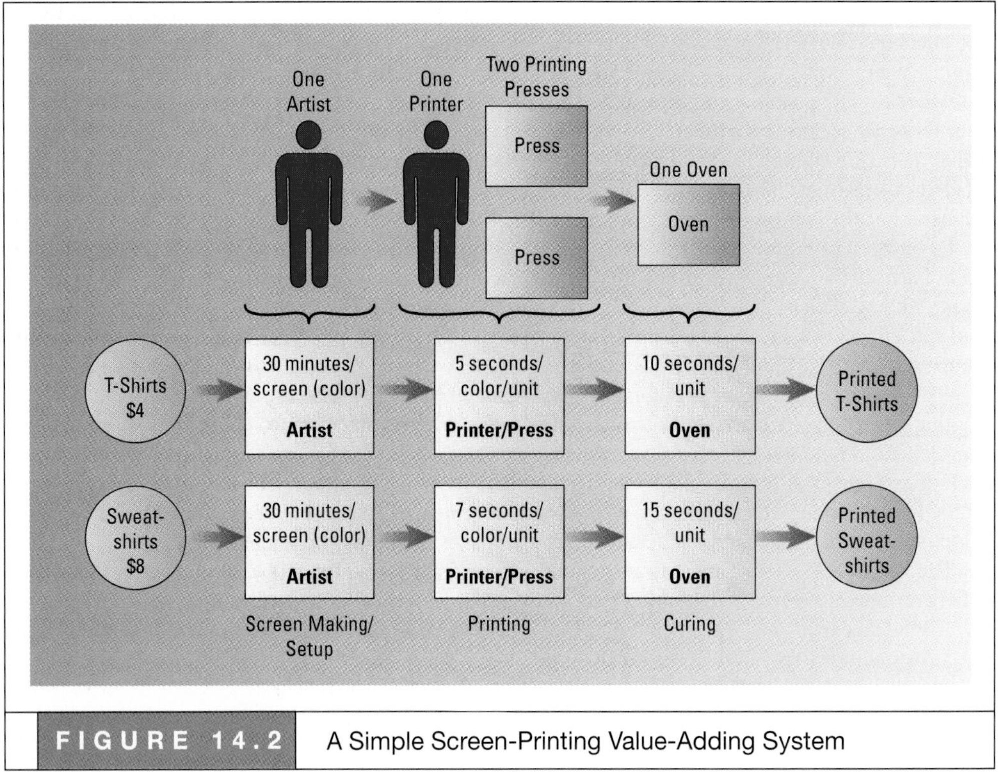

FIGURE 14.2 A Simple Screen-Printing Value-Adding System

The company buys its sweatshirts for $8 and its T-shirts for $4. It sells the sweatshirts for $16 with one-color prints, and $17, $18, and $19 for two-, three-, and four-color prints respectively. T-shirts sell for $10, $11, $12, and $13 for one-, two-, three-, and four-color prints respectively.

Consider the following questions pertaining to the screen-printing operation just described:

- Suppose the sales commission is 10% to 7% of the dollar value of sales (declining as the order size increased) plus an additional 10% for orders from new customers. If you were a salesperson, what kind of jobs would you shoot for? The answer: Based on these incentives, you'd be looking for lots of new customers and you'd be trying to sell them lots of expensive items. You'd be pushing the four-color items and, because of the declining percentage, you wouldn't push too hard for larger jobs. Result: lots of small four-color jobs.
- What effect would your decision have on the printing operation? The answer: Recall that each screen takes 30 minutes to make. Since a four-color job requires four screens, the printing operation can handle only 20 of these each week (and it can only do that if there are no other jobs). As a result, the commission structure would motivate the sales force to sell work that cannot be completed. The firm's revenues would be far lower than they might be otherwise, and friction would develop between marketing and operations.

Obviously, the situation we've just described is not a desirable one. What if the sales commission was 10% of sales for on-time jobs, paid only upon delivery and verification of customer satisfaction? In that case, the sales force would be motivated to sell whatever product would generate the greatest revenue from the printing operation. It wouldn't do the salesperson any good to sell something that could get held up in production. Result: The sales force would be continually trying to assess the status of operational resources and then selling whatever product generates the highest margin per minute at the bottleneck resource.

In regard to the screen-printing operation, Table 14.1 shows the weekly capacity of each resource and the margin per minute or per screen. Depending on the mix of jobs in the facility, the operational bottleneck may be the printer, the printing press, the oven, or the screen-making operation.

For example, suppose that the market potential (perhaps based on the size of the sales force) was around 10,000 units a week, and the typical order size was for 300 units. (That means there will be about 10,000/300 = 33.33 orders per week.) If all of these orders were three- and four-color jobs, screen making and setup would be a system bottleneck. If all of the orders were one-color jobs, oven capacity would be the bottleneck. If the mix was 25 orders each for 400 shirts with three-color designs, printing would be the bottleneck.

TABLE 14.1	Cost Breakdown on T-Shirts and Sweatshirts							
	Sweatshirts				T-Shirts			
Price/Shirt	$16	$17	$18	$19	$10	$11	$12	$13
Cost/Shirt	$8	$8	$8	$8	$4	$4	$4	$4
Margin/Shirt	$8	$9	$10	$11	$6	$7	$8	$9
Screen Making and Setup Capacity (orders per week)	80	40	26.66	20	80	40	26.66	20
Printing Capacity (shirts per week)	20,571	10,285	6,857	5,142	28,800	14,400	9,600	7,200
Oven Capacity (shirts per week)	9,600	9,600	9,600	9,600	14,400	14,400	14,400	14,400
Margin/Screen*	$2,400	$1,350	$1,000	$825	$1,800	$1,050	$800	$675
Margin/Printer Minute	$68.57**	$38.57**	$28.57	$23.57	$72**	$42	$32	$27
Margin/Oven Minute	$32	$36	$40**	$44**	$36	$42	$48**	$54**

*Assumes an average order size of 300 units.

**These margins for the oven and the printer aren't currently attainable, because the printer won't be able to keep up with the oven with three- and four-color images, and the oven won't be able to keep up with the printer with one- and two-color sweatshirts and one-color T-shirts.

When screen making and setup is not the bottleneck, Table 14.1 suggests that the best item to sell would be the two-color T-shirt because at a margin of $42.00 per minute, the margin at the oven and printer is highest. This suggests that $42.00 × 2,400 min/week = $100,800/week could be generated by the system if the sales force could sell 14,400 two-color shirts in 40 or fewer designs. Thus the average order size would need to be 14,400/40 = 360 shirts. (If, as we suggested above, the market is limited to 10,000 shirts because of the size of the sales force, the weekly gross income potential would be only $86,400 (10,000 units × $7.00 margin per unit). Thus, the ability to expand the market would be worth up to $100,800 − $86,400 = $14,400.

Of course, customers will want various designs and not all will be satisfied with two-color prints on T-shirts. The point of the illustration is not to say it is good to turn away customers because they don't want 360 two-color T-shirts. It is not the job of the sales force to make customers conform to the needs of the value-adding system. The example is designed to illustrate that marketing targets for number of colors and job size can be developed from an understanding of operational issues.

Managers would attempt to optimize the revenues generated from the system by aligning sales force incentives and marketing promotions in light of the characteristics of the value-adding system. In doing so, they would make the most of their bottleneck resources. In situations where the market is not limited, some work has to be turned away. Using the logic contained in this example, managers can determine which orders are most desirable. This decision would not occur once and for all time. Rather, based upon the current mix of orders already promised for a given week on the master schedule, management (or the sales force) can prioritize the new order possibilities.

Table 14.2 illustrates a situation where the master schedule for a given week already includes five orders for two-color T-shirts totaling 4,000 shirts and 10 orders for one-color sweatshirts also totaling 4,000 shirts. As you can see, this schedule has the oven most heavily utilized and the screen-making artist has very little work to do. Thus, since the margin per oven minute (shown in Table 14.1) is highest for four-color Ts, it would make sense to promote these shirts for this particular week of the master schedule. Because oven time is getting scarce, not many more shirts can be sold; but there's still plenty of screen making and printing capacity to sell. Thus, orders for multicolored shirts, which are heavy users of such capacity, are desirable in this week.

Table 14.3 illustrates the master schedule in another week. There are 10 orders for a total of 12,000 two-color shirts already scheduled and four orders for a total of 800 four-color sweatshirts. The printer is the most highly utilized resource. With utilization at 98.9%, the weekly capacity is, for all practical purposes, fully committed. Table 14.1 shows that two-color T-shirts provide the highest margin per printer minute. It makes sense, therefore, to give printing priority to the two-color Ts in this situation. If there is any lost time during the week and the full capacity cannot be used, at least the time that has been used will have been dedicated to items with the highest margin per minute.

TABLE 14.2 With the Oven as the Bottleneck: Promote Multicolor Shirts

	Current # of Order	Number of Colors	Total Number of Shirts	Screen Making/ Setup (minutes)	Printing Press (minutes)	Oven (minutes)	Printer (minutes)
T-Shirts	5	2-color	4,000 shirts	300	716	666	666
Sweatshirts	10	1-color	4,000 shirts	300	516	1,000	466
			Total Minutes Required	600	1,232	1,666	1,133
			Total Weekly Capacity	2,400	4,800	2,400	2,400
			Utilization %	25%	25.7%	69.4%	47.16%

TABLE 14.3 With the Printer as the Bottleneck: Give Priority to Two-Color Ts

	Current # of Order	Number of Colors	Total Number of Shirts	Screen Making/ Setup (minutes)	Printing Press (minutes)	Oven (minutes)	Printer (minutes)
T-Shirts	10	2-color	12,000 shirts	600	2,100	2,000	2,000
Sweatshirts	4	4-color	800 shirts	480	453	200	373
			Total Minutes Required	1,080	2,553	2,200	2,373
			Total Weekly Capacity	2,400	4,800	2,400	2,400
			Utilization %	45%	50.2%	91.6%	98.9%

When the screen-making artist is the bottleneck, Table 14.1 suggests it is best to sell one-color jobs because this provides the highest margin per screen. This suggestion makes sense. Who wouldn't sell jobs that make the best use of your scarce resource? Table 14.4 gives another, more specific, example of this situation. It considers a product mix consisting of 10 orders for three-color T-shirts averaging 400 units in size and 11 orders for four-color sweatshirts averaging 200 units in size. If this were the existing demand for a given week, it's clear that the screen-making artist is the most heavily utilized resource. At 92.5% screen-making utilization, you're about to run out of capacity for new work, even though the oven and printing presses are barely being used half of the time. This calls for the sales force to promote large orders for one-color shirts, so that scarce resource can be best leveraged to create additional system revenues by providing work for the underutilized resources.

Finance and accounting majors reading this chapter might be wondering why the company is carrying two printing presses. After all, there is only one printer, and in every example so far, the utilization of the two printing presses has been less than 100%. Having a second press allows the screen-making artist to set up for a printing job while the printer is still working on the prior job. This converts all internal exchange of die (IED) setup tasks to outside exchange of die (OED) setup tasks, which was a primary suggestion of the single minute exchange of dies (SMED) system described in Chapter 13. However, having a second press does tie up capital, require floor space, and eat up maintenance dollars, so the financial types are right to require justification of such an arrangement.

If typical capital justification procedures were used, the second press would have to justify itself on the basis of the revenues it could generate on its own. A common mistake is to look at the utilization of the resource in isolation from the rest of the system to see if it's worth keeping (or buying). So, for example, if the average utilization of each printing press is 52.4%, analysts would say that the second press brings in incremental revenues of only 4.8% (52.4% × 2 = 104.8%, or 4.8% more than one press used continuously). Since Table 14.1 shows that the margin per minute for the printer is at best $42, that means that for 4.8% of 2,400 minutes per week, the second printer brings in incremental revenues of just $42 per minute, or a total of $4,838.40 per week ($42 × .048 × 2,400 = $4,838.40).

Table 14.5 illustrates a hypothetical situation in which there is only one press that is utilized at the rate of 107%. (Actually, the press can't be utilized at more than 100%–this really means that demand exceeds press capacity by 7%.) If a second press were added, the utilization would be 53.5%. (Note that this situation is identical to the one just described, in which the second press, considered in isolation, appears to provide only an additional $4,838.40 per week in revenues.) Because there is only one printer and only one press, however, the number of minutes available for actually printing shirts is reduced by the number of minutes required for setups. Since the setup time per color is 5 minutes, 100 minutes will be required to set up 10 two-color jobs, and 200 minutes to set up 10 four-color jobs. Consequently, though the printer is idle only 6% of the time, the press is unavailable due to setup 300/2,400 = 12.5% of the time. That means that 6.5% (12.5% − 6%) of the week, the printer is idle because of downtime due to setup on the press.

Here is the crux of the matter: Adding a second press would turn that 6.5% of the week into productive time for the printer. In other words, considering the system as a whole, the improvement in the utilization rate resulting from the additional press is not 4.8%, but 6.5% + 4.8% = 11.3%. The incremental revenue resulting from the additional press is 11.3% × 2,400 × $42.00 = $11,390.40 per week. Thus, in synchronous value-adding systems, financial analyses of the need for capital equipment must consider the *systemwide* impact of the resource. Financial managers need to look at the whole value-adding system; that requires an ability to manage across the white spaces.

Compared to virtually any real-world business, this example is quite simple; there are only two types of shirts, only four steps to the process (screen making, setup, printing, and curing), and operation times have been kept simple. Still, this example illustrates the challenges facing managers of such systems. In more complex operational situations, applying the concepts illustrated in this chapter requires the use of sophisticated decision support systems, which have the computing power to handle the required mathematical calculations.

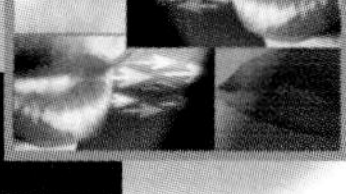

> active poll

What do you think? Voice your opinion and find out what others have to say.

TABLE 14.4 With the Artist as the Bottleneck: Promote Large Orders for Single-Color Shirts

	Current # of Order	Number of Colors	Total Number of Shirts	Screen Making/ Setup (minutes)	Printing Press (minutes)	Oven (minutes)	Printer (minutes)
T-Shirts	10	3-color	4,000 shirts	900	1,165	666	1,000
Sweatshirts	11	4-color	2,200 shirts	1,320	1,246	550	1,026
			Total Minutes Required	2,220	2,411	1,216	2,026
			Total Weekly Capacity	2,400	4,800	2,400	2,400
			Utilization %	92.5%	50.2%	50.6%	84.4%

TABLE 14.5 Making the Case for the Second Printing Press

	Current # of Order	Number of Colors	Total Number of Shirts	Screen Making/ Setup (minutes)	Printing Press (minutes)	Oven (minutes)	Printer (minutes)
T-Shirts	10	2-color	8,000 shirts	600	1,433	1,133	1,333
Sweatshirts	10	4-color	2,000 shirts	1,200	1,133	500	933
			Total Minutes Required	1,800	2,566	1,633	2,266
			Total Weekly Capacity	2,400	2,400	2,400	2,400
			Utilization %	75%	107%	68%	94%

> active concept check

Now let's take a moment to test your knowledge of the concepts you have studied in this section.

Applicability of Synchronous Planning and Control

In general, it makes sense to synchronize system planning and control when operations and demand patterns are too complex for a kanban system to work, and system bottlenecks can be found quickly. In Chapter 13, we noted a number of conditions that limit the effectiveness of the just-in-time (JIT) approach to planning and control. Specifically, kanban systems will not work when the demand pull comes from multiple sources and has not effectively been leveled through master scheduling. Figure 14.3 suggests that when scheduling complexity is introduced in one part of an otherwise simple kanban system, a bottleneck is likely to develop. When that happens, a better-suited option than JIT is needed for system planning and control.

The **theory of constraints** is a general approach that can be used to synchronize value-adding systems containing bottlenecks. You've probably applied this theory without thinking about it at some point in your life. For example, if you've wanted to keep a group of drivers together on the interstate, you've probably put the slowest vehicle (i.e., the team bus) in the front and required the others to follow. The soonest that all of the vehicles can arrive at the destination is determined by the schedule of the bus (bottleneck). When you identified this bottleneck, you subordinated the schedule of all other

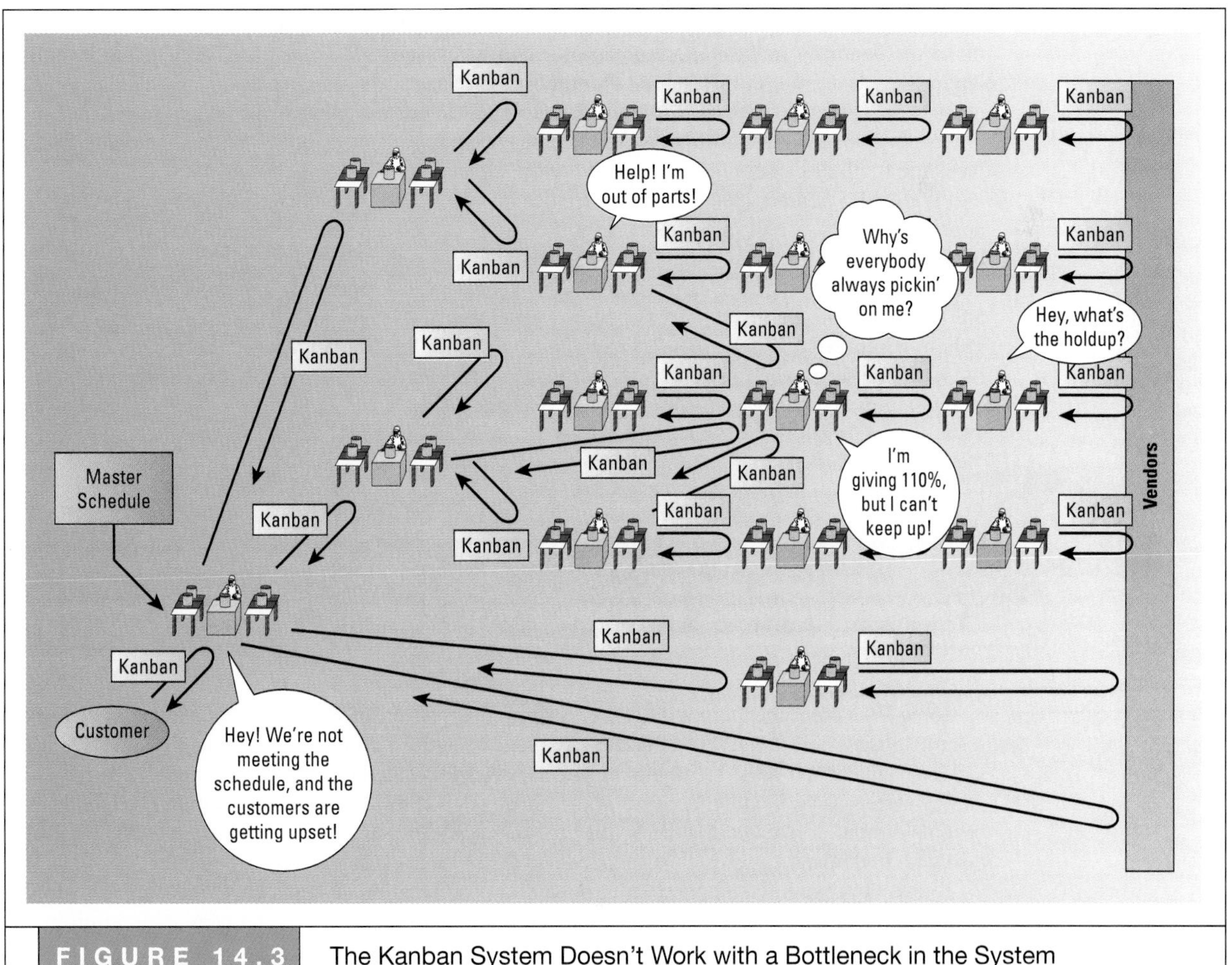

FIGURE 14.3 The Kanban System Doesn't Work with a Bottleneck in the System

Airport hubs, such as this one at Schipol Airport in Holland, have significant excess capacity most of the time. They need to be large, however, to accommodate demand during peak travel holidays (during which time they are the system constraint). Making a hub larger keeps more planes in the air during peak travel days by providing more rapid ground services.

vehicles to it. You might have even attempted to increase the capacity of the bottleneck by towing a trailer of band instruments with another vehicle or taking two smaller buses.

The same principles are in use when families let the youngest child start eating first, so that everyone finishes at the same time, or when an airline boards elderly passengers and families with children first. The time needed to board passengers isn't changed much by this practice, but it does make the boarding process more pleasant for most passengers, since they can wait in the lounge where they are more comfortable. The theory of constraints also applies when a student group decides on a meeting time based on the schedule of the busiest team member or when a small-town university with a large stadium crowd allocates special parking spaces for RVs, cars, and buses at weekend football games.

Figure 14.4 summarizes the characteristics of synchronous planning and control systems. This approach is very useful when demand varies from week to week, the number of product-service bundles is manageable and does not require extensive individual customization, and operational volume is moderate. These characteristics are generally descriptive of batch processes. Also, there are usually some dominant material flows, which carry the lion's share of the system's load, and system complexity is somewhat lessened through limits in product variety. Thus, this approach is likely to be useful wherever customers or materials are batched in order to simplify the scheduling of operations.

active exercise

Take a moment to apply what you've learned.

Some situations are too complex for full implementation of the theory of constraints; we have reserved discussion of such systems for Chapters 15 and 16. Maybe the complexity of the product-service bundle is too great because of the high level of customization that is offered. Maybe the value-adding system is so flexible, because of the need for customization, that capacity requirements have become difficult to predict. Maybe by the time managers find the bottleneck and get a plan in place to deal with it, demand patterns have changed and the bottleneck has moved.

Today, improvements in computing power and information systems have made it easier to find bottleneck(s), interact with customers and suppliers, understand the system capacity requirements for customized work, and at the same time synchronize the value-adding system. The line between systems that can be synchronized (Chapter 14) and those that cannot (Chapter 15) is moving. It is likely that systems that cannot be synchronized today may be synchronized sometime in the

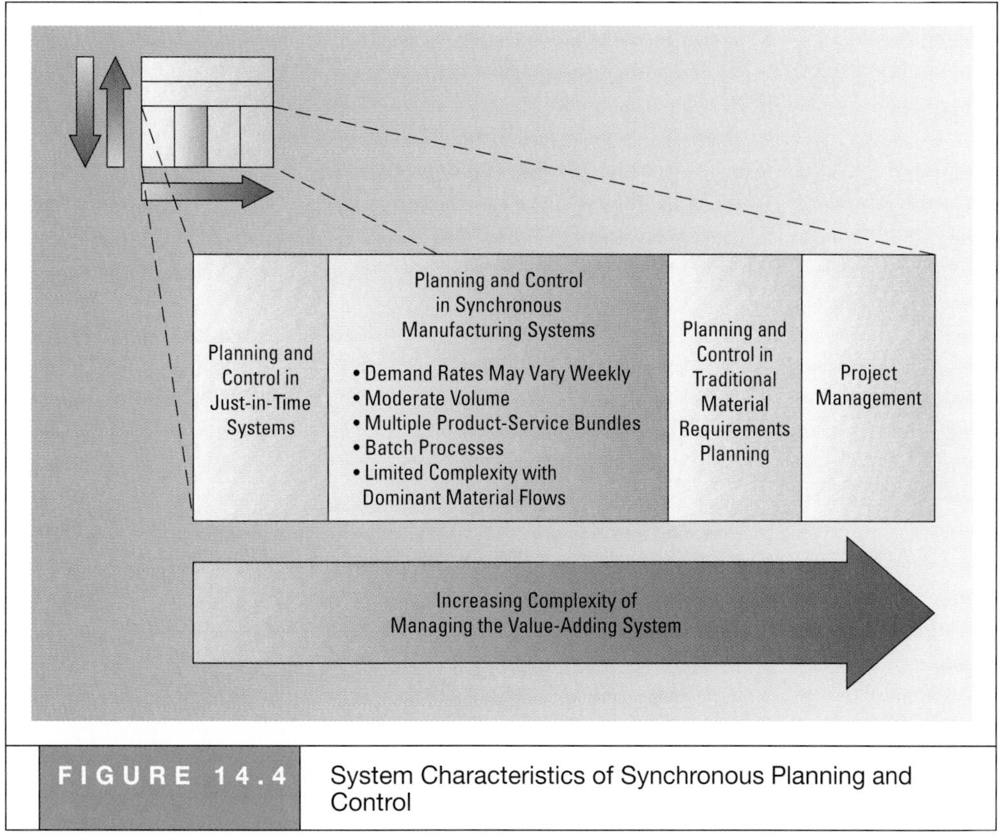

FIGURE 14.4 System Characteristics of Synchronous Planning and Control

future. Companies that can make that kind of improvement will gain a competitive advantage in the marketplace.

Figure 14.5 summarizes short-term planning and control in a synchronous value-adding system. At the master scheduling level, product mix decisions are made. These decisions are about what orders to accept or reject and are based on the orders' profit potential at the system bottleneck. Material plans will then be made to ensure that parts and components are available to support the schedule at the bottleneck. Detailed capacity plans focus on the bottleneck and optimizing throughput at this resource. All operations are synchronized using a *drum-buffer-rope scheduling system* (described later in this chapter). The goal is to maximize throughput while minimizing inventory and operating expense for the given product mix.

While the schedules for various resources can be computed deterministically in a JIT system, in which the master schedule is leveled, that is not possible in a system with enough complexity to require synchronization. According to the theory of constraints, the bottleneck schedule can be arrived at deterministically, but other resources must be scheduled based on probabilistic assumptions (using the "DBR" approach described later in this chapter). The bottleneck is generally scheduled using what is called a **forward finite scheduling** approach. Managers start with current jobs waiting at the bottleneck and assign time to them—from the present onward—based on their priorities. They don't schedule more than the bottleneck can process over a given period. Other resources will have excess capacity; they are scheduled with a **backward infinite scheduling** approach—starting with the time they must arrive at the bottleneck and working backward in time. In other words, the schedule of nonbottleneck resources is determined so as to ensure that work gets to the bottleneck when it is needed. Since these resources have excess capacity, managers aren't concerned about scheduling more work than they can process in a given period.

> active concept check

Now let's take a moment to test your knowledge of the concepts you have studied in this section.

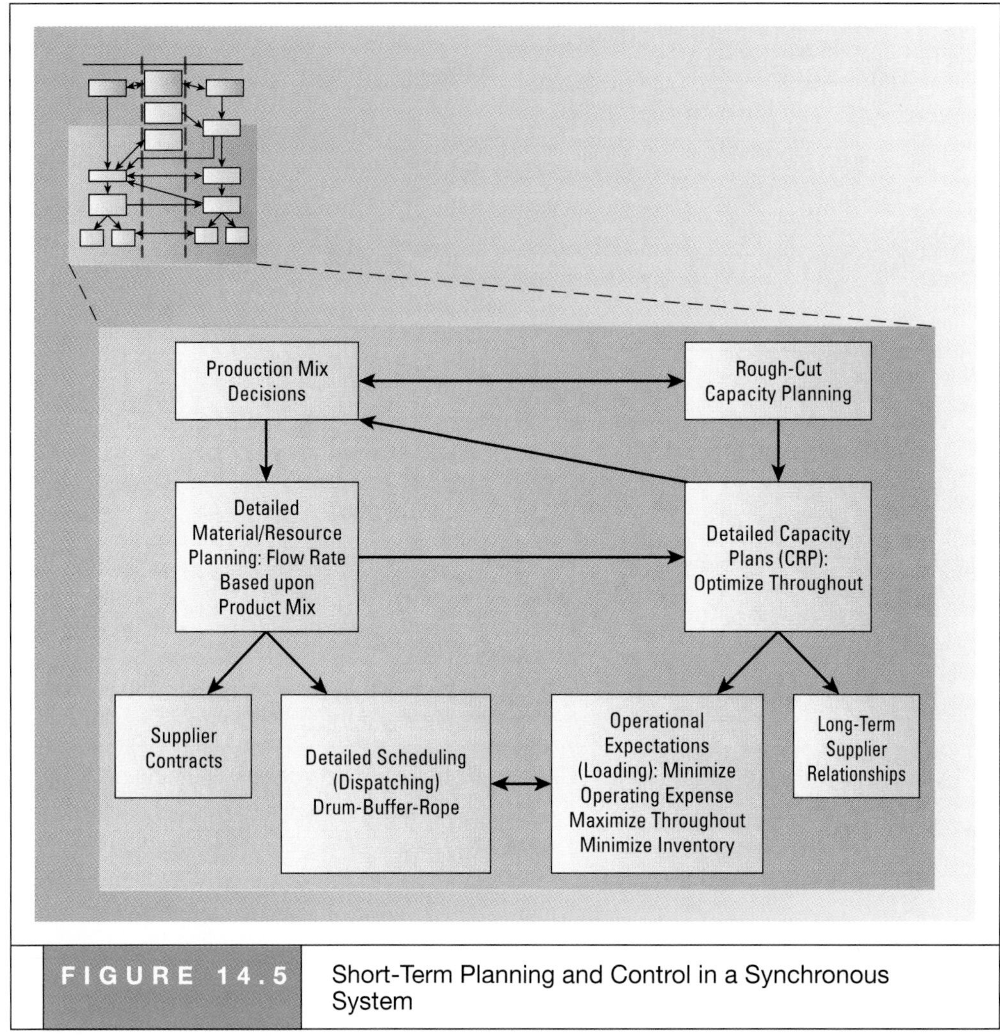

FIGURE 14.5 Short-Term Planning and Control in a Synchronous System

Overview of Synchronous Systems

In the 1980s, Eliyahu Goldratt published a book called *The Goal,* which popularized the principles underlying a software package he had developed called *Optimized Production Technology (OPT).* The book dealt primarily with the importance of bottlenecks in a value-adding system. For example, the lead character in the book, Alex Rogo, learns that an hour lost at a bottleneck is an hour lost for the entire system, while an hour lost at a nonbottleneck is inconsequential. He also learns that it helps not to begin work on jobs that cannot be accommodated at a bottleneck. We saw this principle at work at Tom Jackson's airline, where managers have figured out that if passengers must wait, it's better for them to wait in the lounge than on the airplane or in line at the boarding gate. Similarly, if a customer's order must wait, it's better for it to wait as an unstarted job, with no investment in materials, than as a partially completed order representing a partial investment in materials and processing time. Not only is money tied up when an order waits as work in process, but scheduling flexibility is lost.

Table 14.6 lists the OPT principles that were built into Goldratt's software and highlighted in his book.

PERFORMANCE MEASURES AND CAPACITY ISSUES

One issue that comes up in attempting to synchronize the schedule of resources across an entire facility is the question of how performance will be measured. The traditional approach to operational performance measurement relies on *local performance measures,* in which worker performance and resource utilization are measured against a work standard and resource capacity. In other words, workers are considered to be performing to expectations if they are doing their jobs as fast as we believe they can. Resources are considered to be well managed if the operation is producing the volume of output it is capable of generating. Output is measured in units completed at the individual

TABLE 14.6	The OPT Principles
1.	Balance the flow of materials through the system, not the capacity of resources.
2.	Utilization levels for nonbottleneck resources are not determined based on their own capacity, but by the capacity of the system bottleneck.
3.	Utilization and activation of a resource aren't the same thing. You can create useless WIP by activating a resource. Only useful WIP counts toward utilization.
4.	Any time lost at the bottleneck is lost to the system and cannot be recovered.
5.	Any time saved at a nonbottleneck is irrelevant since it already has time to spare.
6.	The bottleneck is the key to improving throughput or lowering system inventory.
7.	You don't have to complete an order at one work center before you transfer WIP forward allowing the next work center to begin.
8.	Batch sizes aren't set in stone; their size can affect rates of throughput and inventory levels.
9.	Schedules for each resource should simultaneously consider all system constraints. Since the system and its constraints can change over time, schedules change over time and lead-times will also vary.

resource. Similarly, work-in-process inventory is accounted for as an asset whose value increases with each additional operation it passes through. Capacity and, therefore, operating expenses are essentially fixed at the output level individual resources are able to provide.

In synchronous systems, relying too heavily on local performance measures can lead to a frustrating phenomenon called the *hockey stick syndrome,* in which daily output resembles the pattern shown in Figure 14.6. Note the high levels of output at the end of reporting periods, followed by low levels of output for the majority of the reporting period; thus the name *hockey stick syndrome.* You've probably had some experience with this syndrome. For example, you may tend to complete term papers and major projects the weekend or night before they are due. That's probably because for weeks you've been too busy learning about the topic to write it up—or at least that's the explanation your professors get. When the goal changes from learning to showing what you have learned, your rate of output changes dramatically.

Why do companies experience the hockey stick syndrome? When accountants compute local performance measures, they generate information that managers use to make decisions about worker performance, resource utilization, and asset allocation. These decisions ultimately influence workers' pay and the quality of their jobs. As a result, workers and managers are motivated to look good on local performance. But their goal-directed behavior creates problems for anyone who is trying to synchronize operations across an entire system. When decisions are made based on local performance, operations are not synchronized and customers' orders get bottled up in the value-adding system. At the end of the month, when financial performance has to be reported to key stakeholders, managers become very interested in performance measures such as net profit, return on assets (ROA), and cash flow. Unlike the local performance measures that influence employees' behavior for most of the month, these financial measures are *global performance measures:* They indicate the effectiveness of the entire value-adding system, not just one resource. So toward the end of the month, decisions are made with system performance in mind, and the system generates rapid output.

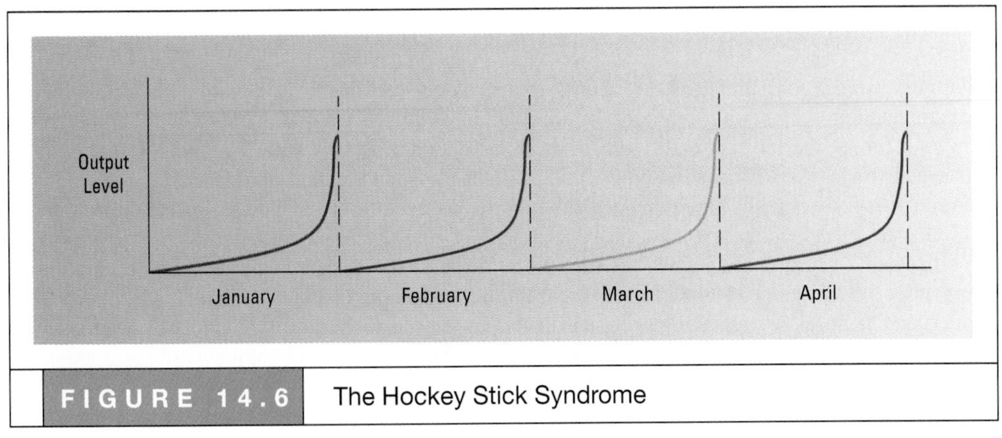

FIGURE 14.6 The Hockey Stick Syndrome

To synchronize operations, local operational performance measures must be replaced with global measures. These broader operational measures should help decision makers and workers to coordinate their activities for the customer's benefit every day of the month, not just when financial results must be reported. Goldratt has suggested that the following three operational performance measures replace traditional local measures:

- **Throughput,** which is the rate at which the system generates money through sales. It is desirable to increase throughput.
- **Inventory,** which is all the money invested in purchasing items the system intends to sell. It is generally desirable to reduce inventory.
- **Operating expense,** which is the money the system spends in converting inventory to throughput. It is generally desirable to reduce operating expense.

These global operational measures differ from local measures in several critically important ways. By definition, they focus on performance of the whole system, not that of individual resources. For example, getting lots of passengers' baggage checked in at Tom's airline creates no throughput. Throughput is only created when satisfied customers collect their baggage and leave the terminal in the city of their destination. Similarly, cutting lots of table legs at Luis's factory would require a large amount of work at one particular work center and would look great on the traditional measures of worker output and resource utilization. On Goldratt's measures, however, it would create no throughput, but instead increase inventory and operating expense. It might even hold back other jobs and thereby reduce throughput, while further increasing inventory and operating expense.

Goldratt's measures are better linked to the global financial measures that become important at the end of the month, because their unit of measurement is money, not output units. Increasing throughput, decreasing operating expense, and decreasing inventory will each lead to an increase in net profit, ROA, and cash flow. Because Goldratt's operational measures are well aligned with the financial measures, companies that utilize these measures throughout the month are less likely to adjust their behavior at the end of financial reporting periods and therefore less likely to suffer from the hockey stick syndrome. A consistent rate of throughput provides a more stable operating environment and improves quality-of-work-life for employees by eliminating the stressful activity that would otherwise occur just prior to reporting deadlines. It can also improve customer satisfaction by reducing leadtimes and making them more predictable.

Ultimately, to use global measures of performance effectively, managers must change their view of resource capacity needs. When performance is measured locally, any activity is presumed to be productive; thus, *resource activation* is confused with *resource utilization.* If Tom's meal catering facility is capable of preparing twice as many meals as needed for his flights, it does no good for that resource to be active 100% of the time. Only half that activity would have practical utility. But if the value-adding system is synchronized, the catering facility cannot create throughput any faster than the system as a whole. The more appropriate view of the capacity of the catering facility is the rate at which the system can create satisfied customers.

active exercise <

Take a moment to apply what you've learned.

COST ACCOUNTING

Like performance measures, cost-accounting practices need to fit the value-adding system to which they are applied. An ongoing problem for accountants and decision makers has been the question of how to estimate the indirect and overhead costs affiliated with particular product-service bundles. Historically, when less computing power was available, cost accountants would apply overhead costs to product-service bundles based on the estimated percentage of overall indirect costs required to support the particular bundle. For example, suppose one of Cheryl's lab technicians tests a variety of different types of samples from four different parts of the hospital. (Let's say they are throat cultures from an outpatient clinic, blood samples from the wellness center, tissue samples from the oncology center, and samples of collagen purchased for use in the plastic surgery practice.) Cost accountants would need to determine how the cost of the lab technician's salary and benefits would be allocated to these four product-service bundles.

Accurate allocation of these costs is essential to good decision making. Suppose the lab technician's time is dominated by time-consuming tissue testing for the oncology clinic, but because the accountants are not lab technicians and don't really know for sure what product-service bundles dominate the technician's schedule, the overhead cost is distributed evenly over the four areas. Cheryl will consider the oncology clinic's services to be more profitable than they really are. Similarly, the other areas will look less profitable than they really are. As a result, when it looks as if the lab is too busy, she will be likely to send wellness, plastic surgery, and outpatient clients to competing hospitals so that lab technicians can concentrate on the oncology. At the end of the accounting period, she will find that the hospital's earnings are lower than expected, and she won't understand why. Cheryl will be particularly confused when she sees the improved performance of her competitors, who will benefit from the work she has sent their way.

With the advent of synchronous value-adding systems, cost accountants have had to develop new approaches that provide more useful information for decision makers. Two of the better-known approaches currently in use are activity-based costing and the balanced scorecard. **Activity-based costing (ABC)** is a managerial accounting approach that rests on the principle that activities cost money and operations consume activities. Cheryl's lab technician, for example, costs money, and his services are consumed in the creation of the various product-service bundles the hospital offers.

ABC seeks to provide greater accuracy in allocating overhead costs to the direct value-adding activities than is possible using the historical percentage allocation method. In this approach, the accountant first enumerates all the overhead activities and their costs. Next, the accountant determines the product-service bundles whose creation consumes these overhead activities. The overhead cost for each product-service bundle is the sum of the costs of the activities consumed in its creation. Though this approach is not conceptually difficult, the level of detail required was prohibitive prior to the advent of modern information systems.

If ABC leads to more accurate estimates of the indirect costs that go along with the creation of each product-service bundle, then it is particularly useful to managers of value-adding systems that contain a bottleneck. These managers have to decide how to ration bottleneck capacity among various product-service bundles. If their indirect cost estimates are not accurate, they might well think they are allocating bottleneck capacity to the most profitable product-service bundles, when they are actually wasting critical capacity on unprofitable items.

Robert Kaplan of the Harvard Business School suggested another managerial accounting approach, the **balanced scorecard,** which includes information about performance in key nonfinancial categories. Part of the idea behind the balanced scorecard is that often the very decisions that optimize short-term financial performance ultimately lead to disappointments in long-term performance. Kaplan's approach suggests that a company should consider its strategic goals in establishing its cost measurement system. Luis's company, which emphasizes flexibility and quality, would use a different scorecard from Fred's, which focuses on cost leadership.

The balanced scorecard might include measures representing the customer perspective, the internal business process, and innovation and learning. For instance, the customer perspective might be measured by customer retention ratios, on-time deliveries, and customer satisfaction surveys. The internal business process perspective might be represented by cycle time, throughput, yield, and quality defect rates. Innovation and learning could be measured by product development lead-time, new product introduction rates, number of employees cross trained, and percentage of sales from new products. Measuring performance from each of these perspectives, in addition to the financial perspective, should help managers to balance various stakeholder concerns.

THE MANAGEMENT PROCESS

The theory of constraints suggests that managers use a five-step process to manage their value-adding system. The five steps are:

1. Identify the system constraints.
2. Determine how to exploit the system contraints.
3. Subordinate every other decision to the decision made in step 2.
4. Elevate the system constraint.
5. If the constraint has changed with the passage of time or the process of moving through steps 1 through 4, go back to step 1.

To see how straightforward this five-step process is, consider the screen-printing example first presented in Figure 14.2. Step 1: We can use Tables 14.1 to 14.5 to identify the constraints, or bottlenecks, by comparing the capacity required at each resource with the capacity available (shown in the tables). Step 2: By finding the margin per unit of the scarce resource (see Table 14.1), we can

About 500 people camped out in a line outside the Eastgate theatre in Portland, Oregon, to get the first tickets to see *Star Wars: The Phantom Menace.* As a company's mix of products and services changes, bottlenecks may develop such as those experienced at ticket windows when a popular band is booked, a big sporting event is announced, or a new movie is released.

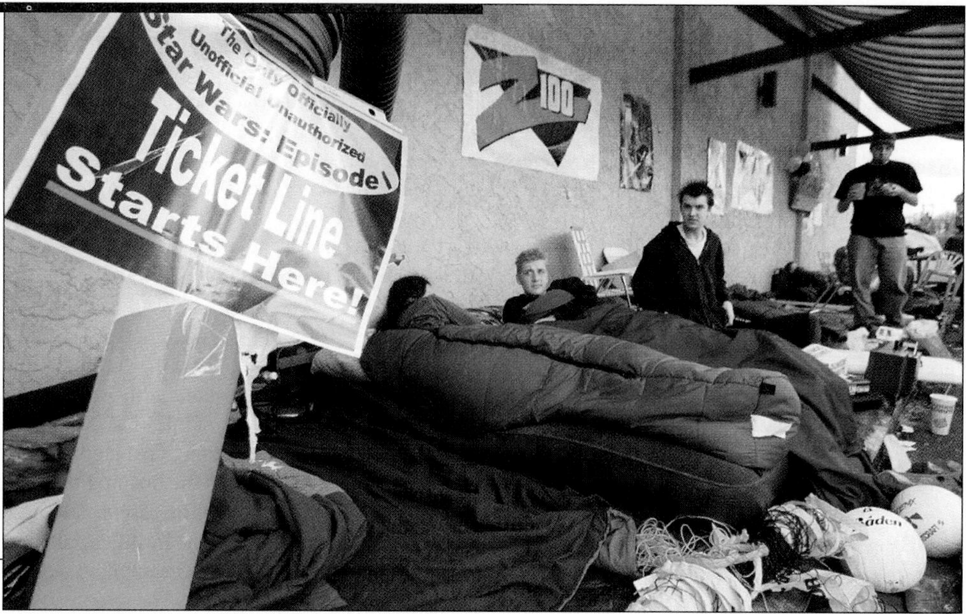

determine how to exploit that constraint. Step 3: In synchronizing the unconstrained activities with the constraint, we will subordinate every other decision to the decision made in step 2. Step 4: If the constraint is a long-standing problem, we can seek ways to elevate it. For example, we might consider buying a second printing press as a way of eliminating a long-standing bottleneck. Step 5: Finally, if the action we took in step 4 alleviates the problem, we should go back to step 1 and identify the new system constraint.

active concept check

Now let's take a moment to test your knowledge of the concepts you have studied in this section.

Supply-Chain Impact of Synchronous Planning and Control

Figure 14.7 indicates some of the ways that synchronous planning and control systems impact the firms that are a company's customers and suppliers in the supply chain.

From the supplier's perspective, several options might be used to improve relations with a customer with a synchronous system. Some of the value the supplier provides could be duplicated in the customer's nonbottleneck operations. At little incremental cost, capacity requirements could be shifted from the supplier to the customer through a temporary outsourcing agreement. Conversely, suppliers can occasionally reduce the customer's bottleneck capacity requirements by providing enhanced product-service bundles. That is what happens when you have pizza delivered rather than going out to eat during final exam week. Suppliers whose revenue potential is limited by customer bottlenecks should consider seeking additional customers for their output. When possible, they should also consider supplying technological alternatives to their customers, so as to reduce the severity of the bottleneck.

From an infrastructural perspective, by far the most important concern for suppliers of customers with synchronous systems is to guarantee the supply of critical bottleneck materials. Additional features and options, better material quality, and price discounts are of little interest to a customer whose bottleneck has been idled by a supply shortage. Guaranteeing the supply of critical materials means that the supplier's scheduling decisions must be synchronized to some extent with the bottleneck schedule. Occasionally, the supply of materials is itself the bottleneck in a value-adding system. In such cases, the supplier needs to work with customers, using the five-step process to make the best use of the limited supply of materials.

Suppliers

Structural Changes

- Expect Temporary Outsourcing of Bottleneck Work
- Seek Complementary Demand Sources (Customers)
- Supply Technology Alternatives to Bottleneck Work
- Provide Capacity Guarantees

Infrastructural Changes

- Improved "Real Time" Communication
- Advance/Delay Delivery of Material Based upon Bottleneck Schedule (i.e., synchronize raw material orders with bottleneck)
- Provide Advance Warning of Problems with Bottleneck Critical Materials

Synchronous Planning and Control

- Five-step focusing process
- Constraint Optimization
- Use Global

Performance Measures

- Maximize Throughput
- Minimize Inventory
- Minimize Operating Expense

Customers

Structural Changes

- Shift Capacity to Nonbottleneck Work Centers
- Consider Additional Suppliers to Ensure Adequate Capacity
- Explore Alternative Technologies That Don't Rely on Bottleneck

Infrastructural Changes

- Get Delivery Guarantees for Bottleneck Processed Items
- Provide Advance Warning of Demand for Bottleneck Processed Items
- Advance/Delay Orders Based upon Bottleneck Schedule (i.e., synchronize orders with bottleneck

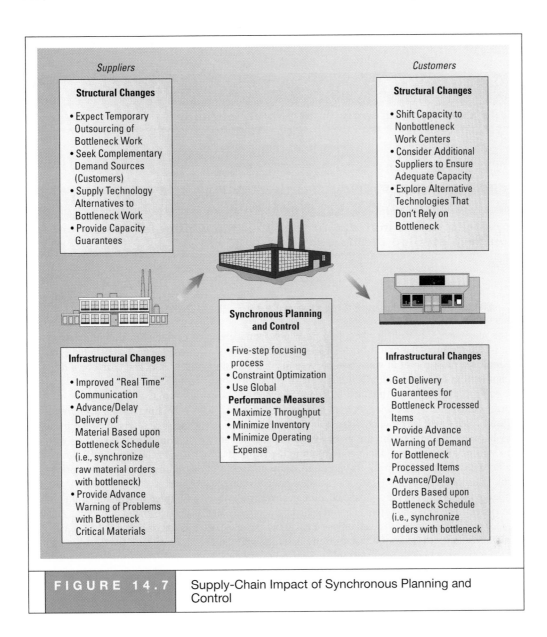

FIGURE 14.7 Supply-Chain Impact of Synchronous Planning and Control

> active example

Take a closer look at the concepts and issues you've been reading about.

From the customer's perspective, several potential structural and infrastructural options need to be considered to reduce the level of dependence on a supplier bottleneck. From a structural perspective, the customer can often shift work from a bottleneck center by changing the make-or-buy decision, and making instead of buying a portion of an item that had been purchased. Other structural changes that can reduce dependence on a supplier bottleneck include seeking additional suppliers and developing alternative technologies that do not require the bottleneck resource.

From an infrastructural perspective, it is important for customers to reserve capacity for their orders in advance. Doing so allows the supplier to assess resource requirements and provide reliable delivery dates. It also provides an opportunity for the customer to interact with the supplier and make decisions about the timing of orders. If as a group, customers are willing to cooperate, it is possible to reduce lead-times and improve customer service by advancing or delaying orders based on demand for the bottleneck capacity. Customer cooperation allows the entire supply chain to be synchronized, not just the company's value-adding system.

active exercise

Take a moment to apply what you've learned.

active concept check

Now let's take a moment to test your knowledge of the concepts you have studied in this section.

Detailed Scheduling: The Drum-Buffer-Rope System

At the most detailed level of scheduling, in which managers must decide who should do what and with which resource, the **drum-buffer-rope system (DBR)** is often used. This is a detailed scheduling approach most useful in value-adding systems that contain a bottleneck. The term *drum* refers to the bottleneck; like a marching band, its rate of throughput sets the pace for all other work centers. The *buffer* is time that is maintained in front of the bottleneck or other strategic points in the system, to make certain the bottleneck never sits idle for lack of work. (This extra time results in an inventory of materials that will accumulate in front of the bottleneck.) Finally, the *rope* refers to communication links between the buffers and the gateway work centers. These communication links keep workers from starting jobs for which there is no room in the buffer. The purpose of the drum-buffer-rope system is to ensure that bottleneck resources are fully utilized and that all other resources work at the pace of the bottleneck.

Figure 14.8 compares the kanban scheduling system described in Chapter 13 with the drum-buffer-rope system. The kanban system is a pull scheduling system; nothing moves from one work center to the next and nothing new is made, unless a customer has used an item and it needs to be replaced. In a kanban system, it is essential that capacity be reasonably balanced throughout the operational system. The master schedule, which establishes the pull rate, must be leveled. The drum-buffer-rope system is a pull and push scheduling system. Work is pulled into the value-adding system based on the schedule at the bottleneck and the expected time needed for it to move from the gateway work center

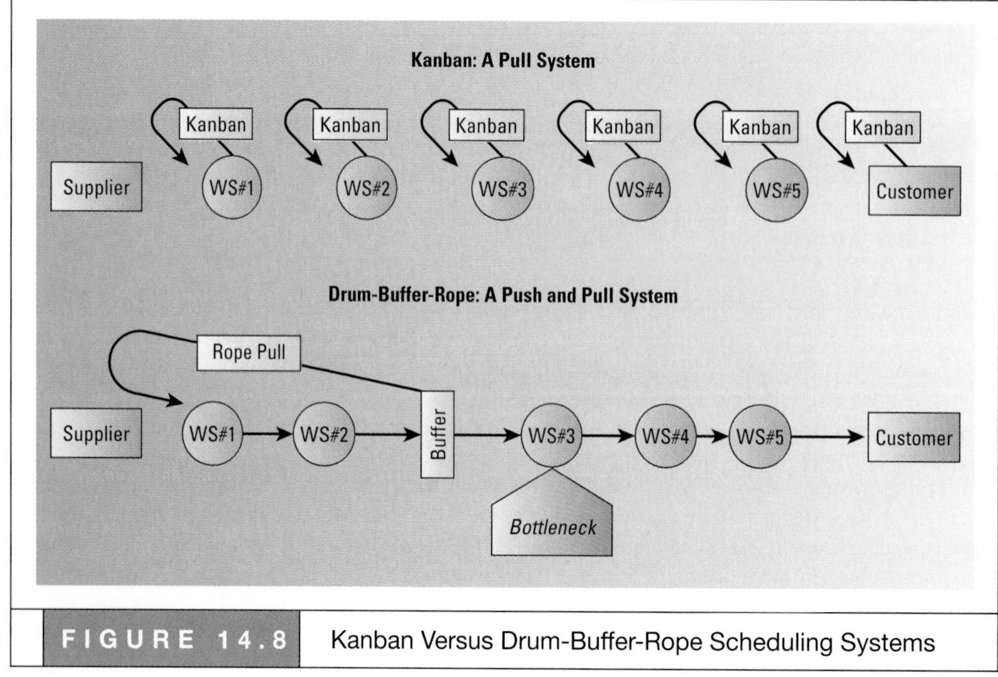

FIGURE 14.8 Kanban Versus Drum-Buffer-Rope Scheduling Systems

to the bottleneck buffer. Once it is in the system, however, orders are pushed through their prescribed routing. Rather than waiting for a free kanban to know what to do, workers will wait for incoming orders and the work-in-process that accompanies them. When employees complete their work on a particular order, they simply send it on to the next station.

Of course, operations rarely are that simple. Figure 14.9 illustrates the drum-buffer-rope scheduling system in a more realistic environment that includes multiple product flows. Notice that the master schedule directly determines the schedule of the bottleneck in addition to the timing of customer shipments. The bottleneck schedule draws work out of the **bottleneck buffer,** which is simply work that is waiting to be processed at the bottleneck. When there is space in the buffer (units of time) for additional work, the communication link symbolized by the rope releases more work into the facility. Since the rate of work at the bottleneck determines the rate at which work enters the facility, no other resource will work at a rate greater than that of the bottleneck. Thus, the bottleneck determines the rate at which all other resources operate.

Figure 14.9 includes three types of buffers: bottleneck buffers (just discussed), assembly buffers, and shipping buffers. An **assembly buffer** is extra time resulting in a collection of work wherever material flows that don't include the bottleneck join work that has been through the bottleneck. These buffers ensure that work doesn't get held up on its way to the customer for want of components or subassemblies that come from another material flow. Ropes from these buffers to the gateway work centers ensure that these resources, which aren't in the bottleneck material flow, nevertheless operate at the pace of the bottleneck.

Many customers would prefer not to receive their shipments early, while many suppliers would like to build in a margin of safety against late delivery of their product-service bundles. The **shipping buffer** is an amount of time (which usually results in an inventory of finished work) used to enhance the probability of correctly timed shipments. It also is useful if there is some bottleneck in outbound logistics or if the market itself is the bottleneck. In such cases, there would be a rope from the shipping buffer to the gateway work center, because it doesn't make any sense to create more product-service bundles than can be shipped or consumed in the marketplace.

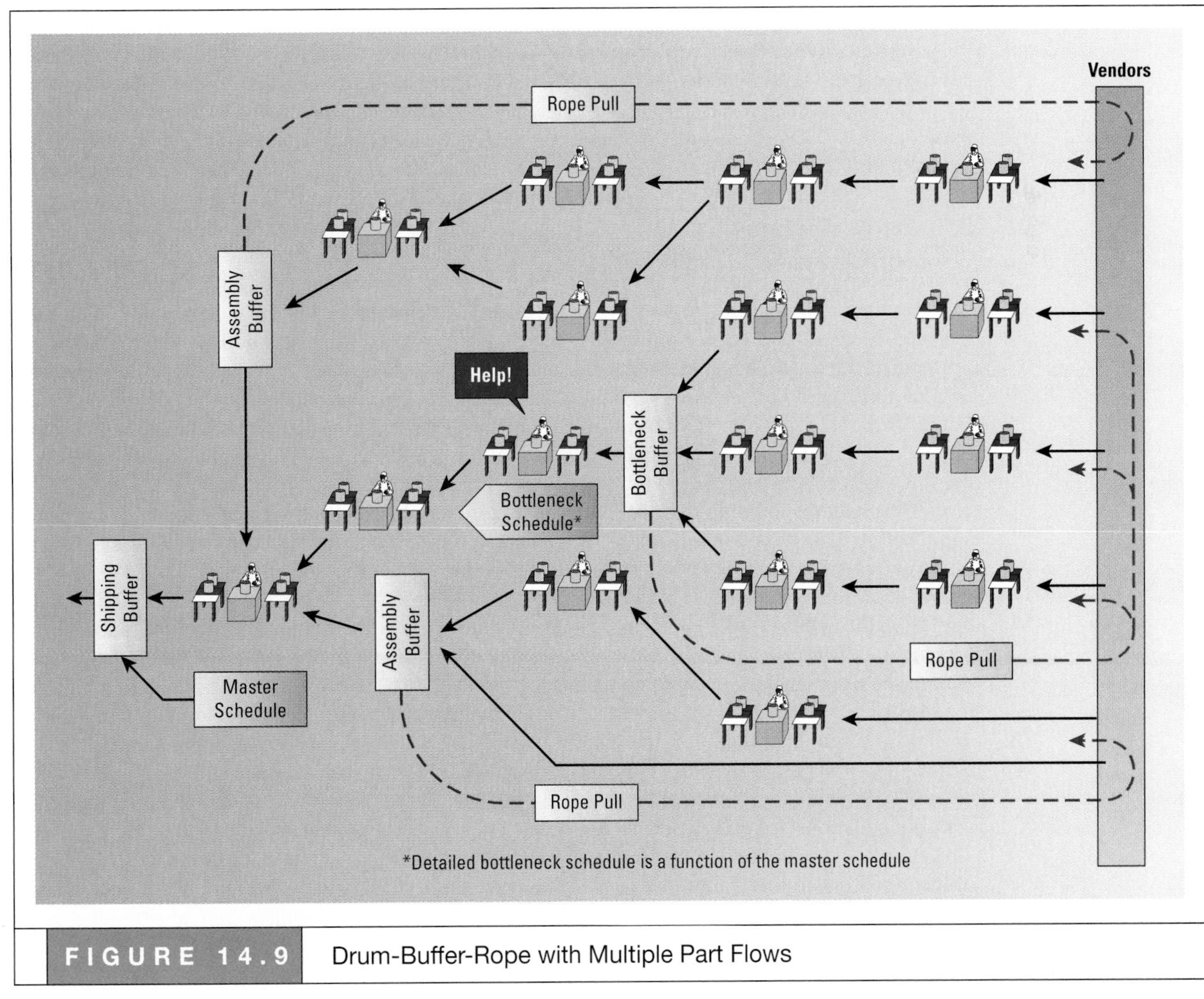

FIGURE 14.9 Drum-Buffer-Rope with Multiple Part Flows

The ships waiting to pass through the Panama Canal illustrate the condition of most bottlenecks. Whether at the Panama Canal, a port facility, on an interstate, or in an industrial facility, bottlenecks can cause frustrating delays. Managers need to anticipate bottlenecks and make appropriate scheduling decisions based on this knowledge. For example, don't send a ship if it can't get through the canal and don't accept an order that can't get through the bottleneck.

Managing buffers is a critical aspect of improving the synchronous system. You'll remember from Chapter 13 that inventory is like water in a river: It helps the system work smoothly, but it hides problems. Since a time buffer is reflected by the inventory required to keep a bottleneck busy for a specified period of time, it helps to ensure that the bottleneck stays busy and the system runs smoothly. Managers who don't want the bottleneck to stop running because of material shortages will want to have a large bottleneck buffer in place "just to be safe." On the other hand, the larger the buffer, the longer the quality feedback loop will be. Suppose you have a two-day buffer at the bottleneck and discover a problem with material while processing it in the bottleneck. Whoever created that material won't hear about the problem for at least two days. Furthermore, the quality of all of the work done during these two days is suspect. The larger the buffer, the longer the required planning horizon. If you reduce your buffer size by two days, the system lead-time required to complete the product-service bundle and the planning horizon will also be shortened. This suggests there is a benefit to keeping buffers as small as possible.

The buffer is basically safety stock. New work is ordered (i.e., brought into the process) based on the expected lead-time between the gateway operation and the bottleneck. The inventory between the gateway operation and the bottleneck includes the work in upstream work centers and the buffer. Essentially, then, the reorder point (i.e., the time to start working on another order) is expected upstream process inventory plus safety stock. In Chapter 12, we suggested that safety stock levels and reorder points could be set based on the lead-time demand distribution and the level of safety desired. In the DBR system, buffer sizes can also be set based on these considerations. The lead-time supply distribution will indicate the mean and variance of the lead-time required for material to travel from the gateway work center to the bottleneck. Based on the relative costs of bottleneck stock-outs and the cost of carrying inventory in the buffer, managers can establish a buffer service level, which is simply a probability that the buffer will stock-out. With this information, the approach to finding safety stock levels discussed in Chapter 12 can be used to determine the appropriate size of a buffer.

Suppose, for example, that it takes an average of three days (with a standard deviation of half a day) from the instant work begins on a job until it shows up at the bottleneck buffer. If no buffer was present and work orders were released exactly three days before their processing was to begin at the bottleneck, the chance of idling the bottleneck would be 50% for each order (a normal distribution of the lead-time is assumed). On the other hand, if the planned buffer was one day (i.e., two standard deviations of the lead-time demand distribution), work orders would be released exactly four days before their processing was to begin. Based on the cumulative normal distribution, which contains about 97.5% of its area to the left of $z = 2.00$, this would reduce the probability of idling the bottleneck to about 2.5% for each order.

You might wonder how anyone would know the variability (or standard deviation) of the time needed for work to travel from the gateway work center to the buffer, especially if the system might bottleneck at a different place each week. In reality, since we are dealing with a situation that is not too complex, most managers are likely to know the variability of their key processes—at least to some extent. We can quickly gauge the system's total upstream variability by adding the variances at all the work centers. The standard deviation of total upstream processing time (i.e., the standard deviation of the lead-time supply distribution) is simply the square root of this sum of variances. This value, in turn, can be used to determine the appropriate size of the buffer.

Figure 14.10 illustrates the effect of inventory levels on the material flow that feeds the bottleneck just described. A similar graph might be drawn for assembly and shipping buffers. In situation A, the plan is for one day's worth of inventory to be in the buffer and three days' worth in process upstream of the bottleneck, for a total of four days' inventory in the upstream portion of the system. But the bottleneck will process one order at a time, and the work will enter the facility one order at a time; thus inventory levels will decrease and increase by the size of the orders, rather than one item at a time. Consequently, at any given moment the upstream inventory level may be somewhat different from the intended level. Situation A simply illustrates the *intended* level of upstream inventories.

In situation B, the buffer has grown larger than intended, while the upstream process inventory is as intended. This situation can only occur if work in the bottleneck has been disrupted and fallen behind schedule. A manager who observes this situation would stop releasing jobs to the gateway workstation until work in the bottleneck caught up. Effort would also be expended to fix the problem that slowed the bottleneck and thereby improve throughput.

Situation C shows more than three days' worth of inventory in upstream processes and a smaller than intended buffer. Managers would realize that there was some upstream process disruption if they observed this inventory situation. They'd try to fix the problem with the upstream resource and might increase the planned buffer to more than one day's worth until they were sure work was back to normal.

In situation D, the upstream work centers have been starved for work because of demand shortages. If there's no order from a customer, no work can be released to upstream work centers. We've included this situation primarily to emphasize that operations is not the only function that can influence the bottleneck schedule.

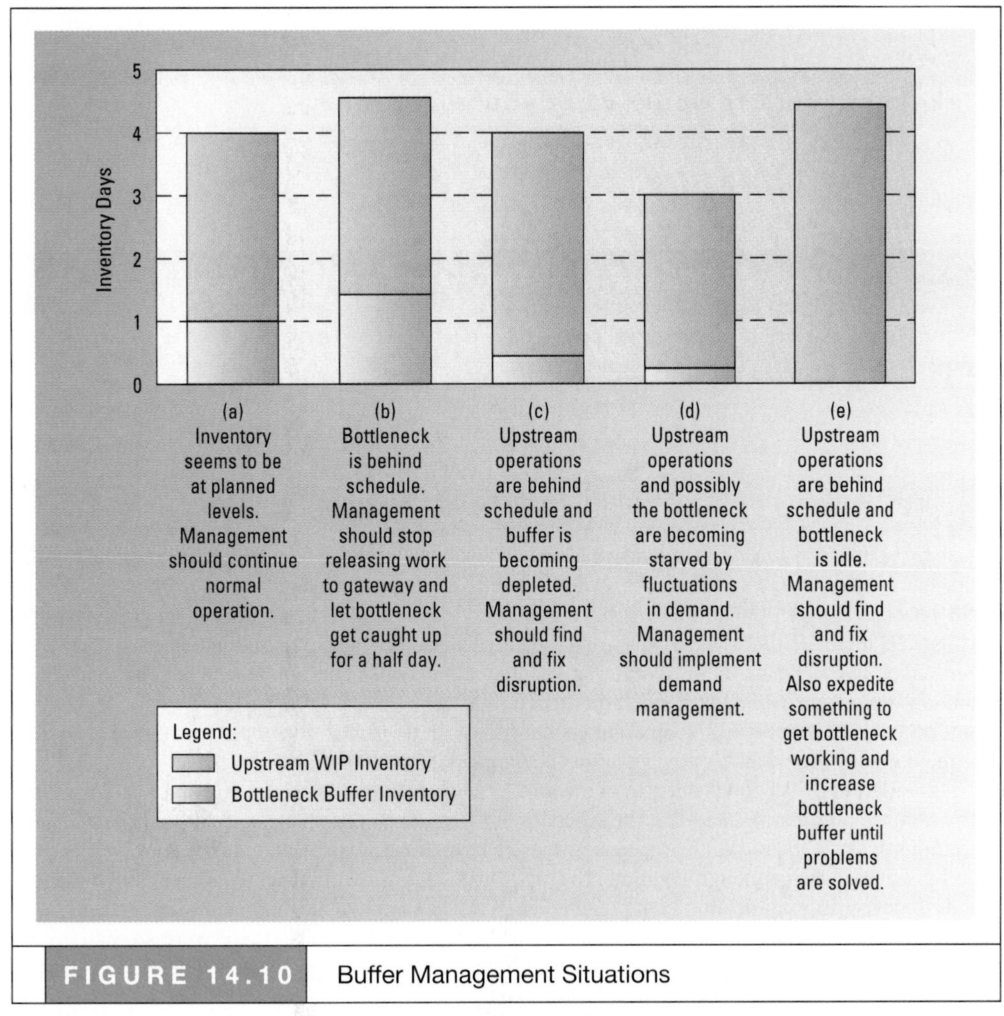

FIGURE 14.10 Buffer Management Situations

Finally, situation E is the situation managers most want to avoid. The upstream problem has not been fixed, and the entire buffer has been used up at the bottleneck. The system's most critical resource has been idled because of process disruptions at an upstream resource. Like an army of ants, workers will be trying to fix the problem that disrupted the upstream resource's schedule. Upstream jobs that can be quickly completed will also be expedited, so that work at the bottleneck will be able to begin again. After such an event, the buffer might be increased until managers are confident of the reliability of upstream resources.

Order sizes are likely to vary depending on customer requirements, so Figure 14.10 doesn't present a fixed order size model. All things being equal, however, the risk of a stock-out is greater with big orders and the system is more difficult to manage. The issue we are alluding to, which is highlighted by OPT principles 7 and 8 in Table 14.6, is batch sizing in the drum-buffer-rope scheduling system. A **production batch size** is the number of items a resource is asked to process with one setup. A **transfer batch size** is the number of items that are moved from one resource to the next on a material routing. If production and/or transfer batch sizes are small, jobs spend less time at each resource. Consequently, the time required for a job to move from a gateway operation to a bottleneck buffer is short and relatively predictable. There is also less inventory in upstream processes.

Typically, for the sake of simplicity, transfer batch sizes and production batch sizes are kept the same, and production batch sizes are determined based on the tradeoff between holding costs and ordering costs at some level of completion. In a DBR system, smaller batches are preferred, because they reduce both inventory levels and the risk of material shortages at the bottleneck. Specifically, it is common to base production order sizes on customer requirements, shown on the master schedule, but to allow transfer batch sizes to be smaller than production batch sizes. Doing so allows an upstream operation to feed a bottleneck, even when all the materials needed to complete a production batch have not been processed. In general, small batch sizes (whether production batches, transfer batches, or both) reduce lead-times and planning horizons, making processes become simpler to manage.

active exercise

Take a moment to apply what you've learned.

active concept check

Now let's take a moment to test your knowledge of the concepts you have studied in this section.

Bottlenecks at the Student Recreation Center

As at any recreation facility, the demand for various venues at the Student Recreation Center (SRC) changes over the year. There are times when basketball games are in full swing from early morning until very late at night. Other times, volleyball nets take up much of the courts and keep the floor just as busy. Yet there are times when you would be hard-pressed to hear a ball bouncing more than a few hours a day. The same is true for swimming, racquetball, exercise equipment, and the Outdoor Pursuit Center. It's also true that the demand varies at certain times of the day. For instance, customers have to wait for many different types of apparatus in the fitness area virtually every afternoon from 4 to 9 PM, but there is very little wait for any apparatus between 8 AM and noon.

The variation in demand is due to a number of factors, including the seasonal nature of student participation, the intramural schedules, the scheduling of special competitions, and seasonal participation in various sports. Obviously, the rec center doesn't have enough space and money to solve the problem by simply buying enough equipment for the busiest hour of the year. This means that the staff needs to devise ways of dealing with potential bottlenecks in any venue and on any apparatus.

One interesting consideration is that of locker availability. Because there were so many recreational opportunities in the center and only one locker room each for men and women, the staff felt that lockers could be the center's most constrained resource. Feeling that convenient availability of locker space was key to full utilization of the facility, the staff originally thought that the lockers would become the bottleneck of the facility. As a result, when the center was first opened:

- Two types of lockers were installed at the center. Changing rooms contained lockers that were available only on a first-come, first-served basis. In addition, there were coin-operated lockers in the public venues. Much like a parking meter, if the key was not returned to these lockers in the specified time, the patron would have to pay more to retrieve their belongings.
- Originally, no long-term locker space was sold to patrons. The lockers were only available while the patron was using the facility. (Long-term rentals would tie up the most critical resource for long periods of time while a patron was absent from the facility.)
- The rec center checked out locks for lockers free of charge along with the towels. Patrons were more likely to return the locks along with their towels when they were done with their workout. If the locks were not returned within several hours, the staff could remove the locks and the contents of the locker. Rules were posted regarding locker use, and the patrons knew that the lockers were not for long-term storage. This also caused the coin-operated locks to remain free as a readily available relief valve when locker space was getting tight. Interestingly, the staff learned that checking out locks was sort of like a drum-buffer-rope mechanism. If locks were not available, patrons would spend less time in the locker room, and locker room throughput was not impeded by congestion.

Over the years the SRC staff has learned that locker space is generally adequate, and their way of allocating locker space has changed. They no longer provide locks for lockers along with towels. It turns out that the process of checking out and collecting locks slowed down the entry and exit process, creating unwanted waiting lines. By not checking out locks, the check-in–checkout bottleneck was removed. Also, a number of lockers can now be rented for long-term use, depending on the seasonal demand factors.

> Integrating Operational Decisions

This chapter is closely linked to Chapters 4 and 7 because decisions about the design of the product-service bundle and the value-adding system determine the level of complexity inherent in planning and control of the system. When product designs allow for some customization within a limited line of products, operational requirements change one week to the next within the constraints established by product design parameters, and the approach to planning and control discussed in this chapter is a good fit. Similarly, when the value-adding system makes use of process layouts with some common product routings, this chapter's approach to planning and control works effectively.

This chapter is also closely tied to Chapters 11 and 12. The broader resource planning and scheduling decisions covered in these chapters establish the level of resources available and what must be accomplished in the short- to intermediate-range. This chapter continues the planning and control process at a more detailed level. It describes the way that TOC-based systems accomplish the detailed scheduling activities that ensure that the requirements of the master schedule are met.

> integrated OM

Take a moment to apply what you've learned.

> Chapter Wrap-Up

To effectively run a synchronous planning and control system, every business function must become concerned with maximizing bottleneck resources. Accountants need to verify that their traditional costing methods are appropriate and revise their approach where necessary. Financial managers have to understand the value-adding system to the extent that they will know the system value of capacity at both bottleneck and nonbottleneck resources. Marketing professionals need to work with customers to make the most of resources with limited capacity. Engineers and others on design teams need to consider the capacity implications of their decisions. Senior managers have to ensure that incentives and performance measurement systems for employees in all of the various functional areas are set up to encourage cooperation and synchronized operations.

Synchronous planning and control systems will only work for certain value-adding systems. They're not a good choice where there is so much complexity that it is difficult to identify the bottleneck quickly enough to synchronize other resources accordingly. On the other hand, where there is no bottleneck because demand has been leveled and resource capacities have been balanced, JIT is a better choice for system planning and control.

The most well-known approach to synchronizing value-adding systems is the theory of constraints developed by Eliyahu Goldratt. The system management principles and five-step focusing process that are based on the theory of constraints were made famous by a book called *The Goal.* Recognition of many of these principles has also begun to impact on cost accounting. At least in part, recently developed approaches to accounting such as activity-based costing and the balanced scorecard owe their acceptance to the awareness of operational issues created by the work of Goldratt and others who have tried to explain synchronous planning and control systems.

In a synchronous planning and control system, detailed decisions about who does what with what resource and when are made with the drum-buffer-rope scheduling approach. The fundamental idea of DBR is that the bottleneck's pace should be the average pace for all resources. Since nonbottleneck resources have excess capacity, it's okay for them to run faster and slower than the bottleneck for short periods of time. Communication ensures that no more work enters the value-adding system than can be handled at the system bottleneck. This guarantees that the average output of nonbottleneck resources can't continually exceed that of the bottleneck. A buffer is used to keep the bottleneck from running out of work, thus preventing wasted time at the system's most critical resource. Buffers are also used to make certain that work that has been processed at the bottleneck is delayed as it proceeds onward to the customer. The entire approach is geared toward maximizing system throughput while minimizing inventory and operating expense.

> end-of-chapter resources

- **Practice Quiz**
- **Key Terms**
- **Solved Problems**
- **Discussion Questions**
- **Problems**
- **Case 14.1: The World's Highest Bottleneck—The Hillary Step**
- **References**
- **Factory Tours**

Planning and Control in Material Requirements Planning Systems

CHAPTER 15

Chapter Outline

What's Ahead

. . . BACK AT THE REC CENTER

"This rec center is well run," Tom blurted out while taking a short break one morning. The group was nearing the middle of the workout, having been there for about half an hour. "I mean, we get here real early, when you would expect things to be slow, but I've come back a few times later in the day or on a weekend with lots of students around and everything still flows smoothly, no glitches." The rest of the group agreed. There were seldom any long waits for machines, plenty of towels, and more than enough staff to help out with a problem, keep things neat, restock whatever was needed, spot somebody on the free weights, offer encouragement, or just make training suggestions. In general, there were people doing the things that needed to be done. The center even seemed to be open longer hours when the demand called for it. He was amazed at how good a handle they seemed to have on planning the center's operation. "Other clubs I've been in haven't been run as well," Tom said. "There never seems to be enough staff, you have to wait a long time for help. Other times, there are plenty of people around looking busy, but they're not doing what you need them to be doing."

"Yeah, I've seen those places too," said Luis, as he started a set of situps on the incline board. "Lots of people, lots of equipment, but you still end up waiting for the stuff you want."

"I see enough of those kinds of headaches at work. Sure glad we don't have it here. Maybe I should take lessons," Tom added with exasperation.

"Sounds like you're not looking forward to working this morning," said Cheryl wiping away the sweat of a 15-minute stint on the treadmill. "Problems?"

"New problems no, just a chronic pain," Tom answered. "We always do it, and we do it as well as anybody, but it's always a pain to get people to the right places at the right time." He said he was always scrambling at the last minute to get a crew somewhere or find enough agents for the gates he needed. " I wish we could run things like this club! Sometimes I almost think it was easier in the old days, you know, before deregulation."

"Hearing this ought to make Fred happy with the plant he's in now," Luis said. "He may have complained about 'plain vanilla' before, but he's got it pretty smooth now—just put people in a job, start the line, and everything goes. No changes, no surprises, real plain, real smooth."

"That's what I mean about deregulation," said Tom. "It used to be a lot simpler to fly the same few routes over and over. We couldn't make it more complicated if we wanted to."

Fred had been listening from a stepper with a sort of smug look growing on his face. "Sounds like you guys want my job!" he laughed.

"Not really, just a little bit of the 'down the line and out the door' simplicity of scheduling it now and then," Luis said.

"It's the complexity of planning, scheduling, and then running a process that gives us headaches," added Cheryl. Luis and Tom nodded in agreement, but she saw a puzzled look on Fred's face. "Even building a simple product with basic technology, like wooden furniture, can be complicated if there are enough orders for enough other products competing for the same resources, changing colors, quantity, design, that kind of stuff."

"And all at the last minute!" Luis added.

"Yeah, Fred, you have us on this one," said Cheryl. "Things are just more complex for Luis and me, even more so than what Tom's talking about. You might have it easy now, but remember what it was like in your old job." Fred had been head of marketing for a division that manufactured all of the newer products and prototypes, a wide variety of things in very small quantities. The group remembered him talking about the same kind of problems, many even worse than what Cheryl and the others seemed concerned about now.

"Yeah, I remember those weekly resource planning meetings. We'd get all the orders together, we'd have 'em all lined up nice and neat," Fred reminisced. "That lasted until the operations people got there. They'd always want to talk about capacity, materials, priorities, and time fences, all kinds of reasons to tell us why they couldn't tell us exactly when we could have what we wanted. Is that what you mean?"

"That's the whole point," Cheryl said. "When you only have a couple of products to produce, even if they are complicated products, it's easy to figure out what it will take to make them. Then you get the resources in place and go to it."

"Okay, I can see what you're talking about when I think of my old job and compare it to this one," said Fred, "but I wonder about something else. Stuff does happen and customers do change their minds. How do you coordinate it all? How do you ever meet your master schedule?"

"Information," said Cheryl.

"That sounds simple," said Fred.

"Believe me, it's not," Cheryl responded. "But think about what you need to know in order to schedule your shop." If you know what the customer wants, how to make it, and can match resources to it, then you have a schedule. In simple value-adding systems, those decisions could be hardwired into the system. It gets tougher as things become more complicated.

"Well, how do you handle it then, Luis?" asked Fred.

"We use something called MRP, or material requirements planning," said Luis. "It's more of an information system." He described how it takes the orders from the customers and, along with the list of components that goes into each product and the routing through the plant for each component, it generates schedules for his work centers. He said it is a great planning tool and helps them be more proactive, to plan ahead. "It's not perfect and it depends on a lot of data from the shop, but it gives us a plan." The data includes some guesswork on the part of management, like how long something will usually take to get through a department, but the more accurate the data put into it, the better the system will help them run the shop. "It's like my drive home on the beltway," said Luis. "When the helicopter report on the radio says an exit is closed or that a wreck has a lane closed somewhere, the best route home still requires some guesswork, but it's a better guess."

"Well I think Tom's right about the rec center. I wonder if there's somebody in a helicopter watching this place right now?" asked Fred, with a smile.

"I don't know about a helicopter, but whatever the system is, I'd like to get some of it for the airlines," said Tom.

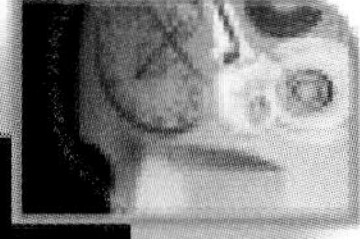

> objectives

Take a moment to familiarize yourself with the key objectives of this chapter.

> gearing up

Before you begin reading this chapter, try a short warm-up activity.

> Introduction

If you've already read Chapters 13 and 14, you are probably getting accustomed to the general flow of this text's chapters on detailed planning and control. Like those chapters, this one looks at short-term operations planning and control. This chapter, however, focuses on very complex value-adding systems, such as job shops, airlines, rental businesses, and hotels. These are environments where each customer's order may be unique and the resources required to satisfy the customer must be—at least in part—probabilistically estimated. Planning and control approaches such as JIT and TOC aren't flexible enough to deal with the managerial tasks required by such complex value-adding systems. In these situations, a system is needed that can identify the quantity and timing of materials required for individual orders and track the progress of those orders through each part of the value-adding system. Systems of this nature used in manufacturing are typically referred to as **material requirements planning (MRP)** systems. Service-oriented systems that perform a similar function are commonly called **yield management systems.**

MRP systems are used to convert customer demand information into operational plans that are useful for the procurement of the parts, components, and subassemblies that go into the product-service bundles on the master schedule. A material requirement is simply something that is needed in order to carry out an order. For example, if your friend were running for student council president, she might ask you to fold, stuff into envelopes, label, stamp, and mail the letters she is sending to off-campus voters. You'd probably think she was crazy if she asked you to do that job without providing the letters, envelopes, labels, or stamps you needed. Those are the material requirements associated with the order she gave. The situation is just the same in business. Employees would think their boss was crazy if they got work orders without the materials necessary to complete the order.

Services that cannot store their capacity in the form of inventory may use yield management systems to perform the same planning function. The process would begin with planning departments determining what services are for sale at what price. For example, an airline might decide on the set of flight schedules and fares to offer in a given period or a hotel may decide the number and types of conferences and events to accommodate. This is much the same as master scheduling in manufacturing environments. Next, yield management systems determine how much of each service-price combination to make available, realizing that each uses a different set of resources. Customers are required to buy and cancel their services through a computer system. Thus, the mix of available service-price combinations and unused capacity is always known. Management can adjust the availability of service-price combinations, in real time, to manage their capacity and maximize their revenues.

This chapter begins with a description of its relevance to students and practitioners in other business functions. Clearly, an asynchronous value-adding system requires less coordination than a synchronous system; nevertheless, the various functions do need to understand the material requirements planning and scheduling process. A brief overview of MRP systems and the environments in which they prove most useful follows. Next, a hypothetical application shows how the material requirements plan flows logically from the master schedule. Discussions of managerial issues in an MRP system, including expediting, lot sizing, and the impact of MRP on the supply chain follow. The chapter closes with a discussion of the most common scheduling approach used in MRP systems, a push system in which each work area is scheduled independently of others.

> Integrating Operations Management with Other Functions

Compared to just-in-time (JIT) and synchronous systems, MRP systems allow for a higher degree of variety in the product-service bundle and far greater variety in the scheduling of each resource from one week to the next. Planners, therefore, must determine exactly what should be done when and at what resource on the basis of specific orders on the master schedule. The JIT approach, in which a group of resources (like an assembly line) are scheduled together, and the synchronous approach, in which all resources are scheduled based on the system bottleneck, are much simpler. The greater complexity of the MRP environment means that there are more decisions to be made, creating a tremendous need for effective communication across the white spaces of the organizational chart—even though the various functions may not coordinate their internal decisions as closely as in other systems. Figure 15.1 highlights some of the cross-functional linkages between this chapter's content and other business functions.

Because an MRP system handles many different product-service bundles, operations personnel must interact frequently with financial managers, accounting personnel, and marketing people in order to establish guidelines for new products. Management must address issues such as new product costing, pricing, and promotion; delivery lead-times; and priorities in material and resource usage.

From a financial perspective, the operational complexity of a system that accommodates variable volumes of a variety of product-service bundles creates some interesting challenges as well. Cash flows both in and out will vary, depending on the mix of orders and the resulting mix of lead-times and profitability. That means managers' budgets and investors' financial forecasts need to be just as flexible. The complexity of the bundle also implies a data-rich financial environment: lots of things to keep up with mean lots of data to enter and maintain. The limited accuracy of such data, along with the complexity of the system, can complicate the auditing task.

Accounting personnel are consulted to establish costing parameters for new products. Management must address issues such as new product costing. This is not ongoing interaction regarding an individual

Chapter Topics \ Functional Areas of Business	Finance	Accounting	Human Resources	Marketing	Engineering	Management Information Systems
Integrating Operations Management with Other Functions	●	●	●	●	●	●
Where to Use MRP Planning and Control	●	●		●	●	●
Overview of a Materials Requirement Planning System			●			●
MRP System Logic					●	●
Managing MRP Systems		●		●	●	●
Supply-Chain Impact of an MRP System				●		●
Detailed Scheduling in an MRP Environment		●		●		●

FIGURE 15.1 Integrating Operations Management with Other Functions

product or product family, but intermittent contact regarding new or redesigned offerings. The flexibility of the operational system and the diversity of product-service bundles accommodated lead to frequent contact between the various business functions.

Where customized items are being made with general purpose equipment you'll find skilled workers. Often, these skills are organized into unions. This can create scheduling difficulties from an operational perspective, and it certainly requires the human resources (HR) area to have personnel who are adept in their relations with the unions. Even if the unions are not a factor, skilled labor is often scarce and especially so during busy times for business. The ability of the HR function to attract and retain skilled workers is critical to the prosperity of the firm.

From a marketing perspective, salespersons need to be able to follow up on customer orders. If operational problems delay time-sensitive orders, operations managers need to be sensitive to customer needs and communicate with marketing personnel. Often, operations managers get wrapped up in their own work and fail to alert sales and service personnel to problems with specific orders, making the marketing people's job difficult. Conversely, given the flexibility inherent in this type of value-adding system, marketing personnel too often assume that operations can perform extremely difficult or time-consuming feats (because they once did something similar). They may make promises to customers that create problems or raise costs in operations. As a consequence, there is often a great deal of conflict and lack of understanding between OM and marketing personnel in this type of system. While marketing personnel need not know how to manage the operational system, the more they know about operations, the more reasonable their customer promises are likely to be.

The engineering function is heavily involved in the design of the product-service bundle. In situations where customization is offered, engineers are involved in figuring out exactly what operational specifications are to be used and what process steps will be required to provide the bundle. The choices they make have a big influence on the quality, cost, and lead-time the customer gets. That means they really need to be familiar with the implications of their choices on the firm's operations and intimately familiar with the managerial issues and planning and control system of the business.

Not surprisingly, information systems are at the heart of any MRP system. From the dawn of business information systems, computers have been used to crunch numbers for material planners. At first, the acronym MRP stood for material requirements planning, which is sometimes referred to today as *little MRP,* or simply *mrp.* Later, a broader information system for manufacturing environments, called **Manufacturing Resources Planning,** became known as *big MRP,* or **MRP II.** These commercially available programs are complete decision support systems. In addition to the MRP module, most contain modules for forecasting, master scheduling, quality control, cost accounting, scheduling, and capacity planning.

In today's client-server environment, in which employees from every function make decisions based on a common database, operations managers rely heavily on information systems (IS) personnel to maintain accurate data and facilitate access to data. IS personnel must meet these expectations while guaranteeing the security and reliability of the information system. Nowadays, MRP II systems aren't talked about so much because of the advent of *enterprise resources planning (ERP)* systems, which more effectively link all functional areas and may be capable of linking customers and suppliers electronically. Thus, IS personnel must meet the information needs of a large and diverse group of users. To do so, they must manage not only across the functional areas within their own firms, but across corporate boundaries as well.

Where to Use MRP Planning and Control

Figure 15.2 illustrates the manufacturing process and common product flows in Luis's furniture factory. Like this illustration, many functionally organized environments have common (or dominant) product flows, but each specific job has its own route through the process. Furthermore, each week the mix of jobs changes. Some of the large jobs will require very little time at each work area per unit. Others may look simple because the parts inventory is small but may nevertheless turn out to be very time consuming. Typically, by the time managers discover a bottleneck, another has developed somewhere else in the facility. Determining how all the jobs will flow through the shop in any week is difficult, then, because a bottleneck could develop at any work center at any time. The complexity of such an environment makes systematic use of the theory of constraints or JIT impractical. As a rule, managers spend little effort trying to coordinate schedules across the entire facility. Rather, each work area schedules the work that has been assigned to that area, for which materials are in stock.

In a make-to-order environment, in which customers can specify the options and delivery schedule of their choice, scheduling and material planning are quite complex. Demand rates are highly variable and small orders are commonplace, so the value delivery system must be flexible enough to deal with

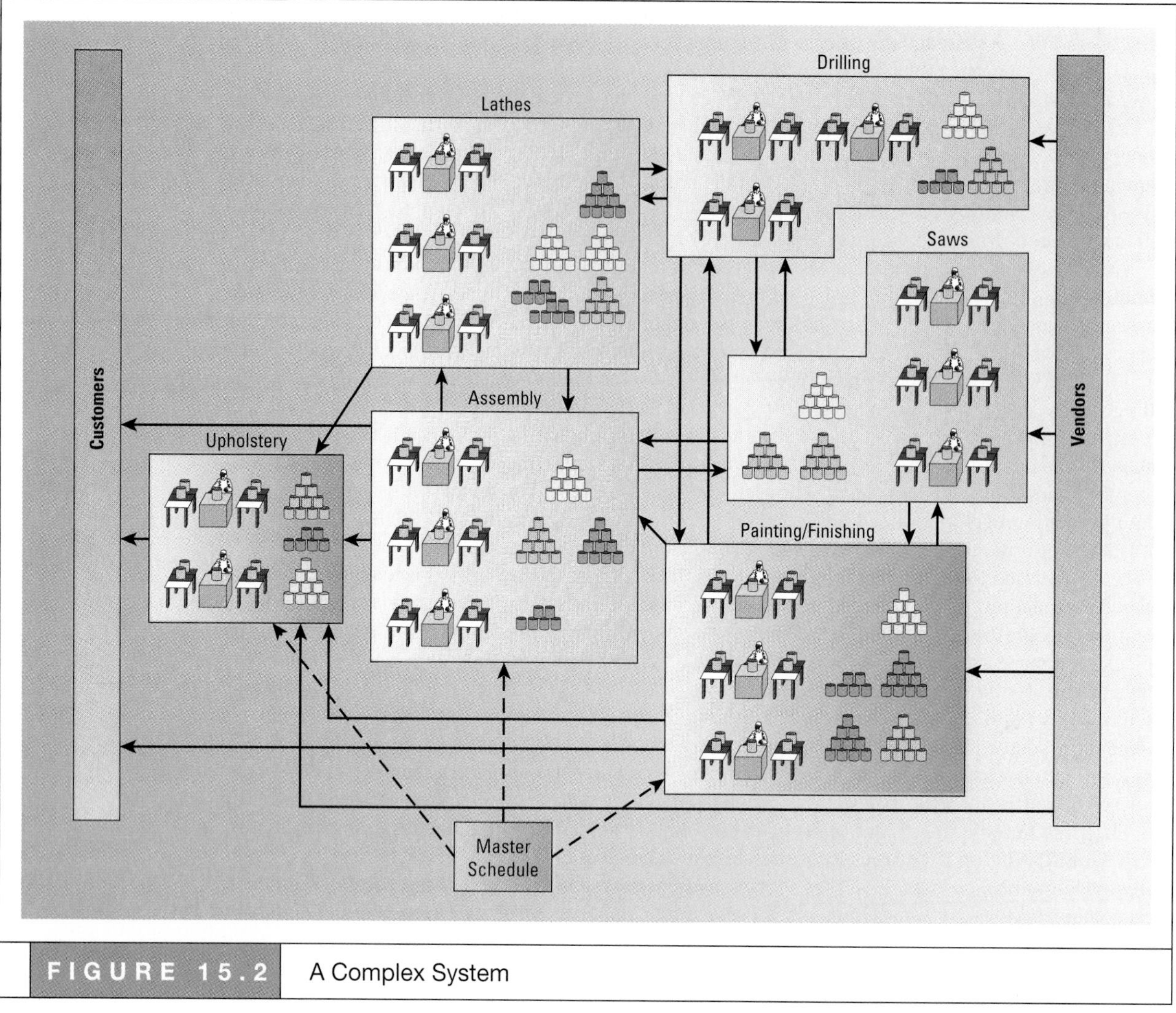

FIGURE 15.2 A Complex System

a wide variety of product-service bundles. The typical process type required in such settings is a job shop or at least a facility with a functional layout. As Figure 15.3 illustrates, MRP systems are best suited for use in such complex environments. The computer system takes information regarding delivery commitments, current inventory levels, and the design of the product-service bundle and converts it into planned orders that can be released for scheduling.

When managerial decision-making tasks become very complex, managers use probabilistic approaches. Think for a moment about how long it takes to complete a typical homework assignment for this class: probably no more than a few hours. But the instructor probably gives you several days to get the job done. The instructor delays the due date sufficiently to allow you time for everything else in your life, without causing you undue hardship. The busier you get, the harder it is for professors to predict how much time you will need to complete the assignment, so they give you a week for a three-hour assignment. That's probably enough time for most students.

The dry cleaner in whose window hangs a sign that says, "In by 10:00 A.M., Ready by 3:00 P.M.—Guaranteed" is taking the same approach. How can the store manager make that promise without knowing how much laundry you've got? (Maybe there aren't many signs like that close to campus dormitories, for good reason.) Basically, the manager has made an assumption about the range of demand for dry cleaning and has estimated the time that would be required under reasonable circumstances to provide same-day service. An unusually large order would create problems.

In all complex value-adding systems, planning and control decisions are much like the case of the professor who is creating a course schedule or the dry cleaner who is stating a guaranteed service cycle time. Generally, managers estimate the time required to complete a job probabilistically and then create a master schedule based on that estimate. Then they calculate the timing of the steps in the value-adding process deterministically.

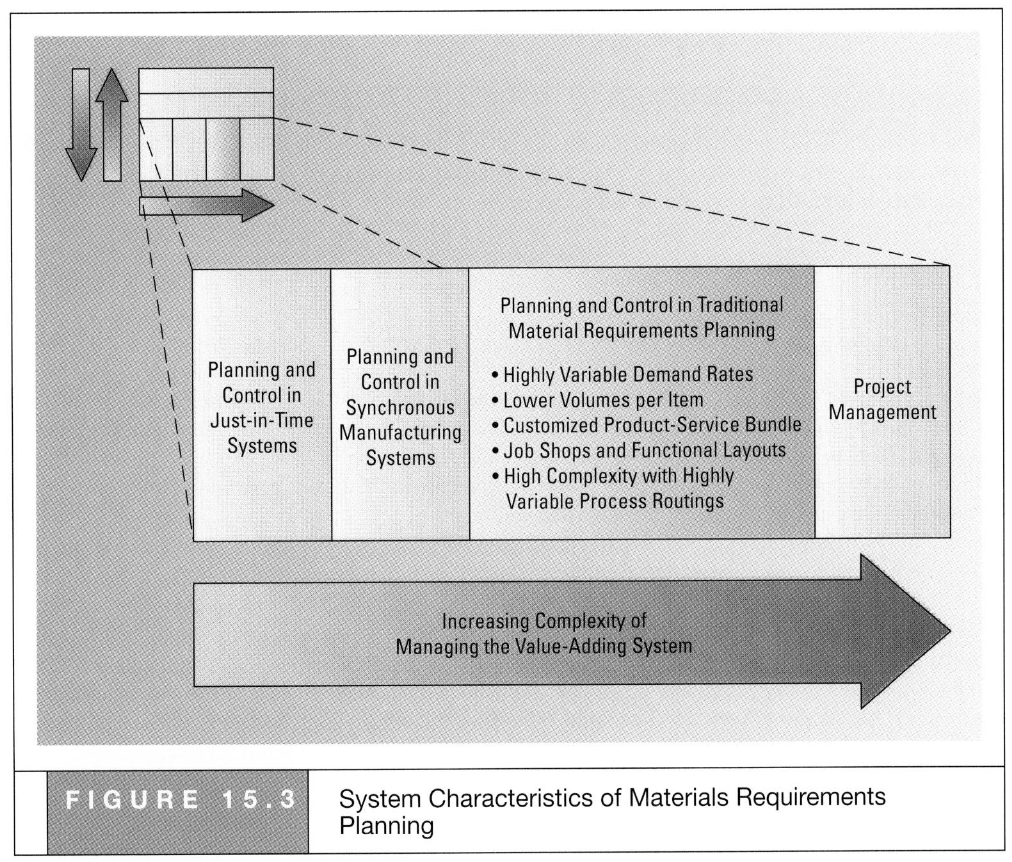

FIGURE 15.3 System Characteristics of Materials Requirements Planning

A skilled worker can form virtually any cylindrical shape with this general purpose metal lathe. Because of the potential variety of jobs, resources of this nature can be very difficult to schedule.

> **active poll**
>
> **What do you think? Voice your opinion and find out what others have to say.**

active concept check

Now let's take a moment to test your knowledge of the concepts you have studied in this section.

Overview of a Material Requirements Planning System

Figure 15.4 summarizes the short-term planning and control activities seen in most MRP systems. In complex environments, the master schedule typically represents those commitments that have been, or are expected to be, made to customers. The near-term portion of this schedule consists almost entirely of order commitments from customers, whereas the more distant portion includes only a few commitments and many expected (or forecasted) orders.

In addition to these independent demand product-service bundles, the master schedule may include certain dependent demand items. For example, if replacement parts are sold to customers, the demand for those parts will be included on the master schedule. In environments in which lead-times are so long that satisfying customer delivery dates usually is not possible or in which group technology has enabled the manufacture of numerous end items from many of the same parts, managers may adopt an assemble-to-order strategy. In these situations, companies may include some of the common parts or modules on the master production schedule. This practice means that common subassemblies are ready for use whenever they are needed, providing customers with more rapid service.

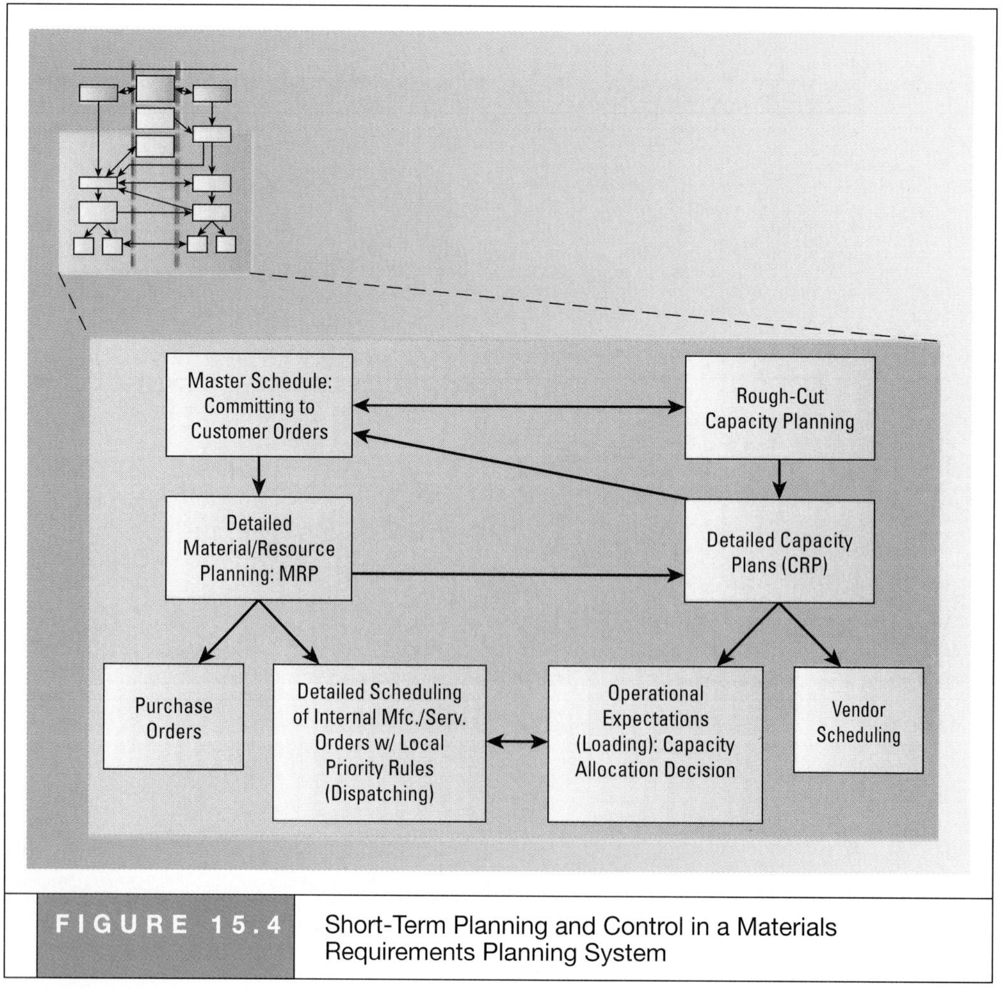

FIGURE 15.4 Short-Term Planning and Control in a Materials Requirements Planning System

MRP programs convert such master scheduling information into plans for all dependent demand items. In other words, taking information about what customers need and when, the programs generate information about when parts, components, and subassemblies will need to be ordered. This information can then be used by MRP planners to allocate both purchase orders and internal shop orders to specific operational resources, a process called **loading.** It can also be used for **capacity requirements planning (CRP),** which alerts managers to capacity shortages resulting from schedules based on the orders planned by MRP systems. If CRP reveals vendor capacity problems, it can be used to help planners determine which vendors should get what orders and when.

If there are so many material requirements in a given week that it is not possible to load all the work on existing resources and vendors, some companies will adjust their master schedules. Companies that can do so based on their CRP output are referred to as **closed loop MRP users** and are said to have *what-if? capability.* This capability allows schedulers to determine the impact of a change in the master schedule on an overutilized work center and it allows a salesperson to determine whether to accept a special rush order. For example, if one of Luis's most important customers were to ask for expedited delivery of a truckload of sofas, the salesperson could determine the feasibility of guaranteeing the desired delivery.

Once the planner actually releases the orders to specific work centers, work teams or area supervisors determine their priority. If material planning has been done correctly, materials will be available to complete the order; they will have been pushed forward from the upstream work center. (That's why you see so much inventory piled up at each work center in Figure 15.2.) Usually, local priority rules are used to schedule, or *dispatch,* the jobs in any work center. The hope is each order will eventually obtain the highest priority in the work center, will be processed, and will move to the next work center on its route. Jobs that get hung up at some point on their route will eventually become critical, at least from the customer's perspective. When that happens, they will usually be expedited. **Expediting** is a process of walking a job through a facility, overriding local scheduling decisions at each point on the route in order to give it top priority. Often, a job that has seen no action in weeks can be completed in hours with an expediter's attention.

> active concept check

Now let's take a moment to test your knowledge of the concepts you have studied in this section.

MRP System Logic

Figure 15.5 describes the basic inputs and outputs of the MRP program. Three primary inputs are shown: the master schedule, the bill of materials, and the inventory status file. As you already know, the master schedule indicates what end items need to be delivered to customers and when. The **bill of materials (BOM)** indicates what parts and subassemblies go into these independent demand items. For each end item, part, and subassembly, the **inventory status file (ISF)** indicates particulars such as inventory on hand, required lead-time, lot size, vendor, and so forth. Using this information, the MRP program generates three types of documents: planned purchase orders, for release to vendors; planned internal orders, for release to workstations within the facility; and exception reports, which indicate a problem that requires a planner's attention—a material shortage or late delivery that threatens the timely completion of some order, for instance. In such cases, the planner must determine how to resolve the problem and take corrective action. If the problem cannot be resolved, the customer must be notified of the expected delay.

Figure 15.6 shows a planning template like the ones used in MRP. Though the numbers in the data rows will vary, the structure of the template remains the same. *Gross requirements* are materials required during a particular week. Their value is calculated from the planned orders for the items of which they are a part. For example, an order for 125 tables would generate a gross requirement for 500 table legs.

Scheduled receipts are deliveries scheduled to be received at the beginning of the week. Figure 15.6 shows a scheduled receipt for 1,000 table legs in the first week; therefore, an order must have been released at some point. *Planned on hand* is inventory that is expected to be available at the beginning of the week. These parts can be used to satisfy some of the gross requirements. In this case, 132 units of inventory are on hand, and the plan appears to be to keep a stock of at least that many on hand at all times.

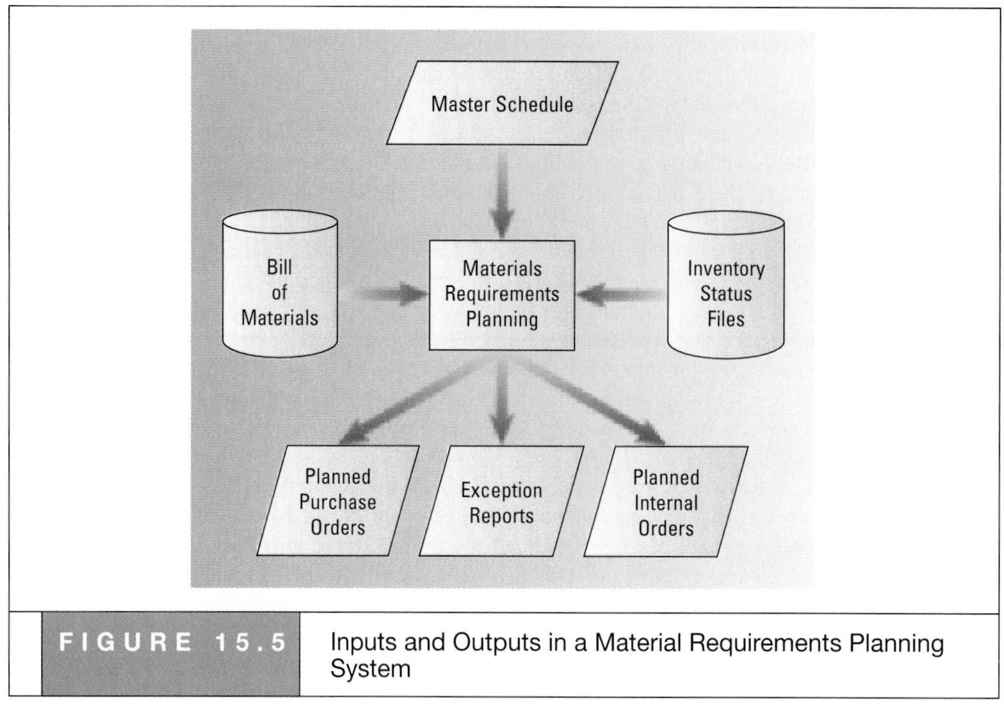

FIGURE 15.5 Inputs and Outputs in a Material Requirements Planning System

Net requirements are calculated from these three amounts, as well as any safety stock the material plan may call for. When the formula *Gross Requirements − Scheduled Receipts − Planned On Hand + desired Safety Stock* yields a positive result, that amount is the net requirement for the week. For example, the gross requirement for table legs in week 5 is 500; there are no scheduled receipts; and 132 table legs are planned on hand. Therefore net requirements in week 5 are 368 table legs. When the result of the "gross to net" calculation is less than or equal to 0, there is no net requirement (a result that is expressed as a 0 on the planning template).

Planned order receipts are determined based on net requirements and a lot-sizing rule. There are many different lot-sizing rules. For example, if a *lot-for-lot (L4L)* lot-sizing rule is being used and the net requirement for table legs is 368, the planned order receipt would be for 368 table legs. If a fixed lot size of 100 table legs is used, the planned order receipt for any net requirement between 0 and 100 would be 100 units; for any net requirement between 101 and 200, it would be 200 units. Sometimes a minimum lot size will be specified. For example, with a minimum lot size of 1,000, the planned order receipt would be large enough to cover the net requirement or 1,000 units, whichever is greater. That is the lot-sizing rule used in Figure 15.6.

Finally, *planned order releases* are directly correlated with planned order receipts: They simply indicate when an order must be released to be received at the planned time. Thus, if the lead-time required to receive an order is one week and the planned order receipt is for 1,000 table legs in week

Week	1	2	3	4	5	6	7	8	9	10
Gross Requirements	500	0	500	0	500	0	500	0	500	0
Scheduled Receipts	1,000									
Planned On Hand 132	132	632	632	132	132	632	632	132	132	632
Net Requirements	0	0	0	0	368	0	0	0	368	0
Planned Order Receipts	0	0	0	0	1,000	0	0	0	1,000	0
Planned Order Releases	0	0	0	1,000	0	0	0	1,000	0	0

FIGURE 15.6 A Material Requirements Planning Template

5, 1,000 table legs would need to be ordered in week 4. When the planned order release is actually executed by an MRP planner, the planned order receipt becomes a scheduled receipt.

> **active exercise**

Take a moment to apply what you've learned.

> **active concept check**

Now let's take a moment to test your knowledge of the concepts you have studied in this section.

An MRP Application

Figure 15.7 presents the set of end items, subassemblies, and components sold by a fictitious company called Bonnie's Candle Shop. Bonnie's assembles wall-and-table-mounted electric candle fixtures in a variety of configurations. The figure shows 12 of the more popular end items, which are referred to as *level (0) items.* Note that level (1) items are used to assemble level (0) items, level (2) items to assemble level (1) items, and so on. In other words, planned order releases for level (0) items would generate gross requirements for level (1) items.

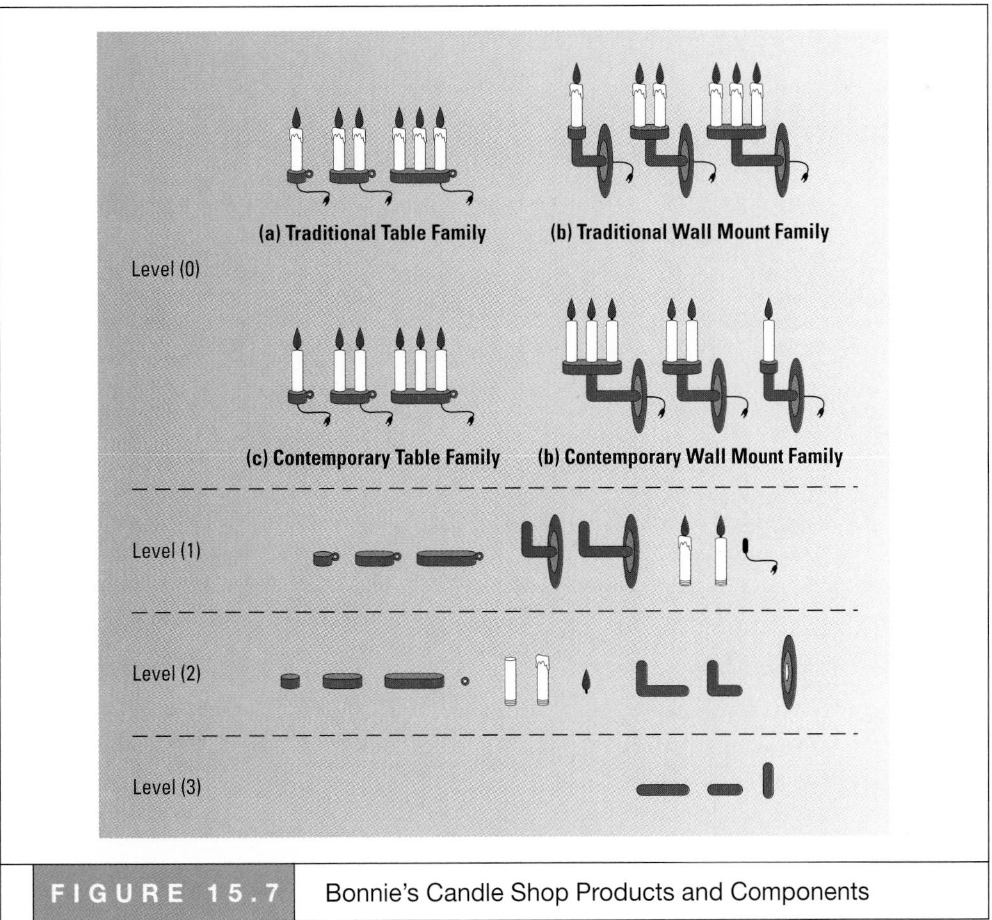

FIGURE 15.7 Bonnie's Candle Shop Products and Components

Figure 15.8 shows pictorial bills of materials for two of the end items Bonnie's sells. These are *low-level-coded BOMs,* which means that each item always appears at the same level of the BOM, regardless of which end item it is being used in. For example, notice that the candle fixture base appears at level (2) on the wall-mounted fixture's BOM, even though it could have been placed at level (1). Because level (2) is the highest level on which the candle fixture base could appear on the BOM for the table-mounted fixture, that part can appear no higher in any other BOM. An alternative way to represent this type of BOM uses indented text. The *indented BOMs* that correspond to the low-level-coded BOMs in Figure 15.8 are shown in Table 15.1.

FROM MASTER SCHEDULE TO MATERIAL PLAN

Figure 15.9 shows the linkage between the master schedule for the end item "Triple-C-Table" (#ct333) and the material plan for that item. The master schedule in this figure shows five orders for the ct333, which represent delivery commitments to customers. These product-service bundles must be provided in L4L fashion. Notice that all the commitments are for some multiple of 75 items, a common situation that results from the size of shipping containers. (The packaging used to ship the ct333 is a box designed to hold 75 fixtures.)

The orders on the master schedule are translated into gross requirements for the item in the bottom portion of Figure 15.9. This part of the material plan details how Bonnie's Candle Shop intends to fulfill its delivery promises. Inventory policies for the ct333 have been captured on the left side of the planning template. The item is assembled in the final assembly workstation in lots of 75 units; the estimated lead-time required to fill an order is one week; current on-hand inventory is 130 units; and the company intends to keep a safety stock of 75 units on hand. Because of the company's lot-sizing policy, whenever the net requirement is positive, enough lots will be ordered to satisfy that demand, and planned order receipts will always be for some multiple of 75.

You might wonder how Bonnie's could end up with 130 units of ct333 planned on hand for week 1. After all, the lot size is 75, and with a safety stock level of 75, you might expect all the numbers in this table to be multiples of 75. If a box holds 75 fixtures, how could Bonnie's end up with a partial box of 55 (130−75) fixtures? This situation is not uncommon and can happen in different ways. Fixtures may have been lost because of quality problems that were discovered during final assembly.

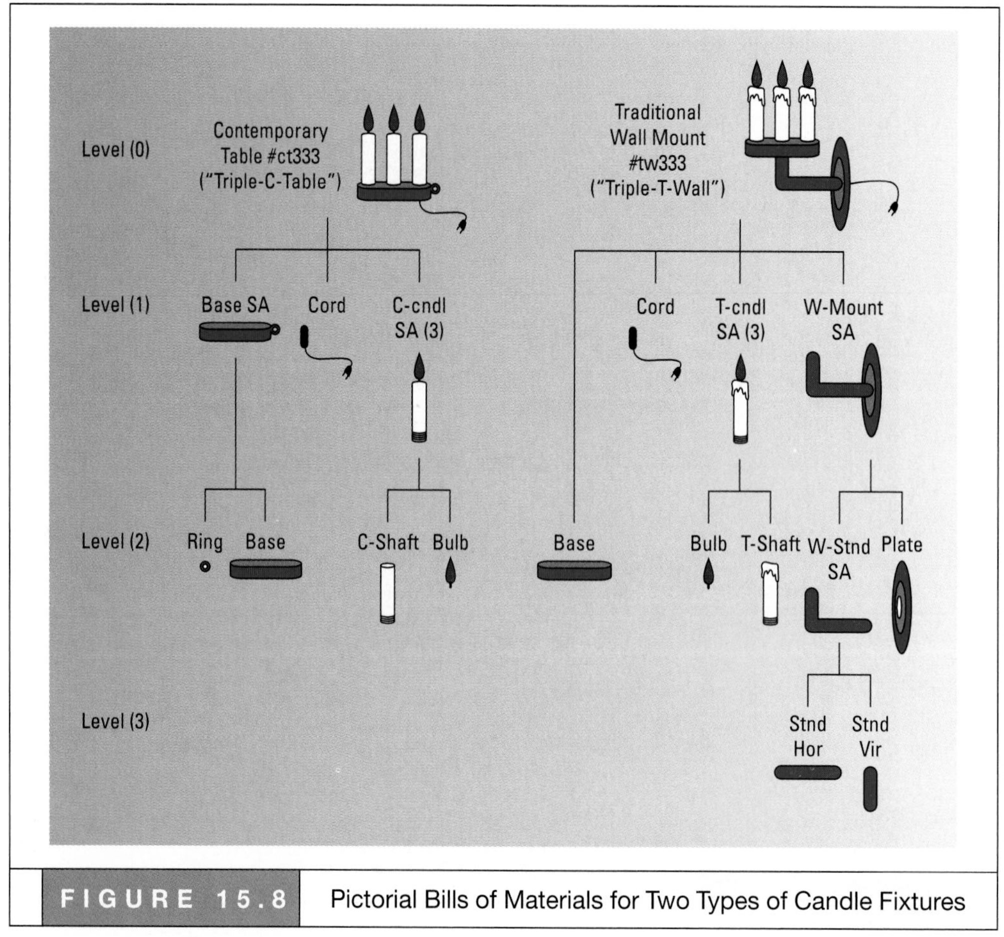

FIGURE 15.8 Pictorial Bills of Materials for Two Types of Candle Fixtures

TABLE 15.1 Indented Bills of Materials for Two Types of Candle Fixtures

Triple-C-Table (#ct333)

- Base Subassembly (Base SA)
    - Ring
    - Base
- Cord
- 3Contemporary Candle Subassembly (C-candle SA)
    - Contemporary Shaft (C-shaft)
    - Bulb

Triple-T-Wall (#tw333)

- Base
- Cord
- 3Traditional Candle Subassembly (T-candle SA)
    - Traditional Shaft (T-shaft)
    - Bulb
- Wall Mount Subassembly (WSA)
    - Plate
    - Arm
        - Vertical Rod (V-rod)
        - Horizontal Rod (H-rod)

Fixtures may have been withdrawn for use as marketing samples, without being noted in the computer system. Or a customer may have returned the unused portion of an order because of quality problems. Suffice to say, even though demand for dependent demand inventory items can be calculated from the requirements for independent demand items, surprises are commonplace. Physical inventory counts seldom match computer records exactly.

Master Schedule										
Week	1	2	3	4	5	6	7	8	9	10
#ct333	500		325		300		250		750	

Work Center	Lot Size	Lead Time	On Hand	Safety Stock	Lower Level Code	Item ID	Week		1	2	3	4	5	6	7	8	9	10
							Gross Requirements		500	0	325	0	300	0	250	0	750	0
							Scheduled Receipts		450									
Final Assembly	75	1	130	75	0	#ct333	Planned On Hand	130	130	80	80	130	130	130	130	105	105	105
							Net Requirements		0	0	320	0	245	0	195	0	720	0
							Planned Order Receipts		0	0	375	0	300	0	225	0	750	0
							Planned Order Releases		0	375	0	300	0	225	0	750	0	0

FIGURE 15.9 Master Schedule and Material Requirements Plan for the Triple-C-Table Fixture Final Assembly

Figure 15.10 shows the rest of the material plan for the ct333. The MRP links the planned order releases for the level (0) ct333 to gross requirements for all the level (1) materials used to make it. Thus, the planned order releases from Figure 15.9 (which are shown in the top rows of Figure 15.10) establish the gross requirements for the base SA, the cord, and the candle SA. Based on these gross requirements, planned order releases for the level (1) items can be determined using the basic MRP formula described earlier. Planned order releases for the level (1) items can then establish the gross requirements for level (2) items. For example, the planned order releases for the base SA are used to determine the gross requirements for ring and base components. So, too, planned order releases for the candle SA determine the gross requirements for shafts and bulbs.

Within each planning template, the MRP logic is essentially the same; only the inventory policies and the resulting numbers differ. For example, while the ct333 has a lot size of 75, the base is ordered in lots of 400 units minimum; the ring is ordered lot-for-lot; and all the other parts have fixed lot sizes ranging from 50 to 4,000 units. Since the cord is a common item in all the light fixtures, not just the

Work Center	Lot Size	Lead Time	On Hand	Safety Stock	Lower Level Code	Item ID	Week		1	2	3	4	5	6	7	8	9	10
Final Assembly	75	1	130	75	0	#ct333	Gross Requirements		500	0	325	0	300	0	250	0	750	0
							Scheduled Receipts		450									
							Planned On Hand	130	130	80	80	130	130	130	130	105	105	105
							Net Requirements		0	0	320	0	245	0	195	0	720	0
							Planned Order Receipts		0	0	375	0	300	0	225	0	750	0
							Planned Order Releases		0	375	0	300	0	225	0	750	0	0
							Week		1	2	3	4	5	6	7	8	9	10
Welding	50	2	410	20	1	Base SA	Gross Requirements		0	375	0	300	0	225	0	750	0	0
							Scheduled Receipts		0									
							Planned On Hand	410	410	410	35	35	35	35	60	60	60	60
							Net Requirements		0	0	0	285	0	210	0	710	0	0
							Planned Order Receipts		0	0	0	300	0	250	0	750	0	0
							Planned Order Releases		0	300	0	250	0	750	0	0	0	0
							Week		1	2	3	4	5	6	7	8	9	10
Purchasing	1,200	2	465	80	1	Cord	Gross Requirements		0	375	0	300	0	225	0	750	0	0
							Scheduled Receipts		0									
							Planned On Hand	465	465	465	90	90	990	990	765	765	1,215	1,215
							Net Requirements		0	0	0	290	0	0	0	65	0	0
							Planned Order Receipts		0	0	0	1,200	0	0	0	1,200	0	0
							Planned Order Releases		0	1,200	0	0	0	1,200	0	0	0	0
							Week		1	2	3	4	5	6	7	8	9	10
Subassembly	1,800	2	240	120	2	C-cndl SA	Gross Requirements		0	1,125	0	900	0	675	0	2,250	0	0
							Scheduled Receipts		0	1,800								
							Planned On Hand	240	240	240	915	915	1,815	1,815	1,140	1,140	690	690
							Net Requirements		0	0	0	105	0	0	0	1,230	0	0
							Planned Order Receipts		0	0	0	1,800	0	0	0	1,800	0	0
							Planned Order Releases		0	1,800	0	0	0	1,800	0	0	0	0

ct333, its lot size is fairly large. This simple example shows the planning for a single end item. By the time the demand for all other end items is considered, the material plan for the cord will include many more large orders. Similarly, the large lot size for bulbs is warranted because bulbs are common to many items. If the rest of the items on the master schedule had been built into this example, the plan would call for many more bulbs to be ordered.

LEAD-TIME AND LOT SIZE

Notice in Figure 15.10 that the gross requirement of 750 units of end item ct333 in week 9 ultimately leads to all of the following planned order releases:

- 750 units of ct333 in week 8
- 750 units of the base SA in week 6

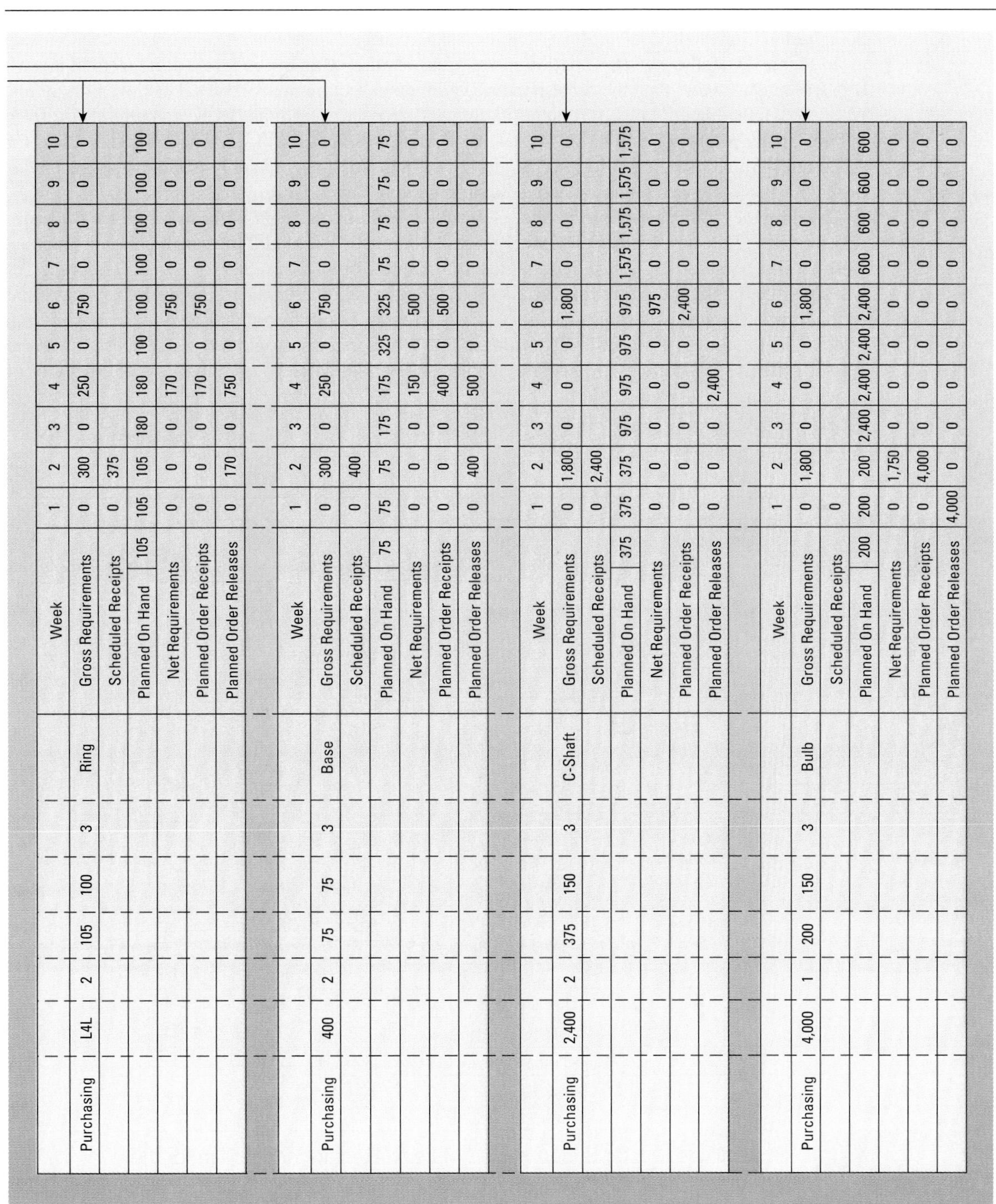

Purchasing	L4L	2	105	100	3	Ring	Week		1	2	3	4	5	6	7	8	9	10
							Gross Requirements		0	300	0	250	0	750	0	0	0	0
							Scheduled Receipts		0	375								
							Planned On Hand	105	105	105	180	180	100	100	100	100	100	100
							Net Requirements		0	0	0	170	0	750	0	0	0	0
							Planned Order Receipts		0	0	0	170	0	750	0	0	0	0
							Planned Order Releases		0	170	0	750	0	0	0	0	0	0

Purchasing	400	2	75	75	3	Base	Week		1	2	3	4	5	6	7	8	9	10
							Gross Requirements		0	300	0	250	0	750	0	0	0	0
							Scheduled Receipts		0	400								
							Planned On Hand	75	75	75	175	175	325	325	75	75	75	75
							Net Requirements		0	0	0	150	0	500	0	0	0	0
							Planned Order Receipts		0	0	0	400	0	500	0	0	0	0
							Planned Order Releases		0	400	0	500	0	0	0	0	0	0

Purchasing	2,400	2	375	150	3	C-Shaft	Week		1	2	3	4	5	6	7	8	9	10
							Gross Requirements		0	1,800	0	0	0	1,800	0	0	0	0
							Scheduled Receipts		0	2,400								
							Planned On Hand	375	375	375	975	975	975	975	1,575	1,575	1,575	1,575
							Net Requirements		0	0	0	0	0	975	0	0	0	0
							Planned Order Receipts		0	0	0	0	0	2,400	0	0	0	0
							Planned Order Releases		0	0	0	2,400	0	0	0	0	0	0

Purchasing	4,000	1	200	150	3	Bulb	Week		1	2	3	4	5	6	7	8	9	10
							Gross Requirements		0	1,800	0	0	0	1,800	0	0	0	0
							Scheduled Receipts		0									
							Planned On Hand	200	200	200	2,400	2,400	2,400	2,400	600	600	600	600
							Net Requirements		0	1,750	0	0	0	0	0	0	0	0
							Planned Order Receipts		0	4,000	0	0	0	0	0	0	0	0
							Planned Order Releases		4,000	0	0	0	0	0	0	0	0	0

FIGURE 15.10 Material Requirements Plan for the Triple-C-Table Fixture

- 1,200 units of the cord in week 6
- 1,800 units of the candle SA in week 6
- 750 units of the ring in week 4
- 500 units of the base in week 4
- 2,400 units of the shaft in week 4

Thus, work on the order actually begins five weeks before its delivery to the customer. If the company is working in a make-to-order mode, it might make sense to tell customers that their orders cannot be changed within five weeks of the due date. But that kind of policy can be hard for customers to understand. A typical order for fixtures might represent only 20 hours worth of work in a value-adding system that employs many people, each working full-time. Indeed, with expediting, such an order might be completed in a day. Why, then, should a customer be satisfied with a five-week lead-time?

An alternative to this approach would be to adopt an assemble-to-order strategy. Two weeks could be cut off the lead-time by keeping a stock of the candle SA and the base SA on hand for use in assembling end items. Demand for these subassemblies could be handled using the reorder point system described in Chapter 12.

In Figure 15.10 the weekly variation in the gross requirements of the level (0) item (final assembly) was much smaller than the corresponding variation in requirements for level (3) inventory items. Even though the material plan for the ct333 showed an order every other week, ranging in size from 250 to 750 items, only one order for the bulb was planned during the 10-week period and that was for 4,000 units. Much like the bullwhip effect described in discussions of supply-chain management earlier in this book, demand tends to become lumpier as you move to lower levels of the BOM.

Leveling the master schedule can help to reduce the lumpiness but will not eliminate the problem. Figures 15.11 and 15.12 show how Figures 15.9 and 15.10 would look if the master schedule were leveled completely. Notice that the material plan for bulbs now calls for two orders in the 10-week period, but the lot-sizing rules still lead to lumpiness in the demand. Figure 15.13 shows that by adding lot-for-lot ordering policies to this perfectly leveled master schedule, managers can remove the lumpiness at lower levels of the BOM. While that approach may make sense in theory, it is of little use in practice, because the whole idea behind MRP is to accommodate a variety of demand patterns and product-service bundles. The complexity of the value-adding systems where

Master Schedule										
Week	1	2	3	4	5	6	7	8	9	10
#ct333	213	213	213	213	213	213	213	213	213	213

Work Center	Lot Size	Lead Time	On Hand	Safety Stock	Lower Level Code	Item ID	Week		1	2	3	4	5	6	7	8	9	10
Final Assembly	75	1	130	75	0	#ct333	Gross Requirements		213	213	213	213	213	213	213	213	213	213
							Scheduled Receipts		225									
							Planned On Hand	130	130	142	79	91	103	115	127	139	76	88
							Net Requirements		0	146	209	197	185	173	161	149	212	200
							Planned Order Receipts		0	150	225	225	225	225	225	150	225	225
							Planned Order Releases		150	225	225	225	225	225	150	225	225	0

FIGURE 15.11 Streamlined Master Schedule and Material Requirements Plan for the Triple-C-Table Fixture Final Assembly

MRP is used can also make it costly to have a level master schedule which requires a large number of very small orders.

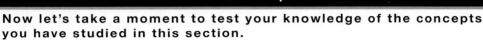

> **active concept check**

Now let's take a moment to test your knowledge of the concepts you have studied in this section.

Managing MRP Systems

While MRP logic is quite simple, MRP systems are actually very difficult to manage. Inventory levels for items at all levels of the BOM are constantly changing: Any worker can remove items from inventory, process and change them, and replace items in inventory. At times, even the most conscientious employees may forget to note their actions on the company computer. Occasionally, workers will purposely understate or overstate their output in order to manipulate their pay or work schedules. As for the bill of materials, when parts are temporarily unavailable, permanent changes may be made to the product without being noted in the computer file. Finally, the master schedule is generally made up of both forecasted demand and customer orders, either of which can change. As a result, the value of an MRP system is quite limited if a company cannot establish order and discipline in its operations and information gathering. One of the primary benefits of an MRP system, in fact, may be that it imposes discipline on complex environments, making them more understandable and manageable.

CHOOSING A SYSTEM

Generally, there are two types of MRP systems, regenerative and net change. *Regenerative MRP systems* typically update the material plan once weekly, usually over the weekend. Thus, orders that have come in during the week, changes in inventory levels that resulted from operations during the week, changes in orders, and shortages resulting from quality problems are not reflected in the material plan until the Monday morning following the change. On Monday morning, the MRP planner receives a clean set of planned orders that reflects all the prior week's activities. The regenerative approach to MRP is justified by the complexity of many manufacturing environments, whose thousands of parts, subassemblies, and end items require a great deal of computer processing time. Usually the plan is relatively close to actual figures throughout the week, and MRP planners can keep track of critical changes in inventory until a fresh computer run has been completed.

In *net change MRP systems,* material plans are updated as new data becomes available. If a material shortage is noted in a shipment from a supplier, the net change system will note it immediately and adjust the material plans for all the items in which it is used. The major benefit of a net change system is this ability to make real-time adjustments. Yet real-time adjustments can also produce **system nervousness,** or problem-causing fluctuation in the material plan. When material plans are not stable and orders change frequently, workers and material planners tend not to trust the information they've been given. They might try to speed up production before an order gets canceled, or delay work on a difficult but important job in the hope it will be canceled or reduced. Alternatively, workers might hide some inventory in order to be prepared for order changes. Such behavior only worsens system nervousness. As a result, the regenerative approach is used more often.

EXPEDITING ORDERS

Many companies that use MRP systems employ expeditors to walk a job through the facility and ensure on-time delivery. If asked, "Do you do any expediting here?" many managers will respond with pride, "Oh yes! Every day. Customer satisfaction is very important to us!" Expediting, however, is a sign that an operation's planning and control system is not working as well as it should. If possible, expediting should be avoided, and the system should be adjusted so that it isn't needed. When expeditors are given the authority to override scheduling decisions in any work area and place a customer's job at the head of the line, they throw a monkey wrench into the company's scheduling system. Expeditors introduce variability into a system that is already difficult enough to manage.

Work Center	Lot Size	Lead Time	On Hand	Safety Stock	Lower Level Code	Item ID	Week	1	2	3	4	5	6	7	8	9	10
Final Assembly	75	1	130	75	0	#ct333	Gross Requirements	213	213	213	213	213	213	213	213	213	213
							Scheduled Receipts	225									
							Planned On Hand 130	130	142	79	91	103	115	127	139	76	88
							Net Requirements	0	146	209	197	185	173	161	149	212	200
							Planned Order Receipts	0	150	225	225	225	225	225	150	225	225
							Planned Order Releases	150	225	225	225	225	225	150	225	225	0
Welding	50	2	410	20	1	Base SA	Gross Requirements	150	225	225	225	225	225	150	225	225	0
							Scheduled Receipts	0									
							Planned On Hand 410	410	260	35	60	35	60	35	35	60	35
							Net Requirements	0	0	210	185	210	185	135	210	185	0
							Planned Order Receipts	0	0	250	200	250	200	150	250	200	0
							Planned Order Releases	250	200	250	200	150	250	200	0	0	0
Purchasing	1,200	2	465	80	1	Cord	Gross Requirements	150	225	225	225	225	225	150	225	225	0
							Scheduled Receipts	0									
							Planned On Hand 465	465	315	90	1,065	840	615	390	240	1,215	990
							Net Requirements	0	0	215	0	0	0	0	65	0	0
							Planned Order Receipts	0	0	1,200	0	0	0	0	1,200	0	0
							Planned Order Releases	1,200	0	0	0	0	1,200	0	0	0	0
Subassembly	1,800	2	240	120	2	C-cndl SA	Gross Requirements	450	675	675	675	675	675	450	675	675	0
							Scheduled Receipts	1,800	0								
							Planned On Hand 240	240	1,590	915	240	1,365	690	1,815	1,365	690	1,815
							Net Requirements	0	0	0	555	0	105	0	0	105	0
							Planned Order Receipts	0	0	0	1,800	0	1,800	0	0	1,800	0
							Planned Order Releases	0	1,800	0	1,800	0	0	1,800	0	0	0

LOT SIZING

The economic order quantity (EOQ) method of determining lot sizes for independent demand inventory items, described in Chapter 12, does not fit the dependent demand situation. The EOQ formula and others similar to it assume a steady state consumption rate and known costs. As we have seen, with dependent demand inventory items, the consumption rate generally is not steady; demand is intermittent and its distribution is lumpy. Furthermore, the decision about lot sizes at one level of the BOM influences the demand at other levels of the BOM. Consequently, the lot-sizing decision is quite complicated; in many situations the optimal lot size is not known.

There are many approaches to lot sizing for dependent demand inventory items. In the example given on pages 648–649, Bonnie's Candle Shop used lot-for-lot, fixed quantity, and minimum quantity lot sizes. Often, the lot-sizing decision in MRP comes down to whether to order this period's net requirement or combine this period's order with the order for next period. Combining orders can reduce ordering (or setup) costs, but a carrying cost may be incurred in the process.

									1	2	3	4	5	6	7	8	9	10
Purchasing	L4L	2	105	100	3	Ring	Week		1	2	3	4	5	6	7	8	9	10
							Gross Requirements		250	200	250	200	150	250	200	0	0	0
							Scheduled Receipts		245	200								
							Planned On Hand	105	105	100	100	100	100	100	100	100	100	100
							Net Requirements		0	0	250	200	150	250	200	0	0	0
							Planned Order Receipts		0	0	250	200	150	250	200	0	0	0
							Planned Order Releases		250	200	150	250	200	0	0	0	0	0

Purchasing	400	2	75	75	3	Base	Week		1	2	3	4	5	6	7	8	9	10
							Gross Requirements		250	200	250	200	150	250	200	0	0	0
							Scheduled Receipts		400	400								
							Planned On Hand	75	75	225	425	175	375	225	375	175	175	175
							Net Requirements		0	0	0	100	0	100	0	0	0	0
							Planned Order Receipts		0	0	0	400	0	400	0	0	0	0
							Planned Order Releases		0	400	0	0	0	0	0	0	0	0

Purchasing	2,400	2	375	150	3	C-shaft	Week		1	2	3	4	5	6	7	8	9	10
							Gross Requirements		0	1,800	0	1,800	0	0	1,800	0	0	0
							Scheduled Receipts		0	2,400								
							Planned On Hand	375	375	375	975	975	1,575	1,575	1,575	2,175	2,175	2,175
							Net Requirements		0	0	0	975	0	0	375	0	0	0
							Planned Order Receipts		0	0	0	2,400	0	0	2,400	0	0	0
							Planned Order Releases		0	2,400	0	0	2,400	0	0	0	0	0

Purchasing	4,000	1	200	150	3	Bulb	Week		1	2	3	4	5	6	7	8	9	10
							Gross Requirements		0	1,800	0	1,800	0	0	1,800	0	0	0
							Scheduled Receipts		0									
							Planned On Hand	200	200	200	2,400	2,400	600	600	600	2,800	2,800	2,800
							Net Requirements		0	1,750	0	0	0	0	1,350	0	0	0
							Planned Order Receipts		0	4,000	0	0	0	0	4,000	0	0	0
							Planned Order Releases		4,000	0	0	0	4,000	0	0	0	0	0

FIGURE 15.12 Streamlined Material Requirements Plan for the Triple-C-Table Fixture

Suppose the net requirements for week 5 are 200 units; the net requirements for week 8, 300 units; and the net requirements for all other weeks, 0. Also suppose the ordering cost is \$200, and the carrying cost per unit per week is \$0.25.

Problem: The manager must decide whether to order 200 units or 500 units.

Solution: If the manager orders 500 units, the company will save \$200 in ordering costs but will also incur 900 "part periods" of inventory carrying cost (for holding 300 units for three weeks). At \$0.25 per unit per week, that would cost *900 × \$.25 = \$225.* In other words, it would be slightly more cost efficient to order 200 units first and another 300 units later.

A variety of different approaches to lot sizing have been employed in MRP environments. Most of them are in some way based on this kind of *part-period balancing* logic.

Work Center	Lot Size	Lead Time	On Hand	Safety Stock	Lower Level Code	Item ID	Week	1	2	3	4	5	6	7	8	9	10
Final Assembly	L4L	1	78	75	0	#ct333	Gross Requirements	213	213	213	213	213	213	213	213	213	213
							Scheduled Receipts	213									
							Planned On Hand 78	78	78	75	75	75	75	75	75	75	75
							Net Requirements	0	210	213	213	213	213	213	213	213	213
							Planned Order Receipts	0	210	213	213	213	213	213	213	213	213
							Planned Order Releases	210	213	213	213	213	213	213	213	213	0
							Week	1	2	3	4	5	6	7	8	9	10
Welding	L4L	2	32	20	1	Base SA	Gross Requirements	210	213	213	213	213	213	213	213	213	0
							Scheduled Receipts	213	213								
							Planned On Hand 32	32	35	35	20	20	20	20	20	20	20
							Net Requirements	0	0	198	213	213	213	213	213	213	0
							Planned Order Receipts	0	0	198	213	213	213	213	213	213	0
							Planned Order Releases	198	213	213	213	213	213	213	0	0	0
							Week	1	2	3	4	5	6	7	8	9	10
Purchasing	L4L	2	85	80	1	Cord	Gross Requirements	210	213	213	213	213	213	213	213	213	0
							Scheduled Receipts	213	213								
							Planned On Hand 85	85	88	88	80	80	80	80	80	80	80
							Net Requirements	0	0	205	213	213	213	213	213	213	0
							Planned Order Receipts	0	0	205	213	213	213	213	213	213	0
							Planned Order Releases	205	213	213	213	213	213	213	0	0	0
							Week	1	2	3	4	5	6	7	8	9	10
Subassembly	L4L	2	125	120	2	C-cndl SA	Gross Requirements	630	639	639	639	639	639	639	639	639	0
							Scheduled Receipts	635	640								
							Planned On Hand 125	125	130	131	120	120	120	120	120	120	120
							Net Requirements	0	0	628	639	639	639	639	639	639	0
							Planned Order Receipts	0	0	628	639	639	639	639	639	639	0
							Planned Order Releases	628	639	639	639	639	639	639	0	0	0

COMBINING MRP WITH JIT AND TOC

Unlike JIT and theory of constraints (TOC), MRP systems don't have any built-in mechanism for reducing inventory over time in order to streamline operations. Think back to the analogy of the rocks and the river (see Figure 13.6): MRP does not place any emphasis on lowering the water level to improve the system. That doesn't mean that quality and improvement are irrelevant. Certainly, one of the most important considerations in an MRP system is whether computers are automating and facilitating unnecessary complexity. If, based on customer preferences, firms find that complexity is not warranted, they should eliminate it and move toward a TOC or JIT system through techniques such as group technology.

Many companies use some combination of MRP, JIT, and TOC in their operations planning and control. For example, highly effective closed loop MRP users can use such a system to guarantee JIT delivery to both internal and external customers. At the Kawasaki plant in Lincoln, Nebraska, JIT is used to schedule the production of roughly a dozen end items, including motorcycles, snowmobiles, and jet skis. MRP is used to do the material planning for these items, as it is in most TOC implementations so that both internal and external suppliers receive advance notice of material requirements on

Purchasing	L4L	2	105	100	3	Ring

Week		1	2	3	4	5	6	7	8	9	10
Gross Requirements		198	213	213	213	213	213	213	0	0	0
Scheduled Receipts		200	215								
Planned On Hand	105	105	107	109	100	100	100	100	100	100	100
Net Requirements		0	0	204	213	213	213	213	0	0	0
Planned Order Receipts		0	0	204	213	213	213	213	0	0	0
Planned Order Releases		204	213	213	213	213	0	0	0	0	0

Purchasing	L4L	2	75	75	3	Base

Week		1	2	3	4	5	6	7	8	9	10
Gross Requirements		198	213	213	213	213	213	213	0	0	0
Scheduled Receipts		200	215								
Planned On Hand	75	75	77	79	75	75	75	75	75	75	75
Net Requirements		0	0	209	213	213	213	213	0	0	0
Planned Order Receipts		0	0	209	213	213	213	213	0	0	0
Planned Order Releases		209	213	213	213	213	213	213	0	0	0

Purchasing	L4L	2	157	150	3	C-shaft

Week		1	2	3	4	5	6	7	8	9	10
Gross Requirements		628	639	639	639	639	639	639	0	0	0
Scheduled Receipts		630	640								
Planned On Hand	157	157	159	160	150	150	150	150	150	150	150
Net Requirements		0	0	629	639	639	639	639	0	0	0
Planned Order Receipts		0	0	629	639	639	639	639	0	0	0
Planned Order Releases		629	639	639	639	639	0	0	0	0	0

Purchasing	L4L	1	172	150	3	Bulb

Week		1	2	3	4	5	6	7	8	9	10
Gross Requirements		628	639	639	639	639	639	639	0	0	0
Scheduled Receipts		630									
Planned On Hand	172	172	174	150	150	150	150	150	150	150	150
Net Requirements		0	615	639	639	639	639	639	0	0	0
Planned Order Receipts		0	615	639	639	639	639	639	0	0	0
Planned Order Releases		615	639	639	639	639	639	0	0	0	0

FIGURE 15.13 Streamlined Material Requirements Plan for the Triple-C-Table Fixture with Reduced Component Lot Sizes

a weekly basis. Product deliveries are scheduled using a JIT pull system. Similarly, a Jergens factory in Cincinnati makes dozens of different soaps and lotions using MRP to schedule weekly material requirements as much as months in advance. Managers can still call a supplier the night before a delivery to adjust the required quantity upward or downward. The actual materials are pulled into the mixing operation using bins that serve as kanbans.

APPLYING MRP IN SERVICE OPERATIONS

While MRP is used primarily to support manufacturing operations, it is applicable to services as well. Many service operations require kits of tools or parts needed to complete a specific task. MRP can be quite useful in that context.

An article in the *Journal of Operations Management* (Steinberg, Khumawala, and Scamell 1982) described how the Park Plaza Hospital in Houston, Texas, used MRP to guarantee adequate supplies for its surgical suite. The data inputs required in this service application closely paralleled the inputs required in a manufacturing environment. Physicians who used the surgical suite were required to schedule their activity well in advance of the time of surgery; cancellations could not occur within a given period of the scheduled operation. This type of schedule was clearly analogous to the master schedule found in any operational context. The particular procedure being performed by a given physician was defined as the level (0) item. The schedule for these level (0) items was obtained by the advance notice that physicians were required to give.

The parallel to the bill of materials in this application was the preference sheet each physician filled out, indicating the instruments preferred for use in each of the procedures being performed. As each surgeon completed this form, the information needed to purchase the lower-level items became available. Since surgical operations cannot be stored, and many surgical instruments are sterilized and reused, inventory considerations were somewhat more complex than in a standard manufacturing operation. To calculate net requirements, managers had to subtract on-hand inventory, scheduled receipts, and sterilized items receipts from the gross requirements for an instrument. Using MRP provided several advantages to the Park Plaza Hospital: the assurance that materials would be available when needed; protection against overinvestment in an inventory of facilitating goods; guidance in formulating and adjusting inventory reordering policies; and a way to analyze and control spending on supplies.

YIELD MANAGEMENT SYSTEMS

Many services are now employing yield management systems in order to more fully utilize their service capacity and maximize their revenue. These information systems require planners to generate a set of paired service-price offerings. They then gather data regarding customer transactions (sales and cancellations) as they occur. Managers are able to modify availability of the service-price offerings on the basis of current information, in order to maximize the revenue they obtain from their use of capacity.

American Airlines pioneered the use of yield management with their SABRE reservation system. At the outset, the airline required that all reservations be made through SABRE. This allowed the company to monitor the sale of seats at particular prices for its own flights and, to some extent, those of competitors. It could then alter the availability of the fares and seats on the basis of real-time demand information. If it looked like there was insufficient demand for the expensive seats, more discounts could be offered. If it seemed that there was strong demand for expensive seats, the number of available discounted seats could be reduced. The system also allows the airline to modify its mix of flights on the basis of weather conditions and other factors that might lead to delays (or other lost revenue events) in particular airports.

active example

Take a closer look at the concepts and issues you've been reading about.

The environments to which yield management systems apply are just as complex as those where MRP is used. One factor that adds complexity for airlines is that of connecting flights. Since passengers can get from point A to point B with many different flight combinations, the airline has to take into account the volume of traffic on each leg of the trip whenever a discount fare is offered. Additional complexity comes from the fact that many services have *perishable inventory.* (Services like hotels and airlines consider the seats on upcoming flights or the rooms for upcoming nights their inventory. Revenue from an unsold seat or hotel room is lost forever if the flight takes off or the reservation date passes.)

The success of yield management at American Airlines has led many other services to adopt the practice. It is most beneficial to service firms with relatively fixed capacity, perishable inventory, ability to sell their service in advance of consumption, ability to segment markets, fluctuating demand, low marginal sales costs, and high marginal costs to change capacity. Indeed yield management is now widely used in the hotel industry, rental businesses, and travel industries—and with the advent of deregulation has even gained a foothold in electrical utilities.[1]

[1]Sheryl E. Kimes, "Yield Management: A Tool for Capacity-Constrained Service Firms," *Journal of Operations Management* 8, no. 4 (October 1989): 348–363.

The growing use of yield management strategies has created new business opportunities and spawned companies that bargain for customers. There are now many clubs and newsletters that advise customers who seek to minimize the price they pay for services that are managed with yield management strategies. Priceline.com, for example, is a web-based business that allows customers to make an offer for a flight, hotel room, or other service within particular timing parameters. Service providers then have the opportunity to accept or reject the customer's bid within a fixed period of time. Recent agreements have given Priceline.com access to 90% of the nation's air travel market with the ability to sell the tickets of every major U.S. airline. (By giving the airlines warrants that can be converted to company stock, Priceline.com also has gained a set of stable institutional investors.)

Yield management allows companies to tailor the use of their capacity to specific customer preference. In Chapter 3, we suggested that companies cannot be all things to all customers and therefore needed to focus their value-adding systems on a specific set of competitive priorities. In the context of yield management, however, an airline can provide different value propositions within the context of one service. For example, airlines can offer cheap fares for customers who just want to get away but don't care so much about when and where they travel. At the same time, they can command top dollar from customers, potentially with identical iteneraries, who have to reach a specific destination and must travel within a specific window of time. The yield management system allows airlines to meet the requirements of both types of customers using their single value-adding system.

> video exercise

Take a moment to apply what you've learned.

> active concept check

Now let's take a moment to test your knowledge of the concepts you have studied in this section.

> Supply-Chain Impact of an MRP System

Figure 15.14 describes some of the supply-chain impacts of MRP planning and control systems. As a rule, MRP users interact with customers and suppliers on an order-by-order basis. Because MRP users make planning and control decisions order by order, they must track orders and monitor quality on the same basis. This approach means there is a lot of information to monitor, and keeping all that information current and accurate is very difficult. Because of the weekly regeneration system most companies use and the decentralized approach to scheduling that is inherent in MRP, total lead-times on customer orders tend to be long.

Careful product design can improve lead-times in an MRP system. The flatter the BOM, the fewer the steps required to create the product-service bundle. Total lead-times are shorter and the system is easier to manage with a flat, wide BOM than with a deep, narrow BOM.

Suppliers of MRP users need to track quality by order, maintain accurate inventory records (so that their shipments don't come up short), and promptly communicate foreseeable shortages or delays. From a structural perspective, suppliers can greatly facilitate their interactions with MRP firms by using information systems that allow them to receive or anticipate orders electronically via some form of electronic data interchange (EDI). Such systems allow customers to obtain updates on an order's progress when needed. Updates to item lead-times, perhaps based on material shortages or capacity considerations, can also be taken into account, and changes in the BOM, inventory status, or schedule can be passed on easily. For all the same reasons that MRP users find a flat BOM beneficial, suppliers do as well.

Like suppliers, customers of MRP users must interact with them one order at a time. They, too, must assess incoming quality order by order, implement compatible information systems, and flatten their BOMs. Unlike suppliers, however, customers drive the MRP system's material planning decisions. Timely and accurate demand information and restraint in changing orders is essential in an MRP customer.

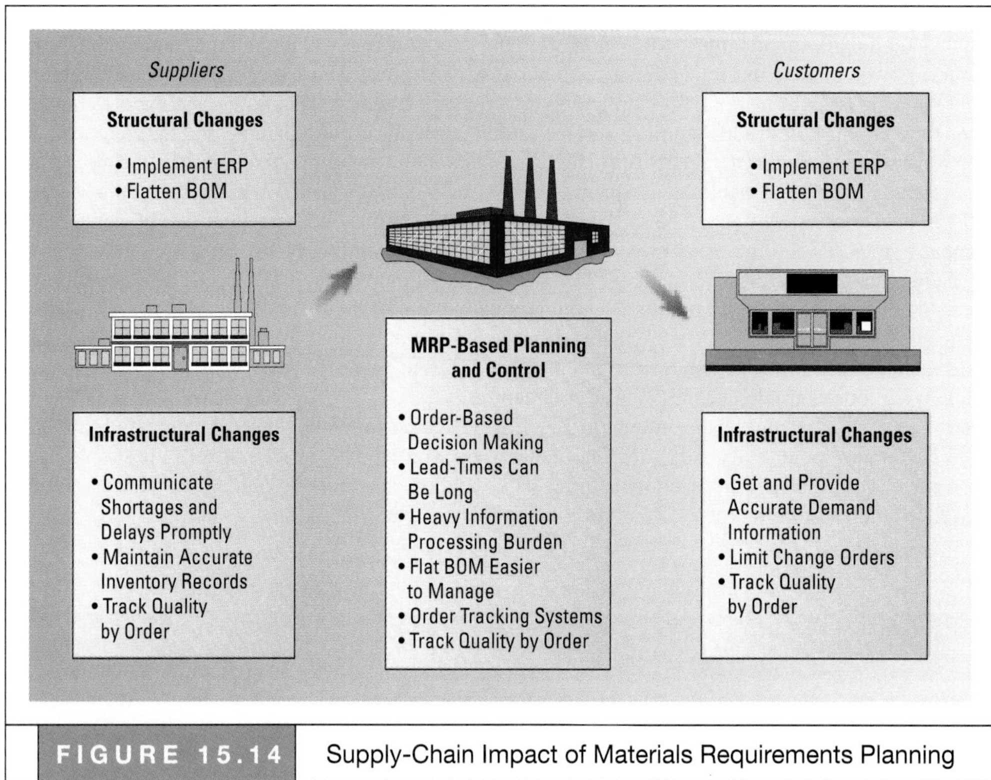

FIGURE 15.14 Supply-Chain Impact of Materials Requirements Planning

active exercise

Take a moment to apply what you've learned.

Detailed Scheduling in an MRP Environment

Once the material requirements have been calculated by the MRP system, orders may be released to specific work centers by the MRP planners. This assignment of work to specific resources is referred to as *loading*. Two approaches to loading exist: finite loading and infinite loading.

Finite loading limits the amount of work that is released to a given work center on the basis of capacity considerations. One simple way to do this is with **input/output control,** a system that monitors the work assigned to a resource (input) and the work completed by a resource (output). Input/output control can also be applied to a group of resources or a whole facility. It is based on the premise that over time, the inputs and outputs at any work center should balance out. If, over an extended period of time, the input rate is greater than the output rate, a large backlog of work will accumulate in the work center. In such a situation, orders should be delayed until the work center has adequate capacity to complete them. A long-term imbalance indicates that more capacity should be added or work should be turned away.

Infinite loading, on the other hand, allows planners to assign jobs to work centers regardless of their available capacity. If other planning and control tasks have been handled effectively—for example, if the aggregate planning process has provided adequate capacity and the master schedule has been leveled—there may be no significant risk of long-term capacity imbalances. Even though a work center may develop a temporary backlog, in the long term it will be able to keep up. Requirements for additional capacity can be discovered and handled through the capacity planning process.

Regardless of the loading approach used, the specific jobs that have been assigned to a work center are generally scheduled based on local considerations. That is, jobs are ranked in terms of the local work center's priorities and worked on in that order. Two basic methods of prioritizing work are local priority rules and Gantt charts.

LOCAL PRIORITY RULES

This process of sequencing jobs through a work center is referred to as **dispatching.** In complex manufacturing environments, a job's characteristics are often used to determine its relative priority. The rules used to assign priorities to jobs based on their characteristics are called **priority rules, dispatching rules,** or **sequencing rules.** In the following sections we will consider several commonly used dispatching rules and their benefits and drawbacks.

First Come, First Served (FCFS)

The first-come, first-served rule is particularly useful in service settings, where the customer considers "cutting in line" unfair. If you are waiting in line at a local restaurant that doesn't take reservations, you would be upset if the town mayor, who arrived after you, was seated before you. On the other hand, FCFS doesn't take into account the urgency of a job based on due date criteria, the importance of a job, efficiency in sequencing jobs, or any other relevant criteria.

Earliest Due Date (EDD)

This earliest due date dispatching rule gives highest priority to the job with the nearest due date, and ranks job priority on that basis alone. Thus, the job that is due tomorrow has a higher priority than the job that is due next week or next month. When customers are particularly sensitive to late deliveries, this rule serves them well, presuming that all jobs have relatively uniform processing times. The weakness of this rule is that it doesn't consider efficiency in sequencing and ignores the time required to complete a job. For example, it will give a higher priority to a job due two days from now that requires one day's work than to a job due three days from now that requires five days' work.

Minimum Slack (MS)

Slack is the difference between the time until a job is due and the processing time required to complete it. Obviously, jobs with negative slack are behind schedule; those jobs might require expediting to get caught up. Under the minimum slack rule, jobs are sequenced based on their slack: Those with the most slack receive the lowest priority and those with the least slack receive the highest priority. Though this sequencing rule was devised to overcome one of the stated weaknesses of EDD, like EDD it ignores efficiency issues.

Critical Ratio (CR)

The critical ratio is the time until a job is due divided by the processing time required to complete it. In the critical ratio rule, jobs are sequenced from lowest CR to highest CR. Those with a CR less than one are considered behind schedule. Like MS, this sequencing rule is meant to overcome one of the stated weaknesses of EDD, but it too ignores efficiency.

Shortest Processing Time (SPT)

The shortest processing time dispatching rule gives highest priority to the job with the shortest processing time, allowing a work center to process a large number of jobs very quickly. This rule generally increases efficiency and can have a very positive effect on an operation's cash flow. In fact, it can be proven mathematically that SPT minimizes average flow time, or the average amount of time that a job spends in a work center, including waiting and processing times. Flow time is highly correlated with inventory levels. For this reason, it can serve as a proxy for efficiency. This rule is especially helpful when a work center is close to the beginning of a job routing, because it allows work to move forward quickly to other work centers. Though minimizing flow time has a positive effect on due date performance, SPT does not explicitly consider due dates in the sequencing of jobs. Thus, if processing times vary, long jobs will receive a low priority and short jobs will continually take precedence over them.

Longest Processing Time (LPT)

The longest processing time sequencing rule is often used by those who want to attack the toughest job first and get it out of the way. Since it is diametrically opposed to SPT, this rule couldn't be recommended based either on efficiency or due date performance. Using LPT in work centers that are early in a job's routing is a bad idea, because the other work centers might become starved for work. For example, in a copy shop with a typesetter and a printer, the time required to print a job is generally independent of the time required to do the typesetting. So if the typesetter picked a really tough job to work on first and took a lot of time to complete it, the printer might quickly run out of work. Indeed, apart from the psychological benefit some workers derive from getting a tough job over with, there is little justification for using LPT.

LOCAL PRIORITY RULES: AN APPLICATION

Figure 15.15 shows the tasks waiting to be scheduled at the paint booth in Luis's factory. Six batches of furniture need to be painted; they vary in size, due date, expected time to completion, and even their location in the work center. Workers might have to move one job aside to get access to another job. This picture illustrates why jobs in complex, functionally organized manufacturing environments typically spend 90% or more of their lead-time waiting in line, and less than 10% of their lead-time actually being worked on. As more jobs arrive at the booth, the competition for this resource intensifies.

Figure 15.16 shows the schedules that result from using various dispatching rules to order the jobs waiting at the paint booth. Notice that the total processing time for all the jobs that have been loaded on the work area, called the **make span,** is 22 hours. Regardless of the sequence in which the six batches are processed, 22 hours worth of work will be required. **Flow time,** or the time a job will spend in the paint booth area, including both waiting time and processing time, *is* affected by the sequencing of jobs. If the crew at the paint booth can complete several jobs quickly, fewer jobs will have a lengthy wait and the flow time will be relatively short. Dividing total flow time by the make span yields the average number of jobs in the system.

In the discussion of sequencing rules starting on page 38, we saw that SPT minimizes average flow time. That result can be seen in Figure 15.16: SPT yields the lowest total flow time, the lowest average flow time, and the lowest average number of jobs in the system. If Luis wants to schedule the paint booth on the basis of efficiency, he will use SPT. If Luis is more concerned about due date performance, he will notice that EDD and MS are better than SPT and will sequence jobs using one of those rules. Interestingly, in this case, SPT provides better due date performance than CR. One downside to using SPT in this setting might arise if the booth must frequently process jobs requiring less than seven hours. Since batch 3 requires seven hours of processing time, it would never move from the back of the line under SPT. Sooner or later, the customer for that job would complain, and batch 3 would have to be expedited.

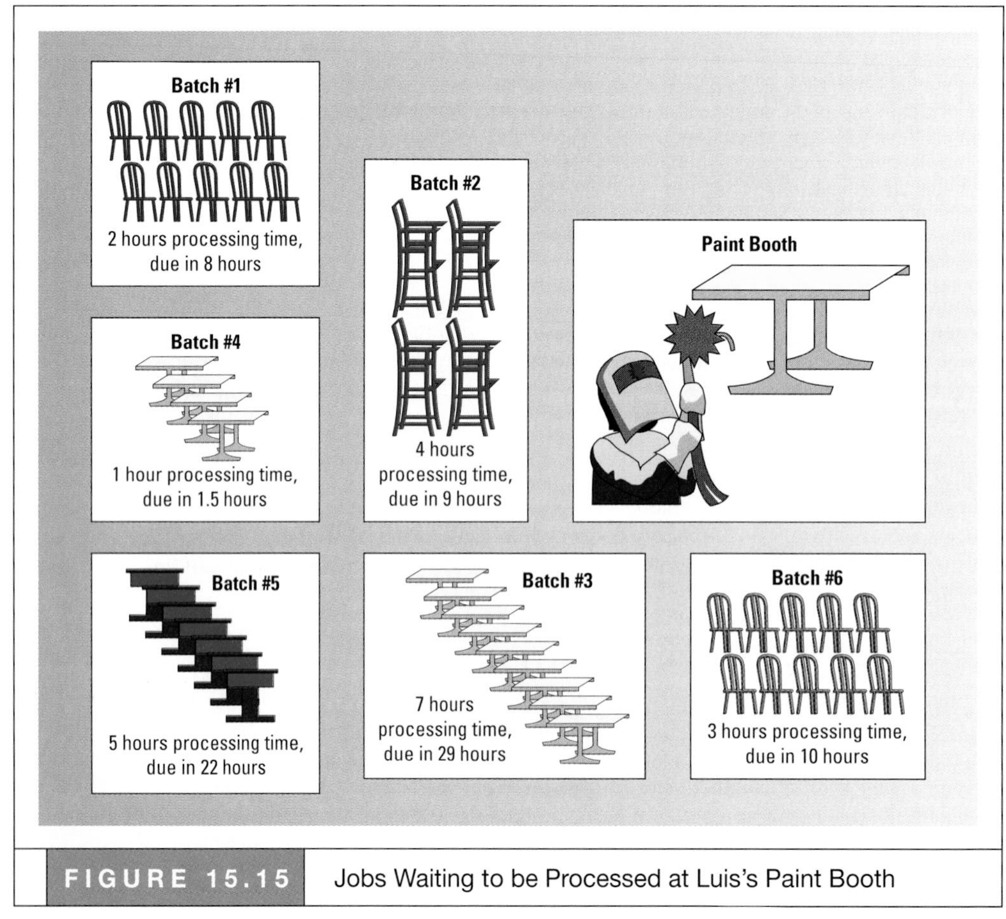

FIGURE 15.15 Jobs Waiting to be Processed at Luis's Paint Booth

(a) First Come, First Served (FCFS)

	Processing Time (hours)	Due (hours from now)	Critical Ratio	Slack (hours)	Flow Time (hours)	Late (hours)
Batch 1	2.00	8.00	**4.00**	6.00	2.00	0.00
Batch 2	4.00	9.00	**2.25**	5.00	6.00	0.00
Batch 3	7.00	29.00	**4.14**	22.00	13.00	0.00
Batch 4	1.00	1.50	**1.50**	0.50	14.00	12.50
Batch 5	5.00	22.00	**4.40**	17.00	19.00	0.00
Batch 6	3.00	10.00	**3.33**	7.00	22.00	12.00
				Total	*76.00*	*24.50*
				Average	*12.67*	*4.08*
Average number of jobs in system				3.45		

(d) Earliest Due Date (EDD)

	Processing Time (hours)	Due (hours from now)	Critical Ratio	Slack (hours)	Flow Time (hours)	Late (hours)
Batch 4	1.00	1.50	**1.50**	0.50	1.00	0.00
Batch 1	2.00	8.00	**4.00**	6.00	3.00	0.00
Batch 2	4.00	9.00	**2.25**	5.00	7.00	0.00
Batch 6	3.00	10.00	**3.33**	7.00	10.00	0.00
Batch 5	5.00	22.00	**4.40**	17.00	15.00	0.00
Batch 3	7.00	29.00	**4.14**	22.00	22.00	0.00
				Total	*58.00*	*0.00*
				Average	*9.67*	*0.00*
Average number of jobs in system				2.64		

(b) Shortest Processing Time (SPT)

	Processing Time (hours)	Due (hours from now)	Critical Ratio	Slack (hours)	Flow Time (hours)	Late (hours)
Batch 4	1.00	1.50	**1.50**	0.50	1.00	0.00
Batch 1	2.00	8.00	**4.00**	6.00	3.00	0.00
Batch 6	3.00	10.00	**3.33**	7.00	6.00	0.00
Batch 2	4.00	9.00	**2.25**	5.00	10.00	1.00
Batch 5	5.00	22.00	**4.40**	17.00	15.00	0.00
Batch 3	7.00	29.00	**4.14**	22.00	22.00	0.00
				Total	*57.00*	*1.00*
				Average	*9.50*	*0.17*
Average number of jobs in system				2.59		

(e) MIN Slack (MS)

	Processing Time (hours)	Due (hours from now)	Critical Ratio	Slack (hours)	Flow Time (hours)	Late (hours)
Batch 4	1.00	1.50	**1.50**	0.50	1.00	0.00
Batch 2	4.00	9.00	**2.25**	5.00	5.00	0.00
Batch 1	2.00	8.00	**4.00**	6.00	7.00	0.00
Batch 6	3.00	10.00	**3.33**	7.00	10.00	0.00
Batch 5	5.00	22.00	**4.40**	17.00	15.00	0.00
Batch 3	7.00	29.00	**4.14**	22.00	22.00	0.00
				Total	*60.00*	*0.00*
				Average	*10.00*	*0.00*
Average number of jobs in system				2.73		

(c) Longest Processing Time (LPT)

	Processing Time (hours)	Due (hours from now)	Critical Ratio	Slack (hours)	Flow Time (hours)	Late (hours)
Batch 3	7.00	29.00	**4.14**	22.00	7.00	0.00
Batch 5	5.00	22.00	**4.40**	17.00	12.00	0.00
Batch 2	4.00	9.00	**2.25**	5.00	16.00	7.00
Batch 6	3.00	10.00	**3.33**	7.00	19.00	9.00
Batch 1	2.00	8.00	**4.00**	6.00	21.00	13.00
Batch 4	1.00	1.50	**1.50**	0.50	22.00	20.50
				Total	*97.00*	*49.50*
				Average	*16.17*	*8.25*
Average number of jobs in system				4.41		

(f) Critical Ratio (CR)

	Processing Time (hours)	Due (hours from now)	Critical Ratio	Slack (hours)	Flow Time (hours)	Late (hours)
Batch 4	1.00	1.50	**1.50**	0.50	1.00	0.00
Batch 2	4.00	9.00	**2.25**	5.00	5.00	0.00
Batch 6	3.00	10.00	**3.33**	7.00	8.00	0.00
Batch 1	2.00	8.00	**4.00**	6.00	10.00	2.00
Batch 3	7.00	29.00	**4.14**	22.00	17.00	0.00
Batch 5	5.00	22.00	**4.40**	17.00	22.00	0.00
				Total	*63.00*	*2.00*
				Average	*10.50*	*0.33*
Average number of jobs in system				2.86		

FIGURE 15.16 Results of Six Different Local Priority Rules

GANTT CHARTS

Schedules can be displayed graphically using **Gantt charts,** or bar graphs that show a resource's scheduled work and available time. Figure 15.17 shows the Gantt chart for Luis's paint booth based on

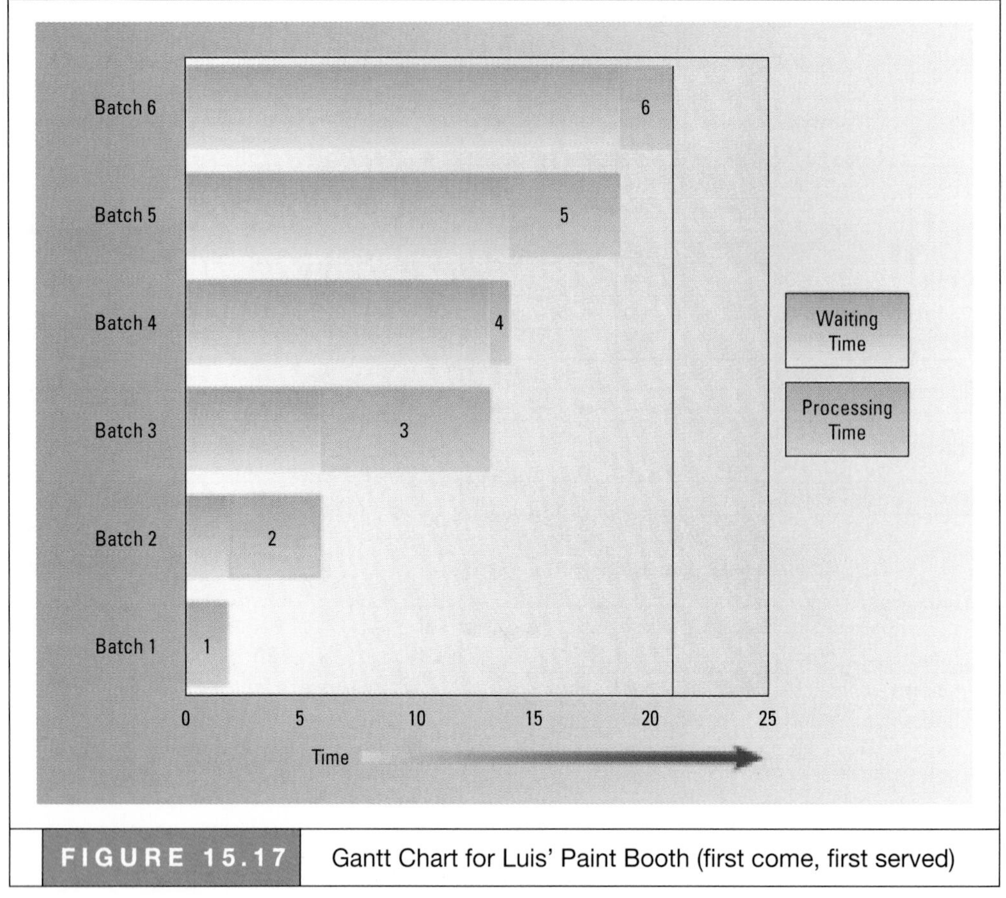

FIGURE 15.17 Gantt Chart for Luis' Paint Booth (first come, first served)

the FCFS rule. This simple figure shows the planned schedule at only one resource. Other versions of Gantt charts include both the planned schedule and time spent at the resource to date, allowing operators to see whether they are behind schedule or ahead.

Multiple resource Gantt charts can also be created to track the progress of a job through its routing. In fact, some companies use a Gantt chart as the weekly plan for their operation, using it to predict and track a job's progress through the factory. A recent development in computerized graphical interfaces, called **leitstands,** allows operations managers to schedule work centers and display multiple resource Gantt charts electronically. With the leitstand, managers can easily play what-if? games and adjust the schedules at individual work centers to improve a facility's performance based on due date performance, average flow time, and cost criteria.

video exercise <

Take a moment to apply what you've learned.

active concept check <

Now let's take a moment to test your knowledge of the concepts you have studied in this section.

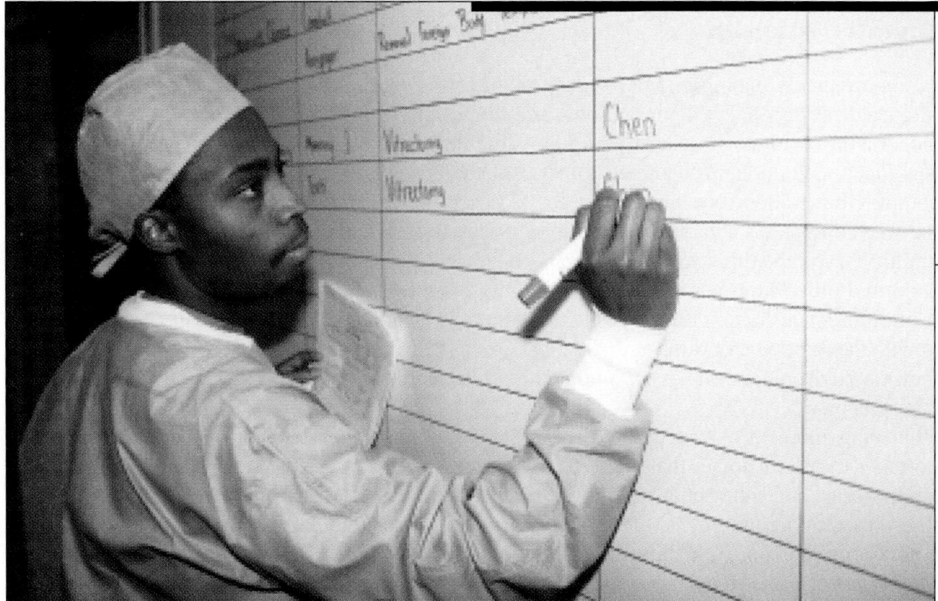

Scheduling in hospitals, like scheduling in other complex service and manufacturing environments, often makes use of Gantt Charts such as the one seen in this photograph.

> Scheduling at Miami's Student Rec Center

At hotels, hospitals and rec centers, the laundry operation is one of the aspects of the business that is most like manufacturing. In fact, the closest thing to a material requirement at the Student Recreation Center is a towel, so material planning doesn't require a lot of effort. Scheduling, on the other hand, is an issue that requires a great deal of attention. At the rec center there are student workers, student supervisors, referees, and full-time employees. All of these individuals are unavailable at certain times and have to be assigned work times in particular venues when they are available. Events such as regional swimming meets, rock wall climbing competitions, student vacations, physical education classes, fitness classes, and intramural competitions must all share these employees and the facilities of the center.

So how do they make certain that there are plenty of workers at all of the right times? Like most other service operations, the answer is a very large Gantt chart, which tracks the use of resources over time. The rec center Gantt chart has a row for each staff slot for each venue and special event. Each column of the chart is an hour that requires staffing. The times when staffing is not required are marked out. The empty cells that remain are filled with workers based on worker availability and, to the extent possible, worker preferences.

> Integrating Operational Decisions

This chapter is closely linked to chapters 4 and 7 because decisions about the design of the product-service bundle and the value-adding system determine the level of complexity inherent in planning and control of the system. When product designs are complex and a high level of product variety is afforded, the MRP system of planning and control described in this chapter is a good fit. Similarly, MRP is a good fit when the value-adding system is process focused and designed to provide a high level of flexibility.

This chapter is also closely tied to chapters 11 and 12. The broader resource planning and scheduling decisions covered in Chapters 11 and 12 establish the level of resources available and what must be accomplished in the short- to intermediate-range. This chapter continues the planning and control process at a more detailed level. It describes the way that MRP systems accomplish the detailed scheduling activities that ensure that the requirements of the master schedule are met.

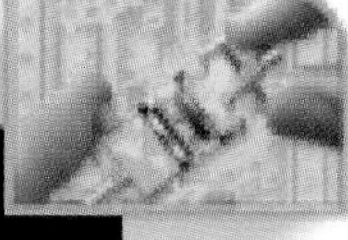

> integrated OM

Take a moment to apply what you've learned.

Chapter Wrap-Up

Material requirements planning (MRP) is a computerized planning and control system that determines the need for dependent demand items and the timing of their orders directly from the master schedule. It is best suited for use in complex value-adding systems such as job shops, where the process is functionally organized and customer expectations are quite diverse.

In complex value-adding systems with a lot of variety in their product-service bundles, communication between operations and other functions is essential. For marketing, making a single sale might entail multiple conversations with finance and operating personnel to price and schedule the customer's desired order. For operations to successfully complete an order, they might need to verify a number of different customer preferences with marketing. Accounting personnel will be challenged to keep up with the multitude of different items that could be inventoried on an ongoing basis. The complexity of the environment makes communication on customer preferences critically important on each order processed.

The planning and control system that generally is used in MRP systems is an order-based system. For each order from a customer that is placed on the master schedule, it determines when to order the parts, components, and subassemblies that are required. Based on the timing of these orders, the system can use capacity requirements planning (CRP) to verify that adequate capacity exists to accomplish the master schedule. Ultimately, all of the orders for end items and the dependent demand items associated with each end item must be released to work centers through a facility loading process. These orders must then be scheduled in each work center.

The MRP logic described in this chapter is straightforward. Gross requirements for independent demand items are found on the master schedule. For other items, gross requirements are a function of planned orders for the items of which they are a part. MRP programs convert gross requirements to net requirements by accounting for planned on-hand inventory and scheduled receipts. When the net requirements are positive, planned receipts will be scheduled by placing an order according to a defined lot-sizing rule. Finally, planned orders have to occur a specified period of time in advance of planned receipts. This period of time—between when orders are placed and when they are received—is called the lead-time.

If the MRP logic is simple, managing in the MRP environment is not. MRP output is only as good as the input data. There is always some uncertainty surrounding the master schedule, inventory records are very difficult to keep up-to-date and accurate, and even bill of materials files can contain faulty information. As a consequence, a major responsibility for management in firms using MRP is to enforce a disciplined approach to decision making and record keeping. In fact, many experts agree that one of the major benefits of MRP is that it forces such discipline on its users.

The primary supply-chain impact of a firm's use of MRP is that interaction with customers and suppliers is generally order driven. Companies need effective order tracking systems in order to field questions of suppliers and customers regarding their business. Quality must be assessed on an order-by-order basis. Payments and terms are also generally handled on an order-by-order basis. Enterprise resources planning systems can help to improve the performance of the supply chain. These systems that allow electronic interaction between companies help by giving decision makers access to more data than they would otherwise see and in a more timely way. Design initiatives that flatten a product-service bundle's BOM are also helpful to customers of a supply chain, because they shorten delivery lead-times.

Detailed scheduling in environments where MRP is used generally happens one work center at a time. Little coordination of schedules across a facility is seen. Instead, jobs are sequenced through individual work centers and the materials are pushed on to the next point in their routing, where they'll eventually meet up with an order. The sequence in which orders are processed is often determined using a local dispatching rule, which is chosen on the basis of the type of performance measurement that is stressed in the work center. For example, if efficiency and cash flow are the primary performance measures, the shortest processing time (SPT) sequencing rule is a logical choice. When due date performance is the primary measure, some other rule such as earliest due date, minimum slack, or critical ratio might be used. Frequently, Gantt charts are also used to display the planned schedule as well as progress against that schedule.

> end-of-chapter resources

- Practice Quiz
- Key Terms
- Solved Problems
- Discussion Questions
- Problems
- Case 15.1: The World's Dirtiest Scheduling Problem
- References
- Factory Tours

Queuing Analysis

SUPPLEMENT F

Supplement Outline

Introduction

Have you ever wondered why the ticket agent at the airline desk can be just sitting there a good part of the day but always have a line when you are late for a plane? Even though, *on average,* the capacity of a service system may be greater than the demands placed on it, a queue or waiting line forms whenever the *current demand* for service exceeds the server's *current capacity* to provide it. While over the course of the day, the agent at the check-in counter has plenty of time to sell tickets and check in baggage for customers flying that day, the random ebbs and flows of customer arrivals will cause a line to form at times and the agent to be idle at other times.

Given the pervasiveness of queues in all sorts of businesses—the line of concertgoers waiting to buy tickets, being on hold or getting a busy signal at a catalog call-in center, or jobs waiting to be processed at a machine center in a factory—structuring a queuing system to provide an optimal, or at least reasonable, balance between customer inconvenience or waiting costs and operational efficiency is a significant design problem for most businesses.

The Components of a Queuing System

As shown in Figure F.1, a queuing system has three basic components: the **calling population,** the **queue** or queues, and the **service facility.** To understand the issues in designing queuing systems and evaluating their performance, we will look at the important characteristics of each.

THE CALLING POPULATION

The calling population or **source** is the set of potential customers for the service. **Customers** can be people, like airline passengers who will be checking in, or things, like jobs waiting to be processed on a machine. The most important characteristic of the calling population is its *size,* which may be either finite or infinite. A population is **finite** if the number of customers is relatively small, such as the five machines an operator is responsible for. A population is considered to be **infinite** if it is large enough that the number of customers already receiving or waiting for service does not affect the rate at which additional customers arrive to get service.

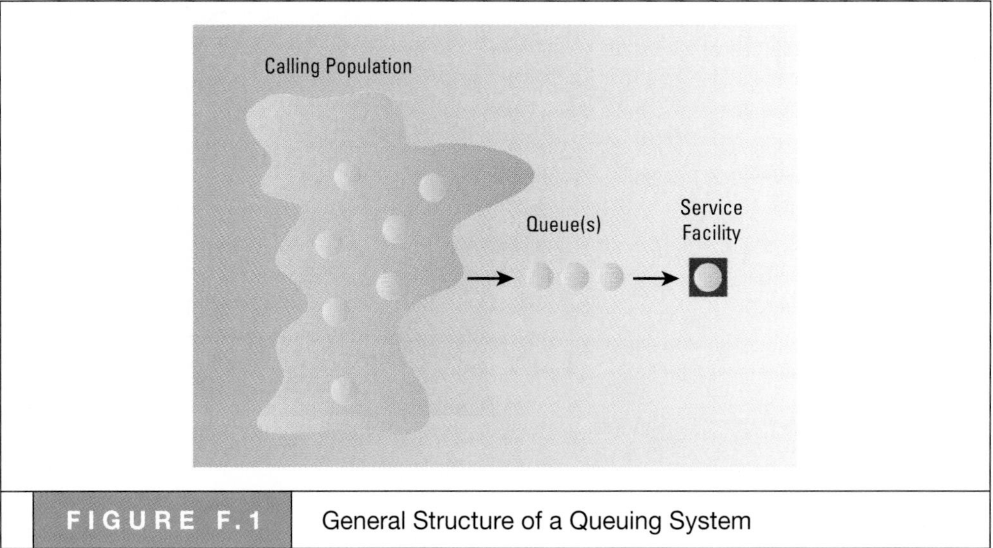

FIGURE F.1 General Structure of a Queuing System

A second important structural characteristic of the calling population is its *composition,* which refers to the classes or types of customers making up the population. Unless an airline has separate check-in counters for its first-class and coach passengers, there will be only one class of customers. On the other hand, a hospital emergency room has at least three types of arrivals: those with relatively minor problems, those with serious injuries or illnesses, and those in life-threatening situations.

Besides these structural characteristics, the calling population has a number of relevant operating characteristics. The most important is the customer **arrival rate** or, if there are multiple customer classes, rates. The arrival rate, which we will represent by the Greek letter λ (lambda), is the average number of customers arriving for service per time period. The average time between arrivals is then $1/\lambda$.

Two other operating characteristics that may be important are balking and group arrivals. Balking is the refusal of an arriving customer to join the queue and wait for service. If customers *arrive in groups* rather than singly (such as, for example, at most good restaurants), then the distribution of group sizes is important.

THE QUEUE OR QUEUES

Assuming the arriving customer stays (doesn't balk) and there is no server available, he or she joins the (or a) queue. The most basic characteristic of queues is the *number.* If there are multiple queues, then the issue of *differentiation* arises: Is there a queue for each type of customer or one for each server? A second important structural characteristic is the *maximum queue length.* In most cases we assume that there is no maximum length. However, an airline reservation system or catalog 800 number has a specific number of telephone lines, some with operators and others (the queue) having customers on hold; when all lines are occupied by callers, any more arriving calls get a busy signal and are turned away (are **rejected** in queuing terminology).

The most important operating characteristic of the queue(s) is the **queue discipline,** the rule used to determine which waiting customer is served next. In many situations, the "fair" rule of **first come, first served** is used, but in other cases it makes more sense to use some other priority rule. As discussed in chapter 15, a job shop's popular rules are "do the shortest available job" (good for minimizing inventories), "do the job with the earliest due date" (good for limiting the number of tardy jobs), and "do the job for our best customer" (good for customer relations).

Other queue operating characteristics that may become important if customers have to wait long times are reneging and jockeying. Similar to balking, reneging occurs when a customer initially joins the queue but leaves before receiving service. **Jockeying** or **line switching** occurs when a customer leaves one queue to join another in the expectation that he or she will get served more quickly (but it never seems to work, does it?).

THE SERVICE FACILITY

Eventually, the waiting customer moves into the service facility, the system that actually delivers the service requested or needed. The basic structural characteristics are the *number* of **servers** and their *configuration.* If there are multiple servers, they may be identical or different. If different, they may service different types of customers, provide different parts of the service, or provide the same service at different rates. Multiple servers may be configured in parallel (next to one another) or in a series (following one another). Each parallel server or series of servers through which a customer might pass is called a **channel.**

The most important operating characteristic of the service facility is the **service rate,** the average number of customers that a server could process in a time period if there were always another customer available. We will represent the service rate by the Greek letter μ (mu), so that the average service time is $1/\mu$. While we usually assume that a server handles one customer at a time, in some cases there may be **batch service,** meaning that multiple customers are processed simultaneously (think of a roller coaster or a kiln in a pottery).

Transient and Steady-State Behavior

As a queuing system operates over time, it passes back and forth through two types of conditions: transient and steady-state behavior. **Transient behavior** is unstable. The length of a queue exhibits a pattern of growth or decline. Waiting times get longer or shorter. Transient behavior occurs whenever the arrival rate changes or the number of servers changes. **Steady-state behavior** is stable. This does not mean that the queue length and waiting time are constant, but that they fluctuate to some extent around constant average levels. Steady-state behavior will occur, in most cases, after a system has operated with constant arrival and service rates for some period of time.

While theoretical models can be developed to describe the transient behavior of some queuing systems (and simulation can be used for others), it is very difficult, requiring sophisticated mathematical techniques. The models to be discussed and illustrated here are for steady-state behavior.

The Basic Single-Server Model (M/M/1)[1]

The most basic queuing model is the basic single-server model, which makes the following assumptions:

1. The calling population is infinite, with only one class of customers.
2. The number of arrivals per time period has a Poisson distribution with rate λ or, equivalently, the time between arrivals has an exponential distribution with average time $1/\lambda$.
3. Service time has an **exponential probability distribution** with rate μ or average time $1/\mu$.
4. There are one server and one queue, which has no maximum length.
5. The queue discipline is first come, first served.
6. There is no balking or reneging.

Given the arrival rate λ and the service rate μ, the equations for the steady-state performance measures for this type of system are given in Table F.1. Looking at these equations, it is obvious that the customer arrival rate must be less than the service rate for this type of system to reach steady-state behavior.

Example F.1

Between noon and 2 P.M., passengers arrive at the check-in counter for Tom's airline at the Flagstaff airport at a rate of $\lambda = 20$ per hour, the actual number of arrivals being Poisson distributed. The single customer service representative takes an average of 2.4 minutes to check a passenger in, for a service rate of $\mu = 25$ per hour, the actual service time having an exponential distribution. (We must be careful to express the arrival rate λ and the service rate μ for the same time period.) Determine the values of the percentage of time the customer service agent is busy, the average number of customers waiting to check in, the average number of customers at the check-in counter, the average amount of time a passenger waits to check in, and the average amount of time a passenger spends at the check-in counter.

[1] M/M/1 is an example of the short form of *Kendall's notation,* the standard notation used for describing queuing models. The short form of Kendall's notation is A/B/C in which A stands for the arrival distribution, B stands for the service time distribution, and C is the number of parallel service channels. For both A and B, the following symbols are used for the different distributions: M (Markov) means that the time has an exponential distribution or the number has a Poisson distribution; D stands for deterministic; G stands for general; and E_k stands for Erlang with parameter value K. It is not necessary to use Kendall's notation to describe a queuing system; it has only been used here to make it easier for you to select the appropriate alternative when using the software.

TABLE F.1 Steady-State Performance Measures for the Basic Queuing Model (M/M/1)

- $\rho = \lambda/\mu$ is the utilization rate or the probability that the server is busy and that an arriving customer will have to wait
- $P(0) = 1 - \rho$ is the probability that the queuing system is empty, with no one receiving or waiting for service
- $P(n) = \rho^n(1 - \rho)$ is the probability that there are *n* customers in the system, receiving or waiting for service
- $L_q = \dfrac{\lambda^2}{\mu(\mu - \lambda)} = \dfrac{\rho^2}{1 - \rho}$ is the mean length of the queue
- $L = \dfrac{\lambda}{\gamma - \lambda} = \dfrac{\rho}{1 - \rho} = L_q + p$ is the mean number of customers in the system, receiving or waiting for service
- $W_q = \dfrac{L_q}{\lambda} = \dfrac{\lambda}{\mu(\mu - \lambda)}$ is the mean time a customer must wait before being served
- $W = \dfrac{L}{\lambda} = W_q + \dfrac{1}{\mu} = \dfrac{1}{\mu - \lambda}$ is the mean time that a customer spends in the system, waiting for or receiving service

Solution:

Since passengers arrive randomly and the amount of time needed to process the passengers varies greatly, with most passengers requiring very little time and a few passengers taking a very long time, exponential distributions are appropriate for the interarrival and check-in times. There is a single customer service agent on duty, so the basic M/M/1 queuing model is appropriate for this situation.

Based on the timing information (parameter values) given, the average values of the queuing system performance characteristics (using the equations in Table F.1) are:

- The customer service agent is busy $\rho = \lambda/\mu = .80$ or 80% of the time, so 80% of arriving passengers have to wait to check in.
- There is an average of $L_q = \dfrac{\lambda^2}{\mu(\mu - \lambda)} = \dfrac{20^2}{25(25 - 20)} = 3.2$ passengers waiting to check in at any given time.
- There is an average of $L = \dfrac{\lambda}{\mu - \lambda} = \dfrac{20}{25 - 20} = 4.0$ passengers at the check-in counter at any given time.
- A passenger waits for an average of $W_q = \dfrac{\lambda}{\mu(\mu - \lambda)} = \dfrac{20}{25(25 - 20)} = .16$ hours or 9.6 minutes to check in.
- A passenger spends an average of $W = \dfrac{1}{\mu - \lambda} = \dfrac{1}{25 - 20} = .20$ hours or 12 minutes at the check-in counter.

active exercise <

Take a moment to apply what you've learned.

As an alternative to using the equations given in Table F.1 to determine the values of the performance characteristics of a queuing system, we can use computer software, like the Excelpom add-in for Excel. Exhibit F.1 shows the Excelpom input and output screen for Example F.1.

ADDITIONAL SINGLE SERVER QUEUING MODELS

While the basic single-server queuing model described above has proven to be quite useful in practice, there are many situations in which the assumption of exponentially distributed service times is not a reasonable approximation to reality. Two other single-server models, both of which assume **Poisson**

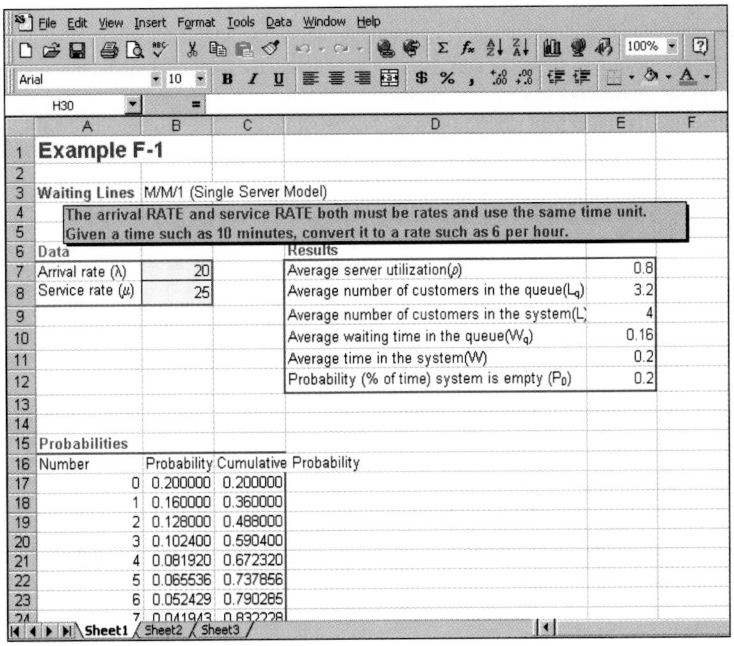

File Edit View Insert Format Tools Data Window Help

Arial 10 H30

	A	B	C	D	E
1	**Example F-1**				
2					
3	**Waiting Lines**	M/M/1 (Single Server Model)			
4	The arrival RATE and service RATE both must be rates and use the same time unit.				
5	Given a time such as 10 minutes, convert it to a rate such as 6 per hour.				
6	Data			Results	
7	Arrival rate (λ)	20		Average server utilization(ρ)	0.8
8	Service rate (μ)	25		Average number of customers in the queue(L_q)	3.2
9				Average number of customers in the system(L)	4
10				Average waiting time in the queue(W_q)	0.16
11				Average time in the system(W)	0.2
12				Probability (% of time) system is empty (P_0)	0.2
13					
14					
15	Probabilities				
16	Number	Probability	Cumulative Probability		
17	0	0.200000	0.200000		
18	1	0.160000	0.360000		
19	2	0.128000	0.488000		
20	3	0.102400	0.590400		
21	4	0.081920	0.672320		
22	5	0.065536	0.737856		
23	6	0.052429	0.790285		
24	7	0.041943	0.832228		

Sheet1 / Sheet2 / Sheet3

EXHIBIT F.1 (Prepared using Prentice Hall's Excel OM software)

arrivals but allow for other types of service time distributions, are the *general service time* distribution model (M/G/1 in Kendall's notation) and the *constant* or *deterministic* service time model (M/D/1). The performance equations for these two models are given in Tables F.2 and F.3, respectively. Both models are also available in the Excelpom software.

TABLE F.2 Steady-State Performance Measures for the Single-Server General Service Time Queuing Model (M/G/1)

The basic equation for this model, which is for the mean length of the queue, L_q, is the **Pollaczek-Kinchine** equation:

- $L_q = \frac{\lambda^2\sigma^2 + \rho^2}{2(1 - \rho)}$ where $\rho = \lambda/\mu$ and σ is the standard deviation of the service time
- $L = L_q + \rho$
- $W_q = L_q/\lambda$
- $W = L/\lambda = W_q + 1/\mu$

TABLE F.3 Steady-State Performance Measures for the Single-Server Deterministic Service Time Queuing Model (M/D/I)

As in Tables F.1 and F.2, $\rho = \lambda/\mu$. Setting $\sigma = 0$ in the equation for L_q in Table F.3, we get:

- $L_q = \frac{\rho^2}{2(1 - \rho)}$

The equations for the other performance measures are the same as in Table F.2.

- $L = L_q + \rho$
- $W_q = L_q/\lambda$
- $W = L/\lambda = W_q + 1/\mu$

Example F.2

Harry's Truck Stop has a single diesel pump. Trucks arrive for fuel on an average of three per hour or 0.05 per minute, Poisson distributed. The time to fill a truck's tank averages 12 minutes, with a standard deviation of 2 minutes. Determine the values for the percentage of time that the pump will be in use, the average number of trucks waiting to use the pump, the average number of trucks at the station, the average amount of time a truck waits to use the pump, and the average amount of time a truck spends at the station.

Solution:
Exhibit F.2 shows the Excelpom input and output screen for this general service time distribution (M/G/1) model. Using 1 minute as the basic unit of time, we have $\lambda = .05$ and $\mu = 1/12 = .08333$. From Exhibit F.2, or by using the equations in Table F.2, we determine that:

- The pump will be in use $\rho = \lambda/\mu = .05/.08333 = .6$ or 60% of the time.
- There will be an average of trucks waiting to use the pump.
- There will be an average of $L_q = \dfrac{\lambda^2\sigma^2 + \rho^2}{2(1-\rho)} = \dfrac{(.05)^2(2)^2 + (.6)^2}{2(1-.6)} = \dfrac{.37}{.8} = 0.4625$ trucks using or waiting for the pump.
- A truck will wait an average of $W_q = L_q/\lambda = 0.4625/.05 = 9.25$ minutes before using the pump.
- A truck will spend an average of $L = L/\lambda = 1.0625/.05 = 21.25$ minutes waiting for or using the pump.

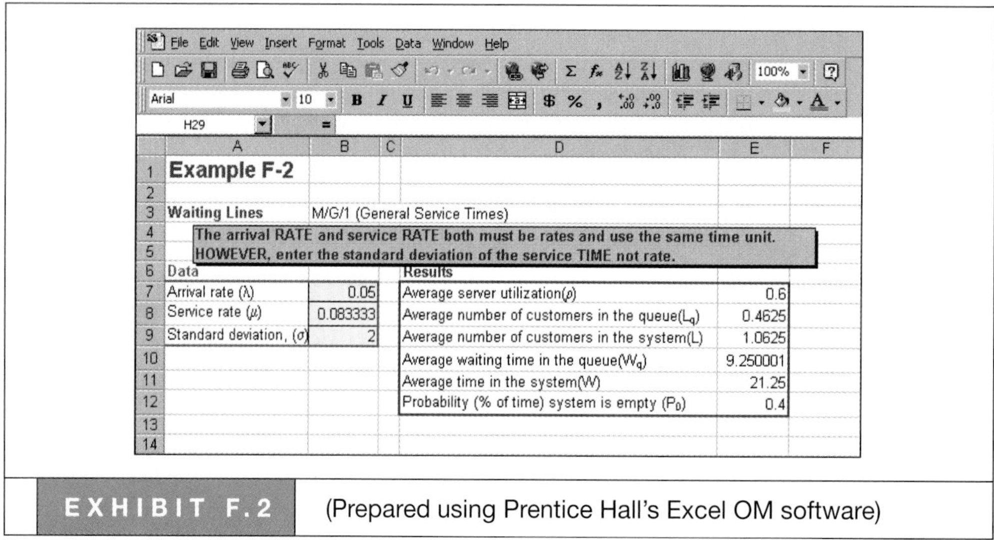

	A	B	C	D	E	F
1	**Example F-2**					
2						
3	**Waiting Lines**	M/G/1 (General Service Times)				
4		The arrival RATE and service RATE both must be rates and use the same time unit.				
5		HOWEVER, enter the standard deviation of the service TIME not rate.				
6	Data			Results		
7	Arrival rate (λ)	0.05		Average server utilization(ρ)	0.6	
8	Service rate (μ)	0.083333		Average number of customers in the queue(L_q)	0.4625	
9	Standard deviation, (σ)	2		Average number of customers in the system(L)	1.0625	
10				Average waiting time in the queue(W_q)	9.250001	
11				Average time in the system(W)	21.25	
12				Probability (% of time) system is empty (P_0)	0.4	
13						
14						

EXHIBIT F.2 (Prepared using Prentice Hall's Excel OM software)

active exercise

Take a moment to apply what you've learned.

Example F.3

A gas station has a single-stall automatic car wash that takes exactly 2.4 minutes to wash a car, so the service rate is $\mu = 25$ per hour. Cars arrive to use the car wash on an average of one every 3 minutes, Poisson distributed, for an arrival rate of $\lambda = 20$ per hour. Determine the percentage of time the car wash is busy, the average number of cars waiting to use the car wash, the average number of cars at the car wash, the average amount of time a car waits before being washed, and the average amount of time a car spends at the car wash.

File Edit View Insert Format Tools Data Window Help

	A	B	C	D	E	F
1	**Example F-3**					
2						
3	**Waiting Lines**	M/D/1 (Constant Service Times)				
4		The arrival RATE and service RATE both must be rates and use the same time unit.				
5		Given a time such as 10 minutes, convert it to a rate such as 6 per hour.				
6	Data			Results		
7	Arrival rate (λ)	20		Average server utilization(ρ)	0.8	
8	Service rate (μ)	25		Average number of customers in the queue(L_q)	1.6	
9				Average number of customers in the system(L)	2.4	
10				Average waiting time in the queue(W_q)	0.08	
11				Average time in the system(W)	0.12	
12				Probability (% of time) system is empty (P_0)	0.2	
13						
14						

EXHIBIT F.3 (Prepared using Prentice Hall's Excel OM software)

Solution:
Exhibit F.3 shows the Excelpom input and output screen for this deterministic service time (M/D/1) example. From Exhibit F.3, or by using the equations in Table F.3, we determine that:

- The car wash will be busy $\rho = \lambda/\mu = 20/25 = .8$ or 80% of the time.
- There will be an average of $L_q = \frac{\rho^2}{2(1-\rho)} = \frac{(.80)^2}{2(1-.8)} = \frac{.64}{.4} = 1.6$ cars waiting to use the car wash.
- There will be an average of $L = L_q = 1.6 + .8 = 2.4$ cars using or waiting for the car wash.
- A car will wait on average $Wq = L_q/\lambda = 1.6/20 = .08$ hours or 4.8 minutes before using the car wash.
- A car will spend an average of $W = L/\lambda = 2.4/20 = .12$ hours or 7.2 minutes waiting for or using the car wash.

> **active exercise**

Take a moment to apply what you've learned.

Note that while ρ, the percentage utilization, for the car wash is exactly the same as at the airline check-in counter in Example F.1, which has the same arrival and service rates, the values for the "waiting" performance measures (L_q and W_q) are exactly half of those in Example F.1. It is service time variability that accounts for much of the waiting in a queuing system.

The Multiple-Server Exponential Service Time Model (M/M/S)

The conditions for applying this model are identical to those given for the basic single-server model, except that there are S parallel, identical servers, each of which is called a *channel.* All arriving customers wait in a single line. When a customer reaches the head of the line, it goes to the first available server. (Think of the way most bank lobbies are set up, as contrasted with the way most supermarkets are set up.)

The formulas for the steady-state performance characteristics of a multiple-server exponential service time model, given in Table F.4, are more complicated than those for the single-server model. The first step is to find the value of P(0), the probability that the system is completely empty, from the equation given. For example, if $\lambda = 2$, $\mu = 1$, and $S = 4$, then $\rho = .50$ and the value of P(0) is .1304 and the system will be completely empty just over 13% of the time.

As with the other models, an alternative to using the equations in Table F.4 is to use computer software, such as Excelpom.

TABLE F.4 Steady-State Performance Measures for the Multiple-Server Exponential Service Time Model (M/M/S)

- $(0) = \dfrac{1}{\displaystyle\sum_{j=0}^{S-1} \frac{(S\rho)^j}{j!} + \frac{(S\rho)^S}{S!(1-\rho)}}$

  where $\rho = \lambda/S\mu$ is the percentage utilization of each server, which must be less than 1.0. This means that λ must be less than $S\mu$, the aggregate service capacity of the system.

- $P(n) = \dfrac{(S\rho)^n}{n!}P(0)$ for $0 \leq n \leq S$
- $P(n) = \dfrac{(S\rho)^n}{S!S^{n-s}}P(0)$ for $n \leq S$
- $P(\text{system busy}) = P(n \geq S) = \dfrac{(S\rho)^S P(0)}{S!(1-\rho)}$
- $L_q = \dfrac{\rho(S\rho)^S P(0)}{S!(1-\rho)^2} = \left(\dfrac{\rho}{1-\rho}\right)P(\text{system busy})$
- $L = L_q + S\rho = L_q + \lambda/\mu$
- $W_q = L_q/\lambda$
- $W = L/\lambda = W_q + 1/\mu$

Example F.4

While the number of passengers on Tom's airline is low enough between noon and 2 P.M. that one customer service agent can keep up with the check-ins (see Example F.1), the airline operates more flights during the early morning and late afternoon hours as business travelers leave to get to their appointments in other cities and return home at the end of their trips. Between 5 P.M. and 7 P.M., passengers arrive for check-in at the airline's check-in counter at the Flagstaff airport at a rate of 70 per hour. Determine the minimum number of agents that must be on duty for the system to reach steady-state conditions and the values of the standard queuing performance measures with that number of agents.

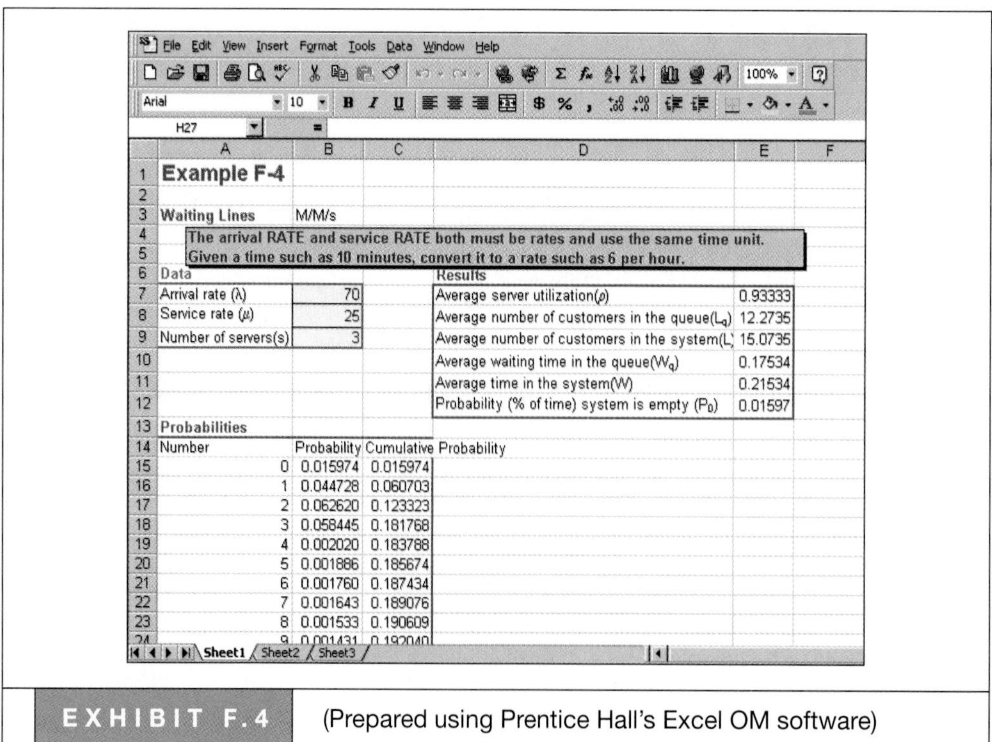

Example F-4

Waiting Lines M/M/s

The arrival RATE and service RATE both must be rates and use the same time unit. Given a time such as 10 minutes, convert it to a rate such as 6 per hour.

Data		Results	
Arrival rate (λ)	70	Average server utilization(ρ)	0.93333
Service rate (μ)	25	Average number of customers in the queue(L_q)	12.2735
Number of servers(s)	3	Average number of customers in the system(L)	15.0735
		Average waiting time in the queue(W_q)	0.17534
		Average time in the system(W)	0.21534
		Probability (% of time) system is empty (P_0)	0.01597

Probabilities

Number	Probability	Cumulative Probability
0	0.015974	0.015974
1	0.044728	0.060703
2	0.062620	0.123323
3	0.058445	0.181768
4	0.002020	0.183788
5	0.001886	0.185674
6	0.001760	0.187434
7	0.001643	0.189076
8	0.001533	0.190609
9	0.001431	0.192040

EXHIBIT F.4 (Prepared using Prentice Hall's Excel OM software)

Solution:

Since each passenger requires an average of 2.4 minutes to check in (μ = 25 per hour), having only one agent on duty is not an option. The line would grow longer and longer, with many unhappy passengers. To be able to reach steady-state conditions, the total service capacity ($S\mu$) must be greater than the arrival rate (λ). Thus, based on $\lambda < S\mu$ or $70 < 25S$, a minimum of S = 3 agents is required.

Exhibit F.4 shows the Excelpom input/output screen for this example. We see that, with S = 3 agents, the servers are busy ρ = 93.33% of the time, there is an average of L_q = 12.27 passengers waiting to check in, and those passengers wait for an average of W_q = .175 hours, or 10.5 minutes. Also, there is an average of L = 15.07 total passengers at the check-in counter, and those passengers are there for an average of W = .215 hours or 12.9 minutes.

> active exercise

Take a moment to apply what you've learned.

> Finite Queue Models

The models discussed so far all assume that there is no limit to how long the queue may become. In some cases, however, there will be a maximum allowable number of waiting customers due to physical constraints or policy limitations. If this is the case, then any customers arriving when the queue is full will be turned away (*rejected* in queuing terminology) and, as a result, their business may be lost.

The conditions for applying this model are identical to those for the multiple-server model (M/M/S) discussed, except there is a maximum of K customers in the system at any time, S of which would be in service and the rest in the queue, which has a maximum length of K-S. The equations for the steady-state operating characteristics for the single-server system with a finite queue are given in Table F.5.[2]

TABLE F.5 Steady-State Performance Measures for the Multiple-Server Finite-Queue Model

- $P(0) = \dfrac{1-\rho}{1-\rho^{k+1}}$ for $\rho = \lambda/\mu = 1$
- $P(0) = \dfrac{1}{K+1}$ for $\rho = 1$
- $P(n) = \rho^n P(0)$ for $n \leq K$
- $P(K) = P(\text{rejection}) = P(\text{lost call}) = \rho^K P(0)$
- $\dfrac{r}{1-r} - \dfrac{(K+1)r^{K+1}}{1-r^{K+1}}$ for $\rho \neq 1$
- $L = \dfrac{K}{2}$ for $p = 1$
- $L_q = L - (1 - P(0))$
- $W_q = \dfrac{L_q}{\lambda(1 - P(K))}$
- $W = W_q + \dfrac{1}{\mu}$

[2]The equations for the comparable multiple-server model are more complicated and are not given here. That model is, however, available in many software packages, including Excelpom.

Example F.5

Tom's airline operates a telephone information and reservation service with a single operator who controls three telephone lines. Two calls can be placed on hold while the operator speaks to a third customer. Additional callers receive a busy signal. Calls come in on an average of one every 2 minutes, Poisson distributed ($\lambda = 0.5$ per minute). Service requires an average of 1.5 minutes, exponentially distributed ($\mu = .6667$ per minute). Determine the values of the standard queuing performance measures for this system.

Solution:

As shown in the Excelpom input/output screen in Exhibit F.5, the operating characteristics of this system, which has $\rho = \lambda/\mu = .5/.6667 = .75$, are:

- The operator is idle and no one is waiting P(0) = .3657 or 36.57% of the time.
- The probability that a caller will receive a busy signal and be rejected or lost is P(K) = P(3) = .1543.
- The mean number of callers in the system, either on hold or speaking to the operator, is L = 1.149.
- The mean number of callers on hold is Lq = .515.
- The mean time a caller spends on hold is Wq = 1.218 minutes.
- The mean time a caller spends on the phone, either on hold or speaking to the operator, is W = 2.718 minutes.

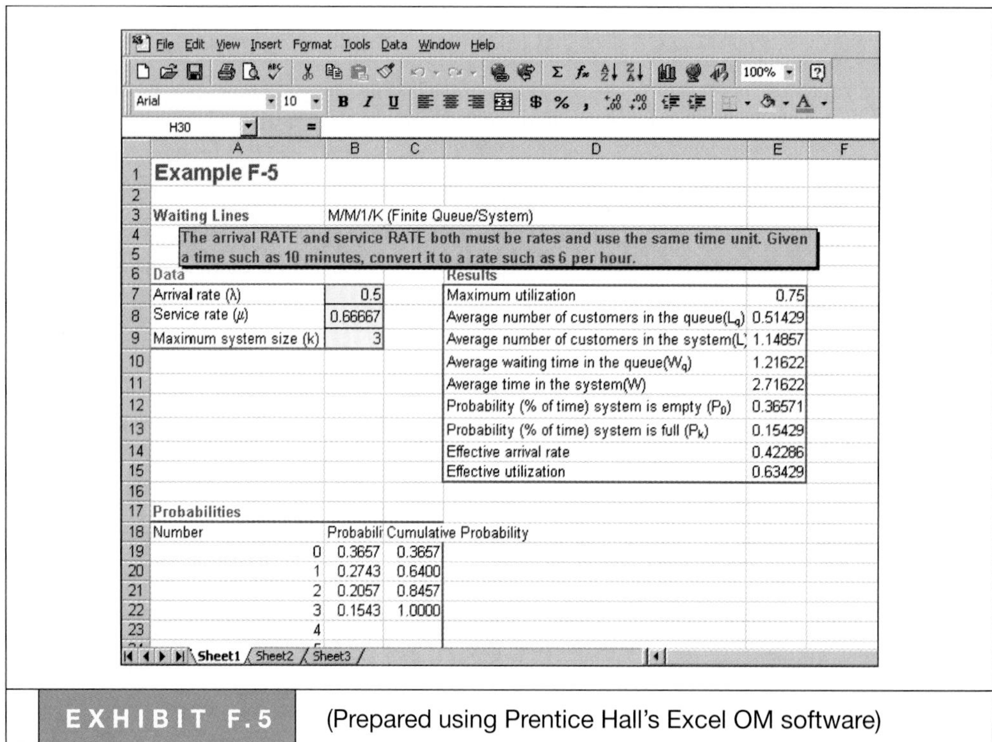

Example F-5

Waiting Lines — M/M/1/K (Finite Queue/System)

The arrival RATE and service RATE both must be rates and use the same time unit. Given a time such as 10 minutes, convert it to a rate such as 6 per hour.

Data	
Arrival rate (λ)	0.5
Service rate (μ)	0.66667
Maximum system size (k)	3

Results	
Maximum utilization	0.75
Average number of customers in the queue(L_q)	0.51429
Average number of customers in the system(L)	1.14857
Average waiting time in the queue(W_q)	1.21622
Average time in the system(W)	2.71622
Probability (% of time) system is empty (P_0)	0.36571
Probability (% of time) system is full (P_k)	0.15429
Effective arrival rate	0.42286
Effective utilization	0.63429

Probabilities

Number	Probability	Cumulative Probability
0	0.3657	0.3657
1	0.2743	0.6400
2	0.2057	0.8457
3	0.1543	1.0000
4		

EXHIBIT F.5 (Prepared using Prentice Hall's Excel OM software)

Finite Population Models

In some cases the calling population is so small that you cannot assume that it is infinite, thus a finite population model must be used. The model given here assumes:

1. Each of the N population members has a Poisson arrival rate of λ per period when not in the queue or receiving service.
2. Each server has a service rate of μ per period, the actual service time having an exponential distribution.
3. The queue discipline for the single queue is first come, first served.
4. There is no balking or reneging.

TABLE F.6 Steady-State Performance Measures for the Single-Server Finite Population Model

- $P(0) = \dfrac{1}{\sum_{i=0}^{N} \dfrac{N!}{(N-i)!}\rho^i}$ *where* $\rho = \lambda/\mu$
- $P(n) = \dfrac{N!}{(N-n)!}\rho^n P(0)$ *for* $n \leq N$
- $L = N - \dfrac{1}{\rho}(1 - P(0))$
- $\lambda_e = \lambda(N - L)$ is the **effective arrival rate,** recognizing that, on average, there are only $N - L$ population members available to call for service.
- $W = L/\lambda_e$
- $Wq = W - 1/\mu$
- $L_q = \lambda_e W_q$

The equations for the steady-state operating characteristics are given in Table F.6.[3]

Example F.6

A repairperson maintains three machines. Each machine operates for an average of four hours before breaking down, the number of failures per operating hour per machine having a Poisson distribution. It takes the repairperson an average of 1 hour to repair a machine, the repair time having an exponential distribution. Determine the values of the standard queuing performance measures for this system.

Solution:
With $N = 3$ machines, $\lambda = 0.25$ breakdowns per operating hour per machine, and $\mu = 1$ repair per hour, the steady-state operating characteristics for this system, shown in the Excelpom input/output screen in Exhibit F.6, are:

- $P(0) = .4507$ is the probability that all machines are working, so the repairperson is idle 45% of the time and busy 55% of the time.
- The mean number of machines not operating is $L = .8028$, so the mean number of machines operating is $N - L = 2.1972$.
- The mean time a machine is not operating is $W = 1.4615$ hours.
- The mean time a machine waits to be repaired is $Wq = .4615$ hours.
- The mean number of machines waiting to be repaired is $L_q = .2535$.

> active exercise

Take a moment to apply what you've learned.

Designing Queuing Systems

Designing a queuing system involves choosing one or more system characteristics that you can control. Examples of such characteristics include: the rate of service, the number of servers, the number of queues, the maximum queue length, the size of a finite population, and the service discipline.

The two basic approaches to designing a queuing system are:

1. design to meet a performance standard
2. design to minimize the combined cost of providing service and of not providing enough service

[3] As with the finite queue model just discussed, the equations for the multiple-server version of this model are more complicated and are not given here. However, that model is available in many software packages, including Excelpom.

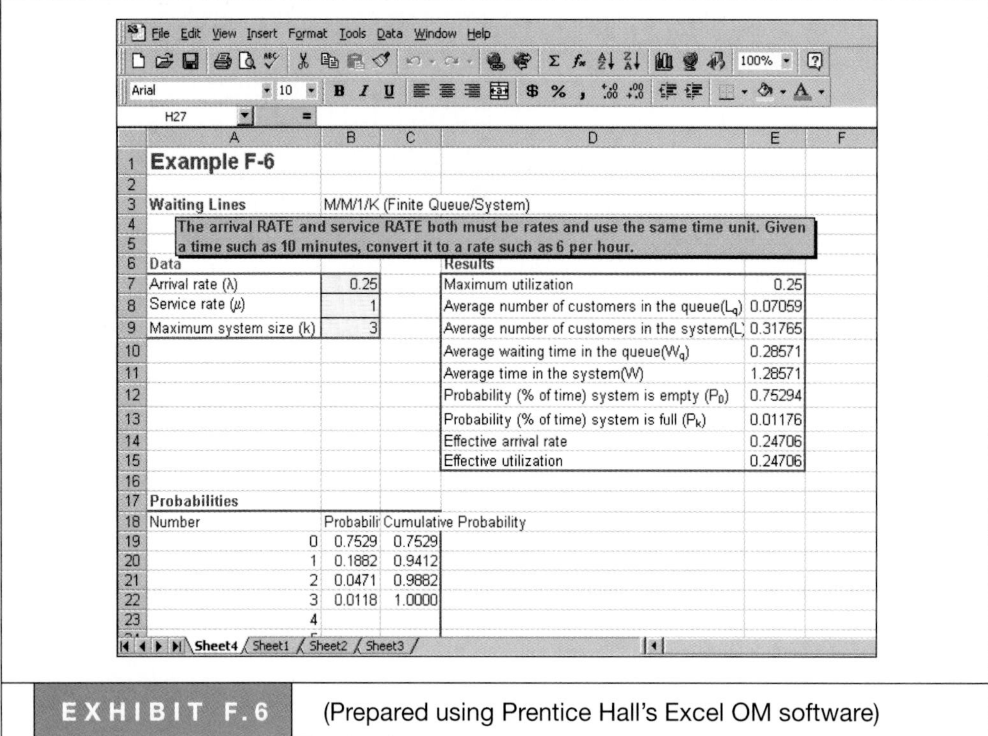

	A	B	C	D	E
1	**Example F-6**				
2					
3	**Waiting Lines**	M/M/1/K (Finite Queue/System)			
4	The arrival RATE and service RATE both must be rates and use the same time unit. Given				
5	a time such as 10 minutes, convert it to a rate such as 6 per hour.				
6	Data			Results	
7	Arrival rate (λ)	0.25		Maximum utilization	0.25
8	Service rate (μ)	1		Average number of customers in the queue(L_q)	0.07059
9	Maximum system size (k)	3		Average number of customers in the system(L)	0.31765
10				Average waiting time in the queue(W_q)	0.28571
11				Average time in the system(W)	1.28571
12				Probability (% of time) system is empty (P_0)	0.75294
13				Probability (% of time) system is full (P_k)	0.01176
14				Effective arrival rate	0.24706
15				Effective utilization	0.24706
16					
17	**Probabilities**				
18	Number	Probabili	Cumulative Probability		
19	0	0.7529	0.7529		
20	1	0.1882	0.9412		
21	2	0.0471	0.9882		
22	3	0.0118	1.0000		
23	4				

EXHIBIT F.6 (Prepared using Prentice Hall's Excel OM software)

DESIGN TO MEET A SERVICE STANDARD

While it is generally possible to determine the cost of providing a specific level of service capacity, it is often not possible to readily determine the costs incurred as a result of customers having to wait or being rejected for service. In such cases, management might specify one or more service performance standards to be met. The objective is then to determine the least expensive system that will meet those performance standards. An example would be the determination of the number and location of ambulances so as to be able to answer 90% of all calls within a specified time, such as 10 minutes.

Example F.7

Refer to Example F.4. During the evening busy period, passengers for Tom's airline at the Flagstaff airport have to wait for an average of .175 hours or 10.5 minutes to check in when there are S = 3 agents on duty. Airline management would like to reduce the average waiting time for check-in to no more than 5 minutes. How many agents would have to be on duty to meet this service standard?

Solution:

In Example F.4 we determined that, during the evening busy period, $\lambda = 70$ per hour and $\mu = 25$ per hour. The Excelpom input/output screen for S = 4 agents is shown in Exhibit F.7. We see that with S = 4 agents the average time spent in the queue is $W_q = 0.014$ hours or 0.86 minutes. Since this is less than the desired service standard of no more than 5 minutes, four agents will be sufficient.

active exercise

Take a moment to apply what you've learned.

DESIGN TO MINIMIZE TOTAL SYSTEM COST

The total cost of a queuing system consists of: (1) the cost of providing service capacity, and (2) the cost of not providing enough capacity. The cost of providing capacity usually consists of the costs of

File Edit View Insert Format Tools Data Window Help

Arial 10 100%

H29 =

	A	B	C	D	E	F
1	**Example F-7**					
2						
3	**Waiting Lines**	M/M/s				
4	The arrival RATE and service RATE both must be rates and use the same time unit.					
5	Given a time such as 10 minutes, convert it to a rate such as 6 per hour.					
6	**Data**			**Results**		
7	Arrival rate (λ)	70		Average server utilization(ρ)	0.7	
8	Service rate (μ)	25		Average number of customers in the queue(L_q)	1.00019	
9	Number of servers(s)	4		Average number of customers in the system(L)	3.80019	
10				Average waiting time in the queue(W_q)	0.01429	
11				Average time in the system(W)	0.05429	
12				Probability (% of time) system is empty (P_0)	0.05021	
13	**Probabilities**					
14	Number	Probability	Cumulative Probability			
15	0	0.050212	0.050212			
16	1	0.140594	0.190806			
17	2	0.196831	0.387637			
18	3	0.183709	0.571346			
19	4	0.128596	0.699942			
20	5	0.000352	0.700294			
21	6	0.000246	0.700540			
22	7	0.000172	0.700712			
23	8	0.000121	0.700833			
24	9	0.000084	0.700917			

Sheet1 / Sheet2 / Sheet3

EXHIBIT F.7 (Prepared using Prentice Hall's Excel OM software)

servers and the cost of queue spaces. The cost of not providing enough capacity typically includes the costs of customers having to wait, which may include the cost of their lost business in the future, and the cost of lost current customers due to balking, reneging, or rejection. Assuming these costs can be determined, the two types of costs can be added together, as shown in Figure F.2, and an optimal service capacity can be determined.

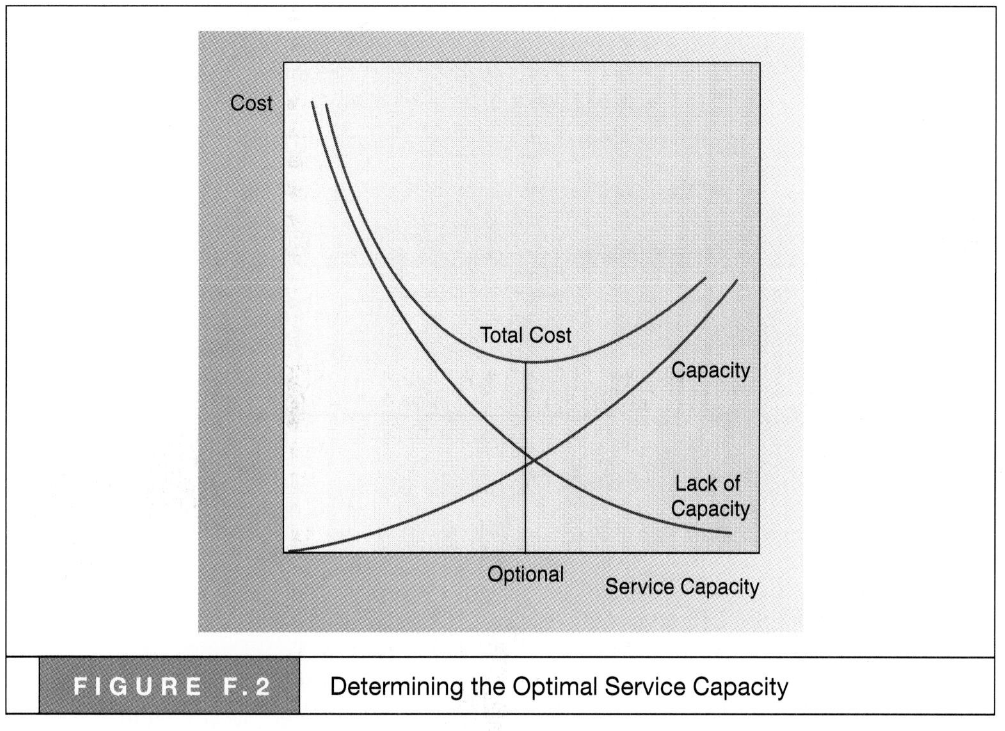

FIGURE F.2 Determining the Optimal Service Capacity

Example F.8

Refer to Examples F.4 and F.7. The cost of having a customer service agent on duty at the Flagstaff airport during the evening busy period is $25 per hour. The airline's management estimates that the cost of making a passenger wait to check in is $50 per hour. How many agents should be on duty during this time to minimize the total cost of the system?

Solution:
We assume that there is no cost of providing waiting spaces (arriving passengers simply queue up in the lobby area), so the cost of providing service capacity is simply the cost of the agents who are on duty:

$$\text{Cost of service capacity} = C_sS = \$25S \text{ per hour.}$$

We assume that there will be no current loss of business due to balking or reneging and, with no limit to the length of the queue, there will be no rejection, so the cost of not providing sufficient capacity is simply the waiting cost for the customers in the system:

$$\text{Cost of insufficient capacity} = C_wL = \$50L \text{ per hour.}$$

Thus, the total cost per hour of operating the system is:

$$\text{Total cost} = \$25S + \$50L.$$

The minimum total cost can be found by determining the total cost for various values of S and comparing them.

- *S = 3:* In Example F.4 we determined that, with S = 3, L = 15.0735. The total cost per hour for operating the check-in counter with S = 3 agents is:

$$\text{Total Cost} = \$25S + \$50L = \$25(3) + \$50(15.0735) = \$75 + \$753.68 = \$828.68$$

- *S = 4:* Exhibit F.7 shows that with S = 4, L = 3.80019. The total cost per hour for operating the check-in counter with S = 4 agents is:

$$\text{Total Cost} = \$25(4) + \$50(3.80019) = \$100 + \$190.01 = \$290.01$$

- *S = 5:* Exhibit F.8 shows that with S = 5, L = 3.0412. The total cost per hour for operating the check-in counter with S = 5 agents is:

$$\text{Total Cost} = \$25(5) + \$50(3.0412) = \$125 + \$152.06 = \$277.06$$

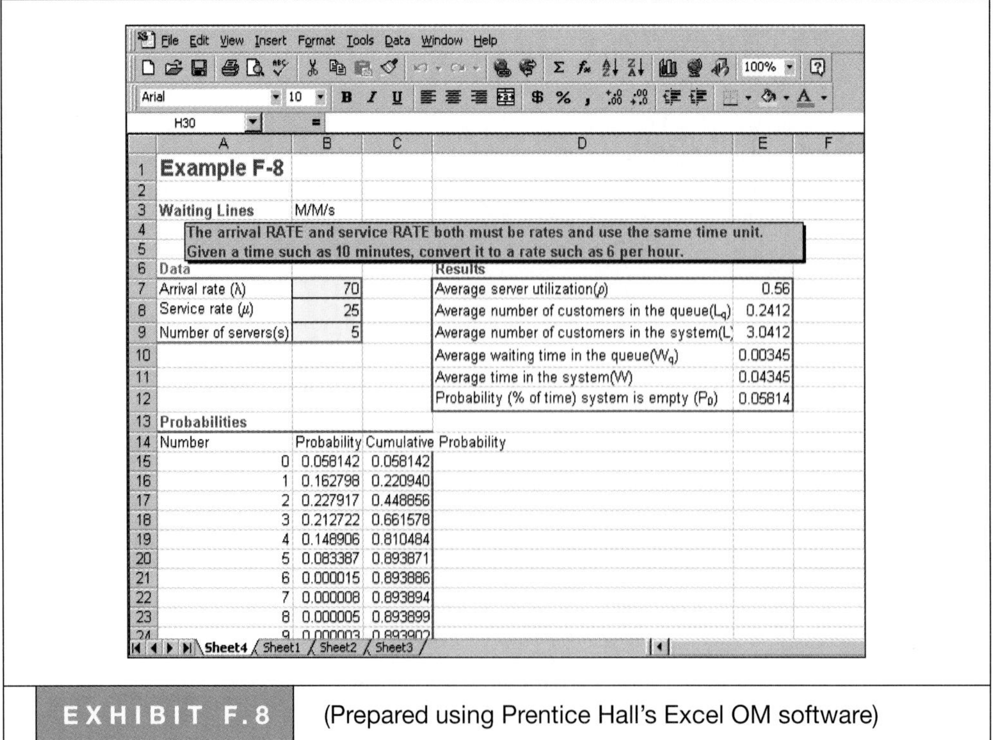

EXHIBIT F.8 (Prepared using Prentice Hall's Excel OM software)

- $S > 6$: Referring to the equations in Table F.4, we see that the equation for L consists of two terms: L_q, which depends on the value of S, and λ/μ, which does not. In this example, $\lambda/\mu = 70/25 = 2.8$. No matter how much an additional agent reduces L_q, L cannot be less than 2.8 and the waiting cost component of total cost cannot be reduced below $50(2.8) = $140. There is no point in adding a sixth agent, since doing so will add an additional $25 to the capacity cost while reducing the waiting cost by no more than $152.06 − $140 = $12.06. The optimal number of agents on duty during the evening busy period is, therefore, five.

> active exercise

Take a moment to apply what you've learned.

> Supplement Wrap-Up

A queue is a waiting line. Queues form whenever the current demand for service exceeds the server's current capacity to provide service. The usual objective of queuing analysis is to design an efficient system that balances operational efficiency and customer inconvenience.

The queuing models given in this supplement provide equations for the steady-state operating characteristics of queuing systems that have Poisson arrivals and one of several different service time distributions. Models are given for the basic exponential service model and its multiple-server extension. Models are also given for single-server models with general or deterministic service times and for exponential service times when there is a finite population or a finite maximum queue length. The operating characteristic values derived from these models can be used to design queuing systems to either meet a specified service standard or minimize the total cost of operating the system, that total cost being the sum of the cost of providing capacity and the cost of providing insufficient capacity.

> end-of-supplement resources

- **Practice Quiz**
- **Key Terms**
- **Solved Problems**
- **Discussion Questions**
- **Problems**

CHAPTER 16

Project Management

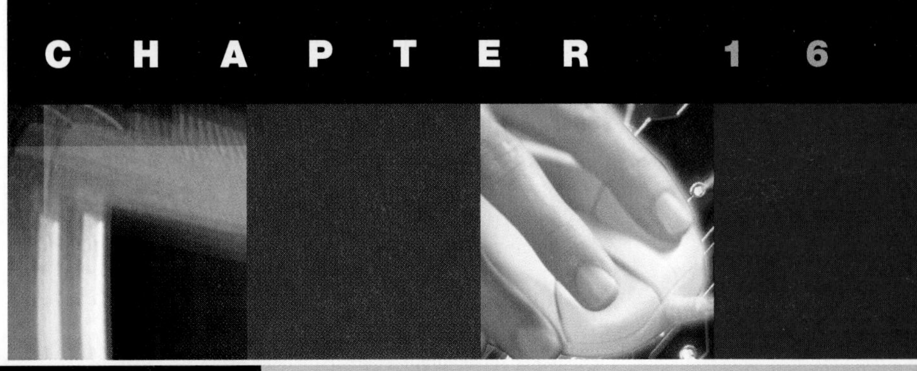

Chapter Outline

What's Ahead

. . . BACK AT THE REC CENTER

Fred was preparing to leave the rec center early. He hadn't said much all morning but as he was on his way to the locker room, Luis asked him why he was leaving already. "I've got to get in early this morning. I have to meet with my team on this software implementation stuff again," he said. Fred had mentioned this project off and on—mostly off—for several months. His company was planning to bring a new software system on line that would help them coordinate their entire supply chain. He had called it SAP but that was the brand name; other times he called it ERP or enterprise resource planning software. It was a big deal for his company; it had set up teams of consultants from the software vendor, internal MIS staff who had experience with software implementation, third-party vendors, as well as staff from the various departments who would work with the software when it was up and running. That's where Fred came into the picture a few months earlier. His team had met a few times to sketch out the basic requirements of the system and to stake out some implementation parameters—but not much had happened for a few months. Now, as his mood indicated, things were heating up quickly.

"That was all of a sudden!" Luis said with surprise. "I just asked you about the project last week."

"Yeah, you said there wasn't much going on with that anymore," said Tom.

"There wasn't," answered Fred, stopping to sit down on the bench next to the steppers that Luis and Tom were using. "Now everything is in a rush. This whole project has been nothing but hurry up and wait."

"Sounds like military planning to me!" laughed Tom. "But I'll bet there's some bigger picture that you're just seeing part of."

"You're probably right," Fred sighed as he looked at his watch. "I just have a hard time understanding why things can be so slow one minute and then there's a super important deadline the next. You gotta remember, this whole thing is still a year or so away from when it's supposed to go on-line."

"Maybe you're slack," laughed Luis as he worked his legs.

"Say what?!" asked Fred as he looked up, surprised, at Luis.

"I think," said Cheryl as she tuned into the conversation, "what he's saying is that when it comes to implementing a system like that, some things have to follow a tight schedule to get the whole thing done on time and others don't. It's the ones that are tight, well, they're critical. Those that don't, well, they have slack."

"It's like building a house," said Luis. He described how his brother-in-law, a general contractor, builds a house. He used the plumbing as an example. As soon as the basement is excavated, the plumber has to rough in all the main floor drains and sewer taps before the concrete walls can be poured. There is usually a tight window for that, as nothing else can really happen until it's completed. "Then they're not needed until most of the frame is up. That can be as much as a month or more," he said. At that point, it is important for them to put the water and drain lines into the walls. "All the plumbing, electrical, heating, and air-conditioning people are really pushed so the dry wall people can get in and finish the walls." They then have to wait until the house is almost finished to set the fixtures, toilets, and showers. Luis explained that sometime between getting all the lines into the wall and setting the fixtures, the plumber and his brother-in-law have to order the actual fixtures to be used. "Orders only require a minimum of a week to arrive," he said. "Finishing the walls, painting, you know all that stuff takes a lot longer, so there's a lot of 'slack' to when that order has to be placed."

Fred could see what Luis meant. Some things need to happen before others can be done. There may be some slack time in between when somebody or something is needed at one point in the project and the time they must come back later in the project. "I guess it's up to the plumber to find something to do in between," said Fred.

"That's a good point," said Cheryl. "That means guys like that have to be flexible and juggle their time between jobs."

"These kind of systems guys must have had five or six irons in the fire," Fred laughed. He described how the systems people from his company and the vendor's people on his team were also on teams together at other plants. They were always talking about different jobs they were juggling all concurrently and all at different stages of completion.

"I guess they're just different from the system guys I'm used to working with," said Fred. "I mean, I'm used to IT guys I see everyday. The guys that keep us up and running, they think just like the rest of us in my plant. They see the world in the time it takes a pager to get through the line and on to the customer—you know hours and days. These guys were really different. They're looking months and years down the road."

"That's another good point," said Cheryl. "They need a way to be looking farther down the road than most of us do in our jobs."

"Oh, they have a system," said Fred. He described how they came in a few months earlier and spent some time looking around and asking a lot of questions. Then they were gone. He said they came back a few weeks later to do some preliminary training and to ask more questions and then left again. There wasn't much going on with the team over the last few weeks. Now they're back with some new people and a very tight schedule. "It just seems like they'd be better off doing one thing at a time and seeing it through. It's more like what I'm used to," Fred added.

"I'll bet it's like the plumbers," said Luis. "They probably had some things done in the beginning and then got out of the way. Something else had to happen next, and now they're back and making more work for you." Tom and Cheryl nodded their agreement.

"Yeah, I guess so. They did give some of the guys in my area a 'to do' list as they were leaving the first time. They needed some information. They wanted things reorganized a bit, nothing big. I guess we must have got it done on time," Fred said.

"And then they came back?" asked Luis.

"Yeah, they did," answered Fred. He began to realize that there wouldn't have been much for them to do while his people were getting their "to do" list together, so they likely were at some other plant making use of the time with another team. "I guess they do need to juggle a few of those 'hurry up and wait' type jobs," he said.

"If they had stayed there, they'd have been slack. Nothing to do," said Luis.

"Besides," asked Cheryl, "after they left the second time, remember, after the training, did any of their people stay behind? Was anybody still there working on putting the software up?"

"I get it," interjected Tom. "All the time Fred thought nothing was going on, the consultants were waiting on Fred's people to do their part, or like the second time, waiting for the techies to get the software up and running."

"So what you're saying is that the next time I'm stuck in the middle of highway construction and it doesn't look like anybody's doing anything, I shouldn't start yelling about wasted tax dollars," Fred laughed. He had stayed longer than he was expecting. He got up from where he was sitting and headed to the men's locker room. "I should remember, it's all part of some bigger plan."

> objectives

Take a moment to familiarize yourself with the key objectives of this chapter.

> gearing up

Before you begin reading this chapter, try a short warm-up activity.

> Introduction

In this chapter, we cover value-adding systems that are designed to both develop and deliver customer-specified product-service bundles. A **project** is by definition a set of tasks that is completed only once. In other words, every project is unique. We tend to notice big civil engineering projects and associate project management with the skills required to accomplish them. But when we study project management, we'll miss the broader picture if we focus only on things like building the Great Wall of China, the Eiffel Tower, the Suez Canal, or the International Space Station. In reality, projects are a part of daily life for each of us, and project management skills are useful in a wide variety of situations. Many businesses add their value by completing projects for their customers: social services agencies, consulting firms, accounting firms, engineering firms, construction firms, advertising agencies, law firms, framing shops, caterers, and artists. The work that such businesses complete is one of a kind, usually done to the specifications of the customer, with a great deal of interaction along the way.

In this chapter, we'll discuss the way that personnel from various functions work together in project-oriented organizations to satisfy their customers. If you've gone through this text in the order that the chapters appear, you are probably convinced by now that no single function—including operations management—exists in a vacuum. To effectively satisfy customers, employees from every functional area must work together effectively. Project management is no different.

We'll also discuss project management organizations. A company that exists primarily to manage projects is much different from the kinds of companies we've discussed so far. Project managing companies must deal with much more uncertainty than most, because they're generally working on jobs that have never before been done. These jobs are often of critical importance to their customers, though those customers may have difficulty defining exactly what they need. Finally, projects present many challenges in regard to workforce management. Skilled workers and experts must work together to understand the scope of the entire project. In completing the project, they will work themselves out of a job.

Since project management organizations and their workforces are different from other organizations, the body of knowledge applied by project managers is somewhat different from that required in other organizations. Much as your approach to a major team project differs from the approach you take to prepare for daily quizzes, the skills and knowledge called for in project management are unique. They form a generally accepted source of expertise called the *project management body of knowledge (PMBOK).*

Projects follow a life cycle including four stages. During the first stage, the need for the project is established, alternatives are considered, and consensus is built around one specific alternative. During the second stage, plans for project implementation are developed. During the third phase, the project itself is under way. During the fourth stage, the project is completed, payments to the project provider are finalized, and the customer begins to use the value provided by the project. Regardless of the project type, whether it's a building, an accounting project, or information system development and installation, these stages of the project life cycle will occur. Further, project managers can anticipate the different managerial challenges associated with each stage.

A project activity may be critical to the timely completion of the project or have virtually no impact on the completion time. The criticality of an activity changes as a project moves forward and sequences of activities get ahead of schedule or behind schedule. Detailed project scheduling is, therefore, necessary to ensure timely completion within budgetary constraints. In many cases, this detailed scheduling makes use of computer modeling techniques that can identify which resources (workers and equipment) to use for a given task at a given point in the project's development.

Finally, in this chapter we provide an overview of planning and control in project management organizations. Even more than managers of the MRP systems described in the last chapter, project managers must keep up with a large number of details. Since resources may be assigned simultaneously to multiple projects, detailed records must be kept on both a project-by-project basis and an aggregate basis. Thus, the planning and control schemes used to manage multiple projects must adapt to progress updates and reassign resources accordingly. The fact that projects are often managed under severe pressure to meet deadlines makes the issue of resource assignment among multiple projects a particularly difficult and important task.

> Integrating Operations Management with Other Functions

As with other product-service bundles, each project has consumers and providers. Like many services, and unlike most manufacturing operations, project consumers often provide at least part of the project. For example, lawyers' and accountants' clients provide information and objectives for the project whose value they consume.

Occasionally, projects are completed and consumed by a single function within a business. Financial managers must occasionally prepare studies of the value of subsidiaries if they were to be spun-off as independent companies or the value of privately held companies in an initial public offering (IPO). Or they might have to restructure a firm's finances in light of new tax laws or corporate opportunities. Accountants might have to set up the books for a new division, audit projects, or prepare a tax return. Human resource managers might have to select and install a new employee database, design a new compensation system, or evaluate a variety of alternative training programs. Marketing people oversee advertising projects for their company, engineers consult on projects to expand capacity, and many MIS professionals are constantly occupied in building, installing, or updating computer systems.

Figure 16.1 illustrates the links between the various functions of a business and the major topics covered in this chapter. Since most functions are providers or consumers of projects at some time or other, the boxes in Figure 16.1 could all be filled with circles, indicating that every part of this chapter is meaningful to every function. Instead, Figure 16.1 shows which aspects of project management are important to the ongoing responsibilities of various functions. In other words, it indicates the role of various functions in providing projects:

- *Finance.* Because cost control is a critical issue in project management, finance is a critical function in the management of projects. Cost management is part of the project manager's core body of knowledge. It plays a role in each stage of the project life cycle, as well as in project planning and control (there may be a financial cost to expediting a project).
- *Accounting.* Most of the work done by accountants is project work. This is true whether the accountant is employed by a large public accounting firm, a smaller accounting service, or a corporate accounting department. As such, this chapter's sections on the project management body of knowledge and the project life cycle are likely to be of particular interest to accounting majors.
- *Human resources.* All in all, it's people who drive a project's success. As such, the human resources function is critical, especially to the successful management of multiple projects. Human resources management is a part of the project manager's core body of knowledge.
- *Marketing.* The characteristics of project management organizations described in this chapter are very familiar to marketing professionals, for this form of organization is common in advertising agencies and promotional firms. Furthermore, to ensure they gain and retain the support of all interested parties, projects must be marketed; not just during the conceptual phase but throughout the project life cycle.
- *Engineering.* More than any other function, engineers add to a firm's operations by managing projects. Whether they are designing the product-service bundle or the value-adding system, developing or installing and repairing new technologies and applications, engineers do their core work in the form of projects.
- *Management information systems.* MIS professionals, who normally support existing computer systems, must occasionally select and implement new software packages. In addition, the software they maintain may include some kind of project management application. Consequently, they must understand the project planning and scheduling process that is used by others in their organization.

Chapter Topics / Functional Areas of Business	Finance	Accounting	Human Resources	Marketing	Engineering	Management Information Systems
Integrating Operations Management with Other Functions	●	●	●	●	●	●
Characteristics of the Project Management Organization			●	●	●	
The Project Management Body of Knowledge	●	●	●		●	●
The Project Management Life-Cycle	●	●	●	●	●	
Planning and Control in Project Management	●		●		●	●
Detailed Scheduling Using Network Modeling			●		●	●

FIGURE 16.1 Integrating Operations Management with Other Functions

Characteristics of the Project Management Organization

Virtually every organization must manage some type of project from time to time, but some organizations are in the business of managing projects: engineering and construction firms, audit firms, consulting firms, law partnerships, research and development labs, insurance underwriters, medical claims processors, and the like. As Figure 16.2 suggests, this kind of company is quite unique in many respects. Workers move from project to project, often from location to location. On each project, they might work with a different group of people. While their expertise is of great value to clients, they often have difficulty communicating with clients without resorting to technical jargon.

From an organizational perspective, teams are common in project management companies. This type of structure makes a lot of sense, because while projects come and go, the employees remain. Workers need to retain some core organizational position, or identity, as they move from project to project. Figure 16.3 shows the traditional *matrix organization* that is often found in project management firms. With a **matrix structure,** employees may be assigned to one or more projects at a given time, but their home department will remain the same.

The matrix structure allows a company to develop and retain core capabilities and functional excellence. It also allows managers to classify and track personnel assigned to multiple projects. Each person has a department boss and a project boss. The project manager's job is to oversee and coordinate the work of personnel from various functions on the project. If a project manager has a problem with any function's performance on the project, he or she can take up the issue with the department manager. No employee should be able to complain of having too many projects to work on. It's the department boss's job to assign workers to specific projects and make sure their cumulative work loads are not excessive. The department boss also oversees contract pricing and scheduling to make sure the department's capacity is not exceeded.

Figures 16.4 and 16.5 show two alternative team structures, a hierarchical structure and a customer-driven structure. With a **hierarchical team structure** (Figure 16.4), the team might remain largely the same as projects come and go. Thus, project workers would always report to the same project manager, who would in turn report to a senior manager, probably the regional director. Compared to the matrix structure, the hierarchical structure is less flexible. Instead of individuals or departments

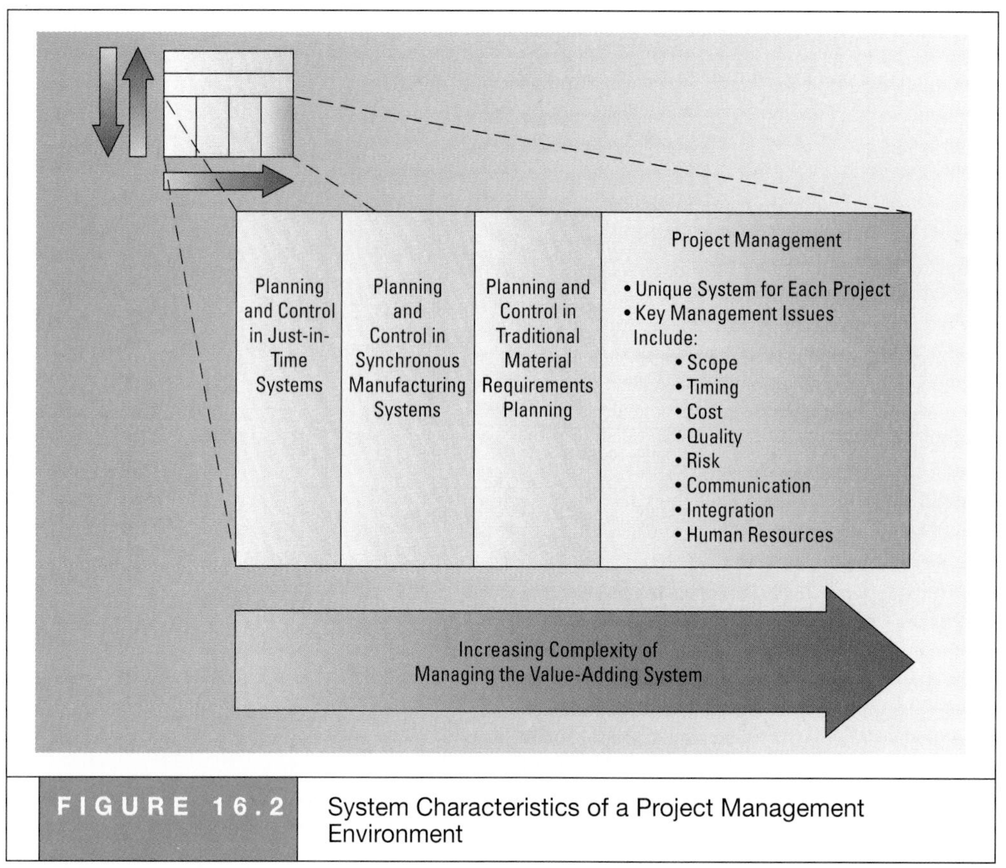

FIGURE 16.2 System Characteristics of a Project Management Environment

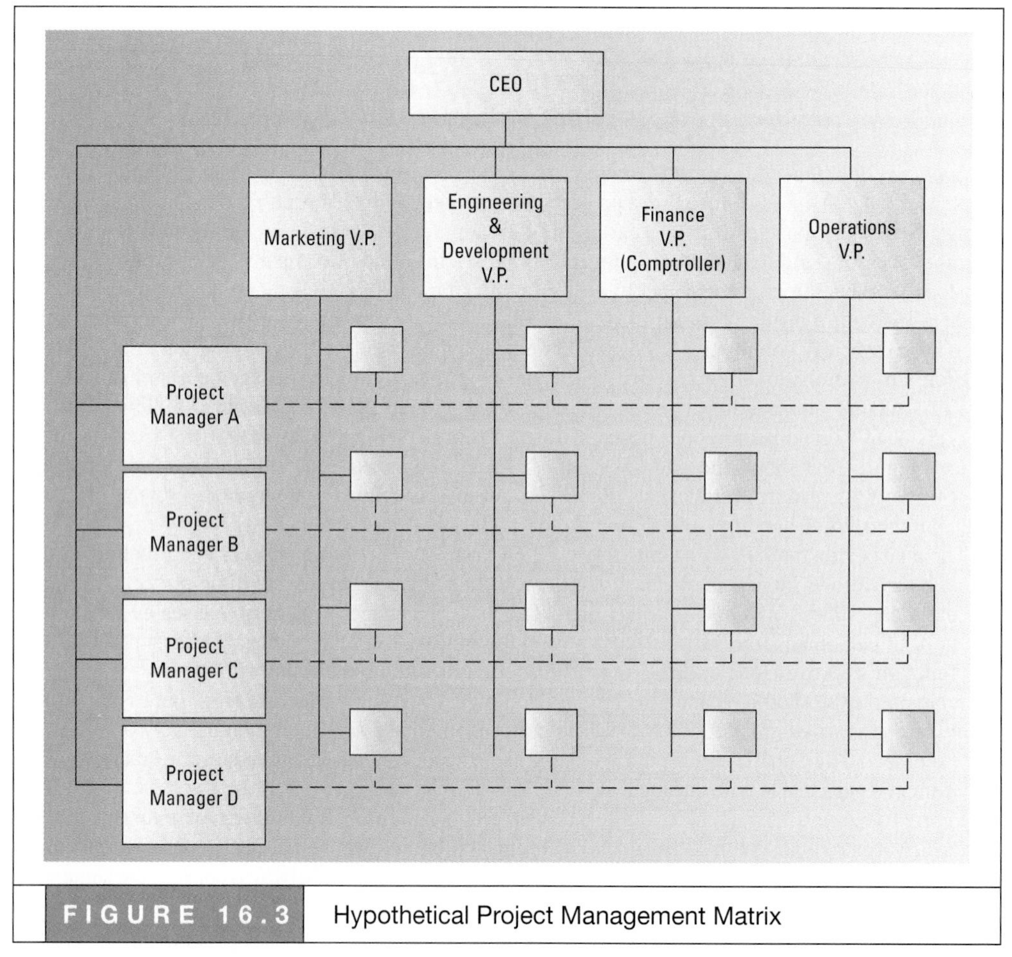

FIGURE 16.3 Hypothetical Project Management Matrix

Regional Director
Manager of Sales and Estimating
Director of Engineering
Human Resource Manager
Financial Comptroller
Project Team A
Highway 75 Resurfacing Project Manager
Contracts and Procurement
Scheduling and Time Management
Quality, Safety, and Compliance
Cost Management and Accounting
Human Resources
Subcontractors
Skilled Trades and Laborers
Project Team B
Thomas Tucker Corporate Office Construction Project Manager
Contracts and Procurement
Scheduling and Time Management
Quality, Safety, and Compliance
Cost Management and Accounting
Human Resources
Subcontractors
Skilled Trades and Laborers

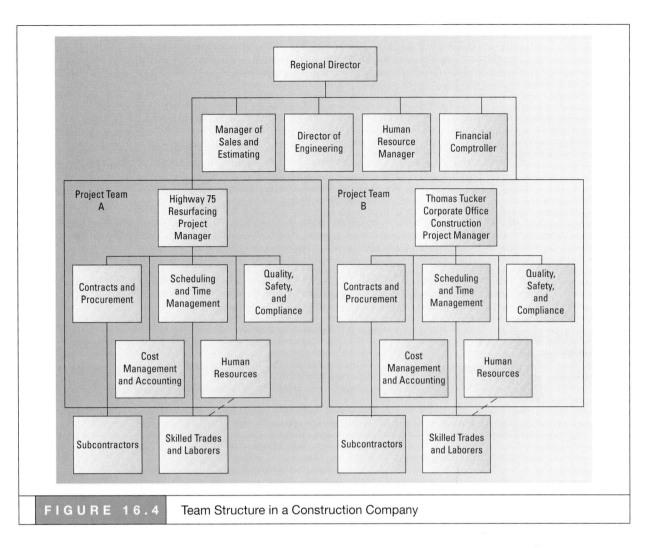

FIGURE 16.4 Team Structure in a Construction Company

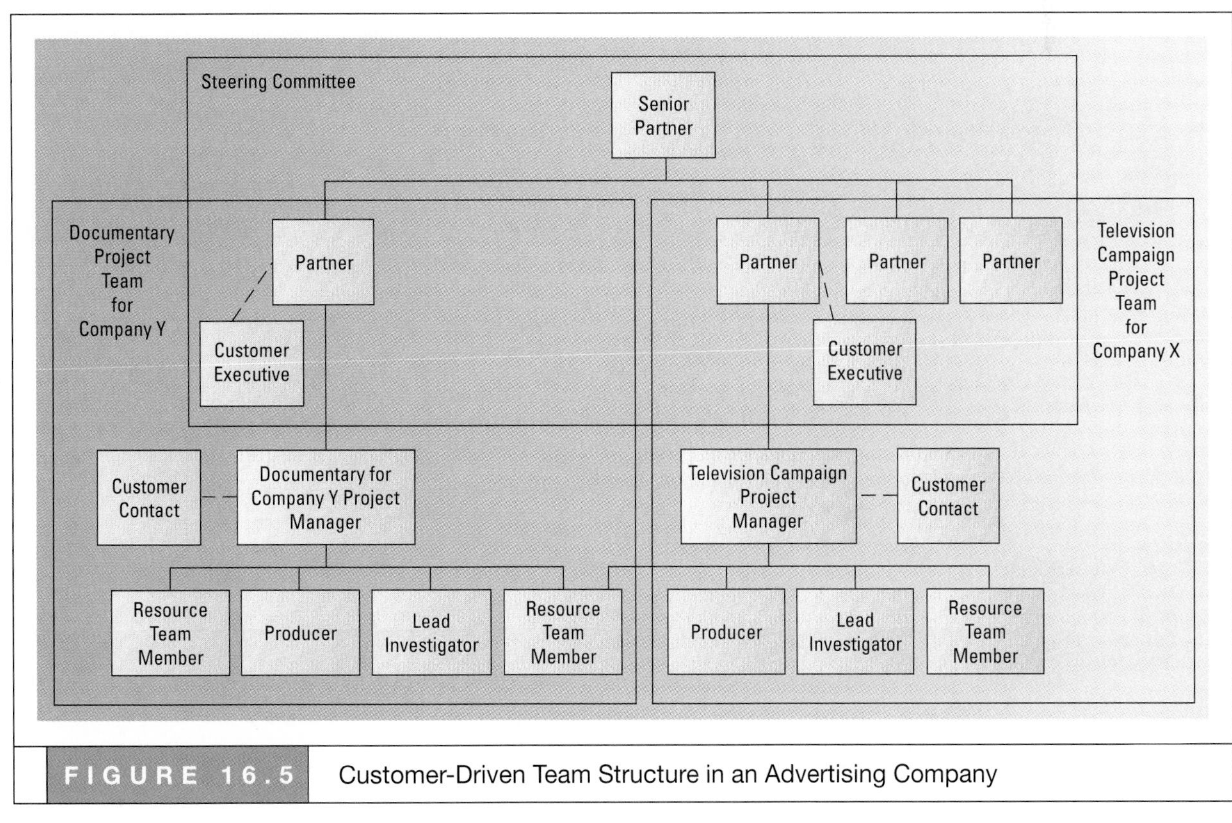

FIGURE 16.5 Customer-Driven Team Structure in an Advertising Company

developing functional capabilities, the team develops expertise with particular types of projects. For example, a large law firm might create standing teams devoted to environmental practice, banking regulations, personal injury, labor law, incorporation, and so on. If the firm runs out of a particular type of work, however, and new cases are not well matched to a team's expertise, a whole team of lawyers might well need to move on.

With a **customer-driven team structure** (Figure 16.5), projects come and go, but the type of customer (rather than the type of project) remains largely the same. As customers become familiar with the team they are working with, they can ask the team to take on a variety of projects. For example, an advertising agency might create a project team devoted exclusively to one client's account. The team might create a broadcast media campaign for one division in the client company, a web-promotion strategy for another, a print campaign for a third, and an overall marketing strategy for the corporation as a whole. Often, team leaders (the partners) in this type of structure, taken together, represent the company's entire steering team. The steering team, which is headed by a senior executive or partner in the firm, is responsible for coordinating the efforts of the various customer-driven teams and creating opportunities for them to learn from each other. If any employees serve on more than one team, it is the steering team's job to ensure that they are not overburdened.

Regardless of the type of structure a project management organization has, all projects share certain tasks and progress through a common life cycle. The next three sections outline the similarities among projects and give an example from Miami University's Student Recreation Center; the final two sections illustrate some popular management techniques.

active concept check <

Now let's take a moment to test your knowledge of the concepts you have studied in this section.

The Project Management Body of Knowledge

Table 16.1 summarizes the project management body of knowledge (PMBOK), which was developed by the Project Management Institute (PMI). With almost 40,000 members worldwide, PMI is the professional organization for project managers; it offers project management professional (PMP) certification to managers who can demonstrate their mastery of the project management body of knowledge. Project management professionals are capable of managing a variety of different projects.

active example <

Take a closer look at the concepts and issues you've been reading about.

Notice that the PMBOK covers a wide area of expertise. It includes the detail-oriented aspects of project scheduling and budgeting, as well as the broad conceptual tasks of specifying a project's scope and integrating a project with existing systems. Not all projects will require the manager to apply every aspect of this body of knowledge, but the well-trained project manager should be prepared to cope with all these tasks.

active example <

Take a closer look at the concepts and issues you've been reading about.

TABLE 16.1 The Project Management Body of Knowledge (PMBOK)	
PMBOK Area	**Key Task(s)**
Scope Management	Defining what's got to be done (and what's not to be done) in order to complete the project. Often, clients have difficulty in defining this themselves—though they think they know what they want, it may be difficult for them to formally express that and cover all aspects. Project managers with functional expertise and experience in previous projects can be very helpful.
Quality Management	Establishing metrics and standards to ensure that the client's expectations are met and making sure that the work is meeting those standards as it progresses. This area requires clear communication in subcontracting.
Cost Management	Establishing a project budget and making sure that the project stays within that budget. It's important to have checkpoints where project progress and expenses are evaluated relative to projections.
Contract Management/ Procurement Management	Establishing and monitoring expectations of subcontractors. Purchasing or renting materials, equipment, training, and other resources as dictated by the project scope, quality standards, and cost structure.
Time Management	Scheduling work in order to complete the project in a timely manner. There may be penalties for late completion or rewards for early delivery. Project managers need to determine the value of time and find ways to use resources so that time is not lost and opportunities for improving the schedule are utilized.
Risk Management	Identifying potential project disruptions, their severity, ways to prevent their occurrence, and contingency plans should they arise. Risk management means more than buying an insurance policy; something that basic shouldn't be overlooked.
Human Resources Management	Getting the right people assigned to the project at the right time. This area includes performance appraisal, discipline, compliance with labor law, and so on.
Communication Management	Keeping everyone on the same page with regard to the project. This area encompasses establishing regular team meeting times, creating formal communication channels such as e-mail, memos, newsletters, and web sites, and establishing the needed informal channels of communication.
Project Integration Management	Fitting the project into existing organizations. For example, if the project is a new computer system, it has to be fit into the company where it will be used. That means that "before," during, and "after" the project, or from the beginning to the end of the project's life cycle, the manager needs to be thinking about what will work in the environment where it will be deployed.

> active concept check

Now let's take a moment to test your knowledge of the concepts you have studied in this section.

> Projects at Miami's Student Rec Center

Day-to-day operations at the Miami's (Ohio) Student Recreation Center (SRC) resemble those of a service-oriented job shop: A large number of students come to the center on a regular basis to use the established venues in ways that fit their personal needs. Nevertheless, many unique projects take place throughout the semester, in the form of special events that must be coordinated with daily operations. These special events may include private parties sponsored by fraternities, sororities, or other student groups; NCAA diving championships; wall-climbing competitions; high school proms; and a variety of swimming competitions. In addition, the Outdoor Pursuit Center (OPC), housed inside the rec center, facilitates ad hoc activities and excursions on an individual or small group basis. These one-time events must be planned, scheduled, and managed in such a way as to maximize their contribution to the SRC's mission and minimize their adverse impact on ongoing activities. Many of them add to the center's revenue stream and help to fill up the center's schedule in otherwise slow periods (such as university holidays).

Whether an SRC administrator is planning a regional swimming and diving meet or a student worker at the OPC is helping a sorority to plan a white-water rafting trip, an understanding of the project management body of knowledge (PMBOK) is essential. With planning duties split between staff and patrons, guidelines for managing these projects and assigning specific responsibilities are also essential. Responsibilities include defining the scope of the event, establishing measures of success or quality, managing costs, purchasing or otherwise securing the necessary equipment or materials, organizing and coordinating the preparation for and execution of the event, identifying and managing the risks associated with the event, dealing with human resource issues, communicating information about events, and, finally, integrating the events into the SRC's daily operation. Managing these steps is not at all unlike managing the construction of a new building or filming a movie. The effective use of the PMBOK to enhance the value-adding system is not limited to the production of a tangible product or profit-seeking businesses.

active poll <

What do you think? Voice your opinion and find out what others have to say.

The most significant project for many businesses is the design of their product-service bundle and the value-adding system with which it will be delivered. Here Boeing uses a fixed-position assembly process to build their 737-200 model aircraft.

The Project Management Life Cycle

Projects have a life cycle much like that shown in Figure 16.6. As a project progresses through the four stages of its life cycle, the relative importance of the PMBOK areas changes.

In the first stage, the period of conceptual study, the primary required outcome is an organizational commitment to the project. This period, which can last for a long time, can raise numerous political and resource issues. The authors' university, for example, recently installed a $19 million fiber-optic data and video transmission network. The first calls for such a network came in the mid-1980s. Many issues had to be debated: Would the network cover all the buildings on campus, including dormitories and administrative buildings, or just academic buildings? If it covered the dorms, would each resident have an outlet or would there be only one outlet per room? Would the network be capable of carrying entertainment programming as well as educational channels? If so, would separate networks be required for various types of media? What bandwidth would be needed? Would the university operate the network or would an outside company operate it for profit? Finally, how would the school finance the network? These are only a few of the questions with which the university community had to come to terms. Ultimately, the university president and board of trustees came to a consensus on the desired characteristics and capabilities and decided to install the network. In terms of Figure 16.6, their decision marked the end of the conceptual phase in the project's life cycle, which lasted roughly a decade.

Next, a team of technical experts and administrators began the development process by writing a request for proposals (RFP). This request defined the scope of the project, indicating the university's needs and specifying the number of outlets, length of cable, and preferred standards and technologies for bidding purposes. It also specified an upper limit for bids on the project, a time limit for its completion, and the quality and performance measures that would be applied. Further development took place as the bidders began to consider how they would complete the project and what various alternatives would cost. For over a year, the development team conferred with potential bidders. The resulting proposals varied slightly, as did their price tags. Finally, in January of 1996, the university accepted a bid and created a joint enterprise with NEC, which agreed to build the network for about

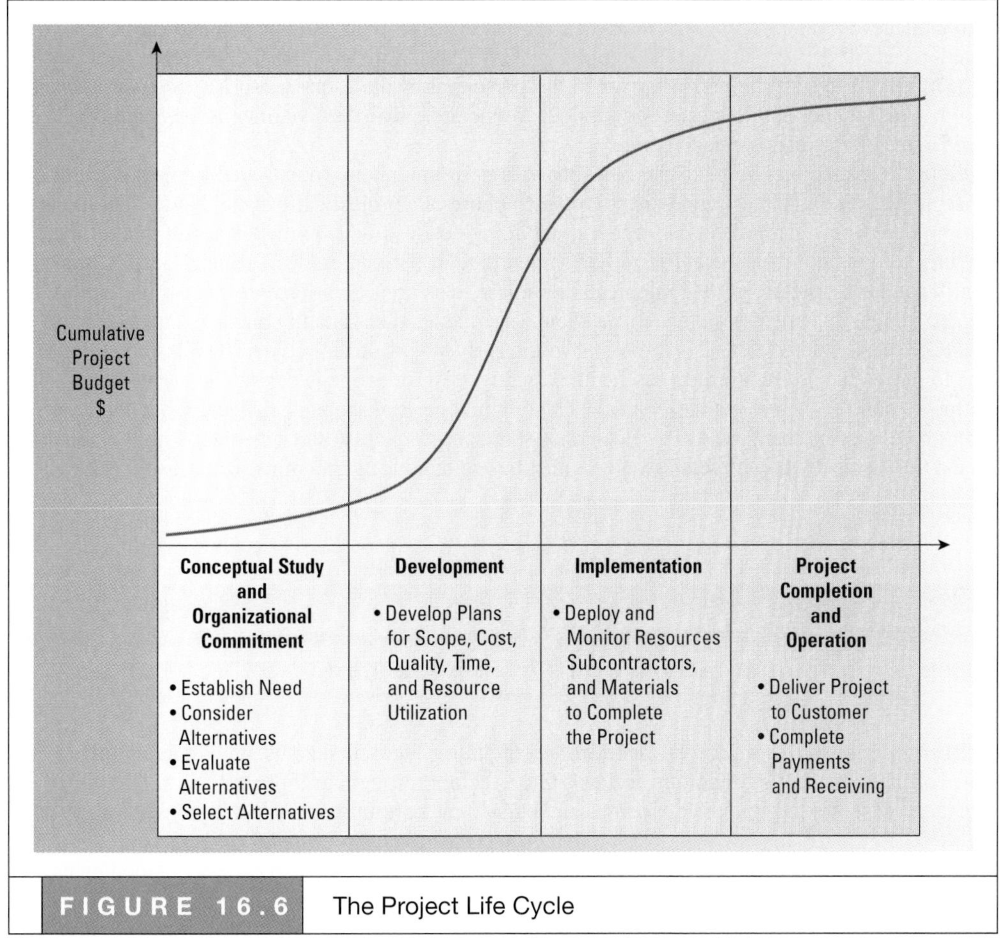

FIGURE 16.6 The Project Life Cycle

Each patient is a project. Developing and implementing recovery plans for critically injured patients requires health care professionals to use project management skills.

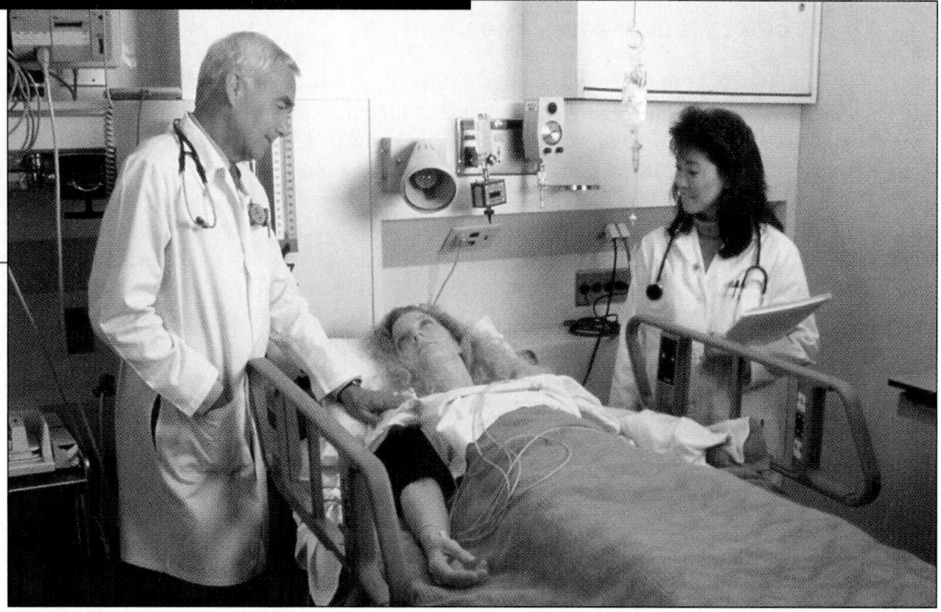

25% of its construction cost. In return, NEC would share in the revenues from the programming delivered over the network. In terms of Figure 16.6, this decision marked the end of the development phase of the project's life cycle.

During 1996 and 1997, an NEC project team worked with a university project manager to install the campus network. Various subcontractors were engaged to develop blueprints of the conduit and outlets; run underground cables; install cable buses, cable, and outlets; test the installations; and so on. At this point, a lot of money was being spent, so monitoring the cost, quality, and schedule established during the development phase was important. The network installation and testing were finally completed in early 1998. At that point the implementation phase of the project was complete, and the project team began to turn the network over to the personnel of the joint enterprise. Today, the project team has disbanded, but the network continues to operate. NEC will continue to receive shared revenue payments for many years to come.

Figure 16.6 also lists some of the cost management, time management, quality management, and conceptual development tasks that are part of each phase of a project's life cycle. Notice that the early work in developing the project concept and obtaining cost estimates, schedules, and quality metrics provides a foundation for the entire project. Even though the cumulative financial outlays are most significant during the project's implementation phase, cost considerations are critical throughout the project. Similar statements could be made about time management, quality management, and so on. In fact, each area of the PMBOK is important in the early stages of the project. It follows that the best time to make changes in a project's schedule, quality, cost, or scope is during the early stages. Once the foundation for the project has been set, changing its general scope is difficult. Once the development phase is over, changing the particulars of scope, cost, quality, and schedule is not just difficult but extremely costly. In particular, changes must be limited during the implementation phase.

video exercise

Take a moment to apply what you've learned.

Over the course of a project, estimates for cost, quality, and schedule become more and more certain. For that reason it is important to track these factors throughout a project. As for cost, project managers must look beyond their expenses and budget and carefully evaluate the progress of the project itself. Figure 16.7a shows the cumulative cost projections for a typical project. Notice that the project cost is only an estimate; the actual cost may be higher or lower than expected. Good managers will evaluate a project periodically and assess the risk of running over budget before the project can be completed. If the worst-case scenario is not tenable and the risk substantial, the project manager would be well advised to inquire whether the plan should be modified or even scrapped.

Figure 16.7b illustrates the many considerations in controlling project costs. It shows a common situation: The cumulative cost to date exceeds the budgeted cost to date. In other words, project managers have spent more money than they expected to. The monetary difference between the cumulative cost and the expected cost is referred to as the **current budget shortfall.** Note that even though the project is over budget, it is behind schedule: The value of the completed work, also called the **earned value,** is less than the budgeted expense. The difference between the budgeted cost to date and the earned value to date represents a variance from projected costs, which is called the **scheduled value shortfall.** The amount of time the project is running behind schedule is called the **project delay.** Managers must be concerned with both a current budget shortfall and a scheduled value shortfall, which together comprise the current **total cost overrun.** This analysis of project progress and expenditures relative to project targets is called **earned value analysis.**

Figure 16.7c shows how cost projections can be updated in the middle of the implementation phase. Notice that the projected (current expected) cost curve begins where the current cumulative

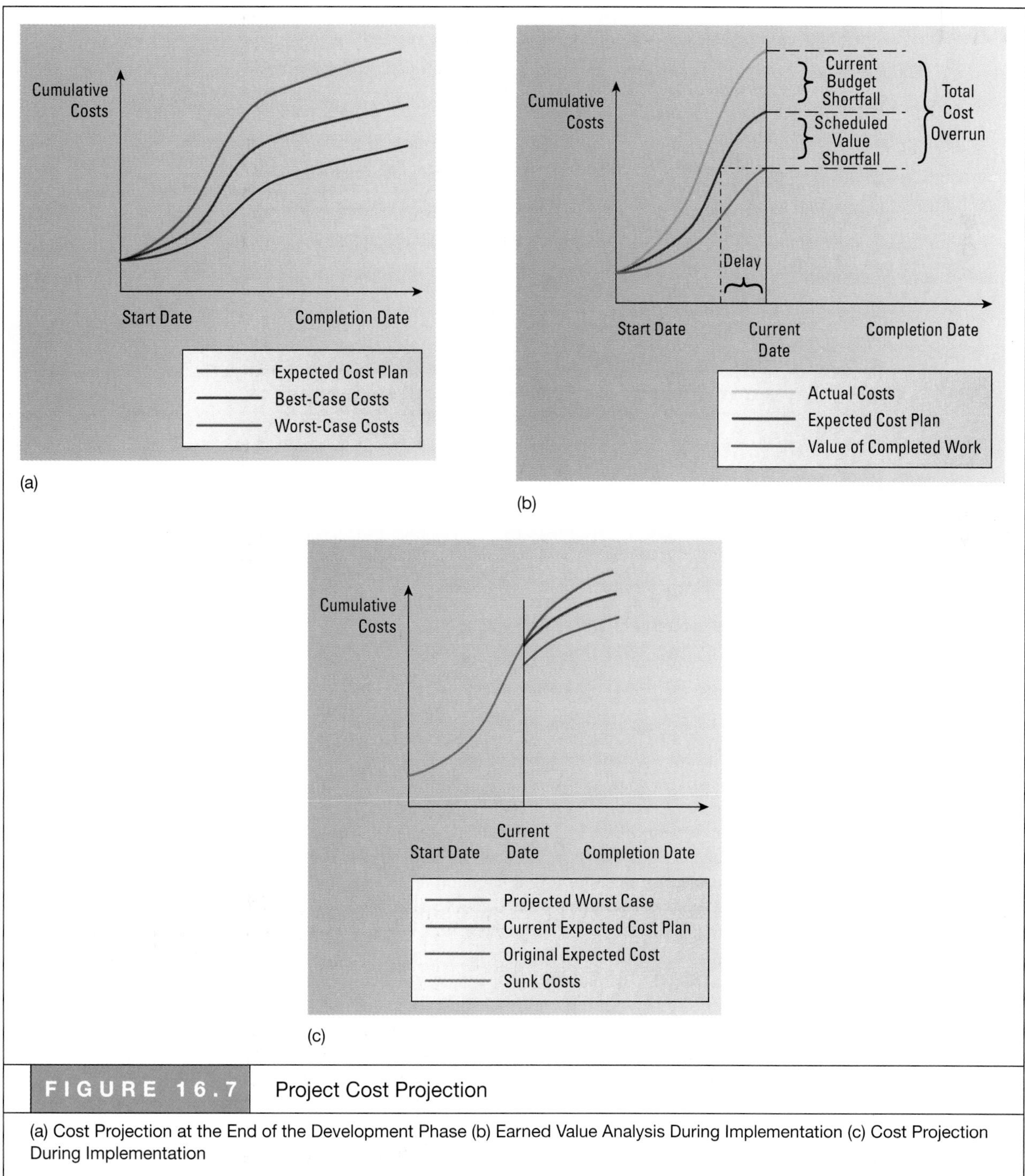

FIGURE 16.7 Project Cost Projection

(a) Cost Projection at the End of the Development Phase (b) Earned Value Analysis During Implementation (c) Cost Projection During Implementation

expenses curve ends. The money that has been spent so far is called the **sunk cost**—that is, it represents an expenditure that can't be recovered. Since some information is gained regarding actual costs as the project progresses, the cost range from best case to worst case will continue to narrow as the project nears completion. Managers must continually evaluate and reevaluate a project's costs. If a cost overrun becomes large enough, they may need to downsize or modify the project. It may even be necessary, after millions or billions of dollars have been spent on the project, to pull the plug on it. Sunk costs are not considered in these forward-looking decisions; they are irrelevant. One example of a project whose plug was pulled in the middle of the implementation phase is the Superconducting Super Collider (SSC), a government-funded nuclear accelerator that was under construction in Texas when it was canceled. (The Case Study at the end of this chapter provides a detailed description of the SSC.)

At the time of this writing, the International Space Station (ISS) was also under scrutiny. Russia, whose economy was very weak, was demanding $60 million to complete the first module and $600 million more to complete the project. NASA's position was that using Russia's established capacities and capabilities would actually cost far less than for the United States to go it alone. But in the U.S. Congress, even the strongest supporters of the ISS were hesitant to commit that much cash. So the new cost estimates appeared to be sinking the project.

Not just large construction projects get scrapped because of cost overruns. Many legal battles are dropped or settled out of court because of mounting costs. Research and development (R&D) projects can be high-risk ventures from the start, so many of them never make it past the R to the D. Too, managers frequently back away from productivity improvement projects—from business process reengineering and TQM to computer system upgrades and equipment replacement. You have probably started some projects in your own back yard and never finished them because of a midstream reevaluation of the costs.

video exercise

Take a moment to apply what you've learned.

active concept check

Now let's take a moment to test your knowledge of the concepts you have studied in this section.

Planning and Control in Project Management

Figure 16.8 illustrates some of the issues in supply-chain management (SCM) that confront project managers. Despite the fact that projects are unique and happen only once, SCM concepts are relevant to project management. Many large projects are completed only after the creation of several levels of subprojects, each with its own subcontractors. For example, an advertising agency that is managing a large one-time media campaign might subcontract the print campaign. The subcontractor, in turn, would probably subcontract the artwork and writing. The advertising agency probably would also subcontract the printing of flyers, sportswear, and other documents to vendors who might then outsource some of it. In other words, projects have supply chains of their own.

Since projects tend to be plagued by uncertainty, subcontractors and vendors need to be flexible in their scheduling, so they can respond to changing demands. But they can also benefit by structuring their contracts so as to financially reward their flexibility. The project's customer must likewise be flexible, providing schedule openings for the project when needed. For example, a software development and installation project would require the customer to provide windows of time for the project team to assess the system requirements, test software modules, conduct dry runs of the new system, run it parallel to the legacy system, and train workers in how to use it. The customer would also need to write formal statements of scope and accountability for the project manager and team.

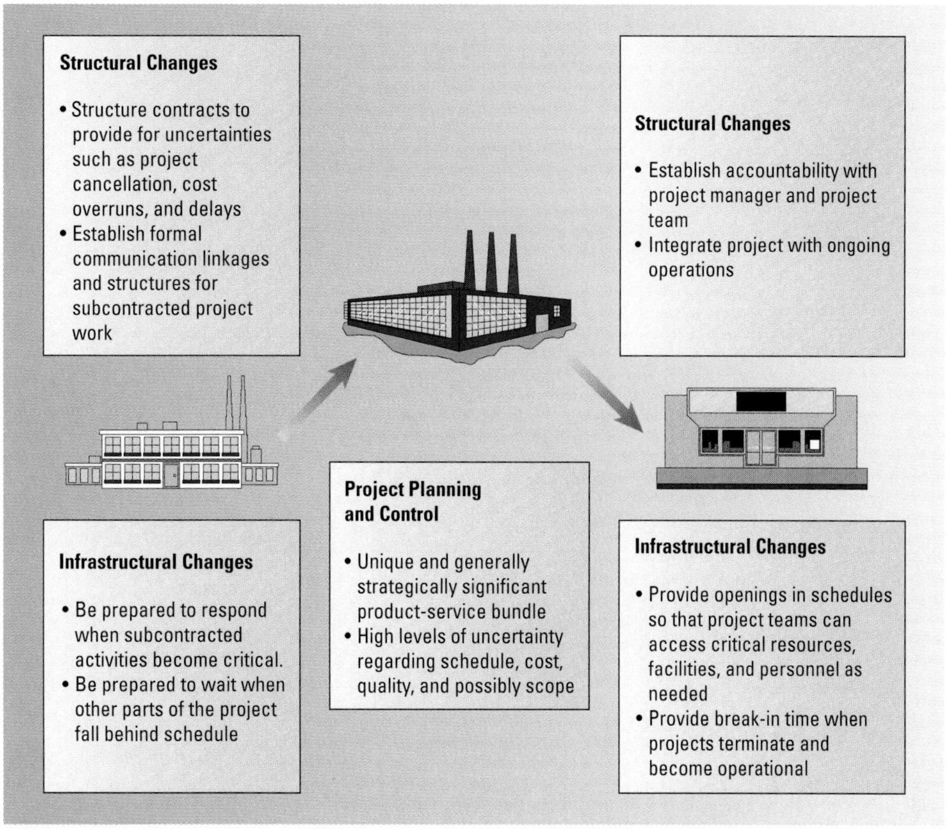

Structural Changes

- Structure contracts to provide for uncertainties such as project cancellation, cost overruns, and delays
- Establish formal communication linkages and structures for subcontracted project work

Structural Changes

- Establish accountability with project manager and project team
- Integrate project with ongoing operations

Project Planning and Control

- Unique and generally strategically significant product-service bundle
- High levels of uncertainty regarding schedule, cost, quality, and possibly scope

Infrastructural Changes

- Be prepared to respond when subcontracted activities become critical.
- Be prepared to wait when other parts of the project fall behind schedule

Infrastructural Changes

- Provide openings in schedules so that project teams can access critical resources, facilities, and personnel as needed
- Provide break-in time when projects terminate and become operational

FIGURE 16.8 Supply-Chain Impact in a PM Environment

Such scheduling issues are a part of time management in the PMBOK. Figure 16.9 presents an overview of time management activities for companies whose product-service bundle comes in the form of projects. At the master scheduling level, managers must estimate the amount of work to be done on a weekly or monthly basis, while taking into consideration all the other projects the company has contracted to complete. The total workload is also an important consideration when bidding on and accepting new contracts. If there is a time conflict between two or more projects, all of which require a given resource, managers must think about turning down some work or finding other ways to get it done.

One way to resolve such scheduling conflicts is to delay a project that is not critical in favor of one that is. **Critical activities** are those on which the scheduled completion of the project depends; they cannot be delayed without delaying the entire project. Critical activities, in other words, have no **slack time** (which is the duration that an activity can be delayed without delaying the project's completion). **Noncritical activities** do have slack time: Their start or finish dates can be delayed without delaying the completion of the project.

While this concept may sound simple, applying it can become quite complicated. Every project has a set of sequentially related critical activities, called the **critical path,** that determines how long the project will take to complete. But as work on a project progresses, some activities may be delayed and others may proceed ahead of schedule. Therefore the critical path can change as the project moves forward. Activities that are critical can become noncritical, while activities that once had slack time can become critical.

If critical activities in separate projects are competing for resources, managers may try to "crash" one or more of the activities in order to deploy their resources more effectively. **Crashing** is finding a way to complete an activity more quickly than expected. It can be done by assigning more workers to an activity, using more or better equipment, approving more overtime, and so on. When a company has a number of projects on the master schedule, effectively deploying resources among them is a real challenge.

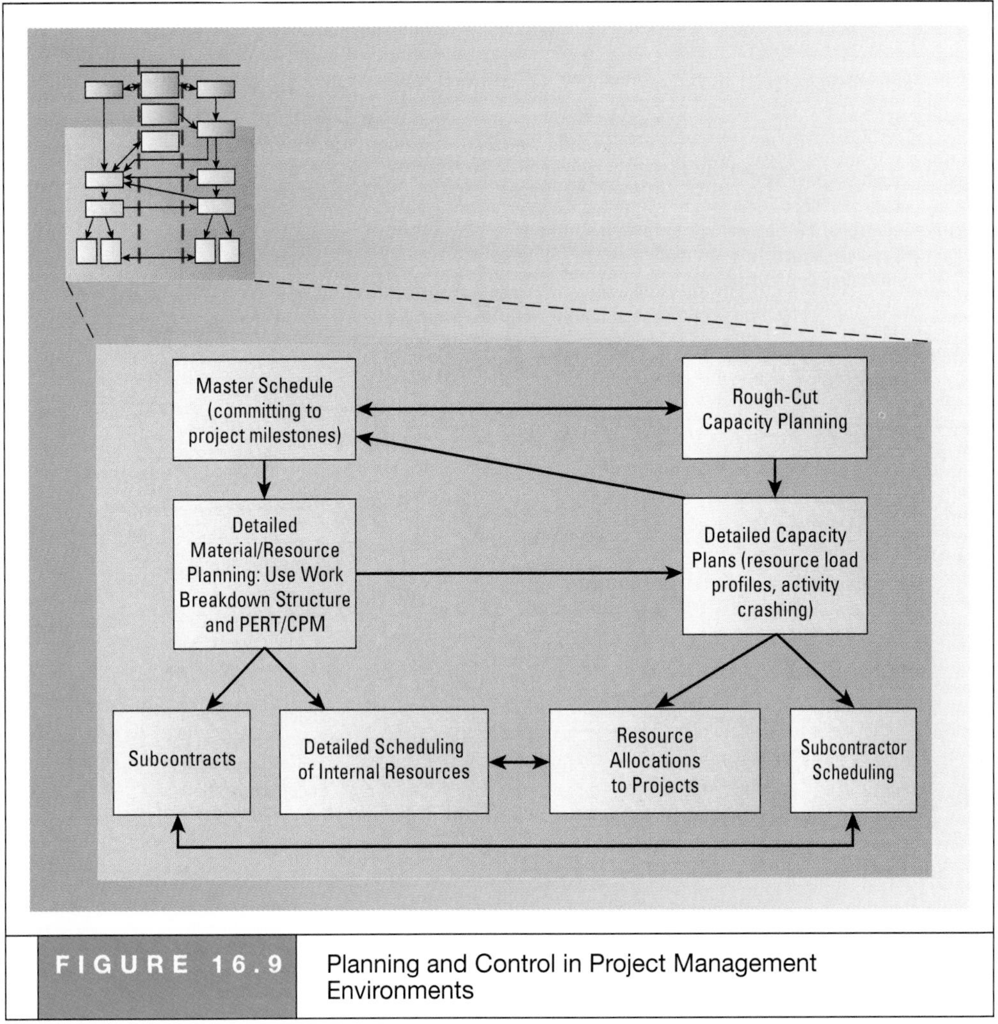

FIGURE 16.9 Planning and Control in Project Management Environments

Project managers use two techniques to manage time and resources and break down the schedule into individual tasks. One is a network planning technique called **PERT,** which stands for **program evaluation and review technique,** and the other is **CPM,** for **critical path method.** Developed in the 1960s, both are network modeling approaches to time management. Originally, the only significant difference between the two was that PERT allowed the expected duration of any activity to be expressed as a probability distribution, while CPM didn't. The two techniques are similar enough that many people use the terms interchangeably.

Currently available project management software, such as *MS-Project,* is based on this type of network modeling. Once the project network has been constructed, the software can be used to update the network and monitor progress, quality conformance, and costs. Since MS-Project can track resources that are shared among multiple projects, it is extremely useful for making detailed capacity plans and allocating resources. Decisions about when subcontracted work and in-house activities should be completed and which activities should be crashed and which delayed are made much more easily with such programs. Recently, Eliyahu Goldratt, the developer of the theory of constraints has developed a number of perspectives that are useful in managing projects. Given that projects contain multiple constraints, Goldratt's "Critical Chain Project Management" builds on the kind of network analysis and project management support provided by MS-Project.

active concept check

Now let's take a moment to test your knowledge of the concepts you have studied in this section.

Detailed Scheduling Using Network Modeling

Detailed scheduling of projects begins with the identification of the specific activities that must be completed. A **work breakdown structure (WBS),** which is a top-down view of the tasks included in a project, can be very useful in this process. Much like a bill of materials, the WBS breaks the project down into subprojects and then into sub-subprojects, until it is reduced to the most basic work units that can be scheduled. These basic work units, which are referred to as **project activities,** are related in various ways to the other activities in the project. **Parallel** (or **independent) activities** are those that can be conducted simultaneously. **Dependent activities** are those that must be completed in a particular sequence—that is, one activity must be completed before another can begin. For example, in home construction, the land can be cleared while a request for a building permit is being processed. Those two tasks are independent activities. But the foundation cannot be poured until a building permit has been issued; those two tasks are dependent activities.

Figure 16.10 shows a simplified WBS for a political campaign. An actual WBS can be quite large, because it generally includes the subprojects to be handled by subcontractors in addition to all the individual activities in the project. While the activities in each subproject need not be listed, all the activities that will *not* be subcontracted should be. A complete enumeration of the project's activities is needed to estimate costs and create a **precedence table,** or a list of all the activities and their sequential relationships.

Figure 16.11 shows a precedence table for the political campaign outlined in Figure 16.10. It was created using MS-Project, Microsoft's project management software. For the sake of simplicity, Figure 16.11 doesn't include all the activities listed on the WBS in Figure 16.10. Notice the column that lists the predecessors for each activity. This column shows which tasks must be completed before other activities may begin.

Based on the information in the precedence table, the software can generate various graphical representations of the project. Notice the right-hand portion of Figure 16.11, a scrollable window that displays a Gantt chart. Figure 16.12 shows the complete Gantt chart for this project. The arrows on the chart indicate the precedence relationships between various activities. Such charts can display both planned and actual progress on a project's activities. They can also highlight the critical path by displaying critical activities in a different color.

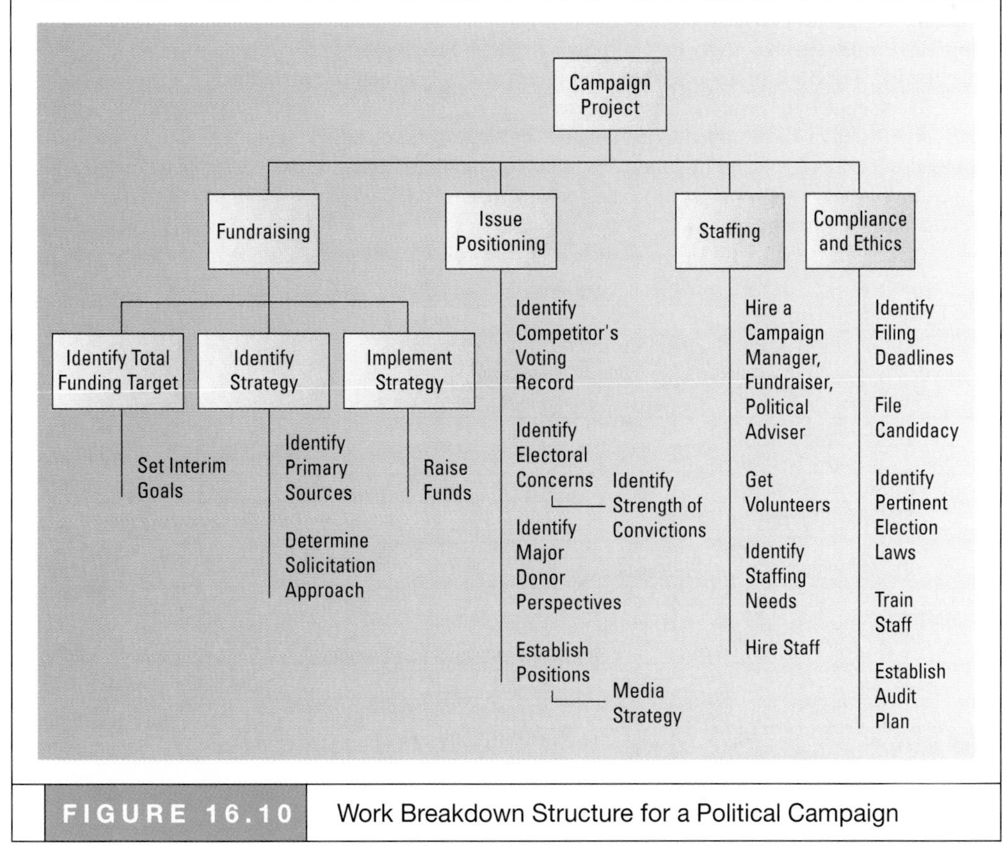

FIGURE 16.10 Work Breakdown Structure for a Political Campaign

ID	Task Name	Duration	Start	Finish	Predecessors	Resource Names
1	Hire Manager	10	Fri 10/9/98	Thu 10/22/98		Candidate
2	Hire Fundraiser	10	Fri 10/23/98	Thu 11/5/98	1	Candidate, Manager
3	Hire Political Adviser	10	Fri 10/23/98	Thu 11/5/98	1	Candidate, Manager
4	Hire Staff	30	Fri 10/23/98	Thu 12/3/98	1	Manager
5	Get Volunteers	30	Fri 12/4/98	Thu 1/14/99	4	Staff
6	Establish Positions	60	Fri 11/6/98	Thu 1/28/99	3	Candidate, Political Adviser
7	Compliance and Ethics Training	2	Fri 1/15/99	Mon 1/18/99	2, 3, 5	Candidate, Political Adviser, Fundraiser, Staff, Volunteers
8	Begin Fundraising	0	Fri 1/18/98	Mon 1/18/99	7	
9	Raise Funds	300	Tue 1/19/99	Mon 3/13/00	8	Fundraiser
10	Implement Campaign Strategy	300	Fri 1/29/99	Thu 3/23/00	7, 6	Candidate, Manager, Staff, Volunteers
11	Vote	0	Thu 3/23/00	Thu 3/23/00	10, 9	Candidate, Manager, Political Adviser, Staff, Volunteers
12						
13						
14						
15						
16						
17						

FIGURE 16.11 Precedence Table for the Political Campaign

Notice that in Figures 16.11 and 16.12, the activities "begin fundraising" and "vote" have a duration of zero days. These less-than-brief activities are called **dummy activities** or **milestones.** Including such activities on the chart is sometimes necessary in order to keep the precedence of activities clear. In this case, the "begin fundraising" dummy had to be added because while fundraising takes a long time, the campaign strategy cannot be implemented until fundraising has begun. In other words, though beginning the activity of fundraising is not an activity in itself, other activities must wait on this milestone. Similarly, the "vote" dummy activity had to be added because it is the milestone that marks the latest possible completion of the project. All activities must be completed by that date.

Figure 16.13 shows a PERT project network for the political campaign, which was also created using MS-Project. Each activity that is shown on the project's precedence table shows up as a *node* in this network. The *arcs,* or arrows, show the precedences between the activities. MS-Project includes five fields on each node, which allow users to display information about activities directly on the diagram. Figure 16.13 shows an activity's name, predecessors, duration, start, and finish. The critical activities and critical path are highlighted with color and bold boxes; dummy activities are highlighted with a double box. As a project moves forward, the boxed activities change color to show that progress has been made.

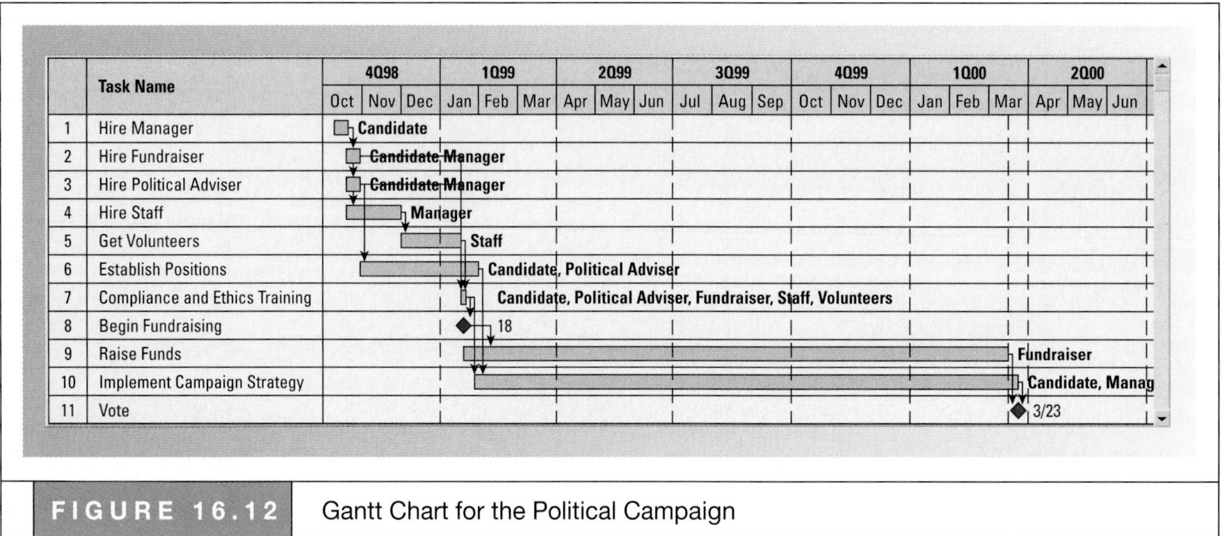

FIGURE 16.12 Gantt Chart for the Political Campaign

Compliance and Ethics Training
2, 3, 5 | 2d
Fri 1/15/99 | Mon 1/18/99

Hire Fundraiser
1 | 10d
Fri 10/23/98 | Thu 11/5/98

Begin Fundraising
7 | 0d
Mon 1/18/99 | Mon 1/18/99

Hire Manager
| 10d
Fri 10/9/98 | Thu 10/22/99

Hire Staff
1 | 30d
Fri 10/23/98 | Thu 12/3/98

Get Volunteers
4 | 30d
Fri 12/4/98 | Thu 1/14/99

Raise Funds
8 | 300d
Tue 1/19/99 | Mon 3/13/00

Hire Political Adviser
1 | 10d
Fri 10/23/98 | Thu 11/15/98

Establish Positions
3 | 60d
Fri 11/6/98 | Thu 1/28/99

Implement Campaign Strategy
7, 6 | 300d
Fri 1/29/99 | Thu 3/23/00

Vote
10, 9 | 0d
Thu 3/23/00 | Thu 3/23/00

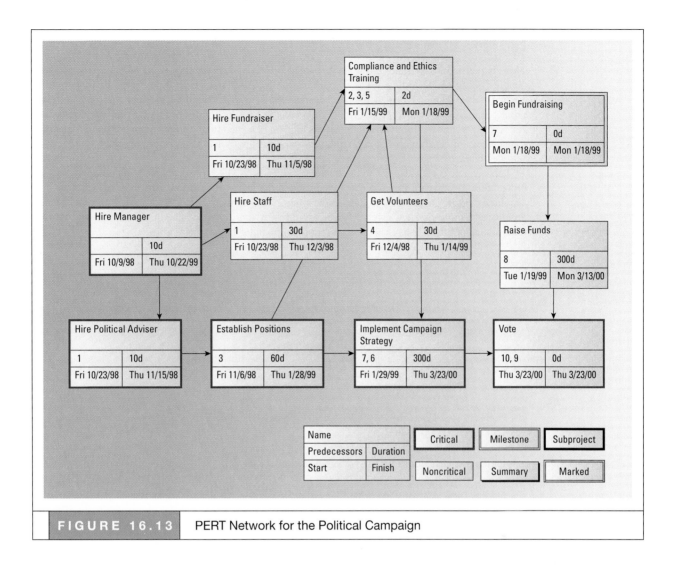

Name
Predecessors | Duration
Start | Finish

Critical
Milestone
Subproject
Noncritical
Summary
Marked

FIGURE 16.13 PERT Network for the Political Campaign

In addition to its time management features, MS-Project can be used to project, track, and control costs and resource requirements. For each resource, such as the campaign manager, fundraiser, or political adviser, data on capacity, cost, accrual rates, and work schedule can be entered into the project database. Once the resource requirements across all projects in the system have been compiled, the software can indicate when resources are overcommitted and when they are undercommitted. It can also generate resource-specific work calendars. For example, the campaign manager could print out a work calendar for the fundraiser. Finally, as the actual activities of project personnel are recorded in the database, the software can be used to track the project's accrued costs.

> active example

Take a closer look at the concepts and issues you've been reading about.

> active concept check

Now let's take a moment to test your knowledge of the concepts you have studied in this section.

Integrating Operational Decisions

This chapter is closely linked to 4 and 7 because decisions about the design of the product-service bundle and the value-adding system determine the level of complexity inherent in the planning and control of the system. When each customer receives a completely unique product-service bundle, the project management concepts described in this chapter are a good fit. Similarly, project management concepts apply most directly to organizations that are designed to use professional expertise—possibly in teams or a matrix organizational structure—to offer their customers a completely unique product-service bundle.

This chapter is also closely tied to Chapters 11 and 12. The broader resource planning and scheduling decisions covered in those chapters establish the level of resources available and what must be accomplished in the short- to intermediate-range. This chapter continues the planning and control process at a more detailed level. It describes the way that detailed scheduling activities ensure the requirements of the master schedule are met in companies that manage projects.

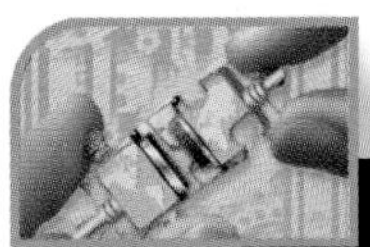

integrated OM

Take a moment to apply what you've learned.

Chapter Wrap-Up

In this chapter, we've covered a topic that is often taught as a course on its own. Project management is important to virtually every type of organization and in virtually every functional area of business. There are, however, some organizations that are all about managing projects. For example, many construction companies do only custom work and every job is a new project. Similarly, though scientific organizations have some ongoing operations, they are really in the business of advancing the frontiers of knowledge one research project at a time. Advertising agencies, consulting firms, law partnerships, and many other professional organizations are also generally primarily in a project management business. It's common to find matrix and team structures in companies that are simultaneously handling a large number of projects.

There is a recognized body of knowledge for project managers. This project management body of knowledge (PMBOK) includes scope management, quality management, cost management, time management, risk management, human resources management, communication management, and project integration management. This broad range of knowledge reflects the fact that a project manager has to manage all aspects of a unique value-adding system. In ongoing operations, unlike projects, these tasks might be divided among functional departments.

Projects typically have a life cycle comprised of four stages: conceptual study, development, implementation, and completion. Although all areas of the PMBOK are important at each stage, the first and second stage set the foundation for the third. While most of the money is spent during the third stage, the decisions made during the earlier stages drive the costs incurred during the implementation phase. Even projects that get canceled midstream because of fund shortages or other reasons must be terminated in some way. In that sense, all projects go through all the stages of the project life cycle.

Even though projects are unique and happen only once, the concept of supply-chain management is relevant to them. Large projects require subcontractors, and those subcontractors may in turn employ subcontractors and vendors of their own. Project management teams also have customers. Generally speaking, flexibility in scheduling is most needed from project subcontractors, while access to information and resources is most needed from the project's customers.

Planning and control presents special challenges in project-oriented organizations. Managers need to keep up with several projects at once and coordinate the use of their human resources and equipment across all of them. Many use work breakdown structures to identify all the activities required to complete a project. After determining the precedence relationships among those activities, they create a network model of the project that shows where their attention is most needed. Software packages such as MS-Project provide computerized graphical displays of these planning aids, which are a great help to managers in keeping up with costs, resource allocations, schedules, and critical activities.

> end-of-chapter resources

- Practice Quiz
- Key Terms
- Discussion Questions
- Case 16.1: The Superconducting Super Collider (SSC) Project
- References
- Factory Tours

TABLE G.2	Early Start and Finish Times for Furniture Factory Expansion Project			
Activity	**Immediate Predecessors**	**Times (weeks)**	**Early Start**	**Early Finish**
A	—	3	0	3
B	A	2	3	5
C	A	4	3	7
D	C	3	7	10
E	C	4	7	11
F	B, D, E	10	11	21
G	A	12	3	15
H	F, G	3	21	24

- Activity F has three predecessors—B, D, and E—so F can start as soon as all three are finished: ES_F = maximum $\{EF_B, EF_D, EF_E\}$ = maximum {5, 10, 11} = 11. F takes 10 weeks, so F can finish as early as the end of week 21 ($EF_F = ES_F + t_F = 11 + 10 = 21$).
- Activity G has one predecessor, A, so G can start as soon as A is finished: $ES_G = EF_A = 3$. G takes 12 weeks, so G can finish as early as the end of week 15 ($EF_G = ES_G + t_G = 3 + 12 = 15$).
- Activity H has two predecessors—F and G—so H can start as soon as both are finished: ES_H = maximum $\{EF_F, EF_G\}$ = maximum {21, 15} = 21. H takes 3 weeks, so H can finish as early as the end of week 24 ($EF_H = ES_H + t_H = 21 + 3 = 24$).

> active exercise

Take a moment to apply what you've learned.

LATE START AND FINISH TIMES

The late times for an activity are based on the assumption that all activities will be delayed as much as possible. An activity's **late finish time (LF)** is the latest time by which it must be completed if the end of the project is not to be delayed beyond its desired completion time. Its **late start time (LS)** is the time by which it must start if it is to be completed in its expected time and is to be finished by its late finish time. Since an activity must be finished in time for all of its successors to be completed by the desired ending time of the project, its late finish time must be no later than the late start time of each of its successors. The late finish and start times of any activity ("act") may be computed from the following formulas:

LF_{act} = minimum $\{LS_{suc1}, ..., LS_{sucj}\}$, where activity "suc1", ..., "sucj" are the immediate successors of activity "act"

$LS_{act} = LF_{act} - t_{act}$, where t_{act} is the time required to complete "act"

Example G.2

Use the immediate predecessors and activity time information given in Table G.1 (see Example G.1) to determine the late start and finish times for the furniture factory expansion project. Assume that the company wants to complete the project as soon as possible.

Solution:

The activities, their immediate predecessors, and their times are listed in Table G.3, along with their late start and finish times computed using the equations for LF_{act} and LS_{act}. The computations were actually done in the reverse of the order shown in the table, beginning with the last activity or activities in the project and working back to the beginning.

TABLE G.3	Late Start and Finish Times for Furniture Factory Expansion Project			
Activity	**Immediate Predecessors**	**Time (weeks)**	**Late Start**	**Late Finish**
A	—	3	0	3
B	A	2	9	11
C	A	4	3	7
D	C	3	8	11
E	C	4	7	11
F	B, D, E	10	11	21
G	A	12	9	21
H	F, G	3	21	24

- Activity H has no successors, so it must end at the desired completion time of the project. Assuming the company wants to complete the project as soon as possible, the desired completion time for the project is the same as the early finish time for H ($LF_H = EF_H = 24$). H takes 3 weeks, so it must start no later than the end of week 21 ($LS_H = LF_H - t_H = 24 - 3 = 21$).
- Activity G has one successor, H, so G must end in time for H to start ($LF_G = LS_H = 21$). G takes 12 weeks, so G must start no later than the end of week 9 ($LS_G = LF_G - t_G = 21 - 12 = 9$).
- Activity F has one successor, H, so F must end in time for H to start ($LF_F = LS_H = 21$). F takes 10 weeks, so F must start no later than the end of week 11 ($LS_F = LF_F - t_F = 21 - 10 = 11$).
- Activity E has one successor, F, so E must end in time for F to start ($LF_E = LS_F = 11$). E takes 4 weeks, so E must start no later than the end of week 7 ($LS_E = LF_E - t_E = 11 - 4 = 7$).
- Activity D has one successor, F, so D must end in time for F to start ($LF_D = LS_F = 11$). D takes 3 weeks, so D must start no later than the end of week 8 ($LS_D = LF_D - t_D = 11 - 3 = 8$).
- Activity C has two successors—D and E—so C must end in time for both to start (LF_C = minimum $\{LS_D, LS_E\}$ = minimum $\{8, 7\} = 7.$). C takes 4 weeks, so C must start no later than the end of week 3 ($LS_C = LF_C - t_C = 7 - 4 = 3$).
- Activity B has one successor, F, so B must end in time for F to start ($LF_B = LS_F = 11$). B takes 2 weeks, so B must start no later than the end of week 9 ($LS_B = L_B - t_B = 11 - 2 = 9$).
- Activity A has three successors—B, C, and G—so A must end in time for all three to start (LF_A = minimum $\{LS_B, LS_C, LS_G\}$ = minimum $\{9, 3, 9\} = 3$). A takes 3 weeks, so A must start immediately ($LS_A = LF_A - t_A = 3 - 3 = 0$).

active exercise

Take a moment to apply what you've learned.

SLACK OR FLOAT

If you compare the early start (or finish) times in Table G.2 with the late start (or finish) times in Table G.3 (see Table G.4), you will notice that for some activities they are the same and for others they are different. The difference between an activity's late and early start times (or between its late and early finish times), called its **slack** or **float,**[2] is the amount of time by which the activity's start or

[2]This is sometimes called *total slack* or *total float* to distinguish it from other types of slack or float that have more restricted meanings. Since we will only discuss total slack or float, we will drop the "total."

completion can be delayed without delaying the project's completion. Slack can be computed using the equation:

$$TS_{act} = LS_{act} - ES_{act} = LF_{act} - EF_{act}$$

Example G.3

Use the early start and finish times given in Table G.2 and the late start and finish times given in Table G.3 to determine the slack for each of the activities in the furniture factory expansion project described in Example G.1.

Solution:
The information in Tables G.2 and G.3 has been combined in Table G.4. The slack times were computed using the equation for $TS_{act.}$ For example:

$$TS_A = LS_A - ES_A = 0 - 0 = 0 \text{ or } = LF_A - EF_A = 3 - 3 = 0 \text{ and } TS_B = LS_B - ES_B = 9 - 3 = 6 \text{ or } = LF_B - EF_B = 11 - 5 = 6.$$

TABLE G.4 Activity Timing for Furniture Factory Expansion Project

Activity	Immediate Predecessors	Time (weeks)	Early Start	Early Finish	Late Start	Late Finish	Slack
A	—	3	0	3	0	3	0
B	A	2	3	5	9	11	6
C	A	4	3	7	3	7	0
D	C	3	7	10	8	11	1
E	C	4	7	11	7	11	0
F	B, D, E	10	11	21	11	21	0
G	A	12	3	15	9	21	6
H	F, G	3	21	24	21	24	0

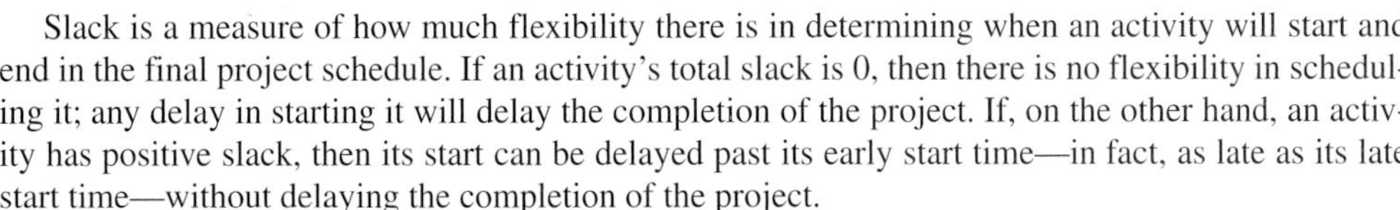

> active exercise

Take a moment to apply what you've learned.

Slack is a measure of how much flexibility there is in determining when an activity will start and end in the final project schedule. If an activity's total slack is 0, then there is no flexibility in scheduling it; any delay in starting it will delay the completion of the project. If, on the other hand, an activity has positive slack, then its start can be delayed past its early start time—in fact, as late as its late start time—without delaying the completion of the project.

The problem with using slack as an indicator of scheduling flexibility is that it is shared by successive activities. While this is not an issue in the furniture factory expansion project, it is in the simple project summarized in Table G.5 and Figure G.2. While activities C and D each have two weeks of slack, it should be fairly obvious that they are the same two weeks. If the start of C is delayed at all,

TABLE G.5 Simple Network Example to Illustrate Slack

Activity	Immediate Predecessors	Time (weeks)	Early Start	Early Finish	Late Start	Late Finish	Slack
A	—	5	0	5	0	5	0
B	A	4	5	9	5	9	0
C	—	3	0	3	2	5	2
D	C	4	3	7	5	9	2

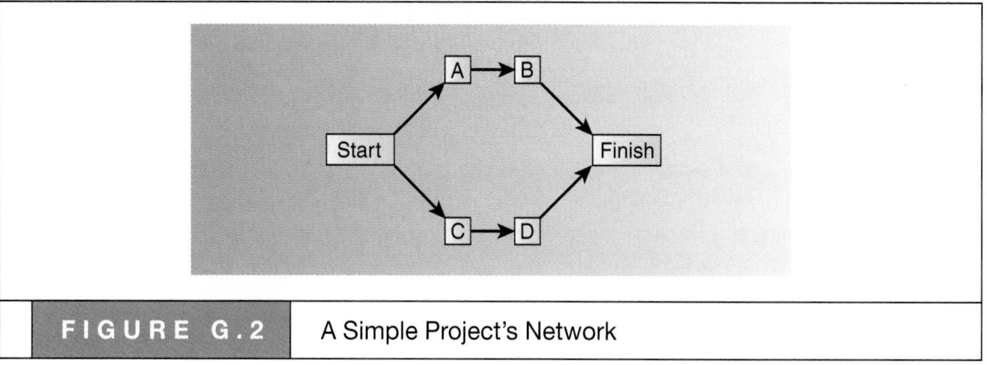

FIGURE G.2 A Simple Project's Network

then the start of D will be delayed by the same amount of time, cutting into the time by which the start of D can be delayed *beyond the amount by which its start is delayed due to the delay in C.*

THE CRITICAL PATH

One of the most important ideas in PERT and CPM is the **critical path.** The critical path for a project is the longest path[3] through its network. Since it is possible, subject to the precedence restrictions and the availability of required resources, to carry out two or more activities simultaneously, the amount of time required to complete the project is *not* the sum of the activity times, but the *length of the critical path.* This assumes, of course, that all activities on the critical path are started and completed within the time limits established by their early and late start and finish times. Because the critical path is the longest path, it is the set of sequential activities with minimum total slack. If the late finish time for the final activity in the project is the same as its early finish time, then all the activities on the critical path will have zero total slack.

Example G.4

Use Figure G.1 and Table G.4 to determine the critical path for the furniture factory expansion project described in Example G.1.

Solution:
Looking at Figure G.1, we see that there are four paths through the project network. Ignoring start and finish, which appear on all paths and are dummy activities taking 0 time, the paths and their lengths in weeks are:

Path	*Length*
A–B–F–H	3 + 2 + 10 + 3 = 18
A–C–D–F–H	3 + 4 + 3 + 10 + 3 = 23
A–C–E–F–H	3 + 4 + 4 + 10 + 3 = 24
A–G–H	3 + 12 + 3 = 18

The critical (longest) path is A–C–E–F–H with a length of 24 weeks, so the project will take 24 weeks. Looking at Table G.4, we see that these are the activities for which slack equals 0.

active exercise 

Take a moment to apply what you've learned.

Although we have referred to *the* critical path, it is important to note that there may be more than one path with the longest length. In this case there will be two or more critical paths, which may be completely distinct or may have some activities in common.

[3]A path in a network is a connected series of nodes. For example, Start–A–B–Finish and Start–C–D–Finish are paths in Figure G.3.

USING EXCEL TO MAKE THE COMPUTATIONS

There are many professional software packages for implementing PERT and CPM, including MS Project. However, it is also possible to use a standard spreadsheet, such as Excel, to do the calculations. While there are a variety of ways of using a spreadsheet to do the calculations, we will use the simplest: implementing the equations given earlier in this supplement. This requires inserting formulas that compute the activities' early and late start and finish times and slack times into specific cells of the spreadsheet. An Excel spreadsheet for the furniture factory expansion project is developed in Example G.5.

Example G.5

Develop a spreadsheet model to determine the early and late start and finish times and slack times for the furniture factory expansion project, using the immediate predecessors and activity timing information given in Table G.1 (see Example G.1).

Solution:
The Excel spreadsheet for this project is shown in Exhibit G.1. The activity, description, immediate predecessors, and activity time columns are taken directly from Table G.1. The actual contents of the cells in rows 5 through 12 of the early start, early finish, late start, late finish, and slack columns (columns E through I of the spreadsheet) are formulas that implement the equations given in the text, leading to the numbers displayed in those cells. For example:

E10: = maximum (F6, F8, F9) to give the early start time for activity F
F10: = E10 + D10 to give the early finish time for activity F
H5: = minimum (G6, G7, G11) to give the late finish time for activity A
G5: = H5 − D5 to give the late start time for activity A
I5: = G5 − E5 to give the slack time for activity A

The only exceptions to the use of these formulas are the cells E5, which is set equal to 0, and H12, which contains = F12 so that the project will be completed as early as possible.

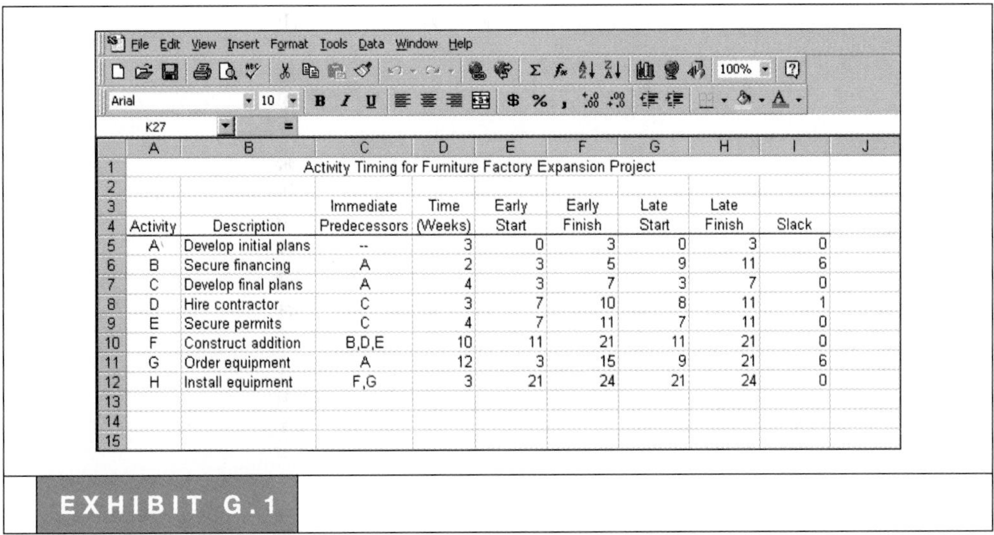

Activity Timing for Furniture Factory Expansion Project

Activity	Description	Immediate Predecessors	Time (Weeks)	Early Start	Early Finish	Late Start	Late Finish	Slack
A	Develop initial plans	--	3	0	3	0	3	0
B	Secure financing	A	2	3	5	9	11	6
C	Develop final plans	A	4	3	7	3	7	0
D	Hire contractor	C	3	7	10	8	11	1
E	Secure permits	C	4	7	11	7	11	0
F	Construct addition	B,D,E	10	11	21	11	21	0
G	Order equipment	A	12	3	15	9	21	6
H	Install equipment	F,G	3	21	24	21	24	0

EXHIBIT G.1

> active exercise

Take a moment to apply what you've learned.

Time-Cost Tradeoffs or Project Crashing

Suppose that a schedule has been developed for a project. For one reason or another, the project manager decides that it is going to take longer than would be desirable. As examples:

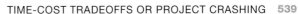

- A platform is being erected for the use of the speakers at a political rally; if the platform is not ready by the time the speeches are scheduled, it will be of no use.
- The contract for constructing a new office building includes a penalty clause for completion after a specified due date or a bonus clause for completion before that date.
- The overhaul of a chemical plant requires that it be shut down while the maintenance is being performed. Since no product will be produced during that time, profits will be lost.
- A company is developing a new product; the longer the development process takes, the more likely that a competitor will bring a similar product to market first, thus reducing the company's profits from the new product.

Often, by using additional personnel or other resources to complete an activity, or by doing an activity in a different, more expensive way, one can reduce the time required for the project, thereby meeting a desired deadline or saving costs that are determined by the length of the project.

One of the original features of CPM was a procedure for determining how best to trade off increased activity costs for reduced project time. This **time-cost tradeoff** process is commonly called **project crashing.** To conduct a project crashing analysis, we need, for each activity, three kinds of information:

1. The **normal time** for the activity and its associated **normal cost.** This will generally be the lowest cost way of doing the activity.
2. The minimum or **crash time** for the activity and its associated **crash cost.** This faster, higher cost way will require either additional resources or a different, more expensive way of doing the activity.
3. The functional relationship relating time and cost between these two extremes.

To illustrate the meaning of this last requirement, consider the four time/cost relationships shown in Figure G.3. The usual assumption, and the one we will use here, is shown in Figure G.3a, where the tradeoff between reduced time and increased cost is linear. That is, any percentage of the time reduction can be obtained by paying the same percentage of the cost increase. The relationships shown in

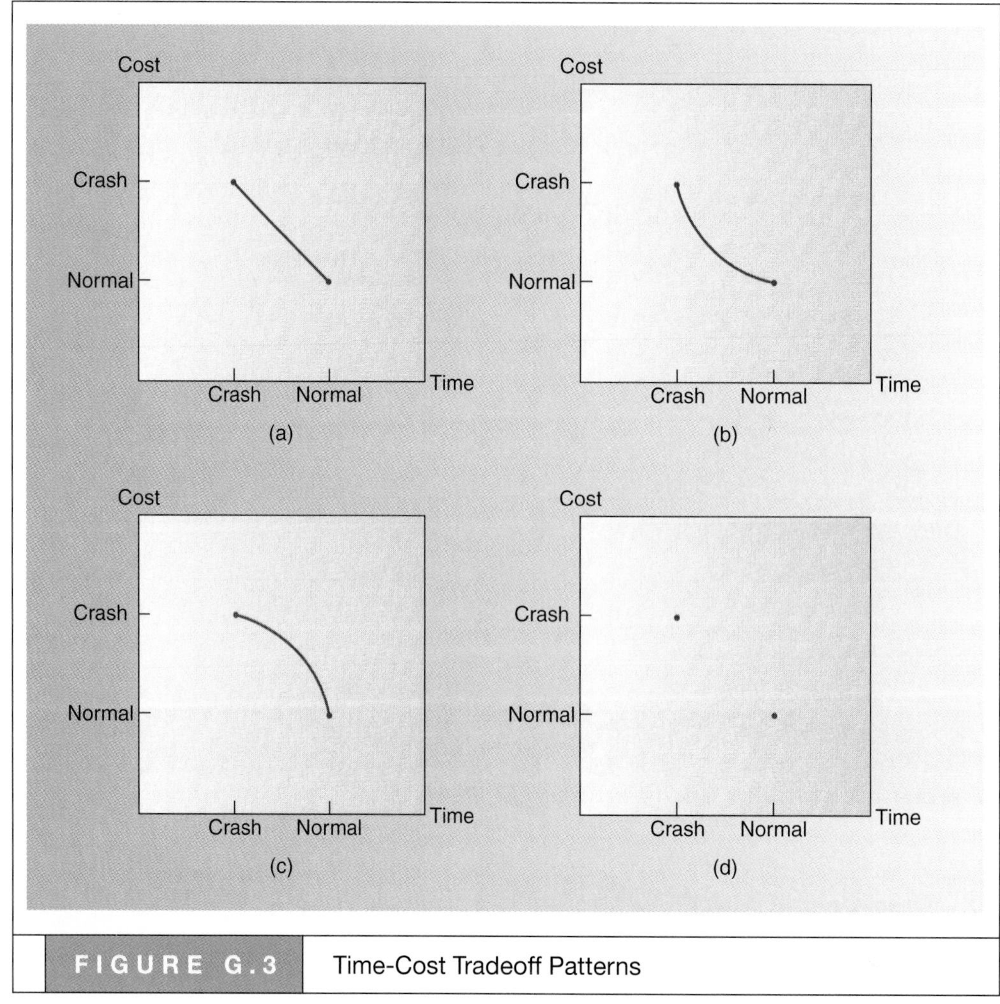

FIGURE G.3 Time-Cost Tradeoff Patterns

parts b and c of Figure G.3 also allow for achieving any amount of the potential time reduction, but the relationship between time and cost is nonlinear. In Figure G.3b, additional time reductions cost greater amounts of money. In Figure G.3c, the relationship is reversed; additional time reductions cost lesser amounts of money. Finally, Figure G.3d shows a discrete relationship, in which there are only two choices for time and cost. The activity may be done in either the long-time/low-cost way or in the short-time/high-cost way; there is no in between.

There are three different, but related, sets of questions that one might ask about project crashing:

1. Which activities should be crashed and by how much in order to get to a specified project length at minimum cost?
2. What is the minimum length for the project, and which activities should be crashed and by how much in order to get to that length at minimum cost?
3. Considering both activity and project costs, what is the optimal project length, and which activities should be crashed and by how much in order to get to that length at minimum cost?

When working with small projects for which the linear time/cost tradeoff assumption can be made, such as the ones we are considering here, the standard methods for answering all three sets of questions are based on the same approach, marginal analysis, conducted as follows:

1. For each activity, determine the marginal cost to crash it by dividing the difference between the crash and normal costs by the difference between the normal and crash times.
2. From among those activities that it makes sense to crash, identify that activity or set of activities that has the lowest marginal cost to crash.
3. Crash the chosen activity or set of activities by:
   a) the maximum amount possible,
   b) the amount required to reach the desired project length, or
   c) until another project path becomes a critical path, whichever is smaller.
4. Repeat steps 2 and 3 as often as necessary.

Steps 2 and 3 of this process require a little more explanation. Which activities does it make sense to crash? To begin with, it only makes sense to consider activities that can be crashed, i.e., that are longer than their crash times. Beyond that, identifying activities that are candidates for crashing and limiting the amount by which the selected activity or activities should be crashed are based on the following two principles:

1. It only makes sense to crash activities that are on the critical path since the length of the project is determined by the length of the critical path. Reducing the length of any activity not on the critical path will not reduce the length of the project.
2. If there is more than one critical path, their lengths must all be reduced simultaneously or the length of the project will not change. This may be done by crashing one activity that is on all the critical paths or by crashing a set of activities that includes one from every critical path.

Example G.6

The board of the hospital at which Cheryl is the administrator has decided that the hospital must upgrade its utility backup systems by adding a water storage tank and building an emergency utilities center with a generator and a pump connected to the water tank. Table G.6 contains the information about the normal and crash times (in weeks) and normal and crash costs (in $1,000s) developed by the hospital's engineering office. The AON network for the project is shown in Figure G.4.

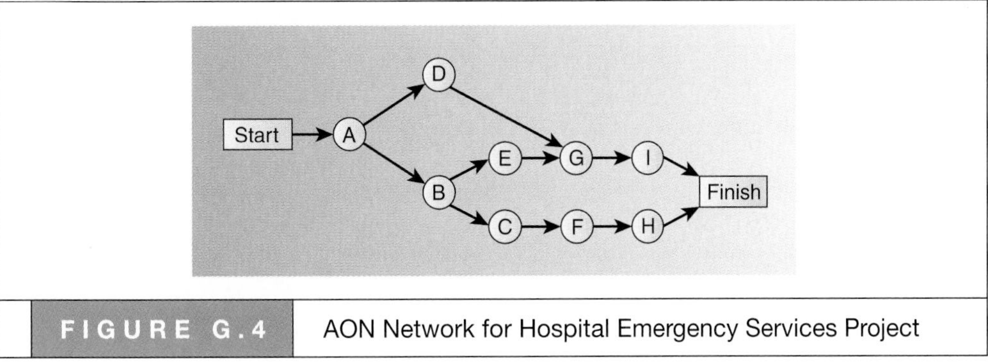

FIGURE G.4 AON Network for Hospital Emergency Services Project

TABLE G.6	Activity Information for Hospital Emergency Services Project					
Activity	**Description**	**Immediate Predecessors**	**Normal Time**	**Normal Cost**	**Crash Time**	**Crash Cost**
A	Prepare site	—	3	30	2	45
B	Construct building	A	8	150	5	210
C	Install generator	B	3	40	2	50
D	Install water tank	A	5	60	3	70
E	Install pump	B	4	25	2	30
F	Connect generator	C	2	18	1	27
G	Connect pump	D, E	3	20	2	28
H	Test electric system	F	3	15	2	21
I	Test water system	G	2	20	2	20

a. Determine how long it will take and how much it will cost to construct and test the emergency systems if all activities are done in their normal time and at normal cost. Identify the critical path.

b. Determine which activities should be crashed and by how much if the hospital wants to have the emergency facility in operation within 16 weeks.

c. Determine the shortest amount of time in which the facility could be ready. Determine which activities should be crashed and by how much to be ready in this amount of time.

d. Because the current backup facilities are in such poor condition, the hospital board has decided it is prudent to rent temporary truck-mounted equipment until the new facility is ready. The cost of this temporary equipment will be $5,000 per week. Recognizing this, determine the amount of time that the hospital should take for this project and the activities that should be crashed, and by how much if the board wants to minimize the combined cost of completing the project and providing emergency backup facilities until the permanent facilities are ready.

Solution:

a. The early and late start and finish times and slack times if all activities are done in their normal times are shown in Table G.7. The project will take 20 weeks. Adding up the normal costs, the project will cost 378, or $378,000. The critical path is A–B–E–G–I.

b. The first step in determining which activities to crash is to find the marginal crashing cost per week for each activity by dividing the difference between the crash and normal costs by the difference between the normal and crash times. The results are shown in Table G.8.

First crashing: The activities on the critical path are A, B, E, G, and I. Of these activities, the one with the lowest marginal crashing cost is E, with a marginal cost of 2.5 or $2,500 per week. Crash E by one week, at which point there are two critical paths, the original one and A–B–C–F–H. The project time is now 19 weeks.

TABLE G.7	Activity Timing for Hospital Emergency Services Project						
Activity	**Immediate Predecessors**	**Time (weeks)**	**Early Start**	**Early Finish**	**Late Start**	**Late Finish**	**Slack**
A	—	3	0	3	0	3	0
B	A	8	3	11	3	11	0
C	B	3	11	14	12	15	1
D	A	5	3	8	10	15	7
E	B	4	11	15	11	15	0
F	C	2	14	16	15	17	1
G	D, E	3	15	18	15	18	0
H	F	3	16	19	17	20	1
I	G	2	18	20	18	20	0

TABLE G.8	Marginal Crashing Costs for Hospital Emergency Services Project				
Activity	**Normal Time**	**Normal Cost**	**Crash Time**	**Crash Cost**	**ΔC/ΔT**
A	3	30	2	45	15
B	8	150	5	210	20
C	3	40	2	50	10
D	5	60	3	70	5
E	4	25	2	30	2.5
F	2	18	1	27	9
G	3	20	2	28	8
H	3	15	2	21	6
I	2	20	2	20	—

Second crashing: Since there are two critical paths, we can either crash one activity that is on both paths (the two possibilities are A and B) or crash a pair of activities, including one from each path (the possibilities are C, F or H combined with E or G, since I cannot be crashed). The less expensive of the single activities to crash is A at a marginal cost of 15 per week. The least expensive pair of activities to crash is E and H at a combined cost of 2.5 + 6 = 8.5. Crash E and H by one week each, at which point both E and H have reached their limits. The project time is now 18 weeks and the same two paths are still both critical.

Third crashing: Since the same two paths are critical, we have the same choices as to what to crash except that neither E nor H can be crashed anymore, so the possible pairs are either C or F combined with G. The less expensive of the single activities is A at a marginal cost of 15 per week. The less expensive pair of activities to crash is F and G at a combined cost of 9 + 8 = 17. Crash A by one week, at which point A has reached its limit. The project time is now 17 weeks and the same two paths are still both critical.

Fourth crashing: Since the same two paths are critical and A cannot be crashed any further, we can either crash B, at a marginal cost of 20 per week, or the lower cost pair, F and G, at a cost of 17 per week. Crash F and G each by one week, at which point the desired project time of 16 weeks has been reached. Also, G has now reached its minimum time and the same two paths are still critical.

Summarizing the results of these four crashes, the minimum cost way of completing the project in 16 weeks is to crash E by two weeks and A, F, G, and H each by one week. The added cost from crashing is 43, or $43,000, for a total project cost of 378 + 43 = 421, or $421,000.

c. Continue the process started in part b until the project's length cannot be reduced any further.

Fifth crashing: At this point there are still two critical paths, A–B–E–G–I and A–B–C–F–H. Since A, E, F, G, and H are all being done in their crash times, the only way of reducing the length of both paths simultaneously is to crash B at a marginal cost of 20 per week. B can be crashed by a maximum of three weeks, which reduces the length of the project to 13 weeks at an added cost of 60. At this point the only critical-path activity that can still be crashed is C, but doing so will only reduce the length of the path A–B–C–F–H, not the length of the project. Adding this information to the summary at the end of part b, we find that the minimum project time is 13 weeks. The minimum cost way of reaching this length is to crash B by three weeks, E by two weeks, and A, F, G, and H each by one week. The added cost from crashing in this way is 103, for a total cost of 378 + 103 = 481, or $481,000. The entire series of crashes for parts b and c is summarized in Table G.9.

d. Refer to Table G.9. At a project length of 20 weeks (no crashing), the total cost, in $1,000s, is 378 + 20(5) = 378 + 100 = 478, or $478,000. If the project is crashed to 19 weeks, the total cost is 380.5 + 19(5) = 475.5. If the project is crashed to 18 weeks, the total cost is 389 + 18(5) = 479. Crashing the project to 17 weeks or less will cost even more since the added crashing cost will be more than the amount saved by not having to rent the emergency backup equipment. Thus, the optimal length of the project, considering both the cost of completing the project and the cost of providing emergency backup facilities, is 19 weeks at a cost of 475.5, or $475,500.

TABLE G.9	Summary of Crashing for Hospital Emergency Services Project		
Project Length	**Activity to Crash**	**Added Cost**	**Total Cost**
20	—	0	378.0
19	E	2.5	380.5
18	E, H	8.5	389.0
17	A	15	404.0
16	F, G	17	421.0
15	B	20	441.0
14	B	20	461.0
13	B	20	481.0

active exercise

Take a moment to apply what you've learned.

Notice that activity D, install water tank, was not crashed at all, even though its marginal crashing cost is the second lowest of all the activities. Looking at the slack values in Table G.7 shows us why: Activity D has so much slack that it never becomes part of a critical path, no matter how much other activities are crashed. This illustrates the first of the two principles stated for selecting activities to be crashed: It only makes sense to crash activities that are on the critical path since the length of the project is determined by the length of the critical path.

Probability In PERT Networks

So far in this supplement we have assumed that the time for an activity is deterministic—that is, we know exactly how long it will take to complete each activity. However, it is often impossible to say how long an activity will take, even with reasonable (if not exact) accuracy. To accommodate uncertainty about an activity's length, the original version of PERT used three time estimates for the length of each activity, rather than the single time estimate of CPM. These three estimates, which we shall denote as *o, m,* and *p,* are the **optimistic,** most likely, and **pessimistic** estimates of how long the activity will take.

Based on the characteristics of beta distributions, an activity's three time estimates are combined, using the following formulas, to estimate the mean and standard deviation of its duration:

$$\mu_i = \frac{o_i + 4m_i + p_i}{6} \qquad s_i = \frac{p_i - o_i}{6}$$

Assuming that the activities' durations are independent, their means and standard deviations may be combined, using the following formulas, to obtain a mean and variance for the length of the project:

$$\mu_P = \Sigma\mu_j \qquad \sigma_p^2 = \Sigma\sigma_j^2$$

where, for both μ_P, the mean time for the project, and σ_p^2, the variance of the project time, the summation is only for those activities on the critical path.

Once the project time's mean and variance have been determined from these formulas, the probability of completing the project within any specified amount of time can be computed by using the standard normal probability approach:

$$P(T_P \leq t_0) = P\left(Z \leq \frac{t_0 - \mu_P}{\sigma_P}\right)$$

TABLE G.10 Activity Information for New Product Development Project

Activity	Description	Immediate Predecessors	Activity Time Estimates Optimistic	Most Likely	Pessimistic
A	Initial design	—	12	16	26
B	Survey market	A	6	9	18
C	Build prototype	A	8	10	18
D	Test prototype	C	2	3	4
E	Redesign product	B, D	3	4	11
F	Market testing	E	6	8	10
G	Set up production	F	15	20	25

Example G.7

The electronics company for which Fred works has been discussing developing a new personal communication device. The product development committee has put together the list of activities and time estimates (in weeks) shown in Table G.10.

a. Find the mean and standard deviation of the time to complete each of the project's activities.

b. Using the activities' mean completion times, find the expected early and late start and finish times for the activities. Determine the critical path and its expected length.

c. Find the probability that the project will be completed in no more than 50 weeks; in more than 60 weeks.

Solution:

a. The means and standard deviations of the times to complete the activities are shown in Table G.11. For example, the mean and standard deviation of the time to complete activity A are computed as follows:

$$\mu_A = \frac{o_A + 4m_A + p_A}{6} = \frac{12 + 4(16) + 26}{6}$$

$$= \frac{102}{6} = 17.0$$

$$\sigma_A = \frac{p_A - o_A}{6} = \frac{26 - 12}{6} = \frac{14}{6} = 2.3333$$

b. The expected early and late start times and slacks for the activities are given in Table G.12. The critical path is A–C–D–E–F–G, with an expected length of 52 weeks.

c. The expected project completion time is the sum of the expected completion times of the activities on the critical path:

$$\mu_P = \mu_A + \mu_C + \mu_D + \mu_E + \mu_F + \mu_G = 17 + 11 + 3 + 5 + 8 + 8 = 52 \text{ weeks}$$

TABLE G.11 Means and Standard Deviations of Activity Completion Times for New Product Development Project

Activity	Optimistic	Activity Time Estimates Most Likely	Pessimistic	Mean Time	Standard Deviation
A	12	16	26	17	2.3333
B	6	9	18	10	2.0000
C	8	10	18	11	1.6667
D	2	3	4	3	0.3333
E	3	4	11	5	1.3333
F	6	8	10	8	0.6667
G	15	20	25	8	0.6667

TABLE G.12 Activity Timing for New Product Development Project

Activity	Immediate Predecessors	Time (weeks)	Early Start	Early Finish	Late Start	Late Finish	Slack
A	—	17	0	17	0	17	0
B	A	10	17	27	21	31	4
C	A	11	17	28	17	28	0
D	C	3	28	31	28	31	0
E	B, D	5	31	36	31	36	0
F	E	8	36	44	36	44	0
G	F	8	44	52	44	52	0

The variance of the project completion time is the sum of the variances of the completion times of the activities on the critical path:

$$\sigma_P^2 = \sigma_A^2 = \sigma_C^2 = \sigma_D^2 = \sigma_E^2 = \sigma_F^2 = \sigma_G^2$$

$$= (2.3333)^2 + (1.6667)^2 + (0.3333)^2 + (1.3333)^2 + (0.6667)^2 + (0.6667)^2$$

$$= 5.4444 + 2.7778 + 0.1111 + 1.7778 + 0.4444 + 0.4444$$

$$= 10.9998 \text{ weeks}^2$$

The standard deviation of the project completion time is the square root of the variance:

$$\mu_P = \sqrt{10.9998} = 3.3166 \text{ weeks}$$

The probability that the project will be completed within 50 weeks is:

$$P(T_p \leq 50) = P\left(Z \leq \frac{50 - \mu_P}{\sigma_p}\right) = P\left(Z \leq \frac{50 - 52}{3.3166}\right)$$

$$= P(Z \leq -0.60) = .2743$$

The probability that the project will take more than 60 weeks is:

$$P(T_p > 60) = P\left(Z > \frac{60 - \mu_P}{\sigma_p}\right) = P\left(Z > \frac{60 - 52}{3.3166}\right)$$

$$= P(Z > 2.41) = .0080$$

active exercise

Take a moment to apply what you've learned.

Often there will be at least one additional path through the network with an expected length almost as long as the critical path. If such a path has a fairly high standard deviation, then there will be a reasonably high probability that when the project is actually done, this other path will turn out to be longer than the one identified as the critical path. Thus, the probability that the project will be completed by a specified time is not the probability that the "critical path" will be completed by that time, but the probability that *all* the paths through the network will be completed by that time. If these paths are completely independent of one another, then the project probability can be computed as the product of the path probabilities, each computed in the same way as the "critical path" probability. Unfortunately, however, the paths typically are not completely independent of one another because they have some activities in common. In this case, the only reasonable, although expensive, approach to estimating the project time probability distribution is simulation.

Supplement Wrap-Up

A project is a well-defined set of interdependent activities, all of which must be completed for the project to be finished. PERT/CPM are network-based methods for planning, scheduling, and controlling projects. Using CPM, a single time estimate is made for each activity. Since one of the original concepts of PERT was that activity times would be uncertain, three time estimates were made for each: an optimistic estimate, a most likely estimate, and a pessimistic estimate. A probability distribution was fit to these three points, and the mean and standard deviation of the activity's time were computed.

Using the precedence relationships and the time estimates for the activities, early and late start and finish times for the activities can be calculated and used to set a project schedule. If the early and late start (or finish) times for an activity differ, then that activity has slack or float, meaning that there is flexibility in its scheduling. The longest connected path of events through the network is identified as the critical path. Activities on this path have minimum slack and it is the length of this path that determines how long the project will take to complete.

A feature of the original version of CPM was time-cost tradeoffs or project crashing. Using the normal time and cost estimates and the crash time and cost estimates for each activity on the critical path or paths, it is possible to determine which activities should be crashed (shortened at an increase in cost) and by how much in order to, at minimum cost, complete the project at some specified time, in the minimum time, or at the optimal time.

A feature of the original version of PERT was probability analysis for the project. This could then be used to find the probability that the project would be completed within any specified amount of time. In many cases, however, this procedure underestimates the true probability since key assumptions on which the procedure is based are frequently violated.

> end-of-supplement resources

- **Practice Quiz**
- **Key Terms**
- **Solved Problems**
- **Discussion Questions**
- **Problems**

INDEX

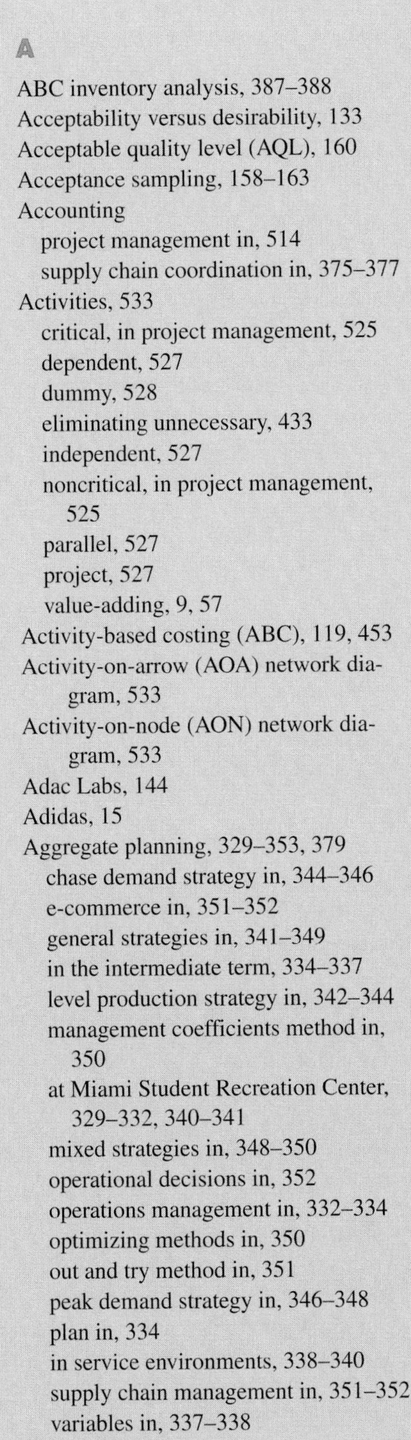

C

D

E

M

Q

T

U

V

W

X

Y

Z

PHOTO CREDITS

CHAPTER 1: page 2, Getty Images, Inc. (top), Getty Images, Inc. (middle), Getty Images, Inc. (bottom); page 3, Getty Images, Inc.; page 10, AP/Wide World Photos.

CHAPTER 3: page 62, PhotoEdit (bottom left), Corbis/Stock Market (bottom right); page 69, Getty Images, Inc.; page 77, Getty Images, Inc.

CHAPTER 4: page 117, Corbis/Stock Market; page 121, Ron Kimball Photography.

CHAPTER 5: page 126, Corbis/SABA Press Photos, Inc.; page 145, U.S. Department of Commerce.

CHAPTER 6: page 157, PhotoEdit; page 171, Getty Images, Inc.

CHAPTER 7: page 201, AP/Wide World Photos; page 206, Getty Images, Inc.; page 207, Cincinnati Machine.

CHAPTER 8: page 231, PhotoEdit; page 234, Getty Images, Inc.

CHAPTER 9: page 281, AP/Wide World Photos; page 285, Corbis/SABA Press Photos, Inc.; page 289, Getty Images, Inc.; page 304, The Image Works.

CHAPTER 10: page 314, Stock Boston; page 320, Custom Medical Stock Photo, Inc.; page 323, Getty Images, Inc.

CHAPTER 11: page 339, PhotoEdit; page 341, Peter Arnold, Inc.; page 346, Getty Images, Inc.

CHAPTER 13: page 416, Churchill & Klehr Photography; page 419, Ford Motor Company; page 434, Corbis/Stock Market.

CHAPTER 14: page 448, Index Stock Imagery, Inc.; page 454, AP/Wide World Photos; page 458, CORBIS.

CHAPTER 15: page 469, The Image Works; page 491, Getty Images, Inc.

CHAPTER 16: page 520, Getty Images, Inc.; page 522, Custom Medical Stock Photo, Inc.